סידור קורן לימות החול • נוסח אשכנז

The Koren Weekday Siddur • Nusaḥ Ashkenaz

קורן ירושלים

THE MAGERMAN EDITION

סידור קורן
אני תפילה לימות החול

THE KOREN
ANI TEFILLA WEEKDAY SIDDUR

WITH TRANSLATION BY
Rabbi Lord Jonathan Sacks שליט״א

AND COMMENTARY BY
Rabbi Dr. Jay Goldmintz

•

KOREN PUBLISHERS JERUSALEM

The Koren Ani Tefilla Weekday Siddur
Third Hebrew/English Ashkenaz Edition, 2018
Combined American/Canadian Edition

Koren Publishers Jerusalem Ltd.
POB 4044, Jerusalem 91040, ISRAEL
POB 8531, New Milford, CT 06776, USA

www.korenpub.com

Koren Tanakh Font © 1962, 2018 Koren Publishers Jerusalem Ltd.
Koren Siddur Font and text design © 1981, 2018 Koren Publishers Jerusalem Ltd.
English translation © 2006, 2009, 2014 Jonathan Sacks
English commentary © 2014 Jay Goldmintz
Temple diagram (page xxiii) © 2006, Gal m, http://commons.wikimedia.org/wiki/
File:Temple_sketch2.png

The English translation and commentary in this edition are based on the English translation
and commentary first published in Great Britain in 2006 in the Authorised Daily Prayer
Book of the United Hebrew Congregations of the Commonwealth: New Translation
and Commentary by Chief Rabbi Jonathan Sacks, (Fourth Edition, Compilation
© United Synagogue) by Collins, a division of HarperCollins Publishers, London.

The creation of this Siddur was made possible with the generous support
of Torah Education in Israel.

Printed in the United States of America

Standard Size, Hardcover, ISBN 978 965 301 668 2
Compact Size, Soft cover, ISBN 978 965 301 694 1

ATA04

וְשִׁנַּנְתָּם לְבָנֶיךָ

Dedicated to my wife,
Debra צביה אהובה
and our children,
Elijah Matthew מנחם מנדל
Zachary Noah יצחק אבנר
Sydney Rachel אלקה שיינה
Lexie Belle רחל לאה

In celebration
of our joint and individual journeys
toward a better understanding of Torah
and our relationship to Hashem.

David Magerman

CONTENTS

PREFACE

It is with great excitement that we present to you the Magerman Edition of the *Koren Ani Tefilla Weekday Siddur*, an engaging and thoughtful siddur for the inquiring high-school student and thoughtful adult alike. This Siddur is part of the Magerman Series of appropriately designed siddurim for students from first to twelfth grade, and beyond. Each siddur has been created to inspire and develop connections to prayer and to God. These goals are achieved through encouraging personal reflection, spiritual and emotional connection, and cognitive learning.

It is always a privilege to collaborate on a project with those who share our commitment and enthusiasm for bringing out the beauty of *Tefilla*. We are grateful to Debra and David Magerman for their critical support and encouragement, and for enabling the creation of this and all the volumes in the series. On behalf of the students who will use this Siddur, we are forever in your debt.

We are fortunate to benefit from a world-class Educational Editorial Board assisting us in the building of this program. We would like to thank the Board's Chairman, Dr. Scott Goldberg of Yeshiva University; Rabbi Adam Englander of the Hillel Day School of Boca Raton; Rabbi Dr. Jay Goldmintz of the Azrieli Graduate School; and Rabbi Boruch Sufrin of the Harkham Hillel Hebrew Academy of Beverly Hills. Their broad knowledge and experience provided the framework to structure the program.

We wish to thank Rabbi Sacks for his foreword and translation, and his ongoing support for this project. Special thanks go to Rabbi Dr. Jay Goldmintz who provided the vision for this Siddur, and its exceptional commentary. The small but highly professional team at Koren was led by Dr. Daniel Rose, Director of Educational Projects, and included Rabbi David Fuchs and Rabbi Ḥanan Benayahu, who reviewed the

◂ *tefillot*

tefillot; Esther Be'er who designed and typeset the text; Rachel Meghnagi, our Language Editor; and Tani Bayer, our Art Director.

It is our sincere hope and prayer that this Siddur will provide a platform for the educational and spiritual growth of present and upcoming generations of committed Jews.

Matthew Miller, Publisher
Jerusalem, 5774 (2014)

FOREWORD

Philosophers speculate about God. Scientists argue about God. Theologians theorize about God. We as Jews do something simpler and ultimately more profound. We talk to God. We bring Him our thanks and our hopes, our fears and our dreams. That conversation is what we call prayer, and Jews have engaged in it ever since the days of Abraham. The Siddur, the book you have in your hand, grew out of those conversations. Every time we pray we become part of the long dialogue between earth and heaven that has lasted now for almost four thousand years. Prayer was our ancestors' source of strength, and when we learn to pray it becomes ours also.

This new Siddur was designed for you and others like you, as you begin to wonder why we pray as we do, why in these words not those, how the various elements that make up a service relate to each other, and how these ancient texts relate to us in the present, in the immediacy of our lives. I hope you will enjoy this new Koren edition with its multiple commentaries and beautiful design. I wish it had existed when I was growing up, but in those days we tended to take prayer for granted. We prayed because Jews pray. Our parents did. So did our grandparents. So did countless generations before them. We didn't ask questions. We didn't read commentaries. We just prayed, often not really understanding what we were doing. I think that the new approach is better, because the more we understand what we say, the more deeply we enter into the act of prayer, and the more profoundly it changes us.

If I were to try to summarize briefly what prayer is, I would call it a journey in three stages. The first stage is *opening our eyes to wonder*. We are here, but we might not have been. The universe exists in almost infinite dimensions, as does the earth in all its sublime beauty. Scientists are just beginning to understand how finely tuned the universe had to be for stars, planets and life to emerge. Biologists, having mapped the human genome,

◀ are just

are just beginning to understand how complex the human body is. There is wonder here, and the opening sequences of prayer give expression to that wonder in the majestic poetry we call *Pesukei DeZimra*, "the verses of praise." In these poems, mostly taken from the last chapters of *Sefer Tehillim*, we move from creation to the Creator, from the universe to God, Architect of the universe. It is almost as if we were taking a rocket journey into space, seeing the earth in all its beauty while traveling beyond it.

The second stage, beginning with *Barekhu* and ending with *Kaddish Titkabal* after the *Amida*, is *approaching the presence of God*. This is a difficult idea and each of us has to find our own way of thinking about it. Imagine this, for example. You have been invited to meet the President (or King or Queen) of your country. It is a huge honor, and as the day approaches, you find yourself full of excitement. You prepare yourself. You dress in your best clothes. You rehearse exactly how you are going to conduct yourself and what you are going to say. The day comes. You enter the building. You are taken through many rooms and corridors until you finally find yourself face to face with the most powerful person in the country. You have to pinch yourself to make sure that this is really happening; it is not just a dream. Whatever is said and whatever is left unsaid, the memory of that encounter will stay with you for a lifetime.

That, multiplied a billion times over, is what it means to be in the presence of God. Only the fact that we do it several times a day, every day, takes away some of the wonder. Yet that is what is happening when, for example, we say the *Amida*. We are having a direct, personal encounter with the Creator of the universe. God, who has seven billion people to worry about, three million other life forms, and a hundred billion galaxies, *cares about us*, personally and individually. That may just be the most remarkable, empowering idea in the entire history of human thought. We matter. We count. God created us in love, and in love He listens to us as we declare our needs and ask for His help. In that moment we are rescued from insignificance and powerlessness. We are here because we are loved by God Himself. If we are fully open to it – and this may take years of practice and concentration – that encounter is life-changing.

Finally, from the second *Ashrei* to *Aleinu*, we come back down to earth, a little different than we were before we began the journey. We have seen the beauty of the created world. We have had a personal meeting with the

Creator Himself. And now we know there is work to do, because there is much in the world around us that is not as it should be. There is poverty, sickness, loneliness and injustice. People are cruel to one another. There is too much conflict and too little love. God wants us to bring a little of His light into other people's lives. He wants us to become "His partners in the work of creation." He has given us a sacred mission, to show by the way we live that God exists and that His existence makes a difference. Meeting God helps us become, in some small way, a little more like God, by doing acts of *tzedek umishpat, ḥesed veraḥamim*, righteousness and justice, kindness and compassion. We are small; God is great. But by opening ourselves to One so much greater than us, we become greater than we would have been if all we cared about was ourselves.

Those are the three phases of *Shaḥarit*, the Morning Prayer, and they correspond to the three ways in which we come to know God: through *creation* (the universe and its wonders), *revelation* (direct experience of the Divine Presence), and *redemption* (God's work in making the world more loving and just). *Minḥa* and *Ma'ariv*, the Afternoon and Evening prayers, have a somewhat different and more abridged structure.

Prayer matters. It changes the world because it changes us. It brings the Divine Presence into our lives and gives us strength we didn't know we had. It is to the soul (the mind, the self, our inner life) what exercise is to the body. Like exercise, it is important that we do it daily at set times, and like exercise, it makes us healthier (though in a different way) and more highly charged with positive energy. Prayer aligns us with the creative energies that run through the universe, the energies we call life and love, the supreme gifts of God.

So I hope you use this Siddur not just to pray but also to reflect on what we are doing when we pray. May God hear and answer all your prayers, and may we be worthy of the great challenge He has set us: of being His children, His ambassadors, His partners in creating a world worthy of His Presence. May He bless us, helping us to become a blessing to those whose lives we touch.

Rabbi Lord Jonathan Sacks
Ḥanukka 5774 (December 2013)

INTRODUCTION

There is an inherent tension that exists in our form of worship. On the one hand, we are encouraged to pour out our hearts to Hashem in a very personal way, to carry on a private dialogue with Him, to acknowledge His role in our own lives, to confide in Him, to ask for help and support – it is what the Rabbis called *avoda shebalev*, service of the heart – emotional, spontaneous, heartfelt.

On the other hand, for a variety of reasons, prayer has also become a ritual, a standardized fixed text with a myriad number of rules associated with it: what exactly one must say, when one should bow, when to stand or sit, when to speak and when not. At times, it can feel for some like it is entirely *avoda* – service, to be sure, but not a lot of heart.

But the truth is that, as the name indicates, *avoda shebalev* is supposed to be a combination of the two. The text is one that has developed over millennia. It contains unique contributions from almost every major Jewish community in Jewish history, as well as different elements of Jewish philosophy, history, language, law and custom. It is made up of prayers that we are all supposed to say both because of the importance of those contents and because prayer is not only an individual activity but a communal one as well. There is added power, effectiveness and holiness when a community prays together in a single voice. That's the "we're-all-together-on-the-same page" aspect. How, then, does one make one's prayer more personal?

Aside from adding one's own prayers, which one is indeed encouraged to do, one solution lies in the standardized text itself. Certainly, the words of the prayers are supposed to be understood literally but, at the same time, their meaning need not end there. Rather, the words can have almost whatever additional meaning we give them. This is because although the words themselves may not change, we do. Sometimes we are more tired, sometimes more awake, sometimes more in need, sometimes

◀ more thankful

more thankful. Each of us comes to *Tefilla* with different experiences and backgrounds, at different stages of our lives and our development, at different times of the day with different needs, moods and desires. The prayer does not change, but the pray-er does.

And so this commentary and guide has been designed to help you create your own meaning. The prayer book has a particular path that leads to a personal and communal encounter with Hashem – that is why it is called a siddur, from the Hebrew word *seder*, which means order or pattern, making sure that we all get to the same destination together as a community. Each one of the legs of the journey has its own function and style, its own theme and rhythm. But how we experience it along the way, what meaning we take from it or bring to it, is up to each and every one of us.

The commentary for this Siddur is thus divided into different sections, each designed to help connect to the text in a different way. Even so, some of the comments do not easily lend themselves to precise categorization, as the fixed and the fluid, the past and the present, the intellectual and the emotional can meld together as different sides of the same coin.

TRANSLATION

There is first and foremost the accessible and elegant translation of Rabbi Lord Jonathan Sacks, which has been included because gaining fluency in the meanings of words is but one prerequisite for more meaningful prayer.

BIUR TEFILLA – ביאור תפילה

The *Biur Tefilla* helps in gaining a thorough understanding of the text and context of the prayers. It examines the micro-understanding of a specific word or phrase in the text of the *Tefilla*, as well as presenting a wider understanding of the historical background of the *Tefilla*, and its place in the context of the overall structure of the service.

IYYUN TEFILLA – עיון תפילה

Iyyun Tefilla explores the deeper meaning behind the *tefillot*, taking a broader approach to the text. It presents a macro-understanding of the prayers, including philosophical and theological approaches to *Tefilla* in general and the text in particular.

HILKHOT TEFILLA – הלכות תפילה

This section ensures that one is aware of the ritual requirements surrounding the mitzva to pray. These comments are interspersed throughout the Siddur as well as concentrated in an appendix at the back which focuses on the laws of daily prayer and changes that need to be made during the course of the year.

ANI TEFILLA – אני תפילה

The expressed aim of the *Ani Tefilla* sections is to encourage connection to the *tefillot* in a direct and personal way. It is hoped this will be achieved through encouraging the reader to consider the prayers in an experiential way through inspiring and thought-provoking quotes and narratives, as well as through a process of personal creative thinking.

The name for this section derives from a statement made by King David in *Tehillim* 109:4 which says: וַאֲנִי תְפִלָּה. This could be translated as "I pray"; but it could also mean "I am prayer." At its best, prayer is an extension of the person who says it. It is shaped by who you are and what thoughts, emotions, memories, moods, feelings and expression you bring to it. The words of the Siddur, then, are not only to be taken literally, they are also signposts to help generate the range of thoughts and emotions and associations that reside within you on any given day. Think and feel beyond the words.

FREQUENTLY ASKED QUESTIONS

In addition, I have appended a section on frequently asked questions about *Tefilla* that I have heard from students and adults over the years (although adults are unfortunately often much more shy about asking difficult questions). The answers to these questions are purposely brief. They should be considered introductions rather than comprehensive and complete. As Hillel said to the person who wanted to learn the entire Torah at once, "*Tzeh ulmad*, go and learn" (*Shabbat* 30a). For rest assured that during the last two thousand years, you are not the only one to have these questions, and others have no doubt come up with more if not better answers than I.

SOME SUGGESTIONS FOR ENHANCING ONE'S KAVANA

Despite our sincere attempts to make the words more meaningful, there can be times when the demands and distractions of everyday life can

◂ make it

make it difficult to focus. One needs to find ways to recharge one's spiritual batteries. This section contains some practical suggestions from over the ages, for the challenge is not a new one. It faces everyone, even the most practiced and well-intentioned.

TORAH READING

We read the Torah twice a week in order to learn it together anew as a community and to relive the Sinai experience. Unfortunately, in the rush to move on with our day, the message can sometimes get lost. And so, for each *aliya*, I have added a question for your consideration. Sometimes it is to highlight a fact, sometimes the goal is to trigger further thought. Always, the purpose is to help one focus a little more on this, our *Etz Ḥayyim*, our Tree of Life.

SHEMONEH ESREH

This particular prayer is the climax of any service and so it deserves special attention. Especially when one knows the prayer by heart or one is in a particular rush, the words can fly by without getting much consideration. In an attempt to get one to slow down, each blessing has been placed on its own page to encourage greater focus on the words, themes and meaning than one might otherwise apply. Recognizing, too, that one might want to approach this experience in different ways on different days, we have designed three different formats. In *Shaḥarit*, the text appears with a full commentary. In *Minḥa*, the page is otherwise left blank, without commentary, in order to encourage you to direct your own thoughts either through reflection or by actually writing them down or posting them on the page. In *Ma'ariv*, we have provided a traditional continuous format for someone who wishes to say the prayer with greater fluency. Each format can be used for any service although one must be careful to make the appropriate changes when necessary. Ribbons have been supplied to help you keep your place.

AUTHORS CITED

The commentary draws on numerous sources, some traditional, some not. Brief biographies of the authors cited are appended in order to give one a sense of the person in his or her historical context. Every effort has

◂ been made

been made to provide proper attribution. If there have been omissions or errors, please let us know.

BIBLIOGRAPHY

Numerous books and articles have been written on the Siddur and on *Tefilla*. It would be impractical to list them all. Instead, a brief list of some noteworthy books has been added for those who wish to continue learning on their own.

Finally, it is important to note that the comments found throughout this Siddur are not intended to be the only possibilities for understanding or interpretation. Some are my own, some are selected from the numerous commentaries that have been written on or about the Siddur. Ultimately, it is our hope and prayer that you will write your own commentary every day.

> *Tefilla* is expressed in the personality of the individual. If you wish to know something of a person's character – watch him at prayer. (Rav Yehuda Amital, Rosh Yeshivat Har Etzion)

A NOTE ON THE CURRENT EDITION

This is essentially a weekday siddur, intended to help enhance one's prayers on a daily basis, day in and day out. Even so, the lines of demarcation of what constitutes weekday cannot be drawn so precisely since there are so many occasions throughout the year when the text changes to accommodate the Jewish calendar. There have therefore been requests for a siddur that contains these many changes (e.g. Ḥol HaMo'ed, *Seliḥot* and the like), even though they appear infrequently, in order for the siddur to be a steadier companion throughout the year. For now, however, the commentary is focused primarily on the regular daily prayers.

Acknowledgments

To the extent that this work is an outgrowth of my own personal development, I owe a long overdue word of thanks to Rabbi Dr. David Eliach, a master teacher and educator who first inspired me over thirty-five years ago to think and teach beyond the words of the Siddur. My thanks to some of my former students who provided suggestions, encouragement

◂ or feedback

or feedback, especially when I first began thinking about this project. Among them: Gabi Agus, Sarah Emmerich, Eliza Ezrapour, Chloe Fein, Alison Goldberg, Esther Malka Issever, Sara Malamut, Sarah Marlowe, Deborah Pollack, Yossi Quint, Nina Rohr, Ethan Stein, Zach Weiner and Josh Wildes. My thanks go as well to Dr. Scott Goldberg for first involving me in this project and additionally to Dr. David Pelcovitz for his ongoing interest and support of my work. To Mrs. Rivka Kahan, Rabbi Dr. Barry Kislowicz, Rebbetzin Peshi Neuburger and Rabbi Dr. Gil Perl who each provided their own encouragement or support to see this project to its end.

Special thanks to Dr. Daniel Rose, Director of Educational Projects at Koren who served as project coordinator and a welcome virtual *ḥavruta*; his influence, educational sensitivity and editorial contributions can be found in numerous places in this work. Thanks, as well, to Koren editor Rabbi David Fuchs for his meticulous care in reviewing portions of the commentary and making important suggestions for changes in both form and content, to Rachel Meghnagi for her careful editing of my text, and to Esther Be'er for the complicated task of typesetting and making all of the pieces come together. Particular heartfelt thanks to Matthew Miller, Publisher of Koren, whose gracious spirit made itself felt from the moment I met him informally years ago and only further intensified when we became reacquainted only months ago. We are all in his debt for his lasting contribution to the world of Jewish books.

May the prayers that emanate from this Siddur's use be a merit for the memory of my father ז״ל, and my father-in-law ז״ל, and for the continued health of my mother and my mother-in-law whose influence and love have been so profound. To my children and grandchildren who have each provided inspiration in their own inimitable way and whose lives attest to the reality that my prayers are answered. And above all to my wife, whose commitment to *Tefilla* has been an inspiration for all of us and whose ongoing daily support lies at the foundation of all of my work. Rabbi Akiva spoke on behalf of my entire family when he said, "What's mine and yours is really hers."

Rabbi Jay Goldmintz Ed.D.
Teaneck, NJ, 5774 (2014)

THE STRUCTURE OF SHAḤARIT*

Recall that the word Siddur means "arrangement" or "order." To the untrained eye, it may seem like just a random collection of verses and sentences but, in truth, there is an order that is designed to take one on a step-by-step journey toward a rendezvous with God. How all of the pieces fit together is a question to which you can provide your own answer. On this page and the next are the brief outlines of just two possibilities.

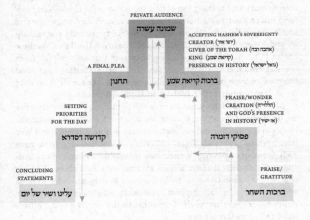

PRIVATE AUDIENCE
שמונה עשרה

ACCEPTING HASHEM'S SOVEREIGNTY
CREATOR (יוצר אור)
GIVER OF THE TORAH (אהבה רבה)
KING (קריאת שמע)
PRESENCE IN HISTORY (גואל ישראל)

A FINAL PLEA
תחנון   ברכות קריאת שמע

PRAISE/WONDER
CREATION (הללויה)
AND GOD'S PRESENCE
IN HISTORY (אז ישיר)

SETTING
PRIORITIES
FOR THE DAY

קדושה דסדרא   פסוקי דזמרה

CONCLUDING
STATEMENTS

עלינו ושיר של יום   ברכות השחר

PRAISE/
GRATITUDE

---

* Based on a diagram conceived by Rabbi Moshe Drelich.

Service of the heart

Rav Shimon Schwab (d. 1995) the leader of the German Jewish community in Washington Heights for close to 40 years, suggests that our "service of the heart" (עבודה שבלב) corresponds to the Service (עבודה) in the *Beit HaMikdash*. All of *Shaḥarit* can therefore be seen as a symbolic path toward a private meeting with God.

What follows is but a brief summary of his more detailed and poetic description.

1. The *Ezrat Nashim* – the place where everyone congregated before the doors opened. Corresponds to things said before *Shaḥarit* begins:
אדון עולם, נטילת ידים, אשר יצר, אלקי נשמה.

2. The 15 steps leading up to the *Ezrat Yisrael*. Corresponds to the 15 ברכות השחר.

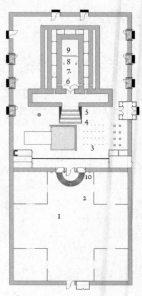

3. The *Ezrat Kohanim*, location of the *Mizbe'aḥ* (Altar). Corresponds to the *Korbanot* section.

4. Steps leading from the *Ezrat Kohanim* to the *Ulam*. The 12 steps plus the platform correspond to the 13 *midot* of Rabbi Yishmael.

5. The *Ulam* or antechamber. Corresponds to *Pesukei DeZimra*.

6. The *Heikhal* or Holy Place, location of the *Shulḥan* and *Menora*. Corresponds to the two blessings before *Shema*, one which focuses on the material world (יוצר אור) and the other on the spiritual (אהבה רבה).

7. The *Mizbe'aḥ HaKetoret* – the Incense Altar, corresponding to the *Shema*.

◄ 8. The *Parokhet*

8. The *Parokhet* – the curtain adjoining the *Kodesh HaKodashim*. Corresponds to the blessing of *geula* which must be attached to *Shemoneh Esreh*.

9. The *Kodesh HaKodashim* – the innermost sanctum where one is alone with God. Corresponds to *Shemoneh Esreh*.

10. At the conclusion of the *Shemoneh Esreh*, we take three steps back, past the *Heikhal*, the *Ulam*, to the *Azara*, where we stop for the Repetition of the *Shemoneh Esreh*.

11. From there we continue backwards, reciting the remainder of the service, finding ourselves back in the *Ezrat Nashim* where we first began our journey.

אני תפילה לימות החול

ANI TEFILLA FOR WEEKDAYS

ימי חול
WEEKDAYS

Shaḥarit

*The following order of prayers and blessings, which departs from that of most prayer books,
is based on the consensus of recent halakhic authorities. See laws 144–152.*

ON WAKING

*On waking, our first thought should be that we are in the presence of God. Since
we are forbidden to speak God's name until we have washed our hands, the
following prayer is said, which, without mentioning God's name, acknowledges
His presence and gives thanks for a new day and for the gift of life.*

מוֹדֶה I thank You, living and eternal King,
for giving me back my soul in mercy.
Great is Your faithfulness.

*Wash hands and say the following blessings.
Some have the custom to say "Wisdom begins" below at this point.*

בָּרוּךְ Blessed are You, Lᴏʀᴅ our God, King of the Universe,
who has made us holy through His commandments,
and has commanded us about washing hands.ᴬᴮᴴ

Some say:

רֵאשִׁית חָכְמָה Wisdom begins in awe of the Lᴏʀᴅ; all who fulfill [His com- *Ps. 111*
mandments] gain good understanding; His praise is ever-lasting. The Torah *Deut. 33*
Moses commanded us is the heritage of the congregation of Jacob. Listen, my *Prov. 1*
son, to your father's instruction, and do not forsake your mother's teaching.
May the Torah be my faith and Almighty God my help. Blessed be the name
of His glorious kingdom for ever and all time.

---

to ourselves that our actions today
must also contain an element of
sanctity.
**How will I use my hands today
to serve a higher purpose?**

HILKHOT TEFILLA · הלכות תפילה
The custom is to say these blessings after wak-
ing in the morning but, if one did not, then they
may be recited before communal services begin.

שחרית

The following order of prayers and blessings, which departs from that of most prayer books,
is based on the consensus of recent halakhic authorities. See laws 144–152.

השכמת הבוקר

On waking, our first thought should be that we are in the presence of God. Since
we are forbidden to speak God's name until we have washed our hands, the
following prayer is said, which, without mentioning God's name, acknowledges
His presence and gives thanks for a new day and for the gift of life.

men מוֹדֶה /women מוֹדָה/ אֲנִי לְפָנֶיךָ מֶלֶךְ חַי וְקַיָּם

שֶׁהֶחֱזַרְתָּ בִּי נִשְׁמָתִי בְּחֶמְלָה

רַבָּה אֱמוּנָתֶךָ.

Wash hands and say the following blessings.
Some have the custom to say רֵאשִׁית חָכְמָה below at this point.

בָּרוּךְ אַתָּה יהוה אֱלֹהֵינוּ מֶלֶךְ הָעוֹלָם

אֲשֶׁר קִדְּשָׁנוּ בְּמִצְוֹתָיו וְצִוָּנוּ עַל נְטִילַת יָדָיִם.אבה

Some say:

רֵאשִׁית חָכְמָה יִרְאַת יהוה, שֵׂכֶל טוֹב לְכָל־עֹשֵׂיהֶם, תְּהִלָּתוֹ עֹמֶדֶת לָעַד: תהלים קיא
תּוֹרָה צִוָּה־לָנוּ מֹשֶׁה, מוֹרָשָׁה קְהִלַּת יַעֲקֹב: שְׁמַע בְּנִי מוּסַר אָבִיךָ וְאַל־תִּטֹּשׁ דברים ל״ג
תּוֹרַת אִמֶּךָ: תּוֹרָה תְּהֵא אֱמוּנָתִי, וְאֵל שַׁדַּי בְּעֶזְרָתִי. בָּרוּךְ שֵׁם כְּבוֹד מַלְכוּתוֹ משלי א׳
לְעוֹלָם וָעֶד.

אני תפילה · ANI TEFILLA

עַל נְטִילַת יָדָיִם — *Washing hands.*
Water is life giving. We wash our hands in the
morning in order to remind ourselves that each
day we are born anew. I am thankful to God to be
able to start all over again (Rashba).

**How would I like my today to be different from
my yesterday?**

ביאור תפילה · BIUR TEFILLA

עַל נְטִילַת יָדָיִם — *Washing hands.*
We wash our hands with a ves-
sel rather than directly from the
faucet, for that is how the *kohanim* did it in the *Beit HaMikdash*
(*Shemot* 30:17-21). We thereby signal

בָּרוּךְ Blessed are You, LORD our God, King of the Universe,
who formed man[IA] in wisdom
and created in him many orifices and cavities.
It is revealed and known before the throne of Your glory
that were one of them to be ruptured or blocked,
it would be impossible to survive and stand before You.
Blessed are You, LORD,
Healer of all flesh who does wondrous deeds.

אֱלֹהַי My God,
the soul[IB] You placed within me is pure.
You created it, You formed it, You breathed it into me,
and You guard it while it is within me.
One day You will take it from me,
and restore it to me in the time to come.
As long as the soul is within me, I will thank You,
LORD my God and God of my ancestors,
Master of all works, LORD of all souls.
Blessed are You, LORD,
who restores souls to lifeless bodies.

בָּרוּךְ אַתָּה יהוה אֱלֹהֵינוּ מֶלֶךְ הָעוֹלָם
אֲשֶׁר יָצַר אֶת הָאָדָם בְּחָכְמָה
וּבָרָא בוֹ נְקָבִים נְקָבִים, חֲלוּלִים חֲלוּלִים.
גָּלוּי וְיָדוּעַ לִפְנֵי כִסֵּא כְבוֹדֶךָ
שֶׁאִם יִפָּתֵחַ אֶחָד מֵהֶם אוֹ יִסָּתֵם אֶחָד מֵהֶם
אִי אֶפְשָׁר לְהִתְקַיֵּם וְלַעֲמֹד לְפָנֶיךָ.
בָּרוּךְ אַתָּה יהוה, רוֹפֵא כָל בָּשָׂר וּמַפְלִיא לַעֲשׂוֹת.

אֱלֹהַי

נְשָׁמָה שֶׁנָּתַתָּ בִּי טְהוֹרָה הִיא.
אַתָּה בְרָאתָהּ, אַתָּה יְצַרְתָּהּ, אַתָּה נְפַחְתָּהּ בִּי
וְאַתָּה מְשַׁמְּרָהּ בְּקִרְבִּי, וְאַתָּה עָתִיד לִטְּלָהּ מִמֶּנִּי
וּלְהַחֲזִירָהּ בִּי לֶעָתִיד לָבוֹא.
כָּל זְמַן שֶׁהַנְּשָׁמָה בְקִרְבִּי, מוֹדֶה/ *men* *women* מוֹדָה/ אֲנִי לְפָנֶיךָ
יהוה אֱלֹהַי וֵאלֹהֵי אֲבוֹתַי
רִבּוֹן כָּל הַמַּעֲשִׂים, אֲדוֹן כָּל הַנְּשָׁמוֹת.
בָּרוּךְ אַתָּה יהוה, הַמַּחֲזִיר נְשָׁמוֹת לִפְגָרִים מֵתִים.

IYUN TEFILLA · עיון תפילה

אֲשֶׁר יָצַר – *Who formed man.* Imagine what it would be like not to be able to go to the bathroom! Imagine the pain or discomfort, the inability to focus on anything else in one's life. And yet for all of its complexity and all of its importance, precisely because it is something that is so natural and so everyday and so private, we take it for granted. And precisely because we have a tendency to take it for granted, the Siddur tries to get us to focus upon it first thing in the morning. Blessings are opportunities to not take life for granted.

ANI TEFILLA · אני תפילה

אֲשֶׁר יָצַר – *Who formed man.*

I could prove God statistically. Take the human body alone – the chances that all the functions of an individual would just happen is a statistical monstrosity.

(Attributed to pollster George Gallup, *Readers Digest*, October 1943)

TZITZIT

The following blessing is said before putting on tzitzit. Neither it nor the subsequent prayer is said by those who wear a tallit. The blessing over the latter exempts the former. See laws 153–159.

בָּרוּךְ Blessed are You, LORD our God, King of the Universe,
who has made us holy through His commandments,
and has commanded us about the command of tasseled garments.

After putting on tzitzit, say:

יְהִי רָצוֹן May it be Your will, LORD my God and God of my ancestors,
that the commandment of the tasseled garment be considered before You
as if I had fulfilled it in all its specifics, details and intentions,
as well as the 613 commandments dependent on it, Amen, Selah.

BLESSINGS OVER THE TORAH

In Judaism, study is greater even than prayer. So, before beginning to pray, we engage in a miniature act of study, preceded by the appropriate blessings. The blessings are followed by brief selections from Scripture, Mishna and Gemara, the three foundational texts of Judaism.

בָּרוּךְ Blessed are You, LORD our God, King of the Universe,
who has made us holy through His commandments,
and has commanded us to engage in study
of the words of Torah.
Please, LORD our God, make the words of Your Torah
sweet in our mouths and in the mouths of Your people,
the house of Israel,
so that we, our descendants (and their descendants)
and the descendants of Your people, the house of Israel,
may all know Your name
and study Your Torah for its own sake.
Blessed are You, LORD, who teaches Torah to His people Israel.

who studied did so for the respect it would bring them or just for the intellectual challenge or for some other reward. As a result, Torah was devalued perhaps in their own eyes as well as in the eyes of others. In our own day, the equivalent might be studying Torah solely for grades or so that others might see us in a particular way. Saying *Birkhot HaTorah* first thing in the morning is thus a reminder that the things we are going to study today are a value in their own right.

לבישת ציצית

The following blessing is said before putting on a טלית קטן. Neither it nor יְהִי רָצון is said
by those who wear a טלית. The blessing over the latter exempts the former. See laws 153–159.

בָּרוּךְ אַתָּה יהוה אֱלֹהֵינוּ מֶלֶךְ הָעוֹלָם
אֲשֶׁר קִדְּשָׁנוּ בְּמִצְוֹתָיו וְצִוָּנוּ עַל מִצְוַת צִיצִת.

After putting on the טלית קטן, say:

יְהִי רָצוֹן מִלְּפָנֶיךָ, יהוה אֱלֹהַי וֵאלֹהֵי אֲבוֹתַי
שֶׁתְּהֵא חֲשׁוּבָה מִצְוַת צִיצִית לְפָנֶיךָ
כְּאִלּוּ קִיַּמְתִּיהָ בְּכָל פְּרָטֶיהָ וְדִקְדּוּקֶיהָ וְכַוָּנוֹתֶיהָ
וְתַרְיַ״ג מִצְוֹת הַתְּלוּיוֹת בָּהּ, אָמֵן סֶלָה.

ברכות התורה[ע]

In Judaism, study is greater even than prayer. So, before beginning to pray, we engage in a
miniature act of study, preceded by the appropriate blessings. The blessings are followed
by brief selections from תנ״ך, משנה and גמרא, the three foundational texts of Judaism.

בָּרוּךְ אַתָּה יהוה אֱלֹהֵינוּ מֶלֶךְ הָעוֹלָם
אֲשֶׁר קִדְּשָׁנוּ בְּמִצְוֹתָיו וְצִוָּנוּ לַעֲסֹק בְּדִבְרֵי תוֹרָה.
וְהַעֲרֶב נָא יהוה אֱלֹהֵינוּ אֶת דִּבְרֵי תוֹרָתְךָ
בְּפִינוּ וּבְפִי עַמְּךָ בֵּית יִשְׂרָאֵל
וְנִהְיֶה אֲנַחְנוּ וְצֶאֱצָאֵינוּ (וְצֶאֱצָאֵי צֶאֱצָאֵינוּ)
וְצֶאֱצָאֵי עַמְּךָ בֵּית יִשְׂרָאֵל
כֻּלָּנוּ יוֹדְעֵי שְׁמֶךָ וְלוֹמְדֵי תוֹרָתֶךָ לִשְׁמָהּ.
בָּרוּךְ אַתָּה יהוה, הַמְלַמֵּד תּוֹרָה לְעַמּוֹ יִשְׂרָאֵל.

IYUN TEFILLA • עיון תפילה

ברכות התורה – *Blessings over the Torah.*
Rabbi.Yehuda (*Nedarim* 81a) claims that the
Beit HaMikdash was destroyed because
people did not recite the *Birkhot HaTorah*
before they learned. Why such a huge

consequence for such a seemingly small
omission? Rabbeinu Yona suggests that it
was because the lack of a recitation of the
blessing means that Torah was not being
studied as a religious value. Perhaps those

בָּרוּךְ Blessed are You, LORD our God, King of the Universe,
who has chosen us from all the peoples
and given us His Torah.
Blessed are You, LORD, Giver of the Torah.

יְבָרֶכְךָ May the LORD bless you[B] and protect you.   *Num. 6*
May the LORD make His face shine on you
and be gracious to you.
May the LORD turn His face toward you
and grant you peace.

אֵלּוּ These are the things   *Mishna*
for which there is no fixed measure: *Pe'ah 1:1*
    the corner of the field, first-fruits,
    appearances before the LORD
    [on festivals, with offerings],
    acts of kindness and the study of Torah.

אֵלּוּ These are the things   *Shabbat*
whose fruits we eat in this world   *127a*
but whose full reward awaits us
in the World to Come:
    honoring parents; acts of kindness;
    arriving early at the house of study
    morning and evening;
    hospitality to strangers; visiting the sick;
    helping the needy bride; attending to the dead;
    devotion in prayer;
    and bringing peace between people –
but the study of Torah is equal to them all.

---

ately after the recitation of the blessing. The next three paragraphs thus represent selections respectively from Torah, Mishna, and Gemara, thereby symbolically incorporating all of the Written Torah and the Oral Torah into our learning – for its own sake.

בָּרוּךְ אַתָּה יהוה אֱלֹהֵינוּ מֶלֶךְ הָעוֹלָם
אֲשֶׁר בָּחַר בָּנוּ מִכָּל הָעַמִּים
וְנָתַן לָנוּ אֶת תּוֹרָתוֹ.
בָּרוּךְ אַתָּה יהוה, נוֹתֵן הַתּוֹרָה.

במדבר ו

יְבָרֶכְךָ יהוה וְיִשְׁמְרֶךָ:
יָאֵר יהוה פָּנָיו אֵלֶיךָ וִיחֻנֶּךָּ:
יִשָּׂא יהוה פָּנָיו אֵלֶיךָ וְיָשֵׂם לְךָ שָׁלוֹם:

משנה,
פאה א: א

אֵלּוּ דְבָרִים שֶׁאֵין לָהֶם שִׁעוּר
הַפֵּאָה וְהַבִּכּוּרִים וְהָרְאָיוֹן
וּגְמִילוּת חֲסָדִים וְתַלְמוּד תּוֹרָה.

שבת קכז.

אֵלּוּ דְבָרִים שֶׁאָדָם אוֹכֵל פֵּרוֹתֵיהֶם בָּעוֹלָם הַזֶּה
וְהַקֶּרֶן קַיֶּמֶת לוֹ לָעוֹלָם הַבָּא
וְאֵלּוּ הֵן
כִּבּוּד אָב וָאֵם, וּגְמִילוּת חֲסָדִים
וְהַשְׁכָּמַת בֵּית הַמִּדְרָשׁ שַׁחֲרִית וְעַרְבִית
וְהַכְנָסַת אוֹרְחִים, וּבִקּוּר חוֹלִים
וְהַכְנָסַת כַּלָּה, וּלְוָיַת הַמֵּת
וְעִיּוּן תְּפִלָּה
וַהֲבָאַת שָׁלוֹם בֵּין אָדָם לַחֲבֵרוֹ
וְתַלְמוּד תּוֹרָה כְּנֶגֶד כֻּלָּם.

BIUR TEFILLA · ביאור תפילה

יְבָרֶכְךָ יהוה – *May the Lord bless you.* We just recited blessings over Torah study. In order

to ensure that the blessings not be in vain, the custom is to "learn" some Torah immedi-

TALLIT

Say the following meditation before putting on the tallit. Meditations before the fulfillment of mitzvot are to ensure that we do so with the requisite intention (kavana). This particularly applies to mitzvot whose purpose is to induce in us certain states of mind, as is the case with tallit and tefillin, both of which are external symbols of inward commitment to the life of observance of the mitzvot.

בָּרְכִי נַפְשִׁי Bless the LORD, my soul. LORD, my God, You are very great, *Ps. 104*
clothed in majesty and splendor, wrapped in a robe of light, spreading
out the heavens like a tent.

Some say:

For the sake of the unification of the Holy One, blessed be He, and His Divine
Presence, in reverence and love, to unify the name *Yod-Heh* with *Vav-Heh* in perfect
unity in the name of all Israel.

I am about to wrap myself in this tasseled garment (tallit). So may my soul, my 248
limbs and 365 sinews be wrapped in the light of the tassel (*hatzitzit*) which amounts
to 613 [commandments]. And just as I cover myself with a tasseled garment in this
world, so may I be worthy of rabbinical dress and a fine garment in the World to
Come in the Garden of Eden. Through the commandment of tassels may my life's-
breath, spirit, soul and prayer be delivered from external impediments, and may the
tallit spread its wings over them like an eagle stirring up its nest, hovering over its *Deut. 32*
young. May the commandment of the tasseled garment be considered before the
Holy One, blessed be He, as if I had fulfilled it in all its specifics, details and intentions, as well as the 613 commandments dependent on it, Amen, Selah.

Before wrapping oneself in the tallit, say:

בָּרוּךְ Blessed are You, LORD our God, King of the Universe,
who has made us holy through His commandments,
and has commanded us to wrap ourselves
in the tasseled garment.

*According to the Shela (R. Isaiah Horowitz), one should say
these verses after wrapping oneself in the tallit:*

מַה־יָּקָר How precious is Your loving-kindness, O God, *Ps. 36*
and the children of men find refuge under the shadow of Your wings.
They are filled with the rich plenty of Your House.
You give them drink from Your river of delights.
For with You is the fountain of life; in Your light, we see light.
Continue Your loving-kindness to those who know You,
and Your righteousness to the upright in heart.

עטיפת טלית

Say the following meditation before putting on the טלית. *Meditations before the fulfillment of* מצות *are to ensure that we do so with the requisite intention* (כונה). *This particularly applies to* מצות *whose purpose is to induce in us certain states of mind, as is the case with* טלית *and* תפילין, *both of which are external symbols of inward commitment to the life of observance of the* מצות.

תהלים קד

בָּרְכִי נַפְשִׁי אֶת־יהוה, יהוה אֱלֹהַי גָּדַלְתָּ מְּאֹד, הוֹד וְהָדָר לָבָשְׁתָּ:
עֹטֶה־אוֹר כַּשַּׂלְמָה, נוֹטֶה שָׁמַיִם כַּיְרִיעָה:

Some say:

לְשֵׁם יִחוּד קֻדְשָׁא בְּרִיךְ הוּא וּשְׁכִינְתֵּהּ בִּדְחִילוּ וּרְחִימוּ, לְיַחֵד שֵׁם י״ה בו״ה בְּיִחוּדָא שְׁלִים בְּשֵׁם כָּל יִשְׂרָאֵל.

הֲרֵינִי מִתְעַטֵּף בַּצִּיצִית. כֵּן תִּתְעַטֵּף נִשְׁמָתִי וּרְמַ״ח אֵבָרַי וּשְׁסַ״ה גִידַי בְּאוֹר הַצִּיצִית הָעוֹלָה תַּרְיַ״ג. וּכְשֵׁם שֶׁאֲנִי מִתְכַּסֶּה בְּטַלִּית בָּעוֹלָם הַזֶּה, כָּךְ אֶזְכֶּה לַחֲלוּקָא דְרַבָּנָן וּלְטַלִּית נָאֶה לָעוֹלָם הַבָּא בְּגַן עֵדֶן. וְעַל יְדֵי מִצְוַת צִיצִית תִּצַּל נַפְשִׁי רוּחִי וְנִשְׁמָתִי וּתְפִלָּתִי מִן הַחִיצוֹנִים. וְהַטַּלִּית תִּפְרֹשׂ כְּנָפֶיהָ עֲלֵיהֶם וְתַצִּילֵם,

דברים לב

כְּנֶשֶׁר יָעִיר קִנּוֹ, עַל גּוֹזָלָיו יְרַחֵף: וּתְהֵא חֲשׁוּבָה מִצְוַת צִיצִית לִפְנֵי הַקָּדוֹשׁ בָּרוּךְ הוּא, כְּאִלּוּ קִיַּמְתִּיהָ בְּכָל פְּרָטֶיהָ וְדִקְדּוּקֶיהָ וְכַוָּנוֹתֶיהָ וְתַרְיַ״ג מִצְוֹת הַתְּלוּיוֹת בָּהּ, אָמֵן סֶלָה.

Before wrapping oneself in the טלית, *say:*

בָּרוּךְ אַתָּה יהוה אֱלֹהֵינוּ מֶלֶךְ הָעוֹלָם
אֲשֶׁר קִדְּשָׁנוּ בְּמִצְוֹתָיו וְצִוָּנוּ לְהִתְעַטֵּף בַּצִּיצִית.

According to the Shela (R. Isaiah Horowitz), one should say these verses after wrapping oneself in the טלית:

תהלים לו

מַה־יָּקָר חַסְדְּךָ אֱלֹהִים, וּבְנֵי אָדָם בְּצֵל כְּנָפֶיךָ יֶחֱסָיוּן:
יִרְוְיֻן מִדֶּשֶׁן בֵּיתֶךָ, וְנַחַל עֲדָנֶיךָ תַשְׁקֵם:
כִּי־עִמְּךָ מְקוֹר חַיִּים, בְּאוֹרְךָ נִרְאֶה־אוֹר:
מְשֹׁךְ חַסְדְּךָ לְיֹדְעֶיךָ, וְצִדְקָתְךָ לְיִשְׁרֵי־לֵב:

TEFILLIN[H]

Some say the following meditation before putting on the tefillin.

For the sake of the unification of the Holy One, blessed be He, and His Divine Presence, in reverence and love, to unify the name *Yod-Heh* with *Vav-Heh* in perfect unity in the name of all Israel.

By putting on the tefillin I hereby intend to fulfill the commandment of my Creator who commanded us to wear tefillin, as it is written in His Torah: "Bind them as a sign on your hand, and they shall be an emblem *Deut. 6* on the center of your head." They contain these four sections of the Torah: one beginning with *Shema* [Deut. 6:4–9]; another with *Vehaya im shamo'a* [ibid. 11:13–21]; the third with *Kadesh Li* [Ex. 13:1–10]; and the fourth with *Vehaya ki yevi'akha* [ibid. 13:11–16]. These proclaim the uniqueness and unity of God, blessed be His name in the world. They also remind us of the miracles and wonders which He did for us when He brought us out of Egypt, and that He has the power and the dominion over the highest and the lowest to deal with them as He pleases. He commanded us to place one of the tefillin on the arm in memory of His "outstretched arm" (of redemption), setting it opposite the heart, to subject the desires and designs of our heart to His service, blessed be His name. The other is to be on the head, opposite the brain, so that my mind, whose seat is in the brain, together with my other senses and faculties, may be subjected to His service, blessed be His name. May the spiritual influence of the commandment of the tefillin be with me so that I may have a long life, a flow of holiness, and sacred thoughts, free from any suggestion of sin or iniquity. May the evil inclination neither incite nor entice us, but leave us to serve the LORD, as it is in our hearts to do.

And may it be Your will, LORD our God and God of our ancestors, that the commandment of tefillin be considered before You as if I had fulfilled it in all its specifics, details and intentions, as well as the 613 commandments dependent on it, Amen, Selah.

an idea and to have that idea realized. Speaking between placement of the two is prohibited by halakha (*Orah Hayyim* 25:9) because this interruption represents a dis-connect between thought and action. Many Jews express identification with Judaism, but they do not act as Jews, reflecting this very difference. (Rabbi Soloveitchik)

הַנָּחַת תְּפִילִין

Some say the following meditation before putting on the תפילין.

לְשֵׁם יִחוּד קֻדְשָׁא בְּרִיךְ הוּא וּשְׁכִינְתֵּהּ בִּדְחִילוּ וּרְחִימוּ, לְיַחֵד שֵׁם י״ה בּו״ה בְּיִחוּדָא שְׁלִים בְּשֵׁם כָּל יִשְׂרָאֵל.

הִנְנִי מְכַוֵּן בַּהֲנָחַת תְּפִילִין לְקַיֵּם מִצְוַת בּוֹרְאִי, שֶׁצִּוָּנוּ לְהָנִיחַ תְּפִילִין, כַּכָּתוּב בְּתוֹרָתוֹ: וּקְשַׁרְתָּם לְאוֹת עַל יָדֶךָ, וְהָיוּ לְטֹטָפֹת בֵּין עֵינֶיךָ: וְהֵן אַרְבַּע פָּרָשִׁיּוֹת אֵלּוּ, שְׁמַע, וְהָיָה אִם שָׁמֹעַ, קַדֶּשׁ לִי, וְהָיָה כִּי יְבִאֲךָ, שֶׁיֵּשׁ בָּהֶם יִחוּדוֹ וְאַחְדּוּתוֹ יִתְבָּרַךְ שְׁמוֹ בָּעוֹלָם, וְשֶׁנִּזְכּוֹר נִסִּים וְנִפְלָאוֹת שֶׁעָשָׂה עִמָּנוּ בְּהוֹצִיאוֹ אוֹתָנוּ מִמִּצְרָיִם, וַאֲשֶׁר לוֹ הַכֹּחַ וְהַמֶּמְשָׁלָה בָּעֶלְיוֹנִים וּבַתַּחְתּוֹנִים לַעֲשׂוֹת בָּהֶם כִּרְצוֹנוֹ. וְצִוָּנוּ לְהָנִיחַ עַל הַיָּד לְזִכָּרוֹן זְרוֹעַ הַנְּטוּיָה, וְשֶׁהִיא נֶגֶד הַלֵּב, לְשַׁעְבֵּד בָּזֶה תַּאֲוֹת וּמַחְשְׁבוֹת לִבֵּנוּ לַעֲבוֹדָתוֹ יִתְבָּרַךְ שְׁמוֹ. וְעַל הָרֹאשׁ נֶגֶד הַמֹּחַ, שֶׁהַנְּשָׁמָה שֶׁבְּמֹחִי עִם שְׁאָר חוּשַׁי וְכֹחוֹתַי כֻּלָּם יִהְיוּ מְשֻׁעְבָּדִים לַעֲבוֹדָתוֹ, יִתְבָּרַךְ שְׁמוֹ. וּמִשֶּׁפַע מִצְוַת תְּפִילִין יִתְמַשֵּׁךְ עָלַי לִהְיוֹת לִי חַיִּים אֲרוּכִים וְשֶׁפַע קֹדֶשׁ וּמַחְשָׁבוֹת קְדוֹשׁוֹת בְּלִי הִרְהוּר חֵטְא וְעָוֹן כְּלָל, וְשֶׁלֹּא יְפַתֵּנוּ וְלֹא יִתְגָּרֶה בָּנוּ יֵצֶר הָרָע, וְיַנִּיחֵנוּ לַעֲבֹד אֶת יהוה כַּאֲשֶׁר עִם לְבָבֵנוּ.

וִיהִי רָצוֹן מִלְּפָנֶיךָ, יהוה אֱלֹהֵינוּ וֵאלֹהֵי אֲבוֹתֵינוּ, שֶׁתְּהֵא חֲשׁוּבָה מִצְוַת הֲנָחַת תְּפִילִין לִפְנֵי הַקָּדוֹשׁ בָּרוּךְ הוּא, כְּאִלּוּ קִיַּמְתִּיהָ בְּכָל פְּרָטֶיהָ וְדִקְדּוּקֶיהָ וְכַוָּנוֹתֶיהָ וְתַרְיַ״ג מִצְוֹת הַתְּלוּיוֹת בָּהּ, אָמֵן סֶלָה.

HILKHOT TEFILLA · הלכות תפילה

הֲנָחַת תְּפִילִין *– Tefillin.* In Ashkenazic practice, the two tefillin each have their own blessing because each one represents something different. The one for the arm represents

the world of action; the one for the head, the world of thought. The success of man is actualized through the merging of thought and action, through his ability to conceive

דברים ו

*Stand and place the hand-tefillin on the biceps of the left arm (or right arm if you
are left-handed), angled toward the heart, and before tightening the strap, say:*

בָּרוּךְ Blessed are You, LORD our God, King of the Universe,
who has made us holy through His commandments,
and has commanded us to put on tefillin.

*Wrap the strap of the hand-tefillin seven times around the arm.
Place the head-tefillin above the hairline, centered between the eyes, and say quietly:*

בָּרוּךְ Blessed are You, LORD our God, King of the Universe,
who has made us holy through His commandments,
and has commanded us about the commandment of tefillin.

Adjust the head-tefillin and say:

בָּרוּךְ Blessed be the name of His glorious kingdom
for ever and all time.

Some say:
From Your wisdom, God most high, grant me [wisdom],
and from Your understanding, give me understanding.
May Your loving-kindness be greatly upon me,
and in Your might may my enemies and those who rise against me be subdued.
Pour Your goodly oil on the seven branches of the menora
so that Your good flows down upon Your creatures.
You open Your hand, and satisfy every living thing with favor.   *Ps. 145*

Wind the strap of the hand-tefillin three times around the middle finger, saying:

וְאֵרַשְׂתִּיךְ I will betroth you to Me for ever;   *Hos. 2*
I will betroth you to Me in righteousness and justice,
loving-kindness and compassion;
I will betroth you to Me in faithfulness;
and you shall know the LORD.

After putting on the tefillin, say the following:

וַיְדַבֵּר The LORD spoke to Moses, saying, "Consecrate to Me every   *Ex. 13*
firstborn male. The first offspring of every womb among the Israelites,
whether man or beast, belongs to Me." Then Moses said to the people,

Stand and place the תפילין של יד *on the biceps of the left arm (or right arm if you are left-handed), angled toward the heart, and before tightening the strap, say:*

בָּרוּךְ אַתָּה יהוה אֱלֹהֵינוּ מֶלֶךְ הָעוֹלָם
אֲשֶׁר קִדְּשָׁנוּ בְּמִצְוֹתָיו
וְצִוָּנוּ לְהָנִיחַ תְּפִלִּין.

Wrap the strap of the תפילין של יד *seven times around the arm.*
Place the תפילין של ראש *above the hairline, centered between the eyes, and say quietly:*

בָּרוּךְ אַתָּה יהוה אֱלֹהֵינוּ מֶלֶךְ הָעוֹלָם
אֲשֶׁר קִדְּשָׁנוּ בְּמִצְוֹתָיו
וְצִוָּנוּ עַל מִצְוַת תְּפִלִּין.

Adjust the תפילין של ראש *and say:*

בָּרוּךְ שֵׁם כְּבוֹד מַלְכוּתוֹ לְעוֹלָם וָעֶד

Some say:

וּמֵחָכְמָתְךָ אֵל עֶלְיוֹן תַּאֲצִיל עָלַי, וּמִבִּינָתְךָ תְּבִינֵנִי
וּבְחַסְדְּךָ תַּגְדִּיל עָלַי, וּבִגְבוּרָתְךָ תַּצְמִית אוֹיְבַי וְקָמַי.
וְשֶׁמֶן הַטּוֹב תָּרִיק עַל שִׁבְעָה קְנֵי הַמְּנוֹרָה
לְהַשְׁפִּיעַ טוּבְךָ לִבְרִיּוֹתֶיךָ.
פּוֹתֵחַ אֶת־יָדֶךָ וּמַשְׂבִּיעַ לְכָל־חַי רָצוֹן:

תהלים
קמה

Wind the strap of the תפילין של יד *three times around the middle finger, saying:*

וְאֵרַשְׂתִּיךְ לִי לְעוֹלָם
וְאֵרַשְׂתִּיךְ לִי בְּצֶדֶק וּבְמִשְׁפָּט וּבְחֶסֶד וּבְרַחֲמִים:
וְאֵרַשְׂתִּיךְ לִי בֶּאֱמוּנָה, וְיָדַעַתְּ אֶת־יהוה:

הושע ב

After putting on the תפילין, *say the following:*

וַיְדַבֵּר יהוה אֶל־מֹשֶׁה לֵּאמֹר: קַדֶּשׁ־לִי כָל־בְּכוֹר, פֶּטֶר כָּל־רֶחֶם
בִּבְנֵי יִשְׂרָאֵל, בָּאָדָם וּבַבְּהֵמָה, לִי הוּא: וַיֹּאמֶר מֹשֶׁה אֶל־הָעָם,

שמות יג

"Remember this day on which you left Egypt, the slave-house, when the Lord brought you out of it with a mighty hand. No leaven shall be eaten. You are leaving on this day, in the month of Aviv. When the Lord brings you into the land of the Canaanites, Hittites, Amorites, Hivites and Jebusites, the land He swore to your ancestors to give you, a land flowing with milk and honey, you are to observe this service in this same month. For seven days you shall eat unleavened bread, and make the seventh day a festival to the Lord. Unleavened bread shall be eaten throughout the seven days. No leavened bread may be seen in your possession, and no leaven shall be seen anywhere within your borders. On that day you shall tell your son, 'This is because of what the Lord did for me when I left Egypt.' [These words] shall also be a sign on your hand, and a reminder above your forehead, so that the Lord's Torah may always be in your mouth, because with a mighty hand the Lord brought you out of Egypt. You shall therefore keep this statute at its appointed time from year to year."

וְהָיָה After the Lord has brought you into the land of the Canaanites, as He swore to you and your ancestors, and He has given it to you, you shall set apart for the Lord the first offspring of every womb. All the firstborn males of your cattle belong to the Lord. Every firstling donkey you shall redeem with a lamb. If you do not redeem it, you must break its neck. Every firstborn among your sons you must redeem. If, in time to come, your son asks you, "What does this mean?" you shall say to him, "With a mighty hand the Lord brought us out of Egypt, out of the slave-house. When Pharaoh stubbornly refused to let us leave, the Lord killed all the firstborn in the land of Egypt, both man and beast. That is why I sacrifice to the Lord the first male offspring of every womb, and redeem all the firstborn of my sons." [These words] shall be a sign on your hand and as an emblem above your forehead, that with a mighty hand the Lord brought us out of Egypt.

זָכוֹר אֶת־הַיּוֹם הַזֶּה, אֲשֶׁר יְצָאתֶם מִמִּצְרַיִם מִבֵּית עֲבָדִים, כִּי בְּחֹזֶק יָד הוֹצִיא יהוה אֶתְכֶם מִזֶּה, וְלֹא יֵאָכֵל חָמֵץ: הַיּוֹם אַתֶּם יֹצְאִים, בְּחֹדֶשׁ הָאָבִיב: וְהָיָה כִי־יְבִיאֲךָ יהוה אֶל־אֶרֶץ הַכְּנַעֲנִי וְהַחִתִּי וְהָאֱמֹרִי וְהַחִוִּי וְהַיְבוּסִי, אֲשֶׁר נִשְׁבַּע לַאֲבֹתֶיךָ לָתֶת לָךְ, אֶרֶץ זָבַת חָלָב וּדְבָשׁ, וְעָבַדְתָּ אֶת־הָעֲבֹדָה הַזֹּאת בַּחֹדֶשׁ הַזֶּה: שִׁבְעַת יָמִים תֹּאכַל מַצֹּת, וּבַיּוֹם הַשְּׁבִיעִי חַג לַיהוה: מַצּוֹת יֵאָכֵל אֵת שִׁבְעַת הַיָּמִים, וְלֹא־יֵרָאֶה לְךָ חָמֵץ וְלֹא־יֵרָאֶה לְךָ שְׂאֹר, בְּכָל־גְּבֻלֶךָ: וְהִגַּדְתָּ לְבִנְךָ בַּיּוֹם הַהוּא לֵאמֹר, בַּעֲבוּר זֶה עָשָׂה יהוה לִי בְּצֵאתִי מִמִּצְרָיִם: וְהָיָה לְךָ לְאוֹת עַל־יָדְךָ וּלְזִכָּרוֹן בֵּין עֵינֶיךָ, לְמַעַן תִּהְיֶה תּוֹרַת יהוה בְּפִיךָ, כִּי בְּיָד חֲזָקָה הוֹצִאֲךָ יהוה מִמִּצְרָיִם: וְשָׁמַרְתָּ אֶת־הַחֻקָּה הַזֹּאת לְמוֹעֲדָהּ, מִיָּמִים יָמִימָה:

וְהָיָה כִּי־יְבִאֲךָ יהוה אֶל־אֶרֶץ הַכְּנַעֲנִי כַּאֲשֶׁר נִשְׁבַּע לְךָ וְלַאֲבֹתֶיךָ, וּנְתָנָהּ לָךְ: וְהַעֲבַרְתָּ כָל־פֶּטֶר־רֶחֶם לַיהוה, וְכָל־פֶּטֶר שֶׁגֶר בְּהֵמָה אֲשֶׁר יִהְיֶה לְךָ הַזְּכָרִים, לַיהוה: וְכָל־פֶּטֶר חֲמֹר תִּפְדֶּה בְשֶׂה, וְאִם־לֹא תִפְדֶּה וַעֲרַפְתּוֹ, וְכֹל בְּכוֹר אָדָם בְּבָנֶיךָ תִּפְדֶּה: וְהָיָה כִּי־יִשְׁאָלְךָ בִנְךָ מָחָר, לֵאמֹר מַה־זֹּאת, וְאָמַרְתָּ אֵלָיו, בְּחֹזֶק יָד הוֹצִיאָנוּ יהוה מִמִּצְרַיִם מִבֵּית עֲבָדִים: וַיְהִי כִּי־הִקְשָׁה פַרְעֹה לְשַׁלְּחֵנוּ, וַיַּהֲרֹג יהוה כָּל־בְּכוֹר בְּאֶרֶץ מִצְרַיִם, מִבְּכֹר אָדָם וְעַד־בְּכוֹר בְּהֵמָה, עַל־כֵּן אֲנִי זֹבֵחַ לַיהוה כָּל־פֶּטֶר רֶחֶם הַזְּכָרִים, וְכָל־בְּכוֹר בָּנַי אֶפְדֶּה: וְהָיָה לְאוֹת עַל־יָדְכָה וּלְטוֹטָפֹת בֵּין עֵינֶיךָ, כִּי בְּחֹזֶק יָד הוֹצִיאָנוּ יהוה מִמִּצְרָיִם:

PREPARATION FOR PRAYER

On entering the synagogue:

HOW GOODLY

Num. 24

are your tents, Jacob, your dwelling places, Israel.
As for me,

Ps. 5

in Your great loving-kindness,
I will come into Your House.
I will bow down to Your holy Temple
in awe of You.
Lord, I love the habitation of Your House,

Ps. 26

the place where Your glory dwells.

As for me,
I will bow in worship;

> I will bend the knee
> before the Lord my Maker.

As for me,
may my prayer come to You, Lord,

Ps. 69

> at a time of favor.
> God, in Your great loving-kindness,
> answer me with Your faithful salvation.

הכנה לתפילה

On entering the בית כנסת:

במדבר כד

מַה־טֹּבוּ

אֹהָלֶיךָ יַעֲקֹב, מִשְׁכְּנֹתֶיךָ יִשְׂרָאֵל:

תהלים ה

וַאֲנִי בְּרֹב חַסְדְּךָ אָבוֹא בֵיתֶךָ
אֶשְׁתַּחֲוֶה אֶל־הֵיכַל־קָדְשְׁךָ
בְּיִרְאָתֶךָ:

תהלים כו

יהוה אָהַבְתִּי מְעוֹן בֵּיתֶךָ
וּמְקוֹם מִשְׁכַּן כְּבוֹדֶךָ:

וַאֲנִי אֶשְׁתַּחֲוֶה

וְאֶכְרָעָה
אֲבָרְכָה לִפְנֵי יהוה עֹשִׂי.

וַאֲנִי תְפִלָּתִי־לְךָ יהוה

תהלים סט

עֵת רָצוֹן
אֱלֹהִים בְּרָב־חַסְדֶּךָ
עֲנֵנִי בֶּאֱמֶת יִשְׁעֶךָ:

The following poems, on this page and the next, both from the Middle Ages,
are summary statements of Jewish faith, orienting us to the spiritual contours
of the world that we actualize in the mind by the act of prayer.

LORD OF THE UNIVERSE,
who reigned before the birth of any thing –

When by His will all things were made
then was His name proclaimed King.

And when all things shall cease to be
He alone will reign in awe.

He was, He is, and He shall be
glorious for evermore.

He is One, there is none else,
alone, unique, beyond compare;

Without beginning, without end,
His might, His rule are everywhere.

He is my God; my Redeemer lives.
He is the Rock on whom I rely –

My banner and my safe retreat,
my cup, my portion when I cry.

Into His hand my soul I place,
when I awake and when I sleep.

The LORD is with me, I shall not fear;
body and soul from harm will He keep.

The following poems, on this page and the next, both from the Middle Ages,
are summary statements of Jewish faith, orienting us to the spiritual contours
of the world that we actualize in the mind by the act of prayer.

אֲדוֹן עוֹלָם

אֲשֶׁר מָלַךְ בְּטֶרֶם כָּל־יְצִיר נִבְרָא.

לְעֵת נַעֲשָׂה בְחֶפְצוֹ כֹּל אֲזַי מֶלֶךְ שְׁמוֹ נִקְרָא.

וְאַחֲרֵי כִּכְלוֹת הַכֹּל לְבַדּוֹ יִמְלֹךְ נוֹרָא.

וְהוּא הָיָה וְהוּא הֹוֶה וְהוּא יִהְיֶה בְּתִפְאָרָה.

וְהוּא אֶחָד וְאֵין שֵׁנִי לְהַמְשִׁיל לוֹ לְהַחְבִּירָה.

בְּלִי רֵאשִׁית בְּלִי תַכְלִית וְלוֹ הָעֹז וְהַמִּשְׂרָה.

וְהוּא אֵלִי וְחַי גּוֹאֲלִי וְצוּר חֶבְלִי בְּעֵת צָרָה.

וְהוּא נִסִּי וּמָנוֹס לִי מְנָת כּוֹסִי בְּיוֹם אֶקְרָא.

בְּיָדוֹ אַפְקִיד רוּחִי בְּעֵת אִישָׁן וְאָעִירָה.

וְעִם רוּחִי גְּוִיָּתִי יהוה לִי וְלֹא אִירָא.

GREAT

is the living God and praised.
He exists, and His existence is beyond time.

He is One, and there is no unity like His.
Unfathomable, His oneness is infinite.

He has neither bodily form nor substance;
His holiness is beyond compare.

He preceded all that was created.
He was first: there was no beginning to His beginning.

Behold He is Master of the Universe; and every creature
shows His greatness and majesty.

The rich flow of His prophecy He gave
to His treasured people in whom He gloried.

Never in Israel has there arisen another like Moses,
a prophet who beheld God's image.

God gave His people a Torah of truth
by the hand of His prophet, most faithful of His House.

God will not alter or change His law
for any other, for eternity.

He sees and knows our secret thoughts;
as soon as something is begun, He foresees its end.

He rewards people with loving-kindness according to their deeds;
He punishes the wicked according to his wickedness.

At the end of days He will send our Messiah
to redeem those who await His final salvation.

God will revive the dead in His great loving-kindness.
Blessed for evermore is His glorious name!

יִגְדַּל

אֱלֹהִים חַי וְיִשְׁתַּבַּח, נִמְצָא וְאֵין עֵת אֶל מְצִיאוּתוֹ.

אֶחָד וְאֵין יָחִיד כְּיִחוּדוֹ, נֶעְלָם וְגַם אֵין סוֹף לְאַחְדוּתוֹ.

אֵין לוֹ דְּמוּת הַגּוּף וְאֵינוֹ גוּף, לֹא נַעֲרֹךְ אֵלָיו קְדֻשָּׁתוֹ.

קַדְמוֹן לְכָל דָּבָר אֲשֶׁר נִבְרָא, רִאשׁוֹן וְאֵין רֵאשִׁית לְרֵאשִׁיתוֹ.

הִנּוֹ אֲדוֹן עוֹלָם, וְכָל נוֹצָר יוֹרֶה גְדֻלָּתוֹ וּמַלְכוּתוֹ.

שֶׁפַע נְבוּאָתוֹ נְתָנוֹ אֶל־אַנְשֵׁי סְגֻלָּתוֹ וְתִפְאַרְתּוֹ.

לֹא קָם בְּיִשְׂרָאֵל כְּמֹשֶׁה עוֹד נָבִיא וּמַבִּיט אֶת תְּמוּנָתוֹ.

תּוֹרַת אֱמֶת נָתַן לְעַמּוֹ אֵל עַל יַד נְבִיאוֹ נֶאֱמַן בֵּיתוֹ.

לֹא יַחֲלִיף הָאֵל וְלֹא יָמִיר דָּתוֹ לְעוֹלָמִים לְזוּלָתוֹ.

צוֹפֶה וְיוֹדֵעַ סְתָרֵינוּ, מַבִּיט לְסוֹף דָּבָר בְּקַדְמָתוֹ.

גּוֹמֵל לְאִישׁ חֶסֶד כְּמִפְעָלוֹ, נוֹתֵן לְרָשָׁע רָע כְּרִשְׁעָתוֹ.

יִשְׁלַח לְקֵץ יָמִין מְשִׁיחֵנוּ לִפְדוֹת מְחַכֵּי קֵץ יְשׁוּעָתוֹ.

מֵתִים יְחַיֶּה אֵל בְּרֹב חַסְדּוֹ, בָּרוּךְ עֲדֵי עַד שֵׁם תְּהִלָּתוֹ.

MORNING BLESSINGS IH

The following blessings are said aloud by the Leader, but each individual should say them quietly as well. It is our custom to say them standing.

בָּרוּךְ Blessed are You, LORD our God,
King of the Universe,
who gives the heart understanding[B]
to distinguish day from night.

Blessed are You, LORD our God,
King of the Universe,
who has not made me a heathen.

Blessed are You, LORD our God,
King of the Universe,
who has not made me a slave.[A]

BIUR TEFILLA · ביאור תפילה

אֲשֶׁר נָתַן לַשֶּׂכְוִי בִינָה – *Who gives the heart understanding.* The word שֶׂכְוִי can mean rooster or it can mean the human heart. An animal with a brain the size of a pea, and

the most intelligent species on the planet nevertheless share an intuitive sense of the world. There are different ways to "know" something to be true.

ANI TEFILLA · אני תפילה

שֶׁלֹּא עָשַׂנִי עָבֶד – *Who has not made me a slave.*
One day, and for days thereafter, in the Kovno Ghetto during the Nazi oppression, the hazan Rabbi Avraham Yosef was leading the prayers, and when he got to this blessing he cried aloud to God in a bitter voice:

"How can I recite this blessing to You when we are imprisoned this way? How can I, a slave, recite the blessing of a free man, when death hangs over me, when I have no bread to eat? How can I recite the blessing 'who did not make me a slave?' I would be making fun of God were I to say

it! My mouth and my heart would not be in accord." Rabbi Ephraim Oshry responded that the blessing is a reference to the fact that a Canaanite slave is not permitted to do mitzvot; that is why one thanks God, for the opportunity to do more mitzvot than others may be obligated to do. The blessing is therefore not about physical slavery at all but about spirituality. As such, Heaven forbid that one should stop saying this blessing! Let us be reminded and let the enemy see that despite the fact that they work us like slaves, we are still free, free to do mitzvot, and free to serve our Creator. (*Responsa MiMa'amakim* III:6)

ברכות השחר‏עה

The following blessings are said aloud by the שליח ציבור, but each individual
should say them quietly as well. It is our custom to say them standing.

בָּרוּךְ אַתָּה יהוה אֱלֹהֵינוּ מֶלֶךְ הָעוֹלָם
אֲשֶׁר נָתַן לַשֶּׂכְוִי בִינָהֻ
לְהַבְחִין בֵּין יוֹם וּבֵין לָיְלָה.
בָּרוּךְ אַתָּה יהוה אֱלֹהֵינוּ מֶלֶךְ הָעוֹלָם
שֶׁלֹּא עָשַׂנִי גּוֹי.
בָּרוּךְ אַתָּה יהוה אֱלֹהֵינוּ מֶלֶךְ הָעוֹלָם
שֶׁלֹּא עָשַׂנִי עָבֶד.א

IYUN TEFILLA · עיון תפילה

ברכות השחר – *Morning Blessings.* The Gemara (*Berakhot* 60b) rules that one should recite a blessing of praise upon every act related to getting up in the morning. These *berakhot*, with some exceptions, are what constitute the 15 *Birkhot HaShaḥar* that appear here. Yet according to current practice, these blessings are unlike most other similar ones. For in general, we recite certain blessings of praise or thanks, *after* having experienced something, such as an act of nature (e.g., the blessing on hearing thunder) or eating (*Birkat HaMazon*) or the like. In the present case, however, we recite these blessings even if we have not experienced the occurrence ourselves. For example, if one were blind, one would still recite the

blessing of פּוֹקֵחַ עִוְרִים, "Who opens the eyes of the blind"; if one was sick and stayed in one's pajamas all day, one would still recite מַלְבִּישׁ עֲרֻמִּים, "Who clothes the naked," etc. We thus begin our day with blessings for the many natural things in our lives that we and others derive benefit from. Imagine if you were unable to see, or couldn't straighten up in the morning, or didn't have clothes to wear; what would your life be like? Someone who reflects upon these things is able to start each day with a new appreciation for the things that we otherwise tend to take for granted. Each day is a new day, even if at first it may have felt the same as the day before. Each day represents a fresh slate, a new beginning.

HILKHOT TEFILLA · הלכות תפילה

ברכות השחר – *Morning Blessings.* Given the reasons for these *berakhot*, one should ideally recite them at home after one washes in the morning. Nevertheless, in

many communities they are the first thing recited aloud by the *ḥazan*, to which the listeners should respond *Amen.* (*Shulḥan Arukh*, 46:1-2)

Blessed are You, LORD our God,
King of the Universe,

men: who has not made me a woman.

women: who has made me according to His will.

Blessed are You, LORD our God,
King of the Universe,
who gives sight to the blind.^A

Blessed are You, LORD our God,
King of the Universe,
who clothes the naked.¹

Blessed are You, LORD our God,
King of the Universe,
who sets captives free.¹

Blessed are You, LORD our God,
King of the Universe,
who raises those bowed down.

Blessed are You, LORD our God,
King of the Universe,
who spreads the earth above the waters.

---

them with clothes since they were embarrassed by their nakedness. They had given
in to their desires which then changed their
perception of the world. Clothes remind us
that we are not animals, that we can restrain
ourselves with modesty. Another word for
clothes is בֶּגֶד, the same root as the word
"traitor." Clothes remind us not to betray our
superiority over the animals.

מַתִּיר אֲסוּרִים – *Who sets captives free*. This
blessing was said when one stretched for
the first time in the morning. The ability to
stretch one's limbs should never be taken
for granted. At the same time, is there some
habit to which you feel bound? If I could
only stop being lazy, overeating, staying up
so late, wasting my time... This blessing says
that freedom from bad habits is possible.

בָּרוּךְ אַתָּה יהוה אֱלֹהֵינוּ מֶלֶךְ הָעוֹלָם
men שֶׁלֹּא עָשַׂנִי אִשָּׁה.
women שֶׁעָשַׂנִי כִּרְצוֹנוֹ.

בָּרוּךְ אַתָּה יהוה אֱלֹהֵינוּ מֶלֶךְ הָעוֹלָם
פּוֹקֵחַ עִוְרִים.ᴬ

בָּרוּךְ אַתָּה יהוה אֱלֹהֵינוּ מֶלֶךְ הָעוֹלָם
מַלְבִּישׁ עֲרֻמִּים.ᵛ

בָּרוּךְ אַתָּה יהוה אֱלֹהֵינוּ מֶלֶךְ הָעוֹלָם
מַתִּיר אֲסוּרִים.ᵛ

בָּרוּךְ אַתָּה יהוה אֱלֹהֵינוּ מֶלֶךְ הָעוֹלָם
זוֹקֵף כְּפוּפִים.

בָּרוּךְ אַתָּה יהוה אֱלֹהֵינוּ מֶלֶךְ הָעוֹלָם
רוֹקַע הָאָרֶץ עַל הַמָּיִם.

ANI TEFILLA · אני תפילה

פּוֹקֵחַ עִוְרִים – *Who gives sight to the blind.*
Try closing your eyes tight. Then open them. Then say this blessing.

עיון תפילה · IYUN TEFILLA

מַלְבִּישׁ עֲרֻמִּים – *Who clothes the naked.* On one level, we must be thankful that unlike so many other people in the world, we have clothes to wear, often an amazing collection of clothes when others have but one outfit they wear all of the time. But as well, we can be reminded that in an act of *ḥesed*, after Adam and Ḥava sinned, Hashem provided

Blessed are You, LORD our God,
   King of the Universe,
   who has provided me with all I need.[IA]

Blessed are You, LORD our God,
   King of the Universe,
   who makes firm the steps of man.[I]

Blessed are You, LORD our God,
   King of the Universe,
   who girds Israel with strength.[B]

Blessed are You, LORD our God,
   King of the Universe,
   who crowns Israel with glory.

Blessed are You, LORD our God,
   King of the Universe,
   who gives strength to the weary.

IYUN TEFILLA · עיון תפילה

הַמֵּכִין מִצְעֲדֵי גָבֶר – *Who makes firm the steps of man.* Hashem cares about each individual and what you can accomplish in this world. He therefore grants each person only a certain number of steps in life. Make each step you take count today (based on *Shomer Emunim*, *hashgaḥa pratit*). The ability to walk comes from Him; the direction you take is up to you.

BIUR TEFILLA · ביאור תפילה

אוֹזֵר יִשְׂרָאֵל בִּגְבוּרָה – *Who girds Israel with strength.* This blessing literally means "who girds Israel with heroism," which is different from the request for strength. "Heroic action means sacrificial action; if one does not sacrifice, he cannot be called a hero. A Jew may not be strong physically, but he can engage in heroic activity, and, indeed, has been engaging in heroic action for millennia... Jewish existence has been a heroic existence. Even today, our task is to defy everybody, which is a very difficult job and demands a great deal of heroism" (Rabbi J.B. Soloveitchik).

בָּרוּךְ אַתָּה יהוה אֱלֹהֵינוּ מֶלֶךְ הָעוֹלָם
שֶׁעָשָׂה לִי כָּל צָרְכִּי.ᵃᵛ

בָּרוּךְ אַתָּה יהוה אֱלֹהֵינוּ מֶלֶךְ הָעוֹלָם
הַמֵּכִין מִצְעֲדֵי גָבֶר.ᵛ

בָּרוּךְ אַתָּה יהוה אֱלֹהֵינוּ מֶלֶךְ הָעוֹלָם
אוֹזֵר יִשְׂרָאֵל בִּגְבוּרָה.ᵇ

בָּרוּךְ אַתָּה יהוה אֱלֹהֵינוּ מֶלֶךְ הָעוֹלָם
עוֹטֵר יִשְׂרָאֵל בְּתִפְאָרָה.

בָּרוּךְ אַתָּה יהוה אֱלֹהֵינוּ מֶלֶךְ הָעוֹלָם
הַנּוֹתֵן לַיָּעֵף כֹּחַ.

IYUN TEFILLA · עיון תפילה

שֶׁעָשָׂה לִי כָּל צָרְכִּי – Who has provided me with all I need. Almost all of the blessings are in the present tense yet this one is expressed in the past tense. Why not say "who gives me all I need"? Oftentimes sadness, hardship, and misfortune may appear to be filling up our lives but it truly is only later, further on down the road, that we can see that it all happened for a reason. Only then can we thank Hashem for what previously seemed to have been bad. A man could have found what seemed to be the perfect job: great pay, great loca-

tion, and great facilities. He goes in for an interview, thinks he got the job, gets excited, and then finds out that he did not get the position. He is distraught, upset, and quite puzzled. Why would he want to thank God for all He does? Only after he gets his new job with better pay, a better location, and better facilities can he thank God for not granting him his originally desired position. Only then can he distinguish the forest from the trees. The Siddur helps give perspective to our lives. (Based on Rabbi A. Twerski)

ANI TEFILLA · אני תפילה

שֶׁעָשָׂה לִי כָּל צָרְכִּי – Who has provided me with all I need.
In early life, Rabbi Yehiel Mikhel of Zlotchov lived in great poverty but he was always happy. Someone once asked him:

"Rabbi, how can you pray every day 'Who provided me with all I need' when you surely lack everything a man has need of!"

He replied: "My need is, most likely, to be poor, and that is what I have been supplied with."

בָּרוּךְ Blessed are You, LORD our God, King of the Universe,
who removes sleep from my eyes and slumber from my eyelids.
And may it be Your will, LORD our God
and God of our ancestors, to accustom us to Your Torah,[B]
and make us attached to Your commandments.
Lead us not into error, transgression, iniquity,[B] temptation or disgrace.
Do not let the evil instinct dominate us.
Keep us far from a bad man and a bad companion.[A]
Help us attach ourselves to the good instinct and to good deeds
and bend our instincts to be subservient to You.
Grant us, this day and every day, grace, loving-kindness
and compassion in Your eyes and in the eyes of all who see us,
and bestow loving-kindness upon us.
Blessed are You, LORD,
who bestows loving-kindness on His people Israel.[I]

יְהִי רָצוֹן May it be Your will, LORD my God and God of my ancestors, to save
me today and every day, from the arrogant and from arrogance itself, from a
bad man, a bad friend, a bad neighbor, a bad mishap, a destructive adversary,
a harsh trial and a harsh opponent, whether or not he is a son of the covenant.

Berakhot 16b

BIUR TEFILLA · ביאור תפילה

לֹא לִידֵי חֵטְא וְלֹא לִידֵי עֲבֵרָה וְעָוֹן – *Not into error, transgression, iniquity.* A חֵטְא is a sin which one commits by accident; an עֲבֵרָה is a transgression, a sin which one commits over and over again until it becomes habitual to the point that it seems totally permissible. An עָוֹן is a sin which is done on purpose, knowing that it is wrong. Each kind of sin stands on its own, yet it is also possible that each one eventually leads to the other. (Rabbi Schwab)

ANI TEFILLA · אני תפילה

וּמֵחָבֵר רָע – *A bad companion.*
What is a bad friend? If he or she is really a friend, then how could they be bad?

IYUN TEFILLA · עיון תפילה

גּוֹמֵל חֲסָדִים טוֹבִים לְעַמּוֹ יִשְׂרָאֵל – *Who bestows loving-kindness on His people Israel.* There is a rule that the theme at the end of a "long" blessing must relate to the theme at the opening of the blessing. What is the connection here? We began by acknowledging that Hashem relieves us of sleepiness. We conclude by acknowledging that our ability to begin a new day, refreshed and alert, even if we are tired, is an act of ḥesed by God (Rabbeinu Tam, *Berakhot 46a*). Each day is a new adventure to be embraced and appreciated.

בָּרוּךְ אַתָּה יהוה אֱלֹהֵינוּ מֶלֶךְ הָעוֹלָם
הַמַּעֲבִיר שֵׁנָה מֵעֵינַי וּתְנוּמָה מֵעַפְעַפָּי.
וִיהִי רָצוֹן מִלְּפָנֶיךָ יהוה אֱלֹהֵינוּ וֵאלֹהֵי אֲבוֹתֵינוּ
שֶׁתַּרְגִּילֵנוּ בְּתוֹרָתֶךָ, וְדַבְּקֵנוּ בְּמִצְוֹתֶיךָ
וְאַל תְּבִיאֵנוּ לֹא לִידֵי חֵטְא
וְלֹא לִידֵי עֲבֵרָה וְעָוֹן
וְלֹא לִידֵי נִסָּיוֹן וְלֹא לִידֵי בִזָּיוֹן
וְאַל תַּשְׁלֶט בָּנוּ יֵצֶר הָרָע
וְהַרְחִיקֵנוּ מֵאָדָם רָע וּמֵחָבֵר רָע
וְדַבְּקֵנוּ בְּיֵצֶר הַטּוֹב וּבְמַעֲשִׂים טוֹבִים
וְכֹף אֶת יִצְרֵנוּ לְהִשְׁתַּעְבֶּד לָךְ
וּתְנֵנוּ הַיּוֹם וּבְכָל יוֹם לְחֵן וּלְחֶסֶד וּלְרַחֲמִים
בְּעֵינֶיךָ, וּבְעֵינֵי כָל רוֹאֵינוּ
וְתִגְמְלֵנוּ חֲסָדִים טוֹבִים.
בָּרוּךְ אַתָּה יהוה, גּוֹמֵל חֲסָדִים טוֹבִים לְעַמּוֹ יִשְׂרָאֵל.

ברכות טז: יְהִי רָצוֹן מִלְּפָנֶיךָ יהוה אֱלֹהַי וֵאלֹהֵי אֲבוֹתַי, שֶׁתַּצִּילֵנִי הַיּוֹם וּבְכָל יוֹם
מֵעַזֵּי פָנִים וּמֵעַזּוּת פָּנִים, מֵאָדָם רָע, וּמֵחָבֵר רָע, וּמִשָּׁכֵן רָע, וּמִפֶּגַע רָע,
וּמִשָּׂטָן הַמַּשְׁחִית, מִדִּין קָשֶׁה, וּמִבַּעַל דִּין קָשֶׁה בֵּין שֶׁהוּא בֶן בְּרִית וּבֵין
שֶׁאֵינוֹ בֶן בְּרִית.

BIUR TEFILLA · ביאור תפילה

שֶׁתַּרְגִּילֵנוּ בְּתוֹרָתֶךָ – To accustom us to Your Torah. We ask that Hashem "accustom us to Torah" or "make Torah habitual for us." Perhaps it is a reference to the studying of Torah or perhaps it is about living our lives according to Torah values and com-

mandments. Regardless, these things come about only when they become habits for us, things that we practice every day. "We are what we repeatedly do," said Aristotle. "Excellence, then, is not an act, but a habit."

THE BINDING OF ISAAC

On the basis of Jewish mystical tradition, some have the custom of saying daily the biblical passage recounting the Binding of Isaac, the supreme trial of faith in which Abraham demonstrated his love of God above all other loves. Some omit and continue with "A person should" on page 38.

Our God and God of our ancestors, remember us with a favorable memory, and recall us with a remembrance of salvation and compassion from the highest of high heavens. Remember, LORD our God, on our behalf, the love of the ancients, Abraham, Isaac and Yisrael Your servants; the covenant, the loving-kindness, and the oath You swore to Abraham our father on Mount Moriah, and the Binding, when he bound Isaac his son on the altar, as is written in Your Torah:

It happened after these things that God tested Abraham. He *Gen. 22* said to him, "Abraham!" "Here I am," he replied. He said, "Take your son, your only son, Isaac, whom you love, and go to the land of Moriah and offer him there as a burnt-offering on one of the mountains which I shall say to you." Early the next morning Abraham rose and saddled his donkey and took his two lads with him, and Isaac his son, and he cut wood for the burnt-offering, and he set out for the place of which God had told him. On the third day Abraham looked up and saw the place from afar. Abraham said to his lads, "Stay here with the donkey while I and the boy go on ahead. We will worship and we will return to you." Abraham took the wood for the burnt-offering and placed it on Isaac his son, and he took in his hand the fire and the knife, and the two of them went together. Isaac said to Abraham his father, "Father?" and he said "Here I am, my son." And he said, "Here are the fire and the wood, but where is the sheep for the burnt-offering?" Abraham said, "God will see to the sheep for the burnt-offering, my son." And the two of them went together. They came

פרשת העקדה

On the basis of Jewish mystical tradition, some have the custom of saying daily the biblical passage recounting the Binding of Isaac, the supreme trial of faith in which Abraham demonstrated his love of God above all other loves. Some omit and continue with לְעוֹלָם יְהֵא אָדָם *on page 39.*

אֱלֹהֵינוּ וֵאלֹהֵי אֲבוֹתֵינוּ, זָכְרֵנוּ בְּזִכְּרוֹן טוֹב לְפָנֶיךָ, וּפָקְדֵנוּ בִּפְקֻדַּת יְשׁוּעָה וְרַחֲמִים מִשְּׁמֵי שְׁמֵי קֶדֶם, וּזְכָר לָנוּ יהוה אֱלֹהֵינוּ, אַהֲבַת הַקַּדְמוֹנִים אַבְרָהָם יִצְחָק וְיִשְׂרָאֵל עֲבָדֶיךָ, אֶת הַבְּרִית וְאֶת הַחֶסֶד וְאֶת הַשְּׁבוּעָה שֶׁנִּשְׁבַּעְתָּ לְאַבְרָהָם אָבִינוּ בְּהַר הַמּוֹרִיָּה, וְאֶת הָעֲקֵדָה שֶׁעָקַד אֶת יִצְחָק בְּנוֹ עַל גַּבֵּי הַמִּזְבֵּחַ, כַּכָּתוּב בְּתוֹרָתֶךָ:

בראשית כב

וַיְהִי אַחַר הַדְּבָרִים הָאֵלֶּה, וְהָאֱלֹהִים נִסָּה אֶת־אַבְרָהָם, וַיֹּאמֶר אֵלָיו אַבְרָהָם, וַיֹּאמֶר הִנֵּנִי: וַיֹּאמֶר קַח־נָא אֶת־בִּנְךָ אֶת־יְחִידְךָ אֲשֶׁר־אָהַבְתָּ, אֶת־יִצְחָק, וְלֶךְ־לְךָ אֶל־אֶרֶץ הַמֹּרִיָּה, וְהַעֲלֵהוּ שָׁם לְעֹלָה עַל אַחַד הֶהָרִים אֲשֶׁר אֹמַר אֵלֶיךָ: וַיַּשְׁכֵּם אַבְרָהָם בַּבֹּקֶר, וַיַּחֲבֹשׁ אֶת־חֲמֹרוֹ, וַיִּקַּח אֶת־שְׁנֵי נְעָרָיו אִתּוֹ וְאֵת יִצְחָק בְּנוֹ, וַיְבַקַּע עֲצֵי עֹלָה, וַיָּקָם וַיֵּלֶךְ אֶל־הַמָּקוֹם אֲשֶׁר־אָמַר־לוֹ הָאֱלֹהִים: בַּיּוֹם הַשְּׁלִישִׁי וַיִּשָּׂא אַבְרָהָם אֶת־עֵינָיו וַיַּרְא אֶת־הַמָּקוֹם מֵרָחֹק: וַיֹּאמֶר אַבְרָהָם אֶל־נְעָרָיו, שְׁבוּ־לָכֶם פֹּה עִם־הַחֲמוֹר, וַאֲנִי וְהַנַּעַר נֵלְכָה עַד־כֹּה, וְנִשְׁתַּחֲוֶה וְנָשׁוּבָה אֲלֵיכֶם: וַיִּקַּח אַבְרָהָם אֶת־עֲצֵי הָעֹלָה וַיָּשֶׂם עַל־יִצְחָק בְּנוֹ, וַיִּקַּח בְּיָדוֹ אֶת־הָאֵשׁ וְאֶת־הַמַּאֲכֶלֶת, וַיֵּלְכוּ שְׁנֵיהֶם יַחְדָּו: וַיֹּאמֶר יִצְחָק אֶל־אַבְרָהָם אָבִיו, וַיֹּאמֶר אָבִי, וַיֹּאמֶר הִנֶּנִּי בְנִי, וַיֹּאמֶר, הִנֵּה הָאֵשׁ וְהָעֵצִים, וְאַיֵּה הַשֶּׂה לְעֹלָה: וַיֹּאמֶר אַבְרָהָם, אֱלֹהִים יִרְאֶה־לּוֹ הַשֶּׂה לְעֹלָה, בְּנִי, וַיֵּלְכוּ שְׁנֵיהֶם יַחְדָּו: וַיָּבֹאוּ אֶל־הַמָּקוֹם אֲשֶׁר אָמַר־לוֹ

to the place God had told him about, and Abraham built there an altar and arranged the wood and bound Isaac his son and laid him on the altar on top of the wood. He reached out his hand and took the knife to slay his son. Then an angel of the Lord called out to him from heaven, "Abraham! Abraham!" He said, "Here I am." He said, "Do not reach out your hand against the boy; do not do anything to him, for now I know that you fear God, because you have not held back your son, your only son, from Me." Abraham looked up and there he saw a ram caught in a thicket by its horns, and Abraham went and took the ram and offered it as a burnt-offering instead of his son. Abraham called that place "The Lord will see," as is said to this day, "On the mountain of the Lord He will be seen." The angel of the Lord called to Abraham a second time from heaven, and said, "By Myself I swear, declares the Lord, that because you have done this and have not held back your son, your only son, I will greatly bless you and greatly multiply your descendants, as the stars of heaven and the sand of the seashore, and your descendants shall take possession of the gates of their enemies. Through your descendants, all the nations of the earth will be blessed, because you have heeded My voice." Then Abraham returned to his lads, and they rose and went together to Beersheba, and Abraham stayed in Beersheba.

Master of the Universe, just as Abraham our father suppressed his compassion to do Your will wholeheartedly, so may Your compassion suppress Your anger from us and may Your compassion prevail over Your other attributes. Deal with us, Lord our God, with the attributes of loving-kindness and compassion, and in Your great goodness may Your anger be turned away from Your people, Your city, Your land and Your inheritance. Fulfill in us, Lord our God, the promise You made in Your Torah through the hand of Moses Your servant, as it is said: "I will remember My covenant with Jacob, *Lev. 26* and also My covenant with Isaac, and also My covenant with Abraham I will remember, and the land I will remember."

הָאֱלֹהִים, וַיִּבֶן שָׁם אַבְרָהָם אֶת־הַמִּזְבֵּחַ וַיַּעֲרֹךְ אֶת־הָעֵצִים,
וַיַּעֲקֹד אֶת־יִצְחָק בְּנוֹ, וַיָּשֶׂם אֹתוֹ עַל־הַמִּזְבֵּחַ מִמַּעַל לָעֵצִים:
וַיִּשְׁלַח אַבְרָהָם אֶת־יָדוֹ, וַיִּקַּח אֶת־הַמַּאֲכֶלֶת, לִשְׁחֹט אֶת־
בְּנוֹ: וַיִּקְרָא אֵלָיו מַלְאַךְ יהוה מִן־הַשָּׁמַיִם, וַיֹּאמֶר אַבְרָהָם
אַבְרָהָם, וַיֹּאמֶר הִנֵּנִי: וַיֹּאמֶר אַל־תִּשְׁלַח יָדְךָ אֶל־הַנַּעַר,
וְאַל־תַּעַשׂ לוֹ מְאוּמָה, כִּי עַתָּה יָדַעְתִּי כִּי־יְרֵא אֱלֹהִים אַתָּה,
וְלֹא חָשַׂכְתָּ אֶת־בִּנְךָ אֶת־יְחִידְךָ מִמֶּנִּי: וַיִּשָּׂא אַבְרָהָם אֶת־
עֵינָיו, וַיַּרְא וְהִנֵּה־אַיִל, אַחַר נֶאֱחַז בַּסְּבַךְ בְּקַרְנָיו, וַיֵּלֶךְ
אַבְרָהָם וַיִּקַּח אֶת־הָאַיִל, וַיַּעֲלֵהוּ לְעֹלָה תַּחַת בְּנוֹ: וַיִּקְרָא
אַבְרָהָם שֵׁם־הַמָּקוֹם הַהוּא יהוה יִרְאֶה, אֲשֶׁר יֵאָמֵר הַיּוֹם
בְּהַר יהוה יֵרָאֶה: וַיִּקְרָא מַלְאַךְ יהוה אֶל־אַבְרָהָם שֵׁנִית
מִן־הַשָּׁמַיִם: וַיֹּאמֶר, בִּי נִשְׁבַּעְתִּי נְאֻם־יהוה, כִּי יַעַן אֲשֶׁר
עָשִׂיתָ אֶת־הַדָּבָר הַזֶּה, וְלֹא חָשַׂכְתָּ אֶת־בִּנְךָ אֶת־יְחִידֶךָ:
כִּי־בָרֵךְ אֲבָרֶכְךָ, וְהַרְבָּה אַרְבֶּה אֶת־זַרְעֲךָ כְּכוֹכְבֵי הַשָּׁמַיִם,
וְכַחוֹל אֲשֶׁר עַל־שְׂפַת הַיָּם, וְיִרַשׁ זַרְעֲךָ אֵת שַׁעַר אֹיְבָיו:
וְהִתְבָּרְכוּ בְזַרְעֲךָ כֹּל גּוֹיֵי הָאָרֶץ, עֵקֶב אֲשֶׁר שָׁמַעְתָּ בְּקֹלִי:
וַיָּשָׁב אַבְרָהָם אֶל־נְעָרָיו, וַיָּקֻמוּ וַיֵּלְכוּ יַחְדָּו אֶל־בְּאֵר שָׁבַע,
וַיֵּשֶׁב אַבְרָהָם בִּבְאֵר שָׁבַע:

רִבּוֹנוֹ שֶׁל עוֹלָם, כְּמוֹ שֶׁכָּבַשׁ אַבְרָהָם אָבִינוּ אֶת רַחֲמָיו לַעֲשׂוֹת רְצוֹנְךָ
בְּלֵבָב שָׁלֵם, כֵּן יִכְבְּשׁוּ רַחֲמֶיךָ אֶת כַּעַסְךָ מֵעָלֵינוּ וְיִגֹּלּוּ רַחֲמֶיךָ עַל מִדּוֹתֶיךָ.
וְתִתְנַהֵג עִמָּנוּ יהוה אֱלֹהֵינוּ בְּמִדַּת הַחֶסֶד וּבְמִדַּת הָרַחֲמִים, וּבְטוּבְךָ הַגָּדוֹל
יָשׁוּב חֲרוֹן אַפְּךָ מֵעַמְּךָ וּמֵעִירְךָ וּמֵאַרְצְךָ וּמִנַּחֲלָתֶךָ. וְקַיֶּם לָנוּ יהוה אֱלֹהֵינוּ
אֶת הַדָּבָר שֶׁהִבְטַחְתָּנוּ בְּתוֹרָתֶךָ עַל יְדֵי מֹשֶׁה עַבְדֶּךָ, כָּאָמוּר: וְזָכַרְתִּי ויקרא כו
אֶת־בְּרִיתִי יַעֲקוֹב וְאַף אֶת־בְּרִיתִי יִצְחָק, וְאַף אֶת־בְּרִיתִי אַבְרָהָם אֶזְכֹּר,
וְהָאָרֶץ אֶזְכֹּר:

ACCEPTING THE SOVEREIGNTY OF HEAVEN

לְעוֹלָם A person should always be God-fearing, privately and publicly, acknowledging the truth and speaking it in his heart.
He should rise early and say:

Tanna DeVei Eliyahu, ch. 21

> Master of all worlds,[1]
> not because of our righteousness
> do we lay our pleas before You,
> but because of Your great compassion.

Dan. 9

What are we?
What are our lives?
What is our loving-kindness?
What is our righteousness?
What is our salvation?
What is our strength?
What is our might?
What shall we say before You,
LORD our God and God of our ancestors?
Are not all the mighty like nothing before You,
the men of renown as if they had never been,
the wise as if they know nothing,
and the understanding as if they lack intelligence?
For their many works are in vain,
and the days of their lives like a fleeting breath before You.
The pre-eminence of man over the animals is nothing,[8]
for all is but a fleeting breath.

Eccl. 3

BIUR TEFILLA · ביאור תפילה

וּמוֹתַר הָאָדָם מִן־הַבְּהֵמָה אָיִן – *The pre-eminence of man over the animals is nothing.*
The word אָיִן means "nothing." But there

are those who suggest that the three letters can be read as an acronym for אָדָם יֵשׁ נְשָׁמָה – the preeminence of man over the animal is that man has a soul.

קבלת עול מלכות שמים

תנא דבי
אליהו,
פרק כא

לְעוֹלָם יְהֵא אָדָם יְרֵא שָׁמַיִם בְּסֵתֶר וּבַגָּלוּי
וּמוֹדֶה עַל הָאֱמֶת, וְדוֹבֵר אֱמֶת בִּלְבָבוֹ
וְיַשְׁכֵּם וְיֹאמַר

דניאל ט

רִבּוֹן כָּל הָעוֹלָמִים‏ּ
לֹא עַל־צִדְקוֹתֵינוּ אֲנַחְנוּ מַפִּילִים תַּחֲנוּנֵינוּ לְפָנֶיךָ
כִּי עַל־רַחֲמֶיךָ הָרַבִּים:

מָה אָנוּ, מֶה חַיֵּינוּ, מֶה חַסְדֵּנוּ, מַה צִּדְקוֹתֵינוּ
מַה יְשׁוּעָתֵנוּ, מַה כֹּחֵנוּ, מַה גְּבוּרָתֵנוּ
מַה נֹּאמַר לְפָנֶיךָ, יהוה אֱלֹהֵינוּ וֵאלֹהֵי אֲבוֹתֵינוּ
הֲלֹא כָל־הַגִּבּוֹרִים כְּאַיִן לְפָנֶיךָ
וְאַנְשֵׁי הַשֵּׁם כְּלֹא הָיוּ
וַחֲכָמִים כִּבְלִי מַדָּע, וּנְבוֹנִים כִּבְלִי הַשְׂכֵּל
כִּי רֹב מַעֲשֵׂיהֶם תֹּהוּ, וִימֵי חַיֵּיהֶם הֶבֶל לְפָנֶיךָ
וּמוֹתַר הָאָדָם מִן־הַבְּהֵמָה אָיִן‏ּ
כִּי הַכֹּל הָבֶל:

קהלת ג

IYUN TEFILLA · עיון תפילה

רִבּוֹן כָּל הָעוֹלָמִים – *Master of all worlds.* The prayer is divided into two parts. In the first, we are reminded that we are but creatures with our weaknesses and faults; in the second, we are reminded that we are chosen by Hashem for greatness. According to Rabbi Bunim of Peshis-ha, everyone should have two pockets, each containing a slip of paper. On one should be written: "I am but dust and ashes," and on the other: "The world was created for me." Sometimes we must reach into one pocket; other times we must reach into the other. The secret of living comes from knowing when to reach into each.

אֲבָל Yet we are Your people, the children of Your covenant,
the children of Abraham, Your beloved,
to whom You made a promise on Mount Moriah;
the offspring of Isaac his only one who was bound on the altar;
the congregation of Jacob Your firstborn son
whom – because of the love with which You loved him
and the joy with which You rejoiced in him –
You called Yisrael and Yeshurun.

לְפִיכָךְ Therefore it is our duty
to thank You, and to praise, glorify, bless, sanctify
and give praise and thanks to Your name.
Happy are we, how good is our portion,
how lovely our fate, how beautiful our heritage.

▸ Happy are we who, early and late,
evening and morning,
say twice each day –

> Listen, Israel: the LORD is our God, the LORD is One.   Deut. 6
>
> *Quietly:* Blessed be the name of His glorious kingdom for ever and all time.

Some congregations say the entire first paragraph of the Shema (below) at this point.
If there is a concern that the Shema will not be recited within the prescribed
time, then all three paragraphs should be said. See law 169.

Love the LORD your God with all your heart, with all your soul, and with all your
might. These words which I command you today shall be on your heart. Teach them
repeatedly to your children, speaking of them when you sit at home and when you
travel on the way, when you lie down and when you rise. Bind them as a sign on your
hand, and they shall be an emblem between your eyes. Write them on the doorposts
of your house and gates.

אַתָּה הוּא It was You who existed
before the world was created,
it is You now that the world has been created.
It is You in this world
and You in the World to Come.

אֲבָל אֲנַחְנוּ עַמְּךָ בְּנֵי בְרִיתֶךָ

בְּנֵי אַבְרָהָם אֹהַבְךָ שֶׁנִּשְׁבַּעְתָּ לּוֹ בְּהַר הַמּוֹרִיָּה

זֶרַע יִצְחָק יְחִידוֹ שֶׁנֶּעֱקַד עַל גַּבֵּי הַמִּזְבֵּחַ

עֲדַת יַעֲקֹב בִּנְךָ בְּכוֹרֶךָ

שֶׁמֵּאַהֲבָתְךָ שֶׁאָהַבְתָּ אוֹתוֹ, וּמִשִּׂמְחָתְךָ שֶׁשָּׂמַחְתָּ בּוֹ

קָרֵאתָ אֶת שְׁמוֹ יִשְׂרָאֵל וִישֻׁרוּן.

לְפִיכָךְ אֲנַחְנוּ חַיָּבִים לְהוֹדוֹת לְךָ וּלְשַׁבֵּחֲךָ וּלְפָאֶרְךָ

וּלְבָרֵךְ וּלְקַדֵּשׁ וְלָתֵת שֶׁבַח וְהוֹדָיָה לִשְׁמֶךָ.

אַשְׁרֵינוּ, מַה טּוֹב חֶלְקֵנוּ, וּמַה נָּעִים גּוֹרָלֵנוּ, וּמַה יָּפָה יְרֻשָּׁתֵנוּ.

◂ אַשְׁרֵינוּ, שֶׁאֲנַחְנוּ מַשְׁכִּימִים וּמַעֲרִיבִים עֶרֶב וָבֹקֶר

וְאוֹמְרִים פַּעֲמַיִם בְּכָל יוֹם

שְׁמַע יִשְׂרָאֵל, יְהוָה אֱלֹהֵינוּ, יְהוָה אֶחָד: דברים ו

Quietly
בָּרוּךְ שֵׁם כְּבוֹד מַלְכוּתוֹ לְעוֹלָם וָעֶד.

Some congregations say the entire first paragraph of the שמע (below) at this point.
If there is a concern that the שמע will not be recited within the prescribed
time, then all three paragraphs should be said. See law 169.

וְאָהַבְתָּ אֵת יְהוָה אֱלֹהֶיךָ, בְּכָל־לְבָבְךָ, וּבְכָל־נַפְשְׁךָ, וּבְכָל־מְאֹדֶךָ: וְהָיוּ הַדְּבָרִים
הָאֵלֶּה, אֲשֶׁר אָנֹכִי מְצַוְּךָ הַיּוֹם, עַל־לְבָבֶךָ: וְשִׁנַּנְתָּם לְבָנֶיךָ, וְדִבַּרְתָּ בָּם, בְּשִׁבְתְּךָ
בְּבֵיתֶךָ, וּבְלֶכְתְּךָ בַדֶּרֶךְ, וּבְשָׁכְבְּךָ וּבְקוּמֶךָ: וּקְשַׁרְתָּם לְאוֹת עַל־יָדֶךָ וְהָיוּ לְטֹטָפֹת
בֵּין עֵינֶיךָ: וּכְתַבְתָּם עַל־מְזֻזוֹת בֵּיתֶךָ וּבִשְׁעָרֶיךָ:

אַתָּה הוּא עַד שֶׁלֹּא נִבְרָא הָעוֹלָם

אַתָּה הוּא מִשֶּׁנִּבְרָא הָעוֹלָם.

אַתָּה הוּא בָּעוֹלָם הַזֶּה

וְאַתָּה הוּא לָעוֹלָם הַבָּא.

▸ Sanctify Your name
through those who sanctify Your name,
and sanctify Your name
throughout Your world.
By Your salvation may our pride be exalted;
raise high our pride.
Blessed are You, LORD,
who sanctifies His name among the multitudes.

אַתָּה הוּא You are the LORD our God
in heaven and on earth, and in the highest heaven of heavens.
Truly, You are the first and You are the last,
and besides You there is no god.
Gather those who hope in You
from the four quarters of the earth.
May all mankind recognize and know
that You alone are God
over all the kingdoms on earth.

You made the heavens and the earth,
the sea and all they contain.
Who among all the works of Your hands,
above and below,
can tell You what to do?

Heavenly Father, deal kindly with us
for the sake of Your great name
by which we are called,
and fulfill for us, LORD our God,
that which is written:
> "At that time I will bring you home,   *Zeph. 3*
> and at that time I will gather you,
> for I will give you renown
> and praise among all the peoples of the earth
> when I bring back your exiles before your eyes,
> says the LORD."

‹ קַדֵּשׁ אֶת שִׁמְךָ עַל מַקְדִּישֵׁי שְׁמֶךָ
וְקַדֵּשׁ אֶת שִׁמְךָ בְּעוֹלָמֶךָ
וּבִישׁוּעָתְךָ תָּרוּם וְתַגְבִּיהַ קַרְנֵנוּ.
בָּרוּךְ אַתָּה יהוה
הַמְקַדֵּשׁ אֶת שְׁמוֹ בָּרַבִּים.

אַתָּה הוּא יהוה אֱלֹהֵינוּ
בַּשָּׁמַיִם וּבָאָרֶץ וּבִשְׁמֵי הַשָּׁמַיִם הָעֶלְיוֹנִים.
אֱמֶת, אַתָּה הוּא רִאשׁוֹן, וְאַתָּה הוּא אַחֲרוֹן
וּמִבַּלְעָדֶיךָ אֵין אֱלֹהִים.
קַבֵּץ קֹוֶיךָ מֵאַרְבַּע כַּנְפוֹת הָאָרֶץ.
יַכִּירוּ וְיֵדְעוּ כָּל בָּאֵי עוֹלָם
כִּי אַתָּה הוּא הָאֱלֹהִים לְבַדְּךָ לְכֹל מַמְלְכוֹת הָאָרֶץ.

אַתָּה עָשִׂיתָ אֶת הַשָּׁמַיִם וְאֶת הָאָרֶץ
אֶת הַיָּם וְאֶת כָּל אֲשֶׁר בָּם
וּמִי בְּכָל מַעֲשֵׂי יָדֶיךָ בָּעֶלְיוֹנִים אוֹ בַתַּחְתּוֹנִים
שֶׁיֹּאמַר לְךָ מַה תַּעֲשֶׂה.

אָבִינוּ שֶׁבַּשָּׁמַיִם, עֲשֵׂה עִמָּנוּ חֶסֶד
בַּעֲבוּר שִׁמְךָ הַגָּדוֹל שֶׁנִּקְרָא עָלֵינוּ
וְקַיֵּם לָנוּ יהוה אֱלֹהֵינוּ
מַה שֶּׁכָּתוּב:

צפניה ג

בָּעֵת הַהִיא אָבִיא אֶתְכֶם, וּבָעֵת קַבְּצִי אֶתְכֶם
כִּי־אֶתֵּן אֶתְכֶם לְשֵׁם וְלִתְהִלָּה בְּכֹל עַמֵּי הָאָרֶץ
בְּשׁוּבִי אֶת־שְׁבוּתֵיכֶם לְעֵינֵיכֶם
אָמַר יהוה:

OFFERINGS B

The sages held that, in the absence of the Temple, studying the laws of sacrifices is the equivalent of offering them. Hence the following texts. There are different customs as to how many passages are to be said, and one should follow the custom of one's congregation. The minimum requirement is to say the verses relating to The Daily Sacrifice on the next page.

THE BASIN

The Lord spoke to Moses, saying: Make a bronze basin, with its   *Ex. 30* bronze stand for washing, and place it between the Tent of Meeting and the altar, and put water in it. From it, Aaron and his sons are to wash their hands and feet. When they enter the Tent of Meeting, they shall wash with water so that they will not die; likewise when they approach the altar to minister, presenting a fire-offering to the Lord. They must wash their hands and feet so that they will not die. This shall be an everlasting ordinance for Aaron and his descendants throughout their generations.

TAKING OF THE ASHES

The Lord spoke to Moses, saying: Instruct Aaron and his sons,   *Lev. 6* saying, This is the law of the burnt-offering. The burnt-offering shall remain on the altar hearth throughout the night until morning, and the altar fire shall be kept burning on it. The priest shall then put on his linen garments, and linen breeches next to his body, and shall remove the ashes of the burnt-offering that the fire has consumed on the altar and place them beside the altar. Then he shall take off these clothes and put on others, and carry the ashes outside the camp to a clean place. The fire on the altar must be kept burning; it must not go out. Each morning the priest shall burn wood on it, and prepare on it the burnt-offering and burn the fat of the peace-offerings. A perpetual fire must be kept burning on the altar; it must not go out.

(אִיזֶהוּ מְקוֹמָן) and Gemara (רַבִּי יִשְׁמָעֵאל אוֹמֵר)
(Tosafot, *Kiddushin* 30a).

סדר הקרבנות – *Offerings.* The word *korban* shares the same root as the word *karov*, meaning closeness. The sacrifices are de-

signed to bring one closer to God, as is their recitation. Nevertheless, with perhaps one exception, their inclusion in one's prayers is not generally considered obligatory, although it is still common for most of them to be recited.

סדר הקרבנות¹

> חז״ל *held that, in the absence of the Temple, studying the laws of sacrifices is the equivalent of offering them. Hence the following texts. There are different customs as to how many passages are to be said, and one should follow the custom of one's congregation. The minimum requirement is to say the verses relating to the* קרבן תמיד *on the next page.*

פרשת הכיור

שמות ל ׀ וַיְדַבֵּר יהוה אֶל־מֹשֶׁה לֵּאמֹר: וְעָשִׂיתָ כִּיּוֹר נְחֹשֶׁת וְכַנּוֹ נְחֹשֶׁת לְרָחְצָה, וְנָתַתָּ אֹתוֹ בֵּין־אֹהֶל מוֹעֵד וּבֵין הַמִּזְבֵּחַ, וְנָתַתָּ שָׁמָּה מָיִם: וְרָחֲצוּ אַהֲרֹן וּבָנָיו מִמֶּנּוּ אֶת־יְדֵיהֶם וְאֶת־רַגְלֵיהֶם: בְּבֹאָם אֶל־אֹהֶל מוֹעֵד יִרְחֲצוּ־מַיִם, וְלֹא יָמֻתוּ, אוֹ בְגִשְׁתָּם אֶל־הַמִּזְבֵּחַ לְשָׁרֵת, לְהַקְטִיר אִשֶּׁה לַיהוה: וְרָחֲצוּ יְדֵיהֶם וְרַגְלֵיהֶם וְלֹא יָמֻתוּ, וְהָיְתָה לָהֶם חָק־עוֹלָם, לוֹ וּלְזַרְעוֹ לְדֹרֹתָם:

פרשת תרומת הדשן

ויקרא ו ׀ וַיְדַבֵּר יהוה אֶל־מֹשֶׁה לֵּאמֹר: צַו אֶת־אַהֲרֹן וְאֶת־בָּנָיו לֵאמֹר, זֹאת תּוֹרַת הָעֹלָה, הִוא הָעֹלָה עַל מוֹקְדָה עַל־הַמִּזְבֵּחַ כָּל־הַלַּיְלָה עַד־הַבֹּקֶר, וְאֵשׁ הַמִּזְבֵּחַ תּוּקַד בּוֹ: וְלָבַשׁ הַכֹּהֵן מִדּוֹ בַד, וּמִכְנְסֵי־בַד יִלְבַּשׁ עַל־בְּשָׂרוֹ, וְהֵרִים אֶת־הַדֶּשֶׁן אֲשֶׁר תֹּאכַל הָאֵשׁ אֶת־הָעֹלָה, עַל־הַמִּזְבֵּחַ, וְשָׂמוֹ אֵצֶל הַמִּזְבֵּחַ: וּפָשַׁט אֶת־בְּגָדָיו, וְלָבַשׁ בְּגָדִים אֲחֵרִים, וְהוֹצִיא אֶת־הַדֶּשֶׁן אֶל־מִחוּץ לַמַּחֲנֶה, אֶל־מָקוֹם טָהוֹר: וְהָאֵשׁ עַל־הַמִּזְבֵּחַ תּוּקַד־בּוֹ, לֹא תִכְבֶּה, וּבִעֵר עָלֶיהָ הַכֹּהֵן עֵצִים בַּבֹּקֶר בַּבֹּקֶר, וְעָרַךְ עָלֶיהָ הָעֹלָה, וְהִקְטִיר עָלֶיהָ חֶלְבֵי הַשְּׁלָמִים: אֵשׁ, תָּמִיד תּוּקַד עַל־הַמִּזְבֵּחַ, לֹא תִכְבֶּה:

ביאור תפילה • BIUR TEFILLA

סדר הקרבנות – *Offerings.* The Gemara (*Ta'anit* 27b; *Megilla* 31b) raises the question of how people will be able to atone if we can no longer bring sacrifices in the *Beit HaMikdash*. The answer is provided in the name of Hashem: "If they read [about the sacrifices] before Me, I will count it as if they offered them before Me, and I will forgive them for their sins."

Similarly elsewhere (*Menaḥot* 110a) *Hazal* tell us that in the absence of the *Beit HaMik-dash*, the recitation of the *korbanot* will be tantamount to actually offering them. Hence it has become customary to read the descriptions of the different *korbanot* as they appear in *Torah Shebikhtav* and *Torah Shebe'al Peh*, the Written and Oral Law. There are selections from each of Torah (תָּמִיד), Mishna

May it be Your will, Lord our God and God of our ancestors, that You have compassion on us and pardon us all our sins, grant atonement for all our iniquities and forgive all our transgressions. May You rebuild the Temple swiftly in our days so that we may offer You the continual-offering that it may atone for us as You have prescribed for us in Your Torah through Moses Your servant, from the mouthpiece of Your glory, as it is said:

THE DAILY SACRIFICE

וַיְדַבֵּר The Lord said to Moses,[H] "Command the Israelites and tell them: 'Be careful to offer to Me at the appointed time My food-offering consumed by fire, as an aroma pleasing to Me.' Tell them: 'This is the fire-offering you shall offer to the Lord – two lambs a year old without blemish, as a regular burnt-offering each day. Prepare one lamb in the morning and the other toward evening, together with a meal-offering of a tenth of an ephah of fine flour mixed with a quarter of a hin of oil from pressed olives. This is the regular burnt-offering instituted at Mount Sinai as a pleasing aroma, a fire-offering made to the Lord. Its libation is to be a quarter of a hin [of wine] with each lamb, poured in the Sanctuary as a libation of strong drink to the Lord. Prepare the second lamb in the afternoon, along with the same meal-offering and libation as in the morning. This is a fire-offering, an aroma pleasing to the Lord.'" *Num. 28*

וְשָׁחַט He shall slaughter it at the north side of the altar before the Lord, and Aaron's sons the priests shall sprinkle its blood against the altar on all sides. *Lev. 1*

May it be Your will, Lord our God and God of our ancestors,
that this recitation be considered accepted and favored before You
as if we had offered the daily sacrifice at its appointed time and place,
according to its laws.

It is You, Lord our God, to whom our ancestors offered fragrant incense
when the Temple stood, as You commanded them through Moses Your prophet,
as is written in Your Torah:

---

day corresponds to three periods related to the sacrifice of the daily *Tamid* offering (*Berakhot* 26b). *Tamid* means consistency, a reflection of the daily service in the *Beit HaMikdash* and the daily service of the heart that we perform today.

יְהִי רָצוֹן מִלְּפָנֶיךָ יהוה אֱלֹהֵינוּ וֵאלֹהֵי אֲבוֹתֵינוּ, שֶׁתְּרַחֵם עָלֵינוּ, וְתִמְחָל לָנוּ עַל כָּל חַטֹּאתֵינוּ וּתְכַפֵּר לָנוּ עַל כָּל עֲוֹנוֹתֵינוּ וְתִסְלַח לָנוּ עַל כָּל פְּשָׁעֵינוּ, וְתִבְנֶה בֵּית הַמִּקְדָּשׁ בִּמְהֵרָה בְיָמֵינוּ, וְנַקְרִיב לְפָנֶיךָ קָרְבַּן הַתָּמִיד שֶׁיְּכַפֵּר בַּעֲדֵנוּ, כְּמוֹ שֶׁכָּתַבְתָּ עָלֵינוּ בְּתוֹרָתֶךָ עַל יְדֵי מֹשֶׁה עַבְדֶּךָ מִפִּי כְבוֹדֶךָ, כָּאָמוּר

פרשת קרבן התמיד

וַיְדַבֵּר יהוה אֶל־מֹשֶׁה לֵּאמֹר: צַו אֶת־בְּנֵי יִשְׂרָאֵל וְאָמַרְתָּ
אֲלֵהֶם, אֶת־קָרְבָּנִי לַחְמִי לְאִשַּׁי, רֵיחַ נִיחֹחִי, תִּשְׁמְרוּ לְהַקְרִיב
לִי בְּמוֹעֲדוֹ: וְאָמַרְתָּ לָהֶם, זֶה הָאִשֶּׁה אֲשֶׁר תַּקְרִיבוּ לַיהוה,
כְּבָשִׂים בְּנֵי־שָׁנָה תְמִימִם שְׁנַיִם לַיּוֹם, עֹלָה תָמִיד: אֶת־הַכֶּבֶשׂ
אֶחָד תַּעֲשֶׂה בַבֹּקֶר, וְאֵת הַכֶּבֶשׂ הַשֵּׁנִי תַּעֲשֶׂה בֵּין הָעַרְבָּיִם:
וַעֲשִׂירִית הָאֵיפָה סֹלֶת לְמִנְחָה, בְּלוּלָה בְּשֶׁמֶן כָּתִית רְבִיעִת
הַהִין: עֹלַת תָּמִיד, הָעֲשֻׂיָה בְּהַר סִינַי, לְרֵיחַ נִיחֹחַ אִשֶּׁה לַיהוה:
וְנִסְכּוֹ רְבִיעִת הַהִין לַכֶּבֶשׂ הָאֶחָד, בַּקֹּדֶשׁ הַסֵּךְ נֶסֶךְ שֵׁכָר לַיהוה:
וְאֵת הַכֶּבֶשׂ הַשֵּׁנִי תַּעֲשֶׂה בֵּין הָעַרְבָּיִם, כְּמִנְחַת הַבֹּקֶר וּכְנִסְכּוֹ
תַּעֲשֶׂה, אִשֵּׁה רֵיחַ נִיחֹחַ לַיהוה:

במדבר כח

וְשָׁחַט אֹתוֹ עַל יֶרֶךְ הַמִּזְבֵּחַ צָפֹנָה לִפְנֵי יהוה, וְזָרְקוּ בְּנֵי אַהֲרֹן
הַכֹּהֲנִים אֶת־דָּמוֹ עַל־הַמִּזְבֵּחַ, סָבִיב:

ויקרא א

יְהִי רָצוֹן מִלְּפָנֶיךָ, יהוה אֱלֹהֵינוּ וֵאלֹהֵי אֲבוֹתֵינוּ
שֶׁתְּהֵא אֲמִירָה זוֹ חֲשׁוּבָה וּמְקֻבֶּלֶת וּמְרֻצָּה לְפָנֶיךָ
כְּאִלּוּ הִקְרַבְנוּ קָרְבַּן הַתָּמִיד בְּמוֹעֲדוֹ וּבִמְקוֹמוֹ וּכְהִלְכָתוֹ.

אַתָּה הוּא יהוה אֱלֹהֵינוּ שֶׁהִקְטִירוּ אֲבוֹתֵינוּ לְפָנֶיךָ אֶת קְטֹרֶת הַסַּמִּים בִּזְמַן שֶׁבֵּית
הַמִּקְדָּשׁ הָיָה קַיָּם, כַּאֲשֶׁר צִוִּיתָ אוֹתָם עַל יְדֵי מֹשֶׁה נְבִיאֶךָ, כַּכָּתוּב בְּתוֹרָתֶךָ:

HILKHOT TEFILLA • הלכות תפילה

וַיְדַבֵּר יהוה אֶל־מֹשֶׁה – *The LORD said to Moses.* Of all of the sacrifices mentioned in this section, the one describing the *Korban Tamid* is

the one considered most obligatory (Rema 48:1). It is of special significance because the timing of the three prayer services in the

THE INCENSE

The LORD said to Moses: Take fragrant spices – balsam, onycha, galba- *Ex. 30*
num and pure frankincense, all in equal amounts – and make a fragrant
blend of incense, the work of a perfumer, well mixed, pure and holy.
Grind it very finely and place it in front of the [Ark of] Testimony in the
Tent of Meeting, where I will meet with you. It shall be most holy to you.

And it is said:

Aaron shall burn fragrant incense on the altar every morning when he
cleans the lamps. He shall burn incense again when he lights the lamps
toward evening so that there will be incense before the LORD at all times,
throughout your generations.

The rabbis taught: How was the incense prepared? It weighed 368 manehs, 365 cor- *Keritot 6a*
responding to the number of days in a solar year, a maneh for each day, half to be
offered in the morning and half in the afternoon, and three additional manehs from
which the High Priest took two handfuls on Yom Kippur. These were put back into
the mortar on the day before Yom Kippur and ground again very thoroughly so as
to be extremely fine. The incense contained eleven kinds of spices: balsam, onycha,
galbanum and frankincense, each weighing seventy manehs; myrrh, cassia, spikenard and saffron, each weighing sixteen manehs; twelve manehs of costus, three of
aromatic bark; nine of cinnamon; nine kabs of Carsina lye; three seahs and three
kabs of Cyprus wine. If Cyprus wine was not available, old white wine might be
used. A quarter of a kab of Sodom salt, and a minute amount of a smoke-raising
herb. Rabbi Nathan the Babylonian says: also a minute amount of Jordan amber. If
one added honey to the mixture, he rendered it unfit for sacred use. If he omitted
any one of its ingredients, he is guilty of a capital offence.

Rabban Simeon ben Gamliel says: "Balsam" refers to the sap that drips from the
balsam tree. The Carsina lye was used for bleaching the onycha to improve it. The
Cyprus wine was used to soak the onycha in it to make it pungent. Though urine is
suitable for this purpose, it is not brought into the Temple out of respect.

It was taught, Rabbi Nathan says: While it was being ground, another would say,
"Grind well, well grind," because the [rhythmic] sound is good for spices. If it was
mixed in half-quantities, it is fit for use, but we have not heard whether this applies
to a third or a quarter. Rabbi Judah said: The general rule is that if it was made in the
correct proportions, it is fit for use even if made in half-quantity, but if he omitted
any one of its ingredients, he is guilty of a capital offence.

It was taught, Bar Kappara says: Once every sixty or seventy years, the accumulated *JT Yoma 4:5*
surpluses amounted to half the yearly quantity. Bar Kappara also taught: If a minute
quantity of honey had been mixed into the incense, no one could have resisted the
scent. Why did they not put honey into it? Because the Torah says, "For you are not *Lev. 2*
to burn any leaven or honey in a fire-offering made to the LORD."

פרשת הקטורת

וַיֹּאמֶר יהוה אֶל־מֹשֶׁה, קַח־לְךָ סַמִּים נָטָף וּשְׁחֵלֶת וְחֶלְבְּנָה, סַמִּים וּלְבֹנָה **שמות ל**
זַכָּה, בַּד בְּבַד יִהְיֶה: וְעָשִׂיתָ אֹתָהּ קְטֹרֶת, רֹקַח מַעֲשֵׂה רוֹקֵחַ, מְמֻלָּח, טָהוֹר
קֹדֶשׁ: וְשָׁחַקְתָּ מִמֶּנָּה הָדֵק, וְנָתַתָּה מִמֶּנָּה לִפְנֵי הָעֵדֻת בְּאֹהֶל מוֹעֵד אֲשֶׁר
אִוָּעֵד לְךָ שָׁמָּה, קֹדֶשׁ קָדָשִׁים תִּהְיֶה לָכֶם:

וְנֶאֱמַר

וְהִקְטִיר עָלָיו אַהֲרֹן קְטֹרֶת סַמִּים, בַּבֹּקֶר בַּבֹּקֶר בְּהֵיטִיבוֹ אֶת־הַנֵּרֹת
יַקְטִירֶנָּה: וּבְהַעֲלֹת אַהֲרֹן אֶת־הַנֵּרֹת בֵּין הָעַרְבַּיִם יַקְטִירֶנָּה, קְטֹרֶת תָּמִיד
לִפְנֵי יהוה לְדֹרֹתֵיכֶם:

תָּנוּ רַבָּנָן: פִּטּוּם הַקְּטֹרֶת כֵּיצַד, שְׁלֹשׁ מֵאוֹת וְשִׁשִּׁים וּשְׁמוֹנָה מָנִים הָיוּ בָהּ. שְׁלֹשׁ **כריתות ו**
מֵאוֹת וְשִׁשִּׁים וַחֲמִשָּׁה כְּמִנְיַן יְמוֹת הַחַמָּה, מָנֶה לְכָל יוֹם, פְּרָס בְּשַׁחֲרִית וּפְרָס
בֵּין הָעַרְבַּיִם, וּשְׁלֹשָׁה מָנִים יְתֵרִים שֶׁמֵּהֶם מַכְנִיס כֹּהֵן גָּדוֹל מְלֹא חָפְנָיו בְּיוֹם
הַכִּפּוּרִים, וּמַחֲזִירָן לְמַכְתֶּשֶׁת בְּעֶרֶב יוֹם הַכִּפּוּרִים וְשׁוֹחֲקָן יָפֶה יָפֶה, כְּדֵי שֶׁתְּהֵא
דַקָּה מִן הַדַּקָּה. וְאַחַד עָשָׂר סַמָּנִים הָיוּ בָהּ, וְאֵלּוּ הֵן: הַצֳּרִי, וְהַצִּפֹּרֶן, וְהַחֶלְבְּנָה,
וְהַלְּבוֹנָה מִשְׁקַל שִׁבְעִים שִׁבְעִים מָנֶה, מֹר, וּקְצִיעָה, שִׁבֹּלֶת נֵרְדְּ, וְכַרְכֹּם מִשְׁקַל
שִׁשָּׁה עָשָׂר שִׁשָּׁה עָשָׂר מָנֶה, הַקֹּשְׁטְ שְׁנֵים עָשָׂר, קִלּוּפָה שְׁלֹשָׁה, קִנָּמוֹן תִּשְׁעָה,
בֹּרִית כַּרְשִׁינָה תִּשְׁעָה קַבִּין, יֵין קַפְרִיסִין סְאִין תְּלָת וְקַבִּין תְּלָתָא, וְאִם לֹא מָצָא
יֵין קַפְרִיסִין, מֵבִיא חֲמַר חִוַּרְיָן עַתִּיק. מֶלַח סְדוֹמִית רֹבַע, מַעֲלֶה עָשָׁן כָּל שֶׁהוּא.
רַבִּי נָתָן הַבַּבְלִי אוֹמֵר: אַף כִּפַּת הַיַּרְדֵּן כָּל שֶׁהוּא, וְאִם נָתַן בָּהּ דְּבַשׁ פְּסָלָהּ, וְאִם
חִסַּר אַחַד מִכָּל סַמָּנֶיהָ, חַיָּב מִיתָה.

רַבָּן שִׁמְעוֹן בֶּן גַּמְלִיאֵל אוֹמֵר: הַצֳּרִי אֵינוֹ אֶלָּא שְׂרָף הַנּוֹטֵף מֵעֲצֵי הַקְּטָף. בֹּרִית
כַּרְשִׁינָה שֶׁשָּׁפִין בָּהּ אֶת הַצִּפֹּרֶן כְּדֵי שֶׁתְּהֵא נָאָה, יֵין קַפְרִיסִין שֶׁשּׁוֹרִין בּוֹ אֶת
הַצִּפֹּרֶן כְּדֵי שֶׁתְּהֵא עַזָּה, וַהֲלֹא מֵי רַגְלַיִם יָפִין לָהּ, אֶלָּא שֶׁאֵין מַכְנִיסִין מֵי רַגְלַיִם
בַּמִּקְדָּשׁ מִפְּנֵי הַכָּבוֹד.

תַּנְיָא, רַבִּי נָתָן אוֹמֵר: כְּשֶׁהוּא שׁוֹחֵק אוֹמֵר, הָדֵק הֵיטֵב הֵיטֵב הָדֵק, מִפְּנֵי שֶׁהַקּוֹל
יָפֶה לַבְּשָׂמִים. פִּטְּמָהּ לַחֲצָאִין כְּשֵׁרָה, לִשְׁלִישׁ וְלִרְבִיעַ לֹא שָׁמַעְנוּ. אָמַר רַבִּי יְהוּדָה:
זֶה הַכְּלָל, אִם כְּמִדָּתָהּ כְּשֵׁרָה לַחֲצָאִין, וְאִם חִסַּר אַחַד מִכָּל סַמָּנֶיהָ חַיָּב מִיתָה.

תַּנְיָא, בַּר קַפָּרָא אוֹמֵר: אַחַת לְשִׁשִּׁים אוֹ לְשִׁבְעִים שָׁנָה הָיְתָה בָאָה שֶׁל שִׁירַיִם **ירושלמי**
לַחֲצָאִין. וְעוֹד תָּנֵי בַּר קַפָּרָא: אִלּוּ הָיָה נוֹתֵן בָּהּ קוֹרְטוֹב שֶׁל דְּבַשׁ אֵין אָדָם יָכוֹל **יומא ד,**
לַעֲמֹד מִפְּנֵי רֵיחָהּ, וְלָמָּה אֵין מְעָרְבִין בָּהּ דְּבַשׁ, מִפְּנֵי שֶׁהַתּוֹרָה אָמְרָה: כִּי כָל־שְׂאֹר **הלכה ה** **ויקרא ב**
וְכָל־דְּבַשׁ לֹא־תַקְטִירוּ מִמֶּנּוּ אִשֶּׁה לַיהוה:

The following three verses are each said three times:

The LORD of hosts is with us; the God of Jacob is our stronghold, Selah. *Ps. 46*
LORD of hosts, happy is the one who trusts in You. *Ps. 84*
LORD, save! May the King answer us on the day we call. *Ps. 20*

You are my hiding place; You will protect me from distress and surround me with *Ps. 32*
songs of salvation, Selah. Then the offering of Judah and Jerusalem will be pleasing *Mal. 3*
to the LORD as in the days of old and as in former years.

THE ORDER OF THE PRIESTLY FUNCTIONS

Abaye related the order of the daily priestly functions in the name of tradition and *Yoma 33a*
in accordance with Abba Shaul: The large pile [of wood] comes before the second
pile for the incense; the second pile for the incense precedes the laying in order
of the two logs of wood; the laying in order of the two logs of wood comes before
the removing of ashes from the inner altar; the removing of ashes from the inner
altar precedes the cleaning of the five lamps; the cleaning of the five lamps comes
before the blood of the daily offering; the blood of the daily offering precedes the
cleaning of the [other] two lamps; the cleaning of the two lamps comes before the
incense-offering; the incense-offering precedes the burning of the limbs; the
burning of the limbs comes before the meal-offering; the meal-offering
precedes the pancakes; the pancakes come before the wine-libations; the wine-
libations precede the additional offerings; the additional offerings come before
the [frankincense] censers; the censers precede the daily afternoon offering; as
it is said, "On it he shall arrange burnt-offerings, and on it he shall burn the fat of *Lev. 6*
the peace-offerings" – "on it" [the daily offering] all the offerings were completed.

Please, by the power of Your great right hand, set the captive nation free.
Accept Your people's prayer. Strengthen us, purify us, You who are revered.
Please, mighty One, guard like the pupil of the eye those who seek Your unity.
Bless them, cleanse them, have compassion on them,
grant them Your righteousness always.
Mighty One, Holy One, in Your great goodness guide Your congregation.
Only One, exalted One, turn to Your people, who proclaim Your holiness.
Accept our plea and heed our cry, You who know all secret thoughts.
 Blessed be the name of His glorious kingdom for ever and all time.

Master of the Universe, You have commanded us to offer the daily sacrifice at its
appointed time with the priests at their service, the Levites on their platform, and
the Israelites at their post. Now, because of our sins, the Temple is destroyed and
the daily sacrifice discontinued, and we have no priest at his service, no Levite
on his platform, no Israelite at his post. But You said: "We will offer in place of *Hos. 14*
bullocks [the prayer of] our lips." Therefore may it be Your will, LORD our God
and God of our ancestors, that the prayer of our lips be considered, accepted and
favored before You as if we had offered the daily sacrifice at its appointed time
and place, according to its laws.

The following three verses are each said three times:

תהלים מו

יהוה צְבָאוֹת עִמָּנוּ, מִשְׂגָּב לָנוּ אֱלֹהֵי יַעֲקֹב סֶלָה:

תהלים פד

יהוה צְבָאוֹת, אַשְׁרֵי אָדָם בֹּטֵחַ בָּךְ:

תהלים כ

יהוה הוֹשִׁיעָה, הַמֶּלֶךְ יַעֲנֵנוּ בְיוֹם־קָרְאֵנוּ:

תהלים לב

אַתָּה סֵתֶר לִי, מִצַּר תִּצְּרֵנִי, רָנֵּי פַלֵּט תְּסוֹבְבֵנִי סֶלָה:

מלאכי ג

וְעָרְבָה לַיהוה מִנְחַת יְהוּדָה וִירוּשָׁלָ‍ִם כִּימֵי עוֹלָם וּכְשָׁנִים קַדְמֹנִיּוֹת:

סדר המערכה

יומא לג

אַבָּיֵי הֲוָה מְסַדֵּר סֵדֶר הַמַּעֲרָכָה מִשְּׁמָא דִגְמָרָא, וְאַלִּבָּא דְאַבָּא שָׁאוּל: מַעֲרָכָה גְדוֹלָה קוֹדֶמֶת לְמַעֲרָכָה שְׁנִיָּה שֶׁל קְטֹרֶת, וּמַעֲרָכָה שְׁנִיָּה שֶׁל קְטֹרֶת קוֹדֶמֶת לְסִדּוּר שְׁנֵי גִזְרֵי עֵצִים, וְסִדּוּר שְׁנֵי גִזְרֵי עֵצִים קוֹדֵם לְדִשּׁוּן מִזְבֵּחַ הַפְּנִימִי, וְדִשּׁוּן מִזְבֵּחַ הַפְּנִימִי קוֹדֵם לַהֲטָבַת חָמֵשׁ נֵרוֹת, וַהֲטָבַת חָמֵשׁ נֵרוֹת קוֹדֶמֶת לְדַם הַתָּמִיד, וְדַם הַתָּמִיד קוֹדֵם לַהֲטָבַת שְׁתֵּי נֵרוֹת, וַהֲטָבַת שְׁתֵּי נֵרוֹת קוֹדֶמֶת לִקְטֹרֶת, וּקְטֹרֶת קוֹדֶמֶת לְאֵבָרִים, וְאֵבָרִים לְמִנְחָה, וּמִנְחָה לַחֲבִתִּין, וַחֲבִתִּין לִנְסָכִין, וּנְסָכִין לְמוּסָפִין, וּמוּסָפִין לְבָזִיכִין, וּבָזִיכִין קוֹדְמִין לְתָמִיד שֶׁל בֵּין הָעַרְבָּיִם. שֶׁנֶּאֱמַר: וְעָרַךְ עָלֶיהָ הָעֹלָה,

ויקרא ו

וְהִקְטִיר עָלֶיהָ חֶלְבֵי הַשְּׁלָמִים: עָלֶיהָ הַשְׁלֵם כָּל הַקָּרְבָּנוֹת כֻּלָּם.

אָנָּא, בְּכֹחַ גְּדֻלַּת יְמִינְךָ, תַּתִּיר צְרוּרָה.

קַבֵּל רִנַּת עַמְּךָ, שַׂגְּבֵנוּ, טַהֲרֵנוּ, נוֹרָא.

נָא גִבּוֹר, דּוֹרְשֵׁי יִחוּדְךָ כְּבָבַת שָׁמְרֵם.

בָּרְכֵם, טַהֲרֵם, רַחֲמֵם, צִדְקָתְךָ תָּמִיד גָּמְלֵם.

חֲסִין קָדוֹשׁ, בְּרֹב טוּבְךָ נַהֵל עֲדָתֶךָ.

יָחִיד גֵּאֶה, לְעַמְּךָ פְּנֵה, זוֹכְרֵי קְדֻשָּׁתֶךָ.

שַׁוְעָתֵנוּ קַבֵּל וּשְׁמַע צַעֲקָתֵנוּ, יוֹדֵעַ תַּעֲלוּמוֹת.

בָּרוּךְ שֵׁם כְּבוֹד מַלְכוּתוֹ לְעוֹלָם וָעֶד.

רִבּוֹן הָעוֹלָמִים, אַתָּה צִוִּיתָנוּ לְהַקְרִיב קָרְבַּן הַתָּמִיד בְּמוֹעֲדוֹ וְלִהְיוֹת כֹּהֲנִים בַּעֲבוֹדָתָם וּלְוִיִּם בְּדוּכָנָם וְיִשְׂרָאֵל בְּמַעֲמָדָם, וְעַתָּה בַּעֲו‍ֹנוֹתֵינוּ חָרַב בֵּית הַמִּקְדָּשׁ וּבָטֵל הַתָּמִיד וְאֵין לָנוּ לֹא כֹהֵן בַּעֲבוֹדָתוֹ וְלֹא לֵוִי בְּדוּכָנוֹ וְלֹא יִשְׂרָאֵל בְּמַעֲמָדוֹ,

הושע יד

וְאַתָּה אָמַרְתָּ: וּנְשַׁלְּמָה פָרִים שְׂפָתֵינוּ: לָכֵן יְהִי רָצוֹן מִלְּפָנֶיךָ יהוה אֱלֹהֵינוּ וֵאלֹהֵי אֲבוֹתֵינוּ, שֶׁיְּהֵא שִׂיחַ שִׂפְתוֹתֵינוּ חָשׁוּב וּמְקֻבָּל וּמְרֻצֶּה לְפָנֶיךָ, כְּאִלּוּ הִקְרַבְנוּ קָרְבַּן הַתָּמִיד בְּמוֹעֲדוֹ וּבִמְקוֹמוֹ וּכְהִלְכָתוֹ.

On Rosh Ḥodesh:

וּבְרָאשֵׁי חָדְשֵׁיכֶם On your new moons, present as a burnt-offering to the LORD, two young bulls, one ram, and seven yearling lambs without blemish. There shall be a meal-offering of three-tenths of an ephah of fine flour mixed with oil for each bull, two-tenths of an ephah of fine flour mixed with oil for the ram, and one-tenth of an ephah of fine flour mixed with oil for each lamb. This is the burnt-offering – a fire-offering of pleasing aroma to the LORD. Their libations shall be: half a hin of wine for each bull, a third of a hin for the ram, and a quarter of a hin for each lamb. This is the monthly burnt-offering to be made at each new moon throughout the year. One male goat should be offered as a sin-offering to God, in addition to the regular daily burnt-offering and its libation.

Num. 28

LAWS OF OFFERINGS, MISHNA ZEVAHIM

אֵיזֶהוּ מְקוֹמָן What is the location for sacrifices? The holiest offerings were slaughtered on the north side. The bull and he-goat of Yom Kippur were slaughtered on the north side. Their blood was received in a sacred vessel on the north side, and had to be sprinkled between the poles [of the Ark], toward the veil [screening the Holy of Holies], and on the golden altar. [The omission of] one of these sprinklings invalidated [the atonement ceremony]. The leftover blood was to be poured onto the western base of the outer altar. If this was not done, however, the omission did not invalidate [the ceremony].

Zevaḥim Ch. 5

The bulls and he-goats that were completely burnt were slaughtered on the north side, their blood was received in a sacred vessel on the north side, and had to be sprinkled toward the veil and on the golden altar. [The omission of] one of these sprinklings invalidated [the ceremony]. The leftover blood was to be poured onto the western base of the outer altar. If this was not done, however, the omission did not invalidate [the ceremony]. All these offerings were burnt where the altar ashes were deposited.

The communal and individual sin-offerings – these are the communal sin-offerings: the he-goats offered on Rosh Ḥodesh and Festivals were slaughtered on the north side, their blood was received in a sacred vessel on the north side, and required four sprinklings, one on each of the four corners of the altar. How was this done? The priest ascended the ramp and turned [right] onto the surrounding ledge. He came to the southeast corner, then went to the northeast, then to the northwest, then to the southwest. The leftover blood he poured onto the southern

בראש חודש:

במדבר כח

וּבְרָאשֵׁי חָדְשֵׁיכֶם תַּקְרִיבוּ עֹלָה לַיהוה, פָּרִים בְּנֵי־בָקָר שְׁנַיִם, וְאַיִל אֶחָד, כְּבָשִׂים בְּנֵי־שָׁנָה שִׁבְעָה, תְּמִימִם: וּשְׁלֹשָׁה עֶשְׂרֹנִים סֹלֶת מִנְחָה בְּלוּלָה בַשֶּׁמֶן לַפָּר הָאֶחָד, וּשְׁנֵי עֶשְׂרֹנִים סֹלֶת מִנְחָה בְּלוּלָה בַשֶּׁמֶן לָאַיִל הָאֶחָד: וְעִשָּׂרֹן עִשָּׂרוֹן סֹלֶת מִנְחָה בְּלוּלָה בַשֶּׁמֶן לַכֶּבֶשׂ הָאֶחָד, עֹלָה רֵיחַ נִיחֹחַ, אִשֶּׁה לַיהוה: וְנִסְכֵּיהֶם, חֲצִי הַהִין יִהְיֶה לַפָּר, וּשְׁלִישִׁת הַהִין לָאַיִל, וּרְבִיעִת הַהִין לַכֶּבֶשׂ יָיִן, זֹאת עֹלַת חֹדֶשׁ בְּחָדְשׁוֹ לְחָדְשֵׁי הַשָּׁנָה: וּשְׂעִיר עִזִּים אֶחָד לְחַטָּאת לַיהוה, עַל־עֹלַת הַתָּמִיד יֵעָשֶׂה, וְנִסְכּוֹ:

דיני זבחים

זבחים
פרק ה

אֵיזֶהוּ מְקוֹמָן שֶׁל זְבָחִים. ∘ קָדְשֵׁי קָדָשִׁים שְׁחִיטָתָן בַּצָּפוֹן. פַּר וְשָׂעִיר שֶׁל יוֹם הַכִּפּוּרִים, שְׁחִיטָתָן בַּצָּפוֹן, וְקִבּוּל דָּמָן בִּכְלִי שָׁרֵת בַּצָּפוֹן, וְדָמָן טָעוּן הַזָּיָה עַל בֵּין הַבַּדִּים, וְעַל הַפָּרֹכֶת, וְעַל מִזְבַּח הַזָּהָב. מַתָּנָה אַחַת מֵהֶן מְעַכָּבֶת. שְׁיָרֵי הַדָּם הָיָה שׁוֹפֵךְ עַל יְסוֹד מַעֲרָבִי שֶׁל מִזְבֵּחַ הַחִיצוֹן, אִם לֹא נָתַן לֹא עִכֵּב.

פָּרִים הַנִּשְׂרָפִים וּשְׂעִירִים הַנִּשְׂרָפִים, שְׁחִיטָתָן בַּצָּפוֹן, וְקִבּוּל דָּמָן בִּכְלִי שָׁרֵת בַּצָּפוֹן, וְדָמָן טָעוּן הַזָּיָה עַל הַפָּרֹכֶת וְעַל מִזְבַּח הַזָּהָב. מַתָּנָה אַחַת מֵהֶן מְעַכָּבֶת. שְׁיָרֵי הַדָּם הָיָה שׁוֹפֵךְ עַל יְסוֹד מַעֲרָבִי שֶׁל מִזְבֵּחַ הַחִיצוֹן, אִם לֹא נָתַן לֹא עִכֵּב. אֵלּוּ וָאֵלּוּ נִשְׂרָפִין בְּבֵית הַדָּשֶׁן.

חַטֹּאת הַצִּבּוּר וְהַיָּחִיד. אֵלּוּ הֵן חַטֹּאת הַצִּבּוּר: שְׂעִירֵי רָאשֵׁי חֳדָשִׁים וְשֶׁל מוֹעֲדוֹת. שְׁחִיטָתָן בַּצָּפוֹן, וְקִבּוּל דָּמָן בִּכְלִי שָׁרֵת בַּצָּפוֹן, וְדָמָן טָעוּן אַרְבַּע

עיון תפילה ∙ IYUN TEFILLA

אֵיזֶהוּ מְקוֹמָן שֶׁל זְבָחִים – *What is the location for sacrifices.* This particular chapter of Mishna was chosen because in all of its *mishnayot* there is not a single disagreement reported among the sages, reflecting perhaps the accuracy of its transmission, and the fact that peace is a value with which to begin one's day.

base. [The meat of these offerings], prepared in any manner, was eaten within the [courtyard] curtains, by males of the priest-hood, on that day and the following night, until midnight.

The burnt-offering was among the holiest of sacrifices. It was slaughtered on the north side, its blood was received in a sacred vessel on the north side, and required two sprinklings [at opposite corners of the altar], making four in all. The offering had to be flayed, dismembered and wholly consumed by fire.

The communal peace-offerings and the guilt-offerings – these are the guilt-offerings: the guilt-offering for robbery; the guilt-offering for profane use of a sacred object; the guilt-offering [for violating] a betrothed maidservant; the guilt-offering of a Nazirite [who had become defiled by a corpse]; the guilt-offering of a leper [at his cleansing]; and the guilt-offering in case of doubt. All these were slaughtered on the north side, their blood was received in a sacred vessel on the north side, and required two sprinklings [at opposite corners of the altar], making four in all. [The meat of these offerings], prepared in any manner, was eaten within the [courtyard] curtains, by males of the priesthood, on that day and the following night, until midnight.

The thanksgiving-offering and the ram of a Nazirite were offerings of lesser holiness. They could be slaughtered anywhere in the Temple court, and their blood required two sprinklings [at opposite corners of the altar], making four in all. The meat of these offerings, prepared in any manner, was eaten anywhere within the city [Jerusalem], by anyone during that day and the following night until midnight. This also applied to the portion of these sacrifices [given to the priests], except that the priests' portion was only to be eaten by the priests, their wives, children and servants.

Peace-offerings were [also] of lesser holiness. They could be slaughtered anywhere in the Temple court, and their blood required two sprinklings [at opposite corners of the altar], making four in all. The meat of these offerings, prepared in any manner, was eaten anywhere within the city [Jerusalem], by anyone, for two days and one night. This also applied to the portion of these sacrifices [given to the priests], except that the priests' portion was only to be eaten by the priests, their wives, children and servants.

The firstborn and tithe of cattle and the Pesaḥ lamb were sacrifices of lesser holiness. They could be slaughtered anywhere in the Temple court, and their blood required only one sprinkling, which had to be done at the base of the altar. They differed in their consumption: the firstborn was eaten only by priests, while the tithe could be eaten by anyone. Both could be eaten anywhere within the city, prepared in any manner, during two days and one night. The Pesaḥ lamb had to be eaten that night until midnight. It could only be eaten by those who had been numbered for it, and eaten only roasted.

מַתָּנוֹת עַל אַרְבַּע קְרָנוֹת. כֵּיצַד, עָלָה בַכֶּבֶשׁ, וּפָנָה לַסּוֹבֵב, וּבָא לוֹ לְקֶרֶן דְּרוֹמִית מִזְרָחִית, מִזְרָחִית צְפוֹנִית, צְפוֹנִית מַעֲרָבִית, מַעֲרָבִית דְּרוֹמִית. שְׁיָרֵי הַדָּם הָיָה שׁוֹפֵךְ עַל יְסוֹד דְּרוֹמִי. וְנֶאֱכָלִין לִפְנִים מִן הַקְּלָעִים, לְזִכְרֵי כְהֻנָּה, בְּכָל מַאֲכָל, לְיוֹם וָלַיְלָה עַד חֲצוֹת.

הָעוֹלָה קֹדֶשׁ קָדָשִׁים. שְׁחִיטָתָהּ בַּצָּפוֹן, וְקִבּוּל דָּמָהּ בִּכְלִי שָׁרֵת בַּצָּפוֹן, וְדָמָהּ טָעוּן שְׁתֵּי מַתָּנוֹת שֶׁהֵן אַרְבַּע, וּטְעוּנָה הֶפְשֵׁט וְנִתּוּחַ, וְכָלִיל לָאִשִּׁים.

זִבְחֵי שַׁלְמֵי צִבּוּר וַאֲשָׁמוֹת. אֵלּוּ הֵן אֲשָׁמוֹת: אֲשַׁם גְּזֵלוֹת, אֲשַׁם מְעִילוֹת, אֲשַׁם שִׁפְחָה חֲרוּפָה, אֲשַׁם נָזִיר, אֲשַׁם מְצֹרָע, אָשָׁם תָּלוּי. שְׁחִיטָתָן בַּצָּפוֹן, וְקִבּוּל דָּמָן בִּכְלִי שָׁרֵת בַּצָּפוֹן, וְדָמָן טָעוּן שְׁתֵּי מַתָּנוֹת שֶׁהֵן אַרְבַּע, וְנֶאֱכָלִין לִפְנִים מִן הַקְּלָעִים, לְזִכְרֵי כְהֻנָּה, בְּכָל מַאֲכָל, לְיוֹם וָלַיְלָה עַד חֲצוֹת.

הַתּוֹדָה וְאֵיל נָזִיר קָדָשִׁים קַלִּים. שְׁחִיטָתָן בְּכָל מָקוֹם בָּעֲזָרָה, וְדָמָן טָעוּן שְׁתֵּי מַתָּנוֹת שֶׁהֵן אַרְבַּע, וְנֶאֱכָלִין בְּכָל הָעִיר, לְכָל אָדָם, בְּכָל מַאֲכָל, לְיוֹם וָלַיְלָה עַד חֲצוֹת. הַמּוּרָם מֵהֶם כַּיּוֹצֵא בָהֶם, אֶלָּא שֶׁהַמּוּרָם נֶאֱכָל לַכֹּהֲנִים, לִנְשֵׁיהֶם, וְלִבְנֵיהֶם וּלְעַבְדֵיהֶם.

שְׁלָמִים קָדָשִׁים קַלִּים. שְׁחִיטָתָן בְּכָל מָקוֹם בָּעֲזָרָה, וְדָמָן טָעוּן שְׁתֵּי מַתָּנוֹת שֶׁהֵן אַרְבַּע, וְנֶאֱכָלִין בְּכָל הָעִיר, לְכָל אָדָם, בְּכָל מַאֲכָל, לִשְׁנֵי יָמִים וְלַיְלָה אֶחָד. הַמּוּרָם מֵהֶם כַּיּוֹצֵא בָהֶם, אֶלָּא שֶׁהַמּוּרָם נֶאֱכָל לַכֹּהֲנִים, לִנְשֵׁיהֶם, וְלִבְנֵיהֶם וּלְעַבְדֵיהֶם.

הַבְּכוֹר וְהַמַּעֲשֵׂר וְהַפֶּסַח קָדָשִׁים קַלִּים. שְׁחִיטָתָן בְּכָל מָקוֹם בָּעֲזָרָה, וְדָמָן טָעוּן מַתָּנָה אֶחָת, וּבִלְבַד שֶׁיִּתֵּן כְּנֶגֶד הַיְסוֹד. שִׁנָּה בַּאֲכִילָתָן, הַבְּכוֹר נֶאֱכָל לַכֹּהֲנִים וְהַמַּעֲשֵׂר לְכָל אָדָם, וְנֶאֱכָלִין בְּכָל הָעִיר, בְּכָל מַאֲכָל, לִשְׁנֵי יָמִים וְלַיְלָה אֶחָד. הַפֶּסַח אֵינוֹ נֶאֱכָל אֶלָּא בַלַּיְלָה, וְאֵינוֹ נֶאֱכָל אֶלָּא עַד חֲצוֹת, וְאֵינוֹ נֶאֱכָל אֶלָּא לִמְנוּיָו, וְאֵינוֹ נֶאֱכָל אֶלָּא צָלִי.

THE INTERPRETIVE PRINCIPLES OF RABBI YISHMAEL

רַבִּי יִשְׁמָעֵאל Rabbi Yishmael says:

The Torah is expounded by thirteen principles:

 1. An inference from a lenient law to a strict one, and vice versa.
 2. An inference drawn from identical words in two passages.
 3. A general principle derived from one text or two related texts.
 4. A general law followed by specific examples
    [where the law applies exclusively to those examples].
 5. A specific example followed by a general law
    [where the law applies to everything implied in the general statement].
 6. A general law followed by specific examples
    and concluding with a general law:
    here you may infer only cases similar to the examples.
 7. When a general statement requires clarification by a specific example,
    or a specific example requires clarification by a general statement
    [then rules 4 and 5 do not apply].
 8. When a particular case, already included in the general statement,
    is expressly mentioned to teach something new,
    that special provision applies to all other cases
    included in the general statement.
 9. When a particular case, though included in the general statement,
    is expressly mentioned with a provision similar to the general law,
    such a case is singled out to lessen the severity of the law,
    not to increase it.
10. When a particular case, though included in the general statement,
    is explicitly mentioned with a provision differing from the general law,
    it is singled out to lessen in some respects, and in others to increase,
    the severity of the law.
11. When a particular case, though included in the general statement,
    is explicitly mentioned with a new provision,
    the terms of the general statement no longer apply to it,
    unless Scripture indicates explicitly that they do apply.
12. A matter elucidated from its context, or from the following passage.
13. Also, when two passages [seem to] contradict each other,
    [they are to be elucidated by] a third passage that reconciles them.

May it be Your will, Lord our God and God of our ancestors, that the Temple be speedily rebuilt in our days, and grant us our share in Your Torah. And may we serve You there in reverence, as in the days of old and as in former years.

ברייתא דרבי ישמעאל

רַבִּי יִשְׁמָעֵאל אוֹמֵר: בִּשְׁלֹשׁ עֶשְׂרֵה מִדּוֹת הַתּוֹרָה נִדְרֶשֶׁת

א מִקַּל וָחֹמֶר

ב וּמִגְּזֵרָה שָׁוָה

ג מִבִּנְיַן אָב מִכָּתוּב אֶחָד, וּמִבִּנְיַן אָב מִשְּׁנֵי כְתוּבִים

ד מִכְּלָל וּפְרָט

ה מִפְּרָט וּכְלָל

ו כְּלָל וּפְרָט וּכְלָל, אִי אַתָּה דָן אֶלָּא כְּעֵין הַפְּרָט

ז מִכְּלָל שֶׁהוּא צָרִיךְ לִפְרָט, וּמִפְּרָט שֶׁהוּא צָרִיךְ לִכְלָל

ח כָּל דָּבָר שֶׁהָיָה בִּכְלָל, וְיָצָא מִן הַכְּלָל לְלַמֵּד
לֹא לְלַמֵּד עַל עַצְמוֹ יָצָא
אֶלָּא לְלַמֵּד עַל הַכְּלָל כֻּלּוֹ יָצָא

ט כָּל דָּבָר שֶׁהָיָה בִּכְלָל, וְיָצָא לִטְעֹן טַעַן אֶחָד שֶׁהוּא כְעִנְיָנוֹ
יָצָא לְהָקֵל וְלֹא לְהַחֲמִיר

י כָּל דָּבָר שֶׁהָיָה בִּכְלָל, וְיָצָא לִטְעֹן טַעַן אַחֵר שֶׁלֹּא כְעִנְיָנוֹ
יָצָא לְהָקֵל וּלְהַחֲמִיר

יא כָּל דָּבָר שֶׁהָיָה בִּכְלָל, וְיָצָא לִדּוֹן בַּדָּבָר הֶחָדָשׁ
אִי אַתָּה יָכוֹל לְהַחֲזִירוֹ לִכְלָלוֹ
עַד שֶׁיַּחֲזִירֶנּוּ הַכָּתוּב לִכְלָלוֹ בְּפֵרוּשׁ

יב דָּבָר הַלָּמֵד מֵעִנְיָנוֹ, וְדָבָר הַלָּמֵד מִסּוֹפוֹ

יג וְכֵן שְׁנֵי כְתוּבִים הַמַּכְחִישִׁים זֶה אֶת זֶה
עַד שֶׁיָּבוֹא הַכָּתוּב הַשְּׁלִישִׁי וְיַכְרִיעַ בֵּינֵיהֶם.

יְהִי רָצוֹן מִלְּפָנֶיךָ, יהוה אֱלֹהֵינוּ וֵאלֹהֵי אֲבוֹתֵינוּ, שֶׁיִּבָּנֶה בֵּית הַמִּקְדָּשׁ
בִּמְהֵרָה בְיָמֵינוּ, וְתֵן חֶלְקֵנוּ בְּתוֹרָתֶךָ, וְשָׁם נַעֲבָדְךָ בְּיִרְאָה כִּימֵי עוֹלָם
וּכְשָׁנִים קַדְמוֹנִיּוֹת.

THE RABBIS' KADDISH[B]

The following prayer, said by mourners, requires the presence of a minyan. A transliteration can be found on page 920.

Mourner: יִתְגַּדַּל **Magnified and sanctified**
may His great name be,
in the world He created by His will.
May He establish His kingdom in your lifetime
and in your days,
and in the lifetime of all the house of Israel,
swiftly and soon –
and say: Amen.

All: May His great name[A] be blessed for ever and all time.

Mourner: Blessed and praised,
glorified and exalted,
raised and honored,
uplifted and lauded
be the name of the Holy One,
blessed be He,

---

whereas this version of the prayer is said by an individual.

Kaddish DeRabbanan (Rabbis') includes a prayer for scholars and is recited at the conclusion of a section of public learning of Rabbinic literature – Halakha, Aggada, Gemara.

Its ancient origins are attested to by the unusual language which is a combination of Hebrew and a form of Aramaic used millennia ago. So important was the prayer considered, so especially inspiring is the one line at its center, that it is one of those that can only be said with a minyan (a *davar shebikedusha* – דְּבַר שֶׁבִּקְדֻשָּׁה).

קדיש דרבנן *

*The following prayer, said by mourners, requires the presence of a מִנְיָן.
A transliteration can be found on page 920.*

אבל יִתְגַּדַּל וְיִתְקַדַּשׁ שְׁמֵהּ רַבָּא (קהל: אָמֵן)
בְּעָלְמָא דִּי בְרָא כִרְעוּתֵהּ
וְיַמְלִיךְ מַלְכוּתֵהּ
בְּחַיֵּיכוֹן וּבְיוֹמֵיכוֹן וּבְחַיֵּי דְכָל בֵּית יִשְׂרָאֵל
בַּעֲגָלָא וּבִזְמַן קָרִיב
וְאִמְרוּ אָמֵן. (קהל: אָמֵן)

קהל
ואבל יְהֵא שְׁמֵהּ רַבָּא * מְבָרַךְ לְעָלַם וּלְעָלְמֵי עָלְמַיָּא.

אבל יִתְבָּרַךְ וְיִשְׁתַּבַּח וְיִתְפָּאַר וְיִתְרוֹמַם וְיִתְנַשֵּׂא
וְיִתְהַדָּר וְיִתְעַלֶּה וְיִתְהַלָּל
שְׁמֵהּ דְּקֻדְשָׁא בְּרִיךְ הוּא (קהל: בְּרִיךְ הוּא)

INTRODUCTION TO KADDISH

There are four variations of this prayer in the siddur.

The shorter one, called Ḥatzi (Half) Kaddish, serves to separate between sections of the service; it acts as a transition. Despite its name, this is the oldest and original version.

Kaddish Titkabal or Shalem (Full) has three extra lines at the end, added during the times of the Geonim, which speak of the acceptance of our prayers. It is usually recited to mark a conclusion of a service defined

here as one involving Seliḥot or the Shemoneh Esreh (even if some other prayers like Taḥanun or Uva LeTziyon were subsequently attached to the end of the Shemoneh Esreh).

Kaddish Yatom (of the Orphan) is recited on behalf of someone who has passed away. The text is similar to Kaddish Shalem except that it is missing the primary line of Titkabal, which asks for the acceptance of our prayers, since that is reserved for a Ḥazan on behalf of the congregation

beyond any blessing,
song, praise and consolation
uttered in the world –
and say: Amen.

To Israel, to the teachers,
their disciples
and their disciples' disciples,
and to all who engage in the study of Torah,
in this (*in Israel add:* holy) place or elsewhere,
may there come to them and you great peace,
grace, kindness and compassion,
long life, ample sustenance and deliverance,
from their Father in Heaven –
and say: Amen.

May there be
great peace from heaven,
and (good) life
for us and all Israel –
and say: Amen.

Bow, take three steps back, as if taking leave of the Divine Presence,
then bow, first left, then right, then center, while saying:

May He who makes peace in His high places,
in His compassion make peace
for us and all Israel –
and say: Amen.

On Hoshana Raba, and in many communities outside Israel (and in Israel)
on Yom HaAtzma'ut and Yom Yerushalayim,
continue Shaharit on page 474.

לְעֵלָּא מִן כָּל בִּרְכָתָא

‏/בעשרת ימי תשובה: לְעֵלָּא לְעֵלָּא מִכָּל בִּרְכָתָא/

וְשִׁירָתָא, תֻּשְׁבְּחָתָא וְנֶחֱמָתָא, דַּאֲמִירָן בְּעָלְמָא

וְאִמְרוּ אָמֵן. (קהל: אָמֵן.)

עַל יִשְׂרָאֵל וְעַל רַבָּנָן

וְעַל תַּלְמִידֵיהוֹן וְעַל כָּל תַּלְמִידֵי תַלְמִידֵיהוֹן

וְעַל כָּל מָאן דְּעָסְקִין בְּאוֹרַיְתָא

דִּי בְאַתְרָא (בארץ ישראל: קַדִּישָׁא) הָדֵין, וְדִי בְכָל אֲתַר וַאֲתַר

יְהֵא לְהוֹן וּלְכוֹן שְׁלָמָא רַבָּא

חִנָּא וְחִסְדָּא, וְרַחֲמֵי, וְחַיֵּי אֲרִיכֵי, וּמְזוֹנֵי רְוִיחֵי

וּפֻרְקָנָא מִן קֳדָם אֲבוּהוֹן דִּי בִשְׁמַיָּא

וְאִמְרוּ אָמֵן. (קהל: אָמֵן.)

יְהֵא שְׁלָמָא רַבָּא מִן שְׁמַיָּא

וְחַיִּים (טוֹבִים) עָלֵינוּ וְעַל כָּל יִשְׂרָאֵל

וְאִמְרוּ אָמֵן. (קהל: אָמֵן.)

Bow, take three steps back, as if taking leave of the Divine Presence,
then bow, first left, then right, then center, while saying:

עֹשֶׂה שָׁלוֹם/בעשרת ימי תשובה: הַשָּׁלוֹם/ בִּמְרוֹמָיו

הוּא יַעֲשֶׂה בְרַחֲמָיו שָׁלוֹם, עָלֵינוּ וְעַל כָּל יִשְׂרָאֵל

וְאִמְרוּ אָמֵן. (קהל: אָמֵן.)

On הושענא רבה *(and in* חוץ לארץ *and in many communities in* ארץ ישראל *on* יום העצמאות *and* יום ירושלים*,* שחרית *continue on page 475.*

A PSALM BEFORE VERSES OF PRAISE

מִזְמוֹר שִׁיר A psalm of David.   *Ps. 30*
A song for the dedication of the House.[B]
I will exalt You, LORD, for You have lifted me up,
   and not let my enemies rejoice over me.
LORD, my God, I cried to You for help and You healed me.
LORD, You lifted my soul from the grave;
   You spared me from going down to the pit.
Sing to the LORD, you His devoted ones,
   and give thanks to His holy name.
For His anger is for a moment, but His favor for a lifetime.
At night there may be weeping, but in the morning there is joy.
When I felt secure, I said, "I shall never be shaken."
LORD, when You favored me,
   You made me stand firm as a mountain,
   but when You hid Your face, I was terrified.
To You, LORD, I called; I pleaded with my LORD:
"What gain would there be if I died and went down to the grave?
   Can dust thank You? Can it declare Your truth?
Hear, LORD, and be gracious to me; LORD, be my help."
▸ You have turned my sorrow into dancing.
You have removed my sackcloth and clothed me with joy,
   so that my soul may sing to You and not be silent.
LORD my God, for ever will I thank You.

---

as an adequate substitute. We dedicate ourselves since we cannot yet dedicate the *Beit HaMikdash*. On the other hand, perhaps it has nothing to do with what precedes. Instead, we sometimes come to prayer too upset or not in the mood to pray and therefore not open to the messages of *Pesukei*

DeZimra that the world is a beautiful place protected by God. King David reminds us that he, too, went through sadness and despair yet awoke to the possibility of happiness and a sense of security because of his awareness of God's presence in his life. (Based on Rabbi E. Munk)

מזמור לפני פסוקי דזמרה

מִזְמוֹר שִׁיר־חֲנֻכַּת הַבַּיִת לְדָוִד:

אֲרוֹמִמְךָ יהוה כִּי דִלִּיתָנִי, וְלֹא־שִׂמַּחְתָּ אֹיְבַי לִי:

יהוה אֱלֹהָי, שִׁוַּעְתִּי אֵלֶיךָ וַתִּרְפָּאֵנִי:

יהוה, הֶעֱלִיתָ מִן־שְׁאוֹל נַפְשִׁי, חִיִּיתַנִי מִיָּרְדִי־בוֹר:

זַמְּרוּ לַיהוה חֲסִידָיו, וְהוֹדוּ לְזֵכֶר קָדְשׁוֹ:

כִּי רֶגַע בְּאַפּוֹ, חַיִּים בִּרְצוֹנוֹ, בָּעֶרֶב יָלִין בֶּכִי וְלַבֹּקֶר רִנָּה:

וַאֲנִי אָמַרְתִּי בְשַׁלְוִי, בַּל־אֶמּוֹט לְעוֹלָם:

יהוה, בִּרְצוֹנְךָ הֶעֱמַדְתָּה לְהַרְרִי עֹז

הִסְתַּרְתָּ פָנֶיךָ הָיִיתִי נִבְהָל:

אֵלֶיךָ יהוה אֶקְרָא, וְאֶל־אֲדֹנָי אֶתְחַנָּן:

מַה־בֶּצַע בְּדָמִי, בְּרִדְתִּי אֶל שָׁחַת

הֲיוֹדְךָ עָפָר, הֲיַגִּיד אֲמִתֶּךָ:

שְׁמַע־יהוה וְחָנֵּנִי, יהוה הֱיֵה־עֹזֵר לִי:

הָפַכְתָּ מִסְפְּדִי לְמָחוֹל לִי, פִּתַּחְתָּ שַׂקִּי, וַתְּאַזְּרֵנִי שִׂמְחָה:

לְמַעַן יְזַמֶּרְךָ כָבוֹד וְלֹא יִדֹּם, יהוה אֱלֹהַי, לְעוֹלָם אוֹדֶךָּ:

ביאור תפילה · BIUR TEFILLA

מִזְמוֹר שִׁיר־חֲנֻכַּת הַבַּיִת לְדָוִד – *A psalm of David. A song for the dedication of the House.* The inclusion of chapter 30 of *Tehillim* is a relatively late addition to the Ashkenazi siddur, first appearing around the seventeenth century. But on the surface the prayer may be said to serve as a transition between the

two parts of the service. On the one hand, one tradition has it that it was sung at the time of the inauguration of the First *Beit HaMikdash*. Having just completed a long recitation of the various sacrifices, we conclude with this reminder and hope that the prayers which we are about to offer serve

MOURNER'S KADDISH

The following prayer, said by mourners, requires the presence of a minyan.
A transliteration can be found on page 921.

Mourner: יִתְגַּדַּל Magnified and sanctified
may His great name be,
in the world He created by His will.
May He establish His kingdom
in your lifetime and in your days,
and in the lifetime of all the house of Israel,
swiftly and soon –
and say: Amen.

All: May His great name be blessed
for ever and all time.

Mourner: Blessed and praised,
glorified and exalted,
raised and honored,
uplifted and lauded
be the name of the Holy One,
blessed be He,
beyond any blessing,
song, praise and consolation
uttered in the world –
and say: Amen.

May there be great peace from heaven,
and life for us and all Israel –
and say: Amen.

Bow, take three steps back, as if taking leave of the Divine Presence,
then bow, first left, then right, then center, while saying:
May He who makes peace in His high places,
make peace for us and all Israel –
and say: Amen.

קדיש יתום

The following prayer, said by mourners, requires the presence of a מנין.
A transliteration can be found on page 921.

אבל: יִתְגַּדַּל וְיִתְקַדַּשׁ שְׁמֵהּ רַבָּא (קהל: אָמֵן)

בְּעָלְמָא דִּי בְרָא כִרְעוּתֵהּ

וְיַמְלִיךְ מַלְכוּתֵהּ

בְּחַיֵּיכוֹן וּבְיוֹמֵיכוֹן וּבְחַיֵּי דְכָל בֵּית יִשְׂרָאֵל

בַּעֲגָלָא וּבִזְמַן קָרִיב

וְאִמְרוּ אָמֵן. (קהל: אָמֵן)

קהל ואבל: יְהֵא שְׁמֵהּ רַבָּא מְבָרַךְ לְעָלַם וּלְעָלְמֵי עָלְמַיָּא.

אבל: יִתְבָּרַךְ וְיִשְׁתַּבַּח וְיִתְפָּאַר

וְיִתְרוֹמַם וְיִתְנַשֵּׂא וְיִתְהַדָּר וְיִתְעַלֶּה וְיִתְהַלָּל

שְׁמֵהּ דְּקֻדְשָׁא בְּרִיךְ הוּא (קהל: בְּרִיךְ הוּא)

לְעֵלָּא מִן כָּל בִּרְכָתָא /בעשרת ימי תשובה: לְעֵלָּא לְעֵלָּא מִכָּל בִּרְכָתָא/

וְשִׁירָתָא, תֻּשְׁבְּחָתָא וְנֶחֱמָתָא

דַּאֲמִירָן בְּעָלְמָא

וְאִמְרוּ אָמֵן. (קהל: אָמֵן)

יְהֵא שְׁלָמָא רַבָּא מִן שְׁמַיָּא

וְחַיִּים, עָלֵינוּ וְעַל כָּל יִשְׂרָאֵל

וְאִמְרוּ אָמֵן. (קהל: אָמֵן)

Bow, take three steps back, as if taking leave of the Divine Presence,
then bow, first left, then right, then center, while saying:

עֹשֶׂה שָׁלוֹם /בעשרת ימי תשובה: הַשָּׁלוֹם/ בִּמְרוֹמָיו

הוּא יַעֲשֶׂה שָׁלוֹם עָלֵינוּ וְעַל כָּל יִשְׂרָאֵל

וְאִמְרוּ אָמֵן. (קהל: אָמֵן)

PESUKEI DEZIMRA

*The introductory blessing to the Pesukei DeZimra (Verses of Praise) is said standing.
There is a custom to hold the two front tzitziot of the tallit until the end of the blessing
at "songs of praise" (on page 70) whereupon they are kissed and released. From
the beginning of this prayer to the end of the Amida, conversation is forbidden.*

Some say:

I hereby prepare my mouth to thank, praise and laud my Creator,
for the sake of the unification of the Holy One,
blessed be He, and His Divine Presence,
through that which is hidden and concealed, in the name of all Israel.

---

is to cut away the thoughts and feelings that get in the way of our ability to
grow spiritually. Reciting these verses
is designed to prepare our souls for the
encounter that we are hopefully to have
with Hashem during the *Shemoneh Esreh*. We first need to nurture our soul, to
give it fresh air to breathe and the space
to be able to come to the fore, before
the demands of our day send it back
into the recesses of our being. *Pesukei
DeZimra* is an opportunity to get back
in touch with the core of who we are
and before whom we stand.

The goal here, then, is to get into
the mood, to get focused. As such, it
is all about quality not quantity. Go
slow. Skip parts if necessary in order to
maintain your own slower pace (see
the guide on what to do when you are
pressed for time, in the Halakha section, law 174). Our sages tell us that we
should utter each word as if it were a
valuable coin being counted. Make the
words count.

HILKHOT TEFILLA · הלכות תפילה

בָּרוּךְ שֶׁאָמַר – *Blessed is He who spoke.*
The following is the opening blessing of
Pesukei DeZimra. It is generally recited while
standing. If you are running out of time, you
should minimally say this prayer before moving on to *Ashrei*.

If one understands the purpose of the different parts of *Pesukei DeZimra* as being a single unit of praise that is designed to prepare us
psychologically and spiritually for *Shemoneh
Esreh*, then one can appreciate the fact that
Halakha deems it important that its recitation
not be interrupted by unnecessary speech.
Its identity as a single unit of praise is indicated by the
opening blessing we are about to recite and
the similar concluding blessing at the end of
Yishtabaḥ, thereby making *Pesukei DeZimra*
one long blessing of praise. This is also the
reason why during its recitation one may respond *Amen* on hearing someone else's blessing, since *Amen*, too, is considered a song of
praise, something that cannot be said of
extraneous conversation.

פסוקי דזמרה

The introductory blessing to the פסוקי דזמרה is said standing. There is a custom to hold the two front ציצית of the טלית until the end of the blessing at בְּתִשְׁבָּחוֹת (on page 71) whereupon they are kissed and released. From the beginning of this prayer to the end of the עמידה, conversation is forbidden.

Some say:

הֲרֵינִי מְזַמֵּן אֶת פִּי לְהוֹדוֹת וּלְהַלֵּל וּלְשַׁבֵּחַ אֶת בּוֹרְאִי
לְשֵׁם יִחוּד קֻדְשָׁא בְּרִיךְ הוּא וּשְׁכִינְתֵּהּ
עַל יְדֵי הַהוּא טָמִיר וְנֶעְלָם בְּשֵׁם כָּל יִשְׂרָאֵל.

AN INTRODUCTION TO THE INTRODUCTION – PESUKEI DEZIMRA

Praying isn't always easy – especially in the morning; especially when you have been up late the night before. The Rabbis understood that even in the best of times, prayer required psyching yourself, getting into the mood or the zone that is familiar to athletes before they play or performers before they go on stage. That's what *Pesukei DeZimra* is: the prelude to *tefilla*. It is a kind of prayer before one prays.

The Rabbis mandated, based upon a request that Moshe made to God, that before one asks anything of God, one should first praise Him.

When I was younger, I cynically thought that this was like trying to bribe God, to butter Him up before I got what I wanted. Yet it gnawed at me: if God is so great, does He really need my praise?! It wasn't until later that I realized that in fact God doesn't need our praise; we do.

If we're going to ask God for something, don't we need to first acknowledge the good that we already have from Him? Don't we need to acknowledge what He is capable of doing for us? Don't we need to first remind ourselves of the beauty of creation, the wonder of the cosmos, the miracle of life, the marvel of God's presence in our history? Only when we know before whom we are standing, when we can admit what His power is relative to our own, can we dare to ask. That's what these seemingly random verses of song, *Pesukei DeZimra*, are supposed to accomplish.

That is why the *Menorat HaMaor* once suggested that the word used here for "song" is related to another Hebrew word, a homonym – זֶמֶר – meaning "to prune." When one wants a plant to grow to be healthy and strong, one often needs to prune it, to cut back the limbs or foliage that prevent it from getting the full measure of air and light required for continued sustenance. So, too, in *Pesukei DeZimra* our goal

BLESSED IS HE WHO SPOKE [B]

and the world came into being, blessed is He.

Blessed is He who creates the universe.

Blessed is He who speaks and acts.

Blessed is He who decrees and fulfills.

Blessed is He who shows compassion to the earth.

Blessed is He who shows compassion to all creatures.

Blessed is He who gives a good reward
to those who fear Him.

Blessed is He who lives for ever and exists to eternity.

Blessed is He who redeems and saves.

Blessed is His name.

---

praying. But note that it's not just about the fact that He created the world, but the *way* in which He created it: simply by uttering His desire to do so. Recall the phrase at the beginning of *Bereshit*, "And God *said*, 'Let there be...' And there was..." Hashem simply willed the world into existence through speech.

But it doesn't end there. The second line, בָּרוּךְ עוֹשֶׂה בְרֵאשִׁית, refers not to the world in general but specifically to the rest of creation. In fact, over and over again in the following verses in *Bereshit* (according to Ḥazal ten times in total), God spoke and the different parts of creation came into being. But what is especially noteworthy is the dif-

ference between the verb tense here and in the previous line. Do you see it? The verb here is in the present tense whereas the previous line is in the past tense. Perhaps that's because the initial creation of the world happened only once, but if you look around you, you can see the world being re-created every day: the dawn of a new day, the birth of a baby, the changing of the seasons – all point to ongoing creation. That's why בָּרוּךְ עוֹשֶׂה בְרֵאשִׁית is written in the present tense, because if I would just open my eyes (sleepy as they may be this time of morning) I would realize how amazing the world is.

IYUN TEFILLA · עיון תפילה

בָּרוּךְ שֶׁאָמַר – *Blessed is He who spoke.* There has been much written about this prayer, the meaning of each one of the phrases, the philosophical content of each, and the like. Suffice it to say that what we have

here is a series of statements that go to the essence of our beliefs about God and the way He runs the universe. In fact, if you look at all of the rest of the statements in this introductory paragraph, you will see that each can

This IYUN TEFILLA continues on page 71.

בָּרוּךְ
שֶׁאָמַר בע
וְהָיָה הָעוֹלָם, בָּרוּךְ הוּא.

בָּרוּךְ עוֹשֶׂה בְרֵאשִׁית

בָּרוּךְ אוֹמֵר וְעוֹשֶׂה

בָּרוּךְ גּוֹזֵר וּמְקַיֵּם

בָּרוּךְ מְרַחֵם עַל הָאָרֶץ

בָּרוּךְ מְרַחֵם עַל הַבְּרִיּוֹת

בָּרוּךְ מְשַׁלֵּם שָׂכָר טוֹב לִירֵאָיו

בָּרוּךְ חַי לָעַד וְקַיָּם לָנֶצַח

בָּרוּךְ פּוֹדֶה וּמַצִּיל

בָּרוּךְ שְׁמוֹ

BIUR TEFILLA · בִּיאוּר תְּפִילָה

בָּרוּךְ שֶׁאָמַר – *Blessed is He who spoke.*
The origin of this prayer is shrouded in mystery. One source claims that a note fell down from heaven upon which this prayer was written. In fact, it may date as far back as the *Tanna'im* but the legend attests to the mystical content of the prayer as well. So holy was this prayer considered, so important was it deemed to be an introduction to *Pesukei DeZimra*, that there are reports of some communities in medieval Germany that used to spend one full hour reciting it. (And you thought *tefilla* today takes a long time!)

בָּרוּךְ שֶׁאָמַר – *Blessed is He who spoke.*
The first section of the *tefilla*, which you can easily tell consists of a number of repetitions of the word בָּרוּךְ (ten of them if you don't include בָּרוּךְ הוּא, which is part of Hashem's name and not a blessing) followed by some descriptions of what Hashem can do and does.

In the very first one, for example, בָּרוּךְ שֶׁאָמַר וְהָיָה הָעוֹלָם בָּרוּךְ הוּא, we declare that Hashem created the world. Sounds like an appropriate way to start off *tefilla*, no? After all, if we are about to pray, it makes sense for us to remind ourselves to whom we are

Blessed are You, LORD our God, King of the Universe,
God, compassionate Father, extolled by the mouth of His people,
praised and glorified by the tongue of His devoted ones
and those who serve Him.
With the songs of Your servant David[B]
we will praise You, O LORD our God.
With praises and psalms
we will magnify and praise You, glorify You,
Speak Your name and proclaim Your kingship,
our King, our God, ▸ the only One, Giver of life to the worlds,
the King whose great name is praised
and glorified to all eternity.
Blessed are You, LORD,
the King extolled with songs of praise.[B]

ANI TEFILLA · אני תפילה

*But just a few days before my arrest, I received
[a book of Psalms from my wife, which the
authorities confiscated from me] … It took
me three years to fight, to force authorities
to give me this book… It was difficult for me
to read, with my [limited] knowledge of Hebrew, this ancient language where you cannot even understand where is the end of the
sentence. It was difficult to understand, but
when you are reading day after day, you understand a word here, a word there, a phrase
here, a phrase there, you compare, and some
moment you start understanding. I remember the first psalm which I suddenly understood, the phrase which I understood was
[Hebrew], "And when I go through the valley of
death, I'll fear no evil, because You are with me."
It was such a powerful feeling, as if King David
himself, together with my wife, together with
my friends, came to prison to save me from
this, and to support me. Suddenly all these
connections of thousands of years are restored,*

*and you feel exactly as King David, 3000 years
ago, wrote this. This was sending me a message to be strong… That was a very powerful
feeling, and it gave me a lot of strength. I felt
all the time that if this book of psalms was
with me, nothing would happen. I fought
each time they took it from me: I was on hunger strikes, I spent hundreds of days on hunger
strikes and in punishment cells, in order not to
permit them to take it from me. Even when I
was released, and I still didn't know that I was
released, but I was brought to the airplane
from the prison, and they took all the clothes,
and gave me different ones, and I suddenly
understood that maybe some big changes
are happening, but my book of psalms was
not with me. I was so scared to be without it
that I lay in the snow and refused to enter the
airplane until they brought it back to me. And
that's the only piece of property with which I
came to freedom from Soviet prison. (Natan
Sharansky)*

בָּרוּךְ אַתָּה יהוה אֱלֹהֵינוּ מֶלֶךְ הָעוֹלָם
הָאֵל הָאָב הָרַחֲמָן הַמְהֻלָּל בְּפִי עַמּוֹ
מְשֻׁבָּח וּמְפֹאָר בִּלְשׁוֹן חֲסִידָיו וַעֲבָדָיו
וּבְשִׁירֵי דָוִד עַבְדֶּךָ נְהַלֶּלְךָ יהוה אֱלֹהֵינוּ.
בִּשְׁבָחוֹת וּבִזְמִירוֹת, נְגַדֶּלְךָ וּנְשַׁבֵּחֲךָ וּנְפָאֶרְךָ
וְנַזְכִּיר שִׁמְךָ וְנַמְלִיכְךָ מַלְכֵּנוּ אֱלֹהֵינוּ, יָחִיד חֵי הָעוֹלָמִים
מֶלֶךְ, מְשֻׁבָּח וּמְפֹאָר עֲדֵי עַד שְׁמוֹ הַגָּדוֹל
בָּרוּךְ אַתָּה יהוה, מֶלֶךְ מְהֻלָּל בַּתִּשְׁבָּחוֹת.

---

be interpreted to reflect a different important belief that we hold dear. In effect, the siddur is directing us at this very beginning of prayer to re-call and reflect upon before whom we stand.

This is heady stuff: to think about God, to feel His presence, to reflect upon his name, His attributes, what He has done, what He continues to do, how He treats us every day... It's amazing that it only took those people in medieval Germany an hour to say this whole thing with *kavana*. How long does it take you?

ביאור תפילה • BIUR TEFILLA

בָּרוּךְ שֶׁאָמַר – *Blessed is He who spoke.*
The prayer really consists of two parts. The second part is, in effect, a *berakha* that we recite before saying *Pesukei DeZimra*. You can find that section because it begins and ends with the traditional formula of בָּרוּךְ אַתָּה... In it, we declare that we are about to praise Hashem using the psalms of King David which mostly speak about the beauty of creation that we too often take for granted. In fact, from here until *Yishtabaḥ*, the concluding bless-ing of *Pesukei DeZimra*, we recite 13 paragraphs of praise, the same number of times that the word בָּרוּךְ appears in this introductory prayer.

BIUR TEFILLA • ביאור תפילה

וּבְשִׁירֵי דָוִד עַבְדֶּךָ – *With the songs of Your servant David.* This is a reference to King David and the songs referred to are the psalms that we know as the book of *Tehillim* which he authored. This opening blessing thus says that we will praise God specifically using David's *Tehillim* and it therefore alludes to the core of *Pesukei DeZimra*, namely, the last six chapters of the book of *Tehillim* which we will begin to say a little later on, starting with the prayer *Ashrei*.

מֶלֶךְ מְהֻלָּל בַּתִּשְׁבָּחוֹת – *The King extolled with songs of praise.* This blessing sets the tone for *Pesukei DeZimra*, namely, praising Hashem. As we mentioned above, Hash-em doesn't need our praises. We need them.

הוֹדוּ לַיהוה Thank the Lord,[B] call on His name, make His acts *1 Chr. 16* known among the peoples. Sing to Him, make music to Him, tell of all His wonders. Glory in His holy name; let the hearts of those who seek the Lord rejoice. Search out the Lord and His strength; seek His presence at all times. Remember the wonders He has done, His miracles, and the judgments He pronounced. Descendants of Yisrael His servant, sons of Jacob His chosen ones: He is the Lord our God. His judgments are throughout the earth. Remember His covenant for ever, the word He commanded for a thousand generations. He made it with Abraham, vowed it to Isaac, and confirmed it to Jacob as a statute and to Israel as an everlasting covenant, saying, "To you I will give the land of Canaan as your allotted heritage." You were then small in number, few, strangers there, wandering from nation to nation, from one kingdom to another, but He let no man oppress them, and for their sake He rebuked kings: "Do not touch My anointed ones, and do My prophets no harm." Sing to the Lord, all the earth; proclaim His salvation daily. Declare His glory among the nations, His marvels among all the peoples. For great is the Lord and greatly to be praised; He is awesome beyond all heavenly powers. ▸ For all the gods of the peoples are mere idols; it was the Lord who made the heavens.

Before Him are majesty and splendor; there is strength and beauty in His holy place. Render to the Lord, families of the peoples, render to the Lord honor and might. Render to the Lord the glory due to His name; bring an offering and come before Him; bow

---

the *Beit HaMikdash* was built by King Solomon. At that point, different sacrifices and songs were instituted.

This historical information explains the difference between Ashkenazic and Sephardic practice regarding this prayer. Sephardim associate it with the sacrifices and therefore recite it before the prayer of *Ba-*

rukh She'amar which marks the beginning of *Pesukei DeZimra*. Ashkenazim, however, associate it with the *Tehillim* composed and recited by David since, once the *Beit HaMikdash* was built, this prayer was no longer said with the sacrifices and thus stands on its own as a song of David (*Beit Yosef* 50, *Tur* 51).

הוֹדוּ לַיהוה קִרְאוּ בִשְׁמוֹ, הוֹדִיעוּ בָעַמִּים עֲלִילֹתָיו: שִׁירוּ לוֹ,
זַמְּרוּ־לוֹ, שִׂיחוּ בְּכָל־נִפְלְאוֹתָיו: הִתְהַלְלוּ בְּשֵׁם קָדְשׁוֹ, יִשְׂמַח לֵב
מְבַקְשֵׁי יהוה: דִּרְשׁוּ יהוה וְעֻזּוֹ, בַּקְּשׁוּ פָנָיו תָּמִיד: זִכְרוּ נִפְלְאֹתָיו
אֲשֶׁר עָשָׂה, מֹפְתָיו וּמִשְׁפְּטֵי־פִיהוּ: זֶרַע יִשְׂרָאֵל עַבְדּוֹ, בְּנֵי יַעֲקֹב
בְּחִירָיו: הוּא יהוה אֱלֹהֵינוּ בְּכָל־הָאָרֶץ מִשְׁפָּטָיו: זִכְרוּ לְעוֹלָם
בְּרִיתוֹ, דָּבָר צִוָּה לְאֶלֶף דּוֹר: אֲשֶׁר כָּרַת אֶת־אַבְרָהָם, וּשְׁבוּעָתוֹ
לְיִצְחָק: וַיַּעֲמִידֶהָ לְיַעֲקֹב לְחֹק, לְיִשְׂרָאֵל בְּרִית עוֹלָם: לֵאמֹר,
לְךָ אֶתֵּן אֶרֶץ־כְּנָעַן, חֶבֶל נַחֲלַתְכֶם: בִּהְיוֹתְכֶם מְתֵי מִסְפָּר,
כִּמְעַט וְגָרִים בָּהּ: וַיִּתְהַלְּכוּ מִגּוֹי אֶל־גּוֹי, וּמִמַּמְלָכָה אֶל־עַם
אַחֵר: לֹא־הִנִּיחַ לְאִישׁ לְעָשְׁקָם, וַיּוֹכַח עֲלֵיהֶם מְלָכִים: אַל־
תִּגְּעוּ בִּמְשִׁיחָי, וּבִנְבִיאַי אַל־תָּרֵעוּ: שִׁירוּ לַיהוה כָּל־הָאָרֶץ,
בַּשְּׂרוּ מִיּוֹם־אֶל־יוֹם יְשׁוּעָתוֹ: סַפְּרוּ בַגּוֹיִם אֶת־כְּבוֹדוֹ, בְּכָל־
הָעַמִּים נִפְלְאֹתָיו: כִּי גָדוֹל יהוה וּמְהֻלָּל מְאֹד, וְנוֹרָא הוּא
עַל־כָּל־אֱלֹהִים: ‹ כִּי כָּל־אֱלֹהֵי הָעַמִּים אֱלִילִים, וַיהוה שָׁמַיִם
עָשָׂה:

הוֹד וְהָדָר לְפָנָיו, עֹז וְחֶדְוָה בִּמְקֹמוֹ: הָבוּ לַיהוה מִשְׁפְּחוֹת
עַמִּים, הָבוּ לַיהוה כָּבוֹד וָעֹז: הָבוּ לַיהוה כְּבוֹד שְׁמוֹ, שְׂאוּ
מִנְחָה וּבֹאוּ לְפָנָיו, הִשְׁתַּחֲווּ לַיהוה בְּהַדְרַת־קֹדֶשׁ: חִילוּ מִלְּפָנָיו

ביאור תפילה · BIUR TEFILLA

הוֹדוּ לַיהוה – *Thank the Lord.* The first set of verses was recited by David and actually come from *Divrei HaYamim* I 16:8–36. Once the Ark had been returned by the Pelishtim, David built a special enclosure in Yerusha-

layim to protect it there. A special *Tamid* sacrifice in its honor was instituted, once in the morning and once in the evening, each with its own song sung by a choir of *Levi'im*. And thus it was for 43 years until

down to the LORD in the splendor of holiness. Tremble before Him, all the earth; the world stands firm, it will not be shaken. Let the heavens rejoice and the earth be glad; let them declare among the nations, "The LORD is King." Let the sea roar, and all that is in it; let the fields be jubilant, and all they contain. Then the trees of the forest will sing for joy before the LORD, for He is coming to judge the earth. Thank the LORD for He is good; His loving-kindness is for ever. Say: "Save us, God of our salvation; gather us and rescue us from the nations, to acknowledge Your holy name and glory in Your praise. Blessed is the LORD, God of Israel, from this world to eternity." And let all the people say "Amen" and "Praise the LORD."

▸ Exalt the LORD our God and bow before His footstool: He is *Ps. 99* holy. Exalt the LORD our God and bow at His holy mountain; for holy is the LORD our God.

He is compassionate. He forgives iniquity and does not destroy. *Ps. 78* Repeatedly He suppresses His anger, not rousing His full wrath. You, LORD: do not withhold Your compassion from me. May Your *Ps. 40* loving-kindness and truth always guard me. Remember, LORD, *Ps. 25* Your acts of compassion and love, for they have existed for ever. Ascribe power to God, whose majesty is over Israel and whose *Ps. 68* might is in the skies. You are awesome, God, in Your holy places. It is the God of Israel who gives might and strength to the people, may God be blessed. God of retribution, LORD, God of retribu- *Ps. 94* tion, appear. Arise, Judge of the earth, to repay the arrogant their just deserts. Salvation belongs to the LORD; may Your blessing *Ps. 3* rest upon Your people, Selah! ▸ The LORD of hosts is with us, the *Ps. 46* God of Jacob is our stronghold, Selah! LORD of hosts, happy is *Ps. 84* the one who trusts in You. LORD, save! May the King answer us *Ps. 20* on the day we call.

Save Your people and bless Your heritage; tend them and carry *Ps. 28* them for ever. Our soul longs for the LORD; He is our Help and *Ps. 33* Shield. For in Him our hearts rejoice, for in His holy name we

כָּל־הָאָרֶץ, אַף־תִּכּוֹן תֵּבֵל בַּל־תִּמּוֹט: יִשְׂמְחוּ הַשָּׁמַיִם וְתָגֵל הָאָרֶץ, וְיֹאמְרוּ בַגּוֹיִם יְהוָה מָלָךְ: יִרְעַם הַיָּם וּמְלֹאוֹ, יַעֲלֹז הַשָּׂדֶה וְכָל־אֲשֶׁר־בּוֹ: אָז יְרַנְּנוּ עֲצֵי הַיָּעַר, מִלִּפְנֵי יְהוָה, כִּי־בָא לִשְׁפֹּט אֶת־הָאָרֶץ: הוֹדוּ לַיהוָה כִּי טוֹב, כִּי לְעוֹלָם חַסְדּוֹ: וְאִמְרוּ, הוֹשִׁיעֵנוּ אֱלֹהֵי יִשְׁעֵנוּ, וְקַבְּצֵנוּ וְהַצִּילֵנוּ מִן־הַגּוֹיִם, לְהֹדוֹת לְשֵׁם קָדְשֶׁךָ, לְהִשְׁתַּבֵּחַ בִּתְהִלָּתֶךָ: בָּרוּךְ יְהוָה אֱלֹהֵי יִשְׂרָאֵל מִן־הָעוֹלָם וְעַד־הָעֹלָם, וַיֹּאמְרוּ כָל־הָעָם אָמֵן, וְהַלֵּל לַיהוָה:

‹ רוֹמְמוּ יְהוָה אֱלֹהֵינוּ וְהִשְׁתַּחֲווּ לַהֲדֹם רַגְלָיו, קָדוֹשׁ הוּא: ‫תהלים צט‬
רוֹמְמוּ יְהוָה אֱלֹהֵינוּ וְהִשְׁתַּחֲווּ לְהַר קָדְשׁוֹ, כִּי־קָדוֹשׁ יְהוָה
אֱלֹהֵינוּ:

וְהוּא רַחוּם, יְכַפֵּר עָוֹן וְלֹא־יַשְׁחִית, וְהִרְבָּה לְהָשִׁיב אַפּוֹ, ‫תהלים עח‬
וְלֹא־יָעִיר כָּל־חֲמָתוֹ: אַתָּה יְהוָה לֹא־תִכְלָא רַחֲמֶיךָ מִמֶּנִּי, חַסְדְּךָ ‫תהלים מ‬
וַאֲמִתְּךָ תָּמִיד יִצְּרוּנִי: זְכֹר־רַחֲמֶיךָ יְהוָה וַחֲסָדֶיךָ, כִּי מֵעוֹלָם ‫תהלים כה‬
הֵמָּה: תְּנוּ עֹז לֵאלֹהִים, עַל־יִשְׂרָאֵל גַּאֲוָתוֹ, וְעֻזּוֹ בַּשְּׁחָקִים: ‫תהלים סח‬
נוֹרָא אֱלֹהִים מִמִּקְדָּשֶׁיךָ, אֵל יִשְׂרָאֵל הוּא נֹתֵן עֹז וְתַעֲצֻמוֹת
לָעָם, בָּרוּךְ אֱלֹהִים: אֵל־נְקָמוֹת יְהוָה, אֵל נְקָמוֹת הוֹפִיעַ: ‫תהלים צד‬
הִנָּשֵׂא שֹׁפֵט הָאָרֶץ, הָשֵׁב גְּמוּל עַל־גֵּאִים: לַיהוָה הַיְשׁוּעָה, ‫תהלים ג‬
עַל־עַמְּךָ בִרְכָתֶךָ סֶּלָה: ‹ יְהוָה צְבָאוֹת עִמָּנוּ, מִשְׂגָּב לָנוּ אֱלֹהֵי ‫תהלים מו‬
יַעֲקֹב סֶלָה: יְהוָה צְבָאוֹת, אַשְׁרֵי אָדָם בֹּטֵחַ בָּךְ: יְהוָה הוֹשִׁיעָה, ‫תהלים פד‬
‫תהלים כ‬
הַמֶּלֶךְ יַעֲנֵנוּ בְיוֹם־קָרְאֵנוּ:

הוֹשִׁיעָה אֶת־עַמֶּךָ, וּבָרֵךְ אֶת־נַחֲלָתֶךָ, וּרְעֵם וְנַשְּׂאֵם עַד־ ‫תהלים כח‬
הָעוֹלָם: נַפְשֵׁנוּ חִכְּתָה לַיהוָה, עֶזְרֵנוּ וּמָגִנֵּנוּ הוּא: כִּי־בוֹ יִשְׂמַח ‫תהלים לג‬

have trusted. May Your loving-kindness, LORD, be upon us, as we
have put our hope in You. Show us, LORD, Your loving-kindness *Ps. 85*
and grant us Your salvation. Arise, help us and redeem us for the *Ps. 44*
sake of Your love. I am the LORD your God who brought you *Ps. 81*
up from the land of Egypt: open your mouth wide and I will fill
it. Happy is the people for whom this is so; happy is the people *Ps. 144*
whose God is the LORD. ▸ As for me, I trust in Your loving-kind- *Ps. 13*
ness; my heart rejoices in Your salvation. I will sing to the LORD
for He has been good to me.

The following psalm recalls the thanksgiving-offering in Temple times.
It is not said on Erev Pesaḥ, on Ḥol HaMo'ed Pesaḥ, or Erev Yom Kippur
since no thanksgiving-offerings were brought on these days.
To emphasize its sacrificial nature, the custom is to say it standing.

מִזְמוֹר A psalm of thanksgiving.ᴵᴬ Shout joyously to the LORD, *Ps. 100*
all the earth. Serve the LORD with joy. Come before Him
with jubilation. Know that the LORD is God. He made us
and we are His. We are His people and the flock He tends.
Enter His gates with thanksgiving, His courts with praise.
Thank Him and bless His name. ▸ For the LORD is good,
His loving-kindness is everlasting, and His faithfulness is
for every generation.

מִזְמוֹר לְתוֹדָה – *A psalm of thanksgiving.* We
go through a myriad of potential disasters
every day. We are surrounded by germs; we
cross the street in busy traffic; our car brakes
are supposed to stop our vehicle when we
press them but they could just as easily
not do so; accidents happen around us all
of the time and we walk away unscathed.
Think about your morning thus far, about

your trip to get here, about the things that
could have gone wrong, but didn't. We go
about our lives as if nothing could have happened…or will happen. We take such things
for granted. This prayer is part of the anti-
dote to that lack of awareness. What might
have gone wrong? What didn't go wrong?
What do I have to be thankful for? Now
say this prayer of thanks.

תהלים פה
תהלים מד

לָ֫נוּ, כִּי בְשֵׁם קָדְשׁוֹ בָטָ֑חְנוּ: יְהִי־חַסְדְּךָ יהוה עָלֵ֑ינוּ, כַּאֲשֶׁר יִחַ֥לְנוּ לָךְ: הַרְאֵנוּ יהוה חַסְדֶּ֑ךָ, וְיֶשְׁעֲךָ תִּתֶּן־לָנוּ: קוּמָ֥ה עֶזְרָ֥תָה

תהלים פא

לָּ֫נוּ, וּפְדֵ֥נוּ לְמַ֥עַן חַסְדֶּ֑ךָ: אָנֹכִ֨י יהוה אֱלֹהֶ֗יךָ הַֽמַּעַלְךָ מֵאֶ֥רֶץ מִצְרָ֑יִם, הַרְחֶב־פִּ֝֗יךָ וַאֲמַלְאֵֽהוּ: אַשְׁרֵ֥י הָעָ֗ם שֶׁכָּ֥כָה לּ֑וֹ, אַשְׁרֵ֥י

תהלים יג

הָעָ֗ם שֶׁיהוה אֱלֹהָֽיו: ◄ וַאֲנִ֤י בְּחַסְדְּךָ בָטַ֗חְתִּי, יָגֵ֥ל לִבִּי֮ בִּישׁוּעָתֶ֥ךָ, אָשִׁ֥ירָה לַֽיהוה, כִּ֖י גָמַ֣ל עָלָֽי:

The following psalm recalls the קָרְבַּן תּוֹדָה *in Temple times.*
It is not said on עֶרֶב יוֹם כִּפּוּר *or* חוֹל הַמּוֹעֵד פֶּסַח, עֶרֶב פֶּסַח,
since no קוּרְבְּנוֹת תּוֹדָה *were brought on these days.*
To emphasize its sacrificial nature, the custom is to say it standing.

תהלים ק

מִזְמ֥וֹר לְתוֹדָ֗ה,ᵃ הָרִ֥יעוּ לַֽיהוה כָּל־הָאָֽרֶץ: עִבְד֣וּ אֶת־ יהוה בְּשִׂמְחָ֑ה, בֹּ֥אוּ לְ֝פָנָ֗יו בִּרְנָנָֽה: דְּע֗וּ כִּֽי־יהוה ה֤וּא אֱלֹהִ֗ים, הֽוּא־עָ֭שָׂנוּ וְל֣וֹ אֲנַ֑חְנוּ, עַ֝מּ֗וֹ וְצֹ֣אן מַרְעִיתֽוֹ: בֹּ֤אוּ שְׁעָרָ֨יו בְּתוֹדָ֗ה, חֲצֵרֹתָ֥יו בִּתְהִלָּ֑ה, הֽוֹדוּ־ל֗וֹ, בָּרְכ֥וּ שְׁמֽוֹ: ◄ כִּי־ט֣וֹב יהוה, לְעוֹלָ֥ם חַסְדּ֑וֹ, וְעַד־דֹּ֥ר וָ֝דֹ֗ר אֱמוּנָתֽוֹ:

מִזְמוֹר לְתוֹדָה – *A psalm of thanksgiving.* Rashi believes that the saying of this prayer is directly related to the sacrifice known as the *Korban Toda* which was brought in the *Beit HaMikdash*. The circumstances for bringing this sacrifice are fairly well known: "Four kinds of people are supposed to bring this kind of sacrifice: someone who survives an ocean voyage, a journey through the desert, an illness, or a period of time in prison" (*Berakhot* 54b).

Imagine if you had been in such a situation. Did you turn to God and say "If You just get me through this, I promise I'll…" And when the moment of danger passed, were you filled with elation and just wanted to scream in thanks? Or did you forget to give thanks altogether? The Torah commanded that on such occasions we go to the *Beit HaMikdash* to give thanks to Hashem, for, no matter what the circumstances of our delivery, we believe that behind it all Hashem is there pulling the strings.

יְהִי כְבוֹד May the Lord's glory[IAB] be for ever; may the Lord rejoice *Ps. 104*
in His works. May the Lord's name be blessed, now and for ever. *Ps. 113*
From the rising of the sun to its setting, may the Lord's name be
praised. The Lord is high above all nations; His glory is above the
heavens. Lord, Your name is for ever. Your renown, Lord, is for all *Ps. 135*
generations. The Lord has established His throne in heaven; His *Ps. 103*
kingdom rules all. Let the heavens rejoice and the earth be glad. Let *1 Chr. 16*
them say among the nations, "The Lord is King." The Lord is King,
the Lord was King, the Lord will be King for ever and all time. The *Ps. 10*
Lord is King for ever and all time; nations will perish from His land.
The Lord foils the plans of nations; He frustrates the intentions of *Ps. 33*
peoples. Many are the intentions in a person's mind, but the Lord's *Prov. 19*
plan prevails. The Lord's plan shall stand for ever, His mind's intent *Ps. 33*
for all generations. For He spoke and it was; He commanded and
it stood firm. For the Lord has chosen Zion; He desired it for His *Ps. 132*
dwelling. For the Lord has chosen Jacob as His own, Israel as His *Ps. 135*
special treasure. For the Lord will not abandon His people; nor will *Ps. 94*
He forsake His heritage. ‣ He is compassionate. He forgives iniquity *Ps. 78*
and does not destroy. Repeatedly He suppresses His anger, not rousing His full wrath. Lord, save! May the King answer us on the day *Ps. 20*
we call.

INTRODUCTION TO THE LAST SIX PSALMS

What follows next is the "core" of *Pesukei DeZimra*, the oldest and most significant parts of this section of *tefilla*. Rabbi J.B. Soloveitchik suggested that it derives from the practice reported in the Gemara (*Berakhot* 30b), wherein the pious men of old would wait for an hour before praying *Shemoneh Esreh* in order to properly collect and direct their thoughts. They recited psalms of praise in keeping with the directive of Rav Simlai (*Berakhot* 32a) that one must first praise Hashem and only afterwards ask for one's needs.

This next section we are about to say comprises a discrete unit since, rather than being seemingly random verses, it consists of the last six psalms of the book of *Tehillim* (chapters 145–150), as if to say that with their recitation, it is as if we recited the entire book of praises. Even so, these psalms share a common theme; they are a kind of *Hallel* in which Hashem reveals Himself not through miracles but through the forces of nature that surround us daily. Nourishment of one's faith lies in the everyday, not in supernatural wonders. As Rabbi Soloveitchik once noted, is there truly any greater miracle than the sun rising in the morning?

תהלים קד
תהלים קג

יְהִי כְבוֹדבש יהוה לְעוֹלָם, יִשְׂמַח יהוה בְּמַעֲשָׂיו: יְהִי שֵׁם יהוה
מְבֹרָךְ, מֵעַתָּה וְעַד־עוֹלָם: מִמִּזְרַח־שֶׁמֶשׁ עַד־מְבוֹאוֹ, מְהֻלָּל

תהלים קלה

שֵׁם יהוה: רָם עַל־כָּל־גּוֹיִם יהוה, עַל הַשָּׁמַיִם כְּבוֹדוֹ: יהוה שִׁמְךָ

תהלים קג

לְעוֹלָם, יהוה זִכְרְךָ לְדֹר־וָדֹר: יהוה בַּשָּׁמַיִם הֵכִין כִּסְאוֹ, וּמַלְכוּתוֹ

דברי הימים
א' טז

בַּכֹּל מָשָׁלָה: יִשְׂמְחוּ הַשָּׁמַיִם וְתָגֵל הָאָרֶץ, וְיֹאמְרוּ בַגּוֹיִם יהוה

תהלים י

מָלָךְ: יהוה מֶלֶךְ, יהוה מָלָךְ, יהוה יִמְלֹךְ לְעֹלָם וָעֶד: יהוה מֶלֶךְ

תהלים לג

עוֹלָם וָעֶד, אָבְדוּ גוֹיִם מֵאַרְצוֹ: יהוה הֵפִיר עֲצַת־גּוֹיִם, הֵנִיא

משלי יט

מַחְשְׁבוֹת עַמִּים: רַבּוֹת מַחֲשָׁבוֹת בְּלֶב־אִישׁ, וַעֲצַת יהוה הִיא

תהלים לג

תָקוּם: עֲצַת יהוה לְעוֹלָם תַּעֲמֹד, מַחְשְׁבוֹת לִבּוֹ לְדֹר וָדֹר: כִּי הוּא

תהלים קלב

אָמַר וַיֶּהִי, הוּא־צִוָּה וַיַּעֲמֹד: כִּי־בָחַר יהוה בְּצִיּוֹן, אִוָּהּ לְמוֹשָׁב לוֹ:

תהלים קלה
תהלים צד

כִּי־יַעֲקֹב בָּחַר לוֹ יָהּ, יִשְׂרָאֵל לִסְגֻלָּתוֹ: כִּי לֹא־יִטֹּשׁ יהוה עַמּוֹ,

תהלים עח

וְנַחֲלָתוֹ לֹא יַעֲזֹב: וְהוּא רַחוּם, יְכַפֵּר עָוֹן וְלֹא־יַשְׁחִית, וְהִרְבָּה

תהלים כ

לְהָשִׁיב אַפּוֹ, וְלֹא־יָעִיר כָּל־חֲמָתוֹ: יהוה הוֹשִׁיעָה, הַמֶּלֶךְ יַעֲנֵנוּ
בְיוֹם־קָרְאֵנוּ:

יְהִי כְבוֹד — *May the Lord's glory.* "May Hashem's glory be forever; may Hashem rejoice in His works." Hashem's "glory" parallels "His works" and is thus a reference to creation. The Gemara says that when an angel uttered this verse at the time of creation, all of the plants began to emerge (*Hullin* 60a). The phrase thus introduces the theme of God's presence in nature that will be at the center of *Pesukei DeZimra.*

יְהִי כְבוֹד — *May the Lord's glory.* The Gemara (*Berakhot* 10a) notes that "there is no artist like God."

Where can I see Hashem's artistry this morning?

יְהִי כְבוֹד — *May the Lord's glory.* Numbers: There is a tradition that in this prayer there are 21 references to Hashem's name, paralleling the 21 verses in the prayer of *Ashrei* which follows (*Tehilla* 145). Can you find the 21? (Hint: most are explicit; one is hidden in the initials of the first four words of one of the verses.)

*The line beginning with "You open Your hand" should be said with special
concentration, representing as it does the key idea of this Psalm, and of Pesukei
DeZimra as a whole, that God is the creator and sustainer of all. Some have
the custom to touch the hand-tefillin at °, and the head-tefillin at °°.*

אַשְׁרֵי Happy are those who dwell in Your House;ᴬᴮ

    they shall continue to praise You, Selah!

Ps. 84

Happy are the people for whom this is so;

    happy are the people whose God is the Lᴏʀᴅ.

Ps. 144

A song of praise by David.

Ps. 145

  א I will exalt You, my God, the King,

    and bless Your name for ever and all time.

  ב Every day I will bless You,

    and praise Your name for ever and all time.

  ג Great is the Lᴏʀᴅ and greatly to be praised;

    His greatness is unfathomable.

  ד One generation will praise Your works to the next,ᴬ

    and tell of Your mighty deeds.

ANI TEFILLA · אני תפילה

דּוֹר לְדוֹר יְשַׁבַּח מַעֲשֶׂיךָ – *One generation
will praise Your works to the next*. Every
generation passes its firsthand experience along to the next generation. We
are who we are thanks to the traditions
passed along to us by our parents, grandparents and previous generations (Radak).
**What has the previous generation
contributed to my development and
growth as a person and as a Jew?**

דּוֹר לְדוֹר יְשַׁבַּח מַעֲשֶׂיךָ – *One generation will
praise Your works to the next*. Every generation
is capable of uncovering scientific knowledge
that was unavailable to its predecessors, so
that in each generation it is possible to gain an
even better and more accurate understanding
and appreciation of God's world (Malbim).
**What inventions or discoveries have pre-
vious generations enabled me to benefit
from?**

ANI TEFILLA · אני תפילה

*Imagine a king who asks his servant to go
up to the attic. If the servant doesn't jump up
from the ground to the attic in a single leap,
the king won't be angry. He expects that the
servant will need to go up a ladder, one rung
at a time. That, then, is what Hashem demands of us; to raise ourselves, in steps, one
rung at a time. (Rabbi Ḥayyim of Volozhin)*

The line beginning with פוֹתֵחַ אֶת יָדֶךָ should be said with special concentration,
representing as it does the key idea of this psalm, and of פסוקי דזמרה as a
whole, that God is the creator and sustainer of all. Some have the custom
to touch the תפילין של יד at °, and the תפילין של ראש at °°.

תהלים פד

אַשְׁרֵי יוֹשְׁבֵי בֵיתֶךָ,°° עוֹד יְהַלְלוּךָ סֶּלָה:

תהלים קמד

אַשְׁרֵי הָעָם שֶׁכָּכָה לּוֹ, אַשְׁרֵי הָעָם שֶׁיהוה אֱלֹהָיו:

תהלים קמה

תְּהִלָּה לְדָוִד

אֲרוֹמִמְךָ אֱלוֹהַי הַמֶּלֶךְ, וַאֲבָרְכָה שִׁמְךָ לְעוֹלָם וָעֶד:

בְּכָל־יוֹם אֲבָרְכֶךָ, וַאֲהַלְלָה שִׁמְךָ לְעוֹלָם וָעֶד:

גָּדוֹל יהוה וּמְהֻלָּל מְאֹד, וְלִגְדֻלָּתוֹ אֵין חֵקֶר:

דּוֹר לְדוֹר יְשַׁבַּח מַעֲשֶׂיךָ,° וּגְבוּרֹתֶיךָ יַגִּידוּ:

ANI TEFILLA · אני תפילה

אַשְׁרֵי יוֹשְׁבֵי בֵיתֶךָ – *Happy are those who dwell in Your House.* Happy are those who take time out every morning to get back in touch with You and with themselves.

Research shows that people who pray regularly are healthier, have greater coping skills and resilience than those who don't. In short, they can indeed be happier.

BIUR TEFILLA · ביאור תפילה

אַשְׁרֵי יוֹשְׁבֵי בֵיתֶךָ – *Happy are those who dwell in Your House.* This verse is from *Tehilla* 84:5 and the next one is from *Tehilla* 144:15. They were added as a prelude to *Tehilla* 145 but the combination is known as *Ashrei*. Rabbi Soloveitchik once suggested that they were added because, viewed in context, they are a declaration of a longing to be in God's presence, just as Jews felt it during the times of the *Beit HaMikdash*. The language is therefore similar to the very

first verse of *Tehillim* which also begins with the word אַשְׁרֵי. But *Hazal* added a verse at the end of this prayer that is not part of the original psalm and thereby makes the last word הַלְלוּיָה. Stylistically it is thus similar to the end of the book of *Tehillim* (and all of the ones we are about to say) which also ends with הַלְלוּיָה. This psalm thus reflects the entire book of *Tehillim* both in substance (the acrostic representing the entire *Alef-Beit*) and in form.

ה On the glorious splendor of Your majesty I will meditate,
  and on the acts of Your wonders.

ו They shall talk of the power of Your awesome deeds,
  and I will tell of Your greatness.

ז They shall recite the record of Your great goodness,
  and sing with joy of Your righteousness.|

ח The Lord is gracious and compassionate,
  slow to anger and great in loving-kindness.

ט The Lord is good to all,|
  and His compassion extends to all His works.

י All Your works shall thank You,|ᴬ Lord,
  and Your devoted ones shall bless You.

כ They shall talk of the glory of Your kingship,
  and speak of Your might.

ל To make known to mankind His mighty deeds
  and the glorious majesty of His kingship.

מ Your kingdom is an everlasting kingdom,
  and Your reign is for all generations.

ס The Lord supports all who fall,|
  and raises all who are bowed down.

ע All raise their eyes to You in hope,
  and You give them their food in due season.

יוֹדוּךָ יהוה כָּל מַעֲשֶׂיךָ – *All Your works shall thank You.* The moon and stars, the sea creatures, the deserts, the mountains and valleys, the vegetation and trees and animals and insects and birds; a song to God emanates from all of them. (*Tehillot Hashem*)

ANI TEFILLA · אני תפילה

יוֹדוּךָ יהוה כָּל מַעֲשֶׂיךָ – *All Your works shall thank You.*
Imagine yourself in a place where you have heard nature sing.

IYUN TEFILLA · עיון תפילה

סוֹמֵךְ יהוה לְכָל הַנֹּפְלִים – *The Lord supports all who fall.* Even people who sin – Hashem supports them so that they do not fall even further (Maharsha). Remember that self improvement is always possible.

הֲדַר כְּבוֹד הוֹדֶֽךָ, וְדִבְרֵי נִפְלְאֹתֶֽיךָ אָשִֽׂיחָה:

וֶעֱזוּז נוֹרְאֹתֶֽיךָ יֹאמֵֽרוּ, וּגְדֻלָּתְךָ אֲסַפְּרֶֽנָּה:

זֵֽכֶר רַב־טוּבְךָ יַבִּֽיעוּ, וְצִדְקָתְךָ יְרַנֵּֽנוּ:

חַנּוּן וְרַחוּם יהוה, אֶֽרֶךְ אַפַּֽיִם וּגְדָל־חָֽסֶד:

טוֹב־יהוה לַכֹּל, וְרַחֲמָיו עַל־כָּל־מַעֲשָׂיו:

יוֹדֽוּךָ יהוה כָּל־מַעֲשֶֽׂיךָ, וַחֲסִידֶֽיךָ יְבָרְכֽוּכָה:

כְּבוֹד מַלְכוּתְךָ יֹאמֵֽרוּ, וּגְבוּרָתְךָ יְדַבֵּֽרוּ:

לְהוֹדִֽיעַ לִבְנֵי הָאָדָם גְּבוּרֹתָיו, וּכְבוֹד הֲדַר מַלְכוּתוֹ:

מַלְכוּתְךָ מַלְכוּת כָּל־עֹלָמִים, וּמֶמְשַׁלְתְּךָ בְּכָל־דּוֹר וָדֹר:

סוֹמֵךְ יהוה לְכָל־הַנֹּפְלִים, וְזוֹקֵף לְכָל־הַכְּפוּפִים:

עֵינֵי־כֹל אֵלֶֽיךָ יְשַׂבֵּֽרוּ, וְאַתָּה נוֹתֵן־לָהֶם אֶת־אָכְלָם בְּעִתּוֹ:

וְצִדְקָתְךָ יְרַנֵּנוּ – *And sing with joy of Your righteousness.* Tzedaka may be understood as righteousness or charity. I sing with joy to Hashem, because when I think about it, everything good that I have in my life is really just a result of His charity and ḥesed. (Malbim)

טוֹב־יהוה לַכֹּל – *The Lᴏʀᴅ is good to all.*

"God is good to all, and His compassion extends to all His works." Therefore, so too should we be careful to preserve animal life unless it is to protect ourselves or for some other worthwhile purpose. (Radak)

"God is good to all, and His compassion extends to all His works." Therefore, so too should we act this way toward people who are not of our faith, to visit their sick and bury their dead and to support their poor. (Rambam)

Even when seemingly bad things happen, one must believe that ultimately there is some good that will result, for "God is good... to all His works." (Me'am Loez)

"God's mercy is in all of His creations." He has implanted His mercy in each of us so that we too can act toward others with compassion. (Bereshit Raba 33:3)

פ °You open Your hand,ᴴᴬ °°and satisfy every living thing with favor.

צ The Lᴏʀᴅ is righteous in all His ways,ᐟ and kind in all He does.ᐟ

ק The Lᴏʀᴅ is close to all who call on Him,ᐟ
  to all who call on Him in truth.

ר He fulfills the will of those who revere Him;
  He hears their cry and saves them.

ש The Lᴏʀᴅ guards all who love Him,
  but all the wicked He will destroy.

ת ‣ My mouth shall speak the praise of the Lᴏʀᴅ,
  and all creatures shall bless His holy name for ever and all time.

We will bless the Lᴏʀᴅ now and for ever. Halleluya!

Ps. 115

---

sensitive to the people around me, I realized that there were a lot of people who were starving in the world and it made me wonder whether in fact God really was satisfying all of the needs of every living thing. I continued to say the verse, but I had my nagging doubts.

It was only later that I came to believe that perhaps God provides all of the resources necessary for all of the world's needs, but it is man's fault that those resources are not shared fairly. And so, whenever I recited the verse, I asked myself what I was doing to ensure that people in need were being helped.

After all, if I want God to provide for my needs, shouldn't I be doing my share to provide for others? Perhaps my role was to be an agent for God's generosity to those around me. And every time I praised God, I also challenged myself to be a better person.

And then, while I became more sensitive to the needs of others, I became more aware of how much I already have in my own life, how many of my needs are already satisfied, how much I take for granted and how I am so fortunate and in many ways so very, very rich.

And then I realized that maybe Mr. Deutsch was right after all.

IYUN TEFILLA · עיון תפילה

צַדִּיק יהוה בְּכָל־דְּרָכָיו – *The Lᴏʀᴅ is righteous in all His ways.* And should one wonder why some people have some things while others do not, know that Hashem gives each according to his unique needs, just as a doctor does not give the same medicine to each person. (Ibn Ezra)

וְחָסִיד בְּכָל־מַעֲשָׂיו – *And kind in all He does.* If a person is punished, one can look at it as a

lack of kindness; alternatively, it is possible that he is getting less of a punishment than he really deserves. (Me'am Loez)

קָרוֹב יהוה לְכָל־קֹרְאָיו – *The Lᴏʀᴅ is close to all who call on Him.* To all those who call out to Him in sincerity." God is close to everyone who calls out to Him; but only those who are sincere walk away realizing that He is close. (Rabbi S.R. Hirsch)

°פּוֹתֵחַ אֶת־יָדֶ֑ךָ,ʰᵃ °°וּמַשְׂבִּיעַ לְכָל־חַי רָצוֹן:

צַדִּיק יהוה בְּכָל־דְּרָכָיו,ᵛ וְחָסִיד בְּכָל־מַעֲשָׂיו:ᵛ

קָרוֹב יהוה לְכָל־קֹרְאָיו,ᵛ לְכֹל אֲשֶׁר יִקְרָאֻֽהוּ בֶאֱמֶת:

רְצוֹן־יְרֵאָיו יַעֲשֶׂה, וְאֶת־שַׁוְעָתָם יִשְׁמַע, וְיוֹשִׁיעֵם:

שׁוֹמֵר יהוה אֶת־כָּל־אֹהֲבָיו, וְאֵת כָּל־הָרְשָׁעִים יַשְׁמִיד:

‹ תְּהִלַּת יהוה יְדַבֶּר־פִּי, וִיבָרֵךְ כָּל־בָּשָׂר שֵׁם קָדְשׁוֹ לְעוֹלָם וָעֶד:

וַאֲנַֽחְנוּ נְבָרֵךְ יָהּ מֵעַתָּה וְעַד־עוֹלָם, הַלְלוּיָהּ:

תהלים קטו

HILKHOT TEFILLA • הלכות תפילה

פּוֹתֵחַ אֶת־יָדֶֽךָ — *You open Your hand.*
So critical is this verse that the *Shulḥan Arukh* says
(51:7) that if one did not recite it with proper *kavana*,
then one must go back and repeat it again, apparently because it contains the essence of *Pesukei
DeZimra*. Why do you think this is so?

ANI TEFILLA • אני תפילה

פּוֹתֵחַ אֶת־יָדֶֽךָ — *You open Your
hand.*
Anyone who says this verse in the
context of this prayer is guaranteed a place in the World to Come.
(*Berakhot* 4b)

ANI TEFILLA • אני תפילה

פּוֹתֵחַ אֶת־יָדֶֽךָ — *You open Your hand.*
When I was in elementary school, my teacher
Mr. Deutsch told us that if we just said the
phrase from Ashrei, **פּוֹתֵחַ אֶת־יָדֶֽךָ וּמַשְׂבִּיעַ
לְכָל־חַי רָצוֹן,** *"You open Your hand, and satisfy
every living thing with favor,"* then we would
grow up to be very rich. As a young child, I
understood it almost as a magic formula:
acknowledge God's ability to make you rich,
tell Him so as if you really mean it, and you
will get rich. No doubt, this interpretation is
one of the things that kept me saying that
phrase with any amount of *kavana* any time
I prayed, even as I mumbled the rest of the
words of the prayer.

As I grew older, I realized two things: the
first was that prayer didn't really work that

way. It is not a magic incantation that you
recite and then, poof, you get what you want,
even if you pray really, really hard. And so I
thought that Mr. Deutsch had really just led
me on. But secondly, I came to learn that this
prayer appears not in a section related to requests, *bakashot*, but that it was in a section
of the siddur that is related to *shevaḥ*, giving
praise to Hashem. In other words, I wasn't necessarily supposed to be asking for anything
at all at this point in the service but rather
was supposed to be praising God for giving
all people the food that they need. And so I
thought of the corn fields and wheat fields
that make this country so rich and so prosperous and praised God for that.

As I grew yet older and became more

הַלְלוּיָהּ Halleluya! Praise the Lord, my soul. I will praise the Lord *Ps. 146* all my life; I will sing to my God as long as I live. Put not your trust in princes, or in mortal man who cannot save. His breath expires, he returns to the earth; on that day his plans come to an end. Happy is he whose help is the God of Jacob, whose hope is in the Lord his God who made heaven and earth, the sea and all they contain; He who keeps faith for ever. He secures justice for the oppressed. He gives food to the hungry. The Lord sets captives free. The Lord gives sight to the blind. The Lord raises those bowed down. The Lord loves the righteous. The Lord protects the stranger. He gives courage to the orphan and widow. He thwarts the way of the wicked.
▸ The Lord shall reign for ever. He is your God, Zion, for all generations. Halleluya!

---

day his plans come to an end." Man is finite. God is eternal. Whose values and plans will last longer?

אַשְׁרֵי שֶׁאֵל יַעֲקֹב בְּעֶזְרוֹ – *Happy is he whose help is the God of Jacob.* He is called the God of Yaakov here because Yaakov (see *Bereshit* 34:10) represents the survival of the Jewish people long after the other nations of the world have disappeared (Sforno). God has continued to watch over us. History proves it.

עֹשֶׂה מִשְׁפָּט לַעֲשׁוּקִים – *He secures justice for the oppressed.* Someone who sets out to harm another, very often inadvertently

ends up helping him. The brothers of Yosef thought they were oppressing him when, in fact, their plot against him played right into God's plan. (Rabbi Yosef Albo)

נֹתֵן לֶחֶם לָרְעֵבִים – *He gives food to the hungry.* There is hunger that comes from not eating, and there is the hunger of the soul that comes from being out of touch. God can satisfy both.

יהוה פֹּקֵחַ עִוְרִים – *The Lord gives sight to the blind.* There are those whose eyesight is 20/20, yet they can still be described as being blind. Belief in God can open one's eyes.

ANI TEFILLA · אני תפילה

When I went to the moon, I was as pragmatic a test pilot, engineer, and scientist as any of my colleagues... But there was another aspect to my experience during Apollo 14, and it con-

tradicted the "pragmatic engineer" attitude. It began with the breathtaking experience of seeing planet Earth floating in the vastness of space...the presence of divinity became almost

This ANI TEFILLA continues on page 89.

תהלים קמו

הַלְלוּיָהּ, הַלְלִי נַפְשִׁי אֶת־יהוה: אֲהַלְלָה יהוה בְּחַיָּי,‏ אֲזַמְּרָה לֵאלֹהַי בְּעוֹדִי: אַל־תִּבְטְחוּ בִנְדִיבִים,‏ בְּבֶן־אָדָם שֶׁאֵין לוֹ תְשׁוּעָה: תֵּצֵא רוּחוֹ,‏ יָשֻׁב לְאַדְמָתוֹ, בַּיּוֹם הַהוּא אָבְדוּ עֶשְׁתֹּנוֹתָיו: אַשְׁרֵי שֶׁאֵל יַעֲקֹב בְּעֶזְרוֹ,‏ שִׂבְרוֹ עַל־יהוה אֱלֹהָיו: עֹשֶׂה שָׁמַיִם וָאָרֶץ, אֶת־הַיָּם וְאֶת־כָּל־אֲשֶׁר־בָּם, הַשֹּׁמֵר אֱמֶת לְעוֹלָם: עֹשֶׂה מִשְׁפָּט לָעֲשׁוּקִים,‏ נֹתֵן לֶחֶם לָרְעֵבִים, יהוה מַתִּיר אֲסוּרִים: יהוה פֹּקֵחַ עִוְרִים,‏ יהוה זֹקֵף כְּפוּפִים, יהוה אֹהֵב צַדִּיקִים: יהוה שֹׁמֵר אֶת־גֵּרִים, יָתוֹם וְאַלְמָנָה יְעוֹדֵד, וְדֶרֶךְ רְשָׁעִים יְעַוֵּת: ‏יִמְלֹךְ יהוה לְעוֹלָם, אֱלֹהַיִךְ צִיּוֹן לְדֹר וָדֹר, הַלְלוּיָהּ:

עיון תפילה • IYUN TEFILLA

הַלְלִי נַפְשִׁי אֶת־יהוה — *Praise the Lord, my soul.* Besides the human soul, there is no other creation that is able to recognize God's presence in the world. (Rabbi S.R. Hirsch)

אֲהַלְלָה יהוה בְּחַיָּי — *I will praise the Lord all my life.* "I will praise Hashem while I live; I will sing praises to my God while I have my being."

The verse can also be read: "I will praise Hashem for the fact that I am alive and I will sing praises for the fact that He also watches over me" (Malbim).

No matter what else is going on in my life, I have much to be thankful for.

אני תפילה • ANI TEFILLA

אֲהַלְלָה יהוה בְּחַיָּי — *I will praise the Lord all my life.*

Compare these interpretations:

I will praise Hashem as long as I am alive. (Meiri)

I will praise Hashem while I still have my health. (Roke'ah)

I will praise Hashem with the way I live my life.

Which of these speaks most to you today?

עיון תפילה • IYUN TEFILLA

אַל־תִּבְטְחוּ בִנְדִיבִים — *Put not your trust in princes.* King David, himself a monarch and a wealthy man, warns us that only God is worthy of our trust; people who are wealthier than us may seem to "have it all," but money and prestige can disappear quickly. Faith in God is the only way to maintain one's true self-worth.

תֵּצֵא רוּחוֹ — *His breath expires.* "His breath expires, he returns to the earth; on that

הַלְלוּיָהּ **Halleluya!** How good it is to sing songs to our God; how *Ps. 147*
pleasant and fitting to praise Him. The LORD rebuilds Jerusalem.
He gathers the scattered exiles of Israel. He heals the brokenheart-
ed¹ and binds up their wounds. He counts the number of the stars,ᴬ¹
calling each by name. Great is our LORD and mighty in power; His
understanding has no limit.¹ The LORD gives courage to the humble,
but casts the wicked to the ground. Sing to the LORD in thanks;
make music to our God on the harp.¹ He covers the sky with clouds.
He provides the earth with rain and makes grass grow on the hills.ᴬ
He gives food to the cattle and to the ravens when they cry. He does
not take delight in the strength of horses nor pleasure in the fleetness of man.¹ The LORD takes pleasure in those who fear Him, who
put their hope in His loving care. Praise the LORD, Jerusalem;¹ sing
to your God, Zion, for He has strengthened the bars of your gates
and blessed your children in your midst. He has brought peace to
your borders, and satisfied you with the finest wheat. He sends His

---

לְתְבוּנָתוֹ אֵין מִסְפָּר – *His understanding has no limit.* The full capacity of one's understanding cannot be measured by standardized tests such as SATs or IQs. And what is true of man is all the more true of God. (Based on Rabbi S.R. Hirsch)

זַמְּרוּ לֵאלֹהֵינוּ בְכִנּוֹר – *Make music to our God on the harp.* Song and music are both instruments for praising Hashem. They both can express emotions of thanks when words might otherwise fail. Sing.

הַמַּצְמִיחַ הָרִים חָצִיר – *Makes grass grow on the hills.*
Have you ever seen lush foliage, green

pastures, mountains covered with clouds and vegetation? Imagine yourself there now.

לֹא־בְשׁוֹקֵי הָאִישׁ יִרְצֶה – *Nor pleasure in the fleetness of man.* The true value of a person is not in his physical prowess, but in how much he fears God. Even if he has athletic talents, he needs to acknowledge that those come from Hashem.

שַׁבְּחִי יְרוּשָׁלַם אֶת־יהוה – *Praise the LORD, Jerusalem.* "Sing to your God, Zion, for He has strengthened the bars of your gates and blessed your children in your midst." Since 1948, the Jewish people have had sovereignty over Jerusalem.

הַלְלוּיָהּ, כִּי־טוֹב זַמְּרָה אֱלֹהֵינוּ, כִּי־נָעִים נָאוָה תְהִלָּה: בּוֹנֵה
יְרוּשָׁלַ֫͏ִם יהוה, נִדְחֵי יִשְׂרָאֵל יְכַנֵּס: הָרֹפֵא לִשְׁבוּרֵי לֵב, וּמְחַבֵּשׁ
לְעַצְּבוֹתָם: מוֹנֶה מִסְפָּר לַכּוֹכָבִים,ᵛ לְכֻלָּם שֵׁמוֹת יִקְרָא:ᵛ גָּדוֹל
אֲדוֹנֵינוּ וְרַב־כֹּחַ, לִתְבוּנָתוֹ אֵין מִסְפָּר:ᵛ מְעוֹדֵד עֲנָוִים יהוה,
מַשְׁפִּיל רְשָׁעִים עֲדֵי־אָרֶץ: עֱנוּ לַיהוה בְּתוֹדָה, זַמְּרוּ לֵאלֹהֵינוּ
בְכִנּוֹר:ᵛ הַמְכַסֶּה שָׁמַיִם בְּעָבִים, הַמֵּכִין לָאָרֶץ מָטָר, הַמַּצְמִיחַ
הָרִים חָצִיר: נוֹתֵן לִבְהֵמָה לַחְמָהּ, לִבְנֵי עֹרֵב אֲשֶׁר יִקְרָאוּ: לֹא
בִגְבוּרַת הַסּוּס יֶחְפָּץ, לֹא־בְשׁוֹקֵי הָאִישׁ יִרְצֶה:ᵛ רוֹצֶה יהוה
אֶת־יְרֵאָיו, אֶת־הַמְיַחֲלִים לְחַסְדּוֹ: שַׁבְּחִי יְרוּשָׁלַ֫ם אֶת־יהוה,ᵛ
הַלְלִי אֱלֹהַיִךְ צִיּוֹן: כִּי־חִזַּק בְּרִיחֵי שְׁעָרָיִךְ, בֵּרַךְ בָּנַיִךְ בְּקִרְבֵּךְ:
הַשָּׂם־גְּבוּלֵךְ שָׁלוֹם, חֵלֶב חִטִּים יַשְׂבִּיעֵךְ: הַשֹּׁלֵחַ אִמְרָתוֹ אָרֶץ,

---

palpable, and I knew that life in the universe was not just an accident based on random processes... It was knowledge gained through private subjective awareness, but it was – and still is – every bit as real as the objective data upon which, say, the navigational program or the communications system was based.
(Captain Edgar D. Mitchell)

עיון תפילה · IYUN TEFILLA

הָרֹפֵא לִשְׁבוּרֵי לֵב – *He heals the brokenhearted.* Sometimes when other people cannot understand you, Hashem is the only One who can.

אני תפילה · ANI TEFILLA

מוֹנֶה מִסְפָּר לַכּוֹכָבִים – *He counts the number of the stars.* Imagine yourself in a place where you have seen a star-filled sky. Close your eyes. Count them.

עיון תפילה · IYUN TEFILLA

מוֹנֶה מִסְפָּר לַכּוֹכָבִים – *He counts the number of the stars.* Hashem counts each one of His creations because He cares about them. (Rashi)

Every person has a star in the heavens which corresponds to him and shines according to the actions of that person. (*Midrash Shoher Tov* 148:1)

Hashem knows the name of every one of His creations – including me.

commandment to earth; swiftly runs His word. He spreads snow like fleece,[A] sprinkles frost like ashes, scatters hail like crumbs. Who can stand His cold? He sends His word and melts them; He makes the wind blow and the waters flow. ▸ He has declared His words to Jacob, His statutes and laws to Israel. He has done this for no other nation; such laws they do not know. Halleluya![A]

הַלְלוּיָה Halleluya! Praise the LORD from the heavens,[B] praise Him *Ps. 148* in the heights. Praise Him, all His angels; praise Him, all His hosts. Praise Him, sun and moon; praise Him, all shining stars. Praise Him, highest heavens and the waters above the heavens. Let them praise the name of the LORD, for He commanded and they were created. He established them for ever and all time, issuing a decree

---

ANI TEFILLA · אני תפילה

Think about the complexity of creation as you know it from biology or any of the other physical sciences. Close your eyes and imagine being in a place where you were once overwhelmed by the beauty, symmetry and complexity of nature.

IYUN TEFILLA · עיון תפילה

הַלְלוּיָה, הַלְלוּ אֶת־יהוה מִן־הַשָּׁמַיִם – *Halleluya! Praise the LORD from the heavens.* This psalm describes the entire universe in dynamic terms. Borrowing heavily from the terminology and images used in *Bereshit*, the psalm in both content and structure reflects one who is overcome by the realization of the varied yet unified nature of the world around us. The first section begins "Praise Hashem from the heavens"; the second section begins "Praise Hashem from the earth"; the concluding section begins "His majesty is above [both] the earth and the heavens."

ANI TEFILLA · אני תפילה

At a meeting of Alcoholics Anonymous (AA), a man related that he had been sober for seven years.

"I walked out on my first contact with AA. They were talking about having a Higher Power, and I was an avowed atheist. When I could not get sober, I returned and said that I want to join the program, but I don't want any of the God talk, and they said 'Okay.' They told me I had to get a sponsor, which I did, and my

This ANI TEFILLA continues on page 93.

עַד־מְהֵרָה יָרוּץ דְּבָרוֹ: הַנֹּתֵן שֶׁלֶג כַּצֶּמֶר,* כְּפוֹר כָּאֵפֶר יְפַזֵּר:
מַשְׁלִיךְ קַרְחוֹ כְפִתִּים, לִפְנֵי קָרָתוֹ מִי יַעֲמֹד: יִשְׁלַח דְּבָרוֹ וְיַמְסֵם,
יַשֵּׁב רוּחוֹ יִזְּלוּ־מָיִם: ‹ מַגִּיד דְּבָרָו לְיַעֲקֹב, חֻקָּיו וּמִשְׁפָּטָיו
לְיִשְׂרָאֵל: לֹא עָשָׂה כֵן לְכָל־גּוֹי, וּמִשְׁפָּטִים בַּל־יְדָעוּם, הַלְלוּיָהּ:*

תהלים קמח

הַלְלוּיָהּ, הַלְלוּ אֶת־יהוה מִן־הַשָּׁמַיִם,* הַלְלוּהוּ בַּמְּרוֹמִים:
הַלְלוּהוּ כָל־מַלְאָכָיו, הַלְלוּהוּ כָּל־צְבָאָו: הַלְלוּהוּ שֶׁמֶשׁ וְיָרֵחַ,
הַלְלוּהוּ כָּל־כּוֹכְבֵי אוֹר: הַלְלוּהוּ שְׁמֵי הַשָּׁמַיִם, וְהַמַּיִם אֲשֶׁר מֵעַל
הַשָּׁמַיִם: יְהַלְלוּ אֶת־שֵׁם יהוה, כִּי הוּא צִוָּה וְנִבְרָאוּ: וַיַּעֲמִידֵם
לָעַד לְעוֹלָם, חָק־נָתַן וְלֹא יַעֲבוֹר: הַלְלוּ אֶת־יהוה מִן־הָאָרֶץ,

---

ANI TEFILLA · אני תפילה

הַנֹּתֵן שֶׁלֶג כַּצֶּמֶר — *He spreads snow like fleece.* The next three verses speak of Hashem's control over precipitation and the weather, which can have both positive and negative effects on man. The religious personality sees God's hand in the cycle of nature; "when the snow melts...the waters flow," and the cycle of life continues.

Look outside. What is the weather like today? Don't take it for granted.

BIUR TEFILLA · ביאור תפילה

הַלְלוּיָהּ, הַלְלוּ אֶת־יהוה מִן־הַשָּׁמַיִם — *Halleluya! Praise the Lᴏʀᴅ from the heavens.* The diversity of creation is highlighted by the listing of creations. In the first section (verses 1–6) they are listed according to their stature, moving mostly from "higher" to "lower." In the second section, the reverse is true: the creations are listed from the bottom of the sea up to the sky and back down again but according to their stature not their place. Especially toward the end, one sees movement from the inanimate (mountains) to the animate (animals) to mankind. Indeed, even within each category there is an attempt to convey a sense of all of its members by the use of opposites (fire and hail etc.). The all-encompassing nature of the description in both sections is emphasized by the recurring use of the word כָּל. It is as if the reader is immersed in all of the parts of creation. Man, reflecting upon the world around him, is overwhelmed by its diversity and complexity. At the same time, however, man is called upon to recognize the thread which ties together all of these diverse elements: namely, the One who created them all.

that will never change. Praise the LORD from the earth: sea monsters and all the deep seas; fire and hail, snow and mist, storm winds that obey His word; mountains and all hills, fruit trees and all cedars; wild animals and all cattle, creeping things and winged birds; kings of the earth and all nations, princes and all judges on earth; youths and maidens, old and young. ▸ Let them praise the name of the LORD,^A for His name alone is sublime; His majesty is above earth and heaven. He has raised the pride of His people, for the glory of all His devoted ones, the children of Israel, the people close to Him. Halleluya!

הַלְלוּיָהּ Halleluya! Sing to the LORD a new song,^| His praise in the   *Ps. 149*
assembly of the devoted. Let Israel rejoice in its Maker; let the children of Zion exult in their King. Let them praise His name with dancing; sing praises to Him with timbrel and harp. For the LORD delights in His people; He adorns the humble with salvation. Let the devoted revel in glory; let them sing for joy on their beds. Let high praises of God be in their throats, and a two-edged sword in their hand: to impose retribution on the nations, punishment on the peoples, ▸ binding their kings with chains, their nobles with iron fetters, carrying out the judgment written against them. This is the glory of all His devoted ones. Halleluya!

ANI TEFILLA · אני תפילה

One night I dreamed I was walking on the beach with God. I saw many scenes from my life flash across the sky. In each scene I noticed footprints in the sand. Sometimes there were two sets of footprints and sometimes there was only one.

This bothered me because I noticed that during the low periods in my life, when I was suffering from anguish, sorrow or defeat, I could see only one set of footprints, so I said

to God, "You promised me that if I followed You, You would walk with me always. But I have noticed that during the most trying periods of my life there has been only one set of footprints in the sand. Why, when I have needed You most, have You not been there for me?"

God replied, "The years when you have seen only one set of footprints, my child, is when I carried you." (Author unknown)

תַּנִּינִים וְכָל־תְּהֹמוֹת: אֵשׁ וּבָרָד שֶׁלֶג וְקִיטוֹר, רוּחַ סְעָרָה עֹשָׂה דְבָרוֹ: הֶהָרִים וְכָל־גְּבָעוֹת, עֵץ פְּרִי וְכָל־אֲרָזִים: הַחַיָּה וְכָל־בְּהֵמָה, רֶמֶשׂ וְצִפּוֹר כָּנָף: מַלְכֵי־אֶרֶץ וְכָל־לְאֻמִּים, שָׂרִים וְכָל־שֹׁפְטֵי אָרֶץ: בַּחוּרִים וְגַם־בְּתוּלוֹת, זְקֵנִים עִם־נְעָרִים: ◀ יְהַלְלוּ אֶת־שֵׁם יהוה,ֿ כִּי־נִשְׂגָּב שְׁמוֹ לְבַדּוֹ, הוֹדוֹ עַל־אֶרֶץ וְשָׁמָיִם: וַיָּרֶם קֶרֶן לְעַמּוֹ, תְּהִלָּה לְכָל־חֲסִידָיו, לִבְנֵי יִשְׂרָאֵל עַם קְרֹבוֹ, הַלְלוּיָהּ:

תהלים קמט

הַלְלוּיָהּ, שִׁירוּ לַיהוה שִׁיר חָדָשׁ,ֿ תְּהִלָּתוֹ בִּקְהַל חֲסִידִים: יִשְׂמַח יִשְׂרָאֵל בְּעֹשָׂיו, בְּנֵי־צִיּוֹן יָגִילוּ בְמַלְכָּם: יְהַלְלוּ שְׁמוֹ בְמָחוֹל, בְּתֹף וְכִנּוֹר יְזַמְּרוּ־לוֹ: כִּי־רוֹצֶה יהוה בְּעַמּוֹ, יְפָאֵר עֲנָוִים בִּישׁוּעָה: יַעְלְזוּ חֲסִידִים בְּכָבוֹד, יְרַנְּנוּ עַל־מִשְׁכְּבוֹתָם: רוֹמְמוֹת אֵל בִּגְרוֹנָם, וְחֶרֶב פִּיפִיּוֹת בְּיָדָם: לַעֲשׂוֹת נְקָמָה בַּגּוֹיִם, תּוֹכֵחוֹת בַּלְאֻמִּים: לֶאְסֹר מַלְכֵיהֶם בְּזִקִּים, וְנִכְבְּדֵיהֶם בְּכַבְלֵי בַרְזֶל: לַעֲשׂוֹת בָּהֶם מִשְׁפָּט כָּתוּב, הָדָר הוּא לְכָל־חֲסִידָיו, הַלְלוּיָהּ:

---

sponsor told me I had to pray every day. I said:
'Hold it! I was assured that I would not be bothered about God.' My sponsor said, 'Look here, do you want to get sober or stay drunk? If you want to get sober, you're going to pray every day.'
"Well, I prayed every day, but I didn't pray to God because I didn't believe in God. But when I prayed, that reminded me that I was not God."
The first step in recovery from addiction and in the effort to achieve a relationship with God, is humility, the realization that we are not God. Only then can we have emuna. Until then, our prayers may only help us realize that we are not God. (Rabbi A.J. Twerski)

IYUN TEFILLA · עיון תפילה

הַלְלוּיָהּ, שִׁירוּ לַיהוה שִׁיר חָדָשׁ – Halleluya! Sing to the Lᴏʀᴅ a new song. Each of us is called upon to create our own personal praise of Hashem's presence in our lives. Each day we should create our own new song. Alternatively, each day we are different than we were the day before and so our song is a new one, unlike the one we sang yesterday, not because the words are different but because we are.
What's your song today?

הַלְלוּיָהּ Halleluya! Praise God in His holy place; Ps. 150
praise Him in the heavens of His power.
Praise Him for His mighty deeds;
praise Him for His surpassing greatness.¹
Praise Him with blasts of the shofar;
praise Him with the harp and lyre.
Praise Him with timbrel and dance;
praise Him with strings and flute.
Praise Him with clashing cymbals;
praise Him with resounding cymbals.
▸ Let all that breathes praise the Lᴏʀᴅ. Halleluya!¹
Let all that breathes praise the Lᴏʀᴅ. Halleluya!ᴮ

עיון תפילה · IYUN TEFILLA

כָּל הַנְּשָׁמָה תְּהַלֵּל יָהּ – *Let all that breathes praise the Lᴏʀᴅ.* Words, music and song are all but modes of expression for that which lies at our core – the human soul. It is like "an inner drive that breaks out like a flame inside a volcano, but cannot do so in the form of words or logical sentences" (Rabbi J.B. Soloveitchik). Alternatively, the word for soul is related to the word for breath (נשימה) – wherever we are, we should look for God's presence in our lives and celebrate with every breath we take.

ביאור תפילה · BIUR TEFILLA

כָּל הַנְּשָׁמָה תְּהַלֵּל יָהּ – *Let all that breathes praise the Lᴏʀᴅ.* The repetition of the final sentence is a traditional way of conveying the fact that this represents the conclusion of a section; here it marks the end of the last chapter of *Tehillim*, the core of *Pesukei DeZimra* (Tur 51, *Sefer Pardes*).

אני תפילה · ANI TEFILLA

We can only pray the way prayer is supposed to be when we recognize that in fact the soul is always praying.

Without stop, the soul soars and yearns for its Beloved. It is at the time of outward prayer [as we are doing now], that the perpetual prayer of the soul reveals itself in the realm of action.

This is prayer's pleasure and joy, its glory and beauty. It is like a rose, opening its elegant petals toward the dew, facing the rays of the sun as they shine over it with the sun's light. (Rabbi A.I. Kook)

My soul is always praying. Now is the time to hear its voice.

הַלְלוּיָהּ, הַלְלוּ־אֵל בְּקָדְשׁוֹ‏

הַלְלוּהוּ בִּרְקִיעַ עֻזּוֹ:

הַלְלוּהוּ בִגְבוּרֹתָיו

הַלְלוּהוּ כְּרֹב גֻּדְלוֹ:‏

הַלְלוּהוּ בְּתֵקַע שׁוֹפָר

הַלְלוּהוּ בְּנֵבֶל וְכִנּוֹר:

הַלְלוּהוּ בְּתֹף וּמָחוֹל

הַלְלוּהוּ בְּמִנִּים וְעֻגָב:

הַלְלוּהוּ בְצִלְצְלֵי־שָׁמַע

הַלְלוּהוּ בְּצִלְצְלֵי תְרוּעָה:

‏› כֹּל הַנְּשָׁמָה תְּהַלֵּל יָהּ, הַלְלוּיָהּ:‏

כֹּל הַנְּשָׁמָה תְּהַלֵּל יָהּ, הַלְלוּיָהּ:‏

עיון תפילה • IYUN TEFILLA

הַלְלוּ־אֵל בְּקָדְשׁוֹ – *Halleluya! Praise God in His holy place. praise Him in the heavens.* His holy place is the *Beit HaMikdash* and represents God's revelation to man in the moral sphere. The heavens represent His revelation to man in the world of nature (Rabbi S.R. Hirsch). The study of Torah represents man's education about what God wants in the moral sphere; the study of the sciences represents man's education about God's presence in the physical sphere.

Science can be a religious quest.

הַלְלוּהוּ כְּרֹב גֻּדְלוֹ – *Praise Him for His surpassing greatness.* One might think one should continue to praise with words. However, sometimes words are inadequate to express how beautiful, complex, and overwhelming the beauty of the world and its creations can be. Did you ever witness something so amazing that it was indescribable? And so, when words fail, sometimes only music and song can best express what our heart is feeling. What follows, then, is reference to a variety of ancient musical instruments whose sounds are sometimes better equipped to express the praise we feel.

בָּרוּךְ Blessed be the LORD for ever.^B Amen and Amen. *Ps. 89*

Blessed from Zion be the LORD who dwells in Jerusalem. Halleluya! *Ps. 135*

Blessed be the LORD, God of Israel, who alone does wonders. *Ps. 72*

▸ Blessed be His glorious name for ever,
and may all the earth be filled with His glory.
Amen and Amen.^B

Stand until after "Bless the LORD" on page 108.

וַיְבָרֶךְ David blessed the LORD^A in front of the entire assembly. *1 Chr. 29*
David said, "Blessed are You, LORD, God of our father Yisrael, for
ever and ever. Yours, LORD, are the greatness and the power, the
glory, majesty and splendor, for everything in heaven and earth is
Yours. Yours, LORD, is the kingdom; You are exalted as Head over all.
Both riches and honor are in Your gift and You reign over all things.
In Your hand are strength and might. It is in Your power to make
great and give strength to all. Therefore, our God, we thank You
and praise Your glorious name." You alone are the LORD.^B *Neh. 9*

---

at this point to set aside money to donate
to *tzedaka* (*Magen Avraham* 51). In so doing,
we state our awareness that the money that
we have, no matter the amount, is a gift
from God. My giving some of it to others
is an acknowledgment that He also gives

to me. The prevalent custom is to stand for
these verses, perhaps because the practice
of some was to stand when doing a mitzva
like giving *tzedaka*, or because people
once stood in honor of others who came
to collect it.

ANI TEFILLA · אני תפילה

וַיְבָרֶךְ דָּוִיד אֶת יהוה – *David blessed
the LORD.*
*Rabbi Elazar would give a coin
to a poor person and only then
would he begin to pray (Bava
Batra 10a).*
If you haven't set aside some
money for *tzedaka*, do so now.
To ask for help one should be prepared to give help.

BIUR TEFILLA · ביאור תפילה

אַתָּה הוּא יהוה לְבַדֶּךָ – *You alone are the LORD.* What
follows in the next prayers is a brief history of
our relationship with Hashem from Creation until
the splitting of the Sea at the time of the exodus.
This represents a shift from focusing primarily on
Hashem's presence in nature to Hashem's presence in history. The bridge between the two is
Avraham who, according to one tradition, discovered Hashem in nature and then went on to find
His place in human affairs.

בָּרוּךְ יהוה לְעוֹלָם, אָמֵן וְאָמֵן:

בָּרוּךְ יהוה מִצִּיּוֹן, שֹׁכֵן יְרוּשָׁלֶָם, הַלְלוּיָהּ:

בָּרוּךְ יהוה אֱלֹהִים אֱלֹהֵי יִשְׂרָאֵל, עֹשֵׂה נִפְלָאוֹת לְבַדּוֹ:

וּבָרוּךְ שֵׁם כְּבוֹדוֹ לְעוֹלָם, וְיִמָּלֵא כְבוֹדוֹ אֶת־כָּל־הָאָרֶץ

אָמֵן וְאָמֵן:

Stand until after בָּרְכוּ *on page 109.*

וַיְבָרֶךְ דָּוִיד אֶת־יהוה לְעֵינֵי כָּל־הַקָּהָל, וַיֹּאמֶר דָּוִיד, בָּרוּךְ

אַתָּה יהוה, אֱלֹהֵי יִשְׂרָאֵל אָבִינוּ, מֵעוֹלָם וְעַד־עוֹלָם: לְךָ יהוה

הַגְּדֻלָּה וְהַגְּבוּרָה וְהַתִּפְאֶרֶת וְהַנֵּצַח וְהַהוֹד, כִּי־כֹל בַּשָּׁמַיִם

וּבָאָרֶץ, לְךָ יהוה הַמַּמְלָכָה וְהַמִּתְנַשֵּׂא לְכֹל לְרֹאשׁ: וְהָעֹשֶׁר

וְהַכָּבוֹד מִלְּפָנֶיךָ, וְאַתָּה מוֹשֵׁל בַּכֹּל, וּבְיָדְךָ כֹּחַ וּגְבוּרָה, וּבְיָדְךָ

לְגַדֵּל וּלְחַזֵּק לַכֹּל: וְעַתָּה אֱלֹהֵינוּ מוֹדִים אֲנַחְנוּ לָךְ, וּמְהַלְלִים

לְשֵׁם תִּפְאַרְתֶּךָ: אַתָּה־הוּא יהוה לְבַדֶּךָ, אַתָּ עָשִׂיתָ

BIUR TEFILLA · ביאור תפילה

בָּרוּךְ יהוה לְעוֹלָם – *Blessed be the* LORD *for ever.* The prayers which follow add other dimensions to the *Pesukei DeZimra*. As they are not directly a part of the core *Tehillim* we just concluded, the Maharam would recite the following series of verses, reminiscent of the language of a closing blessing, in order to separate the two sections. (Abudarham)

אָמֵן וְאָמֵן – *Amen and Amen.* The word *amen* can have two meanings:
(a) a declaration – I agree with everything that was just said;
(b) a prayer – I pray that everything that was just said will come true. (*Tzeluta DeAvraham*)

HILKHOT TEFILLA · הלכות תפילה

וַיְבָרֶךְ דָּוִיד אֶת יהוה – *David blessed the* LORD. These verses of thanks were recited by King David toward the end of his life when he had amassed the wealth necessary to build the *Beit HaMikdash* that would be constructed by his son. As a result, there is a custom

You made the heavens, even the highest heavens, and all their hosts, the earth and all that is on it, the seas and all they contain. You give life to them all, and the hosts of heaven worship You. ▸ You are the LORD God who chose Abram^A and brought him out of Ur of the Chaldees, changing his name to Abraham. You found his heart faithful toward You, ◂ and You made a covenant with him to give to his descendants the land of the Canaanites, Hittites, Amorites, Perizzites, Jebusites and Girgashites. You fulfilled Your promise for You are righteous. You saw the suffering of our ancestors in Egypt. You heard their cry at the Sea of Reeds. You sent signs and wonders against Pharaoh, all his servants and all the people of his land, because You knew how arrogantly the Egyptians treated them. You created for Yourself renown that remains to this day. ▸ You divided the sea before them, so that they passed through the sea on dry land, but You cast their pursuers into the depths, like a stone into mighty waters.

וַיּוֹשַׁע That day the LORD saved Israel from the hands of the Egyptians, and Israel saw the Egyptians lying dead on the seashore. ▸ When Israel saw the great power^i the LORD had displayed against the Egyptians, the people feared the LORD, and believed in the LORD and in His servant, Moses. *Ex. 14*

---

be your seed," so shall be the history of your people, your children. Your great destiny is just as enigmatic and mysterious and incomprehensible as the great story of the heavens.

Why try to rationalize it? ... The story of your people is the story of the heavens; no one will ever be able to understand it. (Rabbi J.B. Soloveitchik)

IYUN TEFILLA · עיון תפילה

וַיַּרְא יִשְׂרָאֵל אֶת הַיָּד הַגְּדֹלָה – *When Israel saw the great power.* But were there not times subsequently when *Benei Yisrael* did not believe in Hashem?! What happened to their faith? If faith is not something that is binary, an either/or proposition. Instead, faith is akin to an analog signal that varies with different intensities and strengths

at different points in one's life. (Rabbi S. Aviner)

Indeed, it can be argued that a faith that relies upon supernatural miracles is inferior. The stronger faith is the one that sees the miracles in the everyday.
What miracles surround your life this morning?

אֶת־הַשָּׁמַיִם, שְׁמֵי הַשָּׁמַיִם וְכָל־צְבָאָם, הָאָרֶץ וְכָל־אֲשֶׁר עָלֶיהָ,
הַיַּמִּים וְכָל־אֲשֶׁר בָּהֶם, וְאַתָּה מְחַיֶּה אֶת־כֻּלָּם, וּצְבָא הַשָּׁמַיִם לְךָ
מִשְׁתַּחֲוִים: ◄ אַתָּה הוּא יהוה הָאֱלֹהִים אֲשֶׁר בָּחַרְתָּ בְּאַבְרָם,
וְהוֹצֵאתוֹ מֵאוּר כַּשְׂדִּים, וְשַׂמְתָּ שְּׁמוֹ אַבְרָהָם: וּמָצָאתָ אֶת־
לְבָבוֹ נֶאֱמָן לְפָנֶיךָ, ◄ וְכָרוֹת עִמּוֹ הַבְּרִית לָתֵת אֶת־אֶרֶץ הַכְּנַעֲנִי
הַחִתִּי הָאֱמֹרִי וְהַפְּרִזִּי וְהַיְבוּסִי וְהַגִּרְגָּשִׁי, לָתֵת לְזַרְעוֹ, וַתָּקֶם
אֶת־דְּבָרֶיךָ, כִּי צַדִּיק אָתָּה: וַתֵּרֶא אֶת־עֳנִי אֲבֹתֵינוּ בְּמִצְרָיִם,
וְאֶת־זַעֲקָתָם שָׁמַעְתָּ עַל־יַם־סוּף: וַתִּתֵּן אֹתֹת וּמֹפְתִים בְּפַרְעֹה
וּבְכָל־עֲבָדָיו וּבְכָל־עַם אַרְצוֹ, כִּי יָדַעְתָּ כִּי הֵזִידוּ עֲלֵיהֶם, וַתַּעַשׂ־
לְךָ שֵׁם כְּהַיּוֹם הַזֶּה: ◄ וְהַיָּם בָּקַעְתָּ לִפְנֵיהֶם, וַיַּעַבְרוּ בְתוֹךְ־הַיָּם
בַּיַּבָּשָׁה, וְאֶת־רֹדְפֵיהֶם הִשְׁלַכְתָּ בִמְצוֹלֹת כְּמוֹ־אֶבֶן, בְּמַיִם עַזִּים:

שמות יד

וַיּוֹשַׁע יהוה בַּיּוֹם הַהוּא אֶת־יִשְׂרָאֵל מִיַּד מִצְרָיִם, וַיַּרְא יִשְׂרָאֵל
אֶת־מִצְרַיִם מֵת עַל־שְׂפַת הַיָּם: וַיַּרְא יִשְׂרָאֵל אֶת־הַיָּד הַגְּדֹלָה
אֲשֶׁר עָשָׂה יהוה בְּמִצְרַיִם, וַיִּירְאוּ הָעָם אֶת־יהוה, וַיַּאֲמִינוּ
בַּיהוה וּבְמֹשֶׁה עַבְדּוֹ:

ANI TEFILLA · אני תפילה

When Avraham was a lad, when he was a shepherd and remained in the field at night, he couldn't sleep because he was restless. He could not understand the cosmos; the grandeur of the cosmic drama puzzled him. Chaldea [Ur Kasdim] was the land where astronomy was born. They were the first ones to describe the skies, draw maps of the heavens. Avraham counted the stars; he discovered God with the stars. When a sensitive and refined person lifts his eyes and watches the stars and the heavenly drama, he begins to

think of the enormous distances and is confronted by the Ein Sof, by infinity, by endlessness itself. The sensitive soul will sense the complete worthlessness of man in comparison with infinity and will finally find God in the infinite spaces separating galaxies and stars...

God tells Avraham not merely to count the stars, but to try to comprehend them. Can you enumerate the stars, Avraham? Can you explain the cosmic drama, the flying nebulae on the outskirts of the universe? ... "So shall

אָז יָשִׁיר־מֹשֶׁה Then Moses and the Israelites sang[HA] this song to   *Ex. 15*
the Lord, saying:
I will sing to the Lord, for He has triumphed gloriously;
horse and rider He has hurled into the sea.
The Lord is my strength and song; He has become my salvation.
This is my God, and I will beautify Him,
my father's God, and I will exalt Him.
The Lord is a Master of war; Lord is His name.
Pharaoh's chariots and army He cast into the sea;
the best of his officers drowned in the Sea of Reeds.
The deep waters covered them;
they went down to the depths like a stone.
Your right hand, Lord, is majestic in power.
Your right hand, Lord, shatters the enemy.
In the greatness of Your majesty, You overthrew those who rose
against You.
You sent out Your fury; it consumed them like stubble.
By the blast of Your nostrils the waters piled up.
The surging waters stood straight like a wall;
the deeps congealed in the heart of the sea.
The enemy said, "I will pursue. I will overtake. I will divide the spoil.
My desire shall have its fill of them.
I will draw my sword. My hand will destroy them."
You blew with Your wind; the sea covered them.
They sank in the mighty waters like lead.
Who is like You, Lord, among the mighty?
Who is like You – majestic in holiness, awesome in glory,
working wonders?

---

all lifted up the hems of their clothes to
keep them from getting wet, for it actually seemed to them that they had gone
down into the Sea which had split before
them. Such is the power of imagination
during tefilla.

שמות טו

אָז יָשִׁיר־מֹשֶׁה וּבְנֵי יִשְׂרָאֵל אֶת־הַשִּׁירָה הַזֹּאת לַיהוה, וַיֹּאמְרוּ

סוּס ‖ לֵאמֹר, אָשִׁירָה לַיהוה כִּי־גָאֹה גָּאָה,

וְרֹכְבוֹ רָמָה בַיָּם: עָזִּי וְזִמְרָת יָהּ וַיְהִי־לִי

אֱלֹהֵי ‖ לִישׁוּעָה, זֶה אֵלִי וְאַנְוֵהוּ,

אָבִי וַאֲרֹמְמֶנְהוּ: יהוה אִישׁ מִלְחָמָה, יהוה

וּמִבְחַר ‖ שְׁמוֹ: מַרְכְּבֹת פַּרְעֹה וְחֵילוֹ יָרָה בַיָּם,

כְּמוֹ־ ‖ שָׁלִשָׁיו טֻבְּעוּ בְיַם־סוּף: תְּהֹמֹת יְכַסְיֻמוּ, יָרְדוּ בִמְצוֹלֹת

אָבֶן: יְמִינְךָ יהוה נֶאְדָּרִי בַּכֹּחַ,

יהוה תִּרְעַץ אוֹיֵב: וּבְרֹב גְּאוֹנְךָ תַּהֲרֹס

וּבְרוּחַ ‖ קָמֶיךָ, תְּשַׁלַּח חֲרֹנְךָ יֹאכְלֵמוֹ כַּקַּשׁ:

נִצְּבוּ כְמוֹ־נֵד ‖ אַפֶּיךָ נֶעֶרְמוּ מַיִם,

אָמַר ‖ נֹזְלִים, קָפְאוּ תְהֹמֹת בְּלֶב־יָם:

אוֹיֵב אֶרְדֹּף, אַשִּׂיג, אֲחַלֵּק שָׁלָל, תִּמְלָאֵמוֹ

נַשְׁפְתָּ ‖ נַפְשִׁי, אָרִיק חַרְבִּי תּוֹרִישֵׁמוֹ יָדִי:

בְרוּחֲךָ כִּסָּמוֹ יָם, צָלֲלוּ כַּעוֹפֶרֶת בְּמַיִם

מִי ‖ אַדִּירִים: מִי־כָמֹכָה בָּאֵלִם יהוה,

כָּמֹכָה נֶאְדָּר בַּקֹּדֶשׁ, נוֹרָא תְהִלֹּת עֹשֵׂה

ANI TEFILLA · אני תפילה

Then Moses and the Israelites sang. Once, Rabbi Shmelke of Nikolsburg said the Song at the Sea as Ḥazan with such power that when the congregation recited with him the verses about the crossing of the Reed Sea, they

HILKHOT TEFILLA · הלכות תפילה

אָז יָשִׁיר־מֹשֶׁה וּבְנֵי יִשְׂרָאֵל – *Then Moses and the Israelites sang.* One should say the Song at the Sea with great joy, and imagine that at that very moment he crossed through it and was liberated. And if one does so, then all of his sins will be forgiven (*Mishna Berura* 51:17). In other words, this is not just about reciting or retelling the event; it is about reliving it.

You stretched out Your right hand,
     the earth swallowed them.
In Your loving-kindness, You led the people You redeemed.
     In Your strength, You guided them to Your holy abode.
Nations heard and trembled;
     terror gripped Philistia's inhabitants.
The chiefs of Edom were dismayed,
     Moab's leaders were seized with trembling,
     the people of Canaan melted away.
Fear and dread fell upon them.
     By the power of Your arm, they were still as stone –
     until Your people crossed, LORD,
     until the people You acquired crossed over.
You will bring them and plant them
     on the mountain of Your heritage –
     the place, LORD, You made for Your dwelling,
     the Sanctuary, LORD, Your hands established.
     The LORD will reign for ever and all time.

The LORD will reign for ever and all time.
The LORD's kingship is established for ever and to all eternity.

When Pharaoh's horses, chariots and riders went into the sea,
     the LORD brought the waters of the sea back over them,
     but the Israelites walked on dry land through the sea.

▸ For kingship is the LORD's   *Ps. 22*
    and He rules over the nations.
    Saviors shall go up to Mount Zion   *Ob. 1*
    to judge Mount Esau,
    and the LORD's shall be the kingdom.

    Then the LORD shall be King over all the earth;   *Zech. 14*
    on that day the LORD shall be One and His name One,

    (as it is written in Your Torah, saying:
    Listen, Israel: the LORD is our God, the LORD is One.)   *Deut. 6*

פֶּלֶא: נָטִיתָ יְמִינְךָ תִּבְלָעֵמוֹ אָרֶץ: נָחִיתָ

בְחַסְדְּךָ עַם־זוּ גָאָלְתָּ, נֵהַלְתָּ בְעָזְּךָ אֶל־נְוֵה

קָדְשֶׁךָ: שָׁמְעוּ עַמִּים יִרְגָּזוּן, חִיל

אָחַז יֹשְׁבֵי פְּלָשֶׁת: אָז נִבְהֲלוּ אַלּוּפֵי

אֱדוֹם, אֵילֵי מוֹאָב יֹאחֲזֵמוֹ רָעַד, נָמֹגוּ

כֹּל יֹשְׁבֵי כְנָעַן: תִּפֹּל עֲלֵיהֶם אֵימָתָה

וָפַחַד, בִּגְדֹל זְרוֹעֲךָ יִדְּמוּ כָּאָבֶן, עַד־

יַעֲבֹר עַמְּךָ יהוה, עַד־יַעֲבֹר עַם־זוּ

קָנִיתָ: תְּבִאֵמוֹ וְתִטָּעֵמוֹ בְּהַר נַחֲלָתְךָ, מָכוֹן

לְשִׁבְתְּךָ פָּעַלְתָּ יהוה, מִקְּדָשׁ אֲדֹנָי כּוֹנְנוּ

יָדֶיךָ: יהוה ׀ יִמְלֹךְ לְעֹלָם וָעֶד:

יהוה יִמְלֹךְ לְעֹלָם וָעֶד.

יהוה מַלְכוּתֵהּ קָאֵם לְעָלַם וּלְעָלְמֵי עָלְמַיָּא.

כִּי

בָא סוּס פַּרְעֹה בְּרִכְבּוֹ וּבְפָרָשָׁיו בַּיָּם, וַיָּשֶׁב יהוה עֲלֵהֶם אֶת־מֵי

הַיָּם, וּבְנֵי יִשְׂרָאֵל הָלְכוּ בַיַּבָּשָׁה בְּתוֹךְ הַיָּם:

◂ כִּי לַיהוה הַמְּלוּכָה וּמֹשֵׁל בַּגּוֹיִם: תהלים כב

וְעָלוּ מוֹשִׁעִים בְּהַר צִיּוֹן לִשְׁפֹּט אֶת־הַר עֵשָׂו עובדיה א

וְהָיְתָה לַיהוה הַמְּלוּכָה:

וְהָיָה יהוה לְמֶלֶךְ עַל־כָּל־הָאָרֶץ זכריה יד

בַּיּוֹם הַהוּא יִהְיֶה יהוה אֶחָד וּשְׁמוֹ אֶחָד:

(וּבְתוֹרָתְךָ כָּתוּב לֵאמֹר, שְׁמַע יִשְׂרָאֵל, יהוה אֱלֹהֵינוּ יהוה אֶחָד:) דברים ו

יִשְׁתַּבַּח May Your name be praised[BH]
for ever, our King,
the great and holy God,
King in heaven and on earth.
For to You,
LORD our God and God of our ancestors,
it is right to offer song and praise,
hymn and psalm,
strength and dominion,
eternity, greatness and power,
song of praise and glory,
holiness and kingship,
▸ blessings and thanks,
from now and for ever.
Blessed are You, LORD,
God and King,
exalted in praises,
God of thanksgivings,
Master of wonders,
who delights in hymns of song,
King, God, Giver of life to the worlds.[B]

Yishtabaḥ at the end. As such, no interruptions are generally permitted. What about between *Yishtabaḥ* and *Barekhu*? If the first unit (*Pesukei DeZimra*) is complete, and the next unit (*Birkhot Keriat Shema*) has not yet begun, should any talking be permitted? There are those authorities who say it is not (Rif on *Berakhot* 23a; Rosh 5, 5; *Kol Bo*, *siman* 4). Their reasoning is because if *Pesukei DeZimra* is really intended as the praise one should say before one prays, then isn't it contradictory to interrupt that process? After all, traveling on a straight path it makes no sense to take a detour, especially one that will get in the way of reaching one's destination with the right frame of mind. Why work so hard getting into the mood, only to get sidetracked and have to start over? Nevertheless, one sees that interrupting at this point, between units, is probably different from interrupting in the middle of a unit itself, and so some communities have the practice to allow certain interruptions (such as the recitation of *Shir HaMa'alot*) that are still related to the act of prayer or some other community related need (See Rema and *Mishna Berura* 54:3).

יִשְׁתַּבַּח

שִׁמְךָ לָעַד, מַלְכֵּנוּ

הָאֵל הַמֶּלֶךְ הַגָּדוֹל וְהַקָּדוֹשׁ בַּשָּׁמַיִם וּבָאָרֶץ

כִּי לְךָ נָאֶה, יהוה אֱלֹהֵינוּ וֵאלֹהֵי אֲבוֹתֵינוּ

שִׁיר וּשְׁבָחָה, הַלֵּל וְזִמְרָה

עֹז וּמֶמְשָׁלָה, נֶצַח, גְּדֻלָּה וּגְבוּרָה

תְּהִלָּה וְתִפְאֶרֶת, קְדֻשָּׁה וּמַלְכוּת

‹ בְּרָכוֹת וְהוֹדָאוֹת, מֵעַתָּה וְעַד עוֹלָם.

בָּרוּךְ אַתָּה יהוה

אֵל מֶלֶךְ גָּדוֹל בַּתִּשְׁבָּחוֹת

אֵל הַהוֹדָאוֹת

אֲדוֹן הַנִּפְלָאוֹת

הַבּוֹחֵר בְּשִׁירֵי זִמְרָה

מֶלֶךְ, אֵל, חַי הָעוֹלָמִים.

BIUR TEFILLA · ביאור תפילה

יִשְׁתַּבַּח שִׁמְךָ – *May Your name be praised.* It is said that the 15 nouns here correspond to the 15 steps leading from one part of the *Beit HaMikdash* to another. As we conclude this part of the service, we get one step closer to our personal encounter with Hashem in the *Shemoneh Esreh*.

מֶלֶךְ, אֵל, חַי הָעוֹלָמִים – *King, God, Giver of life to the worlds.* At the beginning of *Pesukei DeZimra* we said that we would praise Hashem and make His name great in our eyes via the recitation of *Tehillim*: בְּשִׁבְחוֹת...נְגַדֶּלְךָ. We conclude here by saying that, thanks to our focusing on the *Tehillim* that we just said, we are now more aware of how great You are: מֶלֶךְ גָּדוֹל בַּתִּשְׁבָּחוֹת.

HILKHOT TEFILLA · הלכות תפילה

יִשְׁתַּבַּח שִׁמְךָ – *May Your name be praised.* As we have noted, *Pesukei DeZimra* is a single unit bounded by the blessing *Barukh She'amar* at the beginning and the blessing

Between Rosh HaShana and Yom Kippur, and on Hoshana Raba,
many congregations open the Ark and say this psalm responsively, verse by verse.

שִׁיר הַמַּעֲלוֹת A song of ascents. From the depths I have called to You, LORD. Ps. 130
LORD, hear my voice; let Your ears be attentive to my plea. If You, LORD,
should keep account of sins, O LORD, who could stand? But with You there
is forgiveness, that You may be held in awe. I wait for the LORD, my soul
waits, and in His word I put my hope. My soul waits for the LORD more
than watchmen wait for the morning, more than watchmen wait for the
morning. Israel, put your hope in the LORD, for with the LORD there is
loving-kindness, and great is His power to redeem. It is He who will redeem
Israel from all their sins.

HALF KADDISH

Leader: יִתְגַּדַּל Magnified and sanctified may His great name be,
in the world He created by His will.
May He establish His kingdom
in your lifetime and in your days,
and in the lifetime of all the house of Israel,
swiftly and soon – and say: Amen.

All: May His great name^A be blessed for ever and all time.

Leader: Blessed and praised, glorified and exalted,
raised and honored, uplifted and lauded
be the name of the Holy One, blessed be He,
beyond any blessing,
song, praise and consolation
uttered in the world – and say: Amen.

---

we try to raise ourselves up, something we particularly commit ourselves to during the days between
Rosh HaShana and Yom Kippur. During this period,
we call to Hashem "from the depths" – the depths
of our being, the depths of our desire to improve
ourselves, to be closer to Him than we normally are.
Alternatively, writes Elie Wiesel, despite our sometimes deep inability to see Your Presence in our
lives, we anyway call out to You; we believe in You.

ANI TEFILLA · אני תפילה

יְהֵא שְׁמֵהּ רַבָּא – *May His great
name.* Whoever says *yeheh shemeh raba...* with all his strength, the
Heavenly Court rips up any negative decree against him (*Shabbat*
119b). "With all his strength" – with
his complete concentration (Rashi).

During the הושענא רבה, and on ימי תשובה עשרת,
many congregations open the ארון קודש and say this psalm responsively, verse by verse.

שִׁיר הַמַּעֲלוֹת,ּ מִמַּעֲמַקִּים קְרָאתִיךָ יהוה: אֲדֹנָי שִׁמְעָה בְקוֹלִי, תִּהְיֶינָה אָזְנֶיךָ קַשֻּׁבוֹת לְקוֹל תַּחֲנוּנָי: אִם־עֲוֹנוֹת תִּשְׁמָר־יָהּ, אֲדֹנָי מִי יַעֲמֹד: כִּי־עִמְּךָ הַסְּלִיחָה, לְמַעַן תִּוָּרֵא: קִוִּיתִי יהוה קִוְּתָה נַפְשִׁי, וְלִדְבָרוֹ הוֹחָלְתִּי: נַפְשִׁי לַאדֹנָי, מִשֹּׁמְרִים לַבֹּקֶר, שֹׁמְרִים לַבֹּקֶר: יַחֵל יִשְׂרָאֵל אֶל יהוה, כִּי־עִם־יהוה הַחֶסֶד, וְהַרְבֵּה עִמּוֹ פְדוּת: וְהוּא יִפְדֶּה אֶת־יִשְׂרָאֵל, מִכֹּל עֲוֹנֹתָיו:

תהלים קל

חֲצִי קַדִּישׁ

ש״ץ: יִתְגַּדַּל וְיִתְקַדַּשׁ שְׁמֵהּ רַבָּא (קהל: אָמֵן)
בְּעָלְמָא דִּי בְרָא כִרְעוּתֵהּ
וְיַמְלִיךְ מַלְכוּתֵהּ
בְּחַיֵּיכוֹן וּבְיוֹמֵיכוֹן וּבְחַיֵּי דְכָל בֵּית יִשְׂרָאֵל
בַּעֲגָלָא וּבִזְמַן קָרִיב, וְאִמְרוּ אָמֵן. (קהל: אָמֵן)

קהל
ושׁ״ץ: יְהֵא שְׁמֵהּ רַבָּא* מְבָרַךְ לְעָלַם וּלְעָלְמֵי עָלְמַיָּא.

ש״ץ: יִתְבָּרַךְ וְיִשְׁתַּבַּח וְיִתְפָּאַר וְיִתְרוֹמַם וְיִתְנַשֵּׂא וְיִתְהַדָּר וְיִתְעַלֶּה וְיִתְהַלָּל
שְׁמֵהּ דְּקֻדְשָׁא בְּרִיךְ הוּא (קהל: בְּרִיךְ הוּא)
לְעֵלָּא מִן כָּל בִּרְכָתָא / בעשרת ימי תשובה: לְעֵלָּא לְעֵלָּא מִכָּל בִּרְכָתָא/
וְשִׁירָתָא, תֻּשְׁבְּחָתָא וְנֶחֱמָתָא
דַּאֲמִירָן בְּעָלְמָא, וְאִמְרוּ אָמֵן. (קהל: אָמֵן)

עיון תפילה · IYUN TEFILLA

שִׁיר הַמַּעֲלוֹת – *A song of ascents.* This is actually one of 15 consecutive chapters of *Tehillim* (120–134) which are each introduced as being "a song of ascents." Some have suggested that the ascent is a literal one, from exile up to Israel, or up to the *Beit HaMikdash.* Rabbi S.R. Hirsch (on *Tehillim* 120:1) maintains that it is also a spiritual one, as

BLESSINGS OF THE SHEMA

The following blessing and response are said only in the presence of a minyan.
They represent a formal summons to the congregation to engage in an act of collective
prayer. The custom of bowing at this point is based on 1 Chronicles 29:20, "David said
to the whole assembly, 'Now bless the LORD your God.' All the assembly blessed the
LORD God of their fathers and bowed their heads low to the LORD and the King."
The Leader says the following, bowing at "Bless," standing straight at "the LORD."
The congregation, followed by the Leader, responds, bowing at "Bless,"
standing straight at "the LORD."

Leader: # BLESS

the LORD, the blessed One.

Congregation: Bless the LORD, the blessed One,
for ever and all time.

Leader: Bless the LORD, the blessed One,
for ever and all time.

I'm not in the mood, or am having a difficult time focusing, the presence of other people helps me to get into the right frame of mind. I allow myself to be drawn in to their devotion or excitement or participation.

And so the *Ḥazan* here issues an invitation to the entire congregation to join him in the recitation of the *berakhot* of *Keriat Shema* which are about to follow. In effect, he says, "Please join me so that I am not saying this alone, but rather we can all say this together as a community. Join with me, and

have the intention to sanctify God's name, to fulfill the commandment regarding the recitation of the *Shema*. Join me, so that I can help you and you can help me. We're on the verge of entering the palace of the *Shemoneh Esreh*; let's go together." Implied here as well is the thought that if for some reason you are having a particularly difficult time focusing today, then listen to me, answer *Amen* to the blessings of the *Shema* and to the *Shema* itself. We thus transform our prayer from being not only a private affair but a communal one as well.

קריאת שמע וברכותיה

The following blessing and response are said only in the presence of a מִנְיָן.
They represent a formal summons to the קָהָל to engage in an act of collective prayer.
The custom of bowing at this point is based on דברי הימים א' כט, כ, "David said
to the whole assembly, 'Now bless the LORD your God.' All the assembly blessed the
LORD God of their fathers and bowed their heads low to the LORD and the King."
The שְׁלִיחַ צִבּוּר says the following, bowing at בָּרְכוּ, standing straight at ה. The קָהָל,
followed by the שְׁלִיחַ צִבּוּר, responds, bowing at בָּרוּךְ, standing straight at ה.

שׁ״ץ: בָּרְכוּ

אֶת יהוה הַמְבֹרָךְ.

קהל: בָּרוּךְ יהוה הַמְבֹרָךְ לְעוֹלָם וָעֶד.

שׁ״ץ: בָּרוּךְ יהוה הַמְבֹרָךְ לְעוֹלָם וָעֶד.

INTRODUCTION TO BAREKHU

Until this point, although we have been praying with a *minyan*, the truth is that our prayer has been relatively individualistic. The service until now has been a warm-up exercise, a way for us to begin to get into the right frame of mind for the prayers which are to come, especially the *Shemoneh Esreh*. At this point, then, we move one step closer to our encounter with Hashem by formally joining together with the rest of the *tzibbur* or congregation.

One benefit of joining with others is that I am sometimes able to get "into it" much better, when everyone around me is doing the same thing, than when I am alone. Have you ever been to a sporting event or a concert and looked around at the thousands of people surrounding you, all experiencing the same emotions as you at that moment? That can be such a powerful experience. We aspire to that same experience in communal prayer. If

*The custom is to sit from this point until the Amida, since the predominant
emotion of this section of the prayers is love rather than awe.
Conversation is forbidden until after the Amida.*

בָּרוּךְ Blessed are You, LORD our God, King of the Universe,
who forms light and creates darkness,[B] makes peace and creates all.[B]   *Is. 45*

הַמֵּאִיר In compassion He gives light to the earth and its inhabitants,[I]
and in His goodness continually renews the work of creation,[A]
day after day.[I]
How numerous are Your works, LORD;[A]   *Ps. 104*
You made them all in wisdom;
the earth is full of Your creations.

---

of the planet is dependent upon His *raḥamim*
(mercy).

מְחַדֵּשׁ בְּכָל יוֹם – *Renews the work of creation,
day after day.* Creation was not a one-time
event. It happens anew every day; one need
only open one's eyes to the miracle of it all. The
sun comes up, the flowers reappear, babies are
born. Creation is dynamic and ongoing; life is
beautiful.

If at the beginning of the blessing
there was a refutation of there being more
than one God, here the siddur refutes the
idea advanced by the Greek philosopher
Aristotle that God created the world
and walked away. Instead, Hashem's
presence is always felt, if one only looks
for it.
**Where have I seen it thus far today?
Where can I see it?**

תָּמִיד מַעֲשֵׂה בְרֵאשִׁית – *Renews the work of
creation.*
*Rav Schwab relates that when he flew overseas
in the early days of aviation, they flew close to
the ocean and he recited the blessing "Oseh
Ma'aseh Bereshit" that one is obligated to say
when one sees an unusual aspect of nature.
The first time he flew on a jet, though, he was
above the clouds for the first time in his life and
was even more amazed when he said these
words of prayer. He went back to Rav Breuer
and told him that he never had such kavana.
Rav Breuer said that he has the same kavana
when he looks at a flower.*

מַה־רַבּוּ מַעֲשֶׂיךָ יהוה – *How numerous are
Your works, LORD.*
*People ask me every day if I get bored of
delivering children, or if the deliveries become routine. I can say quite assuredly that
the opposite is true: the more I see and the
more I know, the more I am aware how miraculous it is each and every time. In fact, I
probably am more in awe of the birth than
the parents are. I tell patients every day that
there are billions of ways the reproductive
process can go wrong. The fact that it
ever goes right is a miracle.* (Dr. Nathan S.
Fox, MD)

The custom is to sit from this point until the עֲמִידָה, since the predominant emotion of this section of the prayers is love rather than awe. Conversation is forbidden until after the עֲמִידָה.

בָּרוּךְ אַתָּה יהוה אֱלֹהֵינוּ מֶלֶךְ הָעוֹלָם

יוֹצֵר אוֹר וּבוֹרֵא חֹשֶׁךְ, עֹשֶׂה שָׁלוֹם וּבוֹרֵא אֶת הַכֹּל.ב

המֵּאִיר לָאָרֶץ וְלַדָּרִים עָלֶיהָ בְּרַחֲמִיםע

וּבְטוּבוֹ מְחַדֵּשׁ בְּכָל יוֹםע תָּמִיד מַעֲשֵׂה בְרֵאשִׁית.א

מָה־רַבּוּ מַעֲשֶׂיךָ יהוה,א כֻּלָּם בְּחָכְמָה עָשִׂיתָ

מָלְאָה הָאָרֶץ קִנְיָנֶךָ:

ישעיה מה

תהלים קד

BIUR TEFILLA · ביאור תפילה

יוֹצֵר אוֹר וּבוֹרֵא חֹשֶׁךְ – *Who forms light and creates darkness.* Continuing the theme of *Pesukei DeZimra*, the theme of this first blessing before the *Shema* is "Hashem as Creator." From the beginning, we acknowledge that He is the One solely responsible for the world as we know it in all of its perfect harmony. At the same time, the blessing slides a step further into the theme of a similar relationship that Hashem has with the heavenly world, where He is also acknowledged as Creator. There is thus a balance between the lower world and the upper, which means that the whole universe is in harmony. The blessing thereby serves as an important prelude to our recitation of the *Shema* where we are called upon to declare His Oneness.

וּבוֹרֵא אֶת הַכֹּל – *And creates all.* There are those who say that the phrasing of this blessing was chosen specifically to deny the claim of those believers in ancient religions who thought there was a god of light and a god of darkness, one who reigned when good things happened and one who reigned when bad things happened. Interestingly, the phrasing is taken from a verse in *Yishayahu* but was actually changed here. The original says that God "makes peace and creates evil," whereas here the Rabbis changed the ending to say "makes peace and creates everything" (*Yishayahu* 45:7). The lesson is clear as we approach the *Shema* – there is only one God.

IYUN TEFILLA · עיון תפילה

הַמֵּאִיר לָאָרֶץ וְלַדָּרִים עָלֶיהָ בְּרַחֲמִים – *In compassion He gives light to the earth and its inhabitants.* If the sun were closer to the Earth, we would be like Venus – the oceans would boil away. If it were further away, we would be like Mars – the oceans would be frozen. We would no longer be in what astronomers call a Goldilocks Zone, a place that is situated in just the right location relative to its star. The continued existence

He is the King exalted alone since the beginning of time –
praised, glorified and elevated since the world began.
Eternal God,

> in Your great compassion, have compassion on us,
> Lord of our strength, Rock of our refuge,
> Shield of our salvation, You are our stronghold.

The blessed God,[B] great in knowledge,[A]
prepared and made the rays of the sun.
He who is good formed glory for His name,
surrounding His power with radiant stars.[I]
The leaders of His hosts, the holy ones, exalt the Almighty,[I]
constantly proclaiming God's glory and holiness.[A]

---

to God: "I don't know the prayers. All I know is the letters of the Alef-Beit. Please take the letters and turn them into the right words to reflect what I feel in my heart." The Ba'al

Shem Tov said that the boy's prayer not only broke through the gates of heaven, but enabled everyone else's prayers to enter as well.

IYUN TEFILLA · עיון תפילה

מְאוֹרוֹת נָתַן סְבִיבוֹת עֻזּוֹ – Surrounding His power with radiant stars. God is hidden behind His creations. On the one hand, one might think this means that He cannot be found. On the other hand, one can also say that if you want to know God, look carefully at all of His creations. As the Rambam (Yesodei HaTorah 2:2) says:

> What is the path [a person should take to attain] love and fear of Him? When a person contemplates His wondrous and great deeds and creations and appreciates His infinite wisdom that surpasses all comparison, he will immediately love, praise, and glorify [Him], yearning with tremendous desire to know [God's] great name, as David stated: "My soul thirsts for Hashem, for the living God" [Psalms 42:3].

Seen in this light, the siddur may be un-

derstood to mean that astronomy, biology, anatomy and the like can all be used as vehicles for getting to know God better. **When you read about these subjects, do you see them as aspects of human knowledge or as a way to come to a better knowledge of God?**

פְּנוֹת צְבָאָיו קְדוֹשִׁים, רוֹמְמֵי שַׁדַּי – The leaders of His hosts, the holy ones, exalt the Almighty. Only the angels can recognize God's attribute of שַׁדַּי. The meaning of this name is found in Ḥagiga 12a: "During the Creation of the universe, it was constantly expanding until God demanded that it stop." When we look through telescopes we think the universe is ever expanding, but no earthly creature knows where it stops. For us, it remains a mystery. Look at photos of outer space. You can feel the mystery (Rabbi S. Schwab).

The ANI TEFILLA is on page 115.

הַמֶּלֶךְ הַמְרוֹמָם לְבַדּוֹ מֵאָז
הַמְשֻׁבָּח וְהַמְפֹאָר וְהַמִּתְנַשֵּׂא מִימוֹת עוֹלָם.
אֱלֹהֵי עוֹלָם
בְּרַחֲמֶיךָ הָרַבִּים רַחֵם עָלֵינוּ
אֲדוֹן עֻזֵּנוּ, צוּר מִשְׂגַּבֵּנוּ
מָגֵן יִשְׁעֵנוּ, מִשְׂגָּב בַּעֲדֵנוּ.
אֵל בָּרוּךְ גְּדוֹל דֵּעָה*
הֵכִין וּפָעַל זָהֳרֵי חַמָּה
טוֹב יָצַר כָּבוֹד לִשְׁמוֹ
מְאוֹרוֹת נָתַן סְבִיבוֹת עֻזּוֹ
פִּנּוֹת צְבָאָיו קְדוֹשִׁים, רוֹמְמֵי שַׁדַּי
תָּמִיד מְסַפְּרִים כְּבוֹד אֵל וּקְדֻשָּׁתוֹ.*

ביאור תפילה · BIUR TEFILLA

אֵל בָּרוּךְ – *The blessed God.* This is the first instance thus far in the siddur where a prayer is written out as an alphabetical acrostic incorporating all 22 letters of the Hebrew alphabet. It is one of a number of prayers that are constructed this way, including this prayer's parallel "sister" prayer said on Shabbat morning – אֵל אָדוֹן.

Why are certain prayers constructed this way? There is no one correct answer. One possibility comes from the experience that some of us have had of being in a place that was of such overwhelming beauty, a place that filled us with such awe, that we

could not adequately describe it. There is a word here for every letter of the alphabet, but these are just representatives for every word in the entire language that we could possibly use to describe the feelings that we have at this moment. It's not only about what the words mean but about how they help us feel.

Alternatively, the blessing grapples with the old question of why did God bring the world into being? The letters of the *Alef-Beit* symbolize the written word of the Torah, the demands of which bring purpose and meaning to our world (Rabbi I. Wohlgemuth).

אני תפילה · ANI TEFILLA

אֵל בָּרוּךְ גְּדוֹל דֵּעָה – *The blessed God, great in knowledge.*

A young illiterate boy came to shul and

wanted to pray but had never been taught how to read. And so he simply recited the *Alef-Beit* over and over again. He then said

Be blessed, LORD our God, for the magnificence of Your handiwork
and for the radiant lights You have made.
May they glorify You, Selah!

תִּתְבָּרַךְ May You be blessed,
our Rock, King and Redeemer, Creator of holy beings.[1]
May Your name be praised for ever,
our King, Creator of the ministering angels,
all of whom stand in the universe's heights,
proclaiming together, in awe, aloud,
the words of the living God, the eternal King.
They are all beloved, all pure, all mighty,
and all perform in awe and reverence the will of their Maker.

▸ All open their mouths in holiness and purity, with song and psalm,
and bless, praise, glorify,
revere, sanctify and declare the sovereignty[A] of – ◂
The name of the great, mighty and awesome God and King,
holy is He.

IYUN TEFILLA · עיון תפילה

בּוֹרֵא קְדוֹשִׁים – *Creator of holy beings.* What
goes on in our world of ongoing creation
takes place in the upper worlds as well.
While focusing on the skies above us, the
blessing now shifts from the physical world
to the spiritual world, from the sun and the
moon and the stars to the angels, the Seraphim and Ophanim. Our knowledge of these
angels comes from the prophetic visions of
Yishayahu and Yehezkel, and therefore our
understanding is limited. But the blessing
assures us that there is such a world, one

which in many ways parallels our own.
Alternatively, in Hebrew, the word "angel"
and the word for "emissary" are the same,
in which case we could say that aspects
of nature are themselves the angels/emis-
saries of Hashem. Thus, the sun and moon
and stars are "angels," that is, emissaries
and servants of God, who obey His will and sing
His praises, as it were, just by the way they
function.

**When was the last time you listened
to their song? Listen to it now if you can.**

ANI TEFILLA · אני תפילה

וּמְבָרְכִים וּמְשַׁבְּחִים וּמְפָאֲרִים וּמַעֲרִיצִים וּמַקְדִּישִׁים
וּמַמְלִיכִים – *And bless, praise, glorify, revere,
sanctify and declare the sovereignty.* There
are six verbs here listed in rapid succes-
sion. It has been suggested that these re-

flect the six wings that Yishayahu
saw on each one of the angels in his
vision.

**Close your eyes. What does it sound
like?**

תִּתְבָּרַךְ יהוה אֱלֹהֵינוּ
עַל שֶׁבַח מַעֲשֵׂה יָדֶיךָ.
וְעַל מְאוֹרֵי אוֹר שֶׁעָשִׂיתָ
יְפָאֲרוּךָ סֶּלָה.

תִּתְבָּרַךְ

צוּרֵנוּ מַלְכֵּנוּ וְגוֹאֲלֵנוּ, בּוֹרֵא קְדוֹשִׁים ּ
יִשְׁתַּבַּח שִׁמְךָ לָעַד
מַלְכֵּנוּ, יוֹצֵר מְשָׁרְתִים
וַאֲשֶׁר מְשָׁרְתָיו כֻּלָּם עוֹמְדִים בְּרוּם עוֹלָם
וּמַשְׁמִיעִים בְּיִרְאָה יַחַד בְּקוֹל
דִּבְרֵי אֱלֹהִים חַיִּים וּמֶלֶךְ עוֹלָם.
כֻּלָּם אֲהוּבִים, כֻּלָּם בְּרוּרִים, כֻּלָּם גִּבּוֹרִים
וְכֻלָּם עוֹשִׂים בְּאֵימָה וּבְיִרְאָה רְצוֹן קוֹנָם
◂ וְכֻלָּם פּוֹתְחִים אֶת פִּיהֶם בִּקְדֻשָּׁה וּבְטָהֳרָה
בְּשִׁירָה וּבְזִמְרָה
וּמְבָרְכִים וּמְשַׁבְּחִים וּמְפָאֲרִים
וּמַעֲרִיצִים וּמַקְדִּישִׁים וּמַמְלִיכִים ◂
אֶת שֵׁם הָאֵל הַמֶּלֶךְ הַגָּדוֹל, הַגִּבּוֹר וְהַנּוֹרָא
קָדוֹשׁ הוּא.

ANI TEFILLA · אני תפילה

תָּמִיד מְסַפְּרִים כְּבוֹד אֵל וְקִדֻּשָׁתוֹ –
*Constantly proclaiming God's glory
and holiness.* If life seems hum-
drum and boring sometimes, it is
because of our perception. The

world is in constant motion. Nature is constantly
in flux. Beauty and the miraculous surround us
all of the time. As Keats wrote "The poetry of the
earth is never dead." The siddur reminds us to open
our eyes.

▸ All accept on themselves, one from another,
  the yoke of the kingdom of heaven,[i]
  granting permission to one another[j]
  to sanctify the One who formed them, in serene spirit,
  pure speech and sweet melody.
  All, as one, proclaim His holiness,
  saying in awe:

> *All say aloud:* Holy, holy, holy[H] is the LORD of hosts;
> the whole world is filled with His glory.

Is. 6

▸ Then the Ophanim and the Holy Ḥayyot, with a roar of noise,
  raise themselves toward the Seraphim and,
  facing them, give praise, saying:

> *All say aloud:* Blessed is the LORD's glory from His place.[i]

Ezek. 3

HILKHOT TEFILLA · הלכות תפילה

קָדוֹשׁ, קָדוֹשׁ, קָדוֹשׁ – Holy, holy, holy. This section of the prayer is known in halakhic literature as the "sitting *Kedusha*" (קְדֻשָּׁה דִּישִׁיבָה) as opposed to the "standing *Kedusha*" (קְדֻשָּׁה דַּעֲמִידָה) which is found in *Shemoneh Esreh*. What distinguishes the two is that in this one we do not actually sanctify God's name, otherwise we would not be able to

sit down when reciting it, nor would we be able to say it without a *minyan* as normally required in a דָּבָר שֶׁבִּקְדֻשָּׁה (a prayer of such sanctity that it requires a *minyan*); rather, we merely describe the way that the angels praise Him and sanctify His name. The description is one step removed from our own experience.

IYUN TEFILLA · עיון תפילה

קָדוֹשׁ, קָדוֹשׁ, קָדוֹשׁ... בָּרוּךְ כְּבוֹד – Holy, holy, holy… Blessed is the LORD's glory. The two primary lines of the *Kedusha* contain a contradiction of sorts. On the one hand, God is distant, unfathomable, beyond anything we can understand or relate to – קָדוֹשׁ, קָדוֹשׁ, קָדוֹשׁ. The distance between infinity and mortality is too huge for us to cross. On the other hand, it says that God is nearby – בָּרוּךְ כְּבוֹד יהוה מִמְּקוֹמוֹ. He is located in a particular place, able to be perceived and

praised. His presence thus fills the entire universe and yet He can be found in one place. He is *Kadosh* in a way that we cannot fathom; on the other hand, the whole world is filled with His glory. How can He be far and yet be here? Yet this is precisely the relationship we have with Him. Like a parent who is far away; we can feel very close despite the distance. And we can send messages and thereby maintain our relationship even though

This IYUN TEFILLA continues on page 119.

‹ וְכֻלָּם מְקַבְּלִים עֲלֵיהֶם עֹל מַלְכוּת שָׁמַיִם זֶה מִזֶּה ּ

וְנוֹתְנִים רְשׁוּת זֶה לָזֶה ּ

לְהַקְדִּישׁ לְיוֹצְרָם בְּנַחַת רוּחַ

בְּשָׂפָה בְרוּרָה וּבִנְעִימָה

קְדֻשָּׁה כֻלָּם כְּאֶחָד

עוֹנִים וְאוֹמְרִים בְּיִרְאָה

All say aloud קָדוֹשׁ, קָדוֹשׁ, קָדוֹשׁ יהוה צְבָאוֹת   ישעיהו

מְלֹא כָל־הָאָרֶץ כְּבוֹדוֹ:

‹ וְהָאוֹפַנִּים וְחַיּוֹת הַקֹּדֶשׁ בְּרַעַשׁ גָּדוֹל מִתְנַשְּׂאִים לְעֻמַּת שְׂרָפִים

לְעֻמָּתָם מְשַׁבְּחִים וְאוֹמְרִים

All say aloud בָּרוּךְ כְּבוֹד־יהוה מִמְּקוֹמוֹ:   יחזקאל ג

ביאור תפילה · BIUR TEFILLA

וְכֻלָּם מְקַבְּלִים עֲלֵיהֶם עֹל מַלְכוּת שָׁמַיִם זֶה מִזֶּה — *All accept on themselves, one from another, the yoke of the kingdom of heaven.* Just as there is a unity and balance in the physical world, so too is there unity in the spiritual world. Here the emissaries gather together, as it were, to take upon themselves the yoke

of heaven, **קַבָּלַת עֹל מַלְכוּת שָׁמַיִם**, just as we are about to do in the first paragraph of the *Shema*. And they do so as a prelude to sanctifying God's name in the *Kedusha*, just as we will do in the *Shemoneh Esreh*. In our collective praise, the upper and lower worlds, the physical and the spiritual, will be united.

עיון תפילה · IYUN TEFILLA

וְנוֹתְנִים רְשׁוּת זֶה לָזֶה — *Granting permission to one another.* "They give permission to one another." In the spiritual world there is no place for selfishness. At first, they defer to one another, "You go first." "No, it's really ok, you go first." But in the end, they join together as one, **כְּאֶחָד**, in keeping with the theme of the *Shema* that we are about to say. The Midrash says that herein lies a challenge to all of us — to get rid of our selfishness in all aspects of life, both physical and spiritual.

אני תפילה · ANI TEFILLA

From the angels one learns that spirituality can be found in acknowledging the holiness of the other person. For in the other person I recognize that all of us are created in the image of Hashem. As one anonymous person wrote:

"I searched for God but could not find Thee. I searched for myself but could not find me. I searched for the other and there I found all three."

לְאֵל To the blessed[B] God they offer melodies.
To the King, living and eternal God,
they say psalms and proclaim praises.

> For it is He alone
> who does mighty deeds
> and creates new things,
> who is Master of battles,
> and sows righteousness,
> who makes salvation grow
> and creates cures,
> who is revered in praises,
> LORD of wonders,

who in His goodness,
continually renews the work of creation,
day after day,
as it is said:

> "[Praise] Him who made the great lights,   *Ps. 136*
> for His love endures for ever."[B]

▸ May You make a new light shine over Zion,[B]
and may we all soon be worthy of its light.
Blessed are You, LORD,
who forms the radiant lights.

BIUR TEFILLA · ביאור תפילה	ANI TEFILLA · אני תפילה
אוֹר חָדָשׁ עַל צִיּוֹן תָּאִיר – *May You make a new light shine over Zion.* It is not clear what this "new light" is. In *Bereshit* it says that God created light before He created the luminaries. According to *Ḥazal*, this therefore refers not to the light that we know but to one that was subsequently hidden from man for some future time. Here we pray for its restoration. Others suggest that it is a metaphoric light, the light of redemption or the restoration of the entire Jewish people to the Land.	*It is told that Rabbi Menachem Mendel Morgenstern, known as the Kotzker Rebbe, once asked a group of scholars "Where does God live?" They laughed and replied, "Doesn't it say that the whole world is filled with His glory!" But the Kotzker Rebbe then responded to his own question:* *"God lives wherever man decides to let Him in."*

לָאֵל בָּרוּךְ נְעִימוֹת יִתֵּנוּ, לְמֶלֶךְ אֵל חַי וְקַיָם
זְמִירוֹת יֹאמֵרוּ וְתִשְׁבָּחוֹת יַשְׁמִיעוּ
כִּי הוּא לְבַדּוֹ
פּוֹעֵל גְּבוּרוֹת, עוֹשֶׂה חֲדָשׁוֹת
בַּעַל מִלְחָמוֹת, זוֹרֵעַ צְדָקוֹת
מַצְמִיחַ יְשׁוּעוֹת, בּוֹרֵא רְפוּאוֹת
נוֹרָא תְהִלּוֹת, אֲדוֹן הַנִּפְלָאוֹת
הַמְחַדֵּשׁ בְּטוּבוֹ בְּכָל יוֹם תָּמִיד מַעֲשֵׂה בְרֵאשִׁית
כָּאָמוּר

תהלים קלו

לְעֹשֵׂה אוֹרִים גְּדֹלִים, כִּי לְעוֹלָם חַסְדּוֹ:

‹ אוֹר חָדָשׁ עַל צִיּוֹן תָּאִיר וְנִזְכֶּה כֻלָּנוּ מְהֵרָה לְאוֹרוֹ.
בָּרוּךְ אַתָּה יהוה, יוֹצֵר הַמְּאוֹרוֹת.

---

sometimes the gap which separates seems huge.

Alternatively, there are times when belief is very difficult, when God cannot be seen. Yet at other times, belief is easy and natural, times when God feels close. Sometimes we feel one way, sometimes we feel the other. Both are natural.

BIUR TEFILLA • ביאור תפילה

לָאֵל בָּרוּךְ – *To the blessed.* As the blessing draws to a close, we return to the original theme. The angels sing about the wonderful things that God continues to do for the entire universe, including us, through His involvement in the ongoing creation of the world.

Each of the expressions can be understood to reflect some aspect of His role in nature or in human affairs. For example:

פּוֹעֵל גְּבוּרוֹת, *He does mighty deeds* – He is the force behind hurricanes and man's ability to conquer space.

עוֹשֶׂה חֲדָשׁוֹת, *He creates new things* – from the cotton gin to the microchip.

בַּעַל מִלְחָמוֹת, *He is Master of battles* – the force behind successful human military strategy, victory and defeat.

אֲדוֹן הַנִּפְלָאוֹת, *He is Lord of wonders* – from the Seven Wonders of the World to the birth of a baby.

Look around you right now. Where can His hand be seen?

אַהֲבָה You have loved us with great love,[B] LORD our God,
and with surpassing compassion
have You had compassion on us.[1]
Our Father, our King,
for the sake of our ancestors who trusted in You,
and to whom You taught the laws of life,
be gracious also to us and teach us.
Our Father, compassionate Father,
ever compassionate,
have compassion on us.
Instill in our hearts
the desire to understand[B] and discern,
to listen, learn and teach,
to observe, perform and fulfill
all the teachings of Your Torah in love.

IYUN TEFILLA · עיון תפילה

חֶמְלָה גְדוֹלָה וִיתֵרָה חָמַלְתָּ עָלֵינוּ – *And with
surpassing compassion have You had compassion on us.* The only person in the Torah
who is described as having the kind of com-

passion meant by חֶמְלָה was the daughter of
Pharaoh (*Shemot* 2:6), who had pity on the
baby she found. Hashem, You have had that
kind of compassion for us.

BIUR TEFILLA · ביאור תפילה

לְהָבִין – *understanding* the difficult theoretical
issues of Torah study.

וּלְהַשְׂכִּיל – *understanding* in order to be able to
carry out in practice what we learn in theory.

לִשְׁמֹעַ – *listening* to the Rabbis as the qualified
interpreters of Torah tradition.

לִלְמֹד – we have to review our *learning* until it
becomes part of our Torah knowledge.

וּלְלַמֵּד – *teaching/sharing our knowledge*
with others.

לִשְׁמֹר – *guarding/reviewing* our knowledge lest we forget it.

וְלַעֲשׂוֹת – *performing/carrying out* the commandments.

וּלְקַיֵּם – *fulfilling* the commandments in a
meaningful way. (Rabbi I. Wohlgemuth)

אַהֲבָה רַבָּה³ אֲהַבְתָּנוּ, יהוה אֱלֹהֵינוּ
חֶמְלָה גְדוֹלָה וִיתֵרָה חָמַלְתָּ עָלֵינוּ.ᵛ
אָבִינוּ מַלְכֵּנוּ
בַּעֲבוּר אֲבוֹתֵינוּ שֶׁבָּטְחוּ בְךָ
וַתְּלַמְּדֵם חֻקֵּי חַיִּים
כֵּן תְּחָנֵּנוּ וּתְלַמְּדֵנוּ.
אָבִינוּ, הָאָב הָרַחֲמָן, הַמְרַחֵם
רַחֵם עָלֵינוּ
וְתֵן בְּלִבֵּנוּ לְהָבִין² וּלְהַשְׂכִּיל
לִשְׁמֹעַ, לִלְמֹד וּלְלַמֵּד
לִשְׁמֹר וְלַעֲשׂוֹת, וּלְקַיֵּם⁵
אֶת כָּל דִּבְרֵי תַלְמוּד תּוֹרָתֶךָ בְּאַהֲבָה.

אַהֲבָה רַבָּה – *Great love.* The first blessing, *Yotzer Or*, focused on Hashem's role as Creator. Its theme was quite universalistic. This second blessing, however, is more particularistic, moving us one step closer to focusing on our special relationship with Hashem. That unique relationship is exemplified by the Torah, which was given to us as a gift. Just as a groom presents his bride with a ring under the *huppa*, so, too, Hashem gave us the Torah at Sinai. This relationship also carries with it certain responsibilities, including the requirement to declare our belief in Him as the One God, which we will do shortly in the *Shema*.

אַהֲבָה רַבָּה – *Great love.* רַבָּה in this context could mean not only "great" but also "constantly increasing" (Rabbi S. Schwab). His love is manifest in the fact that He helped expand the understanding of Torah over time. Torah has been at the center of Jewish intellectual history and Jewish identity for millennia. In each generation, scholars and lay people alike have expanded and enhanced our appreciation of its depth, beauty, and relevance to contemporary life. And the older we get, the more mature is our ability to understand and to appreciate what a gift it is. Appreciate Torah as our families did in previous generations.

Enlighten our eyes in Your Torah[B]
and let our hearts cling to Your commandments.[B]
Unite our hearts to love and revere Your name,[B]
so that we may never be ashamed.
And because we have trusted
in Your holy, great and revered name,
may we be glad and rejoice in Your salvation.

At this point, gather the four tzitziot of the tallit, holding them in the left hand.

Bring us back in peace from the four quarters of the earth
and lead us upright to our land.
▸ For You are a God who performs acts of salvation,
and You chose us from all peoples and tongues,
bringing us close to Your great name for ever in truth,
that we may thank You
and proclaim Your oneness in love.
Blessed are You, LORD,
who chooses His people Israel in love.

INTRODUCTION TO KERIAT SHEMA

In the first blessing, *Yotzer Or*, we focused on God as Creator; in the second it was the God of Israel. In the first, God is distant; in the second He is close. In the first, our relationship is marked by awe and wonder, or יִרְאָה; in the second it is marked by love, אַהֲבָה. Having experienced both emotions, we are now ready to speak about the Unity of God. (Rabbi M. Angel)

Contrary to popular belief, the *Shema* is not a prayer, as is commonly understood, as much as it is a declaration. That's why it is not called תְּפִלַּת שְׁמַע but rather קְרִיאַת שְׁמַע, for it is similar to reading a proclamation. Think of it a little like a national anthem. We sing it as much for ourselves as for anyone else. Rabbi Yitzḥak Arama in *Akedat Yitzḥak* (58:1) explains that it is a de-

scription of the roots of faith upon which prayer and belief are built. If in much of the rest of prayer man talks to God, here God talks to man. "Listen Israel" to what He has to say.

The first paragraph is about קַבָּלַת עֹל מַלְכוּת שָׁמַיִם – accepting God as the ultimate ruler in one's life.

The second paragraph is about קַבָּלַת עֹל מִצְוֹת – accepting the responsibility of doing mitzvot.

The first paragraph focuses on love.

The second paragraph focuses on awe and the concept of reward and punishment.

The first paragraph is in the singular.

The second paragraph is in the plural.

The path to accepting God in one's life is through love not fear.

This INTRODUCTION *continues on page 125.*

וְהָאֵר עֵינֵינוּ בְּתוֹרָתֶךָ, וְדַבֵּק לִבֵּנוּ בְּמִצְוֹתֶיךָ
וְיַחֵד לְבָבֵנוּ לְאַהֲבָה וּלְיִרְאָה אֶת שְׁמֶךָ
וְלֹא נֵבוֹשׁ לְעוֹלָם וָעֶד.
כִּי בְשֵׁם קָדְשְׁךָ הַגָּדוֹל וְהַנּוֹרָא בָּטָחְנוּ
נָגִילָה וְנִשְׂמְחָה בִּישׁוּעָתֶךָ.

At this point, gather the four ציצית *of the* טלית, *holding them in the left hand.*

וַהֲבִיאֵנוּ לְשָׁלוֹם מֵאַרְבַּע כַּנְפוֹת הָאָרֶץ
וְתוֹלִיכֵנוּ קוֹמְמִיּוּת לְאַרְצֵנוּ.
כִּי אֵל פּוֹעֵל יְשׁוּעוֹת אָתָּה
וּבָנוּ בָחַרְתָּ מִכָּל עַם וְלָשׁוֹן
וְקֵרַבְתָּנוּ לְשִׁמְךָ הַגָּדוֹל סֶלָה, בֶּאֱמֶת
לְהוֹדוֹת לְךָ וּלְיַחֶדְךָ בְּאַהֲבָה.
בָּרוּךְ אַתָּה יהוה, הַבּוֹחֵר בְּעַמּוֹ יִשְׂרָאֵל בְּאַהֲבָה.

BIUR TEFILLA • ביאור תפילה

וְהָאֵר עֵינֵינוּ בְּתוֹרָתֶךָ – *Enlighten our eyes in Your Torah.*
We declare our willingness to learn the To-rah for which you chose us. The two bless-ings of *Keriat Shema* are thus connected: the first blessing spoke of the lights of creation which help our physical lives. Here we speak about the enlightenment of Torah, a key to our spiritual lives.

וְדַבֵּק לִבֵּנוּ בְּמִצְוֹתֶיךָ – *And let our hearts cling*

to Your commandments. We not only want to learn Torah but to actualize it in our lives through the mitzvot.

וְיַחֵד לְבָבֵנוּ לְאַהֲבָה וּלְיִרְאָה אֶת שְׁמֶךָ – *Unite our hearts to love and revere Your name.* And through Torah and mitzvot we wish to unify our hearts in both love and awe. Chosen-ness, Torah, mitzvot, love, awe, unity, the Land – these are all themes that we will further describe in the *Shema*.

IYUN TEFILLA • עיון תפילה

The Maggid of Mezeritch said that the *Shema* is not a command to love God, nor is it a way to manipulate yourself into thinking you do. Rather it is a call

for mindfulness. Be mindful. Hashem is our God. If you get that, says the Mag-gid, then *ve'ahavta* will be an inevitable result.

The Shema must be said with intense concentration. In the first paragraph one should accept, with love, the sovereignty of God; in the second, the mitzvot as the will of God. The end of the third paragraph constitutes fulfillment of the mitzva to remember, morning and evening, the exodus from Egypt. See laws 175–183.

When not praying with a minyan, say:

God, faithful King!

The following verse should be said aloud, while covering the eyes with the right hand:

Listen, Israel: the LORD is our God, the LORD is One.

Deut. 6

Quietly: Blessed be the name of His glorious kingdom for ever and all time.

BIUR TEFILLA · ביאור תפילה

שְׁמַע יִשְׂרָאֵל – Listen, Israel.
"Know" (Rabbi Sa'adia Gaon)
"Believe and accept" (*Hovot HaLevavot, ot* 5)
"Hear and understand" (Abudarham, *ot* 17)
"Listen, Israel" (Rabbi J. Sacks)
Which one do you need to emphasize most today?

IYUN TEFILLA · עיון תפילה

The covering of one's eyes during the recitation of the sentence beginning *Shema Yisrael* is to indicate our exclusion of every possible argument for not accepting *HaKadosh Barukh Hu* – and there are thousands of them. (Rabbi S. Schwab)

ANI TEFILLA · אני תפילה

שְׁמַע יִשְׂרָאֵל – Listen, Israel.
Rabbi Eliezer Silver, a leader of American Orthodox Jewry in the twentieth century, was president of the Va'ad Hatzala or the Rescue Committee for Jews who survived the Shoah. In that capacity he traveled in post-war Europe looking for Jewish children who had ended up in non-Jewish orphanages, most often sponsored by the Church. In one such case he came to an orphanage in Alsace Lorraine asking if there were Jewish children there. He was told that there were none or that they could not be identified as such; their origins

were unknown and they themselves had forgotten where they were from. Rabbi Silver insisted that he nevertheless be permitted to see the children and he was finally allowed to do so for a few moments before their bedtime. He walked into a room filled with beds of children preparing to go to sleep. He called out "Shema Yisrael Hashem Elokeinu Hashem Ehad" and immediately a young child cried out "Mommy!" Soon other voices joined in as children began to come forward crying out for their mothers. "These children are mine," he said to the priest. "I will take them now."

The שמע must be said with intense concentration. In the first paragraph one should accept, with love, the sovereignty of God; in the second, the מצות as the will of God. The end of the third paragraph constitutes fulfillment of the מצוה to remember, morning and evening, the exodus from Egypt. See laws 175–183.

When not praying with a מנין, say:

אֵל מֶלֶךְ נֶאֱמָן

The following verse should be said aloud, while covering the eyes[v] *with the right hand:*

דברים ו

שְׁמַע יִשְׂרָאֵל, יהוה אֱלֹהֵינוּ, יהוה ׀ אֶחָד:

Quietly בָּרוּךְ שֵׁם כְּבוֹד מַלְכוּתוֹ לְעוֹלָם וָעֶד.

The path to accepting the mitzvot is through reward and punishment.

WHY THESE DIFFERENCES?
Love of God is a matter for the individual who strives to attain it through self-perfection, whilst the acceptance of the yoke of the mitzvot and their fulfillment is only conceivable in human society. Robinson Crusoe living on his desert island isolated from human society could indeed have implemented "you should love Hashem your God," but he could not have fulfilled "if you [plural] listen to my commandments" which, for the most part, relate to the life of man amidst society and his bonds with his family, friends, the state, and the human race. (Nechama Leibowitz)

The third paragraph contains the mitzva to recall the exodus from Egypt, another basic tenet of Jewish life, without which the Jewish people would have disappeared from the stage of history. It also contains a reference to *tzitzit*, as well as a reminder that our eyes and our hearts can sometimes mislead us.

In sum, it has been suggested that *Birkhot HaShahar* are about Hashem's providence over our individual lives, *Pesukei DeZimra* are about Hashem's mastery over the world, and *Keriat Shema* is about our relationship with the God of Israel. The first paragraph of the *Shema* focuses on Hashem as King – similar to the theme of the first blessing of *Birkhot Keriat Shema;* the second paragraph of the *Shema* speaks of Hashem's unique relationship with the Jewish people – similar to the theme of the second blessing of *Birkhot Keriat Shema*. The third paragraph speaks to Hashem's involvement in history, just like the third blessing of *Birkhot Keriat Shema*.

Step by step we move closer to our personal encounter with Hashem in the *Shemoneh Esreh* where all of these themes, and more, will come together. We are almost there.

Touch the hand-tefillin at ° and the head-tefillin at °°.

וְאָהַבְתָּ Love the Lord your God with all your heart, with all your   *Deut. 6*
soul, and with all your might. These words which I command you
today shall be on your heart. Teach them repeatedly to your children, speaking of them when you sit at home and when you travel
on the way, when you lie down and when you rise. °Bind them as
a sign on your hand, and °°they shall be an emblem between your
eyes. Write them on the doorposts of your house and gates.

Touch the hand-tefillin at ° and the head-tefillin at °°.

וְהָיָה If you indeed heed My commandments with which I charge   *Deut. 11*
you today, to love the Lord your God and worship Him with all
your heart[B] and with all your soul, I will give rain in your land in its
season, the early and late rain; and you shall gather in your grain,
wine and oil. I will give grass in your field for your cattle, and you
shall eat and be satisfied. Be careful lest your heart be tempted and
you go astray and worship other gods, bowing down to them. Then
the Lord's anger will flare against you and He will close the heavens so that there will be no rain. The land will not yield its crops,
and you will perish swiftly from the good land that the Lord is
giving you. Therefore, set these, My words, on your heart and soul.
°Bind them as a sign on your hand, °°and they shall be an emblem
between your eyes. Teach them to your children, speaking of them

---

phrase as, "You shall love Hashem your God
with all of your *very-muchness*." This would
refer to the extra talents or abilities which
HaKadosh Barukh Hu has given a person,
מְאֹד, more than that which he has given to
other people. Examples would be utilizing

one's great intelligence or musical or artis-
tic ability, or building skills, to demonstrate
his love for *HaKadosh Barukh Hu*. (Rabbi S.
Schwab)
**Which part of my מְאֹד can I better use to-
day to enhance my spirituality?**

IYUN TEFILLA · עיון תפילה

וּלְעָבְדוֹ, בְּכָל לְבַבְכֶם – *And worship Him with
all your heart.*

What is service of the heart? *Tefilla.* (*Ta'anit
2a*)

Touch the תפילין של יד *at* °*and the* תפילין של ראש *at* °°.

דברים⁰ וְאָהַבְתָּ⁰ אֵת יְהוָה אֱלֹהֶיךָ, בְּכָל־לְבָבְךָ וּבְכָל־נַפְשְׁךָ וּבְכָל־
מְאֹדֶךָ: וְהָיוּ הַדְּבָרִים הָאֵלֶּה, אֲשֶׁר אָנֹכִי מְצַוְּךָ הַיּוֹם, עַל־
לְבָבֶךָ: וְשִׁנַּנְתָּם לְבָנֶיךָ וְדִבַּרְתָּ בָּם, בְּשִׁבְתְּךָ בְּבֵיתֶךָ וּבְלֶכְתְּךָ
בַדֶּרֶךְ, וּבְשָׁכְבְּךָ וּבְקוּמֶךָ: °וּקְשַׁרְתָּם לְאוֹת עַל־יָדֶךָ °°וְהָיוּ
לְטֹטָפֹת בֵּין עֵינֶיךָ: וּכְתַבְתָּם עַל־מְזֻזוֹת בֵּיתֶךָ וּבִשְׁעָרֶיךָ:

Touch the תפילין של יד *at* °*and the* תפילין של ראש *at* °°.

דברים⁰⁰ וְהָיָה אִם־שָׁמֹעַ תִּשְׁמְעוּ אֶל־מִצְוֹתַי אֲשֶׁר אָנֹכִי מְצַוֶּה אֶתְכֶם
הַיּוֹם, לְאַהֲבָה אֶת־יְהוָה אֱלֹהֵיכֶם וּלְעָבְדוֹ, בְּכָל־לְבַבְכֶם וּבְכָל־
נַפְשְׁכֶם: וְנָתַתִּי מְטַר־אַרְצְכֶם בְּעִתּוֹ, יוֹרֶה וּמַלְקוֹשׁ, וְאָסַפְתָּ
דְגָנֶךָ וְתִירֹשְׁךָ וְיִצְהָרֶךָ: וְנָתַתִּי עֵשֶׂב בְּשָׂדְךָ לִבְהֶמְתֶּךָ, וְאָכַלְתָּ
וְשָׂבָעְתָּ: הִשָּׁמְרוּ לָכֶם פֶּן־יִפְתֶּה לְבַבְכֶם, וְסַרְתֶּם וַעֲבַדְתֶּם
אֱלֹהִים אֲחֵרִים וְהִשְׁתַּחֲוִיתֶם לָהֶם: וְחָרָה אַף־יְהוָה בָּכֶם, וְעָצַר
אֶת־הַשָּׁמַיִם וְלֹא־יִהְיֶה מָטָר, וְהָאֲדָמָה לֹא תִתֵּן אֶת־יְבוּלָהּ,
וַאֲבַדְתֶּם מְהֵרָה מֵעַל הָאָרֶץ הַטֹּבָה אֲשֶׁר יְהוָה נֹתֵן לָכֶם:
וְשַׂמְתֶּם אֶת־דְּבָרַי אֵלֶּה עַל־לְבַבְכֶם וְעַל־נַפְשְׁכֶם, °וּקְשַׁרְתֶּם
אֹתָם לְאוֹת עַל־יֶדְכֶם, °°וְהָיוּ לְטוֹטָפֹת בֵּין עֵינֵיכֶם: וְלִמַּדְתֶּם

IYUN TEFILLA · עיון תפילה

וְאָהַבְתָּ – *Love.* How does one come to love
God? By studying His Torah and by studying
nature, for through His creations, one comes
to better understand and know the Creator.

And you should love Hashem. The Kotzker rebbe once called over one of his followers
whom he heard reciting the Shma. Tell me
the truth, he said, when you said v'ahavta, is

it really Hashem you love or yourself? When
someone says "I love fish" it's not really the fish
he loves, but himself! So too here, do you love
Hashem or do you love yourself? (Sneh Bo'er
BeKotzk p. 110)

מְאֹדֶךָ – *Your might.* The phrase literally
means "very much." I would translate the

when you sit at home and when you travel on the way, when you lie down and when you rise. Write them on the doorposts of your house and gates, so that you and your children may live long in the land that the LORD swore to your ancestors to give them, for as long as the heavens are above the earth.

Hold the tzitziot in the right hand also (some transfer to the right hand), kissing them at °.

וַיֹּאמֶר The LORD spoke to Moses, saying: Speak to the Israelites   Num. 15
and tell them to make °tassels on the corners of their garments
for all generations. They shall attach to the °tassel at each corner
a thread of blue. This shall be your °tassel, and you shall see it
and remember all of the LORD's commandments and keep them,
not straying after your heart and after your eyes,^ following your
own sinful desires. Thus you will be reminded to keep all My
commandments, and be holy to your God. I am the LORD your
God, who brought you out of the land of Egypt' to be your God.
I am the LORD your God.

°True^B –

The Leader repeats:
▸ The LORD your God is true –

BIUR TEFILLA · ביאור תפילה

אֱמֶת – *True.* We now begin the third and final *berakha* before the *Shemoneh Esreh*, called *Birkat Geula*, referring to our being freed from Egypt. The last paragraph of the *Shema* served as an introduction to this theme in its declaration that God took us out of Egypt in order to be His people. The blessing here conveys the point that it wasn't just that He gave us our freedom at that one point in history, but, like a parent, He continued to watch over us and protect us. This relationship is highlighted by the subsequent threat at *Yam Suf* and the destruction of our enemies in light of overwhelming odds, a phenomenon that has repeated itself numerous times throughout our history. Here we therefore emphasize not the God of Creation (*Yotzer or*), or the God of Sinai (*Ahava raba*), but the God of history who remains a powerful force in our personal and collective lives.

אֹתָם אֶת־בְּנֵיכֶם לְדַבֵּר בָּם, בְּשִׁבְתְּךָ בְּבֵיתֶךָ וּבְלֶכְתְּךָ בַדֶּרֶךְ,
וּֽבְשָׁכְבְּךָ וּבְקוּמֶךָ: וּכְתַבְתָּם עַל־מְזוּזוֹת בֵּיתֶךָ וּבִשְׁעָרֶיךָ: לְמַעַן
יִרְבּוּ יְמֵיכֶם וִימֵי בְנֵיכֶם עַל הָֽאֲדָמָה אֲשֶׁר נִשְׁבַּע יהוה לַאֲבֹתֵיכֶם
לָתֵת לָהֶם, כִּימֵי הַשָּׁמַיִם עַל־הָאָֽרֶץ:

Hold the ציצית *in the right hand also (*some transfer to the right hand), kissing them at* °.

במדבר טו

וַיֹּאמֶר יהוה אֶל־מֹשֶׁה לֵּאמֹר: דַּבֵּר אֶל־בְּנֵי יִשְׂרָאֵל וְאָמַרְתָּ
אֲלֵהֶם, וְעָשׂוּ לָהֶם °צִיצִת עַל־כַּנְפֵי בִגְדֵיהֶם לְדֹרֹתָם, וְנָתְנוּ °עַל־
צִיצִת הַכָּנָף פְּתִיל תְּכֵלֶת: וְהָיָה לָכֶם °לְצִיצִת, וּרְאִיתֶם אֹתוֹ
וּזְכַרְתֶּם אֶת־כָּל־מִצְוֹת יהוה וַעֲשִׂיתֶם אֹתָם, וְלֹא תָתֻרוּ אַחֲרֵי
לְבַבְכֶם וְאַחֲרֵי עֵֽינֵיכֶם, אֲשֶׁר־אַתֶּם זֹנִים אַחֲרֵיהֶם: לְמַעַן תִּזְכְּרוּ
וַעֲשִׂיתֶם אֶת־כָּל־מִצְוֹתָי, וִהְיִיתֶם קְדֹשִׁים לֵאלֹֽהֵיכֶם: אֲנִי יהוה
אֱלֹֽהֵיכֶם, אֲשֶׁר הוֹצֵאתִי אֶתְכֶם מֵאֶרֶץ מִצְרַיִם, לִהְיוֹת לָכֶם
לֵאלֹהִים, אֲנִי יהוה אֱלֹהֵיכֶם:

°אֱמֶת׃

The שליח ציבור *repeats:*

◄ יהוה אֱלֹהֵיכֶם אֱמֶת

ANI TEFILLA · אני תפילה

וְלֹא תָתֻרוּ אַחֲרֵי לְבַבְכֶם – *Not straying after your heart and after your eyes.* "You should not wander after your hearts and your eyes."

Do your eyes follow your heart or do you let your heart follow your eyes?

IYUN TEFILLA · עיון תפילה

אֲנִי יהוה אֱלֹֽהֵיכֶם, אֲשֶׁר הוֹצֵאתִי אֶתְכֶם מֵאֶרֶץ מִצְרַיִם – *I am the Lord your God, who brought you out of the land of Egypt.* In an age when might triumphed over right, the Torah

records one of the great turning points in the human story, when the Creator of heaven and earth intervened in defense of the powerless. (Rabbi J. Sacks)

וְיַצִּיב **And firm**, established and enduring, right, faithful,
beloved, cherished, delightful, pleasant,
awesome, mighty, perfect, accepted,
good and beautiful[i]
is this faith[B] for us for ever.

True   is the eternal God, our King,
Rock of Jacob, Shield of our salvation.
He exists and His name exists
through all generations.
His throne is established,
His kingship and faithfulness endure for ever.

At °, kiss the tzitziot and release them.

His words live and persist,
faithful and desirable
°for ever and all time.

‣ So they were for our ancestors, so they are for us,
and so they will be for our children
and all our generations
and for all future generations
of the seed of Israel, Your servants. ◂

---

are about to have a private audience with
Him. Imagine yourself 15 steps away.

Alternatively, it has been suggested that
including the word אֱמֶת there are 16 adjec-

tives corresponding to the 16 verses from
Shema to the end of the second paragraph.
We declare each one of those verses to be
true (*Etz Yosef*).

BIUR TEFILLA · ביאור תפילה

הַדָּבָר הַזֶּה – *Is this faith.* There are numerous
adjectives added here, all of which describe
"הַדָּבָר הַזֶּה.""What is "this thing?"Most likely it is
a reference to the final theme we mentioned
in the *Shema*, namely, we hereby reaffirm
our belief in the fact that "I am Hashem your

God who took you out of Egypt." It is thus
a reference to our belief in the historical
truth of the exodus (*Tosafot, Berakhot* 12a).
Alternatively, there are those who say it is a
reference to our belief in Hashem, that it was
He who took us out (*Emek Berakha*).

וְיַצִּיב, וְנָכוֹן וְקַיָּם, וְיָשָׁר וְנֶאֱמָן

וְאָהוּב וְחָבִיב, וְנֶחְמָד וְנָעִים

וְנוֹרָא וְאַדִּיר, וּמְתֻקָּן וּמְקֻבָּל

וְטוֹב וְיָפֶה°

הַדָּבָר הַזֶּה° עָלֵינוּ לְעוֹלָם וָעֶד.

אֱמֶת אֱלֹהֵי עוֹלָם מַלְכֵּנוּ

צוּר יַעֲקֹב מָגֵן יִשְׁעֵנוּ

לְדוֹר וָדוֹר הוּא קַיָּם וּשְׁמוֹ קַיָּם

וְכִסְאוֹ נָכוֹן

וּמַלְכוּתוֹ וֶאֱמוּנָתוֹ לָעַד קַיֶּמֶת.

At °, kiss the ציצית *and release them.*

וּדְבָרָיו חַיִּים וְקַיָּמִים, נֶאֱמָנִים וְנֶחְמָדִים

°לָעַד וּלְעוֹלְמֵי עוֹלָמִים

‹ עַל אֲבוֹתֵינוּ וְעָלֵינוּ

עַל בָּנֵינוּ וְעַל דּוֹרוֹתֵינוּ

וְעַל כָּל דּוֹרוֹת זֶרַע יִשְׂרָאֵל עֲבָדֶיךָ. ‹

IYUN TEFILLA · עיון תפילה

There are 15 adjectives here connected with one another by the conjunction "and," thus indicating that they are intended to form a single unit. This 15 is reminiscent of the 15 chapters of *Tehillim* composed by King David which begin with the phrase שִׁיר הַמַּעֲלוֹת (song of *ascents*), which in turn are reminiscent of the 15 steps in the *Beit HaMikdash* leading from the outer courtyard to the inner courtyard, as well as

the 15 מַעֲלוֹת טוֹבוֹת (rising levels of favors) which Hashem did for us during and after the exodus mentioned in *Dayeinu* in the Haggada (Abudarham). These allusions remind us that we are moving ever closer to the encounter with Hashem in the *Shemoneh Esreh*.

Imagine yourself at the bottom of a long staircase or at the end of a long hallway leading up to the office of the King. You

For the early and the later generations
this faith has proved good and enduring for ever –
True and faithful, an irrevocable law.

True You are the LORD: our God and God of our ancestors,
➤ our King and King of our ancestors,
our Redeemer and Redeemer of our ancestors,
our Maker,
Rock of our salvation,
our Deliverer and Rescuer:
this has ever been Your name.
There is no God but You.

עֶזְרַת You have always been the help of our ancestors,
Shield and Savior of their children after them
in every generation.
Your dwelling is in the heights of the universe,
and Your judgments and righteousness
reach to the ends of the earth.
Happy is the one who obeys Your commandments
and takes to heart Your teaching and Your word.

True You are the Master of Your people
and a mighty King who pleads their cause.

True You are the first and You are the last.
Besides You, we have no king,
redeemer or savior.

---

knew them all to be true because they saw "Truth" when God revealed Himself to them. We approach faith based upon their experiences which they handed down to us. But we can also have our own absolute faith that the Torah is true, for it has proven itself as the foundation of the laws of civilization, from one generation to the next, and it will never disappear.

עַל הָרִאשׁוֹנִים וְעַל הָאַחֲרוֹנִים ‏ע

דָּבָר טוֹב וְקַיָּם לְעוֹלָם וָעֶד

אֱמֶת וֶאֱמוּנָה, חֹק וְלֹא יַעֲבֹר.

אֱמֶת שָׁאַתָּה הוּא יהוה אֱלֹהֵינוּ וֵאלֹהֵי אֲבוֹתֵינוּ

‏‹ מַלְכֵּנוּ מֶלֶךְ אֲבוֹתֵינוּ

גּוֹאֲלֵנוּ גּוֹאֵל אֲבוֹתֵינוּ

יוֹצְרֵנוּ צוּר יְשׁוּעָתֵנוּ

פּוֹדֵנוּ וּמַצִּילֵנוּ מֵעוֹלָם שְׁמֶךָ

אֵין אֱלֹהִים זוּלָתֶךָ.

עֶזְרַת אֲבוֹתֵינוּ אַתָּה הוּא מֵעוֹלָם

מָגֵן וּמוֹשִׁיעַ לִבְנֵיהֶם אַחֲרֵיהֶם בְּכָל דּוֹר וָדוֹר.

בְּרוּם עוֹלָם מוֹשָׁבֶךָ

וּמִשְׁפָּטֶיךָ וְצִדְקָתְךָ עַד אַפְסֵי אָרֶץ.

אַשְׁרֵי אִישׁ שֶׁיִּשְׁמַע לְמִצְוֹתֶיךָ

וְתוֹרָתְךָ וּדְבָרְךָ יָשִׂים עַל לִבּוֹ.

אֱמֶת אַתָּה הוּא אָדוֹן לְעַמֶּךָ

וּמֶלֶךְ גִּבּוֹר לָרִיב רִיבָם.

אֱמֶת אַתָּה הוּא רִאשׁוֹן וְאַתָּה הוּא אַחֲרוֹן

וּמִבַּלְעָדֶיךָ אֵין לָנוּ מֶלֶךְ גּוֹאֵל וּמוֹשִׁיעַ.

IYUN TEFILLA • עיון תפילה

עַל הָרִאשׁוֹנִים וְעַל הָאַחֲרוֹנִים — *For the early and the later generations.* There are some

mitzvot in the Torah that make sense to us, and others that do not. Our ancestors

From Egypt You redeemed us,[B] LORD our God,
and from the slave-house You delivered us.
All their firstborn You killed,
but Your firstborn You redeemed.
You split the Sea of Reeds
and drowned the arrogant.
You brought Your beloved ones across.
The water covered their foes;   *Ps. 106*
not one of them was left.

For this, the beloved ones praised and exalted God,
the cherished ones sang psalms, songs and praises,
blessings and thanksgivings to the King,
the living and enduring God.
High and exalted, great and awesome,
He humbles the haughty and raises the lowly,
freeing captives and redeeming those in need,
helping the poor
and answering His people when they cry out to Him.

Stand in preparation for the Amida. Take three steps back before beginning the Amida.

▸ Praises to God Most High,
the Blessed One who is blessed.
Moses and the children of Israel
recited to You a song with great joy,
and they all exclaimed:
        "Who is like You, LORD, among the mighty?   *Ex. 15*
        Who is like You, majestic in holiness,
        awesome in praises, doing wonders?"

---

erful was that experience that they burst
into song and praise of Hashem, just as
we are about to do in the first three blessings of the *Shemoneh Esreh*. We thus fulfill the Rabbis' insistence that we precede
our prayer by recalling that we were freed
from Egypt and saved as a people (סוֹמֵךְ
גְּאֻלָּה לִתְפִלָּה).

מִמִּצְרַיִם גְּאַלְתָּנוּ, יהוה אֱלֹהֵינוּ
וּמִבֵּית עֲבָדִים פְּדִיתָנוּ
כָּל בְּכוֹרֵיהֶם הָרָגְתָּ, וּבְכוֹרְךָ גָּאַלְתָּ
וְיַם סוּף בָּקַעְתָּ
וְזֵדִים טִבַּעְתָּ
וִידִידִים הֶעֱבַרְתָּ
וַיְכַסּוּ־מַיִם צָרֵיהֶם, אֶחָד מֵהֶם לֹא נוֹתָר:

תהלים קו

עַל זֹאת שִׁבְּחוּ אֲהוּבִים, וְרוֹמְמוּ אֵל
וְנָתְנוּ יְדִידִים זְמִירוֹת, שִׁירוֹת וְתִשְׁבָּחוֹת
בְּרָכוֹת וְהוֹדָאוֹת לְמֶלֶךְ אֵל חַי וְקַיָּם
רָם וְנִשָּׂא, גָּדוֹל וְנוֹרָא
מַשְׁפִּיל גֵּאִים וּמַגְבִּיהַּ שְׁפָלִים
מוֹצִיא אֲסִירִים, וּפוֹדֶה עֲנָוִים וְעוֹזֵר דַּלִּים
וְעוֹנֶה לְעַמּוֹ בְּעֵת שַׁוְּעָם אֵלָיו.

Stand in preparation for the עמידה. *Take three steps back before beginning the* עמידה.

◂ תְּהִלּוֹת לְאֵל עֶלְיוֹן, בָּרוּךְ הוּא וּמְבֹרָךְ
מֹשֶׁה וּבְנֵי יִשְׂרָאֵל
לְךָ עָנוּ שִׁירָה בְּשִׂמְחָה רַבָּה
וְאָמְרוּ כֻלָּם
מִי־כָמֹכָה בָּאֵלִם, יהוה
מִי כָּמֹכָה נֶאְדָּר בַּקֹּדֶשׁ, נוֹרָא תְהִלֹּת, עֹשֵׂה פֶלֶא:

שמות טו

BIUR TEFILLA · ביאור תפילה

מִמִּצְרַיִם גְּאַלְתָּנוּ – *From Egypt You redeemed us.* The Torah says that when Israel saw the

splitting of the *Yam Suf*, they "believed in God and in Moshe His servant." So pow-

▸ With a new song, the redeemed people praised
Your name at the seashore.
Together they all gave thanks, proclaimed Your kingship,
and declared:

> "The LORD shall reign for ever and ever." *Ex. 15*

Congregants should end the following blessing together with the Leader so as to be able to move directly from the words "redeemed Israel" to the Amida, without the interruption of saying Amen.

▸ צוּר יִשְׂרָאֵל Rock of Israel! Arise to the help of Israel.
Deliver, as You promised, Judah and Israel.

> Our Redeemer, the LORD of hosts is His name, *Is. 47*
> the Holy One of Israel.

Blessed are You, LORD, who redeemed Israel.

INTRODUCTION TO THE AMIDA: THE STRUCTURE OF THE SHEMONEH ESREH

There are nineteen blessings that comprise the *Shemoneh Esreh*. They are known by the following names:

1. אבות – Patriarchs
2. גבורות – Divine Might
3. קדושת שם – Holiness
4. דעת – Knowledge
5. תשובה – Repentance
6. סליחה – Forgiveness
7. גאולה – Redemption
8. רפואה – Healing
9. ברכת השנים – Prosperity
10. קיבוץ גלויות – Ingathering of Exiles
11. משפט – Justice
12. ברכת המינים – Against Informers
13. על הצדיקים – The Righteous
14. בנין ירושלים – Rebuilding Jerusalem
15. מלכות בית דוד – Kingdom of David
16. שומע תפלה – Response to Prayer
17. עבודה – Temple Service
18. מודים – Thanksgiving
19. שלום – Peace

Numerous attempts have been made to define the overall structure of the prayer. The most traditional division is the following: the first three blessings consist of praise/שֶׁבַח; the middle thirteen blessings constitute requests/בַּקָּשׁוֹת and the final three blessings are thanks/הוֹדָאָה.

This is the way that Rabbi Ḥanina (*Berakhot* 34a) characterized this structure: "The first blessings are like a servant who organizes his praise before his master; the middle blessings are like a servant who requests his allotment from his master; and the last blessings are like a servant who received his allotment from his master and takes his leave."

As we have mentioned before, one begins with describing Hashem's relation-

This INTRODUCTION *continues on page 139.*

‹ שִׁירָה חֲדָשָׁה שִׁבְּחוּ גְאוּלִים
לְשִׁמְךָ עַל שְׂפַת הַיָּם
יַחַד כֻּלָּם הוֹדוּ וְהִמְלְיכוּ
וְאָמְרוּ

יהוה יִמְלֹךְ לְעֹלָם וָעֶד:

שמות טו

The קהל should end the following blessing together with the שליח ציבור so as to be able to move
directly from the words גָּאַל יִשְׂרָאֵל to the עמידה, without the interruption of saying אמן.

‹ צוּר יִשְׂרָאֵל, קוּמָה בְּעֶזְרַת יִשְׂרָאֵל
וּפְדֵה כִנְאֻמֶךָ יְהוּדָה וְיִשְׂרָאֵל.
גֹּאֲלֵנוּ יהוה צְבָאוֹת שְׁמוֹ, קְדוֹשׁ יִשְׂרָאֵל:
בָּרוּךְ אַתָּה יהוה, גָּאַל יִשְׂרָאֵל.

ישעיה מז

Rabbi Yose ben Elyakim testified in the name
of the holy community of Jerusalem:
If one joins the blessing of Geula to the

Tefilla [Shemoneh Esreh], he will not meet
with any mishap for the whole of the day.
(Berakhot 9b)

IYUN TEFILLA · עיון תפילה

We know these events took place because they
have been passed along to us by our parents and
their parents going back to the moment when it
all happened. We are living only a short period of
time after the Holocaust, though there are people
who deny it ever took place. It is all the more under-
standable that there are those who would deny the
exodus and the splitting of the Sea. Yet, says Rabbi
Yehuda HaLevi, our tradition has been unbroken
and our historical experience ever since has proven
over and over again that God has been an ongoing
presence in our history, even if He is sometimes
hard to see.

ANI TEFILLA · אני תפילה

At this point we transport ourselves in time, seeing ourselves
as having been there at the moment of liberation. Imagine the
joy, the gratitude, the sense of
awe and wonder, the sense of
intimacy with Hashem and with
one another.
Close your eyes and imagine
actually coming into contact
with the Presence of the Di-
vine. Now begin the *Shemoneh*
Esreh.

THE AMIDA

There are three formats of the Amida offered in this Siddur. The Amida of Shaḥarit includes commentary; in the Amida of Minḥa (on page 280) one may add one's own commentary; the Amida of Maʾariv (on page 360) is in the traditional form.

The Amida until "in former years" on page 192, is said standing with feet together. The Amida is said silently, following the precedent of Hannah when she prayed for a child (1 Sam. 1:13). If there is a minyan, it is repeated aloud by the Leader. Take three steps forward, as if formally entering the place of the Divine Presence. At the points indicated by ˈ, bend the knees at the first word, bow at the second, and stand straight before saying God's name.

O Lᴏʀᴅ, open my lips,ᴮᴬ so that my mouth may declare Your praise.   Ps. 51

---

ask for prosperity in ברכת השנים. The same is true for all of the other blessings as well, as long as one does not forgo the text of the blessing and as long as one keeps within the theme of that blessing (Shulḥan Arukh 119:1). Any request that doesn't seem to fit into the theme of an existing blessing may be included in שומע תפלה. In short, there is a tremendous amount of room for personal expression.

We conclude with three blessings whose primary theme is thanks, like a servant who departs from his master, grateful for the audience, relieved that he has had the opportunity to express his innermost thoughts, confident that his prayers have been heard and hopeful that they will be answered.

For more on the *Amida* go to page 869.

BIUR TEFILLA · ביאור תפילה

אֲדֹנָי, שְׂפָתַי תִּפְתָּח – *O Lᴏʀᴅ , open my lips.* This is actually a verse from *Tehillim*, (51) recited by King David in the wake of his sin with Batsheva. Knowing that Hashem does not want sacrifices or ritual offerings empty of heartfelt emotion or a change in one's behavior, he asks that Hashem help him to open his mouth in sincere prayer.

Other approaches to this verse include:

Forgive me, Hashem, so that my prayer will be acceptable. (Rashi)

Help me, Hashem, so that I may pray with kavana so that my prayers will be accepted. In effect, this is a prayer for proper prayer. (Rabbeinu Yona)

Help me, Hashem, to feel dependent enough upon You to want to pray out of a true sense of need.

Help me, Hashem, to feel other people's sense of sorrow and pain, without my having to actually suffer these, so that I may pray to You out of a true sense of need. (Rabbi Tzaddok of Lublin)

ANI TEFILLA · אני תפילה

אֲדֹנָי, שְׂפָתַי תִּפְתָּח – *O Lᴏʀᴅ , open my lips.* A rabbi was seen coming late to shul on a regular basis, despite the fact that he was also regularly seen up and about from the time

of sunrise early in the morning. When asked what he was doing during all of that time, he responded: "I pray that I may be able to pray." **Pray for a moment before you pray.**

עמידה

There are three formats of the עמידה offered in this Siddur. The Amida of שחרית includes commentary; in the עמידה of מנחה (on page 281) one may add one's own commentary; the עמידה of מעריב (on page 361) is in the traditional form.

The עמידה until קְדֻשׁוֹת on page 193, is said standing with feet together. The עמידה is said silently, following the precedent of Hannah when she prayed for a child (שמואל א' א', י ג,א). If there is a מנין, it is repeated aloud by the שליח צבור. Take three steps forward, as if formally entering the place of the Divine Presence. At the points indicated by ˅, bend the knees at the first word, bow at the second, and stand straight before saying God's name.

תהלים נא

אֲדֹנָי, שְׂפָתַי תִּפְתָּח,בא וּפִי יַגִּיד תְּהִלָּתֶךָ:

---

ship with us and His power over the world, not because Hashem needs our praise, but because before one can ask for something, one needs to first acknowledge His ability to grant such requests. I need to first remind myself of who Hashem is, what role He plays in the world, and only then can I truly stand before Him as a servant before his master.

The requests speak to a central feature of prayer. Yet to see prayer as only this is to do an injustice to the concept of *tefilla*, which can be very different than prayer. Many Jewish philosophers have suggested that *tefilla* is less for God than it is for man. It is a way for me to understand myself, to clarify my values and priorities, to get me to change. Rabbi S.R. Hirsch famously suggested that this is why the word *tefilla* is derived from the root פלל which refers to judging or clarifying a matter. The Hebrew reflexive verb לְהִתְפַּלֵּל would thus mean "to judge oneself" or "to clarify things for oneself," and denotes "to step out of active life in order to attempt to gain a true judgment about oneself, that is, about one's ego, about one's relationship to God and the world, and of God and the world to oneself" (Hirsch, *Horev*). The middle blessings are therefore not only opportunities to ask things of Hashem but also opportunities for asking things of ourselves.

There have been many attempts to understand the internal structure of the middle blessings. Are the various blessings related? Are they listed in a particular way? There are those who suggest that the first set of six refer to individual needs and the second set to communal ones, with the last blessing (שמע תפילה) being a summative one. Some have seen the blessings to be sequential (e.g., one needs health before one asks for material prosperity) and that perhaps there is even a symmetrical and causal relationship among them (e.g., blessing 4 must precede blessing 5, but it also is linked to blessing 10; 6 precedes 7 but is linked to blessing 11 etc.) (cited in Abudarham). An additional explanation has a further internal division in which blessings 4–6 refer to spiritual needs, and 7–9 refer to physical needs, while 10–12 refer to national rebuilding, and 13–15 are components of their realization.

Regardless, there is a tradition that each of the blessings can also be understood as a category within which one can subsume one's related needs. So, for example, one can break from the text of the blessing of רְפָאֵנוּ, ideally toward the end (*Mishna Berura* 119:3), to insert one's own personal plea for someone, before going back to finish the text of the blessing itself. So, too, if one wanted to

PATRIARCHS[IA]

בָּרוּךְ Blessed are You, LORD our God and God of our fathers,[BA] God of Abraham, God of Isaac and God of Jacob;[B] the great, mighty and awesome God, God Most High, who bestows acts of loving-kindness and creates all, who remembers the loving-kindness of the fathers and will bring a Redeemer to their children's children for the sake of His name, in love.

> *Between Rosh* Remember us for life, O King who desires life,
> *HaShana &* and write us in the book of life –
> *Yom Kippur:* for Your sake, O God of life.

King, Helper, Savior, Shield:[A]
Blessed are You, LORD, Shield of Abraham.

BIUR TEFILLA · ביאור תפילה

אֱלֹהֵינוּ וֵאלֹהֵי אֲבוֹתֵינוּ – *Our God and God of our fathers.* The blessing says "our God and God of our fathers." Why does it say both? Isn't it the same God?!

The Ba'al Shem Tov answered that our knowledge of God comes from two sources: (1) our parents and the way they raised us, and (2) the knowledge of God we acquire on our own by ourselves as we mature.

ANI TEFILLA · אני תפילה

וֵאלֹהֵי אֲבוֹתֵינוּ – *God of our fathers.*
How did your parents or family convey to you a sense of Jewish tradition? Have this in mind when you say וֵאלֹהֵי אֲבוֹתֵינוּ.

How have you tried to make your knowledge of God your own? Have this in mind when you say אֱלֹהֵינוּ.

אֱלֹהֵינוּ וֵאלֹהֵי אֲבוֹתֵינוּ – *Our God and God of our fathers.*
Did you ever have difficulty relating to the existence of God? Some people find strength in recalling that Hashem has had a historical relationship with the Jewish people going

all the way back to the Avot, that is, with our Fathers and with our fathers.
What event or phenomenon in Jewish history gives you reason to believe?

מֶלֶךְ עוֹזֵר וּמוֹשִׁיעַ וּמָגֵן – *King, Helper, Savior, Shield.*
How has Hashem been a King, Helper, Savior and Shield for the Jewish people in the past? Today?

How has Hashem been that in your family's life?

How has Hashem been that in your own life? What do I have to be grateful for?

אבות

אבות^א

בָּרוּךְ אַתָּה יהוה, אֱלֹהֵינוּ וֵאלֹהֵי אֲבוֹתֵינוּ,^{בּא}
אֱלֹהֵי אַבְרָהָם, אֱלֹהֵי יִצְחָק, וֵאלֹהֵי יַעֲקֹב,^ג
הָאֵל הַגָּדוֹל הַגִּבּוֹר וְהַנּוֹרָא, אֵל עֶלְיוֹן,
גּוֹמֵל חֲסָדִים טוֹבִים, וְקֹנֵה הַכֹּל
וְזוֹכֵר חַסְדֵי אָבוֹת
וּמֵבִיא גוֹאֵל לִבְנֵי בְנֵיהֶם לְמַעַן שְׁמוֹ בְּאַהֲבָה.

בעשרת ימי תשובה: זָכְרֵנוּ לְחַיִּים, מֶלֶךְ חָפֵץ בַּחַיִּים
וְכָתְבֵנוּ בְּסֵפֶר הַחַיִּים, לְמַעַנְךָ אֱלֹהִים חַיִּים.

מֶלֶךְ עוֹזֵר וּמוֹשִׁיעַ וּמָגֵן.^א
בָּרוּךְ אַתָּה יהוה, מָגֵן אַבְרָהָם.

אבות – **PATRIARCHS.** The *Shulḥan Arukh* says about this blessing that one should have *kavana* in one's heart for the meaning of the words that one says with one's mouth. Also one should imagine that the *Shekhina* is standing right in front of your eyes and you should therefore remove all foreign thoughts which might distract you. You should think that you are standing before a human king or president, in which case you would be very careful about what you say and you would make sure that it was expressed well and with proper intention. All the more so if you are standing in front of the King of kings, *HaKadosh Barukh Hu*, the One who knows all of man's thoughts...

אבות – *PATRIARCHS.*
If you could meet the President of the United States, how would you act? What would you say? **You are standing in front of the President of the world.**

What do you want to say?

אבות – *PATRIARCHS.* The *Sefat Emet*, a Rebbe of the Ger Hasidim, wrote that there is a spark of the *Avot* that resides in each and every one of us. That is why the *Shem-oneh Esreh* begins with referring to them, for it is through them that we can more easily come to cleave to Hashem. **Which sparks of the *Avot* can you recognize in your-self?**

DIVINE MIGHT

אַתָּה גִבּוֹר You are eternally mighty,[A] LORD.
You give life to the dead[B] and have great power to save.

The phrase "He makes the wind blow and the rain fall" is said from Simhat Torah until Pesah. In Israel the phrase "He causes the dew to fall" is said from Pesah until Shemini Atzeret.

In fall & winter: He makes the wind blow and the rain fall.
In Israel, in spring & summer: He causes the dew to fall.

He sustains the living with loving-kindness,
and with great compassion revives the dead.
He supports the fallen, heals the sick, sets captives free,
and keeps His faith with those who sleep in the dust.
Who is like You, Master of might,
and who can compare to You,
O King who brings death and gives life,[A] and makes salvation grow?

Between Rosh HaShana & Yom Kippur: Who is like You, compassionate Father,
who remembers His creatures in compassion, for life?

Faithful are You to revive the dead.
Blessed are You, LORD, who revives the dead.

When saying the Amida silently, continue with "You are holy" on page 146.

---

of Hashem's power over the physical world than that. Even so, many have suggested alternative possibilities for the meaning of the phrase "gives life to the dead."

Which interpretation appeals to you the most today?

(1) He supports and cures those who were at death's door whom doctors said could not be cured. Hashem thus revives the dead in this way. (Abudarham)

(2) By virtue of the fact that He provides good to those who are still alive, this provides life/satisfaction to those who are dead. (Tiferet Shlomo)

(3) Hashem grants life to those who are downcast or enveloped by sadness, who may feel like they are dead.

(4) Hashem sends rain on a regular basis which revives life on earth.

(5) Hashem enables us to awake every morning when we are otherwise like dead people.

Rabbi Avraham Weinberg, a leader of the Hasidim of Slonim, noted that the phrase סוֹמֵךְ נוֹפְלִים – "who raises those who fall," is written in the present tense and not in the past tense. From here one learns that no matter how many times you may have stumbled or fallen, Hashem is still there every day, in the present, to support you and make sure that you can get up again. Every day brings with it new hope for a fresh beginning.

גבורות

אַתָּה גִּבּוֹר לְעוֹלָם,* אֲדֹנָי
מְחַיֵּה מֵתִים² אַתָּה, רַב לְהוֹשִׁיעַ

The phrase מַשִּׁיב הָרוּחַ *is said from* שמחת תורה *until* פסח.
In ארץ ישראל *the phrase* מוֹרִיד הַטָּל *is said from* פסח *until* שמיני עצרת.

בחורף: מַשִּׁיב הָרוּחַ וּמוֹרִיד הַגֶּשֶׁם / בארץ ישראל בקיץ: מוֹרִיד הַטָּל.

מְכַלְכֵּל חַיִּים בְּחֶסֶד, מְחַיֵּה מֵתִים בְּרַחֲמִים רַבִּים
סוֹמֵךְ נוֹפְלִים, וְרוֹפֵא חוֹלִים, וּמַתִּיר אֲסוּרִים
וּמְקַיֵּם אֱמוּנָתוֹ לִישֵׁנֵי עָפָר.
מִי כָמוֹךָ, בַּעַל גְּבוּרוֹת, וּמִי דּוֹמֶה לָּךְ
מֶלֶךְ, מֵמִית וּמְחַיֶּה* וּמַצְמִיחַ יְשׁוּעָה.

בעשרת ימי תשובה: מִי כָמוֹךָ אַב הָרַחֲמִים, זוֹכֵר יְצוּרָיו לְחַיִּים בְּרַחֲמִים.

וְנֶאֱמָן אַתָּה לְהַחֲיוֹת מֵתִים.
בָּרוּךְ אַתָּה יהוה, מְחַיֵּה הַמֵּתִים.

When saying the עמידה *silently, continue with* אַתָּה קָדוֹשׁ *on page 147.*

ANI TEFILLA · אני תפילה

אַתָּה גִּבּוֹר לְעוֹלָם — *You are eternally mighty* . Have you ever been in a place in nature where you felt the presence of God? Have you ever witnessed a natural phenomenon when you felt like there was a force or Presence that was beyond you?
Close your eyes. Imagine yourself there now.

מְכַלְכֵּל חַיִּים בְּחֶסֶד — *He sustains the living with loving-kindness.* The Ḥafetz Ḥayyim

once wrote that the fulfillment of our prayers is dependent upon our actions. If we do acts of Ḥesed for other people, then it is much more likely that Hashem will do acts of Ḥesed for us (*Ahavat Ḥesed* II:6). For how can we ask Him to do something for us that we ourselves are not prepared to do for others?
What Ḥesed did you do for someone yesterday?

   Whom can you reach out to today?

BIUR TEFILLA · ביאור תפילה

מְחַיֵּה מֵתִים — *Who revives the dead.* The *berakha* mentions the cardinal Jewish belief

in the revival of the dead no less than five times, for there can be no greater example

KEDUSHA^{BI}

During the Leader's Repetition, the following is said standing
with feet together, rising on the toes at the words indicated by ◆.

Cong. then   נְקַדֵּשׁ We will sanctify Your name on earth,
Leader: as they sanctify it in the highest heavens,
             as is written by Your prophet,
             "And they [the angels] call to one another saying: Is. 6

Cong. then   ◆"Holy, ◆holy, ◆holy^A is the LORD of hosts
Leader: the whole world is filled with His glory."
             Those facing them say "Blessed – "

Cong. then   ◆"Blessed is the LORD's glory from His place."   Ezek. 3
Leader: And in Your holy Writings it is written thus:

Cong. then   ◆"The LORD shall reign for ever. He is your God, Zion,   Ps. 146
Leader: from generation to generation, Halleluya!"

Leader: From generation to generation we will declare Your greatness,
             and we will proclaim Your holiness for evermore.
             Your praise, our God, shall not leave our mouth forever,
             for You, God, are a great and holy King. Blessed are You, LORD,
             the holy God. / *Between Rosh HaShana & Yom Kippur:* the holy King./

The Leader continues with "You grace humanity" on page 148.

ANI TEFILLA · אני תפילה

קָדוֹשׁ, קָדוֹשׁ קָדוֹשׁ – *Holy, holy, holy.* Rudolph Otto was a famous German scholar of religion. In 1911, he traveled to Morocco and visited a small synagogue on Shabbat. He wrote:

I have heard the Sanctus, sanctus, sanctus of the cardinals in Saint Peter's, the Swiat, swiat, swiat in the cathedral in the Kremlin, and the Hagios, hagios, hagios of the patriarch in Jerusalem. In whatever language these words are spoken, the most sublime words that

human lips have ever uttered, they always seize one in the deepest ground of the soul, arousing and stirring with a mighty shudder the mystery of the otherworldly that sleeps therein. That happens here more than anywhere else, here in this deserted place, where they resound in the language in which Isaiah first heard them and on the lips of this people whose heritage they initially were. (Rudolph Otto, *Autobiographical and Social Essays,* ed. Gregory D. Alles [The Hague: Mouton, 1996], 81)

קְדוּשָׁה‏‎*ב

During חזרת הש״ץ*, the following is said standing
with feet together, rising on the toes at the words indicated by* ^.

קהל
then
ש״ץ: נְקַדֵּשׁ אֶת שִׁמְךָ בָּעוֹלָם
כְּשֵׁם שֶׁמַּקְדִּישִׁים אוֹתוֹ בִּשְׁמֵי מָרוֹם

ישעיה ו

כַּכָּתוּב עַל יַד נְבִיאֶךָ, וְקָרָא זֶה אֶל־זֶה וְאָמַר

קהל
then
ש״ץ: ^קָדוֹשׁ, ^קָדוֹשׁ, ^קָדוֹשׁ יהוה צְבָאוֹת
מְלֹא כָל־הָאָרֶץ כְּבוֹדוֹ:
לְעֻמָּתָם בָּרוּךְ יֹאמֵרוּ

יחזקאל ג

קהל
then
ש״ץ: ^בָּרוּךְ כְּבוֹד־יהוה מִמְּקוֹמוֹ:
וּבְדִבְרֵי קָדְשְׁךָ כָּתוּב לֵאמֹר

תהלים קמו

קהל
then
ש״ץ: ^יִמְלֹךְ יהוה לְעוֹלָם, אֱלֹהַיִךְ צִיּוֹן לְדֹר וָדֹר, הַלְלוּיָהּ:

ש״ץ: לְדוֹר וָדוֹר נַגִּיד גָּדְלֶךָ
וּלְנֵצַח נְצָחִים קְדֻשָּׁתְךָ נַקְדִּישׁ
וְשִׁבְחֲךָ אֱלֹהֵינוּ מִפִּינוּ לֹא יָמוּשׁ לְעוֹלָם וָעֶד
כִּי אֵל מֶלֶךְ גָּדוֹל וְקָדוֹשׁ אָתָּה.
בָּרוּךְ אַתָּה יהוה, הָאֵל הַקָּדוֹשׁ./‏‎בעשרת ימי תשובה: הַמֶּלֶךְ הַקָּדוֹשׁ.‏‎/

The שליח ציבור *continues with* אַתָּה חוֹנֵן *on page 149.*

קְדוּשָׁה – KEDUSHA. An Introduction to *Kedusha* can be found on page 872.

עיון תפילה · IYUN TEFILLA

קְדוּשָׁה – KEDUSHA. In the *Kedusha* we move beyond the priestly prayer-as-sacrifice and the prophetic prayer-as-dialogue, to prayer as a mystic experience. So holy is it that in Israel in ancient times it was said only on Shabbat and festivals [*Sanhedrin* 37b; *Massekhet Soferim* 20:3]. The *Zohar* interprets Jacob's vision of a ladder stretching from earth to heaven, with angels ascending and descending (Gen. 28:12) as a metaphor for prayer, and this, too, is part of the meaning of *Kedusha*. We have climbed the ladder from earth to heaven. As the Leader repeats the prayer on behalf of the entire community, we reach the summit of religious experience. (Rabbi J. Sacks)

HOLINESS

אַתָּה קָדוֹשׁ You are holy[BIA] and Your name is holy,
and holy ones praise You daily, Selah![B]
Blessed are You, LORD,
the holy God. / *Between Rosh HaShana & Yom Kippur:* the holy King./

(If forgotten, repeat the Amida.)

---

placed within you a spark of My own *kedusha*, the *Tzelem Elokim*, which is the ability of the human being to overpower and separate himself from his *yetzer hara*. Just as *HaKadosh Barukh Hu* is *kadosh* above and not bound by His nature, He has imbued the human being with a similar power of *kedusha*: that of being able to transcend his own urges and inclinations, and separate himself from them. **What inclination can I try to overcome just once today?**

The Ramban says that we can be-come holy by living a life of balance. **How can you balance your life a little today?**

אַתָּה קָדוֹשׁ – *You are holy.* The Alsheikh HaKadosh asks: Just because God is holy, why should that mean that I should be holy? After all, I am not like Him! The an-swer is that Hashem gave us the ability to be holy by living a life that separates us, enriches us, and makes us special. By living our lives this way, we acknowledge His be-ing holy, to ourselves and to others.

ANI TEFILLA · אני תפילה

אַתָּה קָדוֹשׁ – *You are holy.*
What one act can I do today that will reflect my living a life of *kedusha*?

In my interactions with a non-Jew today, how can I be a representa-tive of a life lived apart?

In my interactions with others today, how can I reflect the *kedusha* of Hashem?

BIUR TEFILLA · ביאור תפילה

וּקְדוֹשִׁים בְּכָל יוֹם יְהַלְלוּךָ סֶּלָה – *And holy ones praise You daily, Selah.* Who are the "holy ones?" Two possibilities: (a) the angels, (b) we Jews. **Which interpretation appeals to you most today?**

Alternatively, perhaps both are possible. We Jews are meant to strive to be like angels. **Close your eyes. Imagine yourself to be an angel.**

קדושת השם

אַתָּה קָדוֹשׁﬞﬞﬞ וְשִׁמְךָ קָדוֹשׁ
וּקְדוֹשִׁים בְּכָל יוֹם יְהַלְלוּךָ סֶּלָה.ﬞ
בָּרוּךְ אַתָּה יהוה, הָאֵל הַקָּדוֹשׁ./בעשרת ימי תשובה: הַמֶּלֶךְ הַקָּדוֹשׁ.

(If forgotten, repeat the עמידה.)

אַתָּה קָדוֹשׁ — *You are holy.* What does the word קָדוֹשׁ really mean? At its core, the word is derived from the Hebrew word for "separation." The Hebrew word for betrothal, "קִדּוּשִׁין," for example, suggests that, once engaged, the woman is off limits or *separated* from any other man who may want to marry her. Similarly, קָדוֹשׁ which we say on Friday night is designed to establish that we are acknowledging that Shabbat is a day *separate* from all others. Finally, there is the *parasha* in the Torah of קְדֹשִׁים תִּהְיוּ — the commandment that the Jewish people be *separate* from all other nations.

Based on this, the meaning of the pres-

ent blessing becomes clear: we declare Hashem as being *Kadosh* – totally separate, not only from man but from all life as we know it. Here we acknowledge that He is indescribable, seemingly distant, and beyond anything we can imagine. After having praised Hashem in history (the first blessing – *Avot*) and in nature (the second blessing – *Gevurot*), we here admit that those descriptions are limited and that, in the end, He is beyond our understanding.

This is the meaning of the declaration at the beginning of the blessing which states simply "You are *Kadosh*." There is simply no better way to describe how indescribable You really are.

אַתָּה קָדוֹשׁ — *You are holy.*
Parashat Kedoshim begins: קְדֹשִׁים תִּהְיוּ כִּי קָדוֹשׁ אֲנִי יהוה — we need to be holy because Hashem is holy. Rabbi Shimon Schwab

wrote that here Hashem asks that we separate ourselves from our *yetzer hara* (inclination to act badly) because Hashem is קָדוֹשׁ, that is, you can be *kadosh* because I have

KNOWLEDGE^{IA}

אַתָּה חוֹנֵן You grace humanity with knowledge^{BA}
and teach mortals understanding.^B

In Ma'ariv on Motza'ei Shabbat and Motza'ei Yom Tov add "You have graced us" on page 362.

Grace us with the knowledge, understanding
and discernment that come from You.
Blessed are You, LORD,
who graciously grants knowledge.

---

infer and make deductions based upon the knowledge one has acquired. In this blessing we ask for both, for as the Mishna in *Avot* (3:21) says, "If there is no בִּינָה, there can be no דֵּעַת; and if there is no דֵּעַת, then there can be no בִּינָה."

What does it mean to have one without the other?

What added knowledge would I like to pray for today?

What added understanding would I like to pray for today?

דֵּעַת – *Knowledge.* On Saturday night during *Ma'ariv*, a special blessing is inserted here which serves as a kind of verbal *Havdala*. The Gemara (Yerushalmi, *Berakhot* 5:2) explains that this *Havdala* was inserted into this particular blessing because "if there is

no understanding, one can make no distinctions [*havdala*]."

What distinctions can I make in my life today between the holy and the secular?

What aspect of my life today can I make holy?

אַתָּה חוֹנֵן לְאָדָם דֵּעַת – *You grace humanity with knowledge.* This is the only one of the middle *berakhot* of the *Shemoneh Esreh* that begins with a declarative statement of praise, namely, "You grace humanity with knowledge..." All of the other *berakhot* simply begin with a request. What makes this particular request so important that it requires us to begin by declaring that Hashem gives us the very thing that we are asking for? Consider one possibility: without intellect, prayer would be impossible.

אַתָּה חוֹנֵן לְאָדָם דֵּעַת – *You grace humanity with knowledge.* If one has trouble remembering what one has learned, one should

spend some extra time on the blessing of אַתָּה חוֹנֵן. (Rashi, *Avoda Zara* 8a)

דעת[א]

אַתָּה חוֹנֵן לְאָדָם דַּעַת[בא]
וּמְלַמֵּד לֶאֱנוֹשׁ בִּינָה.[ב]

In מעריב on מוצאי שבת and מוצאי יום טוב add אַתָּה חוֹנַנְתָּנוּ on page 363.

חָנֵּנוּ מֵאִתְּךָ דֵּעָה בִּינָה וְהַשְׂכֵּל.
בָּרוּךְ אַתָּה יהוה, חוֹנֵן הַדָּעַת.

עיון תפילה • IYUN TEFILLA

דעת – *KNOWLEDGE.* Unlike any other creation on earth, man is created in the image
of God. What is the image of God? According to some, it refers to man's intelligence,
his ability to think. Hence the opening of

the blessing declares that Hashem gave
intelligence to Adam/Man. It was an act
of grace (חֵן) not just to Adam but to all of
humanity (אֱנוֹשׁ).

אני תפילה • ANI TEFILLA

דעת – *KNOWLEDGE.*
**Why did God give man intelligence? For what
purpose?**

How has mankind used human intelligence for positive purposes?

How has mankind used human intelligence for negative purposes?

How can I use my intelligence today?

There are those who say that these
words refer not just to the physical
realm but to the spiritual realm as
well.
**What spiritual knowledge would I
like to pray for today?**

What spiritual understanding
would I like to pray for today?

ביאור תפילה • BIUR TEFILLA

דַּעַת... בִּינָה – *Knowledge... understanding.*
What is the difference between knowledge
(דַּעַת) and understanding (בִּינָה)? One pos-

sibility is that knowledge refers to basic
information; understanding refers to the
ability to manipulate that information, to

REPENTANCE

הֲשִׁיבֵנוּ Bring us back,[1A] our Father,[1]
to Your Torah.
Draw us near, our King,
to Your service.
Lead us back to You in perfect repentance.[B]
Blessed are You, LORD, who desires repentance.

---

roots, my legacy." So too when a Jew becomes preoccupied with frivolous things, if after some time he decides to return, he is not embarrassed to do so for he says, "I am returning to my inheritance, my roots." That is why we say אָבִינוּ – for we are like a son returning to his inheritance which he received from his Father.

ANI TEFILLA · אני תפילה

הֲשִׁיבֵנוּ – Bring us back.
Which part of my spiritual inheritance have I been ignoring?

What will be my attitude to Torah study today?

How can I live more of a Torah life today?

BIUR TEFILLA · ביאור תפילה

וְהַחֲזִירֵנוּ בִּתְשׁוּבָה שְׁלֵמָה לְפָנֶיךָ – Lead us back to You in perfect repentance. לְפָנֶיךָ – this word literally means "in front of You." One must always believe that Hashem is there in front of you. Sforno says that people do not repent because they think that it is futile, because they feel that Hashem is not always there. In truth, says Sforno, bad things sometimes

happen not because of the absence of Hashem, but because people do not recognize His presence.

Close your eyes and imagine that you are actually standing in His presence.

What can I do today to be more conscious of His presence?

ANI TEFILLA · אני תפילה

A young boy is found crying by his grandfather. "Why are you crying?" asks the old man. "Grandfather," the child responds, "I was playing hide-and-seek with my friends, and I was

hiding but no one came to find me!"

Tears welled up in the old man's eyes, and he said, "My child, that is what Hashem says, 'I am hiding, and people don't try to find Me.'"

תשובה

הֲשִׁיבֵנוּ‪*‬ אָבִינוּ‪*‬ לְתוֹרָתֶךָ
וְקָרְבֵנוּ מַלְכֵּנוּ לַעֲבוֹדָתֶךָ
וְהַחֲזִירֵנוּ בִּתְשׁוּבָה שְׁלֵמָה לְפָנֶיךָ.‪*‬
בָּרוּךְ אַתָּה יהוה, הָרוֹצֶה בִּתְשׁוּבָה.

הֲשִׁיבֵנוּ – *Bring us back.* Asking for the ability to "return" to a destination implies that we want to go back to a place where we have been before. What is that place?

Rav Simlai (*Nidda* 30b) suggests that when a child is in the womb the knowledge of the entire Torah is implanted within him. Just before birth, however, an angel comes and taps him on the mouth (hence that small indentation in the middle of our upper lip) and the child is thereby made to

forget everything. According to some, this is the meaning of the request to "return us," that is, return us to the state of knowing the entire Torah.

Alternatively, I know who I am or have the potential to be when I am at my best, both as a person and as a Jew. I just haven't been able to actualize that as often or as fully as I would like. Today I would like to move one step closer. Help me.

הֲשִׁיבֵנוּ – *Bring us back.* The Ba'al HaTanya, the founder of Lubavitch, said that you should imagine two people standing back to back. They can't be much closer together than that, but neither could they be further away from one another. One needs to stand face to face. *Teshuva* means "to return." People tend to think that God is very far away. It's not true – He's right behind you. All you need to do is turn around. **What can I do to "turn around" today?**

הֲשִׁיבֵנוּ אָבִינוּ – *Bring us back, our Father.* We pray that we should be dear to You like a son is to a father. There is a midrash (*Shemot Raba* 33:7) which states that this may be compared to the son of a king, a prince, who was taken captive overseas as a young child until he became steeped in the ways of the foreigners. If after many years he would seek to return to his father, he would not be ashamed to do so, for he would say, "I am returning to my inheritance, my

FORGIVENESS[A]

Strike the left side of the chest at °.

סְלַח לָנוּ Forgive us, our Father,[1]
for we have °sinned.
Pardon us, our King,[A]
for we have °transgressed;[BA]
for You pardon and forgive.
Blessed are You, LORD,
the gracious One who repeatedly forgives.

Is there a difference in the reaction of your father versus your friend?

Did your parent ever forgive you for something you did even if you didn't necessarily deserve it?

Imagine that you break someone's computer. You need to ask forgiveness. But you also need to pay back the damage. Imagine that he pardons you and tells you to forget about the payment. Here we ask God for both. The first is about asking for forgiveness because we have hurt our relationship with our Father. But we also ask for pardon from the consequences; that's our relationship with Him as King (Rabbi D. Aaron).

The word חָטָא in Tanakh is also used as a term in archery for missing the target. As such, a sin is not a catastrophe but a reason to redouble one's efforts to focus and correct one's aim.
How will I do that today?

סְלִיחָה – *Forgiveness.*
What does it feel like to be insulted or to be wronged? When was the last time it happened to you? Do you recall how you felt when someone did something to you intentionally? Unintentionally? How do you think God feels?

When was the last time you had the chance to do a mitzva and you passed it up?

What amends can I make today?

סְלִיחָה – *Forgiveness.* If a friend were to forgive you and then you did it again, he wouldn't be so quick to forgive you again, and certainly not after the third or fourth time. Not so Hashem. Every time you sin, forgiveness is possible. (Ba'al HaTanya)

The Hebrew word for past is *kedem.* The word for progress is *lehitkadem.* In Judaism, progress doesn't always mean going on to something new but rather returning to oneself, to one's past.

When we lose sight of our own godliness, we lose contact with our true selves. This requires a return. (Rabbi D. Aaron)

Prayer changes the world because it changes us. (Rabbi J. Sacks)

סליחה^א

Strike the left side of the chest at °.

סְלַח לָנוּ אָבִינוּ^ע כִּי °חָטָאנוּ
מְחַל לָנוּ מַלְכֵּנוּ^א כִּי °פָשָׁעְנוּ^{בא}
כִּי מוֹחֵל וְסוֹלֵחַ אָתָּה.
בָּרוּךְ אַתָּה יהוה, חַנּוּן הַמַּרְבֶּה לִסְלֹחַ.

עיון תפילה · IYUN TEFILLA

סְלַח לָנוּ אָבִינוּ — *Forgive us, our Father.* Only this blessing and the one that precedes it emphasize Hashem as "Father." "Why? The Tur (*OḤ* 115) explains that we remind Hashem that it is a father's obligation to teach rather than simply punish his child. So, too, we ask Hashem here to have mercy, to be kind to us, just as a father would be forgiving of a child, and to teach us how to return to Him.

ביאור תפילה · BIUR TEFILLA

כִּי חָטָאנוּ... כִּי פָשָׁעְנוּ — *For we have sinned...for we have transgressed.*

Two types of sins are described here:
A חֵטְא is a sin that is committed inadvertently.
A פֶּשַׁע is a sin which is committed intentionally.

Note the parallels:
סְלַח לָנוּ אָבִינוּ כִּי חָטָאנוּ ← סְלַח = total forgiveness
חֵטְא = unintentional sin
מְחַל לָנוּ מַלְכֵּנוּ כִּי פָשָׁעְנוּ ← מְחַל = partial forgiveness
פֶּשַׁע = intentional sin

Why does one phrase address Hashem as Father and the other as King?

Which kind of sin does the entire blessing end with? Why?

אני תפילה · ANI TEFILLA

כִּי חָטָאנוּ... כִּי פָשָׁעְנוּ — *For we have sinned...for we have transgressed.*
What חֵטְא **might you have committed in the last 24 hours?**

What פֶּשַׁע **might you have committed in the last 24 hours?**

אָבִינוּ... מַלְכֵּנוּ — *Our Father... Our King.* Imagine that you sin against a friend and ask forgiveness and he grants it to you. Imagine the same when you ask forgiveness from your father.

REDEMPTION[BA]

רְאֵה **Look on our affliction,**[IA] plead our cause,[I]
and redeem us soon for Your name's sake,

---

them and did not look away. He came
closer to them than He otherwise
might, had they not prayed at that
moment.
**What do you want Hashem to "see" in
your life?**
     Are there people in your life who
would want you to really "see" them?
     When was the last time that you
"saw" someone's pain?

רְאֵה בְעָנְיֵנוּ – *Look on our affliction.* The root
of the word עָנְיֵנוּ is the same one that the
Torah uses for the five "afflictions" of Yom
Kippur. They are things that we are deprived
of, things that make us feel uncomfortable.
**What things make you uncomfortable,
that you wish were not a part of your
life?**

רְאֵה בְעָנְיֵנוּ – *Look on our affliction.* Rabbi
Elimelekh Szapira of Grodzisk explained
that we ask that Hashem not only see our
afflictions but that He sees "*into our afflictions*" (as indicated here by the letter ב).
This is because we know that in our heart
of hearts, in the essence of our being, we
want to be closer to Hashem and to do the

right thing. But externally we are not always
able to be that way, to live our daily lives
that way. And so we ask Hashem here to see
what is really going on beneath the surface,
at the core of our being. Please, see into
my heart and how much I am bothered by
the lack of consistency in my life. Help me
help myself.

וְרִיבָה רִיבֵנוּ – *Plead our cause.* Why should
we be asking Hashem to fight our battles?
There are some Hasidic masters who maintain that the battle we seek help with is the
battle with our own *yetzer hara* (evil inclination). This is the bad side of us that gets

in our way, that we give in to sometimes
when we know we shouldn't. Here we ask
Hashem's help to overcome it.
**What battles have you been fighting with
your own *yetzer hara*? Ask Hashem for
help.**

גְּאוּלָה[כא]

רְאֵה בְעָנְיֵנוּ,[כב] וְרִיבָה רִיבֵנוּ[כא]
וּגְאָלֵנוּ מְהֵרָה לְמַעַן שְׁמֶךָ

BIUR TEFILLA · ביאור תפילה

גְּאוּלָה – *REDEMPTION*. The Hebrew word for "redemption" – גְּאוּלָה – often refers to that time in the future predicted by the prophets when the Jewish people will be whole again in its own Land. The problem is that this theme is already touched upon in later blessings of *Shemoneh Esreh*. Here, then, it must mean something else, especially since this section of *Shemoneh Esreh* focuses more on individual concerns. What does it mean?

Redemption can mean to set someone loose from bondage, to free them from the limitations that prevent them from reaching self-fulfillment. The blessing could therefore refer to the suffering of those individuals who are actually in prison or being persecuted in some way or, alternatively, it could refer to personal suffering or other misfortunes, or other factors which you find limiting in your life.

ANI TEFILLA · אני תפילה

גְּאוּלָה – *REDEMPTION*. Are there individual Jews you know of who are in jail or being persecuted for their Jewishness?

Think about them when you say this *tefilla*. What are the afflictions, misfortunes, absences in your own life that you think would make you more whole?

IYUN TEFILLA · עיון תפילה

רְאֵה בְעָנְיֵנוּ – *Look on our affliction*. Why do we ask God to "see" our afflictions; after all, doesn't He see everything?

Compare this to the story we cite in the Haggada, when *Benei Yisrael* were suffering under the yoke of the Egyptians and finally called out to Hashem for help. Note what

the verse says (*Shemot* 2:24–25), "And God heard their mourning, and God recalled His covenant with Avraham, Yitzhak and Yaakov; and God *saw* the children of Israel, and God *knew*."

What was it that Hashem saw? Rashi explains that He paid close attention to

for You are a powerful Redeemer.[B]
Blessed are You, LORD, the Redeemer of Israel.[B]

On Fast Days the Leader adds:

עֲנֵנוּ Answer us, LORD, answer us' on our Fast Day, for we are in great distress. Look not at our wickedness. Do not hide Your face from us and do not ignore our plea. Be near to our cry; please let Your loving-kindness comfort us. Even before we call to You, answer us, as is said, "Before they call, I will answer. While they are still speaking, I will hear." For You, LORD, are the One who answers in time of distress, redeems and rescues in all times of trouble and anguish. Blessed are You, LORD, who answers in time of distress. *Is. 65*

---

fast and so one adds it during *Minḥa*. The Ḥazan nevertheless recites it here because he is praying on behalf of the congregation and we assume that there will always be at least ten people who are fasting. (Rabbi I. Wohlgemuth)

IYUN TEFILLA · עיון תפילה

עֲנֵנוּ יהוה עֲנֵנוּ – *Answer us, LORD, answer us.* There are days when the Jewish people fast because of calamities that befell us, in order to arouse our hearts and to open our eyes to the need to repent. This is designed to help us focus on our own misdeeds and those of our ancestors which were similar to ours, to the point that we were all affected by those calamities; the purpose of this memorializing is therefore in order for us to change our ways. The primary goal then is not the fasting itself; rather, fasting is but a preparation for our changing something within ourselves. Therefore, those people who fast but spend their time doing frivolous things not in keeping with the spirit of the day, have grabbed onto what is secondary and have abandoned that which is essential (based on *Ḥayyei Adam* 2:133).

ANI TEFILLA · אני תפילה

What can I try to improve about myself today?

כִּי גוֹאֵל חָזָק אָתָּה.ְּ
בָּרוּךְ אַתָּה יהוה, גּוֹאֵל יִשְׂרָאֵל.ְּ

On Fast Days the שליח ציבור adds:

עֲנֵנוּ יהוה עֲנֵנוּ בְּיוֹם צוֹם תַּעֲנִיתֵנוּ, כִּי בְצָרָה גְדוֹלָה אֲנַחְנוּ. אַל תֵּפֶן אֶל רִשְׁעֵנוּ, וְאַל תַּסְתֵּר פָּנֶיךָ מִמֶּנּוּ, וְאַל תִּתְעַלַּם מִתְּחִנָּתֵנוּ. הֱיֵה נָא קָרוֹב לְשַׁוְעָתֵנוּ, יְהִי נָא חַסְדְּךָ לְנַחֲמֵנוּ, טֶרֶם נִקְרָא אֵלֶיךָ עֲנֵנוּ, כַּדָּבָר שֶׁנֶּאֱמַר: וְהָיָה טֶרֶם יִקְרָאוּ וַאֲנִי אֶעֱנֶה, עוֹד הֵם מְדַבְּרִים וַאֲנִי אֶשְׁמָע: כִּי אַתָּה יהוה הָעוֹנֶה בְּעֵת צָרָה, פּוֹדֶה וּמַצִּיל בְּכָל עֵת צָרָה וְצוּקָה. בָּרוּךְ אַתָּה יהוה, הָעוֹנֶה בְּעֵת צָרָה.

ישעיה סה

ביאור תפילה · BIUR TEFILLA

כִּי גוֹאֵל חָזָק אָתָּה – *For You are a powerful Redeemer.* You can operate above nature, You can turn the tide, just as You did in Egypt when You redeemed *Benei Yisrael.* So too, I acknowledge that You can change what now seems to be the natural course of nature, and redeem me.

בָּרוּךְ... גּוֹאֵל יִשְׂרָאֵל – *Blessed... the Redeemer of Israel.* Note that in the blessing before

the *Shemoneh Esreh,* the conclusion was גָּאַל יִשְׂרָאֵל in the past tense, whereas here it says גּוֹאֵל יִשְׂרָאֵל in the present tense. Why? The blessing before the *Shemoneh Esreh* refers to the redemption that took place in the past, in Egypt, whereas here we reaffirm Hashem's redemption of us each and every day.

How can I look at the coming day as a redeeming experience?

הלכות תפילה · HILKHOT TEFILLA

עֲנֵנוּ יהוה עֲנֵנוּ – *Answer us, Lord, answer us.* If there is a *minyan* of people fasting, then the *Ḥazan* recites this in the Repetition. It is recited in this particular blessing because of the theme of Hashem helping us, redeeming us (גָּאַלְנוּ), in our moment of need (צָרָה).

Although the *tefilla* was originally said three times during the day, the concern was that if someone said it in the morning and had to break his fast later in the day, then he would have said this blessing in vain. Once one fasts until later in the day, however, the likelihood is that he will complete the

HEALING

רְפָאֵנוּ Heal us, LORD, and we shall be healed.
Save us and we shall be saved,[BA]
for You are our praise.
Bring complete recovery for all our ailments,

The following prayer for a sick person may be said here:
May it be Your will, O LORD my God and God of my ancestors, that You
speedily send a complete recovery from heaven, a healing of both soul and
body, to the patient (*name*), son/daughter of (*mother's name*) among the
other afflicted of Israel.

---

for You, God, King, are a faithful and compassionate Healer.
Blessed are You, LORD, Healer of the sick of His people Israel.

---

friend) who was obviously in physical
pain? Who was obviously in emotional
pain?

What ability do I have to help relieve
someone of their pain or discomfort today? What is holding me back?

רְפָאֵנוּ יהוה וְנֵרָפֵא – *Heal us, LORD, and we shall
be healed.*

Do I suffer from a spiritual illness?
What doesn't feel right?
If you were to speak to Hashem
about the fact that you don't feel well
spiritually, what would you ask for? Try it
now.

Assuming my prayer would be answered, what responsibility might that
then confer upon me?

ANI TEFILLA · אני תפילה

Praying on behalf of another person is a fulfillment of the commandment of *ve'ahavta
lere'akha kamokha* וְאָהַבְתָּ לְרֵעֲךָ כָּמוֹךָ – and
you should love your neighbor as yourself.
(*Yesod VeShoresh HaAvoda* 5:4)

Rabbi Isaac the son of Rabbi Judah said: Let
one always pray for mercy not to fall sick; for
if he falls sick he is asked to show by what
merit he should be healed. (*Shabbat* 32a)

One cannot always know what is going
on inside one's own body. We know today
that one's immune system is constantly at
work, even when it is under siege yet the
symptoms may not be felt for days or weeks
or months or even years. One must therefore always pray not only for others, but for
oneself, for a person who experiences a
miracle is not always aware that he is living
that miracle.

רפואה

רְפָאֵנוּ יהוה וְנֵרָפֵא*
הוֹשִׁיעֵנוּ וְנִוָּשֵׁעָה, כִּי תְהִלָּתֵנוּ אָתָּה
וְהַעֲלֵה רְפוּאָה שְׁלֵמָה לְכָל מַכּוֹתֵינוּ

The following prayer for a sick person may be said here:

יְהִי רָצוֹן מִלְּפָנֶיךָ יהוה אֱלֹהַי וֵאלֹהֵי אֲבוֹתַי, שֶׁתִּשְׁלַח מְהֵרָה רְפוּאָה שְׁלֵמָה
מִן הַשָּׁמַיִם רְפוּאַת הַנֶּפֶשׁ וּרְפוּאַת הַגּוּף לַחוֹלֶה/לַחוֹלָה *name of patient*
בֶּן/בַּת *mother's name* בְּתוֹךְ שְׁאָר חוֹלֵי יִשְׂרָאֵל.

כִּי אֵל מֶלֶךְ רוֹפֵא נֶאֱמָן וְרַחֲמָן אָתָּה.
בָּרוּךְ אַתָּה יהוה, רוֹפֵא חוֹלֵי עַמּוֹ יִשְׂרָאֵל.

ביאור תפילה • BIUR TEFILLA

רְפָאֵנוּ יהוה וְנֵרָפֵא – *Heal us, Lord, and we shall be healed.* Perhaps the prayer is not speaking only about physical illness, but psychological illness or spiritual illness as well. The Etz Yosef suggests that whereas in physical illness we simply ask Hashem for a cure and we are passive agents, when it comes to spiritual illness, the cure does not come on its own. Hashem will respond to our prayer

for restoring our spiritual health, but after that it is up to us. The soul cannot be cured unless we ourselves take an active part, a willing part, a purposeful part in changing the way we feel or think or act. But starting out can be difficult – we therefore ask Hashem to first help us get going, to do His part – רְפָאֵנוּ – and we promise that we will then do our part – וְנֵרָפֵא.

אני תפילה • ANI TEFILLA

רְפָאֵנוּ יהוה וְנֵרָפֵא – *Heal us, Lord, and we shall be healed.*
A doctor was once thanked by a patient for saving her life. "Don't thank me," said the doctor, "I'm only His messenger."
What role does man play in the relief of human suffering?

What call to action might this blessing represent? What might it be demanding not of God but of me?

When was the last time you did *bikur holim*?

When was the last time I reached out to help an acquaintance (not a close

PROSPERITY^{AB}

The phrase "Grant dew and rain as a blessing" is said from December 5th (in the year before a civil leap year, December 6th) until Pesaḥ. In Israel, it is said from the 7th of Marḥeshvan. The phrase "Grant blessing" is said from Ḥol HaMo'ed Pesaḥ until December 4th (in the year before a civil leap year, December 5th). In Israel it is said through the 6th of Marḥeshvan.

בָּרֵךְ Bless this year for us,^A LORD our God,
and all its types of produce for good.^B

In winter: Grant dew and rain as a blessing^B

In other seasons: Grant blessing

on the face of the earth,
and from its goodness satisfy us,^{IB}
blessing our year as the best of years.
Blessed are You, LORD, who blesses the years.

---

swer: I should distinguish between what I want versus what I really need.

A person should consider that he has what he needs and he needs what he already has.

וְשַׂבְּעֵנוּ מִטּוּבֶךְ\מִטּוּבָהּ – *And from its/Your goodness satisfy us.* There are two different versions of this blessing in various siddurim.

This Siddur has וְשַׂבְּעֵנוּ מִטּוּבָהּ which means "satisfy us from its [=the Land's] goodness."

Other siddurim have the phrase וְשַׂבְּעֵנוּ מִטּוּבֶךְ which means "satisfy us from Your goodness."

What do you think is the basis behind the two different versions?

The Hasidic leader, Rabbi Simḥa Bunim of Peshischa, was once asked: How was the serpent cursed by being told that he would have to eat the dust of the earth all the days of his life? What type of punishment is this? After all, dust is plentiful and therefore the serpent will never lack sustenance! To this, Rabbi Simḥa Bunim replied: The very fact that the serpent is always provided for and there is no need whatsoever for it to have to turn to Hashem, this is a punishment! Man, on the other hand, whom Hashem loves and wants to benefit by having contact with him, does not always have everything he needs. The necessities of life will lead him to pray and thereby enable him to derive a relationship with God.

בִּרְכַּת הַשָּׁנִיםᵃᵇ

The phrase וְתֵן טַל וּמָטָר לִבְרָכָה *is said from December 5th (in the year before a civil leap year, December 6th) until* פסח. *In* אֶרֶץ יִשְׂרָאֵל, *it is said from* מרחשון ז'. *The phrase* וְתֵן בְּרָכָה *is said from* חוֹל הַמּוֹעֵד פסח *until December 4th (in the year before a civil leap year, December 5th). In* אֶרֶץ יִשְׂרָאֵל *it is said through* מרחשון ר'.

בָּרֵךְ עָלֵינוּᵃ יהוה אֱלֹהֵינוּ אֶת הַשָּׁנָה הַזֹּאת
וְאֶת כָּל מִינֵי תְבוּאָתָהּ, לְטוֹבָהᵇ
בחורף וְתֵן טַל וּמָטָרᵃ לִבְרָכָה / בִּקַּיִץ וְתֵן בְּרָכָה
עַל פְּנֵי הָאֲדָמָה, וְשַׂבְּעֵנוּ מִטּוּבָהּᵃᵇ
וּבָרֵךְ שְׁנָתֵנוּ כַּשָּׁנִים הַטּוֹבוֹת.
בָּרוּךְ אַתָּה יהוה, מְבָרֵךְ הַשָּׁנִים.

BIUR TEFILLA · בִּיאוּר תְּפִילָּה

לְטוֹבָה — *For good.* Isn't a blessing always something always "good"? Why add this word?

Sometimes the material things we acquire are not necessarily "good" for us.

Can you think of things you have asked for in the past that ultimately were not really in your best interests? We therefore ask that whatever we do acquire has only positive and not negative influences.

וְתֵן טַל וּמָטָר — *Grant dew and rain as a blessing.* Note that our request for rain in the winter is a request most specifically related to the climate of Israel, where rain in the winter months can mean the difference between an abundance of crops and famine. This is but one of the many places in the Siddur that reflects our millennia-old connection to the Land. **Imagine yourself standing in a field or an open-air market in Israel. Now think about the need for rain.**

IYUN TEFILLA · עִיּוּן תְּפִילָּה

וְשַׂבְּעֵנוּ מִטּוּבָהּ — *And from its goodness satisfy us.* A verse in *Kohelet* 5:9 says: אֹהֵב כֶּסֶף לֹא יִשְׂבַּע כֶּסֶף – "The person who loves money will never get enough money." There is a midrash (*Kohelet Raba* 1:32) which says that this is because a person leaves this world having fulfilled only half of his desires – if

he has 100, then he wants 200; if he has 200, then he wants 400. In other words, we are insatiable – we always want more than we have.

Based on this, what do you think is the meaning of the word in the blessing: וְשַׂבְּעֵנוּ – "and satisfy/satiate us"? One an-

INGATHERING OF EXILES

תְּקַע Sound the great shofar[8] for our freedom,
raise high the banner to gather our exiles,[8]
and gather us together from the four quarters of the earth.[A]
Blessed are You, LORD,
who gathers the dispersed of His people Israel.[A]

What kind of "shofar" do you think would rally the Jewish people around a return to Israel today?

What could I do to bring the ingathering to Israel to reality?

מְקַבֵּץ נִדְחֵי עַמּוֹ יִשְׂרָאֵל – *Who gathers the dispersed of His people Israel.* Rabbi Shimon Schwab notes that we are separated from one another not only geographically but ideologically as well. All Jews do not necessarily believe the same thing; not all Jews practice Judaism in the same way. Even within the Orthodox community there can be disagreement about practices and

views of the world. And so here we ask that all Jews come together to see the commonalities which unite us, so that we may no longer be exiled from ourselves as a people.

In a similar vein, Rabbi Soloveitchik used to note that in the gas chambers there was no distinction made between religious Jews and secular ones, between the learned and the unlearned. All Jews share a common fate.

What can I do today to focus on what I have in common with the Jews around me, rather than on what makes us different?

מְקַבֵּץ נִדְחֵי עַמּוֹ יִשְׂרָאֵל – *Who gathers the dispersed of His people Israel.* Rabbi Menaḥem Naḥum Twersky of Chernobyl, a student of the Ba'al Shem Tov, once suggested that there are two kinds of *galut* (exile). There is the general exile of the Jewish people

among the nations of the world, but there is also a private exile, wherein each person feels like he is alone, with his own private trials and tribulations.

How do you wish your life could "come together" for you?

A reporter for ABC News once asked Rabbi David Aaron why Jews were drawn to the

Land of Israel. He responded: "I don't know. Why are salmon drawn upstream?"

קבוץ גלויות

תְּקַע בְּשׁוֹפָר גָּדוֹל² לְחֵרוּתֵנוּ

וְשָׂא נֵס לְקַבֵּץ גָּלֻיּוֹתֵינוּ²

וְקַבְּצֵנוּ יַחַד מֵאַרְבַּע כַּנְפוֹת הָאָרֶץ.ⁿ

בָּרוּךְ אַתָּה יהוה, מְקַבֵּץ נִדְחֵי עַמּוֹ יִשְׂרָאֵל.ᵛ

ביאור תפילה · BIUR TEFILLA

תְּקַע בְּשׁוֹפָר גָּדוֹל – *Sound the great shofar.* The phrase is based upon a verse in *Yishayahu* (27:13) which says than on that day in the future a big shofar will be blown and all of the lost Jews will come to the Land of Israel. We pray that now is the time of "our freedom" and ask Hashem that He blow the great shofar.

וְשָׂא נֵס לְקַבֵּץ גָּלֻיּוֹתֵינוּ – *Raise high the banner to gather our exiles.* The word *nes* can mean "banner" or it can mean "miracle."

The State of Israel's population has doubled a number of times since 1948. Since independence, more than three million people have immigrated there "from the four corners of the earth." For the first time in millennia, there are more Jews living in Israel than in any other country in the world. Jerusalem is the leading center of absorption. The miracle of the "ingathering of exiles" has been taking place before our very eyes.

אני תפילה · ANI TEFILLA

וְקַבְּצֵנוּ יַחַד מֵאַרְבַּע כַּנְפוֹת הָאָרֶץ – *And gather us together from the four quarters of the earth.* There are still pockets of "lost" Jews in the world who want to live in Israel, but who are prevented from doing so because of the lack of political freedom or economic freedom. Pray for them.

There are millions of Jews who are "lost" not geographically or physically, but spiritually; Jews who do not know they are Jewish, or do not appreciate their Jewishness. Pray for them to actively rejoin the Jewish people.

Can you think of times in Jewish history when Jews had the opportunity to live in Israel but gave up the opportunity?

What does the State of Israel mean to you?

What prayers do you have for the State as the national homeland of the Jewish people?

For the first time in millennia, the Jewish people has its own sovereign state, with its own Jewish holidays and Jewish flavor. Yet there are still millions of Jews who live outside of the homeland.

JUSTICE[B]

הָשִׁיבָה Restore our judges as at first,
and our counselors as at the beginning,
and remove from us sorrow and sighing.[B]
May You alone, Lord, reign over us
with loving-kindness and compassion,[A] and vindicate us in justice.
Blessed are You, Lord,
the King who loves righteousness and justice.[BA]

/ *Between Rosh HaShana & Yom Kippur, end the blessing:* **the King of justice.**/

According to the Malbim, מִשְׁפָּט refers to the strict letter of the law; in other words, whatever the rule and its consequence, someone should be judged and held accountable. צְדָקָה on the other hand, refers to the extenuating circumstances that may have been present; that even though the law requires one thing, the special considerations of time or place or the individual requires that the rules be bent. Here we ask Hashem to balance both the letter of the law and its spirit, צְדָקָה וּמִשְׁפָּט.

בְּחֶסֶד וּבְרַחֲמִים – *Loving-kindness and compassion.* What would it mean for me to judge someone בְּחֶסֶד וּבְרַחֲמִים today? **Whom have I treated unjustly in the last 24 hours?**

Whom have I misjudged in the last 24 hours?

בְּחֶסֶד וּבְרַחֲמִים – *Loving-kindness and compassion.* There is no hope for a society, even a religious one, that corrupts social justice. **How can I volunteer to help increase social justice in the world?**

(Be informed, write a postcard, raise consciousness, attend a rally, donate to a cause, stand up when I see someone being treated inappropriately even by a friend or colleague...)

צְדָקָה וּמִשְׁפָּט – *Righteousness and justice.* **Were you ever judged unfairly because someone was strictly following the letter of the rules?**

Whom can I judge with a little more צְדָקָה today?

בָּרוּךְ אַתָּה יהוה מֶלֶךְ אוֹהֵב צְדָקָה וּמִשְׁפָּט – *Blessed are You, Lord, the King who loves righteousness and justice.* The conclusion suggests not only that Hashem loves צְדָקָה וּמִשְׁפָּט but also that He loves *the people who do* צְדָקָה וּמִשְׁפָּט.

The Sefat Emet (Shofetim 5647) suggested that every person needs to assume the attributes of a judge, the ability to understand truth as it is found in Torah and Talmud, and through that to be able to rule over himself.

הַשָּׁבַת הַמִּשְׁפָּטⁱ
הָשִׁיבָה שׁוֹפְטֵינוּ כְּבָרִאשׁוֹנָה וְיוֹעֲצֵינוּ כְּבַתְּחִלָּה
וְהָסֵר מִמֶּנּוּ יָגוֹן וַאֲנָחָהⁱⁱ
וּמְלֹךְ עָלֵינוּ אַתָּה יהוה לְבַדְּךָ בְּחֶסֶד וּבְרַחֲמִיםˣ
וְצַדְּקֵנוּ בַּמִּשְׁפָּט.
בָּרוּךְ אַתָּה יהוה
מֶלֶךְ אוֹהֵב צְדָקָה וּמִשְׁפָּט.ⁱˣ / בעשרת ימי תשובה: הַמֶּלֶךְ הַמִּשְׁפָּט./

הַשָּׁבַת הַמִּשְׁפָּט – JUSTICE. Why does this blessing follow the previous one about the ingathering of the exiles?

In the previous one, we essentially ask for the revival of the Jewish State. But here we say that having a State is not enough; it must be one that is founded on the principles of Hashem's justice and compassion.

Imagine living in a society that was even more just and compassionate than it is now.

In what ways would it look different? Pray for it.

הָשִׁיבָה שׁוֹפְטֵינוּ – Restore our judges. "Our people need leaders," said Rabbi S.R. Hirsch, "men who will champion the truth..."
Pray for the success of such leaders.

הָשִׁיבָה שׁוֹפְטֵינוּ – Restore our judges. Rebbe Yose ben Elisha said: If you see a genera-tion upon whom befall many tragedies, go and check the judges of Israel. For every calamity that comes to the world only hap-pens because of the actions of the judges of Israel... They are evil, but they trust in God. (Shabbat 139a)

יָגוֹן וַאֲנָחָה – Sorrow and sighing. What's the difference between יָגוֹן and אֲנָחָה?

The son of the Gaon of Vilna suggested that אֲנָחָה refers to the kind of pain and suffering that is inflicted upon one by an enemy or outside force; יָגוֹן refers to the sad-ness that one can sometimes experience from within.

Think of someone you know of who is in pain. Pray for them.

Can I think of anyone whose "sorrow and sighing" I might be able to help re-lieve today, even a little?

צְדָקָה וּמִשְׁפָּט – Righteousness and justice. What's the difference between them?

AGAINST INFORMERS

וְלַמַּלְשִׁינִים For the slanderers let there be no hope,
and may all wickedness perish in an instant.
May all Your people's enemies swiftly be cut down.
May You swiftly uproot, crush, cast down
and humble the arrogant swiftly in our days.
Blessed are You, LORD,
who destroys enemies and humbles the arrogant.

BIUR TEFILLA · ביאור תפילה

ברכת המינים – *AGAINST INFORMERS*. The Gemara (*Sanhedrin* 11a) says that when the time came to compose this prayer, the Rabbis all turned to a man by the name of Shmuel HaKatan (lit. Shmuel the Small). Why was he called "the small" if he was great enough to be acknowledged by all of the Rabbis? The answer may lie precisely in his being considered "small," not in physical size, but in reference to his humility. Only a humble person may have the correct frame of mind to distinguish between the sin and the sinner. This is borne out by the fact that in *Pirkei Avot* (4:19) it says that "Shmuel HaKatan used to say: Do not rejoice at the downfall of your enemies." Perhaps only a humble person could appropriately compose a prayer that asks that Hashem "humble the arrogant."

Do I know any arrogant people?

How can I increase my own humility today?

ANI TEFILLA · אני תפילה

The story is told that the Gaon of Vilna was riding in a wagon and the wagon driver allowed the horse to veer off to the side and ride through the garden of a non-Jew. The non-Jew came running over to the wagon and started hitting the Gaon. The Gaon later said that it was on the tip of his tongue to say "It's not my fault, it's the fault of the wagon driver; why are you hitting me?!" But he did not do so because he thought he would be guilty of being a מַלְשִׁין *– one who informs on other Jews – for after all, it was an accident, and even if it wasn't, at most the wagon driver should have to pay damages instead of get-* *ting hit. And so the Gaon took the beating without saying anything. (Ḥafetz Ḥayyim, Shem Olam, Ḥelek beit)*

The Ba'al Shem Tov said that true humility takes place inside a person. A king once went on a short trip but instructed his coach and horseman to go ahead of him while he walked behind them. When asked to explain, he said that he was trying to display his humility to his people. A wise man told him: "Humility is not something one advertises to other people. Rather, the true test is to sit inside the coach and still be humble."

ברכת המינים בּיא

וְלַמַּלְשִׁינִים אַל תְּהִי תִקְוָה, וְכָל הָרִשְׁעָה כְּרֶגַע תֹּאבֵד
וְכָל אוֹיְבֵי עַמְּךָ מְהֵרָה יִכָּרֵתוּ
וְהַזֵּדִים מְהֵרָה תְעַקֵּר וּתְשַׁבֵּר וּתְמַגֵּר וְתַכְנִיעַ בִּמְהֵרָה בְיָמֵינוּ.
בָּרוּךְ אַתָּה יהוה, שׁוֹבֵר אוֹיְבִים וּמַכְנִיעַ זֵדִים.

ברכת המינים – *AGAINST INFORMERS*. Although *Shemoneh Esreh* means 18, the truth
is that there are 19 blessings in total. According to many, this particular blessing is the
nineteenth, and was added at a later date.
Historically, this blessing was created to address those who worked against the Jewish
community in Roman times. Since then, the
blessing continued to be said against any
enemy who would undermine Judaism and
the Jewish people.

ברכת המינים – *AGAINST INFORMERS*. There
are variants of this text which also include a
prayer against מִינִים and מְשֻׁמָּדִים, disbeliev-
ers and apostates who would work with
authorities against the Jewish religion. As
such, this blessing is not just about physical threats to the Jewish people, but spiritual threats as well.
**What forces around you could be inter-
preted as trying to undermine Judaism
today? Have them in mind.**

ברכת המינים – *AGAINST INFORMERS*. The Gemara
(*Berakhot* 10a) relates that Rabbi Meir was once being harassed by a man in his community, and he
was therefore praying for God to destroy this person
who was harassing him. Beruria, Rabbi Meir's wife,
renowned for her Torah knowledge, corrected him,
pointing out, "The verse in *Tehillim* [104:35] says: יִתַּמּוּ
חַטָּאִים מִן הָאָרֶץ – Let *sins* be wiped out from the
earth.' It doesn't say, 'Let *sinners* be wiped out.'" We
do not seek vengeance or violence; we seek an end
to the existence of "רִשְׁעָה" – wickedness. Hence the
blessing does not say "may all the wicked perish" but,
rather, "may all wickedness perish."
**What can I do today to help eradicate the sin
that comes through slandering other people?**

ברכת המינים – *AGAINST INFORMERS*.
The *Ya'arot Devash* (*Helek* 1, *derush*
1) says that with the recitation of
this blessing one fulfils the mitzva
to remember Amalek. The eradication of the Jewish people was a
goal of Amalek. Have them in mind,
for as Rabbi Soloveitchik has said,
Amalek is not necessarily a people,
but an ideology that still exists in
modern times.
**What enemies can I think of who
are trying to undermine the Jewish people in the present? Have
them in mind.**

THE RIGHTEOUS

עַל הַצַּדִּיקִים To the righteous,[BA] the pious,
the elders of Your people the house of Israel,
the remnant of their scholars,
the righteous converts, and to us,
may Your compassion be aroused, LORD our God.
Grant a good reward[A] to all who sincerely trust in Your name.
Set our lot with them,[A]
so that we may never be ashamed,[B] for in You we trust.
Blessed are You, LORD,
who is the support and trust of the righteous.

עַל הַצַּדִּיקִים – *To the Righteous.* There are people in your life who are older and wiser just because they have lived life and experienced things.
Who are these people in your life? What do you wish you could learn from them?

עַל הַצַּדִּיקִים – *To the Righteous.* The simple but true fact of life is that you become like those with whom you closely associate – for the good and for the bad (see Rashi on *Bemidbar* 3:29, 38).

שָׂכָר טוֹב – *Grant a good reward.* Note that in the blessing we ask for a "good reward." **Did you ever get a "bad reward" – something** that you wanted badly but turned out to be not so great after all?

How does one tell the difference between a good reward and a bad one?

What kind of good reward would you like to pray for today?

וְשִׂים חֶלְקֵנוּ עִמָּהֶם – *Set our lot with them.* We ask that "You set our lot with them" – that we be associated with the categories of people who are working on themselves spiritually.
Do I associate with those kinds of people?

Do people look at me that way?

What one thing can I do today to change?

BIUR TEFILLA · ביאור תפילה

וּלְעוֹלָם לֹא נֵבוֹשׁ – *So that we may never be ashamed.* Some say that this refers to the World to Come when we stand before Hashem and we get to see all of our actions, good and bad, laid out before us for all to see.
What can I do today to avoid adding something to my profile that will ultimately make me embarrassed?

עַל הַצַּדִּיקִים

עַל הַצַּדִּיקִים^{בּא} וְעַל הַחֲסִידִים, וְעַל זִקְנֵי עַמְּךָ בֵּית יִשְׂרָאֵל
וְעַל פְּלֵיטַת סוֹפְרֵיהֶם, וְעַל גֵּרֵי הַצֶּדֶק, וְעָלֵינוּ
יֶהֱמוּ רַחֲמֶיךָ יהוה אֱלֹהֵינוּ
וְתֵן שָׂכָר טוֹב^א לְכָל הַבּוֹטְחִים בְּשִׁמְךָ בֶּאֱמֶת
וְשִׂים חֶלְקֵנוּ עִמָּהֶם,^א וּלְעוֹלָם לֹא נֵבוֹשׁ^ב כִּי בְךָ בָּטָחְנוּ.
בָּרוּךְ אַתָּה יהוה, מִשְׁעָן וּמִבְטָח לַצַּדִּיקִים.

ביאור תפילה · BIUR TEFILLA

עַל הַצַּדִּיקִים – *To the Righteous.* After having prayed for the physical restoration of the State, and for the establishment of a system of justice, we now turn to the prayer for spiritual leadership and redemption in which each of us has a part to play. For sovereignty in our own state to work we not only need a justice system but also strong spiritual leadership, and it is to this that we now turn our attention. Look at the list of categories of people who are described at the beginning of the *tefilla.* There are those who say that the list appears in descending order.

הַצַּדִּיקִים – the truly righteous who do everything possible that a servant of Hashem can do.
הַחֲסִידִים – the pious, those who go beyond the letter of the law and do more than is required.

זִקְנֵי יִשְׂרָאֵל – the elders, not only in age but in wisdom born of life experience.
סוֹפְרֵיהֶם – the people who spend their lives teaching Torah to others.
גֵּרֵי הַצֶּדֶק – the converts who join Judaism because they truly believe in Torah.
וְעָלֵינוּ – and on us, the everyday, ordinary Jew, who, while not the same as the other people on the list, nevertheless has an important contribution to make.

עַל הַצַּדִּיקִים – *To the Righteous.* Earlier, we said the blessing for our physical sustenance. Here, says Rabbi S.R. Hirsch, we ask for the spiritual sustenance of the nation. **How could I contribute to the spiritual well-being of the community today?**

אני תפילה · ANI TEFILLA

עַל הַצַּדִּיקִים – *To the Righteous.*
Can you think of a different person for each one of these categories for whom you could pray today?

Do you know any converts? Why do you think they get special mention here?

What do you think your spiritual contribution could be to the community?

Ask Hashem for help.

REBUILDING JERUSALEM[B]

וְלִירוּשָׁלַיִם To Jerusalem, Your city,[A]
may You return in compassion,[B]
and may You dwell in it[A] as You promised.
May You rebuild it rapidly in our days[B]
as an everlasting structure,
and install within it soon the throne of David.*
Blessed are You, LORD, who builds Jerusalem.

*At Minḥa, on Tisha B'Av all conclude with "Console" on page 310.

Think of a beautiful place you have seen or heard of in Jerusalem. Imagine yourself there now.

וְלִירוּשָׁלַיִם עִירְךָ – To Jerusalem, Your city. Rabbi Yehoshua ben Levi said, "HaKadosh

Barukh Hu said to Israel: You caused the destruction of My House and the exile of My children. Inquire of the welfare of Yerushalayim and I will grant you peace." (Derekh Eretz Zuta, Perek HaShalom)

Pray for the peace of Yerushalayim.

BIUR TEFILLA · ביאור תפילה

בְּרַחֲמִים תָּשׁוּב – May You return in compassion. Wherever the Jews went into exile, the Shekhina went with them (Megilla 29a). In this berakha we ask Hashem to return the Shekhina to Yerushalayim.

בְּיָמֵינוּ – In our days. Rabbi Naftali of Ropshitz explained that the phrase "in our days" may also be translated "with our days." In other words, may the Beit HaMikdash be rebuilt with the way we spend

our days, that is, every mitzva we do, how we spend each and every day has the potential to contribute to the rebuilding of Jerusalem and the Beit HaMikdash. It has also been pointed out that this is the reason that the blessing ends in the present tense: every day we can contribute to its rebuilding.

What can I do today to help move one step closer to the rebuilding of Yerushalayim?

ANI TEFILLA · אני תפילה

וְתִשְׁכֹּן בְּתוֹכָהּ – And may You dwell in it. Rav Aḥa said, "The Shekhina never departs from the Western Wall of the Beit HaMikdash." (Tanḥuma Shemot)

"In Tel Aviv I feel like a 16-year-old Israeli. In Jerusalem I feel like a 3000-year-old Jew." (A sixteen-year-old boy from Yerushalayim)

בניין ירושלים‎

וְלִירוּשָׁלַיִם עִירְךָ‎ בְּרַחֲמִים תָּשׁוּב‎ב‎
וְתִשְׁכּוֹן בְּתוֹכָהּ‎ כַּאֲשֶׁר דִּבַּרְתָּ‎
וּבְנֵה אוֹתָהּ בְּקָרוֹב בְּיָמֵינוּ‎ג‎ בִּנְיַן עוֹלָם‎
וְכִסֵּא דָוִד מְהֵרָה לְתוֹכָהּ תָּכִין.*‎
בָּרוּךְ אַתָּה יהוה, בּוֹנֵה יְרוּשָׁלָיִם.‎

*At מנחה, on תשעה באב, all conclude with נַחֵם on page 311.

BIUR TEFILLA • ביאור תפילה

בניין ירושלים — *REBUILDING JERUSALEM.* For thousands of years the Jewish people has mourned the destruction of Jerusalem. Every single day, in our prayers, when we say *Birkat HaMazon*, at weddings, and on holy days, we have always declared our connection to Yerushalayim. "Let my tongue cling to the roof of my mouth if I do not remember you, if I do not consider Jerusalem my highest joy" (*Tehillim* 137).

There are actually three interrelated requests in this blessing:

(a) The return to Jerusalem and the *Beit HaMikdash* being rebuilt.
(b) The dwelling of the *Shekhina* there.
(c) That the monarchy be reestablished there.

The desire is expressed not just for the rebuilding of the *Beit HaMikdash* itself but for the residence of the *Shekhina* there. Hence the fact that we have Yerushalayim in our hands today is not a sufficient fulfillment of the request in the blessing.

ANI TEFILLA • אני תפילה

וְלִירוּשָׁלַיִם עִירְךָ – *To Jerusalem, Your city.* The first part of the name Yerushalayim is traditionally understood to come from the Hebrew word יראה, "will be seen" – meaning Hashem will be seen there. **Have you ever been to Yerushalayim? Have you ever felt something special there? Try to recapture those feelings.**

Imagine that you are standing at the **Kotel. You can feel the warm rays of the sun on your neck. You reach out to** touch the stones of the wall. They are cool and smooth.

Close your eyes. What do you want to say?

וְלִירוּשָׁלַיִם עִירְךָ – *To Jerusalem, Your city.* The Rabbis said (*Kiddushin* 49b) that there are ten measures of beauty that descended to this world. Nine of them belong to Yerushalayim and one went to the rest of the world. Whoever has not seen Yerushalayim in her glory has never seen a beautiful city in his life.

KINGDOM OF DAVID[BI]

אֶת צֶמַח **May the offshoot of Your servant David soon flower,[B]**
and may his pride be raised high by Your salvation,
for we wait for Your salvation all day.[ABI]
Blessed are You, LORD, who makes the glory of salvation flourish.

---

progress. The road to the Mashiaḥ is not only about the goal of getting there; it's about the process, and the progress we make to get there. (Rabbi E. Bick)

What can I do today to make progress toward a more perfect world?

BIUR TEFILLA · ביאור תפילה

כִּי לִישׁוּעָתְךָ קִוִּינוּ כָּל הַיּוֹם – *For we wait for Your salvation all day.* In all of the other blessings, we ask Hashem for something because He is the One who is capable of effecting it (i.e., "because You are a Redeemer," "because

You are a faithful and merciful Healer.") In this blessing, however, we explain our request for redemption not because He is a Redeemer but because "we wait for Your salvation all day." The promise lies within each of us.

IYUN TEFILLA · עיון תפילה

כִּי לִישׁוּעָתְךָ קִוִּינוּ כָּל הַיּוֹם – *For we wait for Your salvation all day.* The mitzva here may well lie not only in belief in the Mashiaḥ, but in the *anticipation* of his coming. Like a soldier standing lookout in a tower awaiting relief, he is ever vigilant, ever hopeful, even when he cannot see anything on the horizon. (Rabbi A.I. Kook)

מלכות בית דוד – *KINGDOM OF DAVID.* There are those who suggest that in ancient Israel

this blessing about the Mashiaḥ and the previous blessing about the restoration of the *Beit HaMikdash* were merged into one since they share the same theme. The Jews of Babylonia split it into two. Rabbi Soloveitchik suggested that it was because they feared that when they went into exile they would be pressured by other religious beliefs who believed that the Messiah had already come. This blessing, then, is also a plea for keeping our identity even in the Diaspora.

ANI TEFILLA · אני תפילה

Trees only bear fruit after the seedling has been cultivated and nourished. So, too, in relationships, meaningfulness comes about only after a period of growth. Friendship has to be cultivated in order to be meaningful

and lasting. Love needs to be nourished in order for it to flourish and not stagnate. Knowledge cannot come about through impatience. So, too, with tefilla.

מלכות בית דוד בע

אֶת צֶמַח דָּוִד עַבְדְּךָ מְהֵרָה תַצְמִיחַ,ּ
וְקַרְנוֹ תָּרוּם בִּישׁוּעָתֶךָ
כִּי לִישׁוּעָתְךָ קִוִּינוּ כָּל הַיּוֹם.אבע
בָּרוּךְ אַתָּה יהוה, מַצְמִיחַ קֶרֶן יְשׁוּעָה.

ביאור תפילה • BIUR TEFILLA

מלכות בית דוד – *KINGDOM OF DAVID.*
This blessing is essentially a prayer for
the coming of Mashiaḥ. King David, the
paradigm of a leader who combined the
political and the religious, was promised
that the monarchy would always belong
to his family. Here we pray for the restoration of that period of time when the
world in which we live is balanced by
leadership that combines a knowledge
of politics with the morality and spiritual
values of religiosity.

How have today's political leaders
succeeded politically but failed morally?

אֶת צֶמַח דָּוִד עַבְדְּךָ מְהֵרָה תַצְמִיחַ – *May the offshoot of Your servant David soon flower.* Why do
we use the imagery of "flowering" and "flourish-
ing" like plants?

There are two possible answers:

First, the process of growth is such that a
seed is planted in the ground, rots, and from
its decay grows anew something greater than
what was planted. The world we live in is simply
a preparation for a greater world yet to come.

Second, a plant doesn't grow all at once
but in increments. So too, will Israel's redemption come in increments, slowly, step by step,
measured in years and not in minutes.

אני תפילה • ANI TEFILLA

כִּי לִישׁוּעָתְךָ קִוִּינוּ כָּל הַיּוֹם – *For we wait for
Your salvation all day.*
How can I see the coming of Mashiaḥ as
being more possible today than 100 years
ago?

What can I do today to bring Mashiaḥ
closer?

כִּי לִישׁוּעָתְךָ קִוִּינוּ כָּל הַיּוֹם – *For we wait for
Your salvation all day.* Rava said: When one
comes to the next world for judgment, one
will be asked, "Were you honest in business,
did you establish set times for learning Torah? Did you have a family? Did you antici-

pate the redemption?" This is your chance:
anticipate. (*Shabbat* 31a)

כִּי לִישׁוּעָתְךָ קִוִּינוּ כָּל הַיּוֹם – *For we wait for
Your salvation all day.* There is a student
who always earns marks in the 90s. There
is another student who always gets in the
70s. On the next test, the first student gets
a mark of 95 but the second student gets
a mark in the 80s. In absolute terms, the first
student is the better student. But in relative
terms, the second student has made more
progress. Salvation is not about achieving
perfection; it's about being on the road of

RESPONSE TO PRAYER

שְׁמַע קוֹלֵנוּ Listen to our voice,[BIA] LORD our God.
Spare us and have compassion on us,
and in compassion and favor accept our prayer,
for You, God, listen to prayers and pleas.[BA]
Do not turn us away, O our King,
empty-handed from Your presence,[B]*

*At Minḥa, at this point on fast days, the congregation adds "Answer us" on page 314.
In times of drought in Israel, some add "And answer us" on page 684.

for You listen with compassion to the prayer of Your people Israel.
Blessed are You, LORD, who listens to prayer.

---

plural, as opposed to the previous reference to תְּפִלָּתֵנוּ, meaning "our prayer" in the singular. This is because the prayers mentioned here refer not only to the prayers of the individual, and not only to the prayers of the other Jews in your *minyan*, and not only to the prayers of all Jews, but to the prayers of all mankind as well. (Rabbi S. Schwab)
What prayer might you have in common with the rest of humanity?
What prayer can I offer for the entire human race today?

כִּי אֵל שׁוֹמֵעַ תְּפִלּוֹת וְתַחֲנוּנִים אָתָּה – For You, God, listen to prayers and pleas. Listen to the prayer of all Israel, lest my own individual prayer is found lacking in some way. May my prayer be considered as part of theirs.

וּמִלְּפָנֶיךָ מַלְכֵּנוּ רֵיקָם אַל תְּשִׁיבֵנוּ – Do not turn us away, O our King, empty-handed from Your presence. This could mean, "Please give us at least something we asked for," or it could mean, "Let our prayers not be empty of content. Let us leave You with at least a meaningful prayer to our credit" (Rabbi S.R. Hirsch). Make this prayer meaningful.

I thought I knew something about prayer, but I found out otherwise. I was at the Kotel saying Tehillim and thinking that I was really praying. I saw a blind man being led down to the Kotel. He ran his fingers over the stones, feeling thousands of years of history. Then he kissed the Wall, and began talking to God. He spoke very rapidly, and I could not understand anything he said. Abruptly he stopped, paused momentarily, then said, "Ok, I told you about that yesterday," and resumed his communication. I realized that he was really communicating with God, and knew that He listened. I resumed saying Tehillim, but with a much different *kavana*. (Rabbi A.J. Twerski)

The ANI TEFILLA on שובע תפילה continues on page 177.

שומע תפילה
שְׁמַע קוֹלֵנוּ‏בּ‏עא יהוה אֱלֹהֵינוּ
חוּס וְרַחֵם עָלֵינוּ, וְקַבֵּל בְּרַחֲמִים וּבְרָצוֹן אֶת תְּפִלָּתֵנוּ
כִּי אֵל שׁוֹמֵעַ תְּפִלּוֹת וְתַחֲנוּנִים אָתָּה‏בּא
וּמִלְּפָנֶיךָ מַלְכֵּנוּ רֵיקָם אַל תְּשִׁיבֵנוּ‏‏ג‏‏*

*At מנחה, at this point on fast days, the קהל adds עֲנֵנוּ on page 315.
In times of drought in אֶרֶץ יִשְׂרָאֵל, some add וְעֲנֵנוּ on page 685.

כִּי אַתָּה שׁוֹמֵעַ תְּפִלַּת עַמְּךָ יִשְׂרָאֵל בְּרַחֲמִים.
בָּרוּךְ אַתָּה יהוה, שׁוֹמֵעַ תְּפִלָּה.

שְׁמַע קוֹלֵנוּ – **Listen to our voice.** Listen, even if we ourselves have not understood all of the messages of the words we have just said in the previous blessings. (*Etz Yosef*)

"Listen to our voice" – even if we could not muster all of the correct *kavana* for the words because it is so hard to focus and so many other thoughts interfere. (*Siaḥ Yitzḥak*)

שְׁמַע קוֹלֵנוּ – **Listen to our voice.** "Prayer...is a dialogue not a monologue. A dialogue exists when one person addresses another, even if the other is temporarily silent.... In praying, we do not seek a response to a particular request as much as we desire a fel-

lowship with God" (Rabbi J.B. Soloveitchik). Hashem is like a friend on the other end of the phone who doesn't always speak. But there is comfort in knowing that He is always listening whenever we want to speak to Him. Hashem is always a שׁוֹמֵעַ תְּפִלָּה.

שְׁמַע קוֹלֵנוּ – **Listen to our voice.** We ask Hashem to "listen to the sound of our voices." When the Jews suffered all of those years of slavery in Egypt, what was it that finally caused God to remember His covenant and to set the exodus in motion? The answer: "And the children of Israel sighed by reason of the bondage, and they cried, and their cry came up to God by reason

of the bondage" (Shemot 2:23). God heard their voices, their pain, their sighing. Not their words. Sometimes, if we have the right *kavana*, just using the right voice can be enough.
Don't just read the words; use your voice.

כִּי אֵל שׁוֹמֵעַ תְּפִלּוֹת – **For You, God, listen to prayers.** Here the word תְּפִלּוֹת is in the

TEMPLE SERVICE^B

רְצֵה Find favor,^B LORD our God,
in Your people Israel and their prayer.^B
Restore the service to Your most holy House,
and accept in love^B and favor
the fire-offerings^B of Israel and their prayer.
May the service of Your people Israel
always find favor with You.

---

moved you to become a better person today?

How can I make myself a better person and a better Jew today?

הָעֲבוֹדָה – *The service.* The עֲבוֹדָה could be a reference to general worship in the *Beit HaMikdash* (דְּבִיר בֵּיתֶךָ).

The עֲבוֹדָה could be a reference to the specific *Avoda* of Yom Kippur performed by the *Kohen Gadol* in the Holy of Holies. (דְּבִיר בֵּיתֶךָ refers to the place where the word [דִּבּוּר] of God is heard.)

The עֲבוֹדָה could be a reference to the prayers which were offered then and which we offer now, the עֲבוֹדָה שֶׁבַּלֵּב, the service of the heart.

Which interpretation speaks to you today?

וְאִשֵּׁי – *The fire-offerings.* This could refer to the fire-*offerings* in the *Beit HaMikdash.*

We ask that the Temple service be restored. Prayers there are different than our prayers here. How?

וְאִשֵּׁי could refer to the martyrs of Israel (from the word אִישׁ) who sacrificed their lives for Your name. Accept their sacrifice and their prayers. (*Tosafot Menaḥḥot* 110a)

וְאִשֵּׁי could refer to the fire that was always lit on the Altar. So, too, in the heart of every Jew there is a hidden flame that seeks to cleave to Hashem that is never extinguished.

Which interpretation speaks to you today?

בְּאַהֲבָה – *In love.* "Love" could describe the prayers – we ask that the prayers we offer out of love should be accepted.

"Love" could describe the acceptance – we ask that the prayers we offer should be accepted with love.

עבודה⁸

רְצֵה⁸ יהוה⁸ אֱלֹהֵינוּ בְּעַמְּךָ יִשְׂרָאֵל וּבִתְפִלָּתָם⁸
וְהָשֵׁב אֶת הָעֲבוֹדָה⁸ לִדְבִיר בֵּיתֶךָ
וְאִשֵּׁי⁸ יִשְׂרָאֵל וּתְפִלָּתָם בְּאַהֲבָה תְקַבֵּל בְּרָצוֹן
וּתְהִי לְרָצוֹן תָּמִיד עֲבוֹדַת יִשְׂרָאֵל עַמֶּךָ.

As a friend of mine once explained to me, people are unhappy because they want what they cannot have, and they don't want what they already have. We can alleviate this cycle of negativity in two ways. First, we must learn to want what we already have and be grateful to God. If we don't, we will not be ready to receive anything more. Next, we need to learn to desire what God wants to give us. When our will is aligned with God's will, and we sincerely ask for what God has wanted to give us all along, then His blessings flow freely into our lives. (Rabbi D. Aaron)

עבודה – TEMPLE SERVICE. This is the first of the final three blessings of the Shemoneh Esreh, the birkhot hodaya, blessings of thanks. What they all have in common, despite elements of additional requests, is the acknowledgment of and gratitude to Hashem for the personal and communal relationship we have with Him.

רְצֵה – Find favor. Here we ask that our prayers be found acceptable in terms of their content. Here we ask that our prayers be found acceptable in terms of their sincerity.

וּבִתְפִלָּתָם – And their prayer. We first ask Hashem to find favor in "Your people," and only afterwards in "their prayers." This is to teach us that if we make a sincere effort to make our own lives worthy, to become better people and better Jews, only then can we hope that our prayers will be found worthy. (Rabbi S.R. Hirsch)

How have your prayers until this point

On Rosh Ḥodesh and Ḥol HaMo'ed, say:

אֱלֹהֵינוּ Our God and God of our ancestors, may there rise, come, reach, appear, be favored, heard, regarded and remembered before You, our recollection and remembrance, as well as the remembrance of our ancestors, and of the Messiah son of David Your servant, and of Jerusalem Your holy city, and of all Your people the house of Israel – for deliverance and well-being, grace, loving-kindness and compassion, life and peace, on this day of:

> *On Rosh Ḥodesh:* Rosh Ḥodesh.
>
> *On Pesaḥ:* the Festival of Matzot.
>
> *On Sukkot:* the Festival of Sukkot.

On it remember us, LORD our God, for good; recollect us for blessing, and deliver us for life. In accord with Your promise of salvation and compassion, spare us and be gracious to us; have compassion on us and deliver us, for our eyes are turned to You because You, God, are a gracious and compassionate King.

וְתֶחֱזֶינָה And may our eyes witness[B]
Your return to Zion in compassion.
Blessed are You, LORD, who restores His Presence to Zion.[B]

ANI TEFILLA · אני תפילה

Make a picture in your mind when you are praying that you are really standing in Israel and in the Holy Temple and that you are actually seeing everything with your own eyes.... And when you imagine this is so, that you are standing in Israel, you will achieve great clarity in your prayer. (Rabbi Elimelech of Lizhensk)

IYUN TEFILLA · עיון תפילה

וְיִפָּקֵד וְיִזָּכֵר – *Regarded and remembered.* Why is there so much discussion here about remembering; after all, does Hashem really forget anything? Rather, just as there are distractions which cause us to be unable to recall things we really know, so too there are things about our actions which act as barriers to Hashem's "remembering" the good things that we do. For example,

each person is born with his own unique potential which he must realize on his own. We ask that Hashem remember (וְיִפָּקֵד) the potential that we have and that he recall (וְיִזָּכֵר) the good deeds we have done to try to realize that potential. Rosh Ḥodesh and the holy days are times for introspection, for that, too, is a form of service of the heart.

On ראש חודש and חול המועד, say:

אֱלֹהֵינוּ וֵאלֹהֵי אֲבוֹתֵינוּ, יַעֲלֶה וְיָבֹא וְיַגִּיעַ, וְיֵרָאֶה וְיֵרָצֶה וְיִשָּׁמַע,
וְיִפָּקֵד וְיִזָּכֵר זִכְרוֹנֵנוּ וּפִקְדוֹנֵנוּ וְזִכְרוֹן אֲבוֹתֵינוּ, וְזִכְרוֹן מָשִׁיחַ בֶּן
דָּוִד עַבְדֶּךָ, וְזִכְרוֹן יְרוּשָׁלַיִם עִיר קָדְשֶׁךָ, וְזִכְרוֹן כָּל עַמְּךָ בֵּית
יִשְׂרָאֵל, לְפָנֶיךָ, לִפְלֵיטָה לְטוֹבָה, לְחֵן וּלְחֶסֶד וּלְרַחֲמִים, לְחַיִּים
וּלְשָׁלוֹם בְּיוֹם

בראש חודש: רֹאשׁ הַחֹדֶשׁ / בפסח: חַג הַמַּצּוֹת / בסוכות: חַג הַסֻּכּוֹת
הַזֶּה. זָכְרֵנוּ יהוה אֱלֹהֵינוּ בּוֹ לְטוֹבָה, וּפָקְדֵנוּ בוֹ לִבְרָכָה, וְהוֹשִׁיעֵנוּ
בוֹ לְחַיִּים. וּבִדְבַר יְשׁוּעָה וְרַחֲמִים, חוּס וְחָנֵּנוּ וְרַחֵם עָלֵינוּ וְהוֹשִׁיעֵנוּ,
כִּי אֵלֶיךָ עֵינֵינוּ, כִּי אֵל מֶלֶךְ חַנּוּן וְרַחוּם אָתָּה.

וְתֶחֱזֶינָה עֵינֵינוּ בְּשׁוּבְךָ לְצִיּוֹן בְּרַחֲמִים.
בָּרוּךְ אַתָּה יהוה
הַמַּחֲזִיר שְׁכִינָתוֹ לְצִיּוֹן.

וְתֶחֱזֶינָה עֵינֵינוּ – *And may our eyes witness.*
An alternative translation is "and may You
enable us to see." The existence of the State
of Israel can be seen as a sign that You are a

presence in history and that the State is the
beginning of Your return to Zion. May You
enable our eyes to see Israel not only as a political entity, but as the miracle that it really is.

הַמַּחֲזִיר שְׁכִינָתוֹ לְצִיּוֹן – *Who restores His Presence to Zion.* I thank You Hashem because
I know that You will return Your Presence
to Jerusalem. I only pray that it be sooner
rather than later.

While this *berakha* is found in the final
section of the *Amida*, the section of "Thanks,"
it sounds like a request for the restoration

of the Temple service, which more appropriately belongs in the middle section, and
it can be argued these themes are already
found there. However, if we approach this
as a statement of faith rather than a request,
that we have total faith that this will happen,
and we merely desire it in a speedy fashion,
then it certainly belongs here.

THANKSGIVING

Bow at the first nine words.

מוֹדִים We give thanks to You,^{BA}
for You are the LORD our God
and God of our ancestors
for ever and all time.
You are the Rock of our lives,
Shield of our salvation
from generation to generation.
We will thank You and
declare Your praise for our lives,^B
which are entrusted into Your hand;
for our souls,^B
which are placed in Your charge;
for Your miracles^B
which are with us every day;
and for Your wonders^B and favors^B
at all times, evening,
morning and midday.
You are good –
for Your compassion never fails.
You are compassionate –
for Your loving-
kindnesses never cease.
We have always
placed our hope in You.

During the Leader's Repetition,
the congregation says quietly:

מוֹדִים We give thanks^B to You,
for You are the LORD
our God
and God of our ancestors,
God of all flesh,
who formed us
and formed the universe.
Blessings and thanks are due
to Your great and holy name
for giving us life
and sustaining us.
May You continue
to give us life and sustain us;
and may You gather
our exiles
to Your holy courts,
to keep Your decrees,
do Your will and serve You
with a perfect heart,
for it is for us
to give You thanks.
Blessed be God
to whom
thanksgiving is due.

---

ed. I know that there is more to me as a person than my physical body.

וְעַל נִסֶּיךָ – *For Your miracles.* We thank You for the everyday miracles in our lives of which we are not aware, for example, a virus I did not catch, a moment when my life was imperiled on my way here today but I walked by, totally unaware.

וְעַל נִפְלְאוֹתֶיךָ – *And for Your wonders.* We thank You for the everyday wonders to which we may be oblivious. I will not take for granted the vibrant life which surrounds me.

וְטוֹבוֹתֶיךָ – *And favors.* We thank You even for the things which seem bad, because ultimately we know that You want good to emerge from them.

ANI TEFILLA on מוֹדִים is on page 182. BIUR TEFILLA on מוֹדִים דרבנן is on page 185.

הוֹדָאָה

Bow at the first five words.

מוֹדִים אֲנַחְנוּ לָךְ בֹּא

שָׁאַתָּה הוּא יהוה אֱלֹהֵינוּ

וֵאלֹהֵי אֲבוֹתֵינוּ לְעוֹלָם וָעֶד.

צוּר חַיֵּינוּ, מָגֵן יִשְׁעֵנוּ

אַתָּה הוּא לְדוֹר וָדוֹר.

נוֹדֶה לְּךָ וּנְסַפֵּר תְּהִלָּתֶךָ

עַל חַיֵּינוּ בּ הַמְּסוּרִים בְּיָדֶךָ

וְעַל נִשְׁמוֹתֵינוּ בּ הַפְּקוּדוֹת לָךְ

וְעַל נִסֶּיךָ בּ שֶׁבְּכָל יוֹם עִמָּנוּ

וְעַל נִפְלְאוֹתֶיךָ בּ וְטוֹבוֹתֶיךָ בּ

שֶׁבְּכָל עֵת

עֶרֶב וָבֹקֶר וְצָהֳרָיִם.

הַטּוֹב, כִּי לֹא כָלוּ רַחֲמֶיךָ

וְהַמְרַחֵם, כִּי לֹא תַמּוּ חֲסָדֶיךָ

מֵעוֹלָם קִוִּינוּ לָךְ.

חזרת הש״ץ, During
the קָהל says quietly:

מוֹדִים בּ אֲנַחְנוּ לָךְ

שָׁאַתָּה הוּא יהוה אֱלֹהֵינוּ

וֵאלֹהֵי אֲבוֹתֵינוּ

אֱלֹהֵי כָל בָּשָׂר

יוֹצְרֵנוּ, יוֹצֵר בְּרֵאשִׁית.

בְּרָכוֹת וְהוֹדָאוֹת

לְשִׁמְךָ הַגָּדוֹל וְהַקָּדוֹשׁ

עַל שֶׁהֶחֱיִיתָנוּ וְקִיַּמְתָּנוּ.

כֵּן תְּחַיֵּינוּ וּתְקַיְּמֵנוּ

וְתֶאֱסֹף גָּלֻיּוֹתֵינוּ

לְחַצְרוֹת קָדְשֶׁךָ

לִשְׁמֹר חֻקֶּיךָ

וְלַעֲשׂוֹת רְצוֹנֶךָ וּלְעָבְדְּךָ

בְּלֵבָב שָׁלֵם

עַל שֶׁאֲנַחְנוּ מוֹדִים לָךְ.

בָּרוּךְ אֵל הַהוֹדָאוֹת.

מוֹדִים אֲנַחְנוּ לָךְ – *We give thanks to You.* The word מוֹדִים can mean "thank" in which case the sense is that we thank You for all of the good that there is in our lives.

The word can mean "acknowledge" in which case the sense is that we acknowledge that You are our God and the God of our ancestors. We acknowledge that God exists based upon all of the good things we have in our lives.

Do I want to thank God today or to acknowledge His existence?

עַל חַיֵּינוּ – *For our lives.* We thank You for our physical life. I will not take my physical health for granted. There are so many people who are worse off than me.

וְעַל נִשְׁמוֹתֵינוּ – *For our souls.* We thank You for our souls which animate our bodies.

I will not take my spiritual life for grant-

On Ḥanukka:

עַל הַנִּסִּים [We thank You also] for the miracles,[8] the redemption, the mighty deeds, the salvations, and the victories in battle which You performed for our ancestors in those days, at this time.

בִּימֵי מַתִּתְיָהוּ In the days of Mattityahu, son of Yoḥanan, the High Priest, the Hasmonean, and his sons, the wicked Greek kingdom rose up against Your people Israel to make them forget Your Torah and to force them to transgress the statutes of Your will. It was then that You in Your great compassion stood by them in the time of their distress. You championed their cause, judged their claim, and avenged their wrong. You delivered the strong into the hands of the weak, the many into the hands of the few, the impure into the hands of the pure, the wicked into the hands of the righteous, and the arrogant into the hands of those who were engaged in the study of Your Torah. You made for Yourself great and holy renown in Your world, and for Your people Israel You performed a great salvation and redemption as of this very day. Your children then entered the holiest part of Your House, cleansed Your Temple, purified Your Sanctuary, kindled lights in Your holy courts, and designated these eight days of Ḥanukka for giving thanks and praise to Your great name.

Continue with "For all these things."

BIUR TEFILLA · ביאור תפילה

מוֹדִים דרבנן — *THE RABBIS' MODIM.* The Gemara (*Sota* 40a) asks what the congregation is supposed to recite when the *Ḥazan* reaches this point. Yet why ask? After all, in no other blessing during the *Ḥazan's* repetition of the *Shemoneh Esreh* is there a different blessing that we ourselves say; the *Ḥazan* is our emissary for all of those other blessings. Why might it be different here? One answer was offered by Abudarham: because when it comes to saying "thank you" one cannot appoint a messenger. Each of us must offer thanks in our own personal way.

BIUR TEFILLA · ביאור תפילה

עַל הַנִּסִּים — *For the miracles.* In the times of Mattityahu, the enemy wanted to force us to "forget" the Torah, to "abandon our laws" and customs; in effect, they wanted us to assimilate. The threat was completely spiritual. In the times of Mordekhai and Esther, the enemy wanted "to kill and annihilate" us. The threat was completely physical. In every generation there have been those who have continued to seek to attack us spiritually or physically. Yet, as a people, we have miraculously survived so that we can stand here today proud and tall. Be thankful.

בחנוכה:

עַל הַנִּסִּים וְעַל הַפֻּרְקָן וְעַל הַגְּבוּרוֹת וְעַל הַתְּשׁוּעוֹת וְעַל הַמִּלְחָמוֹת שֶׁעָשִׂיתָ לַאֲבוֹתֵינוּ בַּיָּמִים הָהֵם בַּזְּמַן הַזֶּה.

בִּימֵי מַתִּתְיָהוּ בֶן יוֹחָנָן כֹּהֵן גָּדוֹל חַשְׁמוֹנַאי וּבָנָיו, כְּשֶׁעָמְדָה מַלְכוּת יָוָן הָרְשָׁעָה עַל עַמְּךָ יִשְׂרָאֵל לְהַשְׁכִּיחָם תּוֹרָתֶךָ וּלְהַעֲבִירָם מֵחֻקֵּי רְצוֹנֶךָ, וְאַתָּה בְּרַחֲמֶיךָ הָרַבִּים עָמַדְתָּ לָהֶם בְּעֵת צָרָתָם, רַבְתָּ אֶת רִיבָם, דַּנְתָּ אֶת דִּינָם, נָקַמְתָּ אֶת נִקְמָתָם, מָסַרְתָּ גִבּוֹרִים בְּיַד חַלָּשִׁים, וְרַבִּים בְּיַד מְעַטִּים, וּטְמֵאִים בְּיַד טְהוֹרִים, וּרְשָׁעִים בְּיַד צַדִּיקִים, וְזֵדִים בְּיַד עוֹסְקֵי תוֹרָתֶךָ, וּלְךָ עָשִׂיתָ שֵׁם גָּדוֹל וְקָדוֹשׁ בְּעוֹלָמֶךָ, וּלְעַמְּךָ יִשְׂרָאֵל עָשִׂיתָ תְּשׁוּעָה גְדוֹלָה וּפֻרְקָן כְּהַיּוֹם הַזֶּה. וְאַחַר כֵּן בָּאוּ בָנֶיךָ לִדְבִיר בֵּיתֶךָ, וּפִנּוּ אֶת הֵיכָלֶךָ, וְטִהֲרוּ אֶת מִקְדָּשֶׁךָ, וְהִדְלִיקוּ נֵרוֹת בְּחַצְרוֹת קָדְשֶׁךָ, וְקָבְעוּ שְׁמוֹנַת יְמֵי חֲנֻכָּה אֵלּוּ, לְהוֹדוֹת וּלְהַלֵּל לְשִׁמְךָ הַגָּדוֹל.

Continue with וְעַל כֻּלָּם.

ANI TEFILLA • אני תפילה

מוֹדִים אֲנַחְנוּ לָךְ — *We give thanks to You.* In short, one can thank God here for anything and everything: the people in our lives who care about us, our family, our relatives, our friends and acquaintances, the mate-

rial comforts we have, the air we breathe. Sometimes we do not appreciate things enough until they are gone. Don't wait. Be thankful.
What is on your list today?

ANI TEFILLA • אני תפילה

The story is told of two angels who were assigned the task of going around the world to collect people's prayers. Each one set out with a bag, determined to beat the other one out. At the end of the prescribed time, one angel returned with a bag that was bulging, he was bent over from the burden of his load. The other angel, however, clearly did not have the same success. His bag was half empty, or, at best, half full, and as he turned his bag over to empty it, it became clear that he had returned with a paltry

sum of prayers. What accounted for the difference?

It turns out that they were collecting different prayers. The first angel was collecting only those prayers which contained requests, people's expressions of the things they wanted or thought they wanted or thought they needed. The other angel, however, the one with the emptier bag, only collected prayers of thanks. The point of the story is clear. We simply do not thank as much as we could, as much as we should.

On Purim:

עַל הַנִּסִּים [We thank You also] for the miracles, the redemption, the mighty deeds, the salvations, and the victories in battle which You performed for our ancestors in those days, at this time.

בִּימֵי מָרְדְּכַי In the days of Mordekhai and Esther, in Shushan the capital, the wicked Haman rose up against them and sought to destroy, slay and extermi- *Esther 3* nate all the Jews, young and old, children and women, on one day, the thirteenth day of the twelfth month, which is the month of Adar, and to plunder their possessions. Then You in Your great compassion thwarted his counsel, frustrated his plans, and caused his scheme to recoil on his own head, so that they hanged him and his sons on the gallows.

Continue with "For all these things."

וְעַל כֻּלָּם For all these things may Your name be blessed and exalted, our King, continually, for ever and all time.

Between Rosh HaShana And write, for a good life,
& Yom Kippur: all the children of Your covenant.

Let all that lives thank You, Selah! and praise Your name in truth, God, our Savior and Help, Selah!
Blessed are You, LORD, whose name is "the Good"
and to whom thanks are due.

The following is said by the Leader during the Repetition of the Amida, except in a house of mourning and on Tisha B'Av. In Israel, if Kohanim bless the congregation, turn to page 684.

Our God and God of our fathers, bless us with the threefold blessing in the Torah, written by the hand of Moses Your servant and pronounced by Aaron and his sons the priests, Your holy people, as it is said:[B]

May the LORD bless you and protect you. *Num. 6*
Cong: May it be Your will.
May the LORD make His face shine on you and be gracious to you.
Cong: May it be Your will.
May the LORD turn His face toward you, and grant you peace.
Cong: May it be Your will.

---

with Hashem at the center, and each phrase has 3, 5 and 7 words respectively, symbolizing the incremental growth inherent in each blessing (*berakha*), like a spring of water (*bereikha*) which bubbles up and gives life.

בפורים:
עַל הַנִּסִּים וְעַל הַפֻּרְקָן וְעַל הַגְּבוּרוֹת וְעַל הַתְּשׁוּעוֹת וְעַל הַמִּלְחָמוֹת שֶׁעָשִׂיתָ לַאֲבוֹתֵינוּ בַּיָּמִים הָהֵם בַּזְּמַן הַזֶּה.

אסתר ג
בִּימֵי מָרְדְּכַי וְאֶסְתֵּר בְּשׁוּשַׁן הַבִּירָה, כְּשֶׁעָמַד עֲלֵיהֶם הָמָן הָרָשָׁע, בִּקֵּשׁ לְהַשְׁמִיד לַהֲרֹג וּלְאַבֵּד אֶת־כָּל־הַיְּהוּדִים מִנַּעַר וְעַד־זָקֵן טַף וְנָשִׁים בְּיוֹם אֶחָד, בִּשְׁלוֹשָׁה עָשָׂר לְחֹדֶשׁ שְׁנֵים־עָשָׂר, הוּא־חֹדֶשׁ אֲדָר, וּשְׁלָלָם לָבוֹז: וְאַתָּה בְּרַחֲמֶיךָ הָרַבִּים הֵפַרְתָּ אֶת עֲצָתוֹ, וְקִלְקַלְתָּ אֶת מַחֲשַׁבְתּוֹ, וַהֲשֵׁבוֹתָ לּוֹ גְּמוּלוֹ בְּרֹאשׁוֹ, וְתָלוּ אוֹתוֹ וְאֶת בָּנָיו עַל הָעֵץ.

Continue with וְעַל כֻּלָּם.

וְעַל כֻּלָּם יִתְבָּרַךְ וְיִתְרוֹמַם שִׁמְךָ מַלְכֵּנוּ תָּמִיד לְעוֹלָם וָעֶד.

בעשרת ימי תשובה: וּכְתֹב לְחַיִּים טוֹבִים כָּל בְּנֵי בְרִיתֶךָ.

וְכֹל הַחַיִּים יוֹדְוּךָ סֶּלָה, וִיהַלְלוּ אֶת שִׁמְךָ בֶּאֱמֶת הָאֵל יְשׁוּעָתֵנוּ וְעֶזְרָתֵנוּ סֶלָה. בָּרוּךְ אַתָּה יהוה, הַטּוֹב שִׁמְךָ וּלְךָ נָאֶה לְהוֹדוֹת.

The following is said by the שליח ציבור during חזרת הש״ץ, except in a house of mourning and on תשעה באב. In ארץ ישראל say ברכת כהנים turn to page 685.

אֱלֹהֵינוּ וֵאלֹהֵי אֲבוֹתֵינוּ, בָּרְכֵנוּ בַּבְּרָכָה הַמְשֻׁלֶּשֶׁת בַּתּוֹרָה, הַכְּתוּבָה עַל יְדֵי מֹשֶׁה עַבְדֶּךָ, הָאֲמוּרָה מִפִּי אַהֲרֹן וּבָנָיו כֹּהֲנִים עַם קְדוֹשֶׁיךָ, כָּאָמוּר:
במדבר ו

יְבָרֶכְךָ יהוה וְיִשְׁמְרֶךָ: קהל: כֵּן יְהִי רָצוֹן
יָאֵר יהוה פָּנָיו אֵלֶיךָ וִיחֻנֶּךָּ: קהל: כֵּן יְהִי רָצוֹן
יִשָּׂא יהוה פָּנָיו אֵלֶיךָ וְיָשֵׂם לְךָ שָׁלוֹם: קהל: כֵּן יְהִי רָצוֹן

ברכת כהנים – BIRKAT KOHANIM. In the times of the Beit HaMikdash, after the sacrifices were offered, the kohanim would fulfill the positive commandment of blessing the people (Bemidbar 6:22–26.; Vayikra 9:22).

Ultimately, however, it is understood that the blessing comes from Hashem, whose love for Israel is manifest in the blessings that we receive in our daily lives all around us. Note that each phrase has two verbs

PEACE

In Shaharit:

שִׂים שָׁלוֹם Grant peace,[ABI] goodness and blessing, grace, loving-kindness and compassion[B] to us and all Israel Your people. Bless us, our Father, all as one, with the light of Your face, for by the light of Your face[B] You have given us, LORD our God, the Torah of life and love of kindness, righteousness, blessing, compassion, life and peace. May it be good in Your eyes to bless Your people Israel at every time, in every hour, with Your peace.

In Minḥa and Ma'ariv:

שָׁלוֹם רָב Grant great peace[BIA] to Your people Israel for ever, for You are the sovereign LORD of all peace; and may it be good in Your eyes to bless Your people Israel at every time, at every hour, with Your peace.

שִׂים שָׁלוֹם – *Grant peace.* Where there is anger, there cannot be peace. In a place where there is holiness, anger cannot exist. Therefore we ask Hashem to help us not be angry so that peace and holiness can reign.

שִׂים שָׁלוֹם – *Grant peace.* Shalom comes about when everyone knows his or her place in the world, where there is no struggle because there is acceptance of others.

Can you think of someone whom you might have a hard time accepting? What small change can you try to make today in your relationship?

שִׂים שָׁלוֹם – *Grant peace.* When one says this blessing, one should have in mind the mitzva of וְאָהַבְתָּ לְרֵעֲךָ כָּמוֹךָ – love your neighbor as yourself (*Ya'arot Devash*). **Whom can I have in mind for this mitzva today?**

חֵן וָחֶסֶד וְרַחֲמִים – *Grace, loving-kindness and compassion.*

Ḥen, grace, is when the receiver finds favor in the eyes of the giver.

Ḥesed comes from the generosity of the giver, whether the recipient deserves it or not. Raḥamim, mercy, is granted when it is not deserved. **Which ones are most relevant for me today?**

בְּאוֹר פָּנֶיךָ – *With the light of Your face.* "Bless us with the light of Your face" – this could be a request to God to stop hiding from us. The Ba'al HaTanya wrote that we are asking Him to enlighten us with belief in Him so that we can live with the clear understanding that everything comes from Him, and that He should reveal Himself to us in our daily lives. Peace can come from that knowledge. **How can I try harder to see the presence of God somewhere in my life today?**

ברכת שלום

In שחרית:	In מעריב and מנחה:

שִׂים שָׁלוֹם‎אבע טוֹבָה וּבְרָכָה

חֵן וָחֶסֶד וְרַחֲמִים‎ב

עָלֵינוּ וְעַל כָּל יִשְׂרָאֵל עַמֶּךָ.

בָּרְכֵנוּ אָבִינוּ כֻּלָּנוּ כְּאֶחָד בְּאוֹר פָּנֶיךָ

כִּי בְאוֹר פָּנֶיךָ‎ג נָתַתָּ לָּנוּ יהוה אֱלֹהֵינוּ

תּוֹרַת חַיִּים וְאַהֲבַת חֶסֶד

וּצְדָקָה וּבְרָכָה

וְרַחֲמִים וְחַיִּים וְשָׁלוֹם.

וְטוֹב בְּעֵינֶיךָ לְבָרֵךְ אֶת עַמְּךָ יִשְׂרָאֵל

בְּכָל עֵת וּבְכָל שָׁעָה בִּשְׁלוֹמֶךָ.

שָׁלוֹם רָב

עַל יִשְׂרָאֵל עַמְּךָ

תָּשִׂים לְעוֹלָם

כִּי אַתָּה הוּא

מֶלֶךְ אָדוֹן

לְכָל הַשָּׁלוֹם.

וְטוֹב בְּעֵינֶיךָ

לְבָרֵךְ אֶת עַמְּךָ יִשְׂרָאֵל

בְּכָל עֵת וּבְכָל שָׁעָה

בִּשְׁלוֹמֶךָ.

ANI TEFILLA · אני תפילה

שִׂים שָׁלוֹם – *Grant peace.* One vision of peace is surely that all Jews live together harmoniously. Although no one person can unify the world, every person is still obligated to feel united and connected to *Klal Yisrael.* (Rinat Ḥayyim)

To whom in my world could I feel more connected than I do?

שִׂים שָׁלוֹם – *Grant peace.* With whom am I angry?

I resolve to let my anger go so that I can feel more complete, so that the other person can feel more complete, so that the world can be more complete.

There can be no inner peace and no peace with others in a place where there is jealousy.

I resolve not to be jealous of others today.

There can be no inner peace or peace with others where there is unhealthy competitiveness.

I resolve not to be competitive today in an unhealthy way.

BIUR TEFILLA · ביאור תפילה

שִׂים שָׁלוֹם – *Grant peace.* Shalom is related to the word *shalem,* meaning "whole" or "complete." There cannot be peace unless people feel complete within themselves; until they are at peace with their physical selves, their ethical selves, their emotional selves. We ask Hashem to help us become more complete people today so that we may be at peace with ourselves and with others.

What can I do today to make myself into a more complete person physically? Ethically? Emotionally? Religiously?

Between   In the book of life, blessing, peace and prosperity,
Rosh HaShana   may we and all Your people the house of Israel
& Yom Kippur: be remembered and written before You
                 for a good life, and for peace.*

Blessed are You, LORD, who blesses His people Israel with peace.[A]

*Between Rosh HaShana and Yom Kippur
outside Israel, many end the blessing:
Blessed are You, LORD, who makes peace.

The following verse concludes the Leader's Repetition of the Amida.
Some also say it here as part of the silent Amida.

May the words of my mouth[H] and the meditation of my heart   Ps. 19
find favor before You, LORD, my Rock and Redeemer.

---

declare Your praise." Now at the conclusion, we therefore say this parallel request: "May the words of my mouth and the meditation of my heart find favor..." We thus begin and end the prayer with a very personal request (unlike all of the other blessings, these words are in the singular and not the plural) that our prayers be heard, both those uttered aloud and those expressed in the inner recesses of our soul.

The question is whether this verse is part and parcel of the *Shemoneh Esreh* itself or, given that it is not really a blessing and given that it is in the singular and not the plural, whether it is part of a private supplication. The practical difference would be if, for example, you had not yet said the verse but had already concluded *Sim Shalom* and, in the meantime, the rest of the congregation had reached *Kedusha*; would you respond or would you have to remain silent because you haven't really finished *Shemoneh Esreh* yet?

At the same time, there developed a practice to add even more supplications after the *Tefilla* was over as will be explained in the *Tahanun* prayer found below. One such supplication, *Elokai Netzor* which appears next, was authored by one of the last of the Amoraim, Mar the son of Ravina (fifth century CE), and it was ultimately incorporated into the fixed text. Note that toward the end he includes this concluding verse of יִהְיוּ לְרָצוֹן. As such, where exactly does *Shemoneh Esreh* end – after *Sim Shalom*? after the recitation of the verse יִהְיוּ לְרָצוֹן the first time? after the recitation of *Elokai Netzor*?

The *Shulḥan Arukh* (122:1) rules that one should not utter any interruption until one has said יִהְיוּ לְרָצוֹן. The Rema disagrees, clearly believing that one's *Shemoneh Esreh* already formally concluded after *Sim Shalom*. The *Mishna Berura* suggests that one should say the verse יִהְיוּ לְרָצוֹן twice, once here and once in *Elokai Netzor* in order to remove oneself from doubt.

בעשרת ימי תשובה: בְּסֵפֶר חַיִּים, בְּרָכָה וְשָׁלוֹם, וּפַרְנָסָה טוֹבָה
נִזָּכֵר וְנִכָּתֵב לְפָנֶיךָ, אֲנַחְנוּ וְכָל עַמְּךָ בֵּית יִשְׂרָאֵל
לְחַיִּים טוֹבִים וּלְשָׁלוֹם.*

בָּרוּךְ אַתָּה יהוה, הַמְבָרֵךְ אֶת עַמּוֹ יִשְׂרָאֵל בַּשָּׁלוֹם.א

*During the עשרת ימי תשובה in חוץ לארץ, many end the blessing:

בָּרוּךְ אַתָּה יהוה, עוֹשֵׂה הַשָּׁלוֹם.

The following verse concludes the חזרת הש"ץ.
Some also say it here as part of the silent עמידה.

תהלים יט

יִהְיוּ לְרָצוֹן אִמְרֵי־פִיא וְהֶגְיוֹן לִבִּי לְפָנֶיךָ, יהוה צוּרִי וְגֹאֲלִי:

ANI TEFILLA · אני תפילה

If you saw somebody pulling a boat to the shore and were mistaken about mechanics and motion, you might think that he was pulling the shore to the boat. That's what prayer is like. You think that you're pulling God to you, but in fact, if you pray well, you pull yourself to God. (Attributed to Yehuda Aryeh MiModena)

ANI TEFILLA · אני תפילה

הַמְבָרֵךְ אֶת עַמּוֹ יִשְׂרָאֵל בַּשָּׁלוֹם – Who blesses His people Israel with peace. One of God's names is "Peace" (Shabbat 10b). That is one meaning of the greeting Shalom Aleikhem – May peace be upon you. May Hashem's name be upon you. Without peace, there is nothing.

IYUN TEFILLA · עיון תפילה

יִהְיוּ לְרָצוֹן אִמְרֵי־פִי – May the words of my mouth. The verse comes from the nineteenth chapter of Tehillim. Just as King David uttered this verse after reciting 18 psalms, so, too, do we express the same sentiment after reciting the prayer known as the Eighteen Blessings (Berakhot 9b).

HILKHOT TEFILLA · הלכות תפילה

יִהְיוּ לְרָצוֹן אִמְרֵי־פִי – May the words of my mouth. The Gemara Berakhot 9b says that one should conclude one's Shemoneh Esreh

with this verse from Tehillim 19 just as one began one's prayer with the words, "Hashem, open my lips so that my mouth may

Berakhot
17a

אֱלֹהַי My God,
guard[BI] my tongue from evil and my lips from deceitful speech.
To those who curse me, let my soul be silent;[BA]
may my soul be to all like the dust.
Open my heart to Your Torah
and let my soul pursue Your commandments.
As for all who plan evil against me,
swiftly thwart their counsel and frustrate their plans.

> Act for the sake of Your name;
> act for the sake of Your right hand;
> act for the sake of Your holiness;
> act for the sake of Your Torah.

---

with the owner of the donkey; for the owner might sit by the wayside and say "Okay, since you are obligated to lift up your fellow man's donkey, you lift it up while I sit back and watch." Hence the Gemara says "you must lift it *with him*," meaning, the owner of the donkey must participate.

So, too, in our case, said the Ḥafetz Ḥayyim, if we ask Hashem to help unload us from this sin, then Hashem may say, "Help Me by doing your share, otherwise I am under no obligation to help you."

BIUR TEFILLA · ביאור תפילה

וְלִמְקַלְלַי נַפְשִׁי תִדֹּם – *To those who curse me, let my soul be silent.* Perhaps this is a reference to being on the receiving end of לָשׁוֹן הָרֵע; if I am ever put in that position where people speak about me or against me, I hope I have the strength not to answer them in kind; otherwise, I will be no different than they are, and my prayer will now be meaningless.

ANI TEFILLA · אני תפילה

וְלִמְקַלְלַי נַפְשִׁי תִדֹּם – *To those who curse me, let my soul be silent.* One sees from here that one of the goals of prayer is to imbue you with a sense of serenity, of being at peace with yourself. When people make you angry or insult you or get on your bad side, there is something to be said for not allowing that to ruin your day or create within you a feeling of

anger or resentment or a desire for revenge. Let their taunts not bother me, says this *tefilla*. I am better than that. My self-esteem comes from within me not from what others think of me. It is their pettiness. There are more important things in life to get upset about. Seen in this light, when you walk away from *tefilla*, you walk away transformed.

ברכות יז.

אֱלֹהַי

נְצֹר^{כ״ו} לְשׁוֹנִי מֵרָע וּשְׂפָתַי מִדַּבֵּר מִרְמָה

וְלִמְקַלְלַי נַפְשִׁי תִדֹּם,^{כ״ז} וְנַפְשִׁי כֶּעָפָר לַכֹּל תִּהְיֶה.

פְּתַח לִבִּי בְּתוֹרָתֶךָ, וּבְמִצְוֹתֶיךָ תִּרְדּוֹף נַפְשִׁי.

וְכָל הַחוֹשְׁבִים עָלַי רָעָה

מְהֵרָה הָפֵר עֲצָתָם וְקַלְקֵל מַחֲשַׁבְתָּם.

עֲשֵׂה לְמַעַן שְׁמֶךָ

עֲשֵׂה לְמַעַן יְמִינֶךָ

עֲשֵׂה לְמַעַן קְדֻשָּׁתֶךָ

עֲשֵׂה לְמַעַן תּוֹרָתֶךָ.

BIUR TEFILLA · ביאור תפילה

אֱלֹהַי, נְצֹר — *My God, guard.*
The major theme of this concluding prayer is the request that we be protected against the sin of לָשׁוֹן הָרַע, evil speech. Think about what negative effects לָשׁוֹן הָרַע has upon us, our relationships, and our daily lives. Think about it enough, suffer from it once, try not speaking it for any length of time, and you'll begin to understand why we need God's help.

IYUN TEFILLA · עיון תפילה

אֱלֹהַי, נְצֹר — *My God, guard.* The Ḥafetz Ḥayyim once said:

To be sure, in this prayer we ask Hashem for His help. We ask Him to help us not speak לָשׁוֹן הָרַע and not speak lies. But do we do our part? Do we expend energy to "protect our tongue from speaking evil and our lips from uttering deceit?"
Do we do our part?

And if we do not do our part, then how can we possibly ask Him for His help? For we have learned that there is a law (*Devarim* 22:4) that if you see someone's donkey fallen under too heavy a load, you must help the owner pick it up. And the verse says הָקֵם תָּקִים עִמּוֹ — you shall surely lift it *with him*. From here the Gemara in *Bava Metzia* 32b says it must happen "with him," meaning

That Your beloved ones may be delivered,[B]   *Ps. 60*
save with Your right hand and answer me.

May the words of my mouth and the meditation of my heart   *Ps. 19*
find favor before You, LORD, my Rock and Redeemer.

Bow, take three steps back, then bow, first left, then right, then center, while saying:

May He who makes peace in His high places,
make peace for us and all Israel –
and say: Amen.

יְהִי רָצוֹן May it be Your will, LORD our God and God of our ancestors,
that the Temple be rebuilt speedily in our days,
and grant us a share in Your Torah.
And there we will serve You with reverence,
as in the days of old and as in former years.
Then the offering of Judah and Jerusalem will be pleasing to the LORD   *Mal. 3*
as in the days of old and as in former years.

When praying with a minyan, the Amida is repeated aloud by the Leader.

On days when Taḥanun is said (see page 200), start Taḥanun on page 208.
On Mondays and Thursdays start Taḥanun on page 200.
In Israel, on days on which Taḥanun is said, some say Viduy and
the Thirteen Attributes of Divine Compassion on page 686.

On fast days (except Tisha B'Av) most congregations say Seliḥot
on page 590 before Avinu Malkenu on page 194.

Between Rosh HaShana and Yom Kippur (but not on Erev Yom Kippur,
unless it falls on Friday), say Avinu Malkenu on page 194.

On Rosh Ḥodesh, Ḥanukka, Ḥol HaMo'ed, Yom HaAtzma'ut and
Yom Yerushalayim, say Hallel on page 442.

On other days when Taḥanun is not said (see page 200),
the Leader says Half Kaddish on page 214.

---

as we say on Shabbat רְצֵה וְהַחֲלִיצֵנוּ in ברכת
(הזמון). If so, then in this prayer I am asking

that Hashem allow me to achieve mental rest,
a release from pressure, tension, and worry.

תהלים ס

לְמַעַן יֵחָלְצוּן יְדִידֶיךָ, הוֹשִׁיעָה יְמִינְךָ וַעֲנֵנִי:

תהלים יט

יִהְיוּ לְרָצוֹן אִמְרֵי־פִי וְהֶגְיוֹן לִבִּי לְפָנֶיךָ, יהוה צוּרִי וְגֹאֲלִי:

Bow, take three steps back, then bow, first left, then right, then center, while saying:

עֹשֶׂה שָׁלוֹם/*בעשרת ימי תשובה:* הַשָּׁלוֹם/ בִּמְרוֹמָיו
הוּא יַעֲשֶׂה שָׁלוֹם עָלֵינוּ וְעַל כָּל יִשְׂרָאֵל, וְאִמְרוּ אָמֵן.

יְהִי רָצוֹן מִלְּפָנֶיךָ יהוה אֱלֹהֵינוּ וֵאלֹהֵי אֲבוֹתֵינוּ
שֶׁיִּבָּנֶה בֵּית הַמִּקְדָּשׁ בִּמְהֵרָה בְיָמֵינוּ
וְתֵן חֶלְקֵנוּ בְּתוֹרָתֶךָ
וְשָׁם נַעֲבָדְךָ בְּיִרְאָה כִּימֵי עוֹלָם וּכְשָׁנִים קַדְמוֹנִיּוֹת.

מלאכי ג

וְעָרְבָה לַיהוה מִנְחַת יְהוּדָה וִירוּשָׁלָיִם כִּימֵי עוֹלָם וּכְשָׁנִים קַדְמוֹנִיּוֹת:

When praying with a מנין, the עמידה is repeated aloud by the שליח ציבור.

On days when תחנון is said (see page 201), start תחנון on page 209.
On Mondays and Thursdays start תחנון on page 201.
In ארץ ישראל, on days on which תחנון is said,
some say וידוי and the י"ג מדות on page 687.

On fast days (except תשעה באב) most congregations say
סליחות on page 591 before אבינו מלכנו on page 195.

During the עשרת ימי תשובה (but not on ערב יום כיפור,
unless it falls on Friday), say אבינו מלכנו on page 195.

On יום ירושלים and יום העצמאות, חול המועד, חנוכה, ראש חודש,
say הלל on page 443.

On other days when תחנון is not said (see page 201),
the שליח ציבור says חצי קדיש on page 215.

ביאור תפילה · BIUR TEFILLA

לְמַעַן יֵחָלְצוּן יְדִידֶיךָ – *That Your beloved ones may be delivered.* The Meiri suggests that the word יֵחָלְצוּן comes not from the word "to free," but rather from the word "to rest" (just

AVINU MALKENU [BA]

*On fast days (except Tisha B'Av) most congregations say Seliḥot
on page 590 before Avinu Malkenu.*

*Between Rosh HaShana and Yom Kippur (but not on Erev Yom
Kippur, unless it falls on Friday), say Avinu Malkenu below.*

The Ark is opened.

אָבִֽינוּ מַלְכֵּֽנוּ Our Father, our King, we have sinned before You.

Our Father, our King, we have no king but You.

Our Father, our King, deal kindly with us for the sake of Your name.

Our Father our King, /*bless us with / a good year.

> /*Between Rosh HaShana & Yom Kippur: renew for us/

Our Father, our King, nullify all harsh decrees against us.

Our Father, our King, nullify the plans of those who hate us.

Our Father, our King, thwart the counsel of our enemies.

Our Father, our King, rid us of every oppressor and adversary.

Our Father, our King, close the mouths of our adversaries and accusers.

Our Father, our King, eradicate pestilence, sword, famine,
> captivity and destruction, iniquity and eradication
> from the people of Your covenant.

Our Father, our King, withhold the plague from Your heritage.

Our Father, our King, forgive and pardon all our iniquities.

---

nation to not observe mitzvot that made no sense to him. In short, he had faith, a faith born of his own struggles. A lesson to all of us as we are about ask for Hashem's help.

ANI TEFILLA · אני תפילה

אָבִֽינוּ מַלְכֵּֽנוּ – *Our Father, our King.*
The story is told about a young prince whose father, the king, was also his teacher. Whenever the boy misbehaved, the king would be very hard on him. One day the father found the boy at home in tears and asked him why he was crying so intensely. The prince responded: "My teacher is too hard on me." His father replied, "I will speak to your teacher." Sometimes Hashem can relate to us as a king meting out punishment that we deserve; but we ask that he also relate to us to the extent possible with the compassion of a father, and so we say, "My Father, my King."

אָבִינוּ מַלְכֵּנוּ בא

On fast days (except תשעה באב) most congregations say סליחות
on page 591 before אבינו מלכנו.
During the עשרת ימי תשובה (but not on ערב יום כיפור,
unless it falls on Friday), say אבינו מלכנו below.

The ארון קודש *is opened.*

אָבִינוּ מַלְכֵּנוּ, חָטָאנוּ לְפָנֶיךָ.

אָבִינוּ מַלְכֵּנוּ, אֵין לָנוּ מֶלֶךְ אֶלָּא אָתָּה.

אָבִינוּ מַלְכֵּנוּ, עֲשֵׂה עִמָּנוּ לְמַעַן שְׁמֶךָ.

אָבִינוּ מַלְכֵּנוּ, בָּרֵךְ/ בעשרת ימי תשובה: חַדֵּשׁ/ עָלֵינוּ שָׁנָה טוֹבָה.

אָבִינוּ מַלְכֵּנוּ, בַּטֵּל מֵעָלֵינוּ כָּל גְּזֵרוֹת קָשׁוֹת.

אָבִינוּ מַלְכֵּנוּ, בַּטֵּל מַחְשְׁבוֹת שׂוֹנְאֵינוּ.

אָבִינוּ מַלְכֵּנוּ, הָפֵר עֲצַת אוֹיְבֵינוּ.

אָבִינוּ מַלְכֵּנוּ, כַּלֵּה כָּל צַר וּמַשְׂטִין מֵעָלֵינוּ.

אָבִינוּ מַלְכֵּנוּ, סְתֹם פִּיּוֹת מַשְׂטִינֵינוּ וּמְקַטְרִגֵינוּ.

אָבִינוּ מַלְכֵּנוּ, כַּלֵּה דֶבֶר וְחֶרֶב וְרָעָב וּשְׁבִי וּמַשְׁחִית וְעָוֹן וּשְׁמַד
מִבְּנֵי בְרִיתֶךָ.

אָבִינוּ מַלְכֵּנוּ, מְנַע מַגֵּפָה מִנַּחֲלָתֶךָ.

אָבִינוּ מַלְכֵּנוּ, סְלַח וּמְחַל לְכָל עֲוֹנוֹתֵינוּ.

ביאור תפילה · BIUR TEFILLA

אָבִינוּ מַלְכֵּנוּ — *Our Father, our King.* This very ancient prayer is recited on days related to repentance, particularly on fast days and the days between Rosh HaShana and Yom Kippur. The Gemara (*Ta'anit* 25b) relates that there was a horrible drought and the prayers for relief were not answered until Rabbi Akiva got up and recited the intro-

ductory formula for this prayer, whereupon it began to rain. And what made his prayer more effective than those of others? One possibility offered is that it was because, as a *ba'al teshuva*, he had to forge his own relationship with Hashem, rather than rely first upon a religious upbringing. Another possibility is that he overcame his own initial incli-

Our Father, our King, wipe away and remove our transgressions and sins
from Your sight.

Our Father, our King, erase in Your abundant mercy all records of our sins.

The following nine sentences are said responsively, first by the Leader, then by the congregation:

Our Father, our King, bring us back to You in perfect repentance.

Our Father, our King, send a complete healing to the sick of Your people.

Our Father, our King, tear up the evil decree against us.

Our Father, our King, remember us with a memory of favorable deeds
before You.

Between Rosh HaShana and Yom Kippur:

Our Father, our King, write us in the book of good life.

Our Father, our King, write us in the book of redemption and
salvation.

Our Father, our King, write us in the book of livelihood and
sustenance.

Our Father, our King, write us in the book of merit.

Our Father, our King, write us in the book of pardon and
forgiveness.

On Fast Days:

Our Father, our King, remember us for a good life.

Our Father, our King, remember us for redemption and
salvation.

Our Father, our King, remember us for livelihood and
sustenance.

Our Father, our King, remember us for merit.

Our Father, our King, remember us for pardon and forgiveness.

End of responsive reading.

Our Father, our King, let salvation soon flourish for us.

Our Father, our King, raise the honor of Your people Israel.

Our Father, our King, raise the honor of Your anointed.

Our Father, our King, fill our hands with Your blessings.

Our Father, our King, fill our storehouses with abundance.

אָבִינוּ מַלְכֵּנוּ, מְחֵה וְהַעֲבֵר פְּשָׁעֵינוּ וְחַטֹּאתֵינוּ מִנֶּגֶד עֵינֶיךָ.

אָבִינוּ מַלְכֵּנוּ, מְחֹק בְּרַחֲמֶיךָ הָרַבִּים כָּל שִׁטְרֵי חוֹבוֹתֵינוּ.

The following nine sentences are said responsively, first by the שְׁלִיחַ ציבור, then by the קָהָל:

אָבִינוּ מַלְכֵּנוּ, הַחֲזִירֵנוּ בִּתְשׁוּבָה שְׁלֵמָה לְפָנֶיךָ.

אָבִינוּ מַלְכֵּנוּ, שְׁלַח רְפוּאָה שְׁלֵמָה לְחוֹלֵי עַמֶּךָ.

אָבִינוּ מַלְכֵּנוּ, קְרַע רֹעַ גְּזַר דִּינֵנוּ.

אָבִינוּ מַלְכֵּנוּ, זָכְרֵנוּ בְּזִכָּרוֹן טוֹב לְפָנֶיךָ.

During the עשרת ימי תשובה:

אָבִינוּ מַלְכֵּנוּ, כָּתְבֵנוּ בְּסֵפֶר חַיִּים טוֹבִים.

אָבִינוּ מַלְכֵּנוּ, כָּתְבֵנוּ בְּסֵפֶר גְּאֻלָּה וִישׁוּעָה.

אָבִינוּ מַלְכֵּנוּ, כָּתְבֵנוּ בְּסֵפֶר פַּרְנָסָה וְכַלְכָּלָה.

אָבִינוּ מַלְכֵּנוּ, כָּתְבֵנוּ בְּסֵפֶר זְכֻיּוֹת.

אָבִינוּ מַלְכֵּנוּ, כָּתְבֵנוּ בְּסֵפֶר סְלִיחָה וּמְחִילָה.

On Fast Days:

אָבִינוּ מַלְכֵּנוּ, זָכְרֵנוּ לְחַיִּים טוֹבִים.

אָבִינוּ מַלְכֵּנוּ, זָכְרֵנוּ לִגְאֻלָּה וִישׁוּעָה.

אָבִינוּ מַלְכֵּנוּ, זָכְרֵנוּ לְפַרְנָסָה וְכַלְכָּלָה.

אָבִינוּ מַלְכֵּנוּ, זָכְרֵנוּ לִזְכֻיּוֹת.

אָבִינוּ מַלְכֵּנוּ, זָכְרֵנוּ לִסְלִיחָה וּמְחִילָה.

End of responsive reading.

אָבִינוּ מַלְכֵּנוּ, הַצְמַח לָנוּ יְשׁוּעָה בְּקָרוֹב.

אָבִינוּ מַלְכֵּנוּ, הָרֵם קֶרֶן יִשְׂרָאֵל עַמֶּךָ.

אָבִינוּ מַלְכֵּנוּ, הָרֵם קֶרֶן מְשִׁיחֶךָ.

אָבִינוּ מַלְכֵּנוּ, מַלֵּא יָדֵינוּ מִבִּרְכוֹתֶיךָ.

אָבִינוּ מַלְכֵּנוּ, מַלֵּא אֲסָמֵינוּ שָׂבָע.

Our Father, our King, hear our voice, pity and be compassionate to us.

Our Father, our King, accept, with compassion and favor, our prayer.

Our Father, our King, open the gates of heaven to our prayer.

Our Father, our King, remember that we are dust.

Our Father, our King, please do not turn us away from You empty-handed.

Our Father, our King, may this moment be a moment of compassion
and a time of favor before You.

Our Father, our King, have pity on us, our children and our infants.

Our Father, our King, act for the sake of those who were killed
for Your holy name.ᴬ

Our Father, our King, act for the sake of those who were slaughtered
for proclaiming Your Unity.

Our Father, our King, act for the sake of those
who went through fire and water
to sanctify Your name.

Our Father, our King, avenge before our eyes
the spilt blood of Your servants.

Our Father, our King, act for Your sake, if not for ours.

Our Father, our King, act for Your sake, and save us.

Our Father, our King, act for the sake of Your abundant compassion.

Our Father, our King, act for the sake of Your great, mighty and awesome
name by which we are called.

▸ Our Father, our King, be gracious to us and answer us, though we have
no worthy deeds; act with us in charity and
loving-kindness and save us.

The Ark is closed.

שֵׁם קׇדְשֶׁךָ and יִחוּדֶךָ? The Holocaust survivor
answered his own question by explaining
that when the Nazis marched into a town,
they assembled 100 men and lined them
up in front of a river. One soldier with a machine gun started shooting from the right
side of the line and moved his gun toward
the left until he killed all of the men. When
the shooting began, all of the men started

reciting the *Shema* together. The people on
the right were killed as they said "*Hashem
Elokeinu*"; they did not manage to finish the
verse. Those people were הֲרוּגִים עַל שֵׁם קׇדְשֶׁךָ
(they died saying God's name). The people
further left managed to stay alive for long
enough to say "*Hashem eḥad;*" they died עַל
יִחוּדֶךָ (for Your Unity). Rav Itzikel could not
stop crying after hearing this.

אָבִינוּ מַלְכֵּנוּ, שְׁמַע קוֹלֵנוּ, חוּס וְרַחֵם עָלֵינוּ.

אָבִינוּ מַלְכֵּנוּ, קַבֵּל בְּרַחֲמִים וּבְרָצוֹן אֶת תְּפִלָּתֵנוּ.

אָבִינוּ מַלְכֵּנוּ, פְּתַח שַׁעֲרֵי שָׁמַיִם לִתְפִלָּתֵנוּ.

אָבִינוּ מַלְכֵּנוּ, זְכֹר כִּי עָפָר אֲנָחְנוּ.

אָבִינוּ מַלְכֵּנוּ, נָא אַל תְּשִׁיבֵנוּ רֵיקָם מִלְּפָנֶיךָ.

אָבִינוּ מַלְכֵּנוּ, תְּהֵא הַשָּׁעָה הַזֹּאת שְׁעַת רַחֲמִים
וְעֵת רָצוֹן מִלְּפָנֶיךָ.

אָבִינוּ מַלְכֵּנוּ, חֲמֹל עָלֵינוּ וְעַל עוֹלָלֵינוּ וְטַפֵּנוּ.

אָבִינוּ מַלְכֵּנוּ, עֲשֵׂה לְמַעַן הֲרוּגִים עַל שֵׁם קָדְשֶׁךָ.ⁿ

אָבִינוּ מַלְכֵּנוּ, עֲשֵׂה לְמַעַן טְבוּחִים עַל יִחוּדֶךָ.

אָבִינוּ מַלְכֵּנוּ, עֲשֵׂה לְמַעַן בָּאֵי בָאֵשׁ וּבַמַּיִם עַל קִדּוּשׁ שְׁמֶךָ.

אָבִינוּ מַלְכֵּנוּ, נְקֹם לְעֵינֵינוּ נִקְמַת דַּם עֲבָדֶיךָ הַשָּׁפוּךְ.

אָבִינוּ מַלְכֵּנוּ, עֲשֵׂה לְמַעַנְךָ אִם לֹא לְמַעֲנֵנוּ.

אָבִינוּ מַלְכֵּנוּ, עֲשֵׂה לְמַעַנְךָ וְהוֹשִׁיעֵנוּ.

אָבִינוּ מַלְכֵּנוּ, עֲשֵׂה לְמַעַן רַחֲמֶיךָ הָרַבִּים.

אָבִינוּ מַלְכֵּנוּ, עֲשֵׂה לְמַעַן שִׁמְךָ הַגָּדוֹל הַגִּבּוֹר וְהַנּוֹרָא
שֶׁנִּקְרָא עָלֵינוּ.

‹ אָבִינוּ מַלְכֵּנוּ, חָנֵּנוּ וַעֲנֵנוּ, כִּי אֵין בָּנוּ מַעֲשִׂים
עֲשֵׂה עִמָּנוּ צְדָקָה וָחֶסֶד וְהוֹשִׁיעֵנוּ.

The ארון קודש *is closed.*

ANI TEFILLA • אני תפילה

עֲשֵׂה לְמַעַן הֲרוּגִים עַל שֵׁם קָדְשֶׁךָ – *Act for the sake of those who were killed for Your holy name.*

The story is told that a Holocaust survivor asked Rav Itzikel from Antwerp the fol-

lowing question: We say in *Avinu Malkenu* "הֲרוּגִים עַל שֵׁם קָדְשֶׁךָ, those who were killed for Your holy name," and then "טְבוּחִים עַל יִחוּדֶךָ, slaughtered for proclaiming Your Unity." Why do we say two distinct phrases,

TAHANUN

On Mondays and Thursdays, when Tahanun is said, begin with "He is compassionate"
below. On other days when Tahanun is said, begin with "David said" on page 208.

Tahanun is not said on: Rosh Hodesh, Hanukka, Tu BiShvat, the 14th and 15th of Adar I, Purim
and Shushan Purim, in the month of Nisan, Yom HaAtzma'ut, the 14th of Iyar (Pesah Sheni),
Lag BaOmer, Yom Yerushalayim, from Rosh Hodesh Sivan through the day after Shavuot (in
Israel through 12th of Sivan), Tisha B'Av, Tu B'Av, Erev Rosh HaShana, and from Erev Yom
Kippur through the day after Simhat Torah (in Israel through Rosh Hodesh Marheshvan).

Tahanun is also not said: on the morning of a Brit Mila, either where the brit will take place
or where the father, Sandek or Mohel are present; if a groom is present (and some say a bride)
on the day of his wedding or during the week of Sheva Berakhot; in a house of mourning.

In Israel on days on which Tahanun is said, say Viduy and the
Thirteen Attributes of Divine Compassion on page 686

The following until "David said" on page 208 is said standing.

וְהוּא רַחוּם **He is compassionate.** He forgives iniquity and does not destroy. *Ps. 78*
Repeatedly He suppresses His anger, not rousing His full wrath. LORD, do
not withhold Your compassion from us. May Your loving-kindness and
truth always protect us. Save us, LORD our God, and gather us from among *Ps. 106*
the nations, that we may give thanks to Your holy name and glory in Your
praise. If You, LORD, should keep account of sins, O LORD, who could stand? *Ps. 130*
But with You is forgiveness, that You may be revered. Do not deal with us
according to our sins; do not repay us according to our iniquities. Though *Jer. 14*
our iniquities testify against us, LORD, act for Your name's sake. Remember, *Ps. 25*
LORD, Your compassion and loving-kindness, for they are everlasting. May *Ps. 20*

---

regularly, both as individuals and as a nation,
and that we are in need of God's help.

וְהוּא רַחוּם is one of those prayers of profound beauty, and the depth of individual
and national longing that the prayer ex-
presses is sometimes lost with a recitation
that is too quick and cursory.

While the source of the prayer is not
known for certain, there are a number of
differing traditions. One of the most famous,
and the one that may be closest to the historical truth, can be found in the siddur of
the Roke'ah (Rabbi Elazar of Worms, one
of the Torah giants of his generation), al-

though the story itself was already known
in the times of the Geonim, centuries before.

Vespasian drove three groups of dis-
tinguished Jerusalemites into exile. He
placed each group in a separate ship
without any navigator, and they trav-
eled as far as Europe: one group arriving
at Lyon, another at Arles and the third at
Bordeaux. This last group was cordially re-
ceived by the local duke. He allotted them
fields and vineyards and they lived there
peacefully for a long time, until that duke
died and a new king arose over them. He

This INTRODUCTION continues on page 203.

סדר תחנון

On Mondays and Thursdays, when תחנון *is said, begin with* וְהוּא רַחוּם *below.*
On other days when תחנון *is said, begin with* וַיֹּאמֶר דָּוִד *on page 209.*

תחנון *is not said on:* פורים (אדר א', the 14th and 15th of* חנוכה, ראש חודש, ט"ו בשבט, *and*
שושן פורים, *in the month of* ניסן (פסח שני) אייר, the 14th of* יום העצמאות, ל"ג בעומר, *through*
ירושלים ראש חודש סיון (in* ארץ ישראל *through* שבועות, the day after* יום ירושלים, *through*
the day after שמחת תורה (in* ארץ ישראל *through* ער ראש חודש, ער יום כיפור, *and from* ט' באב, תשעה באב, ער*).

תחנון *is also not said: on the morning of a* ברית מילה, *either where the* ברית *will take place*
or where the father, סנדק *or* מוהל *are present; if a* חתן *is present (and some say a* כלה)
on the day of his wedding or during the week of שבע ברכות; *in a house of mourning.*

In ארץ ישראל *on days on which* תחנון *is said, say* וידוי
and the י"ג מדות *on page 687*

The following until וַיֹּאמֶר דָּוִד *on page 209 is said standing.*

תהלים עח וְהוּא רַחוּם, יְכַפֵּר עָוֹן וְלֹא־יַשְׁחִית, וְהִרְבָּה לְהָשִׁיב אַפּוֹ וְלֹא־יָעִיר כָּל־
חֲמָתוֹ: אַתָּה יהוה לֹא־תִכְלָא רַחֲמֶיךָ מִמֶּנִּי, חַסְדְּךָ וַאֲמִתְּךָ תָּמִיד יִצְּרוּנִי.
תהלים קל הוֹשִׁיעֵנוּ יהוה אֱלֹהֵינוּ וְקַבְּצֵנוּ מִן־הַגּוֹיִם, לְהוֹדוֹת לְשֵׁם קָדְשֶׁךָ, לְהִשְׁתַּבֵּחַ
תהלים קל בִּתְהִלָּתֶךָ: אִם־עֲוֹנוֹת תִּשְׁמָר־יָהּ, אֲדֹנָי מִי יַעֲמֹד: כִּי־עִמְּךָ הַסְּלִיחָה לְמַעַן
ירמיה יד תִּוָּרֵא: לֹא כַחֲטָאֵינוּ תַּעֲשֶׂה לָּנוּ, וְלֹא כַעֲוֹנוֹתֵינוּ תִּגְמֹל עָלֵינוּ. אִם־עֲוֹנֵינוּ
תהלים כה עָנוּ בָנוּ, יהוה עֲשֵׂה לְמַעַן שְׁמֶךָ: זְכֹר־רַחֲמֶיךָ יהוה וַחֲסָדֶיךָ, כִּי מֵעוֹלָם
תהלים כ הֵמָּה: יַעַנְךָ יהוה בְּיוֹם צָרָה, יְשַׂגֶּבְךָ שֵׁם אֱלֹהֵי יַעֲקֹב. יהוה הוֹשִׁיעָה,

---

INTRODUCTION TO THE "LONG TAHANUN" OF MONDAYS AND THURSDAYS

Mondays and Thursdays have long been known as fortuitous days in Jewish life, marked especially as days that are worthy of prayers being answered. The most famous Thursday-Monday combination took place when Moshe Rabbeinu went up Mount Sinai a second time to get the commandments after *Benei Yisrael* erred the first time; according to tradition, Moshe went up the mountain on a Thursday and came back down with the second Tablets on a Monday (Tur, 134). Ever since, Mon-

days and Thursdays have been known as יְמֵי רָצוֹן, days that are particularly favorable for getting a positive response from Hashem, especially in response to requests for forgiveness and atonement. So advantageous were these days for repentance that another tradition is to fast every Monday and Thursday, as if each were a mini Yom Kippur!

As a result, Mondays and Thursdays became days for adding lots of prayers that focus on our recognition that we sin all too

the LORD answer us when we are in distress; may the name of Jacob's God protect us. LORD, save! May the King answer us when we call. Our Father, our King, be gracious to us and answer us, though we have no worthy deeds; act charitably with us for Your name's sake. LORD our God, hear the sound of our pleas. Remember for us the covenant of our ancestors, and save us for Your name's sake.

וְעַתָּה And now, My LORD, our God, who took Your people out of the land   *Dan. 9*
of Egypt with a mighty hand, creating for Yourself renown to this day: we have sinned and acted wrongly. LORD, in keeping with all Your righteousness, please turn Your wrath and anger away from Jerusalem, Your holy mountain. Because of our sins and the iniquities of our ancestors, Jerusalem and Your people have become the scorn of all those around us. And now, our God, heed Your servant's prayer and pleas, and let Your face shine on Your desolate Sanctuary, for Your sake, O LORD. Incline Your ear, my God, and hear. Open Your eyes and see our desolation and that of the city called by Your name. Not because of our righteousness do we lay our pleas before You, but because of Your great compassion. LORD, hear! LORD, forgive! LORD, listen and act! Do not delay – for Your sake, my God, because Your city and Your people are called by Your name.

אָבִינוּ Our Father, compassionate Father, show us a sign for good, and gather our scattered ones from the four quarters of the earth. Let all the nations recognize and know that You are the LORD our God. And now, LORD, You   *Is. 64*
are our Father. We are the clay and You are our Potter; we are all the work of Your hand. Save us for the sake of Your name, our Rock, our King and our Redeemer. Pity Your people, LORD. Let not Your heritage become an object   *Joel 2*
of scorn, a byword among nations. Why should they say among the peoples, "Where is their God?" We know we have sinned and that there is no one to stand up for us. Let Your great name stand up for us in time of trouble. We know we have no merits of our own: therefore deal with us charitably for Your name's sake. As a father has compassion on his children, so, LORD, have compassion on us, and save us for the sake of Your name. Have mercy

---

All of these prayers are culled from as many as 58 biblical sources, although in fewer than half are the verses quoted verbatim. The rest are merely modeled, in respect of their language, on biblical sentences. The expressions, "our Father, our King," "Merciful and gracious," "Save us for Your name's sake," "Look down..." (*Habet, habita*) especially, keep being repeated. There are 13 words in the sentence *Vehu Raḥum*, corresponding, perhaps, to the 13 *Middot*: *Hashem Hashem Kel Raḥum* etc.

הַמֶּלֶךְ יַעֲנֵנוּ בְיוֹם־קָרְאֵנוּ: אָבִינוּ מַלְכֵּנוּ, חָנֵּנוּ וַעֲנֵנוּ, כִּי אֵין בָּנוּ מַעֲשִׂים, צְדָקָה עֲשֵׂה עִמָּנוּ לְמַעַן שְׁמֶךָ. אֲדוֹנֵינוּ אֱלֹהֵינוּ, שְׁמַע קוֹל תַּחֲנוּנֵינוּ, וּזְכָר לָנוּ אֶת בְּרִית אֲבוֹתֵינוּ וְהוֹשִׁיעֵנוּ לְמַעַן שְׁמֶךָ.

וְעַתָּה אֲדֹנָי אֱלֹהֵינוּ, אֲשֶׁר הוֹצֵאתָ אֶת־עַמְּךָ מֵאֶרֶץ מִצְרַיִם בְּיָד חֲזָקָה דניאל ט וַתַּעַשׂ־לְךָ שֵׁם כַּיּוֹם הַזֶּה, חָטָאנוּ רָשָׁעְנוּ: אֲדֹנָי, כְּכָל־צִדְקֹתֶךָ יָשָׁב־נָא אַפְּךָ וַחֲמָתְךָ, מֵעִירְךָ יְרוּשָׁלַיִם הַר־קָדְשֶׁךָ, כִּי בַחֲטָאֵינוּ וּבַעֲוֹנוֹת אֲבֹתֵינוּ, יְרוּשָׁלַיִם וְעַמְּךָ לְחֶרְפָּה לְכָל־סְבִיבֹתֵינוּ: וְעַתָּה שְׁמַע אֱלֹהֵינוּ אֶל־תְּפִלַּת עַבְדְּךָ וְאֶל־תַּחֲנוּנָיו, וְהָאֵר פָּנֶיךָ עַל־מִקְדָּשְׁךָ הַשָּׁמֵם, לְמַעַן אֲדֹנָי: הַטֵּה אֱלֹהַי אָזְנְךָ וּשֲׁמָע, פְּקַח עֵינֶיךָ וּרְאֵה שֹׁמְמֹתֵינוּ וְהָעִיר אֲשֶׁר־נִקְרָא שִׁמְךָ עָלֶיהָ, כִּי לֹא עַל־צִדְקֹתֵינוּ אֲנַחְנוּ מַפִּילִים תַּחֲנוּנֵינוּ לְפָנֶיךָ, כִּי עַל־רַחֲמֶיךָ הָרַבִּים: אֲדֹנָי שְׁמָעָה, אֲדֹנָי סְלָחָה, אֲדֹנָי הַקְשִׁיבָה וַעֲשֵׂה אַל־תְּאַחַר, לְמַעַנְךָ אֱלֹהַי, כִּי־שִׁמְךָ נִקְרָא עַל־עִירְךָ וְעַל־עַמֶּךָ:

אָבִינוּ הָאָב הָרַחֲמָן, הַרְאֵנוּ אוֹת לְטוֹבָה וְקַבֵּץ נְפוּצוֹתֵינוּ מֵאַרְבַּע כַּנְפוֹת הָאָרֶץ. יַכִּירוּ וְיֵדְעוּ כָּל הַגּוֹיִם כִּי אַתָּה יהוה הוּא אֱלֹהֵינוּ. וְעַתָּה יהוה אָבִינוּ ישעיה סד אַתָּה, אֲנַחְנוּ הַחֹמֶר וְאַתָּה יֹצְרֵנוּ וּמַעֲשֵׂה יָדְךָ כֻּלָּנוּ: הוֹשִׁיעֵנוּ לְמַעַן שְׁמֶךָ, צוּרֵנוּ מַלְכֵּנוּ וְגוֹאֲלֵנוּ. חוּסָה יהוה עַל־עַמֶּךָ, וְאַל־תִּתֵּן נַחֲלָתְךָ יואל ב לְחֶרְפָּה לִמְשָׁל־בָּם גּוֹיִם, לָמָּה יֹאמְרוּ בָעַמִּים אַיֵּה אֱלֹהֵיהֶם: יְדַעְנוּ כִּי חָטָאנוּ וְאֵין מִי יַעֲמֹד בַּעֲדֵנוּ, שִׁמְךָ הַגָּדוֹל יַעֲמָד־לָנוּ בְּעֵת צָרָה. יָדַעְנוּ כִּי אֵין בָּנוּ מַעֲשִׂים, צְדָקָה עֲשֵׂה עִמָּנוּ לְמַעַן שְׁמֶךָ. כְּרַחֵם אָב עַל בָּנִים כֵּן תְּרַחֵם יהוה עָלֵינוּ, וְהוֹשִׁיעֵנוּ לְמַעַן שְׁמֶךָ. חֲמֹל עַל עַמֶּךָ, רַחֵם עַל

---

imposed new restrictions upon them and they suffered very much. Among them were two brothers, Joseph and Benjamin, and their cousin, Samuel. They cried out to God in their distress, fasted, donned sackcloth on their flesh, and the three together composed the Vehu Raḥum prayer. Joseph is designated as the composer of the first part, Vehu Raḥum, to the end

of the paragraph Habet Na, which also ends with the words Vehu Raḥum. The second part, from Ana Melekh to the end of the paragraph Raḥum, the last words of which are Raḥum Ata, was composed by Samuel. The third part, from Ein Ka-mokha to the end of the paragraph beginning with Hapote'aḥ, was composed by Benjamin.

on Your people; have compassion for Your heritage; take pity in Your great compassion. Be gracious to us and answer us, for righteousness is Yours, LORD. Always You do wondrous things.

הַבֶּט נָא Please look, please swiftly have compassion for Your people for Your name's sake. In Your great compassion, LORD our God, have pity and compassion, and rescue the flock You tend. Let us not be ruled by wrath, for our eyes are turned toward You. Save us for Your name's sake. Have compassion on us for the sake of Your covenant. Look and answer us in time of trouble, for Yours, LORD, is the power to save. Our hope is in You, God of forgiveness. Please forgive, good and forgiving God, for You are a gracious, compassionate God and King.

אָנָא מֶלֶךְ Please, gracious and compassionate King, remember and call to mind the Covenant between the Pieces [with Abraham] and let the binding of his only son [Isaac] appear before You for Israel's sake. Our Father, our King, be gracious to us and answer us, for we are called by Your great name. You who work miracles at all times, deal with us according to Your loving-kindness. Gracious and compassionate One, look and answer us in time of trouble, for salvation is Yours, LORD. Our Father, our King, our Refuge, do not act with us according to our evil deeds. Remember, LORD, Your tender mercies and Your love. Save us in Your great goodness, and have mercy on us, for we have no other god but You, our Rock. Do not abandon us, LORD our God, do not be distant from us, for we are worn out by the sword and captivity, pestilence and plague, and by every trouble and sorrow. Rescue us, for in You lies our hope. Put us not to shame, LORD our God. Let Your face shine upon us. Remember for us the covenant of our ancestors and save us for Your name's sake. See our troubles and heed the voice of our prayer, for You heed the prayer of every mouth.

אֵל רַחוּם וְחַנּוּן O Compassionate and gracious God, have compassion on us and on all Your works, for there is none like You, LORD our God. Please, we beg You, forgive our sins, our Father, our King, our Rock, our Redeemer, living and eternal God, mighty in strength, loving and good to all Your works, for You are the LORD our God. O God, slow to anger and full of compassion, act with us according to Your great compassion and save us for Your name's sake. Hear our prayer, our King, and save us from our enemies' hands. Heed our prayer, our King, and save us from all distress and sorrow. You are our Father, our King. We are called by Your name. Do not desert us. Do not abandon us, our Father. Do not cast us away, our Creator. Do not forget us, our Maker – for You are a gracious and compassionate God and King.

נַחֲלָתֶךָ, חוּסָה נָּא כְּרֹב רַחֲמֶיךָ, חָנֵּנוּ וַעֲנֵנוּ. כִּי לְךָ יהוה הַצְּדָקָה, עֹשֵׂה נִפְלָאוֹת בְּכָל עֵת.

הַבֶּט נָא, רַחֵם נָּא עַל עַמְּךָ מְהֵרָה לְמַעַן שְׁמֶךָ בְּרַחֲמֶיךָ הָרַבִּים יהוה אֱלֹהֵינוּ. חוּס וְרַחֵם וְהוֹשִׁיעָה צֹאן מַרְעִיתֶךָ, וְאַל יִמְשָׁל בָּנוּ קָצֶף, כִּי לְךָ עֵינֵינוּ תְלוּיוֹת. הוֹשִׁיעֵנוּ לְמַעַן שְׁמֶךָ. רַחֵם עָלֵינוּ לְמַעַן בְּרִיתֶךָ. הַבִּיטָה וַעֲנֵנוּ בְּעֵת צָרָה, כִּי לְךָ יהוה הַיְשׁוּעָה. בְּךָ תוֹחַלְתֵּנוּ אֱלוֹהַּ סְלִיחוֹת, אָנָּא סְלַח נָא אֵל טוֹב וְסַלָּח, כִּי אֵל מֶלֶךְ חַנּוּן וְרַחוּם אָתָּה.

אָנָּא מֶלֶךְ חַנּוּן וְרַחוּם, זְכֹר וְהַבֵּט לִבְרִית בֵּין הַבְּתָרִים, וְתֵרָאֶה לְפָנֶיךָ עֲקֵדַת יָחִיד לְמַעַן יִשְׂרָאֵל. אָבִינוּ מַלְכֵּנוּ, חָנֵּנוּ וַעֲנֵנוּ, כִּי שִׁמְךָ הַגָּדוֹל נִקְרָא עָלֵינוּ. עֹשֵׂה נִפְלָאוֹת בְּכָל עֵת, עֲשֵׂה עִמָּנוּ כְּחַסְדֶּךָ. חַנּוּן וְרַחוּם, הַבִּיטָה וַעֲנֵנוּ בְּעֵת צָרָה, כִּי לְךָ יהוה הַיְשׁוּעָה. אָבִינוּ מַלְכֵּנוּ מַחֲסֵנוּ, אַל תַּעַשׂ עִמָּנוּ כְּרֹעַ מַעֲלָלֵינוּ. זְכֹר רַחֲמֶיךָ יהוה וַחֲסָדֶיךָ, וּכְרֹב טוּבְךָ הוֹשִׁיעֵנוּ. וַחֲמָל נָא עָלֵינוּ, כִּי אֵין לָנוּ אֱלוֹהַּ אַחֵר מִבַּלְעָדֶיךָ צוּרֵנוּ. אַל תַּעַזְבֵנוּ יהוה אֱלֹהֵינוּ אַל תִּרְחַק מִמֶּנּוּ. כִּי נַפְשֵׁנוּ קָצְרָה, מֵחֶרֶב וּמִשְּׁבִי וּמִדֶּבֶר וּמִמַּגֵּפָה. וּמִכָּל צָרָה וְיָגוֹן הַצִּילֵנוּ, כִּי לְךָ קִוִּינוּ. וְאַל תַּכְלִימֵנוּ יהוה אֱלֹהֵינוּ, וְהָאֵר פָּנֶיךָ בָּנוּ, וּזְכֹר לָנוּ אֶת בְּרִית אֲבוֹתֵינוּ וְהוֹשִׁיעֵנוּ לְמַעַן שְׁמֶךָ. רְאֵה בְּצָרוֹתֵינוּ, וּשְׁמַע קוֹל תְּפִלָּתֵנוּ, כִּי אַתָּה שׁוֹמֵעַ תְּפִלַּת כָּל פֶּה.

אֵל רַחוּם וְחַנּוּן, רַחֵם עָלֵינוּ וְעַל כָּל מַעֲשֶׂיךָ, כִּי אֵין כָּמוֹךָ יהוה אֱלֹהֵינוּ. אָנָּא שָׂא נָא פְשָׁעֵינוּ, אָבִינוּ מַלְכֵּנוּ צוּרֵנוּ וְגֹאֲלֵנוּ, אֵל חַי וְקַיָּם הֶחָסִין בַּכֹּחַ, חָסִיד וְטוֹב עַל כָּל מַעֲשֶׂיךָ, כִּי אַתָּה הוּא יהוה אֱלֹהֵינוּ. אֵל אֶרֶךְ אַפַּיִם וּמָלֵא רַחֲמִים, עֲשֵׂה עִמָּנוּ כְּרֹב רַחֲמֶיךָ, וְהוֹשִׁיעֵנוּ לְמַעַן שְׁמֶךָ. שְׁמַע מַלְכֵּנוּ תְּפִלָּתֵנוּ, וּמִיַּד אוֹיְבֵינוּ הַצִּילֵנוּ. שְׁמַע מַלְכֵּנוּ תְּפִלָּתֵנוּ, וּמִכָּל צָרָה וְיָגוֹן הַצִּילֵנוּ. אָבִינוּ מַלְכֵּנוּ אַתָּה, וְשִׁמְךָ עָלֵינוּ נִקְרָא. אַל תַּנִּיחֵנוּ, אַל תַּעַזְבֵנוּ אָבִינוּ וְאַל תִּטְּשֵׁנוּ וְאַל תִּשְׁכָּחֵנוּ בּוֹרְאֵנוּ וְאַל תַּשְׁחִיתֵנוּ יוֹצְרֵנוּ, כִּי אֵל מֶלֶךְ חַנּוּן וְרַחוּם אָתָּה.

אֵין כָּמֽוֹךָ **There is none like You** in grace and compassion, LORD our God. There is none like You, God, slow to anger and abounding in loving-kindness and truth. Save us in Your great compassion; rescue us from storm and turmoil. Remember Your servants Abraham, Isaac and Jacob; do not attend to our stubbornness, wickedness and sinfulness. Turn from Your fierce anger, and relent from the evil meant for Your people. Remove from us the scourge of death, for You are compassionate. This is Your way, to show unearned loving-kindness to every generation. Have pity on Your people, LORD, and save us from Your wrath. Remove from us the scourge of plague and the harsh decree, for You are the Guardian of Israel. You are right, my LORD, and we are shamefaced. How can we complain? What can we say? What can we plead? How can we justify ourselves? Let us search our ways and examine them and return to You, for Your right hand is outstretched to receive those who return. Please, LORD, please save. Please, LORD, please send success. Please, LORD, answer us when we call. For You, LORD, we wait. For You, LORD, we hope. For You, LORD, we long. Do not be silent while we suffer, for the nations are saying, "Their hope is lost." To You alone every knee must bend, and those who hold themselves high bow down.

Ex. 32

Ps. 118

הַפּוֹתֵֽחַ יָד **You who hold out** an open hand of repentance to receive transgressors and sinners – our soul is overwhelmed by our great sorrow. Do not forget us for ever. Arise and save us, for we seek refuge in You. Our Father, our King, though we lack righteousness and good deeds, remember for us the covenant of our fathers, and our testimonies daily that "The LORD is One." Look on our affliction, for many are our sufferings and heartaches. Have pity on us, LORD, in the land of our captivity. Do not pour out Your wrath on us, for we are Your people, the children of Your covenant. God, see how low our glory has sunk among the nations. They abhor us as if we were impure. How long will Your strength be captive, and Your glory in the hand of the foe? Arouse Your strength and zeal against Your enemies. Let them be shamed and deprived of power. Let not our hardships seem small to You. Swiftly may Your compassion reach us in the day of our distress. If not for our sake, act for Yours, so that the memory of our survivors be not destroyed. Be gracious to the nation who, in constant love, proclaim twice daily the unity of Your name, saying, "Listen, Israel, the LORD is our God, the LORD is One."

Deut. 6

According to the Tur, Rabbi Yaakov ben Asher, that's the meaning of *Nefilat Apayim* or "falling down on one's face" immediately after the *Shemoneh Esreh*. You've just finished asking for everything, you've just finished saying everything there was to say, but somehow words have failed you and now there's nothing left to do but throw

This INTRODUCTION continues on page 209.

אֵין כָּמוֹךָ חַנּוּן וְרַחוּם יהוה אֱלֹהֵינוּ, אֵין כָּמוֹךָ אֵל אֶרֶךְ אַפַּיִם וְרַב חֶסֶד
וֶאֱמֶת. הוֹשִׁיעֵנוּ בְּרַחֲמֶיךָ הָרַבִּים, מֵרַעַשׁ וּמֵרֹגֶז הַצִּילֵנוּ. זְכֹר לַעֲבָדֶיךָ
לְאַבְרָהָם לְיִצְחָק וּלְיַעֲקֹב, אַל תֵּפֶן אֶל קָשְׁיֵנוּ וְאֶל רִשְׁעֵנוּ וְאֶל חַטָּאתֵנוּ.

שמות לב שׁוּב מֵחֲרוֹן אַפֶּךָ, וְהִנָּחֵם עַל הָרָעָה לְעַמֶּךָ: וְהָסֵר מִמֶּנּוּ מַכַּת הַמָּוֶת כִּי
רַחוּם אָתָּה, כִּי כֵן דַּרְכֶּךָ, עֹשֶׂה חֶסֶד חִנָּם בְּכָל דּוֹר וָדוֹר. חוּסָה יהוה עַל
עַמֶּךָ וְהַצִּילֵנוּ מִזַּעְמֶךָ, וְהָסֵר מִמֶּנּוּ מַכַּת הַמַּגֵּפָה וּגְזֵרָה קָשָׁה, כִּי אַתָּה
שׁוֹמֵר יִשְׂרָאֵל. לְךָ אֲדֹנָי הַצְּדָקָה וְלָנוּ בֹּשֶׁת הַפָּנִים: מַה נִּתְאוֹנֵן, מַה נֹּאמַר,

דניאל ט מַה נְּדַבֵּר וּמַה נִּצְטַדָּק. נַחְפְּשָׂה דְרָכֵינוּ וְנַחְקֹרָה וְנָשׁוּבָה אֵלֶיךָ, כִּי יְמִינְךָ
פְּשׁוּטָה לְקַבֵּל שָׁבִים. אָנָּא יהוה הוֹשִׁיעָה נָּא, אָנָּא יהוה הַצְלִיחָה נָּא:

תהלים קיח אָנָּא יהוה עֲנֵנוּ בְיוֹם קָרְאֵנוּ. לְךָ יהוה חִכִּינוּ, לְךָ יהוה קִוִּינוּ, לְךָ יהוה
נְיַחֵל. אַל תֶּחֱשֶׁה וּתְעַנֵּנוּ, כִּי נֶאֶמְרוּ גוֹיִם, אָבְדָה תִקְוָתָם. כָּל בֶּרֶךְ וְכָל
קוֹמָה, לְךָ לְבַד תִּשְׁתַּחֲוֶה.

הַפּוֹתֵחַ יָד בִּתְשׁוּבָה לְקַבֵּל פּוֹשְׁעִים וְחַטָּאִים, נִבְהֲלָה נַפְשֵׁנוּ מֵרֹב עִצְּבוֹנֵנוּ.
אַל תִּשְׁכָּחֵנוּ נֶצַח, קוּמָה וְהוֹשִׁיעֵנוּ כִּי חָסִינוּ בָךְ. אָבִינוּ מַלְכֵּנוּ, אִם אֵין
בָּנוּ צְדָקָה וּמַעֲשִׂים טוֹבִים, זְכָר לָנוּ אֶת בְּרִית אֲבוֹתֵינוּ וְעֵדוֹתֵנוּ בְּכָל
יוֹם יהוה אֶחָד. הַבִּיטָה בְעָנְיֵנוּ, כִּי רַבּוּ מַכְאוֹבֵינוּ וְצָרוֹת לְבָבֵנוּ. חוּסָה
יהוה עָלֵינוּ בְּאֶרֶץ שִׁבְיֵנוּ, וְאַל תִּשְׁפֹּךְ חֲרוֹנְךָ עָלֵינוּ, כִּי אֲנַחְנוּ עַמְּךָ בְּנֵי
בְרִיתֶךָ. אֵל, הַבִּיטָה, דַּל כְּבוֹדֵנוּ בַגּוֹיִם וְשִׁקְּצוּנוּ כְּטֻמְאַת הַנִּדָּה. עַד מָתַי
עֻזְּךָ בַּשֶּׁבִי, וְתִפְאַרְתְּךָ בְּיַד צָר. עוֹרְרָה גְבוּרָתְךָ וְקִנְאָתְךָ עַל אוֹיְבֶיךָ. הֵם
יֵבֹשׁוּ וְיֵחַתּוּ מִגְּבוּרָתָם. וְאַל יִמְעֲטוּ לְפָנֶיךָ תְּלָאוֹתֵינוּ, מַהֵר יְקַדְּמוּנוּ רַחֲמֶיךָ
בְּיוֹם צָרָתֵנוּ. וְאִם לֹא לְמַעֲנֵנוּ, לְמַעַנְךָ פְּעָל, וְאַל תַּשְׁחִית זֵכֶר שְׁאֵרִיתֵנוּ,

דברים ו וְחָן אִם הַמְּיַחֲדִים שִׁמְךָ פַּעֲמַיִם בְּכָל יוֹם תָּמִיד בְּאַהֲבָה, וְאוֹמְרִים, שְׁמַע
יִשְׂרָאֵל, יהוה אֱלֹהֵינוּ, יהוה אֶחָד:

INTRODUCTION TO TAḤANUN – תחנון: נפילת אפים

Did you ever try to say something important, but couldn't get the words out just right?

Did you ever try to say something, but couldn't say it with enough feeling or passion?

Did you ever have an emotion so deep (love, frustration, anger) that you couldn't even speak, but needed to physically act out by giving someone a hug or throwing yourself onto your bed?

LOWERING THE HEAD

On Sundays, Tuesdays, Wednesdays and Fridays, begin Taḥanun here.
The following, until "We do not know" on page 214, is said sitting. When praying
in a place where there is a Torah scroll, one should lean forward, resting one's
head on the left arm (unless you are wearing tefillin on the left arm, in which case
rest on the right arm out of respect for the tefillin), until "in sudden shame."

וַיֹּאמֶר דָּוִד David said[ʰ] to Gad, "I am in great distress.   *II Sam. 24*
Let us fall into God's hand, for His mercy is great;
but do not let me fall into the hand of man."

Compassionate and gracious One, I have sinned before You.
LORD, full of compassion, have compassion on me and accept my pleas.

LORD, do not rebuke me in Your anger or chastise me in Your wrath. Be gracious   *Ps. 6*
to me,[ᴮ] LORD, for I am weak. Heal me, LORD,[ᴮ] for my bones are in agony.[ᴮ] My
soul is in anguish, and You, O LORD – how long? Turn, LORD, set my soul free;
save me for the sake of Your love. For no one remembers You when he is dead.
Who can praise You from the grave? I am weary with my sighing.[ᴵ] Every night
I drench my bed, I soak my couch with my tears. My eye grows dim from grief,
worn out because of all my foes. Leave me, all you evildoers, for the LORD has
heard the sound of my weeping.[ᴬ] The LORD has heard[ᴵ] my pleas. The LORD will
accept my prayer. All my enemies will be shamed and utterly dismayed. They will
turn back in sudden shame.

Sit upright.

The Tefilla continues on page 212.

---

of Moshe's life and leadership, you can just
imagine how heartfelt, how desperate, how
pleading was that prayer. That's *Taḥanun*.

There's a verse in *Mishlei* (18:23) which
says: תַּחֲנוּנִים יְדַבֶּר רָשׁ וְעָשִׁיר יַעֲנֶה עַזּוֹת –
"The poor person speaks entreatingly
(*taḥanunim*)…" Did you ever see a home-
less person on the street asking for some
money for a cup of coffee? Did you ever
encounter a poor person at the *Kotel* asking
for *tzedaka*, and you were truly moved by

the sense of need the person seemed to
convey? Did you ever have someone stand
outside your door asking for a small amount
and you felt so badly for them because of
the way they spoke to you or appeared to
you that you felt like you just had to give
them something? How did these needy
people present themselves? How did they
speak? How did they act?
**Imagine yourself the poor person. Now
say *Taḥanun*.**

HILKHOT TEFILLA · הלכות תפילה

וַיֹּאמֶר דָּוִד – *David said*. Ḥazal learn that
there is a prohibition from the Torah to fully
prostrate oneself on a stone floor. This is

learned from the verse: "You shall not make
idols for yourselves, neither shall you raise
up an engraved image or a pillar, neither

This HILKHOT TEFILLA continues on page 211. The commentary on Psalm 6 is on page 210.

נפילת אפים

On Sundays, Tuesdays, Wednesdays and Fridays, begin תחנון *here.*
The following, until וַאֲנַחְנוּ לֹא נֵדַע *on page 215, is said sitting. When praying*
in a place where there is a סֵפֶר תּוֹרָה, *one should lean forward, resting one's*
head on the left arm (unless you are wearing תְּפִילִין *on the left arm, in which*
case rest on the right arm out of respect for the tefillin), until יָבֹשׁוּ רָגַע.

שמואל ב, כד

וַיֹּאמֶר דָּוִד אֶל־גָּד, צַר־לִי מְאֹד
נִפְּלָה־נָּא בְיַד־יהוה, כִּי־רַבִּים רַחֲמָו, וּבְיַד־אָדָם אַל־אֶפֹּלָה:

רַחוּם וְחַנּוּן, חָטָאתִי לְפָנֶיךָ:

יהוה מָלֵא רַחֲמִים, רַחֵם עָלַי וְקַבֵּל תַּחֲנוּנָי:

תהלים ו

יהוה, אַל־בְּאַפְּךָ תוֹכִיחֵנִי, וְאַל־בַּחֲמָתְךָ תְיַסְּרֵנִי: חָנֵּנִי יהוה, כִּי אֻמְלַל אָנִי,
רְפָאֵנִי יהוה, כִּי נִבְהֲלוּ עֲצָמָי: וְנַפְשִׁי נִבְהֲלָה מְאֹד, וְאַתָּ יהוה, עַד־מָתָי:
שׁוּבָה יהוה, חַלְּצָה נַפְשִׁי, הוֹשִׁיעֵנִי לְמַעַן חַסְדֶּךָ: כִּי אֵין בַּמָּוֶת זִכְרֶךָ, בִּשְׁאוֹל
מִי יוֹדֶה־לָּךְ: יָגַעְתִּי בְּאַנְחָתִי, אַשְׂחֶה בְכָל־לַיְלָה מִטָּתִי, בְּדִמְעָתִי עַרְשִׂי
אַמְסֶה: עָשְׁשָׁה מִכַּעַס עֵינִי, עָתְקָה בְּכָל־צוֹרְרָי: סוּרוּ מִמֶּנִּי כָּל־פֹּעֲלֵי אָוֶן,
כִּי־שָׁמַע יהוה קוֹל בִּכְיִי: שָׁמַע יהוה תְּחִנָּתִי, יהוה תְּפִלָּתִי יִקָּח: יֵבֹשׁוּ
וְיִבָּהֲלוּ מְאֹד כָּל־אֹיְבָי, יָשֻׁבוּ יֵבֹשׁוּ רָגַע:

Sit upright.
The תְּפִילָה *continues on page 213.*

---

your body down and prostrate yourself before the Creator of the Universe who knows and understands all.

Apparently prayer isn't just something you do with your heart alone. You can do it with your body too. In fact, what we do with our bodies can have an effect on our hearts. (Why stand for the national anthem?) At other times, our heart comes first – you feel so strongly about something that you just have to physically display your emotion, for example, jump for joy, stand at attention, throw yourself on your bed.

That seems to be what the Tur is saying: during *tefilla* we resort to different physical displays of emotion, and if we don't

feel that emotion, the physical action is supposed to help us to feel it – to get us in the mood. Throughout *Keriat Shema* and its *berakhot*, we remain seated. Then, in the *Shemoneh Esreh*, standing upright is the appropriate posture – that, after all, is why it is called the *Amida*. There is but one physical pose left to express ourselves, namely falling to the ground and throwing ourselves, as it were, at Hashem's mercy. That's *Tahanun*.

Interestingly, much about this prayer is learned from Moshe Rabbeinu. In particular, note that in *Parashat VaEt-hanan*, Moshe pleads with Hashem to permit him to enter the Promised Land. If you recall the story

ביאור תפילה • BIUR TEFILLA

חָנֵּנִי יהוה – *Be gracious to me, Lord.* Note the word חָנֵּנִי (find favor, or חֵן) is related to the word תַּחֲנוּן. Find another related word later in this psalm.

רְפָאֵנִי יהוה – *Heal me, Lord.* There are those who say that the word רְפָאֵנִי asks for a cure from a physical illness. Others say it refers to spiritual illness.

Which do you think is more in keeping with the rest of the psalm?

כִּי נִבְהֲלוּ עֲצָמָי – *For my bones are in agony.* Note that the translation which appears here translates the word נִבְהֲלוּ differently in this verse and the next verse.

Why? Would you have done the same?

עיון תפילה • IYUN TEFILLA

יָגַעְתִּי בְּאַנְחָתִי – *I am weary with my sighing.* This verse refers specifically to crying in one's bed at night.

Why does it use this analogy? Did you ever cry at night? What for? Did you ever cry to God at night? What for?

Radak suggests that this expression is used because, (a) one is so worried and in pain that one cries oneself to sleep every night; (b) it is harder to bear things at night than it is during the day; (c) at night everyone else is asleep and one can cry in the privacy of one's room without anyone else seeing or hearing.

Which, if any, of these means the most to you today?

אני תפילה • ANI TEFILLA

קוֹל בִּכְיִי – *The sound of my weeping.* To what may this be compared? To a wealthy man who bought his son very expensive clothes. The young man walked outside in the clothes in order to show off in front of his friends, and he jumped into a muddy puddle and dirtied his clothes. The boy said: Better that I should go personally and tell my father that I ruined my clothes, than he should hear about it from others. And so it happened.

When he came to his father and admitted his wrongdoing, his father forgave him. That is the same thing that the poet said to his enemies: *סוּרוּ מִמֶּנִּי כָּל־פֹּעֲלֵי אָוֶן, כִּי שָׁמַע יהוה קוֹל בִּכְיִי.* (Me'am Loez)

Explain the parable: (a) Who is the king? (b) Who is the son? (c) What does the muddy puddle represent? (d) What do the expensive clothes represent? (e) What is the cause of the crying in the psalm?

עיון תפילה • IYUN TEFILLA

שָׁמַע יהוה – *The Lord has heard.* Verse 10 from this chapter of *Tehillim* (beginning with the words שָׁמַע יהוה) is very positive in outlook. It may well be that verse 10 corresponds to,

and is a response to, verse 3 (beginning with the words חָנֵּנִי יהוה – look in the Hebrew. Can you spot the recurring root? How is it a response?

shall you place any figured stone in your land, to bow down to it; for I am Hashem your God" (*Vayikra* 26:1). The Gemara (*Megilla* 22b) concludes from this that one may not fully prostrate oneself on a stone floor other than that of the *Beit HaMikdash*: "אֲבָל אַתָּה מִשְׁתַּחֲוֶה עַל אֲבָנִים שֶׁל בֵּית הַמִּקְדָּשׁ אִי אַתָּה מִשְׁתַּחֲוֶה בְּאַרְצְכֶם"

Needless to say, the Gemara and subsequent authorities don't leave it at that. For example, what constitutes prostrating oneself? (Answer: כְּרִיעָה refers to bowing; קִדָּה refers to bowing down on the floor and covering one's face; הִשְׁתַּחֲוָיָה is considered getting down on the floor and extending one's hands and legs.) Which one is forbidden? And where? And on what kind of floor? And why? Is it forbidden because it is a pagan practice? Or is it forbidden because you may not do a *Beit HaMikdash*-like act outside of the *Beit HaMikdash*?

The bottom line is that except for Yom Kippur and Rosh HaShana, we never bow down on the floor. But then how is one supposed to do *Taḥanun*, given that its very definition is to "fall on one's face"?! The custom therefore developed instead to compromise by bowing one's head down on one's arm, usually tilted to the side, and covering one's face with something. It's a kind of symbolic "falling on one's face," or נְפִילַת אַפַּיִם.

Now just as your face is hidden when you lie face-down on the floor, so, too, ideally, should one's face be covered during *Taḥanun*. But here, too, we compromise by making sure that there is still some kind of separation between our head and the surface. That's one reason why many people make sure to wear long sleeves when they pray, because there are authorities which suggest that if you try to

cover a body part (your face) with a body part (your bare arm) that's not really the kind of external separator that is required. (Similarly, there are those who say that men shouldn't use their hand on their head instead of a *kippa* in order to make a blessing.) So next time you see someone struggling to pull their short sleeve down further to cover their arm, know that it's not their arm they are worried about, but their נְפִילַת אַפַּיִם.

One generally leans on one's left side, for that is the way of "free men and kings" (Rabbi Hai Gaon), as we do during the Pesaḥ Seder, although the Ashkenazi *minhag* is for men to lean on the right side when tefillin are on their left, so as not to "embarrass" the tefillin (Rema 131:1). Still, there are some who lean on the left hand regardless (the Vilna Gaon, Rabbi J.B. Soloveitchik).

There is a widespread custom not to "fall down" unless there is a *sefer Torah* present, since we learn the "falling down" from King David, who did so in the presence of a *sefer Torah*. Others suggest that having printed *sefarim* in the vicinity would also suffice. Interestingly, if you are in Jerusalem (perhaps only the Old City), then you are always considered to be in front of *Aron Hashem*, and so no *sefer Torah* is necessary.

Because of the somber mood of the prayer that focuses on our frailties, *Taḥanun* is not recited on festive days or days of great gladness, thus leading to frequent disputes in *shul*s as to what days would qualify. For example, Hasidim often don't say it on the day of the *yahrtzeit* of a great *tzaddik* (considered a festive rather than a sad day from a kabbalistic perspective), although there are those who disagree with this practice.

On Mondays and Thursdays, say the following.
On other days, continue with "Guardian of Israel" below.

> LORD, God of Israel, turn away from Your fierce anger,
> and relent from the evil against Your people.

Look down from heaven and see how we have become an object of scorn and derision among the nations. We are regarded as sheep led to the slaughter, to be killed, destroyed, beaten and humiliated. Yet, despite all this, we have not forgotten Your name. Please do not forget us.

> LORD, God of Israel, turn away from Your fierce anger,
> and relent from the evil against Your people.

Strangers say, "You have no hope or expectation." Be gracious to the nation whose hope is in Your name. O Pure One, bring our deliverance close. We are exhausted. We are given no rest. May Your compassion suppress Your anger against us. Please turn away from Your fierce anger, and have compassion on the people You chose as Your own.

> LORD, God of Israel, turn away from Your fierce anger,
> and relent from the evil against Your people.

Have pity on us, LORD, in Your compassion, and do not hand us over to cruel oppressors. Why should the nations say, "Where is their God now?" For Your own sake, deal kindly with us, and do not delay. Please turn away from Your fierce anger, and have compassion on the people You chose as Your own.

> LORD, God of Israel, turn away from Your fierce anger,
> and relent from the evil against Your people.

Heed our voice and be gracious. Do not abandon us into the hand of our enemies to blot out our name. Remember what You promised our fathers: "I will make your descendants as many as the stars of heaven" – yet now we are only a few left from many. Yet, despite all this, we have not forgotten Your name. Please do not forget us.

> LORD, God of Israel, turn away from Your fierce anger,
> and relent from the evil against Your people.

Help us, God of our salvation, for the sake of the glory of Your name. Save us and   *Ps. 79*
pardon our sins for Your name's sake.

> LORD, God of Israel, turn away from Your fierce anger,
> and relent from the evil against Your people.

On all days continue here:

שׁוֹמֵר יִשְׂרָאֵל Guardian of Israel, guard the remnant of Israel,
> and let not Israel perish, who declare, "Listen, Israel."

Guardian of a unique nation, guard the remnant of a unique people,
> and let not that unique nation perish, who proclaim the unity
> of Your name [saying], "The LORD is our God, the LORD is One."

On Mondays and Thursdays, say the following.
On other days, continue with שׁוֹמֵר יִשְׂרָאֵל *below.*

יהוה אֱלֹהֵי יִשְׂרָאֵל, שׁוּב מֵחֲרוֹן אַפֶּךָ וְהִנָּחֵם עַל הָרָעָה לְעַמֶּךָ.

הַבֵּט מִשָּׁמַיִם וּרְאֵה כִּי הָיִינוּ לַעַג וָקֶלֶס בַּגּוֹיִם, נֶחְשַׁבְנוּ כַּצֹּאן לַטֶּבַח יוּבָל, לַהֲרֹג וּלְאַבֵּד וּלְמַכָּה וּלְחֶרְפָּה. וּבְכָל זֹאת שִׁמְךָ לֹא שָׁכָחְנוּ, נָא אַל תִּשְׁכָּחֵנוּ.

יהוה אֱלֹהֵי יִשְׂרָאֵל, שׁוּב מֵחֲרוֹן אַפֶּךָ וְהִנָּחֵם עַל הָרָעָה לְעַמֶּךָ.

זָרִים אוֹמְרִים אֵין תּוֹחֶלֶת וְתִקְוָה, חֹן אֹם לְשִׁמְךָ מְקַוֶּה, טָהוֹר יְשׁוּעָתֵנוּ קָרְבָה, יָגַעְנוּ וְלֹא הוּנַח לָנוּ, רַחֲמֶיךָ יִכְבְּשׁוּ אֶת כַּעַסְךָ מֵעָלֵינוּ. אָנָּא שׁוּב מֵחֲרוֹנְךָ וְרַחֵם סְגֻלָּה אֲשֶׁר בָּחָרְתָּ.

יהוה אֱלֹהֵי יִשְׂרָאֵל, שׁוּב מֵחֲרוֹן אַפֶּךָ וְהִנָּחֵם עַל הָרָעָה לְעַמֶּךָ.

חוּסָה יהוה עָלֵינוּ בְּרַחֲמֶיךָ, וְאַל תִּתְּנֵנוּ בִּידֵי אַכְזָרִים. לָמָּה יֹאמְרוּ הַגּוֹיִם אַיֵּה נָא אֱלֹהֵיהֶם, לְמַעַנְךָ עֲשֵׂה עִמָּנוּ חֶסֶד וְאַל תְּאַחַר. אָנָּא שׁוּב מֵחֲרוֹנְךָ וְרַחֵם סְגֻלָּה אֲשֶׁר בָּחָרְתָּ.

יהוה אֱלֹהֵי יִשְׂרָאֵל, שׁוּב מֵחֲרוֹן אַפֶּךָ וְהִנָּחֵם עַל הָרָעָה לְעַמֶּךָ.

קוֹלֵנוּ תִשְׁמַע וְתָחֹן, וְאַל תִּטְּשֵׁנוּ בְּיַד אֹיְבֵינוּ לִמְחוֹת אֶת שְׁמֵנוּ. זְכֹר אֲשֶׁר נִשְׁבַּעְתָּ לַאֲבוֹתֵינוּ כְּכוֹכְבֵי הַשָּׁמַיִם אַרְבֶּה אֶת זַרְעֲכֶם, וְעַתָּה נִשְׁאַרְנוּ מְעַט מֵהַרְבֵּה. וּבְכָל זֹאת שִׁמְךָ לֹא שָׁכָחְנוּ, נָא אַל תִּשְׁכָּחֵנוּ.

יהוה אֱלֹהֵי יִשְׂרָאֵל, שׁוּב מֵחֲרוֹן אַפֶּךָ וְהִנָּחֵם עַל הָרָעָה לְעַמֶּךָ.

עָזְרֵנוּ אֱלֹהֵי יִשְׁעֵנוּ עַל־דְּבַר כְּבוֹד־שְׁמֶךָ, וְהַצִּילֵנוּ וְכַפֵּר עַל־חַטֹּאתֵינוּ לְמַעַן שְׁמֶךָ: תהלים עט

יהוה אֱלֹהֵי יִשְׂרָאֵל, שׁוּב מֵחֲרוֹן אַפֶּךָ וְהִנָּחֵם עַל הָרָעָה לְעַמֶּךָ.

On all days continue here:

שׁוֹמֵר יִשְׂרָאֵל, שְׁמֹר שְׁאֵרִית יִשְׂרָאֵל, וְאַל יֹאבַד יִשְׂרָאֵל הָאוֹמְרִים שְׁמַע יִשְׂרָאֵל.

שׁוֹמֵר גּוֹי אֶחָד, שְׁמֹר שְׁאֵרִית עַם אֶחָד, וְאַל יֹאבַד גּוֹי אֶחָד הַמְיַחֲדִים שִׁמְךָ, יהוה אֱלֹהֵינוּ יהוה אֶחָד.

Guardian of a holy nation, guard the remnant of that holy people,
and let not the holy nation perish, who three times repeat
the threefold declaration of holiness to the Holy One.

You who are conciliated by calls for compassion and placated by pleas,
be conciliated and placated toward an afflicted generation,
for there is no other help.

Our Father, our King, be gracious to us and answer us, though we have no
worthy deeds; act with us in charity and loving-kindness and save us.

Stand at ^.

וַאֲנַחְנוּ We do not know ^what to do, but our eyes are turned to You. Remem- *11 Chr. 12*
ber, LORD, Your compassion and loving-kindness, for they are everlasting. *Ps. 25*
May Your loving-kindness, LORD, be with us, for we have put our hope in *Ps. 33*
You. Do not hold against us the sins of those who came before us. May Your *Ps. 79*
mercies meet us swiftly, for we have been brought very low. Be gracious to us, *Ps. 123*
LORD, be gracious to us, for we are sated with contempt. In wrath, remember *Hab. 3*
mercy. He knows our nature; He remembers that we are dust. ▸ Help us, God *Ps. 103*
of our salvation, for the sake of the glory of Your name. Save us and grant *Ps. 79*
atonement for our sins for Your name's sake.

HALF KADDISH

Leader: יִתְגַּדַּל Magnified and sanctified may His great name be,
in the world He created by His will.
May He establish His kingdom in your lifetime and in your days,
and in the lifetime of all the house of Israel,
swiftly and soon – and say: Amen.

All: May His great name^ be blessed for ever and all time.

Leader: Blessed and praised, glorified and exalted,
raised and honored, uplifted and lauded
be the name of the Holy One, blessed be He,
beyond any blessing, song, praise and consolation
uttered in the world – and say: Amen.

יְהֵא שְׁמֵהּ רַבָּא – *May His great name.* Whoever says *yeheh shemeh raba...* with all his
strength, the Heavenly Court rips up any

negative decree against him (*Shabbat* 119b).
"With all his strength" – with all of one's heart
and soul (*Mishna Berura* 56:1).

שׁוֹמֵר גּוֹי קָדוֹשׁ, שְׁמֹר שְׁאֵרִית עַם קָדוֹשׁ, וְאַל יֹאבַד גּוֹי קָדוֹשׁ
הַמְשַׁלְּשִׁים בְּשָׁלֹשׁ קְדֻשּׁוֹת לְקָדוֹשׁ.

מִתְרַצֶּה בְּרַחֲמִים וּמִתְפַּיֵּס בְּתַחֲנוּנִים, הִתְרַצֶּה וְהִתְפַּיֵּס לְדוֹר עָנִי
כִּי אֵין עוֹזֵר.

אָבִינוּ מַלְכֵּנוּ, חָנֵּנוּ וַעֲנֵנוּ, כִּי אֵין בָּנוּ מַעֲשִׂים
עֲשֵׂה עִמָּנוּ צְדָקָה וָחֶסֶד וְהוֹשִׁיעֵנוּ.

Stand at ^.

<table>
<tr><td>דברי
הימים ב' כ"ב
תהלים כה
תהלים ל"ג
תהלים קכ"ג</td><td>וַאֲנַחְנוּ לֹא נֵדַע מַה־נַּעֲשֶׂה, כִּי עָלֶיךָ עֵינֵינוּ: זְכֹר־רַחֲמֶיךָ יהוה וַחֲסָדֶיךָ,
כִּי מֵעוֹלָם הֵמָּה: יְהִי־חַסְדְּךָ יהוה עָלֵינוּ, כַּאֲשֶׁר יִחַלְנוּ לָךְ: אַל־תִּזְכָּר־לָנוּ</td></tr>
<tr><td>תהלים קכ"ט</td><td>עֲוֹנֹת רִאשֹׁנִים, מַהֵר יְקַדְּמוּנוּ רַחֲמֶיךָ, כִּי דַלּוֹנוּ מְאֹד: חָנֵּנוּ יהוה חָנֵּנוּ,</td></tr>
<tr><td>חבקוק ג'
תהלים קל
תהלים ע"ט</td><td>כִּי־רַב שָׂבַעְנוּ בוּז: בְּרֹגֶז רַחֵם תִּזְכּוֹר: כִּי־הוּא יָדַע יִצְרֵנוּ, זָכוּר כִּי־עָפָר
אֲנָחְנוּ: ◦ עָזְרֵנוּ אֱלֹהֵי יִשְׁעֵנוּ עַל־דְּבַר כְּבוֹד־שְׁמֶךָ, וְהַצִּילֵנוּ וְכַפֵּר עַל־
חַטֹּאתֵינוּ לְמַעַן שְׁמֶךָ:</td></tr>
</table>

חצי קדיש

שׁ״ץ: יִתְגַּדַּל וְיִתְקַדַּשׁ שְׁמֵהּ רַבָּא (קהל: אָמֵן)
בְּעָלְמָא דִּי בְרָא כִרְעוּתֵהּ
וְיַמְלִיךְ מַלְכוּתֵהּ
בְּחַיֵּיכוֹן וּבְיוֹמֵיכוֹן וּבְחַיֵּי דְכָל בֵּית יִשְׂרָאֵל
בַּעֲגָלָא וּבִזְמַן קָרִיב, וְאִמְרוּ אָמֵן. (קהל: אָמֵן)

קהל: יְהֵא שְׁמֵהּ רַבָּא◦ מְבָרַךְ לְעָלַם וּלְעָלְמֵי עָלְמַיָּא.
ושׁ״ץ:

שׁ״ץ: יִתְבָּרַךְ וְיִשְׁתַּבַּח וְיִתְפָּאַר וְיִתְרוֹמַם וְיִתְנַשֵּׂא
וְיִתְהַדָּר וְיִתְעַלֶּה וְיִתְהַלָּל
שְׁמֵהּ דְּקֻדְשָׁא בְּרִיךְ הוּא (קהל: בְּרִיךְ הוּא)
לְעֵלָּא מִן כָּל בִּרְכָתָא /בעשרת ימי תשובה: לְעֵלָּא לְעֵלָּא מִכָּל בִּרְכָתָא/
וְשִׁירָתָא, תֻּשְׁבְּחָתָא וְנֶחֱמָתָא
דַּאֲמִירָן בְּעָלְמָא, וְאִמְרוּ אָמֵן. (קהל: אָמֵן)

REMOVING THE TORAH FROM THE ARK

On Mondays and Thursdays, Rosh Ḥodesh, Ḥol HaMo'ed, Ḥanukka, Purim and Fast Days,
the Torah is read when a minyan is present. On Yom HaAtzma'ut that is not Thursday, the
Haftara on page 584 is read. On all other days, continue with "Happy are those" on page 240.

Before taking the Torah out of the Ark, on Mondays and Thursdays, stand
while reciting "God, slow to anger." It is not said on Rosh Ḥodesh, Ḥol HaMo'ed,
Erev Pesaḥ, Ḥanukka, the 14th and 15th of Adar I, Purim and Shushan Purim,
Yom HaAtzma'ut, Yom Yerushalayim, Tisha B'Av or in a house of mourning, and
in Israel on Isru Ḥag. Most people say both paragraphs; some say only the first.

God, slow to anger, abounding in loving-kindness and truth, do not rebuke us in Your anger. Have pity on Your people, LORD, and save us from all evil. We have sinned against You, LORD. Please forgive in accordance with Your great compassion, God.	God, slow to anger, full of compassion, do not hide Your face from us. Have pity on the remnant of Israel Your people, LORD, and deliver us from all evil. We have sinned against You, LORD. Please forgive in accordance with Your great compassion, God.

The Ark is opened and the congregation stands. All say:

וַיְהִי בִּנְסֹעַ **Whenever the Ark set out, Moses would say,**
"Arise, LORD, and may Your enemies be scattered.
May those who hate You flee before You."
For the Torah shall come forth from Zion,
and the word of the LORD from Jerusalem.
Blessed is He who in His holiness
gave the Torah to His people Israel.

Num. 10

Is. 2

---

and not the learning, of Torah). The mere act of reading or hearing it sanctifies the listener. In doing so, I attach myself to my people, my tradition, my God. I am a part of something bigger than myself and I am uplifted.

אֵל אֶרֶךְ אַפַּיִם – *God, slow to anger.* Many suggest that this *Keriat HaTorah* represents a kind of reenactment of the giving of the Torah at Sinai. If so, then perhaps this intro-

ductory passage of supplication to Hashem can be reminiscent of the days in which *Benei Yisrael* prepared for receiving the Torah, days no doubt filled with a sense of excitement and anticipation. Recall how very young children often approach the open *Aron Kodesh* for the first time, in awe and wonder at the beauty and the pageantry. There is no reason to lose that feeling. There is no reason to lose that feeling just because we are older.

הוצאת ספר תורה

On Mondays and Thursdays, פורים, חנוכה, חל המועד, ראש חדש and Fast Days,
the תורה is read when a מנין is present. On יום העצמאות that is not Thursday, the
הפטרה on page 585 is read. On all other days, continue with אשרי on page 241.

Before taking the תורה out of the ארון קדש, on Mondays and Thursdays, stand while reciting
אל ארך אפים. It is not said on: ראש חדש, חל המועד, חנוכה, ערב פסח, the 14th and 15th of
אדר א', פורים and שושן פורים, יום העצמאות, תשעה באב, ירושלים יום or in a house of mourning,
and in ארץ ישראל on חג אסרו. Most people say both paragraphs, some say only the first.

אֵל אֶרֶךְ אַפַּיִם וּמָלֵא רַחֲמִים	אֵל אֶרֶךְ אַפַּיִם וְרַב חֶסֶד וֶאֱמֶת
אַל תַּסְתֵּר פָּנֶיךָ מִמֶּנּוּ	אַל בְּאַפְּךָ תוֹכִיחֵנוּ
חְוּסָה יהוה עַל שְׁאֵרִית יִשְׂרָאֵל עַמֶּךָ	חְוּסָה יהוה עַל עַמֶּךָ
וְהַצִּילֵנוּ מִכָּל רָע.	וְהוֹשִׁיעֵנוּ מִכָּל רָע.
חָטָאנוּ לְךָ אָדוֹן	חָטָאנוּ לְךָ אָדוֹן
סְלַח נָא כְּרֹב רַחֲמֶיךָ אֵל.	סְלַח נָא כְּרֹב רַחֲמֶיךָ אֵל.

The ארון קדש is opened and the קהל stands. All say:

במדברי

וַיְהִי בִּנְסֹעַ הָאָרֹן וַיֹּאמֶר מֹשֶׁה
קוּמָה יהוה וְיָפֻצוּ אֹיְבֶיךָ וְיָנֻסוּ מְשַׂנְאֶיךָ מִפָּנֶיךָ:

ישעיה ב

כִּי מִצִּיּוֹן תֵּצֵא תוֹרָה וּדְבַר־יהוה מִירוּשָׁלָםִ:
בָּרוּךְ שֶׁנָּתַן תּוֹרָה לְעַמּוֹ יִשְׂרָאֵל בִּקְדֻשָּׁתוֹ.

עִיּוּן תְּפִלָּה • IYUN TEFILLA

קְרִיאַת הַתּוֹרָה – *PUBLIC READING OF THE
TORAH.* Education in Jewish life has always
been democratic. It is not only for the elite
but for every person, rich or poor. Amaz-
ingly, universal schooling has been a part
of Jewish life for close to 2000 years. So it
should come as no surprise that from the
very outset Moshe instituted that the Torah
be read publicly three times a week (*Bava
Kama* 82a), not just to keep the content

of Torah alive, for that would happen in
schools and private study regardless, but,
rather, to remind us as a community that
Torah is our life, as water is to a thirsty
person, as water is to fish. We cannot live
without it. According to Rabbi Soloveitchik,
that is why there is not necessarily a need
to even understand this public Torah reading or to learn from it (perhaps that is why it
is simply called *Keriat HaTorah*: the reading,

Blessed is the name[B] of the Master of the Universe. Blessed is Your crown and Your place.   *Zohar,*
May Your favor always be with Your people Israel. Show Your people the salvation of Your   *Vayak-hel*
right hand in Your Temple. Grant us the gift of Your good light, and accept our prayers in
mercy. May it be Your will to prolong our life in goodness. May I be counted among the
righteous, so that You will have compassion on me and all that is mine
and all that is Your people Israel's. You feed all; You sustain all; You rule over all; You rule
over kings, for sovereignty is Yours. I am a servant of the Holy One, blessed be He, before
whom and before whose glorious Torah I bow at all times. Not in man do I trust, nor on
any angel do I rely, but on the God of heaven who is the God of truth, whose Torah is truth,
whose prophets speak truth, and who abounds in acts of love and truth. ▸ In Him I trust,
and to His holy and glorious name I offer praises. May it be Your will to open my heart to
the Torah, and to fulfill the wishes of my heart and of the hearts of all Your people Israel
for good, for life, and for peace.

> *The Leader takes the Torah scroll in his right arm, bows toward the Ark and says:*

Magnify the LORD[B] with me, and let us exalt His name together.   *Ps. 34*

> *The Ark is closed. The Leader carries the Torah scroll to the bima and the congregation says:*

לְךָ Yours, LORD, are the greatness and the power, the glory and the   *1 Chr. 29*
majesty and splendor, for everything in heaven and earth is Yours.
Yours, LORD, is the kingdom; You are exalted as Head over all.

רוֹמְמוּ Exalt the LORD our God and bow to His footstool; He is holy.   *Ps. 99*
Exalt the LORD our God, and bow at His holy mountain, for holy is
the LORD our God.

אַב הָרַחֲמִים May the Father of compassion have compassion on the
people borne by Him. May He remember the covenant with the
mighty [patriarchs], and deliver us from evil times. May He reproach
the evil instinct in the people carried by Him, and graciously grant
that we be an everlasting remnant. May He fulfill in good measure our
requests for salvation and compassion.

גַּדְּלוּ לַיהוה – *Magnify the LORD.* This call to
the congregation by the *Ḥazan* urges us
to be uplifted by the presence and revelation of the Torah. Symbolically, there is a
custom for him to physically raise the Torah
up accordingly. The phrase has six words
which, according to one opinion, symbolize the series of six steps that the bearers of
the Ark took when David led the amazing

celebration of the repossession of the Ark
(*Shmuel* II 6:13). Others point to the fact
that the phrase has 26 letters, the *gema-
tria* or numerical equivalent of the name
of Hashem. All of these traditions simply
try to convey the joy, pride and awe that
it is possible to feel at this moment, if only
we would allow ourselves not to take it for
granted. Give in to the moment.

בְּרִיךְ שְׁמֵהּ דְּמָרֵא עָלְמָא, בְּרִיךְ כִּתְרָךְ וְאַתְרָךְ. יְהֵא רְעוּתָךְ עִם עַמָּךְ יִשְׂרָאֵל לְעָלַם, וּפֻרְקַן יְמִינָךְ אַחֲזֵי לְעַמָּךְ בְּבֵית מַקְדְּשָׁךְ, וּלְאַמְטוֹיֵי לָנָא מִטּוּב נְהוֹרָךְ, וּלְקַבֵּל צְלוֹתָנָא בְּרַחֲמִין. יְהֵא רַעֲוָא קֳדָמָךְ דְּתוֹרִיךְ לָן חַיִּין בְּטִיבוּ, וְלֶהֱוֵי אֲנָא פְקִידָא בְּגוֹ צַדִּיקַיָּא, לְמִרְחַם עָלַי וּלְמִנְטַר יָתִי וְיָת כָּל דִּי לִי וְדִי לְעַמָּךְ יִשְׂרָאֵל. אַנְתְּ הוּא זָן לְכֹלָּא וּמְפַרְנֵס לְכֹלָּא, אַנְתְּ הוּא שַׁלִּיט עַל כֹּלָּא, אַנְתְּ הוּא דְּשַׁלִּיט עַל מַלְכַיָּא, וּמַלְכוּתָא דִּילָךְ הִיא. אֲנָא עַבְדָּא דְקֻדְשָׁא בְּרִיךְ הוּא, דְּסָגֵדְנָא קַמֵּהּ וּמִקַּמֵּי דִּיקַר אוֹרַיְתֵהּ בְּכָל עִדָּן וְעִדָּן. לָא עַל אֱנָשׁ רָחִיצְנָא וְלָא עַל בַּר אֱלָהִין סָמִיכְנָא, אֶלָּא בֶּאֱלָהָא דִשְׁמַיָּא, דְּהוּא אֱלָהָא קְשׁוֹט, וְאוֹרַיְתֵהּ קְשׁוֹט, וּנְבִיאוֹהִי קְשׁוֹט, וּמַסְגֵּא לְמֶעְבַּד טַבְוָן וּקְשׁוֹט. ◀ בֵּהּ אֲנָא רָחִיץ, וְלִשְׁמֵהּ קַדִּישָׁא יַקִּירָא אֲנָא אֵמַר תֻּשְׁבְּחָן. יְהֵא רַעֲוָא קֳדָמָךְ דְּתִפְתַּח לִבַּאי בְּאוֹרַיְתָא, וְתַשְׁלִים מִשְׁאֲלִין דְּלִבַּאי וְלִבָּא דְכָל עַמָּךְ יִשְׂרָאֵל לְטָב וּלְחַיִּין וְלִשְׁלָם.

זוהר ויקהל

The שְׁלִיחַ צִבּוּר *takes the* סֵפֶר תּוֹרָה *in his right arm, bows toward the* אֲרוֹן קוֹדֶשׁ *and says:*

גַּדְּלוּ לַיהוה אִתִּי וּנְרוֹמְמָה שְׁמוֹ יַחְדָּו:

תהלים לד

The אֲרוֹן קוֹדֶשׁ *is closed. The* שְׁלִיחַ צִבּוּר *carries the* סֵפֶר תּוֹרָה *to the* בִּימָה *and the* קָהָל *says:*

לְךָ יהוה הַגְּדֻלָּה וְהַגְּבוּרָה וְהַתִּפְאֶרֶת וְהַנֵּצַח וְהַהוֹד, כִּי־כֹל בַּשָּׁמַיִם וּבָאָרֶץ, לְךָ יהוה הַמַּמְלָכָה וְהַמִּתְנַשֵּׂא לְכֹל לְרֹאשׁ:

דברי הימים א, כט

רוֹמְמוּ יהוה אֱלֹהֵינוּ וְהִשְׁתַּחֲווּ לַהֲדֹם רַגְלָיו, קָדוֹשׁ הוּא: רוֹמְמוּ יהוה אֱלֹהֵינוּ וְהִשְׁתַּחֲווּ לְהַר קָדְשׁוֹ, כִּי־קָדוֹשׁ יהוה אֱלֹהֵינוּ:

תהילים צט

אַב הָרַחֲמִים הוּא יְרַחֵם עַם עֲמוּסִים, וְיִזְכֹּר בְּרִית אֵיתָנִים, וְיַצִּיל נַפְשׁוֹתֵינוּ מִן הַשָּׁעוֹת הָרָעוֹת, וְיִגְעַר בְּיֵצֶר הָרָע מִן הַנְּשׂוּאִים, וְיָחֹן אוֹתָנוּ לִפְלֵיטַת עוֹלָמִים, וִימַלֵּא מִשְׁאֲלוֹתֵינוּ בְּמִדָּה טוֹבָה יְשׁוּעָה וְרַחֲמִים.

BIUR TEFILLA • ביאור תפילה

בְּרִיךְ שְׁמֵהּ — *Blessed is the name.* Added to the service by kabbalists about four centuries ago or more, this prayer is really a quote from the *Zohar* which says that "when the congregation takes the Torah from the Ark to read from it, the Gates of Mercy are

opened in heaven and love is awakened on high; therefore this prayer should be spoken." Thus this prayer makes use, as it were, of a favorable circumstance to pray for the fulfillment of our hearts' deepest desires. (Rabbi E. Munk)

The Torah scroll is placed on the bima and the Gabbai calls a Kohen to the Torah.

May His kingship over us be soon revealed and made manifest. May He be gracious to our surviving remnant, the remnant of His people the house of Israel in grace, loving-kindness, compassion and favor, and let us say: Amen. Let us all render greatness to our God and give honor to the Torah. *Let the Kohen come forward. Arise (*name* son of *father's name*), the Kohen.

*If no Kohen is present, a Levi or Yisrael is called up as follows:
/As there is no Kohen, arise (*name* son of *father's name*) in place of a Kohen./

Blessed is He who, in His holiness, gave the Torah to His people Israel.

Congregation followed by the Gabbai:
You who cling to the LORD your God are all alive today.   *Deut. 4*

Another suggestion is that it is as if one is actually *receiving* the Torah on Mount Sinai (*Orkhot Ḥayyim*). And yet another suggestion is that there is a need to hold onto any article over which one is reciting a blessing, similar to a *lulav* (*Beit Yosef*). The custom is to keep holding at least one of the handles until one is completely finished with one's *aliya*.

5. The Gemara (*Megilla* 32a) relates a dispute about how one should recite the blessings. Rabbi Meir was concerned that if you look into the *sefer Torah* when reciting the blessings, people might think that the blessings were actually printed inside the Torah and were part of the Torah itself. Those who follow his opinion therefore suggest that one turn one's head to the left (*Magen Avraham* 139:8) or the right (*Arukh HaShulḥan* 139:13), or close one's eyes (*Ḥayyei Adam*), or do anything but look down. Rabbi Yehuda, on the other hand, said that you don't really need to worry about that since most people know the blessings are separate from the Torah itself; therefore, just recite the blessing however you want.

6. Reciting *Barekhu* is in effect an invitation to the community to join with you in learning Torah together, with you as their representative. They, in turn, answer in order to convey their presence and their participation. It is therefore important to recite the words loudly enough so that everyone (or at least a *minyan*'s worth) can hear you.

7. Ideally, each person is supposed to read the Torah portion for his own *aliya*. But if that were always enforced, then some people who could not read it accurately might be embarrassed (Ran), or he might read it with so many errors that those present would not be fulfilling their obligation to hear the Torah reading (Rosh), or a person who could not read Hebrew would never get an *aliya*, nor could a blind person. As such, the custom evolved to have a *ba'al keria*, who would be in charge of the reading and act as a *shaliaḥ* or messenger for the person getting the *aliya*. Nevertheless, there is a custom that the person getting an *aliya* should do his best to read along in a whisper with the *ba'al keria* as if to fulfill his own obligation to read,

The ספר תורה *is placed on the* שולחן *and the* גבאי *calls a* כהן *to the* תורה.

וְתִגָּלֶה וְתֵרָאֶה מַלְכוּתוֹ עָלֵינוּ בִּזְמַן קָרוֹב, וְיָחֹן פְּלֵיטָתֵנוּ וּפְלֵיטַת עַמּוֹ בֵּית יִשְׂרָאֵל לְחֵן וּלְחֶסֶד וּלְרַחֲמִים וּלְרָצוֹן וְנֹאמַר אָמֵן. הַכֹּל הָבוּ גֹדֶל לֵאלֹהֵינוּ וּתְנוּ כָבוֹד לַתּוֹרָה. *כֹּהֵן קְרָב, יַעֲמֹד* (פלוני בן פלוני) *הַכֹּהֵן.*

If no כהן *is present, a* לוי *or* ישראל *is called up as follows:*

/אֵין כָּאן כֹּהֵן, יַעֲמֹד (פלוני בן פלוני) בִּמְקוֹם כֹּהֵן./

בָּרוּךְ שֶׁנָּתַן תּוֹרָה לְעַמּוֹ יִשְׂרָאֵל בִּקְדֻשָּׁתוֹ.

followed by the גבאי: קהל

דברים ד

וְאַתֶּם הַדְּבֵקִים בַּיהוה אֱלֹהֵיכֶם חַיִּים כֻּלְּכֶם הַיּוֹם:

HILKHOT TEFILLA · הלכות תפילה

A GUIDE TO GETTING AN ALIYA

1. Getting an *aliya* is a big deal. It's important to recall that the *kavod* (honor) is not only yours but the Torah's. In fact Rabbi Yehuda (*Berakhot* 55a) suggested that, except in certain extenuating circumstances, one's life might be shortened, God forbid, if one turns down an *aliya*. After all, the Torah is described as (*Devarim* 30:20) – כִּי הוּא חַיֶּיךָ וְאֹרֶךְ יָמֶיךָ – "Torah is your life and the length of your days." Why would you want to give it up?

2. In order to show your love of the Torah and what an honor it is to get an *aliya*, and in order that everyone else doesn't have to wait unnecessarily long until you get from your seat to the *bima*, the custom is to take the shortest route to the Torah. If you are equidistant from both sides of the *bima*, the custom is to go up on the right side and leave via the left side. This is just because there is a preference in Judaism for the right (*Yoma* 15b). Hence, some halakhic authorities prefer that you always go up

the right side even if it is further away from you (*Hatam Sofer* OḤ 187). The prophet Yeḥezkel (46:9) noted that in the *Beit HaMikdash* the custom was to enter via one gate and leave via another. Consider this *aliya*, then, a kind of *going up* to the *Beit HaMikdash*.

3. Since you are about to "read" the Torah, it makes sense to see exactly what you are about to "read" before making the blessing. That's why there is a custom for the *ba'al keria* to show you the place where your *aliya* begins. There is another custom to make a motion to touch that spot with one's tallit or some other material and then kiss it in order to display one's love of Torah and one's excitement at this opportunity.

4. There is a custom to hold onto the wooden handles which are called the *Etzei Ḥayyim* or "Trees (lit. wood) of Life." (Recall the verse [*Mishlei* 3:18] עֵץ־חַיִּים הִיא לַמַּחֲזִיקִים בָּהּ...) – "It is a tree of life to those who grasp it.") One reason may be purely practical – you need to open the Torah to find the place (*Megilla* 32a).

The appropriate Torah portions are to be found from page 696.

The Reader shows the oleh the section to be read.
The oleh touches the scroll at that place with the tzitzit of his tallit,
which he then kisses. Holding the handles of the scroll, he says:

Oleh: Bless⁸ the LORD, the blessed One.

Cong: Bless the LORD, the blessed One, for ever and all time.

Oleh: Bless the LORD, the blessed One, for ever and all time.

Blessed are You, LORD our God,
King of the Universe,
who has chosen us from all peoples
and has given us His Torah.
Blessed are You, LORD, Giver of the Torah.

After the reading, the oleh says:

Oleh: Blessed are You, LORD our God,
King of the Universe,
who has given us the Torah of truth,
planting everlasting life in our midst.
Blessed are You, LORD, Giver of the Torah.

---

which the traditional reply is בָּרוּךְ תִּהְיֶה (barukh tihiyeh), "May you be blessed." In Sepharadi tradition, the greeting is חֲזַק וּבָרוּךְ (ḥazak ubarukh) "may your

strength be increased and may you be blessed," to which the traditional reply is חֲזַק וֶאֱמָץ (ḥazak ve'ematz) "Be strong and courageous."

BIUR TEFILLA · ביאור תפילה

בָּרְכוּ – *Bless.* Here the person getting the *aliya* invites us all to join in with him. Indeed, there was a time when there was only one blessing cited before the first *aliya* and a second blessing recited only at the end of all of the *aliyot* as if it were one long reading in which all were involved

(*Megilla* 4a). Today, each individual recites two blessings. The first refers to "His [God's] Torah" while the second seems to suggest that the Torah is now a part of us. Perhaps that is the goal of this reading; namely, that we should walk away feeling like it is part of us.

The appropriate תורה portions are to be found from page 696.

The קורא shows the עולה the section to be read.
The עולה touches the ספר תורה at that place with the ציצת of his טלית,
which he then kisses. Holding the handles of the ספר תורה, he says:

עולה: בָּרְכוּ אֶת יהוה הַמְבֹרָךְ.

קהל: בָּרוּךְ יהוה הַמְבֹרָךְ לְעוֹלָם וָעֶד.

עולה: בָּרוּךְ יהוה הַמְבֹרָךְ לְעוֹלָם וָעֶד.

בָּרוּךְ אַתָּה יהוה, אֱלֹהֵינוּ מֶלֶךְ הָעוֹלָם
אֲשֶׁר בָּחַר בָּנוּ מִכָּל הָעַמִּים
וְנָתַן לָנוּ אֶת תּוֹרָתוֹ.
בָּרוּךְ אַתָּה יהוה, נוֹתֵן הַתּוֹרָה.

After the קריאת התורה, the עולה says:

עולה: בָּרוּךְ אַתָּה יהוה אֱלֹהֵינוּ מֶלֶךְ הָעוֹלָם
אֲשֶׁר נָתַן לָנוּ תּוֹרַת אֱמֶת
וְחַיֵּי עוֹלָם נָטַע בְּתוֹכֵנוּ.
בָּרוּךְ אַתָּה יהוה, נוֹתֵן הַתּוֹרָה.

---

and so as to reinforce that the blessing he said was on his own reading.

8. Upon completion of the final blessing, the custom is to remain at the *bima* standing beside the *gabbai* until the completion of the next *aliya*. This is considered a fulfillment of giving honor to the Torah by not abandoning it prematurely (*Levush*). While theoretically one could leave once the next person getting an *aliya* is standing in front of the Torah, the custom is to wait until the end of his *aliya* and to try to get back to one's seat before the next *aliya* so that

one does not miss any of the reading (*Magen Avraham* 141:8).

9. When returning to one's seat, the custom is to take the longest route back, as if to symbolize your sadness at leaving the Torah (*Levush*) or lest it look like you are trying to make a hasty getaway (*Arukh HaShulḥan*). If the routes are equidistant, then leave from the opposite side you came from.

10. Finally, it is customary for people to wish you a יִישַׁר כֹּחַ (*yishar ko'aḥ/koḥakha*), "may your strength be increased" or "more power to you," to

One who has survived a situation of danger says:

Blessed are You, LORD our God, King of the Universe,
who bestows good on the unworthy, who has bestowed on me much good.

The congregation responds:

Amen. May He who bestowed much good on you
continue to bestow on you much good, Selah.

Special blessings and memorial prayers may be said at this point (below and next page).

FOR A SICK MAN

May He who blessed our fathers, Abraham, Isaac and Jacob, Moses and
Aaron, David and Solomon, bless and heal one who is ill, (*sick person's name,
son of mother's name*), on whose behalf (*name of the one making the offering*)
is making a contribution to charity. As a reward for this, may the Holy One,
blessed be He, be filled with compassion for him, to restore his health, cure
him, strengthen and revive him, sending him a swift and full recovery from
heaven to all his 248 organs and 365 sinews, amongst the other sick ones in
Israel, a healing of the spirit and a healing of the body, now, swiftly and soon,
and let us say: Amen.

FOR A SICK WOMAN

May He who blessed our fathers, Abraham, Isaac and Jacob, Moses and
Aaron, David and Solomon, bless and heal one who is ill, (*sick person's name,
daughter of mother's name*), on whose behalf (*name of the one making the
offering*) is making a contribution to charity. As a reward for this, may the
Holy One, blessed be He, be filled with compassion for her, to restore her
health, cure her, strengthen and revive her, sending her a swift and full
recovery from heaven to all her organs and sinews, amongst the other sick
ones in Israel, a healing of the spirit and a healing of the body, now, swiftly
and soon, and let us say: Amen.

For a male close relative:

אֵל מָלֵא רַחֲמִים God, full of mercy, who dwells on high, grant fitting rest on
the wings of the Divine Presence, in the heights of the holy and the pure who
shine like the radiance of heaven, to the soul of (*name son of father's name*)
who has gone to his eternal home, and to this I pledge (without formal vow)
to give charity in his memory, may his resting place be in the Garden of
Eden. Therefore, Master of compassion, shelter him in the shadow of Your
wings forever and bind his soul in the bond of everlasting life. The LORD is
his heritage; may he rest in peace, and let us say: Amen.

One who has survived a situation of danger says:

בָּרוּךְ אַתָּה יהוה אֱלֹהֵינוּ מֶלֶךְ הָעוֹלָם
הַגּוֹמֵל לְחַיָּבִים טוֹבוֹת, שֶׁגְּמָלַנִי כָּל טוֹב.

The קהל responds:

אָמֵן. מִי שֶׁגְּמָלְךָ כָּל טוֹב הוּא, יִגְמָלְךָ כָּל טוֹב, סֶלָה.

Special שברי מי and memorial prayers may be said at this point (below and next page).

מי שברך לחולה

מִי שֶׁבֵּרַךְ אֲבוֹתֵינוּ אַבְרָהָם יִצְחָק וְיַעֲקֹב, מֹשֶׁה וְאַהֲרֹן דָּוִד וּשְׁלֹמֹה הוּא
יְבָרֵךְ וִירַפֵּא אֶת הַחוֹלֶה (פלוני בן פלונית) בַּעֲבוּר שֶׁ(פלוני בן פלוני) נוֹדֵר צְדָקָה
בַּעֲבוּרוֹ. בִּשְׂכַר זֶה הַקָּדוֹשׁ בָּרוּךְ הוּא יִמָּלֵא רַחֲמִים עָלָיו לְהַחֲלִימוֹ
וּלְרַפֹּאתוֹ וּלְהַחֲזִיקוֹ וּלְהַחֲיוֹתוֹ וְיִשְׁלַח לוֹ מְהֵרָה רְפוּאָה שְׁלֵמָה מִן הַשָּׁמַיִם
לִרְמַ״ח אֵבָרָיו וּשְׁסַ״ה גִידָיו בְּתוֹךְ שְׁאָר חוֹלֵי יִשְׂרָאֵל, רְפוּאַת הַנֶּפֶשׁ
וּרְפוּאַת הַגּוּף, הַשְׁתָּא בַּעֲגָלָא וּבִזְמַן קָרִיב, וְנֹאמַר אָמֵן.

מי שברך לחולה

מִי שֶׁבֵּרַךְ אֲבוֹתֵינוּ אַבְרָהָם יִצְחָק וְיַעֲקֹב, מֹשֶׁה וְאַהֲרֹן דָּוִד וּשְׁלֹמֹה הוּא
יְבָרֵךְ וִירַפֵּא אֶת הַחוֹלָה (פלונית בת פלונית) בַּעֲבוּר שֶׁ(פלוני בן פלוני) נוֹדֵר צְדָקָה
בַּעֲבוּרָהּ. בִּשְׂכַר זֶה הַקָּדוֹשׁ בָּרוּךְ הוּא יִמָּלֵא רַחֲמִים עָלֶיהָ לְהַחֲלִימָהּ
וּלְרַפֹּאתָהּ וּלְהַחֲזִיקָהּ וּלְהַחֲיוֹתָהּ וְיִשְׁלַח לָהּ מְהֵרָה רְפוּאָה שְׁלֵמָה מִן
הַשָּׁמַיִם לְכָל אֵבָרֶיהָ וּלְכָל גִּידֶיהָ בְּתוֹךְ שְׁאָר חוֹלֵי יִשְׂרָאֵל, רְפוּאַת הַנֶּפֶשׁ
וּרְפוּאַת הַגּוּף, הַשְׁתָּא בַּעֲגָלָא וּבִזְמַן קָרִיב, וְנֹאמַר אָמֵן.

For a male close relative:

אֵל מָלֵא רַחֲמִים, שׁוֹכֵן בַּמְּרוֹמִים, הַמְצֵא מְנוּחָה נְכוֹנָה עַל כַּנְפֵי הַשְּׁכִינָה,
בְּמַעֲלוֹת קְדוֹשִׁים וּטְהוֹרִים, כְּזֹהַר הָרָקִיעַ מַזְהִירִים, לְנִשְׁמַת (פלוני בן פלוני)
שֶׁהָלַךְ לְעוֹלָמוֹ, בַּעֲבוּר שֶׁבְּלִי נֶדֶר צְדָקָה בְּעַד הַזְכָּרַת נִשְׁמָתוֹ, בְּגַן
עֵדֶן תְּהֵא מְנוּחָתוֹ. לָכֵן, בַּעַל הָרַחֲמִים יַסְתִּירֵהוּ בְּסֵתֶר כְּנָפָיו לְעוֹלָמִים,
וְיִצְרֹר בִּצְרוֹר הַחַיִּים אֶת נִשְׁמָתוֹ, יהוה הוּא נַחֲלָתוֹ, וְיָנוּחַ בְּשָׁלוֹם עַל
מִשְׁכָּבוֹ, וְנֹאמַר אָמֵן.

For a female close relative:

אֵל מָלֵא רַחֲמִים God, full of mercy, who dwells on high, grant fitting rest on the wings of the Divine Presence, in the heights of the holy and the pure who shine like the radiance of heaven, to the soul of (*name* daughter of *father's name*) who has gone to her eternal home, and to this I pledge (without formal vow) to give charity in her memory, may her resting place be in the Garden of Eden. Therefore, Master of compassion, shelter her in the shadow of Your wings forever and bind her soul in the bond of everlasting life. The LORD is her heritage; may she rest in peace, and let us say: Amen.

HALF KADDISH

After the Reading of the Torah, the Reader says Half Kaddish:

Reader: יִתְגַּדַּל Magnified and sanctified may His great name be,
in the world He created by His will.
May He establish His kingdom in your lifetime and in your days,
and in the lifetime of all the house of Israel,
swiftly and soon – and say: Amen.

All: May His great name^A be blessed for ever and all time.

Reader: Blessed and praised, glorified and exalted,
raised and honored, uplifted and lauded
be the name of the Holy One, blessed be He,
beyond any blessing, song, praise and consolation
uttered in the world – and say: Amen.

The Torah scroll is lifted and the congregation says:

וְזֹאת הַתּוֹרָה This is the Torah   *Deut. 4*
that Moses placed before the children of Israel,
at the LORD's commandment, by the hand of Moses.   *Num. 9*

Some add: It is a tree of life to those who grasp it,   *Prov. 3*
and those who uphold it are happy.
Its ways are ways of pleasantness, and all its paths are peace.
Long life is at its right hand; at its left, riches and honor.
It pleased the LORD for the sake of [Israel's] righteousness,   *Is. 42*
to make the Torah great and glorious.

ANI TEFILLA · אני תפילה

יְהֵא שְׁמֵהּ רַבָּא – *May His great name.* Whoever says *yeheh shemeh raba...* with all his strength, the Heavenly Court rips up any negative decree against him (*Shabbat* 119b). "With all his strength" – in a loud voice (Tosafot).

For a female close relative:

אֵל מָלֵא רַחֲמִים, שׁוֹכֵן בַּמְּרוֹמִים, הַמְצֵא מְנוּחָה נְכוֹנָה עַל כַּנְפֵי הַשְּׁכִינָה, בְּמַעֲלוֹת קְדוֹשִׁים וּטְהוֹרִים, כְּזֹהַר הָרָקִיעַ מַזְהִירִים, לְנִשְׁמַת (פלונית בת פלוני) שֶׁהָלְכָה לְעוֹלָמָהּ, בַּעֲבוּר שֶׁבְּלִי נֶדֶר צְדָקָה בְּעַד הַזְכָּרַת נִשְׁמָתָהּ, בְּגַן עֵדֶן תְּהֵא מְנוּחָתָהּ. לָכֵן, בַּעַל הָרַחֲמִים יַסְתִּירֶהָ בְּסֵתֶר כְּנָפָיו לְעוֹלָמִים, וְיִצְרֹר בִּצְרוֹר הַחַיִּים אֶת נִשְׁמָתָהּ, יהוה הוּא נַחֲלָתָהּ, וְתָנוּחַ בְּשָׁלוֹם עַל מִשְׁכָּבָהּ, וְנֹאמַר אָמֵן.

חצי קדיש

After the קריאת התורה, *the* קורא *says* :חצי קדיש

קורא: יִתְגַּדַּל וְיִתְקַדַּשׁ שְׁמֵהּ רַבָּא (קהל: אָמֵן)
בְּעָלְמָא דִּי בְרָא כִרְעוּתֵהּ
וְיַמְלִיךְ מַלְכוּתֵהּ
בְּחַיֵּיכוֹן וּבְיוֹמֵיכוֹן וּבְחַיֵּי דְכָל בֵּית יִשְׂרָאֵל
בַּעֲגָלָא וּבִזְמַן קָרִיב, וְאִמְרוּ אָמֵן. (קהל: אָמֵן)

קורא
וקהל: יְהֵא שְׁמֵהּ רַבָּא* מְבָרַךְ לְעָלַם וּלְעָלְמֵי עָלְמַיָּא.

קורא: יִתְבָּרַךְ וְיִשְׁתַּבַּח וְיִתְפָּאַר וְיִתְרוֹמַם וְיִתְנַשֵּׂא
וְיִתְהַדָּר וְיִתְעַלֶּה וְיִתְהַלָּל שְׁמֵהּ דְּקֻדְשָׁא בְּרִיךְ הוּא (קהל: בְּרִיךְ הוּא)
לְעֵלָּא מִן כָּל בִּרְכָתָא / בעשרת ימי תשובה: לְעֵלָּא לְעֵלָּא מִכָּל בִּרְכָתָא/
וְשִׁירָתָא, תֻּשְׁבְּחָתָא וְנֶחֱמָתָא
דַּאֲמִירָן בְּעָלְמָא, וְאִמְרוּ אָמֵן. (קהל: אָמֵן)

The ספר תורה *is lifted and the* קהל *says:*

דברים ד   וְזֹאת הַתּוֹרָה אֲשֶׁר־שָׂם מֹשֶׁה לִפְנֵי בְּנֵי יִשְׂרָאֵל:
במדבר ט   עַל־פִּי יהוה בְּיַד־מֹשֶׁה:

משלי ג   *Some add*
עֵץ־חַיִּים הִיא לַמַּחֲזִיקִים בָּהּ וְתֹמְכֶיהָ מְאֻשָּׁר:
דְּרָכֶיהָ דַרְכֵי־נֹעַם וְכָל־נְתִיבוֹתֶיהָ שָׁלוֹם:
אֹרֶךְ יָמִים בִּימִינָהּ, בִּשְׂמֹאולָהּ עֹשֶׁר וְכָבוֹד:
ישעיה מב   יהוה חָפֵץ לְמַעַן צִדְקוֹ יַגְדִּיל תּוֹרָה וְיַאְדִּיר:

On those Mondays and Thursdays when Taḥanun is said,
the Leader says the following while the Torah scroll is being bound:

יְהִי רָצוֹן May it be the will of our Father in heaven
to establish (the Temple), home of our life,
and to restore His Presence to our midst,
swiftly in our days –
and let us say: Amen.

יְהִי רָצוֹן May it be the will of our Father in heaven
to have compassion on us and our remnant,
and to keep destruction and plague away from us
and from all His people the house of Israel –
and let us say: Amen.

יְהִי רָצוֹן May it be the will of our Father in heaven
to preserve among us the sages of Israel:
them, their wives, their sons and daughters,
their disciples and their disciples' disciples,
in all their dwelling places –
and let us say: Amen.

יְהִי רָצוֹן May it be the will of our Father in heaven
that we may hear and be given good tidings
of salvation and consolation,
and that our dispersed be gathered
from the four quarters of the earth –
and let us say: Amen.

All:

אַחֵינוּ As for our brothers of the whole house of Israel
who are in distress or captivity, on sea or land,
may the All-Present have compassion on them
and lead them from distress to relief,
from darkness to light,
and from oppression to freedom,
now, swiftly and soon –
and let us say: Amen.

On those Mondays and Thursdays when תחנון is said,
the שליח ציבור says the following while the ספר תורה is being bound:

יְהִי רָצוֹן מִלְּפְנֵי אָבִינוּ שֶׁבַּשָּׁמַיִם
לְכוֹנֵן אֶת בֵּית חַיֵּינוּ
וּלְהָשִׁיב אֶת שְׁכִינָתוֹ בְּתוֹכֵנוּ
בִּמְהֵרָה בְיָמֵינוּ, וְנֹאמַר אָמֵן.

יְהִי רָצוֹן מִלְּפְנֵי אָבִינוּ שֶׁבַּשָּׁמַיִם
לְרַחֵם עָלֵינוּ וְעַל פְּלֵיטָתֵנוּ
וְלִמְנֹעַ מַשְׁחִית וּמַגֵּפָה מֵעָלֵינוּ
וּמֵעַל כָּל עַמּוֹ בֵּית יִשְׂרָאֵל, וְנֹאמַר אָמֵן.

יְהִי רָצוֹן מִלְּפְנֵי אָבִינוּ שֶׁבַּשָּׁמַיִם
לְקַיֵּם בָּנוּ חַכְמֵי יִשְׂרָאֵל
הֵם וּנְשֵׁיהֶם וּבְנֵיהֶם וּבְנוֹתֵיהֶם
וְתַלְמִידֵיהֶם וְתַלְמִידֵי תַלְמִידֵיהֶם
בְּכָל מְקוֹמוֹת מוֹשְׁבוֹתֵיהֶם, וְנֹאמַר אָמֵן.

יְהִי רָצוֹן מִלְּפְנֵי אָבִינוּ שֶׁבַּשָּׁמַיִם
שֶׁנִּשְׁמַע וְנִתְבַּשֵּׂר בְּשׂוֹרוֹת טוֹבוֹת, יְשׁוּעוֹת וְנֶחָמוֹת
וִיקַבֵּץ נִדָּחֵינוּ מֵאַרְבַּע כַּנְפוֹת הָאָרֶץ, וְנֹאמַר אָמֵן.

All:

אַחֵינוּ כָּל בֵּית יִשְׂרָאֵל
הַנְּתוּנִים בְּצָרָה וּבַשִּׁבְיָה
הָעוֹמְדִים בֵּין בַּיָּם וּבֵין בַּיַּבָּשָׁה
הַמָּקוֹם יְרַחֵם עֲלֵיהֶם וְיוֹצִיאֵם מִצָּרָה לִרְוָחָה
וּמֵאֲפֵלָה לְאוֹרָה, וּמִשִּׁעְבּוּד לִגְאֻלָּה
הַשְׁתָּא בַּעֲגָלָא וּבִזְמַן קָרִיב, וְנֹאמַר אָמֵן.

The prayer for the Welfare of the Canadian Government is on the next page.

PRAYER FOR THE WELFARE OF THE AMERICAN GOVERNMENT

The Leader says the following:

הַנּוֹתֵן תְּשׁוּעָה May He who gives salvation to kings and dominion to princes, whose kingdom is an everlasting kingdom, who delivers His servant David from the evil sword, who makes a way in the sea and a path through the mighty waters, bless and protect, guard and help, exalt, magnify and uplift the President, Vice President and all officials of this land. May the Supreme King of kings in His mercy put into their hearts and the hearts of all their counselors and officials, to deal kindly with us and all Israel. In their days and in ours, may Judah be saved and Israel dwell in safety, and may the Redeemer come to Zion. May this be His will, and let us say: Amen.

PRAYER FOR THE SAFETY OF THE AMERICAN MILITARY

The Leader says the following:

אַדִּיר בַּמָּרוֹם God on high who dwells in might, the King to whom peace belongs, look down from Your holy habitation and bless the soldiers of the American military forces who risk their lives for the sake of peace on earth. Be their shelter and stronghold, and let them not falter. Give them the strength and courage to thwart the plans of the enemy and end the rule of evil. May their enemies be scattered and their foes flee before them, and may they rejoice in Your salvation. Bring them back safely to their homes, as is written: "The LORD *Ps. 121* will guard you from all harm, He will guard your life. The LORD will guard your going and coming, now and for evermore." And may there be fulfilled for us the verse: "Nation shall not lift up sword against *Is. 2* nation, nor shall they learn war any more." Let all the inhabitants on earth know that sovereignty is Yours and Your name inspires awe over all You have created – and let us say: Amen.

_____

Think about the opportunities that this country has given you, your family, your people. Keep these in mind when you recite this prayer.

The prayer for the Welfare of the Canadian Government is on the next page.

תפילה לשלום המלכות

The שליח ציבור says the following:

הַנּוֹתֵן תְּשׁוּעָה לַמְּלָכִים וּמֶמְשָׁלָה לַנְּסִיכִים, מַלְכוּתוֹ מַלְכוּת כָּל עוֹלָמִים, הַפּוֹצֶה אֶת דָּוִד עַבְדּוֹ מֵחֶרֶב רָעָה, הַנּוֹתֵן בַּיָּם דֶּרֶךְ וּבְמַיִם עַזִּים נְתִיבָה, הוּא יְבָרֵךְ וְיִשְׁמֹר וְיִנְצֹר וְיַעֲזֹר וִירוֹמֵם וִיגַדֵּל וִינַשֵּׂא לְמַעְלָה אֶת הַנָּשִׂיא וְאֶת מִשְׁנֵהוּ וְאֶת כָּל שָׂרֵי הָאָרֶץ הַזֹּאת. מֶלֶךְ מַלְכֵי הַמְּלָכִים, בְּרַחֲמָיו יִתֵּן בְּלִבָּם וּבְלֵב כָּל יוֹעֲצֵיהֶם וְשָׂרֵיהֶם לַעֲשׂוֹת טוֹבָה עִמָּנוּ וְעִם כָּל יִשְׂרָאֵל. בִּימֵיהֶם וּבְיָמֵינוּ תִּוָּשַׁע יְהוּדָה, וְיִשְׂרָאֵל יִשְׁכֹּן לָבֶטַח, וּבָא לְצִיּוֹן גּוֹאֵל. וְכֵן יְהִי רָצוֹן, וְנֹאמַר אָמֵן.

תפילה לשלום חיילי צבא ארצות הברית

The שליח ציבור says the following:

אַדִּיר בַּמָּרוֹם שׁוֹכֵן בִּגְבוּרָה, מֶלֶךְ שֶׁהַשָּׁלוֹם שֶׁלּוֹ, הַשְׁקִיפָה מִמְּעוֹן קָדְשֶׁךָ, וּבָרֵךְ אֶת חַיְלֵי צְבָא אַרְצוֹת הַבְּרִית, הַמְחָרְפִים נַפְשָׁם בְּלֶכְתָּם לָשִׂים שָׁלוֹם בָּאָרֶץ. הֱיֵה נָא לָהֶם מַחֲסֶה וּמָעוֹז, וְאַל תִּתֵּן לַמּוֹט רַגְלָם, חַזֵּק יְדֵיהֶם וְאַמֵּץ רוּחָם לְהָפֵר עֲצַת אוֹיֵב וּלְהַעֲבִיר מֶמְשֶׁלֶת זָדוֹן, יָפוּצוּ אוֹיְבֵיהֶם וְיָנוּסוּ מְשַׂנְאֵיהֶם מִפְּנֵיהֶם, וְיִשְׂמְחוּ בִּישׁוּעָתֶךָ. הֲשִׁיבֵם בְּשָׁלוֹם אֶל בֵּיתָם, כַּכָּתוּב בִּדְבָרֵי קָדְשֶׁךָ: יְהוָה תהלים קכא יִשְׁמָרְךָ מִכָּל רָע, יִשְׁמֹר אֶת נַפְשֶׁךָ: יְהוָה יִשְׁמָר צֵאתְךָ וּבוֹאֶךָ, מֵעַתָּה וְעַד עוֹלָם: וְקַיֵּם בָּנוּ מִקְרָא שֶׁכָּתוּב: לֹא יִשָּׂא גוֹי אֶל גּוֹי חֶרֶב, ישעיה ב וְלֹא יִלְמְדוּ עוֹד מִלְחָמָה: וְיֵדְעוּ כָּל יוֹשְׁבֵי תֵבֵל כִּי לְךָ מְלוּכָה יָאֵתָה, וְשִׁמְךָ נוֹרָא עַל כָּל מַה שֶּׁבָּרֵאתָ. וְנֹאמַר אָמֵן.

ANI TEFILLA · אני תפילה

"Seek the peace of the city to which I have exiled you, and pray to God for its sake." (Yirmiyahu 29:7).

Rabbi Ḥanina the deputy [High] Priest said: "Pray for the welfare of the government for if not for its fear, a person would swallow his fellow live." (Pirkei Avot 3:2)

PRAYER FOR THE WELFARE OF THE CANADIAN GOVERNMENT

The Leader says the following:

הַנּוֹתֵן תְּשׁוּעָה May He who gives salvation to kings and dominion to princes, whose kingdom is an everlasting kingdom, who delivers His servant David from the evil sword, who makes a way in the sea and a path through the mighty waters, bless and protect, guard and help, exalt, magnify and uplift the Prime Minister and all the elected and appointed officials of Canada. May the Supreme King of kings in His mercy put into their hearts and the hearts of all their counselors and officials, to deal kindly with us and all Israel. In their days and in ours, may Judah be saved and Israel dwell in safety, and may the Redeemer come to Zion. May this be His will, and let us say: Amen.

PRAYER FOR THE SAFETY OF THE CANADIAN MILITARY FORCES

The Leader says the following:

אַדִּיר בַּמָּרוֹם God on high who dwells in might, the King to whom peace belongs, look down from Your holy habitation and bless the soldiers of the Canadian Forces who risk their lives for the sake of peace on earth. Be their shelter and stronghold, and let them not falter. Give them the strength and courage to thwart the plans of the enemy and end the rule of evil. May their enemies be scattered and their foes flee before them, and may they rejoice in Your salvation. Bring them back safely to their homes, as is written: "The LORD will guard you from all harm, He will *Ps. 121* guard your life. The LORD will guard your going and coming, now and for evermore." And may there be fulfilled for us the verse: "Nation shall *Is. 2* not lift up sword against nation, nor shall they learn war any more." Let all the inhabitants on earth know that sovereignty is Yours and Your name inspires awe over all You have created – and let us say: Amen.

תפילה לשלום המלכות

The שליח ציבור *says the following:*

הַנּוֹתֵן תְּשׁוּעָה לַמְּלָכִים וּמֶמְשָׁלָה לַנְּסִיכִים, מַלְכוּתוֹ מַלְכוּת כָּל
עוֹלָמִים, הַפּוֹצֶה אֶת דָּוִד עַבְדּוֹ מֵחֶרֶב רָעָה, הַנּוֹתֵן בַּיָּם דֶּרֶךְ וּבְמַיִם
עַזִּים נְתִיבָה, הוּא יְבָרֵךְ וְיִשְׁמֹר וְיִנְצֹר וְיַעֲזֹר וִירוֹמֵם וִיגַדֵּל וִינַשֵּׂא
לְמַעְלָה אֶת רֹאשׁ הַמֶּמְשָׁלָה וְאֶת כָּל שָׂרֵי הָאָרֶץ הַזֹּאת. מֶלֶךְ
מַלְכֵי הַמְּלָכִים, בְּרַחֲמָיו יִתֵּן בְּלִבָּם וּבְלֵב כָּל יוֹעֲצֵיהֶם וְשָׂרֵיהֶם
לַעֲשׂוֹת טוֹבָה עִמָּנוּ וְעִם כָּל יִשְׂרָאֵל. בִּימֵיהֶם וּבְיָמֵינוּ תִּוָּשַׁע יְהוּדָה,
וְיִשְׂרָאֵל יִשְׁכֹּן לָבֶטַח, וּבָא לְצִיּוֹן גּוֹאֵל. וְכֵן יְהִי רָצוֹן, וְנֹאמַר אָמֵן.

תפילה לשלום חיילי צבא קנדה

The שליח ציבור *says the following:*

אַדִּיר בַּמָּרוֹם שׁוֹכֵן בִּגְבוּרָה, מֶלֶךְ שֶׁהַשָּׁלוֹם שֶׁלּוֹ, הַשְׁקִיפָה מִמְּעוֹן
קָדְשְׁךָ, וּבָרֵךְ אֶת חַיְלֵי צְבָא קַנָדָה, הַמְחָרְפִים נַפְשָׁם בְּלֶכְתָּם לָשִׂים
שָׁלוֹם בָּאָרֶץ. הֱיֵה נָא לָהֶם מַחֲסֶה וּמָעוֹז, וְאַל תִּתֵּן לַמּוֹט רַגְלָם, חַזֵּק
יְדֵיהֶם וְאַמֵּץ רוּחָם לְהָפֵר עֲצַת אוֹיֵב וּלְהַעֲבִיר מֶמְשֶׁלֶת זָדוֹן, יָפוּצוּ
אוֹיְבֵיהֶם וְיָנוּסוּ מְשַׂנְאֵיהֶם מִפְּנֵיהֶם, וְיִשְׂמְחוּ בִּישׁוּעָתֶךָ. הֲשִׁיבֵם
תהלים קכא — בְּשָׁלוֹם אֶל בֵּיתָם, כַּכָּתוּב בְּדִבְרֵי קָדְשֶׁךָ: יהוה יִשְׁמָרְךָ מִכָּל־רָע,
יִשְׁמֹר אֶת־נַפְשֶׁךָ: יהוה יִשְׁמָר־צֵאתְךָ וּבוֹאֶךָ, מֵעַתָּה וְעַד־עוֹלָם:
ישעיה ב — וְקַיֵּם בָּנוּ מִקְרָא שֶׁכָּתוּב: לֹא־יִשָּׂא גוֹי אֶל־גּוֹי חֶרֶב, וְלֹא־יִלְמְדוּ
עוֹד מִלְחָמָה: וְיֵדְעוּ כָּל יוֹשְׁבֵי תֵבֵל כִּי לְךָ מְלוּכָה יָאָתָה, וְשִׁמְךָ
נוֹרָא עַל כָּל מַה שֶּׁבָּרָאתָ. וְנֹאמַר אָמֵן.

PRAYER FOR THE STATE OF ISRAEL[BA]

The Leader says the following prayer:

אָבִינוּ שֶׁבַּשָּׁמַיִם Heavenly Father, Israel's Rock and Redeemer,¹ bless the State of Israel, the first flowering of our redemption.¹ Shield it under the wings of Your loving-kindness and spread over it the Tabernacle of Your peace.¹ Send Your light and truth to its leaders, ministers and counselors, and direct them with good counsel before You.

Strengthen the hands of the defenders of our Holy Land; grant them deliverance, our God, and crown them with the crown of victory. Grant peace in the land and everlasting joy to its inhabitants.

As for our brothers, the whole house of Israel, remember them in all the lands of our (*In Israel say:* their) dispersion, and swiftly lead us (*In Israel say:* them) upright to Zion Your city, and Jerusalem Your dwelling place, as is written in the Torah of Moses Your servant: "Even if you are scattered to the furthermost lands under the heavens, from there the LORD your God will gather you and take you back. The LORD your God will bring you to the land your ancestors possessed and you will possess it; and He will make you more prosperous and numerous than your ·*Deut. 30*

צוּר יִשְׂרָאֵל וְגוֹאֲלוֹ – *Israel's Rock and Redeemer.* Note the names of Hashem that are used here. Why were these chosen?

When the Declaration of Independence was being drafted in 1948 there was much controversy over whether to include God's name in the text. Secular Zionists were offended at the notion that the achievements of Zionism should be attributed to God, and Religious Zionists were insistent that they should be. The compromise was to include the term "צוּר יִשְׂרָאֵל," a name of God that can also be interpreted in other ways. Now reflect on why the Chief Rabbis in 1948 chose these two names in their prayer for the state.

רֵאשִׁית צְמִיחַת גְּאֻלָּתֵנוּ – *The first flowering of our redemption.* The phrase which

declares that Israel is "the first flowering of our redemption" is one that some have objected to, especially those who would claim that the State of Israel has no religious significance, and they therefore leave out the prayer altogether. Still others have objected to the wish that all Jews eventually settle there. We believe, however, that the modern State, for all of its faults, is the instrument through which Hashem will bring the Jewish people its redemption. For the first time in 2000 years we live in our own sovereign state; that fact alone is cause for thanks and for hope.

סֻכַּת שְׁלוֹמֶךָ – *The Tabernacle of Your peace.* Why do you think it is called the "*sukka*" of peace? What does a *sukka* represent?

תפילה לשלום מדינת ישראל

תפילה לשלום מדינת ישראל

The שליח ציבור *says the following prayer:*

אָבִינוּ שֶׁבַּשָּׁמַיִם, צוּר יִשְׂרָאֵל וְגוֹאֲלוֹ, בָּרֵךְ אֶת מְדִינַת יִשְׂרָאֵל,
רֵאשִׁית צְמִיחַת גְּאֻלָּתֵנוּ. הָגֵן עָלֶיהָ בְּאֶבְרַת חַסְדֶּךָ וּפְרֹשׂ עָלֶיהָ
סֻכַּת שְׁלוֹמֶךָ, וּשְׁלַח אוֹרְךָ וַאֲמִתְּךָ לְרָאשֶׁיהָ, שָׂרֶיהָ וְיוֹעֲצֶיהָ,
וְתַקְּנֵם בְּעֵצָה טוֹבָה מִלְּפָנֶיךָ.

חַזֵּק אֶת יְדֵי מְגִנֵּי אֶרֶץ קָדְשֵׁנוּ, וְהַנְחִילֵם אֱלֹהֵינוּ יְשׁוּעָה וַעֲטֶרֶת
נִצָּחוֹן תְּעַטְּרֵם, וְנָתַתָּ שָׁלוֹם בָּאָרֶץ וְשִׂמְחַת עוֹלָם לְיוֹשְׁבֶיהָ.

וְאֶת אַחֵינוּ כָּל בֵּית יִשְׂרָאֵל, פְּקָד נָא בְּכָל אַרְצוֹת פְּזוּרֵינוּ, וְתוֹלִיכֵנוּ
/בארץ ישראל: פְּזוּרֵיהֶם, וְתוֹלִיכֵם/ מְהֵרָה קוֹמְמִיּוּת לְצִיּוֹן עִירֶךָ וְלִירוּשָׁלַיִם
מִשְׁכַּן שְׁמֶךָ, כַּכָּתוּב בְּתוֹרַת מֹשֶׁה עַבְדֶּךָ: אִם־יִהְיֶה נִדַּחֲךָ בִּקְצֵה
הַשָּׁמַיִם, מִשָּׁם יְקַבֶּצְךָ יהוה אֱלֹהֶיךָ וּמִשָּׁם יִקָּחֶךָ: וֶהֱבִיאֲךָ יהוה
אֱלֹהֶיךָ אֶל־הָאָרֶץ אֲשֶׁר־יָרְשׁוּ אֲבֹתֶיךָ וִירִשְׁתָּהּ, וְהֵיטִבְךָ וְהִרְבְּךָ

דברים ל

ביאור תפילה · BIUR TEFILLA

תפילה לשלום מדינת ישראל – *PRAYER FOR
THE STATE OF ISRAEL.* The Prayer for the State
of Israel was written by Chief Rabbis Herzog
and Uziel in 1948 (allegedly with some mi-
nor revisions made by Noble Laureate Shai

Agnon). This prayer is a modern contribution to the ongoing millennial development
of the siddur as a microcosm of Jewish history, wherein each generation adds its own
concerns and aspirations.

אני תפילה · ANI TEFILLA

תפילה לשלום מדינת ישראל – *PRAYER FOR
THE STATE OF ISRAEL.*
*Once I sat on the steps by a gate at David's
Tower, I placed my two heavy baskets at my
side. A group of tourists was standing around
their guide and I became their target marker.
"You see that man with the baskets? Just right
of his head there's an arch from the Roman*

*period. Just right of his head." "But he's mov-
ing, he's moving!" I said to myself: redemption will come only if their guide tells them,
"You see that arch from the Roman period? It's
not important: but next to it, left and down a
bit, there sits a man who's bought fruit and
vegetables for his family." (Yehuda Amichai,
Tourists)*

ancestors. Then the LORD your God will open up your heart and the heart of your descendants, to love the LORD your God with all your heart and with all your soul, that you may live."

Unite our hearts to love and revere Your name and observe all the words of Your Torah, and swiftly send us Your righteous anointed one of the house of David, to redeem those who long for Your salvation.

Appear in Your glorious majesty over all the dwellers on earth, and let all who breathe declare: The LORD God of Israel is King and His kingship has dominion over all. Amen, Selah.

PRAYER FOR ISRAEL'S DEFENSE FORCES[A]

The Leader says the following prayer:

מִי שֶׁבֵּרַךְ May He who blessed our ancestors, Abraham, Isaac and Jacob, bless the members of Israel's Defense Forces and its security services who stand guard over our land and the cities of our God from the Lebanese border to the Egyptian desert, from the Mediterranean sea to the approach of the Aravah, and wherever else they are, on land, in air and at sea. May the LORD make the enemies who rise against us be struck down before them. May the Holy One, blessed be He, protect and deliver them from all trouble and distress, affliction and illness, and send blessing and success to all the work of their hands. May He subdue our enemies under them and crown them with deliverance and victory. And may there be fulfilled in them the verse, "It is the LORD your God who goes with you to fight for you against your enemies, to deliver you." And let us say: Amen.   *Deut. 20*

---

with laughter and good cheer as they thanked us for coming and we thanked them for their service. When it came time to part company, one of them, a seemingly non-religious soldier, turned to me and on behalf of his comrades asked that we provide them with a blessing. I was stunned and speechless. What could I, someone from the Diaspora, who had never served in the army, say to these young men? Suddenly, one of my students stepped in and began to recite the Prayer for the Israel Defense Forces. The rest of the students quickly joined in, for they all knew it by heart after reciting it regularly in school. A bunch of young people from a day school in New York joined together in a common bond with a bunch of young people on the front lines of battle half a world away. A couple of the soldiers in the jeep had tears in their eyes. And so did I. Through this tefilla we became one.

מֵאֲבֹתֶיךָ: וּמָל יהוה אֱלֹהֶיךָ אֶת־לְבָבְךָ וְאֶת־לְבַב זַרְעֶךָ, לְאַהֲבָה אֶת־יהוה אֱלֹהֶיךָ בְּכָל־לְבָבְךָ וּבְכָל־נַפְשְׁךָ, לְמַעַן חַיֶּיךָ:

וְיַחֵד לְבָבֵנוּ לְאַהֲבָה וּלְיִרְאָה אֶת שְׁמֶךָ, וְלִשְׁמֹר אֶת כָּל דִּבְרֵי תוֹרָתֶךָ, וּשְׁלַח לָנוּ מְהֵרָה בֶן דָּוִד מְשִׁיחַ צִדְקֶךָ, לִפְדּוֹת מְחַכֵּי קֵץ יְשׁוּעָתֶךָ:

וְהוֹפַע בַּהֲדַר גְּאוֹן עֻזֶּךָ עַל כָּל יוֹשְׁבֵי תֵבֵל אַרְצֶךָ וְיֹאמַר כֹּל אֲשֶׁר נְשָׁמָה בְאַפּוֹ, יהוה אֱלֹהֵי יִשְׂרָאֵל מֶלֶךְ וּמַלְכוּתוֹ בַּכֹּל מָשֳׁלָה, אָמֵן סֶלָה.

The שליח ציבור says the following prayer:

מִי שֶׁבֵּרַךְ אֲבוֹתֵינוּ אַבְרָהָם יִצְחָק וְיַעֲקֹב הוּא יְבָרֵךְ אֶת חַיָּלֵי צְבָא הַהֲגָנָה לְיִשְׂרָאֵל וְאַנְשֵׁי כֹּחוֹת הַבִּטָּחוֹן, הָעוֹמְדִים עַל מִשְׁמַר אַרְצֵנוּ וְעָרֵי אֱלֹהֵינוּ, מִגְּבוּל הַלְּבָנוֹן וְעַד מִדְבַּר מִצְרַיִם וּמִן הַיָּם הַגָּדוֹל עַד לְבוֹא הָעֲרָבָה וּבְכָל מָקוֹם שֶׁהֵם, בַּיַּבָּשָׁה, בָּאֲוִיר וּבַיָּם. יִתֵּן יהוה אֶת אוֹיְבֵינוּ הַקָּמִים עָלֵינוּ נִגָּפִים לִפְנֵיהֶם. הַקָּדוֹשׁ בָּרוּךְ הוּא יִשְׁמֹר וְיַצִּיל אֶת חַיָּלֵינוּ מִכָּל צָרָה וְצוּקָה וּמִכָּל נֶגַע וּמַחֲלָה, וְיִשְׁלַח בְּרָכָה וְהַצְלָחָה בְּכָל מַעֲשֵׂי יְדֵיהֶם. יַדְבֵּר שׂוֹנְאֵינוּ תַּחְתֵּיהֶם וִיעַטְּרֵם בְּכֶתֶר יְשׁוּעָה וּבַעֲטֶרֶת נִצָּחוֹן. וִיקֻיַּם בָּהֶם הַכָּתוּב: כִּי יהוה אֱלֹהֵיכֶם הַהֹלֵךְ עִמָּכֶם לְהִלָּחֵם לָכֶם עִם־אֹיְבֵיכֶם לְהוֹשִׁיעַ אֶתְכֶם: וְנֹאמַר אָמֵן.

דברים כ

מי שברך לחיילי צה״ל – *PRAYER FOR ISRAEL'S DEFENSE FORCES.*
I was touring the Israeli-Lebanese border with

some students when a group of Israeli soldiers on patrol in a jeep and personnel carrier stopped to greet us. The encounter was filled

RETURNING THE TORAH TO THE ARK

The Ark is opened. The Leader takes the Torah scroll and says:

יְהַלְלוּ Let them praise the name of the LORD,   *Ps. 148*
    for His name alone is sublime.

The congregation responds:

הוֹדוֹ His majesty is above earth and heaven.
    He has raised the horn of His people,
    for the glory of all His devoted ones,
    the children of Israel, the people close to Him.
    Halleluya!

As the Torah scroll is returned to the Ark, say:

לְדָוִד מִזְמוֹר A psalm of David. The earth is the LORD's and all it contains, *Ps. 24*
the world and all who live in it. For He founded it on the seas and established it on the streams. Who may climb the mountain of the LORD?
Who may stand in His holy place? He who has clean hands and a pure
heart, who has not taken My name in vain, or sworn deceitfully. He shall
receive blessing from the LORD, and just reward from God, his salvation.
This is a generation of those who seek Him, the descendants of Jacob
who seek Your presence, Selah! Lift up your heads, O gates; be uplifted,
eternal doors, so that the King of glory may enter. Who is the King of
glory? It is the LORD, strong and mighty, the LORD mighty in battle. Lift
up your heads, O gates; lift them up, eternal doors, so that the King of
glory may enter. Who is He, the King of glory? The LORD of hosts, He
is the King of glory, Selah!

As the Torah scroll is placed into the Ark, say:

וּבְנֻחֹה יֹאמַר When the Ark came to rest, Moses would say: "Return, O   *Num. 10*
LORD, to the myriad thousands of Israel." Advance, LORD, to Your resting   *Ps. 132*
place, You and Your mighty Ark. Your priests are clothed in righteousness,
and Your devoted ones sing in joy. For the sake of Your servant David,
do not reject Your anointed one. For I give you good instruction; do not   *Prov. 4*
forsake My Torah. It is a tree of life to those who grasp it, and those who   *Prov. 3*
uphold it are happy. Its ways are ways of pleasantness, and all its paths
are peace. ▸ Turn us back, O LORD, to You, and we will return. Renew   *Lam. 5*
our days as of old.

The Ark is closed.

הכנסת ספר תורה

The *ארון קודש* is opened. The *שליח ציבור* takes the *ספר תורה* *and says:*

תהלים קמח

יְהַלְלוּ אֶת־שֵׁם יהוה, כִּי נִשְׂגָּב שְׁמוֹ, לְבַדּוֹ

The *קהל* *responds:*

הוֹדוֹ עַל־אֶרֶץ וְשָׁמָיִם:
וַיָּרֶם קֶרֶן לְעַמּוֹ
תְּהִלָּה לְכָל־חֲסִידָיו
לִבְנֵי יִשְׂרָאֵל עַם קְרֹבוֹ, הַלְלוּיָהּ:

As the *ספר תורה* is returned to the *ארון קודש*, *say:*

תהלים כד

לְדָוִד מִזְמוֹר, לַיהוה הָאָרֶץ וּמְלוֹאָהּ, תֵּבֵל וְיֹשְׁבֵי בָהּ: כִּי־הוּא עַל־
יַמִּים יְסָדָהּ, וְעַל־נְהָרוֹת יְכוֹנְנֶהָ: מִי־יַעֲלֶה בְהַר־יהוה, וּמִי־יָקוּם
בִּמְקוֹם קָדְשׁוֹ: נְקִי כַפַּיִם וּבַר־לֵבָב, אֲשֶׁר לֹא־נָשָׂא לַשָּׁוְא נַפְשִׁי
וְלֹא נִשְׁבַּע לְמִרְמָה: יִשָּׂא בְרָכָה מֵאֵת יהוה, וּצְדָקָה מֵאֱלֹהֵי יִשְׁעוֹ:
זֶה דּוֹר דֹּרְשָׁו, מְבַקְשֵׁי פָנֶיךָ, יַעֲקֹב, סֶלָה: שְׂאוּ שְׁעָרִים רָאשֵׁיכֶם,
וְהִנָּשְׂאוּ פִּתְחֵי עוֹלָם, וְיָבוֹא מֶלֶךְ הַכָּבוֹד: מִי זֶה מֶלֶךְ הַכָּבוֹד, יהוה
עִזּוּז וְגִבּוֹר, יהוה גִּבּוֹר מִלְחָמָה: שְׂאוּ שְׁעָרִים רָאשֵׁיכֶם, וּשְׂאוּ פִּתְחֵי
עוֹלָם, וְיָבֹא מֶלֶךְ הַכָּבוֹד: מִי הוּא זֶה מֶלֶךְ הַכָּבוֹד, יהוה צְבָאוֹת
הוּא מֶלֶךְ הַכָּבוֹד, סֶלָה:

As the *ספר תורה* is placed into the *ארון קודש*, *say:*

במדברי
תהלים קלב

וּבְנֻחֹה יֹאמַר, שׁוּבָה יהוה רִבְבוֹת אַלְפֵי יִשְׂרָאֵל: קוּמָה יהוה
לִמְנוּחָתֶךָ, אַתָּה וַאֲרוֹן עֻזֶּךָ: כֹּהֲנֶיךָ יִלְבְּשׁוּ־צֶדֶק, וַחֲסִידֶיךָ יְרַנֵּנוּ:

משלי ד
משלי ג
איכה ה

בַּעֲבוּר דָּוִד עַבְדֶּךָ אַל־תָּשֵׁב פְּנֵי מְשִׁיחֶךָ: כִּי לֶקַח טוֹב נָתַתִּי לָכֶם,
תּוֹרָתִי אַל־תַּעֲזֹבוּ: עֵץ־חַיִּים הִיא לַמַּחֲזִיקִים בָּהּ, וְתֹמְכֶיהָ מְאֻשָּׁר:
דְּרָכֶיהָ דַרְכֵי־נֹעַם וְכָל־נְתִיבוֹתֶיהָ שָׁלוֹם: ◂ הֲשִׁיבֵנוּ יהוה אֵלֶיךָ וְנָשׁוּבָה,
חַדֵּשׁ יָמֵינוּ כְּקֶדֶם:

The *ארון קודש* is closed.

CONCLUSION OF THE SERVICE

Some have the custom to touch the hand-tefillin at °, and the head-tefillin at °°.

אַשְׁרֵי **Happy**[ß] are those who dwell in Your House;   Ps. 84
they shall continue to praise You, Selah!
Happy are the people for whom this is so;   Ps. 144
happy are the people whose God is the LORD.

The prayer thus ensures that one begins one's day with Torah learning before venturing out of *shul*.

A second theory, presented in the name of Rashi, suggests that there was a time when the government would not permit Jews to say the *Kedusha* in the *Shemoneh Esreh* because the Jews rejected the understanding of the threefold repetition of *kadosh* as a reference to different manifestations of God. They therefore sent spies into the *shul* at that time to make sure it was not recited. By the end of the service, however, the spies had left and so the congregants slipped in this *Kedusha* in order to be able to sanctify God's name before starting one's day (*Sefer HaPardes*). *Kedusha* follows a specific order, or *seder*, and therefore it is known as *Kedusha deSidra*.

Finally, there is another theory which suggests that there were people who came late to *shul* (can you believe that?!) and thus missed saying the *Kedusha* in the *Shemoneh Esreh*. These people were generally the more unlearned and therefore the *Kedusha* was translated into the vernacular so that they would understand it. Indeed, the entire prayer may be a kind of summary of the *Shemoneh Esreh* (God's name is mentioned 18 times) (Abudarham). Its insertion at this

point in the service ensures that before we embark on our day, we come together as a community to sanctify God's name.

There are a few parts to this very ancient prayer. The first part speaks about the coming of the Redeemer, a fitting hope to have before one walks away from *tefilla* to begin one's day, especially after the allusion that we just made in Psalm 20 to the fact that life can have its sad or tragic moments.

Another section refers to Torah study. Before leaving *shul* to begin our day we restate the importance of learning as a core value, reflecting our millennia-old commitment to Torah as that which has kept us alive as a people. Indeed, Rabbi Meir Simḥa of Dvinsk suggested that this is the difference between this *Kedusha* and the other ones we have recited. In *Pesukei DeZimra* we described the *Kedusha* that the angels say on high; in the repetition of the *Shemoneh Esreh* we said the *Kedusha* as if we were angels ourselves; here, we create *Kedusha* through our Torah study, a sound that not even the angels can make (*Meshekh Ḥokhma Vayikra* 19).

But the sum total of the prayer seems to point toward putting one's faith in God and His Torah. In a world in which people are often asking "Why was I created?" or "What is the purpose of life?" Judaism's response

The continuation of this INTRODUCTION *and* BIUR TEFILLA *on* אַשְׁרֵי *are on page 243.*

סיום התפילה

Some have the custom to touch the תפילין של יד *at* °, *and the* תפילין של ראש *at* °°.

תהלים פד

אַשְׁרֵי° יוֹשְׁבֵי בֵיתֶךָ, עוֹד יְהַלְלוּךָ סֶּלָה:

תהלים קמד

אַשְׁרֵי הָעָם שֶׁכָּכָה לּוֹ, אַשְׁרֵי הָעָם שֶׁיהוה אֱלֹהָיו:

INTRODUCTION TO KEDUSHA DESIDRA: קדושה דסדרא

The service begins to draw to a close. *Shemoneh Esreh* is over, *Kaddish* has been recited to complete the previous section, and we now move toward the final segment. The entire section is called by the prayer which concludes it, known as *Kedusha deSidra*, literally "the *Kedusha* of the order," the most important part of which is, as one would imagine, the *Kedusha* that is recited with its Aramaic translation. The section actually consists of three parts. The first is *Ashrei*, repeated here for a second time in *Shaharit*, in keeping with the Talmud's statement that "whoever says *Ashrei* three times a day is guaranteed a place in the World to Come" (*Berakhot* 4b). The third recitation will take place at *Minha*. Indeed, just as in *Minha* we have *Ashrei* followed by the *Kedusha* of *Shemoneh Esreh*, so too, here, we have *Ashrei* followed by the *Kedusha deSidra*. *Ashrei* describes a perfect world, an ideal state in which all of the world is in harmony; a fitting way to view the beginning of one's day.

The second component of this section is Psalm 20. This particular psalm also exudes confidence and optimism that all of our prayers will be answered (יְמַלֵּא יהוה כָּל מִשְׁאֲלוֹתֶיךָ). Indeed, it has been suggested that this twentieth psalm is the culmination of the previous 19 in *Sefer Tehillim*, and thus serves as a fitting summary here for a different 19, namely, the 19 blessings of the *Shemoneh Esreh* that we just recited. Because of its suggestion that God will even answer us on a *yom tzara*, a day of distress, it is omitted on holidays which cannot be characterized in such a negative way. Conversely, it is also omitted in the house of a mourner because we do not want to add to the distress which is already felt.

The final prayer in the section is the prayer from which the section derives its name: *Kedusha deSidra*. While the Gemara itself mentions this *tefilla* ("The world subsists on the *Kedusha deSidra*" – *Sota* 49a), it is not clear why it was instituted. The oldest explanation is that of Rabbi Natronai Gaon, who said that in Talmudic times before leaving *shul* they learned Torah together, which included the recitation of verses and their translation into the vernacular, which was Aramaic. Unfortunately, time constraints eventually dictated that this learning be curtailed and all that remains are some representative parts of Tanakh, specifically the sections that we know as *Kedusha*. A block of time dedicated to learning is known as a *seder*, hence this section became known as *Kedusha deSidra*, or the *Kedusha* which follows a *seder* of learning (*Teshuvot HaGeonim*).

A song of praise by David.

Ps. 145

א I will exalt You, my God, the King,
　　and bless Your name for ever and all time.

ב Every day I will bless You,
　　and praise Your name for ever and all time.

ג Great is the LORD and greatly to be praised;
　　His greatness is unfathomable.

ד One generation will praise Your works to the next,
　　and tell of Your mighty deeds.

ה On the glorious splendor of Your majesty I will meditate,
　　and on the acts of Your wonders.

ו They shall talk of the power of Your awesome deeds,
　　and I will tell of Your greatness.

ז They shall recite the record of Your great goodness,
　　and sing with joy of Your righteousness.

ח The LORD is gracious and compassionate,
　　slow to anger and great in loving-kindness.

ט The LORD is good to all,
　　and His compassion extends to all His works.

י All Your works shall thank You, LORD,
　　and Your devoted ones shall bless You.

כ They shall talk of the glory of Your kingship,
　　and speak of Your might.

ל To make known to mankind His mighty deeds
　　and the glorious majesty of His kingship.

מ Your kingdom is an everlasting kingdom,
　　and Your reign is for all generations.

ס The LORD supports all who fall,
　　and raises all who are bowed down.

ע All raise their eyes to You in hope,
　　and You give them their food in due season.

out our day. Numerous studies have correlations that indicate that people who pray are better able to cope with the challenges that each day brings. Belief brings relief.

תְּהִלָּה לְדָוִד

אֲרוֹמִמְךָ אֱלוֹהַי הַמֶּלֶךְ, וַאֲבָרְכָה שִׁמְךָ לְעוֹלָם וָעֶד:

בְּכָל־יוֹם אֲבָרְכֶךָּ, וַאֲהַלְלָה שִׁמְךָ לְעוֹלָם וָעֶד:

גָּדוֹל יהוה וּמְהֻלָּל מְאֹד, וְלִגְדֻלָּתוֹ אֵין חֵקֶר:

דּוֹר לְדוֹר יְשַׁבַּח מַעֲשֶׂיךָ, וּגְבוּרֹתֶיךָ יַגִּידוּ:

הֲדַר כְּבוֹד הוֹדֶךָ, וְדִבְרֵי נִפְלְאֹתֶיךָ אָשִׂיחָה:

וֶעֱזוּז נוֹרְאֹתֶיךָ יֹאמֵרוּ, וּגְדֻלָּתְךָ אֲסַפְּרֶנָּה:

זֵכֶר רַב־טוּבְךָ יַבִּיעוּ, וְצִדְקָתְךָ יְרַנֵּנוּ:

חַנּוּן וְרַחוּם יהוה, אֶרֶךְ אַפַּיִם וּגְדָל־חָסֶד:

טוֹב־יהוה לַכֹּל, וְרַחֲמָיו עַל־כָּל־מַעֲשָׂיו:

יוֹדוּךָ יהוה כָּל־מַעֲשֶׂיךָ, וַחֲסִידֶיךָ יְבָרְכוּכָה:

כְּבוֹד מַלְכוּתְךָ יֹאמֵרוּ, וּגְבוּרָתְךָ יְדַבֵּרוּ:

לְהוֹדִיעַ לִבְנֵי הָאָדָם גְּבוּרֹתָיו, וּכְבוֹד הֲדַר מַלְכוּתוֹ:

מַלְכוּתְךָ מַלְכוּת כָּל־עֹלָמִים, וּמֶמְשַׁלְתְּךָ בְּכָל־דּוֹר וָדֹר:

סוֹמֵךְ יהוה לְכָל־הַנֹּפְלִים, וְזוֹקֵף לְכָל־הַכְּפוּפִים:

עֵינֵי־כֹל אֵלֶיךָ יְשַׂבֵּרוּ, וְאַתָּה נוֹתֵן־לָהֶם אֶת־אָכְלָם בְּעִתּוֹ:

---

is that each of us is unique and was created for a specific purpose, even if we are not yet aware of what that purpose is. We have an identity that binds us to thousands of years of tradition and commitment, and faith which assures us that a bright future lies ahead. Life, especially a life in which one

has pride for one's identity, is full of beauty and meaning, even as some individual days can seem overbearing and difficult. The person who puts his or her faith in God knows that such setbacks are temporary and can be overcome. Thus fortified, one can begin a new day.

BIUR TEFILLA · ביאור תפילה

אַשְׁרֵי – *Happy.* There are no requests here. The prayer speaks only of Hashem's watching

out for the world, and so we now remind ourselves that He will continue to do so through-

פ ˚You open Your hand,
˚˚and satisfy every living thing with favor.
צ The LORD is righteous in all His ways,
and kind in all He does.
ק The LORD is close to all who call on Him,
to all who call on Him in truth.
ר He fulfills the will of those who revere Him;
He hears their cry and saves them.
ש The LORD guards all who love Him,
but all the wicked He will destroy.
ת ‣ My mouth shall speak the praise of the LORD,
and all creatures shall bless His holy name for ever and all time.

We will bless the LORD now and for ever. Halleluya!   *Ps. 115*

*Omit on Rosh Ḥodesh, Ḥol HaMo'ed, Erev Pesaḥ, Erev Yom Kippur, Ḥanukka,
the 14th and 15th of Adar I, Purim and Shushan Purim, Yom HaAtzma'ut,
Yom Yerushalayim, Tisha B'Av, or in a house of mourning, and in Israel on Isru Ḥag.*

לַמְנַצֵּחַ For the conductor of music. A psalm of David.ᴮ May the LORD   *Ps. 20*
answer you when you are in distress; may the name of Jacob's God
protect you. May He send you help from the Sanctuary and support
from Zion. May He remember all your meal-offerings and accept
your burnt-offerings, Selah! May He give you your heart's desire and
make all your plans succeed. We will shout for joy at Your salvation
and lift a banner in the name of our God. May the LORD grant all your
requests. Now I know that the LORD saves His anointed; He answers
him from His holy heaven with the saving power of His right hand.
Some trust in chariots, others in horses, but we call on the name of
the LORD our God. They were brought to their knees and fell, but we
rose up and stood firm. ‣ LORD, save! May the King answer us on the
day we call.

---

that no such device is reliable. The ultimate
answer on the battlefield of war and of
life lies elsewhere. Our greatest enemy is

our own lack of faith and optimism that
things will work out; our greatest source of
strength lies above.

°פּוֹתֵחַ אֶת־יָדֶךָ, °°וּמַשְׂבִּיעַ לְכָל־חַי רָצוֹן:

צַדִּיק יהוה בְּכָל־דְּרָכָיו, וְחָסִיד בְּכָל־מַעֲשָׂיו:

קָרוֹב יהוה לְכָל־קֹרְאָיו, לְכֹל אֲשֶׁר יִקְרָאֻהוּ בֶאֱמֶת:

רְצוֹן־יְרֵאָיו יַעֲשֶׂה, וְאֶת־שַׁוְעָתָם יִשְׁמַע, וְיוֹשִׁיעֵם:

שׁוֹמֵר יהוה אֶת־כָּל־אֹהֲבָיו, וְאֵת כָּל־הָרְשָׁעִים יַשְׁמִיד:

‹ תְּהִלַּת יהוה יְדַבֶּר פִּי, וִיבָרֵךְ כָּל־בָּשָׂר שֵׁם קָדְשׁוֹ לְעוֹלָם וָעֶד:

וַאֲנַחְנוּ נְבָרֵךְ יָהּ מֵעַתָּה וְעַד־עוֹלָם, הַלְלוּיָהּ:

תהלים קטו

Omit on חנוכה, ערב יום כיפור ,ערב פסח, חול המועד ,ראש חודש,
יום העצמאות, שושן פורים <i>and</i> פורים אדר א' <i>of</i> the 14th and 15th
אסרו חג <i>on</i> ארץ ישראל, תשעה באב, יום ירושלים, <i>or in a house of mourning, and in</i></div>

תהלים כ

לַמְנַצֵּחַ מִזְמוֹר לְדָוִד: יַעַנְךָ יהוה בְּיוֹם צָרָה, יְשַׂגֶּבְךָ שֵׁם אֱלֹהֵי

יַעֲקֹב: יִשְׁלַח־עֶזְרְךָ מִקֹּדֶשׁ, וּמִצִּיּוֹן יִסְעָדֶךָּ: יִזְכֹּר כָּל־מִנְחֹתֶךָ,

וְעוֹלָתְךָ יְדַשְּׁנֶה סֶּלָה: יִתֶּן־לְךָ כִלְבָבֶךָ, וְכָל־עֲצָתְךָ יְמַלֵּא: נְרַנְּנָה

בִּישׁוּעָתֶךָ, וּבְשֵׁם־אֱלֹהֵינוּ נִדְגֹּל, יְמַלֵּא יהוה כָּל־מִשְׁאֲלוֹתֶיךָ:

עַתָּה יָדַעְתִּי כִּי הוֹשִׁיעַ יהוה מְשִׁיחוֹ, יַעֲנֵהוּ מִשְּׁמֵי קָדְשׁוֹ, בִּגְבֻרוֹת

יֵשַׁע יְמִינוֹ: אֵלֶּה בָרֶכֶב וְאֵלֶּה בַסּוּסִים, וַאֲנַחְנוּ בְּשֵׁם־יהוה אֱלֹהֵינוּ

נַזְכִּיר: הֵמָּה כָּרְעוּ וְנָפָלוּ, וַאֲנַחְנוּ קַּמְנוּ וַנִּתְעוֹדָד: ‹ יהוה הוֹשִׁיעָה,

הַמֶּלֶךְ יַעֲנֵנוּ בְיוֹם־קָרְאֵנוּ:

BIUR TEFILLA · ביאור תפילה	IYUN TEFILLA · עיון תפילה
לַמְנַצֵּחַ מִזְמוֹר לְדָוִד — *For the conductor of music. A psalm of David.* The psalm reassures a king (David) that as he goes out to do battle, Hashem will be with him. We too are encouraged to believe the same thing as we are about to begin our day.	**וַאֲנַחְנוּ בְּשֵׁם־יהוה אֱלֹהֵינוּ נַזְכִּיר** — *But we call on the name of the LORD our God.* Nations have too often believed that their success lies in the development of the ultimate weapon, from horses and chariots to a nuclear arsenal. Yet we Jews are reminded

*In a house of mourning and on Tisha B'Av omit the verse beginning
"As for Me" and continue with "You are the Holy One."*

וּבָא לְצִיּוֹן גּוֹאֵל "A redeemer will come to Zion,   *Is. 59*
to those in Jacob who repent of their sins," declares the Lord.
"As for Me, this is My covenant with them," says the Lord.
"My spirit, that is on you,
and My words I have placed in your mouth
will not depart from your mouth,
or from the mouth of your children,
or from the mouth of their descendants from this time on
and for ever," says the Lord.

▸ You are the Holy One, enthroned on the praises of Israel.   *Ps. 22*
And (the angels) call to one another, saying, "Holy, holy, holy   *Is. 6*
is the Lord of hosts; the whole world is filled with His glory."
And they receive permission from one another, saying: *Targum Yonatan Is. 6*
"Holy in the highest heavens, home of His Presence; holy on earth,
the work of His strength; holy for ever and all time is the Lord of hosts;
the whole earth is full of His radiant glory."

▸ Then a wind lifted me up and I heard behind me   *Ezek. 3*
the sound of a great noise, saying,
"Blessed is the Lord's glory from His place."
Then a wind lifted me up and I heard behind me   *Targum Yonatan Ezek. 3*
the sound of a great tempest of those who uttered praise, saying,
"Blessed is the Lord's glory from the place of the home of His Presence."

The Lord shall reign for ever and all time.   *Ex. 15*
The Lord's kingdom is established for ever and all time.   *Targum Onkelos Ex. 15*

יהוה Lord, God of Abraham, Isaac and Yisrael, our ancestors, may You   *1 Chr. 29*
keep this for ever so that it forms the thoughts in Your people's heart,
and directs their heart toward You. He is compassionate. He forgives   *Ps. 78*
iniquity and does not destroy. Repeatedly He suppresses His anger,
not rousing His full wrath. For You, my Lord, are good and forgiving,   *Ps. 86*
abundantly kind to all who call on You. Your righteousness is eternally   *Ps. 119*

---

residence of the Divine. The second "holy" re-   of His creation. The third "holy" refers to God's
fers to God's holiness on earth, the residence   holiness in time, forever and ever.

In a house of mourning and on תשעה באב *omit the verse*
beginning וַאֲנִי זֹאת בְּרִיתִי *and continue with* וְאַתָּה קָדוֹשׁ.

וּבָא לְצִיּוֹן גּוֹאֵל, וּלְשָׁבֵי פֶשַׁע בְּיַעֲקֹב, נְאֻם יהוה:

וַאֲנִי זֹאת בְּרִיתִי אוֹתָם, אָמַר יהוה

רוּחִי אֲשֶׁר עָלֶיךָ וּדְבָרַי אֲשֶׁר־שַׂמְתִּי בְּפִיךָ

לֹא־יָמוּשׁוּ מִפִּיךָ וּמִפִּי זַרְעֲךָ וּמִפִּי זֶרַע זַרְעֲךָ

אָמַר יהוה, מֵעַתָּה וְעַד־עוֹלָם:

ישעיה נט

▶ וְאַתָּה קָדוֹשׁ יוֹשֵׁב תְּהִלּוֹת יִשְׂרָאֵל: וְקָרָא זֶה אֶל־זֶה וְאָמַר
קָדוֹשׁ, קָדוֹשׁ, קָדוֹשׁ יהוה צְבָאוֹת, מְלֹא כָל־הָאָרֶץ כְּבוֹדוֹ:

תהלים כב
ישעיה ו

וּמְקַבְּלִין דֵּין מִן דֵּין וְאָמְרִין, קַדִּישׁ בִּשְׁמֵי מְרוֹמָא עִלָּאָה בֵּית שְׁכִינְתֵּהּ
קַדִּישׁ עַל אַרְעָא עוֹבַד גְּבוּרְתֵּהּ, קַדִּישׁ לְעָלַם וּלְעָלְמֵי עָלְמַיָּא
יהוה צְבָאוֹת, מַלְיָא כָל אַרְעָא זִיו יְקָרֵהּ.

תרגום
יונתן
ישעיה ו

▶ וַתִּשָּׂאֵנִי רוּחַ, וָאֶשְׁמַע אַחֲרַי קוֹל רַעַשׁ גָּדוֹל
בָּרוּךְ כְּבוֹד־יהוה מִמְּקוֹמוֹ:

יחזקאל ג

וּנְטָלַתְנִי רוּחָא, וּשְׁמָעִית בַּתְרַי קָל זֵיעַ סַגִּיא, דִּמְשַׁבְּחִין וְאָמְרִין
בְּרִיךְ יְקָרָא דַיהוה מֵאֲתַר בֵּית שְׁכִינְתֵּהּ.

תרגום
יונתן
יחזקאל ג

יהוה יִמְלֹךְ לְעֹלָם וָעֶד:

שמות טו

יהוה מַלְכוּתֵהּ קָאֵם לְעָלַם וּלְעָלְמֵי עָלְמַיָּא.

תרגום
אונקלוס
שמות טו

יהוה אֱלֹהֵי אַבְרָהָם יִצְחָק וְיִשְׂרָאֵל אֲבֹתֵינוּ, שָׁמְרָה־זֹאת לְעוֹלָם
לְיֵצֶר מַחְשְׁבוֹת לְבַב עַמֶּךָ, וְהָכֵן לְבָבָם אֵלֶיךָ: וְהוּא רַחוּם יְכַפֵּר
עָוֹן וְלֹא־יַשְׁחִית, וְהִרְבָּה לְהָשִׁיב אַפּוֹ, וְלֹא־יָעִיר כָּל־חֲמָתוֹ:
כִּי־אַתָּה אֲדֹנָי טוֹב וְסַלָּח, וְרַב־חֶסֶד לְכָל־קֹרְאֶיךָ: צִדְקָתְךָ

דברי הימים
א׳ כט
תהלים עח
תהלים פו

עִיּוּן תְּפִלָּה · IYUN TEFILLA

קָדוֹשׁ, קָדוֹשׁ, קָדוֹשׁ – *Holy, holy, holy.* Why
does the verse from *Yishayahu* repeat the

word *kadosh* three times? The first "holy" refers to God's holiness in heaven above, the

righteous, and Your Torah is truth. Grant truth to Jacob, loving-kindness *Mic. 7*
to Abraham, as You promised our ancestors in ancient times. Blessed *Ps. 68*
is my LORD for day after day He burdens us [with His blessings];¹ God.
is our salvation, Selah! The LORD of hosts is with us; the God of Jacob *Ps. 46*
is our refuge, Selah! LORD of hosts, happy is the one who trusts in You. *Ps. 84*
LORD, save!ᴬ May the King answer us on the day we call. *Ps. 20*

בָּרוּךְ Blessed is He, our God, who created us for His glory, separating
us from those who go astray; who gave us the Torah of truth, planting
within us eternal life. May He open our heart to His Torah, imbuing
our heart with the love and awe of Him, that we may do His will and
serve Him with a perfect heart, so that we neither toil in vain nor give
birth to confusion.

יְהִי רָצוֹן May it be Your will, O LORD our God and God of our ancestors,
that we keep Your laws in this world, and thus be worthy to live, see and
inherit goodness and blessing in the Messianic Age and in the life of the
World to Come. So that my soul may sing to You and not be silent. LORD, *Ps. 30*
my God, for ever I will thank You. Blessed is the man who trusts in the *Jer. 17*
LORD, whose trust is in the LORD alone. Trust in the LORD for evermore, *Is. 26*
for God, the LORD, is an everlasting Rock. ▸ Those who know Your name *Ps. 9*
trust in You, for You, LORD, do not forsake those who seek You. The LORD *Is. 42*
desired, for the sake of Israel's merit, to make the Torah great and glorious.

*On Rosh Ḥodesh and Ḥol HaMo'ed, the Leader says Half Kaddish, page 226. The service
then continues with Musaf for Rosh Ḥodesh on page 458. for Ḥol HaMo'ed on page 502.*

On other days, the Leader continues with Full Kaddish on the next page.

ANI TEFILLA · אני תפילה

*A pauper once encountered a wealthy man
on the street and begged him for some
money. The rich man said that he hadn't
enough with him but if the pauper were to
come to his home that evening, he would
give him even more than he asked for. The
wealthy man waited all night but the pauper did not come. The next day, the rich man
was accosted by the same pauper who once
again pleaded with him for money. Again the
wealthy man told him to come to his home*

*and again the poor man did not show up. The
next day, the pauper found the potential benefactor once more, but this time the wealthy
man laughed at him that he was a liar and a
charlatan.*

*Every day we ask Hashem in our prayers
for the ability to understand and learn and live
Torah. And He is willing to help us with that
and more. He asks only one thing: we need to
show up and be willing to do so earnestly and
honestly. (Ḥafetz Ḥayyim)*

מיכה ז

צֶדֶק לְעוֹלָם וְתוֹרָתְךָ אֱמֶת: תִּתֵּן אֱמֶת לְיַעֲקֹב, חֶסֶד לְאַבְרָהָם,

תהלים סח

אֲשֶׁר־נִשְׁבַּעְתָּ לַאֲבֹתֵינוּ מִימֵי קֶדֶם: בָּרוּךְ אֲדֹנָי יוֹם יוֹם יַעֲמָס־

תהלים מו

לָנוּ, הָאֵל יְשׁוּעָתֵנוּ סֶלָה: יהוה צְבָאוֹת עִמָּנוּ, מִשְׂגָּב לָנוּ אֱלֹהֵי

תהלים פד
תהלים כ

יַעֲקֹב סֶלָה: יהוה צְבָאוֹת, אַשְׁרֵי אָדָם בֹּטֵחַ בָּךְ: יהוה הוֹשִׁיעָה,•

הַמֶּלֶךְ יַעֲנֵנוּ בְיוֹם־קָרְאֵנוּ:

בָּרוּךְ הוּא אֱלֹהֵינוּ שֶׁבְּרָאָנוּ לִכְבוֹדוֹ, וְהִבְדִּילָנוּ מִן הַתּוֹעִים,
וְנָתַן לָנוּ תּוֹרַת אֱמֶת, וְחַיֵּי עוֹלָם נָטַע בְּתוֹכֵנוּ. הוּא יִפְתַּח לִבֵּנוּ
בְּתוֹרָתוֹ, וְיָשֵׂם בְּלִבֵּנוּ אַהֲבָתוֹ וְיִרְאָתוֹ וְלַעֲשׂוֹת רְצוֹנוֹ וּלְעָבְדוֹ
בְּלֵבָב שָׁלֵם, לְמַעַן לֹא נִיגַע לָרִיק וְלֹא נֵלֵד לַבֶּהָלָה.

תהלים ל

יְהִי רָצוֹן מִלְּפָנֶיךָ יהוה אֱלֹהֵינוּ וֵאלֹהֵי אֲבוֹתֵינוּ, שֶׁנִּשְׁמֹר חֻקֶּיךָ
בָּעוֹלָם הַזֶּה, וְנִזְכֶּה וְנִחְיֶה וְנִרְאֶה וְנִירַשׁ טוֹבָה וּבְרָכָה, לִשְׁנֵי

ירמיה יז

יְמוֹת הַמָּשִׁיחַ וּלְחַיֵּי הָעוֹלָם הַבָּא. לְמַעַן יְזַמֶּרְךָ כָבוֹד וְלֹא יִדֹּם,

ישעיה כו

יהוה אֱלֹהַי, לְעוֹלָם אוֹדֶךָּ: בָּרוּךְ הַגֶּבֶר אֲשֶׁר יִבְטַח בַּיהוה, וְהָיָה

תהלים ט
ישעיה מב

יהוה מִבְטַחוֹ: בִּטְחוּ בַיהוה עֲדֵי־עַד, כִּי בְּיָהּ יהוה צוּר עוֹלָמִים:

‹ וְיִבְטְחוּ בְךָ יוֹדְעֵי שְׁמֶךָ, כִּי לֹא־עָזַבְתָּ דֹרְשֶׁיךָ, יהוה: יהוה חָפֵץ
לְמַעַן צִדְקוֹ, יַגְדִּיל תּוֹרָה וְיַאְדִּיר:

On חצי קדיש says שליח ציבור, the חול המועד and ראש חודש, page 227.
The service then continues with מוסף for ראש חודש on page 459. for חול המועד on page 503.

On other days the שליח ציבור continues with קדיש שלם on the next page.

עיון תפילה · IYUN TEFILLA	אני תפילה · ANI TEFILLA

IYUN TEFILLA · עיון תפילה

יַעֲמָס־לָנוּ – *He burdens us [with His blessings].* Yet how many of us focus on the things we don't have instead? Think of all of the good things in your life that others do not have. They would look at us and say that we are burdened with blessings. We need to recognize it too. What do I have that many others do not?

ANI TEFILLA · אני תפילה

יהוה הוֹשִׁיעָה – *Lord, save.* The verse says: Don't worry, Hashem will save us, take care of us, He loves us and will answer us on the day we call out to Him. He listens to us, He is connected to us (Rabbi S. Aviner). It has always been so. I have reason to be optimistic.

FULL KADDISH

Leader: **יִתְגַּדַּל** Magnified and sanctified may His great name be,
in the world He created by His will.
May He establish His kingdom in your lifetime
and in your days,
and in the lifetime of all the house of Israel,
swiftly and soon –
and say: Amen.

All: May His great name^A be blessed for ever and all time.

Leader: Blessed and praised, glorified and exalted,
raised and honored, uplifted and lauded be
the name of the Holy One, blessed be He,
beyond any blessing,
song, praise and consolation uttered in the world –
and say: Amen.

*On Tisha B'Av, omit the next verse and continue
with "May there be great peace."*

May the prayers and pleas of all Israel
be accepted by their Father in heaven –
and say: Amen.

May there be great peace from heaven,
and life for us and all Israel –
and say: Amen.

*Bow, take three steps back, as if taking leave of the Divine Presence,
then bow, first left, then right, then center, while saying:*

May He who makes peace in His high places,
make peace for us and all Israel –
and say: Amen.

ANI TEFILLA · אני תפילה

יְהֵא שְׁמֵהּ רַבָּא – *May His great name.* Whoever says *yeheh shemeh raba...* with all his
strength, the Heavenly Court rips up any

negative decree against him (*Shabbat* 119b).
"With all his strength" – one should enunciate the words clearly (Maharal).

קדיש שלם

ש״ץ: יִתְגַּדַּל וְיִתְקַדַּשׁ שְׁמֵהּ רַבָּא (קהל: אָמֵן)

בְּעָלְמָא דִּי בְרָא כִרְעוּתֵהּ

וְיַמְלִיךְ מַלְכוּתֵהּ

בְּחַיֵּיכוֹן וּבְיוֹמֵיכוֹן וּבְחַיֵּי דְכָל בֵּית יִשְׂרָאֵל

בַּעֲגָלָא וּבִזְמַן קָרִיב, וְאִמְרוּ אָמֵן. (קהל: אָמֵן)

קהל   יְהֵא שְׁמֵהּ רַבָּאᵃ מְבָרַךְ לְעָלַם וּלְעָלְמֵי עָלְמַיָּא.
ושׁ״ץ:

ש״ץ: יִתְבָּרַךְ וְיִשְׁתַּבַּח וְיִתְפָּאַר

וְיִתְרוֹמַם וְיִתְנַשֵּׂא וְיִתְהַדָּר וְיִתְעַלֶּה וְיִתְהַלָּל

שְׁמֵהּ דְּקֻדְשָׁא בְּרִיךְ הוּא (קהל: בְּרִיךְ הוּא)

לְעֵלָּא מִן כָּל בִּרְכָתָא

/בעשרת ימי תשובה: לְעֵלָּא לְעֵלָּא מִכָּל בִּרְכָתָא/

וְשִׁירָתָא, תֻּשְׁבְּחָתָא וְנֶחֱמָתָא

דַּאֲמִירָן בְּעָלְמָא, וְאִמְרוּ אָמֵן. (קהל: אָמֵן)

On תשעה באב, *omit the next verse and continue with* יְהֵא שְׁלָמָא.

תִּתְקַבֵּל צְלוֹתְהוֹן וּבָעוּתְהוֹן דְּכָל יִשְׂרָאֵל

קֳדָם אֲבוּהוֹן דִּי בִשְׁמַיָּא, וְאִמְרוּ אָמֵן. (קהל: אָמֵן)

יְהֵא שְׁלָמָא רַבָּא מִן שְׁמַיָּא

וְחַיִּים, עָלֵינוּ וְעַל כָּל יִשְׂרָאֵל, וְאִמְרוּ אָמֵן. (קהל: אָמֵן)

Bow, take three steps back, as if taking leave of the Divine Presence,
then bow, first left, then right, then center, while saying:

עֹשֶׂה שָׁלוֹם /בעשרת ימי תשובה: הַשָּׁלוֹם/ בִּמְרוֹמָיו

הוּא יַעֲשֶׂה שָׁלוֹם עָלֵינוּ וְעַל כָּל יִשְׂרָאֵל

וְאִמְרוּ אָמֵן. (קהל: אָמֵן)

Stand while saying Aleinu. Bow at ˙.

עָלֵינוּ It is our duty[B] to praise the Master of all,
and ascribe greatness to the Author of creation,
who has not made us like the nations of the lands
nor placed us like the families of the earth;
who has not made our portion like theirs,
nor our destiny like all their multitudes.
(For they worship vanity and emptiness,
and pray to a god who cannot save.)
˙But we bow in worship
and thank the Supreme King of kings,
the Holy One, blessed be He,
who extends the heavens and establishes the earth,
whose throne of glory is in the heavens above,
and whose power's Presence is in the highest of heights.
He is our God; there is no other.
Truly He is our King, there is none else,
as it is written in His Torah:
"You shall know and take to heart this day
that the LORD is God, in heaven above and on earth below.
There is no other."

Deut. 4

---

misguided. The second paragraph, however, lays out our dream for the future, a time when all of the people of the world will accept God's sovereignty and adopt the basic standards of morality and justice exemplified in the seven laws of Noah (Rabbi S.R. Hirsch). How will this happen? When we ourselves become the most religious, moral, and just people that we can be. Unlike other nations, who want to accomplish their mission via military conquest, we hope to spread our message by leading exemplary lives. In short, the more particular we are in how we live our lives, the more universal is our message. As we get ready to leave *shul* for the "outside" world, we remind ourselves that our goal is not simply to pray, but to live a prayerful life.

Stand while saying עָלֵינוּ. *Bow at* ׳.

עָלֵינוּ לְשַׁבֵּחַ לַאֲדוֹן הַכֹּל, לָתֵת גְּדֻלָּה לְיוֹצֵר בְּרֵאשִׁית

שֶׁלֹּא עָשָׂנוּ כְּגוֹיֵי הָאֲרָצוֹת, וְלֹא שָׂמָנוּ כְּמִשְׁפְּחוֹת הָאֲדָמָה

שֶׁלֹּא שָׂם חֶלְקֵנוּ כָּהֶם וְגוֹרָלֵנוּ כְּכָל הֲמוֹנָם.

(שֶׁהֵם מִשְׁתַּחֲוִים לְהֶבֶל וָרִיק וּמִתְפַּלְּלִים אֶל אֵל לֹא יוֹשִׁיעַ.)

וַאֲנַחְנוּ כּוֹרְעִים וּמִשְׁתַּחֲוִים וּמוֹדִים

לִפְנֵי מֶלֶךְ מַלְכֵי הַמְּלָכִים, הַקָּדוֹשׁ בָּרוּךְ הוּא

שֶׁהוּא נוֹטֶה שָׁמַיִם וְיוֹסֵד אָרֶץ

וּמוֹשַׁב יְקָרוֹ בַּשָּׁמַיִם מִמַּעַל

וּשְׁכִינַת עֻזּוֹ בְּגָבְהֵי מְרוֹמִים.

הוּא אֱלֹהֵינוּ, אֵין עוֹד.

אֱמֶת מַלְכֵּנוּ, אֶפֶס זוּלָתוֹ

כַּכָּתוּב בְּתוֹרָתוֹ

וְיָדַעְתָּ הַיּוֹם וַהֲשֵׁבֹתָ אֶל־לְבָבֶךָ

כִּי יהוה הוּא הָאֱלֹהִים בַּשָּׁמַיִם מִמַּעַל וְעַל־הָאָרֶץ מִתַּחַת

אֵין עוֹד:

דברים ד

ביאור תפילה · BIUR TEFILLA

עָלֵינוּ — *It is our duty.* The appearance of this prayer as the conclusion of the service is a relatively late development of the past 500 years, even though the prayer itself is at least three times that age. It is comprised of two paragraphs which in effect lay out two

themes, one particularistic and the other universalistic. In the first, we declare that we are the Chosen People. We believe in one God who alone is the Creator of heaven and earth and He chose us above all other nations whose beliefs are simply untrue or

Therefore, we place our hope in You, Lord our God,
that we may soon see the glory of Your power,
when You will remove abominations from the earth,
and idols will be utterly destroyed,
when the world will be perfected
under the sovereignty of the Almighty,
when all humanity will call on Your name,
to turn all the earth's wicked toward You.
All the world's inhabitants will realize and know
that to You every knee must bow and every tongue swear loyalty.
Before You, Lord our God, they will kneel and bow down
and give honor to Your glorious name.
They will all accept the yoke of Your kingdom,
and You will reign over them soon and for ever.
For the kingdom is Yours,
and to all eternity You will reign in glory,
as it is written in Your Torah:
"The Lord will reign for ever and ever."   *Ex. 15*

▸ And it is said:
"Then the Lord shall be King over all the earth;   *Zech. 14*
on that day the Lord shall be One and His name One."

Some add:

Have no fear of sudden terror or of the ruin when it overtakes the wicked.   *Prov. 3*
Devise your strategy, but it will be thwarted; propose your plan,   *Is. 8*
but it will not stand, for God is with us.
When you grow old, I will still be the same.   *Is. 46*
When your hair turns gray, I will still carry you.
I made you, I will bear you, I will carry you, and I will rescue you.

---

too, are a nation with a mission. But unlike others who would influence the world
through the use of military force, we seek
to influence the world through the force of
who we are as people. We seek to be role
models of morality and ethics, religiosity
and spirituality. We will improve the world
by improving ourselves. As I change myself,
I can change the world. What one thing can
I do today to live up to this mission?

עַל כֵּן נְקַוֶּה לְּךָ יהוה אֱלֹהֵינוּ, לִרְאוֹת מְהֵרָה בְּתִפְאֶרֶת עֻזֶּךָ,
לְהַעֲבִיר גִּלּוּלִים מִן הָאָרֶץ, וְהָאֱלִילִים כָּרוֹת יִכָּרֵתוּן,
לְתַקֵּן עוֹלָם בְּמַלְכוּת שַׁדַּי.
וְכָל בְּנֵי בָשָׂר יִקְרְאוּ בִשְׁמֶךָ, לְהַפְנוֹת אֵלֶיךָ כָּל רִשְׁעֵי אָרֶץ.
יַכִּירוּ וְיֵדְעוּ כָּל יוֹשְׁבֵי תֵבֵל,
כִּי לְךָ תִּכְרַע כָּל בֶּרֶךְ, תִּשָּׁבַע כָּל לָשׁוֹן.
לְפָנֶיךָ יהוה אֱלֹהֵינוּ יִכְרְעוּ וְיִפֹּלוּ, וְלִכְבוֹד שִׁמְךָ יְקָר יִתֵּנוּ,
וִיקַבְּלוּ כֻלָּם אֶת עֹל מַלְכוּתֶךָ,
וְתִמְלֹךְ עֲלֵיהֶם מְהֵרָה לְעוֹלָם וָעֶד.
כִּי הַמַּלְכוּת שֶׁלְּךָ הִיא וּלְעוֹלְמֵי עַד תִּמְלֹךְ בְּכָבוֹד,
כַּכָּתוּב בְּתוֹרָתֶךָ, יהוה יִמְלֹךְ לְעֹלָם וָעֶד:
◂ וְנֶאֱמַר, וְהָיָה יהוה לְמֶלֶךְ עַל־כָּל־הָאָרֶץ
בַּיּוֹם הַהוּא יִהְיֶה יהוה אֶחָד וּשְׁמוֹ אֶחָד:

שמות טו
זכריה יד

Some add:

משלי ג
אַל־תִּירָא מִפַּחַד פִּתְאֹם וּמִשֹּׁאַת רְשָׁעִים כִּי תָבֹא:
ישעיה ח
עֻצוּ עֵצָה וְתֻפָר, דַּבְּרוּ דָבָר וְלֹא יָקוּם, כִּי עִמָּנוּ אֵל:
ישעיה מו
וְעַד־זִקְנָה אֲנִי הוּא, וְעַד־שֵׂיבָה אֲנִי אֶסְבֹּל
אֲנִי עָשִׂיתִי וַאֲנִי אֶשָּׂא וַאֲנִי אֶסְבֹּל וַאֲמַלֵּט:

ANI TEFILLA · אני תפילה

Every nation needs a reason to exist and many find in that reason a sense of mission that they want to bring to the rest of the world. America wanted to "make the world safe for democracy" and Britain once claimed that its influence was so vast that "the sun never set on the British Empire." The Soviet Union once wanted to unite all of the world's workers under the banner of Communism, and in most recent years there have been terror groups who sought to impose their views on other nations. We,

MOURNER'S KADDISH

The following prayer, said by mourners, requires the presence of a minyan.
A transliteration can be found on page 921.

Mourner: יִתְגַּדַּל Magnified and sanctified
may His great name be,
in the world He created by His will.
May He establish His kingdom
in your lifetime and in your days,
and in the lifetime of all the house of Israel,
swiftly and soon –
and say: Amen.

All: May His great name be blessed
for ever and all time.

Mourner: Blessed and praised,
glorified and exalted,
raised and honored,
uplifted and lauded
be the name of the Holy One,
blessed be He,
beyond any blessing, song,
praise and consolation
uttered in the world –
and say: Amen.

May there be great peace from heaven,
and life for us and all Israel –
and say: Amen.

Bow, take three steps back, as if taking leave of the Divine Presence,
then bow, first left, then right, then center, while saying:
May He who makes peace in His high places,
make peace for us and all Israel –
and say: Amen.

קדיש יתום

The following prayer, said by mourners, requires the presence of a מנין.
A transliteration can be found on page 921.

אבל יִתְגַּדַּל וְיִתְקַדַּשׁ שְׁמֵהּ רַבָּא (קהל: אָמֵן)
בְּעָלְמָא דִּי בְרָא כִרְעוּתֵהּ
וְיַמְלִיךְ מַלְכוּתֵהּ
בְּחַיֵּיכוֹן וּבְיוֹמֵיכוֹן וּבְחַיֵּי דְכָל בֵּית יִשְׂרָאֵל
בַּעֲגָלָא וּבִזְמַן קָרִיב
וְאִמְרוּ אָמֵן. (קהל: אָמֵן)

קהל
ואבל
יְהֵא שְׁמֵהּ רַבָּא מְבָרַךְ לְעָלַם וּלְעָלְמֵי עָלְמַיָּא.

אבל יִתְבָּרַךְ וְיִשְׁתַּבַּח וְיִתְפָּאַר
וְיִתְרוֹמַם וְיִתְנַשֵּׂא וְיִתְהַדָּר וְיִתְעַלֶּה וְיִתְהַלָּל
שְׁמֵהּ דְּקֻדְשָׁא בְּרִיךְ הוּא (קהל: בְּרִיךְ הוּא)

לְעֵלָּא מִן כָּל בִּרְכָתָא
/בעשרת ימי תשובה: לְעֵלָּא לְעֵלָּא מִכָּל בִּרְכָתָא/

וְשִׁירָתָא, תֻּשְׁבְּחָתָא וְנֶחָמָתָא
דַּאֲמִירָן בְּעָלְמָא
וְאִמְרוּ אָמֵן. (קהל: אָמֵן)

יְהֵא שְׁלָמָא רַבָּא מִן שְׁמַיָּא
וְחַיִּים, עָלֵינוּ וְעַל כָּל יִשְׂרָאֵל
וְאִמְרוּ אָמֵן. (קהל: אָמֵן)

Bow, take three steps back, as if taking leave of the Divine Presence,
then bow, first left, then right, then center, while saying:

עֹשֶׂה שָׁלוֹם/ בעשרת ימי תשובה: הַשָּׁלוֹם/ בִּמְרוֹמָיו
הוּא יַעֲשֶׂה שָׁלוֹם עָלֵינוּ וְעַל כָּל יִשְׂרָאֵל
וְאִמְרוּ אָמֵן. (קהל: אָמֵן)

THE DAILY PSALM

One of the following psalms is said on the appropriate day of the week as indicated.
After the psalm, the Mourner's Kaddish on page 256 is said.

After the Daily Psalm, on Rosh Ḥodesh, add Barekhi Nafshi, page 266 (in
Israel, some only say Barekhi Nafshi). On Ḥanukka, add Psalm 30, page 62
followed by Mourner's Kaddish. From the second day of Rosh Ḥodesh Elul
through Shemini Atzeret (in Israel, through Hoshana Raba), add Psalm 27
on page 270. In a house of mourning the service concludes on page 272.

Sunday: Today is the first day of the week,[B]
            on which the Levites used to say this psalm in the Temple:

לְדָוִד מִזְמוֹר A psalm of David. The earth is the LORD's and all it contains,[i] the   *Ps. 24*
world and all who live in it. For He founded it on the seas and established it
on the streams. Who may climb the mountain of the LORD? Who may stand
in His holy place? He who has clean hands and a pure heart, who has not
taken My name in vain or sworn deceitfully. He shall receive a blessing from

---

and consequently the other days do
not have their own names, but only
numbers. Our week is, in effect, all
about getting to Shabbat. As such,
we refer to them as "the first day
of the week/Shabbat," "the second
day of the week/Shabbat," etc. On
each day we are thereby reminded
that Shabbat rest and re-creation
are just around the corner. Hang
in there!

BIUR TEFILLA · ביאור תפילה

הַיּוֹם יוֹם רִאשׁוֹן בְּשַׁבָּת – *Today is the first day of the*
week. Hashem is the Creator, not in the remote
heavens but on earth. Especially when we might
enter into the beginning of the week wanting to
conquer the world, it behooves us to recall that
the world is not of our making. And how does
one acknowledge this? By being a person who
has "clean hands and a pure heart." What a great
challenge for the week ahead!

IYUN TEFILLA · עיון תפילה

לַיהוה הָאָרֶץ וּמְלוֹאָהּ – *The earth is the LORD's*
and all it contains. The Gemara (Berakhot
35a) asks, "But is there not a contradiction to
this from another verse which says (Tehillim
115:16) 'And Hashem gave the land to man.'
Does the land belong to God or to man?"

To which the Gemara answers: "The earth
belongs to God. But when man makes a
blessing on food before he eats it, then the
earth belongs to man." Blessings are how
we get permission for, and take ownership
of, what does not belong to us.

שיר של יום

One of the following psalms is said on the appropriate day of the week as indicated.
After the psalm, קדיש יתום on page 257 is said.

After שיר של יום, on ראש חודש, add בָּרְכִי נַפְשִׁי, page 267 (in אֶרֶץ יִשְׂרָאֵל, some only say
בָּרְכִי נַפְשִׁי). On חנוכה, add מִזְמוֹר שִׁיר־חֲנֻכַּת הַבַּיִת, page 63 followed by קדיש יתום. From the
second day of ראש חודש אֱלוּל through שמיני עצרת (in אֶרֶץ יִשְׂרָאֵל, through הושענא רבה),
add לְדָוִד, יהוה אוֹרִי on page 271. In a house of mourning the service concludes on page 273.

Sunday הַיּוֹם יוֹם רִאשׁוֹן בְּשַׁבָּת, שֶׁבּוֹ הָיוּ הַלְוִיִּם אוֹמְרִים בְּבֵית הַמִּקְדָּשׁ:

תהלים כד לְדָוִד מִזְמוֹר, לַיהוה הָאָרֶץ וּמְלוֹאָהּ, תֵּבֵל וְיֹשְׁבֵי בָהּ: כִּי־הוּא עַל־יַמִּים
יְסָדָהּ, וְעַל־נְהָרוֹת יְכוֹנְנֶהָ: מִי־יַעֲלֶה בְהַר־יהוה, וּמִי־יָקוּם בִּמְקוֹם
קָדְשׁוֹ: נְקִי כַפַּיִם וּבַר־לֵבָב, אֲשֶׁר לֹא־נָשָׂא לַשָּׁוְא נַפְשִׁי, וְלֹא נִשְׁבַּע
לְמִרְמָה: יִשָּׂא בְרָכָה מֵאֵת יהוה, וּצְדָקָה מֵאֱלֹהֵי יִשְׁעוֹ: זֶה דּוֹר דֹּרְשָׁו,

---

INTRODUCTION: שיר של יום – THE DAILY PSALM

In the times of the *Beit HaMikdash*, during the offering of the daily *Korban Tamid*, the *Levi'im* were charged with providing musical accompaniment, singing a different chapter of *Tehillim* each day (Mishna *Tamid* 7:3–4). Why these particular chapters were chosen is really not so clear. The Gemara (*Rosh HaShana* 31a) suggests that each daily chapter reflects a different theme of each corresponding day of creation. Later sources have suggested that there is a cumulative theme that connects them all, while still others have focused on the independent message of each. We have followed the latter by suggesting a lesson that one can take away as one greets the new day. Nevertheless, examine them carefully and create your own meaning.

What they all certainly have in common is the introduction, which calls upon us to identify the days not by their secular name (many of which are pagan in origin, e.g., Sunday is the day of the sun; Monday, the day of the moon...) but rather by their relationship to Shabbat. The Ramban (on *Shemot* 20:8) notes that this is in fulfillment of the Torah's commandment to "remember the Sabbath day" constantly, even throughout the week. If a person were to be lost in the desert and lose track of time, he is supposed to begin counting the days and observe the seventh as Shabbat, for all revolves around that day. Indeed, it has been suggested that the first three days of the week draw a certain holiness from the previous Shabbat, while the last three days are drawn to the holiness of the next (*Hayyei Adam* II:1).

Given how central a role Shabbat plays in our personal and religious lives, all of the other days of the week revolve around it,

the LORD, and just reward from the God of his salvation. This is a generation of those who seek Him, the descendants of Jacob who seek Your presence, Selah! Lift up your heads, O gates; be uplifted, eternal doors, so that the King of glory may enter. Who is the King of glory? It is the LORD, strong and mighty, the LORD mighty in battle. Lift up your heads, O gates; lift them up, eternal doors, that the King of glory may enter. ▸ Who is He, the King of glory? The LORD of hosts, He is the King of glory, Selah!

Mourner's Kaddish (page 256)

Monday: Today is the second day of the week,[B]
on which the Levites used to say this psalm in the Temple:

שִׁיר מִזְמוֹר A song. A psalm of the sons of Korah. Great is the LORD and *Ps. 48* greatly to be praised in the city of God, on His holy mountain – beautiful in its heights, joy of all the earth, Mount Zion on its northern side, city of the great King. In its citadels God is known as a stronghold. See how the kings joined forces, advancing together. They saw, they were astounded, they panicked, they fled. There fear seized them, like the pains of a woman giving birth, like ships of Tarshish wrecked by an eastern wind. What we had heard, now we have seen, in the city of the LORD of hosts, in the city of our God. May God preserve it for ever, Selah! In the midst of Your Temple, God, we meditate on Your love. As is Your name, God, so is Your praise: it reaches to the ends of the earth. Your right hand is filled with righteousness. Let Mount Zion rejoice, let the towns of Judah be glad, because of Your judgments. Walk around Zion and encircle it.[A] Count its towers, note its strong walls, view its citadels, so that you may tell a future generation ▸ that this is God, our God, for ever and ever. He will guide us for evermore.

Mourner's Kaddish (page 256)

A score of conquerors have held it as their choicest prize; and more than a dozen times has it been utterly destroyed. The Babylonians burnt it, and deported its population; the Romans slew a million of its inhabitants, razed it to the ground, passed the ploughshare over it, and strewed its furrows with salt; Hadrian banished its very name from the lips of men, changed it to Aelia Capitolina, and prohibited any Jew from entering its precincts on pain of death. Persians and Arabs, Barbarians and Crusaders and Turks took it and retook it, ravaged it and burnt it; and yet, marvelous to relate, it ever rises from its ashes to renewed life and glory. It is the Eternal City of the Eternal People. (Rabbi J.H. Hertz)

מְבַקְשֵׁי פָנֶיךָ יַעֲקֹב סֶלָה: שְׂאוּ שְׁעָרִים רָאשֵׁיכֶם, וְהִנָּשְׂאוּ פִּתְחֵי עוֹלָם,
וְיָבוֹא מֶלֶךְ הַכָּבוֹד: מִי זֶה מֶלֶךְ הַכָּבוֹד, יְהוָה עִזּוּז וְגִבּוֹר, יְהוָה גִּבּוֹר
מִלְחָמָה: שְׂאוּ שְׁעָרִים רָאשֵׁיכֶם, וּשְׂאוּ פִּתְחֵי עוֹלָם, וְיָבֹא מֶלֶךְ הַכָּבוֹד:
‹ מִי הוּא זֶה מֶלֶךְ הַכָּבוֹד, יְהוָה צְבָאוֹת הוּא מֶלֶךְ הַכָּבוֹד סֶלָה:

קדיש יתום (*page 257*)

Monday הַיּוֹם יוֹם שֵׁנִי בְּשַׁבָּת,‹ שֶׁבּוֹ הָיוּ הַלְוִיִּם אוֹמְרִים בְּבֵית הַמִּקְדָּשׁ:

תהלים מח

שִׁיר מִזְמוֹר לִבְנֵי־קֹרַח: גָּדוֹל יְהוָה וּמְהֻלָּל מְאֹד, בְּעִיר אֱלֹהֵינוּ, הַר־
קָדְשׁוֹ: יְפֵה נוֹף מְשׂוֹשׂ כָּל־הָאָרֶץ, הַר־צִיּוֹן יַרְכְּתֵי צָפוֹן, קִרְיַת מֶלֶךְ
רָב: אֱלֹהִים בְּאַרְמְנוֹתֶיהָ נוֹדַע לְמִשְׂגָּב: כִּי־הִנֵּה הַמְּלָכִים נוֹעֲדוּ, עָבְרוּ
יַחְדָּו: הֵמָּה רָאוּ כֵּן תָּמָהוּ, נִבְהֲלוּ נֶחְפָּזוּ: רְעָדָה אֲחָזָתַם שָׁם, חִיל
כַּיּוֹלֵדָה: בְּרוּחַ קָדִים תְּשַׁבֵּר אֳנִיּוֹת תַּרְשִׁישׁ: כַּאֲשֶׁר שָׁמַעְנוּ כֵּן רָאִינוּ,
בְּעִיר־יְהוָה צְבָאוֹת, בְּעִיר אֱלֹהֵינוּ, אֱלֹהִים יְכוֹנְנֶהָ עַד־עוֹלָם סֶלָה:
דִּמִּינוּ אֱלֹהִים חַסְדֶּךָ, בְּקֶרֶב הֵיכָלֶךָ: כְּשִׁמְךָ אֱלֹהִים כֵּן תְּהִלָּתְךָ עַל־
קַצְוֵי־אֶרֶץ, צֶדֶק מָלְאָה יְמִינֶךָ: יִשְׂמַח הַר־צִיּוֹן, תָּגֵלְנָה בְּנוֹת יְהוּדָה,
לְמַעַן מִשְׁפָּטֶיךָ: סֹבּוּ צִיּוֹן וְהַקִּיפוּהָ,‹ סִפְרוּ מִגְדָּלֶיהָ: שִׁיתוּ לִבְּכֶם
לְחֵילָה, פַּסְּגוּ אַרְמְנוֹתֶיהָ, לְמַעַן תְּסַפְּרוּ לְדוֹר אַחֲרוֹן: ‹ כִּי זֶה אֱלֹהִים
אֱלֹהֵינוּ עוֹלָם וָעֶד, הוּא יְנַהֲגֵנוּ עַל־מוּת:

קדיש יתום (*page 257*)

ביאור תפילה • BIUR TEFILLA

הַיּוֹם יוֹם שֵׁנִי בְּשַׁבָּת – *Today is the second day of the week.* If yesterday we declared

Hashem as our Master, today we declare Israel and Jerusalem as our place.

אני תפילה • ANI TEFILLA

סֹבּוּ צִיּוֹן וְהַקִּיפוּהָ – *Walk around Zion and encircle it.*

Do I see Israel as a destination or as my destiny?

Tuesday: Today is the third day of the week,¹
on which the Levites used to say this psalm in the Temple:

מִזְמוֹר לְאָסָף A psalm of Asaph. God stands in the divine assembly. Among the judges He delivers judgment.¹ How long will you judge unjustly, showing favor to the wicked? Selah. Do justice to the weak and the orphaned. Vindicate the poor and destitute. Rescue the weak and needy. Save them from the hand of the wicked. They do not know nor do they understand. They walk about in darkness while all the earth's foundations shake. I once said, "You are like gods, all of you, are sons of the Most High." But you shall die like mere men, you will fall like any prince. ‣ Arise, O Lord, judge the earth, for all the nations are Your possession. *Ps. 82*

Mourner's Kaddish (page 256)

Wednesday: Today is the fourth day of the week,¹
on which the Levites used to say this psalm in the Temple:

אֵל־נְקָמוֹת God of retribution, Lord, God of retribution, appear! Rise up, Judge of the earth. Repay to the arrogant what they deserve. How long shall the wicked, Lord, how long shall the wicked triumph? They pour out insolent words. All the evildoers are full of boasting. They crush Your people, Lord, and oppress Your inheritance. They kill the widow and the stranger. They murder the orphaned. They say, "The Lord does not see. The God of Jacob pays no heed." Take heed, you most brutish people. You fools, when will you grow wise? Will He who implants the ear not hear? Will He who formed the eye not see? Will He who disciplines nations – He who teaches man knowledge – not punish? The Lord knows that the thoughts of man are a mere fleeting breath. Happy is the man whom You discipline, Lord, the one You instruct in Your Torah, giving him tranquility in days of trouble, until a pit is dug for the *Ps. 94*

IYUN TEFILLA · עיון תפילה

הַיּוֹם יוֹם רְבִיעִי בְּשַׁבָּת – *Today is the fourth day of the week.* For all of the justice that we try to pursue in this world, the reality is that evil still exists; in trying to become like gods, men can become beasts. And we may sometimes wonder why it is that the wicked seem to succeed and flourish as often as they do. All one can do is have faith that Hashem has a plan and rest assured that the evil and corrupt will be eradicated. For my part, I will continue to believe in and stand up for what is right, as I begin a day that may be marked by individuals or nations who seek my downfall. It is my faith that will carry me through. That may be why two verses from the next psalm in *Tehillim* were added to this one, for they indicate two related notions. The first is that no matter what the challenge, one must always be optimistic about the future; faith allows one to always see the bright side. Hold on to that! In addition, these two verses are also the first two verses of the *Kabbalat Shabbat* service on Friday night, as if to say: "Shabbat is coming! Hold on to that!"

Tuesday הַיּוֹם יוֹם שְׁלִישִׁי בְּשַׁבָּת, שֶׁבּוֹ הָיוּ הַלְוִיִּם אוֹמְרִים בְּבֵית הַמִּקְדָּשׁ:

מִזְמוֹר לְאָסָף, אֱלֹהִים נִצָּב בַּעֲדַת־אֵל, בְּקֶרֶב אֱלֹהִים יִשְׁפֹּט: עַד־מָתַי תהלים פב
תִּשְׁפְּטוּ־עָוֶל, וּפְנֵי רְשָׁעִים תִּשְׂאוּ־סֶלָה: שִׁפְטוּ־דָל וְיָתוֹם, עָנִי וָרָשׁ
הַצְדִּיקוּ: פַּלְּטוּ־דַל וְאֶבְיוֹן, מִיַּד רְשָׁעִים הַצִּילוּ: לֹא יָדְעוּ וְלֹא יָבִינוּ,
בַּחֲשֵׁכָה יִתְהַלָּכוּ, יִמּוֹטוּ כָּל־מוֹסְדֵי אָרֶץ: אֲנִי־אָמַרְתִּי אֱלֹהִים אַתֶּם,
וּבְנֵי עֶלְיוֹן כֻּלְּכֶם: אָכֵן כְּאָדָם תְּמוּתוּן, וּכְאַחַד הַשָּׂרִים תִּפֹּלוּ: ◀ קוּמָה
אֱלֹהִים שָׁפְטָה הָאָרֶץ, כִּי־אַתָּה תִנְחַל בְּכָל־הַגּוֹיִם:

קדיש יתום (page 257)

Wednesday הַיּוֹם יוֹם רְבִיעִי בְּשַׁבָּת, שֶׁבּוֹ הָיוּ הַלְוִיִּם אוֹמְרִים בְּבֵית הַמִּקְדָּשׁ:

אֵל־נְקָמוֹת יְהוָה, אֵל נְקָמוֹת הוֹפִיעַ: הִנָּשֵׂא שֹׁפֵט הָאָרֶץ, הָשֵׁב גְּמוּל תהלים צד
עַל־גֵּאִים: עַד־מָתַי רְשָׁעִים, יְהוָה, עַד־מָתַי רְשָׁעִים יַעֲלֹזוּ: יַבִּיעוּ יְדַבְּרוּ
עָתָק, יִתְאַמְּרוּ כָּל־פֹּעֲלֵי אָוֶן: עַמְּךָ יְהוָה יְדַכְּאוּ, וְנַחֲלָתְךָ יְעַנּוּ: אַלְמָנָה
וְגֵר יַהֲרֹגוּ, וִיתוֹמִים יְרַצֵּחוּ: וַיֹּאמְרוּ לֹא יִרְאֶה־יָּהּ, וְלֹא־יָבִין אֱלֹהֵי יַעֲקֹב:
בִּינוּ בֹּעֲרִים בָּעָם, וּכְסִילִים מָתַי תַּשְׂכִּילוּ: הֲנֹטַע אֹזֶן הֲלֹא יִשְׁמָע, אִם־
יֹצֵר עַיִן הֲלֹא יַבִּיט: הֲיֹסֵר גּוֹיִם הֲלֹא יוֹכִיחַ, הַמְלַמֵּד אָדָם דָּעַת: יְהוָה
יֹדֵעַ מַחְשְׁבוֹת אָדָם, כִּי־הֵמָּה הָבֶל: אַשְׁרֵי הַגֶּבֶר אֲשֶׁר־תְּיַסְּרֶנּוּ יָּהּ,
וּמִתּוֹרָתְךָ תְלַמְּדֶנּוּ: לְהַשְׁקִיט לוֹ מִימֵי רָע, עַד יִכָּרֶה לָרָשָׁע שָׁחַת:

עיון תפילה · IYUN TEFILLA

הַיּוֹם יוֹם שְׁלִישִׁי בְּשַׁבָּת – Today is the third of the week. The place spoken of yesterday can only be realized when it is built upon principles of fairness and justice for all. Today we declare our understanding that a just society is one that must be founded upon religious principles, for as long as laws are dependent solely on people, they are subject to change according to human whim and self-interest. The laws of God, however, cannot ever be changed.

What can I do on this day of the week to be more conscious of the need to judge fairly?

בְּקֶרֶב אֱלֹהִים יִשְׁפֹּט – Among the judges He delivers judgment. A judge should always remember that when he sits in judgment of other people, he does not sit alone. God sits there with him, among the judges, listening and watching (Midrash Shoher Tov). Good advice for the rest of us as well. If I should judge someone today or be judgmental, I must remember Who is looking over my shoulder.

wicked. For the LORD will not forsake His people, nor abandon His heritage. Judgment shall again accord with justice, and all the upright in heart will follow it. Who will rise up for me against the wicked? Who will stand up for me against wrongdoers? Had the LORD not been my help, I would soon have dwelt in death's silence. When I thought my foot was slipping, Your loving-kindness, LORD, gave me support. When I was filled with anxiety, Your consolations soothed my soul. Can a corrupt throne be allied with You? Can injustice be framed into law? They join forces against the life of the righteous, and condemn the innocent to death. But the LORD is my stronghold, my God is the Rock of my refuge. He will bring back on them their wickedness, and destroy them for their evil deeds. The LORD our God will destroy them.

‣ Come, let us sing for joy to the LORD; let us shout aloud to the Rock of our salvation. Let us greet Him with thanksgiving, shout aloud to Him with songs of praise. For the LORD is the great God, the King great above all powers. *Ps. 95*

Mourner's Kaddish (page 256)

Thursday: Today is the fifth day of the week,[B]
on which the Levites used to say this psalm in the Temple:

לַמְנַצֵּחַ For the conductor of music. On the Gittit. By Asaph. Sing for joy to God, our strength. Shout aloud to the God of Jacob. Raise a song, beat the drum, play the sweet harp and lyre. Sound the shofar on the new moon, on our feast day when the moon is hidden. For it is a statute for Israel, an ordinance of the God of Jacob. He established it as a testimony for Joseph when He went forth against the land of Egypt, where I heard a language that I did not know. I relieved his shoulder of the burden. His hands were freed from the builder's basket. In distress you called and I rescued you. I answered you from the secret place of thunder; I tested you at the waters of Meribah, Selah! Hear, My people, and I will warn you. Israel, if you would only listen to Me! Let there be no strange god among you.[B] Do not bow down to an alien god. I am the LORD your God who brought you out of the land of Egypt. Open your mouth wide and I will fill it. But My people would not listen to Me. Israel would have none of Me. So I left them to their stubborn hearts, letting them follow their *Ps. 81*

---

our part of the covenant? The week is not over. There is still time.

לֹא־יִהְיֶה בְךָ אֵל זָר – *Let there be no strange god among you.* This phrase can also be read "Let there be no strange god *within*

you. "What strange god exists in the human body? The answer – the evil inclination (*Shabbat* 105b).

Alternatively, the Kotzker Rebbe used to paraphrase the verse as "Let God not be a stranger in you."

כִּי לֹא־יִטֹּשׁ יהוה עַמּוֹ, וְנַחֲלָתוֹ לֹא יַעֲזֹב: כִּי־עַד־צֶדֶק יָשׁוּב מִשְׁפָּט, וְאַחֲרָיו כָּל־יִשְׁרֵי־לֵב: מִי־יָקוּם לִי עִם־מְרֵעִים, מִי־יִתְיַצֵּב לִי עִם־פֹּעֲלֵי אָוֶן: לוּלֵי יהוה עֶזְרָתָה לִּי, כִּמְעַט שָׁכְנָה דוּמָה נַפְשִׁי: אִם־אָמַרְתִּי מָטָה רַגְלִי, חַסְדְּךָ יהוה יִסְעָדֵנִי: בְּרֹב שַׂרְעַפַּי בְּקִרְבִּי, תַּנְחוּמֶיךָ יְשַׁעַשְׁעוּ נַפְשִׁי: הַיְחָבְרְךָ כִּסֵּא הַוּוֹת, יֹצֵר עָמָל עֲלֵי־חֹק: יָגוֹדּוּ עַל־נֶפֶשׁ צַדִּיק, וְדָם נָקִי יַרְשִׁיעוּ: וַיְהִי יהוה לִי לְמִשְׂגָּב, וֵאלֹהַי לְצוּר מַחְסִי: וַיָּשֶׁב עֲלֵיהֶם אֶת־אוֹנָם, וּבְרָעָתָם יַצְמִיתֵם, יַצְמִיתֵם יהוה אֱלֹהֵינוּ:

תהלים צה
‹ לְכוּ נְרַנְּנָה לַיהוה, נָרִיעָה לְצוּר יִשְׁעֵנוּ: נְקַדְּמָה פָנָיו בְּתוֹדָה, בִּזְמִרוֹת נָרִיעַ לוֹ: כִּי אֵל גָּדוֹל יהוה, וּמֶלֶךְ גָּדוֹל עַל־כָּל־אֱלֹהִים:

קדיש יתום *(page 257)*

Thursday הַיּוֹם יוֹם חֲמִישִׁי בְּשַׁבָּת, שֶׁבּוֹ הָיוּ הַלְוִיִּם אוֹמְרִים בְּבֵית הַמִּקְדָּשׁ:

תהלים פא
לַמְנַצֵּחַ עַל־הַגִּתִּית לְאָסָף: הַרְנִינוּ לֵאלֹהִים עוּזֵּנוּ, הָרִיעוּ לֵאלֹהֵי יַעֲקֹב: שְׂאוּ־זִמְרָה וּתְנוּ־תֹף, כִּנּוֹר נָעִים עִם־נָבֶל: תִּקְעוּ בַחֹדֶשׁ שׁוֹפָר, בַּכֵּסֶה לְיוֹם חַגֵּנוּ: כִּי חֹק לְיִשְׂרָאֵל הוּא, מִשְׁפָּט לֵאלֹהֵי יַעֲקֹב: עֵדוּת בִּיהוֹסֵף שָׂמוֹ, בְּצֵאתוֹ עַל־אֶרֶץ מִצְרָיִם, שְׂפַת לֹא־יָדַעְתִּי אֶשְׁמָע: הֲסִירוֹתִי מִסֵּבֶל שִׁכְמוֹ, כַּפָּיו מִדּוּד תַּעֲבֹרְנָה: בַּצָּרָה קָרָאתָ וָאֲחַלְּצֶךָּ, אֶעֶנְךָ בְּסֵתֶר רַעַם, אֶבְחָנְךָ עַל־מֵי מְרִיבָה סֶלָה: שְׁמַע עַמִּי וְאָעִידָה בָּךְ, יִשְׂרָאֵל אִם־תִּשְׁמַע־לִי: לֹא־יִהְיֶה בְךָ אֵל זָר, וְלֹא תִשְׁתַּחֲוֶה לְאֵל נֵכָר: אָנֹכִי יהוה אֱלֹהֶיךָ, הַמַּעַלְךָ מֵאֶרֶץ מִצְרָיִם, הַרְחֶב־פִּיךָ וַאֲמַלְאֵהוּ: וְלֹא־שָׁמַע עַמִּי לְקוֹלִי, וְיִשְׂרָאֵל לֹא־אָבָה לִי: וָאֲשַׁלְּחֵהוּ בִּשְׁרִירוּת

BIUR TEFILLA · בִּיאוּר תְּפִלָּה

הַיּוֹם יוֹם חֲמִישִׁי בְּשַׁבָּת – *Today is the fifth day of the week.* As the week begins to draw to a close, and we move closer to Shabbat, there may be reason to celebrate. The psalm begins with a joyous call to sing to God, and to prepare for a revelation comparable to Rosh

HaShana, when He answered the prayers of the matriarchs and others (*Rosh HaShana* 8a; 11a). At the same time, in the second section, we are reminded not to rest upon our laurels. Are we ready to hear what He wants from us? Have we been living up to

own devices. If only My people would listen to Me, if Israel would walk in My ways, I would soon subdue their enemies, and turn My hand against their foes. Those who hate the LORD would cower before Him and their doom would last for ever. ‣ He would feed Israel with the finest wheat – with honey from the rock I would satisfy you.

Mourner's Kaddish (page 256)

Friday: Today is the sixth day of the week,ⁱ
on which the Levites used to say this psalm in the Temple:

יהוה מָלָךְ The LORD reigns. He is robed in majesty. The LORD is robed, girded with strength. The world is firmly established; it cannot be moved. Your throne stands firm as of old; You are eternal. Rivers lift up, LORD, rivers lift up their voice, rivers lift up their crashing waves. Mightier than the noise of many waters, than the mighty waves of the sea is the LORD on high. ‣ Your testimonies are very sure;ᴮ holiness adorns Your House, LORD, for evermore.

Ps. 93

Mourner's Kaddish (page 256)

On Rosh Ḥodesh, the following psalm is said:

בָּרְכִי נַפְשִׁי Bless the LORD, my soul.ᴮ LORD, my God, You are very great, clothed in majesty and splendor, wrapped in a robe of light. You have spread out the heavens like a tent. He has laid the beams of His lofts in the waters. He makes the clouds His chariot, riding on the wings of the wind. He makes the winds

Ps. 104

What can I do to prepare for Shabbat today, to make it more meaningful?

What can I do beforehand to enhance the spirit of Shabbat tonight?

בָּרְכִי נַפְשִׁי – *Bless the LORD, my soul.* This psalm is a kind of *shir shel yom* for Rosh Ḥodesh, ostensibly because of its reference in verse 19 to "He made the moon to mark the seasons" (*Tur* 423). The chapter is an exquisite celebration of the beauty of nature and an acknowledgment of its Source. Yet if He is present in nature, He certainly abides

in man, which in turn implies that no sinner is beyond redemption (Rabbi Soloveitchik). As the chapter concludes, and as Beruria, the wife of Rabbi Meir explained, it does not say "let sinners vanish from the earth" but, rather, "let sins vanish from the earth." Just as the moon renews itself each month, so, too, can we.

לְבָם, יֵלְכוּ בְּמוֹעֲצוֹתֵיהֶם: לוּ עַמִּי שֹׁמֵעַ לִי, יִשְׂרָאֵל בִּדְרָכַי יְהַלֵּכוּ: כִּמְעַט אוֹיְבֵיהֶם אַכְנִיעַ, וְעַל־צָרֵיהֶם אָשִׁיב יָדִי: מְשַׂנְאֵי יהוה יְכַחֲשׁוּ־לוֹ, וִיהִי עִתָּם לְעוֹלָם: וַיַּאֲכִילֵהוּ מֵחֵלֶב חִטָּה, וּמִצּוּר, דְּבַשׁ אַשְׂבִּיעֶךָ:

(page 257) קדיש יתום

הַיּוֹם יוֹם שִׁשִּׁי בְּשַׁבָּת,ּ שֶׁבּוֹ הָיוּ הַלְוִיִּם אוֹמְרִים בְּבֵית הַמִּקְדָּשׁ *Friday*

תהלים צג

יהוה מָלָךְ, גֵּאוּת לָבֵשׁ, לָבֵשׁ יהוה עֹז הִתְאַזָּר, אַף־תִּכּוֹן תֵּבֵל בַּל־תִּמּוֹט: נָכוֹן כִּסְאֲךָ מֵאָז, מֵעוֹלָם אָתָּה: נָשְׂאוּ נְהָרוֹת יהוה, נָשְׂאוּ נְהָרוֹת קוֹלָם, יִשְׂאוּ נְהָרוֹת דָּכְיָם: מִקֹּלוֹת מַיִם רַבִּים, אַדִּירִים מִשְׁבְּרֵי־יָם, אַדִּיר בַּמָּרוֹם יהוה: עֵדֹתֶיךָ נֶאֶמְנוּ מְאֹד, לְבֵיתְךָ נַאֲוָה־קֹּדֶשׁ, יהוה לְאֹרֶךְ יָמִים:

(page 257) קדיש יתום

On ראש חוֹדֶשׁ, *the following psalm is said:*

תהלים קד

בָּרְכִי נַפְשִׁי אֶת־יהוה, יהוה אֱלֹהַי גָּדַלְתָּ מְּאֹד, הוֹד וְהָדָר לָבָשְׁתָּ: עֹטֶה־אוֹר כַּשַּׂלְמָה, נוֹטֶה שָׁמַיִם כַּיְרִיעָה: הַמְקָרֶה בַמַּיִם עֲלִיּוֹתָיו, הַשָּׂם־עָבִים רְכוּבוֹ, הַמְהַלֵּךְ עַל־כַּנְפֵי־רוּחַ: עֹשֶׂה מַלְאָכָיו רוּחוֹת,

---

עיון תפילה · IYUN TEFILLA

הַיּוֹם יוֹם שִׁשִּׁי בְּשַׁבָּת – *Today is the sixth day of the week*. Today is the remaining day of Creation before Shabbat. Interestingly, although it is the day when, according to tradition, man himself was created, nowhere in this psalm does man appear. Rather, man takes his position as a part of creation to ac-

knowledge the Creator. Shabbat is coming. We will soon be enveloped by that island in time. To appreciate it fully we cannot simply fall into it. We transition into its holiness even now, while the last day of the week is just beginning. The more we prepare, the more we will appreciate her presence.

ביאור תפילה · BIUR TEFILLA

עֵדֹתֶיךָ נֶאֶמְנוּ מְאֹד – *Your testimonies are very sure*. What is this a reference to? The predictions of Your prophets? Your com-

mandments which testify to Your presence in history? The crashing waves of the oceans that testify to Your very existence?

His messengers, flames of fire His ministers. He has fixed the earth on its foundations so that it will never be shaken. You covered it with the deep like a cloak; the waters stood above the mountains. At Your rebuke they fled; at the sound of Your thunder they rushed away, flowing over the hills, pouring down into the valleys to the place You appointed for them. You fixed a boundary they were not to pass, so that they would never cover the earth again. He makes springs flow in the valleys; they make their way between the hills, giving drink to all the beasts of the field; the wild donkeys quench their thirst. The birds of the sky dwell beside them, singing among the foliage. He waters the mountains from His lofts: the earth is sated with the fruit of Your work. He makes grass grow for the cattle, and plants for the use of man, that he may produce bread from the earth, wine to cheer the heart of man, oil to make the face shine, and bread to sustain man's heart. The trees of the LORD drink their fill, the cedars of Lebanon which He planted. There, birds build their nests; the stork makes its home in the cypresses. High hills are for the wild goats; crags are shelter for the badgers. He made the moon to mark the seasons, and makes the sun know when to set. You bring darkness and it is night; then all the beasts of the forests stir. The young lions roar for prey, seeking their food from God. When the sun rises, they slink away and seek rest in their lairs. Man goes out to his work and his labor until evening. How numerous are Your works, LORD; You made them all in wisdom; the earth is full of Your creations. There is the vast, immeasurable sea with its countless swarming creatures, living things great and small. There ships sail. There is Leviathan You formed to sport there. All of them look to You in hope, to give them their food when it is due. What You give them, they gather up. When You open Your hand, they are sated with good. When You hide Your face, they are dismayed. When You take away their breath, they die and return to dust. When You send back Your breath, they are created, giving new life to the earth. May the glory of the LORD be for ever; may the LORD rejoice in His works. When He looks at the earth, it trembles. When He touches the mountains, they pour forth smoke. I will sing to the LORD as long as I live; I will sing psalms to my God all my life. ▸ May my meditation be pleasing to Him; I shall rejoice in the LORD. May sinners vanish from the earth, and the wicked be no more. Bless the LORD, my soul. Halleluya!

Mourner's Kaddish (page 256)

---

of their own special blessings, rather than being subsumed under a broader more general blessing. Each has its own unique qualities.

מְשָׁרְתָיו אֵשׁ לֹהֵט: יָסַד־אֶרֶץ עַל־מְכוֹנֶיהָ, בַּל־תִּמּוֹט עוֹלָם וָעֶד: תְּהוֹם
כַּלְּבוּשׁ כִּסִּיתוֹ, עַל־הָרִים יַעַמְדוּ־מָיִם: מִן־גַּעֲרָתְךָ יְנוּסוּן, מִן־קוֹל רַעַמְךָ
יֵחָפֵזוּן: יַעֲלוּ הָרִים, יֵרְדוּ בְקָעוֹת, אֶל־מְקוֹם זֶה יָסַדְתָּ לָהֶם: גְּבוּל־שַׂמְתָּ
בַּל־יַעֲבֹרוּן, בַּל־יְשֻׁבוּן לְכַסּוֹת הָאָרֶץ: הַמְשַׁלֵּחַ מַעְיָנִים בַּנְּחָלִים, בֵּין
הָרִים יְהַלֵּכוּן: יַשְׁקוּ כָּל־חַיְתוֹ שָׂדָי, יִשְׁבְּרוּ פְרָאִים צְמָאָם: עֲלֵיהֶם עוֹף־
הַשָּׁמַיִם יִשְׁכּוֹן, מִבֵּין עֳפָאיִם יִתְּנוּ־קוֹל: מַשְׁקֶה הָרִים מֵעֲלִיּוֹתָיו, מִפְּרִי
מַעֲשֶׂיךָ תִּשְׂבַּע הָאָרֶץ: מַצְמִיחַ חָצִיר לַבְּהֵמָה, וְעֵשֶׂב לַעֲבֹדַת הָאָדָם,
לְהוֹצִיא לֶחֶם מִן־הָאָרֶץ: וְיַיִן יְשַׂמַּח לְבַב־אֱנוֹשׁ, לְהַצְהִיל פָּנִים מִשָּׁמֶן,
וְלֶחֶם לְבַב־אֱנוֹשׁ יִסְעָד: יִשְׂבְּעוּ עֲצֵי יְהוָה, אַרְזֵי לְבָנוֹן אֲשֶׁר נָטָע:
אֲשֶׁר־שָׁם צִפֳּרִים יְקַנֵּנוּ, חֲסִידָה בְּרוֹשִׁים בֵּיתָהּ: הָרִים הַגְּבֹהִים לַיְּעֵלִים,
סְלָעִים מַחְסֶה לַשְׁפַנִּים: עָשָׂה יָרֵחַ לְמוֹעֲדִים, שֶׁמֶשׁ יָדַע מְבוֹאוֹ: תָּשֶׁת־
חֹשֶׁךְ וִיהִי לָיְלָה, בּוֹ־תִרְמֹשׂ כָּל־חַיְתוֹ־יָעַר: הַכְּפִירִים שֹׁאֲגִים לַטָּרֶף,
וּלְבַקֵּשׁ מֵאֵל אָכְלָם: תִּזְרַח הַשֶּׁמֶשׁ יֵאָסֵפוּן, וְאֶל־מְעוֹנֹתָם יִרְבָּצוּן: יֵצֵא
אָדָם לְפָעֳלוֹ, וְלַעֲבֹדָתוֹ עֲדֵי־עָרֶב: מָה־רַבּוּ מַעֲשֶׂיךָ יְהוָה, כֻּלָּם בְּחָכְמָה
עָשִׂיתָ, מָלְאָה הָאָרֶץ קִנְיָנֶךָ: זֶה הַיָּם גָּדוֹל וּרְחַב יָדָיִם, שָׁם־רֶמֶשׂ וְאֵין
מִסְפָּר, חַיּוֹת קְטַנּוֹת עִם־גְּדֹלוֹת: שָׁם אֳנִיּוֹת יְהַלֵּכוּן, לִוְיָתָן זֶה־יָצַרְתָּ
לְשַׂחֶק־בּוֹ: כֻּלָּם אֵלֶיךָ יְשַׂבֵּרוּן, לָתֵת אָכְלָם בְּעִתּוֹ: תִּתֵּן לָהֶם יִלְקֹטוּן,
תִּפְתַּח יָדְךָ יִשְׂבְּעוּן טוֹב: תַּסְתִּיר פָּנֶיךָ יִבָּהֵלוּן, תֹּסֵף רוּחָם יִגְוָעוּן,
וְאֶל־עֲפָרָם יְשׁוּבוּן: תְּשַׁלַּח רוּחֲךָ יִבָּרֵאוּן, וּתְחַדֵּשׁ פְּנֵי אֲדָמָה: יְהִי
כְבוֹד יְהוָה לְעוֹלָם, יִשְׂמַח יְהוָה בְּמַעֲשָׂיו: הַמַּבִּיט לָאָרֶץ וַתִּרְעָד, יִגַּע
בֶּהָרִים וְיֶעֱשָׁנוּ: אָשִׁירָה לַיהוָה בְּחַיָּי, אֲזַמְּרָה לֵאלֹהַי בְּעוֹדִי: יֶעֱרַב
עָלָיו שִׂיחִי, אָנֹכִי אֶשְׂמַח בַּיהוָה: יִתַּמּוּ חַטָּאִים מִן־הָאָרֶץ, וּרְשָׁעִים
עוֹד אֵינָם, בָּרְכִי נַפְשִׁי אֶת־יְהוָה, הַלְלוּיָהּ:

קדיש יתום (page 257)

עִיּוּן תְּפִלָּה • IYUN TEFILLA

מַצְמִיחַ חָצִיר לַבְּהֵמָה – *He makes grass grow for the cattle.* The Gemara (*Berakhot* 35b) uses these two verses as prooftexts for the fact that wine and bread are each deserving

During the month of Elul (except Erev Rosh HaShana), the shofar is sounded
(some sound the shofar after the psalm below). From the second day of Rosh Ḥodesh Elul
through Shemini Atzeret (in Israel through Hoshana Raba), the following psalm is said:

לְדָוִד By David. The Lᴏʀᴅ is my light[8] and my salvation – whom then shall I   Ps. 27
fear? The Lᴏʀᴅ is the stronghold of my life – of whom shall I be afraid? When
evil men close in on me to devour my flesh, it is they, my enemies and foes,
who stumble and fall. Should an army besiege me, my heart would not fear.
Should war break out against me, still I would be confident. One thing I ask
of the Lᴏʀᴅ, only this do I seek: to live in the House of the Lᴏʀᴅ all the days
of my life, to gaze on the beauty of the Lᴏʀᴅ and worship in His Temple.[For
He will keep me safe in His pavilion on the day of trouble. He will hide me
under the cover of His tent. He will set me high upon a rock. Now my head
is high above my enemies who surround me. I will sacrifice in His tent with
shouts of joy. I will sing and chant praises to the Lᴏʀᴅ. Lᴏʀᴅ, hear my voice
when I call. Be gracious to me and answer me. On Your behalf my heart says,
"Seek My face." Your face, Lᴏʀᴅ, will I seek. Do not hide Your face from me.
Do not turn Your servant away in anger. You have been my help. Do not reject
or forsake me, God, my Savior. Were my father and my mother to forsake
me,[the Lᴏʀᴅ would take me in. Teach me Your way, Lᴏʀᴅ, and lead me on
a level path, because of my oppressors. Do not abandon me to the will of my
foes, for false witnesses have risen against me, breathing violence. ▸ Were it
not for my faith that I shall see the Lᴏʀᴅ's goodness in the land of the living.
Hope in the Lᴏʀᴅ. Be strong and of good courage, and hope in the Lᴏʀᴅ!

Mourner's Kaddish (page 256)

In Israel, "There is none like our God" through "Bless the Lᴏʀᴅ," on page 688, is said:

---

suggested that when we are visitors we notice everything for the first time, and we fall
in love with the experience. As time goes on,
however, the specialness is lost to us and we take things
for granted. So it can sometimes be with
our passion for Jewish life. When we were
young, everything seemed exciting, but as
time wore on our enthusiasm waned. And
so we pray to live in the house of Hashem
as permanent residents, but that our mindset and disposition always be that of the

enthusiastic guest, experiencing all of Jewish life as if for the first time. What can I do
to regain some of the passion I once had?

כִּי־אָבִי וְאִמִּי עֲזָבוּנִי – *Were it my father and my*
mother to forsake me. There are times when
one can feel that, despite the presence of
parents, friends or spouse, one is still very
much alone. Faith enables one to overcome that loneliness, for Hashem is always
there and knows you better than you know
yourself.

During the month of אלול (*except* ערב ראש השנה)*, the* שופר *is sounded (some sound the* שופר *after the psalm below). From the second day of* ראש חודש אלול *through* שמיני עצרת *in* ארץ ישראל *through* הושענא רבה (*in*), *the following psalm is said:*

תהלים כז לְדָוִד, יהוה אוֹרִי וְיִשְׁעִי, מִמִּי אִירָא, יהוה מָעוֹז־חַיַּי, מִמִּי אֶפְחָד: בִּקְרֹב עָלַי מְרֵעִים לֶאֱכֹל אֶת־בְּשָׂרִי, צָרַי וְאֹיְבַי לִי, הֵמָּה כָשְׁלוּ וְנָפָלוּ: אִם־תַּחֲנֶה עָלַי מַחֲנֶה, לֹא־יִירָא לִבִּי, אִם־תָּקוּם עָלַי מִלְחָמָה, בְּזֹאת אֲנִי בוֹטֵחַ: אַחַת שָׁאַלְתִּי מֵאֵת־יהוה, אוֹתָהּ אֲבַקֵּשׁ, שִׁבְתִּי בְּבֵית־יהוה כָּל־יְמֵי חַיַּי, לַחֲזוֹת בְּנְעַם־יהוה, וּלְבַקֵּר בְּהֵיכָלוֹ: כִּי יִצְפְּנֵנִי בְּסֻכֹּה בְּיוֹם רָעָה, יַסְתִּרֵנִי בְּסֵתֶר אָהֳלוֹ, בְּצוּר יְרוֹמְמֵנִי: וְעַתָּה יָרוּם רֹאשִׁי עַל אֹיְבַי סְבִיבוֹתַי, וְאֶזְבְּחָה בְאָהֳלוֹ זִבְחֵי תְרוּעָה, אָשִׁירָה וַאֲזַמְּרָה לַיהוה: שְׁמַע־יהוה קוֹלִי אֶקְרָא, וְחָנֵּנִי וַעֲנֵנִי: לְךָ אָמַר לִבִּי בַּקְּשׁוּ פָנַי, אֶת־פָּנֶיךָ יהוה אֲבַקֵּשׁ: אַל־תַּסְתֵּר פָּנֶיךָ מִמֶּנִּי, אַל תַּט־בְּאַף עַבְדֶּךָ, עֶזְרָתִי הָיִיתָ, אַל־תִּטְּשֵׁנִי וְאַל־תַּעַזְבֵנִי, אֱלֹהֵי יִשְׁעִי: כִּי־אָבִי וְאִמִּי עֲזָבוּנִי, וַיהוה יַאַסְפֵנִי: הוֹרֵנִי יהוה דַּרְכֶּךָ, וּנְחֵנִי בְּאֹרַח מִישׁוֹר, לְמַעַן שׁוֹרְרָי: אַל־תִּתְּנֵנִי בְּנֶפֶשׁ צָרָי, כִּי קָמוּ־בִי עֵדֵי־שֶׁקֶר, וִיפֵחַ חָמָס: לוּלֵא הֶאֱמַנְתִּי לִרְאוֹת בְּטוּב־יהוה בְּאֶרֶץ חַיִּים: קַוֵּה אֶל־יהוה, חֲזַק וְיַאֲמֵץ לִבֶּךָ, וְקַוֵּה אֶל־יהוה:

קדיש יתום (*page 257*)

In ארץ ישראל*,* אֵין כַּאלֹהֵינוּ *through* בָּרְכוּ*, on page 689, is said:*

ביאור תפילה • BIUR TEFILLA

לְדָוִד יהוה אוֹרִי – *By David. The Lord is my light.* Included in the siddur only a few hundred years ago, this *tefilla* is added as a kind of daily *shir shel yom* from Rosh Ḥodesh Elul until Shemini Atzeret.

The psalm has numerous references that are appropriate during this time of year. Find the ones that speak to you the most as you prepare for these Days of Awe.

עיון תפילה • IYUN TEFILLA

וּלְבַקֵּר בְּהֵיכָלוֹ – *And worship in His Temple.* The word *levaker* could be interpreted to mean "to visit," in which case there would be a contradiction: the one thing I ask is to *live* in Your house, yet I also want to visit it. What's the point? Rabbi Soloveitchik once

After the regular service, the following psalm is read in a house of mourning during the shiva week. On those days on which Taḥanun is not said, Psalm 16 (below) is substituted.

לַמְנַצֵּחַ For the conductor of music. Of the sons of Korah. A sacred song. Hear *Ps. 49* this, all you peoples. Listen, all inhabitants of the world, low and high, rich and poor alike. My mouth will speak words of wisdom; the utterance of my heart will give understanding. I listen with care to a parable; I expound my mystery to the music of the harp. Why should I fear when evil days come, when the wickedness of my foes surrounds me, trusting in their wealth, boasting of their great riches? No man can redeem his brother or pay God the price of his release, for the ransom of a life is costly; no payment is ever enough that would let him live for ever, never seeing the grave. For all can see that wise men die, that the foolish and senseless all perish and leave their wealth to others. They think their houses will remain for ever, their dwellings for all generations; they give their names to their estates. But man, despite his splendor, does not endure; he is like the beasts that perish. Such is the fate of the foolish and their followers who approve their words, Selah. Like sheep they are destined for the grave: death will be their shepherd. The upright will rule over them in the morning. Their forms will decay in the grave, far from their mansions. But God will redeem my life from the grave; He will surely take me to Himself, Selah. Do not be overawed when a man grows rich, when the glory of his house increases, for he will take nothing with him when he dies; his wealth will not descend with him. Though while he lived he counted himself blessed – men always praise you when you prosper – he will join the generation of his ancestors who will never again see the light. A man who, despite his splendor, lacks understanding, is like the beasts that perish.

Mourner's Kaddish (page 256)

On those days on which Taḥanun is not said, substitute:

מִכְתָּם לְדָוִד A musical composition of David. Protect me, God, for in You I *Ps. 16* have found refuge. I have said to the LORD: You are my LORD: from You alone comes the good I enjoy. All my delight is in the holy ones, the mighty in the land. Those who run after other gods multiply their sorrows. I shall never offer them libations of blood, nor will their names pass my lips. The LORD is my allotted portion and my cup: You direct my fate. The lines have fallen for me in pleasant places; I am well content with my inheritance. I will bless the LORD who has guided me; at night my innermost being admonishes me. I have set the LORD before me at all times. He is at my right hand: I shall not be shaken. Therefore my heart is glad, my spirit rejoices, and my body rests secure. For You will not abandon me to the grave, nor let Your faithful one see the pit. You will teach me the path of life. In Your presence is fullness of joy; at Your right hand, bliss for evermore.

Mourner's Kaddish (page 256)

After the regular service, the following psalm is read in a house of mourning during the שבעה *week. On those days on which* תחנון *is not said,* תהלים טז *(below) is substituted.*

תהלים מט

לַמְנַצֵּחַ לִבְנֵי־קֹרַח מִזְמוֹר: שִׁמְעוּ־זֹאת כָּל־הָעַמִּים, הַאֲזִינוּ כָּל־יֹשְׁבֵי חָלֶד: גַּם־בְּנֵי אָדָם, גַּם־בְּנֵי־אִישׁ, יַחַד עָשִׁיר וְאֶבְיוֹן: פִּי יְדַבֵּר חָכְמוֹת, וְהָגוּת לִבִּי תְבוּנוֹת: אַטֶּה לְמָשָׁל אָזְנִי, אֶפְתַּח בְּכִנּוֹר חִידָתִי: לָמָּה אִירָא בִּימֵי רָע, עֲוֹן עֲקֵבַי יְסֻבֵּנִי: הַבֹּטְחִים עַל־חֵילָם, וּבְרֹב עָשְׁרָם יִתְהַלָּלוּ: אָח לֹא־פָדֹה יִפְדֶּה אִישׁ, לֹא־יִתֵּן לֵאלֹהִים כָּפְרוֹ: וְיֵקַר פִּדְיוֹן נַפְשָׁם, וְחָדַל לְעוֹלָם: וִיחִי־עוֹד לָנֶצַח, לֹא יִרְאֶה הַשָּׁחַת: כִּי יִרְאֶה חֲכָמִים יָמוּתוּ, יַחַד כְּסִיל וָבַעַר יֹאבֵדוּ, וְעָזְבוּ לַאֲחֵרִים חֵילָם: קִרְבָּם בָּתֵּימוֹ לְעוֹלָם, מִשְׁכְּנֹתָם לְדֹר וָדֹר, קָרְאוּ בִשְׁמוֹתָם עֲלֵי אֲדָמוֹת: וְאָדָם בִּיקָר בַּל־יָלִין, נִמְשַׁל כַּבְּהֵמוֹת נִדְמוּ: זֶה דַרְכָּם, כֵּסֶל לָמוֹ, וְאַחֲרֵיהֶם בְּפִיהֶם יִרְצוּ סֶלָה: כַּצֹּאן לִשְׁאוֹל שַׁתּוּ, מָוֶת יִרְעֵם, וַיִּרְדּוּ בָם יְשָׁרִים לַבֹּקֶר, וְצוּרָם לְבַלּוֹת שְׁאוֹל מִזְּבֻל לוֹ: אַךְ־אֱלֹהִים יִפְדֶּה נַפְשִׁי מִיַּד שְׁאוֹל, כִּי יִקָּחֵנִי סֶלָה: אַל־תִּירָא כִּי־יַעֲשִׁר אִישׁ, כִּי־יִרְבֶּה כְּבוֹד בֵּיתוֹ: כִּי לֹא בְמוֹתוֹ יִקַּח הַכֹּל, לֹא־יֵרֵד אַחֲרָיו כְּבוֹדוֹ: כִּי־נַפְשׁוֹ בְּחַיָּיו יְבָרֵךְ, וְיוֹדֻךָ כִּי־תֵיטִיב לָךְ: תָּבוֹא עַד־דּוֹר אֲבוֹתָיו, עַד־נֵצַח לֹא יִרְאוּ־אוֹר: אָדָם בִּיקָר וְלֹא יָבִין, נִמְשַׁל כַּבְּהֵמוֹת נִדְמוּ:

קדיש יתום *(page 257)*

On those days on which תחנון *is not said, substitute:*

תהלים טז

מִכְתָּם לְדָוִד, שָׁמְרֵנִי אֵל כִּי־חָסִיתִי בָךְ: אָמַרְתְּ לַיהוה, אֲדֹנָי אָתָּה, טוֹבָתִי בַּל־עָלֶיךָ: לִקְדוֹשִׁים אֲשֶׁר־בָּאָרֶץ הֵמָּה, וְאַדִּירֵי כָּל־חֶפְצִי־בָם: יִרְבּוּ עַצְּבוֹתָם אַחֵר מָהָרוּ, בַּל־אַסִּיךְ נִסְכֵּיהֶם מִדָּם, וּבַל־אֶשָּׂא אֶת־שְׁמוֹתָם עַל־שְׂפָתָי: יהוה, מְנָת־חֶלְקִי וְכוֹסִי, אַתָּה תּוֹמִיךְ גּוֹרָלִי: חֲבָלִים נָפְלוּ־לִי בַּנְּעִמִים, אַף־נַחֲלָת שָׁפְרָה עָלָי: אֲבָרֵךְ אֶת־יהוה אֲשֶׁר יְעָצָנִי, אַף־לֵילוֹת יִסְּרוּנִי כִלְיוֹתָי: שִׁוִּיתִי יהוה לְנֶגְדִּי תָמִיד, כִּי מִימִינִי בַּל־אֶמּוֹט: לָכֵן שָׂמַח לִבִּי וַיָּגֶל כְּבוֹדִי, אַף־בְּשָׂרִי יִשְׁכֹּן לָבֶטַח: כִּי לֹא־תַעֲזֹב נַפְשִׁי לִשְׁאוֹל, לֹא־תִתֵּן חֲסִידְךָ לִרְאוֹת שָׁחַת: תּוֹדִיעֵנִי אֹרַח חַיִּים, שֹׂבַע שְׂמָחוֹת אֶת־פָּנֶיךָ, נְעִמוֹת בִּימִינְךָ נֶצַח:

קדיש יתום *(page 257)*

Minḥa for Weekdays

אַשְׁרֵי **Happy**[8] are those who dwell in Your House;
they shall continue to praise You, Selah!   *Ps. 84*

Happy are the people for whom this is so;   *Ps. 144*
happy are the people whose God is the Lord.

A song of praise by David.   *Ps. 145*

א I will exalt You,[ˡ] my God, the King,
  and bless Your name for ever and all time.

ב Every day I will bless You,
  and praise Your name for ever and all time.

ג Great is the Lord and greatly to be praised;
  His greatness is unfathomable.

BIUR TEFILLA · ביאור תפילה

אַשְׁרֵי – *Happy.* In some ways, *Ashrei* here serves the same function as all of *Pesukei DeZimra* did in *Shaḥarit*. It is a prelude to *Tefilla* (the *Shemoneh Esreh*), a way for us to get into the right mindset before our afternoon rendezvous with *HaKadosh Barukh Hu*.

What is that mindset? The Gemara (*Berakhot* 31a) explains that one should not pray out of a sense of frivolity, or sadness, or while carrying on trivial conversation, but rather with a sense of joy. Rashi explains that reminding us of the joy in our lives is exactly the purpose of *Ashrei* – "Hashem protects those who love Him," "Hashem will fulfill the desires of those who are in awe of Him." We are reminded that we are not alone, that we have much to be thankful for. Once we acknowledge that, we are ready to say the *Shemoneh Esreh*. **What do I have to be thankful for this afternoon? Let *Ashrei* point the way.**

IYUN TEFILLA · עיון תפילה

אֲרוֹמִמְךָ – *I will exalt You.* One of the reasons that the Rabbis decreed that this psalm should be said three times a day was because it is written as an acrostic, wherein each line begins with another letter of the *Alef-Beit*. It is as if one is saying, "Any praise I give You is incomplete. Therefore let each letter of the alphabet represent all of the praises that begin with that letter, of which I will offer just one line as an example." In a certain sense, then, the alphabetic listing of words is designed to convey the impression that all words fall short. It's not only about the meaning of the words but the feeling of the *Alef-Beit*.

מנחה לחול

תהלים פד

אַשְׁרֵי יוֹשְׁבֵי בֵיתֶךָ, עוֹד יְהַלְלוּךָ סֶּלָה:

תהלים קמד

אַשְׁרֵי הָעָם שֶׁכָּכָה לּוֹ, אַשְׁרֵי הָעָם שֶׁיהוה אֱלֹהָיו:

תהלים קמה

תְּהִלָּה לְדָוִד

אֲרוֹמִמְךָ אֱלוֹהַי הַמֶּלֶךְ, וַאֲבָרְכָה שִׁמְךָ לְעוֹלָם וָעֶד:

בְּכָל־יוֹם אֲבָרְכֶךָּ, וַאֲהַלְלָה שִׁמְךָ לְעוֹלָם וָעֶד:

גָּדוֹל יהוה וּמְהֻלָּל מְאֹד, וְלִגְדֻלָּתוֹ אֵין חֵקֶר:

INTRODUCTION TO MINḤA

The word *minḥa* can mean an offering or a gift. Already in the twelfth century, Avraham ben Yitzḥak of Narbonne wrote in his work *HaEshkol* that people are so busy all day long at their jobs that they forget to say this important prayer service altogether. And yet, *Ḥazal* said (*Berakhot* 6a) that one should be especially careful about making sure to pray *Minḥa*, for that was the time when the prophet Eliyahu called out to Hashem "Answer me! Answer me!" and his prayers were answered (*Melakhim* I 18:36–38). Apparently, then, *Minḥa* is a time when one's prayers could be particularly effective. Why should this be so? One answer lies in the words of *HaEshkol* cited above. Precisely because *Minḥa* occurs during the most inconvenient time of the day, it is the easiest to ignore. In the morning one gets up refreshed, ready to begin one's day; prayer is natural. So, too, in the evening, the end of the day brings its own mood of reflection. But in the middle of the day, we are so preoccupied with our work and routine that stopping is difficult, if not an outright intrusion (Rabbi Yehoshua ben Alexander HaKohen Falk, *Perisha*). But perhaps that's exactly the point. For that is the time of the day when we would benefit the most from stopping to take stock, to center ourselves Jewishly, to ask ourselves if our day is going the way it should, the way it could, to gain perspective on what's really important in our lives and not what might be filling our time or our minds. Viewed in this light, *Minḥa* is not an intrusion, rather, it is, as its name implies, a gift. If only we would take the time to see it that way. Take the time now.

ד One generation will praise Your works to the next,
and tell of Your mighty deeds.

ה On the glorious splendor of Your majesty I will meditate,
and on the acts of Your wonders.

ו They shall talk of the power of Your awesome deeds,
and I will tell of Your greatness.

ז They shall recite the record of Your great goodness,
and sing with joy of Your righteousness.

ח The Lord is gracious and compassionate,
slow to anger and great in loving-kindness.

ט The Lord is good to all,
and His compassion extends to all His works.

י All Your works shall thank You, Lord,
and Your devoted ones shall bless You.

כ They shall talk of the glory of Your kingship,
and speak of Your might.

ל To make known to mankind His mighty deeds
and the glorious majesty of His kingship.

מ Your kingdom is an everlasting kingdom,
and Your reign is for all generations.

ס The Lord supports all who fall,
and raises all who are bowed down.

ע All raise their eyes to You in hope,
and You give them their food in due season.

פ You open Your hand,
and satisfy every living thing with favor.

צ The Lord is righteous in all His ways,
and kind in all He does.

ק The Lord is close to all who call on Him,
to all who call on Him in truth.

ר He fulfills the will of those who revere Him;
He hears their cry and saves them.

ש The Lord guards all who love Him,
but all the wicked He will destroy.

ת ‣ My mouth shall speak the praise of the Lord,
and all creatures shall bless His holy name for ever and all time.

We will bless the Lord now and for ever. Halleluya!   Ps. 115

דּוֹד לְדָוִד יְשַׁבַּח מַעֲשֶׂיךָ, וּגְבוּרֹתֶיךָ יַגִּידוּ:

הֲדַר כְּבוֹד הוֹדֶךָ, וְדִבְרֵי נִפְלְאֹתֶיךָ אָשִׂיחָה:

וֶעֱזוּז נוֹרְאֹתֶיךָ יֹאמֵרוּ, וּגְדוּלָּתְךָ אֲסַפְּרֶנָּה:

זֵכֶר רַב־טוּבְךָ יַבִּיעוּ, וְצִדְקָתְךָ יְרַנֵּנוּ:

חַנּוּן וְרַחוּם יהוה, אֶרֶךְ אַפַּיִם וּגְדָל־חָסֶד:

טוֹב־יהוה לַכֹּל, וְרַחֲמָיו עַל־כָּל־מַעֲשָׂיו:

יוֹדוּךָ יהוה כָּל־מַעֲשֶׂיךָ, וַחֲסִידֶיךָ יְבָרְכוּכָה:

כְּבוֹד מַלְכוּתְךָ יֹאמֵרוּ, וּגְבוּרָתְךָ יְדַבֵּרוּ:

לְהוֹדִיעַ לִבְנֵי הָאָדָם גְּבוּרֹתָיו, וּכְבוֹד הֲדַר מַלְכוּתוֹ:

מַלְכוּתְךָ מַלְכוּת כָּל־עֹלָמִים, וּמֶמְשַׁלְתְּךָ בְּכָל־דּוֹר וָדֹר:

סוֹמֵךְ יהוה לְכָל־הַנֹּפְלִים, וְזוֹקֵף לְכָל־הַכְּפוּפִים:

עֵינֵי־כֹל אֵלֶיךָ יְשַׂבֵּרוּ, וְאַתָּה נוֹתֵן־לָהֶם אֶת־אָכְלָם בְּעִתּוֹ:

פּוֹתֵחַ אֶת־יָדֶךָ, וּמַשְׂבִּיעַ לְכָל־חַי רָצוֹן:

צַדִּיק יהוה בְּכָל־דְּרָכָיו, וְחָסִיד בְּכָל־מַעֲשָׂיו:

קָרוֹב יהוה לְכָל־קֹרְאָיו, לְכֹל אֲשֶׁר יִקְרָאֻהוּ בֶאֱמֶת:

רְצוֹן־יְרֵאָיו יַעֲשֶׂה, וְאֶת־שַׁוְעָתָם יִשְׁמַע, וְיוֹשִׁיעֵם:

שׁוֹמֵר יהוה אֶת־כָּל־אֹהֲבָיו, וְאֵת כָּל־הָרְשָׁעִים יַשְׁמִיד:

‹ תְּהִלַּת יהוה יְדַבֶּר־פִּי, וִיבָרֵךְ כָּל־בָּשָׂר שֵׁם קָדְשׁוֹ לְעוֹלָם וָעֶד:

וַאֲנַחְנוּ נְבָרֵךְ יָהּ מֵעַתָּה וְעַד־עוֹלָם, הַלְלוּיָהּ:

תהלים קמה

ANI TEFILLA · אני תפילה

"Imagine a man," said the Ba'al Shem Tov, "whose business hounds him through many streets and across the marketplace the entire day. He almost forgets that there is a Maker of the world. Only when Minha comes along does he remember: 'I must pray.' And then, *from the bottom of his heart, he heaves a sigh of regret that he has spent his day on vain and idle matters, and he runs into a side street and stands there and prays. God holds him dear, very dear, and his prayer pierces the firmament."*

HALF KADDISH

Leader: יִתְגַּדַּל Magnified and sanctified may His great name be,
in the world He created by His will.
May He establish His kingdom
in your lifetime and in your days,
and in the lifetime of all the house of Israel,
swiftly and soon – and say: Amen.

All: May His great name[A] be blessed for ever and all time.

Leader: Blessed and praised, glorified and exalted,
raised and honored, uplifted and lauded
be the name of the Holy One, blessed be He,
beyond any blessing,
song, praise and consolation
uttered in the world – and say: Amen.

On fast days, go to Removing the Torah from the Ark on page 216.
The Torah reading and Haftara for fast days are on page 746. After
the Torah is returned to the Ark, the Leader says Half Kaddish.

Shaḥarit we gave a number of suggestions for the kinds of ways to expand your *kavana* for each one of the blessings. Here, we provide you with an alternative strategy, namely, to write down your own personal thoughts, associations, requests, hopes and dreams. Fill in the blank spaces, either figuratively or literally. Use an erasable pencil or post a temporary note so that you can make changes over time to reflect the fact that you yourself change over time. Such additions, however, should not act as a distraction (see Rema 90:23). Alternatively, just leave the spaces blank and fill them in with your mind.

The Ben Ish Ḥai (*Ḥayyei Sara* 17) reports that there were those who wrote the word

tefillin on every page of their siddur so that they would not lose sight of the fact that they were wearing them, and could thereby recall their holiness.

Rabbi Meir Margoliot (Ostrog; d. 1790) and his brother were devoted students of the Ba'al Shem Tov. He said to them: "You are very beloved to me. Ask me for anything and I will do it for you." They responded: "Do what you think is best." He said: "I have a handwritten siddur that I use every day. Write your names and the name of your mother next to any blessing in the *Shemoneh Esreh* and I will have you in mind." They wrote their names next to the blessing of שׁוֹמֵעַ תְּפִלָּה (*Emunat Tzaddikim* pp. 7–8).

חצי קדיש

ש״ץ יִתְגַּדַּל וְיִתְקַדַּשׁ שְׁמֵהּ רַבָּא (קהל: אָמֵן)

בְּעָלְמָא דִּי בְרָא כִרְעוּתֵהּ

וְיַמְלִיךְ מַלְכוּתֵהּ

בְּחַיֵּיכוֹן וּבְיוֹמֵיכוֹן וּבְחַיֵּי דְכָל בֵּית יִשְׂרָאֵל

בַּעֲגָלָא וּבִזְמַן קָרִיב, וְאִמְרוּ אָמֵן. (קהל: אָמֵן)

קהל
 וש״ץ יְהֵא שְׁמֵהּ רַבָּא* מְבָרַךְ לְעָלַם וּלְעָלְמֵי עָלְמַיָּא.

ש״ץ יִתְבָּרַךְ וְיִשְׁתַּבַּח וְיִתְפָּאַר וְיִתְרוֹמַם וְיִתְנַשֵּׂא

וְיִתְהַדָּר וְיִתְעַלֶּה וְיִתְהַלָּל

שְׁמֵהּ דְּקֻדְשָׁא בְּרִיךְ הוּא (קהל: בְּרִיךְ הוּא)

לְעֵלָּא מִן כָּל בִּרְכָתָא

/ בעשרת ימי תשובה: לְעֵלָּא לְעֵלָּא מִכָּל בִּרְכָתָא/

וְשִׁירָתָא, תֻּשְׁבְּחָתָא וְנֶחֱמָתָא

דַּאֲמִירָן בְּעָלְמָא, וְאִמְרוּ אָמֵן. (קהל: אָמֵן)

*On fast days, go to הוצאת ספר תורה on page 217.
The תורה reading and הפטרה for fast days are on page 746. After the
תורה is returned to the ארון קודש, the שליח ציבור says חצי קדיש.*

ANI TEFILLA • אני תפילה

יְהֵא שְׁמֵהּ רַבָּא — *May His great name.* Whoever says *yeheh shemeh raba...* with all his
strength, the Heavenly Court rips up any

negative decree against him (*Shabbat* 119b).
"With all his strength" – with all of your physical strength. (Ritva)

INTRODUCTION TO THE MINHA AMIDA

Tefilla is supposed to be a time of reflection
about personal as well as communal issues.
The standardized text of the siddur provides

guidelines for what to be thinking about,
but that still leaves room for lots of personal
input (see our Introduction to this Siddur). In

THE AMIDA

There are three formats of the Amida offered in this Siddur. The Amida of Shaḥarit includes commentary (on page 138); in the Amida of Minḥa one may add one's own commentary; the Amida of Ma'ariv (on page 360) is in the traditional form.

The Amida, until "in former years" on page 326, is said silently, standing with feet together. If there is a minyan, the Amida is repeated aloud by the Leader. Take three steps forward and at the points indicated by ˙, bend the knees at the first word, bow at the second, and stand straight before saying God's name.

When I proclaim the Lord's name, give glory to our God.   *Deut. 32*

O Lord, open my lips,^ so that my mouth may declare Your praise.   *Ps. 51*

עמידה

There are three formats of the עמידה offered in this סידור. The שחרית of עמידה includes commentary (on page 139); in the עמידה of מנחה one may add one's own commentary; the עמידה of מעריב (on page 361) is in the traditional form.

The עמידה, until קדמוניות on page 327, is said silently, standing with feet together. If there is a מנין, the עמידה is repeated aloud by the שליח ציבור. Take three steps forward and at the points indicated by ׳, bend the knees at the first word, bow at the second, and stand straight before saying God's name.

דברים לב

כִּי שֵׁם יהוה אֶקְרָא, הָבוּ גֹדֶל לֵאלֹהֵינוּ:

תהלים נא

אֲדֹנָי, שְׂפָתַי תִּפְתָּח,׳ וּפִי יַגִּיד תְּהִלָּתֶךָ:

ANI TEFILLA · אני תפילה

אֲדֹנָי, שְׂפָתַי תִּפְתָּח – *O LORD, open my lips.* The Gemara (*Berakhot* 32b) says that the Ḥasidim Rishonim would spend an hour on the *Shemoneh Esreh*. If there are 3600 seconds in an hour and about 500 words in *Shemoneh Esreh*, that would mean one word every seven seconds (Rabbi A. Kaplan). That may not be realistic for you right now, but the lesson is clear – slow down!

PATRIARCHS

בָּרוּךְ Blessed are You, LORD our God and God of our fathers,
God of Abraham, God of Isaac and God of Jacob;
the great, mighty and awesome God, God Most High,
who bestows acts of loving-kindness and creates all,
who remembers the loving-kindness of the fathers
and will bring a Redeemer to their children's children
for the sake of His name, in love.

Between Rosh Remember us for life, O King who desires life,
HaShana & and write us in the book of life –
Yom Kippur: for Your sake, O God of life.

King, Helper, Savior, Shield:
Blessed are You, LORD,
Shield of Abraham.

אָבוֹת

בָּרוּךְ אַתָּה יהוה, אֱלֹהֵינוּ וֵאלֹהֵי אֲבוֹתֵינוּ

אֱלֹהֵי אַבְרָהָם, אֱלֹהֵי יִצְחָק, וֵאלֹהֵי יַעֲקֹב

הָאֵל הַגָּדוֹל הַגִּבּוֹר וְהַנּוֹרָא, אֵל עֶלְיוֹן

גּוֹמֵל חֲסָדִים טוֹבִים, וְקֹנֵה הַכֹּל

וְזוֹכֵר חַסְדֵי אָבוֹת

וּמֵבִיא גוֹאֵל לִבְנֵי בְנֵיהֶם לְמַעַן שְׁמוֹ בְּאַהֲבָה.

בעשרת ימי תשובה: זָכְרֵנוּ לְחַיִּים, מֶלֶךְ חָפֵץ בַּחַיִּים

וְכָתְבֵנוּ בְּסֵפֶר הַחַיִּים, לְמַעַנְךָ אֱלֹהִים חַיִּים.

מֶלֶךְ עוֹזֵר וּמוֹשִׁיעַ וּמָגֵן.

בָּרוּךְ אַתָּה יהוה, מָגֵן אַבְרָהָם.

DIVINE MIGHT

אַתָּה גִבּוֹר You are eternally mighty, LORD.
You give life to the dead and have great power to save.

*The phrase "He makes the wind blow and the rain fall" is added
from Simḥat Torah until Pesaḥ. In Israel the phrase "He causes the
dew to fall" is added from Pesaḥ until Shemini Atzeret.*

In fall & winter: He makes the wind blow and the rain fall.

*In Israel, in spring
& summer:* He causes the dew to fall.

He sustains the living with loving-kindness,
and with great compassion revives the dead.
He supports the fallen, heals the sick,
sets captives free,
and keeps His faith with those who sleep in the dust.
Who is like You, Master of might,
and who can compare to You,
O King who brings death and gives life,
and makes salvation grow?

*Between Rosh HaShana
& Yom Kippur:* Who is like You, compassionate Father,
who remembers His creatures in compassion, for life?

Faithful are You to revive the dead.
Blessed are You, LORD, who revives the dead.

When saying the Amida silently, continue with "You are holy" on page 288.

גְּבוּרוֹת

אַתָּה גִּבּוֹר לְעוֹלָם, אֲדֹנָי

מְחַיֵּה מֵתִים אַתָּה, רַב לְהוֹשִׁיעַ

The phrase מַשִּׁיב הָרוּחַ *is added from* שמחת תורה *until* פסח.
In ארץ ישראל *the phrase* מוֹרִיד הַטָּל *is added from* פסח *until* שמיני עצרת.

בארץ ישראל בקיץ: **מוֹרִיד הַטָּל** / בחורף: **מַשִּׁיב הָרוּחַ וּמוֹרִיד הַגֶּשֶׁם**

מְכַלְכֵּל חַיִּים בְּחֶסֶד, מְחַיֵּה מֵתִים בְּרַחֲמִים רַבִּים

סוֹמֵךְ נוֹפְלִים, וְרוֹפֵא חוֹלִים, וּמַתִּיר אֲסוּרִים

וּמְקַיֵּם אֱמוּנָתוֹ לִישֵׁנֵי עָפָר.

מִי כָמִוֹךָ, בַּעַל גְּבוּרוֹת

וּמִי דּוֹמֶה לָּךְ

מֶלֶךְ, מֵמִית וּמְחַיֶּה וּמַצְמִיחַ יְשׁוּעָה.

בעשרת ימי תשובה: מִי כָמִוֹךָ אַב הָרַחֲמִים
זוֹכֵר יְצוּרָיו לְחַיִּים בְּרַחֲמִים.

וְנֶאֱמָן אַתָּה לְהַחֲיוֹת מֵתִים.

בָּרוּךְ אַתָּה יהוה, מְחַיֵּה הַמֵּתִים.

When saying the עמידה *silently, continue with* אַתָּה קָדוֹשׁ *on page 289.*

KEDUSHA

> *During the Leader's Repetition, the following is said standing*
> *with feet together, rising on the toes at the words indicated by ˄.*

Cong. then נְקַדֵּשׁ We will sanctify Your name on earth,
Leader: as they sanctify it in the highest heavens,
as is written by Your prophet,
"And they [the angels] call to one another saying: *Is. 6*

Cong. then ˄Holy, ˄holy, ˄holy is the LORD of hosts
Leader: the whole world is filled with His glory."
Those facing them say "Blessed – "

Cong. then ˄"Blessed is the LORD's glory from His place." *Ezek. 3*
Leader: And in Your holy Writings it is written thus:

Cong. then ˄"The LORD shall reign for ever. He is your God, Zion, *Ps. 146*
Leader: from generation to generation, Halleluya!"

Leader: From generation to generation
we will declare Your greatness,
and we will proclaim Your holiness for evermore.
Your praise, our God, shall not leave our mouth forever,
for You, God, are a great and holy King.
Blessed are You, LORD,
the holy God. / *Between Rosh HaShana & Yom Kippur:* the holy King./

> *The Leader continues with "You grace humanity" on page 290.*

קדושה

During the חזרת הש״ץ, *the following is said standing*
with feet together, rising on the toes at the words indicated by ּ.

קהל
then
ש״ץ נְקַדֵּשׁ אֶת שִׁמְךָ בָּעוֹלָם, כְּשֵׁם שֶׁמַּקְדִּישִׁים אוֹתוֹ בִּשְׁמֵי מָרוֹם
כַּכָּתוּב עַל יַד נְבִיאֶךָ:

ישעיהו וְקָרָא זֶה אֶל־זֶה וְאָמַר:

קהל
then
ש״ץ קָדוֹשׁ, קָדוֹשׁ, קָדוֹשׁ, יהוה צְבָאוֹת, מְלֹא כָל־הָאָרֶץ כְּבוֹדוֹ:
לְעֻמָּתָם בָּרוּךְ יֹאמֵרוּ

יחזקאל ג
קהל
then
ש״ץ בָּרוּךְ כְּבוֹד־יהוה מִמְּקוֹמוֹ:
וּבְדִבְרֵי קָדְשְׁךָ כָּתוּב לֵאמֹר:

תהלים קמו
קהל
then
ש״ץ יִמְלֹךְ יהוה לְעוֹלָם, אֱלֹהַיִךְ צִיּוֹן לְדֹר וָדֹר, הַלְלוּיָהּ:

ש״ץ לְדוֹר וָדוֹר נַגִּיד גָּדְלֶךָ, וּלְנֵצַח נְצָחִים קְדֻשָּׁתְךָ נַקְדִּישׁ
וְשִׁבְחֲךָ אֱלֹהֵינוּ מִפִּינוּ לֹא יָמוּשׁ לְעוֹלָם וָעֶד
כִּי אֵל מֶלֶךְ גָּדוֹל וְקָדוֹשׁ אָתָּה.
בָּרוּךְ אַתָּה יהוה, הָאֵל הַקָּדוֹשׁ. / בעשרת ימי תשובה: הַמֶּלֶךְ הַקָּדוֹשׁ. /

The שליח ציבור *continues with* אַתָּה חוֹנֵן *on page 291.*

HOLINESS

אַתָּה קָדוֹשׁ You are holy and Your name is holy,
and holy ones praise You daily, Selah!
Blessed are You, LORD,
the holy God. / *Between Rosh HaShana & Yom Kippur:* the holy King./

(*If forgotten, repeat the Amida.*)

קדושת השם

אַתָּה קָדוֹשׁ וְשִׁמְךָ קָדוֹשׁ
וּקְדוֹשִׁים בְּכָל יוֹם יְהַלְלוּךָ סֶּלָה.
בָּרוּךְ אַתָּה יהוה, הָאֵל הַקָּדוֹשׁ./ בעשרת ימי תשובה: הַמֶּלֶךְ הַקָּדוֹשׁ./
(If forgotten, repeat the עמידה*.)*

KNOWLEDGE

אַתָּה חוֹנֵן You grace humanity with knowledge
and teach mortals understanding.

In Ma'ariv on Motza'ei Shabbat and Motza'ei Yom Tov add "You have graced us" on page 362.

Grace us with the knowledge, understanding
and discernment that come from You.
Blessed are You, LORD,
who graciously grants knowledge.

דעת

אַתָּה חוֹנֵן לְאָדָם דַּעַת
וּמְלַמֵּד לֶאֱנוֹשׁ בִּינָה.

In מעריב *on* מוצאי שבת *and* מוצאי יום טוב *add* אַתָּה חוֹנַנְתָּנוּ *on page 363.*

חָנֵּנוּ מֵאִתְּךָ דֵּעָה בִּינָה וְהַשְׂכֵּל.
בָּרוּךְ אַתָּה יהוה, חוֹנֵן הַדָּעַת.

REPENTANCE

הֲשִׁיבֵנוּ Bring us back, our Father, to Your Torah.
Draw us near, our King, to Your service.
Lead us back to You in perfect repentance.
Blessed are You, LORD,
who desires repentance.

תשובה

הֲשִׁיבֵנוּ אָבִינוּ לְתוֹרָתֶךָ
וְקָרְבֵנוּ מַלְכֵּנוּ לַעֲבוֹדָתֶךָ
וְהַחֲזִירֵנוּ בִּתְשׁוּבָה שְׁלֵמָה לְפָנֶיךָ.
בָּרוּךְ אַתָּה יהוה, הָרוֹצֶה בִּתְשׁוּבָה.

FORGIVENESS

Strike the left side of the chest at °.

סְלַח לָנוּ Forgive us, our Father, for we have °sinned.
Pardon us, our King, for we have °transgressed;
for You pardon and forgive.
Blessed are You, LORD,
the gracious One who repeatedly forgives.

סליחה
Strike the left side of the chest at °.

סְלַח לָנוּ אָבִינוּ כִּי °חָטָאנוּ
מְחַל לָנוּ מַלְכֵּנוּ כִּי °פָשָׁעְנוּ
כִּי מוֹחֵל וְסוֹלֵחַ אָתָּה.
בָּרוּךְ אַתָּה יהוה, חַנּוּן הַמַּרְבֶּה לִסְלֹחַ.

REDEMPTION

רְאֵה Look on our affliction, plead our cause,
and redeem us soon for Your name's sake,
for You are a powerful Redeemer.
Blessed are You, LORD,
the Redeemer of Israel.

On fast days the Leader adds:
עֲנֵנוּ Answer us, LORD, answer us on our Fast Day, for we are in great distress.
Look not at our wickedness. Do not hide Your face from us and do not
ignore our plea. Be near to our cry; please let Your loving-kindness comfort
us. Even before we call to You, answer us, as it is said, "Before they call, *Is. 65*
I will answer. While they are still speaking, I will hear." For You, LORD,
are the One who answers in time of distress, redeems and rescues in all
times of trouble and anguish. Blessed are You, LORD, who answers in time
of distress.

גְּאוּלָה

רְאֵה בְעָנְיֵנוּ, וְרִיבָה רִיבֵנוּ
וּגְאָלֵנוּ מְהֵרָה לְמַעַן שְׁמֶךָ
כִּי גּוֹאֵל חָזָק אָתָּה.
בָּרוּךְ אַתָּה יהוה, גּוֹאֵל יִשְׂרָאֵל.

On fast days the שליח ציבור adds:

עֲנֵנוּ יהוה עֲנֵנוּ בְּיוֹם צוֹם תַּעֲנִיתֵנוּ, כִּי בְצָרָה גְדוֹלָה אֲנָחְנוּ. אַל תֵּפֶן אֶל
רִשְׁעֵנוּ, וְאַל תַּסְתֵּר פָּנֶיךָ מִמֶּנּוּ, וְאַל תִּתְעַלַּם מִתְּחִנָּתֵנוּ. הֱיֵה נָא קָרוֹב
לְשַׁוְעָתֵנוּ, יְהִי נָא חַסְדְּךָ לְנַחֲמֵנוּ, טֶרֶם נִקְרָא אֵלֶיךָ עֲנֵנוּ, כַּדָּבָר שֶׁנֶּאֱמַר:
וְהָיָה טֶרֶם יִקְרָאוּ וַאֲנִי אֶעֱנֶה, עוֹד הֵם מְדַבְּרִים וַאֲנִי אֶשְׁמָע: כִּי אַתָּה יהוה   ישעיה סה
הָעוֹנֶה בְּעֵת צָרָה, פּוֹדֶה וּמַצִּיל בְּכָל עֵת צָרָה וְצוּקָה. בָּרוּךְ אַתָּה יהוה,
הָעוֹנֶה בְּעֵת צָרָה.

HEALING

רְפָאֵנוּ Heal us, LORD, and we shall be healed.
Save us and we shall be saved,
for You are our praise.
Bring complete recovery for all our ailments,

_____

The following prayer for a sick person may be said here:
May it be Your will, O LORD my God and God of my ancestors, that You
speedily send a complete recovery from heaven, a healing of both soul and
body, to the patient (*name*), son/daughter of (*mother's name*) among the
other afflicted of Israel.

_____

for You, God, King, are a faithful and compassionate Healer.
Blessed are You, LORD, Healer of the sick of His people Israel.

רפואה

רְפָאֵנוּ יהוה וְנֵרָפֵא
הוֹשִׁיעֵנוּ וְנִוָּשֵׁעָה, כִּי תְהִלָּתֵנוּ אָתָּה
וְהַעֲלֵה רְפוּאָה שְׁלֵמָה לְכָל מַכּוֹתֵינוּ

The following prayer for a sick person may be said here:

יְהִי רָצוֹן מִלְּפָנֶיךָ יהוה אֱלֹהַי וֵאלֹהֵי אֲבוֹתַי, שֶׁתִּשְׁלַח מְהֵרָה רְפוּאָה שְׁלֵמָה
מִן הַשָּׁמַיִם רְפוּאַת הַנֶּפֶשׁ וּרְפוּאַת הַגּוּף לַחוֹלֶה/לַחוֹלָה *name of patient*
בֶּן/בַּת *mother's name* בְּתוֹךְ שְׁאָר חוֹלֵי יִשְׂרָאֵל.

כִּי אֵל מֶלֶךְ רוֹפֵא נֶאֱמָן וְרַחֲמָן אָתָּה.
בָּרוּךְ אַתָּה יהוה, רוֹפֵא חוֹלֵי עַמּוֹ יִשְׂרָאֵל.

PROSPERITY

> *The phrase "Grant dew and rain as a blessing" is said from December 5th*
> *(in the year before a civil leap year, December 6th) until Pesaḥ. In Israel, it*
> *is said from the 7th of Marḥeshvan. The phrase "Grant blessing" is said*
> *from Ḥol HaMo'ed Pesaḥ until December 4th (in the year before a civil leap*
> *year, December 5th). In Israel it is said through the 6th of Marḥeshvan.*

בָּרֵךְ Bless this year for us, LORD our God,
and all its types of produce for good.

In winter: Grant dew and rain as a blessing
In other seasons: Grant blessing

on the face of the earth,
and from its goodness satisfy us,
blessing our year as the best of years.
Blessed are You, LORD, who blesses the years.

ברכת השנים

The phrase וְתֵן טַל וּמָטָר לִבְרָכָה is said from December 5th (in the year before a
civil leap year, December 6th) until פסח. In אֶרֶץ יִשְׂרָאֵל, it is said from
ז בְּמַרְחֶשְׁוָן.
The phrase וְתֵן בְּרָכָה is said from חוֹל הַמּוֹעֵד פסח until December 4th (in the year
before a civil leap year, December 5th). In אֶרֶץ יִשְׂרָאֵל it is said through ז בְּמַרְחֶשְׁוָן.

בָּרֵךְ עָלֵינוּ יהוה אֱלֹהֵינוּ אֶת הַשָּׁנָה הַזֹּאת
וְאֶת כָּל מִינֵי תְבוּאָתָהּ, לְטוֹבָה

בחורף: וְתֵן טַל וּמָטָר לִבְרָכָה / בקיץ: וְתֵן בְּרָכָה

עַל פְּנֵי הָאֲדָמָה, וְשַׂבְּעֵנוּ מִטּוּבָה
וּבָרֵךְ שְׁנָתֵנוּ כַּשָּׁנִים הַטּוֹבוֹת.
בָּרוּךְ אַתָּה יהוה, מְבָרֵךְ הַשָּׁנִים.

INGATHERING OF EXILES

תְּקַע Sound the great shofar for our freedom,
raise high the banner to gather our exiles,
and gather us together from the four quarters of the earth.
Blessed are You, LORD,
who gathers the dispersed of His people Israel.

קבּוּץ גָּלֻיּוֹת

תְּקַע בְּשׁוֹפָר גָּדוֹל לְחֵרוּתֵנוּ

וְשָׂא נֵס לְקַבֵּץ גָּלֻיּוֹתֵינוּ

וְקַבְּצֵנוּ יַחַד מֵאַרְבַּע כַּנְפוֹת הָאָרֶץ.

בָּרוּךְ אַתָּה יהוה, מְקַבֵּץ נִדְחֵי עַמּוֹ יִשְׂרָאֵל.

JUSTICE

הָשִׁיבָה Restore our judges as at first,
and our counselors as at the beginning,
and remove from us sorrow and sighing.
May You alone, LORD,
reign over us with loving-kindness and compassion,
and vindicate us in justice.
Blessed are You, LORD,
the King who loves righteousness and justice.

/ *Between Rosh HaShana & Yom Kippur, end the blessing:* the King of justice./

השבת המשפט

הָשִׁיבָה שׁוֹפְטֵינוּ כְּבָרִאשׁוֹנָה וְיוֹעֲצֵינוּ כְּבַתְּחִלָּה

וְהָסֵר מִמֶּנּוּ יָגוֹן וַאֲנָחָה

וּמְלֹךְ עָלֵינוּ אַתָּה יהוה לְבַדְּךָ בְּחֶסֶד וּבְרַחֲמִים

וְצַדְּקֵנוּ בַּמִּשְׁפָּט.

בָּרוּךְ אַתָּה יהוה

מֶלֶךְ אוֹהֵב צְדָקָה וּמִשְׁפָּט. / בעשרת ימי תשובה: הַמֶּלֶךְ הַמִּשְׁפָּט./

AGAINST INFORMERS

וְלַמַּלְשִׁינִים For the slanderers let there be no hope,
and may all wickedness perish in an instant.
May all Your people's enemies swiftly be cut down.
May You swiftly uproot, crush, cast down
and humble the arrogant swiftly in our days.
Blessed are You, LORD,
who destroys enemies and humbles the arrogant.

ברכת המינים

וְלַמַּלְשִׁינִים אַל תְּהִי תִקְוָה
וְכָל הָרִשְׁעָה כְּרֶגַע תֹּאבֵד
וְכָל אוֹיְבֵי עַמְּךָ מְהֵרָה יִכָּרֵתוּ
וְהַזֵּדִים מְהֵרָה תְעַקֵּר וּתְשַׁבֵּר וּתְמַגֵּר וְתַכְנִיעַ בִּמְהֵרָה בְיָמֵינוּ.
בָּרוּךְ אַתָּה יהוה, שׁוֹבֵר אוֹיְבִים וּמַכְנִיעַ זֵדִים.

THE RIGHTEOUS

עַל הַצַּדִּיקִים To the righteous, the pious,
the elders of Your people the house of Israel,
the remnant of their scholars,
the righteous converts, and to us,
may Your compassion be aroused, LORD our God.
Grant a good reward
to all who sincerely trust in Your name.
Set our lot with them,
so that we may never be ashamed,
for in You we trust.
Blessed are You, LORD,
who is the support and trust of the righteous.

על הצדיקים

עַל הַצַּדִּיקִים וְעַל הַחֲסִידִים

וְעַל זִקְנֵי עַמְּךָ בֵּית יִשְׂרָאֵל

וְעַל פְּלֵיטַת סוֹפְרֵיהֶם

וְעַל גֵּרֵי הַצֶּדֶק, וְעָלֵינוּ

יֶהֱמוּ רַחֲמֶיךָ יהוה אֱלֹהֵינוּ

וְתֵן שָׂכָר טוֹב לְכָל הַבּוֹטְחִים בְּשִׁמְךָ בֶּאֱמֶת

וְשִׂים חֶלְקֵנוּ עִמָּהֶם

וּלְעוֹלָם לֹא נֵבוֹשׁ כִּי בְךָ בָּטָחְנוּ.

בָּרוּךְ אַתָּה יהוה, מִשְׁעָן וּמִבְטָח לַצַּדִּיקִים.

REBUILDING JERUSALEM

וְלִירוּשָׁלַיִם To Jerusalem, Your city,
may You return in compassion,
and may You dwell in it as You promised.
May You rebuild it rapidly in our days
as an everlasting structure,
and install within it soon the throne of David.
*Blessed are You, Lᴏʀᴅ, who builds Jerusalem.

---

*At Minḥa, on Tisha B'Av all conclude as follows:

נַחֵם Console, O Lᴏʀᴅ our God, the mourners of Zion and the mourners of
Jerusalem, and the city that is in sorrow, laid waste, scorned and desolate; that
grieves for the loss of its children, that is laid waste of its dwellings, robbed
of its glory, desolate without inhabitants. She sits with her head covered
like a barren childless woman. Legions have devoured her; idolaters have
taken possession of her; they have put Your people Israel to the sword and
deliberately killed the devoted followers of the Most High. Therefore Zion
weeps bitterly, and Jerusalem raises her voice. My heart, my heart grieves for
those they killed; I am in anguish, I am in anguish for those they killed. For
You, O Lᴏʀᴅ, consumed it with fire, and with fire You will rebuild it in the
future, as is said, "And I Myself will be a wall of fire around it, says the Lᴏʀᴅ,   *Zech. 2*
and I will be its glory within." Blessed are You, Lᴏʀᴅ, who consoles Zion and
rebuilds Jerusalem.

Continue with "May the offshoot" on the next page.

בניין ירושלים

וְלִירוּשָׁלַיִם עִירְךָ בְּרַחֲמִים תָּשׁוּב
וְתִשְׁכֹּן בְּתוֹכָהּ כַּאֲשֶׁר דִּבַּרְתָּ
וּבְנֵה אוֹתָהּ בְּקָרוֹב בְּיָמֵינוּ בִּנְיַן עוֹלָם
וְכִסֵּא דָוִד מְהֵרָה לְתוֹכָהּ תָּכִין.
*בָּרוּךְ אַתָּה יהוה, בּוֹנֵה יְרוּשָׁלָיִם.

---

*At מנחה, on תשעה באב, all conclude as follows:

נַחֵם יהוה אֱלֹהֵינוּ אֶת אֲבֵלֵי צִיּוֹן וְאֶת אֲבֵלֵי יְרוּשָׁלַיִם, וְאֶת הָעִיר הָאֲבֵלָה
וְהַחֲרֵבָה וְהַבְּזוּיָה וְהַשּׁוֹמֵמָה. הָאֲבֵלָה מִבְּלִי בָנֶיהָ, וְהַחֲרֵבָה מִמְּעוֹנוֹתֶיהָ,
וְהַבְּזוּיָה מִכְּבוֹדָהּ, וְהַשּׁוֹמֵמָה מֵאֵין יוֹשֵׁב. וְהִיא יוֹשֶׁבֶת וְרֹאשָׁהּ חָפוּי, כְּאִשָּׁה
עֲקָרָה שֶׁלֹּא יָלָדָה. וַיְבַלְּעוּהָ לִגְיוֹנוֹת, וַיִּירָשׁוּהָ עוֹבְדֵי פְסִילִים, וַיָּטִילוּ אֶת
עַמְּךָ יִשְׂרָאֵל לֶחָרֶב, וַיַּהַרְגוּ בְזָדוֹן חֲסִידֵי עֶלְיוֹן. עַל כֵּן צִיּוֹן בְּמַר תִּבְכֶּה,
וִירוּשָׁלַיִם תִּתֵּן קוֹלָהּ. לִבִּי לִבִּי עַל חַלְלֵיהֶם, מֵעַי מֵעַי עַל חַלְלֵיהֶם, כִּי אַתָּה
יהוה בָּאֵשׁ הִצַּתָּהּ, וּבָאֵשׁ אַתָּה עָתִיד לִבְנוֹתָהּ. כָּאָמוּר: וַאֲנִי אֶהְיֶה לָּהּ, זכריה ב
נְאֻם־יהוה, חוֹמַת אֵשׁ סָבִיב, וּלְכָבוֹד אֶהְיֶה בְתוֹכָהּ: בָּרוּךְ אַתָּה יהוה,
מְנַחֵם צִיּוֹן וּבוֹנֵה יְרוּשָׁלָיִם.

Continue with אֶת צֶמַח on the next page.

KINGDOM OF DAVID

אֶת צֶמַח May the offshoot of Your servant David soon flower,
and may his pride be raised high by Your salvation,
for we wait for Your salvation all day.
Blessed are You, LORD,
who makes the glory of salvation flourish.

משיח בן דוד

אֶת צֶמַח דָּוִד עַבְדְּךָ מְהֵרָה תַצְמִיחַ
וְקַרְנוֹ תָּרוּם בִּישׁוּעָתֶךָ
כִּי לִישׁוּעָתְךָ קִוִּינוּ כָּל הַיּוֹם.
בָּרוּךְ אַתָּה יהוה, מַצְמִיחַ קֶרֶן יְשׁוּעָה.

RESPONSE TO PRAYER

שְׁמַע קוֹלֵנוּ Listen to our voice, LORD our God.
Spare us and have compassion on us,
and in compassion and favor accept our prayer,
for You, God, listen to prayers and pleas.
Do not turn us away, O our King,
empty-handed from Your presence,*
for You listen with compassion
to the prayer of Your people Israel.
Blessed are You, LORD,
who listens to prayer.

---

*At Minḥa, at this point on fast days, the congregation adds "Answer us" below.
In times of drought in Israel, say "And answer us" on page 684.
עֲנֵנוּ Answer us, LORD, answer us on our Fast Day, for we are in great distress.
Look not at our wickedness. Do not hide Your face from us and do not
ignore our plea. Be near to our cry; please let Your loving-kindness comfort
us. Even before we call to You, answer us, as is said, "Before they call, I will
answer. While they are still speaking, I will hear." For You, LORD, are the
One who answers in time of distress, redeems and rescues in all times of
trouble and anguish.   *Continue with "for You listen" above.*

שומע תפלה
שְׁמַע קוֹלֵנוּ יהוה אֱלֹהֵינוּ
חוּס וְרַחֵם עָלֵינוּ
וְקַבֵּל בְּרַחֲמִים וּבְרָצוֹן אֶת תְּפִלָּתֵנוּ
כִּי אֵל שׁוֹמֵעַ תְּפִלּוֹת וְתַחֲנוּנִים אָתָּה
וּמִלְּפָנֶיךָ מַלְכֵּנוּ רֵיקָם אַל תְּשִׁיבֵנוּ*
כִּי אַתָּה שׁוֹמֵעַ תְּפִלַּת עַמְּךָ יִשְׂרָאֵל בְּרַחֲמִים.
בָּרוּךְ אַתָּה יהוה, שׁוֹמֵעַ תְּפִלָּה.

---

*At מנחה, *at this point on fast days, the* קהל *adds* עֲנֵנוּ *below.*
In times of drought in ארץ ישראל, *say* וְעֲנֵנוּ *on page 685.*

עֲנֵנוּ יהוה עֲנֵנוּ בְּיוֹם צוֹם הַתַּעֲנִיתֵנוּ, כִּי בְצָרָה גְדוֹלָה אֲנָחְנוּ. אַל תֵּפֶן אֶל רִשְׁעֵנוּ, וְאַל תַּסְתֵּר פָּנֶיךָ מִמֶּנּוּ, וְאַל תִּתְעַלַּם מִתְּחִנָּתֵנוּ. הֱיֵה נָא קָרוֹב לְשַׁוְעָתֵנוּ, יְהִי נָא חַסְדְּךָ לְנַחֲמֵנוּ, טֶרֶם נִקְרָא אֵלֶיךָ עֲנֵנוּ, כַּדָּבָר שֶׁנֶּאֱמַר: וְהָיָה טֶרֶם יִקְרָאוּ וַאֲנִי אֶעֱנֶה, עוֹד הֵם מְדַבְּרִים וַאֲנִי אֶשְׁמָע: כִּי אַתָּה יהוה הָעוֹנֶה בְּעֵת צָרָה, פּוֹדֶה וּמַצִּיל בְּכָל עֵת צָרָה וְצוּקָה.

Continue with כִּי אַתָּה שׁוֹמֵעַ *above.*

TEMPLE SERVICE

רְצֵה Find favor, Lᴏʀᴅ our God,
in Your people Israel and their prayer.
Restore the service to Your most holy House,
and accept in love and favor
the fire-offerings of Israel and their prayer.
May the service of Your people Israel always find favor with You.

On Rosh Ḥodesh and Ḥol HaMo'ed, say:

אֱלֹהֵינוּ Our God and God of our ancestors, may there rise, come, reach,
appear, be favored, heard, regarded and remembered before You, our recollection and remembrance, as well as the remembrance of our ancestors,
and of the Messiah son of David Your servant, and of Jerusalem Your
holy city, and of all Your people the house of Israel – for deliverance and
well-being, grace, loving-kindness and compassion, life and peace, on
this day of:

On Rosh Ḥodesh: Rosh Ḥodesh.

On Pesaḥ: the Festival of Matzot.

On Sukkot: the Festival of Sukkot.

On it remember us, Lᴏʀᴅ our God, for good; recollect us for blessing,
and deliver us for life. In accord with Your promise of salvation and
compassion, spare us and be gracious to us; have compassion on us and
deliver us, for our eyes are turned to You because You, God, are a gracious
and compassionate King.

וְתֶחֱזֶינָה And may our eyes witness
Your return to Zion in compassion.
Blessed are You, Lᴏʀᴅ, who restores His Presence to Zion.

עבודה

רְצֵה יהוה אֱלֹהֵינוּ בְּעַמְּךָ יִשְׂרָאֵל וּבִתְפִלָּתָם
וְהָשֵׁב אֶת הָעֲבוֹדָה לִדְבִיר בֵּיתֶךָ
וְאִשֵּׁי יִשְׂרָאֵל וּתְפִלָּתָם בְּאַהֲבָה תְקַבֵּל בְּרָצוֹן
וּתְהִי לְרָצוֹן תָּמִיד עֲבוֹדַת יִשְׂרָאֵל עַמֶּךָ.

On חול המועד *and* ראש חודש, *say:*

אֱלֹהֵינוּ וֵאלֹהֵי אֲבוֹתֵינוּ, יַעֲלֶה וְיָבוֹא וְיַגִּיעַ, וְיֵרָאֶה וְיֵרָצֶה וְיִשָּׁמַע,
וְיִפָּקֵד וְיִזָּכֵר זִכְרוֹנֵנוּ וּפִקְדוֹנֵנוּ וְזִכְרוֹן אֲבוֹתֵינוּ, וְזִכְרוֹן מָשִׁיחַ בֶּן
דָּוִד עַבְדֶּךָ, וְזִכְרוֹן יְרוּשָׁלַיִם עִיר קָדְשֶׁךָ, וְזִכְרוֹן כָּל עַמְּךָ בֵּית
יִשְׂרָאֵל, לְפָנֶיךָ, לִפְלֵיטָה לְטוֹבָה, לְחֵן וּלְחֶסֶד וּלְרַחֲמִים, לְחַיִּים
וּלְשָׁלוֹם בְּיוֹם

בראש חודש: רֹאשׁ הַחֹדֶשׁ / בפסח: חַג הַמַּצּוֹת / בסוכות: חַג הַסֻּכּוֹת

הַזֶּה. זָכְרֵנוּ יהוה אֱלֹהֵינוּ בּוֹ לְטוֹבָה, וּפָקְדֵנוּ בוֹ לִבְרָכָה,
וְהוֹשִׁיעֵנוּ בוֹ לְחַיִּים. וּבִדְבַר יְשׁוּעָה וְרַחֲמִים, חוּס וְחָנֵּנוּ וְרַחֵם
עָלֵינוּ וְהוֹשִׁיעֵנוּ, כִּי אֵלֶיךָ עֵינֵינוּ, כִּי אֵל מֶלֶךְ חַנּוּן וְרַחוּם אָתָּה.

וְתֶחֱזֶינָה עֵינֵינוּ בְּשׁוּבְךָ לְצִיּוֹן בְּרַחֲמִים.
בָּרוּךְ אַתָּה יהוה, הַמַּחֲזִיר שְׁכִינָתוֹ לְצִיּוֹן.

THANKSGIVING

Bow at the first nine words.

מוֹדִים We give thanks to You,
for You are the LORD our God
and God of our ancestors
for ever and all time.
You are the Rock of our lives,
Shield of our salvation
from generation to generation.
We will thank You and
declare Your praise for our lives,
which are entrusted into Your hand;
for our souls,
which are placed in Your charge;
for Your miracles
which are with us every day;
and for Your wonders and favors
at all times,
evening, morning and midday.
You are good –
for Your compassion never fails.
You are compassionate –
for Your loving-kindnesses never cease.
We have always placed our hope in You.

*During the Leader's Repetition,
the congregation says quietly:*

מוֹדִים We give thanks to You,
for You are the LORD our God
and God of our ancestors,
God of all flesh,
who formed us
and formed the universe.
Blessings and thanks
are due to Your great
and holy name for giving us
life and sustaining us.
May You continue
to give us life
and sustain us;
and may You gather our
exiles to Your holy courts,
to keep Your decrees,
do Your will and serve You
with a perfect heart,
for it is for us
to give You thanks.
Blessed be God to whom
thanksgiving is due.

הוֹדָאָה

Bow at the first five words.

<table>
<tr><td>

חֲזָרַת הש״ץ, *During the*
the קָהָל *says quietly:*

מוֹדִים אֲנַחְנוּ לָךְ

שָׁאַתָּה הוּא יהוה אֱלֹהֵינוּ

וֵאלֹהֵי אֲבוֹתֵינוּ

אֱלֹהֵי כָל בָּשָׂר

יוֹצְרֵנוּ, יוֹצֵר בְּרֵאשִׁית.

בְּרָכוֹת וְהוֹדָאוֹת

לְשִׁמְךָ הַגָּדוֹל וְהַקָּדוֹשׁ

עַל שֶׁהֶחֱיִיתָנוּ וְקִיַּמְתָּנוּ.

כֵּן תְּחַיֵּנוּ וּתְקַיְּמֵנוּ

וְתֶאֱסֹף גָּלֻיּוֹתֵינוּ

לְחַצְרוֹת קָדְשֶׁךָ

לִשְׁמֹר חֻקֶּיךָ וְלַעֲשׂוֹת רְצוֹנֶךָ

וּלְעָבְדְּךָ בְּלֵבָב שָׁלֵם

עַל שֶׁאֲנַחְנוּ מוֹדִים לָךְ.

בָּרוּךְ אֵל הַהוֹדָאוֹת.

</td><td>

מוֹדִים אֲנַחְנוּ לָךְ

שָׁאַתָּה הוּא יהוה אֱלֹהֵינוּ

וֵאלֹהֵי אֲבוֹתֵינוּ לְעוֹלָם וָעֶד.

צוּר חַיֵּינוּ, מָגֵן יִשְׁעֵנוּ

אַתָּה הוּא לְדוֹר וָדוֹר.

נוֹדֶה לְּךָ וּנְסַפֵּר תְּהִלָּתֶךָ

עַל חַיֵּינוּ הַמְּסוּרִים בְּיָדֶךָ

וְעַל נִשְׁמוֹתֵינוּ הַפְּקוּדוֹת לָךְ

וְעַל נִסֶּיךָ שֶׁבְּכָל יוֹם עִמָּנוּ

וְעַל נִפְלְאוֹתֶיךָ וְטוֹבוֹתֶיךָ

שֶׁבְּכָל עֵת, עֶרֶב וָבֹקֶר וְצָהֳרָיִם.

הַטּוֹב, כִּי לֹא כָלוּ רַחֲמֶיךָ

וְהַמְרַחֵם, כִּי לֹא תַמּוּ חֲסָדֶיךָ

מֵעוֹלָם קִוִּינוּ לָךְ.

</td></tr>
</table>

On Ḥanukka:

עַל הַנִּסִּים [We thank You also] for the miracles, the redemption, the mighty deeds, the salvations, and the victories in battle which You performed for our ancestors in those days, at this time.

בִּימֵי מַתִּתְיָהוּ In the days of Mattityahu, son of Yoḥanan, the High Priest, the Hasmonean, and his sons, the wicked Greek kingdom rose up against Your people Israel to make them forget Your Torah and to force them to transgress the statutes of Your will. It was then that You in Your great compassion stood by them in the time of their distress. You championed their cause, judged their claim, and avenged their wrong. You delivered the strong into the hands of the weak, the many into the hands of the few, the impure into the hands of the pure, the wicked into the hands of the righteous, and the arrogant into the hands of those who were engaged in the study of Your Torah. You made for Yourself great and holy renown in Your world, and for Your people Israel You performed a great salvation and redemption as of this very day. Your children then entered the holiest part of Your House, cleansed Your Temple, purified Your Sanctuary, kindled lights in Your holy courts, and designated these eight days of Ḥanukka for giving thanks and praise to Your great name.

Continue with "For all these things."

On Purim:

עַל הַנִּסִּים [We thank You also] for the miracles, the redemption, the mighty deeds, the salvations, and the victories in battle which You performed for our ancestors in those days, at this time.

בִּימֵי מָרְדְּכַי In the days of Mordekhai and Esther, in Shushan the capital, the wicked Haman rose up against them and sought to destroy, slay and exterminate *Esther 3* all the Jews, young and old, children and women, on one day, the thirteenth day of the twelfth month, which is the month of Adar, and to plunder their possessions. Then You in Your great compassion thwarted his counsel, frustrated his plans, and caused his scheme to recoil on his own head, so that they hanged him and his sons on the gallows.

Continue with "For all these things."

בחנוכה:

עַל הַנִּסִּים וְעַל הַפֻּרְקָן וְעַל הַגְּבוּרוֹת וְעַל הַתְּשׁוּעוֹת וְעַל הַמִּלְחָמוֹת
שֶׁעָשִׂיתָ לַאֲבוֹתֵינוּ בַּיָּמִים הָהֵם בַּזְּמַן הַזֶּה.

בִּימֵי מַתִּתְיָהוּ בֶּן יוֹחָנָן כֹּהֵן גָּדוֹל חַשְׁמוֹנַאי וּבָנָיו, כְּשֶׁעָמְדָה מַלְכוּת יָוָן
הָרְשָׁעָה עַל עַמְּךָ יִשְׂרָאֵל לְהַשְׁכִּיחָם תּוֹרָתֶךָ וּלְהַעֲבִירָם מֵחֻקֵּי רְצוֹנֶךָ,
וְאַתָּה בְּרַחֲמֶיךָ הָרַבִּים עָמַדְתָּ לָהֶם בְּעֵת צָרָתָם, רַבְתָּ אֶת רִיבָם, דַּנְתָּ
אֶת דִּינָם, נָקַמְתָּ אֶת נִקְמָתָם, מָסַרְתָּ גִבּוֹרִים בְּיַד חַלָּשִׁים, וְרַבִּים בְּיַד
מְעַטִּים, וּטְמֵאִים בְּיַד טְהוֹרִים, וּרְשָׁעִים בְּיַד צַדִּיקִים, וְזֵדִים בְּיַד עוֹסְקֵי
תוֹרָתֶךָ, וּלְךָ עָשִׂיתָ שֵׁם גָּדוֹל וְקָדוֹשׁ בְּעוֹלָמֶךָ, וּלְעַמְּךָ יִשְׂרָאֵל עָשִׂיתָ
תְּשׁוּעָה גְדוֹלָה וּפֻרְקָן כְּהַיּוֹם הַזֶּה. וְאַחַר כֵּן בָּאוּ בָנֶיךָ לִדְבִיר בֵּיתֶךָ,
וּפִנּוּ אֶת הֵיכָלֶךָ, וְטִהֲרוּ אֶת מִקְדָּשֶׁךָ, וְהִדְלִיקוּ נֵרוֹת בְּחַצְרוֹת קָדְשֶׁךָ,
וְקָבְעוּ שְׁמוֹנַת יְמֵי חֲנֻכָּה אֵלּוּ, לְהוֹדוֹת וּלְהַלֵּל לְשִׁמְךָ הַגָּדוֹל.

Continue with וְעַל כֻּלָּם.

בפורים:

עַל הַנִּסִּים וְעַל הַפֻּרְקָן וְעַל הַגְּבוּרוֹת וְעַל הַתְּשׁוּעוֹת וְעַל הַמִּלְחָמוֹת
שֶׁעָשִׂיתָ לַאֲבוֹתֵינוּ בַּיָּמִים הָהֵם בַּזְּמַן הַזֶּה.

בִּימֵי מָרְדְּכַי וְאֶסְתֵּר בְּשׁוּשַׁן הַבִּירָה, כְּשֶׁעָמַד עֲלֵיהֶם הָמָן הָרָשָׁע,
בִּקֵּשׁ לְהַשְׁמִיד לַהֲרֹג וּלְאַבֵּד אֶת־כָּל־הַיְּהוּדִים מִנַּעַר וְעַד־זָקֵן טַף אסתר ג
וְנָשִׁים בְּיוֹם אֶחָד, בִּשְׁלוֹשָׁה עָשָׂר לְחֹדֶשׁ שְׁנֵים־עָשָׂר, הוּא־חֹדֶשׁ אֲדָר,
וּשְׁלָלָם לָבוֹז: וְאַתָּה בְּרַחֲמֶיךָ הָרַבִּים הֵפַרְתָּ אֶת עֲצָתוֹ, וְקִלְקַלְתָּ אֶת
מַחֲשַׁבְתּוֹ, וַהֲשֵׁבוֹתָ לּוֹ גְּמוּלוֹ בְּרֹאשׁוֹ, וְתָלוּ אוֹתוֹ וְאֶת בָּנָיו עַל הָעֵץ.

Continue with וְעַל כֻּלָּם.

וְעַל כֻּלָּם For all these things may Your name be blessed and exalted, our King, continually, for ever and all time.

Between Rosh HaShana And write, for a good life,
& Yom Kippur: all the children of Your covenant.

Let all that lives thank You, Selah! and praise Your name in truth, God, our Savior and Help, Selah!
ʼBlessed are You, Lord, whose name is "the Good" and to whom thanks are due.

On public fast days only, the following is said by the Leader during
the Repetition of the Amida, except in a house of mourning. In Israel, on Fast Days,
if Kohanim bless the congregation, turn to page 684.

Our God and God of our fathers, bless us with the threefold blessing in the Torah, written by the hand of Moses Your servant and pronounced by Aaron and his sons the priests, Your holy people, as it is said:

May the Lord bless you and protect you.   *Num. 6*
Cong: May it be Your will.
May the Lord make His face shine on you and be gracious to you.
Cong: May it be Your will.
May the Lord turn His face toward you, and grant you peace.
Cong: May it be Your will.

וְעַל כֻּלָּם יִתְבָּרַךְ וְיִתְרוֹמַם שִׁמְךָ מַלְכֵּנוּ תָּמִיד לְעוֹלָם וָעֶד.

בעשרת ימי תשובה: וּכְתֹב לְחַיִּים טוֹבִים כָּל בְּנֵי בְרִיתֶךָ.

וְכֹל הַחַיִּים יוֹדוּךָ סֶּלָה, וִיהַלְלוּ אֶת שִׁמְךָ בֶּאֱמֶת
הָאֵל יְשׁוּעָתֵנוּ וְעֶזְרָתֵנוּ סֶלָה.
בָּרוּךְ אַתָּה יהוה, הַטּוֹב שִׁמְךָ וּלְךָ נָאֶה לְהוֹדוֹת.

On public fast days only, the following is said by the שְׁלִיחַ צִבּוּר during the
חֲזָרַת הַשַּׁץ except in a house of mourning. In אֶרֶץ יִשְׂרָאֵל, on Fast Days,
if כֹּהֲנִים say בִּרְכַּת כֹּהֲנִים turn to page 685.

אֱלֹהֵינוּ וֵאלֹהֵי אֲבוֹתֵינוּ, בָּרְכֵנוּ בַבְּרָכָה הַמְשֻׁלֶּשֶׁת בַּתּוֹרָה
הַכְּתוּבָה עַל יְדֵי מֹשֶׁה עַבְדֶּךָ, הָאֲמוּרָה מִפִּי אַהֲרֹן וּבָנָיו כֹּהֲנִים
עַם קְדוֹשֶׁךָ, כָּאָמוּר:

יְבָרֶכְךָ יהוה וְיִשְׁמְרֶךָ: ‎קהל: כֵּן יְהִי רָצוֹן
במדברו

יָאֵר יהוה פָּנָיו אֵלֶיךָ וִיחֻנֶּךָּ: ‎קהל: כֵּן יְהִי רָצוֹן

יִשָּׂא יהוה פָּנָיו אֵלֶיךָ וְיָשֵׂם לְךָ שָׁלוֹם: ‎קהל: כֵּן יְהִי רָצוֹן

PEACE

In Minḥa and Ma'ariv

שָׁלוֹם רָב Grant great peace[BIA]
to Your people Israel
for ever,
for You are
the sovereign LORD
of all peace;
and may it
be good
in Your eyes
to bless
Your people Israel
at every time,
at every hour,
with Your peace.

In Minḥa on fast days and in Shaḥarit:

שִׂים שָׁלוֹם Grant peace,
goodness and blessing, grace,
loving-kindness and compassion
to us and all Israel Your people.
Bless us, our Father, all as one,
with the light of Your face,
for by the light of Your face
You have given us, LORD our God,
the Torah of life and love of kindness,
righteousness, blessing, compassion,
life and peace.
May it be good in Your eyes
to bless Your people Israel
at every time, in every hour,
with Your peace.

Between Rosh HaShana & Yom Kippur: In the book of life, blessing, peace and prosperity,
may we and all Your people
the house of Israel be remembered
and written before You for a good life, and for peace.*

Blessed are You, LORD, who blesses His people Israel with peace.

*Between Rosh HaShana and Yom Kippur outside Israel, many end the blessing:
Blessed are You, LORD, who makes peace.

שָׁלוֹם רָב – *Grant great peace.* Perhaps because it is later in the day, our appreciation of the need for *shalom* – peace, wholeness – is greater than it was this morning, hence we ask now for an abundance of it.

שָׁלוֹם רָב – *Grant great peace.* The word *shalom* is related to the word *shalem*, meaning whole or complete. Each of us has a purpose in life, a task that makes us complete. **The day is not yet over. How can I still fulfill my potential today?**

בִּרְכַּת שָׁלוֹם

In מנחה *on fast days and in* שחרית:	*In* מעריב *and* מנחה
שִׂים שָׁלוֹם טוֹבָה וּבְרָכָה	שָׁלוֹם רָב בּעֹא
חֵן וָחֶסֶד וְרַחֲמִים	עַל יִשְׂרָאֵל עַמְּךָ תָּשִׂים
עָלֵינוּ וְעַל כָּל יִשְׂרָאֵל עַמֶּךָ.	לְעוֹלָם
בָּרְכֵנוּ אָבִינוּ כֻּלָּנוּ כְּאֶחָד בְּאוֹר פָּנֶיךָ	כִּי אַתָּה הוּא מֶלֶךְ אָדוֹן
כִּי בְאוֹר פָּנֶיךָ נָתַתָּ לָּנוּ יהוה אֱלֹהֵינוּ	לְכָל הַשָּׁלוֹם.
תּוֹרַת חַיִּים וְאַהֲבַת חֶסֶד	וְטוֹב בְּעֵינֶיךָ
וּצְדָקָה וּבְרָכָה וְרַחֲמִים וְחַיִּים וְשָׁלוֹם.	לְבָרֵךְ אֶת עַמְּךָ יִשְׂרָאֵל
וְטוֹב בְּעֵינֶיךָ לְבָרֵךְ אֶת עַמְּךָ יִשְׂרָאֵל	בְּכָל עֵת וּבְכָל שָׁעָה
בְּכָל עֵת וּבְכָל שָׁעָה בִּשְׁלוֹמֶךָ.	בִּשְׁלוֹמֶךָ.

בעשרת ימי תשובה: בְּסֵפֶר חַיִּים, בְּרָכָה וְשָׁלוֹם, וּפַרְנָסָה טוֹבָה
נִזָּכֵר וְנִכָּתֵב לְפָנֶיךָ, אֲנַחְנוּ וְכָל עַמְּךָ בֵּית יִשְׂרָאֵל
לְחַיִּים טוֹבִים וּלְשָׁלוֹם.*

בָּרוּךְ אַתָּה יהוה, הַמְבָרֵךְ אֶת עַמּוֹ יִשְׂרָאֵל בַּשָּׁלוֹם.

During the עשרת ימי תשובה *in* חוץ לארץ, *many end the blessing:*
בָּרוּךְ אַתָּה יהוה, עוֹשֵׂה הַשָּׁלוֹם.

BIUR TEFILLA · ביאור תפילה

שָׁלוֹם רָב — *Grant great peace.* The most common Ashkenazi practice is, except on a fast
day, to change the text of this blessing from
Sim Shalom said in the morning to *Shalom
Rav.* The wording of the morning's *Sim Shalom* is an extension of the themes recited
in the preceding *Birkat Kohanim.* But the

kohanim never give their blessing when
there is a possibility that they might have
been drinking alcohol, hence it is not said in
the afternoon (except on a fast day), which
in turn precludes repeating its themes in
Sim Shalom. Hence a different text, namely
Shalom Rav, is substituted.

The following verse concludes the Leader's Repetition of the Amida.
Some also say it here as part of the silent Amida.

May the words of my mouth and the meditation of my heart   *Ps. 19*
find favor before You, Lord, my Rock and Redeemer.

אֱלֹהַי **My God,**   *Berakhot*
17a
guard my tongue from evil and my lips from deceitful speech.
To those who curse me, let my soul be silent;
may my soul be to all like the dust.
Open my heart to Your Torah and let my soul
pursue Your commandments.
As for all who plan evil against me,
swiftly thwart their counsel and frustrate their plans.
    Act for the sake of Your name; act for the sake of Your right hand;
      act for the sake of Your holiness; act for the sake of Your Torah.
That Your beloved ones may be delivered,   *Ps. 60*
save with Your right hand and answer me.
May the words of my mouth and the meditation of my heart   *Ps. 19*
find favor before You, Lord, my Rock and Redeemer.

Bow, take three steps back, then bow, first left, then right, then center, while saying:
May He who makes peace in His high places,
make peace for us and all Israel – and say: Amen.

יְהִי רָצוֹן **May it be Your will,** Lord our God and God of our ancestors,
that the Temple be rebuilt speedily in our days,
and grant us a share in Your Torah.
And there we will serve You with reverence,
as in the days of old and as in former years.
Then the offering of Judah and Jerusalem will be pleasing to the Lord   *Mal. 3*
as in the days of old and as in former years.

    On days when Taḥanun is not said, the Leader says Full Kaddish on page 335.

The following verse concludes the חזרת הש"ץ.
Some also say it here as part of the silent עמידה.

תהלים יט

יִהְיוּ לְרָצוֹן אִמְרֵי־פִי וְהֶגְיוֹן לִבִּי לְפָנֶיךָ, יהוה צוּרִי וְגֹאֲלִי:

ברכות יז

אֱלֹהַי

נְצֹר לְשׁוֹנִי מֵרָע וּשְׂפָתַי מִדַּבֵּר מִרְמָה

וְלִמְקַלְלַי נַפְשִׁי תִדֹּם, וְנַפְשִׁי כֶּעָפָר לַכֹּל תִּהְיֶה.

פְּתַח לִבִּי בְּתוֹרָתֶךָ, וּבְמִצְוֹתֶיךָ תִּרְדֹּף נַפְשִׁי.

וְכָל הַחוֹשְׁבִים עָלַי רָעָה

מְהֵרָה הָפֵר עֲצָתָם וְקַלְקֵל מַחֲשַׁבְתָּם.

עֲשֵׂה לְמַעַן שְׁמֶךָ, עֲשֵׂה לְמַעַן יְמִינֶךָ

עֲשֵׂה לְמַעַן קְדֻשָּׁתֶךָ, עֲשֵׂה לְמַעַן תּוֹרָתֶךָ.

תהלים ס

לְמַעַן יֵחָלְצוּן יְדִידֶיךָ, הוֹשִׁיעָה יְמִינְךָ וַעֲנֵנִי:

תהלים יט

יִהְיוּ לְרָצוֹן אִמְרֵי־פִי וְהֶגְיוֹן לִבִּי לְפָנֶיךָ, יהוה צוּרִי וְגֹאֲלִי:

Bow, take three steps back, then bow, first left, then right, then center, while saying:

עֹשֶׂה שָׁלוֹם/ בעשרת ימי תשובה: הַשָּׁלוֹם/ בִּמְרוֹמָיו

הוּא יַעֲשֶׂה שָׁלוֹם עָלֵינוּ וְעַל כָּל יִשְׂרָאֵל, וְאִמְרוּ אָמֵן.

יְהִי רָצוֹן מִלְּפָנֶיךָ יהוה אֱלֹהֵינוּ וֵאלֹהֵי אֲבוֹתֵינוּ

שֶׁיִּבָּנֶה בֵּית הַמִּקְדָּשׁ בִּמְהֵרָה בְיָמֵינוּ

וְתֵן חֶלְקֵנוּ בְּתוֹרָתֶךָ

וְשָׁם נַעֲבָדְךָ בְּיִרְאָה כִּימֵי עוֹלָם וּכְשָׁנִים קַדְמֹנִיּוֹת.

מלאכי ג

וְעָרְבָה לַיהוה מִנְחַת יְהוּדָה וִירוּשָׁלָיִם כִּימֵי עוֹלָם וּכְשָׁנִים קַדְמֹנִיּוֹת:

On days when תחנון *is not said, the* שליח ציבור *says* קדיש שלם on page 335.

AVINU MALKENU

Between Rosh HaShana and Yom Kippur and on fast days, except days when
Taḥanun is not said (see list below), Avinu Malkenu (on page 332) is said here.

The Ark is opened.

אָבִינוּ מַלְכֵּנוּ Our Father, our King, we have sinned before You.

Our Father, our King, we have no king but You.

Our Father, our King, deal kindly with us for the sake of Your name.

Our Father our King, /*bless us with / a good year.

/*Between Rosh HaShana & Yom Kippur: renew for us/

Our Father, our King, nullify all harsh decrees against us.

Our Father, our King, nullify the plans of those who hate us.

Our Father, our King, thwart the counsel of our enemies.

Our Father, our King, rid us of every oppressor and adversary.

Our Father, our King, close the mouths of our adversaries and accusers.

Our Father, our King, eradicate pestilence, sword, famine,
captivity and destruction, iniquity and eradication
from the people of Your covenant.

Our Father, our King, withhold the plague from Your heritage.

Our Father, our King, forgive and pardon all our iniquities.

Our Father, our King, wipe away and remove our transgressions and sins
from Your sight.

Our Father, our King, erase in Your abundant mercy all records of our sins.

The following nine sentences are said responsively, first by the Leader, then by the congregation:

Our Father, our King, bring us back to You in perfect repentance.

Our Father, our King, send a complete healing to the sick of Your people.

Our Father, our King, tear up the evil decree against us.

Our Father, our King, remember us with a memory of favorable deeds
before You.

Between Rosh HaShana and Yom Kippur:

Our Father, our King, write us in the book of good life.

Our Father, our King, write us in the book of redemption and
salvation.

Our Father, our King, write us in the book of livelihood and
sustenance.

Our Father, our King, write us in the book of merit.

Our Father, our King, write us in the book of pardon and
forgiveness.

אבינו מלכנו

During the עשרת ימי תשובה *and on fast days, except days when*
תחנון *is not said (see list on page 333),* אבינו מלכנו *is said.*

The ארון קודש *is opened.*

אָבִינוּ מַלְכֵּנוּ, חָטָאנוּ לְפָנֶיךָ.

אָבִינוּ מַלְכֵּנוּ, אֵין לָנוּ מֶלֶךְ אֶלָּא אָתָּה.

אָבִינוּ מַלְכֵּנוּ, עֲשֵׂה עִמָּנוּ לְמַעַן שְׁמֶךָ.

אָבִינוּ מַלְכֵּנוּ, בָּרֵךְ /בעשרת ימי תשובה: חַדֵּשׁ/ עָלֵינוּ שָׁנָה טוֹבָה.

אָבִינוּ מַלְכֵּנוּ, בַּטֵּל מֵעָלֵינוּ כָּל גְּזֵרוֹת קָשׁוֹת.

אָבִינוּ מַלְכֵּנוּ, בַּטֵּל מַחְשְׁבוֹת שׂוֹנְאֵינוּ.

אָבִינוּ מַלְכֵּנוּ, הָפֵר עֲצַת אוֹיְבֵינוּ.

אָבִינוּ מַלְכֵּנוּ, כַּלֵּה כָּל צַר וּמַשְׂטִין מֵעָלֵינוּ.

אָבִינוּ מַלְכֵּנוּ, סְתֹם פִּיּוֹת מַשְׂטִינֵינוּ וּמְקַטְרְגֵינוּ.

אָבִינוּ מַלְכֵּנוּ, כַּלֵּה דֶּבֶר וְחֶרֶב וְרָעָב וּשְׁבִי וּמַשְׁחִית וְעָוֹן וּשְׁמַד מִבְּנֵי בְרִיתֶךָ.

אָבִינוּ מַלְכֵּנוּ, מְנַע מַגֵּפָה מִנַּחֲלָתֶךָ.

אָבִינוּ מַלְכֵּנוּ, סְלַח וּמְחַל לְכָל עֲוֹנוֹתֵינוּ.

אָבִינוּ מַלְכֵּנוּ, מְחֵה וְהַעֲבֵר פְּשָׁעֵינוּ וְחַטֹּאתֵינוּ מִנֶּגֶד עֵינֶיךָ.

אָבִינוּ מַלְכֵּנוּ, מְחֹק בְּרַחֲמֶיךָ הָרַבִּים כָּל שִׁטְרֵי חוֹבוֹתֵינוּ.

The following nine sentences are said responsively, first by the שליח ציבור, *then by the* קהל:

אָבִינוּ מַלְכֵּנוּ, הַחֲזִירֵנוּ בִּתְשׁוּבָה שְׁלֵמָה לְפָנֶיךָ.

אָבִינוּ מַלְכֵּנוּ, שְׁלַח רְפוּאָה שְׁלֵמָה לְחוֹלֵי עַמֶּךָ.

אָבִינוּ מַלְכֵּנוּ, קְרַע רֹעַ גְּזַר דִּינֵנוּ.

אָבִינוּ מַלְכֵּנוּ, זָכְרֵנוּ בְּזִכָּרוֹן טוֹב לְפָנֶיךָ.

During the עשרת ימי תשובה:

אָבִינוּ מַלְכֵּנוּ, כָּתְבֵנוּ בְּסֵפֶר חַיִּים טוֹבִים.

אָבִינוּ מַלְכֵּנוּ, כָּתְבֵנוּ בְּסֵפֶר גְּאֻלָּה וִישׁוּעָה.

אָבִינוּ מַלְכֵּנוּ, כָּתְבֵנוּ בְּסֵפֶר פַּרְנָסָה וְכַלְכָּלָה.

אָבִינוּ מַלְכֵּנוּ, כָּתְבֵנוּ בְּסֵפֶר זְכֻיּוֹת.

אָבִינוּ מַלְכֵּנוּ, כָּתְבֵנוּ בְּסֵפֶר סְלִיחָה וּמְחִילָה.

On Fast Days:

Our Father, our King, remember us for a good life.

Our Father, our King, remember us for redemption and
salvation.

Our Father, our King, remember us for livelihood and
sustenance.

Our Father, our King, remember us for merit.

Our Father, our King, remember us for pardon and forgiveness.

End of responsive reading.

Our Father, our King, let salvation soon flourish for us.

Our Father, our King, raise the honor of Your people Israel.

Our Father, our King, raise the honor of Your anointed.

Our Father, our King, fill our hands with Your blessings.

Our Father, our King, fill our storehouses with abundance.

Our Father, our King, hear our voice, pity and be compassionate to us.

Our Father, our King, accept, with compassion and favor, our prayer.

Our Father, our King, open the gates of heaven to our prayer.

Our Father, our King, remember that we are dust.

Our Father, our King, please do not turn us away from You empty-handed.

Our Father, our King, may this moment be a moment of compassion
and a time of favor before You.

Our Father, our King, have pity on us, our children and our infants.

Our Father, our King, act for the sake of those who were killed
for Your holy name.

Our Father, our King, act for the sake of those who were slaughtered
for proclaiming Your Unity.

Our Father, our King, act for the sake of those
who went through fire and water
to sanctify Your name.

Our Father, our King, avenge before our eyes the spilt blood of Your servants.

Our Father, our King, act for Your sake, if not for ours.

Our Father, our King, act for Your sake, and save us.

Our Father, our King, act for the sake of Your abundant compassion.

Our Father, our King, act for the sake of Your great, mighty and awesome
name by which we are called.

▸ Our Father, our King, be gracious to us and answer us, though we have
no worthy deeds; act with us in charity and
loving-kindness and save us.

The Ark is closed.

On Fast Days:

אָבִינוּ מַלְכֵּנוּ, זָכְרֵנוּ לְחַיִּים טוֹבִים.

אָבִינוּ מַלְכֵּנוּ, זָכְרֵנוּ לִגְאֻלָּה וִישׁוּעָה.

אָבִינוּ מַלְכֵּנוּ, זָכְרֵנוּ לְפַרְנָסָה וְכַלְכָּלָה.

אָבִינוּ מַלְכֵּנוּ, זָכְרֵנוּ לִזְכֻיּוֹת.

אָבִינוּ מַלְכֵּנוּ, זָכְרֵנוּ לִסְלִיחָה וּמְחִילָה.

End of responsive reading.

אָבִינוּ מַלְכֵּנוּ, הַצְמַח לָנוּ יְשׁוּעָה בְּקָרוֹב.

אָבִינוּ מַלְכֵּנוּ, הָרֵם קֶרֶן יִשְׂרָאֵל עַמֶּךָ.

אָבִינוּ מַלְכֵּנוּ, הָרֵם קֶרֶן מְשִׁיחֶךָ.

אָבִינוּ מַלְכֵּנוּ, מַלֵּא יָדֵינוּ מִבִּרְכוֹתֶיךָ.

אָבִינוּ מַלְכֵּנוּ, מַלֵּא אֲסָמֵינוּ שָׂבָע.

אָבִינוּ מַלְכֵּנוּ, שְׁמַע קוֹלֵנוּ, חוּס וְרַחֵם עָלֵינוּ.

אָבִינוּ מַלְכֵּנוּ, קַבֵּל בְּרַחֲמִים וּבְרָצוֹן אֶת תְּפִלָּתֵנוּ.

אָבִינוּ מַלְכֵּנוּ, פְּתַח שַׁעֲרֵי שָׁמַיִם לִתְפִלָּתֵנוּ.

אָבִינוּ מַלְכֵּנוּ, זְכֹר כִּי עָפָר אֲנָחְנוּ.

אָבִינוּ מַלְכֵּנוּ, נָא אַל תְּשִׁיבֵנוּ רֵיקָם מִלְּפָנֶיךָ.

אָבִינוּ מַלְכֵּנוּ, תְּהֵא הַשָּׁעָה הַזֹּאת שְׁעַת רַחֲמִים וְעֵת רָצוֹן מִלְּפָנֶיךָ.

אָבִינוּ מַלְכֵּנוּ, חֲמֹל עָלֵינוּ וְעַל עוֹלָלֵינוּ וְטַפֵּנוּ.

אָבִינוּ מַלְכֵּנוּ, עֲשֵׂה לְמַעַן הֲרוּגִים עַל שֵׁם קָדְשֶׁךָ.

אָבִינוּ מַלְכֵּנוּ, עֲשֵׂה לְמַעַן טְבוּחִים עַל יִחוּדֶךָ.

אָבִינוּ מַלְכֵּנוּ, עֲשֵׂה לְמַעַן בָּאֵי בָאֵשׁ וּבַמַּיִם עַל קִדּוּשׁ שְׁמֶךָ.

אָבִינוּ מַלְכֵּנוּ, נְקֹם לְעֵינֵינוּ נִקְמַת דַּם עֲבָדֶיךָ הַשָּׁפוּךְ.

אָבִינוּ מַלְכֵּנוּ, עֲשֵׂה לְמַעַנְךָ אִם לֹא לְמַעֲנֵנוּ.

אָבִינוּ מַלְכֵּנוּ, עֲשֵׂה לְמַעַנְךָ וְהוֹשִׁיעֵנוּ.

אָבִינוּ מַלְכֵּנוּ, עֲשֵׂה לְמַעַן רַחֲמֶיךָ הָרַבִּים.

אָבִינוּ מַלְכֵּנוּ, עֲשֵׂה לְמַעַן שִׁמְךָ הַגָּדוֹל הַגִּבּוֹר וְהַנּוֹרָא שֶׁנִּקְרָא עָלֵינוּ.

◄ אָבִינוּ מַלְכֵּנוּ, חָנֵּנוּ וַעֲנֵנוּ, כִּי אֵין בָּנוּ מַעֲשִׂים עֲשֵׂה עִמָּנוּ צְדָקָה וָחֶסֶד וְהוֹשִׁיעֵנוּ.

The ‏ארון קודש *is closed.*

TAḤANUN

Taḥanun is not said on Erev Shabbat and Erev Yom Tov. It is also not said on the following days: Rosh Ḥodesh, Ḥanukka, Tu BiShvat, the 14th and 15th of Adar I, Purim and Shushan Purim, Yom HaAtzma'ut, Lag BaOmer, Yom Yerushalayim, Tisha B'Av, Tu B'Av, and the preceding afternoons, the month of Nisan, the 14th of Iyar (Pesaḥ Sheni), from Rosh Ḥodesh Sivan through the day after Shavuot (in Israel through 12th of Sivan), and from Erev Yom Kippur through the day after Simḥat Torah (in Israel through Rosh Ḥodesh Marḥeshvan). Taḥanun is also not said: on the occasion of a Brit Mila, either where the brit will take place or where the father, Sandek or Mohel are present; if a groom is present (and some say, a bride) on the day of his wedding or during the week of Sheva Berakhot; in a house of mourning.

LOWERING THE HEAD

Say while sitting; in the presence of a Torah scroll say until "in sudden shame," leaning forward and resting one's head on the left arm (unless you are wearing tefillin on the left arm, in which case rest on the right arm out of respect for the tefillin).

וַיֹּאמֶר דָּוִד David said to Gad, "I am in great distress.   *II Sam. 24*
Let us fall into God's hand, for His mercy is great;
but do not let me fall into the hand of man."

Compassionate and gracious One, I have sinned before You.
Lᴏʀᴅ, full of compassion, have compassion on me
and accept my pleas.

Lᴏʀᴅ, do not rebuke me in Your anger or chastise me in Your wrath.   *Ps. 6*
Be gracious to me, Lᴏʀᴅ, for I am weak.
Heal me, Lᴏʀᴅ, for my bones are in agony.
My soul is in anguish, and You, O Lᴏʀᴅ – how long?
Turn, Lᴏʀᴅ, set my soul free; save me for the sake of Your love.
For no one remembers You when he is dead.
Who can praise You from the grave? I am weary with my sighing.
Every night I drench my bed, I soak my couch with my tears.
My eye grows dim from grief, worn out because of all my foes.
Leave me, all you evildoers,
for the Lᴏʀᴅ has heard the sound of my weeping.
The Lᴏʀᴅ has heard my pleas. The Lᴏʀᴅ will accept my prayer.
All my enemies will be shamed and utterly dismayed.
They will turn back in sudden shame.

Sit upright.

סדר תחנון

תחנון is not said on ערב שבת *and* ערב יום טוב. *It is also not said on the following days:* שושן פורים *and* פורים, the 14th and 15th of *א' אדר*, ראש חודש, חנוכה, ט"ו בשבט, *and the preceding afternoons, the month of* ניסן, the 14th of *אייר (פסח שני)*, *from* ראש חודש סיון *through the day after* שבועות (in *ארץ ישראל* through *סיון י"ב*), *and from* ערב יום כיפור *through the day after* שמחת תורה (in *ארץ ישראל* through *ראש חודש מרחשון*). תחנון *is also not said: on the occasion of a* ברית מילה, *either where the* ברית *will take place or where the father,* מוהל *or* סנדק *are present; if a* חתן *is present (and some say, a* כלה) *on the day of his wedding or during the week of* שבע ברכות; *in a house of mourning.*

נפילת אפיים

Say while sitting; in the presence of a ספר תורה *say until* יבשו רגע, *leaning forward and resting one's head on the left arm (unless you are wearing tefillin on the left arm, in which case rest on the right arm out of respect for the tefillin).*

שמואל ב' כד

וַיֹּאמֶר דָּוִד אֶל־גָּד, צַר־לִי מְאֹד
נִפְּלָה־נָּא בְיַד־יְהוָה, כִּי־רַבִּים רַחֲמָו, וּבְיַד־אָדָם אַל־אֶפְּלָה:

רַחוּם וְחַנּוּן, חָטָאתִי לְפָנֶיךָ.
יְהוָה מָלֵא רַחֲמִים, רַחֵם עָלַי וְקַבֵּל תַּחֲנוּנָי.

תהלים ו

יְהוָה, אַל־בְּאַפְּךָ תוֹכִיחֵנִי, וְאַל־בַּחֲמָתְךָ תְיַסְּרֵנִי:
חָנֵּנִי יְהוָה, כִּי אֻמְלַל אָנִי, רְפָאֵנִי יְהוָה, כִּי נִבְהֲלוּ עֲצָמָי:
וְנַפְשִׁי נִבְהֲלָה מְאֹד, וְאַתְּ יְהוָה, עַד־מָתָי:
שׁוּבָה יְהוָה, חַלְּצָה נַפְשִׁי, הוֹשִׁיעֵנִי לְמַעַן חַסְדֶּךָ:
כִּי אֵין בַּמָּוֶת זִכְרֶךָ, בִּשְׁאוֹל מִי יוֹדֶה־לָּךְ:
יָגַעְתִּי בְּאַנְחָתִי, אַשְׂחֶה בְכָל־לַיְלָה מִטָּתִי, בְּדִמְעָתִי עַרְשִׂי אַמְסֶה:
עָשְׁשָׁה מִכַּעַס עֵינִי, עָתְקָה בְּכָל־צוֹרְרָי:
סוּרוּ מִמֶּנִּי כָּל־פֹּעֲלֵי אָוֶן, כִּי־שָׁמַע יְהוָה קוֹל בִּכְיִי:
שָׁמַע יְהוָה תְּחִנָּתִי, יְהוָה תְּפִלָּתִי יִקָּח:
יֵבֹשׁוּ וְיִבָּהֲלוּ מְאֹד כָּל־אֹיְבָי, יָשֻׁבוּ יֵבֹשׁוּ רָגַע:

Sit upright.

שׁוֹמֵר יִשְׂרָאֵל Guardian of Israel,
    guard the remnant of Israel,
        and let not Israel perish, who declare, "Listen, Israel."
Guardian of a unique nation, guard the remnant of a unique people,
    and let not that unique nation perish, who proclaim the unity of
        Your name [saying], "The LORD is our God, the LORD is One."
Guardian of a holy nation, guard the remnant of that holy people,
    and let not the holy nation perish, who three times repeat
        the threefold declaration of holiness to the Holy One.
You who are conciliated by calls for compassion and placated by pleas,
    be conciliated and placated toward an afflicted generation,
        for there is no other help.
Our Father, our King, be gracious to us and answer us,
    though we have no worthy deeds;
        act with us in charity and loving-kindness and save us.

Stand at ˄.

וַאֲנַחְנוּ We do not know ˄what to do, but our eyes are turned to You. *11 Chr. 12*
Remember, LORD, Your compassion and loving-kindness, for they are *Ps. 25*
everlasting. May Your loving-kindness, LORD, be with us, for we have put *Ps. 33*
our hope in You. Do not hold against us the sins of those who came before *Ps. 79*
us. May Your mercies meet us swiftly, for we have been brought very low.
Be gracious to us, LORD, be gracious to us, for we are sated with contempt. *Ps. 123*
In wrath, remember mercy. He knows our nature; He remembers that *Hab. 3 / Ps. 103*
we are dust. ‣ Help us, God of our salvation, for the sake of the glory of *Ps. 79*
Your name. Save us and grant atonement for our sins for Your name's sake.

FULL KADDISH

Leader: יִתְגַּדַּל Magnified and sanctified may His great name be,
    in the world He created by His will.
    May He establish His kingdom
    in your lifetime and in your days,
    and in the lifetime of all the house of Israel,
    swiftly and soon – and say: Amen.

All: May His great name be blessed for ever and all time.

שׁוֹמֵר יִשְׂרָאֵל, שְׁמֹר שְׁאֵרִית יִשְׂרָאֵל, וְאַל יֹאבַד יִשְׂרָאֵל
הָאוֹמְרִים שְׁמַע יִשְׂרָאֵל.

שׁוֹמֵר גּוֹי אֶחָד, שְׁמֹר שְׁאֵרִית עַם אֶחָד, וְאַל יֹאבַד גּוֹי אֶחָד
הַמְיַחֲדִים שִׁמְךָ, יהוה אֱלֹהֵינוּ יהוה אֶחָד.

שׁוֹמֵר גּוֹי קָדוֹשׁ, שְׁמֹר שְׁאֵרִית עַם קָדוֹשׁ, וְאַל יֹאבַד גּוֹי קָדוֹשׁ
הַמְשַׁלְּשִׁים בְּשָׁלֹשׁ קְדֻשּׁוֹת לְקָדוֹשׁ.

מִתְרַצֶּה בְּרַחֲמִים וּמִתְפַּיֵּס בְּתַחֲנוּנִים, הִתְרַצֵּה וְהִתְפַּיֵּס לְדוֹר עָנִי
כִּי אֵין עוֹזֵר.

אָבִינוּ מַלְכֵּנוּ, חָנֵּנוּ וַעֲנֵנוּ, כִּי אֵין בָּנוּ מַעֲשִׂים
עֲשֵׂה עִמָּנוּ צְדָקָה וָחֶסֶד וְהוֹשִׁיעֵנוּ.

Stand at ^.

דברי
הימים ב ב
תהלים כה

תהלים לג

תהלים עט

תהלים קכב
חבקוק ג
תהלים ק
תהלים עט

וַאֲנַחְנוּ לֹא נֵדַע יְּמַה־נַּעֲשֶׂה, כִּי עָלֶיךָ עֵינֵינוּ: זְכֹר־רַחֲמֶיךָ יהוה
וַחֲסָדֶיךָ, כִּי מֵעוֹלָם הֵמָּה: יְהִי־חַסְדְּךָ יהוה עָלֵינוּ, כַּאֲשֶׁר יִחַלְנוּ לָךְ:
אַל־תִּזְכָּר־לָנוּ עֲוֹנֹת רִאשֹׁנִים, מַהֵר יְקַדְּמוּנוּ רַחֲמֶיךָ, כִּי דַלּוֹנוּ מְאֹד:
חָנֵּנוּ יהוה חָנֵּנוּ, כִּי־רַב שָׂבַעְנוּ בוּז: בְּרֹגֶז רַחֵם תִּזְכּוֹר: כִּי־הוּא יָדַע
יִצְרֵנוּ, זָכוּר כִּי־עָפָר אֲנָחְנוּ: ‹ עָזְרֵנוּ אֱלֹהֵי יִשְׁעֵנוּ עַל־דְּבַר כְּבוֹד
שְׁמֶךָ, וְהַצִּילֵנוּ וְכַפֵּר עַל־חַטֹּאתֵינוּ לְמַעַן שְׁמֶךָ:

קַדִּישׁ שָׁלֵם

ש״ץ יִתְגַּדַּל וְיִתְקַדַּשׁ שְׁמֵהּ רַבָּא (קהל אָמֵן)

בְּעָלְמָא דִּי בְרָא כִרְעוּתֵהּ

וְיַמְלִיךְ מַלְכוּתֵהּ

בְּחַיֵּיכוֹן וּבְיוֹמֵיכוֹן וּבְחַיֵּי דְּכָל בֵּית יִשְׂרָאֵל

בַּעֲגָלָא וּבִזְמַן קָרִיב, וְאִמְרוּ אָמֵן. (קהל אָמֵן)

קהל
 וש״ץ יְהֵא שְׁמֵהּ רַבָּא מְבָרַךְ לְעָלַם וּלְעָלְמֵי עָלְמַיָּא.

Leader: Blessed and praised,
glorified and exalted, raised and honored,
uplifted and lauded be
the name of the Holy One, blessed be He,
beyond any blessing,
song, praise and consolation
uttered in the world –
and say: Amen.

May the prayers and pleas of all Israel
be accepted by their Father in heaven –
and say: Amen.

May there be great peace from heaven,
and life for us and all Israel –
and say: Amen.

*Bow, take three steps back, as if taking leave of the Divine Presence,
then bow, first left, then right, then center, while saying:*
May He who makes peace in His high places,
make peace for us and all Israel –
and say: Amen.

Stand while saying Aleinu. Bow at ˙.
עָלֵינוּ It is our duty to praise the Master of all,
and ascribe greatness to the Author of creation,
who has not made us like the nations of the lands
nor placed us like the families of the earth;
who has not made our portion like theirs,
nor our destiny like all their multitudes.
(For they worship vanity and emptiness,
and pray to a god who cannot save.)
˙But we bow in worship
and thank the Supreme King of kings,
the Holy One, blessed be He,
who extends the heavens and establishes the earth,

שַ״ץ יִתְבָּרַךְ וְיִשְׁתַּבַּח וְיִתְפָּאַר
וְיִתְרוֹמַם וְיִתְנַשֵּׂא וְיִתְהַדָּר וְיִתְעַלֶּה וְיִתְהַלָּל
שְׁמֵהּ דְּקֻדְשָׁא בְּרִיךְ הוּא (קהל: בְּרִיךְ הוּא)
לְעֵלָּא מִן כָּל בִּרְכָתָא
/בעשרת ימי תשובה: לְעֵלָּא לְעֵלָּא מִכָּל בִּרְכָתָא/
וְשִׁירָתָא, תֻּשְׁבְּחָתָא וְנֶחֱמָתָא
דַּאֲמִירָן בְּעָלְמָא וְאִמְרוּ אָמֵן. (קהל: אָמֵן)

תִּתְקַבַּל צְלוֹתְהוֹן וּבָעוּתְהוֹן דְּכָל יִשְׂרָאֵל
קֳדָם אֲבוּהוֹן דִּי בִשְׁמַיָּא, וְאִמְרוּ אָמֵן. (קהל: אָמֵן)

יְהֵא שְׁלָמָא רַבָּא מִן שְׁמַיָּא
וְחַיִּים, עָלֵינוּ וְעַל כָּל יִשְׂרָאֵל
וְאִמְרוּ אָמֵן. (קהל: אָמֵן)

*Bow, take three steps back, as if taking leave of the Divine Presence,
then bow, first left, then right, then center, while saying:*

עֹשֶׂה שָׁלוֹם /בעשרת ימי תשובה: הַשָּׁלוֹם/ בִּמְרוֹמָיו
הוּא יַעֲשֶׂה שָׁלוֹם עָלֵינוּ
וְעַל כָּל יִשְׂרָאֵל, וְאִמְרוּ אָמֵן. (קהל: אָמֵן)

Stand while saying עָלֵינוּ. Bow at ‏.

עָלֵינוּ לְשַׁבֵּחַ לַאֲדוֹן הַכֹּל, לָתֵת גְּדֻלָּה לְיוֹצֵר בְּרֵאשִׁית
שֶׁלֹּא עָשָׂנוּ כְּגוֹיֵי הָאֲרָצוֹת, וְלֹא שָׂמָנוּ כְּמִשְׁפְּחוֹת הָאֲדָמָה
שֶׁלֹּא שָׂם חֶלְקֵנוּ כָּהֶם וְגוֹרָלֵנוּ כְּכָל הֲמוֹנָם.
(שֶׁהֵם מִשְׁתַּחֲוִים לְהֶבֶל וָרִיק וּמִתְפַּלְלִים אֶל אֵל לֹא יוֹשִׁיעַ.)
וַאֲנַחְנוּ כּוֹרְעִים וּמִשְׁתַּחֲוִים וּמוֹדִים
לִפְנֵי מֶלֶךְ מַלְכֵי הַמְּלָכִים, הַקָּדוֹשׁ בָּרוּךְ הוּא
שֶׁהוּא נוֹטֶה שָׁמַיִם וְיוֹסֵד אָרֶץ

whose throne of glory is in the heavens above,
and whose power's Presence is in the highest of heights.
He is our God; there is no other.
Truly He is our King, there is none else,
as it is written in His Torah:
"You shall know and take to heart this day that the Lord is God,   *Deut. 4*
in heaven above and on earth below. There is no other."

Therefore, we place our hope in You, Lord our God,
that we may soon see the glory of Your power,
when You will remove abominations from the earth,
and idols will be utterly destroyed,
when the world will be perfected
under the sovereignty of the Almighty,
when all humanity will call on Your name,
to turn all the earth's wicked toward You.
All the world's inhabitants will realize and know
that to You every knee must bow
and every tongue swear loyalty.
Before You, Lord our God, they will kneel and bow down
and give honor to Your glorious name.
They will all accept the yoke of Your kingdom,
and You will reign over them soon and for ever.
For the kingdom is Yours,
and to all eternity You will reign in glory,
as it is written in Your Torah:
"The Lord will reign for ever and ever."   *Ex. 15*
▸ And it is said: "Then the Lord shall be King over all the earth;   *Zech. 14*
on that day the Lord shall be One and His name One."

Some add:
Have no fear of sudden terror or of the ruin when it overtakes the wicked.   *Prov. 3*
Devise your strategy, but it will be thwarted; propose your plan,   *Is. 8*
but it will not stand, for God is with us.
When you grow old, I will still be the same.   *Is. 46*
When your hair turns gray, I will still carry you.
I made you, I will bear you, I will carry you, and I will rescue you.

וּמוֹשַׁב יְקָרוֹ בַּשָּׁמַיִם מִמַּעַל

וּשְׁכִינַת עֻזּוֹ בְּגָבְהֵי מְרוֹמִים.

הוּא אֱלֹהֵינוּ, אֵין עוֹד.

אֱמֶת מַלְכֵּנוּ, אֶפֶס זוּלָתוֹ

כַּכָּתוּב בְּתוֹרָתוֹ

וְיָדַעְתָּ הַיּוֹם וַהֲשֵׁבֹתָ אֶל־לְבָבֶךָ   דברים ד

כִּי יְהוָה הוּא הָאֱלֹהִים בַּשָּׁמַיִם מִמַּעַל וְעַל־הָאָרֶץ מִתָּחַת, אֵין עוֹד:

עַל כֵּן נְקַוֶּה לְּךָ יְהוָה אֱלֹהֵינוּ, לִרְאוֹת מְהֵרָה בְּתִפְאֶרֶת עֻזֶּךָ

לְהַעֲבִיר גִּלּוּלִים מִן הָאָרֶץ, וְהָאֱלִילִים כָּרוֹת יִכָּרֵתוּן

לְתַקֵּן עוֹלָם בְּמַלְכוּת שַׁדַּי.

וְכָל בְּנֵי בָשָׂר יִקְרְאוּ בִשְׁמֶךָ לְהַפְנוֹת אֵלֶיךָ כָּל רִשְׁעֵי אָרֶץ.

יַכִּירוּ וְיֵדְעוּ כָּל יוֹשְׁבֵי תֵבֵל

כִּי לְךָ תִּכְרַע כָּל בֶּרֶךְ, תִּשָּׁבַע כָּל לָשׁוֹן.

לְפָנֶיךָ יְהוָה אֱלֹהֵינוּ יִכְרְעוּ וְיִפֹּלוּ, וְלִכְבוֹד שִׁמְךָ יְקָר יִתֵּנוּ

וִיקַבְּלוּ כֻלָּם אֶת עֹל מַלְכוּתֶךָ

וְתִמְלֹךְ עֲלֵיהֶם מְהֵרָה לְעוֹלָם וָעֶד.

כִּי הַמַּלְכוּת שֶׁלְּךָ הִיא וּלְעוֹלְמֵי עַד תִּמְלֹךְ בְּכָבוֹד

כַּכָּתוּב בְּתוֹרָתֶךָ, יְהוָה יִמְלֹךְ לְעֹלָם וָעֶד: שמות טו

◄ וְנֶאֱמַר, וְהָיָה יְהוָה לְמֶלֶךְ עַל־כָּל־הָאָרֶץ   זכריה יד

בַּיּוֹם הַהוּא יִהְיֶה יְהוָה אֶחָד וּשְׁמוֹ אֶחָד:

Some add:

אַל־תִּירָא מִפַּחַד פִּתְאֹם וּמִשֹּׁאַת רְשָׁעִים כִּי תָבֹא: משלי ג

עֻצוּ עֵצָה וְתֻפָר, דַּבְּרוּ דָבָר וְלֹא יָקוּם, כִּי עִמָּנוּ אֵל: ישעיה ח

וְעַד־זִקְנָה אֲנִי הוּא, וְעַד־שֵׂיבָה אֲנִי אֶסְבֹּל   ישעיה מו

אֲנִי עָשִׂיתִי וַאֲנִי אֶשָּׂא וַאֲנִי אֶסְבֹּל וַאֲמַלֵּט:

MOURNER'S KADDISH

The following prayer, said by mourners, requires the presence of a minyan.
A transliteration can be found on page 921.

Mourner: יִתְגַּדַּל **Magnified and sanctified**
may His great name be,
in the world He created by His will.
May He establish His kingdom
in your lifetime
and in your days,
and in the lifetime
of all the house of Israel,
swiftly and soon –
and say: Amen.

All: May His great name be blessed for ever and all time.

Mourner: Blessed and praised,
glorified and exalted,
raised and honored,
uplifted and lauded
be the name of the Holy One,
blessed be He,
beyond any blessing,
song, praise and consolation
uttered in the world –
and say: Amen.

May there be great peace from heaven,
and life for us and all Israel –
and say: Amen.

Bow, take three steps back, as if taking leave of the Divine Presence,
then bow, first left, then right, then center, while saying:

May He who makes peace in His high places,
make peace for us and all Israel –
and say: Amen.

קדיש יתום

The following prayer, said by mourners, requires the presence of a מנין.
A transliteration can be found on page 921.

אבל: יִתְגַּדַּל וְיִתְקַדַּשׁ שְׁמֵהּ רַבָּא (קהל: אָמֵן)
בְּעָלְמָא דִּי בְרָא כִרְעוּתֵהּ
וְיַמְלִיךְ מַלְכוּתֵהּ
בְּחַיֵּיכוֹן וּבְיוֹמֵיכוֹן וּבְחַיֵּי דְּכָל בֵּית יִשְׂרָאֵל
בַּעֲגָלָא וּבִזְמַן קָרִיב
וְאִמְרוּ אָמֵן. (קהל: אָמֵן)

קהל
ואבל: יְהֵא שְׁמֵהּ רַבָּא מְבָרַךְ לְעָלַם וּלְעָלְמֵי עָלְמַיָּא.

אבל: יִתְבָּרַךְ וְיִשְׁתַּבַּח וְיִתְפָּאַר
וְיִתְרוֹמַם וְיִתְנַשֵּׂא וְיִתְהַדָּר וְיִתְעַלֶּה וְיִתְהַלָּל
שְׁמֵהּ דְּקֻדְשָׁא בְּרִיךְ הוּא (קהל: בְּרִיךְ הוּא)
לְעֵלָּא מִן כָּל בִּרְכָתָא
/בעשרת ימי תשובה: לְעֵלָּא לְעֵלָּא מִכָּל בִּרְכָתָא/
וְשִׁירָתָא, תֻּשְׁבְּחָתָא וְנֶחֱמָתָא
דַּאֲמִירָן בְּעָלְמָא
וְאִמְרוּ אָמֵן. (קהל: אָמֵן)

יְהֵא שְׁלָמָא רַבָּא מִן שְׁמַיָּא
וְחַיִּים, עָלֵינוּ וְעַל כָּל יִשְׂרָאֵל
וְאִמְרוּ אָמֵן. (קהל: אָמֵן)

*Bow, take three steps back, as if taking leave of the Divine Presence,
then bow, first left, then right, then center, while saying:*

עֹשֶׂה שָׁלוֹם/בעשרת ימי תשובה: הַשָּׁלוֹם/ בִּמְרוֹמָיו
הוּא יַעֲשֶׂה שָׁלוֹם עָלֵינוּ וְעַל כָּל יִשְׂרָאֵל
וְאִמְרוּ אָמֵן. (קהל: אָמֵן)

Ma'ariv for Weekdays

On Motza'ei Shabbat, many congregations recite Psalms 144 and 67 before Ma'ariv (page 398).

וְהוּא רַחוּם **He is compassionate.**[B]   *Ps. 78*
He forgives iniquity and does not destroy.
Repeatedly He suppresses His anger, not rousing His full wrath.
Lord, save! May the King, answer us on the day we call.   *Ps. 20*

BLESSINGS OF THE SHEMA

*The Leader says the following, bowing at "Bless," standing straight
at "the Lord"; the congregation, followed by the Leader, responds,
bowing at "Bless," standing straight at "the Lord":*

Leader: # BLESS[B]

the Lord, the blessed One.

Congregation: Bless the Lord, the blessed One,
for ever and all time.

Leader: Bless the Lord, the blessed One,
for ever and all time.

---

by joy. "The glory of Yaakov's epiphany is that it happened at night, in the midst of fear and flight (Rabbi J. Sacks).

The nighttime hours are often a time of uncertainty, when the insecurities of our lives rear their heads the most. What better time to search out an encounter with the One who knows us best? Preoccupied with the successes or disappointments of our day, we enter into an intimate conversation with Hashem, finding friendship and support, and, perhaps, a transformative experience.

BIUR TEFILLA · ביאור תפילה

וְהוּא רַחוּם – *He is compassionate.* A number of reasons are offered for this introduction. One of them simply suggests the possibility that we committed some wrong during the course of the day. This introductory statement declares, before we pray, our belief that Hashem will forgive us. This verse was

chosen, it was suggested, because it has 13 words in it, reminiscent of the 13 *Middot* (attributes of forgiveness) of Hashem. In any event, consider it a way to get into the right frame of mind before the *Hazan* calls us together; a way of gathering our thoughts and being mindful. Pause a moment, to focus.

The BIUR TEFILLA *on* בָּרְכוּ *is on page 345.*

מעריב לחול

On מוצאי שבת, many congregations recite Psalms 144 and 67 before מעריב (page 399).

תהלים עח

וְהוּא רַחוּם, יְכַפֵּר עָוֹן וְלֹא־יַשְׁחִית
וְהִרְבָּה לְהָשִׁיב אַפּוֹ, וְלֹא־יָעִיר כָּל־חֲמָתוֹ:

תהלים כ

יהוה הוֹשִׁיעָה, הַמֶּלֶךְ יַעֲנֵנוּ בְיוֹם־קָרְאֵנוּ:

קריאת שמע וברכותיה

The שליח ציבור says the following, bowing at בָּרְכוּ, standing straight at ה'; the קהל,
followed by the שליח ציבור, responds, bowing at בָּרוּךְ, standing straight at ה':

ש״ץ ‏ בָּרְכוּ

אֶת יהוה הַמְבֹרָךְ.

קהל ‏ בָּרוּךְ יהוה הַמְבֹרָךְ לְעוֹלָם וָעֶד.

ש״ץ ‏ בָּרוּךְ יהוה הַמְבֹרָךְ לְעוֹלָם וָעֶד.

INTRODUCTION TO MA'ARIV

The Gemara (*Berakhot* 26b) explains that each one of the three daily services was established by one of the *Avot*. It has often been suggested that the timing also relates to the character of each of the *Avot*. Avraham, the bold and assertive pioneer, is associated with the morning, and thus *Shaḥarit*. Yitzhak, the one who never left Israel, but stayed and worked the Land, is associated with the afternoon and *Minḥa*. Yaakov's life, on the other hand, was filled with trials and tribulations, with uncertainty and clouds of darkness. Yaakov is the one who established *Ma'ariv*.

The phrase the Torah uses is "*vayifga baMakom*," (*Bereshit* 28:11) which in Rabbinic Hebrew could be read to mean, "He bumped into God." There are spiritual experiences we have when we are least expecting them – when we are alone, afraid, thinking of something else altogether. This was Yaakov's vision of prayer. Not everything in the life of the spirit is under our control. The great transformative experiences – love, a sudden sense of beauty, an upsurge of happiness – happen unpredictably and leave us, in Wordsworth's famous words, "surprised

בָּרוּךְ Blessed are You, LORD our God, King of the Universe,
who by His word brings on evenings,
by His wisdom opens the gates of heaven,
with understanding makes time change
and the seasons rotate,
and by His will orders the stars
in their constellations in the sky.
He creates day and night,
rolling away the light before the darkness,
and darkness before the light.
▸ He makes the day pass and brings on night,
distinguishing day from night:
the LORD of hosts is His name.
May the living
and forever enduring God rule over us
for all time.
Blessed are You, LORD,
who brings on evenings.¹

אַהֲבַת עוֹלָם With everlasting love
have You loved Your people, the house of Israel.
You have taught us Torah and commandments,
decrees and laws of justice.

---

descent of darkness which envelops us. The Gemara (*Berakhot* 11b) says that we must recall the attributes of day and night together, for both reflect the miracle of creation and its single source, Hashem, whose unity we will declare momentarily. Night and day; sun and stars; past, present, and future are all part of one continuum. The world is whole and there is a pattern and there is a plan. We need only find our place in it.

ANI TEFILLA · אני תפילה

"The sun descending in the west, / The evening star does shine; / The birds are silent in their nest, / And I must seek for mine." (William Blake)

בָּרוּךְ אַתָּה יהוה אֱלֹהֵינוּ מֶלֶךְ הָעוֹלָם

אֲשֶׁר בִּדְבָרוֹ מַעֲרִיב עֲרָבִים

בְּחָכְמָה פּוֹתֵחַ שְׁעָרִים

וּבִתְבוּנָה מְשַׁנֶּה עִתִּים וּמַחֲלִיף אֶת הַזְּמַנִּים

וּמְסַדֵּר אֶת הַכּוֹכָבִים בְּמִשְׁמְרוֹתֵיהֶם בָּרָקִיעַ כִּרְצוֹנוֹ.

בּוֹרֵא יוֹם וָלָיְלָה

גּוֹלֵל אוֹר מִפְּנֵי חֹשֶׁךְ וְחֹשֶׁךְ מִפְּנֵי אוֹר

וּמַעֲבִיר יוֹם וּמֵבִיא לָיְלָה

וּמַבְדִּיל בֵּין יוֹם וּבֵין לָיְלָה

יהוה צְבָאוֹת שְׁמוֹ.

אֵל חַי וְקַיָּם תָּמִיד, יִמְלֹךְ עָלֵינוּ לְעוֹלָם וָעֶד.

בָּרוּךְ אַתָּה יהוה, הַמַּעֲרִיב עֲרָבִים.ᵛ

אַהֲבַת עוֹלָם בֵּית יִשְׂרָאֵל עַמְּךָ אָהָבְתָּ

תּוֹרָה וּמִצְוֹת, חֻקִּים וּמִשְׁפָּטִים, אוֹתָנוּ לִמַּדְתָּ

BIUR TEFILLA · ביאור תפילה

בָּרוּךְ – *Bless.* Like in *Shaharit*, *Keriat Shema* has two introductory blessings, and as in the morning, the theme of the first is Hashem's revelation in nature, and the theme of the second is Hashem's revelation in Torah. God can be found in both, although in different ways.

בָּרְכוּ – *Bless.* Just as in the morning, as a prelude to the *Shema*, the *Hazan* invites us to join together as a single entity to declare our most basic beliefs and allegiance. Let's support one another. We will declare Him One, as one.

IYUN TEFILLA · עיון תפילה

הַמַּעֲרִיב עֲרָבִים – *Who brings on evenings.* If in the morning we were conscious of the sun and the beginning of the day, here we are aware of the ending of the day and the

Therefore, LORD our God, when we lie down and when we rise up[B]
we will speak of Your decrees, rejoicing in the words of Your Torah
and Your commandments for ever.

▸ For they are our life and the length of our days;
on them will we meditate day and night.[B]
May You never take away Your love from us.
Blessed are You, LORD, who loves His people Israel.

The Shema must be said with intense concentration.
When not with a minyan, say:

God, faithful King!

The following verse should be said aloud, while covering the eyes with the right hand:

Listen, Israel: the LORD is our God, the LORD is One.

Deut. 6

Quietly: Blessed be the name of His glorious kingdom for ever and all time.

וְאָהַבְתָּ Love the LORD your God with all your heart, with all your *Deut. 6*
soul, and with all your might. These words which I command you
today shall be on your heart. Teach them repeatedly to your children, speaking of them when you sit at home and when you travel
on the way, when you lie down and when you rise. Bind them as a
sign on your hand, and they shall be an emblem between your eyes.
Write them on the doorposts of your house and gates.

וְהָיָה If you indeed heed My commandments with which I charge you *Deut. 11*
today, to love the LORD your God and worship Him with all your
heart and with all your soul, I will give rain in your land in its season,

---

to enter the Promised Land, the very first
message to the people was the centrality of
Torah in their lives and the need to *"meditate
upon them day and night*... do not fear and
do not lose resolve, for Hashem is with you

wherever you will go" (*Yehoshua* 1:8–9). By
reciting the *Shema* a second time today, we
fulfill that mandate. And in doing so, we
pray that Hashem will be with us wherever
we will go, physically and emotionally.

עַל כֵּן יהוה אֱלֹהֵינוּ בְּשָׁכְבֵנוּ וּבְקוּמֵנוּ נָשֵׂיחַ בְּחֻקֵּיךָ
וְנִשְׂמַח בְּדִבְרֵי תוֹרָתֶךָ וּבְמִצְוֹתֶיךָ לְעוֹלָם וָעֶד
כִּי הֵם חַיֵּינוּ וְאְרֶךְ יָמֵינוּ
וּבָהֶם נֶהְגֶּה יוֹמָם וָלֵיְלָה.
וְאַהֲבָתְךָ אַל תָּסִיר מִמֶּנּוּ לְעוֹלָמִים.
בָּרוּךְ אַתָּה יהוה, אוֹהֵב עַמּוֹ יִשְׂרָאֵל.

The שמע must be said with intense concentration.

When not with a מנין, say:

אֵל מֶלֶךְ נֶאֱמָן

The following verse should be said aloud, while covering the eyes with the right hand:

שְׁמַע יִשְׂרָאֵל, יהוה אֱלֹהֵינוּ, יהוה ׀ אֶחָד׃
דברים ו

בָּרוּךְ שֵׁם כְּבוֹד מַלְכוּתוֹ לְעוֹלָם וָעֶד.

Quietly

וְאָהַבְתָּ אֵת יהוה אֱלֹהֶיךָ, בְּכָל־לְבָבְךָ וּבְכָל־נַפְשְׁךָ וּבְכָל־
מְאֹדֶךָ׃ וְהָיוּ הַדְּבָרִים הָאֵלֶּה, אֲשֶׁר אָנֹכִי מְצַוְּךָ הַיּוֹם, עַל־לְבָבֶךָ׃
וְשִׁנַּנְתָּם לְבָנֶיךָ וְדִבַּרְתָּ בָּם, בְּשִׁבְתְּךָ בְּבֵיתֶךָ וּבְלֶכְתְּךָ בַדֶּרֶךְ,
וּבְשָׁכְבְּךָ וּבְקוּמֶךָ׃ וּקְשַׁרְתָּם לְאוֹת עַל־יָדֶךָ וְהָיוּ לְטֹטָפֹת בֵּין
עֵינֶיךָ׃ וּכְתַבְתָּם עַל־מְזֻזוֹת בֵּיתֶךָ וּבִשְׁעָרֶיךָ׃
דברים ו

וְהָיָה אִם־שָׁמֹעַ תִּשְׁמְעוּ אֶל־מִצְוֹתַי אֲשֶׁר אָנֹכִי מְצַוֶּה אֶתְכֶם
הַיּוֹם, לְאַהֲבָה אֶת־יהוה אֱלֹהֵיכֶם וּלְעָבְדוֹ, בְּכָל־לְבַבְכֶם וּבְכָל־
דברים יא

BIUR TEFILLA · ביאור תפילה

בְּשָׁכְבֵנוּ וּבְקוּמֵנוּ – *When we lie down and when we rise up.* These two Hebrew words anticipate the words of the *Shema* and the reason that we recite it twice a day: "when you go to sleep and when you rise up."

וּבָהֶם נֶהְגֶּה יוֹמָם וָלֵיְלָה – *On them will we meditate day and night.* The source of this line is a verse from *Yehoshua.* As *Benei Yisrael* were about

the early and late rain; and you shall gather in your grain, wine and oil. I will give grass in your field for your cattle, and you shall eat and be satisfied. Be careful lest your heart be tempted and you go astray and worship other gods, bowing down to them. Then the LORD's anger will flare against you and He will close the heavens so that there will be no rain. The land will not yield its crops, and you will perish swiftly from the good land that the LORD is giving you. Therefore, set these, My words, on your heart and soul. Bind them as a sign on your hand, and they shall be an emblem between your eyes. Teach them to your children, speaking of them when you sit at home and when you travel on the way, when you lie down and when you rise. Write them on the doorposts of your house and gates, so that you and your children may live long in the land that the LORD swore to your ancestors to give them, for as long as the heavens are above the earth.

וַיֹּאמֶר The LORD spoke[H] to Moses, saying: Speak to the Israelites *Num. 15* and tell them to make tassels on the corners of their garments for all generations. They shall attach to the tassel at each corner a thread of blue. This shall be your tassel, and you shall see it and remember all of the LORD's commandments and keep them, not straying after your heart and after your eyes, following your own sinful desires. Thus you will be reminded to keep all My commandments, and be holy to your God. I am the LORD your God, who brought you out of the land of Egypt to be your God. I am the LORD your God.

True –

The Leader repeats:

▸ The LORD your God is true –

HILKHOT TEFILLA · הלכות תפילה

וַיֹּאמֶר – *Spoke.* The primary halakhic function of the third paragraph of the *Shema* at this time is to recall the exodus from Egypt. The exodus is the rationale provided

for many mitzvot in the Torah. It lies at the heart of our chosenness, and at the heart of our need to be empathetic toward others less fortunate.

נַפְשְׁכֶם: וְנָתַתִּי מְטַר־אַרְצְכֶם בְּעִתּוֹ, יוֹרֶה וּמַלְקוֹשׁ, וְאָסַפְתָּ
דְגָנֶךָ וְתִירֹשְׁךָ וְיִצְהָרֶךָ: וְנָתַתִּי עֵשֶׂב בְּשָׂדְךָ לִבְהֶמְתֶּךָ, וְאָכַלְתָּ
וְשָׂבָעְתָּ: הִשָּׁמְרוּ לָכֶם פֶּן־יִפְתֶּה לְבַבְכֶם, וְסַרְתֶּם וַעֲבַדְתֶּם
אֱלֹהִים אֲחֵרִים וְהִשְׁתַּחֲוִיתֶם לָהֶם: וְחָרָה אַף־יְהֹוָה בָּכֶם, וְעָצַר
אֶת־הַשָּׁמַיִם וְלֹא־יִהְיֶה מָטָר, וְהָאֲדָמָה לֹא תִתֵּן אֶת־יְבוּלָהּ,
וַאֲבַדְתֶּם מְהֵרָה מֵעַל הָאָרֶץ הַטֹּבָה אֲשֶׁר יְהֹוָה נֹתֵן לָכֶם:
וְשַׂמְתֶּם אֶת־דְּבָרַי אֵלֶּה עַל־לְבַבְכֶם וְעַל־נַפְשְׁכֶם, וּקְשַׁרְתֶּם
אֹתָם לְאוֹת עַל־יֶדְכֶם, וְהָיוּ לְטוֹטָפֹת בֵּין עֵינֵיכֶם: וְלִמַּדְתֶּם
אֹתָם אֶת־בְּנֵיכֶם לְדַבֵּר בָּם, בְּשִׁבְתְּךָ בְּבֵיתֶךָ וּבְלֶכְתְּךָ בַדֶּרֶךְ,
וּבְשָׁכְבְּךָ וּבְקוּמֶךָ: וּכְתַבְתָּם עַל־מְזוּזוֹת בֵּיתֶךָ וּבִשְׁעָרֶיךָ: לְמַעַן
יִרְבּוּ יְמֵיכֶם וִימֵי בְנֵיכֶם עַל הָאֲדָמָה אֲשֶׁר נִשְׁבַּע יְהֹוָה לַאֲבֹתֵיכֶם
לָתֵת לָהֶם, כִּימֵי הַשָּׁמַיִם עַל־הָאָרֶץ:

בּמדבר טו

וַיֹּאמֶר יְהֹוָה אֶל־מֹשֶׁה לֵּאמֹר: דַּבֵּר אֶל־בְּנֵי יִשְׂרָאֵל וְאָמַרְתָּ
אֲלֵהֶם, וְעָשׂוּ לָהֶם צִיצִת עַל־כַּנְפֵי בִגְדֵיהֶם לְדֹרֹתָם, וְנָתְנוּ
עַל־צִיצִת הַכָּנָף פְּתִיל תְּכֵלֶת: וְהָיָה לָכֶם לְצִיצִת, וּרְאִיתֶם אֹתוֹ
וּזְכַרְתֶּם אֶת־כָּל־מִצְוֹת יְהֹוָה וַעֲשִׂיתֶם אֹתָם, וְלֹא תָתוּרוּ אַחֲרֵי
לְבַבְכֶם וְאַחֲרֵי עֵינֵיכֶם, אֲשֶׁר־אַתֶּם זֹנִים אַחֲרֵיהֶם: לְמַעַן תִּזְכְּרוּ
וַעֲשִׂיתֶם אֶת־כָּל־מִצְוֹתָי, וִהְיִיתֶם קְדֹשִׁים לֵאלֹהֵיכֶם: אֲנִי יְהֹוָה
אֱלֹהֵיכֶם, אֲשֶׁר הוֹצֵאתִי אֶתְכֶם מֵאֶרֶץ מִצְרַיִם, לִהְיוֹת לָכֶם
לֵאלֹהִים, אֲנִי יְהֹוָה אֱלֹהֵיכֶם:

אֱמֶת

The שליח ציבור *repeats:*

‹ יהוה אֱלֹהֵיכֶם אֱמֶת

וֶאֱמוּנָה – and faithful[H] is all this,
and firmly established for us
that He is the LORD our God,
and there is none besides Him,
and that we, Israel, are His people.
He is our King, who redeems us from the hand of kings
and delivers us from the grasp of all tyrants.
He is our God,
who on our behalf repays our foes
and brings just retribution on our mortal enemies;
who performs great deeds beyond understanding
and wonders beyond number;
who kept us alive, not letting our foot slip;   *Ps. 66*
who led us on the high places of our enemies,
raising our pride above all our foes;
who did miracles for us
and brought vengeance against Pharaoh;
who performed signs and wonders
in the land of Ham's children;
who smote in His wrath all the firstborn of Egypt,
and brought out His people Israel from their midst
into everlasting freedom;

---

remains faithful to man, protects his soul overnight, and a miracle takes place in the morning when the soul is restored and he awakes feeling refreshed and invigorated, ready to begin a new day. (Rashi)

HILKHOT TEFILLA · הלכות תפילה

וֶאֱמוּנָה – *Faithful.* Rav says (*Berakhot* 12a) that whoever does not include the theme of *Emet VeEmuna* in the evening prayer does not fulfill his obligation. The assertion is based upon the verse in *Tehillim* (92:3),

"I will tell of Your *ḥesed* in the morning and Your *emuna* (faithfulness) at night. The nighttime is all about Hashem's faithfulness... and our faith.

וֶאֱמוּנָה^{עה} כָּל זֹאת וְקַיָּם עָלֵינוּ

כִּי הוּא יהוה אֱלֹהֵינוּ וְאֵין זוּלָתוֹ

וַאֲנַחְנוּ יִשְׂרָאֵל עַמּוֹ.

הַפּוֹדֵנוּ מִיַּד מְלָכִים

מַלְכֵּנוּ הַגּוֹאֲלֵנוּ מִכַּף כָּל הֶעָרִיצִים.

הָאֵל הַנִּפְרָע לָנוּ מִצָּרֵינוּ

וְהַמְשַׁלֵּם גְּמוּל לְכָל אוֹיְבֵי נַפְשֵׁנוּ.

הָעוֹשֶׂה גְדוֹלוֹת עַד אֵין חֵקֶר, וְנִפְלָאוֹת עַד אֵין מִסְפָּר

הַשָּׂם נַפְשֵׁנוּ בַּחַיִּים

וְלֹא־נָתַן לַמּוֹט רַגְלֵנוּ:

הַמַּדְרִיכֵנוּ עַל בָּמוֹת אוֹיְבֵינוּ

וַיָּרֶם קַרְנֵנוּ עַל כָּל שׂוֹנְאֵינוּ.

הָעוֹשֶׂה לָּנוּ נִסִּים וּנְקָמָה בְּפַרְעֹה

אוֹתוֹת וּמוֹפְתִים בְּאַדְמַת בְּנֵי חָם.

הַמַּכֶּה בְעֶבְרָתוֹ כָּל בְּכוֹרֵי מִצְרָיִם

וַיּוֹצֵא אֶת עַמּוֹ יִשְׂרָאֵל מִתּוֹכָם לְחֵרוּת עוֹלָם.

תהלים סו

עיון תפילה

IYUN TEFILLA

וֶאֱמוּנָה – *And faithful.* Just as in the morning there was a blessing on God's presence in history, so too do we say one here. The difference is that the one in the morning refers specifically to the redemption from Egypt which took place in the past. Here, however, in keeping with the theme of the evening, our focus shifts to the future, about redemption yet to come. (*Magen Avraham*)

וֶאֱמוּנָה – *Faithful.* After a long day of work and pressures, there is no person whose soul does not ache. When the person goes to sleep, the soul rises to heaven and although Hashem orders her to return to the body, she does not wish to do so. Hashem responds: "Man placed his faith in Me at night by placing his soul in My hands for safekeeping." Hashem therefore

who led His children through the divided Reed Sea,
plunging their pursuers and enemies into the depths.
When His children saw His might,
they gave praise and thanks to His name,
‣ and willingly accepted His Sovereignty.
Moses and the children of Israel
then sang a song to You
with great joy,
and they all exclaimed:

> מִי־כָמֹכָה "Who is like You, LORD,   *Ex. 15*
> among the mighty?
> Who is like You, majestic in holiness,
> awesome in praises, doing wonders?"

‣ Your children beheld Your majesty
  as You parted the sea before Moses.
"This is my God!" they responded,
and then said:

> "The LORD shall reign for ever and ever."   *Ex. 15*

‣ And it is said,

> "For the LORD has redeemed Jacob   *Jer. 31*
> and rescued him from a power
> stronger than his own."

Blessed are You, LORD,
who redeemed Israel.

הַשְׁכִּיבֵנוּ Help us lie down, O LORD our God, in peace,
and rise up, O our King, to life.
Spread over us Your canopy of peace.
Direct us with Your good counsel,^A
and save us for the sake of Your name.

הַמַּעֲבִיר בָּנָיו בֵּין גִּזְרֵי יַם סוּף

אֶת רוֹדְפֵיהֶם וְאֶת שׂוֹנְאֵיהֶם בִּתְהוֹמוֹת טִבַּע

וְרָאוּ בָנָיו גְּבוּרָתוֹ, שִׁבְּחוּ וְהוֹדוּ לִשְׁמוֹ

‹ וּמַלְכוּתוֹ בְּרָצוֹן קִבְּלוּ עֲלֵיהֶם.

מֹשֶׁה וּבְנֵי יִשְׂרָאֵל, לְךָ עָנוּ שִׁירָה בְּשִׂמְחָה רַבָּה

וְאָמְרוּ כֻלָּם

שמות טו

מִי־כָמֹכָה בָּאֵלִם יהוה

מִי כָּמֹכָה נֶאְדָּר בַּקֹּדֶשׁ

נוֹרָא תְהִלֹּת עֹשֵׂה פֶלֶא:

‹ מַלְכוּתְךָ רָאוּ בָנֶיךָ, בּוֹקֵעַ יָם לִפְנֵי מֹשֶׁה

זֶה אֵלִי עָנוּ, וְאָמְרוּ

יהוה יִמְלֹךְ לְעֹלָם וָעֶד:

שמות טו

‹ וְנֶאֱמַר

כִּי־פָדָה יהוה אֶת־יַעֲקֹב, וּגְאָלוֹ מִיַּד חָזָק מִמֶּנּוּ:

ירמיהו לא

בָּרוּךְ אַתָּה יהוה, גָּאַל יִשְׂרָאֵל.

הַשְׁכִּיבֵנוּ יהוה אֱלֹהֵינוּ לְשָׁלוֹם

וְהַעֲמִידֵנוּ מַלְכֵּנוּ לְחַיִּים

וּפְרֹשׂ עָלֵינוּ סֻכַּת שְׁלוֹמֶךָ, וְתַקְּנֵנוּ בְּעֵצָה טוֹבָהˣ מִלְּפָנֶיךָ

וְהוֹשִׁיעֵנוּ לְמַעַן שְׁמֶךָ.

אני תפילה · ANI TEFILLA

וְתַקְּנֵנוּ בְּעֵצָה טוֹבָה – *Direct us with Your good counsel.* At night, we are more open to possibilities, more open to divine inspiration. I pray that I will be open to Your direction and advice. (*Iyun Tefilla,* Rabbi Yaakov Tzvi Mecklenburg)

Shield us and remove from us every enemy,
plague, sword, famine and sorrow.
Remove the adversary from before and behind us.[B]
Shelter us in the shadow of Your wings,[A]
for You, God, are our Guardian and Deliverer;
You, God, are a gracious and compassionate King.
▸ Guard our going out and our coming in,
for life and peace, from now and for ever.
Blessed are You, LORD,
who guards His people Israel for ever.

*In Israel in some communities outside Israel
the service continues with Half Kaddish on page 358.*

בָּרוּךְ Blessed be the LORD for ever. Amen and Amen.[B]   Ps. 89

Blessed from Zion be the LORD   Ps. 135
who dwells in Jerusalem. Halleluya!

Blessed be the LORD, God of Israel,   Ps. 72
who alone does wondrous things.
Blessed be His glorious name for ever,
and may the whole earth
be filled with His glory. Amen and Amen.

May the glory of the LORD endure for ever;   Ps. 104
may the LORD rejoice in His works.

May the name of the LORD   Ps. 113
be blessed now and for all time.

corresponding to the 18 blessings of *Shem-oneh Esreh*. Its origin is said to have been a substitute for that prayer during Babylonian times, when synagogues were located outside the city and people were afraid to remain there after dark; as such, this passage was recited in place of the *Shemoneh Esreh* (Abudarham). In a related vein, it may be that latecomers to the service would have ended up praying after everyone else finished, and so this section was added for everyone to say so that the latecomers could catch up; everyone would pray the *Amida* together, and then be able to leave together (Tosafot). It thus served as a kind of *Pesukei DeZimra* for those who recited it. Although social conditions have changed, the prayer was nevertheless retained, although in Israel and in some Diaspora communities it is omitted and the service continues with *Kaddish*.

וְהָגֵן בַּעֲדֵנוּ, וְהָסֵר מֵעָלֵינוּ אוֹיֵב, דֶּבֶר וְחֶרֶב וְרָעָב וְיָגוֹן
וְהָסֵר שָׂטָן מִלְּפָנֵינוּ וּמֵאַחֲרֵינוּ,ּ וּבְצֵל כְּנָפֶיךָ תַּסְתִּירֵנוּ*
כִּי אֵל שׁוֹמְרֵנוּ וּמַצִּילֵנוּ אֵתָּה,
כִּי אֵל מֶלֶךְ חַנּוּן וְרַחוּם אֵתָּה.
‹ וּשְׁמֹר צֵאתֵנוּ וּבוֹאֵנוּ לְחַיִּים וּלְשָׁלוֹם מֵעַתָּה וְעַד עוֹלָם.
בָּרוּךְ אַתָּה יהוה, שׁוֹמֵר עַמּוֹ יִשְׂרָאֵל לָעַד.

In ארץ ישראל *and in some communities outside* ארץ ישראל
the service continues with חצי קדיש *on page 359.*

תהלים פט בָּרוּךְ יהוה לְעוֹלָם, אָמֵן וְאָמֵן:ּ
תהלים קלה בָּרוּךְ יהוה מִצִּיּוֹן, שֹׁכֵן יְרוּשָׁלָיִם, הַלְלוּיָהּ:
תהלים עב בָּרוּךְ יהוה אֱלֹהִים אֱלֹהֵי יִשְׂרָאֵל, עֹשֵׂה נִפְלָאוֹת לְבַדּוֹ:
וּבָרוּךְ שֵׁם כְּבוֹדוֹ לְעוֹלָם
וְיִמָּלֵא כְבוֹדוֹ אֶת־כָּל־הָאָרֶץ, אָמֵן וְאָמֵן:
תהלים קד יְהִי כְבוֹד יהוה לְעוֹלָם, יִשְׂמַח יהוה בְּמַעֲשָׂיו:
תהלים קיג יְהִי שֵׁם יהוה מְבֹרָךְ מֵעַתָּה וְעַד־עוֹלָם:

BIUR TEFILLA · ביאור תפילה

וְהָסֵר שָׂטָן מִלְּפָנֵינוּ וּמֵאַחֲרֵינוּ – *Remove the adversary from before and behind us.* The *Satan* is the evil inclination (*Bava Batra* 16a), the disposition that we sometimes have to do what we know in our heart of hearts we should not do. We therefore ask here for help with our own inclinations which, especially at night, can seem to overwhelm us.

ANI TEFILLA · אני תפילה

וּבְצֵל כְּנָפֶיךָ תַּסְתִּירֵנוּ – *Shelter us in the shadow of Your wings.* Like a mother bird who protects her chicks by gathering them under her wing. The warm embrace of a parent, the feeling of comfort and security that comes with being enveloped, protected and secure. That is what we all long for, no matter how old we are. That is what Hashem provides. Feel enveloped.

BIUR TEFILLA · ביאור תפילה

בָּרוּךְ יהוה לְעוֹלָם אָמֵן וְאָמֵן – *Blessed be the Lord for ever. Amen and Amen.* The source of

this passage is not entirely clear. It contains the four-letter name of Hashem 18 times,

For the sake of His great name *1 Sam. 12*
the LORD will not abandon His people,
for the LORD vowed to make you a people of His own.

When all the people saw [God's wonders] they fell on their faces *1 Kings 18*
and said: "The LORD, He is God; the LORD, He is God."

Then the LORD shall be King over all the earth; *Zech. 14*
on that day the LORD shall be One and His name One.

May Your love, LORD, be upon us, as we have put our hope in You. *Ps. 33*

Save us, LORD our God, gather us *Ps. 106*
and deliver us from the nations,
to thank Your holy name, and glory in Your praise.

All the nations You made shall come and bow before You, LORD, *Ps. 86*
and pay honor to Your name,
for You are great and You perform wonders:
You alone are God.

We, Your people, the flock of Your pasture, will praise You for ever. *Ps. 79*
For all generations we will relate Your praise.

בָּרוּךְ Blessed is the LORD by day, blessed is the LORD by night.
Blessed is the LORD when we lie down;
blessed is the LORD when we rise.
For in Your hand are the souls of the living and the dead,
[as it is written:] "In His hand is every living soul, *Job 12*
and the breath of all mankind."

---

somewhere we forget the reasons that we began the journey, or alternatively we miss important stops along the way. *Tefilla* is a journey. The moment of encounter is upon us. Perhaps what the verse is also telling us is *vayifga baMakom*, not that he encountered the place, but he encountered, *HaMakom*, God. The key to that encounter is the realization that one can return to the spot where "my fathers prayed."

ANI TEFILLA · אני תפילה

Prayer enlightens man about his needs. It tells man the story of hidden hopes and expectations. It teaches him how to behold the vision and how to strive in order to realize this vision, when to be satisfied with what one possesses, when to reach out for more. In a word, man finds his need-awareness, himself, in prayer. (Rabbi J.B. Soloveitchik)

שמואל א, יב
כִּי לֹא־יִטֹּשׁ יהוה אֶת־עַמּוֹ בַּעֲבוּר שְׁמוֹ הַגָּדוֹל
כִּי הוֹאִיל יהוה לַעֲשׂוֹת אֶתְכֶם לוֹ לְעָם:

מלכים א, יח
וַיַּרְא כָּל־הָעָם וַיִּפְּלוּ עַל־פְּנֵיהֶם
וַיֹּאמְרוּ, יהוה הוּא הָאֱלֹהִים, יהוה הוּא הָאֱלֹהִים:

זכריה יד
וְהָיָה יהוה לְמֶלֶךְ עַל־כָּל־הָאָרֶץ
בַּיּוֹם הַהוּא יִהְיֶה יהוה אֶחָד וּשְׁמוֹ אֶחָד:

תהלים לג
יְהִי־חַסְדְּךָ יהוה עָלֵינוּ, כַּאֲשֶׁר יִחַלְנוּ לָךְ:

תהלים קו
הוֹשִׁיעֵנוּ יהוה אֱלֹהֵינוּ, וְקַבְּצֵנוּ מִן־הַגּוֹיִם
לְהֹדוֹת לְשֵׁם קָדְשֶׁךָ, לְהִשְׁתַּבֵּחַ בִּתְהִלָּתֶךָ:

תהלים פו
כָּל־גּוֹיִם אֲשֶׁר עָשִׂיתָ, יָבוֹאוּ וְיִשְׁתַּחֲווּ לְפָנֶיךָ, אֲדֹנָי
וִיכַבְּדוּ לִשְׁמֶךָ:
כִּי־גָדוֹל אַתָּה וְעֹשֵׂה נִפְלָאוֹת, אַתָּה אֱלֹהִים לְבַדֶּךָ:

תהלים עט
וַאֲנַחְנוּ עַמְּךָ וְצֹאן מַרְעִיתֶךָ, נוֹדֶה לְּךָ לְעוֹלָם
לְדוֹר וָדֹר נְסַפֵּר תְּהִלָּתֶךָ:

בָּרוּךְ יהוה בַּיּוֹם, בָּרוּךְ יהוה בַּלַּיְלָה
בָּרוּךְ יהוה בְּשָׁכְבֵנוּ, בָּרוּךְ יהוה בְּקוּמֵנוּ.
כִּי בְיָדְךָ נַפְשׁוֹת הַחַיִּים וְהַמֵּתִים.

איוב יב
אֲשֶׁר בְּיָדוֹ נֶפֶשׁ כָּל־חָי, וְרוּחַ כָּל־בְּשַׂר־אִישׁ:

ANI TEFILLA · אני תפילה

Yaakov, who established *Ma'ariv*, is said to have been journeying from Be'er Sheva to Ḥaran when suddenly "*vayifga bama-kom* – he encountered the place" (*Bereshit* 28:10–11). The Gemara (*Ḥullin* 91b) relates that when he reached Ḥaran it occurred to him that along the way "I passed by

the place where my fathers had prayed. How could I not have prayed there my-self?" And so he returned to that spot, and miraculously the ground between the two places contracted, and that is why the verse immediately says "he encountered the place." Sometimes in our haste to get

Into Your hand I entrust my spirit: Ps. 31
You redeemed me, LORD, God of truth.
Our God in heaven, bring unity to Your name,
establish Your kingdom constantly
and reign over us for ever and all time.

יִרְאוּ **May our eyes see, our hearts rejoice,**
and our souls be glad in Your true salvation,
when Zion is told, "Your God reigns."
The LORD is King, the LORD was King,
the LORD will be King for ever and all time.

▸ For sovereignty is Yours, and to all eternity You will reign in glory,
for we have no king but You.
Blessed are You, LORD,
the King who in His constant glory will reign over us
and all His creation for ever and all time.

HALF KADDISH

Leader: יִתְגַּדַּל **Magnified and sanctified may His great name be,**
in the world He created by His will.
May He establish His kingdom
in your lifetime and in your days,
and in the lifetime of all the house of Israel,
swiftly and soon – and say: Amen.

All: May His great name^ be blessed for ever and all time.

Leader: Blessed and praised, glorified and exalted,
raised and honored, uplifted and lauded
be the name of the Holy One, blessed be He,
beyond any blessing, song, praise and consolation
uttered in the world – and say: Amen.

ANI TEFILLA · אני תפילה

יְהֵא שְׁמֵהּ רַבָּא – *May His great name.* Whoever says *yeheh shemeh raba...* with all his
strength, the Heavenly Court rips up any
negative decree against him (*Shabbat*

119b). "With all his strength" – with all of His
strength, for through the power of one's *tefilla*, one strengthens the hand of Hashem
to destroy the decree. (Maharsha)

בְּיָדְךָ אַפְקִיד רוּחִי, פָּדִיתָה אוֹתִי יהוה אֵל אֱמֶת:
אֱלֹהֵינוּ שֶׁבַּשָּׁמַיִם, יַחֵד שִׁמְךָ וְקַיֵּם מַלְכוּתְךָ תָּמִיד
וּמְלֹךְ עָלֵינוּ לְעוֹלָם וָעֶד.

יִרְאוּ עֵינֵינוּ וְיִשְׂמַח לִבֵּנוּ, וְתָגֵל נַפְשֵׁנוּ בִּישׁוּעָתְךָ בֶּאֱמֶת
בֶּאֱמֹר לְצִיּוֹן מָלַךְ אֱלֹהָיִךְ.
יהוה מֶלֶךְ, יהוה מָלָךְ, יהוה יִמְלֹךְ לְעֹלָם וָעֶד.
‹ כִּי הַמַּלְכוּת שֶׁלְּךָ הִיא, וּלְעוֹלְמֵי עַד תִּמְלֹךְ בְּכָבוֹד
כִּי אֵין לָנוּ מֶלֶךְ אֶלָּא אָתָּה.
בָּרוּךְ אַתָּה יהוה
הַמֶּלֶךְ בִּכְבוֹדוֹ תָּמִיד, יִמְלֹךְ עָלֵינוּ לְעוֹלָם וָעֶד
וְעַל כָּל מַעֲשָׂיו.

חצי קדיש

ש״ץ   יִתְגַּדַּל וְיִתְקַדַּשׁ שְׁמֵהּ רַבָּא (קהל: אָמֵן)
בְּעָלְמָא דִּי בְרָא כִרְעוּתֵהּ
וְיַמְלִיךְ מַלְכוּתֵהּ
בְּחַיֵּיכוֹן וּבְיוֹמֵיכוֹן וּבְחַיֵּי דְכָל בֵּית יִשְׂרָאֵל
בַּעֲגָלָא וּבִזְמַן קָרִיב, וְאִמְרוּ אָמֵן. (קהל: אָמֵן)

קהל   יְהֵא שְׁמֵהּ רַבָּא× מְבָרַךְ לְעָלַם וּלְעָלְמֵי עָלְמַיָּא.
וש״ץ

שׁ״ץ   יִתְבָּרַךְ וְיִשְׁתַּבַּח וְיִתְפָּאַר וְיִתְרוֹמַם וְיִתְנַשֵּׂא
וְיִתְהַדָּר וְיִתְעַלֶּה וְיִתְהַלָּל
שְׁמֵהּ דְּקֻדְשָׁא בְּרִיךְ הוּא (קהל: בְּרִיךְ הוּא)
לְעֵלָּא מִן כָּל בִּרְכָתָא
/ בעשרת ימי תשובה: לְעֵלָּא לְעֵלָּא מִכָּל בִּרְכָתָא/
וְשִׁירָתָא, תֻּשְׁבְּחָתָא וְנֶחֱמָתָא
דַּאֲמִירָן בְּעָלְמָא, וְאִמְרוּ אָמֵן. (קהל: אָמֵן)

THE AMIDA

*For other formats of the Amida see page 138 and page 280. Please follow the
instructions carefully if you are using this layout for Shaharit or Minha. For the
Repetition of the Amida at Shaharit turn to page 138 and at Minha to page 280.*

*The following prayer, until "in former years" on page 378, is said silently, standing with feet
together. Take three steps forward and at the points indicated by ˙, bend the knees at
the first word, bow at the second, and stand straight before saying God's name.*

O Lord, open my lips, so that my mouth may declare Your praise.   *Ps. 51*

PATRIARCHS

˙בָּרוּךְ Blessed are You, Lord our God and God of our fathers,
God of Abraham, God of Isaac and God of Jacob;
the great, mighty and awesome God, God Most High,
who bestows acts of loving-kindness and creates all,
who remembers the loving-kindness of the fathers
and will bring a Redeemer to their children's children
for the sake of His name, in love.

*Between Rosh
HaShana &
Yom Kippur:*
Remember us for life, O King who desires life,
and write us in the book of life –
for Your sake, O God of life.

King, Helper, Savior, Shield:
˙Blessed are You, Lord, Shield of Abraham.

DIVINE MIGHT

אַתָּה גִּבּוֹר You are eternally mighty, Lord.
You give life to the dead
and have great power to save.

*The phrase "He makes the wind blow and the rain fall" is added
from Simhat Torah until Pesah. In Israel the phrase "He causes the
dew to fall" is added from Pesah until Shemini Atzeret.*

In fall & winter: He makes the wind blow and the rain fall.
*In Israel, in spring
& summer:* He causes the dew to fall.

He sustains the living with loving-kindness,
and with great compassion revives the dead.
He supports the fallen, heals the sick, sets captives free,
and keeps His faith with those who sleep in the dust.

עמידה

For other formats of the עמידה see page 139 and page 281. Please follow the
instructions carefully if you are using this layout for שחרית or מנחה. For
שחרית at חזרת הש״ץ turn to page 139 and at מנחה to page 281.
The following prayer, until קדמניות on page 379, is said silently, standing with feet
together. Take three steps forward and at the points indicated by ˈ, bend the knees at
the first word, bow at the second, and stand straight before saying God's name.

תהילים נא

אֲדֹנָי, שְׂפָתַי תִּפְתָּח, וּפִי יַגִּיד תְּהִלָּתֶךָ:

אבות

י֨בָּרוּךְ אַתָּה יהוה, אֱלֹהֵינוּ וֵאלֹהֵי אֲבוֹתֵינוּ

אֱלֹהֵי אַבְרָהָם, אֱלֹהֵי יִצְחָק, וֵאלֹהֵי יַעֲקֹב

הָאֵל הַגָּדוֹל הַגִּבּוֹר וְהַנּוֹרָא, אֵל עֶלְיוֹן

גּוֹמֵל חֲסָדִים טוֹבִים, וְקֹנֵה הַכֹּל

וְזוֹכֵר חַסְדֵי אָבוֹת

וּמֵבִיא גוֹאֵל לִבְנֵי בְנֵיהֶם לְמַעַן שְׁמוֹ בְּאַהֲבָה.

בעשרת ימי תשובה: זָכְרֵנוּ לְחַיִּים, מֶלֶךְ חָפֵץ בַּחַיִּים

וְכָתְבֵנוּ בְּסֵפֶר הַחַיִּים, לְמַעַנְךָ אֱלֹהִים חַיִּים.

מֶלֶךְ עוֹזֵר וּמוֹשִׁיעַ וּמָגֵן.

י֨בָּרוּךְ אַתָּה יהוה, מָגֵן אַבְרָהָם.

גבורות

אַתָּה גִּבּוֹר לְעוֹלָם, אֲדֹנָי

מְחַיֵּה מֵתִים אַתָּה, רַב לְהוֹשִׁיעַ

The phrase מַשִּׁיב הָרוּחַ is added from שמחת תורה until פסח. In ארץ ישראל
the phrase מוֹרִיד הַטָּל is added from פסח until שמיני עצרת.

בחורף: מַשִּׁיב הָרוּחַ וּמוֹרִיד הַגֶּשֶׁם / בארץ ישראל בקיץ: מוֹרִיד הַטָּל

מְכַלְכֵּל חַיִּים בְּחֶסֶד, מְחַיֵּה מֵתִים בְּרַחֲמִים רַבִּים

סוֹמֵךְ נוֹפְלִים, וְרוֹפֵא חוֹלִים, וּמַתִּיר אֲסוּרִים

וּמְקַיֵּם אֱמוּנָתוֹ לִישֵׁנֵי עָפָר.

Who is like You, Master of might,
and who can compare to You,
O King who brings death and gives life,
and makes salvation grow?

Between Rosh HaShana Who is like You, compassionate Father,
& Yom Kippur: who remembers His creatures
in compassion, for life?

Faithful are You to revive the dead.
Blessed are You, LORD, who revives the dead.

HOLINESS

אַתָּה קָדוֹשׁ You are holy and Your name is holy,
and holy ones praise You daily, Selah!
Blessed are You, LORD,
the holy God. / *Between Rosh HaShana & Yom Kippur:* the holy King./
(*If forgotten, repeat the Amida.*)

KNOWLEDGE

אַתָּה חוֹנֵן You grace humanity with knowledge
and teach mortals understanding.

> *On Motza'ei Shabbat and Motza'ei Yom Tov say:*
> אַתָּה חוֹנַנְתָּנוּ You have graced us with the knowledge of Your Torah, and
> taught us to perform the statutes of Your will. You have distinguished, LORD
> our God, between sacred and profane, light and darkness, Israel and the
> nations, and between the seventh day and the six days of work. Our Father,
> our King, may the days approaching us bring peace; may we be free from
> all sin, cleansed from all iniquity, holding fast to our reverence of You. And

Grace us with the knowledge, understanding
and discernment that come from You.
Blessed are You, LORD, who graciously grants knowledge.

REPENTANCE

הֲשִׁיבֵנוּ Bring us back, our Father, to Your Torah.
Draw us near, our King, to Your service.
Lead us back to You in perfect repentance.
Blessed are You, LORD, who desires repentance.

מִי כָמְוֹךָ, בַּעַל גְּבוּרוֹת, וּמִי דְּוֹמֶה לָּךְ
מֶלֶךְ, מֵמִית וּמְחַיֶּה וּמַצְמִיחַ יְשׁוּעָה.

בעשרת ימי תשובה: מִי כָמְוֹךָ אַב הָרַחֲמִים, זוֹכֵר יְצוּרָיו לְחַיִּים בְּרַחֲמִים.

וְנֶאֱמָן אַתָּה לְהַחֲיוֹת מֵתִים.
בָּרוּךְ אַתָּה יהוה, מְחַיֵּה הַמֵּתִים.

קדושת השם
אַתָּה קָדוֹשׁ וְשִׁמְךָ קָדוֹשׁ
וּקְדוֹשִׁים בְּכָל יוֹם יְהַלְלוּךָ סֶּלָה.
בָּרוּךְ אַתָּה יהוה, הָאֵל הַקָּדוֹשׁ./בעשרת ימי תשובה: הַמֶּלֶךְ הַקָּדוֹשׁ./

(*If forgotten, repeat the* עמידה.)

דעת
אַתָּה חוֹנֵן לְאָדָם דַּעַת
וּמְלַמֵּד לֶאֱנוֹשׁ בִּינָה.

On מוצאי שבת *and* מוצאי יום טוב *say:*

אַתָּה חוֹנַנְתָּנוּ לְמַדַּע תּוֹרָתֶךָ, וַתְּלַמְּדֵנוּ לַעֲשׂוֹת חֻקֵּי רְצוֹנֶךָ, וַתַּבְדֵּל
יהוה אֱלֹהֵינוּ בֵּין קֹדֶשׁ לְחֹל, בֵּין אוֹר לְחֹשֶׁךְ, בֵּין יִשְׂרָאֵל לָעַמִּים, בֵּין יוֹם
הַשְּׁבִיעִי לְשֵׁשֶׁת יְמֵי הַמַּעֲשֶׂה. אָבִינוּ מַלְכֵּנוּ, הָחֵל עָלֵינוּ הַיָּמִים הַבָּאִים
לִקְרָאתֵנוּ לְשָׁלוֹם, חֲשׂוּכִים מִכָּל חֵטְא וּמְנֻקִּים מִכָּל עָוֹן וּמְדֻבָּקִים בְּיִרְאָתֶךָ. וְ

חָנֵּנוּ מֵאִתְּךָ דֵּעָה בִּינָה וְהַשְׂכֵּל.
בָּרוּךְ אַתָּה יהוה, חוֹנֵן הַדָּעַת.

תשובה
הֲשִׁיבֵנוּ אָבִינוּ לְתוֹרָתֶךָ
וְקָרְבֵנוּ מַלְכֵּנוּ לַעֲבוֹדָתֶךָ
וְהַחֲזִירֵנוּ בִּתְשׁוּבָה שְׁלֵמָה לְפָנֶיךָ.
בָּרוּךְ אַתָּה יהוה, הָרוֹצֶה בִּתְשׁוּבָה.

FORGIVENESS

Strike the left side of the chest at °.

סְלַח לָנוּ Forgive us, our Father,
for we have °sinned.
Pardon us, our King,
for we have °transgressed;
for You pardon and forgive.
Blessed are You, Lord,
the gracious One who repeatedly forgives.

REDEMPTION

רְאֵה Look on our affliction,
plead our cause,
and redeem us soon for Your name's sake,
for You are a powerful Redeemer.
Blessed are You, Lord,
the Redeemer of Israel.

HEALING

רְפָאֵנוּ Heal us, Lord, and we shall be healed.
Save us and we shall be saved,
for You are our praise.
Bring complete recovery for all our ailments,

The following prayer for a sick person may be said here:
May it be Your will, O Lord my God and God of my ancestors, that You
speedily send a complete recovery from heaven, a healing of both soul and
body, to the patient (*name*), son/daughter of (*mother's name*) among the
other afflicted of Israel.

---

for You, God, King, are a faithful and compassionate Healer.
Blessed are You, Lord,
Healer of the sick of His people Israel.

סליחה

Strike the left side of the chest at °.

סְלַח לָנוּ אָבִינוּ כִּי °חָטָאנוּ

מְחַל לָנוּ מַלְכֵּנוּ כִּי °פָשָׁעְנוּ

כִּי מוֹחֵל וְסוֹלֵחַ אָתָּה.

בָּרוּךְ אַתָּה יהוה, חַנּוּן הַמַּרְבֶּה לִסְלֹחַ.

גאולה

רְאֵה בְעָנְיֵנוּ, וְרִיבָה רִיבֵנוּ

וּגְאָלֵנוּ מְהֵרָה לְמַעַן שְׁמֶךָ

כִּי גוֹאֵל חָזָק אָתָּה.

בָּרוּךְ אַתָּה יהוה, גּוֹאֵל יִשְׂרָאֵל.

רפואה

רְפָאֵנוּ יהוה וְנֵרָפֵא

הוֹשִׁיעֵנוּ וְנִוָּשֵׁעָה

כִּי תְהִלָּתֵנוּ אָתָּה

וְהַעֲלֵה רְפוּאָה שְׁלֵמָה לְכָל מַכּוֹתֵינוּ

The following prayer for a sick person may be said here:

יְהִי רָצוֹן מִלְּפָנֶיךָ יהוה אֱלֹהַי וֵאלֹהֵי אֲבוֹתַי, שֶׁתִּשְׁלַח מְהֵרָה רְפוּאָה שְׁלֵמָה
מִן הַשָּׁמַיִם רְפוּאַת הַנֶּפֶשׁ וּרְפוּאַת הַגּוּף לַחוֹלֶה/לַחוֹלָה *name of patient*
בֶּן/בַּת *mother's name* בְּתוֹךְ שְׁאָר חוֹלֵי יִשְׂרָאֵל.

כִּי אֵל מֶלֶךְ רוֹפֵא נֶאֱמָן וְרַחֲמָן אָתָּה.

בָּרוּךְ אַתָּה יהוה, רוֹפֵא חוֹלֵי עַמּוֹ יִשְׂרָאֵל.

PROSPERITY

*The phrase "Grant dew and rain as a blessing" is said from December 4th
(in the year before a civil leap year, December 5th) until Pesaḥ. In Israel, it
is said from the 7th of Marḥeshvan. The phrase "Grant blessing" is said
from Ḥol HaMo'ed Pesaḥ until December 3rd (in the year before a civil leap
year, December 4th). In Israel it is said through the 6th of Marḥeshvan.*

בָּרֵךְ Bless this year for us, LORD our God,
and all its types of produce for good.

In winter: Grant dew and rain as a blessing

In other seasons: Grant blessing

on the face of the earth,
and from its goodness satisfy us,
blessing our year as the best of years.
Blessed are You, LORD,
who blesses the years.

INGATHERING OF EXILES

תְּקַע Sound the great shofar for our freedom,
raise high the banner to gather our exiles,
and gather us together from the four quarters of the earth.
Blessed are You, LORD,
who gathers the dispersed of His people Israel.

JUSTICE

הָשִׁיבָה Restore our judges as at first,
and our counselors as at the beginning,
and remove from us sorrow and sighing.
May You alone, LORD,
reign over us with loving-kindness and compassion,
and vindicate us in justice.
Blessed are You, LORD,
the King who loves righteousness and justice.
/ *Between Rosh HaShana & Yom Kippur, end the blessing:* the King of justice. /

ברכת השנים

The phrase וְתֵן טַל וּמָטָר לִבְרָכָה *is said from December 4th (in the year before a civil leap year, December 5th) until* פסח. *In* אֶרֶץ יִשְׂרָאֵל, *it is said from* ז מרחשון. *The phrase* וְתֵן בְּרָכָה *is said from* חול המועד פסח *until December 3rd (in the year before a civil leap year, December 4th). In* אֶרֶץ יִשְׂרָאֵל *it is said through* ז מרחשון.

בָּרֵךְ עָלֵינוּ יהוה אֱלֹהֵינוּ אֶת הַשָּׁנָה הַזֹּאת
וְאֶת כָּל מִינֵי תְבוּאָתָהּ, לְטוֹבָה

בחורף: וְתֵן טַל וּמָטָר לִבְרָכָה / בקיץ: וְתֵן בְּרָכָה

עַל פְּנֵי הָאֲדָמָה, וְשַׂבְּעֵנוּ מִטּוּבָהּ
וּבָרֵךְ שְׁנָתֵנוּ כַּשָּׁנִים הַטּוֹבוֹת.
בָּרוּךְ אַתָּה יהוה, מְבָרֵךְ הַשָּׁנִים.

קבוץ גלויות

תְּקַע בְּשׁוֹפָר גָּדוֹל לְחֵרוּתֵנוּ
וְשָׂא נֵס לְקַבֵּץ גָּלֻיּוֹתֵינוּ
וְקַבְּצֵנוּ יַחַד מֵאַרְבַּע כַּנְפוֹת הָאָרֶץ.
בָּרוּךְ אַתָּה יהוה, מְקַבֵּץ נִדְחֵי עַמּוֹ יִשְׂרָאֵל.

השבת המשפט

הָשִׁיבָה שׁוֹפְטֵינוּ כְּבָרִאשׁוֹנָה
וְיוֹעֲצֵינוּ כְּבַתְּחִלָּה
וְהָסֵר מִמֶּנּוּ יָגוֹן וַאֲנָחָה
וּמְלֹךְ עָלֵינוּ אַתָּה יהוה לְבַדְּךָ בְּחֶסֶד וּבְרַחֲמִים
וְצַדְּקֵנוּ בַּמִּשְׁפָּט.
בָּרוּךְ אַתָּה יהוה
מֶלֶךְ אוֹהֵב צְדָקָה וּמִשְׁפָּט. / בעשרת ימי תשובה: הַמֶּלֶךְ הַמִּשְׁפָּט. /

AGAINST INFORMERS

וְלַמַּלְשִׁינִים For the slanderers let there be no hope,
and may all wickedness perish in an instant.
May all Your people's enemies swiftly be cut down.
May You swiftly uproot, crush, cast down
and humble the arrogant swiftly in our days.
Blessed are You, LORD,
who destroys enemies and humbles the arrogant.

THE RIGHTEOUS

עַל הַצַּדִּיקִים To the righteous, the pious,
the elders of Your people the house of Israel,
the remnant of their scholars,
the righteous converts, and to us,
may Your compassion be aroused, LORD our God.
Grant a good reward to all
who sincerely trust in Your name.
Set our lot with them, so that we may never be ashamed,
for in You we trust.
Blessed are You, LORD,
who is the support and trust of the righteous.

REBUILDING JERUSALEM

וְלִירוּשָׁלַיִם To Jerusalem, Your city,
may You return in compassion,
and may You dwell in it as You promised.
May You rebuild it rapidly in our days
as an everlasting structure,
and install within it soon the throne of David.*
Blessed are You, LORD,
who builds Jerusalem.

*At Minḥa on Tisha B'Av, this blessing concludes with "Console" on page 310.

ברכת המינים

וְלַמַּלְשִׁינִים אַל תְּהִי תִקְוָה

וְכָל הָרִשְׁעָה כְּרֶגַע תֹּאבֵד

וְכָל אוֹיְבֵי עַמְּךָ מְהֵרָה יִכָּרֵתוּ

וְהַזֵּדִים מְהֵרָה תְעַקֵּר וּתְשַׁבֵּר וּתְמַגֵּר וְתַכְנִיעַ בִּמְהֵרָה בְיָמֵינוּ.

בָּרוּךְ אַתָּה יהוה, שׁוֹבֵר אוֹיְבִים וּמַכְנִיעַ זֵדִים.

על הצדיקים

עַל הַצַּדִּיקִים וְעַל הַחֲסִידִים

וְעַל זִקְנֵי עַמְּךָ בֵּית יִשְׂרָאֵל

וְעַל פְּלֵיטַת סוֹפְרֵיהֶם

וְעַל גֵּרֵי הַצֶּדֶק, וְעָלֵינוּ

יֶהֱמוּ רַחֲמֶיךָ יהוה אֱלֹהֵינוּ

וְתֵן שָׂכָר טוֹב לְכָל הַבּוֹטְחִים בְּשִׁמְךָ בֶּאֱמֶת

וְשִׂים חֶלְקֵנוּ עִמָּהֶם

וּלְעוֹלָם לֹא נֵבוֹשׁ כִּי בְךָ בָּטָחְנוּ.

בָּרוּךְ אַתָּה יהוה, מִשְׁעָן וּמִבְטָח לַצַּדִּיקִים.

בניין ירושלים

וְלִירוּשָׁלַיִם עִירְךָ בְּרַחֲמִים תָּשׁוּב

וְתִשְׁכֹּן בְּתוֹכָהּ כַּאֲשֶׁר דִּבַּרְתָּ

וּבְנֵה אוֹתָהּ בְּקָרוֹב בְּיָמֵינוּ בִּנְיַן עוֹלָם

וְכִסֵּא דָוִד מְהֵרָה לְתוֹכָהּ תָּכִין.*

*בָּרוּךְ אַתָּה יהוה, בּוֹנֵה יְרוּשָׁלָיִם.

*At מנחה on תשעה באב, this blessing concludes with נַחֵם on page 311.

KINGDOM OF DAVID

אֶת צֶמַח May the offshoot of Your servant David soon flower,
and may his pride be raised high by Your salvation,
for we wait for Your salvation all day.
Blessed are You, LORD,
who makes the glory of salvation flourish.

RESPONSE TO PRAYER

שְׁמַע קוֹלֵנוּ Listen to our voice, LORD our God.
Spare us and have compassion on us,
and in compassion and favor accept our prayer,
for You, God, listen to prayers and pleas.
Do not turn us away, O our King,
empty-handed from Your presence,*

*At Minḥa, at this point on fast days, the congregation adds "Answer us" on page 314.
In times of drought in Israel, some add "And answer us" on page 684.

for You listen with compassion
to the prayer of Your people Israel.
Blessed are You, LORD,
who listens to prayer.

TEMPLE SERVICE

רְצֵה Find favor, LORD our God,
in Your people Israel and their prayer.
Restore the service to Your most holy House,
and accept in love and favor
the fire-offerings of Israel and their prayer.
May the service of Your people Israel
always find favor with You.

On Rosh Ḥodesh and Ḥol HaMo'ed say:
אֱלֹהֵינוּ Our God and God of our ancestors, may there rise, come,
reach, appear, be favored, heard, regarded and remembered before

משיח בן דוד

אֶת צֶמַח דָּוִד עַבְדְּךָ מְהֵרָה תַצְמִיחַ
וְקַרְנוֹ תָּרוּם בִּישׁוּעָתֶךָ
כִּי לִישׁוּעָתְךָ קִוִּינוּ כָּל הַיּוֹם.
בָּרוּךְ אַתָּה יהוה, מַצְמִיחַ קֶרֶן יְשׁוּעָה.

שומע תפלה

שְׁמַע קוֹלֵנוּ יהוה אֱלֹהֵינוּ
חוּס וְרַחֵם עָלֵינוּ
וְקַבֵּל בְּרַחֲמִים וּבְרָצוֹן אֶת תְּפִלָּתֵנוּ
כִּי אֵל שׁוֹמֵעַ תְּפִלּוֹת וְתַחֲנוּנִים אָתָּה
וּמִלְּפָנֶיךָ מַלְכֵּנוּ רֵיקָם אַל תְּשִׁיבֵנוּ*

*At מנחה, *at this point on fast days, the* קהל *adds* עֲנֵנוּ *on page 315.*
In times of drought in ארץ ישראל, *some add* וְעֲנֵנוּ *on page 685.*

כִּי אַתָּה שׁוֹמֵעַ תְּפִלַּת עַמְּךָ יִשְׂרָאֵל בְּרַחֲמִים.
בָּרוּךְ אַתָּה יהוה, שׁוֹמֵעַ תְּפִלָּה.

עבודה

רְצֵה יהוה אֱלֹהֵינוּ בְּעַמְּךָ יִשְׂרָאֵל וּבִתְפִלָּתָם
וְהָשֵׁב אֶת הָעֲבוֹדָה לִדְבִיר בֵּיתֶךָ
וְאִשֵּׁי יִשְׂרָאֵל וּתְפִלָּתָם בְּאַהֲבָה תְקַבֵּל בְּרָצוֹן
וּתְהִי לְרָצוֹן תָּמִיד עֲבוֹדַת יִשְׂרָאֵל עַמֶּךָ.

On ראש חודש *and* חול המועד *say:*

אֱלֹהֵינוּ וֵאלֹהֵי אֲבוֹתֵינוּ, יַעֲלֶה וְיָבוֹא וְיַגִּיעַ, וְיֵרָאֶה וְיֵרָצֶה וְיִשָּׁמַע,
וְיִפָּקֵד וְיִזָּכֵר זִכְרוֹנֵנוּ וּפִקְדוֹנֵנוּ וְזִכְרוֹן אֲבוֹתֵינוּ, וְזִכְרוֹן מָשִׁיחַ בֶּן

You, our recollection and remembrance, as well as the remembrance of our ancestors, and of the Messiah son of David Your servant, and of Jerusalem Your holy city, and of all Your people the house of Israel – for deliverance and well-being, grace, loving-kindness and compassion, life and peace, on this day of:

> *On Rosh Ḥodesh:* Rosh Ḥodesh.
>
> *On Pesaḥ:* the Festival of Matzot.
>
> *On Sukkot:* the Festival of Sukkot.

On it remember us, Lord our God, for good; recollect us for blessing, and deliver us for life. In accord with Your promise of salvation and compassion, spare us and be gracious to us; have compassion on us and deliver us, for our eyes are turned to You because You, God, are a gracious and compassionate King.

וְתֶחֱזֶינָה And may our eyes witness Your return
to Zion in compassion.
Blessed are You, Lord,
who restores His Presence to Zion.

THANKSGIVING

Bow at the first nine words.

מוֹדִים We give thanks to You,
for You are the Lord our God and God of our ancestors
for ever and all time.
You are the Rock of our lives,
Shield of our salvation from generation to generation.
We will thank You and declare Your praise for our lives,
which are entrusted into Your hand; for our souls,
which are placed in Your charge; for Your miracles
which are with us every day;
and for Your wonders and favors
at all times, evening, morning and midday.
You are good – for Your compassion never fails.
You are compassionate – for Your loving-kindnesses never cease.
We have always placed our hope in You.

דָּוִד עַבְדֶּךָ, וְזִכְרוֹן יְרוּשָׁלַיִם עִיר קָדְשֶׁךָ, וְזִכְרוֹן כָּל עַמְּךָ בֵּית יִשְׂרָאֵל, לְפָנֶיךָ, לִפְלֵיטָה לְטוֹבָה, לְחֵן וּלְחֶסֶד וּלְרַחֲמִים, לְחַיִּים וּלְשָׁלוֹם בְּיוֹם

בראש חודש: **רֹאשׁ הַחֹדֶשׁ** / בפסח: **חַג הַמַּצּוֹת** / בסוכות: **חַג הַסֻּכּוֹת**

הַזֶּה. זָכְרֵנוּ יהוה אֱלֹהֵינוּ בּוֹ לְטוֹבָה, וּפָקְדֵנוּ בוֹ לִבְרָכָה, וְהוֹשִׁיעֵנוּ בוֹ לְחַיִּים. וּבִדְבַר יְשׁוּעָה וְרַחֲמִים, חוּס וְחָנֵּנוּ וְרַחֵם עָלֵינוּ וְהוֹשִׁיעֵנוּ, כִּי אֵלֶיךָ עֵינֵינוּ, כִּי אֵל מֶלֶךְ חַנּוּן וְרַחוּם אָתָּה.

וְתֶחֱזֶינָה עֵינֵינוּ בְּשׁוּבְךָ לְצִיּוֹן בְּרַחֲמִים.
בָּרוּךְ אַתָּה יהוה, הַמַּחֲזִיר שְׁכִינָתוֹ לְצִיּוֹן.

הוֹדָאָה

Bow at the first five words.

מוֹדִים אֲנַחְנוּ לָךְ
שָׁאַתָּה הוּא יהוה אֱלֹהֵינוּ וֵאלֹהֵי אֲבוֹתֵינוּ לְעוֹלָם וָעֶד.
צוּר חַיֵּינוּ, מָגֵן יִשְׁעֵנוּ
אַתָּה הוּא לְדוֹר וָדוֹר.
נוֹדֶה לְּךָ וּנְסַפֵּר תְּהִלָּתֶךָ
עַל חַיֵּינוּ הַמְּסוּרִים בְּיָדֶךָ
וְעַל נִשְׁמוֹתֵינוּ הַפְּקוּדוֹת לָךְ
וְעַל נִסֶּיךָ שֶׁבְּכָל יוֹם עִמָּנוּ
וְעַל נִפְלְאוֹתֶיךָ וְטוֹבוֹתֶיךָ
שֶׁבְּכָל עֵת, עֶרֶב וָבֹקֶר וְצָהֳרָיִם.
הַטּוֹב, כִּי לֹא כָלוּ רַחֲמֶיךָ וְהַמְרַחֵם
כִּי לֹא תַמּוּ חֲסָדֶיךָ
מֵעוֹלָם קִוִּינוּ לָךְ.

On Hanukka:

עַל הַנִּסִּים [We thank You also] for the miracles, the redemption, the mighty deeds, the salvations, and the victories in battle which You performed for our ancestors in those days, at this time.

בִּימֵי מַתִּתְיָהוּ In the days of Mattityahu, son of Yoḥanan, the High Priest, the Hasmonean, and his sons, the wicked Greek kingdom rose up against Your people Israel to make them forget Your Torah and to force them to transgress the statutes of Your will. It was then that You in Your great compassion stood by them in the time of their distress. You championed their cause, judged their claim, and avenged their wrong. You delivered the strong into the hands of the weak, the many into the hands of the few, the impure into the hands of the pure, the wicked into the hands of the righteous, and the arrogant into the hands of those who were engaged in the study of Your Torah. You made for Yourself great and holy renown in Your world, and for Your people Israel You performed a great salvation and redemption as of this very day. Your children then entered the holiest part of Your House, cleansed Your Temple, purified Your Sanctuary, kindled lights in Your holy courts, and designated these eight days of Ḥanukka for giving thanks and praise to Your great name.

Continue with "For all these things."

On Purim:

עַל הַנִּסִּים [We thank You also] for the miracles, the redemption, the mighty deeds, the salvations, and the victories in battle which You performed for our ancestors in those days at this time.

בִּימֵי מָרְדְּכַי In the days of Mordekhai and Esther, in Shushan the capital, the wicked Haman rose up against them and sought to destroy, slay and exterminate all the Jews, young and old, children and women, on one day, the thirteenth day of the twelfth month, which is the month of Adar, and to plunder their possessions. Then You in Your great compassion thwarted his counsel, frustrated his plans, and caused his scheme to recoil on his own head, so that they hanged him and his sons on the gallows.

Esther 3

Continue with "For all these things."

וְעַל כֻּלָּם For all these things may Your name be blessed and exalted, our King, continually, for ever and all time.

Between Rosh HaShana And write, for a good life,
& Yom Kippur: all the children of Your covenant.

Let all that lives thank You, Selah! and praise Your name in truth, God, our Savior and Help, Selah!
Blessed are You, Lord, whose name is "the Good" and to whom thanks are due.

בחנוכה:

עַל הַנִּסִּים וְעַל הַפֻּרְקָן וְעַל הַגְּבוּרוֹת וְעַל הַתְּשׁוּעוֹת וְעַל הַמִּלְחָמוֹת
שֶׁעָשִׂיתָ לַאֲבוֹתֵינוּ בַּיָּמִים הָהֵם בַּזְּמַן הַזֶּה.

בִּימֵי מַתִּתְיָהוּ בֶּן יוֹחָנָן כֹּהֵן גָּדוֹל חַשְׁמוֹנַאי וּבָנָיו, כְּשֶׁעָמְדָה מַלְכוּת יָוָן
הָרְשָׁעָה עַל עַמְּךָ יִשְׂרָאֵל לְהַשְׁכִּיחָם תּוֹרָתֶךָ וּלְהַעֲבִירָם מֵחֻקֵּי רְצוֹנֶךָ,
וְאַתָּה בְּרַחֲמֶיךָ הָרַבִּים עָמַדְתָּ לָהֶם בְּעֵת צָרָתָם, רַבְתָּ אֶת רִיבָם, דַּנְתָּ
אֶת דִּינָם, נָקַמְתָּ אֶת נִקְמָתָם, מָסַרְתָּ גִבּוֹרִים בְּיַד חַלָּשִׁים, וְרַבִּים בְּיַד
מְעַטִּים, וּטְמֵאִים בְּיַד טְהוֹרִים, וּרְשָׁעִים בְּיַד צַדִּיקִים, וְזֵדִים בְּיַד עוֹסְקֵי
תוֹרָתֶךָ, וּלְךָ עָשִׂיתָ שֵׁם גָּדוֹל וְקָדוֹשׁ בְּעוֹלָמֶךָ, וּלְעַמְּךָ יִשְׂרָאֵל עָשִׂיתָ
תְּשׁוּעָה גְדוֹלָה וּפֻרְקָן כְּהַיּוֹם הַזֶּה. וְאַחַר כֵּן בָּאוּ בָנֶיךָ לִדְבִיר בֵּיתֶךָ,
וּפִנּוּ אֶת הֵיכָלֶךָ, וְטִהֲרוּ אֶת מִקְדָּשֶׁךָ, וְהִדְלִיקוּ נֵרוֹת בְּחַצְרוֹת קָדְשֶׁךָ,
וְקָבְעוּ שְׁמוֹנַת יְמֵי חֲנֻכָּה אֵלּוּ, לְהוֹדוֹת וּלְהַלֵּל לְשִׁמְךָ הַגָּדוֹל.

Continue with וְעַל כֻּלָּם.

בפורים:

עַל הַנִּסִּים וְעַל הַפֻּרְקָן וְעַל הַגְּבוּרוֹת וְעַל הַתְּשׁוּעוֹת וְעַל הַמִּלְחָמוֹת
שֶׁעָשִׂיתָ לַאֲבוֹתֵינוּ בַּיָּמִים הָהֵם בַּזְּמַן הַזֶּה.

אסתר ג בִּימֵי מָרְדְּכַי וְאֶסְתֵּר בְּשׁוּשַׁן הַבִּירָה, כְּשֶׁעָמַד עֲלֵיהֶם הָמָן הָרָשָׁע,
בִּקֵּשׁ לְהַשְׁמִיד לַהֲרֹג וּלְאַבֵּד אֶת־כָּל־הַיְּהוּדִים מִנַּעַר וְעַד־זָקֵן טַף
וְנָשִׁים בְּיוֹם אֶחָד, בִּשְׁלוֹשָׁה עָשָׂר לְחֹדֶשׁ שְׁנֵים־עָשָׂר, הוּא־חֹדֶשׁ אֲדָר,
וּשְׁלָלָם לָבוֹז: וְאַתָּה בְּרַחֲמֶיךָ הָרַבִּים הֵפַרְתָּ אֶת עֲצָתוֹ, וְקִלְקַלְתָּ אֶת
מַחֲשַׁבְתּוֹ, וַהֲשֵׁבוֹתָ לּוֹ גְּמוּלוֹ בְּרֹאשׁוֹ, וְתָלוּ אוֹתוֹ וְאֶת בָּנָיו עַל הָעֵץ.

Continue with וְעַל כֻּלָּם.

וְעַל כֻּלָּם יִתְבָּרַךְ וְיִתְרוֹמַם שִׁמְךָ מַלְכֵּנוּ תָּמִיד לְעוֹלָם וָעֶד.

בעשרת ימי תשובה: וּכְתֹב לְחַיִּים טוֹבִים כָּל בְּנֵי בְרִיתֶךָ.

וְכֹל הַחַיִּים יוֹדוּךָ סֶּלָה, וִיהַלְלוּ אֶת שִׁמְךָ בֶּאֱמֶת
הָאֵל יְשׁוּעָתֵנוּ וְעֶזְרָתֵנוּ סֶלָה.
בָּרוּךְ אַתָּה יהוה, הַטּוֹב שִׁמְךָ וּלְךָ נָאֶה לְהוֹדוֹת.

PEACE

In Minḥa and Ma'ariv

שָׁלוֹם רָב Grant
great peace
to Your people Israel
for ever,
for You are
the sovereign LORD
of all peace;
and may it
be good
in Your eyes
to bless
Your people Israel
at every time,
at every hour,
with Your peace.

In Shaḥarit and in Minḥa on fast days:

שִׂים שָׁלוֹם Grant peace,
goodness and blessing, grace,
loving-kindness and compassion
to us and all Israel Your people.
Bless us, our Father, all as one,
with the light of Your face,
for by the light of Your face
You have given us, LORD our God,
the Torah of life and love of kindness,
righteousness, blessing, compassion,
life and peace.
May it be good in Your eyes
to bless Your people Israel
at every time, in every hour,
with Your peace.

Between Rosh HaShana & Yom Kippur: In the book of life, blessing, peace and prosperity, may we and all Your people the house of Israel be remembered and written before You for a good life, and for peace.*

Blessed are You, LORD, who blesses His people Israel with peace.

*Between Rosh HaShana and Yom Kippur outside Israel, many end the blessing:
Blessed are You, LORD, who makes peace.

Some say the following verse:

May the words of my mouth and the meditation of my heart
find favor before You, LORD, my Rock and Redeemer.

Ps. 19

אֱלֹהַי My God,
guard my tongue from evil and my lips from deceitful speech.
To those who curse me, let my soul be silent;
may my soul be to all like the dust.
Open my heart to Your Torah
and let my soul pursue Your commandments.
As for all who plan evil against me,
swiftly thwart their counsel and frustrate their plans.

Berakhot 17a

ברכת שלום

In מנחה and in שחרית on fast days:	In מעריב and מנחה
שִׂים שָׁלוֹם טוֹבָה וּבְרָכָה	שָׁלוֹם רָב
חֵן וָחֶסֶד וְרַחֲמִים	עַל יִשְׂרָאֵל עַמְּךָ
עָלֵינוּ וְעַל כָּל יִשְׂרָאֵל עַמֶּךָ.	תָּשִׂים לְעוֹלָם
בָּרְכֵנוּ אָבִינוּ כֻּלָּנוּ כְּאֶחָד בְּאוֹר פָּנֶיךָ	כִּי אַתָּה הוּא
כִּי בְאוֹר פָּנֶיךָ נָתַתָּ לָּנוּ יהוה אֱלֹהֵינוּ	מֶלֶךְ אָדוֹן
תּוֹרַת חַיִּים וְאַהֲבַת חֶסֶד	לְכָל הַשָּׁלוֹם.
וּצְדָקָה וּבְרָכָה וְרַחֲמִים	וְטוֹב בְּעֵינֶיךָ
וְחַיִּים וְשָׁלוֹם.	לְבָרֵךְ אֶת עַמְּךָ יִשְׂרָאֵל
וְטוֹב בְּעֵינֶיךָ לְבָרֵךְ אֶת עַמְּךָ יִשְׂרָאֵל	בְּכָל עֵת וּבְכָל שָׁעָה
בְּכָל עֵת וּבְכָל שָׁעָה בִּשְׁלוֹמֶךָ.	בִּשְׁלוֹמֶךָ.

בעשרת ימי תשובה: בְּסֵפֶר חַיִּים, בְּרָכָה וְשָׁלוֹם, וּפַרְנָסָה טוֹבָה
נִזָּכֵר וְנִכָּתֵב לְפָנֶיךָ, אֲנַחְנוּ וְכָל עַמְּךָ בֵּית יִשְׂרָאֵל
לְחַיִּים טוֹבִים וּלְשָׁלוֹם.*

בָּרוּךְ אַתָּה יהוה, הַמְבָרֵךְ אֶת עַמּוֹ יִשְׂרָאֵל בַּשָּׁלוֹם.

*During the עשרת ימי תשובה in חוץ לארץ, many end the blessing:
בָּרוּךְ אַתָּה יהוה, עוֹשֶׂה הַשָּׁלוֹם.

Some say the following verse:
תהלים יט
יִהְיוּ לְרָצוֹן אִמְרֵי־פִי וְהֶגְיוֹן לִבִּי לְפָנֶיךָ, יהוה צוּרִי וְגֹאֲלִי:

ברכות יז.
אֱלֹהַי
נְצֹר לְשׁוֹנִי מֵרָע וּשְׂפָתַי מִדַּבֵּר מִרְמָה
וְלִמְקַלְלַי נַפְשִׁי תִדֹּם, וְנַפְשִׁי כֶּעָפָר לַכֹּל תִּהְיֶה.
פְּתַח לִבִּי בְּתוֹרָתֶךָ, וּבְמִצְוֹתֶיךָ תִּרְדֹּף נַפְשִׁי.
וְכָל הַחוֹשְׁבִים עָלַי רָעָה, מְהֵרָה הָפֵר עֲצָתָם וְקַלְקֵל מַחֲשַׁבְתָּם.

Act for the sake of Your name; act for the sake of Your right hand;
    act for the sake of Your holiness; act for the sake of Your Torah.

That Your beloved ones may be delivered,   *Ps. 60*
save with Your right hand and answer me.

May the words of my mouth   *Ps. 19*
and the meditation of my heart find favor before You,
LORD, my Rock and Redeemer.

Bow, take three steps back, then bow, first left, then right, then center, while saying:

May He who makes peace in His high places,
make peace for us and all Israel – and say: Amen.

יְהִי רָצוֹן May it be Your will, LORD our God and God of our ancestors,
that the Temple be rebuilt speedily in our days, and grant us a share in Your Torah.
And there we will serve You with reverence,
as in the days of old and as in former years.

Then the offering of Judah and Jerusalem   *Mal. 3*
will be pleasing to the LORD as in the days of old and as in former years.

When praying with a minyan, the Amida is repeated aloud by the Leader.
at Shaharit on page 138 and at Minha on page 280.

On Motza'ei Shabbat (except when Yom Tov or Erev Pesah falls in the following week), the
Leader continues with Half Kaddish on page 400, then "May the pleasantness" on page 400.
On Motza'ei Shabbat when Yom Tov falls in the following week, the service continues on page 406.
On other evenings the Leader says Full Kaddish:

FULL KADDISH

Leader: יִתְגַּדַּל Magnified and sanctified may His great name be,
in the world He created by His will.
May He establish His kingdom
in your lifetime and in your days,
and in the lifetime of all the house of Israel,
swiftly and soon – and say: Amen.

All: May His great name be blessed for ever and all time.

Leader: Blessed and praised, glorified and exalted,
raised and honored, uplifted and lauded be
the name of the Holy One, blessed be He,

עֲשֵׂה לְמַעַן שְׁמֶךָ, עֲשֵׂה לְמַעַן יְמִינֶךָ

עֲשֵׂה לְמַעַן קְדֻשָּׁתֶךָ, עֲשֵׂה לְמַעַן תּוֹרָתֶךָ.

תהלים ס

לְמַעַן יֵחָלְצוּן יְדִידֶיךָ, הוֹשִׁיעָה יְמִינְךָ וַעֲנֵנִי:

תהלים יט

יִהְיוּ לְרָצוֹן אִמְרֵי־פִי וְהֶגְיוֹן לִבִּי לְפָנֶיךָ, יהוה צוּרִי וְגֹאֲלִי:

Bow, take three steps back, then bow, first left, then right, then center, while saying:

עֹשֶׂה שָׁלוֹם/ בעשרת ימי תשובה: הַשָּׁלוֹם/ בִּמְרוֹמָיו

הוּא יַעֲשֶׂה שָׁלוֹם עָלֵינוּ וְעַל כָּל יִשְׂרָאֵל, וְאִמְרוּ אָמֵן.

יְהִי רָצוֹן מִלְּפָנֶיךָ יהוה אֱלֹהֵינוּ וֵאלֹהֵי אֲבוֹתֵינוּ

שֶׁיִּבָּנֶה בֵּית הַמִּקְדָּשׁ בִּמְהֵרָה בְיָמֵינוּ, וְתֵן חֶלְקֵנוּ בְּתוֹרָתֶךָ

וְשָׁם נַעֲבָדְךָ בְּיִרְאָה כִּימֵי עוֹלָם וּכְשָׁנִים קַדְמֹנִיּוֹת.

מלאכי ג

וְעָרְבָה לַיהוה מִנְחַת יְהוּדָה וִירוּשָׁלָיִם כִּימֵי עוֹלָם וּכְשָׁנִים קַדְמֹנִיּוֹת:

When praying with a מנין, *the* עמידה *is repeated aloud by the* שליח ציבור
at שחרית *on page 139 and at* מנחה *on page 281.*

On מוצאי שבת (except when יום טוב or ערב פסח falls in the following week),
the שליח ציבור *continues with* חצי קדיש *on page 401, then* וִיהִי נֹעַם *on page 401.*
On מוצאי שבת *when* יום טוב *falls in the following week, the service continues on page 407.*
On other evenings the שליח ציבור *says* קדיש שלם:

קדיש שלם

ש״ץ: יִתְגַּדַּל וְיִתְקַדַּשׁ שְׁמֵהּ רַבָּא (קהל: אָמֵן)

בְּעָלְמָא דִּי בְרָא כִרְעוּתֵהּ, וְיַמְלִיךְ מַלְכוּתֵהּ

בְּחַיֵּיכוֹן וּבְיוֹמֵיכוֹן וּבְחַיֵּי דְכָל בֵּית יִשְׂרָאֵל

בַּעֲגָלָא וּבִזְמַן קָרִיב, וְאִמְרוּ אָמֵן. (קהל: אָמֵן)

קהל
 וש״ץ: יְהֵא שְׁמֵהּ רַבָּא מְבָרַךְ לְעָלַם וּלְעָלְמֵי עָלְמַיָּא.

ש״ץ: יִתְבָּרַךְ וְיִשְׁתַּבַּח וְיִתְפָּאַר וְיִתְרוֹמַם וְיִתְנַשֵּׂא

וְיִתְהַדָּר וְיִתְעַלֶּה וְיִתְהַלָּל

שְׁמֵהּ דְּקֻדְשָׁא בְּרִיךְ הוּא (קהל: בְּרִיךְ הוּא)

beyond any blessing,
song, praise and consolation
uttered in the world – and say: Amen.

May the prayers and pleas of all Israel
be accepted by their Father in heaven –
and say: Amen.

May there be great peace from heaven,
and life for us and all Israel –
and say: Amen.

Bow, take three steps back, as if taking leave of the Divine Presence,
then bow, first left, then right, then center, while saying:

May He who makes peace in His high places,
make peace for us and all Israel –
and say: Amen.

On Yom HaAtzma'ut (in Israel and many communities outside Israel)
the service continues with "Listen, Israel" on page 580.
From the second night of Pesaḥ until the night before Shavuot, the Omer is counted here (page 388).
On Purim, Megillat Esther is read; on Tisha B'Av, Megillat Eikha is read.

Stand while saying Aleinu. Bow at ˙.

עָלֵינוּ It is our duty to praise the Master of all,
and ascribe greatness to the Author of creation,
who has not made us like the nations of the lands
nor placed us like the families of the earth;
who has not made our portion like theirs,
nor our destiny like all their multitudes.
(For they worship vanity and emptiness,
and pray to a god who cannot save.)
˙But we bow in worship and thank the Supreme King of kings,
the Holy One, blessed be He,
who extends the heavens and establishes the earth,
whose throne of glory is in the heavens above,
and whose power's Presence is in the highest of heights.

לְעֵלָּא מִן כָּל בִּרְכָתָא

/בעשרת ימי תשובה: לְעֵלָּא לְעֵלָּא מִכָּל בִּרְכָתָא/

וְשִׁירָתָא, תֻּשְׁבְּחָתָא וְנֶחֱמָתָא

דַּאֲמִירָן בְּעָלְמָא, וְאִמְרוּ אָמֵן. (קהל: אָמֵן)

תִּתְקַבֵּל צְלוֹתְהוֹן וּבָעוּתְהוֹן דְּכָל יִשְׂרָאֵל

קֳדָם אֲבוּהוֹן דִּי בִשְׁמַיָּא, וְאִמְרוּ אָמֵן. (קהל: אָמֵן)

יְהֵא שְׁלָמָא רַבָּא מִן שְׁמַיָּא

וְחַיִּים, עָלֵינוּ וְעַל כָּל יִשְׂרָאֵל, וְאִמְרוּ אָמֵן. (קהל: אָמֵן)

*Bow, take three steps back, as if taking leave of the Divine Presence,
then bow, first left, then right, then center, while saying:*

עֹשֶׂה שָׁלוֹם /בעשרת ימי תשובה: הַשָּׁלוֹם/ בִּמְרוֹמָיו

הוּא יַעֲשֶׂה שָׁלוֹם עָלֵינוּ

וְעַל כָּל יִשְׂרָאֵל, וְאִמְרוּ אָמֵן. (קהל: אָמֵן)

On חוץ לארץ (in ארץ ישראל and many communities in יום העצמאות)
the service continues with שמע ישראל on page 581.
From the second night of פסח until the night before שבועות, the עומר is counted here (page 389).
On פורים, מגילת אסתר is read; on תשעה באב, מגילת איכה is read.

Stand while saying עלינו. Bow at ˙.

עָלֵינוּ לְשַׁבֵּחַ לַאֲדוֹן הַכֹּל, לָתֵת גְּדֻלָּה לְיוֹצֵר בְּרֵאשִׁית
שֶׁלֹּא עָשָׂנוּ כְּגוֹיֵי הָאֲרָצוֹת, וְלֹא שָׂמָנוּ כְּמִשְׁפְּחוֹת הָאֲדָמָה
שֶׁלֹּא שָׂם חֶלְקֵנוּ כָּהֶם, וְגוֹרָלֵנוּ כְּכָל הֲמוֹנָם.
(שֶׁהֵם מִשְׁתַּחֲוִים לְהֶבֶל וָרִיק וּמִתְפַּלְלִים אֶל אֵל לֹא יוֹשִׁיעַ.)
˙וַאֲנַחְנוּ כּוֹרְעִים וּמִשְׁתַּחֲוִים וּמוֹדִים
לִפְנֵי מֶלֶךְ מַלְכֵי הַמְּלָכִים, הַקָּדוֹשׁ בָּרוּךְ הוּא
שֶׁהוּא נוֹטֶה שָׁמַיִם וְיוֹסֵד אָרֶץ
וּמוֹשַׁב יְקָרוֹ בַּשָּׁמַיִם מִמַּעַל, וּשְׁכִינַת עֻזּוֹ בְּגָבְהֵי מְרוֹמִים.

He is our God; there is no other.
Truly He is our King, there is none else,
   as it is written in His Torah:
"You shall know and take to heart this day   *Deut. 4*
   that the LORD is God,
   in heaven above and on earth below.
   There is no other."

Therefore, we place our hope in You, LORD our God,
   that we may soon see the glory of Your power,
   when You will remove abominations from the earth,
   and idols will be utterly destroyed,
   when the world will be perfected
   under the sovereignty of the Almighty,
   when all humanity will call on Your name,
   to turn all the earth's wicked toward You.
All the world's inhabitants will realize and know
   that to You every knee must bow and every tongue swear loyalty.
Before You, LORD our God, they will kneel and bow down
   and give honor to Your glorious name.
They will all accept the yoke of Your kingdom,
   and You will reign over them soon and for ever.
For the kingdom is Yours,
   and to all eternity You will reign in glory,
   as it is written in Your Torah:
"The LORD will reign for ever and ever."   *Ex. 15*
▸ And it is said: "Then the LORD shall be King over all the earth;   *Zech. 14*
   on that day the LORD shall be One and His name One."

Some add:

Have no fear of sudden terror or of the ruin when it overtakes the wicked.   *Prov. 3*
Devise your strategy, but it will be thwarted; propose your plan,   *Is. 8*
   but it will not stand, for God is with us.
When you grow old, I will still be the same.   *Is. 46*
When your hair turns gray, I will still carry you.
I made you, I will bear you, I will carry you, and I will rescue you.

הוּא אֱלֹהֵינוּ, אֵין עוֹד.
אֱמֶת מַלְכֵּנוּ, אֶפֶס זוּלָתוֹ
כַּכָּתוּב בְּתוֹרָתוֹ

דברים ד

וְיָדַעְתָּ הַיּוֹם וַהֲשֵׁבֹתָ אֶל־לְבָבֶךָ
כִּי יהוה הוּא הָאֱלֹהִים בַּשָּׁמַיִם מִמַּעַל וְעַל־הָאָרֶץ מִתָּחַת
אֵין עוֹד:

עַל כֵּן נְקַוֶּה לְּךָ יהוה אֱלֹהֵינוּ
לִרְאוֹת מְהֵרָה בְּתִפְאֶרֶת עֻזֶּךָ
לְהַעֲבִיר גִּלּוּלִים מִן הָאָרֶץ, וְהָאֱלִילִים כָּרוֹת יִכָּרֵתוּן
לְתַקֵּן עוֹלָם בְּמַלְכוּת שַׁדַּי.
וְכָל בְּנֵי בָשָׂר יִקְרְאוּ בִשְׁמֶךָ לְהַפְנוֹת אֵלֶיךָ כָּל רִשְׁעֵי אָרֶץ.
יַכִּירוּ וְיֵדְעוּ כָּל יוֹשְׁבֵי תֵבֵל
כִּי לְךָ תִּכְרַע כָּל בֶּרֶךְ, תִּשָּׁבַע כָּל לָשׁוֹן.
לְפָנֶיךָ יהוה אֱלֹהֵינוּ יִכְרְעוּ וְיִפֹּלוּ, וְלִכְבוֹד שִׁמְךָ יְקָר יִתֵּנוּ
וִיקַבְּלוּ כֻלָּם אֶת עֹל מַלְכוּתֶךָ
וְתִמְלֹךְ עֲלֵיהֶם מְהֵרָה לְעוֹלָם וָעֶד.
כִּי הַמַּלְכוּת שֶׁלְּךָ הִיא וּלְעוֹלְמֵי עַד תִּמְלֹךְ בְּכָבוֹד

שמות טו

כַּכָּתוּב בְּתוֹרָתֶךָ, יהוה יִמְלֹךְ לְעֹלָם וָעֶד:

זכריה יד

‹ וְנֶאֱמַר, וְהָיָה יהוה לְמֶלֶךְ עַל־כָּל־הָאָרֶץ
בַּיּוֹם הַהוּא יִהְיֶה יהוה אֶחָד וּשְׁמוֹ אֶחָד:

Some add:

משלי ג

אַל־תִּירָא מִפַּחַד פִּתְאֹם וּמִשֹּׁאַת רְשָׁעִים כִּי תָבֹא:

ישעיה ח

עֻצוּ עֵצָה וְתֻפָר, דַּבְּרוּ דָבָר וְלֹא יָקוּם, כִּי עִמָּנוּ אֵל:

ישעיה מו

וְעַד־זִקְנָה אֲנִי הוּא, וְעַד־שֵׂיבָה אֲנִי אֶסְבֹּל
אֲנִי עָשִׂיתִי וַאֲנִי אֶשָּׂא וַאֲנִי אֶסְבֹּל וַאֲמַלֵּט:

MOURNER'S KADDISH

The following prayer, said by mourners, requires the presence of a minyan.
A transliteration can be found on page 921.

Mourner: יִתְגַּדַּל Magnified and sanctified
may His great name be,
in the world He created by His will.
May He establish His kingdom
in your lifetime
and in your days,
and in the lifetime of all the house of Israel,
swiftly and soon –
and say: Amen.

All: May His great name be blessed
for ever and all time.

Mourner: Blessed and praised,
glorified and exalted,
raised and honored,
uplifted and lauded
be the name of the Holy One,
blessed be He,
beyond any blessing,
song, praise and consolation
uttered in the world –
and say: Amen.

May there be great peace from heaven,
and life for us and all Israel –
and say: Amen.

Bow, take three steps back, as if taking leave of the Divine Presence,
then bow, first left, then right, then center, while saying:
May He who makes peace in His high places,
make peace for us and all Israel –
and say: Amen.

קדיש יתום

The following prayer, said by mourners, requires the presence of a מִנְיָן.
A transliteration can be found on page 921.

אבל יִתְגַּדַּל וְיִתְקַדַּשׁ שְׁמֵהּ רַבָּא (קהל: אָמֵן)
בְּעָלְמָא דִּי בְרָא כִרְעוּתֵהּ
וְיַמְלִיךְ מַלְכוּתֵהּ
בְּחַיֵּיכוֹן וּבְיוֹמֵיכוֹן וּבְחַיֵּי דְכָל בֵּית יִשְׂרָאֵל
בַּעֲגָלָא וּבִזְמַן קָרִיב
וְאִמְרוּ אָמֵן. (קהל: אָמֵן)

קהל יְהֵא שְׁמֵהּ רַבָּא מְבָרַךְ לְעָלַם וּלְעָלְמֵי עָלְמַיָּא.
ואבל:

אבל: יִתְבָּרַךְ וְיִשְׁתַּבַּח וְיִתְפָּאַר
וְיִתְרוֹמַם וְיִתְנַשֵּׂא וְיִתְהַדָּר וְיִתְעַלֶּה וְיִתְהַלָּל
שְׁמֵהּ דְּקֻדְשָׁא בְּרִיךְ הוּא (קהל: בְּרִיךְ הוּא)
לְעֵלָּא מִן כָּל בִּרְכָתָא
/בעשרת ימי תשובה: לְעֵלָּא לְעֵלָּא מִכָּל בִּרְכָתָא/
וְשִׁירָתָא, תֻּשְׁבְּחָתָא וְנֶחֱמָתָא
דַּאֲמִירָן בְּעָלְמָא
וְאִמְרוּ אָמֵן. (קהל: אָמֵן)

יְהֵא שְׁלָמָא רַבָּא מִן שְׁמַיָּא
וְחַיִּים, עָלֵינוּ וְעַל כָּל יִשְׂרָאֵל
וְאִמְרוּ אָמֵן. (קהל: אָמֵן)

Bow, take three steps back, as if taking leave of the Divine Presence,
then bow, first left, then right, then center, while saying:

עֹשֶׂה שָׁלוֹם/ בעשרת ימי תשובה: הַשָּׁלוֹם/ בִּמְרוֹמָיו
הוּא יַעֲשֶׂה שָׁלוֹם עָלֵינוּ וְעַל כָּל יִשְׂרָאֵל
וְאִמְרוּ אָמֵן. (קהל: אָמֵן)

*From the second day of Rosh Ḥodesh Elul through Shemini Atzeret
(in Israel through Hoshana Raba), the following psalm is said:*

לְדָוִד By David. The Lord is my light and my salvation – whom then   *Ps. 27*
shall I fear? The Lord is the stronghold of my life – of whom shall I be
afraid? When evil men close in on me to devour my flesh, it is they, my
enemies and foes, who stumble and fall. Should an army besiege me, my
heart would not fear. Should war break out against me, still I would be
confident. One thing I ask of the Lord, only this do I seek: to live in the
House of the Lord all the days of my life, to gaze on the beauty of the
Lord and worship in His Temple. For He will keep me safe in His pavilion
on the day of trouble. He will hide me under the cover of His tent. He will
set me high upon a rock. Now my head is high above my enemies who
surround me. I will sacrifice in His tent with shouts of joy. I will sing and
chant praises to the Lord. Lord, hear my voice when I call. Be gracious
to me and answer me. On Your behalf my heart says, "Seek My face." Your
face, Lord, will I seek. Do not hide Your face from me. Do not turn Your
servant away in anger. You have been my help. Do not reject or forsake me,
God, my Savior. Were my father and my mother to forsake me, the Lord
would take me in. Teach me Your way, Lord, and lead me on a level path,
because of my oppressors. Do not abandon me to the will of my foes, for
false witnesses have risen against me, breathing violence. ‣ Were it not
for my faith that I shall see the Lord's goodness in the land of the living.
Hope in the Lord. Be strong and of good courage, and hope in the Lord!

Mourner's Kaddish (on previous page)

From the second day of חודש אלול ראש שמיני עצרת through
(in ארץ ישראל through הושענא רבה), the following psalm is said:

תהלים כז

לְדָוִד, יהוה אוֹרִי וְיִשְׁעִי, מִמִּי אִירָא, יהוה מָעוֹז־חַיַּי, מִמִּי אֶפְחָד: בִּקְרֹב
עָלַי מְרֵעִים לֶאֱכֹל אֶת־בְּשָׂרִי, צָרַי וְאֹיְבַי לִי, הֵמָּה כָשְׁלוּ וְנָפָלוּ: אִם־
תַּחֲנֶה עָלַי מַחֲנֶה, לֹא־יִירָא לִבִּי, אִם־תָּקוּם עָלַי מִלְחָמָה, בְּזֹאת אֲנִי
בוֹטֵחַ: אַחַת שָׁאַלְתִּי מֵאֵת־יהוה, אוֹתָהּ אֲבַקֵּשׁ, שִׁבְתִּי בְּבֵית־יהוה
כָּל־יְמֵי חַיַּי, לַחֲזוֹת בְּנֹעַם־יהוה, וּלְבַקֵּר בְּהֵיכָלוֹ: כִּי יִצְפְּנֵנִי בְּסֻכֹּה בְּיוֹם
רָעָה, יַסְתִּרֵנִי בְּסֵתֶר אָהֳלוֹ, בְּצוּר יְרוֹמְמֵנִי: וְעַתָּה יָרוּם רֹאשִׁי עַל אֹיְבַי
סְבִיבוֹתַי, וְאֶזְבְּחָה בְאָהֳלוֹ זִבְחֵי תְרוּעָה, אָשִׁירָה וַאֲזַמְּרָה לַיהוה: שְׁמַע־
יהוה קוֹלִי אֶקְרָא, וְחָנֵּנִי וַעֲנֵנִי: לְךָ אָמַר לִבִּי בַּקְּשׁוּ פָנָי, אֶת־פָּנֶיךָ יהוה
אֲבַקֵּשׁ: אַל־תַּסְתֵּר פָּנֶיךָ מִמֶּנִּי, אַל תַּט־בְּאַף עַבְדֶּךָ, עֶזְרָתִי הָיִיתָ, אַל־
תִּטְּשֵׁנִי וְאַל־תַּעַזְבֵנִי, אֱלֹהֵי יִשְׁעִי: כִּי־אָבִי וְאִמִּי עֲזָבוּנִי, וַיהוה יַאַסְפֵנִי:
הוֹרֵנִי יהוה דַּרְכֶּךָ, וּנְחֵנִי בְּאֹרַח מִישׁוֹר, לְמַעַן שׁוֹרְרָי: אַל־תִּתְּנֵנִי בְּנֶפֶשׁ
צָרָי, כִּי קָמוּ־בִי עֵדֵי־שֶׁקֶר, וִיפֵחַ חָמָס: לוּלֵא הֶאֱמַנְתִּי לִרְאוֹת בְּטוּב־
יהוה בְּאֶרֶץ חַיִּים: קַוֵּה אֶל־יהוה, חֲזַק וְיַאֲמֵץ לִבֶּךָ, וְקַוֵּה אֶל־יהוה:

קדיש יתום (on previous page)

COUNTING OF THE OMER^{BA}

*The Omer is counted each night from the second night of Pesah
until the night before Shavuot. See laws 97–99.
Some say the following meditation before the blessing:*
For the sake of the unification of the Holy One, blessed be He,
and His Divine Presence, in reverence and love,
to unify the name *Yod-Heh* with *Vav-Heh*
in perfect unity in the name of all Israel.

הִנְנִי I am prepared and ready to fulfill the positive commandment of Counting the Omer, as is written in the Torah, "You shall count seven complete   Lev. 23
weeks from the day following the [Pesah] rest day, when you brought the
Omer as a wave-offering. To the day after the seventh week you shall count
fifty days. Then you shall present a meal-offering of new grain to the Lord."
May the pleasantness of the Lord our God be upon us. Establish for us the   Ps. 90
work of our hands, O establish the work of our hands.

בָּרוּךְ Blessed are You, Lord our God,
King of the Universe,
who has made us holy through His commandments,
and has commanded us about counting the Omer.

---

before a vacation, before seeing a friend or a loved one. People often count down the days and weeks before a life milestone such as a bar mitzva or a wedding. Counting is a way to mark time, to express our hopes and our longing. *Sefirat HaOmer,* the daily counting of the days and weeks from Pesah to Shavuot, is that kind of counting. For without Shavuot, Pesah would be meaningless. The giving of the Torah was the reason for our liberation, the essence of who we are as a people, our definition of ourselves. The giving of the Torah changed the course of history, and not just for the Jews. Shavuot is thus our spiritual birthday, the true source of our freedom, a rendezvous with an old friend, the marriage of the Jewish people with God. We count the days and weeks to

express our excitement or to remind ourselves to get excited.

The Hagim are not just holidays whose task is to commemorate the past and provide opportunity for recreation; rather, they are holy days whose task is to reenact and to re-create. Especially because Shavuot has fewer symbols and rituals associated with it than say, Pesah or Sukkot, it may need even more preparation. As we know, most special events are made special because we prepare for them. The more we prepare, the more we anticipate, the more meaningful is the event when it finally arrives. How can I better prepare for the coming of the giving of the Torah? What can I do to make this coming Shavuot more meaningful? The counting of the Omer can be a beginning.

סדר ספירת העומר א״ב

The עומר *is counted each night from the second night of* פסח
until the night before שבועות. *See laws 97–99.*
Some say the following meditation before the blessing:

לְשֵׁם יִחוּד קֻדְשָׁא בְּרִיךְ הוּא וּשְׁכִינְתֵּהּ בִּדְחִילוּ וּרְחִימוּ
לְיַחֵד שֵׁם י״ה בו״ה בְּיִחוּדָא שְׁלִים בְּשֵׁם כָּל יִשְׂרָאֵל.

הִנְנִי מוּכָן וּמְזֻמָּן לְקַיֵּם מִצְוַת עֲשֵׂה שֶׁל סְפִירַת הָעְמֶר. כְּמוֹ שֶׁכָּתוּב בַּתּוֹרָה,
וּסְפַרְתֶּם לָכֶם מִמָּחֳרַת הַשַּׁבָּת, מִיּוֹם הֲבִיאֲכֶם אֶת־עְמֶר הַתְּנוּפָה, שֶׁבַע
שַׁבָּתוֹת תְּמִימֹת תִּהְיֶינָה: עַד מִמָּחֳרַת הַשַּׁבָּת הַשְּׁבִיעִת תִּסְפְּרוּ חֲמִשִּׁים
יוֹם, וְהִקְרַבְתֶּם מִנְחָה חֲדָשָׁה לַיהוה: וִיהִי נֹעַם אֲדֹנָי אֱלֹהֵינוּ עָלֵינוּ, וּמַעֲשֵׂה
יָדֵינוּ כּוֹנְנָה עָלֵינוּ, וּמַעֲשֵׂה יָדֵינוּ כּוֹנְנֵהוּ:

ויקרא כג

תהלים צ

בָּרוּךְ אַתָּה יהוה אֱלֹהֵינוּ מֶלֶךְ הָעוֹלָם
אֲשֶׁר קִדְּשָׁנוּ בְּמִצְוֺתָיו וְצִוָּנוּ עַל סְפִירַת הָעְמֶר.

BIUR TEFILLA · ביאור תפילה

ספירת העומר – *COUNTING OF THE OMER.* In the days of the *Beit HaMikdash*, on the first day after Pesah, an offering was brought consisting of an *omer* (a unit of measurement, approximately 2–4 liters) of barley. Before this offering, any grains from new crops (*hadash*) were not permitted to be eaten. The Torah says that the next 49 days – seven weeks – of the "waving of the *omer*" were to be counted until the arrival of Shavuot, when another offering was brought to mark the beginning of the grain harvest. This is what became known as the period of the counting (*sefira*) of the *omer*. When the *Beit HaMikdash* was destroyed, the Rabbis mandated that we continue the practice of counting.

As for the requirement not to eat from crops that were planted before Pesah until the day after Pesah (*hadash*), it is generally accepted that this rule is independent of the existence of the *Beit HaMikdash*; it continues to be observed both in Israel and in the Diaspora, where people carefully calculate the dates of the growing and harvesting of the grains grown in their country and used in different products to make sure that they only eat from older crops (*yashan*). Others maintain that this is an act of piety that is untenable for most people and rely upon a more lenient *halakhic* view.

ANI TEFILLA · אני תפילה

ספירת העומר – *COUNTING OF THE OMER.* Do you recall the last time you counted the

days before an important event in your life? Perhaps it was the days before a birthday,

16 Nisan

1. Today is the first day
   of the Omer.

17 Nisan

2. Today is the second day
   of the Omer.

18 Nisan

3. Today is the third day
   of the Omer.

19 Nisan

4. Today is the fourth day
   of the Omer.

20 Nisan

5. Today is the fifth day
   of the Omer.

21 Nisan

6. Today is the sixth day
   of the Omer.

22 Nisan

7. Today is the seventh day,
   making one week
   of the Omer.

23 Nisan

8. Today is the eighth day,
   making one week and one day
   of the Omer.

24 Nisan

9. Today is the ninth day,
   making one week and two days
   of the Omer.

25 Nisan

10. Today is the tenth day,
    making one week and three
    days of the Omer.

26 Nisan

11. Today is the eleventh day,
    making one week
    and four days
    of the Omer.

27 Nisan

12. Today is the twelfth day,
    making one week
    and five days
    of the Omer.

28 Nisan

13. Today is the thirteenth day,
    making one week
    and six days
    of the Omer.

29 Nisan

14. Today is the fourteenth day,
    making two weeks
    of the Omer.

30 Nisan, 1st day Rosh Ḥodesh

15. Today is the fifteenth day,
    making two weeks
    and one day
    of the Omer.

1 Iyar, 2nd day Rosh Ḥodesh

16. Today is the sixteenth day,
    making two weeks
    and two days
    of the Omer.

2 Iyar

17. Today is the seventeenth day,
    making two weeks
    and three days
    of the Omer.

טז בניסן

1. הַיּוֹם יוֹם אֶחָד בָּעֹמֶר.
חסד שבחסד

יז בניסן

2. הַיּוֹם שְׁנֵי יָמִים בָּעֹמֶר.
גבורה שבחסד

יח בניסן

3. הַיּוֹם שְׁלֹשָׁה יָמִים בָּעֹמֶר.
תפארת שבחסד

יט בניסן

4. הַיּוֹם אַרְבָּעָה יָמִים בָּעֹמֶר.
נצח שבחסד

כ בניסן

5. הַיּוֹם חֲמִשָּׁה יָמִים בָּעֹמֶר.
הוד שבחסד

כא בניסן

6. הַיּוֹם שִׁשָּׁה יָמִים בָּעֹמֶר.
יסוד שבחסד

כב בניסן

7. הַיּוֹם שִׁבְעָה יָמִים
שֶׁהֵם שָׁבוּעַ אֶחָד בָּעֹמֶר.
מלכות שבחסד

כג בניסן

8. הַיּוֹם שְׁמוֹנָה יָמִים
שֶׁהֵם שָׁבוּעַ אֶחָד וְיוֹם אֶחָד
בָּעֹמֶר.
חסד שבגבורה

כד בניסן

9. הַיּוֹם תִּשְׁעָה יָמִים
שֶׁהֵם שָׁבוּעַ אֶחָד וּשְׁנֵי יָמִים
בָּעֹמֶר.
גבורה שבגבורה

כה בניסן

10. הַיּוֹם עֲשָׂרָה יָמִים
שֶׁהֵם שָׁבוּעַ אֶחָד וּשְׁלֹשָׁה
יָמִים בָּעֹמֶר.   תפארת שבגבורה

כו בניסן

11. הַיּוֹם אַחַד עָשָׂר יוֹם
שֶׁהֵם שָׁבוּעַ אֶחָד וְאַרְבָּעָה
יָמִים בָּעֹמֶר.   נצח שבגבורה

כז בניסן

12. הַיּוֹם שְׁנֵים עָשָׂר יוֹם
שֶׁהֵם שָׁבוּעַ אֶחָד וַחֲמִשָּׁה
יָמִים בָּעֹמֶר.   הוד שבגבורה

כח בניסן

13. הַיּוֹם שְׁלֹשָׁה עָשָׂר יוֹם
שֶׁהֵם שָׁבוּעַ אֶחָד וְשִׁשָּׁה יָמִים
בָּעֹמֶר.   יסוד שבגבורה

כט בניסן

14. הַיּוֹם אַרְבָּעָה עָשָׂר יוֹם
שֶׁהֵם שְׁנֵי שָׁבוּעוֹת
בָּעֹמֶר.   מלכות שבגבורה

ל בניסן, א' דראש חודש

15. הַיּוֹם חֲמִשָּׁה עָשָׂר יוֹם
שֶׁהֵם שְׁנֵי שָׁבוּעוֹת וְיוֹם אֶחָד
בָּעֹמֶר.   חסד שבתפארת

א באייר, ב' דראש חודש

16. הַיּוֹם שִׁשָּׁה עָשָׂר יוֹם
שֶׁהֵם שְׁנֵי שָׁבוּעוֹת וּשְׁנֵי יָמִים
בָּעֹמֶר.   גבורה שבתפארת

ב באייר

17. הַיּוֹם שִׁבְעָה עָשָׂר יוֹם
שֶׁהֵם שְׁנֵי שָׁבוּעוֹת וּשְׁלֹשָׁה
יָמִים בָּעֹמֶר.   תפארת שבתפארת

3 Iyar

18. Today is the eighteenth day,
    making two weeks
    and four days
    of the Omer.

4 Iyar

19. Today is the nineteenth day,
    making two weeks
    and five days
    of the Omer.

5 Iyar, Yom HaAtzma'ut

20. Today is the twentieth day,
    making two weeks
    and six days
    of the Omer.

6 Iyar

21. Today is the twenty-first day,
    making three weeks
    of the Omer.

7 Iyar

22. Today is the twenty-second day,
    making three weeks
    and one day
    of the Omer.

8 Iyar

23. Today is the twenty-third day,
    making three weeks
    and two days
    of the Omer.

9 Iyar

24. Today is the twenty-fourth day,
    making three weeks
    and three days
    of the Omer.

10 Iyar

25. Today is the twenty-fifth day,
    making three weeks
    and four days
    of the Omer.

11 Iyar

26. Today is the twenty-sixth day,
    making three weeks
    and five days
    of the Omer.

12 Iyar

27. Today is the twenty-seventh
    day, making three weeks
    and six days
    of the Omer.

13 Iyar

28. Today is the twenty-eighth day,
    making four weeks
    of the Omer.

14 Iyar, Pesaḥ Sheni

29. Today is the twenty-ninth day,
    making four weeks
    and one day
    of the Omer.

15 Iyar

30. Today is the thirtieth day,
    making four weeks
    and two days
    of the Omer.

16 Iyar

31. Today is the thirty-first day,
    making four weeks
    and three days
    of the Omer.

ג באייר

18. הַיּוֹם שְׁמוֹנָה עָשָׂר יוֹם
שֶׁהֵם שְׁנֵי שָׁבוּעוֹת וְאַרְבָּעָה
יָמִים בָּעֹמֶר.   נצח שבתפארת

ד באייר

19. הַיּוֹם תִּשְׁעָה עָשָׂר יוֹם
שֶׁהֵם שְׁנֵי שָׁבוּעוֹת וַחֲמִשָּׁה
יָמִים בָּעֹמֶר.   הוד שבתפארת

ה באייר, יום העצמאות

20. הַיּוֹם עֶשְׂרִים יוֹם
שֶׁהֵם שְׁנֵי שָׁבוּעוֹת וְשִׁשָּׁה
יָמִים בָּעֹמֶר.   יסוד שבתפארת

ו באייר

21. הַיּוֹם אֶחָד וְעֶשְׂרִים יוֹם
שֶׁהֵם שְׁלֹשָׁה שָׁבוּעוֹת בָּעֹמֶר.
מלכות שבתפארת

ז באייר

22. הַיּוֹם שְׁנַיִם וְעֶשְׂרִים יוֹם
שֶׁהֵם שְׁלֹשָׁה שָׁבוּעוֹת
וְיוֹם אֶחָד בָּעֹמֶר.   חסד שבנצח

ח באייר

23. הַיּוֹם שְׁלֹשָׁה וְעֶשְׂרִים יוֹם
שֶׁהֵם שְׁלֹשָׁה שָׁבוּעוֹת
וּשְׁנֵי יָמִים בָּעֹמֶר.   גבורה שבנצח

ט באייר

24. הַיּוֹם אַרְבָּעָה וְעֶשְׂרִים יוֹם
שֶׁהֵם שְׁלֹשָׁה שָׁבוּעוֹת
וּשְׁלֹשָׁה יָמִים בָּעֹמֶר.
תפארת שבנצח

יא באייר

25. הַיּוֹם חֲמִשָּׁה וְעֶשְׂרִים יוֹם
שֶׁהֵם שְׁלֹשָׁה שָׁבוּעוֹת
וְאַרְבָּעָה יָמִים בָּעֹמֶר.   נצח שבנצח

יא באייר

26. הַיּוֹם שִׁשָּׁה וְעֶשְׂרִים יוֹם
שֶׁהֵם שְׁלֹשָׁה שָׁבוּעוֹת
וַחֲמִשָּׁה יָמִים בָּעֹמֶר.   הוד שבנצח

יב באייר

27. הַיּוֹם שִׁבְעָה וְעֶשְׂרִים יוֹם
שֶׁהֵם שְׁלֹשָׁה שָׁבוּעוֹת
וְשִׁשָּׁה יָמִים בָּעֹמֶר.   יסוד שבנצח

יג באייר

28. הַיּוֹם שְׁמוֹנָה וְעֶשְׂרִים יוֹם
שֶׁהֵם אַרְבָּעָה שָׁבוּעוֹת
בָּעֹמֶר.   מלכות שבנצח

יד באייר, פסח שני

29. הַיּוֹם תִּשְׁעָה וְעֶשְׂרִים יוֹם
שֶׁהֵם אַרְבָּעָה שָׁבוּעוֹת
וְיוֹם אֶחָד בָּעֹמֶר.   חסד שבהוד

טו באייר

30. הַיּוֹם שְׁלֹשִׁים יוֹם
שֶׁהֵם אַרְבָּעָה שָׁבוּעוֹת
וּשְׁנֵי יָמִים בָּעֹמֶר.   גבורה שבהוד

טז באייר

31. הַיּוֹם אֶחָד וּשְׁלֹשִׁים יוֹם
שֶׁהֵם אַרְבָּעָה שָׁבוּעוֹת
וּשְׁלֹשָׁה יָמִים בָּעֹמֶר.
תפארת שבהוד

17 Iyar

32. Today is the thirty-second day,
    making four weeks
    and four days
    of the Omer.

18 Iyar, Lag BaOmer

33. Today is the thirty-third day,
    making four weeks
    and five days
    of the Omer.

19 Iyar

34. Today is the thirty-fourth day,
    making four weeks
    and six days
    of the Omer.

20 Iyar

35. Today is the thirty-fifth day,
    making five weeks
    of the Omer.

21 Iyar

36. Today is the thirty-sixth day,
    making five weeks
    and one day
    of the Omer.

22 Iyar

37. Today is the thirty-seventh day,
    making five weeks
    and two days
    of the Omer.

23 Iyar

38. Today is the thirty-eighth day,
    making five weeks
    and three days
    of the Omer.

24 Iyar

39. Today is the thirty-ninth day,
    making five weeks
    and four days
    of the Omer.

25 Iyar

40. Today is the fortieth day,
    making five weeks
    and five days
    of the Omer.

26 Iyar

41. Today is the forty-first day,
    making five weeks
    and six days
    of the Omer.

27 Iyar

42. Today is the forty-second day,
    making six weeks
    of the Omer.

28 Iyar, Yom Yerushalayim

43. Today is the forty-third day,
    making six weeks
    and one day
    of the Omer.

29 Iyar

44. Today is the forty-fourth day,
    making six weeks
    and two days
    of the Omer.

1 Sivan, Rosh Hodesh

45. Today is the forty-fifth day,
    making six weeks
    and three days
    of the Omer.

כד באייר

39. הַיּוֹם תִּשְׁעָה וּשְׁלֹשִׁים יוֹם
שֶׁהֵם חֲמִשָּׁה שָׁבוּעוֹת
וְאַרְבָּעָה יָמִים בָּעֹמֶר. נצח שביסוד

כה באייר

40. הַיּוֹם אַרְבָּעִים יוֹם
שֶׁהֵם חֲמִשָּׁה שָׁבוּעוֹת
וַחֲמִשָּׁה יָמִים בָּעֹמֶר. הוד שביסוד

כו באייר

41. הַיּוֹם אֶחָד וְאַרְבָּעִים יוֹם
שֶׁהֵם חֲמִשָּׁה שָׁבוּעוֹת
וְשִׁשָּׁה יָמִים בָּעֹמֶר. יסוד שביסוד

כז באייר

42. הַיּוֹם שְׁנַיִם וְאַרְבָּעִים יוֹם
שֶׁהֵם שִׁשָּׁה שָׁבוּעוֹת
בָּעֹמֶר. מלכות שביסוד

כח באייר, יום ירושלים

43. הַיּוֹם שְׁלֹשָׁה וְאַרְבָּעִים יוֹם
שֶׁהֵם שִׁשָּׁה שָׁבוּעוֹת
וְיוֹם אֶחָד בָּעֹמֶר. חסד שבמלכות

כט באייר

44. הַיּוֹם אַרְבָּעָה וְאַרְבָּעִים יוֹם
שֶׁהֵם שִׁשָּׁה שָׁבוּעוֹת
וּשְׁנֵי יָמִים בָּעֹמֶר. גבורה שבמלכות

א בסיון, ראש חודש

45. הַיּוֹם חֲמִשָּׁה וְאַרְבָּעִים יוֹם
שֶׁהֵם שִׁשָּׁה שָׁבוּעוֹת וּשְׁלֹשָׁה
יָמִים בָּעֹמֶר. תפארת שבמלכות

יז באייר

32. הַיּוֹם שְׁנַיִם וּשְׁלֹשִׁים יוֹם
שֶׁהֵם אַרְבָּעָה שָׁבוּעוֹת
וְאַרְבָּעָה יָמִים בָּעֹמֶר. נצח שבהוד

יח באייר, לג בעומר

33. הַיּוֹם שְׁלֹשָׁה וּשְׁלֹשִׁים יוֹם
שֶׁהֵם אַרְבָּעָה שָׁבוּעוֹת
וַחֲמִשָּׁה יָמִים בָּעֹמֶר. הוד שבהוד

יט באייר

34. הַיּוֹם אַרְבָּעָה וּשְׁלֹשִׁים יוֹם
שֶׁהֵם אַרְבָּעָה שָׁבוּעוֹת
וְשִׁשָּׁה יָמִים בָּעֹמֶר. יסוד שבהוד

כ באייר

35. הַיּוֹם חֲמִשָּׁה וּשְׁלֹשִׁים יוֹם
שֶׁהֵם חֲמִשָּׁה שָׁבוּעוֹת
בָּעֹמֶר. מלכות שבהוד

כא באייר

36. הַיּוֹם שִׁשָּׁה וּשְׁלֹשִׁים יוֹם
שֶׁהֵם חֲמִשָּׁה שָׁבוּעוֹת
וְיוֹם אֶחָד בָּעֹמֶר. חסד שביסוד

כב באייר

37. הַיּוֹם שִׁבְעָה וּשְׁלֹשִׁים יוֹם
שֶׁהֵם חֲמִשָּׁה שָׁבוּעוֹת
וּשְׁנֵי יָמִים בָּעֹמֶר. גבורה שביסוד

כג באייר

38. הַיּוֹם שְׁמוֹנָה וּשְׁלֹשִׁים יוֹם
שֶׁהֵם חֲמִשָּׁה שָׁבוּעוֹת
וּשְׁלֹשָׁה יָמִים בָּעֹמֶר. תפארת שביסוד

2 Sivan

46. Today is the forty-sixth day,
    making six weeks and four days
    of the Omer.

3 Sivan

47. Today is the forty-seventh day,
    making six weeks and five days
    of the Omer.

4 Sivan

48. Today is the forty-eighth day,
    making six weeks and six days
    of the Omer.

5 Sivan, Erev Shavuot

49. Today is the forty-ninth day,
    making seven weeks of the
    Omer.

הָרַחֲמָן May the Compassionate One restore the Temple service
to its place speedily in our days. Amen, Selah.

Some add:

לַמְנַצֵּחַ For the conductor of music. With stringed instruments. A psalm, a song. *Ps. 67* May God be gracious to us and bless us. May He make His face shine on us, Selah. Then will Your way be known on earth, Your salvation among all the nations. Let the peoples praise You, God; let all peoples praise You. Let nations rejoice and sing for joy, for You judge the peoples with equity, and guide the nations of the earth, Selah. Let the peoples praise You, God; let all peoples praise You. The earth has yielded its harvest. May God, our God, bless us. God will bless us, and all the ends of the earth will fear Him.

אָנָּא Please, by the power of Your great right hand, set the captive nation free. Accept Your people's prayer. Strengthen us, purify us, You who are revered. Please, mighty One, guard like the pupil of the eye those who seek Your unity. Bless them, cleanse them, have compassion on them, grant them Your righteousness always. Mighty One, Holy One, in Your great goodness guide Your congregation. Only One, exalted One, turn to Your people, who proclaim Your holiness. Accept our plea and heed our cry, You who know all secret thoughts. Blessed be the name of His glorious kingdom for ever and all time.

רִבּוֹנוֹ שֶׁל עוֹלָם Master of the Universe, You commanded us through Your servant Moses to count the Omer, to cleanse our carapaces and impurities, as You have written in Your Torah: "You shall count seven complete weeks from the day *Lev. 23* following the [Pesaḥ] rest day, when you brought the Omer as a wave-offering. To the day after the seventh week, you shall count fifty days." This is so that the souls of Your people Israel may be purified from their uncleanliness. May it also be Your will, LORD our God and God of our ancestors, that in the merit of the Omer count that I have counted today, there may be rectified any defect on my part in the counting of (*insert the appropriate sefira for each day*). May I be cleansed and sanctified with Your holiness on high, and through this may there flow a rich stream through all worlds, to rectify our lives, spirits and souls from any dross and defect, purifying and sanctifying us with Your sublime holiness. Amen, Selah.

The service continues with Aleinu on page 380.

ד בסיון

48. הַיּוֹם שְׁמוֹנָה וְאַרְבָּעִים יוֹם
שֶׁהֵם שִׁשָּׁה שָׁבוּעוֹת וְשִׁשָּׁה
יָמִים בָּעֹמֶר. יסוד שבמלכות

ב בסיון

46. הַיּוֹם שִׁשָּׁה וְאַרְבָּעִים יוֹם
שֶׁהֵם שִׁשָּׁה שָׁבוּעוֹת וְאַרְבָּעָה
יָמִים בָּעֹמֶר. נצח שבמלכות

ה בסיון, ערב שבועות

49. הַיּוֹם תִּשְׁעָה וְאַרְבָּעִים יוֹם
שֶׁהֵם שִׁבְעָה שָׁבוּעוֹת בָּעֹמֶר.
מלכות שבמלכות

ג בסיון

47. הַיּוֹם שִׁבְעָה וְאַרְבָּעִים יוֹם
שֶׁהֵם שִׁשָּׁה שָׁבוּעוֹת וַחֲמִשָּׁה
יָמִים בָּעֹמֶר. הוד שבמלכות

הָרַחֲמָן הוּא יַחֲזִיר לָנוּ עֲבוֹדַת בֵּית הַמִּקְדָּשׁ לִמְקוֹמָהּ
בִּמְהֵרָה בְיָמֵינוּ, אָמֵן סֶלָה.

Some add:

תהלים סז

לַמְנַצֵּחַ בִּנְגִינֹת, מִזְמוֹר שִׁיר: אֱלֹהִים יְחָנֵּנוּ וִיבָרְכֵנוּ, יָאֵר פָּנָיו אִתָּנוּ סֶלָה: לָדַעַת בָּאָרֶץ דַּרְכֶּךָ, בְּכָל־גּוֹיִם יְשׁוּעָתֶךָ: יוֹדוּךָ עַמִּים אֱלֹהִים, יוֹדוּךָ עַמִּים כֻּלָּם: יִשְׂמְחוּ וִירַנְּנוּ לְאֻמִּים, כִּי־תִשְׁפֹּט עַמִּים מִישֹׁר, וּלְאֻמִּים בָּאָרֶץ תַּנְחֵם סֶלָה: יוֹדוּךָ עַמִּים אֱלֹהִים, יוֹדוּךָ עַמִּים כֻּלָּם: אֶרֶץ נָתְנָה יְבוּלָהּ, יְבָרְכֵנוּ אֱלֹהִים אֱלֹהֵינוּ: יְבָרְכֵנוּ אֱלֹהִים, וְיִירְאוּ אוֹתוֹ כָּל־אַפְסֵי־אָרֶץ:

אָנָּא, בְּכֹחַ גְּדֻלַּת יְמִינְךָ, תַּתִּיר צְרוּרָה. קַבֵּל רִנַּת עַמְּךָ, שַׂגְּבֵנוּ, טַהֲרֵנוּ, נוֹרָא. נָא גִבּוֹר, דּוֹרְשֵׁי יִחוּדְךָ כְּבָבַת שָׁמְרֵם. בָּרְכֵם, טַהֲרֵם, רַחֲמֵם, צִדְקָתְךָ תָּמִיד גָּמְלֵם. חֲסִין קָדוֹשׁ, בְּרֹב טוּבְךָ נַהֵל עֲדָתֶךָ. יָחִיד גֵּאֶה, לְעַמְּךָ פְּנֵה, זוֹכְרֵי קְדֻשָּׁתֶךָ. שַׁוְעָתֵנוּ קַבֵּל וּשְׁמַע צַעֲקָתֵנוּ, יוֹדֵעַ תַּעֲלוּמוֹת. בָּרוּךְ שֵׁם כְּבוֹד מַלְכוּתוֹ לְעוֹלָם וָעֶד.

רִבּוֹנוֹ שֶׁל עוֹלָם, אַתָּה צִוִּיתָנוּ עַל יְדֵי מֹשֶׁה עַבְדְּךָ לִסְפֹּר סְפִירַת הָעֹמֶר, כְּדֵי לְטַהֲרֵנוּ מִקְּלִפּוֹתֵינוּ וּמִטֻּמְאוֹתֵינוּ. כְּמוֹ שֶׁכָּתַבְתָּ בְּתוֹרָתֶךָ: וּסְפַרְתֶּם לָכֶם מִמָּחֳרַת הַשַּׁבָּת, מִיּוֹם הֲבִיאֲכֶם אֶת־עֹמֶר הַתְּנוּפָה, שֶׁבַע שַׁבָּתוֹת תְּמִימֹת תִּהְיֶינָה: עַד מִמָּחֳרַת הַשַּׁבָּת הַשְּׁבִיעִת תִּסְפְּרוּ חֲמִשִּׁים יוֹם: כְּדֵי שֶׁיִּטָּהֲרוּ נַפְשׁוֹת עַמְּךָ יִשְׂרָאֵל מִזֻּהֲמָתָם. וּבְכֵן יְהִי רָצוֹן מִלְּפָנֶיךָ יהוה אֱלֹהֵינוּ וֵאלֹהֵי אֲבוֹתֵינוּ, שֶׁבִּזְכוּת סְפִירַת הָעֹמֶר שֶׁסָּפַרְתִּי הַיּוֹם, יְתֻקַּן מַה שֶּׁפָּגַמְתִּי בִּסְפִירָה (insert appropriate ספירה for each day) וְאֶטַּהֵר וְאֶתְקַדֵּשׁ בִּקְדֻשָּׁה שֶׁל מַעְלָה, וְעַל יְדֵי זֶה יֻשְׁפַּע שֶׁפַע רַב בְּכָל הָעוֹלָמוֹת, לְתַקֵּן אֶת נַפְשׁוֹתֵינוּ וְרוּחוֹתֵינוּ וְנִשְׁמוֹתֵינוּ מִכָּל סִיג וּפְגָם, וּלְטַהֲרֵנוּ וּלְקַדְּשֵׁנוּ בִּקְדֻשָּׁתְךָ הָעֶלְיוֹנָה, אָמֵן סֶלָה.

ויקרא כג

The service continues with עָלֵינוּ *on page 381.*

MOTZA'EI SHABBAT

In many congregations, the following two psalms are sung
before Ma'ariv at the end of Shabbat.

לְדָוִד Of David. Blessed is the Lord, my Rock, who trains my hands *Ps. 144* for war, my fingers for battle. He is my Benefactor, my Fortress, my Stronghold and my Refuge, my Shield in whom I trust, He who subdues nations under me. Lord, what is man that You care for him, what are mortals that You think of them? Man is no more than a breath, his days like a fleeting shadow. Lord, part Your heavens and come down; touch the mountains so that they pour forth smoke. Flash forth lightning and scatter them; shoot Your arrows and panic them. Reach out Your hand from on high; deliver me and rescue me from the mighty waters, from the hands of strangers, whose every word is worthless, whose right hands are raised in falsehood. To You, God, I will sing a new song; to You I will play music on a ten-stringed harp. He who gives salvation to kings, who saved His servant David from the cruel sword: may He deliver me and rescue me from the hands of strangers, whose every word is worthless, whose right hands are raised in falsehood. Then our sons will be like saplings, well nurtured in their youth. Our daughters will be like pillars carved for a palace. Our barns will be filled with every kind of provision. Our sheep will increase by thousands, even tens of thousands in our fields. Our oxen will draw heavy loads. There will be no breach in the walls, no going into captivity, no cries of distress in our streets. Happy are the people for whom this is so; happy are the people whose God is the Lord.

לַמְנַצֵּחַ For the conductor of music. With stringed instruments. A psalm, *Ps. 67* a song. May God be gracious to us and bless us. May He make His face shine on us, Selah. Then will Your way be known on earth, Your salvation among all the nations. Let the peoples praise You, God; let all peoples praise You. Let nations rejoice and sing for joy, for You judge the peoples with equity, and guide the nations of the earth, Selah. Let the peoples praise You, God; let all peoples praise You. The earth has yielded its harvest. May God, our God, bless us. God will bless us, and all the ends of the earth will fear Him.

The service continues with Ma'ariv for Weekdays on page 342.

מוצאי שבת

In many congregations, the following two psalms
are sung before מעריב *on* מוצאי שבת.

תהלים קמד

לְדָוִד, בָּרוּךְ יהוה צוּרִי, הַמְלַמֵּד יָדַי לַקְרָב, אֶצְבְּעוֹתַי לַמִּלְחָמָה: חַסְדִּי וּמְצוּדָתִי מִשְׂגַּבִּי וּמְפַלְטִי לִי, מָגִנִּי וּבוֹ חָסִיתִי, הָרוֹדֵד עַמִּי תַחְתָּי: יהוה מָה־אָדָם וַתֵּדָעֵהוּ, בֶּן־אֱנוֹשׁ וַתְּחַשְּׁבֵהוּ: אָדָם לַהֶבֶל דָּמָה, יָמָיו כְּצֵל עוֹבֵר: יהוה הַט־שָׁמֶיךָ וְתֵרֵד, גַּע בֶּהָרִים וְיֶעֱשָׁנוּ: בְּרוֹק בָּרָק וּתְפִיצֵם, שְׁלַח חִצֶּיךָ וּתְהֻמֵּם: שְׁלַח יָדֶיךָ מִמָּרוֹם, פְּצֵנִי וְהַצִּילֵנִי מִמַּיִם רַבִּים, מִיַּד בְּנֵי נֵכָר: אֲשֶׁר פִּיהֶם דִּבֶּר־שָׁוְא, וִימִינָם יְמִין שָׁקֶר: אֱלֹהִים שִׁיר חָדָשׁ אָשִׁירָה לָּךְ, בְּנֵבֶל עָשׂוֹר אֲזַמְּרָה־לָּךְ: הַנּוֹתֵן תְּשׁוּעָה לַמְּלָכִים, הַפּוֹצֶה אֶת־דָּוִד עַבְדּוֹ מֵחֶרֶב רָעָה: פְּצֵנִי וְהַצִּילֵנִי מִיַּד בְּנֵי נֵכָר, אֲשֶׁר פִּיהֶם דִּבֶּר־שָׁוְא, וִימִינָם יְמִין שָׁקֶר: אֲשֶׁר בָּנֵינוּ כִּנְטִעִים, מְגֻדָּלִים בִּנְעוּרֵיהֶם, בְּנוֹתֵינוּ כְזָוִיֹּת, מְחֻטָּבוֹת תַּבְנִית הֵיכָל: מְזָוֵינוּ מְלֵאִים, מְפִיקִים מִזַּן אֶל־זַן, צֹאונֵנוּ מַאֲלִיפוֹת מְרֻבָּבוֹת בְּחוּצוֹתֵינוּ: אַלּוּפֵינוּ מְסֻבָּלִים, אֵין פֶּרֶץ וְאֵין יוֹצֵאת, וְאֵין צְוָחָה בִּרְחֹבֹתֵינוּ: אַשְׁרֵי הָעָם שֶׁכָּכָה לּוֹ, אַשְׁרֵי הָעָם שֶׁיהוה אֱלֹהָיו:

תהלים סז

לַמְנַצֵּחַ בִּנְגִינֹת, מִזְמוֹר שִׁיר: אֱלֹהִים יְחָנֵּנוּ וִיבָרְכֵנוּ, יָאֵר פָּנָיו אִתָּנוּ סֶלָה: לָדַעַת בָּאָרֶץ דַּרְכֶּךָ, בְּכָל־גּוֹיִם יְשׁוּעָתֶךָ: יוֹדוּךָ עַמִּים אֱלֹהִים, יוֹדוּךָ עַמִּים כֻּלָּם: יִשְׂמְחוּ וִירַנְּנוּ לְאֻמִּים, כִּי־תִשְׁפֹּט עַמִּים מִישׁוֹר, וּלְאֻמִּים בָּאָרֶץ תַּנְחֵם סֶלָה: יוֹדוּךָ עַמִּים אֱלֹהִים, יוֹדוּךָ עַמִּים כֻּלָּם: אֶרֶץ נָתְנָה יְבוּלָהּ, יְבָרְכֵנוּ אֱלֹהִים אֱלֹהֵינוּ: יְבָרְכֵנוּ אֱלֹהִים, וְיִירְאוּ אוֹתוֹ כָּל־אַפְסֵי־אָרֶץ:

The service continues with מעריב לחול *on page 343.*

MOTZA'EI SHABBAT

At the conclusion of the Amida on Motza'ei Shabbat (except when Yom Tov or Erev Pesah falls in the following week), the Leader continues with Half Kaddish below, then "May the pleasantness."

HALF KADDISH

Leader: יִתְגַּדַּל Magnified and sanctified may His great name be,
in the world He created by His will.
May He establish His kingdom
in your lifetime and in your days,
and in the lifetime of all the house of Israel,
swiftly and soon –
and say: Amen.

All: May His great name be blessed for ever and all time.

Leader: Blessed and praised, glorified and exalted,
raised and honored, uplifted and lauded
be the name of the Holy One,
blessed be He,
beyond any blessing, song,
praise and consolation
uttered in the world –
and say: Amen.

וִיהִי נֹעַם May the pleasantness of the LORD our God be upon us. *Ps. 90* Establish for us the work of our hands, O establish the work of our hands.

יֹשֵׁב He who lives in the shelter of the Most High dwells in the *Ps. 91* shadow of the Almighty. I say of the LORD, my Refuge and Stronghold, my God in whom I trust, that He will save you from the fowler's snare and the deadly pestilence. With His pinions He will cover you, and beneath His wings you will find shelter; His faithfulness is an encircling shield. You need not fear terror by night,

מוצאי שבת

At the conclusion of the מוצאי שבת on עמידה (except when ערב פסח or יום טוב falls in
the following week), the שליח ציבור continues with חצי קדיש below, then ויהי נעם.

חצי קדיש

ש״ץ יִתְגַּדַּל וְיִתְקַדַּשׁ שְׁמֵהּ רַבָּא (קהל: אָמֵן)
בְּעָלְמָא דִּי בְרָא כִרְעוּתֵהּ
וְיַמְלִיךְ מַלְכוּתֵהּ
בְּחַיֵּיכוֹן וּבְיוֹמֵיכוֹן וּבְחַיֵּי דְּכָל בֵּית יִשְׂרָאֵל
בַּעֲגָלָא וּבִזְמַן קָרִיב, וְאִמְרוּ אָמֵן. (קהל: אָמֵן)

קהל
וש״ץ: יְהֵא שְׁמֵהּ רַבָּא מְבָרַךְ לְעָלַם וּלְעָלְמֵי עָלְמַיָּא.

ש״ץ: יִתְבָּרַךְ וְיִשְׁתַּבַּח וְיִתְפָּאַר וְיִתְרוֹמַם וְיִתְנַשֵּׂא
וְיִתְהַדָּר וְיִתְעַלֶּה וְיִתְהַלָּל
שְׁמֵהּ דְּקֻדְשָׁא בְּרִיךְ הוּא (קהל: בְּרִיךְ הוּא)
לְעֵלָּא מִן כָּל בִּרְכָתָא
/בעשרת ימי תשובה: לְעֵלָּא לְעֵלָּא מִכָּל בִּרְכָתָא/
וְשִׁירָתָא, תֻּשְׁבְּחָתָא וְנֶחֱמָתָא
דַּאֲמִירָן בְּעָלְמָא, וְאִמְרוּ אָמֵן. (קהל: אָמֵן)

תהלים צ
וִיהִי נֹעַם אֲדֹנָי אֱלֹהֵינוּ עָלֵינוּ וּמַעֲשֵׂה יָדֵינוּ כּוֹנְנָה עָלֵינוּ וּמַעֲשֵׂה
יָדֵינוּ כּוֹנְנֵהוּ:

תהלים צא
יֹשֵׁב בְּסֵתֶר עֶלְיוֹן, בְּצֵל שַׁדַּי יִתְלוֹנָן: אֹמַר לַיהוה מַחְסִי וּמְצוּדָתִי,
אֱלֹהַי אֶבְטַח בּוֹ: כִּי הוּא יַצִּילְךָ מִפַּח יָקוּשׁ, מִדֶּבֶר הַוּוֹת:
בְּאֶבְרָתוֹ יָסֶךְ לָךְ, וְתַחַת כְּנָפָיו תֶּחְסֶה, צִנָּה וְסֹחֵרָה אֲמִתּוֹ:
לֹא־תִירָא מִפַּחַד לָיְלָה, מֵחֵץ יָעוּף יוֹמָם: מִדֶּבֶר בָּאֹפֶל יַהֲלֹךְ,

nor the arrow that flies by day; not the pestilence that stalks in darkness, nor the plague that ravages at noon. A thousand may fall at your side, ten thousand at your right hand, but it will not come near you. You will only look with your eyes and see the punishment of the wicked. Because you said, "The LORD is my Refuge," taking the Most High as your shelter, no harm will befall you, no plague come near your tent, for He will command His angels about you, to guard you in all your ways. They will lift you in their hands, lest your foot stumble on a stone. You will tread on lions and vipers; you will trample on young lions and snakes. [God says:] "Because he loves Me, I will rescue him; I will protect him, because he acknowledges My name. When he calls on Me, I will answer him; I will be with him in distress, I will deliver him and bring him honor.
➤ With long life I will satisfy him and show him My salvation.
  With long life I will satisfy him and show him My salvation.

➤ You are the Holy One, enthroned on the praises of Israel.   *Ps. 22*
  And [the angels] call to one another, saying,
  "Holy, holy, holy is the LORD of hosts;   *Is. 6*
  the whole world is filled with His glory."
  And they receive permission from one another, saying: *Targum*
  "Holy in the highest heavens, home of His Presence;   *Yonatan*
  holy on earth, the work of His strength;   *Is. 6*
  holy for ever and all time is the LORD of hosts;
  the whole earth is full of His radiant glory."

➤ Then a wind lifted me up   *Ezek. 3*
  and I heard behind me the sound of a great noise, saying,
  "Blessed is the LORD's glory from His place."
  Then a wind lifted me up and I heard behind me   *Targum*
  the sound of a great tempest of those who uttered praise, saying, *Yonatan*
  "Blessed is the LORD's glory from the place of the home of His Presence." *Ezek. 3*

  The LORD shall reign for ever and all time.   *Ex. 15*
  The LORD's kingdom is established for ever and all time.   *Targum*
                                                                     Onkelos Ex. 15

מִקֶּטֶב יָשׁוּד צָהֳרָיִם: יִפֹּל מִצִּדְּךָ אֶלֶף, וּרְבָבָה מִימִינֶךָ, אֵלֶיךָ
לֹא יִגָּשׁ: רַק בְּעֵינֶיךָ תַבִּיט, וְשִׁלֻּמַת רְשָׁעִים תִּרְאֶה: כִּי־אַתָּה
יהוה מַחְסִי, עֶלְיוֹן שַׂמְתָּ מְעוֹנֶךָ: לֹא־תְאֻנֶּה אֵלֶיךָ רָעָה, וְנֶגַע
לֹא־יִקְרַב בְּאָהֳלֶךָ: כִּי מַלְאָכָיו יְצַוֶּה־לָּךְ, לִשְׁמָרְךָ בְּכָל־דְּרָכֶיךָ:
עַל־כַּפַּיִם יִשָּׂאוּנְךָ, פֶּן־תִּגֹּף בָּאֶבֶן רַגְלֶךָ: עַל־שַׁחַל וָפֶתֶן תִּדְרֹךְ,
תִּרְמֹס כְּפִיר וְתַנִּין: כִּי בִי חָשַׁק וַאֲפַלְּטֵהוּ, אֲשַׂגְּבֵהוּ כִּי־יָדַע
שְׁמִי: יִקְרָאֵנִי וְאֶעֱנֵהוּ, עִמּוֹ אָנֹכִי בְצָרָה, אֲחַלְּצֵהוּ וַאֲכַבְּדֵהוּ:

‹ אֹרֶךְ יָמִים אַשְׂבִּיעֵהוּ, וְאַרְאֵהוּ בִּישׁוּעָתִי:
   אֹרֶךְ יָמִים אַשְׂבִּיעֵהוּ, וְאַרְאֵהוּ בִּישׁוּעָתִי:

תהלים כב

‹ וְאַתָּה קָדוֹשׁ יוֹשֵׁב תְּהִלּוֹת יִשְׂרָאֵל:
   וְקָרָא זֶה אֶל־זֶה וְאָמַר

ישעיהו
קָדוֹשׁ, קָדוֹשׁ, קָדוֹשׁ, יהוה צְבָאוֹת, מְלֹא כָל־הָאָרֶץ כְּבוֹדוֹ:

תרגום יונתן
ישעיהו
וּמְקַבְּלִין דֵּין מִן דֵּין וְאָמְרִין
קַדִּישׁ בִּשְׁמֵי מְרוֹמָא עִלָּאָה בֵּית שְׁכִינְתֵּהּ
קַדִּישׁ עַל אַרְעָא עוֹבַד גְּבוּרְתֵּהּ
קַדִּישׁ לְעָלַם וּלְעָלְמֵי עָלְמַיָּא
יהוה צְבָאוֹת, מַלְיָא כָל אַרְעָא זִיו יְקָרֵהּ.

יחזקאל ג
‹ וַתִּשָּׂאֵנִי רוּחַ, וָאֶשְׁמַע אַחֲרַי קוֹל רַעַשׁ גָּדוֹל
   בָּרוּךְ כְּבוֹד־יהוה מִמְּקוֹמוֹ:

תרגום יונתן
יחזקאל ג
וּנְטָלַתְנִי רוּחָא, וְשִׁמְעִית בַּתְרַי קָל זִיעַ סַגִּיא, דִּמְשַׁבְּחִין וְאָמְרִין
בְּרִיךְ יְקָרָא דַיהוה מֵאֲתַר בֵּית שְׁכִינְתֵּהּ.

שמות טו
יהוה יִמְלֹךְ לְעֹלָם וָעֶד:

תרגום אונקלוס
שמות טו
יהוה מַלְכוּתֵהּ קָאֵם לְעָלַם וּלְעָלְמֵי עָלְמַיָּא.

יהוה LORD, God of Abraham, Isaac and Yisrael, our ancestors, may *1 Chr. 29*
You keep this for ever so that it forms the thoughts in Your people's
heart, and directs their heart toward You. He is compassionate. He *Ps. 78*
forgives iniquity and does not destroy. Repeatedly He suppresses
His anger, not rousing His full wrath. For You, my LORD, are good *Ps. 86*
and forgiving, abundantly kind to all who call on You. Your righ- *Ps. 119*
teousness is eternally righteous, and Your Torah is truth. Grant *Micah 7*
truth to Jacob, loving-kindness to Abraham, as You promised our
ancestors in ancient times. Blessed is my LORD for day after day He *Ps. 68*
burdens us [with His blessings]; God is our salvation, Selah! The *Ps. 46*
LORD of hosts is with us; the God of Jacob is our refuge, Selah!
LORD of hosts, happy is the one who trusts in You. LORD, save! *Ps. 84*
May the King answer us on the day we call. *Ps. 20*

בָּרוּךְ Blessed is He, our God, who created us for His glory, separating us from those who go astray; who gave us the Torah of truth,
planting within us eternal life. May He open our heart to His Torah,
imbuing our heart with the love and awe of Him, that we may do
His will and serve Him with a perfect heart, so that we neither toil
in vain nor give birth to confusion.

יְהִי רָצוֹן May it be Your will, O LORD our God and God of our ancestors, that we keep Your laws in this world, and thus be worthy to live,
see and inherit goodness and blessing in the Messianic Age and in
the life of the World to Come. So that my soul may sing to You and *Ps. 30*
not be silent. LORD, my God, for ever I will thank You. Blessed is *Jer. 17*
the man who trusts in the LORD, whose trust is in the LORD alone.
Trust in the LORD for evermore, for God, the LORD, is an everlast- *Is. 26*
ing Rock. ‣ Those who know Your name trust in You, for You, LORD, *Ps. 9*
do not forsake those who seek You. The LORD desired, for the sake *Is. 42*
of Israel's merit, to make the Torah great and glorious.

יְהוָה אֱלֹהֵי אַבְרָהָם יִצְחָק וְיִשְׂרָאֵל אֲבֹתֵינוּ, שָׁמְרָה־זֹּאת לְעוֹלָם
לְיֵצֶר מַחְשְׁבוֹת לְבַב עַמֶּךָ, וְהָכֵן לְבָבָם אֵלֶיךָ: וְהוּא רַחוּם יְכַפֵּר
עָוֹן וְלֹא־יַשְׁחִית, וְהִרְבָּה לְהָשִׁיב אַפּוֹ, וְלֹא־יָעִיר כָּל־חֲמָתוֹ:
כִּי־אַתָּה אֲדֹנָי טוֹב וְסַלָּח, וְרַב־חֶסֶד לְכָל־קֹרְאֶיךָ: צִדְקָתְךָ
צֶדֶק לְעוֹלָם וְתוֹרָתְךָ אֱמֶת: תִּתֵּן אֱמֶת לְיַעֲקֹב, חֶסֶד לְאַבְרָהָם,
אֲשֶׁר־נִשְׁבַּעְתָּ לַאֲבֹתֵינוּ מִימֵי קֶדֶם: בָּרוּךְ אֲדֹנָי יוֹם יוֹם יַעֲמָס־
לָנוּ, הָאֵל יְשׁוּעָתֵנוּ סֶלָה: יְהוָה צְבָאוֹת עִמָּנוּ, מִשְׂגָּב לָנוּ אֱלֹהֵי
יַעֲקֹב סֶלָה: יְהוָה צְבָאוֹת, אַשְׁרֵי אָדָם בֹּטֵחַ בָּךְ: יְהוָה הוֹשִׁיעָה,
הַמֶּלֶךְ יַעֲנֵנוּ בְיוֹם־קָרְאֵנוּ:

בָּרוּךְ הוּא אֱלֹהֵינוּ שֶׁבְּרָאָנוּ לִכְבוֹדוֹ, וְהִבְדִּילָנוּ מִן הַתּוֹעִים,
וְנָתַן לָנוּ תּוֹרַת אֱמֶת, וְחַיֵּי עוֹלָם נָטַע בְּתוֹכֵנוּ. הוּא יִפְתַּח לִבֵּנוּ
בְּתוֹרָתוֹ, וְיָשֵׂם בְּלִבֵּנוּ אַהֲבָתוֹ וְיִרְאָתוֹ וְלַעֲשׂוֹת רְצוֹנוֹ וּלְעָבְדוֹ
בְּלֵבָב שָׁלֵם, לְמַעַן לֹא נִיגַע לָרִיק וְלֹא נֵלֵד לַבֶּהָלָה.

יְהִי רָצוֹן מִלְּפָנֶיךָ יְהוָה אֱלֹהֵינוּ וֵאלֹהֵי אֲבוֹתֵינוּ, שֶׁנִּשְׁמֹר חֻקֶּיךָ
בָּעוֹלָם הַזֶּה, וְנִזְכֶּה וְנִחְיֶה וְנִרְאֶה וְנִירַשׁ טוֹבָה וּבְרָכָה, לִשְׁנֵי
יְמוֹת הַמָּשִׁיחַ וּלְחַיֵּי הָעוֹלָם הַבָּא. לְמַעַן יְזַמֶּרְךָ כָבוֹד וְלֹא יִדֹּם,
יְהוָה אֱלֹהַי, לְעוֹלָם אוֹדֶךָּ: בָּרוּךְ הַגֶּבֶר אֲשֶׁר יִבְטַח בַּיהוָה,
וְהָיָה יְהוָה מִבְטַחוֹ: בִּטְחוּ בַיהוָה עֲדֵי־עַד, כִּי בְּיָהּ יְהוָה צוּר
עוֹלָמִים: ◂ וְיִבְטְחוּ בְךָ יוֹדְעֵי שְׁמֶךָ, כִּי לֹא־עָזַבְתָּ דֹרְשֶׁיךָ, יְהוָה:
יְהוָה חָפֵץ לְמַעַן צִדְקוֹ, יַגְדִּיל תּוֹרָה וְיַאְדִּיר:

דברי הימים
א׳ כט
תהלים עח
תהלים פו
תהלים קיט
מיכה ז
תהלים סח
תהלים מו
תהלים פד
תהלים כ
תהלים ל
ירמיה יז
ישעיה כו
תהלים ט
ישעיה מב

FULL KADDISH

Leader: יִתְגַּדַּל Magnified and sanctified may His great name be,
in the world He created by His will.
May He establish His kingdom in your lifetime
and in your days,
and in the lifetime of all the house of Israel,
swiftly and soon –
and say: Amen.

All: May His great name be blessed for ever and all time.

Leader: Blessed and praised,
glorified and exalted,
raised and honored,
uplifted and lauded be
the name of the Holy One,
blessed be He,
beyond any blessing,
song, praise and consolation uttered in the world –
and say: Amen.

*On Purim and Tisha B'Av, omit the next verse and
continue with "May there be great peace."*
May the prayers and pleas of all Israel
be accepted by their Father in heaven –
and say: Amen.

May there be great peace from heaven,
and life for us and all Israel –
and say: Amen.

*Bow, take three steps back, as if taking leave of the Divine Presence,
then bow, first left, then right, then center, while saying:*
May He who makes peace in His high places,
make peace for us and all Israel –
and say: Amen.

קדיש שלם

ש״ץ יִתְגַּדַּל וְיִתְקַדַּשׁ שְׁמֵהּ רַבָּא (קהל: אָמֵן)
בְּעָלְמָא דִּי בְרָא כִרְעוּתֵהּ
וְיַמְלִיךְ מַלְכוּתֵהּ
בְּחַיֵּיכוֹן וּבְיוֹמֵיכוֹן וּבְחַיֵּי דְכָל בֵּית יִשְׂרָאֵל
בַּעֲגָלָא וּבִזְמַן קָרִיב, וְאִמְרוּ אָמֵן. (קהל: אָמֵן)

קהל
ושׁ״ץ: יְהֵא שְׁמֵהּ רַבָּא מְבָרַךְ לְעָלַם וּלְעָלְמֵי עָלְמַיָּא.

שׁ״ץ: יִתְבָּרַךְ וְיִשְׁתַּבַּח וְיִתְפָּאַר
וְיִתְרוֹמַם וְיִתְנַשֵּׂא וְיִתְהַדָּר וְיִתְעַלֶּה וְיִתְהַלָּל
שְׁמֵהּ דְּקֻדְשָׁא בְּרִיךְ הוּא (קהל: בְּרִיךְ הוּא)
לְעֵלָּא מִן כָּל בִּרְכָתָא
/בעשרת ימי תשובה: לְעֵלָּא לְעֵלָּא מִכָּל בִּרְכָתָא/
וְשִׁירָתָא, תֻּשְׁבְּחָתָא וְנֶחֱמָתָא
דַּאֲמִירָן בְּעָלְמָא, וְאִמְרוּ אָמֵן. (קהל: אָמֵן)

On פורים and תשעה באב, omit the next verse and continue with יְהֵא שְׁלָמָא.
תִּתְקַבַּל צְלוֹתְהוֹן וּבָעוּתְהוֹן דְּכָל יִשְׂרָאֵל
קֳדָם אֲבוּהוֹן דִּי בִשְׁמַיָּא, וְאִמְרוּ אָמֵן. (קהל: אָמֵן)

יְהֵא שְׁלָמָא רַבָּא מִן שְׁמַיָּא
וְחַיִּים, עָלֵינוּ וְעַל כָּל יִשְׂרָאֵל, וְאִמְרוּ אָמֵן. (קהל: אָמֵן)

Bow, take three steps back, as if taking leave of the Divine Presence,
then bow, first left, then right, then center, while saying:

עֹשֶׂה שָׁלוֹם/בעשרת ימי תשובה: הַשָּׁלוֹם/ בִּמְרוֹמָיו
הוּא יַעֲשֶׂה שָׁלוֹם עָלֵינוּ וְעַל כָּל יִשְׂרָאֵל
וְאִמְרוּ אָמֵן. (קהל: אָמֵן)

Between Pesaḥ and Shavuot the Omer is counted at this point on page 388.
On Ḥanukka, the candles are lit at this point, page 562.
On Tisha B'Av, the following prayers are omitted
and the service continues with Aleinu on page 416.

BIBLICAL VERSES OF BLESSING

וְיִתֶּן־לְךָ **May God give you dew from heaven and the richness of the earth, and** *Gen. 27*
corn and wine in plenty. May peoples serve you and nations bow down to you.
Be lord over your brothers, and may your mother's sons bow down to you. A
curse on those who curse you, but a blessing on those who bless you.

וְאֵל שַׁדַּי **May God Almighty bless you; may He make you fruitful and numerous** *Gen. 28*
until you become an assembly of peoples. May He give you and your descendants the blessing of Abraham, that you may possess the land where you are
now staying, the land God gave to Abraham. This comes from the God of your *Gen. 49*
father – may He help you – and from the Almighty – may He bless you with
blessings of the heaven above and the blessings of the deep that lies below, the
blessings of breast and womb. The blessings of your father surpass the blessings
of my fathers to the bounds of the endless hills. May they rest on the head of
Joseph, on the brow of the prince among his brothers. He will love you and bless *Deut. 7*
you and increase your numbers. He will bless the fruit of your womb and the
fruit of your land: your corn, your wine and oil, the calves of your herds and
the lambs of your flocks, in the land He swore to your fathers to give you. You
will be blessed more than any other people. None of your men or women will
be childless, nor any of your livestock without young. The LORD will keep you
free from any disease. He will not inflict on you the terrible diseases you knew
in Egypt, but He will inflict them on those who hate you.

הַמַּלְאָךְ **May the angel who rescued me from all harm, bless these boys. May they** *Gen. 48*
be called by my name and the names of my fathers Abraham and Isaac, and may
they increase greatly on the earth. The LORD your God has increased your num- *Deut. 1*
bers so that today you are as many as the stars in the sky. May the LORD, God of
your fathers, increase you a thousand times, and bless you as He promised you.

בָּרוּךְ **You will be blessed in the city, and blessed in the field. You will be blessed** *Deut. 28*
when you come in, and blessed when you go out. Your basket and your kneading
trough will be blessed. The fruit of your womb will be blessed, and the crops
of your land, and the young of your livestock, the calves of your herds and
the lambs of your flocks. The LORD will send a blessing on your barns, and on everything you put your hand to. The LORD your God will bless you in the land
He is giving you. The LORD will open for you the heavens, the storehouse of
His bounty, to send rain on your land in season, and to bless all the work of your
hands. You will lend to many nations but will borrow from none. For the LORD *Deut. 15*

Between פסח *and* שבועות *the* עומר *is counted at this point on page 389.*
On חנוכה*, the candles are lit at this point, page 563.*
On תשעה באב*, the following prayers are omitted*
and the service continues with עלינו *on page 417.*

פסוקי ברכה

בראשית כז וְיִתֶּן־לְךָ הָאֱלֹהִים מִטַּל הַשָּׁמַיִם וּמִשְׁמַנֵּי הָאָרֶץ, וְרֹב דָּגָן וְתִירֹשׁ: יַעַבְדוּךָ עַמִּים וְיִשְׁתַּחֲווּ לְךָ לְאֻמִּים, הֱוֵה גְבִיר לְאַחֶיךָ וְיִשְׁתַּחֲווּ לְךָ בְּנֵי אִמֶּךָ, אֹרְרֶיךָ אָרוּר וּמְבָרֲכֶיךָ בָּרוּךְ:

בראשית כח וְאֵל שַׁדַּי יְבָרֵךְ אֹתְךָ וְיַפְרְךָ וְיַרְבֶּךָ, וְהָיִיתָ לִקְהַל עַמִּים: וְיִתֶּן־לְךָ אֶת־ בִּרְכַּת אַבְרָהָם, לְךָ וּלְזַרְעֲךָ אִתָּךְ, לְרִשְׁתְּךָ אֶת־אֶרֶץ מְגֻרֶיךָ אֲשֶׁר־נָתַן אֱלֹהִים לְאַבְרָהָם: בראשית מט מֵאֵל אָבִיךָ וְיַעְזְרֶךָּ וְאֵת שַׁדַּי וִיבָרְכֶךָּ, בִּרְכֹת שָׁמַיִם מֵעָל בִּרְכֹת תְּהוֹם רֹבֶצֶת תָּחַת, בִּרְכֹת שָׁדַיִם וָרָחַם: בִּרְכֹת אָבִיךָ גָּבְרוּ עַל־בִּרְכֹת הוֹרַי עַד־תַּאֲוַת גִּבְעֹת עוֹלָם, תִּהְיֶיןָ לְרֹאשׁ יוֹסֵף וּלְקָדְקֹד דברים ז נְזִיר אֶחָיו: וַאֲהֵבְךָ וּבֵרַכְךָ וְהִרְבֶּךָ, וּבֵרַךְ פְּרִי־בִטְנְךָ וּפְרִי־אַדְמָתֶךָ, דְּגָנְךָ וְתִירֹשְׁךָ וְיִצְהָרֶךָ, שְׁגַר־אֲלָפֶיךָ וְעַשְׁתְּרֹת צֹאנֶךָ, עַל הָאֲדָמָה אֲשֶׁר־נִשְׁבַּע לַאֲבֹתֶיךָ לָתֶת לָךְ: בָּרוּךְ תִּהְיֶה מִכָּל־הָעַמִּים, לֹא־יִהְיֶה בְךָ עָקָר וַעֲקָרָה וּבִבְהֶמְתֶּךָ: וְהֵסִיר יהוה מִמְּךָ כָּל־חֹלִי, וְכָל־מַדְוֵי מִצְרַיִם הָרָעִים אֲשֶׁר יָדַעְתָּ, לֹא יְשִׂימָם בָּךְ, וּנְתָנָם בְּכָל־שֹׂנְאֶיךָ:

בראשית מח הַמַּלְאָךְ הַגֹּאֵל אֹתִי מִכָּל־רָע יְבָרֵךְ אֶת־הַנְּעָרִים, וְיִקָּרֵא בָהֶם שְׁמִי וְשֵׁם דברים א אֲבֹתַי אַבְרָהָם וְיִצְחָק, וְיִדְגּוּ לָרֹב בְּקֶרֶב הָאָרֶץ: יהוה אֱלֹהֵיכֶם הִרְבָּה אֶתְכֶם, וְהִנְּכֶם הַיּוֹם כְּכוֹכְבֵי הַשָּׁמַיִם לָרֹב: יהוה אֱלֹהֵי אֲבוֹתֵכֶם יֹסֵף עֲלֵיכֶם כָּכֶם אֶלֶף פְּעָמִים, וִיבָרֵךְ אֶתְכֶם כַּאֲשֶׁר דִּבֶּר לָכֶם:

דברים כח בָּרוּךְ אַתָּה בָּעִיר, וּבָרוּךְ אַתָּה בַּשָּׂדֶה: בָּרוּךְ אַתָּה בְּבֹאֶךָ, וּבָרוּךְ אַתָּה בְּצֵאתֶךָ: בָּרוּךְ טַנְאֲךָ וּמִשְׁאַרְתֶּךָ: בָּרוּךְ פְּרִי־בִטְנְךָ וּפְרִי אַדְמָתְךָ וּפְרִי בְהֶמְתֶּךָ, שְׁגַר אֲלָפֶיךָ וְעַשְׁתְּרוֹת צֹאנֶךָ: יְצַו יהוה אִתְּךָ אֶת־הַבְּרָכָה בַּאֲסָמֶיךָ וּבְכֹל מִשְׁלַח יָדֶךָ, וּבֵרַכְךָ בָּאָרֶץ אֲשֶׁר־יהוה אֱלֹהֶיךָ נֹתֵן לָךְ: יִפְתַּח יהוה לְךָ אֶת־אוֹצָרוֹ הַטּוֹב אֶת־הַשָּׁמַיִם, לָתֵת מְטַר־אַרְצְךָ בְּעִתּוֹ, דברים טו וּלְבָרֵךְ אֵת כָּל־מַעֲשֵׂה יָדֶךָ, וְהִלְוִיתָ גּוֹיִם רַבִּים וְאַתָּה לֹא תִלְוֶה: כִּי־יהוה

your God will bless you as He has promised: you will lend to many nations but will borrow from none. You will rule over many nations, but none will rule over you. Happy are you, Israel! Who is like you, a people saved by the LORD? He is your Shield and Helper and your glorious Sword. Your enemies will cower before you, and you will tread on their high places. *Deut. 33*

מָחִיתִי I have wiped away your transgressions like a cloud, your sins like the morning mist. Return to Me for I have redeemed you. Sing for joy, O heavens, for the LORD has done this; shout aloud, you depths of the earth; burst into song, you mountains, you forests and all your trees, for the LORD has redeemed Jacob, and will glory in Israel. Our Redeemer, the LORD of hosts is His name, the Holy One of Israel. *Is. 44* *Is. 47*

יִשְׂרָאֵל Israel is saved by the LORD with everlasting salvation. You will never be ashamed or disgraced to time everlasting. You will eat your fill and praise the name of the LORD your God, who has worked wonders for you. Never again shall My people be shamed. Then you will know that I am in the midst of Israel, that I am the LORD your God, and there is no other. Never again will My people be shamed. You will go out in joy and be led out in peace. The mountains and hills will burst into song before you, and all the trees of the field will clap their hands. Behold, God is my salvation, I will trust and not be afraid. The LORD, the LORD, is my strength and my song. He has become my salvation. With joy you will draw water from the springs of salvation. On that day you will say, "Thank the LORD, proclaim His name, make His deeds known among the nations." Declare that His name is exalted. Sing to the LORD, for He has done glorious things; let this be known throughout the world. Shout aloud and sing for joy, you who dwell in Zion, for great in your midst is the Holy One of Israel. On that day they will say, "See, this is our God; we set our hope in Him and He saved us. This is the LORD in whom we hoped; let us rejoice and be glad in His salvation." *Is. 45* *Joel 2* *Is. 55* *Is. 12* *Is. 25*

בֵּית Come, house of Jacob: let us walk in the light of the LORD. He will be the sure foundation of your times; a rich store of salvation, wisdom and knowledge – the fear of the LORD is a person's treasure. In everything he did, David was successful, for the LORD was with him. *Is. 2* *Is. 32* *1 Sam. 18*

פָּדָה He redeemed my soul in peace from the battle waged against me, for the sake of the many who were with me. The people said to Saul, "Shall Jonathan die – he who has brought about this great deliverance in Israel? Heaven forbid! As surely as the LORD lives, not a hair of his head shall fall to the ground, for he did this today with God's help." So the people rescued Jonathan and he did not die. Those redeemed by the LORD shall return; they will enter Zion singing; everlasting joy will crown their heads. Gladness and joy will overtake them, and sorrow and sighing will flee away. *Ps. 55* *1 Sam. 14* *Is. 35*

אֱלֹהֶיךָ בֵּרַכְךָ כַּאֲשֶׁר דִּבֶּר־לָךְ, וְהַעֲבַטְתָּ גּוֹיִם רַבִּים וְאַתָּה לֹא תַעֲבֹט,
וּמָשַׁלְתָּ בְּגוֹיִם רַבִּים וּבְךָ לֹא יִמְשֹׁלוּ: אַשְׁרֶיךָ יִשְׂרָאֵל, מִי כָמוֹךָ, עַם
נוֹשַׁע בַּיהוָה, מָגֵן עֶזְרֶךָ וַאֲשֶׁר־חֶרֶב גַּאֲוָתֶךָ, וְיִכָּחֲשׁוּ אֹיְבֶיךָ לָךְ, וְאַתָּה
עַל־בָּמוֹתֵימוֹ תִדְרֹךְ:
דברים לג

מָחִיתִי כָעָב פְּשָׁעֶיךָ וְכֶעָנָן חַטֹּאותֶיךָ, שׁוּבָה אֵלַי כִּי גְאַלְתִּיךָ: רָנּוּ שָׁמַיִם
כִּי־עָשָׂה יְהוָה, הָרִיעוּ תַּחְתִּיּוֹת אָרֶץ, פִּצְחוּ הָרִים רִנָּה, יַעַר וְכָל־עֵץ בּוֹ,
כִּי־גָאַל יְהוָה יַעֲקֹב וּבְיִשְׂרָאֵל יִתְפָּאָר: גֹּאֲלֵנוּ, יְהוָה צְבָאוֹת שְׁמוֹ, קְדוֹשׁ
יִשְׂרָאֵל:
ישעיה מד
ישעיה מז

יִשְׂרָאֵל נוֹשַׁע בַּיהוָה תְּשׁוּעַת עוֹלָמִים, לֹא־תֵבֹשׁוּ וְלֹא־תִכָּלְמוּ עַד־עוֹלְמֵי
עַד: וַאֲכַלְתֶּם אָכוֹל וְשָׂבוֹעַ, וְהִלַּלְתֶּם אֶת־שֵׁם יְהוָה אֱלֹהֵיכֶם אֲשֶׁר־עָשָׂה
עִמָּכֶם לְהַפְלִיא, וְלֹא־יֵבֹשׁוּ עַמִּי לְעוֹלָם: וִידַעְתֶּם כִּי בְקֶרֶב יִשְׂרָאֵל
אָנִי, וַאֲנִי יְהוָה אֱלֹהֵיכֶם וְאֵין עוֹד, וְלֹא־יֵבֹשׁוּ עַמִּי לְעוֹלָם: כִּי־בְשִׂמְחָה
תֵצֵאוּ וּבְשָׁלוֹם תּוּבָלוּן, הֶהָרִים וְהַגְּבָעוֹת יִפְצְחוּ לִפְנֵיכֶם רִנָּה, וְכָל־עֲצֵי
הַשָּׂדֶה יִמְחֲאוּ־כָף: הִנֵּה אֵל יְשׁוּעָתִי אֶבְטַח, וְלֹא אֶפְחָד, כִּי־עָזִּי וְזִמְרָת
יָהּ יְהוָה, וַיְהִי־לִי לִישׁוּעָה: וּשְׁאַבְתֶּם־מַיִם בְּשָׂשׂוֹן, מִמַּעַיְנֵי הַיְשׁוּעָה:
וַאֲמַרְתֶּם בַּיּוֹם הַהוּא, הוֹדוּ לַיהוָה קִרְאוּ בִשְׁמוֹ, הוֹדִיעוּ בָעַמִּים עֲלִילֹתָיו,
הַזְכִּירוּ כִּי נִשְׂגָּב שְׁמוֹ: זַמְּרוּ יְהוָה כִּי גֵאוּת עָשָׂה, מוּדַעַת זֹאת בְּכָל־
הָאָרֶץ: צַהֲלִי וָרֹנִּי יוֹשֶׁבֶת צִיּוֹן, כִּי־גָדוֹל בְּקִרְבֵּךְ קְדוֹשׁ יִשְׂרָאֵל: וְאָמַר
בַּיּוֹם הַהוּא, הִנֵּה אֱלֹהֵינוּ זֶה קִוִּינוּ לוֹ וְיוֹשִׁיעֵנוּ, זֶה יְהוָה קִוִּינוּ לוֹ, נָגִילָה
וְנִשְׂמְחָה בִּישׁוּעָתוֹ:
ישעיה מה
יואל ב
ישעיה נה
ישעיה יב
ישעיה כה

בֵּית יַעֲקֹב לְכוּ וְנֵלְכָה בְּאוֹר יְהוָה: וְהָיָה אֱמוּנַת עִתֶּיךָ, חֹסֶן יְשׁוּעֹת חָכְמַת
וָדָעַת, יִרְאַת יְהוָה הִיא אוֹצָרוֹ: וַיְהִי דָוִד לְכָל־דְּרָכָו מַשְׂכִּיל, וַיהוָה עִמּוֹ:
ישעיה ב
ישעיה לג
שמואל א יח

פָּדָה בְשָׁלוֹם נַפְשִׁי מִקְּרָב־לִי, כִּי־בְרַבִּים הָיוּ עִמָּדִי: וַיֹּאמֶר הָעָם אֶל־
שָׁאוּל, הֲיוֹנָתָן יָמוּת אֲשֶׁר עָשָׂה הַיְשׁוּעָה הַגְּדוֹלָה הַזֹּאת בְּיִשְׂרָאֵל,
חָלִילָה, חַי־יְהוָה אִם־יִפֹּל מִשַּׂעֲרַת רֹאשׁוֹ אַרְצָה, כִּי־עִם־אֱלֹהִים עָשָׂה
הַיּוֹם הַזֶּה, וַיִּפְדּוּ הָעָם אֶת־יוֹנָתָן וְלֹא־מֵת: וּפְדוּיֵי יְהוָה יְשֻׁבוּן וּבָאוּ צִיּוֹן
בְּרִנָּה, וְשִׂמְחַת עוֹלָם עַל־רֹאשָׁם, שָׂשׂוֹן וְשִׂמְחָה יַשִּׂיגוּ, וְנָסוּ יָגוֹן וַאֲנָחָה:
תהלים נה
שמואל א יד
ישעיה לה

הָפַכְתָּ You have turned my sorrow into dancing. You have removed my sackcloth *Ps. 30* and clothed me with joy. The Lord your God refused to listen to Balaam; in- *Deut. 23* stead the Lord your God turned the curse into a blessing, for the Lord your God loves you. Then maidens will dance and be glad; so too will young men and *Jer. 31* old together; I will turn their mourning into gladness; I will give them comfort and joy instead of sorrow.

בּוֹרֵא I create the speech of lips: Peace, peace to those far and near, says the Lord, *Is. 57* and I will heal them. Then the spirit came upon Amasai, chief of the captains, *1 Chr. 12* and he said: "We are yours, David! We are with you, son of Jesse! Peace, peace to you, and peace to those who help you; for your God will help you." Then David received them and made them leaders of his troop. And you shall say: "To life! *1 Sam. 25* Peace be to you, peace to your household, and peace to all that is yours!" The Lord will give strength to His people; the Lord will bless His people with peace. *Ps. 29*

אָמַר Rabbi Yoḥanan said: Wherever you find the greatness of the Holy One, *Megilla 31a* blessed be He, there you find His humility. This is written in the Torah, repeated in the Prophets, and stated a third time in the Writings. It is written in the Torah: "For the Lord your God is God of gods and Lord of lords, the great, *Deut. 10* mighty and awe-inspiring God, who shows no favoritism and accepts no bribe." Immediately afterwards it is written, "He upholds the cause of the orphan and widow, and loves the stranger, giving him food and clothing." It is repeated in the Prophets, as it says: "So says the High and Exalted One, who lives for ever and *Is. 57* whose name is Holy: I live in a high and holy place, but also with the contrite and lowly in spirit, to revive the spirit of the lowly, and to revive the heart of the contrite." It is stated a third time in the Writings: "Sing to God, make music for *Ps. 68* His name, extol Him who rides the clouds – the Lord is His name – and exult before Him." Immediately afterwards it is written: "Father of the orphans and Justice of widows, is God in His holy habitation."

יְהִי May the Lord our God be with us, as He was with our ancestors. May He *1 Kings 8* never abandon us or forsake us. You who cleave to the Lord your God are all *Deut. 4* alive this day. For the Lord will comfort Zion, He will comfort all her ruins; *Is. 51* He will make her wilderness like Eden, and her desert like a garden of the Lord. Joy and gladness will be found there, thanksgiving and the sound of singing. It *Is. 42* pleased the Lord for the sake of [Israel's] righteousness to make the Torah great and glorious.

שִׁיר הַמַּעֲלוֹת A song of ascents. Happy are all who fear the Lord, who walk in His *Ps. 128* ways. When you eat the fruit of your labor, happy and fortunate are you. Your wife shall be like a fruitful vine within your house; your sons like olive saplings around your table. So shall the man who fears the Lord be blessed. May the Lord bless you from Zion; may you see the good of Jerusalem all the days of your life; and may you live to see your children's children. Peace be on Israel!

תהלים ל
דברים כג

הָפַכְתָּ מִסְפְּדִי לְמָחוֹל לִי, פִּתַּחְתָּ שַׂקִּי, וַתְּאַזְּרֵנִי שִׂמְחָה: וְלֹא־אָבָה יהוה אֱלֹהֶיךָ לִשְׁמֹעַ אֶל־בִּלְעָם, וַיַּהֲפֹךְ יהוה אֱלֹהֶיךָ לְּךָ אֶת־הַקְּלָלָה לִבְרָכָה,

ירמיה לא

כִּי אֲהֵבְךָ יהוה אֱלֹהֶיךָ: אָז תִּשְׂמַח בְּתוּלָה בְּמָחוֹל, וּבַחֻרִים וּזְקֵנִים יַחְדָּו, וְהָפַכְתִּי אֶבְלָם לְשָׂשׂוֹן, וְנִחַמְתִּים, וְשִׂמַּחְתִּים מִיגוֹנָם:

ישעיה נז
דברי
הימים א׳ י״ב

בּוֹרֵא נִיב שְׂפָתָיִם, שָׁלוֹם שָׁלוֹם לָרָחוֹק וְלַקָּרוֹב אָמַר יהוה, וּרְפָאתִיו: וְרוּחַ לָבְשָׁה אֶת־עֲמָשַׂי רֹאשׁ הַשָּׁלִישִׁים, לְךָ דָוִיד וְעִמְּךָ בֶן־יִשַׁי, שָׁלוֹם שָׁלוֹם לְךָ וְשָׁלוֹם לְעֹזְרֶךָ, כִּי עֲזָרְךָ אֱלֹהֶיךָ, וַיְקַבְּלֵם דָּוִיד וַיִּתְּנֵם בְּרָאשֵׁי הַגְּדוּד:

שמואל א׳ כה
תהלים כט

וַאֲמַרְתֶּם כֹּה לֶחָי, וְאַתָּה שָׁלוֹם וּבֵיתְךָ שָׁלוֹם וְכֹל אֲשֶׁר־לְךָ שָׁלוֹם: יהוה עֹז לְעַמּוֹ יִתֵּן, יהוה יְבָרֵךְ אֶת־עַמּוֹ בַשָּׁלוֹם:

מגילה לא

אָמַר רַבִּי יוֹחָנָן: בְּכָל מָקוֹם שֶׁאַתָּה מוֹצֵא גְּדֻלָּתוֹ שֶׁל הַקָּדוֹשׁ בָּרוּךְ הוּא, שָׁם אַתָּה מוֹצֵא עַנְוְתָנוּתוֹ. דָּבָר זֶה כָּתוּב בַּתּוֹרָה, וְשָׁנוּי בַּנְּבִיאִים,

דברים י

וּמְשֻׁלָּשׁ בַּכְּתוּבִים. כָּתוּב בַּתּוֹרָה: כִּי יהוה אֱלֹהֵיכֶם הוּא אֱלֹהֵי הָאֱלֹהִים וַאֲדֹנֵי הָאֲדֹנִים, הָאֵל הַגָּדֹל הַגִּבֹּר וְהַנּוֹרָא, אֲשֶׁר לֹא־יִשָּׂא פָנִים וְלֹא יִקַּח שֹׁחַד: וּכְתִיב בַּתְרֵהּ: עֹשֶׂה מִשְׁפַּט יָתוֹם וְאַלְמָנָה, וְאֹהֵב גֵּר לָתֶת לוֹ לֶחֶם

ישעיה נז

וְשִׂמְלָה: שָׁנוּי בַּנְּבִיאִים, דִּכְתִיב: כִּי כֹה אָמַר רָם וְנִשָּׂא שֹׁכֵן עַד וְקָדוֹשׁ שְׁמוֹ, מָרוֹם וְקָדוֹשׁ אֶשְׁכּוֹן, וְאֶת־דַּכָּא וּשְׁפַל־רוּחַ, לְהַחֲיוֹת רוּחַ שְׁפָלִים

תהלים סח

וּלְהַחֲיוֹת לֵב נִדְכָּאִים: מְשֻׁלָּשׁ בַּכְּתוּבִים, דִּכְתִיב: שִׁירוּ לֵאלֹהִים, זַמְּרוּ שְׁמוֹ, סֹלּוּ לָרֹכֵב בָּעֲרָבוֹת בְּיָהּ שְׁמוֹ, וְעִלְזוּ לְפָנָיו: וּכְתִיב בַּתְרֵהּ: אֲבִי יְתוֹמִים וְדַיַּן אַלְמָנוֹת, אֱלֹהִים בִּמְעוֹן קָדְשׁוֹ:

מלכים א׳ ח
דברים ד
ישעיה נא

יְהִי יהוה אֱלֹהֵינוּ עִמָּנוּ כַּאֲשֶׁר הָיָה עִם־אֲבֹתֵינוּ, אַל־יַעַזְבֵנוּ וְאַל־יִטְּשֵׁנוּ: וְאַתֶּם הַדְּבֵקִים בַּיהוה אֱלֹהֵיכֶם, חַיִּים כֻּלְּכֶם הַיּוֹם: כִּי־נִחַם יהוה צִיּוֹן, נִחַם כָּל־חָרְבֹתֶיהָ, וַיָּשֶׂם מִדְבָּרָהּ כְּעֵדֶן וְעַרְבָתָהּ כְּגַן־יהוה, שָׂשׂוֹן וְשִׂמְחָה יִמָּצֵא

ישעיה מב

בָהּ, תּוֹדָה וְקוֹל זִמְרָה: יהוה חָפֵץ לְמַעַן צִדְקוֹ, יַגְדִּיל תּוֹרָה וְיַאְדִּיר:

תהלים קכח

שִׁיר הַמַּעֲלוֹת, אַשְׁרֵי כָּל־יְרֵא יהוה, הַהֹלֵךְ בִּדְרָכָיו: יְגִיעַ כַּפֶּיךָ כִּי תֹאכֵל, אַשְׁרֶיךָ וְטוֹב לָךְ: אֶשְׁתְּךָ כְּגֶפֶן פֹּרִיָּה בְּיַרְכְּתֵי בֵיתֶךָ, בָּנֶיךָ כִּשְׁתִלֵי זֵיתִים, סָבִיב לְשֻׁלְחָנֶךָ: הִנֵּה כִי־כֵן יְבֹרַךְ גָּבֶר יְרֵא יהוה: יְבָרֶכְךָ יהוה מִצִּיּוֹן, וּרְאֵה בְּטוּב יְרוּשָׁלָםִ, כֹּל יְמֵי חַיֶּיךָ: וּרְאֵה־בָנִים לְבָנֶיךָ, שָׁלוֹם עַל־יִשְׂרָאֵל:

HAVDALA

Some congregations begin Havdala at "Please pay attention" below.
On Motza'ei Yom Tov that is not a Motza'ei Shabbat, the blessings for
the spices and flame are omitted. At the end of Yom Kippur, only the
blessing for the spices is omitted. See laws 246, 247 and 249.

The Leader takes the cup of wine in his right hand, and says:

הִנֵּה Behold, God is my salvation. I will trust and not be afraid. *Is. 12*
The Lord, the Lord, is my strength and my song.
He has become my salvation.
With joy you will draw water from the springs of salvation.
Salvation is the Lord's; on Your people is Your blessing, Selah. *Ps. 3*
The Lord of hosts is with us, the God of Jacob is our stronghold, Selah. *Ps. 46*
Lord of hosts: happy is the one who trusts in You. *Ps. 84*
Lord, save! May the King answer us on the day we call. *Ps. 20*
For the Jews there was light and gladness, joy and honor – *Esther 8*
so may it be for us.
I will lift the cup of salvation and call on the name of the Lord. *Ps. 116*

Please pay attention, my masters.
Blessed are You, Lord our God, King of the Universe,
who creates the fruit of the vine.

Holding the spice box, the Leader says:

Blessed are You, Lord our God, King of the Universe,
who creates the various spices.

The Leader smells the spices and puts the spice box down.
He lifts his hands toward the flame of the Havdala candle, and says:

Blessed are You, Lord our God, King of the Universe,
who creates the lights of fire.

He lifts the cup of wine in his right hand, and says:

Blessed are You, Lord our God, King of the Universe, who distinguishes
between sacred and secular, between light and darkness, between Israel
and the nations, between the seventh day and the six days of work. Blessed
are You, Lord, who distinguishes between sacred and secular.

On Sukkot, if Havdala is made in the sukka, add:
Blessed are You, Lord our God, King of the Universe,
who has made us holy through his commandments
and has commanded us to dwell in the sukka.

הַבְדָּלָה

Some congregations begin הבדלה at סָבְרִי מָרָנָן below.
On מוצאי יום טוב that is not a מוצאי שבת, the blessings for the spices and flame are omitted.
At the end of יום כפור, only the blessing for the spices is omitted. See laws 246, 247 and 249.

The שליח ציבור takes the cup of wine in his right hand, and says:

ישעיה יב

הִנֵּה אֵל יְשׁוּעָתִי אֶבְטַח, וְלֹא אֶפְחָד
כִּי־עָזִּי וְזִמְרָת יָהּ יהוה, וַיְהִי־לִי לִישׁוּעָה:
וּשְׁאַבְתֶּם־מַיִם בְּשָׂשׂוֹן, מִמַּעַיְנֵי הַיְשׁוּעָה:

תהלים ג

לַיהוה הַיְשׁוּעָה, עַל־עַמְּךָ בִרְכָתֶךָ סֶּלָה:

תהלים מו

יהוה צְבָאוֹת עִמָּנוּ, מִשְׂגָּב לָנוּ אֱלֹהֵי יַעֲקֹב סֶלָה:

תהלים פד

יהוה צְבָאוֹת, אַשְׁרֵי אָדָם בֹּטֵחַ בָּךְ:

תהלים כ

יהוה הוֹשִׁיעָה, הַמֶּלֶךְ יַעֲנֵנוּ בְיוֹם־קָרְאֵנוּ:

אסתר ח

לַיְּהוּדִים הָיְתָה אוֹרָה וְשִׂמְחָה וְשָׂשֹׂן וִיקָר: כֵּן תִּהְיֶה לָּנוּ:

תהלים קטז

כּוֹס־יְשׁוּעוֹת אֶשָּׂא, וּבְשֵׁם יהוה אֶקְרָא:

סָבְרִי מָרָנָן

בָּרוּךְ אַתָּה יהוה אֱלֹהֵינוּ מֶלֶךְ הָעוֹלָם, בּוֹרֵא פְּרִי הַגָּפֶן.

Holding the spice box, the שליח ציבור says:

בָּרוּךְ אַתָּה יהוה אֱלֹהֵינוּ מֶלֶךְ הָעוֹלָם, בּוֹרֵא מִינֵי בְשָׂמִים.

The שליח ציבור smells the spices and puts the spice box down.
He lifts his hands toward the flame of the הבדלה candle, and says:

בָּרוּךְ אַתָּה יהוה אֱלֹהֵינוּ מֶלֶךְ הָעוֹלָם, בּוֹרֵא מְאוֹרֵי הָאֵשׁ.

He lifts the cup of wine in his right hand, and says:

בָּרוּךְ אַתָּה יהוה אֱלֹהֵינוּ מֶלֶךְ הָעוֹלָם, הַמַּבְדִּיל בֵּין קֹדֶשׁ לְחֹל,
בֵּין אוֹר לְחֹשֶׁךְ, בֵּין יִשְׂרָאֵל לָעַמִּים, בֵּין יוֹם הַשְּׁבִיעִי לְשֵׁשֶׁת יְמֵי
הַמַּעֲשֶׂה. בָּרוּךְ אַתָּה יהוה, הַמַּבְדִּיל בֵּין קֹדֶשׁ לְחֹל.

On סוכות, if הבדלה is made in the סוכה, add:

בָּרוּךְ אַתָּה יהוה אֱלֹהֵינוּ מֶלֶךְ הָעוֹלָם
אֲשֶׁר קִדְּשָׁנוּ בְּמִצְוֹתָיו וְצִוָּנוּ לֵישֵׁב בַּסֻּכָּה.

Stand while saying Aleinu. Bow at ˎ.

עָלֵינוּ It is our duty to praise the Master of all,
and ascribe greatness to the Author of creation,
who has not made us like the nations of the lands
nor placed us like the families of the earth;
who has not made our portion like theirs,
nor our destiny like all their multitudes.
(For they worship vanity and emptiness,
and pray to a god who cannot save.)
ˎBut we bow in worship and thank the Supreme King of kings,
the Holy One, blessed be He,
who extends the heavens and establishes the earth,
whose throne of glory is in the heavens above,
and whose power's Presence is in the highest of heights.
He is our God; there is no other.
Truly He is our King, there is none else, as it is written in His Torah:
"You shall know and take to heart this day that the LORD is God,   *Deut. 4*
in heaven above and on earth below. There is no other."

Therefore, we place our hope in You, LORD our God,
that we may soon see the glory of Your power,
when You will remove abominations from the earth,
and idols will be utterly destroyed,
when the world will be perfected under the sovereignty of the Almighty,
when all humanity will call on Your name,
to turn all the earth's wicked toward You.
All the world's inhabitants will realize and know
that to You every knee must bow and every tongue swear loyalty.
Before You, LORD our God, they will kneel and bow down
and give honor to Your glorious name.
They will all accept the yoke of Your kingdom,
and You will reign over them soon and for ever.
For the kingdom is Yours, and to all eternity You will reign in glory,
as it is written in Your Torah:
"The LORD will reign for ever and ever."   *Ex. 15*
▸ And it is said: "Then the LORD shall be King over all the earth;   *Zech. 14*
on that day the LORD shall be One and His name One."

Stand while saying עָלֵינוּ. Bow at ⁎.

עָלֵינוּ לְשַׁבֵּחַ לַאֲדוֹן הַכֹּל, לָתֵת גְּדֻלָּה לְיוֹצֵר בְּרֵאשִׁית
שֶׁלֹּא עָשָׂנוּ כְּגוֹיֵי הָאֲרָצוֹת, וְלֹא שָׂמָנוּ כְּמִשְׁפְּחוֹת הָאֲדָמָה
שֶׁלֹּא שָׂם חֶלְקֵנוּ כָּהֶם וְגוֹרָלֵנוּ כְּכָל הֲמוֹנָם.
(שֶׁהֵם מִשְׁתַּחֲוִים לְהֶבֶל וָרִיק וּמִתְפַּלְּלִים אֶל אֵל לֹא יוֹשִׁיעַ.)

⁎וַאֲנַחְנוּ כּוֹרְעִים וּמִשְׁתַּחֲוִים וּמוֹדִים
לִפְנֵי מֶלֶךְ מַלְכֵי הַמְּלָכִים, הַקָּדוֹשׁ בָּרוּךְ הוּא
שֶׁהוּא נוֹטֶה שָׁמַיִם וְיוֹסֵד אָרֶץ
וּמוֹשַׁב יְקָרוֹ בַּשָּׁמַיִם מִמַּעַל
וּשְׁכִינַת עֻזּוֹ בְּגָבְהֵי מְרוֹמִים.
הוּא אֱלֹהֵינוּ, אֵין עוֹד.
אֱמֶת מַלְכֵּנוּ, אֶפֶס זוּלָתוֹ, כַּכָּתוּב בְּתוֹרָתוֹ
וְיָדַעְתָּ הַיּוֹם וַהֲשֵׁבֹתָ אֶל־לְבָבֶךָ

דברים ד

כִּי יהוה הוּא הָאֱלֹהִים בַּשָּׁמַיִם מִמַּעַל וְעַל־הָאָרֶץ מִתָּחַת, אֵין עוֹד:

עַל כֵּן נְקַוֶּה לְךָ יהוה אֱלֹהֵינוּ, לִרְאוֹת מְהֵרָה בְּתִפְאֶרֶת עֻזֶּךָ
לְהַעֲבִיר גִּלּוּלִים מִן הָאָרֶץ, וְהָאֱלִילִים כָּרוֹת יִכָּרֵתוּן
לְתַקֵּן עוֹלָם בְּמַלְכוּת שַׁדַּי.
וְכָל בְּנֵי בָשָׂר יִקְרְאוּ בִשְׁמֶךָ לְהַפְנוֹת אֵלֶיךָ כָּל רִשְׁעֵי אָרֶץ.
יַכִּירוּ וְיֵדְעוּ כָּל יוֹשְׁבֵי תֵבֵל, כִּי לְךָ תִּכְרַע כָּל בֶּרֶךְ, תִּשָּׁבַע כָּל לָשׁוֹן.
לְפָנֶיךָ יהוה אֱלֹהֵינוּ יִכְרְעוּ וְיִפֹּלוּ, וְלִכְבוֹד שִׁמְךָ יְקָר יִתֵּנוּ
וִיקַבְּלוּ כֻלָּם אֶת עֹל מַלְכוּתֶךָ וְתִמְלֹךְ עֲלֵיהֶם מְהֵרָה לְעוֹלָם וָעֶד.
כִּי הַמַּלְכוּת שֶׁלְּךָ הִיא וּלְעוֹלְמֵי עַד תִּמְלֹךְ בְּכָבוֹד
כַּכָּתוּב בְּתוֹרָתֶךָ

שמות טו

יהוה יִמְלֹךְ לְעֹלָם וָעֶד:

זכריה יד

◂ וְנֶאֱמַר, וְהָיָה יהוה לְמֶלֶךְ עַל־כָּל־הָאָרֶץ
בַּיּוֹם הַהוּא יִהְיֶה יהוה אֶחָד וּשְׁמוֹ אֶחָד:

Some add:

Have no fear of sudden terror or of the ruin when it overtakes the wicked.	*Prov. 3*
Devise your strategy, but it will be thwarted; propose your plan,	*Is. 8*
but it will not stand, for God is with us. When you grow old, I will still be the same.	*Is. 46*

When your hair turns gray, I will still carry you. I made you, I will bear you,
I will carry you, and I will rescue you.

MOURNER'S KADDISH

*The following prayer, said by mourners, requires the presence of a minyan.
A transliteration can be found on page 1244.*

Mourner: יִתְגַּדַּל Magnified and sanctified
may His great name be,
in the world He created by His will.
May He establish His kingdom
in your lifetime and in your days,
and in the lifetime of all the house of Israel,
swiftly and soon –
and say: Amen.

All: May His great name be blessed for ever and all time.

Mourner: Blessed and praised, glorified and exalted,
raised and honored, uplifted and lauded
be the name of the Holy One,
blessed be He,
beyond any blessing,
song, praise and consolation
uttered in the world –
and say: Amen.

May there be great peace from heaven,
and life for us and all Israel – and say: Amen.

*Bow, take three steps back, as if taking leave of the Divine Presence,
then bow, first left, then right, then center, while saying:*

May He who makes peace in His high places,
make peace for us and all Israel –
and say: Amen.

Some add:

משלי ג

אַל־תִּירָא מִפַּחַד פִּתְאֹם וּמִשֹּׁאַת רְשָׁעִים כִּי תָבֹא:

ישעיה ח

עֻצוּ עֵצָה וְתֻפָר, דַּבְּרוּ דָבָר וְלֹא יָקוּם, כִּי עִמָּנוּ אֵל:

ישעיה מו

וְעַד־זִקְנָה אֲנִי הוּא, וְעַד־שֵׂיבָה אֲנִי אֶסְבֹּל

אֲנִי עָשִׂיתִי וַאֲנִי אֶשָּׂא וַאֲנִי אֶסְבֹּל וַאֲמַלֵּט:

קדיש יתום

The following prayer, said by mourners, requires the presence of a מִנְיָן.
A transliteration can be found on page 1244.

אבל יִתְגַּדַּל וְיִתְקַדַּשׁ שְׁמֵהּ רַבָּא (קהל: אָמֵן)

בְּעָלְמָא דִּי בְרָא כִרְעוּתֵהּ

וְיַמְלִיךְ מַלְכוּתֵהּ

בְּחַיֵּיכוֹן וּבְיוֹמֵיכוֹן וּבְחַיֵּי דְכָל בֵּית יִשְׂרָאֵל

בַּעֲגָלָא וּבִזְמַן קָרִיב, וְאִמְרוּ אָמֵן. (קהל: אָמֵן)

קהל
ואבל: יְהֵא שְׁמֵהּ רַבָּא מְבָרַךְ לְעָלַם וּלְעָלְמֵי עָלְמַיָּא.

אבל: יִתְבָּרַךְ וְיִשְׁתַּבַּח וְיִתְפָּאַר

וְיִתְרוֹמַם וְיִתְנַשֵּׂא וְיִתְהַדָּר וְיִתְעַלֶּה וְיִתְהַלָּל

שְׁמֵהּ דְּקֻדְשָׁא בְּרִיךְ הוּא (קהל: בְּרִיךְ הוּא)

לְעֵלָּא מִן כָּל בִּרְכָתָא / בעשרת ימי תשובה: לְעֵלָּא לְעֵלָּא מִכָּל בִּרְכָתָא/

וְשִׁירָתָא, תֻּשְׁבְּחָתָא וְנֶחֱמָתָא

דַּאֲמִירָן בְּעָלְמָא, וְאִמְרוּ אָמֵן. (קהל: אָמֵן)

יְהֵא שְׁלָמָא רַבָּא מִן שְׁמַיָּא

וְחַיִּים, עָלֵינוּ וְעַל כָּל יִשְׂרָאֵל, וְאִמְרוּ אָמֵן. (קהל: אָמֵן)

*Bow, take three steps back, as if taking leave of the Divine Presence,
then bow, first left, then right, then center, while saying:*

עֹשֶׂה שָׁלוֹם/ בעשרת ימי תשובה: הַשָּׁלוֹם / בִּמְרוֹמָיו

הוּא יַעֲשֶׂה שָׁלוֹם עָלֵינוּ וְעַל כָּל יִשְׂרָאֵל

וְאִמְרוּ אָמֵן. (קהל: אָמֵן)

From the second day of Rosh Ḥodesh Elul through Shemini Atzeret
(in Israel through Hoshana Raba), the following psalm is said:

לְדָוִד By David. The LORD is my light and my salvation – whom then shall   *Ps. 27*
I fear? The LORD is the stronghold of my life – of whom shall I be afraid?
When evil men close in on me to devour my flesh, it is they, my enemies and
foes, who stumble and fall. Should an army besiege me, my heart would not
fear. Should war break out against me, still I would be confident. One thing
I ask of the LORD, only this do I seek: to live in the House of the LORD all
the days of my life, to gaze on the beauty of the LORD and worship in His
Temple. For He will keep me safe in His pavilion on the day of trouble. He
will hide me under the cover of His tent. He will set me high upon a rock.
Now my head is high above my enemies who surround me. I will sacrifice in
His tent with shouts of joy. I will sing and chant praises to the LORD. LORD,
hear my voice when I call. Be gracious to me and answer me. On Your behalf
my heart says, "Seek My face." Your face, LORD, will I seek. Do not hide Your
face from me. Do not turn Your servant away in anger. You have been my help.
Do not reject or forsake me, God, my Savior. Were my father and my mother
to forsake me, the LORD would take me in. Teach me Your way, LORD, and
lead me on a level path, because of my oppressors. Do not abandon me to
the will of my foes, for false witnesses have risen against me, breathing violence. ▸ Were it not for my faith that I shall see the LORD's goodness in the land
of the living. Hope in the LORD. Be strong and of good courage, and hope in
the LORD!

Mourner's Kaddish (previous page)

From the second day of שמיני עצרת through ראש חודש אלול
(in ארץ ישראל through הושענא רבה), the following psalm is said:

תהלים כז

לְדָוִד, יהוה אוֹרִי וְיִשְׁעִי, מִמִּי אִירָא, יהוה מָעוֹז־חַיַּי, מִמִּי אֶפְחָד: בִּקְרֹב
עָלַי מְרֵעִים לֶאֱכֹל אֶת־בְּשָׂרִי, צָרַי וְאֹיְבַי לִי, הֵמָּה כָשְׁלוּ וְנָפָלוּ: אִם־
תַּחֲנֶה עָלַי מַחֲנֶה, לֹא־יִירָא לִבִּי, אִם־תָּקוּם עָלַי מִלְחָמָה, בְּזֹאת אֲנִי
בוֹטֵחַ: אַחַת שָׁאַלְתִּי מֵאֵת־יהוה, אוֹתָהּ אֲבַקֵּשׁ, שִׁבְתִּי בְּבֵית־יהוה
כָּל־יְמֵי חַיַּי, לַחֲזוֹת בְּנֹעַם־יהוה, וּלְבַקֵּר בְּהֵיכָלוֹ: כִּי יִצְפְּנֵנִי בְּסֻכֹּה
בְּיוֹם רָעָה, יַסְתִּרֵנִי בְּסֵתֶר אָהֳלוֹ, בְּצוּר יְרוֹמְמֵנִי: וְעַתָּה יָרוּם רֹאשִׁי
עַל אֹיְבַי סְבִיבוֹתַי, וְאֶזְבְּחָה בְאָהֳלוֹ זִבְחֵי תְרוּעָה, אָשִׁירָה וַאֲזַמְּרָה
לַיהוה: שְׁמַע־יהוה קוֹלִי אֶקְרָא, וְחָנֵּנִי וַעֲנֵנִי: לְךָ אָמַר לִבִּי בַּקְּשׁוּ פָנָי,
אֶת־פָּנֶיךָ יהוה אֲבַקֵּשׁ: אַל־תַּסְתֵּר פָּנֶיךָ מִמֶּנִּי, אַל תַּט־בְּאַף עַבְדֶּךָ,
עֶזְרָתִי הָיִיתָ, אַל־תִּטְּשֵׁנִי וְאַל־תַּעַזְבֵנִי, אֱלֹהֵי יִשְׁעִי: כִּי־אָבִי וְאִמִּי
עֲזָבוּנִי, וַיהוה יַאַסְפֵנִי: הוֹרֵנִי יהוה דַּרְכֶּךָ, וּנְחֵנִי בְּאֹרַח מִישׁוֹר, לְמַעַן
שׁוֹרְרָי: אַל־תִּתְּנֵנִי בְּנֶפֶשׁ צָרָי, כִּי קָמוּ־בִי עֵדֵי־שֶׁקֶר, וִיפֵחַ חָמָס:‹ לוּלֵא
הֶאֱמַנְתִּי לִרְאוֹת בְּטוּב־יהוה בְּאֶרֶץ חַיִּים: קַוֵּה אֶל־יהוה, חֲזַק וְיַאֲמֵץ
לִבֶּךָ, וְקַוֵּה אֶל־יהוה:

קדיש יתום (previous page)

BLESSING OF THE NEW MOON

*Kiddush Levana, the Blessing of the New Moon, is said between the third
day and the middle day of each month. If possible, it should be said at the
end of Shabbat, under the open sky, and in the presence of a minyan.*

הַלְלוּיָהּ **Halleluya!** Praise the LORD from the heavens, praise Him in *Ps. 148*
the heights. Praise Him, all His angels; praise Him, all His hosts. Praise
Him, sun and moon; praise Him, all shining stars. Praise Him, highest
heavens and the waters above the heavens. Let them praise the name of
the LORD, for He commanded and they were created. He established
them for ever and all time, issuing a decree that will never change.

כִּי־אֶרְאֶה **When I see** Your heavens, the work of Your fingers, the moon *Ps. 8*
and the stars which You have set in place: What is man that You are
mindful of him, the son of man that You care for him?

Look at the moon, then say:

בָּרוּךְ **Blessed** are You, LORD our God, King of the Universe who by
His word created the heavens, and by His breath all their host. He set
for them laws and times, so that they should not deviate from their
appointed task. They are joyous and glad to perform the will of their
Owner, the Worker of truth whose work is truth. To the moon He said
that it should renew itself as a crown of beauty for those He carried
from the womb [Israel], for they are destined to be renewed like it, and
to praise their Creator for the sake of His glorious majesty. Blessed are
You, LORD, who renews the months.

The following five verses are each said three times:
Blessed is He who formed you; blessed is He who made you;
blessed is He who owns you; blessed is He who created you.

The following verse is said rising on the toes.
Just as I leap toward you but cannot touch you,
so may none of my enemies be able to touch me to do me harm.

May fear and dread fall upon them; *Ex. 15*
by the power of Your arm may they be still as stone.

May they be still as stone through the power of Your arm,
when dread and fear fall upon them.

קידוש לבנה

קידוש לבנה, the Blessing of the New Moon, is said between the third day
and the middle day of each month. If possible, it should be said at the
end of שבת, under the open sky, and in the presence of a מנין.

תהלים קמח הַלְלוּיָהּ, הַלְלוּ אֶת־יהוה מִן הַשָּׁמַיִם, הַלְלוּהוּ בַּמְּרוֹמִים: הַלְלוּהוּ
כָל־מַלְאָכָיו, הַלְלוּהוּ כָּל־צְבָאָו: הַלְלוּהוּ שֶׁמֶשׁ וְיָרֵחַ, הַלְלוּהוּ
כָּל־כּוֹכְבֵי אוֹר: הַלְלוּהוּ שְׁמֵי הַשָּׁמָיִם, וְהַמַּיִם אֲשֶׁר מֵעַל הַשָּׁמָיִם:
יְהַלְלוּ אֶת־שֵׁם יהוה, כִּי הוּא צִוָּה וְנִבְרָאוּ: וַיַּעֲמִידֵם לָעַד לְעוֹלָם,
חׇק־נָתַן וְלֹא יַעֲבוֹר:

תהלים ח כִּי־אֶרְאֶה שָׁמֶיךָ מַעֲשֵׂה אֶצְבְּעֹתֶיךָ, יָרֵחַ וְכוֹכָבִים אֲשֶׁר כּוֹנָנְתָּה:
מָה־אֱנוֹשׁ כִּי־תִזְכְּרֶנּוּ, וּבֶן־אָדָם כִּי תִפְקְדֶנּוּ:

Look at the moon, then say:

בָּרוּךְ אַתָּה יהוה אֱלֹהֵינוּ מֶלֶךְ הָעוֹלָם, אֲשֶׁר בְּמַאֲמָרוֹ בָּרָא שְׁחָקִים,
וּבְרוּחַ פִּיו כָּל צְבָאָם, חֹק וּזְמַן נָתַן לָהֶם שֶׁלֹּא יְשַׁנּוּ אֶת תַּפְקִידָם.
שָׂשִׂים וּשְׂמֵחִים לַעֲשׂוֹת רְצוֹן קוֹנָם, פּוֹעֵל אֱמֶת שֶׁפְּעֻלָּתוֹ אֱמֶת.
וְלַלְּבָנָה אָמַר שֶׁתִּתְחַדֵּשׁ, עֲטֶרֶת תִּפְאֶרֶת לַעֲמוּסֵי בָטֶן, שֶׁהֵם
עֲתִידִים לְהִתְחַדֵּשׁ כְּמוֹתָהּ וּלְפָאֵר לְיוֹצְרָם עַל שֵׁם כְּבוֹד מַלְכוּתוֹ.
בָּרוּךְ אַתָּה יהוה, מְחַדֵּשׁ חֳדָשִׁים.

The following five verses are each said three times:

בָּרוּךְ יוֹצְרֵךְ, בָּרוּךְ עוֹשֵׂךְ, בָּרוּךְ קוֹנֵךְ, בָּרוּךְ בּוֹרְאֵךְ.

The following verse is said rising on the toes.

כְּשֵׁם שֶׁאֲנִי רוֹקֵד כְּנֶגְדֵּךְ וְאֵינִי יָכוֹל לִנְגֹּעַ בָּךְ
כָּךְ לֹא יוּכְלוּ כָּל אוֹיְבַי לִנְגֹּעַ בִּי לְרָעָה.

שמות טו תִּפֹּל עֲלֵיהֶם אֵימָתָה וָפַחַד, בִּגְדֹל זְרוֹעֲךָ יִדְּמוּ כָּאָבֶן:
כָּאֶבֶן יִדְּמוּ זְרוֹעֲךָ בִּגְדֹל, וָפַחַד אֵימָתָה עֲלֵיהֶם תִּפֹּל.

David, King of Israel, lives and endures.

Turn to three people and say to each:
Peace upon you.

They respond:
Upon you, peace.

Say three times:
May it be a good sign and a good omen for us and all Israel. Amen.

קוֹל Hark! My beloved! Here he comes, leaping over the mountains, *Song. 2*
bounding over the hills. My beloved is like a gazelle, like a young deer.
There he stands outside our wall, peering in through the windows,
gazing through the lattice.

שִׁיר לַמַּעֲלוֹת A song of ascents. I lift my eyes up to the hills; from where *Ps. 121*
will my help come? My help comes from the LORD, Maker of heaven
and earth. He will not let your foot stumble; He who guards you does
not slumber. See: the Guardian of Israel neither slumbers nor sleeps.
The LORD is your Guardian; the LORD is your Shade at your right hand.
The sun will not strike you by day, nor the moon by night. The LORD
will guard you from all harm; He will guard your life. The LORD will
guard your going and coming, now and for evermore.

הַלְלוּיָהּ Halleluya! Praise God in His holy place; praise Him in the *Ps. 150*
heavens of His power. Praise Him for His mighty deeds; praise Him
for His surpassing greatness. Praise Him with blasts of the ram's horn;
praise Him with the harp and lyre. Praise Him with timbrel and dance;
praise Him with strings and flute. Praise Him with clashing cymbals;
praise Him with resounding cymbals. Let all that breathes praise the
LORD. Halleluya!

תְּנָא In the academy of Rabbi Yishmael it was taught: Were the people *Sanhedrin 42a*
of Israel privileged to greet the presence of their heavenly Father only
once a month, it would have been sufficient for them. Abaye said:
Therefore it [the blessing of the moon] should be said standing. Who *Song. 8*
is this coming up from the desert, leaning on her beloved?

דָּוִד מֶלֶךְ יִשְׂרָאֵל חַי וְקַיָּם.

Turn to three people and say to each:

שָׁלוֹם עֲלֵיכֶם.

They respond:

עֲלֵיכֶם שָׁלוֹם.

Say three times:

סִימָן טוֹב וּמַזָּל טוֹב יְהֵא לָנוּ וּלְכָל יִשְׂרָאֵל, אָמֵן.

קוֹל דּוֹדִי הִנֵּה־זֶה בָּא, מְדַלֵּג עַל־הֶהָרִים, מְקַפֵּץ עַל־הַגְּבָעוֹת: **שיר השירים ב**
דּוֹמֶה דוֹדִי לִצְבִי אוֹ לְעֹפֶר הָאַיָּלִים, הִנֵּה־זֶה עוֹמֵד אַחַר כָּתְלֵנוּ,
מַשְׁגִּיחַ מִן־הַחַלֹּנוֹת, מֵצִיץ מִן־הַחֲרַכִּים:

שִׁיר לַמַּעֲלוֹת, אֶשָּׂא עֵינַי אֶל־הֶהָרִים, מֵאַיִן יָבֹא עֶזְרִי: עֶזְרִי מֵעִם **תהלים קכא**
יהוה, עֹשֵׂה שָׁמַיִם וָאָרֶץ: אַל־יִתֵּן לַמּוֹט רַגְלֶךָ, אַל־יָנוּם שֹׁמְרֶךָ:
הִנֵּה לֹא־יָנוּם וְלֹא יִישָׁן, שׁוֹמֵר יִשְׂרָאֵל: יהוה שֹׁמְרֶךָ, יהוה צִלְּךָ
עַל־יַד יְמִינֶךָ: יוֹמָם הַשֶּׁמֶשׁ לֹא־יַכֶּכָּה, וְיָרֵחַ בַּלָּיְלָה: יהוה יִשְׁמָרְךָ
מִכָּל־רָע, יִשְׁמֹר אֶת־נַפְשֶׁךָ: יהוה יִשְׁמָר־צֵאתְךָ וּבוֹאֶךָ, מֵעַתָּה
וְעַד־עוֹלָם:

הַלְלוּיָהּ, הַלְלוּ־אֵל בְּקָדְשׁוֹ, הַלְלוּהוּ בִּרְקִיעַ עֻזּוֹ: הַלְלוּהוּ בִגְבוּרֹתָיו, **תהלים קנ**
הַלְלוּהוּ כְּרֹב גֻּדְלוֹ: הַלְלוּהוּ בְּתֵקַע שׁוֹפָר, הַלְלוּהוּ בְּנֵבֶל וְכִנּוֹר:
הַלְלוּהוּ בְתֹף וּמָחוֹל, הַלְלוּהוּ בְּמִנִּים וְעֻגָב: הַלְלוּהוּ בְצִלְצְלֵי־שָׁמַע,
הַלְלוּהוּ בְּצִלְצְלֵי תְרוּעָה: כֹּל הַנְּשָׁמָה תְּהַלֵּל יָהּ, הַלְלוּיָהּ:

תָּנָא דְּבֵי רַבִּי יִשְׁמָעֵאל: אִלְמָלֵי לֹא זָכוּ יִשְׂרָאֵל אֶלָּא לְהַקְבִּיל פְּנֵי **סנהדרין מב**
אֲבִיהֶם שֶׁבַּשָּׁמַיִם פַּעַם אַחַת בַּחֹדֶשׁ, דַּיָּם. אָמַר אַבַּיֵּי: הִלְכָּךְ צָרִיךְ
לְמֵימְרָא מְעֻמָּד. מִי זֹאת עֹלָה מִן־הַמִּדְבָּר, מִתְרַפֶּקֶת עַל־דּוֹדָהּ: **שיר השירים ח**

וִיהִי May it be Your will, Lᴏʀᴅ my God and God of my ancestors, to make good the deficiency of the moon, so that it is no longer in its diminished state. May the light of the moon be like the light of the sun and like the light of the seven days of creation as it was before it was diminished, as it says, "The two great luminaries." And may there be fulfilled for us the verse: "They shall seek the Lᴏʀᴅ their God, and David their king." Amen.   *Gen. 1*   *Hos. 3*

לַמְנַצֵּחַ For the conductor of music. With stringed instruments, a psalm.   *Ps. 67*
A song. May God be gracious to us and bless us. May He make His face shine on us, Selah. Then will Your way be known on earth, Your salvation among all the nations. Let the peoples praise You, God; let all peoples praise You. Let nations rejoice and sing for joy, for You judge the peoples with equity, and guide the nations of the earth, Selah. Let the peoples praise You, God; let all peoples praise You. The earth has yielded its harvest. May God, our God, bless us. God will bless us, and all the ends of the earth will fear Him.

The service continues with Aleinu (page 381)
and Mourner's Kaddish (page 385)
followed by "Good are the radiant stars" below.

All sing:
טוֹבִים Good are the radiant stars our God created;
He formed them with knowledge,
understanding and deliberation.
He gave them strength and might
to rule throughout the world.

Full of splendor, radiating light,
beautiful is their splendor throughout the world.
Glad as they go forth, joyous as they return,
they fulfill with awe their Creator's will.

Glory and honor they give to His name,
jubilation and song at the mention of His majesty.
He called the sun into being and it shone with light.
He looked and fashioned the form of the moon.

וִיהִי רָצוֹן מִלְּפָנֶיךָ יהוה אֱלֹהַי וֵאלֹהֵי אֲבוֹתַי, לְמַלֹּאת פְּגִימַת הַלְּבָנָה
וְלֹא יִהְיֶה בָּהּ שׁוּם מִעוּט. וִיהִי אוֹר הַלְּבָנָה כְּאוֹר הַחַמָּה וּכְאוֹר
שִׁבְעַת יְמֵי בְרֵאשִׁית, כְּמוֹ שֶׁהָיְתָה קֹדֶם מִעוּטָהּ, שֶׁנֶּאֱמַר: אֶת־שְׁנֵי **בראשית א**
הַמְּאֹרֹת הַגְּדֹלִים: וְיִתְקַיֶּם בָּנוּ מִקְרָא שֶׁכָּתוּב: וּבִקְשׁוּ אֶת־יהוה **הושע ג**
אֱלֹהֵיהֶם וְאֵת דָּוִיד מַלְכָּם: אָמֵן.

לַמְנַצֵּחַ בִּנְגִינֹת, מִזְמוֹר שִׁיר: אֱלֹהִים יְחָנֵּנוּ וִיבָרְכֵנוּ, יָאֵר פָּנָיו אִתָּנוּ **תהלים סז**
סֶלָה: לָדַעַת בָּאָרֶץ דַּרְכֶּךָ, בְּכָל־גּוֹיִם יְשׁוּעָתֶךָ: יוֹדוּךָ עַמִּים אֱלֹהִים,
יוֹדוּךָ עַמִּים כֻּלָּם: יִשְׂמְחוּ וִירַנְּנוּ לְאֻמִּים, כִּי־תִשְׁפֹּט עַמִּים מִישֹׁר,
וּלְאֻמִּים בָּאָרֶץ תַּנְחֵם סֶלָה: יוֹדוּךָ עַמִּים אֱלֹהִים, יוֹדוּךָ עַמִּים כֻּלָּם:
אֶרֶץ נָתְנָה יְבוּלָהּ, יְבָרְכֵנוּ אֱלֹהִים אֱלֹהֵינוּ: יְבָרְכֵנוּ אֱלֹהִים, וְיִירְאוּ
אֹתוֹ כָּל־אַפְסֵי־אָרֶץ:

The service continues with עָלֵינוּ (page 381) and קדיש יתום
(page 385) followed by טוֹבִים מְאוֹרוֹת below.

All sing:

טוֹבִים מְאוֹרוֹת שֶׁבָּרָא אֱלֹהֵינוּ
יְצָרָם בְּדַעַת בְּבִינָה וּבְהַשְׂכֵּל
כֹּחַ וּגְבוּרָה נָתַן בָּהֶם
לִהְיוֹת מוֹשְׁלִים בְּקֶרֶב תֵּבֵל.

מְלֵאִים זִיו וּמְפִיקִים נֹגַהּ
נָאֶה זִיוָם בְּכָל־הָעוֹלָם
שְׂמֵחִים בְּצֵאתָם וְשָׂשִׂים בְּבוֹאָם
עוֹשִׂים בְּאֵימָה רְצוֹן קוֹנָם.

פְּאֵר וְכָבוֹד נוֹתְנִים לִשְׁמוֹ
צָהֳלָה וְרִנָּה לְזֵכֶר מַלְכוּתוֹ
קָרָא לַשֶּׁמֶשׁ וַיִּזְרַח אוֹר
רָאָה וְהִתְקִין צוּרַת הַלְּבָנָה.

SHEMA BEFORE SLEEP AT NIGHT[B]

הֲרֵינִי I hereby forgive anyone who has angered or provoked me or sinned against me, physically or financially or by failing to give me due respect, or in any other matter relating to me, involuntarily or willingly, inadvertently or deliberately, whether in word or deed: let no one incur punishment because of me.

בָּרוּךְ Blessed are You, LORD our God, King of the Universe,
who makes the bonds of sleep fall on my eyes,[IHB]
and slumber on my eye-lids.
May it be Your will, LORD my God and God of my fathers,
that You make me lie down in peace
and arise in peace.
Let not my imagination, bad dreams or troubling thoughts disturb me.[B]

HILKHOT TEFILLA · הלכות תפילה

הַמַּפִּיל חֶבְלֵי שֵׁנָה עַל עֵינַי – *Who makes the bonds of sleep fall on my eyes.* There are two traditions regarding the recitation of the *Shema* and the blessing. Which should be recited first? Which should be one's final prayer before drifting into sleep? Interestingly, the *Mishna Berura* suggests that it is up to each individual to decide according to one's own level of fatigue – if you

don't think you can stay awake long enough to say the blessing, say it first; otherwise, leave it for the end. Each of us leaves our consciousness of the previous day and the presence of God in our lives in our own way. Also interesting is that unlike almost all other prayers, this one is in the singular, perhaps because it takes place at a most intimate and personal moment in our day.

BIUR TEFILLA · ביאור תפילה

הַמַּפִּיל חֶבְלֵי שֵׁנָה עַל עֵינַי – *Who makes the bonds of sleep fall on my eyes.* We say a blessing on it because sleep is something that man needs. The Midrash (*Bereshit Raba* 9:6) teaches that "*vehineh tov meod*" (and God saw that it was *very* good) is a reference to sleep. With it, man is able to get up in the morning and pursue Torah (Abudarham). Is this a statement of fact or of thanks?

וְאַל יְבַהֲלוּנִי רַעְיוֹנַי וַחֲלוֹמוֹת רָעִים וְהִרְהוּרִים רָעִים – *Let not my imagination, bad dreams or troubling thoughts disturb me.* One's imagination, bad thoughts and bad dreams can shake one to the core at night, causing one to wake up startled, confused and ill at ease, and subsequently leaving one as tired, if not more so, than when one went to sleep. We pray that our sleep is restful and refreshing.

קריאת שמע על המיטהᵇ

הֲרֵינִי מוֹחֵל לְכָל מִי שֶׁהִכְעִיס וְהִקְנִיט אוֹתִי אוֹ שֶׁחָטָא כְּנֶגְדִּי, בֵּין בְּגוּפִי בֵּין בְּמָמוֹנִי בֵּין בִּכְבוֹדִי בֵּין בְּכָל אֲשֶׁר לִי, בֵּין בְּאֹנֶס בֵּין בְּרָצוֹן, בֵּין בְּשׁוֹגֵג בֵּין בְּמֵזִיד, בֵּין בְּדִבּוּר בֵּין בְּמַעֲשֶׂה, וְלֹא יֵעָנֵשׁ שׁוּם אָדָם בְּסִבָּתִי.

בָּרוּךְ אַתָּה יהוה אֱלֹהֵינוּ מֶלֶךְ הָעוֹלָם
הַמַּפִּיל חֶבְלֵי שֵׁנָה עַל עֵינַיᵉⁱ⁻ וּתְנוּמָה עַל עַפְעַפָּי.
וִיהִי רָצוֹן מִלְּפָנֶיךָ, יהוה אֱלֹהַי וֵאלֹהֵי אֲבוֹתַי
שֶׁתַּשְׁכִּיבֵנִי לְשָׁלוֹם וְתַעֲמִידֵנִי לְשָׁלוֹם
וְאַל יְבַהֲלוּנִי רַעְיוֹנַי וַחֲלוֹמוֹת רָעִים וְהִרְהוּרִים רָעִיםᵇ

ביאור תפילה • BIUR TEFILLA

קריאת שמע על המיטה – *Shema before sleep at night.* The Gemara (*Berakhot* 4b) says that, separate from what one said in *Ma'ariv*, one should recite the [first paragraph of the] *Shema* again because of its reference to the timing of its recitation, namely, בְּשָׁכְבְּךָ, when you lie down. As a result there is a special recitation of the *Shema* which is said just before one nods off to sleep. In addition, the Gemara elsewhere (*Berakhot* 60b) mentions a blessing that should be said upon going to sleep. At its core, then, "the bedtime *Shema*" consists of a blessing and the recitation of the *Shema*; all of the other paragraphs represent additional prayers that are an expansion of one's request for protection during the night.

עיון תפילה • IYUN TEFILLA

הַמַּפִּיל חֶבְלֵי שֵׁנָה עַל עֵינַי – *Who makes the bonds of sleep fall on my eyes.* Here it sounds like sleep is something cast upon you, against your will. Some of us would like to stay up all night if we could, but the blessing assures us that sleep is a *ḥesed* provided by Hashem for the benefit of our bodies, and our souls. Alternatively, young children have a fear of the dark, as their imaginations run wild about the dangers. As adults, we often have our own fears and trepidations about the day prior, about the night and day ahead. Sleep is cast upon us to teach us that the dark is to be embraced before the dawn of a new day.

Compare the text above with the text of the blessing that we say in the morning:

בָּרוּךְ אַתָּה יהוה אֱלֹהֵינוּ מֶלֶךְ הָעוֹלָם, הַמַּעֲבִיר שֵׁנָה מֵעֵינַי וּתְנוּמָה מֵעַפְעַפָּי.

Blessed are You, Hashem our God, King of the Universe, who removes sleep from my eyes and slumber from my eyelids.

May my bed be flawless before You.
Enlighten my eyes lest I sleep the sleep of death,[B]
for it is You who illuminates the pupil of the eye.
Blessed are You, LORD, who gives light to the whole world in His glory.[B]

When saying all three paragraphs of Shema, say:
God, faithful King!

The following verse should be said aloud, while covering the eyes with the right hand:

Listen, Israel: the LORD is our God, the LORD is One.

Deut. 6

Quietly: Blessed be the name of His glorious kingdom for ever and all time.

וְאָהַבְתָּ Love the LORD your God with all your heart, with all your soul, and with all your might. These words which I command you today shall be on your heart. Teach them repeatedly to your children, speaking of them when you sit at home and when you travel on the way, when you lie down and when you rise. Bind them as a sign on your hand, and they shall be an emblem between your eyes. Write them on the doorposts of your house and gates.

Deut. 6

וִיהִי May the pleasantness of the LORD our God be upon us. Establish for us the work of our hands, O establish the work of our hands.

Ps. 90

יֹשֵׁב He who lives in the shelter of the Most High dwells in the shadow of the Almighty. I say of God, my Refuge and Stronghold, my LORD in whom I trust, that He will save you from the fowler's snare and the deadly pestilence. With His pinions He will cover you, and beneath His wings you will find shelter; His faithfulness is an encircling shield. You need not fear terror by night, nor

Ps. 91

I will thank Hashem for the restoration of my soul and my reemergence from a state of slumber to a rejuvenated state of being alive.

הַמֵּאִיר לָעוֹלָם כֻּלּוֹ בִּכְבוֹדוֹ – *Who gives light to the whole world in His glory.* The blessing

ends on a note of optimism. Dark as it may seem at night, we will awaken in the morning to acknowledge a new day, illuminated both literally and figuratively by the light which Hashem provides. Such a thought brings comfort, peace and rest.

וּתְהֵא מִטָּתִי שְׁלֵמָה לְפָנֶיךָ

וְהָאֵר עֵינַי פֶּן אִישַׁן הַמָּוֶת, כִּי אַתָּה הַמֵּאִיר לְאִישׁוֹן בַּת עָיִן.

בָּרוּךְ אַתָּה יהוה, הַמֵּאִיר לָעוֹלָם כֻּלּוֹ בִּכְבוֹדוֹ.

When saying all three paragraphs of שמע, say:

אֵל מֶלֶךְ נֶאֱמָן

The following verse should be said aloud, while covering the eyes with the right hand:

דברים ו

שְׁמַע יִשְׂרָאֵל, יהוה אֱלֹהֵינוּ, יהוה ׀ אֶחָד:

Quietly בָּרוּךְ שֵׁם כְּבוֹד מַלְכוּתוֹ לְעוֹלָם וָעֶד.

דברים ו

וְאָהַבְתָּ אֵת יהוה אֱלֹהֶיךָ, בְּכָל־לְבָבְךָ וּבְכָל־נַפְשְׁךָ וּבְכָל־מְאֹדֶךָ: וְהָיוּ הַדְּבָרִים הָאֵלֶּה, אֲשֶׁר אָנֹכִי מְצַוְּךָ הַיּוֹם, עַל־לְבָבֶךָ: וְשִׁנַּנְתָּם לְבָנֶיךָ וְדִבַּרְתָּ בָּם, בְּשִׁבְתְּךָ בְּבֵיתֶךָ וּבְלֶכְתְּךָ בַדֶּרֶךְ, וּבְשָׁכְבְּךָ וּבְקוּמֶךָ: וּקְשַׁרְתָּם לְאוֹת עַל־יָדֶךָ וְהָיוּ לְטֹטָפֹת בֵּין עֵינֶיךָ: וּכְתַבְתָּם עַל־מְזֻזוֹת בֵּיתֶךָ וּבִשְׁעָרֶיךָ:

תהלים צ

וִיהִי נֹעַם אֲדֹנָי אֱלֹהֵינוּ עָלֵינוּ וּמַעֲשֵׂה יָדֵינוּ כּוֹנְנָה עָלֵינוּ וּמַעֲשֵׂה יָדֵינוּ כּוֹנְנֵהוּ:

תהלים צא

יֹשֵׁב בְּסֵתֶר עֶלְיוֹן, בְּצֵל שַׁדַּי יִתְלוֹנָן: אֹמַר לַיהוה מַחְסִי וּמְצוּדָתִי, אֱלֹהַי אֶבְטַח־בּוֹ: כִּי הוּא יַצִּילְךָ מִפַּח יָקוּשׁ, מִדֶּבֶר הַוּוֹת: בְּאֶבְרָתוֹ יָסֶךְ לָךְ, וְתַחַת־כְּנָפָיו תֶּחְסֶה, צִנָּה וְסֹחֵרָה אֲמִתּוֹ: לֹא־תִירָא מִפַּחַד

BIUR TEFILLA • ביאור תפילה

וְהָאֵר עֵינַי פֶּן אִישַׁן הַמָּוֶת – *Enlighten my eyes lest I sleep the sleep of death.* Only at the end does one admit to the biggest fear of them all – lest I not awake in the morning. The apprehension of death is not always present, but the possibility is. Here it receives its due mention, a prelude to the celebratory statement in the morning of *Modeh Ani*, wherein

the arrow that flies by day; not the pestilence that stalks in darkness, nor the plague that ravages at noon. A thousand may fall at your side, ten thousand at your right hand, but it will not come near you. You will only look with your eyes and see the punishment of the wicked. Because you said, "The Lord is my Refuge," taking the Most High as your shelter, no harm will befall you, no plague come near your tent, for He will command His angels about you, to guard you in all your ways. They will lift you in their hands, lest your foot stumble on a stone. You will tread on lions and vipers; you will trample on young lions and snakes. [God says:] "Because he loves Me, I will rescue him; I will protect him, because he acknowledges My name. When he calls on Me, I will answer him; I will be with him in distress, I will deliver him and bring him honor. With long life I will satisfy him and show him My salvation.

With long life I will satisfy him and show him My salvation.

יהוה Lord, how numerous are my enemies, how many rise against me. *Ps. 3* Many say of me: "There is no help for him in God," Selah. But You, Lord, are a shield around me. You are my glory; You raise my head high. I cry aloud to the Lord, and He answers me from His holy mountain, Selah. I lie down to sleep and I wake again, for the Lord supports me. I will not fear the myriad forces ranged against me on all sides. Arise, Lord, save me, O my God; strike all my enemies across the cheek; break the teeth of the wicked. From the Lord comes deliverance; may Your blessing rest upon Your people, Selah.

הַשְׁכִּיבֵנוּ Help us lie down, O Lord our God, in peace, and rise up, O our King, to life. Spread over us Your canopy of peace. Direct us with Your good counsel, and save us for the sake of Your name. Shield us and remove from us every enemy, plague, sword, famine and sorrow. Remove the adversary from before and behind us. Shelter us in the shadow of Your wings, for You, God, are our Guardian and Deliverer; You, God, are a gracious and compassionate King. Guard our going out and our coming in, for life and peace, from now and for ever.

בָּרוּךְ Blessed is the Lord by day, blessed is the Lord by night. Blessed is the Lord when we lie down; blessed is the Lord when we rise. For in Your hand are the souls of the living and the dead, [as it is written:] "In His hand *Job 12* is every living soul, and the breath of all mankind." Into Your hand I entrust *Ps. 31* my spirit: You redeemed me, Lord, God of truth. Our God in heaven, bring unity to Your name, establish Your kingdom constantly and reign over us for ever and all time.

לַיְלָה, מֵחֵץ יָעוּף יוֹמָם: מִדֶּבֶר בָּאֹפֶל יַהֲלֹךְ, מִקֶּטֶב יָשׁוּד צָהֳרָיִם: יִפֹּל מִצִּדְּךָ אֶלֶף, וּרְבָבָה מִימִינֶךָ, אֵלֶיךָ לֹא יִגָּשׁ: רַק בְּעֵינֶיךָ תַבִּיט, וְשִׁלֻּמַת רְשָׁעִים תִּרְאֶה: כִּי־אַתָּה יהוה מַחְסִי, עֶלְיוֹן שַׂמְתָּ מְעוֹנֶךָ: לֹא־תְאֻנֶּה אֵלֶיךָ רָעָה, וְנֶגַע לֹא־יִקְרַב בְּאָהֳלֶךָ: כִּי מַלְאָכָיו יְצַוֶּה־לָּךְ, לִשְׁמָרְךָ בְּכָל־דְּרָכֶיךָ: עַל־כַּפַּיִם יִשָּׂאוּנְךָ, פֶּן־תִּגֹּף בָּאֶבֶן רַגְלֶךָ: עַל־שַׁחַל וָפֶתֶן תִּדְרֹךְ, תִּרְמֹס כְּפִיר וְתַנִּין: כִּי בִי חָשַׁק וַאֲפַלְּטֵהוּ, אֲשַׂגְּבֵהוּ כִּי־יָדַע שְׁמִי: יִקְרָאֵנִי וְאֶעֱנֵהוּ, עִמּוֹ־אָנֹכִי בְצָרָה, אֲחַלְּצֵהוּ וַאֲכַבְּדֵהוּ: אֹרֶךְ יָמִים אַשְׂבִּיעֵהוּ, וְאַרְאֵהוּ בִּישׁוּעָתִי:
אֹרֶךְ יָמִים אַשְׂבִּיעֵהוּ, וְאַרְאֵהוּ בִּישׁוּעָתִי:

תהלים ג

יהוה מָה־רַבּוּ צָרָי, רַבִּים קָמִים עָלָי: רַבִּים אֹמְרִים לְנַפְשִׁי, אֵין יְשׁוּעָתָה לּוֹ בֵאלֹהִים, סֶלָה: וְאַתָּה יהוה מָגֵן בַּעֲדִי, כְּבוֹדִי וּמֵרִים רֹאשִׁי: קוֹלִי אֶל־יהוה אֶקְרָא, וַיַּעֲנֵנִי מֵהַר קָדְשׁוֹ, סֶלָה: אֲנִי שָׁכַבְתִּי וָאִישָׁנָה, הֱקִיצוֹתִי כִּי יהוה יִסְמְכֵנִי: לֹא־אִירָא מֵרִבְבוֹת עָם, אֲשֶׁר סָבִיב שָׁתוּ עָלָי: קוּמָה יהוה, הוֹשִׁיעֵנִי אֱלֹהַי, כִּי־הִכִּיתָ אֶת־כָּל־אֹיְבַי לֶחִי, שִׁנֵּי רְשָׁעִים שִׁבַּרְתָּ: לַיהוה הַיְשׁוּעָה, עַל־עַמְּךָ בִרְכָתֶךָ סֶּלָה:

הַשְׁכִּיבֵנוּ, יהוה אֱלֹהֵינוּ, לְשָׁלוֹם, וְהַעֲמִידֵנוּ, מַלְכֵּנוּ, לְחַיִּים. וּפְרֹשׂ עָלֵינוּ סֻכַּת שְׁלוֹמֶךָ, וְתַקְּנֵנוּ בְּעֵצָה טוֹבָה מִלְּפָנֶיךָ, וְהוֹשִׁיעֵנוּ לְמַעַן שְׁמֶךָ. וְהָגֵן בַּעֲדֵנוּ, וְהָסֵר מֵעָלֵינוּ אוֹיֵב, דֶּבֶר וְחֶרֶב וְרָעָב וְיָגוֹן. וְהָסֵר שָׂטָן מִלְּפָנֵינוּ וּמֵאַחֲרֵינוּ, וּבְצֵל כְּנָפֶיךָ תַּסְתִּירֵנוּ, כִּי אֵל שׁוֹמְרֵנוּ וּמַצִּילֵנוּ אָתָּה, כִּי אֵל מֶלֶךְ חַנּוּן וְרַחוּם אָתָּה. וּשְׁמֹר צֵאתֵנוּ וּבוֹאֵנוּ לְחַיִּים וּלְשָׁלוֹם מֵעַתָּה וְעַד עוֹלָם.

בָּרוּךְ יהוה בַּיּוֹם, בָּרוּךְ יהוה בַּלַּיְלָה, בָּרוּךְ יהוה בְּשָׁכְבֵנוּ, בָּרוּךְ יהוה בְּקוּמֵנוּ. כִּי בְיָדְךָ נַפְשׁוֹת הַחַיִּים וְהַמֵּתִים. אֲשֶׁר בְּיָדוֹ נֶפֶשׁ כָּל־חָי, וְרוּחַ כָּל־בְּשַׂר־אִישׁ: בְּיָדְךָ אַפְקִיד רוּחִי, פָּדִיתָה אוֹתִי יהוה אֵל אֱמֶת: אֱלֹהֵינוּ שֶׁבַּשָּׁמַיִם, יַחֵד שִׁמְךָ וְקַיֵּם מַלְכוּתְךָ תָּמִיד, וּמְלֹךְ עָלֵינוּ לְעוֹלָם וָעֶד.

איוב יב

תהלים לא

יִרְאוּ May our eyes see, our hearts rejoice, and our souls be glad in Your true salvation, when Zion is told, "Your God reigns." The Lord is King, the Lord was King, and the Lord will be King for ever and all time. For sovereignty is Yours, and to all eternity You will reign in glory, for we have no king but You.

הַמַּלְאָךְ May the angel who rescued me from all harm, bless these boys. May *Gen. 48* they be called by my name and the names of my fathers Abraham and Isaac, and may they increase greatly on the earth.

וַיֹּאמֶר He said, "If you listen carefully to the voice of the Lord your God and *Ex. 15* do what is right in His eyes, if you pay attention to His commandments and keep all His statutes, I will not bring on you any of the diseases I brought on the Egyptians, for I am the Lord who heals you." The Lord said to the *Zech. 3* accuser, "The Lord shall rebuke you, accuser. The Lord who has chosen Jerusalem shall rebuke you! Is not this man a burning stick snatched from the fire?" Look! It is Solomon's bed, escorted by sixty warriors, the noblest *Song. 3* of Israel, all of them wearing the sword, experienced in battle, each with his sword at his side, prepared for the terror of the nights.

Say three times:

יְבָרֶכְךָ May the Lord bless you and protect you. *Num. 6*
May the Lord make His face shine on you and be gracious to you.
May the Lord turn His face toward you and grant you peace.

Say three times:

הִנֵּה See – the Guardian of Israel *Ps. 121*
neither slumbers nor sleeps.

Say three times:

לִישׁוּעָתְךָ For Your salvation I hope, Lord. *Gen. 49*
I hope, Lord, for Your salvation.
Lord, for Your salvation I hope.

Say three times:

בְּשֵׁם In the name of the Lord, God of Israel:
may Michael be at my right hand,
Gabriel, at my left;
in front of me, Uriel,
behind me, Raphael;
and above my head the Presence of God.

יִרְאוּ עֵינֵינוּ וְיִשְׂמַח לִבֵּנוּ, וְתָגֵל נַפְשֵׁנוּ בִּישׁוּעָתְךָ בֶּאֱמֶת, בֶּאֱמֹר לְצִיּוֹן מָלַךְ אֱלֹהָיִךְ. יהוה מֶלֶךְ, יהוה מָלָךְ, יהוה יִמְלֹךְ לְעוֹלָם וָעֶד. כִּי הַמַּלְכוּת שֶׁלְּךָ הִיא, וּלְעוֹלְמֵי עַד תִּמְלֹךְ בְּכָבוֹד, כִּי אֵין לָנוּ מֶלֶךְ אֶלָּא אָתָּה.

בראשית מח
הַמַּלְאָךְ הַגֹּאֵל אֹתִי מִכָּל־רָע יְבָרֵךְ אֶת־הַנְּעָרִים, וְיִקָּרֵא בָהֶם שְׁמִי וְשֵׁם אֲבֹתַי אַבְרָהָם וְיִצְחָק, וְיִדְגּוּ לָרֹב בְּקֶרֶב הָאָרֶץ:

שמות טו
וַיֹּאמֶר אִם־שָׁמוֹעַ תִּשְׁמַע לְקוֹל יהוה אֱלֹהֶיךָ, וְהַיָּשָׁר בְּעֵינָיו תַּעֲשֶׂה, וְהַאֲזַנְתָּ לְמִצְוֹתָיו וְשָׁמַרְתָּ כָּל־חֻקָּיו, כָּל־הַמַּחֲלָה אֲשֶׁר־שַׂמְתִּי בְמִצְרַיִם לֹא־אָשִׂים עָלֶיךָ, כִּי אֲנִי יהוה רֹפְאֶךָ:

זכריה ג
וַיֹּאמֶר יהוה אֶל־הַשָּׂטָן, יִגְעַר יהוה בְּךָ הַשָּׂטָן, וְיִגְעַר יהוה בְּךָ הַבֹּחֵר בִּירוּשָׁלָםִ, הֲלוֹא זֶה אוּד מֻצָּל מֵאֵשׁ:

שיר השירים ג
הִנֵּה מִטָּתוֹ שֶׁלִּשְׁלֹמֹה, שִׁשִּׁים גִּבֹּרִים סָבִיב לָהּ, מִגִּבֹּרֵי יִשְׂרָאֵל: כֻּלָּם אֲחֻזֵי חֶרֶב, מְלֻמְּדֵי מִלְחָמָה, אִישׁ חַרְבּוֹ עַל־יְרֵכוֹ מִפַּחַד בַּלֵּילוֹת:

Say three times:

במדבר ו
יְבָרֶכְךָ יהוה וְיִשְׁמְרֶךָ:
יָאֵר יהוה פָּנָיו אֵלֶיךָ וִיחֻנֶּךָּ:
יִשָּׂא יהוה פָּנָיו אֵלֶיךָ וְיָשֵׂם לְךָ שָׁלוֹם:

Say three times:

תהלים קכא
הִנֵּה לֹא־יָנוּם וְלֹא יִישָׁן שׁוֹמֵר יִשְׂרָאֵל:

Say three times:

בראשית מט
לִישׁוּעָתְךָ קִוִּיתִי יהוה:
קִוִּיתִי יהוה לִישׁוּעָתְךָ:
יהוה לִישׁוּעָתְךָ קִוִּיתִי:

Say three times:

בְּשֵׁם יהוה אֱלֹהֵי יִשְׂרָאֵל
מִימִינִי מִיכָאֵל, וּמִשְּׂמֹאלִי גַּבְרִיאֵל
וּמִלְּפָנַי אוּרִיאֵל, וּמֵאֲחוֹרַי רְפָאֵל
וְעַל רֹאשִׁי שְׁכִינַת אֵל.

שִׁיר הַמַּעֲלוֹת A song of ascents. *Ps. 128*

Happy are all who fear the Lᴏʀᴅ, who walk in His ways.

When you eat the fruit of your labor, happy and fortunate are you.

Your wife shall be like a fruitful vine within your house;

your sons like olive saplings around your table.

So shall the man who fears the Lᴏʀᴅ be blessed.

May the Lᴏʀᴅ bless you from Zion;

may you see the good of Jerusalem all the days of your life;

and may you live to see your children's children. Peace be on Israel!

Say three times:

רִגְזוּ Tremble, and do not sin. *Ps. 4*

Search your heart as you lie on your bed, and be silent. Selah.

אֲדוֹן עוֹלָם Lᴏʀᴅ of the Universe,

who reigned before the birth of any thing;

when by His will all things were made,

then was His name proclaimed King.

And when all things shall cease to be,

He alone will reign in awe.

He was, He is, and He shall be glorious for evermore.

He is One, there is none else, alone, unique, beyond compare;

Without beginning, without end, His might, His rule are everywhere.

He is my God; my Redeemer lives.

He is the Rock on whom I rely –

my banner and my safe retreat, my cup, my portion when I cry.

Into His hand my soul I place, when I awake and when I sleep.

The Lᴏʀᴅ is with me, I shall not fear;

body and soul from harm will He keep.

שִׁיר הַמַּעֲלוֹת, אַשְׁרֵי כָּל־יְרֵא יהוה, הַהֹלֵךְ בִּדְרָכָיו:
יְגִיעַ כַּפֶּיךָ כִּי תֹאכֵל, אַשְׁרֶיךָ וְטוֹב לָךְ:
אֶשְׁתְּךָ כְּגֶפֶן פֹּרִיָּה בְּיַרְכְּתֵי בֵיתֶךָ
בָּנֶיךָ כִּשְׁתִלֵי זֵיתִים, סָבִיב לְשֻׁלְחָנֶךָ:
הִנֵּה כִי־כֵן יְבֹרַךְ גָּבֶר יְרֵא יהוה:
יְבָרֶכְךָ יהוה מִצִּיּוֹן, וּרְאֵה בְּטוּב יְרוּשָׁלָֽםִ, כֹּל יְמֵי חַיֶּיךָ:
וּרְאֵה־בָנִים לְבָנֶיךָ, שָׁלוֹם עַל־יִשְׂרָאֵל:

Say three times:

רִגְזוּ וְאַל־תֶּחֱטָֽאוּ
אִמְרוּ בִלְבַבְכֶם עַל־מִשְׁכַּבְכֶם, וְדֹֽמּוּ סֶֽלָה:

אֲדוֹן עוֹלָם אֲשֶׁר מָלַךְ בְּטֶֽרֶם כָּל־יְצִיר נִבְרָא.
לְעֵת נַעֲשָׂה בְחֶפְצוֹ כֹּל אֲזַי מֶֽלֶךְ שְׁמוֹ נִקְרָא.
וְאַחֲרֵי כִּכְלוֹת הַכֹּל לְבַדּוֹ יִמְלֹךְ נוֹרָא.
וְהוּא הָיָה וְהוּא הֹוֶה וְהוּא יִהְיֶה בְּתִפְאָרָה.
וְהוּא אֶחָד וְאֵין שֵׁנִי לְהַמְשִׁיל לוֹ לְהַחְבִּֽירָה.
בְּלִי רֵאשִׁית בְּלִי תַכְלִית וְלוֹ הָעֹז וְהַמִּשְׂרָה.
וְהוּא אֵלִי וְחַי גֹּאֲלִי וְצוּר חֶבְלִי בְּעֵת צָרָה.
וְהוּא נִסִּי וּמָנוֹס לִי מְנָת כּוֹסִי בְּיוֹם אֶקְרָא.
בְּיָדוֹ אַפְקִיד רוּחִי בְּעֵת אִישָׁן וְאָעִֽירָה.
וְעִם רוּחִי גְּוִיָּתִי יהוה לִי וְלֹא אִירָא.

מועדים

MO'ADIM

Blessing on Taking the Lulav

On Sukkot, except on Shabbat, the lulav and etrog are taken before Hallel.

Some say the following:

יְהִי רָצוֹן May it be Your will, Lᴏʀᴅ my God and God of my fathers, that through the fruit of the citron tree, the palm frond, the myrtle branches and willows of the brook, the letters of Your unique name draw close to one another and become united in my hand. Make it known I am called by Your name, so that [evil] will fear to come close to me. When I wave them, may a rich flow of blessings flow from the supreme Source of wisdom to the place of the Tabernacle and the site of the House of our God. May the command of these four species be considered by You as if I had fulfilled it in all its details and roots, as well as the 613 commandments dependent on it, for it is my intention to unify the name of the Holy One, blessed be He, and His Divine Presence, in reverence and love, to unify the name *Yod-Heh* with *Vav-Heh*, in perfect unity in the name of all Israel, Amen. Blessed is the Ps. 89
Lᴏʀᴅ forever, Amen and Amen.

*The lulav is taken in the right hand, with the myrtle leaves on the right,
willow leaves on the left. The etrog is taken in the left hand, with its
pointed end toward the floor. Then say the following blessing:*

בָּרוּךְ Blessed are You, Lᴏʀᴅ our God, King of the Universe,
who has made us holy through His commandments,
and has commanded us about taking the lulav.

On the first day the lulav is taken, add:

בָּרוּךְ Blessed are You, Lᴏʀᴅ our God, King of the Universe,
who has given us life, sustained us and brought us to this time.

*Invert the etrog, so that its pointed end is facing up.
Face the front of the synagogue and wave the lulav and etrog
in the following sequence, three times in each direction:
ahead, right, back, left, up, down.
Continue to hold the lulav and etrog during Hallel.*

סדר נטילת לולב

On סוכות, except on שבת, the לולב and אתרוג are taken before הלל.

Some say the following:

יְהִי רָצוֹן מִלְּפָנֶיךָ יהוה אֱלֹהַי וֵאלֹהֵי אֲבוֹתַי, בִּפְרִי עֵץ הָדָר וְכַפֹּת
תְּמָרִים וַעֲנַף עֵץ עָבוֹת וְעַרְבֵי נָחַל, אוֹתִיּוֹת שִׁמְךָ הַמְיֻחָד תִּקְרַב
אֶחָד אֶל אֶחָד וְהָיוּ לַאֲחָדִים בְּיָדִי, וְלֵידַע אֵיךְ שִׁמְךָ נִקְרָא עָלַי
וְיִירְאוּ מִגֶּשֶׁת אֵלָי. וּבְנַעֲנוּעַי אוֹתָם תַּשְׁפִּיעַ שֶׁפַע בְּרָכוֹת מִדַּעַת
עֶלְיוֹן לְנָוֶה אַפִּרְיוֹן לִמְכוֹן בֵּית אֱלֹהֵינוּ, וּתְהֵא חֲשׁוּבָה לְפָנֶיךָ מִצְוַת
אַרְבָּעָה מִינִים אֵלּוּ כְּאִלּוּ קִיַּמְתִּיהָ בְּכָל פְּרָטוֹתֶיהָ וְשָׁרָשֶׁיהָ וְתַרְיַ"ג
מִצְוֹת הַתְּלוּיוֹת בָּהּ, כִּי כַוָּנָתִי לְיַחֵד לְיַחֲדָא שְׁמָא דְּקֻדְשָׁא בְּרִיךְ הוּא
וּשְׁכִינְתֵּהּ בִּדְחִילוּ וּרְחִימוּ, לְיַחֵד שֵׁם י"ה בו"ה בְּיִחוּדָא שְׁלִים
בְּשֵׁם כָּל יִשְׂרָאֵל, אָמֵן. בָּרוּךְ יהוה לְעוֹלָם, אָמֵן וְאָמֵן:

תהלים פט

The לולב is taken in the right hand, with the הדסים on the right, ערבות on the left. The אתרוג is taken in the left hand, with its pointed end toward the floor. Then say the following blessing:

בָּרוּךְ אַתָּה יהוה אֱלֹהֵינוּ מֶלֶךְ הָעוֹלָם
אֲשֶׁר קִדְּשָׁנוּ בְּמִצְוֹתָיו וְצִוָּנוּ עַל נְטִילַת לוּלָב.

On the first day the לולב is taken, add:

בָּרוּךְ אַתָּה יהוה אֱלֹהֵינוּ מֶלֶךְ הָעוֹלָם
שֶׁהֶחֱיָנוּ וְקִיְּמָנוּ וְהִגִּיעָנוּ לַזְּמַן הַזֶּה.

Invert the אתרוג, so that its pointed end is facing up.
Face the front of the בית כנסת and wave the לולב and אתרוג
in the following sequence, three times in each direction:
ahead, right, back, left, up, down.
Continue to hold the לולב and אתרוג during הלל.

Hallel

On Ḥanukka, Ḥol HaMo'ed Sukkot, Yom HaAtzma'ut and Yom Yerushalayim, Full Hallel is said. On Ḥol HaMo'ed Pesaḥ and on Rosh Ḥodesh Half Hallel is said. See laws 278–279.

בָּרוּךְ Blessed are You, LORD our God, King of the Universe, who has made us holy through His commandments and has commanded us to recite the Hallel.

הַלְלוּיָהּ Halleluya! Servants of the LORD,^ give praise; praise the name of the LORD. Blessed be the name of the LORD now and for evermore. From the rising of the sun to its setting, may the LORD's name be praised. High is the LORD above all nations; His glory is above the

Ps. 113

---

new month as a new start, filled with hope for emerging from the limitations that may hold us back, and with the promise that

Hashem is ever-present to help us out. **What are your hopes for the coming month?**

HILKHOT TEFILLA · הלכות תפילה

Each holiday has its own historical derivation and halakhic status, and this helps determine how much of Hallel is required. The core consists of six successive chapters of *Tehillim* (113–118) with a blessing at the beginning and at the end. Sometimes, the first parts of some of those chapters are omitted, resulting in two versions referred to as "Full Hallel" and "Half/Skipped Hallel." Full Hallel is generally

recited for events of great national import, such as Pesaḥ, Shavuot, Sukkot and Ḥanukka, and, by the decree of the Chief Rabbinate of Israel, on Yom HaAtzma'ut and Yom Yerushalayim as well. Similarly, the shortened version is recited on Rosh Ḥodesh which, while not a holiday in the classic sense, was nevertheless commemorated with the celebration of seeing the new moon.

ANI TEFILLA · אני תפילה

הַלְלוּיָהּ הַלְלוּ עַבְדֵי יהוה – *Halleluya! Servants of the LORD, give praise.* The first three verses speak of Hashem's presence in time – for eternity and in a single day.

The middle three verses speak of Hashem's presence in space – in the universe, and on earth.

The last three verses, speak of Hashem's presence in the lives of man – helping the poor and the childless.

Where can you feel Hashem's presence most today?

סֵדֶר הַלֵּל

On חנוכה, יום העצמאות, חול המועד סוכות, שלם ירושלים, *and* הלל שלם *is said.*
On חול המועד פסח *and on* ראש חודש, בדילוג הלל *is said. See laws 278–279.*

בָּרוּךְ אַתָּה יהוה אֱלֹהֵינוּ מֶלֶךְ הָעוֹלָם
אֲשֶׁר קִדְּשָׁנוּ בְּמִצְוֹתָיו וְצִוָּנוּ לִקְרֹא אֶת הַהַלֵּל.

הַלְלוּיָהּ, הַלְלוּ עַבְדֵי יהוה,∗ הַלְלוּ אֶת־שֵׁם יהוה: יְהִי שֵׁם יהוה
מְבֹרָךְ, מֵעַתָּה וְעַד־עוֹלָם: מִמִּזְרַח־שֶׁמֶשׁ עַד־מְבוֹאוֹ, מְהֻלָּל שֵׁם
יהוה: רָם עַל־כָּל־גּוֹיִם יהוה, עַל הַשָּׁמַיִם כְּבוֹדוֹ: מִי כַּיהוה אֱלֹהֵינוּ,

תהלים קיג

AN INTRODUCTION TO HALLEL

The Talmud (*Pesaḥim* 117a) brings a number of opinions regarding the ancient roots of Hallel. There are those who suggest that it was recited by Moshe and *Benei Yisrael* at the splitting of the Sea, by Yehoshua and *Benei Yisrael* when faced by the kings of Canaan, and by Mordekhai and Esther when they were facing Haman, to name but three occasions. In short, say the sages, it was to be said whenever the Jewish people were redeemed from some potential calamity. In Rabbinic literature it is called *Hallel Mitzri*, or the Egyptian Hallel, based upon the reference in the second paragraph to the exodus from Egypt. The prayer marks our deliverance, often by seemingly supernatural means, throughout our history. "That is why we say it on Yom HaAtzma'ut and Yom Yerushalayim, the two most transformative events of modern Jewish history, in the faith that it is not human beings alone who shape the destiny of our people, but God

working in and through His children" (Rabbi J. Sacks). In Hallel, we praise God's presence in world events, past and present.

Rosh Ḥodesh is not that exact same kind of holy day. Rather, Rosh Ḥodesh marks the beginning of a new month. Recall that the very first commandment that the Israelites were given in Egypt was to sanctify the new moon (*Shemot* 12:1), in effect to enable the measurement and marking of time, and establish the calendar. Each new month is thus not only a natural astrological event, but a psychological and theological one as well. On a national level, the fate of the Jewish people has been compared to the waxing and waning of the moon, from periods of darkness to periods when it fills the world with its reflected light. On a personal level, Rosh Ḥodesh represents a new beginning, one that is filled with optimism about the opportunities for growth and personal enlightenment. As such, we celebrate every

heavens. Who is like the LORD our God, who sits enthroned so high, yet turns so low to see the heavens and the earth? ▸ He raises the poor from the dust and the needy from the refuse heap, giving them a place alongside princes, the princes of His people. He makes the woman in a childless house a happy mother of children. Halleluya!

בְּצֵאת When Israel came out¹ of Egypt, the house of Jacob from a *Ps. 114* people of foreign tongue, Judah became His sanctuary, Israel His dominion. The sea saw and fled; the Jordan turned back. The mountains skipped like rams, the hills like lambs. ▸ Why was it, sea, that you fled? Jordan, why did you turn back? Why, mountains, did you skip like rams, and you, hills, like lambs? It was at the presence of the LORD, Creator of the earth, at the presence of the God of Jacob, who turned the rock into a pool of water, flint into a flowing spring.

Omit on Rosh Ḥodesh (except on Ḥanukka) and on Ḥol HaMo'ed Pesaḥ:

לֹא לָנוּ Not to us, LORD, not to us, but to Your name give glory, for *Ps. 115* Your love, for Your faithfulness. Why should the nations say, "Where now is their God?" Our God is in heaven; whatever He wills He does. Their idols are silver and gold, made by human hands.¹ They have mouths but cannot speak; eyes but cannot see. They have ears but cannot hear; noses but cannot smell. They have hands but cannot feel; feet but cannot walk. No sound comes from their throat. Those who make them become like them; so will all who trust in them. ▸ Israel, trust in the LORD – He is their Help and their Shield. House of

are silver and gold, made by human hands. We cannot always see God. He sometimes seems absent or hidden from our lives. This psalm addresses this frustration by speaking of the folly of idolatry and of placing one's faith in other gods or non-Jewish beliefs. They are called idols, עֲצַבִּים (from the word *itzev*, to make), because they are fashioned by man, but also because they bring sadness (from the word *atzuv*) and

disappointment to their believers. Physical idols and images of gods are easily seen, but their abilities are not manifest. Hashem, however, cannot be physically seen but His actions can be seen everywhere (Rabbi S.R. Hirsch). The search for God is universal and it is a natural inclination to want to see some physical manifestation of Him. Judaism's response is that He cannot be seen but His impact is everywhere. Look around you.

הַמַּגְבִּיהִי לָשָׁבֶת: הַמַּשְׁפִּילִי לִרְאוֹת, בַּשָּׁמַיִם וּבָאָרֶץ: ◌ מְקִימִי
מֵעָפָר דָּל, מֵאַשְׁפֹּת יָרִים אֶבְיוֹן: לְהוֹשִׁיבִי עִם־נְדִיבִים, עִם נְדִיבֵי
עַמּוֹ: מוֹשִׁיבִי עֲקֶרֶת הַבַּיִת, אֵם־הַבָּנִים שְׂמֵחָה, הַלְלוּיָהּ:

תהלים קיד

בְּצֵאת יִשְׂרָאֵל מִמִּצְרָיִם, בֵּית יַעֲקֹב מֵעַם לֹעֵז: הָיְתָה יְהוּדָה
לְקָדְשׁוֹ, יִשְׂרָאֵל מַמְשְׁלוֹתָיו: הַיָּם רָאָה וַיָּנֹס, הַיַּרְדֵּן יִסֹּב לְאָחוֹר:
הֶהָרִים רָקְדוּ כְאֵילִים, גְּבָעוֹת כִּבְנֵי־צֹאן: מַה־לְּךָ הַיָּם כִּי תָנוּס,
הַיַּרְדֵּן תִּסֹּב לְאָחוֹר: הֶהָרִים תִּרְקְדוּ כְאֵילִים, גְּבָעוֹת כִּבְנֵי־צֹאן:
מִלִּפְנֵי אָדוֹן חוּלִי אָרֶץ, מִלִּפְנֵי אֱלוֹהַּ יַעֲקֹב: הַהֹפְכִי הַצּוּר אֲגַם־
מָיִם, חַלָּמִישׁ לְמַעְיְנוֹ־מָיִם:

Omit on ראש חודש (except on חנוכה) and on פסח המועד חול:

תהלים קטו

לֹא לָנוּ יהוה לֹא לָנוּ, כִּי־לְשִׁמְךָ תֵּן כָּבוֹד, עַל־חַסְדְּךָ עַל־אֲמִתֶּךָ: לָמָּה
יֹאמְרוּ הַגּוֹיִם אַיֵּה־נָא אֱלֹהֵיהֶם: וֵאלֹהֵינוּ בַשָּׁמָיִם, כֹּל אֲשֶׁר־חָפֵץ
עָשָׂה: עֲצַבֵּיהֶם כֶּסֶף וְזָהָב, מַעֲשֵׂה יְדֵי אָדָם: פֶּה־לָהֶם וְלֹא יְדַבֵּרוּ,
עֵינַיִם לָהֶם וְלֹא יִרְאוּ: אָזְנַיִם לָהֶם וְלֹא יִשְׁמָעוּ, אַף לָהֶם וְלֹא יְרִיחוּן:
יְדֵיהֶם וְלֹא יְמִישׁוּן, רַגְלֵיהֶם וְלֹא יְהַלֵּכוּ, לֹא־יֶהְגּוּ בִּגְרוֹנָם: כְּמוֹהֶם יִהְיוּ
עֹשֵׂיהֶם, כֹּל אֲשֶׁר־בֹּטֵחַ בָּהֶם: יִשְׂרָאֵל בְּטַח בַּיהוה, עֶזְרָם וּמָגִנָּם

עיון תפילה · IYUN TEFILLA

בְּצֵאת יִשְׂרָאֵל — *When Israel came out.* Hashem is Master both of nature and of human history. No sooner is Israel freed from Egypt, than the entire natural world responds. The "sea saw and fled" by splitting for the Israelites; similarly "the Jordan [River] turned back" when they crossed over into the Promised Land. The natural world is thus a partner in the historical process. The in-

animate world of seas and rivers, mountains and hills, comes alive when seen as part of the continuum of history, at least forty years of which is compressed here into one unified vision.

Have you ever felt in sync with nature? Imagine the whole world that way.

עֲצַבֵּיהֶם כֶּסֶף וְזָהָב, מַעֲשֵׂה יְדֵי אָדָם — *Their idols*

Aaron, trust in the Lord – He is their Help and their Shield. You who fear the Lord, trust in the Lord[B] – He is their Help and their Shield.

יהוה זְכָרָנוּ The Lord remembers us and will bless us. He will bless the house of Israel. He will bless the house of Aaron. He will bless those who fear the Lord, small and great alike. May the Lord give you increase: you and your children. May you be blessed by the Lord, Maker of heaven and earth. ‣ The heavens are the Lord's, but the earth He has given over to mankind.[B] It is not the dead who praise the Lord,[A] nor those who go down to the silent grave. But we will bless the Lord, now and for ever. Halleluya!

Omit on Rosh Ḥodesh (except on Ḥanukka) and on Ḥol HaMo'ed Pesaḥ:

אָהַבְתִּי I love[A] the Lord, for He hears my voice, my pleas. He turns *Ps. 116* His ear to me whenever I call. The bonds of death encompassed me, the anguish of the grave came upon me, I was overcome by trouble and sorrow. Then I called on the name of the Lord: "Lord, I pray, save my life." Gracious is the Lord, and righteous; our God is full of compassion. The Lord protects the simple hearted. When I was brought low, He saved me.[B] My soul, be at peace once more,[A] for the

---

Look around you now. What can you see that is life affirming?

אָהַבְתִּי – *I love.* I stand before Hashem knowing that life has its challenges, troubles and sorrows, both physical and spiritual. Nevertheless, I know that Hashem listens whenever I speak to Him about them. I do not always get the response that I want, but sometimes just knowing that Someone is listening is relief enough.

Hashem is listening right now. What do you want to say to Him?

דַּלּוֹתִי וְלִי יְהוֹשִׁיעַ – *When I was brought low (daloti), He saved me.* The congregation of Israel spoke before the Holy One, blessed be He, Sovereign of the Universe! Though I am poor (dala) in mitzvot, and do not always do what I am supposed to do, nevertheless, I am Yours, my commitment is there, I try my best, and it is fitting that I should be saved (based on *Pesaḥim* 118b).

שׁוּבִי נַפְשִׁי לִמְנוּחָיְכִי – *My soul, be at peace once more.* One can communicate with one's soul. Prayer can be a form of mindfulness and meditation that enables one to get in touch with one's inner being. Focusing on the realization that Hashem has been good to me can provide my soul with inner peace that I often lose track of in the hustle and bustle of my day. Here is such a moment. Focus: My soul, be at peace once again.

הוּא: בֵּית אַהֲרֹן בִּטְחוּ בַיהוה, עֶזְרָם וּמָגִנָּם הוּא: יִרְאֵי יהוה בִּטְחוּ
בַיהוה,ּ עֶזְרָם וּמָגִנָּם הוּא:

יהוה זְכָרָנוּ יְבָרֵךְ, יְבָרֵךְ אֶת־בֵּית יִשְׂרָאֵל, יְבָרֵךְ אֶת־בֵּית אַהֲרֹן:
יְבָרֵךְ יִרְאֵי יהוה, הַקְּטַנִּים עִם־הַגְּדֹלִים: יֹסֵף יהוה עֲלֵיכֶם, עֲלֵיכֶם
וְעַל־בְּנֵיכֶם: בְּרוּכִים אַתֶּם לַיהוה, עֹשֵׂה שָׁמַיִם וָאָרֶץ: ‹ הַשָּׁמַיִם
שָׁמַיִם לַיהוה, וְהָאָרֶץ נָתַן לִבְנֵי־אָדָם:ּ לֹא הַמֵּתִים יְהַלְלוּ־יָהּ,ּ
וְלֹא כָּל־יֹרְדֵי דוּמָה: וַאֲנַחְנוּ נְבָרֵךְ יָהּ, מֵעַתָּה וְעַד־עוֹלָם, הַלְלוּיָהּ:

Omit on (חנוכה) and on (ראש חודש except on):חֹל הַמּוֹעֵד פֶּסַח

אֲהַבְתִּי,ּ כִּי־יִשְׁמַע יהוה, אֶת־קוֹלִי תַּחֲנוּנָי: כִּי־הִטָּה אָזְנוֹ לִי, וּבְיָמַי
אֶקְרָא: אֲפָפוּנִי חֶבְלֵי־מָוֶת, וּמְצָרֵי שְׁאוֹל מְצָאוּנִי, צָרָה וְיָגוֹן אֶמְצָא:
וּבְשֵׁם־יהוה אֶקְרָא, אָנָּה יהוה מַלְּטָה נַפְשִׁי: חַנּוּן יהוה וְצַדִּיק, וֵאלֹהֵינוּ
מְרַחֵם: שֹׁמֵר פְּתָאיִם יהוה, דַּלּוֹתִי וְלִי יְהוֹשִׁיעַ: שׁוּבִי נַפְשִׁי לִמְנוּחָיְכִי,ּ

תהלים קטז

ביאור תפילה · BIUR TEFILLA

יִרְאֵי יהוה בִּטְחוּ בַיהוה — *You who fear the Lord, trust in the Lord.* The verse says that Hashem will bless "those who fear" Him. But it already said He will bless the house of Israel and the house of Aharon – who else is left? A number of possibilities: it is a reference to converts (Rashi); the Torah scholars (Radak); the religious people of other faiths (Ibn Ezra); the righteous people of other faiths (Metzuda).

וְהָאָרֶץ נָתַן לִבְנֵי־אָדָם — *But the earth He has given over to mankind.* "He gave the earth to man," not as a present but as a trust to be guarded and protected. Hashem gave the planet to mankind, not to be used and abused, but to be developed and nurtured. The Torah gives us the earth as a resource for our use (*Bereshit* 1:28), but also with the responsibility to protect and conserve it (ibid. 2:15). Our challenge is to find the appropriate balance between these two (Rabbi J.B. Soloveitchik).

אני תפילה · ANI TEFILLA

לֹא הַמֵּתִים יְהַלְלוּ־יָהּ — *It is not the dead who praise the Lord.* True, life can be filled with tragedy, and the existence of death, natural as it may be, is still a reason for sadness. Yet knowing that such things exist should also be a reminder that every day presents a new opportunity to praise and thank Hashem for life, and for the things that we have. Even if one has a day when one might feel "down" and want to be in "silence," we are reminded that life in its totality is indeed beautiful and worth singing about.

LORD has been good to you. For You have rescued me from death, my eyes from weeping, my feet from stumbling. ▸ I shall walk in the presence of the LORD in the land of the living. I had faith, even when I said, "I am greatly afflicted," even when I said rashly, "All men are liars."

מָה־אָשִׁיב How can I repay the LORD[A] for all His goodness to me? I will lift the cup of salvation and call on the name of the LORD. I will fulfill my vows to the LORD in the presence of all His people. Grievous in the LORD's sight is the death of His devoted ones. Truly, LORD, I am Your servant;[1A] I am Your servant, the son of Your maidservant. You set me free from my chains. ▸ To You I shall bring a thanksgiving-offering and call on the LORD by name. I will fulfill my vows to the LORD in the presence of all His people, in the courts of the House of the LORD, in your midst, Jerusalem. Halleluya!

הַלְלוּ Praise the LORD,[1] all nations; acclaim Him, all you peoples;
for His loving-kindness to us is strong,
and the LORD's faithfulness is everlasting.
Halleluya!

Ps. 117

---

na" ("Hashem, please, save us" [see page 455]) The Rebbe responded, "No, you mis-understood. I wasn't referring to that phrase but to the one which says "Ana Hashem

ki ani avdekha" (Please Hashem, for I am Your servant). First one must commit oneself to the King's service; only then can one presume to call on Him for help.

הַלְלוּ אֶת־יהוה – *Praise the LORD.*

The shortest of all of the psalms, a mere two verses. The psalmist speaks of the universal significance of Israel's history. It is not Israel alone, but all the nations, who will see in the story of this people, something be-yond mere history. "The Jew is the emblem of eternity. He whom neither slaughter nor torture of thousands of years could destroy, he whom neither fire nor sword nor inqui-

sition was able to wipe off the face of the earth, he who was the first to produce the oracles of God, who has been for so long the guardian of prophecy and transmitted it to the rest of the world – such a nation cannot be destroyed. The Jew is everlasting as eternity itself" (Tolstoy). (Rabbi J. Sacks)

Sometimes non-Jews see the miracle of our survival more clearly than we ourselves do (*Pesaḥim* 118b and Rashi).

כִּי־יהוה גָּמַל עָלָיְכִי: כִּי חִלַּצְתָּ נַפְשִׁי מִמָּוֶת, אֶת־עֵינִי מִן־דִּמְעָה, אֶת־
רַגְלִי מִדֶּחִי: אֶתְהַלֵּךְ לִפְנֵי יהוה, בְּאַרְצוֹת הַחַיִּים: הֶאֱמַנְתִּי כִּי אֲדַבֵּר,
אֲנִי עָנִיתִי מְאֹד: אֲנִי אָמַרְתִּי בְחָפְזִי, כָּל־הָאָדָם כֹּזֵב:

מָה־אָשִׁיב לַיהוה,ᵃ כָּל־תַּגְמוּלוֹהִי עָלָי: כּוֹס־יְשׁוּעוֹת אֶשָּׂא, וּבְשֵׁם
יהוה אֶקְרָא: נְדָרַי לַיהוה אֲשַׁלֵּם, נֶגְדָה־נָּא לְכָל־עַמּוֹ: יָקָר בְּעֵינֵי
יהוה, הַמָּוְתָה לַחֲסִידָיו: אָנָּה יהוה כִּי־אֲנִי עַבְדֶּךָ,ᵛ אֲנִי־עַבְדְּךָ
בֶּן־אֲמָתֶךָ, פִּתַּחְתָּ לְמוֹסֵרָי: לְךָ־אֶזְבַּח זֶבַח תּוֹדָה, וּבְשֵׁם יהוה
אֶקְרָא: נְדָרַי לַיהוה אֲשַׁלֵּם, נֶגְדָה־נָּא לְכָל־עַמּוֹ: בְּחַצְרוֹת בֵּית
יהוה, בְּתוֹכֵכִי יְרוּשָׁלָםִ, הַלְלוּיָהּ:

תהלים קיז

הַלְלוּ אֶת־יהוהᵛ כָּל־גּוֹיִם, שַׁבְּחוּהוּ כָּל־הָאֻמִּים:
כִּי גָבַר עָלֵינוּ חַסְדּוֹ, וֶאֱמֶת־יהוה לְעוֹלָם, הַלְלוּיָהּ:

ANI TEFILLA • אני תפילה

מָה־אָשִׁיב לַיהוה – *How can I repay the Lord.* How can I possibly thank Hashem for everything I have? The answer: I can't. For no matter how difficult daily circumstances may be, I still have my life, which Judaism maintains is a supreme gift. The good always, always, outweighs the bad.

IYUN TEFILLA • עיון תפילה

אָנָּה יהוה כִּי־אֲנִי עַבְדֶּךָ – *Truly, Lord, I am Your servant.* I have come to serve You from two directions. First, I am Your servant; I try to do my best on my own, finding my own faith and my own way. Second, I am a product of my mother, whose traditions and teachings shaped me in becoming a Jew. I am thus a servant in my own right and the child of a servant (Radak). Both of those free me from (physical, social, intellectual or spiritual) chains that would otherwise tie me down. For that I am thankful.

ANI TEFILLA • אני תפילה

אָנָּה יהוה כִּי־אֲנִי עַבְדֶּךָ – *Truly, Lord, I am Your servant.* A Hasid came to his Rebbe and asked for direction about how he might get help from Hashem. The Rebbe advised him to say the phrase that begins with the words "Ana Hashem" with all of his strength and devotion. The Hasid returned one day and complained that he had followed the Rebbe's advice but to no avail. The Rebbe asked him, "Which Ana Hashem did you recite?" The Hasid answered, "Ana Hashem hoshia

The following verses are chanted by the Leader.
At the end of each verse, the congregation responds, "Thank the LORD
for He is good; His loving-kindness is for ever."
On Sukkot, the lulav and etrog are waved, three waves for each word of the verse
(except God's name). On the first word, wave forward, then, on subsequent words,
wave right, back, left, up and down respectively. The Leader waves only for the first
two verses. The congregation waves each time the first verse is said in response.

הוֹדוּ Thank the LORD for He is good;[B] His loving-kindness is for ever. Ps. 118

Let Israel say   His loving-kindness is for ever.

Let the house of Aaron say   His loving-kindness is for ever.

Let those who fear the LORD say   His loving-kindness is for ever.

מִן־הַמֵּצַר In my distress I called on the LORD.[A] The LORD answered me
and set me free. The LORD is with me; I will not be afraid. What can
man do to me? The LORD is with me. He is my Helper. I will see the
downfall of my enemies. It is better to take refuge in the LORD than
to trust in man. It is better to take refuge in the LORD than to trust
in princes. The nations all surrounded me, but in the LORD's name I
drove them off. They surrounded me on every side, but in the LORD's
name I drove them off. They surrounded me like bees,[A] they attacked
me as fire attacks brushwood, but in the LORD's name I drove them
off. They thrust so hard against me, I nearly fell, but the LORD came

---

ANI TEFILLA · אני תפילה

מִן־הַמֵּצַר קָרָאתִי יָּהּ – *In my distress I called on
the LORD.*
There were times when I thought my world
was crashing around me, when I could not understand why this was happening to me, to my
family, to people that I cared about. At those
moments, I took strength from the belief that
there must be a bigger plan, that Hashem had
something in mind that I just couldn't see right
now. That belief doesn't always take away the
pain of the moment, but it gives one enough
perspective to take it in stride and to move
on with a sense of optimism. Though I sometimes find myself confined in narrow "straits"

(*metzar*), my knowing that Hashem is there
enables me to realize that there is a bigger,
more "expansive" (*merḥav*) picture.

סַבּוּנִי כִדְבֹרִים – *They surrounded me like bees.*
Sometimes those who attack us appear as a
forest fire that burns the brush all around us;
we see them coming but cannot get out of the
way. Sometimes they appear as bees, attrac-
tive in color, full of life, bearing sweet honey
for us, but if we let our guard down they sting
us and quickly move off. Either way, my faith
provides me with perspective that makes me
strong and resilient.

The following verses are chanted by the שליח ציבור.

At the end of each verse, the קהל *responds:* הֹודוּ לַיהוה כִּי־טֹוב, כִּי לְעֹולָם חַסְדֹּו.

On סוכות, *the* לולב *and* אתרוג *are waved, three waves for each word of the verse (except God's name). On the first word, wave forward, then, on subsequent words, wave right, back, left, up and down respectively. The* שליח ציבור *waves only for the first two verses. The* קהל *waves each time the first verse is said in response.*

תהלים קיח

הֹודוּ לַיהוה כִּי־טֹובֿ   כִּי לְעֹולָם חַסְדֹּו:

יֹאמַר־נָא יִשְׂרָאֵל   כִּי לְעֹולָם חַסְדֹּו:

יֹאמְרוּ־נָא בֵית־אַהֲרֹן   כִּי לְעֹולָם חַסְדֹּו:

יֹאמְרוּ־נָא יִרְאֵי יהוה   כִּי לְעֹולָם חַסְדֹּו:

מִן־הַמֵּצַר קָרָאתִי יָּהּ,ֿ עָנָנִי בַמֶּרְחָב יָהּ: יהוה לִי לֹא אִירָא, מַה־יַּעֲשֶׂה לִי אָדָם: יהוה לִי בְּעֹזְרָי, וַאֲנִי אֶרְאֶה בְשֹׂנְאָי: טֹוב לַחֲסֹות בַּיהוה, מִבְּטֹחַ בָּאָדָם: טֹוב לַחֲסֹות בַּיהוה, מִבְּטֹחַ בִּנְדִיבִים: כָּל־גֹּויִם סְבָבוּנִי, בְּשֵׁם יהוה כִּי אֲמִילַם: סַבּוּנִי גַם־סְבָבוּנִי, בְּשֵׁם יהוה כִּי אֲמִילַם: סַבּוּנִי כִדְבֹרִים,ֿ דֹּעֲכוּ כְּאֵשׁ

BIUR TEFILLA · ביאור תפילה

הֹודוּ לַיהוה כִּי־טֹוב – *Thank the* Lord *for He is good.* The word *hodu* (thank) is related to the name Yehuda, whose mother, Leah, named him thus because she "thanked God" for his birth (Bereshit 29:35). The name "Jew" or "Yehudi" also comes from the name Yehuda (Judah). The implication is clear: to be a Jew means to be thankful.

הֹודוּ לַיהוה כִּי־טֹוב – *Thank the* Lord *for He is good.* The last three of the groups mentioned here are the ones (referred to in Psalm 115 above) who were called upon to have faith that Hashem would protect and help them. It has been suggested that here there are four groups, the first being all of mankind, and that there is a closeness-to-

God hierarchy of sorts from one group to the next (Rashbam). The greater the constant sense that everything comes from God, the more one knows that everything is a gift, the more one knows how fortunate one really is, the more thankful one can be.

How fortunate do you feel today? Give thanks.

הֹודוּ לַיהוה כִּי־טֹוב – *Thank the* Lord *for He is good.* There are two possibilities for what "good" describes. One could be: "Thank God because He is good." Alternatively, "Thank God because all is good" (Ibn Ezra). The two are separate but certainly related. Have one or both in mind.

to my help. The LORD is my strength and my song; He has become my salvation. Sounds of song and salvation resound in the tents of the righteous: "The LORD's right hand has done mighty deeds. The LORD's right hand is lifted high. The LORD's right hand has done mighty deeds." I will not die but live, and tell what the LORD has done. The LORD has chastened me severely, but He has not given me over to death. ‣ Open for me the gates of righteousness that I may enter them and thank the LORD. This is the gateway to the LORD; through it, the righteous shall enter.

אוֹדְךָ I will thank You, for You answered me,[B]
and became my salvation.
I will thank You, for You answered me,
and became my salvation.

The stone the builders rejected[i]
has become the main cornerstone.
The stone the builders rejected
has become the main cornerstone.

This is the LORD's doing; it is wondrous in our eyes.
This is the LORD's doing; it is wondrous in our eyes.

This is the day the LORD has made;
let us rejoice and be glad in it.
This is the day the LORD has made;
let us rejoice and be glad in it.

IYUN TEFILLA · עיון תפילה

אֶבֶן מָאֲסוּ הַבּוֹנִים – *The stone the builders rejected.* There are those who say that the "foundation stone rejected by the builders" is a reference to King David himself who, before he was anointed, was essentially misunderstood by his family, not unlike the way that Yosef was misunderstood by his brothers. David wasn't even considered to be a candidate for leadership. Nevertheless, he went on to become the cornerstone of Jewish sovereignty. One day a shepherd, the next a king of Israel (*Da'at Soferim*). We ignore the strengths of those around us just as we ourselves are sometimes ignored. But Hashem is aware of the potential in each of us, and for that I give thanks.

קוֹצִים, בְּשֵׁם יהוה כִּי אֲמִילַם: דָּחֹה דְחִיתַנִי לִנְפֹּל, וַיהוה עֲזָרָנִי:
עָזִּי וְזִמְרָת יָהּ, וַיְהִי־לִי לִישׁוּעָה: קוֹל רִנָּה וִישׁוּעָה בְּאָהֳלֵי
צַדִּיקִים, יְמִין יהוה עֹשָׂה חָיִל: יְמִין יהוה רוֹמֵמָה, יְמִין יהוה
עֹשָׂה חָיִל: לֹא־אָמוּת כִּי־אֶחְיֶה, וַאֲסַפֵּר מַעֲשֵׂי יָהּ: יַסֹּר יִסְּרַנִּי
יָהּ, וְלַמָּוֶת לֹא נְתָנָנִי: ◂ פִּתְחוּ־לִי שַׁעֲרֵי־צֶדֶק, אָבֹא־בָם אוֹדֶה
יָהּ: זֶה־הַשַּׁעַר לַיהוה, צַדִּיקִים יָבֹאוּ בוֹ:

אוֹדְךָ כִּי עֲנִיתָנִי, וַתְּהִי־לִי לִישׁוּעָה:
אוֹדְךָ כִּי עֲנִיתָנִי, וַתְּהִי־לִי לִישׁוּעָה:

אֶבֶן מָאֲסוּ הַבּוֹנִים, הָיְתָה לְרֹאשׁ פִּנָּה:
אֶבֶן מָאֲסוּ הַבּוֹנִים, הָיְתָה לְרֹאשׁ פִּנָּה:

מֵאֵת יהוה הָיְתָה זֹּאת, הִיא נִפְלָאת בְּעֵינֵינוּ:
מֵאֵת יהוה הָיְתָה זֹּאת, הִיא נִפְלָאת בְּעֵינֵינוּ:

זֶה־הַיּוֹם עָשָׂה יהוה, נָגִילָה וְנִשְׂמְחָה בוֹ:
זֶה־הַיּוֹם עָשָׂה יהוה, נָגִילָה וְנִשְׂמְחָה בוֹ:

BIUR TEFILLA · ביאור תפילה

אוֹדְךָ כִּי עֲנִיתָנִי – *I will thank You, for You answered me.* Although the following nine verses are part of the same preceding Psalm 118, they are treated differently in that each one of them is repeated. This is because, when looking at the structure of the entire psalm, one notices that all of the verses are coupled, in that the theme or language of one is repeated, in one form or another, in the following verse. That is not the case, however, in these nine verses,

each of which stands alone according to many commentators. And so it was decided that, in keeping with the rhythm, tone and theme of the psalm as a whole, each of these verses should be repeated in order to maintain the pattern (Rashi, *Sukka* 38a). The Gemara (*Pesaḥim* 119a) relates that there is also a conversational quality about these verses that lends itself to responsive reading or singing, as may have been done in the *Beit HaMikdash*.

On Sukkot, the lulav and etrog are waved while saying "Lord, please, save us,"
three waves for each word of the verse (except God's name). On the first word,
wave forward and right; third word: back and left; fourth word: up and down.

Leader followed by congregation:

אָנָּא Lord, please, save us.[B]

Lord, please, save us.

Lord, please, grant us success.

Lord, please, grant us success.

בָּרוּךְ Blessed is one who comes in the name of the Lord;[I]
we bless you from the House of the Lord.

Blessed is one who comes in the name of the Lord;
we bless you from the House of the Lord.

The Lord is God; He has given us light.
Bind the festival offering with thick cords
[and bring it] to the horns of the altar.

The Lord is God; He has given us light. Bind the festival offering
with thick cords [and bring it] to the horns of the altar.

You are my God and I will thank You;
You are my God, I will exalt You.

You are my God and I will thank You;
You are my God, I will exalt You.

Thank the Lord for He is good;
His loving-kindness is for ever.[A]

Thank the Lord for He is good;
His loving-kindness is for ever.

IYUN TEFILLA · עיון תפילה	ANI TEFILLA · אני תפילה
בָּרוּךְ הַבָּא בְּשֵׁם יהוה – *Blessed is one who comes in the name of the Lord.* The blessing is given to those who show up. One cannot expect blessings if one does not first do one's part (*Me'am Loez*).	הוֹדוּ לַיהוה כִּי־טוֹב, כִּי לְעוֹלָם חַסְדּוֹ – *Thank the Lord for He is good; His loving-kindness is for ever.* The chapter ends with the exact same phrase with which it began but, hopefully, we can now say it with added meaning.

On סוכות, *the* לולב *and* אתרוג *are waved while saying* אָנָּא יהוה הוֹשִׁיעָה נָּא,
three waves for each word of the verse (except God's name). On the first word,
wave forward and right; third word: back and left; fourth word: up and down.

שליח ציבור *followed by* קהל:

אָנָּא יהוה הוֹשִׁיעָה נָּא:ב

אָנָּא יהוה הוֹשִׁיעָה נָּא:

אָנָּא יהוה הַצְלִיחָה נָּא:

אָנָּא יהוה הַצְלִיחָה נָּא:

בָּרוּךְ הַבָּא בְּשֵׁם יהוה,ג בֵּרַכְנוּכֶם מִבֵּית יהוה:

בָּרוּךְ הַבָּא בְּשֵׁם יהוה, בֵּרַכְנוּכֶם מִבֵּית יהוה:

אֵל יהוה וַיָּאֶר לָנוּ, אִסְרוּ־חַג בַּעֲבֹתִים

עַד־קַרְנוֹת הַמִּזְבֵּחַ:

אֵל יהוה וַיָּאֶר לָנוּ, אִסְרוּ־חַג בַּעֲבֹתִים עַד־קַרְנוֹת הַמִּזְבֵּחַ:

אֵלִי אַתָּה וְאוֹדֶךָּ, אֱלֹהַי אֲרוֹמְמֶךָּ:

אֵלִי אַתָּה וְאוֹדֶךָּ, אֱלֹהַי אֲרוֹמְמֶךָּ:

הוֹדוּ לַיהוה כִּי־טוֹב,א כִּי לְעוֹלָם חַסְדּוֹ:

הוֹדוּ לַיהוה כִּי־טוֹב, כִּי לְעוֹלָם חַסְדּוֹ:

BIUR TEFILLA · ביאור תפילה

אָנָּא יהוה הוֹשִׁיעָה נָּא – *Lord, please, save us.*
Yeshua refers to being freed from things which
constrict us (Malbim) or, alternatively, it could
be a reference to the personal happiness associated with being alive (Rabbi S.R. Hirsch).

Hatzlaḥa, on the other hand, refers
to success in our endeavors. Help from
above, however, only comes about if we
put in the effort to begin with.
Which speaks to you more today?

יְהַלְלוּךְ All Your works will praise You, LORD our God,
and Your devoted ones –
the righteous who do Your will,
together with all Your people the house of Israel –
will joyously thank, bless, praise, glorify,
exalt, revere, sanctify, and proclaim
the sovereignty of Your name, our King.
‣ For it is good to thank You
and fitting to sing psalms to Your name,
for from eternity to eternity You are God.
Blessed are You, LORD,
King who is extolled with praises.

*On Rosh Ḥodesh and Ḥol HaMo'ed, say Full Kaddish on page 251
and continue the service with the Reading of the Torah
on page 216 (on Hoshana Raba on page 496).*

*On Sukkot some say at this point Hoshanot on page 522,
then Full Kaddish on page 250.*

*On weekday Ḥanukka (except Rosh Ḥodesh Tevet), Yom HaAtzma'ut and
Yom Yerushalayim, the service continues with Half Kaddish on page 214.*

יְהַלְלוּךָ יהוה אֱלֹהֵינוּ כָּל מַעֲשֶׂיךָ

וַחֲסִידֶיךָ צַדִּיקִים עוֹשֵׂי רְצוֹנֶךָ

וְכָל עַמְּךָ בֵּית יִשְׂרָאֵל

בְּרִנָּה יוֹדוּ וִיבָרְכוּ וִישַׁבְּחוּ

וִיפָאֲרוּ וִירוֹמְמוּ וְיַעֲרִיצוּ וְיַקְדִּישׁוּ

וְיַמְלִיכוּ אֶת שִׁמְךָ מַלְכֵּנוּ

‹ כִּי לְךָ טוֹב לְהוֹדוֹת וּלְשִׁמְךָ נָאֶה לְזַמֵּר

כִּי מֵעוֹלָם וְעַד עוֹלָם אַתָּה אֵל.

בָּרוּךְ אַתָּה יהוה, מֶלֶךְ מְהֻלָּל בַּתִּשְׁבָּחוֹת.

On חול המועד and ראש חודש, say קדיש שלם on page 251
and continue the service with קריאת התורה on page 217 (on הושענא רבה on page 497).

On סוכות some say at this point הושענות on page 522,
then קדיש שלם on page 251.

On weekday חנוכה and יום העצמאות, (except ראש חודש טבת), יום ירושלים,
the service continues with חצי קדיש on page 215.

Musaf for Rosh Ḥodesh

THE AMIDA

*The following prayer, until "in former years" on page 472, is said silently, standing
with feet together. If there is a minyan, the Amida is repeated aloud by the Leader.
Take three steps forward and at the points indicated by *, bend the knees at the first word,
bow at the second, and stand straight before saying God's name.*

When I proclaim the LORD's name, give glory to our God. *Deut. 32*
O LORD, open my lips, so that my mouth may declare Your praise. *Ps. 51*

PATRIARCHS

*בָּרוּךְ Blessed are You, LORD our God and God of our fathers,
God of Abraham, God of Isaac and God of Jacob;
the great, mighty and awesome God, God Most High,
who bestows acts of loving-kindness and creates all,
who remembers the loving-kindness of the fathers and will bring
a Redeemer to their children's children
for the sake of His name, in love.
King, Helper, Savior, Shield:
*Blessed are You, LORD, Shield of Abraham.

DIVINE MIGHT

אַתָּה גִּבּוֹר You are eternally mighty, LORD.
You give life to the dead and have great power to save.

---

to be declared by man and not by nature. It is about man finding the moon, not about the moon finding man.

Why should this be so? Perhaps because the feeling of renewal does not happen by itself. It is up to us to start anew, it is up to us to see old things in a new light.

Each time the moon finds the sun again, each time it receives its rays of light afresh, God wants His people to find Him again, to be illuminated with fresh rays of His light, wherever and however,

in running their course, they have had to pass through periods of darkness and obscurity. (Rabbi S.R. Hirsch)

Noticing the fresh birth of the new moon is supposed to induce within each of us a similar rejuvenation. When Israel was in Egypt, they were slaves who had no sense of time, since each day was virtually identical to the next: boring, mundane, and wearying. Hence, the very first mitzva we are given as a people is time-consciousness, the ability to master time by the way we mark it and live it.

מוסף לראש חודש

עמידה

The following prayer, until קְדֻשִּׁיּוֹת *on page 473, is said silently, standing*
with feet together. If there is a מִנְיָן*, the* עֲמִידָה *is repeated aloud by the* שְׁלִיחַ צִבּוּר*.*
Take three steps forward and at the points indicated by ׳*, bend the knees at the first word,*
bow at the second, and stand straight before saying God's name.

דברים לב
כִּי שֵׁם יהוה אֶקְרָא, הָבוּ גֹדֶל לֵאלֹהֵינוּ:

תהלים נא
אֲדֹנָי, שְׂפָתַי תִּפְתָּח, וּפִי יַגִּיד תְּהִלָּתֶךָ:

אבות

בָּרוּךְ אַתָּה יהוה, אֱלֹהֵינוּ וֵאלֹהֵי אֲבוֹתֵינוּ
אֱלֹהֵי אַבְרָהָם, אֱלֹהֵי יִצְחָק, וֵאלֹהֵי יַעֲקֹב
הָאֵל הַגָּדוֹל הַגִּבּוֹר וְהַנּוֹרָא, אֵל עֶלְיוֹן
גּוֹמֵל חֲסָדִים טוֹבִים, וְקֹנֵה הַכֹּל, וְזוֹכֵר חַסְדֵי אָבוֹת
וּמֵבִיא גוֹאֵל לִבְנֵי בְנֵיהֶם לְמַעַן שְׁמוֹ בְּאַהֲבָה.
מֶלֶךְ עוֹזֵר וּמוֹשִׁיעַ וּמָגֵן.
בָּרוּךְ אַתָּה יהוה, מָגֵן אַבְרָהָם.

גבורות

אַתָּה גִּבּוֹר לְעוֹלָם, אֲדֹנָי
מְחַיֵּה מֵתִים אַתָּה, רַב לְהוֹשִׁיעַ

INTRODUCTION TO MUSAF ROSH ḤODESH

In the times of the *Beit HaMikdash*, Rosh Ḥodesh had to be declared by the court on the basis of testimony from two witnesses who actually saw the appearance of the first sliver of the moon. This does not mean that the Rabbis did not know how to calculate a real calendar; rather, the Torah mandated that it was only Rosh Ḥodesh if the moon was sighted and the court verified the testimony of witnesses. Indeed, if everyone saw the moon but the court did not yet have time to rule before the next day, then the new month was postponed a day, even though everyone knew it was already Rosh Ḥodesh the previous day (*Rosh HaShana* 25b). In short, the new month was

*The phrase "He makes the wind blow and the rain fall" is added
from Simḥat Torah until Pesaḥ. In Israel the phrase "He causes the
dew to fall" is added from Pesaḥ until Shemini Atzeret.*

In fall & winter: He makes the wind blow and the rain fall.

*In Israel, in spring
& summer:* He causes the dew to fall.

He sustains the living with loving-kindness,
and with great compassion revives the dead.
He supports the fallen, heals the sick, sets captives free,
and keeps His faith with those who sleep in the dust.
Who is like You, Master of might,
and who can compare to You,
O King who brings death and gives life,
and makes salvation grow?
Faithful are You to revive the dead.
Blessed are You, Lord, who revives the dead.

When saying the Amida silently, continue with "You are holy" on the next page.

KEDUSHA

*During the Leader's Repetition, the following is said standing
with feet together, rising on the toes at the words indicated by ^.*

*Cong. then
Leader:* נְקַדֵּשׁ We will sanctify Your name on earth, as they sanctify it
in the highest heavens, as is written by Your prophet,
"And they [the angels] call to one another saying: *Is. 6*

*Cong. then
Leader:* ^"Holy, ^holy, ^holy is the Lord of hosts
the whole world is filled with His glory."
Those facing them say "Blessed – "

*Cong. then
Leader:* ^"Blessed is the Lord's glory from His place."   *Ezek. 3*
And in Your holy Writings it is written thus:

*Cong. then
Leader:* ^"The Lord shall reign for ever. He is your God, Zion,   *Ps. 146*
from generation to generation, Halleluya!"

Leader: From generation to generation we will declare Your greatness,
and we will proclaim Your holiness for evermore.
Your praise, our God, shall not leave our mouth forever,
for You, God, are a great and holy King.
Blessed are You, Lord, the holy God.

The Leader continues with "You have given New Moons" on the next page.

The phrase מַשִּׁיב הָרוּחַ *is added from* שמחת תורה *until* פסח.
In ארץ ישראל *the phrase* מוריד הַטָּל *is added from* פסח *until* שמיני עצרת.

בחוץ: מַשִּׁיב הָרוּחַ וּמוֹרִיד הַגֶּשֶׁם / בארץ ישראל בקיץ: מוֹרִיד הַטָּל

מְכַלְכֵּל חַיִּים בְּחֶסֶד, מְחַיֵּה מֵתִים בְּרַחֲמִים רַבִּים

סוֹמֵךְ נוֹפְלִים, וְרוֹפֵא חוֹלִים, וּמַתִּיר אֲסוּרִים

וּמְקַיֵּם אֱמוּנָתוֹ לִישֵׁנֵי עָפָר.

מִי כָמוֹךָ, בַּעַל גְּבוּרוֹת, וּמִי דוֹמֶה לָּךְ

מֶלֶךְ, מֵמִית וּמְחַיֶּה וּמַצְמִיחַ יְשׁוּעָה.

וְנֶאֱמָן אַתָּה לְהַחֲיוֹת מֵתִים.

בָּרוּךְ אַתָּה יהוה, מְחַיֵּה הַמֵּתִים.

When saying the עמידה *silently, continue with* אַתָּה קָדוֹשׁ *on the next page.*

קדושה

During the חזרת הש״ץ, *the following is said standing*
with feet together, rising on the toes at the words indicated by ˙.

קהל then ש״ץ	נְקַדֵּשׁ אֶת שִׁמְךָ בָּעוֹלָם, כְּשֵׁם שֶׁמַּקְדִּישִׁים אוֹתוֹ בִּשְׁמֵי מָרוֹם
ישעיה ו	כַּכָּתוּב עַל יַד נְבִיאֶךָ: וְקָרָא זֶה אֶל־זֶה וְאָמַר
קהל then ש״ץ	˙קָדוֹשׁ, ˙קָדוֹשׁ, ˙קָדוֹשׁ, יהוה צְבָאוֹת, מְלֹא כָל־הָאָרֶץ כְּבוֹדוֹ:
	לְעֻמָּתָם בָּרוּךְ יֹאמֵרוּ
קהל then ש״ץ	˙בָּרוּךְ כְּבוֹד־יהוה מִמְּקוֹמוֹ:
יחזקאל ג	וּבְדִבְרֵי קָדְשְׁךָ כָּתוּב לֵאמֹר
קהל then ש״ץ	˙יִמְלֹךְ יהוה לְעוֹלָם, אֱלֹהַיִךְ צִיּוֹן לְדֹר וָדֹר, הַלְלוּיָהּ:
תהלים קמו	
ש״ץ	לְדוֹר וָדוֹר נַגִּיד גָּדְלֶךָ, וּלְנֵצַח נְצָחִים קְדֻשָּׁתְךָ נַקְדִּישׁ
	וְשִׁבְחֲךָ אֱלֹהֵינוּ מִפִּינוּ לֹא יָמוּשׁ לְעוֹלָם וָעֶד
	כִּי אֵל מֶלֶךְ גָּדוֹל וְקָדוֹשׁ אָתָּה.
	בָּרוּךְ אַתָּה יהוה הָאֵל הַקָּדוֹשׁ.

The שליח ציבור *continues with* רָאשֵׁי חֳדָשִׁים *on the next page.*

HOLINESS

אַתָּה קָדוֹשׁ You are holy and Your name is holy,
and holy ones praise You daily, Selah!
Blessed are You, LORD, the holy God.

HOLINESS OF THE DAY

רָאשֵׁי חֳדָשִׁים You have given New Moons to Your people
as a time of atonement for all their offspring.[B]
They would bring You offerings of goodwill,
and goats as sin-offerings for atonement.
May it serve as a remembrance for them all,
and a deliverance of their lives from the hand of the enemy.[B]
May You establish a new altar in Zion,
and may we offer on it the New Moon burnt-offering,
and prepare goats in favor.
May we all rejoice in the Temple service,
and may the songs of David Your servant,
be heard in Your city,
chanted before Your altar.
Bestow on them everlasting love,
and remember the covenant of the fathers for their children.

---

root of the sin which *Musaf* of Rosh Ḥodesh serves to correct. Hence it is called *zeman kapara*, a time for atonement. Perhaps it behooves us all, therefore, to consider on this day how we can avoid the sin of lack of awareness, whether of God or of our fellow man.

What can I do differently this month?

BIUR TEFILLA · ביאור תפילה

תּוֹלְדוֹתָם – *Their offspring.*
There are those who say that this is a reference to all of the days of the months, the "offspring" of the month mentioned at the beginning (*Kuzari* 3:5). But there are also those who say it should be taken literally to refer to children, and that Rosh Ḥodesh is therefore a particularly auspicious time

to pray for the welfare of infants (*Da'at Zekenim*).

שׂוֹנֵא – *The enemy.* Who is the enemy who causes our downfall? There are those who say it is the enemy who attacks the Land of Israel (*Ya'avetz*). Others say it is the evil inclination which attacks us all (*Abudarham*).

קדושת השם

אַתָּה קָדוֹשׁ וְשִׁמְךָ קָדוֹשׁ
וּקְדוֹשִׁים בְּכָל יוֹם יְהַלְלוּךָ סֶּלָה.
בָּרוּךְ אַתָּה יהוה, הָאֵל הַקָּדוֹשׁ.

קדושת היום

רָאשֵׁי חֳדָשִׁים לְעַמְּךָ נָתַתָּ
זְמַן כַּפָּרָהᵃ לְכָל תּוֹלְדוֹתָםᵇ
בִּהְיוֹתָם מַקְרִיבִים לְפָנֶיךָ זִבְחֵי רָצוֹן
וּשְׂעִירֵי חַטָּאת לְכַפֵּר בַּעֲדָם.
זִכָּרוֹן לְכֻלָּם יִהְיוּ, וּתְשׁוּעַת נַפְשָׁם מִיַּד שׂוֹנֵא.ᵇ
מִזְבֵּחַ חָדָשׁ בְּצִיּוֹן תָּכִין
וְעוֹלַת רֹאשׁ חֹדֶשׁ נַעֲלֶה עָלָיו
וּשְׂעִירֵי עִזִּים נַעֲשֶׂה בְרָצוֹן
וּבַעֲבוֹדַת בֵּית הַמִּקְדָּשׁ נִשְׂמַח כֻּלָּנוּ
וּבְשִׁירֵי דָוִד עַבְדְּךָ הַנִּשְׁמָעִים בְּעִירֶךָ
הָאֲמוּרִים לִפְנֵי מִזְבְּחֶךָ.
אַהֲבַת עוֹלָם תָּבִיא לָהֶם, וּבְרִית אָבוֹת לַבָּנִים תִּזְכֹּר.

עיון תפילה · IYUN TEFILLA

זְמַן כַּפָּרָה – *A time of atonement.* As will be mentioned later on, a part of the ritual was bringing a sacrifice known as a sin-offering or *ḥatat*. The Gemara (*Shevuot* 2a, 9a) explains that this was intended to atone for the possibility that someone had entered into the *Beit HaMikdash*, or had eaten the meat of offerings, in a defiled state. In the present case, it particularly means that he did so without being conscious of the fact that he had sinned. There are times, in other words, when we are so oblivious or ignorant or insensitive, that we may have committed wrongs which, unbeknownst to us, affect not only ourselves but others as well. This lack of awareness lies at the

וַהֲבִיאֵנוּ Bring us back, with song,
to Zion Your city,
and to Jerusalem Your Sanctuary with everlasting joy.
There we will prepare for You our obligatory offerings:
the regular daily offerings in their order,
and the additional offerings according to their law.

וְאֶת מוּסַף The additional offering of this New Moon day[8]
we will prepare and offer to You
with love according to Your will's commandment,
as You have written for us in Your Torah
by Your own word, through Your servant Moses,
as it is said:

> "On your new moons,   *Num. 28*
>   present as a burnt-offering to the LORD,
>   two young bulls, one ram,
>   and seven yearling lambs
>   without blemish."

וּמִנְחָתָם And their meal-offerings
and wine-libations as ordained:
three-tenths of an ephah for each bull,
two-tenths of an ephah for the ram,
one-tenth of an ephah for each lamb,
wine for the libations,
a male goat for atonement,
and two regular daily offerings
according to their law.

---

casion. Each is therefore worthy of its own special offering to Hashem to mark the significance of the day. This is the service called *Musaf* or "Addition," which on every Shabbat and festival was added to the regular daily sacrificial rite in the time of the *Beit HaMikdash*. Today, in the absence of the *Beit HaMikdash*, we substitute prayers for our sacrifices, as the prophet Hoshea said (14:3): וּנְשַׁלְּמָה פָרִים שְׂפָתֵינוּ – "We will offer in place of bullocks [the prayer of] our lips."

וַהֲבִיאֵנוּ לְצִיּוֹן עִירְךָ בְּרִנָּה
וְלִירוּשָׁלַיִם בֵּית מִקְדָּשְׁךָ בְּשִׂמְחַת עוֹלָם
וְשָׁם נַעֲשֶׂה לְפָנֶיךָ אֶת קָרְבְּנוֹת חוֹבוֹתֵינוּ
תְּמִידִים כְּסִדְרָם וּמוּסָפִים כְּהִלְכָתָם.

וְאֶת מוּסַף יוֹם רֹאשׁ הַחֹדֶשׁ הַזֶּה
נַעֲשֶׂה וְנַקְרִיב לְפָנֶיךָ בְּאַהֲבָה כְּמִצְוַת רְצוֹנֶךָ
כְּמוֹ שֶׁכָּתַבְתָּ עָלֵינוּ בְּתוֹרָתֶךָ
עַל יְדֵי מֹשֶׁה עַבְדֶּךָ מִפִּי כְבוֹדֶךָ
כָּאָמוּר

במדבר כח

וּבְרָאשֵׁי חָדְשֵׁיכֶם תַּקְרִיבוּ עֹלָה לַיהוה
פָּרִים בְּנֵי־בָקָר שְׁנַיִם
וְאַיִל אֶחָד
כְּבָשִׂים בְּנֵי־שָׁנָה שִׁבְעָה
תְּמִימִם:

וּמִנְחָתָם וְנִסְכֵּיהֶם כִּמְדֻבָּר
שְׁלֹשָׁה עֶשְׂרֹנִים לַפָּר
וּשְׁנֵי עֶשְׂרֹנִים לָאָיִל
וְעִשָּׂרוֹן לַכֶּבֶשׂ
וְיַיִן כְּנִסְכּוֹ, וְשָׂעִיר לְכַפֵּר
וּשְׁנֵי תְמִידִים כְּהִלְכָתָם.

ביאור תפילה • BIUR TEFILLA

מוּסַף יוֹם רֹאשׁ הַחֹדֶשׁ הַזֶּה – The additional offering of this New Moon day. Every holy day

has its own special religious significance rooted in a historical event or special oc-

אֱלֹהֵינוּ O God and God of our ancestors,
renew for us the coming month for good and blessing,
joy and gladness, deliverance and consolation,
sustenance and support, life and peace,
pardon of sin and forgiveness of iniquity
(*From Marḥeshvan to Adar* and atonement of transgression).^B
  II in a Jewish leap year
For You have chosen Your people Israel from all nations,
and have instituted for them rules for the New Moon.
Blessed are You, LORD, who sanctifies Israel and the New Moons.^I

TEMPLE SERVICE

רְצֵה Find favor, LORD our God,
in Your people Israel and their prayer.
Restore the service to Your most holy House,
and accept in love and favor
the fire-offerings of Israel and their prayer.
May the service of Your people Israel
always find favor with You
And may our eyes
witness Your return to Zion in compassion.
Blessed are You, LORD, who restores His Presence to Zion.

ANI TEFILLA · אני תפילה

Alexander Herzen (an eighteenth-century Russian writer and thinker) said about the Slavs that they had no history, only geography. The Jews, he said, had the reverse: a great deal of history but all too little geography. Much time, but little space.
What have Jews done with their time? What will you do with yours?

Where does hope come from? It comes from a certain idea about time. So, at any rate, argues Thomas Cahill in his book, *The Gifts of the Jews*. Cahill, a Catholic historian, argues that we owe to the Hebrew Bible one of the great concepts of Western civilization – the idea of linear time. It is in the biblical narrative that, for the first time, we encounter the notion that time itself is the setting of the human journey toward a destination – the Promised Land, the messianic age, the kingdom of heaven. It was this sense of traveling that gave the West its distinctive orientation to the future. (Rabbi J. Sacks)

What are your hopes for the future?

אֱלֹהֵינוּ וֵאלֹהֵי אֲבוֹתֵינוּ
חַדֵּשׁ עָלֵינוּ אֶת הַחֹדֶשׁ הַזֶּה לְטוֹבָה וְלִבְרָכָה
לְשָׂשׂוֹן וּלְשִׂמְחָה, לִישׁוּעָה וּלְנֶחָמָה
לְפַרְנָסָה וּלְכַלְכָּלָה, לְחַיִּים וּלְשָׁלוֹם
לִמְחִילַת חֵטְא וְלִסְלִיחַת עָוֹן
(‏אדר שני to מרחשון From
in a Jewish leap year ‏)⁻ וּלְכַפָּרַת פָּשַׁע‏
כִּי בְעַמְּךָ יִשְׂרָאֵל בָּחַרְתָּ מִכָּל הָאֻמּוֹת
וְחֻקֵּי רָאשֵׁי חֳדָשִׁים לָהֶם קָבָעְתָּ.
בָּרוּךְ אַתָּה יהוה, מְקַדֵּשׁ יִשְׂרָאֵל וְרָאשֵׁי חֳדָשִׁים.⁻

עבודה

רְצֵה יהוה אֱלֹהֵינוּ בְּעַמְּךָ יִשְׂרָאֵל וּבִתְפִלָּתָם
וְהָשֵׁב אֶת הָעֲבוֹדָה לִדְבִיר בֵּיתֶךָ
וְאִשֵּׁי יִשְׂרָאֵל וּתְפִלָּתָם בְּאַהֲבָה תְקַבֵּל בְּרָצוֹן
וּתְהִי לְרָצוֹן תָּמִיד עֲבוֹדַת יִשְׂרָאֵל עַמֶּךָ.
וְתֶחֱזֶינָה עֵינֵינוּ בְּשׁוּבְךָ לְצִיּוֹן בְּרַחֲמִים.
בָּרוּךְ אַתָּה יהוה, הַמַּחֲזִיר שְׁכִינָתוֹ לְצִיּוֹן.

ביאור תפילה · BIUR TEFILLA

וּלְכַפָּרַת פָּשַׁע – *And atonement of transgres-sion*. There are 12 expressions of blessing here,

one for every month of the year. Hence, dur-ing a leap year, an extra expression is added.

עיון תפילה · IYUN TEFILLA

מְקַדֵּשׁ יִשְׂרָאֵל וְרָאשֵׁי חֳדָשִׁים – *Who sancti-fies Israel and the New Moons*. The Gemara (*Beitza* 17a) suggests that the order here is in-structive. God sanctifies Israel first, as it were, and because of that Israel can then sanc-

tify the new moon. Unlike Shabbat, which would be a holy day regardless of our efforts, since God Himself established it, the sanctity of other holy days like Rosh Hodesh is de-pendent upon us. Time is what we make of it.

THANKSGIVING

Bow at the first nine words.

מוֹדִים We give thanks to You,
for You are the LORD our God
and God of our ancestors
for ever and all time.
You are the Rock of our lives,
Shield of our salvation
from generation to generation.
We will thank You and
declare Your praise for our lives,
which are entrusted into Your hand;
for our souls,
which are placed in Your charge;
for Your miracles
which are with us every day;
and for Your wonders and favors
at all times, evening,
morning and midday.
You are good –
for Your compassion never fails.
You are compassionate –
for Your loving-kindnesses never cease.
We have always placed our hope in You.

*During the Leader's Repetition,
the congregation says quietly:*

מוֹדִים We give thanks to You,
for You are the
LORD our God
and God of our ancestors,
God of all flesh,
who formed us
and formed the universe.
Blessings and thanks
are due to Your great
and holy name for giving us
life and sustaining us.
May You continue
to give us life and sustain us;
and may You gather our
exiles to Your holy courts,
to keep Your decrees,
do Your will and serve You
with a perfect heart,
for it is for us
to give You thanks.
Blessed be God to whom
thanksgiving is due.

On Ḥanukka:

עַל הַנִּסִּים [We thank You also] for the miracles, the redemption, the mighty deeds, the salvations, and the victories in battle which You performed for our ancestors in those days, at this time.

בִּימֵי מַתִּתְיָהוּ In the days of Mattityahu, son of Yoḥanan, the High Priest, the Hasmonean, and his sons, the wicked Greek kingdom rose up against Your people Israel to make them forget Your Torah and to force them to transgress the statutes of Your will. It was then that You in Your great compassion stood by them in the time of their distress. You championed their cause, judged their claim, and avenged their wrong. You delivered the strong into the hands of the weak, the many into the hands of the few, the impure into the hands of the pure, the wicked into the hands of the righteous, and the arrogant into the hands of those who

הודאה

Bow at the first five words.

יְמוֹדִים אֲנַחְנוּ לָךְ
שָׁאַתָּה הוּא יהוה אֱלֹהֵינוּ
וֵאלֹהֵי אֲבוֹתֵינוּ לְעוֹלָם וָעֶד.

צוּר חַיֵּינוּ, מָגֵן יִשְׁעֵנוּ
אַתָּה הוּא לְדוֹר וָדוֹר.

נוֹדֶה לְּךָ וּנְסַפֵּר תְּהִלָּתֶךָ
עַל חַיֵּינוּ הַמְּסוּרִים בְּיָדֶךָ
וְעַל נִשְׁמוֹתֵינוּ הַפְּקוּדוֹת לָךְ

וְעַל נִסֶּיךָ שֶׁבְּכָל יוֹם עִמָּנוּ
וְעַל נִפְלְאוֹתֶיךָ וְטוֹבוֹתֶיךָ
שֶׁבְּכָל עֵת, עֶרֶב וָבֹקֶר וְצָהֳרָיִם.

הַטּוֹב, כִּי לֹא כָלוּ רַחֲמֶיךָ
וְהַמְרַחֵם, כִּי לֹא תַמּוּ חֲסָדֶיךָ
מֵעוֹלָם קִוִּינוּ לָךְ.

חורת הש״ץ, During the
says quietly: קהל the

יְמוֹדִים אֲנַחְנוּ לָךְ
שָׁאַתָּה הוּא יהוה אֱלֹהֵינוּ
וֵאלֹהֵי אֲבוֹתֵינוּ
אֱלֹהֵי כָל בָּשָׂר
יוֹצְרֵנוּ, יוֹצֵר בְּרֵאשִׁית.
בְּרָכוֹת וְהוֹדָאוֹת
לְשִׁמְךָ הַגָּדוֹל וְהַקָּדוֹשׁ
עַל שֶׁהֶחֱיִיתָנוּ וְקִיַּמְתָּנוּ.
כֵּן תְּחַיֵּנוּ וּתְקַיְּמֵנוּ
וְתֶאֱסֹף גָּלֻיּוֹתֵינוּ
לְחַצְרוֹת קָדְשֶׁךָ
לִשְׁמוֹר חֻקֶּיךָ וְלַעֲשׂוֹת רְצוֹנֶךָ
וּלְעָבְדְּךָ בְּלֵבָב שָׁלֵם
עַל שֶׁאֲנַחְנוּ מוֹדִים לָךְ.
בָּרוּךְ אֵל הַהוֹדָאוֹת.

בחנוכה:

עַל הַנִּסִּים וְעַל הַפֻּרְקָן וְעַל הַגְּבוּרוֹת וְעַל הַתְּשׁוּעוֹת וְעַל הַמִּלְחָמוֹת
שֶׁעָשִׂיתָ לַאֲבוֹתֵינוּ בַּיָּמִים הָהֵם בַּזְּמַן הַזֶּה.

בִּימֵי מַתִּתְיָהוּ בֶּן יוֹחָנָן כֹּהֵן גָּדוֹל חַשְׁמוֹנַאי וּבָנָיו, כְּשֶׁעָמְדָה מַלְכוּת יָוָן
הָרְשָׁעָה עַל עַמְּךָ יִשְׂרָאֵל לְהַשְׁכִּיחָם תּוֹרָתֶךָ וּלְהַעֲבִירָם מֵחֻקֵּי רְצוֹנֶךָ,
וְאַתָּה בְּרַחֲמֶיךָ הָרַבִּים עָמַדְתָּ לָהֶם בְּעֵת צָרָתָם, רַבְתָּ אֶת רִיבָם, דַּנְתָּ
אֶת דִּינָם, נָקַמְתָּ אֶת נִקְמָתָם, מָסַרְתָּ גִבּוֹרִים בְּיַד חַלָּשִׁים, וְרַבִּים בְּיַד
מְעַטִּים, וּטְמֵאִים בְּיַד טְהוֹרִים, וּרְשָׁעִים בְּיַד צַדִּיקִים, וְזֵדִים בְּיַד עוֹסְקֵי
תוֹרָתֶךָ, וּלְךָ עָשִׂיתָ שֵׁם גָּדוֹל וְקָדוֹשׁ בְּעוֹלָמֶךָ, וּלְעַמְּךָ יִשְׂרָאֵל עָשִׂיתָ

were engaged in the study of Your Torah. You made for Yourself great and holy
renown in Your world, and for Your people Israel You performed a great salvation
and redemption as of this very day. Your children then entered the holiest part
of Your House, cleansed Your Temple, purified Your Sanctuary, kindled lights in
Your holy courts, and designated these eight days of Ḥanukka for giving thanks
and praise to Your great name.

Continue with "For all these things."

וְעַל כֻּלָּם For all these things may Your name be blessed and exalted,
our King, continually, for ever and all time.
Let all that lives thank You, Selah! and praise Your name in truth,
God, our Savior and Help, Selah!
▸Blessed are You, LORD, whose name is "the Good"
and to whom thanks are due.

When saying the Amida silently, continue with "Grant peace" below.

The following is said by the Leader during the Repetition of the Amida.
In Israel, if Kohanim bless the congregation, turn to page 684.

Our God and God of our fathers, bless us with the threefold blessing in the Torah,
written by the hand of Moses Your servant and pronounced by Aaron and his
sons the priests, Your holy people, as it is said:

May the LORD bless you and protect you.   *Num. 6*
Cong: May it be Your will.
May the LORD make His face shine on you and be gracious to you.
Cong: May it be Your will.
May the LORD turn His face toward you, and grant you peace.
Cong: May it be Your will.

The Leader continues with "Grant peace" below.

PEACE

שִׂים שָׁלוֹם Grant peace, goodness and blessing,
grace, loving-kindness and compassion
to us and all Israel Your people.
Bless us, our Father, all as one, with the light of Your face,
for by the light of Your face You have given us, LORD our God,
the Torah of life and love of kindness,
righteousness, blessing, compassion, life and peace.

תְּשׁוּעָה גְדוֹלָה וּפֻרְקָן כְּהַיּוֹם הַזֶּה. וְאַחַר כֵּן בָּאוּ בָנֶיךָ לִדְבִיר בֵּיתֶךָ,
וּפִנּוּ אֶת הֵיכָלֶךָ, וְטִהֲרוּ אֶת מִקְדָּשֶׁךָ, וְהִדְלִיקוּ נֵרוֹת בְּחַצְרוֹת קָדְשֶׁךָ,
וְקָבְעוּ שְׁמוֹנַת יְמֵי חֲנֻכָּה אֵלּוּ, לְהוֹדוֹת וּלְהַלֵּל לְשִׁמְךָ הַגָּדוֹל.

Continue with וְעַל כֻּלָּם

וְעַל כֻּלָּם יִתְבָּרַךְ וְיִתְרוֹמַם שִׁמְךָ מַלְכֵּנוּ תָּמִיד לְעוֹלָם וָעֶד.
וְכָל הַחַיִּים יוֹדוּךָ סֶּלָה, וִיהַלְלוּ אֶת שִׁמְךָ בֶּאֱמֶת
הָאֵל יְשׁוּעָתֵנוּ וְעֶזְרָתֵנוּ סֶלָה.
יָּבָרוּךְ אַתָּה יהוה, הַטּוֹב שִׁמְךָ וּלְךָ נָאֶה לְהוֹדוֹת.

When saying the עמידה *silently, continue with* שים שלום *below.*

The following is said by the שליח ציבור *during the* חזרת הש״ץ.
In ארץ ישראל, if כהנים say ברכת כהנים, *turn to page 685.*

אֱלֹהֵינוּ וֵאלֹהֵי אֲבוֹתֵינוּ, בָּרְכֵנוּ בַבְּרָכָה הַמְשֻׁלֶּשֶׁת בַּתּוֹרָה, הַכְּתוּבָה עַל יְדֵי מֹשֶׁה
עַבְדֶּךָ, הָאֲמוּרָה מִפִּי אַהֲרֹן וּבָנָיו כֹּהֲנִים עַם קְדוֹשֶׁיךָ, כָּאָמוּר

במדברו

יְבָרֶכְךָ יהוה וְיִשְׁמְרֶךָ: קהל: כֵּן יְהִי רָצוֹן
יָאֵר יהוה פָּנָיו אֵלֶיךָ וִיחֻנֶּךָ: קהל: כֵּן יְהִי רָצוֹן
יִשָּׂא יהוה פָּנָיו אֵלֶיךָ וְיָשֵׂם לְךָ שָׁלוֹם: קהל: כֵּן יְהִי רָצוֹן

The שליח ציבור *continues with* שים שלום *below.*

ברכת שלום
שִׂים שָׁלוֹם טוֹבָה וּבְרָכָה
חֵן וָחֶסֶד וְרַחֲמִים עָלֵינוּ וְעַל כָּל יִשְׂרָאֵל עַמֶּךָ
בָּרְכֵנוּ אָבִינוּ כֻּלָּנוּ כְּאֶחָד בְּאוֹר פָּנֶיךָ
כִּי בְאוֹר פָּנֶיךָ נָתַתָּ לָּנוּ יהוה אֱלֹהֵינוּ
תּוֹרַת חַיִּים וְאַהֲבַת חֶסֶד
וּצְדָקָה וּבְרָכָה וְרַחֲמִים וְחַיִּים וְשָׁלוֹם.

May it be good in Your eyes to bless Your people Israel
at every time, in every hour, with Your peace.
Blessed are You, LORD, who blesses His people Israel with peace.

The following verse concludes the Leader's Repetition of the Amida.
Some also say it here as part of the silent Amida.

May the words of my mouth and the meditation of my heart   *Ps. 19*
find favor before You, LORD, my Rock and Redeemer.

אֱלֹהַי **My God,** guard my tongue from evil   *Berakhot*
and my lips from deceitful speech.   *17a*
To those who curse me, let my soul be silent;
may my soul be to all like the dust.
Open my heart to Your Torah
and let my soul pursue Your commandments.
As for all who plan evil against me,
swiftly thwart their counsel and frustrate their plans.
　　Act for the sake of Your name; act for the sake of Your right hand;
　　act for the sake of Your holiness; act for the sake of Your Torah.
That Your beloved ones may be delivered,   *Ps. 60*
save with Your right hand and answer me.
May the words of my mouth and the meditation of my heart   *Ps. 19*
find favor before You, LORD, my Rock and Redeemer.

Bow, take three steps back, then bow, first left, then right, then center, while saying:
May He who makes peace in His high places,
make peace for us and all Israel – and say: Amen.

יְהִי רָצוֹן **May it be Your will,** LORD our God and God of our ancestors,
that the Temple be rebuilt speedily in our days, and grant us a share in Your Torah.
And there we will serve You with reverence, as in the days of old and as in former years.
Then the offering of Judah and Jerusalem   *Mal. 3*
will be pleasing to the LORD as in the days of old and as in former years.

After the Leader's Repetition, the service continues with Full Kaddish (page 250),
followed by Aleinu (page 252), the Daily Psalm (page 258) and Barekhi Nafshi (page 266).

וְטוֹב בְּעֵינֶיךָ לְבָרֵךְ אֶת עַמְּךָ יִשְׂרָאֵל
בְּכָל עֵת וּבְכָל שָׁעָה בִּשְׁלוֹמֶךָ.
בָּרוּךְ אַתָּה יהוה, הַמְבָרֵךְ אֶת עַמּוֹ יִשְׂרָאֵל בַּשָּׁלוֹם.

The following verse concludes the חזרת הש״ץ.
Some also say it here as part of the silent עמידה.

תהלים יט

יִהְיוּ לְרָצוֹן אִמְרֵי־פִי וְהֶגְיוֹן לִבִּי לְפָנֶיךָ, יהוה צוּרִי וְגֹאֲלִי:

ברכות יז

אֱלֹהַי

נְצֹר לְשׁוֹנִי מֵרָע וּשְׂפָתַי מִדַּבֵּר מִרְמָה
וְלִמְקַלְלַי נַפְשִׁי תִדֹּם, וְנַפְשִׁי כֶּעָפָר לַכֹּל תִּהְיֶה.
פְּתַח לִבִּי בְּתוֹרָתֶךָ, וּבְמִצְוֹתֶיךָ תִּרְדֹּף נַפְשִׁי.
וְכָל הַחוֹשְׁבִים עָלַי רָעָה מְהֵרָה הָפֵר עֲצָתָם וְקַלְקֵל מַחֲשַׁבְתָּם.
עֲשֵׂה לְמַעַן שְׁמֶךָ, עֲשֵׂה לְמַעַן יְמִינֶךָ
עֲשֵׂה לְמַעַן קְדֻשָּׁתֶךָ, עֲשֵׂה לְמַעַן תּוֹרָתֶךָ.

תהלים ס

לְמַעַן יֵחָלְצוּן יְדִידֶיךָ, הוֹשִׁיעָה יְמִינְךָ וַעֲנֵנִי:

תהלים יט

יִהְיוּ לְרָצוֹן אִמְרֵי־פִי וְהֶגְיוֹן לִבִּי לְפָנֶיךָ, יהוה צוּרִי וְגֹאֲלִי:

Bow, take three steps back, then bow, first left, then right, then center, while saying:

עֹשֶׂה שָׁלוֹם בִּמְרוֹמָיו
הוּא יַעֲשֶׂה שָׁלוֹם עָלֵינוּ וְעַל כָּל יִשְׂרָאֵל, וְאִמְרוּ אָמֵן.

יְהִי רָצוֹן מִלְּפָנֶיךָ יהוה אֱלֹהֵינוּ וֵאלֹהֵי אֲבוֹתֵינוּ
שֶׁיִּבָּנֶה בֵּית הַמִּקְדָּשׁ בִּמְהֵרָה בְיָמֵינוּ, וְתֵן חֶלְקֵנוּ בְּתוֹרָתֶךָ
וְשָׁם נַעֲבָדְךָ בְּיִרְאָה כִּימֵי עוֹלָם וּכְשָׁנִים קַדְמוֹנִיּוֹת.

מלאכי ג

וְעָרְבָה לַיהוה מִנְחַת יְהוּדָה וִירוּשָׁלָ͏ִם כִּימֵי עוֹלָם וּכְשָׁנִים קַדְמֹנִיּוֹת:

After the חזרת הש״ץ, the service continues with קדיש שלם (page 251),
followed by בָּרְכִי נַפְשִׁי (page 253), שיר של יום (page 259) and עָלֵינוּ (page 267).

Shaḥarit for Hoshana Raba, Yom HaAtzma'ut and Yom Yerushalayim

Begin as on weekdays, from pages 4–60.

On Hoshana Raba and, in many communites, on Yom HaAtzma'ut and Yom Yerushalayim, Pesukei DeZimra of Yom Tov are said.

A PSALM BEFORE VERSES OF PRAISE

מִזְמוֹר שִׁיר A psalm of David.   *Ps. 30*
A song for the dedication of the House.
I will exalt You, LORD, for You have lifted me up,
and not let my enemies rejoice over me.
LORD, my God, I cried to You for help and You healed me.
LORD, You lifted my soul from the grave;
You spared me from going down to the pit.
Sing to the LORD, you His devoted ones,
and give thanks to His holy name.
For His anger is for a moment, but His favor for a lifetime.
At night there may be weeping, but in the morning there is joy.
When I felt secure, I said, "I shall never be shaken."
LORD, when You favored me,
You made me stand firm as a mountain,
but when You hid Your face, I was terrified.
To You, LORD, I called; I pleaded with my LORD:
"What gain would there be if I died and went down to the grave?
Can dust thank You? Can it declare Your truth?
Hear, LORD, and be gracious to me; LORD, be my help."
You have turned my sorrow into dancing.
► You have removed my sackcloth and clothed me with joy,
so that my soul may sing to You and not be silent.
LORD my God, for ever will I thank You.

שחרית להושענא רבה
ליום העצמאות וליום ירושלים

Begin as on weekdays, from pages 5–61.

On הושענא רבה *and, in many communites, on* יום העצמאות
and יום ירושלים, פסוקי דזמרה *of* יום טוב *are said.*

מזמור לפני פסוקי דזמרה

תהלים ל

מִזְמוֹר שִׁיר־חֲנֻכַּת הַבַּיִת לְדָוִד:

אֲרוֹמִמְךָ יהוה כִּי דִלִּיתָנִי, וְלֹא־שִׂמַּחְתָּ אֹיְבַי לִי:

יהוה אֱלֹהָי, שִׁוַּעְתִּי אֵלֶיךָ וַתִּרְפָּאֵנִי:

יהוה, הֶעֱלִיתָ מִן־שְׁאוֹל נַפְשִׁי, חִיִּיתַנִי מִיָּרְדִי־בוֹר:

זַמְּרוּ לַיהוה חֲסִידָיו, וְהוֹדוּ לְזֵכֶר קָדְשׁוֹ:

כִּי רֶגַע בְּאַפּוֹ, חַיִּים בִּרְצוֹנוֹ

בָּעֶרֶב יָלִין בֶּכִי וְלַבֹּקֶר רִנָּה:

וַאֲנִי אָמַרְתִּי בְשַׁלְוִי, בַּל־אֶמּוֹט לְעוֹלָם:

יהוה, בִּרְצוֹנְךָ הֶעֱמַדְתָּה לְהַרְרִי עֹז

הִסְתַּרְתָּ פָנֶיךָ הָיִיתִי נִבְהָל:

אֵלֶיךָ יהוה אֶקְרָא, וְאֶל־אֲדֹנָי אֶתְחַנָּן:

מַה־בֶּצַע בְּדָמִי, בְּרִדְתִּי אֶל שָׁחַת, הֲיוֹדְךָ עָפָר, הֲיַגִּיד אֲמִתֶּךָ:

שְׁמַע־יהוה וְחָנֵּנִי, יהוה הֱיֵה־עֹזֵר לִי:

◄ הָפַכְתָּ מִסְפְּדִי לְמָחוֹל לִי, פִּתַּחְתָּ שַׂקִּי, וַתְּאַזְּרֵנִי שִׂמְחָה:

לְמַעַן יְזַמֶּרְךָ כָבוֹד וְלֹא יִדֹּם

יהוה אֱלֹהָי, לְעוֹלָם אוֹדֶךָּ:

MOURNER'S KADDISH

The following prayer, said by mourners, requires the presence of a minyan.
A transliteration can be found on page 921.

Mourner: יִתְגַּדַּל Magnified and sanctified
may His great name be,
in the world He created by His will.
May He establish His kingdom
in your lifetime and in your days,
and in the lifetime of all the house of Israel,
swiftly and soon –
and say: Amen.

All: May His great name be blessed
for ever and all time.

Mourner: Blessed and praised,
glorified and exalted,
raised and honored,
uplifted and lauded
be the name of the Holy One,
blessed be He,
beyond any blessing,
song, praise and consolation
uttered in the world –
and say: Amen.

May there be great peace from heaven,
and life for us and all Israel –
and say: Amen.

Bow, take three steps back, as if taking leave of the Divine Presence,
then bow, first left, then right, then center, while saying:
May He who makes peace in His high places,
make peace for us and all Israel –
and say: Amen.

קדיש יתום

The following prayer, said by mourners, requires the presence of a מנין.
A transliteration can be found on page 921.

אבל: יִתְגַּדַּל וְיִתְקַדַּשׁ שְׁמֵהּ רַבָּא (קהל: אָמֵן)
בְּעָלְמָא דִּי בְרָא כִרְעוּתֵהּ
וְיַמְלִיךְ מַלְכוּתֵהּ
בְּחַיֵּיכוֹן וּבְיוֹמֵיכוֹן וּבְחַיֵּי דְּכָל בֵּית יִשְׂרָאֵל
בַּעֲגָלָא וּבִזְמַן קָרִיב
וְאִמְרוּ אָמֵן. (קהל: אָמֵן)

קהל
ואבל: יְהֵא שְׁמֵהּ רַבָּא מְבָרַךְ לְעָלַם וּלְעָלְמֵי עָלְמַיָּא.

אבל: יִתְבָּרַךְ וְיִשְׁתַּבַּח וְיִתְפָּאַר
וְיִתְרוֹמַם וְיִתְנַשֵּׂא וְיִתְהַדָּר וְיִתְעַלֶּה וְיִתְהַלָּל
שְׁמֵהּ דְּקֻדְשָׁא בְּרִיךְ הוּא (קהל: בְּרִיךְ הוּא)
לְעֵלָּא מִן כָּל בִּרְכָתָא וְשִׁירָתָא, תֻּשְׁבְּחָתָא וְנֶחֱמָתָא
דַּאֲמִירָן בְּעָלְמָא
וְאִמְרוּ אָמֵן. (קהל: אָמֵן)

יְהֵא שְׁלָמָא רַבָּא מִן שְׁמַיָּא
וְחַיִּים, עָלֵינוּ וְעַל כָּל יִשְׂרָאֵל
וְאִמְרוּ אָמֵן. (קהל: אָמֵן)

Bow, take three steps back, as if taking leave of the Divine Presence,
then bow, first left, then right, then center, while saying:

עֹשֶׂה שָׁלוֹם בִּמְרוֹמָיו
הוּא יַעֲשֶׂה שָׁלוֹם עָלֵינוּ וְעַל כָּל יִשְׂרָאֵל
וְאִמְרוּ אָמֵן. (קהל: אָמֵן)

PESUKEI DEZIMRA

*The following introductory blessing to the Pesukei DeZimra (Verses of Praise) is
said standing, while holding the two front tzitziot of the tallit. They are kissed
and released at the end of the blessing at "songs of praise" (below). From the
beginning of this prayer to the end of the Amida, conversation is forbidden.*

Some say:

I hereby prepare my mouth to thank, praise and laud my Creator, for the sake of the
unification of the Holy One, blessed be He, and His Divine Presence, through that
which is hidden and concealed, in the name of all Israel.

BLESSED IS HE
WHO SPOKE

and the world came into being, blessed is He.

> Blessed is He who creates the universe.
> Blessed is He who speaks and acts.
> Blessed is He who decrees and fulfills.
> Blessed is He who shows compassion to the earth.
> Blessed is He who shows compassion to all creatures.
> Blessed is He who gives a good reward
> to those who fear Him.
> Blessed is He who lives for ever
> and exists to eternity.
> Blessed is He who redeems and saves.
> Blessed is His name.

Blessed are You, Lord our God, King of the Universe, God,
compassionate Father, extolled by the mouth of His people, praised
and glorified by the tongue of His devoted ones and those who
serve Him. With the songs of Your servant David we will praise
You, O Lord our God. With praises and psalms we will magnify
and praise You, glorify You, Speak Your name and proclaim Your
kingship, our King, our God, ‣ the only One, Giver of life to the
worlds the King whose great name is praised and glorified to all
eternity. Blessed are You, Lord, the King extolled with songs
of praise.

פסוקי דזמרה

The following introductory blessing to the פסוקי דזמרה is said standing, while holding the two
front ציצית of the טלית. They are kissed and released at the end of the blessing at בתשבחות
(below). From the beginning of this prayer to the end of the עמידה, conversation is forbidden.

Some say:

הֲרֵינִי מְזַמֵּן אֶת פִּי לְהוֹדוֹת וּלְהַלֵּל וּלְשַׁבֵּחַ אֶת בּוֹרְאִי, לְשֵׁם יִחוּד קֻדְשָׁא בְּרִיךְ
הוּא וּשְׁכִינְתֵּהּ עַל יְדֵי הַהוּא טָמִיר וְנֶעְלָם בְּשֵׁם כָּל יִשְׂרָאֵל.

בָּרוּךְ
שֶׁאָמַר

וְהָיָה הָעוֹלָם, בָּרוּךְ הוּא.

בָּרוּךְ עוֹשֶׂה בְרֵאשִׁית
בָּרוּךְ אוֹמֵר וְעוֹשֶׂה
בָּרוּךְ גּוֹזֵר וּמְקַיֵּם
בָּרוּךְ מְרַחֵם עַל הָאָרֶץ
בָּרוּךְ מְרַחֵם עַל הַבְּרִיּוֹת
בָּרוּךְ מְשַׁלֵּם שָׂכָר טוֹב לִירֵאָיו
בָּרוּךְ חַי לָעַד וְקַיָּם לָנֶצַח
בָּרוּךְ פּוֹדֶה וּמַצִּיל
בָּרוּךְ שְׁמוֹ

בָּרוּךְ אַתָּה יהוה אֱלֹהֵינוּ מֶלֶךְ הָעוֹלָם, הָאֵל הָאָב הָרַחֲמָן
הַמְהֻלָּל בְּפִי עַמּוֹ, מְשֻׁבָּח וּמְפֹאָר בִּלְשׁוֹן חֲסִידָיו וַעֲבָדָיו, וּבְשִׁירֵי
דָוִד עַבְדֶּךָ, נְהַלֶּלְךָ יהוה אֱלֹהֵינוּ. בִּשְׁבָחוֹת וּבִזְמִירוֹת, נְגַדֶּלְךָ
וּנְשַׁבֵּחֲךָ וּנְפָאֶרְךָ, וְנַזְכִּיר שִׁמְךָ וְנַמְלִיכְךָ, מַלְכֵּנוּ אֱלֹהֵינוּ, יָחִיד
חֵי הָעוֹלָמִים, מֶלֶךְ, מְשֻׁבָּח וּמְפֹאָר עֲדֵי עַד שְׁמוֹ הַגָּדוֹל. בָּרוּךְ
אַתָּה יהוה, מֶלֶךְ מְהֻלָּל בַּתִּשְׁבָּחוֹת.

הודו Thank the LORD, call on His name, make His acts known *1 Chr. 16* among the peoples. Sing to Him, make music to Him, tell of all His wonders. Glory in His holy name; let the hearts of those who seek the LORD rejoice. Search out the LORD and His strength; seek His presence at all times. Remember the wonders He has done, His miracles, and the judgments He pronounced. Descendants of Yisrael His servant, sons of Jacob His chosen ones: He is the LORD our God. His judgments are throughout the earth. Remember His covenant for ever, the word He commanded for a thousand generations. He made it with Abraham, vowed it to Isaac, and confirmed it to Jacob as a statute and to Israel as an everlasting covenant, saying, "To you I will give the land of Canaan as your allotted heritage." You were then small in number, few, strangers there, wandering from nation to nation, from one kingdom to another, but He let no man oppress them, and for their sake He rebuked kings: "Do not touch My anointed ones, and do My prophets no harm." Sing to the LORD, all the earth; proclaim His salvation daily. Declare His glory among the nations, His marvels among all the peoples. For great is the LORD and greatly to be praised; He is awesome beyond all heavenly powers. ‣ For all the gods of the peoples are mere idols; it was the LORD who made the heavens.

Before Him are majesty and splendor; there is strength and beauty in His holy place. Render to the LORD, families of the peoples, render to the LORD honor and might. Render to the LORD the glory due to His name; bring an offering and come before Him; bow down to the LORD in the splendor of holiness. Tremble before Him, all the earth; the world stands firm, it will not be shaken. Let the heavens rejoice and the earth be glad; let them declare among the nations, "The LORD is King." Let the sea roar, and all that is in it; let the fields be jubilant, and all they contain. Then the trees of the forest will sing for joy before the LORD, for He is coming to judge the earth. Thank the LORD for He is good; His lovingkindness is for ever. Say: "Save us, God of our salvation; gather us

הוֹדוּ לַיהוה קִרְאוּ בִשְׁמוֹ, הוֹדִיעוּ בָעַמִּים עֲלִילוֹתָיו: שִׁירוּ לוֹ, זַמְּרוּ־לוֹ, שִׂיחוּ בְּכָל־נִפְלְאוֹתָיו: הִתְהַלְלוּ בְּשֵׁם קָדְשׁוֹ, יִשְׂמַח לֵב מְבַקְשֵׁי יהוה: דִּרְשׁוּ יהוה וְעֻזּוֹ, בַּקְּשׁוּ פָנָיו תָּמִיד: זִכְרוּ נִפְלְאוֹתָיו אֲשֶׁר עָשָׂה, מֹפְתָיו וּמִשְׁפְּטֵי־פִיהוּ: זֶרַע יִשְׂרָאֵל עַבְדּוֹ, בְּנֵי יַעֲקֹב בְּחִירָיו: הוּא יהוה אֱלֹהֵינוּ, בְּכָל־הָאָרֶץ מִשְׁפָּטָיו: זִכְרוּ לְעוֹלָם בְּרִיתוֹ, דָּבָר צִוָּה לְאֶלֶף דּוֹר: אֲשֶׁר כָּרַת אֶת־אַבְרָהָם, וּשְׁבוּעָתוֹ לְיִצְחָק: וַיַּעֲמִידֶהָ לְיַעֲקֹב לְחֹק, לְיִשְׂרָאֵל בְּרִית עוֹלָם: לֵאמֹר, לְךָ אֶתֵּן אֶרֶץ־כְּנָעַן, חֶבֶל נַחֲלַתְכֶם: בִּהְיוֹתְכֶם מְתֵי מִסְפָּר, כִּמְעַט וְגָרִים בָּהּ: וַיִּתְהַלְּכוּ מִגּוֹי אֶל־גּוֹי, וּמִמַּמְלָכָה אֶל־עַם אַחֵר: לֹא־הִנִּיחַ לְאִישׁ לְעָשְׁקָם, וַיּוֹכַח עֲלֵיהֶם מְלָכִים: אַל־תִּגְּעוּ בִּמְשִׁיחָי, וּבִנְבִיאַי אַל־תָּרֵעוּ: שִׁירוּ לַיהוה כָּל־הָאָרֶץ, בַּשְּׂרוּ מִיּוֹם־אֶל־יוֹם יְשׁוּעָתוֹ: סַפְּרוּ בַגּוֹיִם אֶת־כְּבוֹדוֹ, בְּכָל־הָעַמִּים נִפְלְאוֹתָיו: כִּי גָדוֹל יהוה וּמְהֻלָּל מְאֹד, וְנוֹרָא הוּא עַל־כָּל־אֱלֹהִים: ◁ כִּי כָּל־אֱלֹהֵי הָעַמִּים אֱלִילִים, וַיהוה שָׁמַיִם עָשָׂה:

הוֹד וְהָדָר לְפָנָיו, עֹז וְחֶדְוָה בִּמְקֹמוֹ: הָבוּ לַיהוה מִשְׁפְּחוֹת עַמִּים, הָבוּ לַיהוה כָּבוֹד וָעֹז: הָבוּ לַיהוה כְּבוֹד שְׁמוֹ, שְׂאוּ מִנְחָה וּבֹאוּ לְפָנָיו, הִשְׁתַּחֲווּ לַיהוה בְּהַדְרַת־קֹדֶשׁ: חִילוּ מִלְּפָנָיו כָּל־הָאָרֶץ, אַף־תִּכּוֹן תֵּבֵל בַּל־תִּמּוֹט: יִשְׂמְחוּ הַשָּׁמַיִם וְתָגֵל הָאָרֶץ, וְיֹאמְרוּ בַגּוֹיִם יהוה מָלָךְ: יִרְעַם הַיָּם וּמְלוֹאוֹ, יַעֲלֹץ הַשָּׂדֶה וְכָל־אֲשֶׁר־בּוֹ: אָז יְרַנְּנוּ עֲצֵי הַיָּעַר, מִלִּפְנֵי יהוה, כִּי־בָא לִשְׁפּוֹט אֶת־הָאָרֶץ: הוֹדוּ לַיהוה כִּי טוֹב, כִּי לְעוֹלָם חַסְדּוֹ: וְאִמְרוּ, הוֹשִׁיעֵנוּ אֱלֹהֵי יִשְׁעֵנוּ, וְקַבְּצֵנוּ וְהַצִּילֵנוּ מִן־הַגּוֹיִם, לְהֹדוֹת

and rescue us from the nations, to acknowledge Your holy name
and glory in Your praise. Blessed is the LORD, God of Israel, from
this world to eternity." And let all the people say "Amen" and "Praise
the LORD."

‣ Exalt the LORD our God and bow before His footstool: He is holy. *Ps. 99*
Exalt the LORD our God and bow at His holy mountain; for holy
is the LORD our God.

He is compassionate. He forgives iniquity and does not destroy. *Ps. 78*
Repeatedly He suppresses His anger, not rousing His full wrath.
You, LORD: do not withhold Your compassion from me. May Your *Ps. 40*
loving-kindness and truth always guard me. Remember, LORD, Your *Ps. 25*
acts of compassion and love, for they have existed for ever. Ascribe *Ps. 68*
power to God, whose majesty is over Israel and whose might is in
the skies. You are awesome, God, in Your holy places. It is the God
of Israel who gives might and strength to the people, may God be
blessed. God of retribution, LORD, God of retribution, appear. *Ps. 94*
Arise, Judge of the earth, to repay the arrogant their just deserts.
Salvation belongs to the LORD; may Your blessing rest upon Your *Ps. 3*
people, Selah! ‣ The LORD of hosts is with us, the God of Jacob is *Ps. 46*
our stronghold, Selah! LORD of hosts, happy is the one who trusts *Ps. 84*
in You. LORD, save! May the King answer us on the day we call. *Ps. 20*

Save Your people and bless Your heritage; tend them and carry *Ps. 28*
them for ever. Our soul longs for the LORD; He is our Help and *Ps. 33*
Shield. For in Him our hearts rejoice, for in His holy name we have
trusted. May Your loving-kindness, LORD, be upon us, as we have
put our hope in You. Show us, LORD, Your loving-kindness and grant *Ps. 85*
us Your salvation. Arise, help us and redeem us for the sake of Your *Ps. 44*
love. I am the LORD your God who brought you up from the land of *Ps. 81*
Egypt: open your mouth wide and I will fill it. Happy is the people *Ps. 144*
for whom this is so; happy is the people whose God the LORD. ‣ As *Ps. 13*
for me, I trust in Your loving-kindness; my heart rejoices in Your
salvation. I will sing to the LORD for He has been good to me.

לְשֵׁם קָדְשֶׁךָ, לְהִשְׁתַּבֵּחַ בִּתְהִלָּתֶךָ: בָּרוּךְ יהוה אֱלֹהֵי יִשְׂרָאֵל מִן הָעוֹלָם וְעַד הָעוֹלָם, וַיֹּאמְרוּ כָל הָעָם אָמֵן, וְהַלֵּל לַיהוה:

תהלים צט

‹ רוֹמְמוּ יהוה אֱלֹהֵינוּ וְהִשְׁתַּחֲווּ לַהֲדֹם רַגְלָיו, קָדוֹשׁ הוּא: רוֹמְמוּ יהוה אֱלֹהֵינוּ וְהִשְׁתַּחֲווּ לְהַר קָדְשׁוֹ, כִּי קָדוֹשׁ יהוה אֱלֹהֵינוּ:

תהלים עח

וְהוּא רַחוּם, יְכַפֵּר עָוֺן וְלֹא יַשְׁחִית, וְהִרְבָּה לְהָשִׁיב אַפּוֹ,

תהלים מ

וְלֹא יָעִיר כָּל חֲמָתוֹ: אַתָּה יהוה לֹא תִכְלָא רַחֲמֶיךָ מִמֶּנִּי, חַסְדְּךָ

תהלים כה

וַאֲמִתְּךָ תָּמִיד יִצְּרוּנִי: זְכֹר רַחֲמֶיךָ יהוה וַחֲסָדֶיךָ, כִּי מֵעוֹלָם

תהלים סח

הֵמָּה: תְּנוּ עֹז לֵאלֹהִים, עַל יִשְׂרָאֵל גַּאֲוָתוֹ, וְעֻזּוֹ בַּשְּׁחָקִים: נוֹרָא אֱלֹהִים מִמִּקְדָּשֶׁיךָ, אֵל יִשְׂרָאֵל הוּא נֹתֵן עֹז וְתַעֲצֻמוֹת

תהלים צד

לָעָם, בָּרוּךְ אֱלֹהִים: אֵל נְקָמוֹת יהוה, אֵל נְקָמוֹת הוֹפִיעַ: הִנָּשֵׂא

תהלים ג

שֹׁפֵט הָאָרֶץ, הָשֵׁב גְּמוּל עַל גֵּאִים: לַיהוה הַיְשׁוּעָה, עַל עַמְּךָ

תהלים מו

בִרְכָתֶךָ סֶּלָה: ‹ יהוה צְבָאוֹת עִמָּנוּ, מִשְׂגָּב לָנוּ אֱלֹהֵי יַעֲקֹב

תהלים פד
תהלים כ

סֶלָה: יהוה צְבָאוֹת, אַשְׁרֵי אָדָם בֹּטֵחַ בָּךְ: יהוה הוֹשִׁיעָה, הַמֶּלֶךְ יַעֲנֵנוּ בְיוֹם קָרְאֵנוּ:

תהלים כח

הוֹשִׁיעָה אֶת עַמֶּךָ, וּבָרֵךְ אֶת נַחֲלָתֶךָ, וּרְעֵם וְנַשְּׂאֵם עַד

תהלים לג

הָעוֹלָם: נַפְשֵׁנוּ חִכְּתָה לַיהוה, עֶזְרֵנוּ וּמָגִנֵּנוּ הוּא: כִּי בוֹ יִשְׂמַח לִבֵּנוּ, כִּי בְשֵׁם קָדְשׁוֹ בָטָחְנוּ: יְהִי חַסְדְּךָ יהוה עָלֵינוּ, כַּאֲשֶׁר

תהלים פה
תהלים מד

יִחַלְנוּ לָךְ: הַרְאֵנוּ יהוה חַסְדֶּךָ, וְיֶשְׁעֲךָ תִּתֶּן לָנוּ: קוּמָה עֶזְרָתָה

תהלים פא

לָּנוּ, וּפְדֵנוּ לְמַעַן חַסְדֶּךָ: אָנֹכִי יהוה אֱלֹהֶיךָ הַמַּעַלְךָ מֵאֶרֶץ

תהלים קמד

מִצְרָיִם, הַרְחֶב פִּיךָ וַאֲמַלְאֵהוּ: אַשְׁרֵי הָעָם שֶׁכָּכָה לּוֹ, אַשְׁרֵי

תהלים יג

הָעָם שֶׁיהוה אֱלֹהָיו: ‹ וַאֲנִי בְּחַסְדְּךָ בָטַחְתִּי, יָגֵל לִבִּי בִּישׁוּעָתֶךָ, אָשִׁירָה לַיהוה, כִּי גָמַל עָלָי:

The custom is to say the following psalm standing.

מִזְמוֹר A psalm of thanksgiving. Shout joyously to the Lᴏʀᴅ, all the *Ps. 100* earth. Serve the Lᴏʀᴅ with joy. Come before Him with jubilation. Know that the Lᴏʀᴅ is God. He made us and we are His. We are His people and the flock He tends. Enter His gates with thanksgiving, His courts with praise. Thank Him and bless His name. ‣ For the Lᴏʀᴅ is good, His loving-kindness is everlasting, and His faithfulness is for every generation.

לַמְנַצֵּחַ For the conductor of music. A psalm of David. The heavens *Ps. 19* declare the glory of God; the skies proclaim the work of His hands. Day to day they pour forth speech; night to night they communicate knowledge. There is no speech, there are no words, their voice is not heard. Yet their music carries throughout the earth, their words to the end of the world. In them He has set a tent for the sun. It emerges like a groom from his marriage chamber, rejoicing like a champion about to run a race. It rises at one end of the heaven and makes its circuit to the other: nothing is hidden from its heat. The Lᴏʀᴅ's Torah is perfect, refreshing the soul. The Lᴏʀᴅ's testimony is faithful, making the simple wise. The Lᴏʀᴅ's precepts are just, gladdening the heart. The Lᴏʀᴅ's commandment is radiant, giving light to the eyes. The fear of the Lᴏʀᴅ is pure, enduring for ever. The Lᴏʀᴅ's judgments are true, altogether righteous. More precious than gold, than much fine gold. They are sweeter than honey, than honey from the comb. Your servant, too, is careful of them, for in observing them there is great reward. Yet who can discern his errors? Cleanse me of hidden faults. Keep Your servant also from willful sins; let them not have dominion over me. Then shall I be blameless, and innocent of grave sin. ‣ May the words of my mouth and the meditation of my heart find favor before You, Lᴏʀᴅ, my Rock and my Redeemer.

לְדָוִד Of David. When he pretended to be insane before Abimelech, *Ps. 34* who drove him away, and he left. I will bless the Lᴏʀᴅ at all times; His praise will be always on my lips. My soul will glory in the Lᴏʀᴅ; let the lowly hear this and rejoice. Magnify the Lᴏʀᴅ with me; let us exalt His name together. I sought the Lᴏʀᴅ, and He answered me; He saved me from all my fears. Those who look to Him are radiant; Their

The custom is to say the following psalm standing.

תהלים ק

מִזְמוֹר לְתוֹדָה, הָרִיעוּ לַיהוה כָּל־הָאָרֶץ: עִבְדוּ אֶת־יהוה בְּשִׂמְחָה,
בְּאוּ לְפָנָיו בִּרְנָנָה: דְּעוּ כִּי־יהוה הוּא אֱלֹהִים, הוּא עָשָׂנוּ וְלוֹ אֲנַחְנוּ,
עַמּוֹ וְצֹאן מַרְעִיתוֹ: בְּאוּ שְׁעָרָיו בְּתוֹדָה, חֲצֵרֹתָיו בִּתְהִלָּה, הוֹדוּ לוֹ,
בָּרְכוּ שְׁמוֹ: ‹ כִּי־טוֹב יהוה, לְעוֹלָם חַסְדּוֹ, וְעַד־דֹּר וָדֹר אֱמוּנָתוֹ:

תהלים יט

לַמְנַצֵּחַ מִזְמוֹר לְדָוִד: הַשָּׁמַיִם מְסַפְּרִים כְּבוֹד־אֵל, וּמַעֲשֵׂה
יָדָיו מַגִּיד הָרָקִיעַ: יוֹם לְיוֹם יַבִּיעַ אֹמֶר, וְלַיְלָה לְּלַיְלָה יְחַוֶּה־
דָּעַת: אֵין־אֹמֶר וְאֵין דְּבָרִים, בְּלִי נִשְׁמָע קוֹלָם: בְּכָל־הָאָרֶץ
יָצָא קַוָּם, וּבִקְצֵה תֵבֵל מִלֵּיהֶם, לַשֶּׁמֶשׁ שָׂם־אֹהֶל בָּהֶם: וְהוּא
כְּחָתָן יֹצֵא מֵחֻפָּתוֹ, יָשִׂישׂ כְּגִבּוֹר לָרוּץ אֹרַח: מִקְצֵה הַשָּׁמַיִם
מוֹצָאוֹ, וּתְקוּפָתוֹ עַל־קְצוֹתָם, וְאֵין נִסְתָּר מֵחַמָּתוֹ: תּוֹרַת יהוה
תְּמִימָה, מְשִׁיבַת נָפֶשׁ, עֵדוּת יהוה נֶאֱמָנָה, מַחְכִּימַת פֶּתִי:
פִּקּוּדֵי יהוה יְשָׁרִים, מְשַׂמְּחֵי־לֵב, מִצְוַת יהוה בָּרָה, מְאִירַת
עֵינָיִם: יִרְאַת יהוה טְהוֹרָה, עוֹמֶדֶת לָעַד, מִשְׁפְּטֵי־יהוה אֱמֶת,
צָדְקוּ יַחְדָּו: הַנֶּחֱמָדִים מִזָּהָב וּמִפַּז רָב, וּמְתוּקִים מִדְּבַשׁ וְנֹפֶת
צוּפִים: גַּם־עַבְדְּךָ נִזְהָר בָּהֶם, בְּשָׁמְרָם עֵקֶב רָב: שְׁגִיאוֹת מִי־
יָבִין, מִנִּסְתָּרוֹת נַקֵּנִי: גַּם מִזֵּדִים חֲשֹׂךְ עַבְדֶּךָ, אַל־יִמְשְׁלוּ־בִי
אָז אֵיתָם, וְנִקֵּיתִי מִפֶּשַׁע רָב: ‹ יִהְיוּ לְרָצוֹן אִמְרֵי־פִי וְהֶגְיוֹן לִבִּי
לְפָנֶיךָ, יהוה, צוּרִי וְגֹאֲלִי:

תהלים לד

לְדָוִד, בְּשַׁנּוֹתוֹ אֶת־טַעְמוֹ לִפְנֵי אֲבִימֶלֶךְ, וַיְגָרְשֵׁהוּ וַיֵּלַךְ: אֲבָרְכָה
אֶת־יהוה בְּכָל־עֵת, תָּמִיד תְּהִלָּתוֹ בְּפִי: בַּיהוה תִּתְהַלֵּל נַפְשִׁי,
יִשְׁמְעוּ עֲנָוִים וְיִשְׂמָחוּ: גַּדְּלוּ לַיהוה אִתִּי, וּנְרוֹמְמָה שְׁמוֹ יַחְדָּו:
דָּרַשְׁתִּי אֶת־יהוה, וְעָנָנִי, וּמִכָּל־מְגוּרוֹתַי הִצִּילָנִי: הִבִּיטוּ אֵלָיו
וְנָהָרוּ, וּפְנֵיהֶם אַל־יֶחְפָּרוּ: זֶה עָנִי קָרָא, וַיהוה שָׁמֵעַ, וּמִכָּל־

faces are never downcast. This poor man called, and the Lord heard; He saved him from all his troubles. The Lord's angel encamps around those who fear Him, and He rescues them. Taste and see that the Lord is good; happy is the man who takes refuge in Him. Fear the Lord, you His holy ones, for those who fear Him lack nothing. Young lions may grow weak and hungry, but those who seek the Lord lack no good thing. Come, my children, listen to me; I will teach you the fear of the Lord. Who desires life, loving each day to see good? Then guard your tongue from evil and your lips from speaking deceit. Turn from evil and do good; seek peace and pursue it. The eyes of the Lord are on the righteous and His ears attentive to their cry; The Lord's face is set against those who do evil, to erase their memory from the earth. The righteous cry out, and the Lord hears them; delivering them from all their troubles. The Lord is close to the brokenhearted, and saves those who are crushed in spirit. Many troubles may befall the righteous, but the Lord delivers him from them all; He protects all his bones, so that none of them will be broken. Evil will slay the wicked; the enemies of the righteous will be condemned. ‣ The Lord redeems His servants; none who take refuge in Him shall be condemned.

תְּפִלָּה לְמֹשֶׁה A prayer of Moses, the man of God. Lord, You have been *Ps. 90* our shelter in every generation. Before the mountains were born, before You brought forth the earth and the world, from everlasting to everlasting You are God. You turn men back to dust, saying, "Return, you children of men." For a thousand years in Your sight are like yesterday when it has passed, like a watch in the night. You sweep men away; they sleep. In the morning they are like grass newly grown: in the morning it flourishes and is new, but by evening it withers and dries up. For we are consumed by Your anger, terrified by Your fury. You have set our iniquities before You, our secret sins in the light of Your presence. All our days pass away in Your wrath, we spend our years like a sigh. The span of our life is seventy years, or if we are strong, eighty years; but the best of them is trouble and sorrow, for they quickly pass, and we fly away. Who can know the force of Your anger? Your wrath matches the fear due to You. Teach us rightly to number our days, that we may

צִרְעָתָיו הוֹשִׁיעוֹ: חֹנֶה מַלְאַךְ־יְהוָה סָבִיב לִירֵאָיו, וַיְחַלְּצֵם: טַעֲמוּ
וּרְאוּ כִּי־טוֹב יְהוָה, אַשְׁרֵי הַגֶּבֶר יֶחֱסֶה־בּוֹ: יְראוּ אֶת־יְהוָה
קְדֹשָׁיו, כִּי־אֵין מַחְסוֹר לִירֵאָיו: כְּפִירִים רָשׁוּ וְרָעֵבוּ, וְדֹרְשֵׁי יְהוָה
לֹא־יַחְסְרוּ כָל־טוֹב: לְכוּ־בָנִים שִׁמְעוּ־לִי, יִרְאַת יְהוָה אֲלַמֶּדְכֶם:
מִי־הָאִישׁ הֶחָפֵץ חַיִּים, אֹהֵב יָמִים לִרְאוֹת טוֹב: נְצֹר לְשׁוֹנְךָ
מֵרָע, וּשְׂפָתֶיךָ מִדַּבֵּר מִרְמָה: סוּר מֵרָע וַעֲשֵׂה־טוֹב, בַּקֵּשׁ שָׁלוֹם
וְרָדְפֵהוּ: עֵינֵי יְהוָה אֶל־צַדִּיקִים, וְאָזְנָיו אֶל־שַׁוְעָתָם: פְּנֵי יְהוָה
בְּעֹשֵׂי רָע, לְהַכְרִית מֵאֶרֶץ זִכְרָם: צָעֲקוּ וַיהוָה שָׁמֵעַ, וּמִכָּל־
צָרוֹתָם הִצִּילָם: קָרוֹב יְהוָה לְנִשְׁבְּרֵי־לֵב, וְאֶת־דַּכְּאֵי־רוּחַ יוֹשִׁיעַ:
רַבּוֹת רָעוֹת צַדִּיק, וּמִכֻּלָּם יַצִּילֶנּוּ יְהוָה: שֹׁמֵר כָּל־עַצְמוֹתָיו, אַחַת
מֵהֵנָּה לֹא נִשְׁבָּרָה: תְּמוֹתֵת רָשָׁע רָעָה, וְשֹׂנְאֵי צַדִּיק יֶאְשָׁמוּ:
‹ פּוֹדֶה יְהוָה נֶפֶשׁ עֲבָדָיו, וְלֹא יֶאְשְׁמוּ כָּל־הַחֹסִים בּוֹ:

תהלים צ

תְּפִלָּה לְמֹשֶׁה אִישׁ־הָאֱלֹהִים, אֲדֹנָי, מָעוֹן אַתָּה הָיִיתָ לָּנוּ בְּדֹר
וָדֹר: בְּטֶרֶם הָרִים יֻלָּדוּ, וַתְּחוֹלֵל אֶרֶץ וְתֵבֵל, וּמֵעוֹלָם עַד־עוֹלָם
אַתָּה אֵל: תָּשֵׁב אֱנוֹשׁ עַד־דַּכָּא, וַתֹּאמֶר שׁוּבוּ בְנֵי־אָדָם: כִּי
אֶלֶף שָׁנִים בְּעֵינֶיךָ, כְּיוֹם אֶתְמוֹל כִּי יַעֲבֹר, וְאַשְׁמוּרָה בַלָּיְלָה:
זְרַמְתָּם, שֵׁנָה יִהְיוּ, בַּבֹּקֶר כֶּחָצִיר יַחֲלֹף: בַּבֹּקֶר יָצִיץ וְחָלָף,
לָעֶרֶב יְמוֹלֵל וְיָבֵשׁ: כִּי־כָלִינוּ בְאַפֶּךָ, וּבַחֲמָתְךָ נִבְהָלְנוּ: שַׁתָּ
עֲוֹנֹתֵינוּ לְנֶגְדֶּךָ, עֲלֻמֵנוּ לִמְאוֹר פָּנֶיךָ: כִּי כָל־יָמֵינוּ פָּנוּ בְעֶבְרָתֶךָ,
כִּלִּינוּ שָׁנֵינוּ כְמוֹ־הֶגֶה: יְמֵי־שְׁנוֹתֵינוּ בָהֶם שִׁבְעִים שָׁנָה, וְאִם
בִּגְבוּרֹת שְׁמוֹנִים שָׁנָה, וְרָהְבָּם עָמָל וָאָוֶן, כִּי־גָז חִישׁ וַנָּעֻפָה:
מִי־יוֹדֵעַ עֹז אַפֶּךָ, וּכְיִרְאָתְךָ עֶבְרָתֶךָ, לִמְנוֹת יָמֵינוּ כֵּן הוֹדַע,
וְנָבִא לְבַב חָכְמָה: שׁוּבָה יְהוָה עַד־מָתָי, וְהִנָּחֵם עַל־עֲבָדֶיךָ:

gain a heart of wisdom. Relent, O Lord! How much longer? Be sorry
for Your servants. Satisfy us in the morning with Your loving-kindness,
that we may sing and rejoice all our days. Grant us joy for as many days
as You have afflicted us, for as many years as we saw trouble. Let Your
deeds be seen by Your servants, and Your glory by their children. ‣ May
the pleasantness of the Lord our God be upon us. Establish for us the
work of our hands, O establish the work of our hands.

יֹשֵׁב בְּסֵתֶר He who lives in the shelter of the Most High dwells in the *Ps. 91*
shadow of the Almighty. I say of the Lord, my Refuge and Stronghold,
my God in whom I trust, that He will save you from the fowler's snare
and the deadly pestilence. With His pinions He will cover you, and
beneath His wings you will find shelter; His faithfulness is an encircling shield. You need not fear terror by night, nor the arrow that flies
by day; not the pestilence that stalks in darkness, nor the plague that
ravages at noon. A thousand may fall at your side, ten thousand at
your right hand, but it will not come near you. You will only look with
your eyes and see the punishment of the wicked. Because you said
"The Lord is my Refuge," taking the Most High as your shelter, no
harm will befall you, no plague will come near your tent, for He will
command His angels about you, to guard you in all your ways. They
will lift you in their hands, lest your foot stumble on a stone. You will
tread on lions and vipers, you will trample on young lions and snakes.
[God says] "Because he loves Me, I will rescue him; I will protect
him, because he acknowledges My name. When he calls on Me, I will
answer him, I will be with him in distress, I will deliver him and bring
him honor. ‣ With long life I will satisfy him, and show him My salvation. With long life I will satisfy him, and show him My salvation."

הַלְלוּיָהּ Halleluya! Praise the name of the Lord. Praise Him, you ser- *Ps. 135*
vants of the Lord who stand in the Lord's House, in the courtyards
of the House of our God. Praise the Lord, for the Lord is good; sing
praises to His name, for it is lovely. For the Lord has chosen Jacob as
His own, Israel as his treasure. For I know that the Lord is great, that
our Lord is above all heavenly powers. Whatever pleases the Lord,
He does, in heaven and on earth, in the seas and all the depths. He

שַׂבְּעֵנוּ בַבֹּקֶר חַסְדֶּךָ, וּנְרַנְּנָה וְנִשְׂמְחָה בְּכָל־יָמֵינוּ: שַׂמְּחֵנוּ
כִּימוֹת עִנִּיתָנוּ, שְׁנוֹת רָאִינוּ רָעָה: יֵרָאֶה אֶל־עֲבָדֶיךָ פָעֳלֶךָ,
וַהֲדָרְךָ עַל־בְּנֵיהֶם: ◊ וִיהִי נֹעַם אֲדֹנָי אֱלֹהֵינוּ עָלֵינוּ, וּמַעֲשֵׂה
יָדֵינוּ כּוֹנְנָה עָלֵינוּ, וּמַעֲשֵׂה יָדֵינוּ כּוֹנְנֵהוּ:

תהלים צא

יֹשֵׁב בְּסֵתֶר עֶלְיוֹן, בְּצֵל שַׁדַּי יִתְלוֹנָן: אֹמַר לַיהוה מַחְסִי
וּמְצוּדָתִי, אֱלֹהַי אֶבְטַח־בּוֹ: כִּי הוּא יַצִּילְךָ מִפַּח יָקוּשׁ, מִדֶּבֶר
הַוּוֹת: בְּאֶבְרָתוֹ יָסֶךְ לָךְ, וְתַחַת־כְּנָפָיו תֶּחְסֶה, צִנָּה וְסֹחֵרָה
אֲמִתּוֹ: לֹא־תִירָא מִפַּחַד לָיְלָה, מֵחֵץ יָעוּף יוֹמָם: מִדֶּבֶר בָּאֹפֶל
יַהֲלֹךְ, מִקֶּטֶב יָשׁוּד צָהֳרָיִם: יִפֹּל מִצִּדְּךָ אֶלֶף, וּרְבָבָה מִימִינֶךָ,
אֵלֶיךָ לֹא יִגָּשׁ: רַק בְּעֵינֶיךָ תַבִּיט, וְשִׁלֻּמַת רְשָׁעִים תִּרְאֶה:
כִּי־אַתָּה יהוה מַחְסִי, עֶלְיוֹן שַׂמְתָּ מְעוֹנֶךָ: לֹא־תְאֻנֶּה אֵלֶיךָ
רָעָה, וְנֶגַע לֹא־יִקְרַב בְּאָהֳלֶךָ: כִּי מַלְאָכָיו יְצַוֶּה־לָךְ, לִשְׁמָרְךָ
בְּכָל־דְּרָכֶיךָ: עַל־כַּפַּיִם יִשָּׂאוּנְךָ, פֶּן־תִּגֹּף בָּאֶבֶן רַגְלֶךָ: עַל־
שַׁחַל וָפֶתֶן תִּדְרֹךְ, תִּרְמֹס כְּפִיר וְתַנִּין: כִּי בִי חָשַׁק וַאֲפַלְּטֵהוּ,
אֲשַׂגְּבֵהוּ כִּי־יָדַע שְׁמִי: יִקְרָאֵנִי וְאֶעֱנֵהוּ, עִמּוֹ אָנֹכִי בְצָרָה,
אֲחַלְּצֵהוּ וַאֲכַבְּדֵהוּ: ◊ אֹרֶךְ יָמִים אַשְׂבִּיעֵהוּ, וְאַרְאֵהוּ בִּישׁוּעָתִי:
אֹרֶךְ יָמִים אַשְׂבִּיעֵהוּ, וְאַרְאֵהוּ בִּישׁוּעָתִי:

תהלים קלה

הַלְלוּיָהּ, הַלְלוּ אֶת־שֵׁם יהוה, הַלְלוּ עַבְדֵי יהוה: שֶׁעֹמְדִים בְּבֵית
יהוה, בְּחַצְרוֹת בֵּית אֱלֹהֵינוּ: הַלְלוּיָהּ כִּי־טוֹב יהוה, זַמְּרוּ לִשְׁמוֹ
כִּי נָעִים: כִּי־יַעֲקֹב בָּחַר לוֹ יָהּ, יִשְׂרָאֵל לִסְגֻלָּתוֹ: כִּי אֲנִי יָדַעְתִּי
כִּי־גָדוֹל יהוה, וַאֲדֹנֵינוּ מִכָּל־אֱלֹהִים: כֹּל אֲשֶׁר־חָפֵץ יהוה עָשָׂה,
בַּשָּׁמַיִם וּבָאָרֶץ, בַּיַּמִּים וְכָל־תְּהֹמוֹת: מַעֲלֶה נְשִׂאִים מִקְצֵה
הָאָרֶץ, בְּרָקִים לַמָּטָר עָשָׂה, מוֹצֵא־רוּחַ מֵאוֹצְרוֹתָיו: שֶׁהִכָּה

raises clouds from the ends of the earth; He sends lightning with the rain; He brings out the wind from His storehouses. He struck down the firstborn of Egypt, of both man and animals. He sent signs and wonders into your midst, Egypt – against Pharaoh and all his servants. He struck down many nations and slew mighty kings: Siḥon, King of the Amorites, Og, King of Bashan, and all the kingdoms of Canaan, giving their land as a heritage, a heritage for His people Israel. Your name, LORD, endures for ever; Your renown, LORD, for all generations. For the LORD will bring justice to His people, and have compassion on His servants. The idols of the nations are silver and gold, the work of human hands. They have mouths, but cannot speak; eyes, but cannot see; ears, but cannot hear; there is no breath in their mouths. Those who make them will become like them: so will all who trust in them. ‣ House of Israel, bless the LORD. House of Aaron, bless the LORD. House of Levi, bless the LORD. You who fear the LORD, bless the LORD. Blessed is the LORD from Zion, He who dwells in Jerusalem. Halleluya!

The custom is to stand for the following psalm.

הוֹדוּ Thank the LORD for He is good;	His loving-kindness is for ever.	Ps. 136
Thank the God of gods,	His loving-kindness is for ever.	
Thank the LORD of lords,	His loving-kindness is for ever.	
To the One who alone		
works great wonders,	His loving-kindness is for ever.	
Who made the heavens with wisdom,	His loving-kindness is for ever.	
Who spread the earth upon the waters,	His loving-kindness is for ever.	
Who made the great lights,	His loving-kindness is for ever.	
The sun to rule by day,	His loving-kindness is for ever.	
The moon and the stars to rule by night;	His loving-kindness is for ever.	
Who struck Egypt		
through their firstborn,	His loving-kindness is for ever.	
And brought out Israel from their midst,	His loving-kindness is for ever.	
With a strong hand		
and outstretched arm,	His loving-kindness is for ever.	

בְּכוֹרֵי מִצְרָיִם, מֵאָדָם עַד־בְּהֵמָה: שָׁלַח אוֹתֹת וּמֹפְתִים בְּתוֹכֵכִי
מִצְרָיִם, בְּפַרְעֹה וּבְכָל־עֲבָדָיו: שֶׁהִכָּה גּוֹיִם רַבִּים, וְהָרַג מְלָכִים
עֲצוּמִים: לְסִיחוֹן מֶלֶךְ הָאֱמֹרִי, וּלְעוֹג מֶלֶךְ הַבָּשָׁן, וּלְכֹל מַמְלְכוֹת
כְּנָעַן: וְנָתַן אַרְצָם נַחֲלָה, נַחֲלָה לְיִשְׂרָאֵל עַמּוֹ: יהוה שִׁמְךָ
לְעוֹלָם, יהוה זִכְרְךָ לְדֹר־וָדֹר: כִּי־יָדִין יהוה עַמּוֹ, וְעַל־עֲבָדָיו
יִתְנֶחָם: עֲצַבֵּי הַגּוֹיִם כֶּסֶף וְזָהָב, מַעֲשֵׂה יְדֵי אָדָם: פֶּה־לָהֶם
וְלֹא יְדַבֵּרוּ, עֵינַיִם לָהֶם וְלֹא יִרְאוּ: אָזְנַיִם לָהֶם וְלֹא יַאֲזִינוּ, אַף
אֵין־יֶשׁ־רוּחַ בְּפִיהֶם: כְּמוֹהֶם יִהְיוּ עֹשֵׂיהֶם, כֹּל אֲשֶׁר־בֹּטֵחַ בָּהֶם:
‹ בֵּית יִשְׂרָאֵל בָּרְכוּ אֶת־יהוה, בֵּית אַהֲרֹן בָּרְכוּ אֶת־יהוה: בֵּית
הַלֵּוִי בָּרְכוּ אֶת־יהוה, יִרְאֵי יהוה בָּרְכוּ אֶת־יהוה: בָּרוּךְ יהוה
מִצִּיּוֹן, שֹׁכֵן יְרוּשָׁלָ͏ִם, הַלְלוּיָהּ:

The custom is to stand for the following psalm.

כִּי לְעוֹלָם חַסְדּוֹ:	הוֹדוּ לַיהוה כִּי־טוֹב	תהלים קלו
כִּי לְעוֹלָם חַסְדּוֹ:	הוֹדוּ לֵאלֹהֵי הָאֱלֹהִים
כִּי לְעוֹלָם חַסְדּוֹ:	הוֹדוּ לַאֲדֹנֵי הָאֲדֹנִים
כִּי לְעוֹלָם חַסְדּוֹ:	לְעֹשֵׂה נִפְלָאוֹת גְּדֹלוֹת לְבַדּוֹ
כִּי לְעוֹלָם חַסְדּוֹ:	לְעֹשֵׂה הַשָּׁמַיִם בִּתְבוּנָה
כִּי לְעוֹלָם חַסְדּוֹ:	לְרֹקַע הָאָרֶץ עַל־הַמָּיִם
כִּי לְעוֹלָם חַסְדּוֹ:	לְעֹשֵׂה אוֹרִים גְּדֹלִים
כִּי לְעוֹלָם חַסְדּוֹ:	אֶת־הַשֶּׁמֶשׁ לְמֶמְשֶׁלֶת בַּיּוֹם
כִּי לְעוֹלָם חַסְדּוֹ:	אֶת־הַיָּרֵחַ וְכוֹכָבִים לְמֶמְשְׁלוֹת בַּלָּיְלָה
כִּי לְעוֹלָם חַסְדּוֹ:	לְמַכֵּה מִצְרַיִם בִּבְכוֹרֵיהֶם
כִּי לְעוֹלָם חַסְדּוֹ:	וַיּוֹצֵא יִשְׂרָאֵל מִתּוֹכָם
כִּי לְעוֹלָם חַסְדּוֹ:	בְּיָד חֲזָקָה וּבִזְרוֹעַ נְטוּיָה

Who split the Reed Sea into parts,	His loving-kindness is for ever.
And made Israel pass through it,	His loving-kindness is for ever.
Casting Pharaoh and his army into the Reed Sea;	His loving-kindness is for ever.
Who led His people through the wilderness;	His loving-kindness is for ever.
Who struck down great kings,	His loving-kindness is for ever.
And slew mighty kings,	His loving-kindness is for ever.
Siḥon, King of the Amorites,	His loving-kindness is for ever.
And Og, King of Bashan,	His loving-kindness is for ever.
And gave their land as a heritage,	His loving-kindness is for ever.
A heritage for His servant Israel;	His loving-kindness is for ever.
Who remembered us in our lowly state,	His loving-kindness is for ever.
And rescued us from our tormentors,	His loving-kindness is for ever.
‣ Who gives food to all flesh,	His loving-kindness is for ever.
Give thanks to the God of heaven.	His loving-kindness is for ever.

רַנְּנוּ Sing joyfully to the Lord, you righteous, for praise from the *Ps. 33* upright is seemly. Give thanks to the Lord with the harp; make music to Him on the ten-stringed lute. Sing Him a new song, play skillfully with shouts of joy. For the Lord's word is right, and all His deeds are done in faith. He loves righteousness and justice; the earth is full of the Lord's loving-kindness. By the Lord's word the heavens were made, and all their starry host by the breath of His mouth. He gathers the sea waters as a heap, and places the deep in storehouses. Let all the earth fear the Lord, and all the world's inhabitants stand in awe of Him. For He spoke, and it was; He commanded, and it stood firm. The Lord foils the plans of nations; He thwarts the intentions of peoples. The Lord's plans stand for ever, His heart's intents for all generations. Happy is the nation whose God is the Lord, the people He has chosen as His own. From heaven the Lord looks down and sees all mankind; from His dwelling place He oversees all who live on earth. He forms the hearts of all, and discerns all their deeds. No king is saved by the size of his army; no warrior is

לְגֹזֵר יַם־סוּף לִגְזָרִים	כִּי לְעוֹלָם חַסְדּוֹ:
וְהֶעֱבִיר יִשְׂרָאֵל בְּתוֹכוֹ	כִּי לְעוֹלָם חַסְדּוֹ:
וְנִעֵר פַּרְעֹה וְחֵילוֹ בְיַם־סוּף	כִּי לְעוֹלָם חַסְדּוֹ:
לְמוֹלִיךְ עַמּוֹ בַּמִּדְבָּר	כִּי לְעוֹלָם חַסְדּוֹ:
לְמַכֵּה מְלָכִים גְּדֹלִים	כִּי לְעוֹלָם חַסְדּוֹ:
וַיַּהֲרֹג מְלָכִים אַדִּירִים	כִּי לְעוֹלָם חַסְדּוֹ:
לְסִיחוֹן מֶלֶךְ הָאֱמֹרִי	כִּי לְעוֹלָם חַסְדּוֹ:
וּלְעוֹג מֶלֶךְ הַבָּשָׁן	כִּי לְעוֹלָם חַסְדּוֹ:
וְנָתַן אַרְצָם לְנַחֲלָה	כִּי לְעוֹלָם חַסְדּוֹ:
נַחֲלָה לְיִשְׂרָאֵל עַבְדּוֹ	כִּי לְעוֹלָם חַסְדּוֹ:
שֶׁבְּשִׁפְלֵנוּ זָכַר לָנוּ	כִּי לְעוֹלָם חַסְדּוֹ:
וַיִּפְרְקֵנוּ מִצָּרֵינוּ	כִּי לְעוֹלָם חַסְדּוֹ:
‹ נֹתֵן לֶחֶם לְכָל־בָּשָׂר	כִּי לְעוֹלָם חַסְדּוֹ:
הוֹדוּ לְאֵל הַשָּׁמָיִם	כִּי לְעוֹלָם חַסְדּוֹ:

רַנְּנוּ צַדִּיקִים בַּיהוה, לַיְשָׁרִים נָאוָה תְהִלָּה: הוֹדוּ לַיהוה בְּכִנּוֹר, תהלים לג
בְּנֵבֶל עָשׂוֹר זַמְּרוּ־לוֹ: שִׁירוּ־לוֹ שִׁיר חָדָשׁ, הֵיטִיבוּ נַגֵּן בִּתְרוּעָה:
כִּי־יָשָׁר דְּבַר־יהוה, וְכָל־מַעֲשֵׂהוּ בֶּאֱמוּנָה: אֹהֵב צְדָקָה וּמִשְׁפָּט,
חֶסֶד יהוה מָלְאָה הָאָרֶץ: בִּדְבַר יהוה שָׁמַיִם נַעֲשׂוּ, וּבְרוּחַ פִּיו
כָּל־צְבָאָם: כֹּנֵס כַּנֵּד מֵי הַיָּם, נֹתֵן בְּאוֹצָרוֹת תְּהוֹמוֹת: יִירְאוּ
מֵיהוה כָּל־הָאָרֶץ, מִמֶּנּוּ יָגוּרוּ כָּל־יֹשְׁבֵי תֵבֵל: כִּי הוּא אָמַר
וַיֶּהִי, הוּא־צִוָּה וַיַּעֲמֹד: יהוה הֵפִיר עֲצַת־גּוֹיִם, הֵנִיא מַחְשְׁבוֹת
עַמִּים: עֲצַת יהוה לְעוֹלָם תַּעֲמֹד, מַחְשְׁבוֹת לִבּוֹ לְדֹר וָדֹר:
אַשְׁרֵי הַגּוֹי אֲשֶׁר־יהוה אֱלֹהָיו, הָעָם בָּחַר לְנַחֲלָה לוֹ: מִשָּׁמַיִם
הִבִּיט יהוה, רָאָה אֶת־כָּל־בְּנֵי הָאָדָם: מִמְּכוֹן־שִׁבְתּוֹ הִשְׁגִּיחַ,

delivered by great strength. A horse is a vain hope for deliverance; despite its great strength, it cannot save. The eye of the Lord is on those who fear Him, on those who place their hope in His unfailing love, to rescue their soul from death, and keep them alive in famine. Our soul waits for the Lord; He is our Help and Shield. ‣ In Him our hearts rejoice, for we trust in His holy name. Let Your unfailing love be upon us, Lord, as we have put our hope in You.

מִזְמוֹר שִׁיר A psalm. A song for the Sabbath day. It is good to thank the Lord and sing psalms to Your name, Most High – to tell of Your loving-kindness in the morning and Your faithfulness at night, to the music of the ten-stringed lyre and the melody of the harp. For You have made me rejoice by Your work, O Lord; I sing for joy at the deeds of Your hands. How great are Your deeds, Lord, and how very deep Your thoughts. A boor cannot know, nor can a fool understand, that though the wicked spring up like grass and all evildoers flourish, it is only that they may be destroyed for ever. But You, Lord, are eternally exalted. For behold Your enemies, Lord, behold Your enemies will perish; all evildoers will be scattered. You have raised my pride like that of a wild ox; I am anointed with fresh oil. My eyes shall look in triumph on my adversaries, my ears shall hear the downfall of the wicked who rise against me. ‣ The righteous will flourish like a palm tree and grow tall like a cedar in Lebanon. Planted in the Lord's House, blossoming in our God's courtyards, they will still bear fruit in old age, and stay vigorous and fresh, proclaiming that the Lord is upright: He is my Rock, in whom there is no wrong. *Ps. 92*

יהוה מָלָךְ The Lord reigns. He is robed in majesty. The Lord is robed, girded with strength. The world is firmly established; it cannot be moved. Your throne stands firm as of old; You are eternal. Rivers lift up, Lord, rivers lift up their voice, rivers lift up their Crashing waves. ‣ Mightier than the noise of many waters, than the mighty waves of the sea is the Lord on high. Your testimonies are very sure; holiness adorns Your House, Lord, for evermore. *Ps. 93*

Continue with the weekday service, from "May the Lord's glory" on page 78.

אֶל כָּל־יֹשְׁבֵי הָאָרֶץ: הַיֹּצֵר יַחַד לִבָּם, הַמֵּבִין אֶל־כָּל־מַעֲשֵׂיהֶם:
אֵין־הַמֶּלֶךְ נוֹשָׁע בְּרָב־חָיִל, גִּבּוֹר לֹא־יִנָּצֵל בְּרָב־כֹּחַ: שֶׁקֶר
הַסּוּס לִתְשׁוּעָה, וּבְרֹב חֵילוֹ לֹא יְמַלֵּט: הִנֵּה עֵין יהוה אֶל־יְרֵאָיו,
לַמְיַחֲלִים לְחַסְדּוֹ: לְהַצִּיל מִמָּוֶת נַפְשָׁם, וּלְחַיּוֹתָם בָּרָעָב: נַפְשֵׁנוּ
חִכְּתָה לַיהוה, עֶזְרֵנוּ וּמָגִנֵּנוּ הוּא: כִּי־בוֹ יִשְׂמַח לִבֵּנוּ, כִּי בְשֵׁם
קָדְשׁוֹ בָטָחְנוּ: יְהִי־חַסְדְּךָ יהוה עָלֵינוּ, כַּאֲשֶׁר יִחַלְנוּ לָךְ:

מִזְמוֹר שִׁיר לְיוֹם הַשַּׁבָּת: טוֹב לְהֹדוֹת לַיהוה, וּלְזַמֵּר לְשִׁמְךָ **תהלים צב**
עֶלְיוֹן: לְהַגִּיד בַּבֹּקֶר חַסְדֶּךָ, וֶאֱמוּנָתְךָ בַּלֵּילוֹת: עֲלֵי־עָשׂוֹר
וַעֲלֵי־נָבֶל, עֲלֵי הִגָּיוֹן בְּכִנּוֹר: כִּי שִׂמַּחְתַּנִי יהוה בְּפָעֳלֶךָ, בְּמַעֲשֵׂי
יָדֶיךָ אֲרַנֵּן: מַה־גָּדְלוּ מַעֲשֶׂיךָ יהוה, מְאֹד עָמְקוּ מַחְשְׁבֹתֶיךָ:
אִישׁ־בַּעַר לֹא יֵדָע, וּכְסִיל לֹא־יָבִין אֶת־זֹאת: בִּפְרֹחַ רְשָׁעִים
כְּמוֹ עֵשֶׂב, וַיָּצִיצוּ כָּל־פֹּעֲלֵי אָוֶן, לְהִשָּׁמְדָם עֲדֵי־עַד: וְאַתָּה
מָרוֹם לְעֹלָם יהוה: כִּי הִנֵּה אֹיְבֶיךָ יהוה, כִּי־הִנֵּה אֹיְבֶיךָ יֹאבֵדוּ,
יִתְפָּרְדוּ כָּל־פֹּעֲלֵי אָוֶן: וַתָּרֶם כִּרְאֵים קַרְנִי, בַּלֹּתִי בְּשֶׁמֶן רַעֲנָן:
וַתַּבֵּט עֵינִי בְּשׁוּרָי, בַּקָּמִים עָלַי מְרֵעִים תִּשְׁמַעְנָה אָזְנָי: צַדִּיק
כַּתָּמָר יִפְרָח, כְּאֶרֶז בַּלְּבָנוֹן יִשְׂגֶּה: שְׁתוּלִים בְּבֵית יהוה, בְּחַצְרוֹת
אֱלֹהֵינוּ יַפְרִיחוּ: עוֹד יְנוּבוּן בְּשֵׂיבָה, דְּשֵׁנִים וְרַעֲנַנִּים יִהְיוּ: לְהַגִּיד
כִּי־יָשָׁר יהוה, צוּרִי, וְלֹא־עַוְלָתָה בּוֹ:

יהוה מָלָךְ, גֵּאוּת לָבֵשׁ, לָבֵשׁ יהוה עֹז הִתְאַזָּר, אַף־תִּכּוֹן תֵּבֵל **תהלים צג**
בַּל־תִּמּוֹט: נָכוֹן כִּסְאֲךָ מֵאָז, מֵעוֹלָם אָתָּה: נָשְׂאוּ נְהָרוֹת יהוה,
נָשְׂאוּ נְהָרוֹת קוֹלָם, יִשְׂאוּ נְהָרוֹת דָּכְיָם: ‹ מִקֹּלוֹת מַיִם רַבִּים,
אַדִּירִים מִשְׁבְּרֵי־יָם, אַדִּיר בַּמָּרוֹם יהוה: עֵדֹתֶיךָ נֶאֶמְנוּ מְאֹד
לְבֵיתְךָ נַאֲוָה־קֹדֶשׁ, יהוה לְאֹרֶךְ יָמִים:

Continue with the weekday service, from יְהִי כְבוֹד *on page 79.*

REMOVING THE TORAH FROM THE ARK
HOSHANA RABA

אֵין כָּמוֹךָ There is none like You among the heavenly powers, *Ps. 86*
LORD, and there are no works like Yours.
Your kingdom is an eternal kingdom, *Ps. 145*
and Your dominion is for all generations.

The LORD is King, the LORD was King,
the LORD shall be King for ever and all time.
The LORD will give strength to His people; *Ps. 29*
the LORD will bless His people with peace.

Father of compassion,
favor Zion with Your goodness; rebuild the walls of Jerusalem. *Ps. 51*
For we trust in You alone, King, God, high and exalted, Master of worlds.

The Ark is opened and the congregation stands. All say:

וַיְהִי בִּנְסֹעַ Whenever the Ark set out, Moses would say, *Num. 10*
"Arise, LORD, and may Your enemies be scattered.
May those who hate You flee before You."
For the Torah shall come forth from Zion, *Is. 2*
and the word of the LORD from Jerusalem.
Blessed is He who in His Holiness gave the Torah to His people Israel.

Say the following verses three times:

יהוה The LORD, the LORD, compassionate and gracious God, *Ex. 34*
slow to anger, abounding in loving-kindness and truth,
extending loving-kindness to a thousand generations,
forgiving iniquity, rebellion and sin, and absolving [the guilty who repent].

Master of the Universe, fulfill my requests for good. Satisfy my desire, grant my request, and pardon me for all my iniquities and all iniquities of the members of my household, with the pardon of loving-kindness and compassion. Purify us from our sins, our iniquities and our transgressions; remember us with a memory of favorable deeds before You and be mindful of us in salvation and compassion. Remember us for a good life, for peace, for livelihood and sustenance, for bread to eat and clothes to wear, for wealth, honor and length of days dedicated to Your Torah and its commandments. Grant us discernment and understanding that we may understand and discern its deep secrets. Send healing for all our pain, and bless all the work of our hands. Ordain for us decrees of good, salvation and consolation, and nullify all hard and harsh decrees against us. And may the hearts of the government, its advisers and ministers / *in Israel:* And may the hearts of our ministers and their advisers, / be favorable toward us. Amen. May this be Your will.

הוצאת ספר תורה
הושענא רבה

תהלים פו

אֵין־כָּמוֹךָ בָאֱלֹהִים, אֲדֹנָי, וְאֵין כְּמַעֲשֶׂיךָ:

תהלים קמה

מַלְכוּתְךָ מַלְכוּת כָּל־עֹלָמִים, וּמֶמְשַׁלְתְּךָ בְּכָל־דּוֹר וָדֹר:

יהוה מֶלֶךְ, יהוה מָלָךְ, יהוה יִמְלֹךְ לְעֹלָם וָעֶד.

תהלים כט

יהוה עֹז לְעַמּוֹ יִתֵּן, יהוה יְבָרֵךְ אֶת־עַמּוֹ בַשָּׁלוֹם:

תהלים נא

אַב הָרַחֲמִים, הֵיטִיבָה בִרְצוֹנְךָ אֶת־צִיּוֹן תִּבְנֶה חוֹמוֹת יְרוּשָׁלָםִ:
כִּי בְךָ לְבַד בָּטָחְנוּ, מֶלֶךְ אֵל רָם וְנִשָּׂא, אֲדוֹן עוֹלָמִים.

The ארון קודש is opened and the קהל stands. All say:

במדבר י

וַיְהִי בִּנְסֹעַ הָאָרֹן וַיֹּאמֶר מֹשֶׁה
קוּמָה יהוה וְיָפֻצוּ אֹיְבֶיךָ וְיָנֻסוּ מְשַׂנְאֶיךָ מִפָּנֶיךָ:

ישעיה ב

כִּי מִצִּיּוֹן תֵּצֵא תוֹרָה וּדְבַר־יהוה מִירוּשָׁלָםִ:
בָּרוּךְ שֶׁנָּתַן תּוֹרָה לְעַמּוֹ יִשְׂרָאֵל בִּקְדֻשָּׁתוֹ.

Say the following verses three times:

שמות לד

יהוה, יהוה, אֵל רַחוּם וְחַנּוּן, אֶרֶךְ אַפַּיִם וְרַב־חֶסֶד וֶאֱמֶת:
נֹצֵר חֶסֶד לָאֲלָפִים, נֹשֵׂא עָוֹן וָפֶשַׁע וְחַטָּאָה, וְנַקֵּה:

רִבּוֹנוֹ שֶׁל עוֹלָם, מַלֵּא מִשְׁאֲלוֹתַי לְטוֹבָה, וְהָפֵק רְצוֹנִי וְתֵן שְׁאֵלָתִי, וּמְחֹל לִי עַל
כָּל עֲוֹנוֹתַי וְעַל כָּל עֲוֹנוֹת אַנְשֵׁי בֵיתִי, מְחִילָה בְּחֶסֶד מְחִילָה בְּרַחֲמִים, וְטַהֲרֵנוּ
מֵחֲטָאֵינוּ וּמֵעֲוֹנוֹתֵינוּ וּמִפְּשָׁעֵינוּ, וְזָכְרֵנוּ בְּזִכְרוֹן טוֹב לְפָנֶיךָ, וּפָקְדֵנוּ בִּפְקֻדַּת יְשׁוּעָה
וְרַחֲמִים. וְזָכְרֵנוּ לְחַיִּים טוֹבִים וּלְשָׁלוֹם, וּפַרְנָסָה וְכַלְכָּלָה, וְלֶחֶם לֶאֱכֹל וּבֶגֶד לִלְבֹּשׁ,
וְעֹשֶׁר וְכָבוֹד, וְאֹרֶךְ יָמִים לַהֲגוֹת בְּתוֹרָתֶךָ וּלְקַיֵּם מִצְוֹתֶיהָ, וְשֵׂכֶל וּבִינָה לְהָבִין
וּלְהַשְׂכִּיל עִמְקֵי סוֹדוֹתֶיהָ. וְהָפֵק רְפוּאָה לְכָל מַכְאוֹבֵינוּ, וּבָרֵךְ כָּל מַעֲשֵׂה יָדֵינוּ,
וּגְזֹר עָלֵינוּ גְּזֵרוֹת טוֹבוֹת יְשׁוּעוֹת וְנֶחָמוֹת, וּבַטֵּל מֵעָלֵינוּ כָּל גְּזֵרוֹת קָשׁוֹת וְרָעוֹת,
וְתֵן בְּלֵב הַמַּלְכוּת וְיוֹעֲצֶיהָ וְשָׂרֶיהָ /בארץ ישראל: וְתֵן בְּלֵב שָׂרֵינוּ וְיוֹעֲצֵינוּ/ עָלֵינוּ לְטוֹבָה.
אָמֵן וְכֵן יְהִי רָצוֹן.

יִהְיוּ **May** the words of my mouth and the meditation of my heart *Ps. 19*
find favor before You, LORD, my Rock and Redeemer.

Say the following verse three times:

וַאֲנִי **As** for me, may my prayer come to You, LORD, *Ps. 69*
at a time of favor. O God, in Your great love,
answer me with Your faithful salvation.

Continue:

Blessed is the name of the Master of the Universe. Blessed is Your crown *Zohar,*
and Your place. May Your favor always be with Your people Israel. Show *Vayak-hel*
Your people the salvation of Your right hand in Your Temple. Grant us the
gift of Your good light, and accept our prayers in mercy. May it be Your will
to prolong our life in goodness. May I be counted among the righteous, so
that You will have compassion on me and protect me and all that is mine and
all that is Your people Israel's. You feed all; You sustain all; You rule over all;
You rule over kings, for sovereignty is Yours. I am a servant of the Holy One,
blessed be He, before whom and before whose glorious Torah I bow at all
times. Not in man do I trust, nor on any angel do I rely, but on the God of
heaven who is the God of truth, whose Torah is truth, whose prophets speak
truth, and who abounds in acts of love and truth. ‣ In Him I trust, and to His
holy and glorious name I offer praises. May it be Your will to open my heart
to the Torah, and to fulfill the wishes of my heart and of the hearts of all Your
people Israel for good, for life, and for peace.

The Leader takes the Torah scroll in his right arm. Leader then congregation:

Listen, Israel: the LORD is our God, the LORD is One. *Deut. 6*

Leader then congregation:

One is our God; great is our Master;
holy and awesome is His name.

The Leader turns to face the Ark, bows and says:

Magnify the LORD with me, and let us exalt His name together. *Ps. 34*

The Ark is closed. The Leader carries the Torah scroll to the bima and the congregation says:

לְךָ **Yours,** LORD, are the greatness and the power, the glory and the *1 Chr. 29*
majesty and splendor, for everything in heaven and earth is Yours.
Yours, LORD, is the kingdom; You are exalted as Head over all.

תהלים יט

יִהְיוּ לְרָצוֹן אִמְרֵי־פִי וְהֶגְיוֹן לִבִּי לְפָנֶיךָ, יהוה צוּרִי וְגֹאֲלִי:

Say the following verse three times:

תהלים סט

וַאֲנִי תְפִלָּתִי־לְךָ יהוה, עֵת רָצוֹן, אֱלֹהִים בְּרָב־חַסְדֶּךָ עֲנֵנִי בֶּאֱמֶת יִשְׁעֶךָ:

Continue:

זוהר ויקהל

בְּרִיךְ שְׁמֵהּ דְּמָרֵא עָלְמָא, בְּרִיךְ כִּתְרָךְ וְאַתְרָךְ. יְהֵא רְעוּתָךְ עִם עַמָּךְ יִשְׂרָאֵל לְעָלַם, וּפֻרְקָן יְמִינָךְ אַחֲזֵי לְעַמָּךְ בְּבֵית מַקְדְּשָׁךְ, וּלְאַמְטוֹיֵי לָנָא מִטּוּב נְהוֹרָךְ, וּלְקַבֵּל צְלוֹתָנָא בְּרַחֲמִין. יְהֵא רַעֲוָא קֳדָמָךְ דְּתוֹרִיךְ לַן חַיִּין בְּטִיבוּ, וְלֶהֱוֵי אֲנָא פְקִידָא בְּגוֹ צַדִּיקַיָּא, לְמִרְחַם עֲלַי וּלְמִנְטַר יָתִי וְיָת כָּל דִּי לִי וְדִי לְעַמָּךְ יִשְׂרָאֵל. אַנְתְּ הוּא זָן לְכֹלָּא וּמְפַרְנֵס לְכֹלָּא, אַנְתְּ הוּא שַׁלִּיט עַל כֹּלָּא, אַנְתְּ הוּא דְּשַׁלִּיט עַל מַלְכַיָּא, וּמַלְכוּתָא דִּילָךְ הִיא. אֲנָא עַבְדָּא דְקֻדְשָׁא בְּרִיךְ הוּא, דְּסָגִדְנָא קַמֵּהּ וּמִקַּמֵּי דִּיקַר אוֹרַיְתֵהּ בְּכָל עִדָּן וְעִדָּן. לָא עַל אֱנָשׁ רָחִיצְנָא וְלָא עַל בַּר אֱלָהִין סָמִיכְנָא, אֶלָּא בֶּאֱלָהָא דִשְׁמַיָּא, דְּהוּא אֱלָהָא קְשׁוֹט, וְאוֹרַיְתֵהּ קְשׁוֹט, וּנְבִיאוֹהִי קְשׁוֹט, וּמַסְגֵּא לְמֶעְבַּד טָבְוָן וּקְשׁוֹט. ◆ בֵּהּ אֲנָא רָחִיץ, וְלִשְׁמֵהּ קַדִּישָׁא יַקִּירָא אֲנָא אֵמַר תֻּשְׁבְּחָן. יְהֵא רַעֲוָא קֳדָמָךְ דְּתִפְתַּח לִבָּאִי בְּאוֹרַיְתָא, וְתַשְׁלִים מִשְׁאֲלִין דְּלִבָּאִי וְלִבָּא דְכָל עַמָּךְ יִשְׂרָאֵל לְטָב וּלְחַיִּין וְלִשְׁלָם.

The שליח ציבור takes the ספר תורה in his right arm. קהל *then* שליח ציבור:

דברים ו

שְׁמַע יִשְׂרָאֵל, יהוה אֱלֹהֵינוּ, יהוה אֶחָד:

קהל *then* שליח ציבור:

אֶחָד אֱלֹהֵינוּ, גָּדוֹל אֲדוֹנֵינוּ, קָדוֹשׁ וְנוֹרָא שְׁמוֹ.

The שליח ציבור turns to face the ארון קודש, bows and says:

תהלים לד

גַּדְּלוּ לַיהוה אִתִּי וּנְרוֹמְמָה שְׁמוֹ יַחְדָּו:

The ארון קודש is closed. The שליח ציבור carries the ספר תורה to the בימה and the קהל *says:*

דברי הימים א' כט

לְךָ יהוה הַגְּדֻלָּה וְהַגְּבוּרָה וְהַתִּפְאֶרֶת וְהַנֵּצַח וְהַהוֹד, כִּי־כֹל בַּשָּׁמַיִם וּבָאָרֶץ, לְךָ יהוה הַמַּמְלָכָה וְהַמִּתְנַשֵּׂא לְכֹל לְרֹאשׁ:

רוֹמְמוּ Exalt the Lᴏʀᴅ our God and bow to His footstool; He is holy. *Ps. 99*
Exalt the Lᴏʀᴅ our God, and bow at His holy mountain, for holy
is the Lᴏʀᴅ our God.

Over all may the name of the Supreme King of kings, the Holy One blessed be
He, be magnified and sanctified, praised and glorified, exalted and extolled, in the
worlds that He has created – this world and the World to Come – in accordance
with His will, and the will of those who fear Him, and the will of the whole house
of Israel. He is the Rock of worlds, Lᴏʀᴅ of all creatures, God of all souls, who
dwells in the spacious heights and inhabits the high heavens of old. His holiness is
over the Ḥayyot and over the throne of glory. Therefore may Your name, Lᴏʀᴅ our
God, be sanctified among us in the sight of all that lives. Let us sing before Him a
new song, as it is written: "Sing to God, make music for His name, extol Him who *Ps. 68*
rides the clouds – the Lᴏʀᴅ is His name – and exult before Him." And may we see
Him eye to eye when He returns to His abode as it is written: "For they shall see *Is. 52*
eye to eye when the Lᴏʀᴅ returns to Zion." And it is said: "Then will the glory of *Is. 40*
the Lᴏʀᴅ be revealed, and all mankind together shall see that the mouth of the
Lᴏʀᴅ has spoken."

Father of mercy, have compassion on the people borne by Him. May He remember
the covenant with the mighty (patriarchs), and deliver us from evil times. May
He reproach the evil instinct in the people by Him, and graciously grant that we
be an eternal remnant. May He fulfil in good measure our requests for salvation
and compassion.

The Torah scroll is placed on the bima and the Gabbai calls a Kohen to the Torah.

וְיַעֲזוֹר May He help, shield and save all who seek refuge in Him, and let us say:
Amen. Let us all render greatness to our God and give honor to the Torah.
*Let the Kohen come forward. Arise (*name* son of *father's name*), the Kohen.

*If no Kohen is present, a Levi or Yisrael is called up as follows:
/As there is no Kohen, arise (name son of father's name) in place of a Kohen./

Blessed is He who, in His holiness, gave the Torah to His people Israel.

The congregation followed by the Gabbai:
You who cling to the Lᴏʀᴅ your God are all alive today. *Deut. 4*

The Torah portion for Hoshana Raba is found on page 773.
For the blessings of the Oleh turn to page 222.

‏רוֹמְמוּ יְהוָה אֱלֹהֵינוּ וְהִשְׁתַּחֲווּ לַהֲדֹם רַגְלָיו, קָדוֹשׁ הוּא: רוֹמְמוּ‏ ‏תהלים צט‏
‏יְהוָה אֱלֹהֵינוּ וְהִשְׁתַּחֲווּ לְהַר קָדְשׁוֹ, כִּי־קָדוֹשׁ יְהוָה אֱלֹהֵינוּ:‏

‏עַל הַכֹּל יִתְגַּדַּל וְיִתְקַדַּשׁ וְיִשְׁתַּבַּח וְיִתְפָּאַר וְיִתְרוֹמַם וְיִתְנַשֵּׂא שְׁמוֹ שֶׁל מֶלֶךְ‏
‏מַלְכֵי הַמְּלָכִים הַקָּדוֹשׁ בָּרוּךְ הוּא בָּעוֹלָמוֹת שֶׁבָּרָא, הָעוֹלָם הַזֶּה וְהָעוֹלָם‏
‏הַבָּא, כִּרְצוֹנוֹ וְכִרְצוֹן יְרֵאָיו וְכִרְצוֹן כָּל בֵּית יִשְׂרָאֵל. צוּר הָעוֹלָמִים, אֲדוֹן כָּל‏
‏הַבְּרִיּוֹת, אֱלוֹהַּ כָּל הַנְּפָשׁוֹת, הַיּוֹשֵׁב בְּמֶרְחֲבֵי מָרוֹם, הַשּׁוֹכֵן בִּשְׁמֵי שְׁמֵי קֶדֶם,‏
‏קְדֻשָּׁתוֹ עַל הַחַיּוֹת, וּקְדֻשָּׁתוֹ עַל כִּסֵּא הַכָּבוֹד. וּבְכֵן יִתְקַדַּשׁ שִׁמְךָ בָּנוּ יְהוָה‏
‏אֱלֹהֵינוּ לְעֵינֵי כָּל חָי, וְנֹאמַר לְפָנָיו שִׁיר חָדָשׁ, כַּכָּתוּב: שִׁירוּ לֵאלֹהִים זַמְּרוּ‏ ‏תהלים סח‏
‏שְׁמוֹ, סֹלּוּ לָרֹכֵב בָּעֲרָבוֹת, בְּיָהּ שְׁמוֹ, וְעִלְזוּ לְפָנָיו: וְנִרְאֵהוּ עַיִן בְּעַיִן בְּשׁוּבוֹ אֶל‏
‏נָוֵהוּ, כַּכָּתוּב: כִּי עַיִן בְּעַיִן יִרְאוּ בְּשׁוּב יְהוָה צִיּוֹן: וְנֶאֱמַר: וְנִגְלָה כְּבוֹד יְהוָה,‏ ‏ישעיה נב‏
‏וְרָאוּ כָל־בָּשָׂר יַחְדָּו כִּי פִּי יְהוָה דִּבֵּר:‏

‏אַב הָרַחֲמִים הוּא יְרַחֵם עַם עֲמוּסִים, וְיִזְכֹּר בְּרִית אֵיתָנִים, וְיַצִּיל נַפְשׁוֹתֵינוּ מִן‏
‏הַשָּׁעוֹת הָרָעוֹת, וְיִגְעַר בְּיֵצֶר הָרָע מִן הַנְּשׂוּאִים, וְיָחֹן אוֹתָנוּ לִפְלֵיטַת עוֹלָמִים,‏
‏וִימַלֵּא מִשְׁאֲלוֹתֵינוּ בְּמִדָּה טוֹבָה יְשׁוּעָה וְרַחֲמִים.‏

The ‏ספר תורה‏ *is placed on the* ‏שׁוּלְחָן‏ *and the* ‏גבאי‏ *calls a* ‏כהן‏ *to the* ‏תורה‏.

‏וְיַעֲזֹר וְיָגֵן וְיוֹשִׁיעַ לְכָל הַחוֹסִים בּוֹ, וְנֹאמַר אָמֵן. הַכֹּל הָבוּ גֹדֶל לֵאלֹהֵינוּ‏
‏וּתְנוּ כָבוֹד לַתּוֹרָה.‏ *‏כֹּהֵן קְרָב, יַעֲמֹד‏ (‏פלוני בֶּן פלוני‏) ‏הַכֹּהֵן.‏

*If no ‏כהן‏ *is present, a* ‏לוי‏ *or* ‏ישראל‏ *is called up as follows:*

‏/אִם כָּאן כֹּהֵן, יַעֲמֹד‏ (‏פלוני בֶּן פלוני‏) ‏בִּמְקוֹם כֹּהֵן./‏

‏בָּרוּךְ שֶׁנָּתַן תּוֹרָה לְעַמּוֹ יִשְׂרָאֵל בִּקְדֻשָּׁתוֹ.‏

The ‏קהל‏ *followed by the* ‏גבאי‏:

‏וְאַתֶּם הַדְּבֵקִים בַּיהוָה אֱלֹהֵיכֶם חַיִּים כֻּלְּכֶם הַיּוֹם:‏ ‏דברים ד‏

The ‏תורה‏ *portion for* ‏הושענא רבה‏ *is found on page 773.*
For the blessings of the ‏עולה‏ *turn to page 223.*

Musaf for Ḥol HaMo'ed

The following prayer, until "in former years" on page 520, is said silently, standing
with feet together. If there is a minyan, the Amida is repeated aloud by the Leader.
Take three steps forward and at the points indicated by ˅, bend the knees at the first word,
bow at the second, and stand straight before saying God's name.

When I proclaim the LORD's name, give glory to our God.   *Deut. 32*
O LORD, open my lips, so that my mouth may declare Your praise.   *Ps. 51*

PATRIARCHS

˅בָּרוּךְ Blessed are You, LORD our God and God of our fathers,
God of Abraham, God of Isaac and God of Jacob;
the great, mighty and awesome God, God Most High,
who bestows acts of loving-kindness and creates all,
who remembers the loving-kindness of the fathers
and will bring a Redeemer to their children's children
for the sake of His name, in love. King, Helper, Savior, Shield:
˅Blessed are You, LORD, Shield of Abraham.

DIVINE MIGHT

אַתָּה גִבּוֹר You are eternally mighty, LORD.
You give life to the dead and have great power to save.

In Israel: He causes the dew to fall.

He sustains the living with loving-kindness,
and with great compassion revives the dead.
He supports the fallen, heals the sick, sets captives free,
and keeps His faith with those who sleep in the dust.
Who is like You, Master of might,
and who can compare to You,
O King who brings death and gives life,
and makes salvation grow?
Faithful are You to revive the dead.
Blessed are You, LORD, who revives the dead.

When saying the Amida silently, continue with "You are holy" on page 506.
The Kedusha for Ḥoshana Raba is on the next page;
the Kedusha for Ḥol HaMo'ed is on page 506.

מוסף לחול המועד

The following prayer, until קְדֻשְׁה *on page 521, is said silently, standing with*
feet together. If there is a מנין*, the* עמידה *is repeated aloud by the* שליח ציבור*.*
Take three steps forward and at the points indicated by ׳*, bend the knees at the first word,*
bow at the second, and stand straight before saying God's name.

דברים לב
תהלים נא

כִּי שֵׁם יהוה אֶקְרָא, הָבוּ גֹדֶל לֵאלֹהֵינוּ:
אֲדֹנָי, שְׂפָתַי תִּפְתָּח, וּפִי יַגִּיד תְּהִלָּתֶךָ:

אבות

יָּבָרוּךְ אַתָּה יהוה, אֱלֹהֵינוּ וֵאלֹהֵי אֲבוֹתֵינוּ
אֱלֹהֵי אַבְרָהָם, אֱלֹהֵי יִצְחָק, וֵאלֹהֵי יַעֲקֹב
הָאֵל הַגָּדוֹל הַגִּבּוֹר וְהַנּוֹרָא, אֵל עֶלְיוֹן
גּוֹמֵל חֲסָדִים טוֹבִים, וְקֹנֵה הַכֹּל, וְזוֹכֵר חַסְדֵי אָבוֹת
וּמֵבִיא גוֹאֵל לִבְנֵי בְנֵיהֶם לְמַעַן שְׁמוֹ בְּאַהֲבָה.
מֶלֶךְ עוֹזֵר וּמוֹשִׁיעַ וּמָגֵן.
יָּבָרוּךְ אַתָּה יהוה, מָגֵן אַבְרָהָם.

גבורות

אַתָּה גִּבּוֹר לְעוֹלָם, אֲדֹנָי
מְחַיֵּה מֵתִים אַתָּה, רַב לְהוֹשִׁיעַ
בארץ ישראל: מוֹרִיד הַטָּל
מְכַלְכֵּל חַיִּים בְּחֶסֶד, מְחַיֵּה מֵתִים בְּרַחֲמִים רַבִּים
סוֹמֵךְ נוֹפְלִים, וְרוֹפֵא חוֹלִים, וּמַתִּיר אֲסוּרִים
וּמְקַיֵּם אֱמוּנָתוֹ לִישֵׁנֵי עָפָר.
מִי כָמוֹךָ, בַּעַל גְּבוּרוֹת, וּמִי דוֹמֶה לָּךְ
מֶלֶךְ, מֵמִית וּמְחַיֶּה וּמַצְמִיחַ יְשׁוּעָה.
וְנֶאֱמָן אַתָּה לְהַחֲיוֹת מֵתִים.
בָּרוּךְ אַתָּה יהוה, מְחַיֵּה הַמֵּתִים.

When saying the עמידה *silently, continue with* אַתָּה קָדוֹשׁ *on page 507.*
The הושענא רבה *for* חול המועד קדושה *is on the next page; the* קדושה *for* חול המועד *is on page 507.*

KEDUSHA FOR HOSHANA RABA

The following is said standing with feet together,
rising on the toes at the words indicated by ⌃.

Cong. then | נַעֲרִיצְךָ We will revere and sanctify You with the words
Leader: | uttered by the holy Seraphim who sanctify Your name
| in the Sanctuary; as is written by Your prophet:
| "They call out to one another, saying: | *Is. 6*

Cong. then | ⌃Holy, ⌃holy, ⌃holy is the Lord of hosts;
Leader: | the whole world is filled with His glory."
| His glory fills the universe.
| His ministering angels ask each other,
| "Where is the place of His glory?"
| Those facing them reply "Blessed –

Cong. then | ⌃"Blessed is the Lord's glory from His place." | *Ezek. 3*
Leader: | From His place may He turn with compassion
| and be gracious to the people who proclaim the unity of His name,
| morning and evening, every day, continually,
| twice each day reciting in love the Shema.

Cong. then | "Listen, Israel, the Lord is our God, the Lord is One." | *Deut. 6*
Leader: | He is our God, He is our Father, He is our King, He is our Savior –
| and He, in His compassion, will let us hear a second time
| in the presence of all that lives, His promise "to be Your God. | *Num. 15*
| I am the Lord your God."

Cong. then | Glorious is our Glorious One, Lord our Master, and glorious is | *Ps. 8*
Leader: | Your name throughout the earth.
| Then the Lord shall be King over all the earth; | *Zech. 14*
| on that day the Lord shall be One and His name One.

Leader: | And in Your holy Writings it is written:

Cong. then | ⌃"The Lord shall reign for ever. He is your God, Zion, | *Ps. 146*
Leader: | from generation to generation, Halleluya!"

Leader: | From generation to generation we will declare Your greatness,
| and we will proclaim Your holiness for evermore.
| Your praise, our God, shall not leave our mouth forever,
| for You, God, are a great and holy King.
| Blessed are You, Lord, the holy God.

The Leader continues with "You have chosen us" on the next page.

קדושה להושענא רבה

The following is said standing
with feet together, rising on the toes at the words indicated by ^.

קהל then
ש״ץ
נַעֲרִיצְךָ וְנַקְדִּישְׁךָ כְּסוֹד שִׂיחַ שַׂרְפֵי קֹדֶשׁ
הַמַּקְדִּישִׁים שִׁמְךָ בַּקֹּדֶשׁ

ישעיה ו
כַּכָּתוּב עַל יַד נְבִיאֶךָ: וְקָרָא זֶה אֶל־זֶה וְאָמַר

קהל then
ש״ץ
^קָדוֹשׁ, ^קָדוֹשׁ, ^קָדוֹשׁ, יהוה צְבָאוֹת, מְלֹא כָל הָאָרֶץ כְּבוֹדוֹ:
כְּבוֹדוֹ מָלֵא עוֹלָם, מְשָׁרְתָיו שׁוֹאֲלִים זֶה לָזֶה, אַיֵּה מְקוֹם כְּבוֹדוֹ
לְעֻמָּתָם בָּרוּךְ יֹאמֵרוּ

יחזקאל ג
קהל then
ש״ץ
^בָּרוּךְ כְּבוֹד־יהוה מִמְּקוֹמוֹ:
מִמְּקוֹמוֹ הוּא יִפֶן בְּרַחֲמִים, וְיָחֹן עַם הַמְיַחֲדִים שְׁמוֹ
עֶרֶב וָבֹקֶר בְּכָל יוֹם תָּמִיד
פַּעֲמַיִם בְּאַהֲבָה שְׁמַע אוֹמְרִים

דברים ו
קהל then
ש״ץ
שְׁמַע יִשְׂרָאֵל, יהוה אֱלֹהֵינוּ, יהוה אֶחָד:
הוּא אֱלֹהֵינוּ, הוּא אָבִינוּ, הוּא מַלְכֵּנוּ, הוּא מוֹשִׁיעֵנוּ

במדבר טו
וְהוּא יַשְׁמִיעֵנוּ בְּרַחֲמָיו שֵׁנִית לְעֵינֵי כָּל חָי, לִהְיוֹת לָכֶם לֵאלֹהִים
אֲנִי יהוה אֱלֹהֵיכֶם:

תהלים ח
קהל then
ש״ץ
אַדִּיר אַדִּירֵנוּ, יהוה אֲדֹנֵינוּ, מָה־אַדִּיר שִׁמְךָ בְּכָל־הָאָרֶץ:
זכריה יד
וְהָיָה יהוה לְמֶלֶךְ עַל־כָּל־הָאָרֶץ
בַּיּוֹם הַהוּא יִהְיֶה יהוה אֶחָד וּשְׁמוֹ אֶחָד:

ש״ץ
וּבְדִבְרֵי קָדְשְׁךָ כָּתוּב לֵאמֹר

תהלים קמו
קהל then
ש״ץ
יִמְלֹךְ יהוה לְעוֹלָם, אֱלֹהַיִךְ צִיּוֹן לְדֹר וָדֹר, הַלְלוּיָהּ:

ש״ץ
לְדוֹר וָדוֹר נַגִּיד גָּדְלֶךָ, וּלְנֵצַח נְצָחִים קְדֻשָּׁתְךָ נַקְדִּישׁ
וְשִׁבְחֲךָ אֱלֹהֵינוּ מִפִּינוּ לֹא יָמוּשׁ לְעוֹלָם וָעֶד
כִּי אֵל מֶלֶךְ גָּדוֹל וְקָדוֹשׁ אָתָּה.
בָּרוּךְ אַתָּה יהוה, הָאֵל הַקָּדוֹשׁ.

The שליח ציבור *continues with* אַתָּה בְחַרְתָּנוּ *on the next page.*

KEDUSHA FOR ḤOL HAMO'ED

During the Leader's Repetition, the following is said standing
with feet together, rising on the toes at the words indicated by ◦.

Cong. then נְקַדֵּשׁ We will sanctify Your name on earth,
Leader: as they sanctify it in the highest heavens,
as is written by Your prophet,
"And they [the angels] call to one another saying: *Is. 6*

Cong. then ◦Holy, ◦holy, ◦holy is the LORD of hosts
Leader: the whole world is filled with His glory."
Those facing them say "Blessed – "

Cong. then ◦"Blessed is the LORD's glory from His place."   *Ezek. 3*
Leader: And in Your holy Writings it is written thus:

Cong. then ◦"The LORD shall reign for ever.   *Ps. 146*
Leader: He is your God, Zion, from generation to generation,
Halleluya!"

Leader: From generation to generation we will declare Your greatness,
and we will proclaim Your holiness for evermore.
Your praise, our God, shall not leave our mouth forever,
for You, God, are a great and holy King.
Blessed are You, LORD, the holy God.

The Leader continues with "You have chosen us" below.

_____

When saying the Amida silently, continue here with "You are holy":

HOLINESS
אַתָּה קָדוֹשׁ You are holy and Your name is holy,
and holy ones praise You daily, Selah!
Blessed are You, LORD, the holy God.

HOLINESS OF THE DAY
אַתָּה בְחַרְתָּנוּ You have chosen us from among all peoples.
You have loved and favored us.
You have raised us above all tongues.
You have made us holy through Your commandments.
You have brought us near, our King, to Your service,
and have called us by Your great and holy name.

קדושה לחול המועד

During the חזרת הש״ץ, *the following is said standing*
with feet together, rising on the toes at the words indicated by ˙.

קהל
then
ש״ץ

נְקַדֵּשׁ אֶת שִׁמְךָ בָּעוֹלָם, כְּשֵׁם שֶׁמַּקְדִּישִׁים אוֹתוֹ בִּשְׁמֵי מָרוֹם
כַּכָּתוּב עַל יַד נְבִיאֶךָ: וְקָרָא זֶה אֶל־זֶה וְאָמַר

ישעיהו

קהל
then
ש״ץ

˙קָדוֹשׁ, קָדוֹשׁ, קָדוֹשׁ, יהוה צְבָאוֹת, מְלֹא כָל־הָאָרֶץ כְּבוֹדוֹ:
לְעֻמָּתָם בָּרוּךְ יֹאמֵרוּ

ישעיה

קהל
then
ש״ץ

˙בָּרוּךְ כְּבוֹד־יהוה מִמְּקוֹמוֹ:
וּבְדִבְרֵי קָדְשְׁךָ כָּתוּב לֵאמֹר

יחזקאל ג

קהל
then
ש״ץ

˙יִמְלֹךְ יהוה לְעוֹלָם, אֱלֹהַיִךְ צִיּוֹן לְדֹר וָדֹר, הַלְלוּיָהּ:

תהלים קמו

ש״ץ

לְדוֹר וָדוֹר נַגִּיד גָּדְלֶךָ, וּלְנֵצַח נְצָחִים קְדֻשָּׁתְךָ נַקְדִּישׁ
וְשִׁבְחֲךָ אֱלֹהֵינוּ מִפִּינוּ לֹא יָמוּשׁ לְעוֹלָם וָעֶד
כִּי אֵל מֶלֶךְ גָּדוֹל וְקָדוֹשׁ אָתָּה.
בָּרוּךְ אַתָּה יהוה, הָאֵל הַקָּדוֹשׁ.

The שליח ציבור *continues with* אַתָּה בְחַרְתָּנוּ *below.*

When saying the עמידה *silently, continue here with* :אַתָּה קָדוֹשׁ

קדושת השם

אַתָּה קָדוֹשׁ וְשִׁמְךָ קָדוֹשׁ, וּקְדוֹשִׁים בְּכָל יוֹם יְהַלְלוּךָ סֶּלָה.
בָּרוּךְ אַתָּה יהוה, הָאֵל הַקָּדוֹשׁ.

קדושת היום

אַתָּה בְחַרְתָּנוּ מִכָּל הָעַמִּים
אָהַבְתָּ אוֹתָנוּ וְרָצִיתָ בָּנוּ
וְרוֹמַמְתָּנוּ מִכָּל הַלְּשׁוֹנוֹת
וְקִדַּשְׁתָּנוּ בְּמִצְוֹתֶיךָ
וְקֵרַבְתָּנוּ מַלְכֵּנוּ לַעֲבוֹדָתֶךָ
וְשִׁמְךָ הַגָּדוֹל וְהַקָּדוֹשׁ עָלֵינוּ קָרָאתָ.

וַתִּתֶּן לָנוּ And You, LORD our God, have given us in love
festivals for rejoicing, holy days and seasons for joy,
this day of:

> *On Pesaḥ:* the festival of Matzot, the time of our freedom
> *On Sukkot:* the festival of Sukkot, our time of rejoicing

a holy assembly in memory of the exodus from Egypt.

וּמִפְּנֵי חֲטָאֵינוּ But because of our sins we were exiled from our land
and driven far from our country.
We cannot go up to appear and bow before You,
and to perform our duties in Your chosen House,
the great and holy Temple that was called by Your name,
because of the hand that was stretched out against Your Sanctuary.
May it be Your will, LORD our God and God of our ancestors,
merciful King,
that You in Your abounding compassion may once more
have mercy on us and on Your Sanctuary,
rebuilding it swiftly and adding to its glory.
Our Father, our King, reveal the glory of Your kingdom to us swiftly.
Appear and be exalted over us in the sight of all that lives.
Bring back our scattered ones from among the nations,
and gather our dispersed people from the ends of the earth.

Lead us to Zion, Your city, in jubilation,
and to Jerusalem, home of Your Temple, with everlasting joy.
There we will prepare for You our obligatory offerings:
the regular daily offerings in their order
and the additional offerings according to their law.
And the additional offering of this day of:

> *On Pesaḥ:* the festival of Matzot.
> *On Sukkot:* the festival of Sukkot.

we will prepare and offer before You in love,
in accord with Your will's commandment,
as You wrote for us in Your Torah
through Your servant Moses, by Your own word, as it is said:

וַתִּתֶּן לָנוּ יהוה אֱלֹהֵינוּ בְּאַהֲבָה, מוֹעֲדִים לְשִׂמְחָה
חַגִּים וּזְמַנִּים לְשָׂשׂוֹן, אֶת יוֹם

פסח: חַג הַמַּצּוֹת הַזֶּה, זְמַן חֵרוּתֵנוּ

בסוכות: חַג הַסֻּכּוֹת הַזֶּה, זְמַן שִׂמְחָתֵנוּ

מִקְרָא קֹדֶשׁ, זֵכֶר לִיצִיאַת מִצְרָיִם.

וּמִפְּנֵי חֲטָאֵינוּ גָּלִינוּ מֵאַרְצֵנוּ, וְנִתְרַחַקְנוּ מֵעַל אַדְמָתֵנוּ
וְאֵין אֲנַחְנוּ יְכוֹלִים לַעֲלוֹת וְלֵרָאוֹת וּלְהִשְׁתַּחֲוֹות לְפָנֶיךָ
וְלַעֲשׂוֹת חוֹבוֹתֵינוּ בְּבֵית בְּחִירָתֶךָ
בַּבַּיִת הַגָּדוֹל וְהַקָּדוֹשׁ שֶׁנִּקְרָא שִׁמְךָ עָלָיו
מִפְּנֵי הַיָּד שֶׁנִּשְׁתַּלְּחָה בְּמִקְדָּשֶׁךָ.
יְהִי רָצוֹן מִלְּפָנֶיךָ יהוה אֱלֹהֵינוּ וֵאלֹהֵי אֲבוֹתֵינוּ, מֶלֶךְ רַחֲמָן
שֶׁתָּשׁוּב וּתְרַחֵם עָלֵינוּ וְעַל מִקְדָּשְׁךָ בְּרַחֲמֶיךָ הָרַבִּים
וְתִבְנֵהוּ מְהֵרָה וּתְגַדֵּל כְּבוֹדוֹ.
אָבִינוּ מַלְכֵּנוּ, גַּלֵּה כְּבוֹד מַלְכוּתְךָ עָלֵינוּ מְהֵרָה
וְהוֹפַע וְהִנָּשֵׂא עָלֵינוּ לְעֵינֵי כָּל חָי
וְקָרֵב פְּזוּרֵינוּ מִבֵּין הַגּוֹיִם, וּנְפוּצוֹתֵינוּ כַּנֵּס מִיַּרְכְּתֵי אָרֶץ.
וַהֲבִיאֵנוּ לְצִיּוֹן עִירְךָ בְּרִנָּה
וְלִירוּשָׁלַיִם בֵּית מִקְדָּשְׁךָ בְּשִׂמְחַת עוֹלָם
וְשָׁם נַעֲשֶׂה לְפָנֶיךָ אֶת קָרְבְּנוֹת חוֹבוֹתֵינוּ
תְּמִידִים כְּסִדְרָם וּמוּסָפִים כְּהִלְכָתָם, וְאֶת מוּסַף יוֹם

פסח: חַג הַמַּצּוֹת הַזֶּה

בסוכות: חַג הַסֻּכּוֹת הַזֶּה

נַעֲשֶׂה וְנַקְרִיב לְפָנֶיךָ בְּאַהֲבָה כְּמִצְוַת רְצוֹנֶךָ
כְּמוֹ שֶׁכָּתַבְתָּ עָלֵינוּ בְּתוֹרָתֶךָ
עַל יְדֵי מֹשֶׁה עַבְדֶּךָ מִפִּי כְבוֹדֶךָ, כָּאָמוּר

On Ḥol HaMo'ed Pesaḥ say:

וְהִקְרַבְתֶּם And you shall bring an offering consumed by fire, a burnt-offering to the   *Num. 28*
LORD: two young bullocks, one ram, and seven yearling male lambs; they shall
be to you unblemished. And their meal-offerings and wine-libations as ordained:
three-tenths of an ephah for each bull, two-tenths of an ephah for the ram, one-
tenth of an ephah for each lamb, wine for the libations, a male goat for atonement,
and two regular daily offerings according to their law.

Continue with "Our God and God of our ancestors" on page 514.

On the first day of Ḥol HaMo'ed Sukkot,
say the following two paragraphs (in Israel say only the first):

וּבַיּוֹם הַשֵּׁנִי On the second day you shall offer twelve young bullocks, two rams,   *Num. 29*
fourteen yearling male lambs without blemish. And their meal-offerings and
wine-libations as ordained: three-tenths of an ephah for each bull, two-tenths of
an ephah for each ram, one-tenth of an ephah for each lamb, wine for the libations,
a male goat for atonement, and two regular daily offerings according to their
law.

וּבַיּוֹם הַשְּׁלִישִׁי On the third day you shall offer eleven bullocks, two rams, four-   *Num. 29*
teen yearling male lambs without blemish. And their meal-offerings and wine-
libations as ordained: three-tenths of an ephah for each bull, two-tenths of an
ephah for the ram, one-tenth of an ephah for each lamb, wine for the libations,
a male goat for atonement, and two regular daily offerings according to their
law.

Continue with "Our God and God of our ancestors" on page 514.

On the second day of Ḥol HaMo'ed Sukkot,
say the following two paragraphs (in Israel say only the first):

וּבַיּוֹם הַשְּׁלִישִׁי On the third day you shall offer eleven bullocks, two rams, fourteen   *Num. 29*
yearling male lambs without blemish. And their meal-offerings and wine-libations
as ordained: three-tenths of an ephah for each bull, two-tenths of an ephah for
each ram, one-tenth of an ephah for each lamb, wine for the libations, a male goat
for atonement, and two regular daily offerings according to their law.

וּבַיּוֹם הָרְבִיעִי On the fourth day you shall offer ten bullocks, two rams, fourteen   *Num. 29*
yearling male lambs without blemish. And their meal-offerings and wine-libations
as ordained: three-tenths of an ephah for each bull, two-tenths of an ephah for
each ram, one-tenth of an ephah for each lamb, wine for the libations, a male goat
for atonement, and two regular daily offerings according to their law.

Continue with "Our God and God of our ancestors" on page 514.

On חול המועד פסח say:

במדבר כח

וְהִקְרַבְתֶּם אִשֶּׁה עֹלָה לַיהוה, פָּרִים בְּנֵי־בָקָר שְׁנַיִם וְאַיִל אֶחָד, וְשִׁבְעָה כְבָשִׂים בְּנֵי שָׁנָה, תְּמִימִם יִהְיוּ לָכֶם: וּמִנְחָתָם וְנִסְכֵּיהֶם כִּמְדֻבָּר, שְׁלֹשָׁה עֶשְׂרֹנִים לַפָּר וּשְׁנֵי עֶשְׂרֹנִים לָאָיִל, וְעִשָּׂרוֹן לַכֶּבֶשׂ, וְיַיִן כְּנִסְכּוֹ, וְשָׂעִיר לְכַפֵּר, וּשְׁנֵי תְמִידִים כְּהִלְכָתָם.

Continue with אֱלֹהֵינוּ וֵאלֹהֵי אֲבוֹתֵינוּ on page 515.

On the first day of חול המועד סוכות,
say the following two paragraphs (in ארץ ישראל say only the first):

במדבר כט

וּבַיּוֹם הַשֵּׁנִי, פָּרִים בְּנֵי־בָקָר שְׁנֵים עָשָׂר, אֵילִם שְׁנָיִם, כְּבָשִׂים בְּנֵי־שָׁנָה אַרְבָּעָה עָשָׂר, תְּמִימִם: וּמִנְחָתָם וְנִסְכֵּיהֶם כִּמְדֻבָּר, שְׁלֹשָׁה עֶשְׂרֹנִים לַפָּר, וּשְׁנֵי עֶשְׂרֹנִים לָאָיִל, וְעִשָּׂרוֹן לַכֶּבֶשׂ, וְיַיִן כְּנִסְכּוֹ, וְשָׂעִיר לְכַפֵּר, וּשְׁנֵי תְמִידִים כְּהִלְכָתָם.

במדבר כט

וּבַיּוֹם הַשְּׁלִישִׁי, פָּרִים עַשְׁתֵּי־עָשָׂר, אֵילִם שְׁנָיִם, כְּבָשִׂים בְּנֵי־שָׁנָה אַרְבָּעָה עָשָׂר, תְּמִימִם: וּמִנְחָתָם וְנִסְכֵּיהֶם כִּמְדֻבָּר, שְׁלֹשָׁה עֶשְׂרֹנִים לַפָּר, וּשְׁנֵי עֶשְׂרֹנִים לָאָיִל, וְעִשָּׂרוֹן לַכֶּבֶשׂ, וְיַיִן כְּנִסְכּוֹ, וְשָׂעִיר לְכַפֵּר, וּשְׁנֵי תְמִידִים כְּהִלְכָתָם.

Continue with אֱלֹהֵינוּ וֵאלֹהֵי אֲבוֹתֵינוּ on page 515.

On the second day of חול המועד סוכות,
say the following two paragraphs (in ארץ ישראל say only the first):

במדבר כט

וּבַיּוֹם הַשְּׁלִישִׁי, פָּרִים עַשְׁתֵּי־עָשָׂר, אֵילִם שְׁנָיִם, כְּבָשִׂים בְּנֵי־שָׁנָה אַרְבָּעָה עָשָׂר, תְּמִימִם: וּמִנְחָתָם וְנִסְכֵּיהֶם כִּמְדֻבָּר, שְׁלֹשָׁה עֶשְׂרֹנִים לַפָּר, וּשְׁנֵי עֶשְׂרֹנִים לָאָיִל, וְעִשָּׂרוֹן לַכֶּבֶשׂ, וְיַיִן כְּנִסְכּוֹ, וְשָׂעִיר לְכַפֵּר, וּשְׁנֵי תְמִידִים כְּהִלְכָתָם.

במדבר כט

וּבַיּוֹם הָרְבִיעִי, פָּרִים עֲשָׂרָה, אֵילִם שְׁנָיִם, כְּבָשִׂים בְּנֵי־שָׁנָה אַרְבָּעָה עָשָׂר, תְּמִימִם: וּמִנְחָתָם וְנִסְכֵּיהֶם כִּמְדֻבָּר, שְׁלֹשָׁה עֶשְׂרֹנִים לַפָּר, וּשְׁנֵי עֶשְׂרֹנִים לָאָיִל, וְעִשָּׂרוֹן לַכֶּבֶשׂ, וְיַיִן כְּנִסְכּוֹ, וְשָׂעִיר לְכַפֵּר, וּשְׁנֵי תְמִידִים כְּהִלְכָתָם.

Continue with אֱלֹהֵינוּ וֵאלֹהֵי אֲבוֹתֵינוּ on page 515.

On the third day of Ḥol HaMo'ed Sukkot,
say the following two paragraphs (in Israel say only the first):

וּבַיּוֹם הָרְבִיעִי On the fourth day you shall offer ten bullocks, two rams, fourteen *Num. 29*
yearling male lambs without blemish. And their meal-offerings and wine-libations
as ordained: three-tenths of an ephah for each bull, two-tenths of an ephah for each
ram, one-tenth of an ephah for each lamb, wine for the libations, a male goat for
atonement, and two regular daily offerings according to their law.

וּבַיּוֹם הַחֲמִישִׁי On the fifth day you shall offer nine bullocks, two rams, fourteen *Num. 29*
yearling male lambs without blemish. And their meal-offerings and wine-libations
as ordained: three-tenths of an ephah for each bull, two-tenths of an ephah for each
ram, one-tenth of an ephah for each lamb, wine for the libations, a male goat for
atonement, and two regular daily offerings according to their law.

Continue with "Our God and God of our ancestors" on the next page.

On the fourth day of Ḥol HaMo'ed Sukkot,
say the following two paragraphs (in Israel say only the first):

וּבַיּוֹם הַחֲמִישִׁי On the fifth day you shall offer nine bullocks, two rams, fourteen *Num. 29*
yearling male lambs without blemish. And their meal-offerings and wine-libations
as ordained: three-tenths of an ephah for each bull, two-tenths of an ephah for each
ram, one-tenth of an ephah for each lamb, wine for the libations, a male goat for
atonement, and two regular daily offerings according to their law.

וּבַיּוֹם הַשִּׁשִּׁי On the sixth day you shall offer eight bullocks, two rams, fourteen *Num. 29*
yearling male lambs without blemish. And their meal-offerings and wine-libations
as ordained: three-tenths of an ephah for each bull, two-tenths of an ephah for each
ram, one-tenth of an ephah for each lamb, wine for the libations, a male goat for
atonement, and two regular daily offerings according to their law.

Continue with "Our God and God of our ancestors" on the next page.

On Hoshana Raba, say the following two paragraphs.
In Israel, say the first paragraph on the fifth day of Ḥol HaMo'ed
and the second on Hoshana Raba.

וּבַיּוֹם הַשִּׁשִּׁי On the sixth day you shall offer eight bullocks, two rams, fourteen *Num. 29*
yearling male lambs without blemish. And their meal-offerings and wine-libations
as ordained: three-tenths of an ephah for each bull, two-tenths of an ephah for each
ram, one-tenth of an ephah for each lamb, wine for the libations, a male goat for
atonement, and two regular daily offerings according to their law.

וּבַיּוֹם הַשְּׁבִיעִי On the seventh day you shall offer seven bullocks, two rams, fourteen *Num. 29*
yearling male lambs without blemish. And their meal-offerings and wine-libations
as ordained: three-tenths of an ephah for each bull, two-tenths of an ephah for each
ram, one-tenth of an ephah for each lamb, wine for the libations, a male goat for
atonement, and two regular daily offerings according to their law.

Continue with "Our God and God of our ancestors" on the next page.

On the third day of סוכות חול המועד,
say the following two paragraphs (in ארץ ישראל *say only the first):*

במדבר כט

וּבַיּוֹם הָרְבִיעִי, פָּרִים עֲשָׂרָה, אֵילִם שְׁנָיִם, כְּבָשִׂים בְּנֵי־שָׁנָה אַרְבָּעָה עָשָׂר תְּמִימִם: וּמִנְחָתָם וְנִסְכֵּיהֶם כַּמְּדֻבָּר, שְׁלֹשָׁה עֶשְׂרֹנִים לַפָּר, וּשְׁנֵי עֶשְׂרֹנִים לָאַיִל, וְעִשָּׂרוֹן לַכֶּבֶשׂ, וְיַיִן כְּנִסְכּוֹ, וְשָׂעִיר לְכַפֵּר, וּשְׁנֵי תְמִידִים כְּהִלְכָתָם.

במדבר כט

וּבַיּוֹם הַחֲמִישִׁי, פָּרִים תִּשְׁעָה, אֵילִם שְׁנָיִם, כְּבָשִׂים בְּנֵי־שָׁנָה אַרְבָּעָה עָשָׂר, תְּמִימִם: וּמִנְחָתָם וְנִסְכֵּיהֶם כַּמְּדֻבָּר, שְׁלֹשָׁה עֶשְׂרֹנִים לַפָּר, וּשְׁנֵי עֶשְׂרֹנִים לָאַיִל, וְעִשָּׂרוֹן לַכֶּבֶשׂ, וְיַיִן כְּנִסְכּוֹ, וְשָׂעִיר לְכַפֵּר, וּשְׁנֵי תְמִידִים כְּהִלְכָתָם.

Continue with אֱלֹהֵינוּ וֵאלֹהֵי אֲבוֹתֵינוּ *on the next page.*

On the fourth day of סוכות חול המועד, *say the following two*
paragraphs (in ארץ ישראל *say only the first):*

במדבר כט

וּבַיּוֹם הַחֲמִישִׁי, פָּרִים תִּשְׁעָה, אֵילִם שְׁנָיִם, כְּבָשִׂים בְּנֵי־שָׁנָה אַרְבָּעָה עָשָׂר תְּמִימִם: וּמִנְחָתָם וְנִסְכֵּיהֶם כַּמְּדֻבָּר, שְׁלֹשָׁה עֶשְׂרֹנִים לַפָּר, וּשְׁנֵי עֶשְׂרֹנִים לָאַיִל, וְעִשָּׂרוֹן לַכֶּבֶשׂ, וְיַיִן כְּנִסְכּוֹ, וְשָׂעִיר לְכַפֵּר, וּשְׁנֵי תְמִידִים כְּהִלְכָתָם.

במדבר כט

וּבַיּוֹם הַשִּׁשִּׁי, פָּרִים שְׁמֹנָה, אֵילִם שְׁנָיִם, כְּבָשִׂים בְּנֵי־שָׁנָה אַרְבָּעָה עָשָׂר, תְּמִימִם: וּמִנְחָתָם וְנִסְכֵּיהֶם כַּמְּדֻבָּר, שְׁלֹשָׁה עֶשְׂרֹנִים לַפָּר, וּשְׁנֵי עֶשְׂרֹנִים לָאַיִל, וְעִשָּׂרוֹן לַכֶּבֶשׂ, וְיַיִן כְּנִסְכּוֹ, וְשָׂעִיר לְכַפֵּר, וּשְׁנֵי תְמִידִים כְּהִלְכָתָם.

Continue with אֱלֹהֵינוּ וֵאלֹהֵי אֲבוֹתֵינוּ *on the next page.*

On הושענא רבה, *say the following two paragraphs.*
In ארץ ישראל, *say the first paragraph on the fifth day of* חול המועד
and the second on הושענא רבה:

במדבר כט

וּבַיּוֹם הַשִּׁשִּׁי, פָּרִים שְׁמֹנָה, אֵילִם שְׁנָיִם, כְּבָשִׂים בְּנֵי־שָׁנָה אַרְבָּעָה עָשָׂר, תְּמִימִם: וּמִנְחָתָם וְנִסְכֵּיהֶם כַּמְּדֻבָּר, שְׁלֹשָׁה עֶשְׂרֹנִים לַפָּר, וּשְׁנֵי עֶשְׂרֹנִים לָאַיִל, וְעִשָּׂרוֹן לַכֶּבֶשׂ, וְיַיִן כְּנִסְכּוֹ, וְשָׂעִיר לְכַפֵּר, וּשְׁנֵי תְמִידִים כְּהִלְכָתָם.

במדבר כט

וּבַיּוֹם הַשְּׁבִיעִי, פָּרִים שִׁבְעָה, אֵילִם שְׁנָיִם, כְּבָשִׂים בְּנֵי־שָׁנָה אַרְבָּעָה עָשָׂר, תְּמִימִם: וּמִנְחָתָם וְנִסְכֵּיהֶם כַּמְּדֻבָּר, שְׁלֹשָׁה עֶשְׂרֹנִים לַפָּר, וּשְׁנֵי עֶשְׂרֹנִים לָאַיִל, וְעִשָּׂרוֹן לַכֶּבֶשׂ, וְיַיִן כְּנִסְכּוֹ, וְשָׂעִיר לְכַפֵּר, וּשְׁנֵי תְמִידִים כְּהִלְכָתָם.

Continue with אֱלֹהֵינוּ וֵאלֹהֵי אֲבוֹתֵינוּ *on the next page.*

אֱלֹהֵינוּ Our God and God of our ancestors,
merciful King, have compassion upon us.
You who are good and do good, respond to our call.
Return to us in Your abounding mercy
for the sake of our fathers who did Your will.
Rebuild Your Temple as at the beginning,
and establish Your Sanctuary on its site.
Let us witness its rebuilding and gladden us by its restoration.
Bring the priests back to their service,
the Levites to their song and music,
and the Israelites to their homes.

וְשָׁם נַעֲלֶה There we will go up and appear and bow before You
on the three pilgrimage festivals, as is written in Your Torah:

> "Three times in the year
> all your males shall appear before the LORD your God
> at the place He will choose:
> on Pesaḥ, Shavuot and Sukkot.
> They shall not appear before the LORD empty-handed.
> Each shall bring such a gift as he can,
> in proportion to the blessing
> that the LORD your God grants you."

Deut. 16

וְהַשִּׂיאֵנוּ Bestow on us, LORD our God,
the blessing of Your festivals
for life and peace, joy and gladness,
as You desired and promised to bless us.
Make us holy through Your commandments
and grant us a share in Your Torah;
satisfy us with Your goodness, gladden us with Your salvation,
and purify our hearts to serve You in truth.
And grant us a heritage, LORD our God,
with joy and gladness Your holy festivals.
May Israel, who sanctify Your name, rejoice in You.
Blessed are You, LORD, who sanctifies Israel, and the festive seasons.

אֱלֹהֵינוּ וֵאלֹהֵי אֲבוֹתֵינוּ
מֶלֶךְ רַחֲמָן רַחֵם עָלֵינוּ, טוֹב וּמֵטִיב הִדָּרֶשׁ לָנוּ
שׁוּבָה אֵלֵינוּ בַּהֲמוֹן רַחֲמֶיךָ, בִּגְלַל אָבוֹת שֶׁעָשׂוּ רְצוֹנֶךָ.
בְּנֵה בֵיתְךָ כְּבַתְּחִלָּה, וְכוֹנֵן מִקְדָּשְׁךָ עַל מְכוֹנוֹ
וְהַרְאֵנוּ בְּבִנְיָנוֹ, וְשַׂמְּחֵנוּ בְּתִקּוּנוֹ
וְהָשֵׁב כֹּהֲנִים לַעֲבוֹדָתָם, וּלְוִיִּם לְשִׁירָם וּלְזִמְרָם
וְהָשֵׁב יִשְׂרָאֵל לִנְוֵיהֶם.

וְשָׁם נַעֲלֶה וְנֵרָאֶה וְנִשְׁתַּחֲוֶה לְפָנֶיךָ בְּשָׁלֹשׁ פַּעֲמֵי רְגָלֵינוּ
כַּכָּתוּב בְּתוֹרָתֶךָ
שָׁלֹשׁ פְּעָמִים בַּשָּׁנָה יֵרָאֶה כָל־זְכוּרְךָ אֶת־פְּנֵי יהוה אֱלֹהֶיךָ   דברים טז
בַּמָּקוֹם אֲשֶׁר יִבְחָר
בְּחַג הַמַּצּוֹת, וּבְחַג הַשָּׁבוּעוֹת, וּבְחַג הַסֻּכּוֹת
וְלֹא יֵרָאֶה אֶת־פְּנֵי יהוה רֵיקָם:
אִישׁ כְּמַתְּנַת יָדוֹ, כְּבִרְכַּת יהוה אֱלֹהֶיךָ אֲשֶׁר נָתַן־לָךְ:

וְהַשִּׂיאֵנוּ יהוה אֱלֹהֵינוּ אֶת בִּרְכַּת מוֹעֲדֶיךָ
לְחַיִּים וּלְשָׁלוֹם, לְשִׂמְחָה וּלְשָׂשׂוֹן
כַּאֲשֶׁר רָצִיתָ וְאָמַרְתָּ לְבָרְכֵנוּ.
קַדְּשֵׁנוּ בְּמִצְוֹתֶיךָ, וְתֵן חֶלְקֵנוּ בְּתוֹרָתֶךָ
שַׂבְּעֵנוּ מִטּוּבֶךָ, וְשַׂמְּחֵנוּ בִּישׁוּעָתֶךָ
וְטַהֵר לִבֵּנוּ לְעָבְדְּךָ בֶּאֱמֶת
וְהַנְחִילֵנוּ יהוה אֱלֹהֵינוּ
בְּשִׂמְחָה וּבְשָׂשׂוֹן מוֹעֲדֵי קָדְשֶׁךָ
וְיִשְׂמְחוּ בְךָ יִשְׂרָאֵל מְקַדְּשֵׁי שְׁמֶךָ.
בָּרוּךְ אַתָּה יהוה, מְקַדֵּשׁ יִשְׂרָאֵל וְהַזְּמַנִּים.

TEMPLE SERVICE

רְצֵה **Find favor, LORD our God,**
in Your people Israel and their prayer.
Restore the service to Your most holy House,
and accept in love and favor
the fire-offerings of Israel and their prayer.
May the service of Your people Israel always find favor with You.
And may our eyes witness Your return to Zion in compassion.
Blessed are You, LORD, who restores His Presence to Zion.

THANKSGIVING

Bow at the first nine words.

מוֹדִים **We give thanks to You,**
for You are the LORD our God
and God of our ancestors
for ever and all time.
You are the Rock of our lives,
Shield of our salvation
from generation to generation.
We will thank You and
declare Your praise for our lives,
which are entrusted into Your hand;
for our souls,
which are placed in Your charge;
for Your miracles
which are with us every day;
and for Your wonders and favors
at all times,
evening, morning and midday.
You are good –
for Your compassion never fails.
You are compassionate –
for Your loving-kindnesses never cease.
We have always placed our hope in You.

*During the Leader's Repetition,
the congregation says quietly:*

מוֹדִים **We give thanks to You,**
for You are the LORD our God
and God of our ancestors,
God of all flesh,
who formed us
and formed the universe.
Blessings and thanks
are due to Your great
and holy name for giving us
life and sustaining us.
May You continue
to give us life and sustain us;
and may You gather
our exiles
to Your holy courts,
to keep Your decrees,
do Your will and serve You
with a perfect heart,
for it is for us
to give You thanks.
Blessed be God
to whom thanksgiving is due.

עבודה

רְצֵה יהוה אֱלֹהֵינוּ בְּעַמְּךָ יִשְׂרָאֵל וּבִתְפִלָּתָם
וְהָשֵׁב אֶת הָעֲבוֹדָה לִדְבִיר בֵּיתֶךָ
וְאִשֵּׁי יִשְׂרָאֵל וּתְפִלָּתָם בְּאַהֲבָה תְקַבֵּל בְּרָצוֹן
וּתְהִי לְרָצוֹן תָּמִיד עֲבוֹדַת יִשְׂרָאֵל עַמֶּךָ.
וְתֶחֱזֶינָה עֵינֵינוּ בְּשׁוּבְךָ לְצִיּוֹן בְּרַחֲמִים.
בָּרוּךְ אַתָּה יהוה, הַמַּחֲזִיר שְׁכִינָתוֹ לְצִיּוֹן.

הודאה

Bow at the first five words.

חזרת הש"ץ *During the* the קהל *says quietly:*	מוֹדִים אֲנַחְנוּ לָךְ
מוֹדִים אֲנַחְנוּ לָךְ	שָׁאַתָּה הוּא יהוה אֱלֹהֵינוּ
שָׁאַתָּה הוּא יהוה אֱלֹהֵינוּ	וֵאלֹהֵי אֲבוֹתֵינוּ לְעוֹלָם וָעֶד.
וֵאלֹהֵי אֲבוֹתֵינוּ	צוּר חַיֵּינוּ, מָגֵן יִשְׁעֵנוּ
אֱלֹהֵי כָל בָּשָׂר	אַתָּה הוּא לְדוֹר וָדוֹר.
יוֹצְרֵנוּ, יוֹצֵר בְּרֵאשִׁית.	נוֹדֶה לְּךָ וּנְסַפֵּר תְּהִלָּתֶךָ
בְּרָכוֹת וְהוֹדָאוֹת	עַל חַיֵּינוּ הַמְּסוּרִים בְּיָדֶךָ
לְשִׁמְךָ הַגָּדוֹל וְהַקָּדוֹשׁ	וְעַל נִשְׁמוֹתֵינוּ הַפְּקוּדוֹת לָךְ
עַל שֶׁהֶחֱיִיתָנוּ וְקִיַּמְתָּנוּ.	וְעַל נִסֶּיךָ שֶׁבְּכָל יוֹם עִמָּנוּ
כֵּן תְּחַיֵּנוּ וּתְקַיְּמֵנוּ	וְעַל נִפְלְאוֹתֶיךָ וְטוֹבוֹתֶיךָ
וְתֶאֱסֹף גָּלֻיּוֹתֵינוּ	שֶׁבְּכָל עֵת
לְחַצְרוֹת קָדְשֶׁךָ	עֶרֶב וָבֹקֶר וְצָהֳרָיִם.
לִשְׁמֹר חֻקֶּיךָ	הַטּוֹב, כִּי לֹא כָלוּ רַחֲמֶיךָ
וְלַעֲשׂוֹת רְצוֹנֶךָ וּלְעָבְדְּךָ	וְהַמְרַחֵם, כִּי לֹא תַמּוּ חֲסָדֶיךָ
בְּלֵבָב שָׁלֵם	מֵעוֹלָם קִוִּינוּ לָךְ.
עַל שֶׁאֲנַחְנוּ מוֹדִים לָךְ.	
בָּרוּךְ אֵל הַהוֹדָאוֹת.	

וְעַל כֻּלָּם For all these things may Your name be blessed and exalted, our King, continually, for ever and all time.

Let all that lives thank You, Selah! and praise Your name in truth, God, our Savior and Help, Selah!

▸Blessed are You, LORD, whose name is "the Good" and to whom thanks are due.

The following is said by the Leader during the Repetition of the Amida,
In Israel, if Kohanim bless the congregation, turn to page 684.

Our God and God of our fathers, bless us with the threefold blessing in the Torah, written by the hand of Moses Your servant and pronounced by Aaron and his sons the priests, Your holy people, as it is said:

May the LORD bless you and protect you. (*Cong:* May it be Your will.)   *Num. 6*

May the LORD make His face shine on you and be gracious to you.
(*Cong:* May it be Your will.)

May the LORD turn His face toward you, and grant you peace.
(*Cong:* May it be Your will.)

PEACE

שִׂים שָׁלוֹם Grant peace, goodness and blessing,
grace, loving-kindness and compassion
to us and all Israel Your people.
Bless us, our Father, all as one, with the light of Your face,
for by the light of Your face You have given us, LORD our God,
the Torah of life and love of kindness,
righteousness, blessing, compassion, life and peace.
May it be good in Your eyes to bless Your people Israel
at every time, in every hour, with Your peace.
Blessed are You, LORD,
who blesses His people Israel with peace.

The following verse concludes the Leader's Repetition of the Amida.
Some also say it here as part of the silent Amida.

May the words of my mouth and the meditation of my heart   *Ps. 19*
find favor before You, LORD, my Rock and Redeemer.

וְעַל כֻּלָּם יִתְבָּרַךְ וְיִתְרוֹמַם שִׁמְךָ מַלְכֵּנוּ תָּמִיד לְעוֹלָם וָעֶד.

וְכֹל הַחַיִּים יוֹדוּךָ סֶּלָה, וִיהַלְלוּ אֶת שִׁמְךָ בֶּאֱמֶת

הָאֵל יְשׁוּעָתֵנוּ וְעֶזְרָתֵנוּ סֶלָה.

בָּרוּךְ אַתָּה יהוה, הַטּוֹב שִׁמְךָ וּלְךָ נָאֶה לְהוֹדוֹת.

The following is said by the שליח ציבור during חזרת הש״ץ.
In ארץ ישראל if כהנים say ברכת כהנים turn to page 685.

אֱלֹהֵינוּ וֵאלֹהֵי אֲבוֹתֵינוּ, בָּרְכֵנוּ בַּבְּרָכָה הַמְשֻׁלֶּשֶׁת בַּתּוֹרָה, הַכְּתוּבָה עַל יְדֵי מֹשֶׁה
עַבְדֶּךָ, הָאֲמוּרָה מִפִּי אַהֲרֹן וּבָנָיו כֹּהֲנִים עַם קְדוֹשֶׁךָ, כָּאָמוּר

במדבר ו

יְבָרֶכְךָ יהוה וְיִשְׁמְרֶךָ: קהל: כֵּן יְהִי רָצוֹן

יָאֵר יהוה פָּנָיו אֵלֶיךָ וִיחֻנֶּךָּ: קהל: כֵּן יְהִי רָצוֹן

יִשָּׂא יהוה פָּנָיו אֵלֶיךָ וְיָשֵׂם לְךָ שָׁלוֹם: קהל: כֵּן יְהִי רָצוֹן

ברכת שלום

שִׂים שָׁלוֹם טוֹבָה וּבְרָכָה

חֵן וָחֶסֶד וְרַחֲמִים, עָלֵינוּ וְעַל כָּל יִשְׂרָאֵל עַמֶּךָ.

בָּרְכֵנוּ אָבִינוּ כֻּלָּנוּ כְּאֶחָד בְּאוֹר פָּנֶיךָ

כִּי בְאוֹר פָּנֶיךָ נָתַתָּ לָּנוּ יהוה אֱלֹהֵינוּ

תּוֹרַת חַיִּים וְאַהֲבַת חֶסֶד

וּצְדָקָה וּבְרָכָה וְרַחֲמִים וְחַיִּים וְשָׁלוֹם.

וְטוֹב בְּעֵינֶיךָ לְבָרֵךְ אֶת עַמְּךָ יִשְׂרָאֵל

בְּכָל עֵת וּבְכָל שָׁעָה בִּשְׁלוֹמֶךָ.

בָּרוּךְ אַתָּה יהוה, הַמְבָרֵךְ אֶת עַמּוֹ יִשְׂרָאֵל בַּשָּׁלוֹם.

The following verse concludes the חזרת הש״ץ.
Some also say it here as part of the silent עמידה.

תהלים יט

יִהְיוּ לְרָצוֹן אִמְרֵי־פִי וְהֶגְיוֹן לִבִּי לְפָנֶיךָ, יהוה צוּרִי וְגֹאֲלִי:

אֱלֹהַי My God,   *Berakhot 17a*
guard my tongue from evil and my lips from deceitful speech.
To those who curse me, let my soul be silent;
may my soul be to all like the dust.
Open my heart to Your Torah and let my soul
pursue Your commandments.
As for all who plan evil against me,
swiftly thwart their counsel and frustrate their plans.

> Act for the sake of Your name;
> act for the sake of Your right hand;
> act for the sake of Your holiness;
> act for the sake of Your Torah.

That Your beloved ones may be delivered,   *Ps. 60*
save with Your right hand and answer me.
May the words of my mouth and the meditation of my heart   *Ps. 19*
find favor before You, LORD, my Rock and Redeemer.

Bow, take three steps back, then bow, first left, then right, then center, while saying:

May He who makes peace in His high places,
make peace for us and all Israel –
and say: Amen.

יְהִי רָצוֹן May it be Your will, LORD our God and God of our ancestors,
that the Temple be rebuilt speedily in our days,
and grant us a share in Your Torah.
And there we will serve You with reverence,
as in the days of old and as in former years.
Then the offering of Judah and Jerusalem will be pleasing to the LORD   *Mal. 3*
as in the days of old and as in former years.

On Ḥol HaMo'ed Sukkot, Hoshanot on the next page are said at this point
(the Hoshanot for Hoshana Raba are on page 526).

On Ḥol HaMo'ed Pesaḥ, Full Kaddish (page 250) is said and
the service continues with Aleinu (page 252).

אֱלֹהַי

ברכות יז.

נְצֹר לְשׁוֹנִי מֵרָע וּשְׂפָתַי מִדַּבֵּר מִרְמָה

וְלִמְקַלְלַי נַפְשִׁי תִדֹּם, וְנַפְשִׁי כֶּעָפָר לַכֹּל תִּהְיֶה.

פְּתַח לִבִּי בְּתוֹרָתֶךָ, וּבְמִצְוֹתֶיךָ תִּרְדֹּף נַפְשִׁי.

וְכָל הַחוֹשְׁבִים עָלַי רָעָה

מְהֵרָה הָפֵר עֲצָתָם וְקַלְקֵל מַחֲשַׁבְתָּם.

עֲשֵׂה לְמַעַן שְׁמֶךָ

עֲשֵׂה לְמַעַן יְמִינֶךָ

עֲשֵׂה לְמַעַן קְדֻשָּׁתֶךָ

עֲשֵׂה לְמַעַן תּוֹרָתֶךָ.

תהלים ס

לְמַעַן יֵחָלְצוּן יְדִידֶיךָ, הוֹשִׁיעָה יְמִינְךָ וַעֲנֵנִי:

תהלים יט

יִהְיוּ לְרָצוֹן אִמְרֵי פִי וְהֶגְיוֹן לִבִּי לְפָנֶיךָ, יהוה צוּרִי וְגֹאֲלִי:

Bow, take three steps back, then bow, first left, then right, then center, while saying:

עֹשֶׂה שָׁלוֹם בִּמְרוֹמָיו

הוּא יַעֲשֶׂה שָׁלוֹם עָלֵינוּ וְעַל כָּל יִשְׂרָאֵל, וְאִמְרוּ אָמֵן.

יְהִי רָצוֹן מִלְּפָנֶיךָ יהוה אֱלֹהֵינוּ וֵאלֹהֵי אֲבוֹתֵינוּ

שֶׁיִּבָּנֶה בֵּית הַמִּקְדָּשׁ בִּמְהֵרָה בְיָמֵינוּ

וְתֵן חֶלְקֵנוּ בְּתוֹרָתֶךָ

וְשָׁם נַעֲבָדְךָ בְּיִרְאָה כִּימֵי עוֹלָם וּכְשָׁנִים קַדְמֹנִיּוֹת.

מלאכי ג

וְעָרְבָה לַיהוה מִנְחַת יְהוּדָה וִירוּשָׁלָ͏ִם כִּימֵי עוֹלָם וּכְשָׁנִים קַדְמֹנִיּוֹת:

On הושענות, חול המועד סוכות, on the next page are said at this point
(the הושענות for הושענא רבה are on page 526).

On חול המועד פסח, קדיש שלם (page 251) is said
and the service continues with עָלֵינוּ (page 253).

הוֹשַׁעְנוֹת

הוֹשַׁעְנוֹת are said after the חֲזָרַת הש״ץ of the מוּסָף עֲמִידָה
(and in some congregations after הַלֵּל) on every day of סוּכּוֹת.
The אֲרוֹן קוֹדֶשׁ is opened, and a סֵפֶר תּוֹרָה is taken to the בִּימָה.
Members of the קָהָל who have a לוּלָב and אֶתְרוֹג make a circuit around
the בִּימָה and say הוֹשַׁעְנוֹת. Mourners do not participate in the circuit.
At the conclusion of the הוֹשַׁעְנוֹת, the סֵפֶר תּוֹרָה is returned to the אֲרוֹן קוֹדֶשׁ, which is then closed.
On הוֹשַׁעְנָא רַבָּה, turn to page 526.

On sixth day	On fifth day	On fourth day	On third day	On second day	If first day of סוּכּוֹת falls on
אֹם נְצוּרָה	אֵל לְמוֹשָׁעוֹת	אֹם אֲנִי חוֹמָה	אֶרֶךְ שׁוֹעֵי	אֶבֶן שְׁתִיָּה	Monday
אָדוֹן הַמּוֹשִׁיעַ	אֹם נְצוּרָה	אֵל לְמוֹשָׁעוֹת	אֶרֶךְ שׁוֹעֵי	אֶבֶן שְׁתִיָּה	Tuesday
אָדוֹן הַמּוֹשִׁיעַ	אֵל לְמוֹשָׁעוֹת	אֶרֶךְ שׁוֹעֵי	אֹם נְצוּרָה	אֶבֶן שְׁתִיָּה	Thursday
אָדוֹן הַמּוֹשִׁיעַ	אֵל לְמוֹשָׁעוֹת	אֶבֶן שְׁתִיָּה	אֶרֶךְ שׁוֹעֵי	לְמַעַן אֲמִתָּךְ	שַׁבָּת

הוֹשַׁע נָא. למַעַנְךָ אֱלֹהֵינוּ הוֹשַׁע נָא
then שְׁלִיחַ צִיבּוּר קָהָל:

הוֹשַׁע נָא. למַעַנְךָ בּוֹרְאֵנוּ הוֹשַׁע נָא
then שְׁלִיחַ צִיבּוּר קָהָל:

הוֹשַׁע נָא. למַעַנְךָ גּוֹאֲלֵנוּ הוֹשַׁע נָא
then שְׁלִיחַ צִיבּוּר קָהָל:

הוֹשַׁע נָא. למַעַנְךָ דּוֹרְשֵׁנוּ הוֹשַׁע נָא
then שְׁלִיחַ צִיבּוּר קָהָל:

הוֹשַׁע נָא

למַעַן אֲמִתָּךְ. למַעַן בְּרִיתָךְ. למַעַן גָּדְלָךְ וְתִפְאַרְתָּךְ. למַעַן דָּתָךְ. למַעַן
הוֹדָךְ. למַעַן וְעוּדָךְ. למַעַן זִכְרָךְ. למַעַן חַסְדָּךְ. למַעַן טוּבָךְ. למַעַן יִחוּדָךְ.

לְמַעַן כְּבוֹדָךְ. לְמַעַן לִמּוּדָךְ. לְמַעַן מַלְכוּתָךְ. לְמַעַן נִצְחָךְ. לְמַעַן סוֹדָךְ.
לְמַעַן עֻזָּךְ. לְמַעַן פְּאֵרָךְ. לְמַעַן צִדְקָתָךְ. לְמַעַן קְדֻשָּׁתָךְ. לְמַעַן רַחֲמֶיךָ
הָרַבִּים. לְמַעַן שְׁכִינָתָךְ. לְמַעַן תְּהִלָּתָךְ. הוֹשַׁע נָא.

Continue with אֲנִי וָהוֹ הוֹשִׁיעָה נָּא *on the next page.*

הוֹשַׁע נָא

אֶבֶן שְׁתִיָּה. בֵּית הַבְּחִירָה. גֹּרֶן אָרְנָן. דְּבִיר הַמֻּצְנָע. הַר הַמּוֹרִיָּה. וְהַר
יֵרָאֶה. וְכֹל תִּפְאַרְתָּךְ. חָנָה דָוִד. טוֹב הַלְּבָנוֹן. יְפֵה נוֹף מְשׂוֹשׂ כָּל
הָאָרֶץ. כְּלִילַת יֹפִי. לִינַת הַצֶּדֶק. מְכוֹן לְשִׁבְתֶּךָ. נָוֶה שַׁאֲנָן. סֻכַּת שָׁלֵם.
עֲלִיַּת שְׁבָטִים. פִּנַּת יִקְרַת. צִיּוֹן הַמְצֻיֶּנֶת. קֹדֶשׁ הַקֳּדָשִׁים. רָצוּף אַהֲבָה.
שְׁכִינַת כְּבוֹדָךְ. תֵּל תַּלְפִּיּוֹת. הוֹשַׁע נָא.

Continue with אֲנִי וָהוֹ הוֹשִׁיעָה נָּא *on the next page.*

הוֹשַׁע נָא

אֶרֶךְ שׁוֹעַ. בְּבֵית שׁוֹעַ. גָּלִיתִי בַצּוֹם פִּשְׁעִי. דְּרַשְׁתִּיךָ בּוֹ לְהוֹשִׁיעִי.
הַקְשִׁיבָה לְקוֹל שַׁוְעִי. וְקוּמָה וְהוֹשִׁיעִי. זְכֹר וְרַחֵם מוֹשִׁיעִי. חַי כֵּן
תְּשַׁעְשְׁעִי. טוֹב בְּאֹנֶק שֶׁעִי. יוֹחֵשׁ מוֹשִׁיעִי. כַּלֵּה מַרְשִׁיעִי. לְבַל עוֹד
יַרְשִׁיעִי. מַהֵר אֱלֹהֵי יִשְׁעִי. נֶצַח לְהוֹשִׁיעִי. שָׂא נָא עֲוֹן רִשְׁעִי. עֲבֹר עַל
פִּשְׁעִי. פְּנֵה נָא לְהוֹשִׁיעִי. צוּר צַדִּיק מוֹשִׁיעִי. קַבֵּל נָא שַׁוְעִי. רוֹמֵם קֶרֶן
יִשְׁעִי. שַׁדַּי מוֹשִׁיעִי. תּוֹפִיעַ וְתוֹשִׁיעִי. הוֹשַׁע נָא.

Continue with אֲנִי וָהוֹ הוֹשִׁיעָה נָּא *on the next page.*

הוֹשַׁע נָא

אֹם אֲנִי חוֹמָה. בָּרָה כַּחַמָּה. גּוֹלָה וְסוּרָה. דָּמְתָה לְתָמָר. הַהֲרוּגָה עָלֶיךָ.
וְנֶחְשֶׁבֶת כְּצֹאן טִבְחָה. זְרוּיָה בֵּין מַכְעִיסֶיהָ. חֲבוּקָה וּדְבוּקָה בָּךְ. טוֹעֶנֶת
עֻלָּךְ. יְחִידָה לְיַחֲדָךְ. כְּבוּשָׁה בַגּוֹלָה. לוֹמֶדֶת יִרְאָתָךְ. מְרוּטַת לֶחִי. נְתוּנָה
לְמַכִּים. סוֹבֶלֶת סִבְלָךְ. עֲנִיָּה סֹעֲרָה. פְּדוּיַת טוֹבִיָּה. צֹאן קָדָשִׁים. קְהִלּוֹת
יַעֲקֹב. רְשׁוּמִים בְּשִׁמְךָ. שׁוֹאֲגִים הוֹשַׁע נָא. תְּמוּכִים עָלֶיךָ. הוֹשַׁע נָא.

Continue with אֲנִי וָהוֹ הוֹשִׁיעָה נָּא *on the next page.*

הוֹשַׁע נָא

אֵל לְמוֹשָׁעוֹת. בְּאַרְבַּע שְׁבוּעוֹת. גָּשִׁים בְּשׁוּעוֹת. דּוֹפְקֵי עֶרֶךְ שׁוּעוֹת.
הוֹגֵי שַׁעֲשׁוּעוֹת. וְחִידוֹת מִשְׁתַּעַשְׁעוֹת. זוֹעֲקִים לְהַשְׁעוֹת. חוֹכֵי יְשׁוּעוֹת.
טְפֵלִים בָּךְ שָׁעוֹת. יוֹדְעֵי בִין שָׁעוֹת. כּוֹרְעֶיךָ בְּשַׁוְּעוֹת. לְהָבִין שְׁמוּעוֹת.
מַפְרְךָ נִשְׁמָעוֹת. נוֹתֵן תְּשׁוּעוֹת. סְפוּרוֹת מַשְׁמָעוֹת. עֵדוֹת מַשְׁמִיעוֹת.
פּוֹעֵל יְשׁוּעוֹת. צַדִּיק נוֹשָׁעוֹת. קְרִיאַת תְּשׁוּעוֹת. רֶגֶשׁ תְּשׁוּאוֹת. שָׁלֹשׁ
שָׁעוֹת. תָּחִישׁ לִתְשׁוּעוֹת. הוֹשַׁע נָא.

Continue with אֲנִי וָהוּ הוֹשִׁיעָה נָּא *below.*

הוֹשַׁע נָא

אֲדוֹן הַמּוֹשִׁיעַ. בִּלְתְּךָ אֵין לְהוֹשִׁיעַ. גִּבּוֹר וְרַב לְהוֹשִׁיעַ. דַּלּוֹתִי וְלִי
יְהוֹשִׁיעַ. הָאֵל הַמּוֹשִׁיעַ. וּמַצִּיל וּמוֹשִׁיעַ. זוֹעֲקֶיךָ תּוֹשִׁיעַ. חוֹכֶיךָ הוֹשִׁיעַ.
טְלָאֶיךָ תַּשְׁבִּיעַ. יְבוּל לְהַשְׁפִּיעַ. כָּל שִׂיחַ תַּדְשֵׁא וְתוֹשִׁיעַ. לְגֵיא בַּל
תַּרְשִׁיעַ. מְגָדִים תַּמְתִּיק וְתוֹשִׁיעַ. נְשִׂיאִים לְהַסִּיעַ. שְׂעִירִים לְהָנִיעַ.
עֲנָנִים מִלְּהַמְנִיעַ. פּוֹתֵחַ יָד וּמַשְׂבִּיעַ. צְמָאֶיךָ תַּשְׂבִּיעַ. קוֹרְאֶיךָ תּוֹשִׁיעַ.
רְחוּמֶיךָ תּוֹשִׁיעַ. שׁוֹחֲרֶיךָ הוֹשִׁיעַ. תְּמִימֶיךָ תּוֹשִׁיעַ. הוֹשַׁע נָא.

Continue with אֲנִי וָהוּ הוֹשִׁיעָה נָּא *below.*

אֲנִי וָהוּ הוֹשִׁיעָה נָּא.

כְּהוֹשַׁעְתָּ אֵלִים בְּלוּד עִמָּךְ.

כֵּן הוֹשַׁע נָא.   בְּצֵאתְךָ לְיֵשַׁע עַמָּךְ.

כְּהוֹשַׁעְתָּ גּוֹי וֵאלֹהִים.

כֵּן הוֹשַׁע נָא.   דְּרוּשִׁים לְיֵשַׁע אֱלֹהִים.

כְּהוֹשַׁעְתָּ הֲמוֹן צְבָאוֹת.

כֵּן הוֹשַׁע נָא.   וְעִמָּם מַלְאֲכֵי צְבָאוֹת.

כְּהוֹשַׁעְתָּ זַכִּים מִבֵּית עֲבָדִים.

כֵּן הוֹשַׁע נָא.   חַנּוּן בְּיָדָם מַעֲבִידִים.

כְּהוֹשַׁעְתָּ טְבוּעִים בְּצוּל גְּזָרִים.

יָקָרְךָ עִמָּם מַעֲבִירִים.   כֵּן הוֹשַׁע נָא.

כְּהוֹשַׁעְתָּ כַּנָּה מְשׁוֹרֶרֶת וַיּוֹשַׁע.

לְגוֹחָהּ מְצֻיֶּנֶת וַיִּוָּשַׁע.   כֵּן הוֹשַׁע נָא.

כְּהוֹשַׁעְתָּ מַאֲמַר וְהוֹצֵאתִי אֶתְכֶם.

נָקוּב וְהוֹצֵאתִי אִתְּכֶם.   כֵּן הוֹשַׁע נָא.

כְּהוֹשַׁעְתָּ סוֹבְבֵי מִזְבֵּחַ.

עוֹמְסֵי עֲרָבָה לְהַקִּיף מִזְבֵּחַ.   כֵּן הוֹשַׁע נָא.

כְּהוֹשַׁעְתָּ פִּלְאֵי אָרוֹן כְּהֻפְשַׁע.

צַעַר פְּלֶשֶׁת בַּחֲרוֹן אַף, וְנוֹשַׁע.   כֵּן הוֹשַׁע נָא.

כְּהוֹשַׁעְתָּ קְהִלּוֹת בָּבֶלָה שִׁלַּחְתָּ.

רַחוּם לְמַעֲנָם שִׁלָּחְתָּ.   כֵּן הוֹשַׁע נָא.

כְּהוֹשַׁעְתָּ שְׁבוּת שִׁבְטֵי יַעֲקֹב.

תָּשׁוּב וְתָשִׁיב שְׁבוּת אָהֳלֵי יַעֲקֹב.   וְהוֹשִׁיעָה נָא.

כְּהוֹשַׁעְתָּ שׁוֹמְרֵי מִצְוֹת וְחוֹכֵי יְשׁוּעוֹת.

אֵל לְמוֹשָׁעוֹת.   וְהוֹשִׁיעָה נָא.

אֲנִי וָהוֹ הוֹשִׁיעָה נָּא.

The ספר תורה is returned to the ארון קודש.

תהלים כח הוֹשִׁיעָה אֶת־עַמֶּךָ, וּבָרֵךְ אֶת־נַחֲלָתֶךָ, וּרְעֵם וְנַשְּׂאֵם עַד־הָעוֹלָם:
מלכים א׳ ח וְיִהְיוּ דְבָרַי אֵלֶּה, אֲשֶׁר הִתְחַנַּנְתִּי לִפְנֵי יְהוָֹה, קְרֹבִים אֶל־
יְהוָֹה אֱלֹהֵינוּ יוֹמָם וָלָיְלָה, לַעֲשׂוֹת מִשְׁפַּט עַבְדּוֹ וּמִשְׁפַּט עַמּוֹ
יִשְׂרָאֵל, דְּבַר־יוֹם בְּיוֹמוֹ: לְמַעַן דַּעַת כָּל־עַמֵּי הָאָרֶץ כִּי יְהוָֹה
הוּא הָאֱלֹהִים, אֵין עוֹד:

The ארון קודש is closed. The service continues on page 251.

הוֹשַׁעֲנוֹת לְהוֹשַׁעֲנָא רַבָּה

It is the custom to leave the אֲרוֹן קוֹדֶשׁ *open until the end of the* הוֹשַׁעֲנוֹת.
All of the סִפְרֵי תוֹרָה *are held on the* בִּימָה. *Members of the* קָהָל *who have a* לוּלָב *and* אֶתְרוֹג
circle the בִּימָה *seven times while the* הוֹשַׁעֲנוֹת *are read. After finishing the first circuit,*
say כִּי־אָמַרְתִּי, *and immediately proceed to make another circuit, saying* אֶבֶן שְׁתִיָּה, *etc.*

קָהָל *then* שְׁלִיחַ צִיבּוּר:

הוֹשַׁע נָא   לְמַעַנְךָ אֱלֹהֵינוּ   הוֹשַׁע נָא.

קָהָל *then* שְׁלִיחַ צִיבּוּר:

הוֹשַׁע נָא   לְמַעַנְךָ בּוֹרְאֵנוּ   הוֹשַׁע נָא.

קָהָל *then* שְׁלִיחַ צִיבּוּר:

הוֹשַׁע נָא   לְמַעַנְךָ גּוֹאֲלֵנוּ   הוֹשַׁע נָא.

קָהָל *then* שְׁלִיחַ צִיבּוּר:

הוֹשַׁע נָא   לְמַעַנְךָ דּוֹרְשֵׁנוּ   הוֹשַׁע נָא.

הוֹשַׁע נָא

First הַקָּפָה:

לְמַעַן אֲמִתָּךְ. לְמַעַן בְּרִיתָךְ. לְמַעַן גָּדְלָךְ וְתִפְאַרְתָּךְ. לְמַעַן דָּתָךְ. לְמַעַן הוֹדָךְ. לְמַעַן וְעוּדָךְ. לְמַעַן זִכְרָךְ. לְמַעַן חַסְדָּךְ. לְמַעַן טוּבָךְ. לְמַעַן יִחוּדָךְ. לְמַעַן כְּבוֹדָךְ. לְמַעַן לִמּוּדָךְ. לְמַעַן מַלְכוּתָךְ. לְמַעַן נִצְחָךְ. לְמַעַן סוֹדָךְ. לְמַעַן עֻזָּךְ. לְמַעַן פְּאֵרָךְ. לְמַעַן צִדְקָתָךְ. לְמַעַן קְדֻשָּׁתָךְ. לְמַעַן רַחֲמֶיךָ הָרַבִּים. לְמַעַן שְׁכִינָתָךְ. לְמַעַן תְּהִלָּתָךְ. הוֹשַׁע נָא.

After circling the בִּימָה *the first time, say:*

כִּי־אָמַרְתִּי עוֹלָם חֶסֶד יִבָּנֶה:

תְּהִלִּים פט

הוֹשַׁע נָא

אֶבֶן שְׁתִיָּה. בֵּית הַבְּחִירָה. גֹּרֶן אָרְנָן. דְּבִיר הַמֻּצְנָע. הַר הַמּוֹרִיָּה. וְהַר יֵרָאֶה. זְבוּל תִּפְאַרְתֶּךָ. חָנָה דָוִד. טוֹב הַלְּבָנוֹן. יְפֵה נוֹף מְשׂוֹשׂ כָּל הָאָרֶץ. כְּלִילַת יֹפִי. לִינַת הַצֶּדֶק. מְכוֹן לְשִׁבְתֶּךָ. נָוֶה שַׁאֲנָן. סֻכַּת שָׁלֵם. עֲלִיַּת שְׁבָטִים. פִּנַּת יִקְרַת. צִיּוֹן הַמְצֻיֶּנֶת. קֹדֶשׁ הַקֳּדָשִׁים. רָצוּף אַהֲבָה. שְׁכִינַת כְּבוֹדֶךָ. תֵּל תַּלְפִּיּוֹת. הוֹשַׁע נָא.

After circling the בימה *the second time, say:*

תהלים פט

לְךָ זְרוֹעַ עִם־גְּבוּרָה, תָּעֹז יָדְךָ תָּרוּם יְמִינֶךָ:

הוֹשַׁע נָא

אֹם אֲנִי חוֹמָה. בָּרָה כַּחַמָּה. גּוֹלָה וְסוּרָה. דְּמָתָה לְתָמָר. הַהֲרוּגָה עָלֶיךָ. וְנֶחְשֶׁבֶת כְּצֹאן טִבְחָה. זְרוּיָה בֵּין מַכְעִיסֶיהָ. חֲבוּקָה וּדְבוּקָה בָּךְ. טוֹעֶנֶת עֻלָּךְ. יְחִידָה לְיַחֲדָךְ. כְּבוּשָׁה בַּגּוֹלָה. לוֹמֶדֶת יִרְאָתֶךָ. מְרוּטַת לֶחִי. נְתוּנָה לְמַכִּים. סוֹבֶלֶת סִבְלָךְ. עֲנִיָּה סֹעֲרָה. פְּדוּיַת טוֹבִיָּה. צֹאן קָדָשִׁים. קְהִלּוֹת יַעֲקֹב. רְשׁוּמִים בְּשִׁמְךָ. שׁוֹאֲגִים הוֹשַׁע נָא. תְּמוּכִים עָלֶיךָ. הוֹשַׁע נָא.

After circling the בימה *the third time, say:*

מיכה ז

תִּתֵּן אֱמֶת לְיַעֲקֹב, חֶסֶד לְאַבְרָהָם:

הוֹשַׁע נָא

אָדוֹן הַמּוֹשִׁיעַ. בִּלְתְּךָ אֵין לְהוֹשִׁיעַ. גִּבּוֹר וְרַב לְהוֹשִׁיעַ. דַּלּוֹתִי וְלִי יְהוֹשִׁיעַ. הָאֵל הַמּוֹשִׁיעַ. וּמֵצִיל וּמוֹשִׁיעַ. זוֹעֲקֶיךָ תּוֹשִׁיעַ. חוֹכֶיךָ הוֹשִׁיעַ. טְלָאֶיךָ תַּשְׂבִּיעַ. יְבוּל לְהַשְׁפִּיעַ. כָּל שִׂיחַ תַּדְשֶׁא וְתוֹשִׁיעַ. לְגֵיא בַל תַּרְשִׁיעַ. מְגָדִים תַּמְתִּיק וְתוֹשִׁיעַ. נְשִׂיאִים לְהָסִּיעַ. שְׂעִירִים לְהָנִיעַ.

עֲנָנִים מִלְּהַמְנִיעַ. פּוֹתֵחַ יָד וּמַשְׂבִּיעַ. צְמֵאֶיךָ תַּשְׂבִּיעַ. קוֹרְאֶיךָ תּוֹשִׁיעַ.
רְחוּמֶיךָ תּוֹשִׁיעַ. שׁוֹחֲרֶיךָ הוֹשִׁיעַ. תְּמִימֶיךָ תּוֹשִׁיעַ. הוֹשַׁע נָא.

After circling the בימה the fourth time, say:

נְעִמוֹת בִּימִינְךָ נֶצַח:

תהלים טז

הוֹשַׁע נָא

Fifth הקפה:

אָדָם וּבְהֵמָה. בָּשָׂר וְרוּחַ וּנְשָׁמָה. גִּיד וְעֶצֶם וְקָרְמָה. דְּמוּת וְצֶלֶם וְרִקְמָה.
הוֹד לַהֶבֶל דָּמָה. וְנִמְשַׁל כַּבְּהֵמוֹת נִדְמָה. זִיו וְתֹאַר וְקוֹמָה. חִדּוּשׁ
פְּנֵי אֲדָמָה. טִיעַת עֲצֵי נְשָׁמָה. יְקָבִים וְקָמָה. כְּרָמִים וְשִׁקְמָה. לְתֵבֵל
הַמְסִימָה. מְטָרוֹת עֹז לְסַמְּמָה. נְשִׂיָּה לְקַיְּמָה. שִׂיחִים לְקוֹמְמָה. עֲדָנִים
לְעָצְמָה. פְּרָחִים לְהַעֲצִימָה. צְמָחִים לְגָשְׁמָה. קָרִים לְזָרְמָה. רְבִיבִים
לְשַׁלְּמָה. שְׁתִיָּה לְרוֹמְמָה. תְּלוּיָה עַל בְּלִימָה. הוֹשַׁע נָא.

After circling the בימה the fifth time, say:

יהוה אֲדֹנֵינוּ מָה־אַדִּיר שִׁמְךָ בְּכָל־הָאָרֶץ
אֲשֶׁר־תְּנָה הוֹדְךָ עַל־הַשָּׁמָיִם:

תהלים ח

הוֹשַׁע נָא

Sixth הקפה:

אֲדָמָה מֵאֵרֶר. בְּהֵמָה מִמְּשַׁכֶּלֶת. גֹּרֶן מִגָּזָם. דָּגָן מִדַּלֶּקֶת. הוֹן מִמְּאֵרָה.
וְאֹכֶל מִמְּהוּמָה. זַיִת מִנָּשֶׁל. חִטָּה מֵחָגָב. טֶרֶף מִגּוֹבַי. יֶקֶב מִיֶּלֶק. כֶּרֶם
מִתּוֹלַעַת. לֶקֶשׁ מֵאַרְבֶּה. מֶגֶד מִצְּלָצַל. נֶפֶשׁ מִבֶּהָלָה. שֶׂבַע מִסְּלְעָם.
עֲדָרִים מִדַּלּוּת. פֵּרוֹת מִשִּׁדָּפוֹן. צֹאן מִצְּמִיתוּת. קָצִיר מִקְּלָלָה. רֹב מֵרָזוֹן.
שִׁבֹּלֶת מִצְּנָמוֹן. תְּבוּאָה מֵחָסִיל. הוֹשַׁע נָא.

After circling the בימה the sixth time, say:

צַדִּיק יהוה בְּכָל־דְּרָכָיו, וְחָסִיד בְּכָל־מַעֲשָׂיו:

תהלים קמה

הוֹשַׁע נָא

:הקפה *Seventh*

לְמַעַן אֵיתָן הַנִּזְרָק בְּלַהַב אֵשׁ.

לְמַעַן בֵּן הַנֶּעֱקַד עַל עֵצִים וָאֵשׁ.

לְמַעַן גִּבּוֹר הַנֶּאֱבַק עִם שַׂר אֵשׁ.

לְמַעַן דְּגָלִים נָחִיתָ בְּאוֹר וַעֲנַן אֵשׁ.

לְמַעַן הֻעֲלָה לַמָּרוֹם, וְנִתְעַלָּה כְּמַלְאֲכֵי אֵשׁ.

לְמַעַן וְהוּא לְךָ כְּסֵאֶן בְּאַרְאֶלֵּי אֵשׁ.

לְמַעַן זֶבֶד דִּבְּרוֹת הַנְּתוּנוֹת מֵאֵשׁ.

לְמַעַן חֻפּוּי יְרִיעוֹת וַעֲנַן אֵשׁ.

לְמַעַן טֶכֶס הַר יָרַדְתָּ עָלָיו בָּאֵשׁ.

לְמַעַן יְדִידוּת בַּיִת אֲשֶׁר אָהַבְתָּ מִשְּׁמֵי אֵשׁ.

לְמַעַן כַּמָּה עַד שָׁקְעָה הָאֵשׁ.

לְמַעַן לָקַח מַחְתַּת אֵשׁ וְהֵסִיר חֲרוֹן אֵשׁ.

לְמַעַן מְקַנֵּא קִנְאָה גְּדוֹלָה בָּאֵשׁ.

לְמַעַן נָף יָדוֹ וְיָרְדוּ אַבְנֵי אֵשׁ.

לְמַעַן שָׁם טָלֶה חָלָב כְּלִיל אֵשׁ.

לְמַעַן עָמַד בַּגֹּרֶן וְנִתְרַצָּה בָאֵשׁ.

לְמַעַן פִּלֵּל בַּעֲזָרָה וְיָרְדָה הָאֵשׁ.

לְמַעַן צִיר עָלָה וְנִתְעַלָּה בְּרֶכֶב וְסוּסֵי אֵשׁ.

לְמַעַן קְדוֹשִׁים מֻשְׁלָכִים בָּאֵשׁ.

לְמַעַן רִבּוֹ רִבְבָן חָז וְנַהֲרֵי אֵשׁ.

לְמַעַן שִׁמְמוֹת עִירְךָ הַשְּׂרוּפָה בָאֵשׁ.

לְמַעַן תּוֹלְדוֹת אַלּוּפֵי יְהוּדָה, תָּשִׂים כְּכִיּוֹר אֵשׁ. הוֹשַׁע נָא.

After circling the בימה the seventh time, say:

דברי הימים א' כט

לְךָ יהוה הַגְּדֻלָּה וְהַגְּבוּרָה וְהַתִּפְאֶרֶת וְהַנֵּצַח וְהַהוֹד, כִּי־כֹל בַּשָּׁמַיִם וּבָאָרֶץ

לְךָ יהוה הַמַּמְלָכָה וְהַמִּתְנַשֵּׂא לְכֹל לְרֹאשׁ:

זכריה יד

וְהָיָה יהוה לְמֶלֶךְ עַל־כָּל־הָאָרֶץ, בַּיּוֹם הַהוּא יִהְיֶה יהוה אֶחָד וּשְׁמוֹ אֶחָד:

דברים ו

וּבְתוֹרָתְךָ כָּתוּב לֵאמֹר: שְׁמַע יִשְׂרָאֵל, יהוה אֱלֹהֵינוּ, יהוה אֶחָד:

בָּרוּךְ שֵׁם כְּבוֹד מַלְכוּתוֹ לְעוֹלָם וָעֶד.

אֲנִי וָהוֹ הוֹשִׁיעָה נָּא.

כְּהוֹשַׁעְתָּ אֵלִים בְּלוּד עִמָּךְ.

בְּצֵאתְךָ לְיֵשַׁע עַמָּךְ.   כֵּן הוֹשַׁע נָא.

כְּהוֹשַׁעְתָּ גּוֹי וֵאלֹהִים.

דְּרוּשִׁים לְיֵשַׁע אֱלֹהִים.   כֵּן הוֹשַׁע נָא.

כְּהוֹשַׁעְתָּ הֲמוֹן צְבָאוֹת.

וְעִמָּם מַלְאֲכֵי צְבָאוֹת.   כֵּן הוֹשַׁע נָא.

כְּהוֹשַׁעְתָּ זַכִּים מִבֵּית עֲבָדִים.

חַנּוּן בְּיָדָם מַעֲבִידִים.   כֵּן הוֹשַׁע נָא.

כְּהוֹשַׁעְתָּ טְבוּעִים בְּצוּל גְּזָרִים.

יְקָרְךָ עִמָּם מַעֲבִירִים.   כֵּן הוֹשַׁע נָא.

כְּהוֹשַׁעְתָּ כַּנָּה מְשׁוֹרֶרֶת וַיּוֹשַׁע.

לְגוֹחָהּ מְצֻיָּנֶת וַיִּוָּשַׁע.   כֵּן הוֹשַׁע נָא.

כְּהוֹשַׁעְתָּ מַאֲמַר וְהוֹצֵאתִי אֶתְכֶם.

נָקוּב וְהוֹצֵאתִי אִתְּכֶם.   כֵּן הוֹשַׁע נָא.

כְּהוֹשַׁעְתָּ סוֹבְבֵי מִזְבֵּחַ.

עוֹמְסֵי עֲרָבָה לְהַקִּיף מִזְבֵּחַ.   כֵּן הוֹשַׁע נָא.

כְּהוֹשַׁעְתָּ פִּלְאֵי אָרוֹן כְּהֻפְשַׁע.

צַעַר פְּלֶשֶׁת בַּחֲרוֹן אַף, וְנוֹשַׁע.   כֵּן הוֹשַׁע נָא.

כְּהוֹשַׁעְתָּ קְהִלּוֹת בָּבֶלָה שִׁלַּחְתָּ.

רַחוּם לְמַעֲנָם שִׁלַּחְתָּ.   כֵּן הוֹשַׁע נָא.

כְּהוֹשַׁעְתָּ שְׁבוּת שִׁבְטֵי יַעֲקֹב.

תָּשׁוּב וְתָשִׁיב שְׁבוּת אָהֳלֵי יַעֲקֹב.   וְהוֹשִׁיעָה נָּא.

כְּהוֹשַׁעְתָּ שׁוֹמְרֵי מִצְוֹת וְחוֹכֵי יְשׁוּעוֹת.

אֵל לַמּוֹשָׁעוֹת.   וְהוֹשִׁיעָה נָּא.

אֲנִי וָהוֹ הוֹשִׁיעָה נָּא.

תְּחָנֵּנוּ בְּרַחֲמִים וּבְחֶמְלָה.	תִּתְּנֵנוּ לְשֵׁם וְלִתְהִלָּה.
תּוּכִירֵנוּ בְּמֵי זֹאת עוֹלָה.	תְּשִׁיבֵנוּ אֶל הַחֶבֶל וְאֶל הַנַּחֲלָה.
תּוֹשִׁיעֵנוּ לְקֵץ הַגְּאֻלָּה.	תְּרוֹמְמֵנוּ לְמַעְלָה לְמָעְלָה.
תְּהַדְּרֵנוּ בְּזִיו הֲמֻלָּה.	תְּקַבְּצֵנוּ לְבֵית הַתְּפִלָּה.
תַּדְבִּיקֵנוּ כְּאֵזוֹר חֲתוּלָה.	תַּצִּיבֵנוּ כְּעֵץ עַל פַּלְגֵי מַיִם שְׁתוּלָה.
תְּגַדְּלֵנוּ בְּיָד הַגְּדוֹלָה.	תִּפְדֵּנוּ מִכָּל נֶגַע וּמַחֲלָה.
תְּבִיאֵנוּ לְבֵיתְךָ בְּרִנָּה וְצָהֳלָה.	תְּעַטְּרֵנוּ בְּאַהֲבָה כְלוּלָה.
תְּאַדְּרֵנוּ בְּיֶשַׁע וְגִילָה.	תְּשַׂמְּחֵנוּ בְּבֵית הַתְּפִלָּה.
תְּאַמְּצֵנוּ בְּרוּחַ וְהַצָּלָה.	תַּנְחִילֵנוּ עַל מֵי מְנוּחוֹת סֶלָה.
תְּלַבְּבֵנוּ בְּבִנְיַן עִירְךָ כְּבַתְּחִלָּה.	תְּמַלְּאֵנוּ חָכְמָה וְשִׂכְלָה.
תְּעוֹרְרֵנוּ לְצִיּוֹן בְּשִׂכְלוּלָה.	תַּלְבִּישֵׁנוּ עֹז וּגְדֻלָּה.
תְּזַכֵּנוּ בְּבִנְיַנְתָּה הָעִיר עַל תִּלָּהּ.	תַּכְתִּירֵנוּ בְּכֶתֶר כְּלוּלָה.
תַּרְבִּיצֵנוּ בְּשָׁשׁוֹן וְגִילָה.	תְּיַשְּׁרֵנוּ בְּאֹרַח סְלוּלָה.
תְּחַזְּקֵנוּ אֱלֹהֵי יַעֲקֹב סֶלָה.	תַּשִּׂיאֵנוּ בְּיֹשֶׁר מְסִלָּה.

הוֹשַׁע נָא.

קהל then שליח ציבור:

אָנָּא, הוֹשִׁיעָה נָּא.

	אָנָּא אֱזוֹן חִין תָּאֵבֵי יִשְׁעֲךָ.
וְהוֹשִׁיעָה נָּא.	בְּעָרְבֵי נַחַל לְשַׁעַשְׁעֲךָ.
	אָנָּא גְּאַל כַּנַּת נְטָעֶךָ.
וְהוֹשִׁיעָה נָּא.	דּוּמָה בְּטָאטְאֲךָ.
	אָנָּא הַבֵּט לִבְרִית טִבְעֶךָ.
וְהוֹשִׁיעָה נָּא.	וּמַחְשַׁכֵּי אֶרֶץ בְּהַטְבִּיעֲךָ.
	אָנָּא זְכֹר לָנוּ אָב יְדָעֲךָ.
וְהוֹשִׁיעָה נָּא.	חַסְדְּךָ לָמוֹ בְּהוֹדִיעֲךָ.

אָנָא טְהוֹרֵי לֵב בְּהַפְלִיאָךְ.

יוֹדֵעַ כִּי הוּא פְלָאָךְ. ושיעה נָא.

אָנָא כַּבִּיר כֹּחַ תֵּן לָנוּ יִשְׁעֶךָ.

לַאֲבוֹתֵינוּ כְּהִשָּׁבְעֶךָ. ושיעה נָא.

אָנָא מַלֵּא מִשְׁאֲלוֹת עַם מְשַׁוְּעֶךָ.

נֶעֱקַד בְּהַר מוֹר כְּמוֹ שׁוֹעֶךָ. ושיעה נָא.

אָנָא סַגֵּב אֶשְׁלֵי נִטְעֶךָ.

עָרִיצִים בַּהֲנִיעֶךָ. ושיעה נָא.

אָנָא פְּתַח לָנוּ אוֹצְרוֹת רִבְעֶךָ.

צִיָּה מֵהֶם בְּהַרְבִּיעֶךָ. ושיעה נָא.

אָנָא קוֹרְאֶיךָ אֶרֶץ בְּרוֹעֶעֶךָ.

רְעֵם בְּטוּב מֵרֵעֶךָ. ושיעה נָא.

אָנָא שְׁעָרֶיךָ תַּעַל מִמַּשּׁוֹאָךְ.

תֵּל תַּלְפִּיּוֹת בְּהַשִּׂיאָךְ. ושיעה נָא.

קהל then שליח ציבור:

אָנָּא, אֵל נָא, הוֹשַׁע נָא וְהוֹשִׁיעָה נָּא.

אֵל נָא תָּעִינוּ כְּשֶׂה אוֹבֵד

שְׁמֵנוּ מִסִּפְרְךָ אַל תְּאַבֵּד הושע נָא וְהוֹשִׁיעָה נָּא.

אֵל נָא רְעֵה אֶת צֹאן הַהֲרֵגָה

קְצוּפָה, וְעָלֶיךָ הֲרוּגָה הושע נָא וְהוֹשִׁיעָה נָּא.

אֵל נָא צֹאנְךָ וְצֹאן מַרְעִיתֶךָ

פְּעֻלָּתְךָ וְרַעְיָתֶךָ הושע נָא וְהוֹשִׁיעָה נָּא.

אֵל נָא עֲנֵי הַצֹּאן

שִׂיחָם עֲנֵה בְּעֵת רָצוֹן הושע נָא וְהוֹשִׁיעָה נָּא.

אֵל נָא נוֹשְׂאֵי לְךָ עַיִן

מִתְקוֹמְמֶיךָ יִהְיוּ כְאַיִן הושע נָא וְהוֹשִׁיעָה נָּא.

אֵל נָא לְמַנֶסְכֵי לְךָ מַיִם

כְּמִמַּעֲנֵי הַיְשׁוּעָה יִשְׁאֲבוּן מַיִם   הוֹשַׁע נָא וְהוֹשִׁיעָה נָּא.

אֵל נָא יַעֲלוּ לְצִיּוֹן מוֹשִׁיעִים

טְפוּלִים בָּךְ וּבְשִׁמְךָ נוֹשָׁעִים   הוֹשַׁע נָא וְהוֹשִׁיעָה נָּא.

אֵל נָא חֲמוּץ בְּגָדִים

וְעִם לַעֲזֹר כָּל בּוֹגְדִים   הוֹשַׁע נָא וְהוֹשִׁיעָה נָּא.

אֵל נָא וְזָכֹר תִּזְכֹּר

הַבְּכוֹרִים בְּלֶחֶךְ וְכֹר   הוֹשַׁע נָא וְהוֹשִׁיעָה נָּא.

אֵל נָא דּוֹרְשֶׁיךָ בְּעַנְפֵי עֲרָבוֹת

גַּעְיָם שְׁעֵה מֵעֲרָבוֹת   הוֹשַׁע נָא וְהוֹשִׁיעָה נָּא.

אֵל נָא בָּרֵךְ בְּעִטּוּר שָׁנָה

אֲמָרַי רְצֵה בְּפִלּוּלִי בְּיוֹם הוֹשַׁעְנָא   הוֹשַׁע נָא וְהוֹשִׁיעָה נָּא.

קהל *then* שליח ציבור:

אָנָּא, אֵל נָא, הוֹשַׁע נָא וְהוֹשִׁיעָה נָּא, אָבִינוּ אָתָּה.

לְמַעַן תָּמִים בְּדוֹרוֹתָיו, הַנִּמְלָט בְּרֹב צִדְקוֹתָיו

מֻצָּל מִשֶּׁטֶף בְּבוֹא מַבּוּל מָיִם.

לְאֹם אֲנִי חוֹמָה   הוֹשַׁע נָא וְהוֹשִׁיעָה נָּא, אָבִינוּ אָתָּה.

לְמַעַן שָׁלֵם בְּכָל מַעֲשִׂים, הַמְנֻסֶּה בַּעֲשָׂרָה נִסִּים

כָּשֵׁר מַלְאָכִים, נָם יֻקַּח נָא מְעַט מָיִם.

לְבָרָה כַּחַמָּה   הוֹשַׁע נָא וְהוֹשִׁיעָה נָּא, אָבִינוּ אָתָּה.

לְמַעַן רַךְ וְיָחִיד נֶחֱנַט פְּרִי לְמֵאָה, זָעַק אַיֵּה הַשֶּׂה לְעֹלָה

בְּשּׂרוּהוּ עֲבָדָיו מָצָאנוּ מָיִם.

לְגוֹלָה וְסוּרָה   הוֹשַׁע נָא וְהוֹשִׁיעָה נָּא, אָבִינוּ אָתָּה.

לְמַעַן קָדַם שְׁאֵת בְּרָכָה, הַנֶּאֱבָק עִם שַׂר וַיּוּכָל לוֹ וַיִּשְׁמַע חִכָּה

מְיֻחָם בְּמַקְלוֹת בְּשִׁקְתוֹת הַמָּיִם.

לְדָמְתָה לְתָמָר   הוֹשַׁע נָא וְהוֹשִׁיעָה נָּא, אָבִינוּ אָתָּה.

לְמַעַן צֶדֶק הֱיוֹת לְךָ לְכֹהֵן, כְּחָתָן פְּאֵר יְכַהֵן
מְנֻסֶּה בְּמַסָּה בְּמֵי מְרִיבַת מָיִם.
לְהָדָר הַטּוֹב   הוֹשַׁע נָא וְהוֹשִׁיעָה נָּא, אָבִינוּ אָתָּה.

לְמַעַן פְּאֵר הֱיוֹת גְּבִיר לְאֶחָיו, יְהוּדָה אֲשֶׁר גָּבַר בְּאֶחָיו
מִסְּפֹר רֹבַע מִדְּלָיו יִזַּל מָיִם.
לֹא לָנוּ כִּי אִם לְמַעַנְךָ   הוֹשַׁע נָא וְהוֹשִׁיעָה נָּא, אָבִינוּ אָתָּה.

לְמַעַן עָנָו מִכֹּל וְנֶאֱמָן, אֲשֶׁר בְּצִדְקוֹ כִּלְכֵּל הָמָן
מָשׁוּךְ לְגוֹאֵל וּמָשׁוּי מִמָּיִם.
לוֹאת הַנִּשְׁקָפָה   הוֹשַׁע נָא וְהוֹשִׁיעָה נָּא, אָבִינוּ אָתָּה.

לְמַעַן שֶׁמְּתוֹ כְּמַלְאֲכֵי מְרוֹמִים, הַלּוֹבֵשׁ אוּרִים וְתֻמִּים
מְצֻוֶּה לָבוֹא בַּמִּקְדָּשׁ בְּקִדּוּשׁ יָדַיִם וְרַגְלַיִם וּרְחִיצַת מָיִם.
לְחוֹלַת אַהֲבָה   הוֹשַׁע נָא וְהוֹשִׁיעָה נָּא, אָבִינוּ אָתָּה.

לְמַעַן נְבִיאָה מְחוֹלַת מַחֲנַיִם, לְכֻמְּהֵי לֵב הֻשְׁמָה עֵינַיִם
לְרַגְלָהּ רָצָה עֲלוֹת וְרֶדֶת בְּאֵר מָיִם.
לְטוֹבוּ אֹהָלָיו   הוֹשַׁע נָא וְהוֹשִׁיעָה נָּא, אָבִינוּ אָתָּה.

לְמַעַן מְשָׁרֵת לֹא מָשׁ מֵאֹהֶל, וְרוּחַ הַקֹּדֶשׁ עָלָיו אָהֵל
בְּעָבְרוֹ בַיַּרְדֵּן נִכְרְתוּ הַמָּיִם.
לְיָפָה וּבָרָה   הוֹשַׁע נָא וְהוֹשִׁיעָה נָּא, אָבִינוּ אָתָּה.

לְמַעַן לִמַּד רְאוֹת לְטוֹבָה אוֹת, זָעַק אַיֵּה נִפְלָאוֹת
מִצָּה טַל מִגִּזָּה מִלֹּא הַסֵּפֶל מָיִם.
לְכַלַּת לְבָנוֹן   הוֹשַׁע נָא וְהוֹשִׁיעָה נָּא, אָבִינוּ אָתָּה.

לְמַעַן כְּלוּלֵי עֲשׂוֹת מִלְחַמְתֶּךָ, אֲשֶׁר בְּיָדָם תִּתָּה יְשׁוּעָתֶךָ
צְרוּפֵי מִגּוֹי בְּלָקְקָם בְּיָדָם מָיִם.
לְלֹא בָגְדוּ בָךְ   הוֹשַׁע נָא וְהוֹשִׁיעָה נָּא, אָבִינוּ אָתָּה.

לְמַעַן יָחִיד צוֹרְרִים דָּשׁ, אֲשֶׁר מֵרֶחֶם לְנָזִיר הֻקְדַּשׁ
מִמַּכְתֵּשׁ לֶחִי הִבְקַעְתָּ לוֹ מָיִם.
לְמַעַן שֵׁם קָדְשֶׁךָ   הוֹשַׁע נָא וְהוֹשִׁיעָה נָּא, אָבִינוּ אָתָּה.

לְמַעַן טוֹב הוֹלֵךְ וְגָדֵל, אֲשֶׁר מַעְשַׁק עֵדָה חָדֵל
בְּשׁוּב עָם מֵחֵטְא צִוָּה שְׁאָב מָיִם.

לְנָאוָה כִּירוּשָׁלָיִם   הוֹשַׁע נָא וְהוֹשִׁיעָה נָּא, אָבִינוּ אָתָּה.

לְמַעַן חִנֵּךְ מְכֻרְכָּר בְּשִׁיר, הַמְלַמֵּד תּוֹרָה בְּכָל כְּלֵי שִׁיר
מִנַּסֵּךְ לְפָנֶיךָ כְּתָאַב שְׁתוֹת מָיִם.

לִשְׁמוֹ בֶן סִבְרָם   הוֹשַׁע נָא וְהוֹשִׁיעָה נָּא, אָבִינוּ אָתָּה.

לְמַעַן זָךְ עָלָה בַסְּעָרָה, הַמַּקְנֵא וּמֵשִׁיב עֶבְרָה
לְפוֹלְלוֹ יָרְדָה אֵשׁ וְלָחֲכָה עָפָר וּמָיִם.

לְעֵינֶיךָ בְּרֵכוֹת   הוֹשַׁע נָא וְהוֹשִׁיעָה נָּא, אָבִינוּ אָתָּה.

לְמַעַן וְשֶׁרֵת בֶּאֱמֶת לְרַבּוֹ, פִּי שְׁנַיִם בְּרוּחוֹ נֶאֱצַל בּוֹ
בְּקַחְתּוֹ מְגַּן נִתְמַלְּאוּ גֵבִים מָיִם.

לְפָצוּ מִי כָמְכָה   הוֹשַׁע נָא וְהוֹשִׁיעָה נָּא, אָבִינוּ אָתָּה.

לְמַעַן הִרְהֵר עֲשׂוֹת רְצוֹנֶךָ, הַמַּכְרִיז תְּשׁוּבָה לְצֹאנֶךָ
אָז בְּבוֹא מֵחָרֵף סְתַם עֵינוֹת מָיִם.

לְצִיּוֹן מִכְלַל יֹפִי   הוֹשַׁע נָא וְהוֹשִׁיעָה נָּא, אָבִינוּ אָתָּה.

לְמַעַן דְּרָשָׁךָ בְּתוֹךְ הַגּוֹלָה, וְסוֹדְךָ לָמוֹ נִגְלָה
בְּלִי לְהִתְגָּאֵל דָּרְשׁוּ זֵרְעוֹנִים וּמָיִם.

לְקוֹרְאֶיךָ בַצָּר   הוֹשַׁע נָא וְהוֹשִׁיעָה נָּא, אָבִינוּ אָתָּה.

לְמַעַן גָּמַר חָכְמָה וּבִינָה, סוֹפֵר מָהִיר מְפַלֵּשׁ אֲמָנָה
מֵחַכְּמֵנוּ אֲמָרִים הַמַּשְׁלִים בְּרַחֲבֵי מָיִם.

לְרַבָּתִי עָם   הוֹשַׁע נָא וְהוֹשִׁיעָה נָּא, אָבִינוּ אָתָּה.

לְמַעַן בָּאֵי לְךָ הַיּוֹם בְּכָל לֵב, שׁוֹפְכִים לְךָ שִׂיחַ בְּלֹא לֵב וָלֵב
שׁוֹאֲלִים מִמְּךָ עֹז מִטְרוֹת מָיִם.

לִשְׁוֹרְרוּ בַיָּם   הוֹשַׁע נָא וְהוֹשִׁיעָה נָּא, אָבִינוּ אָתָּה.

לְמַעַן אוֹמְרֵי יִגְדַּל שְׁמֶךָ, וְהֵם נַחֲלָתְךָ וְעַמֶּךָ
צְמֵאִים לְיִשְׁעֲךָ כְּאֶרֶץ עֲיֵפָה לַמָּיִם.

לְתָרַת לָמוֹ מְנוּחָה   הוֹשַׁע נָא וְהוֹשִׁיעָה נָּא, אָבִינוּ אָתָּה.

קָהָל *then* שָׁלִיחַ צִבּוּר:

הוֹשַׁע נָא, אֵל נָא, אָנָּא הוֹשִׁיעָה נָּא.
הוֹשַׁע נָא, סְלַח נָא, וְהַצְלִיחָה נָּא, וְהוֹשִׁיעֵנוּ אֵל מָעֻזֵּנוּ.

Put down the לוּלָב *and* אֶתְרוֹג *and pick up the* הוֹשַׁעֲנוֹת.

וְהוֹשִׁיעָה נָּא.	תַּעֲנֶה אֱמוּנִים שׁוֹפְכִים לְךָ לֵב כַּמַּיִם
וְהַצְלִיחָה נָּא.	לְמַעַן בָּא בָאֵשׁ וּבַמַּיִם
וְהוֹשִׁיעֵנוּ אֵל מָעֻזֵּנוּ.	גְּזַר וְנַם יֻקַּח נָא מְעַט מַיִם
וְהוֹשִׁיעָה נָּא.	תַּעֲנֶה דְגָלִים גָּזוּ גִּזְרֵי מַיִם
וְהַצְלִיחָה נָּא.	לְמַעַן הֻעֲקַד בְּשַׁעַר הַשָּׁמַיִם
וְהוֹשִׁיעֵנוּ אֵל מָעֻזֵּנוּ.	וְשָׁב וְחָפַר בְּאֵרוֹת מַיִם
וְהוֹשִׁיעָה נָּא.	תַּעֲנֶה זַכִּים חוֹנִים עֲלֵי מַיִם
וְהַצְלִיחָה נָּא.	לְמַעַן חֻלַּק מִפְצָל מַקְלוֹת בְּשִׁקֲתוֹת הַמָּיִם
וְהוֹשִׁיעֵנוּ אֵל מָעֻזֵּנוּ.	טָעַן וְגַל אֶבֶן מִבְּאֵר מַיִם
וְהוֹשִׁיעָה נָּא.	תַּעֲנֶה יְדִידִים נוֹחֲלֵי דָת מְשׁוּלַת מַיִם
וְהַצְלִיחָה נָּא.	לְמַעַן כָּרוּ בְּמִשְׁעֲנוֹתָם מַיִם
וְהוֹשִׁיעֵנוּ אֵל מָעֻזֵּנוּ.	לְהָכִין לָמוֹ וּלְצֶאֱצָאֵימוֹ מַיִם
וְהוֹשִׁיעָה נָּא.	תַּעֲנֶה מִתְחַנְּנִים כְּבִישִׁימוֹן עֲלֵי מַיִם
וְהַצְלִיחָה נָּא.	לְמַעַן נֶאֱמַן בַּיִת מַסְפִּיק לְעַם מַיִם
וְהוֹשִׁיעֵנוּ אֵל מָעֻזֵּנוּ.	סֶלַע הָךְ וַיָּזוּבוּ מַיִם
וְהוֹשִׁיעָה נָּא.	תַּעֲנֶה עוֹנִים עֲלֵי בְאֵר מַיִם
וְהַצְלִיחָה נָּא.	לְמַעַן פָּקַד בְּמֵי מְרִיבַת מַיִם
וְהוֹשִׁיעֵנוּ אֵל מָעֻזֵּנוּ.	צְמֵאִים לְהַשְׁקוֹתָם מַיִם
וְהוֹשִׁיעָה נָּא.	תַּעֲנֶה קְדוֹשִׁים מְנַסְּכִים לְךָ מַיִם
וְהַצְלִיחָה נָּא.	לְמַעַן רֹאשׁ מְשׁוֹרְרִים כְּתָאַב שְׁתוֹת מַיִם
וְהוֹשִׁיעֵנוּ אֵל מָעֻזֵּנוּ.	שָׁב וְנָסַךְ לְךָ מַיִם
וְהוֹשִׁיעָה נָּא.	תַּעֲנֶה שׁוֹאֲלִים בִּרְבוּעַ אֶשְׁלֵי מַיִם
וְהַצְלִיחָה נָּא.	לְמַעַן תֵּל תַּלְפִּיּוֹת מוֹצָא מַיִם
וְהוֹשִׁיעֵנוּ אֵל מָעֻזֵּנוּ.	תִּפְתַּח אֶרֶץ וְתַרְעִיף שָׁמַיִם

קהל *then* שליח ציבור:

רַחֶם נָא קְהַל עֲדַת יְשׁוּרוּן, סְלַח וּמְחַל עֲוֺנָם
וְהוֹשִׁיעֵנוּ אֱלֹהֵי יִשְׁעֵנוּ.

אָז כְּעֵינֵי עֲבָדִים אֶל יַד אֲדוֹנִים
בָּאנוּ לְפָנֶיךָ נְדוֹנִים   וְהוֹשִׁיעֵנוּ אֱלֹהֵי יִשְׁעֵנוּ.

גֵּאֶה אֲדוֹנֵי הָאֲדוֹנִים, נִתְגָּרוּ בָנוּ מְדָנִים
דְּשֵׁנוּ וּבְעֶלְיוֹנוּ זוּלָתְךָ אֲדוֹנִים   וְהוֹשִׁיעֵנוּ אֱלֹהֵי יִשְׁעֵנוּ.

הֵן גָּשְׁנוּ הַיּוֹם בְּתַחֲנוּן, עָדֶיךָ רַחוּם וְחַנּוּן
וְסִפַּרְנוּ נִפְלְאוֹתֶיךָ בְּשִׁנּוּן   וְהוֹשִׁיעֵנוּ אֱלֹהֵי יִשְׁעֵנוּ.

זָבַת חָלָב וּדְבַשׁ, נָא אַל תִּיבַשׁ
חֲשֵׁרַת מַיִם כְּאֵבָה תֶּחֱבַשׁ   וְהוֹשִׁיעֵנוּ אֱלֹהֵי יִשְׁעֵנוּ.

טַעֲנוּ בַשְּׁמָנָה, בְּיַד שִׁבְעָה וּשְׁמוֹנָה
יָשָׁר צַדִּיק אֵל אֱמוּנָה   וְהוֹשִׁיעֵנוּ אֱלֹהֵי יִשְׁעֵנוּ.

כָּרַתָּ בְרִית לָאָרֶץ, עוֹד כָּל יְמֵי הָאָרֶץ
לְבִלְתִּי פֶרֶץ בָּהּ פֶּרֶץ   וְהוֹשִׁיעֵנוּ אֱלֹהֵי יִשְׁעֵנוּ.

מִתְחַנְּנִים עֲלֵי מַיִם, כַּעֲרָבִים עַל יִבְלֵי מָיִם
נָא זְכֹר לָמוֹ נִסּוּךְ הַמָּיִם   וְהוֹשִׁיעֵנוּ אֱלֹהֵי יִשְׁעֵנוּ.

שִׂיחִים בְּדֶרֶךְ מַטְעָתָם, עוֹמְסִים בְּשַׁוְעָתָם
עֲנֵם בְּקוֹל פְּגִיעָתָם   וְהוֹשִׁיעֵנוּ אֱלֹהֵי יִשְׁעֵנוּ.

פּוֹעֵל יְשׁוּעוֹת, פְּנֵה לְפִלּוּלָם שָׁעוֹת
צַדְּקֵם אֵל לְמוֹשָׁעוֹת   וְהוֹשִׁיעֵנוּ אֱלֹהֵי יִשְׁעֵנוּ.

קוֹל רִגְשָׁם תָּשַׁע, תִּפְתַּח אֶרֶץ וְיִפְרוּ יֶשַׁע
רַב לְהוֹשִׁיעַ וְלֹא חָפֵץ רֶשַׁע   וְהוֹשִׁיעֵנוּ אֱלֹהֵי יִשְׁעֵנוּ.

קהל *then* שליח ציבור:

שַׁעֲרֵי שָׁמַיִם פְּתַח, וְאוֹצָרְךָ הַטּוֹב לָנוּ תִּפְתַּח.
תּוֹשִׁיעֵנוּ וְרִיב אַל תְּמַתַּח. וְהוֹשִׁיעֵנוּ אֱלֹהֵי יִשְׁעֵנוּ.

קוֹל מְבַשֵּׂר מְבַשֵּׂר וְאוֹמֵר.

מְבַשֵּׂר וְאוֹמֵר.	אֹמֶן יֶשְׁעֵךְ בָּא, קוֹל דּוֹדִי הִנֵּה זֶה בָּא.
מְבַשֵּׂר וְאוֹמֵר.	בָּא בְּרִבְבוֹת כִּתִּים, לַעֲמֹד עַל הַר הַזֵּיתִים.
מְבַשֵּׂר וְאוֹמֵר.	גִּשְׁתּוֹ בַּשּׁוֹפָר לִתְקֹעַ, תַּחְתָּיו הַר יִבְקַע.
מְבַשֵּׂר וְאוֹמֵר.	דָּפַק וְהֵצִיץ וְזָרַח, וּמָשׁ חֲצִי הָהָר מִמִּזְרָח.
מְבַשֵּׂר וְאוֹמֵר.	הֵקִים מִלּוּל נֶאֱמוֹ, וּבָא הוּא וְכָל קְדוֹשָׁיו עִמּוֹ.
מְבַשֵּׂר וְאוֹמֵר.	וּלְכָל בָּאֵי הָעוֹלָם, בַּת קוֹל יִשָּׁמַע בָּעוֹלָם.
מְבַשֵּׂר וְאוֹמֵר.	זֶרַע עֲמוּסֵי רַחֲמוֹ, נוֹלְדוּ כְּיֶלֶד מִמְּעֵי אִמּוֹ.
מְבַשֵּׂר וְאוֹמֵר.	חָלָה וְיָלְדָה מִי זֹאת, מִי־שָׁמַע כָּזֹאת. ישעיה סו
מְבַשֵּׂר וְאוֹמֵר.	טָהוֹר פָּעַל כָּל אֵלֶּה, מִי רָאָה כָאֵלֶּה. ישעיה סו
מְבַשֵּׂר וְאוֹמֵר.	יֶשַׁע וּזְמַן הוּחַד, הֲיוּחַל אֶרֶץ בְּיוֹם אֶחָד. ישעיה סו
מְבַשֵּׂר וְאוֹמֵר.	כַּבִּיר רוֹם וְתַחַת, אִם־יִוָּלֵד גּוֹי פַּעַם אֶחָת. ישעיה סו
מְבַשֵּׂר וְאוֹמֵר.	לְעֵת יִגְאַל עַמּוֹ נָאוֹר, וְהָיָה לְעֵת־עֶרֶב יִהְיֶה־אוֹר. זכריה יד
מְבַשֵּׂר וְאוֹמֵר.	מוֹשִׁיעִים יַעֲלוּ לְהַר צִיּוֹן, כִּי־חָלָה גַּם־יָלְדָה צִיּוֹן. ישעיה סו
מְבַשֵּׂר וְאוֹמֵר.	נִשְׁמַע בְּכָל גְּבוּלֵךְ, הַרְחִיבִי מְקוֹם אָהֳלֵךְ. ישעיה נד
מְבַשֵּׂר וְאוֹמֵר.	שִׂימִי עַד דַּמֶּשֶׂק מִשְׁכְּנוֹתַיִךְ, קַבְּלִי בָּנַיִךְ וּבְנוֹתָיִךְ.
מְבַשֵּׂר וְאוֹמֵר.	עִלְזִי חֲבַצֶּלֶת הַשָּׁרוֹן, כִּי קָמוּ יְשֵׁנֵי חֶבְרוֹן.
מְבַשֵּׂר וְאוֹמֵר.	פְּנוּ אֵלַי וְהִוָּשְׁעוּ, הַיּוֹם אִם בְּקוֹלִי תִשְׁמָעוּ.
מְבַשֵּׂר וְאוֹמֵר.	צֶמַח אִישׁ צֶמַח שְׁמוֹ, הוּא דָוִד בְּעַצְמוֹ.
מְבַשֵּׂר וְאוֹמֵר.	קוּמוּ כְּפוּשֵׁי עָפָר, הָקִיצוּ וְרַנְּנוּ שֹׁכְנֵי עָפָר. ישעיה כו
מְבַשֵּׂר וְאוֹמֵר.	רַבָּתִי עָם בְּהַמְלִיכוֹ, מִגְדּוֹל יְשׁוּעוֹת מַלְכּוֹ. שמואל ב׳ כב
מְבַשֵּׂר וְאוֹמֵר.	שָׁם רְשָׁעִים לְהַאֲבִיד, עֹשֶׂה־חֶסֶד לִמְשִׁיחוֹ לְדָוִד. שמואל ב׳ כב
מְבַשֵּׂר וְאוֹמֵר.	תְּנָה יְשׁוּעוֹת לְעַם עוֹלָם, לְדָוִד וּלְזַרְעוֹ עַד־עוֹלָם. שמואל ב׳ כב

קוֹל מְבַשֵּׂר מְבַשֵּׂר וְאוֹמֵר.

Beat the הושענות against a chair or the floor five times,
then say the following (see law 41):

תהלים כח

הוֹשִׁיעָה אֶת־עַמֶּךָ, וּבָרֵךְ אֶת־נַחֲלָתֶךָ
וּרְעֵם וְנַשְּׂאֵם עַד־הָעוֹלָם:

מלכים א׳ ח

וְיִהְיוּ דְבָרַי אֵלֶּה, אֲשֶׁר הִתְחַנַּנְתִּי לִפְנֵי יהוה
קְרֹבִים אֶל־יהוה אֱלֹהֵינוּ יוֹמָם וָלָיְלָה
לַעֲשׂוֹת מִשְׁפַּט עַבְדּוֹ וּמִשְׁפַּט עַמּוֹ יִשְׂרָאֵל
דְּבַר־יוֹם בְּיוֹמוֹ:
לְמַעַן דַּעַת כָּל־עַמֵּי הָאָרֶץ כִּי יהוה הוּא הָאֱלֹהִים
אֵין עוֹד:

The ספרי תורה are returned to the ארון קודש, which is then closed.

יְהִי רָצוֹן מִלְּפָנֶיךָ יהוה אֱלֹהֵינוּ וֵאלֹהֵי אֲבוֹתֵינוּ, הַבּוֹחֵר בִּנְבִיאִים טוֹבִים
וּבְמִנְהֲגֵיהֶם הַטּוֹבִים, שֶׁתְּקַבֵּל בְּרַחֲמִים וּבְרָצוֹן אֶת תְּפִלָּתֵנוּ וְהַקָּפוֹתֵינוּ.
וְזָכֵר לָנוּ זְכוּת שִׁבְעַת תְּמִימֶיךָ, וְתָסִיר מְחִצַּת הַבַּרְזֶל הַמַּפְסֶקֶת בֵּינֵינוּ
וּבֵינֶךָ, וְתַאֲזִין שַׁוְעָתֵנוּ, וְתֵיטִיב לָנוּ הַחֲתִימָה, תּוֹלֶה אֶרֶץ עַל בְּלִימָה,
וְתַחְתְּמֵנוּ בְּסֵפֶר חַיִּים טוֹבִים.

וְהַיּוֹם הַזֶּה תִּתֵּן בִּשְׁכִינַת עֻזְּךָ חָמֵשׁ גְּבוּרוֹת מְמֻתָּקוֹת, עַל יְדֵי חֲבִיטַת
עֲרָבָה מִנְהַג נְבִיאֶךָ הַקְּדוֹשִׁים, וְתִתְעוֹרֵר הָאַהֲבָה בֵּינֵיהֶם. וּתְּנַשְּׁקֵנוּ
מִנְּשִׁיקוֹת פִּיךָ, מַמְתֶּקֶת כָּל הַגְּבוּרוֹת וְכָל הַדִּינִין, וְתָאִיר לְשְׁכִינַת
עֻזְּךָ בְּשֵׁם יוּ״ד ה״א וא״ו שֶׁהוּא טַל אוֹרוֹת טַלֶּךָ, וּמִשָּׁם תַּשְׁפִּיעַ שֶׁפַע
לְעַבְדְּךָ הַמִּתְפַּלֵּל לְפָנֶיךָ, שֶׁתַּאֲרִיךְ יָמָיו וְתִמְחָל לוֹ חֲטָאָיו וַעֲוֹנוֹתָיו
וּפְשָׁעָיו. וְתִפְשֹׁט יְמִינְךָ וְיָדְךָ לְקַבְּלוֹ בִּתְשׁוּבָה שְׁלֵמָה לְפָנֶיךָ. וְאוֹצָרְךָ
הַטּוֹב תִּפְתַּח לְהַשְׂבִּיעַ מַיִם נֶפֶשׁ שׁוֹקֵקָה, כְּמוֹ שֶׁכָּתוּב: יִפְתַּח יהוה
לְךָ אֶת־אוֹצָרוֹ הַטּוֹב אֶת־הַשָּׁמַיִם לָתֵת מְטַר־אַרְצְךָ בְּעִתּוֹ, וּלְבָרֵךְ אֶת
כָּל־מַעֲשֵׂה יָדֶךָ: אָמֵן.

דברים כח

The שליח ציבור continues with קדיש שלם on the next page.

FULL KADDISH

Leader: יִתְגַּדַּל Magnified and sanctified
may His great name be,
in the world He created by His will.
May He establish His kingdom
in your lifetime and in your days,
and in the lifetime of all the house of Israel,
swiftly and soon –
and say: Amen.

All: May His great name be blessed for ever and all time.

Leader: Blessed and praised, glorified and exalted,
raised and honored,
uplifted and lauded be the name of the Holy One,
blessed be He,
beyond any blessing, song,
praise and consolation
uttered in the world –
and say: Amen.

May the prayers and pleas of all Israel
be accepted by their Father in heaven –
and say: Amen.

May there be great peace from heaven,
and life for us and all Israel –
and say: Amen.

*Bow, take three steps back, as if taking leave of the Divine Presence,
then bow, first left, then right, then center, while saying:*
May He who makes peace in His high places,
make peace for us and all Israel –
and say: Amen.

קדיש שלם

ש״ץ יִתְגַּדַּל וְיִתְקַדַּשׁ שְׁמֵהּ רַבָּא (קהל: אָמֵן)

בְּעָלְמָא דִּי בְרָא כִרְעוּתֵהּ

וְיַמְלִיךְ מַלְכוּתֵהּ

בְּחַיֵּיכוֹן וּבְיוֹמֵיכוֹן וּבְחַיֵּי דְכָל בֵּית יִשְׂרָאֵל

בַּעֲגָלָא וּבִזְמַן קָרִיב, וְאִמְרוּ אָמֵן. (קהל: אָמֵן)

קהל
 וש״ץ: יְהֵא שְׁמֵהּ רַבָּא מְבָרַךְ לְעָלַם וּלְעָלְמֵי עָלְמַיָּא.

ש״ץ: יִתְבָּרַךְ וְיִשְׁתַּבַּח וְיִתְפָּאַר

וְיִתְרוֹמַם וְיִתְנַשֵּׂא וְיִתְהַדָּר וְיִתְעַלֶּה וְיִתְהַלָּל

שְׁמֵהּ דְּקֻדְשָׁא בְּרִיךְ הוּא (קהל: בְּרִיךְ הוּא)

לְעֵלָּא מִן כָּל בִּרְכָתָא

וְשִׁירָתָא, תֻּשְׁבְּחָתָא וְנֶחֱמָתָא

דַּאֲמִירָן בְּעָלְמָא, וְאִמְרוּ אָמֵן. (קהל: אָמֵן)

תִּתְקַבַּל צְלוֹתְהוֹן וּבָעוּתְהוֹן דְּכָל יִשְׂרָאֵל

קֳדָם אֲבוּהוֹן דִּי בִשְׁמַיָּא, וְאִמְרוּ אָמֵן. (קהל: אָמֵן)

יְהֵא שְׁלָמָא רַבָּא מִן שְׁמַיָּא

וְחַיִּים, עָלֵינוּ וְעַל כָּל יִשְׂרָאֵל, וְאִמְרוּ אָמֵן. (קהל: אָמֵן)

*Bow, take three steps back, as if taking leave of the Divine Presence,
then bow, first left, then right, then center, while saying:*

עֹשֶׂה שָׁלוֹם בִּמְרוֹמָיו

הוּא יַעֲשֶׂה שָׁלוֹם עָלֵינוּ וְעַל כָּל יִשְׂרָאֵל

וְאִמְרוּ אָמֵן. (קהל: אָמֵן)

אֵין כֵּאלֹהֵינוּ There is none like our God, none like our Lᴏʀᴅ,
none like our King, none like our Savior.
Who is like our God? Who is like our Lᴏʀᴅ?
Who is like our King? Who is like our Savior?
We will thank our God, we will thank our Lᴏʀᴅ,
we will thank our King, we will thank our Savior.
Blessed is our God, blessed is our Lᴏʀᴅ,
blessed is our King, blessed is our Savior.
You are our God, You are our Lᴏʀᴅ,
You are our King, You are our Savior.
You are He to whom our ancestors offered the fragrant incense.

פִּטּוּם הַקְּטֹרֶת **The incense mixture** consisted of balsam, onycha, galbanum and *Keritot 6a*
frankincense, each weighing seventy manehs; myrrh, cassia, spikenard and saffron,
each weighing sixteen manehs; twelve manehs of costus, three of aromatic bark;
nine of cinnamon; nine kabs of Carsina lye; three seahs and three kabs of Cyprus
wine. If Cyprus wine was not available, old white wine might be used. A quarter of
a kab of Sodom salt, and a minute amount of a smoke-raising herb. Rabbi Nathan
says: Also a minute amount of Jordan amber. If one added honey to the mixture, he
rendered it unfit for sacred use. If he omitted any one of its ingredients, he is
guilty of a capital offence.

Rabban Shimon ben Gamliel says: "Balsam" refers to the sap that drips from the
balsam tree. The Carsina lye was used for bleaching the onycha to improve it. The
Cyprus wine was used to soak the onycha in it to make it pungent. Though urine
is suitable for this purpose, it is not brought into the Temple out of respect.

These were the psalms which the Levites used to recite in the Temple: On the first *Mishna,*
day of the week they used to say: "The earth is the Lᴏʀᴅ's and all it contains, the *Tamid 7*
world and all who live in it." On the second day they used to say: "Great is the Lᴏʀᴅ *Ps. 24*
and greatly to be praised in the city of God, on His holy mountain." On the third day *Ps. 48*
they used to say: "God stands in the divine assembly. Among the judges He delivers *Ps. 82*
judgment." On the fourth day they used to say: "God of retribution, Lᴏʀᴅ, God *Ps. 94*
of retribution, appear." On the fifth day they used to say: "Sing for joy to God, our *Ps. 81*
strength. Shout aloud to the God of Jacob." On the sixth day they used to say: "The *Ps. 93*
Lᴏʀᴅ reigns: He is robed in majesty; the Lᴏʀᴅ is robed, girded with strength; the
world is firmly established; it cannot be moved." On the Sabbath they used to say:
"A psalm, a song for the Sabbath day" – [meaning] a psalm and song for the time to *Ps. 92*
come, for the day which will be entirely Sabbath and rest for life everlasting.

It was taught in the Academy of Elijah: Whoever studies [Torah] laws every day is *Megilla 28b*
assured that he will be destined for the World to Come, as it is said, "The ways of *Hab. 3*
the world are His" – read not, "ways" [*halikhot*] but "laws" [*halakhot*].

אֵין כֵּאלֹהֵינוּ, אֵין כַּאדוֹנֵינוּ, אֵין כְּמַלְכֵּנוּ, אֵין כְּמוֹשִׁיעֵנוּ.

מִי כֵאלֹהֵינוּ, מִי כַאדוֹנֵינוּ, מִי כְמַלְכֵּנוּ, מִי כְמוֹשִׁיעֵנוּ.

נוֹדֶה לֵאלֹהֵינוּ, נוֹדֶה לַאדוֹנֵינוּ, נוֹדֶה לְמַלְכֵּנוּ, נוֹדֶה לְמוֹשִׁיעֵנוּ.

בָּרוּךְ אֱלֹהֵינוּ, בָּרוּךְ אֲדוֹנֵינוּ, בָּרוּךְ מַלְכֵּנוּ, בָּרוּךְ מוֹשִׁיעֵנוּ.

אַתָּה הוּא אֱלֹהֵינוּ, אַתָּה הוּא אֲדוֹנֵינוּ,

אַתָּה הוּא מַלְכֵּנוּ, אַתָּה הוּא מוֹשִׁיעֵנוּ.

אַתָּה הוּא שֶׁהִקְטִירוּ אֲבוֹתֵינוּ לְפָנֶיךָ אֶת קְטֹרֶת הַסַּמִּים.

פִּטּוּם הַקְּטֹרֶת. הַצֳּרִי, וְהַצִּפֹּרֶן, וְהַחֶלְבְּנָה, וְהַלְּבוֹנָה מִשְׁקַל שִׁבְעִים שִׁבְעִים **כריתות ו** מָנֶה, מֹר, וּקְצִיעָה, שִׁבֹּלֶת נֵרְדְּ, וְכַרְכֹּם מִשְׁקַל שִׁשָּׁה עָשָׂר שִׁשָּׁה עָשָׂר מָנֶה, הַקֹּשְׁטְ שְׁנֵים עָשָׂר, קִלּוּפָה שְׁלֹשָׁה, וְקִנָּמוֹן תִּשְׁעָה, בֹּרִית כַּרְשִׁינָה תִּשְׁעָה קַבִּין, יֵין קַפְרִיסִין סְאִין תְּלָת וְקַבִּין תְּלָתָא, וְאִם אֵין לוֹ יֵין קַפְרִיסִין, מֵבִיא חֲמַר חִוַּרְיָן עַתִּיק. מֶלַח סְדוֹמִית רֹבַע, מַעֲלֶה עָשָׁן כָּל שֶׁהוּא. רַבִּי נָתָן הַבַּבְלִי אוֹמֵר: אַף כִּפַּת הַיַּרְדֵּן כָּל שֶׁהוּא, וְאִם נָתַן בָּהּ דְּבַשׁ פְּסָלָהּ, וְאִם חִסֵּר אֶחָד מִכָּל סַמָּנֶיהָ, חַיָּב מִיתָה.

רַבָּן שִׁמְעוֹן בֶּן גַּמְלִיאֵל אוֹמֵר: הַצֳּרִי אֵינוֹ אֶלָּא שְׂרָף הַנּוֹטֵף מֵעֲצֵי הַקְּטָף. בֹּרִית כַּרְשִׁינָה שֶׁשָּׁפִין בָּהּ אֶת הַצִּפֹּרֶן כְּדֵי שֶׁתְּהֵא נָאָה, יֵין קַפְרִיסִין שֶׁשּׁוֹרִין בּוֹ אֶת הַצִּפֹּרֶן כְּדֵי שֶׁתְּהֵא עַזָּה, וַהֲלֹא מֵי רַגְלַיִם יָפִין לָהּ, אֶלָּא שֶׁאֵין מַכְנִיסִין מֵי רַגְלַיִם בַּמִּקְדָּשׁ מִפְּנֵי הַכָּבוֹד.

הַשִּׁיר שֶׁהַלְוִיִּם הָיוּ אוֹמְרִים בְּבֵית הַמִּקְדָּשׁ: בַּיּוֹם הָרִאשׁוֹן הָיוּ אוֹמְרִים, לַיהוה **משנה תמיד ז** הָאָרֶץ וּמְלוֹאָהּ, תֵּבֵל וְישְׁבֵי בָהּ: בַּשֵּׁנִי הָיוּ אוֹמְרִים, גָּדוֹל יהוה וּמְהֻלָּל מְאֹד, **תהלים כד** בְּעִיר אֱלֹהֵינוּ הַר־קָדְשׁוֹ: בַּשְּׁלִישִׁי הָיוּ אוֹמְרִים, אֱלֹהִים נִצָּב בַּעֲדַת־אֵל, בְּקֶרֶב **תהלים מח** אֱלֹהִים יִשְׁפֹּט: בָּרְבִיעִי הָיוּ אוֹמְרִים, אֵל־נְקָמוֹת יהוה, אֵל נְקָמוֹת הוֹפִיעַ: **תהלים פב** בַּחֲמִישִׁי הָיוּ אוֹמְרִים, הַרְנִינוּ לֵאלֹהִים עוּזֵּנוּ, הָרִיעוּ לֵאלֹהֵי יַעֲקֹב: בַּשִּׁשִּׁי **תהלים צד** הָיוּ אוֹמְרִים, יהוה מָלָךְ גֵּאוּת לָבֵשׁ, לָבֵשׁ יהוה עֹז הִתְאַזָּר, אַף־תִּכּוֹן תֵּבֵל **תהלים פא** בַּל־תִּמּוֹט: בַּשַּׁבָּת הָיוּ אוֹמְרִים, מִזְמוֹר שִׁיר לְיוֹם הַשַּׁבָּת: מִזְמוֹר שִׁיר לֶעָתִיד **תהלים צג** לָבוֹא, לְיוֹם שֶׁכֻּלּוֹ שַׁבָּת וּמְנוּחָה לְחַיֵּי הָעוֹלָמִים. **תהלים צב**

תָּנָא דְּבֵי אֵלִיָּהוּ: כָּל הַשּׁוֹנֶה הֲלָכוֹת בְּכָל יוֹם, מֻבְטָח לוֹ שֶׁהוּא בֶן עוֹלָם הַבָּא, **מגילה כח** שֶׁנֶּאֱמַר הֲלִיכוֹת עוֹלָם לוֹ: אַל תִּקְרֵי הֲלִיכוֹת אֶלָּא הֲלָכוֹת. **חבקוק ג**

Rabbi Elazar said in the name of Rabbi Hanina: The disciples of the sages increase peace in the world, as it is said, "And all your children shall be taught of the LORD, and great shall be the peace of your children [banayikh]." Read not banayikh, "your children," but bonayikh, "your builders." Those who love Your Torah have great peace; there is no stumbling block for them. May there be peace within your ramparts, prosperity in your palaces. For the sake of my brothers and friends, I shall say, "Peace be within you." For the sake of the House of the LORD our God, I will seek your good. ‣ May the LORD grant strength to His people; may the LORD bless His people with peace.

Berakhot 64a
Is. 54
Ps. 119
Ps. 122
Ps. 29

THE RABBIS' KADDISH

The following prayer, said by mourners, requires the presence of a minyan.
A transliteration can be found on page 920.

Mourner: יִתְגַּדַּל Magnified and sanctified may His great name be,
in the world He created by His will.
May He establish His kingdom in your lifetime
and in your days, and in the lifetime of all the house of Israel,
swiftly and soon – and say: Amen.

All: May His great name be blessed for ever and all time.

Mourner: Blessed and praised, glorified and exalted,
raised and honored, uplifted and lauded
be the name of the Holy One, blessed be He,
beyond any blessing, song, praise and consolation
uttered in the world – and say: Amen.

To Israel, to the teachers,
their disciples and their disciples' disciples,
and to all who engage in the study of Torah,
in this (*in Israel add:* holy) place or elsewhere,
may there come to them and you great peace,
grace, kindness and compassion, long life, ample sustenance
and deliverance, from their Father in Heaven – and say: Amen.

May there be great peace from heaven,
and (good) life for us and all Israel – and say: Amen.

Bow, take three steps back, as if taking leave of the Divine Presence,
then bow, first left, then right, then center, while saying:

May He who makes peace in His high places, in His compassion
make peace for us and all Israel – and say: Amen.

The Leader continues with "It is our duty" on page 252.

ברכות סד.
אָמַר רַבִּי אֶלְעָזָר, אָמַר רַבִּי חֲנִינָא: תַּלְמִידֵי חֲכָמִים מַרְבִּים שָׁלוֹם בָּעוֹלָם,
ישעיה נד
שֶׁנֶּאֱמַר, וְכָל־בָּנַֽיִךְ לִמּוּדֵי יהוה, וְרַב שְׁלוֹם בָּנָֽיִךְ: אַל תִּקְרֵי בָּנָֽיִךְ, אֶלָּא בּוֹנָֽיִךְ.
תהלים קיט
תהלים קכב
שָׁלוֹם רָב לְאֹהֲבֵי תוֹרָתֶֽךָ, וְאֵין־לָֽמוֹ מִכְשׁוֹל: יְהִי־שָׁלוֹם בְּחֵילֵֽךְ, שַׁלְוָה
בְּאַרְמְנוֹתָֽיִךְ: לְמַֽעַן אַחַי וְרֵעָי אֲדַבְּרָה־נָּא שָׁלוֹם בָּךְ: לְמַֽעַן בֵּית־יהוה אֱלֹהֵֽינוּ
תהלים כט
אֲבַקְשָׁה טוֹב לָךְ: ‹ יהוה עֹז לְעַמּוֹ יִתֵּן, יהוה יְבָרֵךְ אֶת־עַמּוֹ בַשָּׁלוֹם:

קדיש דרבנן

The following prayer, said by mourners, requires the presence of a מִנְיָן.
A transliteration can be found on page 920.

אבל
יִתְגַּדַּל וְיִתְקַדַּשׁ שְׁמֵהּ רַבָּא (קהל: אָמֵן)

בְּעָלְמָא דִּי בְרָא כִרְעוּתֵהּ

וְיַמְלִיךְ מַלְכוּתֵהּ, בְּחַיֵּיכוֹן וּבְיוֹמֵיכוֹן וּבְחַיֵּי דְכָל בֵּית יִשְׂרָאֵל
בַּעֲגָלָא וּבִזְמַן קָרִיב, וְאִמְרוּ אָמֵן. (קהל: אָמֵן)

קהל
ואבל
יְהֵא שְׁמֵהּ רַבָּא מְבָרַךְ לְעָלַם וּלְעָלְמֵי עָלְמַיָּא.

אבל
יִתְבָּרַךְ וְיִשְׁתַּבַּח וְיִתְפָּאַר וְיִתְרוֹמַם וְיִתְנַשֵּׂא
וְיִתְהַדָּר וְיִתְעַלֶּה וְיִתְהַלָּל שְׁמֵהּ דְּקֻדְשָׁא בְּרִיךְ הוּא (קהל: בְּרִיךְ הוּא)
לְעֵלָּא מִן כָּל בִּרְכָתָא וְשִׁירָתָא, תֻּשְׁבְּחָתָא וְנֶחֱמָתָא
דַּאֲמִירָן בְּעָלְמָא, וְאִמְרוּ אָמֵן. (קהל: אָמֵן)

עַל יִשְׂרָאֵל וְעַל רַבָּנָן, וְעַל תַּלְמִידֵיהוֹן וְעַל כָּל תַּלְמִידֵי תַלְמִידֵיהוֹן
וְעַל כָּל מָאן דְּעָסְקִין בְּאוֹרַיְתָא
דִּי בְאַתְרָא (בארץ ישראל: קַדִּישָׁא) הָדֵין, וְדִי בְכָל אֲתַר וַאֲתַר
יְהֵא לְהוֹן וּלְכוֹן שְׁלָמָא רַבָּא
חִנָּא וְחִסְדָּא, וְרַחֲמֵי, וְחַיֵּי אֲרִיכֵי, וּמְזוֹנֵי רְוִיחֵי
וּפֻרְקָנָא מִן קֳדָם אֲבוּהוֹן דִּי בִשְׁמַיָּא, וְאִמְרוּ אָמֵן. (קהל: אָמֵן)

יְהֵא שְׁלָמָא רַבָּא מִן שְׁמַיָּא
וְחַיִּים (טוֹבִים) עָלֵֽינוּ וְעַל כָּל יִשְׂרָאֵל, וְאִמְרוּ אָמֵן. (קהל: אָמֵן)

*Bow, take three steps back, as if taking leave of the Divine Presence,
then bow, first left, then right, then center, while saying:*

עֹשֶׂה שָׁלוֹם בִּמְרוֹמָיו, הוּא יַעֲשֶׂה בְרַחֲמָיו שָׁלוֹם
עָלֵֽינוּ וְעַל כָּל יִשְׂרָאֵל וְאִמְרוּ אָמֵן. (קהל: אָמֵן)

The שליח ציבור *continues with* עָלֵֽינוּ *on page 253.*

ANNULMENT OF VOWS

On the morning before Rosh HaShana, one should annul
vows before three men, who sit as judges, saying:

שְׁמְעוּ נָא Listen, please, my masters (expert judges): every vow or
oath or prohibition or restriction or ban that I have vowed or sworn,
whether awake or in a dream, or that I swore with one of the holy
names that may not be erased, or by the holy four-letter name of God,
blessed be He, or any naziriteship that I accepted on myself, even
a naziriteship like that of Samson, or any prohibition, even against
enjoyment, whether I forbade it to myself or others, by any expression of prohibition, whether using the language of prohibition or
restriction or ban, or any positive commitment, even to perform a
[non-obligatory] commandment, that I undertook by way of a vow
or voluntary undertaking or oath or naziriteship or any other such
expression, whether it was done by handshake or vow or voluntary
undertaking or commandment-mandated custom I have custom-
arily practiced, or any utterance that I have verbalized, or any non-
obligatory commandment or good practice or conduct I have vowed
and resolved in my heart to do, and have done three times without
specifying that it does not have the force of a vow, whether it relates
to myself or others, both those known to me and those I have already
forgotten – regarding all of them, I hereby express my retroactive regret,
and ask and seek their annulment from you, my eminences. For I fear
that I may stumble and be trapped, Heaven forbid, in the sin of vows,
oaths, naziriteships, bans, prohibitions, restrictions and agreements. I
do not regret, Heaven forbid, the performance of the good deeds I have
done. I regret, rather, having accepted them on myself in the language
of vow, oath, naziriteship, prohibition, ban, restriction, agreement or
acceptance of the heart.

Therefore I request annulment for them all.

I regret all these things I have mentioned, whether they related to mon-
etary matters, or to the body or to the soul.

התרת נדרים

On the morning before ראש השנה, *one should annul vows*
before three men, who sit as judges, saying:

שִׁמְעוּ נָא רַבּוֹתַי (דַּיָּנִים מֻמְחִים), כָּל נֵדֶר אוֹ שְׁבוּעָה אוֹ אִסָּר אוֹ קוֹנָם
אוֹ חֵרֶם שֶׁנָּדַרְתִּי אוֹ נִשְׁבַּעְתִּי בְּהָקִיץ אוֹ בַּחֲלוֹם, אוֹ נִשְׁבַּעְתִּי בְּשֵׁמוֹת
הַקְּדוֹשִׁים שֶׁאֵינָם נִמְחָקִים וּבְשֵׁם הוי"ה בָּרוּךְ הוּא, וְכָל מִינֵי נְזִירוּת
שֶׁקִּבַּלְתִּי עָלַי וַאֲפִלּוּ נְזִירוּת שִׁמְשׁוֹן, וְכָל שׁוּם אִסָּר וַאֲפִלּוּ אִסּוּר הֲנָאָה
שֶׁאָסַרְתִּי עָלַי אוֹ עַל אֲחֵרִים בְּכָל לָשׁוֹן שֶׁל אִסּוּר בֵּין בִּלְשׁוֹן אִסּוּר אוֹ
חֵרֶם אוֹ קוֹנָם, וְכָל שׁוּם קַבָּלָה אֲפִלּוּ שֶׁל מִצְוָה שֶׁקִּבַּלְתִּי עָלַי בֵּין בִּלְשׁוֹן
נֵדֶר בֵּין בִּלְשׁוֹן נְדָבָה בֵּין בִּלְשׁוֹן שְׁבוּעָה בֵּין בִּלְשׁוֹן נְזִירוּת בֵּין בְּכָל
לָשׁוֹן, וְגַם הַנַּעֲשֶׂה בִּתְקִיעַת כָּף. בֵּין כָּל נֵדֶר וּבֵין כָּל נְדָבָה וּבֵין שׁוּם מִנְהַג
שֶׁל מִצְוָה שֶׁנָּהַגְתִּי אֶת עַצְמִי, וְכָל מוֹצָא שְׂפָתַי שֶׁיָּצָא מִפִּי אוֹ שֶׁנָּדַרְתִּי
וְגָמַרְתִּי בְּלִבִּי לַעֲשׂוֹת שׁוּם מִצְוָה מֵהַמִּצְוֹת אוֹ אֵיזוֹ הַנְהָגָה טוֹבָה אוֹ
אֵיזֶה דָבָר טוֹב שֶׁנָּהַגְתִּי שָׁלֹשׁ פְּעָמִים, וְלֹא הִתְנֵיתִי שֶׁיְּהֵא בְּלִי נֵדֶר. הֵן
דָּבָר שֶׁעָשִׂיתִי, הֵן עַל עַצְמִי הֵן עַל אֲחֵרִים, הֵן אוֹתָן הַיְּדוּעִים לִי הֵן אוֹתָן
שֶׁכְּבָר שָׁכַחְתִּי. בְּכֻלְּהוֹן אִתְחֲרַטְנָא בְּהוֹן מֵעִקָּרָא, וְשׁוֹאֵל וּמְבַקֵּשׁ אֲנִי
מִמַּעֲלַתְכֶם הַתָּרָה עֲלֵיהֶם, כִּי יָרֵאתִי פֶּן אֶכָּשֵׁל וְנִלְכַּדְתִּי, חַס וְשָׁלוֹם,
בַּעֲוֹן נְדָרִים וּשְׁבוּעוֹת וּנְזִירוּת וַחֲרָמוֹת וְאִסּוּרִין וְקוֹנָמוֹת וְהַסְכָּמוֹת. וְאֵין
אֲנִי תוֹהֵא, חַס וְשָׁלוֹם, עַל קִיּוּם הַמַּעֲשִׂים הַטּוֹבִים הָהֵם שֶׁעָשִׂיתִי, רַק
אֲנִי מִתְחָרֵט עַל קַבָּלַת הָעִנְיָנִים בִּלְשׁוֹן נֵדֶר אוֹ שְׁבוּעָה אוֹ נְזִירוּת אוֹ
אִסּוּר אוֹ חֵרֶם אוֹ קוֹנָם אוֹ הַסְכָּמָה אוֹ קַבָּלָה בְּלֵב, וּמִתְחָרֵט אֲנִי עַל זֶה
שֶׁלֹּא אָמַרְתִּי הִנְנִי עוֹשֶׂה דָבָר זֶה בְּלִי נֵדֶר וּשְׁבוּעָה וּנְזִירוּת וְחֵרֶם וְאִסּוּר
וְקוֹנָם וְקַבָּלָה בְּלֵב.

לָכֵן אֲנִי שׁוֹאֵל הַתָּרָה בְּכֻלְּהוֹן.

אֲנִי מִתְחָרֵט עַל כָּל הַנִּזְכָּר, בֵּין אִם הָיוּ הַמַּעֲשִׂים מְדַבְּרִים הַנּוֹגְעִים בְּמָמוֹן,
בֵּין מֵהַדְּבָרִים הַנּוֹגְעִים בַּגּוּף, בֵּין מֵהַדְּבָרִים הַנּוֹגְעִים אֶל הַנְּשָׁמָה.

In relation to them all, I regret the language of vow, oath, naziriteship, prohibition, ban, penalty, and acceptance of the heart.

To be sure, according to the law, one who regrets and seeks annulment must specify the vow [from which he seeks release]. But please know, my masters, that it is impossible to specify them, for they are many. I do not seek release from vows that cannot be annulled. Therefore, may it be in your eyes as if I had specified them.

The judges say the following three times:

May all be permitted to you. May all be forgiven you. May all be allowed to you. There is now no vow, oath, naziriteship, ban, prohibition, penalty, ostracism, excommunication, or curse. There is now pardon, forgiveness and atonement. And just as the earthly court has granted permission, so may the heavenly court grant permission.

The one seeking annulment of vows says:

Behold I make a formal declaration before you that I cancel from now onward all vows and all oaths, naziriteships, prohibitions, penalties, bans, agreements and acceptances of the heart that I may accept upon myself, whether awake or in a dream, except a vow to fast that I undertake at the time of the afternoon prayer. If I forget the conditions of this declaration and make a vow from this day onward, as of now I retroactively regret them and declare them to be null and void, without effect or validity, and they shall have no force whatsoever. Regarding them all, I regret them from now and for ever.

בְּכֻלְּהוֹן אֲנִי מִתְחָרֵט עַל לְשׁוֹן נֶדֶר וּשְׁבוּעָה וּנְזִירוּת וְאִסוּר וְחֵרֶם וְקוֹנָם וְקַבָּלָה בְּלֵב.

וְהִנֵּה מִצַּד הַדִּין הַמִּתְחָרֵט וְהַמְבַקֵּשׁ הַתָּרָה צָרִיךְ לִפְרֹט הַנֶּדֶר, אַךְ דְּעוּ נָא רַבּוֹתַי, כִּי אִי אֶפְשָׁר לְפָרְטָם, כִּי רַבִּים הֵם. וְאֵין אֲנִי מְבַקֵּשׁ הַתָּרָה עַל אוֹתָם הַנְּדָרִים שֶׁאֵין לְהַתִּיר אוֹתָם, עַל כֵּן יִהְיוּ נָא בְּעֵינֵיכֶם כְּאִלּוּ הָיִיתִי פוֹרְטָם.

The judges say the following three times:

הַכֹּל יִהְיוּ מֻתָּרִים לָךְ, הַכֹּל מְחוּלִים לָךְ, הַכֹּל שְׁרוּיִים לָךְ. אֵין כָּאן לֹא נֶדֶר וְלֹא שְׁבוּעָה וְלֹא נְזִירוּת וְלֹא חֵרֶם וְלֹא אִסוּר וְלֹא קוֹנָם וְלֹא נִדּוּי וְלֹא שַׁמְתָּא וְלֹא אָרוּר. אֲבָל יֵשׁ כָּאן מְחִילָה וּסְלִיחָה וְכַפָּרָה. וּכְשֵׁם שֶׁמַּתִּירִים בְּבֵית דִּין שֶׁל מַטָּה, כָּךְ יִהְיוּ מַתִּרִים מִבֵּית דִּין שֶׁל מַעְלָה.

The one seeking annulment of vows says:

הֲרֵי אֲנִי מוֹסֵר מוֹדָעָה לִפְנֵיכֶם, וַאֲנִי מְבַטֵּל מִכָּאן וּלְהַבָּא כָּל הַנְּדָרִים וְכָל שְׁבוּעוֹת וּנְזִירוּת וְאִסוּרִין וְקוֹנָמוֹת וַחֲרָמוֹת וְהַסְכָּמוֹת וְקַבָּלָה בְּלֵב שֶׁאֲקַבֵּל עָלַי בְּעַצְמִי, הֵן בְּהָקִיץ הֵן בַּחֲלוֹם, חוּץ מִנִּדְרֵי תַעֲנִית בִּשְׁעַת מִנְחָה. וּבְאִם אֶשְׁכַּח לִתְנַאי מוֹדָעָה הַזֹּאת וְאֶדֹּר מֵהַיּוֹם עוֹד, מֵעַתָּה אֲנִי מִתְחָרֵט עֲלֵיהֶם וּמַתְנֶה עֲלֵיהֶם שֶׁיִּהְיוּ כֻּלָּן בְּטֵלִין וּמְבֻטָּלִין, לָא שְׁרִירִין וְלָא קַיָּמִין, וְלָא יְהוֹן חָלִין כְּלָל וּכְלָל. בְּכֻלָּן אִתְחֲרַטְנָא בְּהוֹן מֵעַתָּה וְעַד עוֹלָם.

KAPAROT

Taking a rooster (men), or a hen (women) in the right hand
(alternatively one may use money), say the following paragraph three times:

בְּנֵי אָדָם Children of men,
those who sat in darkness and the shadow of death,   *Ps. 107*
cruelly bound in iron chains –
He brought them out from darkness
and the shadow of death and broke open their chains.
Some were fools with sinful ways,
and suffered affliction because of their iniquities.
They found all food repulsive, and came close to the gates of death.
Then they cried to the LORD in their trouble,
and He saved them from their distress.
He sent His word and healed them;
He rescued them from their destruction.
Let them thank the LORD for his loving-kindness
and His wondrous deeds for humankind.
If there is one angel out of a thousand in his defense,   *Job 33*
to declare his righteousness on his behalf, He will be gracious to him
and say, "Spare him from going down to the pit; I have found atonement."

A man revolves the rooster around his head and says:

זֶה חֲלִיפָתִי Let this be my exchange, let this be my substitute,
let this rooster go to death
while I go and enter a good, long life and peace.

A woman revolves the hen around her head and says:

זֹאת חֲלִיפָתִי Let this be my exchange, let this be my substitute,
let this hen go to death
while I go and enter a good, long life and peace.

If money is used, then revolve the money around the head and say:

אֵלוּ חֲלִיפָתִי Let this be my exchange, let this be my substitute,
let this money go to charity
while I go and enter a good, long life and peace.

סדר כפרות

*Taking a rooster (men), or a hen (women) in the right hand
(alternatively one may use money), say the following paragraph three times:*

בְּנֵי אָדָם

תהלים קז

יֹשְׁבֵי חֹשֶׁךְ וְצַלְמָוֶת, אֲסִירֵי עֳנִי וּבַרְזֶל:

יוֹצִיאֵם מֵחֹשֶׁךְ וְצַלְמָוֶת, וּמוֹסְרוֹתֵיהֶם יְנַתֵּק:

אֱוִלִים מִדֶּרֶךְ פִּשְׁעָם, וּמֵעֲוֹנֹתֵיהֶם יִתְעַנּוּ:

כָּל־אֹכֶל תְּתַעֵב נַפְשָׁם, וַיַּגִּיעוּ עַד־שַׁעֲרֵי מָוֶת:

וַיִּזְעֲקוּ אֶל־יהוה בַּצַּר לָהֶם, מִמְּצֻקוֹתֵיהֶם יוֹשִׁיעֵם:

יִשְׁלַח דְּבָרוֹ וְיִרְפָּאֵם, וִימַלֵּט מִשְּׁחִיתוֹתָם:

יוֹדוּ לַיהוה חַסְדּוֹ, וְנִפְלְאוֹתָיו לִבְנֵי אָדָם:

איוב לג

אִם־יֵשׁ עָלָיו מַלְאָךְ מֵלִיץ אֶחָד מִנִּי־אָלֶף, לְהַגִּיד לְאָדָם יָשְׁרוֹ:

וַיְחֻנֶּנּוּ, וַיֹּאמֶר פְּדָעֵהוּ מֵרֶדֶת שַׁחַת, מָצָאתִי כֹפֶר:

A man revolves the rooster around his head and says:

זֶה חֲלִיפָתִי, זֶה תְּמוּרָתִי, זֶה כַּפָּרָתִי.

זֶה הַתַּרְנְגוֹל יֵלֵךְ לְמִיתָה

וַאֲנִי אֵלֵךְ וְאֶכָּנֵס לְחַיִּים טוֹבִים אֲרֻכִּים וּלְשָׁלוֹם.

A woman revolves the hen around her head and says:

זֹאת חֲלִיפָתִי, זֹאת תְּמוּרָתִי, זֹאת כַּפָּרָתִי.

זֹאת הַתַּרְנְגֹלֶת תֵּלֵךְ לְמִיתָה

וַאֲנִי אֵלֵךְ וְאֶכָּנֵס לְחַיִּים טוֹבִים אֲרֻכִּים וּלְשָׁלוֹם.

If money is used, then revolve the money around the head and say:

אֵלּוּ חֲלִיפָתִי, אֵלּוּ תְּמוּרָתִי, אֵלּוּ כַּפָּרָתִי.

אֵלּוּ הַמָּעוֹת יֵלְכוּ לִצְדָקָה

וַאֲנִי אֵלֵךְ וְאֶכָּנֵס לְחַיִּים טוֹבִים אֲרֻכִּים וּלְשָׁלוֹם.

VIDUY FOR MINḤA OF EREV YOM KIPPUR

The following is said on Erev Yom Kippur (and by a bride and groom on the eve of their wedding), in the Amida before "My God, guard":

אֱלֹהֵינוּ Our God and God of our fathers,
let our prayer come before You,
and do not hide Yourself from our plea,
for we are not so arrogant or obstinate as to say before You,
Lord, our God and God of our fathers,
we are righteous and have not sinned,
for in truth, we and our fathers have sinned.

Strike the left side of the chest with the right fist while saying each of the sins:

אָשַׁמְנוּ We have sinned, we have acted treacherously,
we have robbed, we have spoken slander.
We have acted perversely, we have acted wickedly,
we have acted presumptuously, we have been violent, we have framed lies.

We have given bad advice, we have deceived, we have scorned,
we have rebelled, we have provoked, we have turned away,
we have committed iniquity, we have transgressed,
we have persecuted, we have been obstinate.

We have acted wickedly, we have corrupted,
we have acted abominably, we have strayed, we have led others astray.

סַרְנוּ We have turned away from Your commandments and good laws,
to no avail, for You are just in all that has befallen us,
for You have acted faithfully while we have done wickedly.

מַה נֹּאמַר What can we say before You, You who dwell on high?
What can we declare before You, You who abide in heaven?
Do You not know all, the hidden and revealed alike?

אַתָּה יוֹדֵעַ You know the mysteries of the universe,
and the hidden secrets of all that lives.
You search the inmost being, and test the heart and mind.
Nothing is hidden from You, nor is anything concealed from Your eyes.
Therefore may it be Your will, Lord our God and God of our fathers,
to grant atonement for all our sins,
forgive all our iniquities,
and pardon all our transgressions.

וידוי למנחה בערב יום הכיפורים

The following is said on ערב יום הכיפורים *(and by a* חתן *and* כלה *on the eve of their wedding), in the Amida before* אֱלֹהַי, נְצֹר:

אֱלֹהֵינוּ וֵאלֹהֵי אֲבוֹתֵינוּ
תָּבוֹא לְפָנֶיךָ תְּפִלָּתֵנוּ, וְאַל תִּתְעַלַּם מִתְּחִנָּתֵנוּ.
שֶׁאֵין אֲנַחְנוּ עַזֵּי פָנִים וּקְשֵׁי עֹרֶף לוֹמַר לְפָנֶיךָ
יהוה אֱלֹהֵינוּ וֵאלֹהֵי אֲבוֹתֵינוּ
צַדִּיקִים אֲנַחְנוּ וְלֹא חָטָאנוּ. אֲבָל אֲנַחְנוּ וַאֲבוֹתֵינוּ חָטָאנוּ.

Strike the left side of the chest with the right fist while saying each of the sins:

אָשַׁמְנוּ, בָּגַדְנוּ, גָּזַלְנוּ, דִּבַּרְנוּ דֹפִי
הֶעֱוִינוּ, וְהִרְשַׁעְנוּ, זַדְנוּ, חָמַסְנוּ, טָפַלְנוּ שֶׁקֶר
יָעַצְנוּ רָע, כִּזַּבְנוּ, לַצְנוּ, מָרַדְנוּ, נִאַצְנוּ, סָרַרְנוּ
עָוִינוּ, פָּשַׁעְנוּ, צָרַרְנוּ, קִשִּׁינוּ עֹרֶף
רָשַׁעְנוּ, שִׁחַתְנוּ, תִּעַבְנוּ, תָּעִינוּ, תִּעְתָּעְנוּ.

סַרְנוּ מִמִּצְוֹתֶיךָ וּמִמִּשְׁפָּטֶיךָ הַטּוֹבִים, וְלֹא שָׁוָה לָנוּ.
וְאַתָּה צַדִּיק עַל כָּל הַבָּא עָלֵינוּ
כִּי אֱמֶת עָשִׂיתָ, וַאֲנַחְנוּ הִרְשָׁעְנוּ.

מַה נֹּאמַר לְפָנֶיךָ יוֹשֵׁב מָרוֹם, וּמַה נְּסַפֵּר לְפָנֶיךָ שׁוֹכֵן שְׁחָקִים
הֲלֹא כָּל הַנִּסְתָּרוֹת וְהַנִּגְלוֹת אַתָּה יוֹדֵעַ.

אַתָּה יוֹדֵעַ רָזֵי עוֹלָם וְתַעֲלוּמוֹת סִתְרֵי כָּל חָי.
אַתָּה חוֹפֵשׂ כָּל חַדְרֵי בָטֶן וּבוֹחֵן כְּלָיוֹת וָלֵב.
אֵין דָּבָר נֶעְלָם מִמֶּךָּ וְאֵין נִסְתָּר מִנֶּגֶד עֵינֶיךָ.
וּבְכֵן, יְהִי רָצוֹן מִלְּפָנֶיךָ, יהוה אֱלֹהֵינוּ וֵאלֹהֵי אֲבוֹתֵינוּ
שֶׁתְּכַפֵּר לָנוּ עַל כָּל חַטֹּאתֵינוּ
וְתִסְלַח לָנוּ עַל כָּל עֲוֹנוֹתֵינוּ
וְתִמְחַל לָנוּ עַל כָּל פְּשָׁעֵינוּ.

Strike the left side of the chest with the right fist while saying each of the sins.

עַל חֵטְא For the sin we have sinned before You under
                                duress or freewill,
and for the sin we have sinned before You in hardness of heart.

For the sin we have sinned before You unwittingly,
and for the sin we have sinned before You by an utterance
                                of our lips.

For the sin we have sinned before You by unchastity,
and for the sin we have sinned before You openly or secretly.

For the sin we have sinned before You knowingly and deceitfully,
and for the sin we have sinned before You in speech.

For the sin we have sinned before You by wronging a neighbor,
and for the sin we have sinned before You by thoughts of the heart.

For the sin we have sinned before You in a gathering
                                for immorality,
and for the sin we have sinned before You by insincere confession.

For the sin we have sinned before You by contempt
                                for parents and teachers,
and for the sin we have sinned before You willfully or in error.

For the sin we have sinned before You by force,
and for the sin we have sinned before You by desecrating Your name.

For the sin we have sinned before You by impure lips,
and for the sin we have sinned before You by foolish speech.

For the sin we have sinned before You by the evil inclination,
and for the sin we have sinned before You knowingly or unwittingly.

For all these, God of forgiveness,
forgive us, pardon us, grant us atonement.

Strike the left side of the chest with the right fist while saying each of the sins.

עַל חֵטְא שֶׁחָטָאנוּ לְפָנֶיךָ בְּאֹנֶס וּבְרָצוֹן
וְעַל חֵטְא שֶׁחָטָאנוּ לְפָנֶיךָ בְּאִמּוּץ הַלֵּב

עַל חֵטְא שֶׁחָטָאנוּ לְפָנֶיךָ בִּבְלִי דָעַת
וְעַל חֵטְא שֶׁחָטָאנוּ לְפָנֶיךָ בְּבִטּוּי שְׂפָתָיִם

עַל חֵטְא שֶׁחָטָאנוּ לְפָנֶיךָ בְּגִלּוּי עֲרָיוֹת
וְעַל חֵטְא שֶׁחָטָאנוּ לְפָנֶיךָ בְּגָלוּי וּבַסֵּתֶר

עַל חֵטְא שֶׁחָטָאנוּ לְפָנֶיךָ בְּדַעַת וּבְמִרְמָה
וְעַל חֵטְא שֶׁחָטָאנוּ לְפָנֶיךָ בְּדִבּוּר פֶּה

עַל חֵטְא שֶׁחָטָאנוּ לְפָנֶיךָ בְּהוֹנָאַת רֵעַ
וְעַל חֵטְא שֶׁחָטָאנוּ לְפָנֶיךָ בְּהִרְהוּר הַלֵּב

עַל חֵטְא שֶׁחָטָאנוּ לְפָנֶיךָ בִּוְעִידַת זְנוּת
וְעַל חֵטְא שֶׁחָטָאנוּ לְפָנֶיךָ בְּוִדּוּי פֶּה

עַל חֵטְא שֶׁחָטָאנוּ לְפָנֶיךָ בְּזִלְזוּל הוֹרִים וּמוֹרִים
וְעַל חֵטְא שֶׁחָטָאנוּ לְפָנֶיךָ בְּזָדוֹן וּבִשְׁגָגָה

עַל חֵטְא שֶׁחָטָאנוּ לְפָנֶיךָ בְּחֹזֶק יָד
וְעַל חֵטְא שֶׁחָטָאנוּ לְפָנֶיךָ בְּחִלּוּל הַשֵּׁם

עַל חֵטְא שֶׁחָטָאנוּ לְפָנֶיךָ בְּטֻמְאַת שְׂפָתָיִם
וְעַל חֵטְא שֶׁחָטָאנוּ לְפָנֶיךָ בְּטִפְשׁוּת פֶּה

עַל חֵטְא שֶׁחָטָאנוּ לְפָנֶיךָ בְּיֵצֶר הָרָע
וְעַל חֵטְא שֶׁחָטָאנוּ לְפָנֶיךָ בְּיוֹדְעִים וּבְלֹא יוֹדְעִים

וְעַל כֻּלָּם אֱלוֹהַּ סְלִיחוֹת סְלַח לָנוּ, מְחַל לָנוּ, כַּפֶּר לָנוּ.

For the sin we have sinned before You by deceit and lies,
and for the sin we have sinned before You by bribery.

For the sin we have sinned before You by scorn,
and for the sin we have sinned before You by evil speech.

For the sin we have sinned before You in business,
and for the sin we have sinned before You with food and drink.

For the sin we have sinned before You by interest and extortion,
and for the sin we have sinned before You by being haughty.

For the sin we have sinned before You by the idle chatter
of our lips,
and for the sin we have sinned before You by prying eyes.

For the sin we have sinned before You by arrogance,
and for the sin we have sinned before You by insolence.

For all these, God of forgiveness,
forgive us, pardon us, grant us atonement.

For the sin we have sinned before You by casting off the yoke,
and for the sin we have sinned before You by perverting judgment.

For the sin we have sinned before You by entrapping a neighbor,
and for the sin we have sinned before You by envy.

For the sin we have sinned before You by lack of seriousness,
and for the sin we have sinned before You by obstinacy.

For the sin we have sinned before You by running to do evil,
and for the sin we have sinned before You by gossip.

עַל חֵטְא שֶׁחָטָאנוּ לְפָנֶיךָ בְּכַחַשׁ וּבְכָזָב
וְעַל חֵטְא שֶׁחָטָאנוּ לְפָנֶיךָ בְּכַפַּת שֹׁחַד

עַל חֵטְא שֶׁחָטָאנוּ לְפָנֶיךָ בְּלָצוֹן
וְעַל חֵטְא שֶׁחָטָאנוּ לְפָנֶיךָ בְּלָשׁוֹן הָרָע

עַל חֵטְא שֶׁחָטָאנוּ לְפָנֶיךָ בְּמַשָּׂא וּבְמַתָּן
וְעַל חֵטְא שֶׁחָטָאנוּ לְפָנֶיךָ בְּמַאֲכָל וּבְמִשְׁתֶּה

עַל חֵטְא שֶׁחָטָאנוּ לְפָנֶיךָ בְּנֶשֶׁךְ וּבְמַרְבִּית
וְעַל חֵטְא שֶׁחָטָאנוּ לְפָנֶיךָ בִּנְטִיַּת גָּרוֹן

עַל חֵטְא שֶׁחָטָאנוּ לְפָנֶיךָ בְּשִׂיחַ שִׂפְתוֹתֵינוּ
וְעַל חֵטְא שֶׁחָטָאנוּ לְפָנֶיךָ בְּשִׁקּוּר עָיִן

עַל חֵטְא שֶׁחָטָאנוּ לְפָנֶיךָ בְּעֵינַיִם רָמוֹת
וְעַל חֵטְא שֶׁחָטָאנוּ לְפָנֶיךָ בְּעַזּוּת מֵצַח

וְעַל כֻּלָּם אֱלוֹהַּ סְלִיחוֹת סְלַח לָנוּ, מְחַל לָנוּ, כַּפֶּר לָנוּ.

עַל חֵטְא שֶׁחָטָאנוּ לְפָנֶיךָ בִּפְרִיקַת עֹל
וְעַל חֵטְא שֶׁחָטָאנוּ לְפָנֶיךָ בִּפְלִילוּת

עַל חֵטְא שֶׁחָטָאנוּ לְפָנֶיךָ בִּצְדִיַּת רֵעַ
וְעַל חֵטְא שֶׁחָטָאנוּ לְפָנֶיךָ בְּצָרוּת עָיִן

עַל חֵטְא שֶׁחָטָאנוּ לְפָנֶיךָ בְּקַלּוּת רֹאשׁ
וְעַל חֵטְא שֶׁחָטָאנוּ לְפָנֶיךָ בְּקַשְׁיוּת עֹרֶף

עַל חֵטְא שֶׁחָטָאנוּ לְפָנֶיךָ בְּרִיצַת רַגְלַיִם לְהָרַע
וְעַל חֵטְא שֶׁחָטָאנוּ לְפָנֶיךָ בִּרְכִילוּת

For the sin we have sinned before You by vain oath,
and for the sin we have sinned before You by baseless hatred.

For the sin we have sinned before You by breach of trust,
and for the sin we have sinned before You by confusion of heart.

For all these, God of forgiveness,
forgive us, pardon us, grant us atonement.

וְעַל חֲטָאִים And for the sins for which we are liable to bring a burnt-
offering,
and for the sins for which we are liable to bring a sin-offering,
and for the sins for which we are liable to bring an offering
according to our means,
and for the sins for which we are liable to bring a guilt-offering
for certain or possible sin,
and for the sins for which we are liable to lashes for rebellion,
and for the sins for which we are liable to forty lashes,
and for the sins for which we are liable to death by the hands of
Heaven,
and for the sins for which we are liable to be cut off and childless,
and for the sins for which we are liable to the four death penalties
inflicted by the court: stoning, burning, beheading and strangling.

For positive and negative commandments,
whether they can be remedied by an act or not,
for sins known to us and for those that are unknown –
for those that are known,
we have already declared them before You and confessed them to You;
and for those that are unknown,
before You they are revealed and known,
as it is said, "The secret things belong to the LORD our God,   *Deut. 29*
but the things that are revealed are for us and our children for ever,
that we may fulfill all the words of this Torah."
For You are He who forgives Israel
and pardons the tribes of Yeshurun in every generation,
and besides You we have no king who pardons and forgives, only You.

עַל חֵטְא שֶׁחָטָאנוּ לְפָנֶיךָ בִּשְׁבוּעַת שָׁוְא
וְעַל חֵטְא שֶׁחָטָאנוּ לְפָנֶיךָ בְּשִׂנְאַת חִנָּם

עַל חֵטְא שֶׁחָטָאנוּ לְפָנֶיךָ בִּתְשׂוּמֶת יָד
וְעַל חֵטְא שֶׁחָטָאנוּ לְפָנֶיךָ בְּתִמָּהוֹן לֵבָב

וְעַל כֻּלָּם אֱלוֹהַּ סְלִיחוֹת סְלַח לָנוּ, מְחַל לָנוּ, כַּפֶּר לָנוּ.

וְעַל חֲטָאִים שֶׁאָנוּ חַיָּבִים עֲלֵיהֶם עוֹלָה
וְעַל חֲטָאִים שֶׁאָנוּ חַיָּבִים עֲלֵיהֶם חַטָּאת
וְעַל חֲטָאִים שֶׁאָנוּ חַיָּבִים עֲלֵיהֶם קָרְבָּן עוֹלֶה וְיוֹרֵד
וְעַל חֲטָאִים שֶׁאָנוּ חַיָּבִים עֲלֵיהֶם אָשָׁם וַדַּאי וְתָלוּי
וְעַל חֲטָאִים שֶׁאָנוּ חַיָּבִים עֲלֵיהֶם מַכַּת מַרְדּוּת
וְעַל חֲטָאִים שֶׁאָנוּ חַיָּבִים עֲלֵיהֶם מַלְקוּת אַרְבָּעִים
וְעַל חֲטָאִים שֶׁאָנוּ חַיָּבִים עֲלֵיהֶם מִיתָה בִּידֵי שָׁמַיִם
וְעַל חֲטָאִים שֶׁאָנוּ חַיָּבִים עֲלֵיהֶם כָּרֵת וַעֲרִירִי
וְעַל חֲטָאִים שֶׁאָנוּ חַיָּבִים עֲלֵיהֶם אַרְבַּע מִיתוֹת בֵּית דִּין
סְקִילָה, שְׂרֵפָה, הֶרֶג, וְחֶנֶק.

עַל מִצְוֹת עֲשֵׂה וְעַל מִצְוֹת לֹא תַעֲשֶׂה.
בֵּין שֶׁיֵּשׁ בָּהּ קוּם עֲשֵׂה וּבֵין שֶׁאֵין בָּהּ קוּם עֲשֵׂה.
אֶת הַגְּלוּיִים לָנוּ וְאֶת שֶׁאֵינָם גְּלוּיִים לָנוּ
אֶת הַגְּלוּיִים לָנוּ, כְּבָר אֲמַרְנוּם לְפָנֶיךָ, וְהוֹדִינוּ לְךָ עֲלֵיהֶם
וְאֶת שֶׁאֵינָם גְּלוּיִים לָנוּ, לְפָנֶיךָ הֵם גְּלוּיִים וִידוּעִים
כַּדָּבָר שֶׁנֶּאֱמַר
הַנִּסְתָּרֹת לַיהוה אֱלֹהֵינוּ
וְהַנִּגְלֹת לָנוּ וּלְבָנֵינוּ עַד־עוֹלָם
לַעֲשׂוֹת אֶת־כָּל־דִּבְרֵי הַתּוֹרָה הַזֹּאת:
כִּי אַתָּה סָלְחָן לְיִשְׂרָאֵל וּמָחֳלָן לְשִׁבְטֵי יְשֻׁרוּן בְּכָל דּוֹר וָדוֹר
וּמִבַּלְעָדֶיךָ אֵין לָנוּ מֶלֶךְ מוֹחֵל וְסוֹלֵחַ אֶלָּא אָתָּה.

דברים כט

אֱלֹהַי My God,
before I was formed I was unworthy,
and now that I have been formed it is as if I had not been formed.
I am dust while alive,
how much more so when I am dead.
See, I am before You like a vessel filled with shame and disgrace.
May it be Your will, LORD my God and God of my fathers,
that I may sin no more,
and as for the sins I have committed before You,
erase them in Your great compassion,
but not by suffering or severe illness.

אֱלֹהַי My God, *Berakhot*
guard my tongue from evil *17a*
and my lips from deceitful speech.
To those who curse me, let my soul be silent;
may my soul be to all like the dust.
Open my heart to Your Torah
and let my soul pursue Your commandments.
As for all who plan evil against me,
swiftly thwart their counsel and frustrate their plans.
     Act for the sake of Your name; act for the sake of Your right hand;
     act for the sake of Your holiness; act for the sake of Your Torah.
That Your beloved ones may be delivered, *Ps. 60*
save with Your right hand and answer me.
May the words of my mouth and the meditation of my heart *Ps. 19*
find favor before You, LORD, my Rock and Redeemer.

Bow, take three steps back, then bow, first left, then right, then center, while saying:
May He who makes peace in His high places,
make peace for us and all Israel – and say: Amen.

יְהִי רָצוֹן May it be Your will, LORD our God and God of our ancestors,
that the Temple be rebuilt speedily in our days,
and grant us a share in Your Torah.
And there we will serve You with reverence,
as in the days of old and as in former years.
Then the offering of Judah and Jerusalem *Mal. 3*
will be pleasing to the LORD as in the days of old and as in former years.

אֱלֹהַי

עַד שֶׁלֹּא נוֹצַרְתִּי אֵינִי כְדַאי

וְעַכְשָׁיו שֶׁנּוֹצַרְתִּי, כְּאִלּוּ לֹא נוֹצַרְתִּי

עָפָר אֲנִי בְּחַיַּי, קַל וָחֹמֶר בְּמִיתָתִי.

הֲרֵי אֲנִי לְפָנֶיךָ כִּכְלִי מָלֵא בּוּשָׁה וּכְלִמָּה.

יְהִי רָצוֹן מִלְּפָנֶיךָ, יהוה אֱלֹהַי וֵאלֹהֵי אֲבוֹתַי

שֶׁלֹּא אֶחֱטָא עוֹד.

וּמַה שֶּׁחָטָאתִי לְפָנֶיךָ, מְחֹק בְּרַחֲמֶיךָ הָרַבִּים

אֲבָל לֹא עַל יְדֵי יִסּוּרִים וָחֳלָיִם רָעִים.

ברכות יז.

אֱלֹהַי

נְצֹר לְשׁוֹנִי מֵרָע וּשְׂפָתַי מִדַּבֵּר מִרְמָה

וְלִמְקַלְלַי נַפְשִׁי תִדֹּם, וְנַפְשִׁי כֶּעָפָר לַכֹּל תִּהְיֶה.

פְּתַח לִבִּי בְּתוֹרָתֶךָ, וּבְמִצְוֹתֶיךָ תִּרְדֹּף נַפְשִׁי.

וְכָל הַחוֹשְׁבִים עָלַי רָעָה

מְהֵרָה הָפֵר עֲצָתָם וְקַלְקֵל מַחֲשַׁבְתָּם.

עֲשֵׂה לְמַעַן שְׁמֶךָ, עֲשֵׂה לְמַעַן יְמִינֶךָ

עֲשֵׂה לְמַעַן קְדֻשָּׁתֶךָ, עֲשֵׂה לְמַעַן תּוֹרָתֶךָ.

תהלים ס

לְמַעַן יֵחָלְצוּן יְדִידֶיךָ, הוֹשִׁיעָה יְמִינְךָ וַעֲנֵנִי:

תהלים יט

יִהְיוּ לְרָצוֹן אִמְרֵי פִי וְהֶגְיוֹן לִבִּי לְפָנֶיךָ, יהוה צוּרִי וְגֹאֲלִי:

Bow, take three steps back, then bow, first left, then right, then center, while saying:

עֹשֶׂה שָׁלוֹם / בעשרת ימי תשובה: הַשָּׁלוֹם / בִּמְרוֹמָיו

הוּא יַעֲשֶׂה שָׁלוֹם עָלֵינוּ וְעַל כָּל יִשְׂרָאֵל וְאִמְרוּ אָמֵן.

יְהִי רָצוֹן מִלְּפָנֶיךָ יהוה אֱלֹהֵינוּ וֵאלֹהֵי אֲבוֹתֵינוּ

שֶׁיִּבָּנֶה בֵּית הַמִּקְדָּשׁ בִּמְהֵרָה בְיָמֵינוּ, וְתֵן חֶלְקֵנוּ בְּתוֹרָתֶךָ

וְשָׁם נַעֲבָדְךָ בְּיִרְאָה כִּימֵי עוֹלָם וּכְשָׁנִים קַדְמוֹנִיּוֹת.

מלאכי ג

וְעָרְבָה לַיהוה מִנְחַת יְהוּדָה וִירוּשָׁלָ‍ִם כִּימֵי עוֹלָם וּכְשָׁנִים קַדְמוֹנִיּוֹת:

SERVICE FOR ḤANUKKA

*On each of the eight nights of Ḥanukka, the lights of the menora are lit: one on the
first night, two on the second, and so on. On the first night, the rightmost branch of
the menora is used; on each subsequent night, an additional light is added to the left.
Each night, the new light is lit first, then the others, moving rightwards. If possible,
the menora should be displayed near a window so that it is visible from the street.*

*The lights are lit using a separate flame known as the shamash. The lighting should
be carried out as soon as possible after nightfall. On Friday night, it must be done
before the beginning of Shabbat. Before lighting the Ḥanukka lights, say:*

בָּרוּךְ **Blessed are You,** Lord **our God, King of the Universe,**
who has made us holy through His commandments,
and has commanded us to light the Ḥanukka lights.

בָּרוּךְ **Blessed are You,** Lord **our God, King of the Universe,**
who performed miracles for our ancestors in those days,
at this time.

On the first night, add:

בָּרוּךְ **Blessed are You,** Lord **our God, King of the Universe,**
who has given us life, sustained us, and brought us to this time.

After lighting the first light, say:

הַנֵּרוֹת הַלָּלוּ **We light these lights**
because of the miracles and wonders,
deliverances and victories
You performed for our ancestors
in those days, at this time,
through Your holy priests.

Throughout the eight days of Ḥanukka
these lights are holy
and we are not permitted
to make any other use of them,
except to look at them,

that we may give thanks and praise to Your great name
for Your miracles, Your wonders and Your deliverances.

*Soferim
ch. 20*

סדר הדלקת נרות חנוכה

On each of the eight nights of חנוכה, the lights of the חנוכיה are lit: one on the
first night, two on the second, and so on. On the first night, the rightmost branch
of the חנוכיה is used; on each subsequent night, an additional light is added to the
left. Each night, the new light is lit first, then the others, moving rightwards. If possible,
the חנוכיה should be displayed near a window so that it is visible from the street.

The lights are lit using a separate flame known as the שמש. The lighting should
be carried out as soon as possible after nightfall. On Friday night, it must be
done before the beginning of שבת. Before lighting the חנוכה lights, say:

בָּרוּךְ אַתָּה יהוה אֱלֹהֵינוּ מֶלֶךְ הָעוֹלָם
אֲשֶׁר קִדְּשָׁנוּ בְּמִצְוֹתָיו וְצִוָּנוּ לְהַדְלִיק נֵר שֶׁל חֲנֻכָּה.

בָּרוּךְ אַתָּה יהוה אֱלֹהֵינוּ מֶלֶךְ הָעוֹלָם
שֶׁעָשָׂה נִסִּים לַאֲבוֹתֵינוּ בַּיָּמִים הָהֵם בַּזְּמַן הַזֶּה.

On the first night, add:

בָּרוּךְ אַתָּה יהוה אֱלֹהֵינוּ מֶלֶךְ הָעוֹלָם
שֶׁהֶחֱיָנוּ וְקִיְּמָנוּ וְהִגִּיעָנוּ לַזְּמַן הַזֶּה.

After lighting the first light, say:

מסכת
סופרים
פרק כ

הַנֵּרוֹת הַלָּלוּ אָנוּ מַדְלִיקִים
עַל הַנִּסִּים וְעַל הַנִּפְלָאוֹת וְעַל הַתְּשׁוּעוֹת וְעַל הַמִּלְחָמוֹת
שֶׁעָשִׂיתָ לַאֲבוֹתֵינוּ בַּיָּמִים הָהֵם בַּזְּמַן הַזֶּה
עַל יְדֵי כֹּהֲנֶיךָ הַקְּדוֹשִׁים.

וְכָל שְׁמוֹנַת יְמֵי חֲנֻכָּה
הַנֵּרוֹת הַלָּלוּ קֹדֶשׁ הֵם
וְאֵין לָנוּ רְשׁוּת לְהִשְׁתַּמֵּשׁ בָּהֶם
אֶלָּא לִרְאוֹתָם בִּלְבָד

כְּדֵי לְהוֹדוֹת וּלְהַלֵּל לְשִׁמְךָ הַגָּדוֹל
עַל נִסֶּיךָ וְעַל נִפְלְאוֹתֶיךָ וְעַל יְשׁוּעָתֶךָ.

After all the lights are lit:

מָעוֹז צוּר **Refuge, Rock** of my salvation:
to You it is a delight to give praise.
Restore my House of prayer, so that there I may offer You thanksgiving.
When You silence the loud-mouthed foe,
Then will I complete, with song and psalm, the altar's dedication.

רָעוֹת **Troubles** sated my soul; my strength was spent with sorrow.
They embittered my life with hardship,
when I was enslaved under Egyptian rule.
But God with His great power brought out His treasured people,
While Pharaoh's host and followers sank like a stone into the deep.

דְּבִיר **He brought me** to His holy abode, but even there I found no rest.
The oppressor came and exiled me,
because I had served strange gods.
I had drunk poisoned wine. I almost perished.
Then Babylon fell, Zerubbabel came: within seventy years I was saved.

כְּרֹת **The Agagite**, son of Hammedatha,
sought to cut down the tall fir tree,
But it became a trap to him, and his arrogance was brought to an end.
You raised the head of the Benjaminite,
and the enemy's name You blotted out.
His many sons and his household You hanged on the gallows.

יְוָנִים **Then the Greeks** gathered against me,
in the days of the Hasmoneans.
They broke down the walls of my towers, and defiled all the oils.
But from the last remaining flask
a miracle was wrought for Your beloved.
Therefore the sages ordained these eight days for song and praise.

חֲשֹׂף **Bare** Your holy arm, and hasten the time of salvation.
Take retribution against the evil nation
on behalf of Your servants,
For the hour [of deliverance] has been too long delayed;
there seems no end to the evil days.
Thrust the enemy into the darkness of death,
and establish for us the seven Shepherds.

After all the lights are lit:

מָעוֹז צוּר יְשׁוּעָתִי   לְךָ נָאֶה לְשַׁבֵּחַ
תִּכּוֹן בֵּית תְּפִלָּתִי   וְשָׁם תּוֹדָה נְזַבֵּחַ
לְעֵת תָּכִין מַטְבֵּחַ   מִצָּר הַמְנַבֵּחַ
אָז אֶגְמֹר   בְּשִׁיר מִזְמוֹר   חֲנֻכַּת הַמִּזְבֵּחַ.

רָעוֹת שָׂבְעָה נַפְשִׁי   בְּיָגוֹן כֹּחִי כָּלָה
חַיַּי מֵרְרוּ בְקֹשִׁי   בְּשִׁעְבּוּד מַלְכוּת עֶגְלָה
וּבְיָדוֹ הַגְּדוֹלָה   הוֹצִיא אֶת הַסְּגֻלָּה
חֵיל פַּרְעֹה   וְכָל זַרְעוֹ   יָרְדוּ כְּאֶבֶן מְצוּלָה.

דְּבִיר קָדְשׁוֹ הֱבִיאַנִי   וְגַם שָׁם לֹא שָׁקַטְתִּי
וּבָא נוֹגֵשׂ וְהִגְלַנִי   כִּי זָרִים עָבַדְתִּי
וְיֵין רַעַל מָסַכְתִּי   כִּמְעַט שֶׁעָבַרְתִּי
קֵץ בָּבֶל   זְרֻבָּבֶל   לְקֵץ שִׁבְעִים נוֹשַׁעְתִּי.

כְּרֹת קוֹמַת בְּרוֹשׁ בִּקֵּשׁ   אֲגָגִי בֶּן הַמְּדָתָא
וְנִהְיָתָה לוֹ לְפַח וּלְמוֹקֵשׁ   וְגַאֲוָתוֹ נִשְׁבָּתָה
רֹאשׁ יְמִינִי נִשֵּׂאתָ   וְאוֹיֵב שְׁמוֹ מָחִיתָ
רֹב בָּנָיו   וְקִנְיָנָיו   עַל הָעֵץ תָּלִיתָ.

יְוָנִים נִקְבְּצוּ עָלַי   אֲזַי בִּימֵי חַשְׁמַנִּים
וּפָרְצוּ חוֹמוֹת מִגְדָּלַי   וְטִמְּאוּ כָּל הַשְּׁמָנִים
וּמִנּוֹתַר קַנְקַנִּים   נַעֲשָׂה נֵס לַשּׁוֹשַׁנִּים
בְּנֵי בִינָה   יְמֵי שְׁמוֹנָה   קָבְעוּ שִׁיר וּרְנָנִים.

חֲשׂוֹף זְרוֹעַ קָדְשֶׁךָ   וְקָרֵב קֵץ הַיְשׁוּעָה
נְקֹם נִקְמַת עֲבָדֶיךָ   מֵאֻמָּה הָרְשָׁעָה
כִּי אָרְכָה לָנוּ הַשָּׁעָה   וְאֵין קֵץ לִימֵי הָרָעָה
דְּחֵה אַדְמוֹן   בְּצֵל צַלְמוֹן   הָקֵם לָנוּ רוֹעִים שִׁבְעָה.

SERVICE FOR PURIM

Before the reading of the Megilla, the congregation stands
and the Reader says the following three blessings:

בָּרוּךְ Blessed are You, LORD our God, King of the Universe,
who has made us holy through His commandments,
and has commanded us about reading the Megilla.

בָּרוּךְ Blessed are You, LORD our God, King of the Universe,
who performed miracles for our ancestors
in those days at this time.

בָּרוּךְ Blessed are You, LORD our God, King of the Universe,
who has given us life, sustained us, and brought us to this time.

The Megilla is read. When the reading is completed, the scroll is rolled up
and, if a minyan is present, the Reader continues:

בָּרוּךְ Blessed are You, LORD our God, King of the Universe,
who pleads our cause, judges our claim, avenges our wrong,
brings retribution to our enemies, and punishes our foes.
Blessed are You, LORD, who on behalf of His people Israel,
exacts punishment from all their foes, the God who brings salvation.

The following is said after the night reading of the Megilla:

אֲשֶׁר הֵנִיא [God] frustrated the plan of the nations,
Thwarted the intentions of the crafty.
An evil man rose up against us,
An arrogant branch of Amalek's tree,
Haughty, rich, he dug his own pit.
His hubris became his own snare.
He was trapped in the trap he set for others.
Seeking to destroy, he was destroyed.
Haman shared his ancestors' hate,
And stirred against children the hostility of brothers.
He did not remember Saul's act of mercy,
his pity for Agag, through which a new enemy was born.
The wicked planned to cut off the righteous,
but the impure were defeated by the pure.

סדר קריאת המגילה בפורים

Before the reading of the מגילה*, the* קהל *stands
and the* קורא *says the following three blessings:*

בָּרוּךְ אַתָּה יהוה אֱלֹהֵינוּ מֶלֶךְ הָעוֹלָם
אֲשֶׁר קִדְּשָׁנוּ בְּמִצְוֹתָיו וְצִוָּנוּ עַל מִקְרָא מְגִלָּה.

בָּרוּךְ אַתָּה יהוה אֱלֹהֵינוּ מֶלֶךְ הָעוֹלָם
שֶׁעָשָׂה נִסִּים לַאֲבוֹתֵינוּ בַּיָּמִים הָהֵם בַּזְּמַן הַזֶּה.

בָּרוּךְ אַתָּה יהוה אֱלֹהֵינוּ מֶלֶךְ הָעוֹלָם
שֶׁהֶחֱיָנוּ וְקִיְּמָנוּ וְהִגִּיעָנוּ לַזְּמַן הַזֶּה.

The מגילה *is read. When the reading is completed, the scroll is rolled up
and, if a* מנין *is present, the* קורא *continues:*

בָּרוּךְ אַתָּה יהוה אֱלֹהֵינוּ מֶלֶךְ הָעוֹלָם
הָרָב אֶת רִיבֵנוּ, וְהַדָּן אֶת דִּינֵנוּ, וְהַנּוֹקֵם אֶת נִקְמָתֵנוּ
וְהַמְשַׁלֵּם גְּמוּל לְכָל אוֹיְבֵי נַפְשֵׁנוּ, וְהַנִּפְרָע לָנוּ מִצָּרֵינוּ.
בָּרוּךְ אַתָּה יהוה
הַנִּפְרָע לְעַמּוֹ יִשְׂרָאֵל מִכָּל צָרֵיהֶם, הָאֵל הַמּוֹשִׁיעַ.

The following is said after the night reading of the מגילה:

אֲשֶׁר הֵנִיא עֲצַת גּוֹיִם, וַיָּפֶר מַחְשְׁבוֹת עֲרוּמִים.
בְּקוּם עָלֵינוּ אָדָם רָשָׁע, נֵצֶר זָדוֹן מִזֶּרַע עֲמָלֵק.
גָּאָה בְעָשְׁרוֹ וְכָרָה לוֹ בּוֹר, וּגְדֻלָּתוֹ יָקְשָׁה לּוֹ לָכֶד.
דִּמָּה בְנַפְשׁוֹ לִלְכֹּד וְנִלְכָּד, בִּקֵּשׁ לְהַשְׁמִיד וְנִשְׁמַד מְהֵרָה.
הָמָן הוֹדִיעַ אֵיבַת אֲבוֹתָיו, וְעוֹרֵר שִׂנְאַת אַחִים לַבָּנִים.
וְלֹא זָכַר רַחֲמֵי שָׁאוּל, כִּי בְחֶמְלָתוֹ עַל אֲגָג נוֹלַד אוֹיֵב.
זָמַם רָשָׁע לְהַכְרִית צַדִּיק, וְנִלְכַּד טָמֵא בִּידֵי טָהוֹר.

[Mordekhai's] goodness overcame the father's [Saul's] error,
　　　but the evil [Haman] piled sin upon sin.
He hid in his heart his cunning schemes,
　　　intent on his evildoing.
He stretched out his hand against God's holy ones;
　　　he spent his wealth to destroy every memory of them.
When Mordekhai saw the wrath go forth,
　　　and Haman's decrees issued in Shushan,
he put on sackcloth, wrapped himself in mourning,
　　　decreed a fast and sat on ashes.
"Who will arise to atone for error,
　　　and find forgiveness for our ancestors' sins?"
A flower blossomed from the palm tree;
　　　Hadassa arose to wake those who slept.
Her servants hastened Haman to come,
　　　to serve him wine with the venom of serpents.
He had risen by his wealth, but fell by his evil.
　　　He made the very gallows by which he was hanged.
All the inhabitants of the world were amazed
　　　When Haman's ploy (*pur*) became our joy (*Purim*).
The righteous was saved from evil hands,
　　　the perpetrator suffered the fate of his intended victim.
They undertook to celebrate Purim,
　　　and to rejoice on it year after year.
You heeded the prayer of Mordekhai and Esther;
　　　and Haman and his sons were hanged on the gallows.

The following is said after both night and morning readings of the Megilla:

שׁוֹשַׁנַּת יַעֲקֹב The lily of Jacob rejoiced and was glad,
When, together, they saw Mordekhai robed in royal blue.
You have been their eternal salvation, their hope in every generation;
To make known that all who hope in You will not be put to shame,
All who trust in You will never be humiliated.
Cursed be Haman who sought to destroy me. Blessed be Mordekhai the Yehudi.
Cursed be Zeresh, wife of him who terrified me.
Blessed be Esther [whose actions saved] me.
Cursed be all the wicked; blessed be all Israel.
And may Ḥarbona, too, be remembered for good.

*After the night reading, Ma'ariv continues with "You are Holy" to "great
and glorious" on pages 246–248. The Leader then continues with Full
Kaddish. The service continues with Aleinu and Mourner's Kaddish.*

In the morning, continue with Ashrei on page 240.

חֶסֶד גָּבַר עַל שִׁגְגַת אָב, וְרָשָׁע הוֹסִיף חֵטְא עַל חֲטָאָיו.

טָמַן בְּלִבּוֹ מַחְשְׁבוֹת עֲרוּמָיו, וַיִּתְמַכֵּר לַעֲשׂוֹת רָעָה.

יָדוֹ שָׁלַח בְּקִדוֹשֵׁי אֵל, כַּסְפּוֹ נָתַן לְהַכְרִית זִכְרָם.

כִּרְאוֹת מָרְדְּכַי כִּי יָצָא קֶצֶף, וְדָתֵי הָמָן נִתְּנוּ בְשׁוּשָׁן.

לָבַשׁ שַׂק וְקָשַׁר מִסְפֵּד וְגָזַר צוֹם וַיֵּשֶׁב עַל הָאֵפֶר.

מִי זֶה יַעֲמֹד לְכַפֵּר שְׁגָגָה, וְלִמְחֹל חַטַּאת עֲוֹן אֲבוֹתֵינוּ.

נֵץ פָּרַח מִלּוּלָב, הֵן הֲדַסָּה עָמְדָה לְעוֹרֵר יְשֵׁנִים.

סָרִיסֶיהָ הִבְהִילוּ לְהָמָן, לְהַשְׁקוֹתוֹ יֵין חֲמַת תַּנִּינִים.

עָמַד בְּעָשְׁרוֹ וְנָפַל בְּרִשְׁעוֹ, עָשָׂה לוֹ עֵץ וְנִתְלָה עָלָיו.

פִּיהֶם פָּתְחוּ כָּל יוֹשְׁבֵי תֵבֵל, כִּי פוּר הָמָן נֶהְפַּךְ לְפוּרֵנוּ.

צַדִּיק נֶחֱלַץ מִיַּד רָשָׁע, אוֹיֵב נִתַּן תַּחַת נַפְשׁוֹ.

קִיְּמוּ עֲלֵיהֶם לַעֲשׂוֹת פּוּרִים וְלִשְׂמֹחַ בְּכָל שָׁנָה וְשָׁנָה.

רָאִיתָ אֶת תְּפִלַּת מָרְדְּכַי וְאֶסְתֵּר, הָמָן וּבָנָיו עַל הָעֵץ תָּלִיתָ.

The following is said after both night and morning readings of the מְגִילָה:

שׁוֹשַׁנַּת יַעֲקֹב צָהֲלָה וְשָׂמֵחָה
בִּרְאוֹתָם יַחַד תְּכֵלֶת מָרְדְּכַי.

תְּשׁוּעָתָם הָיִיתָ לָנֶצַח, וְתִקְוָתָם בְּכָל דּוֹר וָדוֹר.

לְהוֹדִיעַ שֶׁכָּל קֹוֶיךָ לֹא יֵבֹשׁוּ
וְלֹא יִכָּלְמוּ לָנֶצַח כָּל הַחוֹסִים בָּךְ.

אָרוּר הָמָן אֲשֶׁר בִּקֵּשׁ לְאַבְּדִי
בָּרוּךְ מָרְדְּכַי הַיְּהוּדִי.

אֲרוּרָה זֶרֶשׁ אֵשֶׁת מַפְחִידִי
בְּרוּכָה אֶסְתֵּר בַּעֲדִי.

אֲרוּרִים כָּל הָרְשָׁעִים, בְּרוּכִים כָּל יִשְׂרָאֵל
וְגַם חַרְבוֹנָה זָכוּר לַטּוֹב.

After the night reading, מַעֲרִיב *continues with* קָדוֹשׁ וְאַתָּה to וְאַדִּיר on
pages 247–249. *The* שְׁלִיחַ צִבּוּר *then continues with* קַדִּישׁ שָׁלֵם (*omitting
the line* תִּתְקַבַּל). *The service continues with* עָלֵינוּ *and* קַדִּישׁ יָתוֹם.
In the morning, continue with אַשְׁרֵי *on page 241.*

Shaḥarit for Yom HaZikaron

*At the end of Shaḥarit, after Full Kaddish, the Ark is opened
and the following is said by some congregations:*

לַמְנַצֵּחַ For the conductor of music. Upon the death of Labben. A psalm of David. *Ps. 9*

I will thank You, LORD, with all my heart; I will tell of all Your wonders.

I will rejoice and exult in You; I will sing praise to Your name, Most High.

My enemies retreat; they stumble and perish before You.

For You have upheld my case and my cause; You have sat enthroned as
righteous Judge.

You have rebuked nations and destroyed the wicked, blotting out their name
for ever and all time.

The enemy are finished, ruined forever; You have overthrown their cities; even
the memory of them is lost.

But the LORD abides forever; He has established His throne for judgment.

He will judge the world with righteousness, and try the cause of peoples with
justice.

The LORD is a refuge for the oppressed, a stronghold in times of trouble.

Those who know Your name trust in You, for You, LORD, do not forsake those
who seek You.

Sing praise to the LORD who dwells in Zion; tell the peoples of His deeds.

For He who avenges blood remembers; He does not forget the cry of the
afflicted.

Have mercy on me, LORD, see how my enemies afflict me. Lift me up from the
gates of death,

That in the gates of the Daughter of Zion I may tell all Your praises and rejoice
in Your deliverance.

The nations have fallen into the pit they dug; their feet are caught in the net
they hid.

The LORD is known by His justice; the wicked is ensnared by the work of his
own hands. Reflect on this, Selah.

The wicked return to the grave, all the nations that forget God.

The needy will not be forgotten forever, nor the hope of the afflicted ever be
lost.

Arise, LORD, let not man have power; let the nations be judged in Your
presence.

Strike them with fear, LORD; let the nations know they are only men. Selah.

The Ark is closed.

שחרית ליום הזיכרון

At the end of שחרית, *after* קדיש שלם, *the* ארון קודש *is opened
and the following is said by some congregations:*

תהלים ט

לַמְנַצֵּחַ עַל־מוּת לַבֵּן מִזְמוֹר לְדָוִד:

אוֹדֶה יהוה בְּכָל־לִבִּי, אֲסַפְּרָה כָּל־נִפְלְאוֹתֶיךָ:

אֶשְׂמְחָה וְאֶעֶלְצָה בָךְ, אֲזַמְּרָה שִׁמְךָ עֶלְיוֹן:

בְּשׁוּב־אוֹיְבַי אָחוֹר, יִכָּשְׁלוּ וְיֹאבְדוּ מִפָּנֶיךָ:

כִּי־עָשִׂיתָ מִשְׁפָּטִי וְדִינִי, יָשַׁבְתָּ לְכִסֵּא שׁוֹפֵט צֶדֶק:

גָּעַרְתָּ גוֹיִם אִבַּדְתָּ רָשָׁע, שְׁמָם מָחִיתָ לְעוֹלָם וָעֶד:

הָאוֹיֵב תַּמּוּ חֳרָבוֹת לָנֶצַח, וְעָרִים נָתַשְׁתָּ, אָבַד זִכְרָם הֵמָּה:

וַיהוה לְעוֹלָם יֵשֵׁב, כּוֹנֵן לַמִּשְׁפָּט כִּסְאוֹ:

וְהוּא יִשְׁפֹּט־תֵּבֵל בְּצֶדֶק, יָדִין לְאֻמִּים בְּמֵישָׁרִים:

וִיהִי יהוה מִשְׂגָּב לַדָּךְ, מִשְׂגָּב לְעִתּוֹת בַּצָּרָה:

וְיִבְטְחוּ בְךָ יוֹדְעֵי שְׁמֶךָ, כִּי לֹא־עָזַבְתָּ דֹרְשֶׁיךָ, יהוה:

זַמְּרוּ לַיהוה יֹשֵׁב צִיּוֹן, הַגִּידוּ בָעַמִּים עֲלִילוֹתָיו:

כִּי־דֹרֵשׁ דָּמִים אוֹתָם זָכָר, לֹא־שָׁכַח צַעֲקַת עֲנָוִים:

חָנְנֵנִי יהוה רְאֵה עָנְיִי מִשֹּׂנְאָי, מְרוֹמְמִי מִשַּׁעֲרֵי־מָוֶת:

לְמַעַן אֲסַפְּרָה כָּל־תְּהִלָּתֶיךָ, בְּשַׁעֲרֵי בַת־צִיּוֹן אָגִילָה בִּישׁוּעָתֶךָ:

טָבְעוּ גוֹיִם בְּשַׁחַת עָשׂוּ, בְּרֶשֶׁת־זוּ טָמָנוּ נִלְכְּדָה רַגְלָם:

נוֹדַע יהוה מִשְׁפָּט עָשָׂה, בְּפֹעַל כַּפָּיו נוֹקֵשׁ רָשָׁע, הִגָּיוֹן סֶלָה:

יָשׁוּבוּ רְשָׁעִים לִשְׁאוֹלָה, כָּל־גּוֹיִם שְׁכֵחֵי אֱלֹהִים:

כִּי לֹא לָנֶצַח יִשָּׁכַח אֶבְיוֹן, תִּקְוַת עֲנִיִּים תֹּאבַד לָעַד:

קוּמָה יהוה אַל־יָעֹז אֱנוֹשׁ, יִשָּׁפְטוּ גוֹיִם עַל־פָּנֶיךָ:

שִׁיתָה יהוה מוֹרָה לָהֶם, יֵדְעוּ גוֹיִם, אֱנוֹשׁ הֵמָּה סֶּלָה:

The ארון קודש *is closed.*

Memorial Prayer for Fallen Israeli Soldiers

אָבִינוּ שֶׁבַּשָּׁמַיִם Heavenly Father, God, Source of the spirits of all flesh,
remember, we pray You, the pure souls of our sons and daughters
who heroically gave their lives
in defense of the people and the Land.
Swifter than eagles, stronger than lions,
they fought for the liberation of their people and homeland,
sacrificing their lives for Israel's rebirth in its holy land.
They breathed a spirit of strength and courage
into the whole house of Israel,
in the Land and the Diaspora,
inspiring it to go forward toward its redemption and liberation.
Remember them, our God, for good,
together with the myriad holy ones and heroes of Israel from ancient times.
May their souls be bound in the bonds of everlasting life,
may the Garden of Eden be their resting place,
may they rest in peace
and receive their reward at the End of Days.
Amen.

לְדָוִד Of David. Blessed is the LORD, my Rock, who trains my hands for war, *Ps. 144*
my fingers for battle. He is my Benefactor, my Fortress, my Stronghold and my
Refuge, my Shield in whom I trust, He who subdues nations under me. LORD,
what is man that You care for him, what are mortals that You think of them? Man
is no more than a breath, his days like a fleeting shadow. LORD, part Your heavens
and come down; touch the mountains so that they pour forth smoke. Flash forth
lightning and scatter them; shoot Your arrows and panic them. Reach out Your
hand from on high; deliver me and rescue me from the mighty waters, from the
hands of strangers, whose every word is worthless, whose right hands are raised
in falsehood. To You, God, I will sing a new song; to You I will play music on a
ten-stringed harp. He who gives salvation to kings, who saved His servant David
from the cruel sword: may He deliver me and rescue me from the hands of strangers, whose every word is worthless, whose right hands are raised in falsehood.
Then our sons will be like saplings, well nurtured in their youth. Our daughters
will be like pillars carved for a palace. Our barns will be filled with every kind of
provision. Our sheep will increase by thousands, even tens of thousands in our
fields. Our oxen will draw heavy loads. There will be no breach in the walls, no
going into captivity, no cries of distress in our streets. Happy are the people for
whom this is so; happy are the people whose God is the LORD.

Memorial Prayer for Fallen Israeli Soldiers

אָבִינוּ שֶׁבַּשָּׁמַיִם, אֵל אֱלֹהֵי הָרוּחוֹת לְכָל בָּשָׂר
זְכֹר נָא אֶת הַנְּשָׁמוֹת הַזַּכּוֹת וְהַטְּהוֹרוֹת שֶׁל בָּנֵינוּ וּבְנוֹתֵינוּ
אֲשֶׁר הֶעֱרוּ אֶת נַפְשָׁם לָמוּת מוֹת גִּבּוֹרִים
בְּהֵחָלְצָם לְעֶזְרַת הָעָם וְהָאָרֶץ.
מְנַשְּׁרִים קַלּוּ מֵאֲרָיוֹת גָּבֵרוּ
בְּמִלְחַמְתָּם לְמַעַן שִׁחְרוּר עַמָּם וּמוֹלַדְתָּם.
בַּעֲלוֹתָם עַל מִזְבַּח תְּקוּמַת יִשְׂרָאֵל בְּאֶרֶץ קָדְשׁוֹ
הֵפִיחוּ רוּחַ עֹז וּגְבוּרָה בְּכָל בֵּית יִשְׂרָאֵל בָּאָרֶץ וּבַתְּפוּצוֹת
וַיִּתְעוֹרֵר לִקְרַאת גְּאֻלָּתוֹ וּפְדוּת נַפְשׁוֹ.
יִזְכְּרֵם אֱלֹהֵינוּ לְטוֹבָה
עִם רִבְבוֹת אַלְפֵי קְדוֹשֵׁי יִשְׂרָאֵל וְגִבּוֹרָיו מִימֵי עוֹלָם
בִּצְרוֹר הַחַיִּים יִצְרֹר אֶת נִשְׁמָתָם
בְּגַן עֵדֶן תְּהֵא מְנוּחָתָם
וְיָנוּחוּ בְשָׁלוֹם עַל מִשְׁכָּבָם
וְיַעַמְדוּ לְגוֹרָלָם לְקֵץ הַיָּמִין
אָמֵן.

תהלים קמד ‏ לְדָוִד בָּרוּךְ יהוה צוּרִי הַמְלַמֵּד יָדַי לַקְרָב, אֶצְבְּעוֹתַי לַמִּלְחָמָה: חַסְדִּי וּמְצוּדָתִי
מִשְׂגַּבִּי וּמְפַלְטִי לִי מָגִנִּי וּבוֹ חָסִיתִי הָרוֹדֵד עַמִּי תַחְתָּי: יהוה מָה־אָדָם וַתֵּדָעֵהוּ,
בֶּן־אֱנוֹשׁ וַתְּחַשְּׁבֵהוּ: אָדָם לַהֶבֶל דָּמָה יָמָיו כְּצֵל עוֹבֵר: יהוה הַט־שָׁמֶיךָ וְתֵרֵד
גַּע בֶּהָרִים וְיֶעֱשָׁנוּ: בְּרוֹק בָּרָק וּתְפִיצֵם, שְׁלַח חִצֶּיךָ וּתְהֻמֵּם: שְׁלַח יָדֶיךָ מִמָּרוֹם
פְּצֵנִי וְהַצִּילֵנִי מִמַּיִם רַבִּים מִיַּד בְּנֵי נֵכָר: אֲשֶׁר פִּיהֶם דִּבֶּר־שָׁוְא, וִימִינָם יְמִין
שָׁקֶר: אֱלֹהִים שִׁיר חָדָשׁ אָשִׁירָה לָּךְ, בְּנֵבֶל עָשׂוֹר אֲזַמְּרָה־לָּךְ: הַנּוֹתֵן תְּשׁוּעָה
לַמְּלָכִים הַפּוֹצֶה אֶת־דָּוִד עַבְדּוֹ מֵחֶרֶב רָעָה: פְּצֵנִי וְהַצִּילֵנִי מִיַּד בְּנֵי־נֵכָר אֲשֶׁר
פִּיהֶם דִּבֶּר־שָׁוְא וִימִינָם יְמִין שָׁקֶר: אֲשֶׁר בָּנֵינוּ כִּנְטִעִים מְגֻדָּלִים בִּנְעוּרֵיהֶם
בְּנוֹתֵינוּ כְזָוִיֹּת מְחֻטָּבוֹת תַּבְנִית הֵיכָל: מְזָוֵינוּ מְלֵאִים מְפִיקִים מִזַּן אֶל־זַן צֹאונֵנוּ
מַאֲלִיפוֹת מְרֻבָּבוֹת בְּחוּצוֹתֵינוּ: אַלּוּפֵינוּ מְסֻבָּלִים אֵין פֶּרֶץ וְאֵין יוֹצֵאת וְאֵין
צְוָחָה בִּרְחֹבֹתֵינוּ: אַשְׁרֵי הָעָם שֶׁכָּכָה לּוֹ אַשְׁרֵי הָעָם שֶׁיהוה אֱלֹהָיו:

Ma'ariv for Yom HaAtzma'ut

In Israel, and many communities outside Israel, the following is said before Ma'ariv:

הודו Thank the LORD for He is good; His loving-kindness is for ever. Ps. 107
Let those the LORD redeemed say this – those He redeemed from
the enemy's hand, those He gathered from the lands, from east and
west, from north and south. Some lost their way in desert wastelands,
finding no way to a city where they could live. They were hungry and
thirsty, and their spirit grew faint. Then they cried out to the LORD in
their trouble, and He rescued them from their distress. He led them
by a straight path to a city where they could live. Let them thank the
LORD for His loving-kindness and His wondrous deeds for humankind,
for He satisfies the thirsty and fills the hungry with good. Some sat in
darkness and the shadow of death, cruelly bound in iron chains, for
they had rebelled against God's words and despised the counsel of the
Most High. He humbled their hearts with hard labor; they stumbled,
and there was none to help. Then they cried to the LORD in their trouble,
and He saved them from their distress. He brought them out from

---

years of powerlessness is a knock at the
door.

To acknowledge that millions of Jews
from all over the world have come to live in
Israel is to hear the knock at the door.

To acknowledge that there are now
more Jews living in Israel than anywhere
else in the world, is to recognize the knock
at the door.

To see Jewish bus drivers and newspa-
pers and policemen and a Knesset is to hear
the knock at the door.

To acknowledge that Hebrew is once
again the living language of a sovereign
state is to hear the knock at the door.

To see the list of technological and agri-
cultural wonders that the State has already
contributed to the world, is to hear the
knock at the door.

And the list goes on.

Yom HaAtzma'ut is therefore not just a
regular Independence Day celebration but
an acknowledgment that there is something miraculous, something spiritual that
is taking place before our very eyes.

In *Shir HaShirim*, the young woman
finally gets out of bed to answer the door,
only to discover that her beloved has left
in frustration. Will you answer the door in
time?

מעריב ליום העצמאות

In ארץ ישראל, *and many communities in* חוץ לארץ, *the following is said before* מעריב:

תהלים קז

הֹדוּ לַיהוה כִּי־טוֹב, כִּי לְעוֹלָם חַסְדּוֹ: יֹאמְרוּ גְּאוּלֵי יהוה, אֲשֶׁר גְּאָלָם מִיַּד־צָר: וּמֵאֲרָצוֹת קִבְּצָם, מִמִּזְרָח וּמִמַּעֲרָב, מִצָּפוֹן וּמִיָּם: תָּעוּ בַמִּדְבָּר, בִּישִׁימוֹן דָּרֶךְ, עִיר מוֹשָׁב לֹא מָצָאוּ: רְעֵבִים גַּם־צְמֵאִים, נַפְשָׁם בָּהֶם תִּתְעַטָּף: וַיִּצְעֲקוּ אֶל־יהוה בַּצַּר לָהֶם, מִמְּצוּקוֹתֵיהֶם יַצִּילֵם: וַיַּדְרִיכֵם בְּדֶרֶךְ יְשָׁרָה, לָלֶכֶת אֶל־עִיר מוֹשָׁב: יוֹדוּ לַיהוה חַסְדּוֹ, וְנִפְלְאוֹתָיו לִבְנֵי אָדָם: כִּי־הִשְׂבִּיעַ נֶפֶשׁ שֹׁקֵקָה, וְנֶפֶשׁ רְעֵבָה מִלֵּא־טוֹב: יֹשְׁבֵי חֹשֶׁךְ וְצַלְמָוֶת, אֲסִירֵי עֳנִי וּבַרְזֶל: כִּי־הִמְרוּ אִמְרֵי־אֵל, וַעֲצַת עֶלְיוֹן נָאָצוּ: וַיַּכְנַע בֶּעָמָל לִבָּם, כָּשְׁלוּ וְאֵין עֹזֵר: וַיִּזְעֲקוּ אֶל־יהוה

INTRODUCTION TO YOM HAATZMA'UT

Can you hear the knocking at the door? Or are you still sleeping or lazy and cannot be bothered?

Shir HaShirim, written by King Shlomo, is about the deep and passionate love between a man and a woman that is a metaphor for the relationship between Hashem and the Jewish people. There is a passage in which the man comes knocking at the woman's door one night but she doesn't really want to get out of bed to answer him. "I'm undressed already," she protests, "and I've bathed and don't want to get my feet dirty."

Rabbi J.B. Soloveitchik suggested in his essay *Kol Dodi Dofek,* that the modern State

of Israel is comparable to Hashem coming to knock on our door. After two thousand years of being without a state of our own, without a homeland of our own, but nevertheless never giving up our hope and dream that we would return, the Jewish State became a reality in 1948. A student of history would explain its emergence in terms of the Zionist movement of the nineteenth century, the Holocaust, and the international political motivations of nations with competing interests. The religious student of history understands all of these but also sees the hand of God knocking at our door.

To have an army after thousands of

darkness and the shadow of death and broke open their chains. Let them thank the Lord for His loving-kindness and His wondrous deeds for humankind, for He shattered gates of bronze and broke their iron bars. Some were fools with sinful ways, and suffered affliction because of their iniquities. They found all food repulsive, and came close to the gates of death. Then they cried to the Lord in their trouble, and He saved them from their distress. He sent His word and healed them; He rescued them from their destruction. Let them thank the Lord for His loving-kindness and His wondrous deeds for humankind. Let them sacrifice thanksgiving-offerings and tell His deeds with songs of joy. Those who go to sea in ships, plying their trade in the mighty waters, have seen the works of the Lord, His wondrous deeds in the deep. He spoke and stirred up a tempest that lifted high the waves. They rose to the heavens and plunged down to the depths; their souls melted in misery. They reeled and staggered like drunkards; all their skill was to no avail. Then they cried to the Lord in their trouble, and He brought them out of their distress. He stilled the storm to a whisper, and the waves of the sea grew calm. They rejoiced when all was quiet, then He guided them to their destination. Let them thank the Lord for His loving-kindness and His wondrous deeds for humankind. Let them exalt Him in the assembly of the people and praise Him in the council of the elders. He turns rivers into a desert, springs of water into parched land, fruitful land into a salt marsh, because of the wickedness of its inhabitants. He turns the desert into pools of water, parched land into flowing springs; He brings the hungry to live there, they build themselves a town in which to live. They sow fields and plant vineyards that yield a fruitful harvest; He blesses them, and they increase greatly, their herds do not decrease, though they had been few and brought low by oppression, adversity and sorrow. He pours contempt on nobles and makes them wander in a pathless waste. ‣ He lifts the destitute from poverty and enlarges their families like flocks. The upright see and rejoice, but the mouth of all wrongdoers is stopped. Whoever is wise, let him lay these things to heart, and reflect on the loving-kindness of the Lord.

בַּצַּר לָהֶם, מִמְּצֻקוֹתֵיהֶם יוֹשִׁיעֵם: יוֹצִיאֵם מֵחֹשֶׁךְ וְצַלְמָוֶת,
וּמוֹסְרוֹתֵיהֶם יְנַתֵּק: יוֹדוּ לַיהוה חַסְדּוֹ, וְנִפְלְאוֹתָיו לִבְנֵי אָדָם:
כִּי־שִׁבַּר דַּלְתוֹת נְחֹשֶׁת, וּבְרִיחֵי בַרְזֶל גִּדֵּעַ: אֱוִלִים מִדֶּרֶךְ
פִּשְׁעָם, וּמֵעֲוֹנֹתֵיהֶם יִתְעַנּוּ: כָּל־אֹכֶל תְּתַעֵב נַפְשָׁם, וַיַּגִּיעוּ
עַד־שַׁעֲרֵי מָוֶת: וַיִּזְעֲקוּ אֶל־יהוה בַּצַּר לָהֶם, מִמְּצֻקוֹתֵיהֶם
יוֹשִׁיעֵם: יִשְׁלַח דְּבָרוֹ וְיִרְפָּאֵם, וִימַלֵּט מִשְּׁחִיתוֹתָם: יוֹדוּ
לַיהוה חַסְדּוֹ, וְנִפְלְאוֹתָיו לִבְנֵי אָדָם: וְיִזְבְּחוּ זִבְחֵי תוֹדָה וִיסַפְּרוּ
מַעֲשָׂיו בְּרִנָּה: יוֹרְדֵי הַיָּם בָּאֳנִיּוֹת, עֹשֵׂי מְלָאכָה בְּמַיִם רַבִּים:
הֵמָּה רָאוּ מַעֲשֵׂי יהוה, וְנִפְלְאוֹתָיו בִּמְצוּלָה: וַיֹּאמֶר, וַיַּעֲמֵד
רוּחַ סְעָרָה, וַתְּרוֹמֵם גַּלָּיו: יַעֲלוּ שָׁמַיִם, יֵרְדוּ תְהוֹמוֹת, נַפְשָׁם
בְּרָעָה תִתְמוֹגָג: יָחוֹגּוּ וְיָנוּעוּ כַּשִּׁכּוֹר, וְכָל־חָכְמָתָם תִּתְבַּלָּע:
וַיִּצְעֲקוּ אֶל־יהוה בַּצַּר לָהֶם, וּמִמְּצוּקֹתֵיהֶם יוֹצִיאֵם: יָקֵם סְעָרָה
לִדְמָמָה, וַיֶּחֱשׁוּ גַּלֵּיהֶם: וַיִּשְׂמְחוּ כִי־יִשְׁתֹּקוּ, וַיַּנְחֵם אֶל־מְחוֹז
חֶפְצָם: יוֹדוּ לַיהוה חַסְדּוֹ, וְנִפְלְאוֹתָיו לִבְנֵי אָדָם: וִירֹמְמוּהוּ
בִּקְהַל־עָם, וּבְמוֹשַׁב זְקֵנִים יְהַלְלוּהוּ: יָשֵׂם נְהָרוֹת לְמִדְבָּר,
וּמֹצָאֵי מַיִם לְצִמָּאוֹן: אֶרֶץ פְּרִי לִמְלֵחָה, מֵרָעַת יוֹשְׁבֵי בָהּ: יָשֵׂם
מִדְבָּר לַאֲגַם־מַיִם, וְאֶרֶץ צִיָּה לְמֹצָאֵי מָיִם: וַיּוֹשֶׁב שָׁם רְעֵבִים,
וַיְכוֹנְנוּ עִיר מוֹשָׁב: וַיִּזְרְעוּ שָׂדוֹת, וַיִּטְּעוּ כְרָמִים, וַיַּעֲשׂוּ פְּרִי
תְבוּאָה: וַיְבָרֲכֵם וַיִּרְבּוּ מְאֹד, וּבְהֶמְתָּם לֹא יַמְעִיט: וַיִּמְעֲטוּ
וַיָּשֹׁחוּ, מֵעֹצֶר רָעָה וְיָגוֹן: שֹׁפֵךְ בּוּז עַל־נְדִיבִים, וַיַּתְעֵם בְּתֹהוּ
לֹא־דָרֶךְ: • וַיְשַׂגֵּב אֶבְיוֹן מֵעוֹנִי, וַיָּשֶׂם כַּצֹּאן מִשְׁפָּחוֹת: יִרְאוּ
יְשָׁרִים וְיִשְׂמָחוּ, וְכָל־עַוְלָה קָפְצָה פִּיהָ: מִי־חָכָם וְיִשְׁמָר־אֵלֶּה,
וְיִתְבּוֹנְנוּ חַסְדֵי יהוה:

יהוה מָלָךְ **The** Lord reigns, let the earth be glad. Let the many islands   *Ps. 97*
rejoice. Clouds and thick darkness surround Him; righteousness and
justice are the foundation of His throne. Fire goes ahead of Him, con-
suming His enemies on every side. His lightning lights up the world;
the earth sees and trembles. Mountains melt like wax before the Lord,
before the Lord of all the earth. The heavens proclaim His righteousness, and all the peoples see His glory. All who worship images and
boast in idols are put to shame. Bow down to Him, all you heavenly
powers. Zion hears and rejoices, and the towns of Judah are glad
because of Your judgments, Lord. For You, Lord, are supreme over
all the earth; You are exalted far above all heavenly powers. Let those
who love the Lord hate evil, for He protects the lives of His devoted
ones, delivering them from the hand of the wicked. ‣ Light is sown for
the righteous, and joy for the upright in heart. Rejoice in the Lord, you
who are righteous, and give thanks to His holy name.

The Leader and the Congregation say this psalm responsively, verse by verse

מִזְמוֹר **A** Psalm. Sing a new song to the Lord,   *Ps. 98*
for He has done wondrous things;
He has saved by His right hand and His holy arm.
The Lord has made His salvation known;
He has displayed His righteousness in the sight of the nations.
He remembered His loving-kindness and faithfulness
to the house of Israel;
all the ends of the earth have seen the victory of our Lord.
Shout for joy to the Lord, all the earth;
burst into song, sing with joy, play music.
Play music to the Lord on the harp –
on the harp with the sound of singing.
With trumpets and the sound of the shofar,
shout for joy before the Lord, the King.
‣ Let the sea and all that is in it thunder,
the world and all who live in it.
Let the rivers clap their hands, the mountains sing together for joy –
before the Lord, for He is coming to judge the earth.
He will judge the world with justice, and the peoples with equity.

יהוה מָלָךְ תָּגֵל הָאָרֶץ, יִשְׂמְחוּ אִיִּים רַבִּים: עָנָן וַעֲרָפֶל סְבִיבָיו,
צֶדֶק וּמִשְׁפָּט מְכוֹן כִּסְאוֹ: אֵשׁ לְפָנָיו תֵּלֵךְ, וּתְלַהֵט סָבִיב צָרָיו:
הֵאִירוּ בְרָקָיו תֵּבֵל, רָאֲתָה וַתָּחֵל הָאָרֶץ: הָרִים כַּדּוֹנַג נָמַסּוּ
מִלִּפְנֵי יהוה, מִלִּפְנֵי אֲדוֹן כָּל־הָאָרֶץ: הִגִּידוּ הַשָּׁמַיִם צִדְקוֹ,
וְרָאוּ כָל־הָעַמִּים כְּבוֹדוֹ: יֵבֹשׁוּ כָּל־עֹבְדֵי פֶסֶל הַמִּתְהַלְלִים
בָּאֱלִילִים, הִשְׁתַּחֲווּ־לוֹ כָּל־אֱלֹהִים: שָׁמְעָה וַתִּשְׂמַח צִיּוֹן,
וַתָּגֵלְנָה בְּנוֹת יְהוּדָה, לְמַעַן מִשְׁפָּטֶיךָ יהוה: כִּי־אַתָּה יהוה
עֶלְיוֹן עַל־כָּל־הָאָרֶץ, מְאֹד נַעֲלֵיתָ עַל־כָּל־אֱלֹהִים: אֹהֲבֵי יהוה
שִׂנְאוּ רָע, שֹׁמֵר נַפְשׁוֹת חֲסִידָיו, מִיַּד רְשָׁעִים יַצִּילֵם: ‹ אוֹר
זָרֻעַ לַצַּדִּיק, וּלְיִשְׁרֵי־לֵב שִׂמְחָה: שִׂמְחוּ צַדִּיקִים בַּיהוה, וְהוֹדוּ
לְזֵכֶר קָדְשׁוֹ:

The שליח ציבור and the קהל say this psalm responsively, verse by verse

מִזְמוֹר, שִׁירוּ לַיהוה שִׁיר חָדָשׁ כִּי־נִפְלָאוֹת עָשָׂה
הוֹשִׁיעָה־לּוֹ יְמִינוֹ וּזְרוֹעַ קָדְשׁוֹ:
הוֹדִיעַ יהוה יְשׁוּעָתוֹ, לְעֵינֵי הַגּוֹיִם גִּלָּה צִדְקָתוֹ:
זָכַר חַסְדּוֹ וֶאֱמוּנָתוֹ לְבֵית יִשְׂרָאֵל
רָאוּ כָל־אַפְסֵי־אָרֶץ אֵת יְשׁוּעַת אֱלֹהֵינוּ:
הָרִיעוּ לַיהוה כָּל־הָאָרֶץ, פִּצְחוּ וְרַנְּנוּ וְזַמֵּרוּ:
זַמְּרוּ לַיהוה בְּכִנּוֹר, בְּכִנּוֹר וְקוֹל זִמְרָה:
בַּחֲצֹצְרוֹת וְקוֹל שׁוֹפָר, הָרִיעוּ לִפְנֵי הַמֶּלֶךְ יהוה:
‹ יִרְעַם הַיָּם וּמְלֹאוֹ, תֵּבֵל וְיֹשְׁבֵי בָהּ:
נְהָרוֹת יִמְחֲאוּ־כָף, יַחַד הָרִים יְרַנֵּנוּ:
לִפְנֵי־יהוה כִּי בָא לִשְׁפֹּט הָאָרֶץ
יִשְׁפֹּט־תֵּבֵל בְּצֶדֶק, וְעַמִּים בְּמֵישָׁרִים:

It is customary to sing:

הִתְעוֹרְרִי Wake up, wake up,
　　For your light has come: rise, shine!
　　Awake, awake, break out in song,
　　For the LORD's glory is revealed on you.

　　　　This is the day the LORD has made;　　　　*Ps. 118*
　　　　let us rejoice and be glad in it.

לֹא תֵבֹשִׁי Do not be ashamed, do not be confounded.
　　Why be downcast? Why do you mourn?
　　In you the needy of My people find shelter,
　　And the city shall be rebuilt on its hill.

　　　　This is the day the LORD has made;
　　　　let us rejoice and be glad in it.

יָמִין Right and left you shall spread out,
　　And God you will revere.
　　Through the descendant of Peretz,
　　We shall rejoice and we shall be glad.

　　　　This is the day the LORD has made;
　　　　let us rejoice and be glad in it.

Ma'ariv for Weekdays (page 342) is said at this point, in the Yom Tov melody. After Full Kaddish,
the Ark is opened and the following is said responsively by the Leader and congregation.

　　Listen, Israel: the LORD is our God, the LORD is One.　　*Deut. 6*

The following is said three times responsively:

　　　　The LORD, He is God.

The Leader says the following which is repeated by the congregation.

מִי שֶׁעָשָׂה May He who performed miracles for our ancestors and for us,
　　redeeming us from slavery to freedom,
　　grant us a complete redemption soon,
　　and gather in our dispersed people
　　from the four quarters of the earth,
　　so that all Israel may be united in friendship,
　　and let us say: Amen.

The Ark is closed.

It is customary to sing:

הִתְעוֹרְרִי הִתְעוֹרְרִי

כִּי בָא אוֹרֵךְ קֽוּמִי אֽוֹרִי

עֽוּרִי עֽוּרִי, שִׁיר דַּבֵּרִי

כְּבוֹד יהוה עָלַיִךְ נִגְלָה.

זֶה־הַיּוֹם עָשָׂה יהוה, נָגִֽילָה וְנִשְׂמְחָה בוֹ: תהלים קיח

לֹא תֵבֽוֹשִׁי וְלֹא תִכָּלְמִי

מַה תִּשְׁתּוֹחֲחִי וּמַה תֶּהֱמִי

בָּךְ יֶחֱסוּ עֲנִיֵּי עַמִּי

וְנִבְנְתָה עִיר עַל תִּלָּהּ.

זֶה־הַיּוֹם עָשָׂה יהוה, נָגִֽילָה וְנִשְׂמְחָה בוֹ:

יָמִין וּשְׂמֹאל תִּפְרֹֽצִי

וְאֶת יהוה תַּעֲרִֽיצִי

עַל יַד אִישׁ בֶּן פַּרְצִי

וְנִשְׂמְחָה וְנָגִֽילָה.

זֶה־הַיּוֹם עָשָׂה יהוה, נָגִֽילָה וְנִשְׂמְחָה בוֹ:

קַדִּישׁ שָׁלֵם (מעריב לחול page 343) is said at this point, in the יוֹם טוֹב melody. After
the שְׁלִיחַ צִבּוּר and the קָהָל is opened and the following is said responsively by the אֲרוֹן קוֹדֶשׁ.

שְׁמַע יִשְׂרָאֵל, יהוה אֱלֹהֵֽינוּ, יהוה אֶחָד: דברים ו

The following is said three times responsively:

יהוה הוּא הָאֱלֹהִים.

The שְׁלִיחַ צִבּוּר says the following which is repeated by the קָהָל.

מִי שֶׁעָשָׂה נִסִּים לַאֲבוֹתֵֽינוּ וְלָֽנוּ

וּגְאָלָֽנוּ מֵעַבְדוּת לְחֵרוּת

הוּא יִגְאָלֵֽנוּ גְּאֻלָּה שְׁלֵמָה בְּקָרוֹב

וִיקַבֵּץ נִדָּחֵֽינוּ מֵאַרְבַּע כַּנְפוֹת הָאָֽרֶץ

חֲבֵרִים כָּל יִשְׂרָאֵל, וְנֹאמַר אָמֵן.

The אֲרוֹן קוֹדֶשׁ is closed.

The Leader continues:

וְכִי־תָבֹאוּ When you go into battle in your land against an enemy who is attacking you, sound a staccato blast on the trumpets. Then you will be remembered by the LORD your God and you will be delivered from your enemies. On your days of rejoicing – your festivals and new moon celebrations – you shall sound a note on the trumpets over your burnt- and peace-offerings, and they will be a remembrance for you before your God. I am the LORD your God.

Num. 10

The shofar is sounded with a Tekia Gedola and the following is said aloud:

Next year in Jerusalem rebuilt.

All:

May it be Your will, LORD our God and God of our fathers,
That as we have merited to witness the beginning of redemption,
So may we merit to hear the sound of the shofar
of our righteous anointed one, swiftly in our days.

All sing:

שִׁיר הַמַּעֲלוֹת A song of ascents. When the LORD brought back the exiles of Zion we were like people who dream. Then were our mouths filled with laughter, and our tongues with songs of joy. Then was it said among the nations, "The LORD has done great things for them." The LORD did do great things for us and we rejoiced. Bring back our exiles, LORD, like streams in a dry land. May those who sowed in tears, reap in joy. May one who goes out weeping, carrying a bag of seed, come back with songs of joy, carrying his sheaves.

Ps. 126

The Omer is counted (page 388), followed by Aleinu (page 380).

All sing:

אֲנִי מַאֲמִין I believe with perfect faith
in the coming of the Messiah,
and though he may delay,
I wait daily for his coming.

It is customary to greet each other with the following phrase:
Happy festival; to a complete redemption!

The שליח ציבור continues:

במדברי וְכִי־תָבֹאוּ מִלְחָמָה בְּאַרְצְכֶם עַל־הַצַּר הַצֹּרֵר אֶתְכֶם, וַהֲרֵעֹתֶם
בַּחֲצֹצְרֹת, וְנִזְכַּרְתֶּם לִפְנֵי יהוה אֱלֹהֵיכֶם, וְנוֹשַׁעְתֶּם מֵאֹיְבֵיכֶם:
וּבְיוֹם שִׂמְחַתְכֶם וּבְמוֹעֲדֵיכֶם וּבְרָאשֵׁי חָדְשֵׁכֶם, וּתְקַעְתֶּם
בַּחֲצֹצְרֹת עַל עֹלֹתֵיכֶם וְעַל זִבְחֵי שַׁלְמֵיכֶם, וְהָיוּ לָכֶם לְזִכָּרוֹן
לִפְנֵי אֱלֹהֵיכֶם, אֲנִי יהוה אֱלֹהֵיכֶם:

The שופר is sounded with a תקיעה גדולה and the following is said aloud:

לְשָׁנָה הַבָּאָה בִּירוּשָׁלַיִם הַבְּנוּיָה.

All:

יְהִי רָצוֹן מִלְּפָנֶיךָ יהוה אֱלֹהֵינוּ וֵאלֹהֵי אֲבוֹתֵינוּ
שֶׁכְּשֵׁם שֶׁזָּכִינוּ לְאַתְחַלְתָּא דְּגְאֻלָּה
כֵּן נִזְכֶּה לִשְׁמֹעַ קוֹל שׁוֹפָרוֹ שֶׁל מָשִׁיחַ צִדְקֵנוּ בִּמְהֵרָה בְיָמֵינוּ.

All sing:

תהלים קכו שִׁיר הַמַּעֲלוֹת, בְּשׁוּב יהוה אֶת־שִׁיבַת צִיּוֹן, הָיִינוּ כְּחֹלְמִים: אָז יִמָּלֵא שְׂחוֹק
פִּינוּ וּלְשׁוֹנֵנוּ רִנָּה, אָז יֹאמְרוּ בַגּוֹיִם הִגְדִּיל יהוה לַעֲשׂוֹת עִם־אֵלֶּה: הִגְדִּיל
יהוה לַעֲשׂוֹת עִמָּנוּ, הָיִינוּ שְׂמֵחִים: שׁוּבָה יהוה אֶת־שְׁבִיתֵנוּ, כַּאֲפִיקִים
בַּנֶּגֶב: הַזֹּרְעִים בְּדִמְעָה בְּרִנָּה יִקְצֹרוּ: הָלוֹךְ יֵלֵךְ וּבָכֹה נֹשֵׂא מֶשֶׁךְ־הַזָּרַע,
בֹּא־יָבֹא בְרִנָּה נֹשֵׂא אֲלֻמֹּתָיו:

The עומר is counted (page 389), followed by עלינו (page 381).

All sing:

אֲנִי מַאֲמִין בֶּאֱמוּנָה שְׁלֵמָה בְּבִיאַת הַמָּשִׁיחַ
וְאַף עַל פִּי שֶׁיִּתְמַהְמֵהַּ
עִם כָּל זֶה אֲחַכֶּה לּוֹ בְּכָל יוֹם שֶׁיָּבוֹא.

It is customary to greet each other with the following phrase:

מוֹעֲדִים לְשִׂמְחָה לִגְאֻלָּה שְׁלֵמָה

Shaḥarit for Yom HaAtzma'ut

Begin as on weekdays, from pages 4–60.

In Israel, and many congregations outside Israel, Pesukei DeZimra of Yom Tov are said (page 474). Some communities recite Shirat HaYam (page 100) responsively verse by verse. After the Leader's Repetition, Full Hallel (page 442) is said followed by Half Kaddish (page 214). On Thursdays the Torah is read (page 216). On all days, the following Haftara is read.

עוֹד הַיּוֹם This day he will halt at Nob; he will wave his hand, mountain of the daughter of Zion, hill of Jerusalem. See, the sovereign LORD of hosts will lop off the boughs with an axe. The tall trees will be felled, the lofty ones laid low. He will cut down the forest thickets with an axe. Lebanon will fall before the Mighty One. A shoot will grow from the stump of Jesse; from his roots a branch will bear fruit. The spirit of the LORD will rest on him – a spirit of wisdom and understanding, a spirit of counsel and power, a spirit of knowledge and the fear of the LORD, and he will delight in the fear of the LORD. He will not judge by what his eyes see, or decide by what his ears hear; with justice he will judge the poor, and with equity defend humble in the land. He will strike the earth with the rod of his mouth; with the breath of his lips he will slay the wicked. Justice will be his belt and faithfulness the sash around his waist. The wolf will live with the lamb, the leopard will lie down with the kid, the calf and the lion and the yearling together; and a little child will lead them. The cow will graze with the bear, their young will lie down together, and the lion will eat straw like the ox. An infant will play near the cobra's hole, and a young child put his hand into the viper's nest. They will neither harm nor destroy on all My holy mountain, for the earth will be full of the knowledge of the LORD as the waters cover the sea. On that day the stock of Jesse will stand as a banner for the peoples; nations will rally to him, and his place of rest will be glorious. On that day the LORD will reach out His hand

Is. 10:32–12:6

"Of course," replied the rabbi.
To which Rav Bin Nun answered: "And do you not know that it was human beings who planted the wheat, and cut and harvested it, and threshed it, and ground it, baked it and packaged it and marketed it – and without their efforts you would never have had a piece of bread? And yet you still say HaMotzi!"

שחרית ליום העצמאות

Begin as on weekdays, from pages 5–61.

In ארץ ישראל, and many congregations in חוץ לארץ, פסוקי דזמרה of יום טוב are said (page 475).
Some communities recite שירת הים (page 101) responsively verse by verse. After חזרת הש״ץ,
הלל שלם (page 443) is said followed by חצי קדיש (page 215). On Thursdays
the תורה is read (page 217). On all days, the following הפטרה is read.

ישעיה
י:לב–יב:ו

עוֹד הַיּוֹם בְּנֹב לַעֲמֹד יְנֹפֵף יָדוֹ הַר בַּת־צִיּוֹן גִּבְעַת
יְרוּשָׁלָ͏ִם: הִנֵּה הָאָדוֹן יהוה צְבָאוֹת מְסָעֵף פֻּארָה
בְּמַעֲרָצָה וְרָמֵי הַקּוֹמָה גְּדֻעִים וְהַגְּבֹהִים יִשְׁפָּלוּ: וְנִקַּף סִבְכֵי הַיַּעַר
בַּבַּרְזֶל וְהַלְּבָנוֹן בְּאַדִּיר יִפּוֹל: וְיָצָא חֹטֶר מִגֵּזַע יִשָׁי
וְנֵצֶר מִשָּׁרָשָׁיו יִפְרֶה: וְנָחָה עָלָיו רוּחַ יהוה רוּחַ חָכְמָה וּבִינָה רוּחַ
עֵצָה וּגְבוּרָה רוּחַ דַּעַת וְיִרְאַת יהוה: וַהֲרִיחוֹ בְּיִרְאַת יהוה וְלֹא־
לְמַרְאֵה עֵינָיו יִשְׁפּוֹט וְלֹא־לְמִשְׁמַע אָזְנָיו יוֹכִיחַ: וְשָׁפַט בְּצֶדֶק
דַּלִּים וְהוֹכִיחַ בְּמִישׁוֹר לְעַנְוֵי־אָרֶץ וְהִכָּה־אֶרֶץ בְּשֵׁבֶט פִּיו וּבְרוּחַ
שְׂפָתָיו יָמִית רָשָׁע: וְהָיָה צֶדֶק אֵזוֹר מָתְנָיו וְהָאֱמוּנָה אֵזוֹר חֲלָצָיו:
וְגָר זְאֵב עִם־כֶּבֶשׂ וְנָמֵר עִם־גְּדִי יִרְבָּץ וְעֵגֶל וּכְפִיר וּמְרִיא יַחְדָּו
וְנַעַר קָטֹן נֹהֵג בָּם: וּפָרָה וָדֹב תִּרְעֶינָה יַחְדָּו יִרְבְּצוּ יַלְדֵיהֶן וְאַרְיֵה
כַּבָּקָר יֹאכַל־תֶּבֶן: וְשִׁעֲשַׁע יוֹנֵק עַל־חֻר פָּתֶן וְעַל מְאוּרַת צִפְעוֹנִי
גָּמוּל יָדוֹ הָדָה: לֹא־יָרֵעוּ וְלֹא־יַשְׁחִיתוּ בְּכָל־הַר קָדְשִׁי כִּי־מָלְאָה
הָאָרֶץ דֵּעָה אֶת־יהוה כַּמַּיִם לַיָּם מְכַסִּים: וְהָיָה בַּיּוֹם

ANI TEFILLA · אני תפילה

A rabbi once came to Rav Yoel Bin Nun and challenged the latter's contention that the ingathering of the exiles, the huge masses of Jewish immigration from virtually every country in the world to the State of Israel, was nothing less than a miracle of God. Was it not part of the Zionist enterprise, the result of human action in the political realm, including the participation of many secular Jews? How, then, could it be considered an act of God?

Answered Rav Bin Nun: "Do you recite HaMotzi before you eat bread?"

a second time to reclaim the remnant that is left of His people from Assyria, Lower Egypt, Pathros, Cush, Elam, Shinar, Hamath and the islands of the sea. He will raise a banner for the nations and gather the exiles of Israel; He will assemble the scattered people of Judah from the four quarters of the earth. Ephraim's jealousy will vanish, and Judah's harassment will end. Ephraim will not be jealous of Judah, nor will Judah be hostile toward Ephraim. They will swoop down on the slopes of Philistia to the west; together they will plunder the people to the east. Edom and Moab will be subject to them, and the Ammonites shall obey them. The LORD will dry up the gulf of the Egyptian sea; with a scorching wind He will sweep His hand over the Euphrates River. He will break it up into seven streams so that people can cross over in sandals. There will be a highway for the remnant of His people that is left from Assyria, as there was for Israel when they came up from Egypt. In that day you will say: "I will praise You, O LORD. Although You were angry with me, Your anger has turned away and You have comforted me. Surely God is my salvation; I will trust and not be afraid. The LORD, the LORD, is my strength and my song; He has become my salvation." With joy you will draw water from the wells of salvation. In that day you will say: "Give thanks to the LORD, call on His name; make known among the nations what He has done, and proclaim that His name is exalted. Sing to the LORD, for He has done glorious things; let this be known to all the world. Shout aloud and sing for joy, people of Zion, for great is the Holy One of Israel among you."

PRAYER FOR THE STATE OF ISRAEL

The Leader says the following prayer:

אָבִינוּ שֶׁבַּשָּׁמַיִם Heavenly Father, Israel's Rock and Redeemer, bless the State of Israel, the first flowering of our redemption. Shield it under the wings of Your loving-kindness and spread over it the Tabernacle of Your peace. Send Your light and truth to its leaders, ministers and counselors, and direct them with good counsel before You.

הַהוּא שֹׁרֶשׁ יִשַׁי אֲשֶׁר עֹמֵד לְנֵס עַמִּים אֵלָיו גּוֹיִם יִדְרֹשׁוּ וְהָיְתָה
מְנֻחָתוֹ כָּבוֹד: וְהָיָה ׀ בַּיּוֹם הַהוּא יוֹסִיף אֲדֹנָי ׀ שֵׁנִית יָדוֹ
לִקְנוֹת אֶת־שְׁאָר עַמּוֹ אֲשֶׁר יִשָּׁאֵר מֵאַשּׁוּר וּמִמִּצְרַיִם וּמִפַּתְרוֹס
וּמִכּוּשׁ וּמֵעֵילָם וּמִשִּׁנְעָר וּמֵחֲמָת וּמֵאִיֵּי הַיָּם: וְנָשָׂא נֵס לַגּוֹיִם וְאָסַף
נִדְחֵי יִשְׂרָאֵל וּנְפֻצוֹת יְהוּדָה יְקַבֵּץ מֵאַרְבַּע כַּנְפוֹת הָאָרֶץ: וְסָרָה
קִנְאַת אֶפְרַיִם וְצֹרְרֵי יְהוּדָה יִכָּרֵתוּ אֶפְרַיִם לֹא־יְקַנֵּא אֶת־יְהוּדָה
וִיהוּדָה לֹא־יָצֹר אֶת־אֶפְרָיִם: וְעָפוּ בְכָתֵף פְּלִשְׁתִּים יָמָּה יַחְדָּו יָבֹזּוּ
אֶת־בְּנֵי־קֶדֶם אֱדוֹם וּמוֹאָב מִשְׁלוֹחַ יָדָם וּבְנֵי עַמּוֹן מִשְׁמַעְתָּם:
וְהֶחֱרִים יְהוָה אֵת לְשׁוֹן יָם־מִצְרַיִם וְהֵנִיף יָדוֹ עַל־הַנָּהָר בַּעְיָם
רוּחוֹ וְהִכָּהוּ לְשִׁבְעָה נְחָלִים וְהִדְרִיךְ בַּנְּעָלִים: וְהָיְתָה מְסִלָּה
לִשְׁאָר עַמּוֹ אֲשֶׁר יִשָּׁאֵר מֵאַשּׁוּר כַּאֲשֶׁר הָיְתָה לְיִשְׂרָאֵל בְּיוֹם
עֲלֹתוֹ מֵאֶרֶץ מִצְרָיִם: וְאָמַרְתָּ בַּיּוֹם הַהוּא אוֹדְךָ יְהוָה כִּי אָנַפְתָּ בִּי
יָשֹׁב אַפְּךָ וּתְנַחֲמֵנִי: הִנֵּה אֵל יְשׁוּעָתִי אֶבְטַח וְלֹא אֶפְחָד כִּי־עָזִּי
וְזִמְרָת יָהּ יְהוָה וַיְהִי־לִי לִישׁוּעָה: וּשְׁאַבְתֶּם־מַיִם בְּשָׂשׂוֹן מִמַּעַיְנֵי
הַיְשׁוּעָה: וַאֲמַרְתֶּם בַּיּוֹם הַהוּא הוֹדוּ לַיהוָה קִרְאוּ בִשְׁמוֹ הוֹדִיעוּ
בָעַמִּים עֲלִילֹתָיו הַזְכִּירוּ כִּי נִשְׂגָּב שְׁמוֹ: זַמְּרוּ יְהוָה כִּי גֵאוּת עָשָׂה
מוּדַעַת זֹאת בְּכָל־הָאָרֶץ: צַהֲלִי וָרֹנִּי יוֹשֶׁבֶת צִיּוֹן כִּי־גָדוֹל בְּקִרְבֵּךְ
קְדוֹשׁ יִשְׂרָאֵל:

תפילה לשלום מדינת ישראל

The שליח ציבור *says the following prayer:*

אָבִינוּ שֶׁבַּשָּׁמַיִם, צוּר יִשְׂרָאֵל וְגוֹאֲלוֹ, בָּרֵךְ אֶת מְדִינַת יִשְׂרָאֵל,
רֵאשִׁית צְמִיחַת גְּאֻלָּתֵנוּ. הָגֵן עָלֶיהָ בְּאֶבְרַת חַסְדֶּךָ וּפְרֹשׂ עָלֶיהָ
סֻכַּת שְׁלוֹמֶךָ, וּשְׁלַח אוֹרְךָ וַאֲמִתְּךָ לְרָאשֶׁיהָ, שָׂרֶיהָ וְיוֹעֲצֶיהָ,
וְתַקְּנֵם בְּעֵצָה טוֹבָה מִלְּפָנֶיךָ.

Strengthen the hands of the defenders of our Holy Land; grant them deliverance, our God, and crown them with the crown of victory. Grant peace in the land and everlasting joy to its inhabitants.

As for our brothers, the whole house of Israel, remember them in all the lands of our (*In Israel say:* their) dispersion, and swiftly lead us (*In Israel say:* them) upright to Zion Your city, and Jerusalem Your dwelling place, as is written in the Torah of Moses Your servant: "Even if you *Deut. 30* are scattered to the furthermost lands under the heavens, from there the LORD your God will gather you and take you back. The LORD your God will bring you to the land your ancestors possessed and you will possess it; and He will make you more prosperous and numerous than your ancestors. Then the LORD your God will open up your heart and the heart of your descendants, to love the LORD your God with all your heart and with all your soul, that you may live."

Unite our hearts to love and revere Your name and observe all the words of Your Torah, and swiftly send us Your righteous anointed one of the house of David, to redeem those who long for Your salvation.

Appear in Your glorious majesty over all the dwellers on earth, and let all who breathe declare: The LORD God of Israel is King and His kingship has dominion over all. Amen, Selah.

The Memorial Prayer for Fallen Israeli Soldiers (page 572) is said.
The service then continues with Ashrei (page 240) until the end
of Shaharit. At the end of the service, sing:

אֲנִי מַאֲמִין I believe with perfect faith
in the coming of the Messiah,
and though he may delay,
I wait daily for his coming.

YOM YERUSHALAYIM

At Minha before Yom Yerushalayim, Tahanun is omitted. In the evening, Ma'ariv
for weekdays is said in the Yom Tov melody. The Omer is counted. Many
have the custom to add prayers of thanksgiving at the end of Ma'ariv.

In Shaharit, many communities outside Israel and in Israel say
the Pesukei DeZimra of Yom Tov (page 474). After the Leader's Repetition,
Full Hallel (page 442) is said and the regular service continues.

חַזֵּק אֶת יְדֵי מְגִנֵּי אֶרֶץ קָדְשֵׁנוּ, וְהַנְחִילֵם אֱלֹהֵינוּ יְשׁוּעָה וַעֲטֶרֶת נִצָּחוֹן תְּעַטְּרֵם, וְנָתַתָּ שָׁלוֹם בָּאָרֶץ וְשִׂמְחַת עוֹלָם לְיוֹשְׁבֶיהָ.

וְאֶת אַחֵינוּ כָּל בֵּית יִשְׂרָאֵל, פְּקָד נָא בְּכָל אַרְצוֹת פְּזוּרֵינוּ, וְתוֹלִיכֵנוּ /בארץ ישראל: פְּזוּרֵיהֶם, וְתוֹלִיכֵם/ מְהֵרָה קוֹמְמִיּוּת לְצִיּוֹן עִירֶךָ וְלִירוּשָׁלַיִם מִשְׁכַּן שְׁמֶךָ, כַּכָּתוּב בְּתוֹרַת מֹשֶׁה עַבְדֶּךָ: אִם־יִהְיֶה נִדַּחֲךָ בִּקְצֵה דברים ל הַשָּׁמָיִם, מִשָּׁם יְקַבֶּצְךָ יְהוָה אֱלֹהֶיךָ וּמִשָּׁם יִקָּחֶךָ: וֶהֱבִיאֲךָ יְהוָה אֱלֹהֶיךָ אֶל־הָאָרֶץ אֲשֶׁר־יָרְשׁוּ אֲבֹתֶיךָ וִירִשְׁתָּהּ, וְהֵיטִבְךָ וְהִרְבְּךָ מֵאֲבֹתֶיךָ: וּמָל יְהוָה אֱלֹהֶיךָ אֶת־לְבָבְךָ וְאֶת־לְבַב זַרְעֶךָ, לְאַהֲבָה אֶת־יְהוָה אֱלֹהֶיךָ בְּכָל־לְבָבְךָ וּבְכָל־נַפְשְׁךָ, לְמַעַן חַיֶּיךָ:

וְיַחֵד לְבָבֵנוּ לְאַהֲבָה וּלְיִרְאָה אֶת שְׁמֶךָ, וְלִשְׁמֹר אֶת כָּל דִּבְרֵי תוֹרָתֶךָ, וּשְׁלַח לָנוּ מְהֵרָה בֶּן דָּוִד מְשִׁיחַ צִדְקֶךָ, לִפְדּוֹת מְחַכֵּי קֵץ יְשׁוּעָתֶךָ.

וְהוֹפַע בַּהֲדַר גְּאוֹן עֻזֶּךָ עַל כָּל יוֹשְׁבֵי תֵבֵל אַרְצֶךָ וְיֹאמַר כֹּל אֲשֶׁר נְשָׁמָה בְּאַפּוֹ, יְהוָה אֱלֹהֵי יִשְׂרָאֵל מֶלֶךְ וּמַלְכוּתוֹ בַּכֹּל מָשָׁלָה, אָמֵן סֶלָה.

The אזכרה for Fallen Israeli Soldiers (page 573) is said.

The service then continues with אַשְׁרֵי (page 241) until the end of the service. At the end of the service, sing:

אֲנִי מַאֲמִין בֶּאֱמוּנָה שְׁלֵמָה, בְּבִיאַת הַמָּשִׁיחַ
וְאַף עַל פִּי שֶׁיִּתְמַהְמֵהַּ
עִם כָּל זֶה אֲחַכֶּה לּוֹ בְּכָל יוֹם שֶׁיָּבוֹא.

יום חירות ירושלים

At מנחה before יום ירושלים, תחנון is omitted.
In the evening, מעריב לחול is said in the יום טוב melody. The עומר is counted.
Many have the custom to add prayers of thanksgiving at the end of מעריב.

In שחרית many communities in חוץ לארץ and in ארץ ישראל say
הלל שלם, חזרת הש"ץ (page 475). After יום טוב of פסוקי דזמרה
(page 443) is said and the regular service continues.

Seliḥot

Seliḥot are said on Fast Days. On Tisha B'Av, Kinot are said instead.
On the Fast of Gedalya, the Seliḥot for the Ten Days of Repentance are said.

SELIḤOT FOR THE TENTH OF TEVET

סְלַח לָנוּ Forgive us, our Father, for in our great foolishness we have blundered. Pardon us, our King, for our iniquities are many.

אֵל אֶרֶךְ You are a God slow to anger, You are called the Master of Compassion, and You have taught the way of repentance. May You remember today and every day the greatness of Your compassion and kindness, for the sake of the descendants of Your beloved ones. Turn toward us in compassion, for You are the Master of Compassion. We come before You in plea and prayer, as You in ancient times showed the humble one [Moses]. Turn from Your fierce anger, as is written in Your Torah. In the shadow of Your wings may we shelter and abide, as on the day when the Lᴏʀᴅ descended in the cloud. ‣ Overlook sin and wipe away guilt, as on the day when "He stood beside him there." Give ear to our pleading and listen to our speech, as on the day when "he called upon the name of the Lᴏʀᴅ," and in that place is said –

Congregation then Leader:

And the Lᴏʀᴅ passed by before him and proclaimed: *Ex. 34*

All say aloud:

יהוה The Lᴏʀᴅ, the Lᴏʀᴅ, compassionate and gracious God, slow to anger, abounding in loving-kindness and truth, extending loving-kindness to a thousand generations, forgiving iniquity, rebellion and sin, and absolving [the guilty who repent]. Forgive us our iniquity and our sin, and take us as Your inheritance.

Continue:

סְלַח לָנוּ Forgive us, our Father, for we have sinned. Pardon us, our King, for we have transgressed. For You, Lᴏʀᴅ, are good and forgiving, abounding in   *Ps. 86*
loving-kindness to all who call on You.

For with the Lᴏʀᴅ there is loving-kindness, and great is His power to redeem.   *Ps. 130*
Lᴏʀᴅ, save Israel from all its troubles. It is He who will redeem Israel from   *Ps. 25 / Ps. 130*
all its sins. The Lᴏʀᴅ redeems His servants; those who take refuge in Him   *Ps. 34*
shall not be condemned.

כְּרַחֵם As a father has compassion for his children, so, Lᴏʀᴅ, have compassion for us.
Salvation is the Lᴏʀᴅ's; on Your people is Your blessing, Selah!   *Ps. 3*

סליחות

סליחות are said on Fast Days. On תשעה באב, קינות are said instead.
On צום גדליה, the סליחות for the עשרת ימי תשובה are said.

סליחות לעשרה בטבת

סְלַח לָנוּ, אָבִינוּ, כִּי בְרֹב אִוַּלְתֵּנוּ שָׁגִינוּ.
מְחַל לָנוּ, מַלְכֵּנוּ, כִּי רַבּוּ עֲוֹנֵינוּ.

אֵל אֶרֶךְ אַפַּיִם אַתָּה, וּבַעַל הָרַחֲמִים נִקְרֵאתָ, וְדֶרֶךְ תְּשׁוּבָה הוֹרֵיתָ. גְּדֻלַּת
רַחֲמֶיךָ וַחֲסָדֶיךָ, תִּזְכֹּר הַיּוֹם וּבְכָל יוֹם לְזֶרַע יְדִידֶיךָ. תֵּפֶן אֵלֵינוּ בְּרַחֲמִים,
כִּי אַתָּה הוּא בַּעַל הָרַחֲמִים. בְּתַחֲנוּן וּבִתְפִלָּה פָּנֶיךָ נְקַדֵּם, כְּהוֹדַעְתָּ
לֶעָנָו מִקֶּדֶם. מֵחֲרוֹן אַפְּךָ שׁוּב, כְּמוֹ בְתוֹרָתְךָ כָּתוּב. וּבְצֵל כְּנָפֶיךָ נֶחֱסֶה
וְנִתְלוֹנָן, כְּיוֹם וַיֵּרֶד יהוה בֶּעָנָן. ◂ תַּעֲבֹר עַל פֶּשַׁע וְתִמְחֶה אָשָׁם, כְּיוֹם
וַיִּתְיַצֵּב עִמּוֹ שָׁם. תַּאֲזִין שַׁוְעָתֵנוּ וְתַקְשִׁיב מֶנּוּ מַאֲמָר, כְּיוֹם וַיִּקְרָא בְשֵׁם
יהוה, וְשָׁם נֶאֱמַר:

שְׁלִיחַ צִבּוּר then קָהָל:

שמות לד

וַיַּעֲבֹר יהוה עַל פָּנָיו וַיִּקְרָא

All say aloud:

יהוה, יהוה, אֵל רַחוּם וְחַנּוּן, אֶרֶךְ אַפַּיִם, וְרַב־חֶסֶד וֶאֱמֶת: נֹצֵר
חֶסֶד לָאֲלָפִים, נֹשֵׂא עָוֹן וָפֶשַׁע וְחַטָּאָה, וְנַקֵּה: וְסָלַחְתָּ לַעֲוֹנֵנוּ
וּלְחַטָּאתֵנוּ, וּנְחַלְתָּנוּ:

Continue:

תהלים פו

סְלַח לָנוּ אָבִינוּ כִּי חָטָאנוּ, מְחַל לָנוּ מַלְכֵּנוּ כִּי פָשָׁעְנוּ. כִּי־אַתָּה אֲדֹנָי טוֹב
וְסַלָּח, וְרַב־חֶסֶד לְכָל־קֹרְאֶיךָ:

תהלים קל
תהלים כה
תהלים קל
תהלים לד

כִּי־עִם־יהוה הַחֶסֶד, וְהַרְבֵּה עִמּוֹ פְדוּת: פָּדָה אֱלֹהִים אֶת־יִשְׂרָאֵל מִכֹּל
צָרוֹתָיו: וְהוּא יִפְדֶּה אֶת־יִשְׂרָאֵל מִכֹּל עֲוֹנוֹתָיו: פּוֹדֶה יהוה נֶפֶשׁ עֲבָדָיו, וְלֹא
יֶאְשְׁמוּ כָּל־הַחֹסִים בּוֹ:

תהלים ג

כְּרַחֵם אָב עַל בָּנִים, כֵּן תְּרַחֵם יהוה עָלֵינוּ.
לַיהוה הַיְשׁוּעָה, עַל־עַמְּךָ בִרְכָתֶךָ סֶּלָה:

The LORD of hosts is with us, the God of Jacob is our stronghold, Selah! *Ps. 46*
LORD of hosts, happy is the one who trusts in You. *Ps. 84*
LORD, save! May the King answer us on the day we call. *Ps. 20*

▸ Forgive, please, this people's iniquity, *Num. 14*
   in the abundance of Your kindness,
      and as You have forgiven this people from the time of Egypt until now,
      and there it is written:

Congregation then Leader:
   And the LORD said, I have forgiven as you asked.

Continue:

הַטֵּה Give ear, my God and hear; open Your eyes and see our desolation, and *Dan. 9*
the city that bears Your name, for it is not on the strength of our righteousness that we throw down our pleadings before You, but on the strength of
Your great compassion. LORD, hear me; LORD, forgive; LORD, listen and act
and do not delay – for Your sake, my God; for Your city and Your people
bear Your name.

Our God and God of our fathers:

אֶזְכְּרָה I shall recall the anguish that came to me;
He inflicted three blows upon me in this month.
He cut me off, He veered me aside, He beat me –
   but now He has finally drained me out. *Job 16*

On the eighth of the month He darkened my right and my left;
I marked out all three days for fasting.
The king of Greece forced me to write the Torah in his tongue.
   The ploughmen have ploughed across my back;
      they made the furrows long.

I raged, on the ninth, in shame and disgrace,
my mantle of glory and my wreath were taken from me.
The man who gave us the words of Heaven
was torn from us on that day –
   that was Ezra the Scribe.

On the tenth, Ezekiel the Seer, son of Buzi was commanded,
 "Write this happening in the scroll,
   for the remembrance of a people melted away and disgraced;
      write this very day." *Ezek. 24*

תהלים מו
יהוה צְבָאוֹת עִמָּנוּ, מִשְׂגָּב לָנוּ אֱלֹהֵי יַעֲקֹב סֶלָה:

תהלים פד
יהוה צְבָאוֹת, אַשְׁרֵי אָדָם בֹּטֵחַ בָּךְ:

תהלים כ
יהוה הוֹשִׁיעָה, הַמֶּלֶךְ יַעֲנֵנוּ בְיוֹם־קָרְאֵנוּ:

במדבר יד
‹ סְלַח־נָא לַעֲוֹן הָעָם הַזֶּה כְּגֹדֶל חַסְדֶּךָ
וְכַאֲשֶׁר נָשָׂאתָה לָעָם הַזֶּה מִמִּצְרַיִם וְעַד־הֵנָּה:
וְשָׁם נֶאֱמַר

שליח ציבור then קהל:
וַיֹּאמֶר יהוה, סָלַחְתִּי כִּדְבָרֶךָ:

Continue:

דניאל ט
הַטֵּה אֱלֹהַי אָזְנְךָ וּשֲׁמָע, פְּקַח עֵינֶיךָ וּרְאֵה שֹׁמְמֹתֵינוּ וְהָעִיר אֲשֶׁר־נִקְרָא
שִׁמְךָ עָלֶיהָ, כִּי לֹא עַל־צִדְקֹתֵינוּ אֲנַחְנוּ מַפִּילִים תַּחֲנוּנֵינוּ לְפָנֶיךָ, כִּי עַל־
רַחֲמֶיךָ הָרַבִּים: אֲדֹנָי שְׁמָעָה, אֲדֹנָי סְלָחָה, אֲדֹנָי הַקְשִׁיבָה וַעֲשֵׂה אַל־תְּאַחַר,
לְמַעֲנְךָ אֱלֹהַי, כִּי־שִׁמְךָ נִקְרָא עַל־עִירְךָ וְעַל־עַמֶּךָ:

אֱלֹהֵינוּ וֵאלֹהֵי אֲבוֹתֵינוּ

אֶזְכְּרָה מָצוֹק אֲשֶׁר קְרָאַנִי.
בְּשָׁלִישׁ מַכּוֹת בַּחֹדֶשׁ הַזֶּה הִכַּנִי.
גִּדְעַנִי הֱנִיאַנִי הֶכְאַנִי.

איוב טז
אַךְ־עַתָּה הֶלְאָנִי:
דִּכְּאַנִי בִּשְׁמוֹנָה בּוֹ שְׂמָאלִית וִימָנִית.
הֲלֹא שְׁלָשְׁתָּן קְבַעְתִּי תַעֲנִית.
וּמֶלֶךְ יָוָן אֲנָסַנִי לִכְתֹּב דָּת, יְוָנִית.
עַל גַּבֵּי חָרְשׁוּ חוֹרְשִׁים, הֶאֱרִיכוּ מַעֲנִית.
זַעֲמְתִּי בְּתִשְׁעָה בּוֹ בְּכָלְמָה וָחֵפֶר.
חֻשַּׁךְ מֵעָלַי מְעִיל הוֹד וָצֶפֶר.
טָרֹף טֹרַף בּוֹ הַנּוֹתֵן אִמְרֵי שֶׁפֶר.
הוּא עֶזְרָא הַסּוֹפֵר.
יוֹם עֲשִׂירִי, צֻוָּה בֶּן בּוּזִי הַחוֹזֶה.
כְּתָב לְךָ בַּסֵּפֶר הַמַּחֲזֶה.
לְזִכָּרוֹן לְעַם נָמֵס וְנִבְזֶה.

יחזקאל כד
אֶת־עֶצֶם הַיּוֹם הַזֶּה:

The tenth was listed last among the fasts
to show the order of the months.
My own mouth gapes open with weeping and wailing,
and this chronicle of troubles burns within my heart –
　　as the fugitive came to me and said, "The city is crushed."

For these things I have scattered dust upon my face.
I have spoken now of all four –
would that I could shoot an arrow through my heart.
For these great torments, I have dug my own grave.
　　"The LORD is righteous; I have rebelled against His word." *Lam. 1*

I have called out Your name as I grieve my troubles.
Witness my oppression and hear my voice in its entreaty.
Hear my pleading, please, hasten my salvation. *Lam. 3*
　　Do not block Your ears to my sighing, to my cry.

▸ In the month of Tevet I was stricken sorely.
The world changed its course, from where I stand.
I was stubborn, I sinned –
yet may He reveal His goodness to me;
　　the One who told the ocean, "Only thus far, come."

אֵל מֶלֶךְ God, King who sits upon a throne of compassion, who acts with loving-kindness, who pardons the iniquities of His people, passing them before Him in order; who forgives sinners and pardons transgressors; who performs righteousness with all flesh and spirit, do not repay their bad actions in kind. ▸ God, You taught us to speak thirteen attributes: recall for us today the covenant of the thirteen attributes, as You in ancient times showed the humble one [Moses], as is written: The LORD descended in the cloud *Ex. 34* and stood with him there, and proclaimed in the name of the LORD:

Congregation then Leader:

And the LORD passed by before him and proclaimed: *Ex. 34*

All say aloud:

יהוה The LORD, the LORD, compassionate and gracious God, slow to anger, abounding in loving-kindness and truth, extending loving-kindness to a thousand generations, forgiving iniquity, rebellion and sin, and absolving [the guilty who repent]. Forgive us our iniquity and our sin, and take us as Your inheritance.

מִנְּגֹן סֵדֶר חֲדָשִׁים בַּעֲשָׂרָה בּוֹ הָעִיר.

נֶהִי וִילֵל כְּמוֹ פִי אַפְעִיר.

סֵדֶר פֻּרְעָנוּת בְּתוֹךְ לְבָבִי יְבַעִיר.

בְּבֹא אֵלַי הַפָּלִיט לֵאמֹר הֻכְּתָה הָעִיר.

עַל אֵלֶּה, עַל פְּנֵי אֶבֶק זֵרֵיתִי.

פִּצְחִי עַל אַרְבַּעְתָּן, לוֹ חֵץ בִּלְבִּי יָרֵיתִי.

צָרוֹת עַל אֵלֶּה, קֶבֶר לִי כָּרֵיתִי.

איכה א

צַדִּיק הוּא יְהֹוָה, כִּי פִיהוּ מָרֵיתִי:

קָרָאתִי שְׁמֶךָ, מִתְנַחֵם עַל רָעָתִי.

רְאֵה עָנְיִי וּשְׁמַע קוֹל פְּגִיעָתִי.

שְׁמַע תְּחִנָּתִי, חִישׁ נָא יְשׁוּעָתִי.

איכה ג

אַל־תַּעְלֵם אָזְנְךָ לְרַוְחָתִי לְשַׁוְעָתִי:

‏◃ יֶרַח טֵבֵת, מְאֹד לָקִיתִי בוֹ.

וְנִשְׁתַּנּוּ עָלַי סִדְרֵי נְתִיבוֹ.

סָרַרְתִּי, פְּשָׁעְתִּי, יִגְלֶה לִי טוּבוֹ.

הָאוֹמֵר לַיָּם עַד פֹּה תָבוֹא.

אֵל מֶלֶךְ יוֹשֵׁב עַל כִּסֵּא רַחֲמִים, מִתְנַהֵג בַּחֲסִידוּת. מוֹחֵל עֲוֹנוֹת עַמּוֹ, מַעֲבִיר רִאשׁוֹן רִאשׁוֹן. מַרְבֶּה מְחִילָה לַחַטָּאִים, וּסְלִיחָה לַפּוֹשְׁעִים. עֹשֶׂה צְדָקוֹת עִם כָּל בָּשָׂר וָרוּחַ, לֹא כְרָעָתָם תִּגְמֹל. ◃ אֵל, הוֹרֵיתָ לָּנוּ לוֹמַר שְׁלֹשׁ עֶשְׂרֵה, וּזְכֹר לָנוּ הַיּוֹם בְּרִית שְׁלֹשׁ עֶשְׂרֵה, כְּמוֹ שֶׁהוֹדַעְתָּ לֶעָנָו מִקֶּדֶם, כְּמוֹ שֶׁכָּתוּב: וַיֵּרֶד יְהֹוָה בֶּעָנָן, וַיִּתְיַצֵּב עִמּוֹ שָׁם, וַיִּקְרָא בְשֵׁם, יְהֹוָה:

שמות לד

שליח ציבור then קהל:

שמות לד

וַיַּעֲבֹר יְהֹוָה עַל־פָּנָיו וַיִּקְרָא

All say aloud:

יְהֹוָה, יְהֹוָה, אֵל רַחוּם וְחַנּוּן, אֶרֶךְ אַפַּיִם, וְרַב־חֶסֶד וֶאֱמֶת: נֹצֵר חֶסֶד לָאֲלָפִים, נֹשֵׂא עָוֹן וָפֶשַׁע וְחַטָּאָה, וְנַקֵּה: וְסָלַחְתָּ לַעֲוֹנֵנוּ וּלְחַטָּאתֵנוּ, וּנְחַלְתָּנוּ:

Continue:

סְלַח לָנוּ Forgive us, our Father, for we have sinned. Pardon us, our King, for
we have transgressed. For You, LORD, are good and forgiving, abounding
in loving-kindness to all who call on You. *Ps. 86*

God, nations came into Your inheritance, they made Your holy Sanctuary *Ps. 79*
impure, they reduced Jerusalem to ruins. God, wanton people came up
against us and a gang of oppressors sought out our lives, and did not place
You before them.

כְּרַחֵם As a father has compassion for his children,
so, LORD, have compassion for us.
Salvation is the LORD's; on Your people is Your blessing, Selah! *Ps. 3*
The LORD of hosts is with us, the God of Jacob is our stronghold, Selah! *Ps. 46*
LORD of hosts, happy is the one who trusts in You. *Ps. 84*
LORD, save! May the King answer us on the day we call. *Ps. 20*

Our God and God of our fathers:

אֶבֶן הָרֹאשָׁה The Temple, Top Stone,
is laid to ruin and ploughed over,
and the Torah's heirs, Israel, a derision among nations.

Within me an aching heart, sickened and pained –
we are left as if fatherless, become like orphans.

Israel, delicate and refined, fenced by lilies of the Law,
has now become mournful, given over to assailants.

The faithful city has become like a widow,
the countless descendants of Jacob
have been sold for no price.

Refined and delicate, worthy of royalty,
they have been ploughed across in long furrows
over many years and days.

The house of Jacob is given over to plunder,
to jeering and slander,
and the joyous city to plantations of vines.

Doused in poison by lawless ones,
is the people once desired like offerings,
like fragrant incense.

Continue:

תהלים פו   סְלַח לָנוּ אָבִינוּ כִּי חָטָאנוּ, מְחַל לָנוּ מַלְכֵּנוּ כִּי פָשָׁעְנוּ. כִּי־אַתָּה אֲדֹנָי טוֹב
וְסַלָּח, וְרַב־חֶסֶד לְכָל־קֹרְאֶיךָ:

תהלים עט   אֱלֹהִים בָּאוּ גוֹיִם בְּנַחֲלָתֶךָ, טִמְּאוּ אֶת־הֵיכַל קָדְשֶׁךָ, שָׂמוּ אֶת־יְרוּשָׁלַם
לְעִיִּים: אֱלֹהִים, זֵדִים קָמוּ עָלֵינוּ, וַעֲדַת עָרִיצִים בִּקְשׁוּ נַפְשֵׁנוּ, וְלֹא שָׂמוּךָ
לְנֶגְדָּם.

כְּרַחֵם אָב עַל בָּנִים, כֵּן תְּרַחֵם יהוה עָלֵינוּ.

תהלים ג   לַיהוה הַיְשׁוּעָה, עַל־עַמְּךָ בִרְכָתֶךָ סֶּלָה:

תהלים מו   יהוה צְבָאוֹת עִמָּנוּ, מִשְׂגָּב לָנוּ אֱלֹהֵי יַעֲקֹב סֶלָה:

תהלים פד   יהוה צְבָאוֹת, אַשְׁרֵי אָדָם בֹּטֵחַ בָּךְ:

תהלים כ   יהוה הוֹשִׁיעָה, הַמֶּלֶךְ יַעֲנֵנוּ בְיוֹם־קָרְאֵנוּ:

אֱלֹהֵינוּ וֵאלֹהֵי אֲבוֹתֵינוּ

אֶבֶן הָרֹאשָׁה, לְעִיִּים וְלַחֲרִישָׁה
וְנֹחֲלֵי מוֹרָשָׁה, מְנוֹד רֹאשׁ בַּלְאֻמִּים.

בְּקִרְבִּי לֵב נִכְאָב, נִדְוֶה וְנִדְאָב
נִשְׁאַרְנוּ כְּאֵין אָב, וְהָיִינוּ כִּיתוֹמִים.

רַכָּה וַעֲנֻגָּה, בַּשּׁוֹשַׁנִּים סוּגָה
וְעַתָּה הִיא נוּגָה, מְסוּרָה בְּיַד קָמִים.

הָיְתָה כְּאַלְמָנָה, קְרִיָּה נֶאֱמָנָה
וְזֶרַע מִי מָנָה, נִמְכְּרוּ בְּלֹא דָמִים.

מְעֻגָּה וְרַכָּה, צָלְחָה לַמְּלוּכָה
וּמַעֲנִיתָהּ אֲרֻכָּה, זֶה כַּמֶּה שָׁנִים וְיָמִים.

בֵּית יַעֲקֹב לְבִזָּה, לְלַעַג וּלְעִזָּה
וְהָעִיר הָעֶלְיָזָה, לְמַטְּעֵי כְרָמִים.

רְוָיָה תֵרָעֶלָה, בְּיַד בְּנֵי עַוְלָה
הָרְצוּיָה כְעוֹלָה, וְכִקְטֹרֶת הַסַּמִּים.

They have despised and neglected the Torah of Moses Avi-Zanoaḥ,
they can find no rest by night or by day.

Awesome, highest God, may the desire arise in You
to bring a year of recompense for Israel's strife.

Renew our days as of old, Dwelling Place who is our God of old.
And wash our red guilt white as wool; our stains as snow.

▸ Strengthen us in awe of You, and in the keeping of Your Law.
And come to us, in Your salvation, God who is full of compassion.

אֵל מֶלֶךְ God, King who sits upon a throne of compassion, who acts with
loving-kindness, who pardons the iniquities of His people, passing them
before Him in order; who forgives sinners and pardons transgressors; who
performs righteousness with all flesh and spirit, do not repay their bad actions
in kind. ▸ God, You taught us to speak thirteen attributes: recall for us today
the covenant of the thirteen attributes, as You in ancient times showed the
humble one [Moses], as is written: The Lord descended in the cloud and   Ex. 34
stood with him there, and proclaimed in the name of the Lord:

Congregation then Leader:

And the Lord passed by before him and proclaimed: Ex. 34

All say aloud:

יהוה The Lord, the Lord, compassionate and gracious God, slow
to anger, abounding in loving-kindness and truth, extending loving-
kindness to a thousand generations, forgiving iniquity, rebellion and
sin, and absolving [the guilty who repent]. Forgive us our iniquity
and our sin, and take us as Your inheritance.

Continue:

סְלַח לָנוּ Forgive us, our Father, for we have sinned. Pardon us, our King, for
we have transgressed. For You, Lord, are good and forgiving, abounding in   Ps. 86
loving-kindness to all who call on You.

The following is said responsively:

אֲבוֹתַי When my forebears trusted in the name of God, my Rock,
they grew and were successful and also gave forth fruit.
And from the time when they were drawn away
to walk with Him in enmity,
they diminished and diminished until the tenth month.   Gen. 8

מָאֲסָה לְנֹחַ, תּוֹרַת אֲבִי זָנֹחַ
וְלֹא מָצְאָה מָנוֹחַ, לֵילוֹת וְגַם יָמִים.
נוֹרָא אֵל עֶלְיוֹן, מִמְּךָ יְהִי צִבְיוֹן
לְהָשִׁיב לָרִיב צִיּוֹן, שְׁנַת שִׁלּוּמִים.
חַדֵּשׁ יָמֵינוּ כְּקֶדֶם, מְעוֹנָה אֱלֹהֵי קֶדֶם
וְלַבֵּן כַּצֶּמֶר אֹדֶם, וְכַשֶּׁלֶג כְּתָמִים.
‹ חַזְּקֵנוּ בִּירְאָתֶךָ, וּבְקִיּוּם תּוֹרָתֶךָ
וּפָקְדֵנוּ בִּישׁוּעָתֶךָ, אֵל מָלֵא רַחֲמִים.

אֵל מֶלֶךְ יוֹשֵׁב עַל כִּסֵּא רַחֲמִים, מִתְנַהֵג בַּחֲסִידוּת. מוֹחֵל עֲוֹנוֹת עַמּוֹ,
מַעֲבִיר רִאשׁוֹן רִאשׁוֹן. מַרְבֶּה מְחִילָה לַחַטָּאִים, וּסְלִיחָה לַפּוֹשְׁעִים. עֹשֶׂה
צְדָקוֹת עִם כָּל בָּשָׂר וָרוּחַ, לֹא כְרָעָתָם תִּגְמֹל. ‹ אֵל, הוֹרֵיתָ לָּנוּ לוֹמַר שְׁלֹשׁ
עֶשְׂרֵה, וּזְכָר לָנוּ הַיּוֹם בְּרִית שְׁלֹשׁ עֶשְׂרֵה, כְּמוֹ שֶׁהוֹדַעְתָּ לֶעָנָו מִקֶּדֶם,
כְּמוֹ שֶׁכָּתוּב: וַיֵּרֶד יהוה בֶּעָנָן, וַיִּתְיַצֵּב עִמּוֹ שָׁם, וַיִּקְרָא בְשֵׁם, יהוה: שמות לד

שליח ציבור then קהל:

וַיַּעֲבֹר יהוה עַל־פָּנָיו וַיִּקְרָא שמות לד

All say aloud:

יהוה, יהוה, אֵל רַחוּם וְחַנּוּן, אֶרֶךְ אַפַּיִם, וְרַב־חֶסֶד וֶאֱמֶת: נֹצֵר
חֶסֶד לָאֲלָפִים, נֹשֵׂא עָוֹן וָפֶשַׁע וְחַטָּאָה, וְנַקֵּה: וְסָלַחְתָּ לַעֲוֹנֵנוּ
וּלְחַטָּאתֵנוּ, וּנְחַלְתָּנוּ:

Continue:

סְלַח לָנוּ אָבִינוּ כִּי חָטָאנוּ, מְחַל לָנוּ מַלְכֵּנוּ כִּי פָשָׁעְנוּ. כִּי־אַתָּה אֲדֹנָי טוֹב תהלים פו
וְסַלָּח, וְרַב־חֶסֶד לְכָל־קֹרְאֶיךָ:

The following is said responsively:

אֲבוֹתַי כִּי בָטְחוּ בְּשֵׁם אֱלֹהֵי צוּרִי
גָּדְלוּ וְהִצְלִיחוּ וְגַם עָשׂוּ פֶרִי
וּמֵעֵת הֻדְּחוּ וְהָלְכוּ עִמּוֹ קֶרִי
הָיוּ הָלוֹךְ וְחָסוֹר עַד הַחֹדֶשׁ הָעֲשִׂירִי בראשית ח

On the tenth, the king of Babylon laid siege on the city,
and beleaguered it. The chief of the army arrived,
and I was yielded to be trampled,
was tormented in fetters,
and from month to month my harp turned to grief.

Once like the first figs of a new tree,
they were the very first to be destroyed.
They spoke the names of others, and sin closed their destiny.
They did not recognize God's face and were swept off by the flood –
agony like that of a first childbirth, soars up as high as Heaven.

God brought us a day of evil and siege,
ordered enemies about me to harvest my last fruits.
The day my heart was quelled, no strength to resist,
and He said to the prophet,
"Preach this to the rebellious house."

He took the cloak of authority from the judges at the gate.
His rage burned like fire and He raised the crown away,
and He cast down the splendor of the Temple, Forest of Lebanon,
and rushing wind and storm make my flesh bristle and shiver.

Once you were called most beautiful;
now you are darkened,
for you have stumbled over iniquity
and your heart has turned back.
You have been attacked from behind,
have been weakened, once, then twice,
and even the slightest dressing or balm not offered you.

The Righteous One, perfect Rock,
who forgives iniquity almost too great to bear,
flew from the cherubs to the threshold,
and from there to a corner of the roof,
because of the iniquity marked out; the scream of it rose up,
their evil as abundant as a fruit-tree's crop.

The One who weighs the actions of people,
strengthened all my attackers,
for my days had been filled with malignant deeds,

בָּעֲשִׂירִי לַחֹדֶשׁ סָמַךְ מֶלֶךְ בָּבֶל
וְצָר עַל עִיר הַקֹּדֶשׁ, וְנִקְרַב רַב הַחוֹבֵל
נָתַתִּי הֶדֶשׁ וְעִנִּיתִי בַכֶּבֶל
וְהָיָה מַדֵּי חֹדֶשׁ לְאֵבֶל כִּגּוֹרִי.

רֵאשִׁית בְּכוּרָה לְרֵאשִׁית הַחֵרֶם
שֵׁם אֲחֵרִים הַזְכִּירָה, וְהֶעָוֹן גּוֹרֵם
פְּנֵי אֵל לֹא הִכִּירָה, וְשֻׁטְּפָה בְזֶרֶם
צָרָה כְמַבְכִּירָה כָּעֵת בַּמָּרוֹם תַּמְרִיא.

הָאֱלֹהִים הֵבִיא יוֹם רָעָה וּמָצוֹר
צִוָּה צָרֵי סְבִיבַי עוֹלְלֵי לְבַצֹּר
יוֹם הֵרַךְ לְבָבִי וְאֵין כֹּחַ לַעֲצֹר
וַדַּבֵּר אֶל נָבִיא, מְשֹׁל אֶל בֵּית הַמֶּרִי.

מִיּוֹשְׁבֵי שַׁעַר הֶעֱבִיר אַדֶּרֶת
חֲמָתוֹ כְּאֵשׁ בָּעַר, וְהֵרִים עֲטֶרֶת
וּמִלְּבָנוֹן יַעַר הִשְׁלִיךְ תִּפְאֶרֶת
וְרוּחַ סוֹעָה וָסַעַר תְּסַמֵּר שַׂעֲרַת בְּשָׂרִי.

יְפֵיפִית נִמְשָׁלֶת, וְעַתָּה קְדוֹרַנִּית
בְּעָוֹן כִּי כָשַׁלְתְּ, וְלִבֵּךְ אֲחוֹרַנִּית
זְנוּבֵךְ וְנֶחְשַׁלְתְּ רִאשׁוֹנָה וְשֵׁנִית
וְהַחֵל לֹא חִתַּלְתְּ מְעַט צֳרִי.

צַדִּיק הַצּוּר תָּם, נָשָׂא עֲוֹן נִלְאָה
מִכָּרוֹב לְמִפְתָּן, לְפָנַת גַּג דָּאָה
מֵעָוֹן הֻנַּכְתָּם, וְצַעֲקָתָם בָּאָה
רַבָּה רָעָתָם כְּעֵץ עֹשֶׂה פֶרִי.

חֲזַק כָּל קָמַי, תּוֹכֵן הָעֲלִילוֹת
כִּי מָלְאוּ יָמַי בְּרַע מִפְעָלוֹת

and in the shamefulness of my youth
I forgot the good granted me,
and the One who gives me my bread and water,
my flax and my wool.

My attackers opened wide their mouths and swallowed up my legacy.
They overcame me utterly, drank my blood and gulped it down.
Strangers became my enemies, they injured my brothers –
strangers who called out, "Destroy, destroy!"
Descendants of Seir the Horite.

They said, "Come, let us finish them off,
and put an end to their memory."
Jealous, vengeful God, grant retribution;
let them load the burden of their own ruin.
Pay them back for their actions
and have their hopes disgrace them,
like the baker who dreamt his dream
of three baskets of white bread.

My wound was not softened, my bruise enough to kill me,
and my eyes have grown dim with watching for my bright-faced Love.
Is His anger even now not forever forgotten?
Why has He done this; why this burning rage?

This God of mine is compassionate; He shall not forever reject.
The days of my grief have grown long and still my heart sighs.
Return, God, to my tent; do not abandon Your place.
Close the days of my grief. Bring my recompense.

LORD who is the portion allotted me,
come to me quickly, help me,
and loosen my sackcloth,
wrap me around in joy,
and dazzle my darkness with Your light – light up
the twilight I once longed for, for it is You who are my lamp.

Redeem my soul from anguish and sighing,
grant Your people remission, my King and my Holy One.
And turn into relief the fast of Av;
into gladness and joy, the fast of Tammuz and the fast of Tevet.

Continue with "God, King who sits" on page 634.

וּמִבֹּשֶׁת עֲלוּמַי שָׁכַחְתִּי גְמוּלוֹת
נוֹתֵן לַחְמִי וּמֵימַי, פִּשְׁתִּי וְצַמְרִי.

קָמַי פִּיהֶם פָּעֲרוּ וְנַחֲלָתִי בִּלֵּעוּ
מְאֹד עָלַי גָּבְרוּ וְדָמִי שָׁתוּ וְלָעוּ
נָכְרִים עָלַי צָרוּ וְאֶת אַחַי הֵרֵעוּ
הָאוֹמְרִים עָרוּ עָרוּ, בְּנֵי שֵׂעִיר הַחֹרִי.

אָמְרוּ לְכוּ נִכָּלֵם, וְנַשְׁבִּיתָה זִכְרָם
אֵל קַנּוֹא וְנוֹקֵם, גְּמֻלֵם, יִשְׂאוּ אֶת שִׁבְרָם
כְּמַעֲשֵׂיהֶם שַׁלֵּם וְיֵבוֹשׁוּ מִשִּׁבְרָם
כְּאִישׁ חֲלוֹם חוֹלֵם שְׁלֹשָׁה סַלֵּי חֹרִי.

פְּצָעַי לֹא רֻכְּכָה וְחַבּוּרוֹתַי רֶצַח
וְעֵינִי הֻכְהֲתָה, צוֹפָה לְדוֹדִי צַח
הַעוֹד לֹא שָׁכְכָה חֲמָתוֹ לָנֶצַח
עַל מֶה עָשָׂה כָּכָה וּמֶה חֳרִי.

רַחוּם זֶה אֵלִי, אַל לָעַד תִּזְנַח
אָרְכוּ יְמֵי אֶבְלִי וְעוֹד לִבִּי נֶאֱנַח
שׁוּבָה אֵל לְאָהֳלִי, מְקוֹמְךָ אַל תַּנַּח
שַׁלֵּם יְמֵי אֶבְלִי כִּי תָבוֹא עַל שְׂכָרִי.

יהוה מְנָת חֶלְקִי, חוּשָׁה לִּי לְעֶזְרָה
וּפִתַּחְתָּ שַׂקִּי, שִׂמְחָה לִי לְאַזְּרָה
וְתַגִּיהַּ אֶת חָשְׁכִּי בְּאוֹרֶךְ לְהָאִירָה
אֶת נֵשֶׁף חִשְׁקִי, כִּי אַתָּה נֵרִי.

מִיָּגוֹן וַאֲנָחָה, פְּדֵה אֵל אֶת נַפְשִׁי
עֲשֵׂה לְעַמְּךָ הֲנָחָה, מַלְכִּי וּקְדוֹשִׁי
תַּהֲפוֹךְ לִרְוָחָה אֶת צוֹם הַחֲמִישִׁי
לְשָׂשׂוֹן וּלְשִׂמְחָה, צוֹם הָרְבִיעִי וְצוֹם הָעֲשִׂירִי.

Continue with אֵל מֶלֶךְ יוֹשֵׁב on page 635.

SELIHOT FOR THE FAST OF ESTHER

סְלַח לָנוּ Forgive us, our Father, for in our great foolishness we have blundered. Pardon us, our King, for our iniquities are many.

אֵל אֶרֶךְ You are a God slow to anger, You are called the Master of Compassion, and You have taught the way of repentance. May You remember today and every day the greatness of Your compassion and kindness, for the sake of the descendants of Your beloved ones. Turn toward us in compassion, for You are the Master of Compassion. We come before You in plea and prayer, as You in ancient times showed the humble one [Moses]. Turn from Your fierce anger, as is written in Your Torah. In the shadow of Your wings may we shelter and abide, as on the day when the LORD descended in the cloud. ‣ Disregard transgression and erase guilt as on the day You stood with him [Moses] there. Hear our cry and heed our word, as on the day You proclaimed in the name of the LORD, and there it is written:

Congregation then Leader:

And the LORD passed by before him and proclaimed: *Ex. 34*

All say aloud:

יהוה The LORD, the LORD, compassionate and gracious God, slow to anger, abounding in loving-kindness and truth, extending loving-kindness to a thousand generations, forgiving iniquity, rebellion and sin, and absolving [the guilty who repent]. Forgive us our iniquity and our sin, and take us as Your inheritance.

Continue:

סְלַח לָנוּ Forgive us, our Father, for we have sinned. Pardon us, our King, for we have transgressed. For You, LORD, are good and forgiving, abounding in loving-kindness to all who call on You. *Ps. 86*

We have waited patiently for the LORD, and He has turned toward us and heard *Is. 26* our cry. And on the path of Your laws, LORD, we have waited for You, for it is Your name and Your memory that are our souls' desire.

כְּרַחֵם As a father has compassion for his children,
so, LORD, have compassion for us.
Salvation is the LORD's; on Your people is Your blessing, Selah! *Ps. 3*
The LORD of hosts is with us, the God of Jacob is our stronghold, Selah! *Ps. 46*
LORD of hosts, happy is the one who trusts in You. *Ps. 84*
LORD, save! May the King answer us on the day we call. *Ps. 20*

סליחות לתענית אסתר

סְלַח לָנוּ, אָבִינוּ, כִּי בְרֹב אִוַּלְתֵּנוּ שָׁגִינוּ.
מְחַל לָנוּ, מַלְכֵּנוּ, כִּי רַבּוּ עֲוֹנֵינוּ.

אֵל אֶרֶךְ אַפַּיִם אַתָּה, וּבַעַל הָרַחֲמִים נִקְרֵאתָ, וְדֶרֶךְ תְּשׁוּבָה הוֹרֵיתָ. גְּדֻלַּת
רַחֲמֶיךָ וַחֲסָדֶיךָ, תִּזְכֹּר הַיּוֹם וּבְכָל יוֹם לְזֶרַע יְדִידֶיךָ. תֵּפֶן אֵלֵינוּ בְּרַחֲמִים,
כִּי אַתָּה הוּא בַּעַל הָרַחֲמִים. בְּתַחֲנוּן וּבִתְפִלָּה פָּנֶיךָ נְקַדֵּם, כְּהוֹדַעְתָּ
לֶעָנָו מִקֶּדֶם. מֵחֲרוֹן אַפְּךָ שׁוּב, כְּמוֹ בְתוֹרָתְךָ כָּתוּב. וּבְצֵל כְּנָפֶיךָ נֶחֱסֶה
וְנִתְלוֹנָן, כְּיוֹם וַיֵּרֶד יהוה בֶּעָנָן. ◄ תַּעֲבֹר עַל פֶּשַׁע וְתִמְחֶה אָשָׁם, כְּיוֹם
וַיִּתְיַצֵּב עִמּוֹ שָׁם. תַּאֲזִין שַׁוְעָתֵנוּ וְתַקְשִׁיב מֶנּוּ מַאֲמָר, כְּיוֹם וַיִּקְרָא בְשֵׁם
יהוה, וְשָׁם נֶאֱמַר:

שליח צבור then קהל:

שמות לד
וַיַּעֲבֹר יהוה עַל־פָּנָיו וַיִּקְרָא

All say aloud:

יהוה, יהוה, אֵל רַחוּם וְחַנּוּן, אֶרֶךְ אַפַּיִם, וְרַב־חֶסֶד וֶאֱמֶת: נֹצֵר
חֶסֶד לָאֲלָפִים, נֹשֵׂא עָוֹן וָפֶשַׁע וְחַטָּאָה, וְנַקֵּה: וְסָלַחְתָּ לַעֲוֹנֵנוּ
וּלְחַטָּאתֵנוּ, וּנְחַלְתָּנוּ:

Continue:

תהלים פו
סְלַח לָנוּ אָבִינוּ כִּי חָטָאנוּ, מְחַל לָנוּ מַלְכֵּנוּ כִּי פָשָׁעְנוּ. כִּי־אַתָּה אֲדֹנָי טוֹב
וְסַלָּח, וְרַב־חֶסֶד לְכָל־קֹרְאֶיךָ:

ישעיה כו
קַוֵּה קֹוִינוּ יהוה, וַיֵּט אֵלֵינוּ וַיִּשְׁמַע שַׁוְעָתֵנוּ. אַף אֹרַח מִשְׁפָּטֶיךָ יהוה
קִוִּינוּךָ, לְשִׁמְךָ וּלְזִכְרְךָ תַּאֲוַת־נָפֶשׁ:

כְּרַחֵם אָב עַל בָּנִים, כֵּן תְּרַחֵם יהוה עָלֵינוּ.
תהלים ג
לַיהוה הַיְשׁוּעָה, עַל־עַמְּךָ בִרְכָתֶךָ סֶּלָה:
תהלים מו
יהוה צְבָאוֹת עִמָּנוּ, מִשְׂגָּב לָנוּ אֱלֹהֵי יַעֲקֹב סֶלָה:
תהלים פד
יהוה צְבָאוֹת, אַשְׁרֵי אָדָם בֹּטֵחַ בָּךְ:
תהלים כ
יהוה הוֹשִׁיעָה, הַמֶּלֶךְ יַעֲנֵנוּ בְיוֹם־קָרְאֵנוּ:

▸ Forgive, please, this people's iniquity, in the abundance of Your kindness, *Num. 14*
and as You have forgiven this people from the time of Egypt until now,
and there it is written:

Congregation then Leader:

And the LORD said, I have forgiven as you asked.

Continue:

הַטֵּה Give ear, my God and hear; open Your eyes and see our desolation, and the *Dan. 9*
city that bears Your name, for it is not on the strength of our righteousness that we
throw down our pleadings before You, but on the strength of Your great compassion. LORD, hear me; LORD, forgive, LORD, listen and act and do not delay – for
Your sake, my God; for Your city and Your people bear Your name.

Our God and God of our fathers:

אָדָם When a man rose up against us, convulsions of trembling seized us.
When he attached himself to a government of flattery, we almost stumbled and fell.
They cheerfully closed an agreement to sell us,
as a person with an unwanted mound gives it away quite freely
to one with an unwanted pit.
There was no defense.
>> They said, "Come, let us annihilate them from among nations: *Ps. 83*
>> the name of Israel shall be recalled no more."

My eyes turned heavenward and I called on You to curse my enemies:
"Cut off name and remnant; expunge their name, let it rot.
And be Enemy to my enemies; bring them down in the very deceptions
with which they deceived the people of Jacob."
>> And they said, "The LORD will not see; *Ps. 94*
>> the God of Jacob will not comprehend."

Yet God tormented the scattered ones and made them mournful –
but did not mean to destroy them utterly.
They were guilty on the face of things, and so He terrorized them.
By the taking off of a ring, He made them tremble.
But God fulfilled the good of His word, raising them up in the view of nations.
>> "In their enemies' land He did not reject them, *Lev. 26*
>> and did not detest them to the point of destruction."

He revealed the premonition of events for a nation begrimed and scratched over.
He wrote "I shall surely hide (*astir*) Myself" to hint at Esther,
and fragrant "pure myrrh," translated "mar-dokh," to hint at Mordekhai;
all to put an end to Haman on the morrow, "From (*hamin*) the tree" foreshadow-
ing his gallows.
>> "In place of the thorn bush, shall rise up a cypress, *Is. 55*
>> and in place of the nettle, shall rise up myrtle."

‹ סְלַח־נָא לַעֲוֹן הָעָם הַזֶּה כְּגֹדֶל חַסְדֶּךָ

במדבר יד

וְכַאֲשֶׁר נָשָׂאתָה לָעָם הַזֶּה מִמִּצְרַיִם וְעַד־הֵנָּה:

וְשָׁם נֶאֱמַר

שליח ציבור then *קהל*:

וַיֹּאמֶר יהוה, סָלַחְתִּי כִּדְבָרֶךָ:

Continue:

הַטֵּה אֱלֹהַי אָזְנְךָ וּשֲׁמָע, פְּקַח עֵינֶיךָ וּרְאֵה שֹׁמְמֹתֵינוּ וְהָעִיר אֲשֶׁר־נִקְרָא

דניאל ט

שִׁמְךָ עָלֶיהָ, כִּי לֹא עַל־צִדְקֹתֵינוּ אֲנַחְנוּ מַפִּילִים תַּחֲנוּנֵינוּ לְפָנֶיךָ, כִּי עַל־

רַחֲמֶיךָ הָרַבִּים: אֲדֹנָי שְׁמָעָה, אֲדֹנָי סְלָחָה, אֲדֹנָי הַקְשִׁיבָה וַעֲשֵׂה אַל־

תְּאַחַר, לְמַעַנְךָ אֱלֹהַי, כִּי־שִׁמְךָ נִקְרָא עַל־עִירְךָ וְעַל־עַמֶּךָ:

אֱלֹהֵינוּ וֵאלֹהֵי אֲבוֹתֵינוּ

אָדָם בְּקוּם עָלֵינוּ, חֵיל אֲחָזַתְנוּ לְרֶעַד.

בְּהִסְתַּפְּחוֹ לְמַלְכוּת חָנֵף, כִּמְעַט כָּשַׁלְנוּ לְמַעַד.

גָּמְרוּ לְמַכְנֵנוּ כְּתֵל וְחָרִיץ בְּלִי מִסְעָד.

אָמְרוּ לְכוּ וְנַכְחִידֵם מִגּוֹי, וְלֹא־יִזָּכֵר שֵׁם־יִשְׂרָאֵל עוֹד:

תהלים פג

דָּלוּ עֵינֵי לַמָּרוֹם, קְרָאתִיךָ אוֹיְבַי לָקָב.

הִכָּרֵת שֵׁם וּשְׁאָר, וּמְחֵה שֵׁם לְרִקָּב.

וְצַר צוֹרְרִי בְּנִכְלֵיהֶם אֲשֶׁר נִכְלוּ לְיַעֲקֹב.

וַיֹּאמְרוּ, לֹא יִרְאֶה־יָּה, וְלֹא־יָבִין אֱלֹהֵי יַעֲקֹב:

תהלים צד

זֵרוּיִים עָנָה וְצִוָּה, וְלֹא מֶלֶךְ לְכַלּוֹתָם.

חָבוּ לְפָנָיו, וְרָדַם בַּהֲסָרַת טַבַּעַת לְהַחֲלוֹתָם.

טוֹב דְּבָרוֹ הֵקִים לְעֵינֵי הַגּוֹיִם לְהַעֲלוֹתָם.

בְּאֶרֶץ אֹיְבֵיהֶם לֹא־מְאַסְתִּים וְלֹא־גְעַלְתִּים לְכַלֹּתָם:

ויקרא כו

יָדַע רֶמֶז הַקּוֹרוֹת לְעַם מְעֻפָּר וּמְהֻדָּס.

כָּתַב הַסֵּתֶר אֶסְתִּיר וּמַר דְּרוֹר מְפֹרְדָּס.

לָשֶׁבֶת הָמָן מִמַּחֲרָת, הָמָן הָעֵץ קָנָדַס.

תַּחַת הַנַּעֲצוּץ יַעֲלֶה בְרוֹשׁ וְתַחַת הַסִּרְפַּד יַעֲלֶה הֲדַס:

ישעיה נה

The king who listened to lies, dictated accusation and sorrow.
He wrapped himself in priestly clothes, Ahasuerus,
having mistaken his reckoning of the End.
He ordered "other vessels" to be used,
from the Quarry from which the world was hewn;
    and the devil too, came and placed himself among them.   *Job 2*

When the people in Shushan ate of their destroyer's meat,
the king opened his mouth wide to accuse them,
to give them over into the hands of the one who was ready to pay their price.
The Rock, meanwhile, agreed to write a letter to destroy their hope;
    "I said that I would yield them up,   *Deut. 32*
    would put an end to their memory among mankind."

The angels, messengers of peace, wept bitterly, crying out,
"Compassionate One, look to the covenant and do not break it, pushing it away!"
The Torah, too, heard of it and put on clothes of widowhood and sorrow;
    and she laid her hands upon her head and walked along,   *II Sam. 13*
    crying as she went.

[Elijah] The Tishbite wrapped a covering of sackcloth around his waist.
He hurried and told the three fathers who sleep in the Cave of Makhpelah,
and then hastened to the Shepherd, [Moses] –
"What do you mean by sleeping?
    Rouse yourself! Get up and call out to your God –   *Jonah 1*
    perhaps He may change His mind!"

He told [Mordekhai] Bilshan of the pronouncement
that had been sealed in clay – but not in blood.
They learnt from the example of Nineveh
how to overturn anger after a decree;
the son of Kish knocked at the door of the school,
    and covered himself in sackcloth and sat down on the earth.   *Jonah 3*

For three days he gathered the children before him –
thirsty, hidden from by God – so that, in the voice of Jacob,
they might weaken the hand of the bold-faced king.
His hands raised steadily to God, Mordekhai prayed,
"Save us now from insult;
    that he should not come and slaughter us,   *Gen. 32*
    mothers and children together."

Those and those, from all sides, the children of my mighty ones and teachers,
all cried out, and their plea rose up to the LORD.
And God, when those plaintive calls reached Him, asked,
    "And what is this bleating of sheep that meets My ears?"   *I Sam. 15*

מַקְשִׁיב דְּבַר שֶׁקֶר כָּתַב שִׂטְנָה וָעֶצֶב.

נִתְעַטֵּף בְּבִגְדֵי שְׂרָד פְּטָעָה בְּמִנְיָן קֶצֶב.

סֵדֶר לְהִשְׁתַּמֵּשׁ בְּשׁוֹנִים כְּלֵי הַמַּחֲצָב.

איוב ב

וַיָּבוֹא גַם־הַשָּׂטָן בְּתוֹכָם לְהִתְיַצֵּב:

עַם הַנִּמְצָאִים בְּשׁוּשָׁן, בְּאֵלִים מִזְבֵּחַ עוֹכְרָם.

פָּעַר פִּיו לְהַשְׁטִינָם, וּלְהַסְגִּירָם בְּיַד נוֹתֵן מִכְרָם.

צוּר הַסְכֵּם לִכְתֹּב אִגֶּרֶת לְאַבֵּד שִׂבְרָם.

דברים לב

אָמַרְתִּי אַפְאֵיהֶם, אַשְׁבִּיתָה מֵאֱנוֹשׁ זִכְרָם:

קְדוֹשִׁים מַלְאֲכֵי שָׁלוֹם מַר יִבְכְּיוּן בִּצְעָקָה.

רַחוּם הַבֵּט לַבְּרִית וְאַל תָּפֵר לְהַרְחִיקָהּ.

שָׁמְעָה מוֹרָשָׁה, וַתִּלְבַּשׁ בִּגְדֵי אַלְמָנוּת וּמוּעָקָה.

שמואל ב׳ יג

וַתָּשֶׂם יָדָהּ עַל־רֹאשָׁהּ, וַתֵּלֶךְ הָלוֹךְ וְזָעֲקָה:

תִּשְׁבִּי שָׁם אֵזוֹר שַׂק בְּמָתְנָיו תַּחְבֹּשֶׁת.

מַהֵר וְהוֹדִיעַ יְשֵׁנֵי מַכְפֵּל, אָבוֹת שְׁלֹשֶׁת.

נַחַץ לְרוֹעֶה, מַה לְּךָ נִרְדָּם לְהִתְעַשֵּׁת.

יונה א

קוּם קְרָא אֶל־אֱלֹהֶיךָ, אוּלַי יִתְעַשֵּׁת:

חוֹתַם טִיט אֲשֶׁר נַעֲשָׂה, לְבַלְשָׁן סֵפֶר.

מִנְוֵה לָמְדוּ לְאַחֵר גְּזֵרָה כַּעַס לְהָפֵר.

בֶּן קִישׁ הִקִּישׁ דַּלְתוֹת בֵּית הַסֵּפֶר.

יונה ג

וַיְכַס שָׂק, וַיֵּשֶׁב עַל־הָאֵפֶר:

רָבַץ תִּינוֹקוֹת לְפָנַי יָמִים שְׁלֹשָׁה, צְמֵאִים וּמַכְפִּינִם.

בְּקוֹל יַעֲקֹב לַחֲלֹשׁ יְדֵי עַז פָּנִים.

יָדָיו אֱמוּנָה לָאֵל, הַצִּילֵנִי נָא מֵעֲלוּבוֹנִים.

בראשית לב

פֶּן־יָבוֹא וְהִכַּנִי אֵם עַל־בָּנִים:

מִזֶּה אֵלֶּה וּמָזֶּה אֵלֶּה, בְּנֵי אֵיתָנַי וְרַבְנַי.

כֻּלָּם צָעֲקוּ, וַתַּעַל שַׁוְעָתָם אֶל יְהוָה.

יָהּ, לְקוֹל רָצוֹן כְּבוֹא, שָׁאַל לְפָנַי.

שמואל א׳ טו

וּמֶה קוֹל־הַצֹּאן הַזֶּה בְּאָזְנָי:

The shepherd Moses answered Him,
"These are the little ones of the holy offspring.
Lord, save ones condemned to die, from the evil enemy."
The compassion of the Gracious One was stirred,
and He was moved to weep for what had happened.
  And so it was that when the King of Israel read the letter,   *II Kings 5*
  He tore it to pieces.

The Jew suspended sons below and father above.
Each man covered three *amot*; the fourth *amah* above was space exposed.
Mordekhai saw a double revenge, was delighted, and spoke praises:
  "I was returned to my post and he was hanged!"   *Gen. 41*

Esther wrote with emphasis,
that a Hallel of thanks should be read on that day;
and what the beloved ones accepted down below was established above.
A banner shall be raised by those who bear witness,
to make the wonder known now, as it was then.
  And at this time – may relief and salvation rise up for the Jews.   *Esther 4*

אֵל מֶלֶךְ God, King who sits upon a throne of compassion, who acts with loving-kindness, who pardons the iniquities of His people, passing them before Him in order; who forgives sinners and pardons transgressors; who performs righteousness with all flesh and spirit, do not repay their bad actions in kind. God, You taught us to speak thirteen attributes: recall for us today the covenant of the thirteen attributes, as You in ancient times showed the humble one [Moses], as is written: The Lord descended in the cloud and stood with him there, and proclaimed in the name of the Lord:

Congregation then Leader:

And the Lord passed by before him and proclaimed: *Ex. 34*

All say aloud:

יהוה The Lord, the Lord, compassionate and gracious God, slow to anger, abounding in loving-kindness and truth, extending loving-kindness to a thousand generations, forgiving iniquity, rebellion and sin, and absolving [the guilty who repent]. Forgive us our iniquity and our sin, and take us as Your inheritance.

Continue:

סְלַח לָנוּ Forgive us, our Father, for we have sinned. Pardon us, our King, for we have transgressed. For You, Lord, are good and forgiving, abounding in loving-kindness to all who call on You.   *Ps. 86*

רוֹעֶה הֵשִׁיבוּ, הֵם קְטַנֵּי קֹדֶשׁ זֶרַע.

יָהּ, הַצֵּל לְקוּחִים לַמָּוֶת מֵאוֹיֵב הָרַע.

חַנּוּן נִכְמְרוּ רַחֲמָיו וִיבַקֵּשׁ לַבְּכוֹת הַמְּאֹרָע.

מלכים ב ה
וַיְהִי כִּקְרֹא מֶלֶךְ־יִשְׂרָאֵל אֶת־הַסֵּפֶר, וַיִּקְרַע:

יְהוּדִי הוֹקִיעַ, יְלָדָיו לְמַטָּה וַאֲבִיהֶם לְמַעְלָה.

אִישׁ אִישׁ בִּשְׁלֹשׁ אַמּוֹת, וְהָרְבִיעִית אֲוֵיר מְגֻלָּה.

מִשְׁנֶה נְקָם חָזָה, וְשָׁמְעָה וְשָׁח תִּהְלָה.

בראשית מא
אֹתִי הֵשִׁיב עַל־כַּנִּי וְאֹתוֹ תָלָה:

‹ וַתִּכְתֹּב אֶסְתֵּר תֹּקֶף, לִקְרֹא כְּבָהֵלֵּל מְהוֹדִים.

מִלְמַעְלָה קִיְּמוּ מַה שֶּׁקִּבְּלוּ לְמַטָּה דּוֹדִים.

נֵס יְנוֹסֵס לְפַרְסֵם כָּאן פִּלְאוֹ מַסְהִידִים.

אסתר ד
בָּעֵת הַזֹּאת רֶוַח וְהַצָּלָה יַעֲמוֹד לַיְּהוּדִים:

אֵל מֶלֶךְ יוֹשֵׁב עַל כִּסֵּא רַחֲמִים, מִתְנַהֵג בַּחֲסִידוּת. מוֹחֵל עֲוֹנוֹת עַמּוֹ, מַעֲבִיר רִאשׁוֹן רִאשׁוֹן. מַרְבֶּה מְחִילָה לַחַטָּאִים, וּסְלִיחָה לַפּוֹשְׁעִים. עֹשֶׂה צְדָקוֹת עִם כָּל בָּשָׂר וָרוּחַ, לֹא כְרָעָתָם תִּגְמֹל. ‹ אֵל, הוֹרֵיתָ לָּנוּ לוֹמַר שְׁלֹשׁ עֶשְׂרֵה, וּזְכָר לָנוּ הַיּוֹם בְּרִית שְׁלֹשׁ עֶשְׂרֵה, כְּמוֹ שֶׁהוֹדַעְתָּ לֶעָנָו מִקֶּדֶם, כְּמוֹ שֶׁכָּתוּב: וַיֵּרֶד יהוה בֶּעָנָן, וַיִּתְיַצֵּב עִמּוֹ שָׁם, וַיִּקְרָא בְשֵׁם, יהוה:

שליח ציבור then קהל:

שמות לד
וַיַּעֲבֹר יהוה עַל־פָּנָיו וַיִּקְרָא

All say aloud:

יהוה, יהוה, אֵל רַחוּם וְחַנּוּן, אֶרֶךְ אַפַּיִם, וְרַב־חֶסֶד וֶאֱמֶת: נֹצֵר חֶסֶד לָאֲלָפִים, נֹשֵׂא עָוֹן וָפֶשַׁע וְחַטָּאָה, וְנַקֵּה: וְסָלַחְתָּ לַעֲוֹנֵנוּ וּלְחַטָּאתֵנוּ, וּנְחַלְתָּנוּ:

Continue:

תהלים פו
סְלַח לָנוּ אָבִינוּ כִּי חָטָאנוּ, מְחַל לָנוּ מַלְכֵּנוּ כִּי פָשָׁעְנוּ. כִּי־אַתָּה אֲדֹנָי טוֹב וְסַלָּח, וְרַב־חֶסֶד לְכָל־קֹרְאֶיךָ:

כִּי־עִמְּךָ For in You there is a wellspring of life; in Your light shall we see light. *Ps. 36*
As we call You, God of our righteousness, answer us. In a narrow place You
have opened out our horizon; be gracious to us and hear our prayer. And now *Num. 14*
let the strength of the Lᴏʀᴅ be great, as You have said.

כְּרַחֵם As a father has compassion for his children,
so, Lᴏʀᴅ, have compassion for us.
Salvation is the Lᴏʀᴅ's; on Your people is Your blessing, Selah! *Ps. 3*
The Lᴏʀᴅ of hosts is with us, the God of Jacob is our stronghold, Selah! *Ps. 46*
Lᴏʀᴅ of hosts, happy is the one who trusts in You. *Ps. 84*
Lᴏʀᴅ, save! May the King answer us on the day we call. *Ps. 20*

Our God and God of our fathers:

אַתָּה הָאֵל It is You who are the God of wonders.
You have made known among nations
Your terrifying strength.
You redeemed Your people by might from torments,
suppressed their foes with ignominious death.

When the enemy rose to awaken strife,
and seemed about to cut down the exquisite flowers, Israel,
he plotted to measure out into the masters' treasuries,
a hundred times the silver talents
of the sockets in the Tabernacle.

You warned Your lambs
to announce the shekel offering early;
You knew what would be.
You warned us to be punctual,
and to find a way to douse the fire
of ones who sought to burn us.
And so, those once condemned to death –
are marked out for resurrection.

When (for appearances,) they worshiped a narrow image,
they were yielded up to be clipped off:
all those offshoots and grapes.
Traps surrounded them on all sides;
they turned their eyes to You,
they were concealed in Your hiddenness.

כִּי־עִמְּךָ מְקוֹר חַיִּים, בְּאוֹרְךָ נִרְאֶה־אוֹר: בְּקָרְאֵנוּ עֲנֵנוּ אֱלֹהֵי צִדְקֵנוּ,   _{תהלים לו}
בַּצַּר הִרְחַבְתָּ לָּנוּ, חָנֵּנוּ וּשְׁמַע תְּפִלָּתֵנוּ. וְעַתָּה יִגְדַּל־נָא כֹּחַ אֲדֹנָי, כַּאֲשֶׁר   _{במדבר יד}
דִּבַּרְתָּ לֵאמֹר:

כְּרַחֵם אָב עַל בָּנִים, כֵּן תְּרַחֵם יהוה עָלֵינוּ.
לַיהוה הַיְשׁוּעָה, עַל־עַמְּךָ בִרְכָתֶךָ סֶּלָה: _{תהלים ג}
יהוה צְבָאוֹת עִמָּנוּ, מִשְׂגָּב לָנוּ אֱלֹהֵי יַעֲקֹב סֶלָה: _{תהלים מו}
יהוה צְבָאוֹת, אַשְׁרֵי אָדָם בֹּטֵחַ בָּךְ:   _{תהלים פד}
יהוה הוֹשִׁיעָה, הַמֶּלֶךְ יַעֲנֵנוּ בְיוֹם־קָרְאֵנוּ:   _{תהלים כ}

אֱלֹהֵינוּ וֵאלֹהֵי אֲבוֹתֵינוּ

אַתָּה הָאֵל עוֹשֵׂה פְלָאוֹת
בְּעַמִּים הוֹדַעְתָּ עֹז נוֹרָאוֹת
גָּאַלְתָּ בִּזְרוֹעַ עַמְּךָ מְהֻלָּאוֹת
דִּכִּיתָ צָרֵיהֶם בְּמוֹתֵי תַחֲלוּאוֹת.

הָאוֹיֵב בְּקוּמוֹ לְעוֹרֵר מְדָנִים
וְדִמָּה לְהַכְרִית פִּרְחֵי עֲדָנִים
זָמַם לִשְׁקֹל לְגִנְזֵי אֲדוֹנִים
חֲלִיפֵי מֵאַת כִּכְּרֵי אֲדָנִים.

טְלָאֶיךָ הַזְהַרְתָּ שְׁקֵלֵיהֶם לְהַקְדִּים
יָדַעְתָּ הָעֲתִידוֹת וְדָרַשְׁתָּ נִשְׁקָדִים
כִּבּוּי לְהַמְצִיא לְלַהַב יוֹקְדִים
לְקוּחִים לַמָּוֶת לְתָחֵי נִפְקָדִים.

מַסֵּכַה צָרָה בְּעָבְדָם לְפָנִים
נִמְסְרוּ לְהָתֵז קִנְקַנּוֹת גֻּפָנִים
סְבָבוּם מוֹקְשִׁים בְּכָל דְּפָנִים
עֵינֵיהֶם לְךָ תוֹלִים וּבְסִתְרְךָ נִצְפָּנִים.

The lots were overturned,
they ruled over their enemies,
and the gallows was prepared to receive
Haman the Agagite.
God struck and swallowed the façade
of covering that covered,
and He entombed His people's enemies in darkness.

Peace and truth were written on all sides;
power of salvation, steady rock and fortress.
The plunderer was plundered,
he was caught in his own trap.
The one who spoke against me was swept away;
destroyed; eyed disdainfully.

The people made celebrations,
and these were fixed for all generations.
Amalek had entered the Scriptures three times –
how could there be a fourth?
Yet on High it was agreed and here below it was sealed,
and the reason for all that had been fixed,
was inscribed in the scroll.

Your hand is lifted high to forgive sinners.
You set Mordekhai the Jew and Hadassah Esther
in their place as saviors,
and now their righteousness remains forever to delight us,
and the study of their honor
to recall to You those who were saved.

Be zealous for Your name, Awesome and Sanctified One.
Witness Your vineyard, destroyed, trampled;
gather our scattered ones
and their song to You will be renewed.
Sustain them and revive them with the building of the Temple.

▸ And as You did awe-inspiring things in those days,
so perform with us the wonder of salvation for all time.
Find in Your presence our ransom, our appeasement –
God, King who sits upon a throne of compassion.

פּוּר נֶהְפָּךְ בְּאוֹיְבִים לִשְׁלֹט
צְלִיבָה הוּכַן אֲגָגִי לָקְלֹט
קֶלַע וּבְלַע פְּנֵי הַלוֹט הַלוֹט
רִיבִי עִם בְּאַשְׁמַיִם לַעֲלֹט.

שָׁלוֹם וֶאֱמֶת נִכְתַּב מִכָּל צַד
תֹּקֶף יֶשַׁע סֶלַע וּמְצָד
שׁוֹדֵד הַשָּׁדַד וּבְרִשְׁתּוֹ נוֹצַד
מַלְשְׁנִי נִסְחַף נִגְמַת וְנִרְצַד.

עֲשׂוּ שְׂמָחוֹת וְלַדּוֹרוֹת קְבָעוּם
וּמִקְרָאוֹת שְׁלֹשִׁם וְלֹא רְבָעוּם
נִסְכְּמוּ מִמַּעַל וּלְמַטָּה טְבָעוּם
בַּסֵּפֶר נֶחְקַק עַל מָה קְבָעוּם.

רָמָה יָדְךָ לִסְלֹחַ לַפּוֹשְׁעִים
יְהוּדִי וַהֲדַסָּה הֵקַמְתָּ מוֹשִׁיעִים
צִדְקָתָם עוֹמֶדֶת לָעַד לְשַׁעֲשׁוּעִים
חֵקֶר כְּבוֹדָם לְהִזָּכֵר לְנוֹשָׁעִים.

קַנֵּא לְשִׁמְךָ נוֹרָא וְנִקְדָּשׁ
חֲזֵה כַרְמְךָ נֶהֱרָס וְנָדַשׁ
זְרוּיֵינוּ קַבֵּץ וְשִׁיר לְךָ יֻחַדָּשׁ
קַיֵּם וְהַחַיִּים בְּבִנְיַן בֵּית הַמִּקְדָּשׁ.

◄ וְכַעֲשׂוֹתְךָ נוֹרָאוֹת בְּאוֹתָן הַיָּמִים
אִתָּנוּ הַפְלֵא תְּשׁוּעַת עוֹלָמִים
מְצוֹא לְפָנֶיךָ כֹּפֶר וְתַנְחוּמִים
אֵל מֶלֶךְ יוֹשֵׁב עַל כִּסֵּא רַחֲמִים.

God, King who sits upon a throne of compassion, who acts with loving-kindness, who pardons the iniquities of His people, passing them before Him in order; who forgives sinners and pardons transgressors; who performs righteousness with all flesh and spirit, do not repay their bad actions in kind. ‣ God, You taught us to speak thirteen attributes: recall for us today the covenant of the thirteen attributes, as You in ancient times showed the humble one [Moses], as is written: The LORD descended in the cloud and stood with him there, and proclaimed in the name of the LORD:

Congregation then Leader:

And the LORD passed by before him and proclaimed: *Ex. 34*

All say aloud:

יהוה The LORD, the LORD, compassionate and gracious God, slow to anger, abounding in loving-kindness and truth, extending loving-kindness to a thousand generations, forgiving iniquity, rebellion and sin, and absolving [the guilty who repent]. Forgive us our iniquity and our sin, and take us as Your inheritance.

Continue:

סְלַח לָנוּ Forgive us, our Father, for we have sinned. Pardon us, our King, for we have transgressed. For You, LORD, are good and forgiving, abounding in *Ps. 86* loving-kindness to all who call on You.

The following is said responsively:

Small of number we stand pleading before You:
do not block Your ears to the cry of people crushed.
Listen to their entreaty from the Heaven where You dwell,
as You saved Your children
in the days of Myrrh and Myrtle [Mordekhai and Esther].

> On Israel's praises You sit enthroned, hearing their cry,
> listening to their prayer.
> Bringing healing even before the blow,
> counting it out to help the ones You have acquired;
> to settle their homes again.

A foe and enemy fixed his eyes like knives on Israel;
he opened wide his mouth to swallow up the humble man.
He deliberated within him to destroy Mordekhai's great community;
in the letter, he etched his intent to destroy the treasured people.

אֵל מֶלֶךְ יוֹשֵׁב עַל כִּסֵּא רַחֲמִים, מִתְנַהֵג בַּחֲסִידוּת. מוֹחֵל עֲוֹנוֹת עַמּוֹ, מַעֲבִיר רִאשׁוֹן רִאשׁוֹן. מַרְבֶּה מְחִילָה לַחַטָּאִים, וּסְלִיחָה לַפּוֹשְׁעִים. עֹשֶׂה צְדָקוֹת עִם כָּל בָּשָׂר וָרוּחַ, לֹא כְרָעָתָם תִּגְמֹל. ◂ אֵל, הוֹרֵיתָ לָּנוּ לוֹמַר שְׁלֹשׁ עֶשְׂרֵה, וּזְכָר לָנוּ הַיּוֹם בְּרִית שְׁלֹשׁ עֶשְׂרֵה, כְּמוֹ שֶׁהוֹדַעְתָּ לֶעָנָו מִקֶּדֶם, כְּמוֹ שֶׁכָּתוּב: וַיֵּרֶד יְהוָֹה בֶּעָנָן, וַיִּתְיַצֵּב עִמּוֹ שָׁם, וַיִּקְרָא בְשֵׁם, יְהוָֹה:

שליח ציבור then קהל:

שמות לד

וַיַּעֲבֹר יְהוָֹה עַל־פָּנָיו וַיִּקְרָא

All say aloud:

יְהוָֹה, יְהוָֹה, אֵל רַחוּם וְחַנּוּן, אֶרֶךְ אַפַּיִם, וְרַב־חֶסֶד וֶאֱמֶת: נֹצֵר חֶסֶד לָאֲלָפִים, נֹשֵׂא עָוֹן וָפֶשַׁע וְחַטָּאָה, וְנַקֵּה: וְסָלַחְתָּ לַעֲוֹנֵנוּ וּלְחַטָּאתֵנוּ, וּנְחַלְתָּנוּ:

Continue:

תהלים פו

סְלַח לָנוּ אָבִינוּ כִּי חָטָאנוּ, מְחַל לָנוּ מַלְכֵּנוּ כִּי פָשָׁעְנוּ. כִּי־אַתָּה אֲדֹנָי טוֹב וְסַלָּח, וְרַב־חֶסֶד לְכָל־קֹרְאֶיךָ:

The following is said responsively:

בַּמֶּה מִסְפָּר חֲלָיֵנוּ פָּנֶיךָ.
לִישׁוּעַת נְכָאִים אַל תַּעְלֵם אָזְנֶךָ.
הַקְשֵׁב תְּחִנָּתָם מִשְּׁמֵי מְעֹנֶךָ.
כְּבִימֵי מֹר וַהֲדַס הוֹשַׁעְתָּ בָּנֶיךָ.

תְּהִלּוֹת יִשְׂרָאֵל אַתָּה יוֹשֵׁב.
שַׁוְעָתָם מַאֲזִין וְרִנָּתָם קוֹשֵׁב.
רְפָאוֹת לְמַחַץ מַקְדִּים וּמְחַשֵּׁב.
קְנוּיֶיךָ לְהֵיטִיב וּפְנֵיהֶם לְיַשֵּׁב.

צַר וְאוֹיֵב הֶלְטִישׁ עֵינָיו.
פִּיהוּ פָּעַר לִשְׁאָף עֲנָו.
עֲשֶׁת בְּשִׁלּוֹ לְהַשְׁמִיד קְהַל הֲמוֹנָיו.
סֵגֶל לְאַבֵּד חָרַת בְּנִשְׁתְּוָנָיו.

You who take revenge upon foes
and persist in Your claim against enemies;
You measured them out with the very measure
they used against Your loved ones.
The fighter and his descendants were hanged, suspended;
they were strung up together, like fish on a thread.

On the day on which the enemies hoped
to lay carnage among the people You harbor,
the rule was overturned and bodies fell;
they bore the brunt and fury of Your rage –
they were trodden underfoot and washed away.

And so may Your name be raised up, exalted.
Your glory covers all the highest heavens.
As You lift the downtrodden,
those yielded up as plunder,
Your praise fills up the valleys to their very ends.

Consider our thoughts, now,
and witness our suffering.
Rise up, in Your rage, against the bitter enemy.
Master, we have called You from a narrow place.
Please, take us out into the open,
and release us from anguish.

Bring us much, abundant pardon.
Hear our prayer,
and what is crude in us – pass over.
Bring down those who press us
and fill them with horror.
And as for us –
do not forever withhold Your compassion.

Continue with "God, King who sits" on page 634.

נוֹקֵם לְצָרִים וְנוֹטֵר לְאוֹיְבִים.
מְדַדְתָּ מִדָּתָם כְּדֵי לָאֲהוּבִים.
לוֹחֵם וְעֵינָיו הִתְלוּ מְצַלְּבִים.
כְּבַחֲרוֹת דָּגִים חֹרְזוּ תְחוּבִים.

יוֹם אֲשֶׁר שֻׁבְּרוּ צוּרִים.
טֻבְּחָה לָשִׁית בְּעַם נְצוּרִים.
חֻלְּפָה הֲדַת וְנָפְלוּ פְגָרִים.
זֻלְעֲפוּ זַעֲמוּ מֻבְסִים מְגֹרִים.

וּבְכֵן יִתְעַלֶּה שִׁמְךָ וְיִתְנַשָּׂא.
הוֹדְךָ שְׁמֵי שָׁמַיִם כִּסָּה.
דַּכִּים בְּרוֹמְמָךְ נְתוּנִים לִמְשִׁסָּה.
גֵּיא וַאֲפֵסֶיהָ תְּהִלָּתְךָ מְכַסָּה.

בִּינָה הֲגִיגֵנוּ עַתָּה, וּרְאֵה בַצָּר.
בְּאַפְּךָ קוּמָה עַל צוֹרֵר הַצָּר.
אָדוֹן, קְרָאֲנוּךָ מִן הַמֵּצַר.
אָנָּא הוֹצִיאֵנוּ לַמֶּרְחָב וְחַלְּצֵנוּ מִצָּר.

מְאֹד תַּרְבֶּה לָנוּ מְחִילָה.
שְׁמַע תְּפִלָּה, וְהַעֲבֵר תְּפִלָּה.
לוֹחֲצֵינוּ הַמְעֵד וּמַלְּאֵם חַלְחָלָה.
מִמֶּנּוּ רַחֲמֶיךָ לָעַד לֹא תִכְלָא.

Continue with אֵל מֶלֶךְ יוֹשֵׁב on page 635.

SELIḤOT FOR THE SEVENTEENTH OF TAMMUZ

סְלַח לָנוּ Forgive us, our Father, for in our great foolishness we have blundered. Pardon us, our King, for our iniquities are many.

אֵל אֶרֶךְ You are a God slow to anger, You are called the Master of Compassion, and You have taught the way of repentance. May You remember today and every day the greatness of Your compassion and kindness, for the sake of the descendants of Your beloved ones. Turn toward us in compassion, for You are the Master of Compassion. We come before You in plea and prayer, as You in ancient times showed the humble one [Moses]. Turn from Your fierce anger, as is written in Your Torah. In the shadow of Your wings may we shelter and abide, as on the day when the Lord descended in the cloud. ‣ Disregard transgression and erase guilt as on the day You stood with him [Moses] there. Hear our cry and heed our word, as on the day You proclaimed in the name of the Lord, and there it is written:

Congregation then Leader:

And the Lord passed by before him and proclaimed:　　　　　*Ex. 34*

All say aloud:

יהוה The Lord, the Lord, compassionate and gracious God, slow to anger, abounding in loving-kindness and truth, extending loving-kindness to a thousand generations, forgiving iniquity, rebellion and sin, and absolving [the guilty who repent]. Forgive us our iniquity and our sin, and take us as Your inheritance.

Continue:

סְלַח לָנוּ Forgive us, our Father, for we have sinned. Pardon us, our King, for we have transgressed. For You, Lord, are good and forgiving, abounding in *Ps. 86* loving-kindness to all who call on You.

And do not let Him rest, until He establishes, until He makes Jerusalem the *Is. 62* praise of all the earth. For in You there is a wellspring of life; in Your light shall *Ps. 36* we see light. Our God, we are ashamed of our actions, distraught at our sins.

כְּרַחֵם As a father has compassion for his children,
so, Lord, have compassion for us.
Salvation is the Lord's; on Your people is Your blessing, Selah!　　　*Ps. 3*
The Lord of hosts is with us, the God of Jacob is our stronghold, Selah!　*Ps. 46*
Lord of hosts, happy is the one who trusts in You.　　　　　　　*Ps. 84*
Lord, save! May the King answer us on the day we call.　　　　　*Ps. 20*

סליחות לשבעה עשר בתמוז

סְלַח לָנוּ, אָבִינוּ, כִּי בְּרֹב אִוַּלְתֵּנוּ שָׁגֵינוּ.
מְחַל לָנוּ, מַלְכֵּנוּ, כִּי רַבּוּ עֲוֹנֵינוּ.

אֵל אֶרֶךְ אַפַּיִם אַתָּה, וּבַעַל הָרַחֲמִים נִקְרֵאתָ, וְדֶרֶךְ תְּשׁוּבָה הוֹרֵיתָ. גְּדֻלַּת
רַחֲמֶיךָ וַחֲסָדֶיךָ, תִּזְכּוֹר הַיּוֹם וּבְכָל יוֹם לְזֶרַע יְדִידֶיךָ. תֵּפֶן אֵלֵינוּ בְּרַחֲמִים,
כִּי אַתָּה הוּא בַּעַל הָרַחֲמִים. בְּתַחֲנוּן וּבִתְפִלָּה פָּנֶיךָ נְקַדֵּם, כְּהוֹדַעְתָּ
לֶעָנָו מִקֶּדֶם. מֵחֲרוֹן אַפְּךָ שׁוּב, כְּמוֹ בְּתוֹרָתְךָ כָּתוּב. וּבְצֵל כְּנָפֶיךָ נֶחֱסֶה
וְנִתְלוֹנָן, כְּיוֹם וַיֵּרֶד יהוה בֶּעָנָן. ◀ תַּעֲבֹר עַל פֶּשַׁע וְתִמְחֶה אָשָׁם, כְּיוֹם
וַיִּתְיַצֵּב עִמּוֹ שָׁם. תַּאֲזִין שַׁוְעָתֵנוּ וְתַקְשִׁיב מֶנּוּ מַאֲמַר, כְּיוֹם וַיִּקְרָא בְשֵׁם
יהוה, וְשָׁם נֶאֱמַר:

שליח ציבור then קהל:

שמות לד
וַיַּעֲבֹר יהוה עַל פָּנָיו וַיִּקְרָא

All say aloud:

יהוה, יהוה, אֵל רַחוּם וְחַנּוּן, אֶרֶךְ אַפַּיִם, וְרַב חֶסֶד וֶאֱמֶת: נֹצֵר
חֶסֶד לָאֲלָפִים, נֹשֵׂא עָוֹן וָפֶשַׁע וְחַטָּאָה, וְנַקֵּה: וְסָלַחְתָּ לַעֲוֹנֵנוּ
וּלְחַטָּאתֵנוּ, וּנְחַלְתָּנוּ:

Continue:

תהלים פו
סְלַח לָנוּ אָבִינוּ כִּי חָטָאנוּ, מְחַל לָנוּ מַלְכֵּנוּ כִּי פָשָׁעְנוּ. כִּי אַתָּה אֲדֹנָי טוֹב
וְסַלָּח, וְרַב חֶסֶד לְכָל קֹרְאֶיךָ:

ישעיה סב
תהלים לז
וְאַל תִּתְּנוּ דֳמִי לוֹ, עַד יְכוֹנֵן וְעַד יָשִׂים אֶת יְרוּשָׁלַ͏ִם תְּהִלָּה בָּאָרֶץ: כִּי
עִמְּךָ מְקוֹר חַיִּים, בְּאוֹרְךָ נִרְאֶה אוֹר: אֱלֹהֵינוּ, בּשְׁנוּ בְּמַעֲשֵׂינוּ וְנִכְלַמְנוּ
בַּעֲוֹנֵנוּ.

כְּרַחֵם אָב עַל בָּנִים, כֵּן תְּרַחֵם יהוה עָלֵינוּ.

תהלים ג
לַיהוה הַיְשׁוּעָה, עַל עַמְּךָ בִרְכָתֶךָ סֶּלָה:

תהלים מו
יהוה צְבָאוֹת עִמָּנוּ, מִשְׂגָּב לָנוּ אֱלֹהֵי יַעֲקֹב סֶלָה:

תהלים פד
יהוה צְבָאוֹת, אַשְׁרֵי אָדָם בֹּטֵחַ בָּךְ:

תהלים כ
יהוה הוֹשִׁיעָה, הַמֶּלֶךְ יַעֲנֵנוּ בְיוֹם קָרְאֵנוּ:

▸ Forgive, please, this people's iniquity,   *Num. 14*
  in the abundance of Your kindness,
    and as You have forgiven this people from the time of Egypt until now,
  and there it is written:

Congregation then Leader:

    And the Lᴏʀᴅ said, I have forgiven as you asked.

Continue:

הַטֵּה Give ear, my God and hear; open Your eyes and see our desolation, and   *Dan. 9*
the city that bears Your name, for it is not on the strength of our righteousness that we throw down our pleadings before You, but on the strength of
Your great compassion. Lᴏʀᴅ, hear me; Lᴏʀᴅ, forgive; Lᴏʀᴅ, listen and act
and do not delay – for Your sake, my God; for Your city and Your people
bear Your name.

Our God and God of our fathers:

אָתָֽנוּ We come before You, Former of the winds.
In our many iniquities our sighs have grown heavy;
the decrees against us powerful and our screams so many –
      for on the Seventeenth of Tammuz,
      the Tablets were smashed.

We have been exiled from the House of Your choosing;
our judgment was sealed, the decree laid down.
And the light has darkened over us –
      for on the Seventeenth of Tammuz,
      the Torah scroll was burnt.

Our enemies destroyed the Sanctuary,
the Divine Presence fled from Its corner,
and we were yielded up to the hands of the wanton,
to be consumed –
      for on the Seventeenth of Tammuz,
      an idol was set up in the Temple.

We were scattered from city to city,
and old and young of us were seized.
The place of our delight was destroyed,
and fire raged through her –
      for on the Seventeenth of Tammuz
      the city was broken through.

במדבר יד

‹ סְלַח־נָא לַעֲוֹן הָעָם הַזֶּה כְּגֹדֶל חַסְדֶּךָ
וְכַאֲשֶׁר נָשָׂאתָה לָעָם הַזֶּה מִמִּצְרַיִם וְעַד־הֵנָּה:
וְשָׁם נֶאֱמַר:

שליח ציבור then קהל:

וַיֹּאמֶר יהוה, סָלַחְתִּי כִּדְבָרֶךָ:

Continue:

דניאל ט

הַטֵּה אֱלֹהַי אָזְנְךָ וּשֲׁמָע, פְּקַח עֵינֶיךָ וּרְאֵה שֹׁמְמֹתֵינוּ וְהָעִיר אֲשֶׁר־נִקְרָא
שִׁמְךָ עָלֶיהָ, כִּי לֹא עַל־צִדְקֹתֵינוּ אֲנַחְנוּ מַפִּילִים תַּחֲנוּנֵינוּ לְפָנֶיךָ, כִּי
עַל־רַחֲמֶיךָ הָרַבִּים: אֲדֹנָי שְׁמָעָה, אֲדֹנָי סְלָחָה, אֲדֹנָי הַקְשִׁיבָה וַעֲשֵׂה
אַל־תְּאַחַר, לְמַעַנְךָ אֱלֹהַי, כִּי־שִׁמְךָ נִקְרָא עַל־עִירְךָ וְעַל־עַמֶּךָ:

אֱלֹהֵינוּ וֵאלֹהֵי אֲבוֹתֵינוּ

אֲתָנוּ לָךְ יוֹצֵר רוּחוֹת
בְּרֹב עֲוֹנֵינוּ כָּבְדוּ אֲנָחוֹת
גְּזֵרוֹת עַצְמוּ וְרַבּוּ צְרִיחוֹת
כִּי בְּשִׁבְעָה עָשָׂר בְּתַמּוּז נִשְׁתַּבְּרוּ הַלֻּחוֹת.

גָּלִינוּ מִבֵּית הַבְּחִירָה
דִּינֵנוּ נֶחְתַּם וְנִגְזְרָה גְזֵרָה
וְחָשַׁךְ בַּעֲדֵנוּ אוֹרָה
כִּי בְּשִׁבְעָה עָשָׂר בְּתַמּוּז נִשְׂרְפָה הַתּוֹרָה.

הָרְסוּ אוֹיְבֵינוּ הַהֵיכָל
וּבָרְחָה שְׁכִינָה מִזָּוִית הֵיכָל
וְנִמְסַרְנוּ בִּידֵי זֵדִים לְהִתְאַכָּל
כִּי בְּשִׁבְעָה עָשָׂר בְּתַמּוּז הָעֳמַד צֶלֶם בַּהֵיכָל.

זְרוֹנוּ מֵעִיר אֶל עִיר
וְנִלְכַּד מִמֶּנּוּ רַב וְצָעִיר
חָרְבָה מְשׁוֹשֵׂנוּ וְאֵשׁ בָּהּ הַבְעִיר
כִּי בְּשִׁבְעָה עָשָׂר בְּתַמּוּז הֻבְקְעָה הָעִיר.

The lethal foe took hold of our Temple, and the cherubs,
bride and bridegroom were deprived of all their ornament.
Because we angered You
we were given up to destruction –
>   for on the Seventeenth of Tammuz,
>   the daily offering ceased.

All glory and praise there ended.
The enemy drew his sword
and brandished its point against us;
small children and babies were prepared for the slaughter –
>   for on the Seventeenth of Tammuz,
>   the offerings and sacrifices ceased.

We rebelled against the One who inhabits the Heavens,
and so we were dispersed to all the corners of the world.
All our dancing was turned to lament –
>   for on the Seventeenth of Tammuz,
>   the Temple service ended.

We acted obstinately with You
in the discord of tongues,
and so our own tongue has learnt lamentation;
we have been abandoned in countless numbers –
>   for on the Seventeenth of Tammuz,
>   sin decided our destiny.

We have been dispersed and found no relief,
and so our sighs have multiplied within us;
Rock, see how our souls have been bowed low –
>   and turn our Seventeenth of Tammuz
>   into gladness and joy.

We have been obstinate
and many calamities have met us;
and so we have been yielded up to the plunder,
have been pushed into the mud.
See, Lord, and release us from disaster –
>   and turn our Seventeenth of Tammuz
>   into joy and gladness.

טָפַשׁ מִקְדָּשֵׁנוּ צַר הִמְשְׁמִיד
וְנָטַל מֶחְתָּן וְכַלָּה אֶצְעָדָה וְצָמִיד
יַעַן כְּעָסְנוּךָ נִתְּנוּ לְהַשְׁמִיד
כִּי בְשִׁבְעָה עָשָׂר בְּתַמּוּז בֻּטַּל הַתָּמִיד.

כָּלָה מֶנּוּ כָּל הוֹד וָשֶׁבַח
חַרְבּוֹ שָׁלַף אוֹיֵב עָלֵינוּ לְאַבַּח
לִהְיוֹת עוֹלְלִים וְיוֹנְקִים מוּכָנִים לַטֶּבַח
כִּי בְשִׁבְעָה עָשָׂר בְּתַמּוּז בֻּטְּלוּ עוֹלָה וָזָבַח.

מָרַדְנוּ לְשׁוֹכֵן מְעוֹנוֹת
לָכֵן נִתְפַּזַּרְנוּ בְּכָל פִּנּוֹת
נֶהְפַּךְ מְחוֹלֵנוּ לְקִינוֹת
כִּי בְשִׁבְעָה עָשָׂר בְּתַמּוּז בֻּטְּלוּ קָרְבָּנוֹת.

סָרַרְנוּ לְפָנֶיךָ מֵרִיב לְשׁוֹנוֹת
לָכֵן לֻמַּדָה לְשׁוֹנֵנוּ לוֹמַר קִינוֹת
עֻזַּבְנוּ בְּלִי לְהָמְנוֹת
כִּי בְשִׁבְעָה עָשָׂר בְּתַמּוּז גָּרְמוּ לָנוּ עֲוֹנוֹת.

פָּזַרְנוּ בְּלִי מְצוֹא רְוָחָה
לָכֵן רְבַבְתָּה בָּנוּ אֲנָחָה
צוּר רְאֵה נַפְשֵׁנוּ כִּי שָׁחָה
וְשִׁבְעָה עָשָׂר בְּתַמּוּז הֲפָךְ לָנוּ לְשָׂשׂוֹן וּלְשִׂמְחָה.

קִשִּׁינוּ עֹרֶף וְרַבְתָּה בָּנוּ אָסוֹן
לָכֵן נִתַּנּוּ לִמְשִׁסָּה וְרִפְשׁוֹן
רְאֵה יהוה וְחַלְּצֵנוּ מֵאָסוֹן
וְשִׁבְעָה עָשָׂר בְּתַמּוּז הֲפָךְ לָנוּ לְשִׂמְחָה וּלְשָׂשׂוֹן.

‣ Turn to us, You who reside on High,
and gather in our scattered ones from the very ends of the earth.
Say to Zion, "Come, get up," –
and turn our Seventeenth of Tammuz
to a day of salvation and comfort.

אֵל מֶלֶךְ God, King who sits upon a throne of compassion, who acts with loving-kindness, who pardons the iniquities of His people, passing them before Him in order; who forgives sinners and pardons transgressors; who performs righteousness with all flesh and spirit, do not repay their bad actions in kind. ‣ God, You taught us to speak thirteen attributes: recall for us today the covenant of the thirteen attributes, as You in ancient times showed the humble one [Moses], as is written: The LORD descended in the cloud and stood with him there, and proclaimed in the name of the LORD.

Congregation then Leader:
And the LORD passed by before him and proclaimed: Ex. 34

All say aloud:
יהוה The LORD, the LORD, compassionate and gracious God, slow to anger, abounding in loving-kindness and truth, extending loving-kindness to a thousand generations, forgiving iniquity, rebellion and sin, and absolving [the guilty who repent]. Forgive us our iniquity and our sin, and take us as Your inheritance.

Continue:
סְלַח לָנוּ Forgive us, our Father, for we have sinned. Pardon us, our King, for we have transgressed. For You, LORD, are good and forgiving, abounding in   Ps. 86
loving-kindness to all who call on You.

God, do not rest, do not be silent and do not be still, for Your enemies   Ps. 83
clamor and those who hate You hold their heads high. God of retribution,   Ps. 94
LORD; God of retribution, appear

כְּרַחֵם As a father has compassion for his children,
so, LORD, have compassion for us.
Salvation is the LORD's; on Your people is Your blessing, Selah!   Ps. 3
The LORD of hosts is with us, the God of Jacob is our stronghold, Selah!   Ps. 46
LORD of hosts: happy is the one who trusts in You.   Ps. 84
LORD, save! May the King answer us on the day we call.   Ps. 20

‹ שַׁעֲנוּ שׁוֹכֵן רוּמָה

וְקַבֵּץ נְפוּצוֹתֵינוּ מִקְצְווֹת אֲדָמָה

תֹּאמַר לְצִיּוֹן קוּמָה

וְשִׁבְעָה עָשָׂר בְּתַמּוּז הָפָךְ לָנוּ לְיוֹם יְשׁוּעָה וְנֶחָמָה.

אֵל מֶלֶךְ יוֹשֵׁב עַל כִּסֵּא רַחֲמִים, מִתְנַהֵג בַּחֲסִידוּת. מוֹחֵל עֲוֹנוֹת עַמּוֹ,
מַעֲבִיר רִאשׁוֹן רִאשׁוֹן. מַרְבֶּה מְחִילָה לַחַטָּאִים, וּסְלִיחָה לַפּוֹשְׁעִים. עֹשֶׂה
צְדָקוֹת עִם כָּל בָּשָׂר וָרוּחַ, לֹא כְרָעָתָם תִּגְמֹל. ‹ אֵל, הוֹרֵיתָ לָּנוּ לוֹמַר שְׁלֹשׁ
עֶשְׂרֵה, וּזְכֹר לָנוּ הַיּוֹם בְּרִית שְׁלֹשׁ עֶשְׂרֵה, כְּמוֹ שֶׁהוֹדַעְתָּ לֶעָנָו מִקֶּדֶם,
כְּמוֹ שֶׁכָּתוּב: וַיֵּרֶד יהוה בֶּעָנָן, וַיִּתְיַצֵּב עִמּוֹ שָׁם, וַיִּקְרָא בְשֵׁם, יהוה:

שְׁלִיחַ צִבּוּר then קָהָל:

שמות לד
וַיַּעֲבֹר יהוה עַל־פָּנָיו וַיִּקְרָא

All say aloud:

יהוה, יהוה, אֵל רַחוּם וְחַנּוּן, אֶרֶךְ אַפַּיִם, וְרַב־חֶסֶד וֶאֱמֶת: נֹצֵר
חֶסֶד לָאֲלָפִים, נֹשֵׂא עָוֹן וָפֶשַׁע וְחַטָּאָה, וְנַקֵּה: וְסָלַחְתָּ לַעֲוֹנֵנוּ
וּלְחַטָּאתֵנוּ, וּנְחַלְתָּנוּ:

Continue:

תהלים פו
סְלַח לָנוּ אָבִינוּ כִּי חָטָאנוּ, מְחַל לָנוּ מַלְכֵּנוּ כִּי פָשָׁעְנוּ. כִּי־אַתָּה אֲדֹנָי טוֹב
וְסַלָּח, וְרַב־חֶסֶד לְכָל־קֹרְאֶיךָ:

תהלים פג
אֱלֹהִים אַל־דֳּמִי־לָךְ, אַל־תֶּחֱרַשׁ וְאַל־תִּשְׁקֹט אֵל: כִּי־הִנֵּה אוֹיְבֶיךָ יֶהֱמָיוּן,
תהלים צד
וּמְשַׂנְאֶיךָ נָשְׂאוּ רֹאשׁ: אֵל־נְקָמוֹת יהוה, אֵל נְקָמוֹת הוֹפִיעַ:

כְּרַחֵם אָב עַל בָּנִים, כֵּן תְּרַחֵם יהוה עָלֵינוּ.

תהלים ג
לַיהוה הַיְשׁוּעָה, עַל־עַמְּךָ בִרְכָתֶךָ סֶּלָה:

תהלים מו
יהוה צְבָאוֹת עִמָּנוּ, מִשְׂגָּב לָנוּ אֱלֹהֵי יַעֲקֹב סֶלָה:

תהלים פד
יהוה צְבָאוֹת, אַשְׁרֵי אָדָם בֹּטֵחַ בָּךְ:

תהלים כ
יהוה הוֹשִׁיעָה, הַמֶּלֶךְ יַעֲנֵנוּ בְיוֹם־קָרְאֵנוּ:

Our God and God of our fathers:

אָמַר It is bitterly that I weep, over the Hand raised against our ruins.
I blasphemed Him in His House,
in my unfaithfulness and thieving.
The Holy Presence broke out and fled,
flew ten stretches and rose up to the seventh Heaven.

God cut me off, tormented me, burnt me, in the fourth month.
He closed the time set for Him to break those young boys,
who were like boughs just sprouting.
He shot us with His arrows twice, melted and weakened us,
as heedless women wept for Tammuz in the Temple.
He condemned me and became Enemy to me,
then, in the month of Tammuz.

Five traps were laid for me, deep in the Scripture of sufferings sent.
Those people overcame me for my impurity
on the seventeenth of the month.
For I was ensnared like a wretched bride,
unfaithful beneath a wedding canopy of peace and success.
I did not wait for Moses, my shepherd, until the sixth hour,
and the Tablets were smashed.

From His hand was I ornamented
with jewelry of fine gold, brooch and bracelet.
They flowed away on the day of His rage,
when I corrupted my way, and denounced my faith.
I broke off the order of His service and the constant supplies of the altar –
from the Chamber of the Lambs, the daily offering is ended.

Israel is crumbled to pieces, scattered, storm battered, oppressed.
Likened to a ship without a captain, tossed about like a boat.
You have taken her by the head for her sins,
exposed her twice over to mourning and moaning.
Her enemies waged war on her on this day,
and the city was broken through again.

She fled out like a chased gazelle to hide, when none sought her.
They sharpened their tongues, they made her like a lamb,
and left her wool and milk for all takers.
She cries out for the cherished thing with which she was crowned:
the beloved of her eyes eluded her as Apostomus burnt the Torah.

אֱלֹהֵינוּ וֵאלֹהֵי אֲבוֹתֵינוּ

אֲמַר בְּבֶכִי מִפְּנֵי יַד שְׁלוּחָה בְּעִי.
בְּנָאֳצִי בְּתוֹךְ בֵּיתוֹ בִּבְגָדֵי וְקָבְעִי.
גַּח וּבָרַח וְנָסַע עֶשֶׂר וְעָלָה לַשְּׁבִיעִי.
דְּמֵנִי הֱצִיקַנִי הִשִּׁיקַנִי בַּחֹדֶשׁ הָרְבִיעִי.

הֵבִיא מוֹעֵד בִּמְלֵאתוֹ לְשַׁבֵּר בַּחוּרֵי גְמוּז.
וְרַבָּה בוֹ פְעָמִים בְּמִסְמְסוֹס וּמִזְמוּז.
וְבוּלוֹ כְּשַׁר שַׁאֲנַנּוֹת מַבְכוֹת אֶת הַתַּמּוּז.
חַיָּבַנִי וְאֵיבְנִי אֲזַי בְּיֶרַח תַּמּוּז.

טָמְנוּ פַחִים חֲמִשָּׁה בְּמִקְרָא תְּלָאוֹת מְשֻׁלָּחוֹת.
יָכְלוּ לִי בְּשִׁבְעָה עָשָׂר בּוֹ בַּאֲלִיחוֹת.
כִּי נוֹקַשְׁתִּי כְּכַלָּה עֲלוּבָה בְּחָפַת שַׁלְוָה וְהַצְלָחוֹת.
לְרֹעִי לֹא הַמְתַּנְתִּי שֵׁשׁ, וְנִשְׁתַּבְּרוּ הַלֻּחוֹת.

מִידוֹ עָדִיתִי חֲלִי כֶתֶם, אֶצְעָדָה וְצָמִיד.
נִגְרוֹת בְּיוֹם אַפּוֹ, כְּשָׁחֲתוּ דַּרְכִּי לְהַשְׁמִיד.
סֵדֶר עֲבוֹדָתוֹ וְקַיִץ מִזְּבְחוֹ קִצָּתוֹ לְהַעֲמִיד.
עַל כֵּן מִלֶּשְׁכַּת הַטְּלָאִים בָּטַל הַתָּמִיד.

פּוֹר הִתְפּוֹרְרָה וְנִתְפּוֹרָה סָעֲרָה עֲנִיָּה.
צִי נִמְשְׁלָה מִבְּלִי חוֹבֵל, וְנִטְרְפָה כָּאֳנִיָּה.
קָחְתָּה בְּחֶטְאָתָהּ בָּרֹאשָׁה, וּבְכֵפֶל תַּאֲנִיָּה וַאֲנִיָּה.
רִיבוּהָ צָרֶיהָ כְּהַיּוֹם, וַהֻּבְקְעָה הָעִיר בַּשְּׁנִיָּה.

שָׁלְחָה כִּצְבִי מֻדָּח מֵאֵין דּוֹרֵשׁ לְהַסְתִּירָה.
שִׁנְּנוּ לְשׁוֹנָם וּנְתָנוּהָ כֻּשָׁה, צָמְרָה וְחָלְבָּה לְהַתִּירָה.
תִּצְעַק עַל כְּלִי חֶמְדָּה שֶׁבּוֹ נִכְתָּרָה.
תַּחֲמֹד עֵינָהּ נִצָּל כְּשָׂרַף אַפּוֹסְטֹמוֹס הַתּוֹרָה.

A fool cursed those oppressed and broken to vex them;
  he taunted abject people: "They shall be consumed;"
"God shall hide His face from seeing."
  When idols were placed in the Temple,
God avenged one's hand at the hand of the other, a disgusting item consumed.
This, at the time when He gathered anguish over us;
  for an image was set up in the Sanctuary of God.

Miserable and plagued are these children, who were once the very first.
  Their troubles have come close on one another's heels these many years;
stricken as if by the stings of bees and scorpions.
  They think their hope is gone,
that as they sit in this darkness they have no more chance.

‣ Zealous God, in Your restraint toward those who incite You
  they have flourished fat and succulent.
Raise up those who still await You;
  let them stand firm always,
like something planted, or carved out with love.
  It is on fast days that truth and peace are hewn out.
May they become forever times of joy and celebration – festive days.

אֵל מֶלֶךְ God, King who sits upon a throne of compassion, who acts with loving-kindness, who pardons the iniquities of His people, passing them before Him in order; who forgives sinners and pardons transgressors; who performs righteousness with all flesh and spirit, do not repay their bad actions in kind. ‣ God, You taught us to speak thirteen attributes: recall for us today the covenant of the thirteen attributes, as You in ancient times showed the humble one [Moses], as is written: The Lord descended in the cloud and stood with him there, and proclaimed in the name of the Lord:

Congregation then Leader:
And the Lord passed by before him and proclaimed: Ex. 34

All say aloud:
יהוה The Lord, the Lord, compassionate and gracious God, slow to anger, abounding in loving-kindness and truth, extending loving-kindness to a thousand generations, forgiving iniquity, rebellion and sin, and absolving [the guilty who repent]. Forgive us our iniquity and our sin, and take us as Your inheritance.

חֵרֵף עֲשׁוּקִים וּרְצוּצִים בַּעֲבוּר הָרְעִימָם סָכָל.
יְרוּדִים בּוֹהֶיָה לֶאֱכֹל וּבְהַסְתֵּר פָּנִים מִלְּהֵסְתַּכָּל.
יָד הַשָּׁלִים מִכְּנַף שִׁקּוּצִים נֶאֱכָל.
עֵת צָרָה כְּהִתְכַּנֵּס וְהָעֳמַד צֶלֶם בְּהֵיכָל.

דְּווּיִם סְגוּפִים בָּנִים הֶהָיוּ מִקֶּדֶם רִאשׁוֹנִים.
סְמוּכוֹת צָרוֹתֵיהֶם זוֹ לָזוֹ כַּמֶּה שָׁנִים.
לוֹקִים כַּאֲשֶׁר תַּעֲשֶׂינָה הַדְּבוֹרִים, וְהָעֲקְרַבִּים שׁוֹנִים.
הוֹגִים אָבַד שִׂבְרָם וּבָטֵל סִכּוּיִם בָּאִישׁוֹנִים.

‹ אֵל קַנָּא, בְּהִתְאַקֵּק בְּמַקְנִיאֶיךָ דְּשֵׁנִים רְטוּבִים.
מְחַכִּים תָּקִים עוֹמְדִים לְעוֹלָמִים, כִּנְטִיעִים מֻחְטָבִים בַּאֲהָבִים.
הָאֱמֶת וְהַשָּׁלוֹם בְּצוֹמוֹת חֲטוּבִים.
נֵצַח הֱיוֹתָם לְשִׂמְחָה וּלְשָׂשׂוֹן וּלְמוֹעֲדִים טוֹבִים.

אֵל מֶלֶךְ יוֹשֵׁב עַל כִּסֵּא רַחֲמִים, מִתְנַהֵג בַּחֲסִידוּת. מוֹחֵל עֲוֹנוֹת עַמּוֹ,
מַעֲבִיר רִאשׁוֹן רִאשׁוֹן. מַרְבֶּה מְחִילָה לְחַטָּאִים, וּסְלִיחָה לְפוֹשְׁעִים. עֹשֶׂה
צְדָקוֹת עִם כָּל בָּשָׂר וָרוּחַ, לֹא כְרָעָתָם תִּגְמֹל. ‹ אֵל, הוֹרֵיתָ לָּנוּ לוֹמַר שְׁלֹש
עֶשְׂרֵה, וּזְכָר לָנוּ הַיּוֹם בְּרִית שְׁלֹשׁ עֶשְׂרֵה, כְּמוֹ שֶׁהוֹדַעְתָּ לֶעָנָו מִקֶּדֶם,
כְּמוֹ שֶׁכָּתוּב: וַיֵּרֶד יהוה בֶּעָנָן, וַיִּתְיַצֵּב עִמּוֹ שָׁם, וַיִּקְרָא בְשֵׁם, יהוה:

שליח ציבור then קהל:
וַיַּעֲבֹר יהוה עַל פָּנָיו וַיִּקְרָא
שמות לד

All say aloud:

יהוה, יהוה, אֵל רַחוּם וְחַנּוּן, אֶרֶךְ אַפַּיִם, וְרַב חֶסֶד וֶאֱמֶת: נֹצֵר
חֶסֶד לָאֲלָפִים, נֹשֵׂא עָוֹן וָפֶשַׁע וְחַטָּאָה, וְנַקֵּה: וְסָלַחְתָּ לַעֲוֹנֵנוּ
וּלְחַטָּאתֵנוּ, וּנְחַלְתָּנוּ:

Continue:

סְלַח לָנוּ Forgive us, our Father, for we have sinned. Pardon us, our King, for we have transgressed. For You, LORD, are good and forgiving, abounding in *Ps. 86* loving-kindness to all who call on You.

The following is said responsively:

Turn to this prisoner who has been yielded up,
to the hand of Babylon and then of Seir;
to You he has been calling all these years,
and he pleads like a small child,
> on the day the enemy prevailed and the city was broken through.

And so I bow myself and strike my hands together,
on this day of five disasters that scattered me about,
for at the time of the golden calf, the Tablets left me.
And the daily offering was annulled,
and they brought me away in a cage.
And an idol was placed in the Sanctuary that was my crowning glory,
and I was deprived of His counsel.
The meal-offering was ended, and Your Law –
the foe sent it up in flames,
> on the day the enemy prevailed and the city was broken through.

I tremble terribly, I stand horrified, on the day the LORD pushed me aside,
And Sennacherib, the Viper of the north, swept me away like a deluge.
My light grew dark, and Sheshakh [Babylon] too, tossed me about like a ball.
And the hunter stretched out his hand, and the goat of Greece,
the hairy one of Rome,
> on the day the enemy prevailed and the city was broken through.

The glory of my heart, my Stronghold, will Your rage fume forever?
Will You not see this weary nation, blackened as if by the furnace?
Close, with the descendant of Peretz, the breach in my fence,
and, from among the thorns, pick out the lily.
Build the Temple, and return the borders of the Carmel and of Bashan.
And open Your eyes, exact vengeance from Etzer and Dishan.
Judge a people struck dumb, so that the damages be paid,
by the one who destroys, the one who burns –
> on the day the enemy prevailed and the city was broken through.

Continue:

סְלַח לָנוּ אָבִינוּ כִּי חָטָאנוּ, מְחַל לָנוּ מַלְכֵּנוּ כִּי פָשָׁעְנוּ. כִּי־אַתָּה אֲדֹנָי טוֹב תהלים פו
וְסַלָּח, וְרַב־חֶסֶד לְכָל־קֹרְאֶיךָ:

The following is said responsively:

שָׁעָה נֶאֱסַר, אֲשֶׁר נִמְסַר, בְּיַד בָּבֶל וְגַם שֵׂעִיר.
לְךָ יֶהֱמֶה, זֶה כַּמָּה, וְיִתְחַנַּן כְּבֶן צָעִיר.
יוֹם גָּבַר הָאוֹיֵב וַתִּבָּקַע הָעִיר.

לְזֹאת אֶכַּף, וְאֶסְפֹּק כַּף, בְּיוֹם חָמֵשׁ פְּזוּרוֹנִי.
וְעַל רֶגֶל הָעֵגֶל, הַלֻּחוֹת יְצָאוּנִי.
וְגַם הֻשְׁמַד הַתָּמִיד, וּבַסּוּגַר הֻבֵּאתִי.
וְהוּשַׁם אֵלַי בַּהֵיכָל כָּלִיל, וּמֵעֵצָתוֹ כָּלָאֲנִי.
וְהַמִּנְחָה הוּנָחָה, וְדָתְךָ, צָר בָּאֵשׁ הִבְעִיר.
יוֹם גָּבַר הָאוֹיֵב וַתִּבָּקַע הָעִיר.

מְאֹד אֶתְחַל, וְאֶתְחַלְחַל, בְּיוֹם שַׁדַּי דְּחָפַנִי.
וְהַשְּׁפִיפוֹן מִצָּפוֹן, כְּשִׁבֹּלֶת שְׁטָפַנִי.
מְאוֹר חָשַׁךְ, וְגַם שֻׁשַּׁךְ, כְּמוֹ כַדּוּר צְנָפַנִי.
וְהַצַּיִד שָׁלַח יָד, וְהַצָּפִיר וְהַשָּׂעִיר.
יוֹם גָּבַר הָאוֹיֵב וַתִּבָּקַע הָעִיר.

הוֹד לִבִּי וּמִשְׂגַּבִּי, הֲלָעַד אַפְּךָ יֶעְשָׁן.
הֲלֹא תֵרָאֶה עִם נִלְאֶה, אֲשֶׁר הֻשְׁחַר כְּמוֹ כִבְשָׁן.
גְּדֹר פִּרְצִי בְּבֶן פַּרְצִי, וּמֶחֱזָק לְקֶט שׁוֹשָׁן.
בְּנֵה בַיִת זְבוּל, וְהָשֵׁב גְּבוּל הַכַּרְמֶל וְהַבָּשָׁן.
וְעֵין פְּקַח, וְנָקָם קַח מֵאֱצָר וּמִדִּישָׁן.
שְׁפֹט אִלֵּם, וְאָז יְשֻׁלַּם הַמַּבְעֶה וְהַמַּבְעִיר.
יוֹם גָּבַר הָאוֹיֵב וַתִּבָּקַע הָעִיר.

On all days continue:

אֵל מֶלֶךְ God, King who sits upon a throne of compassion, who acts with loving-kindness, who pardons the iniquities of His people, passing them before Him in order; who forgives sinners and pardons transgressors; who performs righteousness with all flesh and spirit, do not repay their bad actions in kind. God, You taught us to speak thirteen attributes: recall for us today the covenant of the thirteen attributes, as You in ancient times showed the humble one [Moses], as is written: The LORD descended in the cloud and stood with him there, and proclaimed in the name of the LORD:

Congregation then Leader:

And the LORD passed by before him and proclaimed: *Ex. 34*

All say aloud:

יהוה The LORD, the LORD, compassionate and gracious God, slow to anger, abounding in loving-kindness and truth, extending loving-kindness to a thousand generations, forgiving iniquity, rebellion and sin, and absolving [the guilty who repent]. Forgive us our iniquity and our sin, and take us as Your inheritance.

Continue:

סְלַח לָנוּ Forgive us, our Father, for we have sinned. Pardon us, our King, for we have transgressed. For You, LORD, are good and forgiving, abounding in loving-kindness to all who call on You.   *Ps. 86*

זְכֹר Remember, LORD, Your compassion and loving-kindness,   *Ps. 25*
for they are everlasting. Remember us, LORD, in favoring Your people;
redeem us with Your salvation.

זְכֹר Remember Your congregation, the one that You acquired long ago,   *Ps. 74*
the tribe of Your inheritance that You redeemed,
this Mount Zion that You have dwelt in.

זְכֹר Remember, LORD, the fondness of Jerusalem; do not forever forget the
love of Zion. You shall rise up and have compassion for Zion,   *Ps. 102*
for now it is right to be gracious, for the time has come.

זְכֹר Remember, LORD, what the Edomites did on the day Jerusalem fell.   *Ps. 137*
They said, "Tear it down, tear it down to its very foundations!"

זְכֹר Remember Abraham, Isaac and Jacob, to whom You swore by Your   *Ex. 32*
own self, when You said to them, "I shall make Your descendants
as numerous as the stars in the sky, and I shall give all this Land that
I spoke of to your descendants, and they shall inherit it forever."

זְכֹר Remember Your servants, Abraham, Isaac and Jacob; do not attend to   *Deut. 9*
the stubbornness of this people, to their wickedness or sinfulness.

On all days continue:

אֵל מֶלֶךְ יוֹשֵׁב עַל כִּסֵּא רַחֲמִים, מִתְנַהֵג בַּחֲסִידוּת. מוֹחֵל עֲוֹנוֹת עַמּוֹ, מַעֲבִיר רִאשׁוֹן רִאשׁוֹן. מַרְבֶּה מְחִילָה לַחַטָּאִים, וּסְלִיחָה לַפּוֹשְׁעִים. עֹשֶׂה צְדָקוֹת עִם כָּל בָּשָׂר וָרוּחַ, לֹא כְרָעָתָם תִּגְמֹל. ‹ אֵל, הוֹרֵיתָ לָּנוּ לוֹמַר שְׁלֹשׁ עֶשְׂרֵה, וּזְכָר לָנוּ הַיּוֹם בְּרִית שְׁלֹשׁ עֶשְׂרֵה, כְּמוֹ שֶׁהוֹדַעְתָּ לֶעָנָו מִקֶּדֶם, כְּמוֹ שֶׁכָּתוּב: וַיֵּרֶד יהוה בֶּעָנָן, וַיִּתְיַצֵּב עִמּוֹ שָׁם, וַיִּקְרָא בְשֵׁם, יהוה:

שליח ציבור then קהל:

שמות לד וַיַּעֲבֹר יהוה עַל פָּנָיו וַיִּקְרָא

All say aloud:

יהוה, יהוה, אֵל רַחוּם וְחַנּוּן, אֶרֶךְ אַפַּיִם, וְרַב חֶסֶד וֶאֱמֶת: נֹצֵר חֶסֶד לָאֲלָפִים, נֹשֵׂא עָוֹן וָפֶשַׁע וְחַטָּאָה, וְנַקֵּה: וְסָלַחְתָּ לַעֲוֹנֵנוּ וּלְחַטָּאתֵנוּ, וּנְחַלְתָּנוּ:

Continue:

תהלים פו סְלַח לָנוּ אָבִינוּ כִּי חָטָאנוּ, מְחַל לָנוּ מַלְכֵּנוּ כִּי פָשָׁעְנוּ. כִּי אַתָּה אֲדֹנָי טוֹב וְסַלָּח, וְרַב חֶסֶד לְכָל קֹרְאֶיךָ:

תהלים כה זְכֹר רַחֲמֶיךָ יהוה וַחֲסָדֶיךָ, כִּי מֵעוֹלָם הֵמָּה:

זָכְרֵנוּ יהוה בִּרְצוֹן עַמֶּךָ, פָּקְדֵנוּ בִּישׁוּעָתֶךָ.

תהלים עד זְכֹר עֲדָתְךָ קָנִיתָ קֶּדֶם, גָּאַלְתָּ שֵׁבֶט נַחֲלָתֶךָ הַר צִיּוֹן זֶה שָׁכַנְתָּ בּוֹ:

זְכֹר יהוה חִבַּת יְרוּשָׁלַיִם, אַהֲבַת צִיּוֹן אַל תִּשְׁכַּח לָנֶצַח:

תהלים קב אַתָּה תָקוּם תְּרַחֵם צִיּוֹן, כִּי עֵת לְחֶנְנָהּ, כִּי בָא מוֹעֵד:

תהלים קלז זְכֹר יהוה לִבְנֵי אֱדוֹם אֵת יוֹם יְרוּשָׁלָיִם הָאֹמְרִים עָרוּ עָרוּ, עַד הַיְסוֹד בָּהּ:

שמות לב זְכֹר לְאַבְרָהָם לְיִצְחָק וּלְיִשְׂרָאֵל עֲבָדֶיךָ, אֲשֶׁר נִשְׁבַּעְתָּ לָהֶם בָּךְ וַתְּדַבֵּר אֲלֵהֶם, אַרְבֶּה אֶת זַרְעֲכֶם כְּכוֹכְבֵי הַשָּׁמָיִם וְכָל הָאָרֶץ הַזֹּאת אֲשֶׁר אָמַרְתִּי אֶתֵּן לְזַרְעֲכֶם, וְנָחֲלוּ לְעֹלָם:

דברים ט זְכֹר לַעֲבָדֶיךָ לְאַבְרָהָם לְיִצְחָק וּלְיַעֲקֹב אַל תֵּפֶן אֶל קְשִׁי הָעָם הַזֶּה וְאֶל רִשְׁעוֹ וְאֶל חַטָּאתוֹ:

אֵל־נָא Please, do not hold against us the sin

Num. 12

that we committed so foolishly, that we have sinned.
We have sinned, our Rock; forgive us, our Creator.

Some say responsively (all continue with "Remember the covenant" on the next page):

אֵל־נָא God, please, heal please, the diseases of this fruitful vine,
ashamed, disgraced and miserable are her fruits.
Redeem her from destruction and from the seeping wound;
> answer us as You answered our father Abraham on Mount Moriah –
>> We have sinned, our Rock;
>> forgive us, our Creator.

Let the flags of the people redeemed by Your revealed arm,
be spared from plague; let them not be cut down,
and answer our call, and desire the creations of Your hands.
> Answer us as You answered our fathers at the Reed Sea –
>> We have sinned, our Rock;
>> forgive us, our Creator.

Reveal now the merit of Abraham and Sarah,
the rock from which we were hewn.
Spare us from rage and lead us on a straight path.
Clear our impurity, and open our eyes to the light of Your Torah.
> Answer us as You answered Joshua at Gilgal –
>> We have sinned, our Rock;
>> forgive us, our Creator.

LORD, witness the ashes of bound Isaac; make our cure spring up.
Put an end to plunder and brokenness, tempest and storm.
Teach us and make us wise with Your perfect word.
> Answer us as You answered Samuel at Mitzpah –
>> We have sinned, our Rock;
>> forgive us, our Creator.

Jacob who emerged perfect from the womb – do not let his roots dry up.
Cleanse us of all stain and blemish, and do not have us wither.
Help us and we shall be saved,
and receive of Your ways of kindness.
> Answer us as You answered Elijah on Mount Carmel –
>> We have sinned, our Rock;
>> forgive us, our Creator.

במדבר יב

אֵל־נָא תָשֵׁת עָלֵינוּ חַטָּאת אֲשֶׁר נוֹאַלְנוּ וַאֲשֶׁר חָטָאנוּ:
חָטָאנוּ צוּרֵנוּ, סְלַח לָנוּ יוֹצְרֵנוּ.

Some say responsively (all continue with זְכֹר לָנוּ בְּרִית *on the next page):*

אֵל נָא, רְפָא נָא תַּחֲלוּאֵי גֶּפֶן פּוֹרִיָּה
בּוֹשָׁה וַחֲפֵדָה, וְאֻמְלַל פִּרְיָהּ
גְּאָלֶהָ מִשַּׁחַת וּמִמַּכָּה טְרִיָּה.
עֲנֵנוּ כְּשֶׁעָנִיתָ לְאַבְרָהָם אָבִינוּ בְּהַר הַמּוֹרִיָּה.
חָטָאנוּ צוּרֵנוּ, סְלַח לָנוּ יוֹצְרֵנוּ.

דְּגָלֵי עָם, פְּדוּיֵי בְּזְרוֹעַ חָשׂוּף
הַצֵּל מִנֶּגֶף וְאַל יִהְיוּ לְשִׁסּוּף
וְתַעֲנֶה קְרִיאָתֵנוּ וּלְמַעֲשֵׂה יָדֶיךָ תִּכְסֹף
עֲנֵנוּ כְּשֶׁעָנִיתָ לַאֲבוֹתֵינוּ עַל יַם סוּף.
חָטָאנוּ צוּרֵנוּ, סְלַח לָנוּ יוֹצְרֵנוּ.

זְכוּת צוּר חָצַב הַיּוֹם לָנוּ תָגֵל
חָשְׁכֵנוּ מֵאֹנֶף וּנְחֵנוּ בְּיֹשֶׁר מַעְגָּל
טַהֵר טֻמְאָתֵנוּ וְלִמְאוֹר תּוֹרָתְךָ עֵינֵינוּ גַל
עֲנֵנוּ כְּשֶׁעָנִיתָ לִיהוֹשֻׁעַ בַּגִּלְגָּל.
חָטָאנוּ צוּרֵנוּ, סְלַח לָנוּ יוֹצְרֵנוּ.

יָהּ, רְאֵה דֶּשֶׁן עָקוּד, וְהַצְמַח לָנוּ תְרוּפָה
כַּלֵּה שֹׁד וָשֶׁבֶר, סַעַר וְסוּפָה
לַמְּדֵנוּ וְחַכְּמֵנוּ אִמְרָתְךָ הַצְּרוּפָה
עֲנֵנוּ כְּשֶׁעָנִיתָ לִשְׁמוּאֵל בַּמִּצְפָּה.
חָטָאנוּ צוּרֵנוּ, סְלַח לָנוּ יוֹצְרֵנוּ.

מַתְמִם מֵרַחֵם, שָׁרָשָׁיו אַל תַּקְמֵל
נַקֵּנוּ מִכֶּתֶם וָשֶׁמֶץ, וְלֹא נֶאֱמַל
סַעֲדֵנוּ וְנִוָּשֵׁעָה, וְאָרְחוֹת חֲסָדֶיךָ נִגְמֹל
עֲנֵנוּ כְּשֶׁעָנִיתָ לְאֵלִיָּהוּ בְּהַר הַכַּרְמֶל.
חָטָאנוּ צוּרֵנוּ, סְלַח לָנוּ יוֹצְרֵנוּ.

Strengthen us by the righteousness of Moses, drawn from water,
and atone our crimes, wanton or foolish.
Free us from the terror of death that thrusts us back,
rule for our salvation; do not let us melt away in our sins.

> Answer us as You answered Jonah in the belly of the fish –
>> We have sinned, our Rock;
>> forgive us, our Creator.

Remember Your devoted Aaron's sanctity,
for the sake of Israel of the pleasing steps.
Awaken Your compassion, for we are doubly stricken.
Return us resolutely to our awe of You, do not expose us.

> Answer us as You answered David, and Solomon his son in Jerusalem –
>> We have sinned, our Rock;
>> forgive us, our Creator.

On the Fast of Esther add:

Answer those who call You; listen out from Your residence.
Hear the cry of those who call out to You, You who listen to the destitute.
Have compassion for Your children, as a father has for his.

> Answer us as You answered Mordekhai and Esther:
>> and on a fifty-cubit gallows they hanged father and sons –
>>> We have sinned, our Rock.
>>> Forgive us, our Creator.

All continue:

זְכֹר Remember the covenant of our fathers, as You have said,
"I shall remember My covenant with Jacob, and My covenant   *Lev. 26*
  with Isaac, and I shall remember My covenant with Abraham,
  and I shall remember the Land."

זְכֹר Remember the covenant of the early ones, as You have said,
"I shall remember for them the covenant of the early ones,   *Lev. 26*
  those I took out of the Land of Egypt before the eyes of the nations,
  in order to be their God: I am the LORD."

עֲשֵׂה Deal kindly with us as You have promised, "Even so, when they are in the   *Lev. 26*
land of their enemies I shall not reject them and shall not detest them to the
point of destruction, to the point of breaking My covenant with them, for I
am the LORD their God." Restore our fortunes, and have compassion for us as
is written, "And God shall restore your fortunes and have compassion for you,   *Deut. 30*
and shall return and gather you in from all the nations among whom the LORD

עוֹדֵדֵנוּ בְּצֶדֶק מָשׁוּי מִמַּיִם, וְכַפֵּר זָדוֹן וּמְשׁוּגָה
פְּדֵנוּ מִמְּהוּמַת מָוֶת, וְאָחוֹר בַּל נְסוּגָה
צַוֵּה יְשׁוּעָתֵנוּ, וּבַעֲוֹנוֹתֵינוּ אַל נִתְמוֹגְגָה
עֲנֵנוּ כְּשֶׁעָנִיתָ לְיוֹנָה בִּמְעֵי הַדָּגָה.
חָטָאנוּ צוּרֵנוּ, סְלַח לָנוּ יוֹצְרֵנוּ.

קִדַּשְׁתָּ אִישׁ חֲסִידֶךָ זְכֹר לִיפַת פַּעֲמַיִם
וְרַחֲמֶיךָ תְּעוֹרֵר כִּי לָקִינוּ בְּכִפְלַיִם
שׁוּבֵנוּ תְּקֵף לְיִרְאָתֶךָ וְלֹא נֶחֱשַׁף שׁוּלַיִם
עֲנֵנוּ כְּשֶׁעָנִיתָ לְדָוִד וְלִשְׁלֹמֹה בְנוֹ בִּירוּשָׁלַיִם.
חָטָאנוּ צוּרֵנוּ, סְלַח לָנוּ יוֹצְרֵנוּ.

On תענית אסתר *add:*

תֵּעָנֶה לְקוֹרְאֶיךָ, וְהַסְכֵּת מִמְּעוֹנִים
תִּשְׁמַע שַׁוְעַת צוֹעֲקֶיךָ, שׁוֹמֵעַ אֶל אֶבְיוֹנִים
תְּרַחֵם עַל בָּנֶיךָ כְּרַחֵם אָב עַל בָּנִים
עֲנֵנוּ כְּמוֹ שֶׁעָנִיתָ לְמָרְדְּכַי וְאֶסְתֵּר
וְתָלוּ עַל עֵץ חֲמִשִּׁים הָאָב עִם בָּנִים.
חָטָאנוּ צוּרֵנוּ, סְלַח לָנוּ יוֹצְרֵנוּ.

All continue:

זְכֹר לָנוּ בְּרִית אָבוֹת כַּאֲשֶׁר אָמַרְתָּ: וְזָכַרְתִּי אֶת־בְּרִיתִי יַעֲקוֹב ויקרא כו
וְאַף אֶת־בְּרִיתִי יִצְחָק וְאַף אֶת־בְּרִיתִי אַבְרָהָם אֶזְכֹּר
וְהָאָרֶץ אֶזְכֹּר:

זְכֹר לָנוּ בְּרִית רִאשׁוֹנִים כַּאֲשֶׁר אָמַרְתָּ: וְזָכַרְתִּי לָהֶם בְּרִית רִאשֹׁנִים ויקרא כו
אֲשֶׁר הוֹצֵאתִי־אֹתָם מֵאֶרֶץ מִצְרַיִם לְעֵינֵי הַגּוֹיִם
לִהְיוֹת לָהֶם לֵאלֹהִים אֲנִי יהוה:

עֲשֵׂה עִמָּנוּ כְּמָה שֶׁהִבְטַחְתָּנוּ: וְאַף גַּם־זֹאת בִּהְיוֹתָם בְּאֶרֶץ אֹיְבֵיהֶם, ויקרא כו
לֹא־מְאַסְתִּים וְלֹא־גְעַלְתִּים לְכַלֹּתָם, לְהָפֵר בְּרִיתִי אִתָּם, כִּי אֲנִי יהוה
אֱלֹהֵיהֶם: הָשֵׁב שְׁבוּתֵנוּ וְרַחֲמֵנוּ כְּמָה שֶׁכָּתוּב: וְשָׁב יהוה אֱלֹהֶיךָ אֶת־ דברים ל

has scattered you." Gather those of us who have been distanced, as is written, "If your distanced ones are at the very ends of the heavens, from there shall the LORD your God gather you; from there shall He bring You." Wipe out our crimes as if they were a cloud, as if they were a haze, as is written, "I have wiped out your crimes like a cloud, and as a haze your sins; come back to Me for I have redeemed you." Wipe out our crimes for Your sake, as You have said, "I, I am the one who shall wipe out your crimes for My sake, and I shall not recall your sins." Whiten our sins as snow and as wool, as is written, "Come now, let us reason together, says the LORD; If your sins are like scarlet, they shall be whitened like snow; should they be as red as crimson, they shall become like wool." Throw over us pure waters and purify us, as is written, "I shall throw pure waters over you and you shall be pure. I shall purify you of all your impurities and of all your idolatry." Have compassion for us and do not destroy us, as is written, "For the LORD your God is a compassionate God; He will not cease to hold you and He will not destroy you, and will not forget the covenant of your fathers that He pledged to them." Circumcise our hearts to love Your name, as is written, "And the LORD will circumcise your heart and the heart of your descendants to love the LORD your God with all your heart and with all your soul, so that you shall live." Let us find You when we seek You, as is written, "And if from there you seek the LORD your God, you shall find Him, when you seek Him out with all your heart and with all your soul." Bring us to Your holy mountain, and let us rejoice in Your house of prayer, as is written, "I shall bring them to My holy mountain, and I shall make them rejoice in My house of prayer; their offerings and their sacrifices will be accepted, desired on My altar, for My House will be called a house of prayer for all peoples."

Deut. 30

Is. 44

Is. 43

Is. 1

Ezek. 36

Deut. 4

Deut. 30

Deut. 4

Is. 56

The Ark is opened. The following until • is said responsively, verse by verse:

שְׁמַע קוֹלֵנוּ Listen to our voice, LORD our God. Spare us and have compassion on us, and in compassion and favor accept our prayer. Turn us back, O LORD, to You, and we will return. Renew our days as of old. Do not cast us away from You, and do not take Your holy spirit from us. Do not cast us away in our old age; when our strength is gone do not desert us.• Do not desert us, LORD; our God, do not be distant from us. Give us a sign of good things, and those who hate us shall see it and be ashamed, for You, LORD, will help us and console us. Hear our speech, LORD, consider our thoughts. May the words of our mouths and the thoughts within our hearts be pleasing to You, LORD, our Rock and our Redeemer. For it is You, LORD, that we have longed for; You shall answer us, LORD our God.

Lam. 5

The Ark is closed.

שְׁבוּתְךָ וְרִחֲמֶךָ, וְשָׁב וְקִבֶּצְךָ מִכָּל־הָעַמִּים אֲשֶׁר הֱפִיצְךָ יהוה אֱלֹהֶיךָ

דברים ל שָׁמָּה: קַבֵּץ נִדָּחֵינוּ כְּמָה שֶׁכָּתוּב: אִם־יִהְיֶה נִדַּחֲךָ בִּקְצֵה הַשָּׁמָיִם, מִשָּׁם

יְקַבֶּצְךָ יהוה אֱלֹהֶיךָ וּמִשָּׁם יִקָּחֶךָ: מְחֵה פְשָׁעֵינוּ כָּעָב וְכֶעָנָן כְּמָה שֶׁכָּתוּב:

ישעיה מד מָחִיתִי כָעָב פְּשָׁעֶיךָ וְכֶעָנָן חַטֹּאותֶיךָ, שׁוּבָה אֵלַי כִּי גְאַלְתִּיךָ: מְחֵה פְשָׁעֵינוּ

ישעיה מג לְמַעַנְךָ כַּאֲשֶׁר אָמַרְתָּ: אָנֹכִי אָנֹכִי הוּא מֹחֶה פְשָׁעֶיךָ לְמַעֲנִי, וְחַטֹּאתֶיךָ

ישעיה א לֹא אֶזְכֹּר: הַלְבֵּן חֲטָאֵינוּ כַּשֶּׁלֶג וְכַצֶּמֶר כְּמָה שֶׁכָּתוּב: לְכוּ־נָא וְנִוָּכְחָה

יֹאמַר יהוה, אִם־יִהְיוּ חֲטָאֵיכֶם כַּשָּׁנִים כַּשֶּׁלֶג יַלְבִּינוּ, אִם־יַאְדִּימוּ כַתּוֹלָע

יחזקאל לו כַּצֶּמֶר יִהְיוּ: זְרֹק עָלֵינוּ מַיִם טְהוֹרִים וְטַהֲרֵנוּ כְּמָה שֶׁכָּתוּב: וְזָרַקְתִּי עֲלֵיכֶם

מַיִם טְהוֹרִים וּטְהַרְתֶּם, מִכֹּל טֻמְאוֹתֵיכֶם וּמִכָּל־גִּלּוּלֵיכֶם אֲטַהֵר אֶתְכֶם:

רַחֵם עָלֵינוּ וְאַל תַּשְׁחִיתֵנוּ כְּמָה שֶׁכָּתוּב: כִּי אֵל רַחוּם יהוה אֱלֹהֶיךָ, לֹא

יַרְפְּךָ וְלֹא יַשְׁחִיתֶךָ, וְלֹא יִשְׁכַּח אֶת־בְּרִית אֲבֹתֶיךָ אֲשֶׁר נִשְׁבַּע לָהֶם: מוֹל

דברים ל אֶת לְבָבֵנוּ לְאַהֲבָה אֶת שְׁמֶךָ כְּמָה שֶׁכָּתוּב: וּמָל יהוה אֱלֹהֶיךָ אֶת־לְבָבְךָ

וְאֶת־לְבַב זַרְעֶךָ, לְאַהֲבָה אֶת־יהוה אֱלֹהֶיךָ בְּכָל־לְבָבְךָ וּבְכָל־נַפְשְׁךָ, לְמַעַן

דברים ד חַיֶּיךָ: הִמָּצֵא לָנוּ בְּבַקָּשָׁתֵנוּ כְּמָה שֶׁכָּתוּב: וּבִקַּשְׁתֶּם מִשָּׁם אֶת־יהוה

אֱלֹהֶיךָ וּמָצָאתָ, כִּי תִדְרְשֶׁנּוּ בְּכָל־לְבָבְךָ וּבְכָל־נַפְשֶׁךָ: תְּבִיאֵנוּ אֶל הַר

ישעיה נו קָדְשֶׁךָ וְשַׂמְּחֵנוּ בְּבֵית תְּפִלָּתֶךָ כְּמָה שֶׁכָּתוּב: וַהֲבִיאוֹתִים אֶל־הַר קָדְשִׁי

וְשִׂמַּחְתִּים בְּבֵית תְּפִלָּתִי, עוֹלֹתֵיהֶם וְזִבְחֵיהֶם לְרָצוֹן עַל־מִזְבְּחִי, כִּי בֵיתִי

בֵּית־תְּפִלָּה יִקָּרֵא לְכָל־הָעַמִּים:

The אֲרוֹן קוֹדֶשׁ is opened. The following until ▸ is said responsively, verse by verse:

שְׁמַע קוֹלֵנוּ, יהוה אֱלֹהֵינוּ, חוּס וְרַחֵם עָלֵינוּ וְקַבֵּל בְּרַחֲמִים וּבְרָצוֹן אֶת

תְּפִלָּתֵנוּ. הֲשִׁיבֵנוּ יהוה אֵלֶיךָ וְנָשׁוּבָה, חַדֵּשׁ יָמֵינוּ כְּקֶדֶם: אַל תַּשְׁלִיכֵנוּ

איכה ה מִלְּפָנֶיךָ, וְרוּחַ קָדְשְׁךָ אַל תִּקַּח מִמֶּנּוּ. אַל תַּשְׁלִיכֵנוּ לְעֵת זִקְנָה, כִּכְלוֹת

כֹּחֵנוּ אַל תַּעַזְבֵנוּ. אַל תַּעַזְבֵנוּ יהוה, אֱלֹהֵינוּ אַל תִּרְחַק מִמֶּנּוּ. עֲשֵׂה

עִמָּנוּ אוֹת לְטוֹבָה, וְיִרְאוּ שׂוֹנְאֵינוּ וְיֵבֹשׁוּ, כִּי אַתָּה יהוה עֲזַרְתָּנוּ וְנִחַמְתָּנוּ.

אֲמָרֵינוּ הַאֲזִינָה יהוה, בִּינָה הֲגִיגֵנוּ. יִהְיוּ לְרָצוֹן אִמְרֵי פִינוּ וְהֶגְיוֹן לִבֵּנוּ

לְפָנֶיךָ, יהוה צוּרֵנוּ וְגֹאֲלֵנוּ. כִּי לְךָ יהוה הוֹחָלְנוּ, אַתָּה תַעֲנֶה אֲדֹנָי אֱלֹהֵינוּ.

The אֲרוֹן קוֹדֶשׁ is closed.

CONFESSION

אֱלֹהֵינוּ Our God and God of our fathers,
let our prayer come before You, and do not hide Yourself from our plea,
for we are not so arrogant or obstinate as to say before You,
LORD, our God and God of our fathers,
we are righteous and have not sinned,
for in truth, we and our fathers have sinned.

Strike the left side of the chest with the right fist while saying each of the sins.

אָשַׁמְנוּ We have been guilty, we have acted treacherously, we have
robbed, we have spoken slander. We have acted perversely, we have
acted wickedly, we have acted presumptuously, we have been violent,
we have framed lies. We have given bad advice, we have deceived, we
have scorned, we have rebelled, we have provoked, we have turned away,
we have committed iniquity, we have transgressed, we have persecuted,
we have been obstinate. We have acted wickedly, we have corrupted,
we have acted abominably, we have strayed, we have led others astray.

סַרְנוּ We have turned away from Your commandments, and good laws, to no
avail, for You are just in all that has befallen us, for You have acted faithfully   *Neh. 9*
while we have done wickedly.

הִרְשַׁעְנוּ We have been wicked and we have done wrong, and so we have not
been saved. Place it in our hearts to abandon the way of wickedness, and
hasten our salvation, as is written by Your prophet, "Let each wicked person   *Is. 55*
abandon his ways, each man of iniquity his thoughts, and let him come back
to the LORD and He will have compassion for him; back to our God for He
will forgive abundantly."

מְשִׁיחַ Your righteous anointed one said to You, "Who can discern his own   *Ps. 19*
mistakes? Cleanse me of my hidden faults." Cleanse us, LORD our God, of all
our sins, and purify us of all our impurities and throw clear waters over us to
purify us, as was written by Your prophet, "I shall throw clear waters over you   *Ezek. 36*
and you shall be pure. I shall purify you of all your impurities and of all your
idolatry." Your people, Your inheritance, famished of Your good, thirsting for
Your loving-kindness, craving Your salvation – they shall recognize and know
that compassion and forgiveness belong to the LORD our God.

*On days when Taḥanun is not said (such as on the morning of a Brit Mila, or when a bridegroom
is present), continue with Avinu Malkenu on page 194 followed by Half Kaddish (page 214).*

וידוי

אֱלֹהֵינוּ וֵאלֹהֵי אֲבוֹתֵינוּ

תָּבֹא לְפָנֶיךָ תְּפִלָּתֵנוּ, וְאַל תִּתְעַלַּם מִתְּחִנָּתֵנוּ.

שֶׁאֵין אֲנוּ עַזֵּי פָנִים וּקְשֵׁי עֹרֶף לוֹמַר לְפָנֶיךָ

יהוה אֱלֹהֵינוּ וֵאלֹהֵי אֲבוֹתֵינוּ, צַדִּיקִים אֲנַחְנוּ וְלֹא חָטָאנוּ.

אֲבָל אֲנַחְנוּ וַאֲבוֹתֵינוּ חָטָאנוּ.

Strike the left side of the chest with the right fist while saying each of the sins.

אָשַׁמְנוּ, בָּגַדְנוּ, גָּזַלְנוּ, דִּבַּרְנוּ דֹפִי. הֶעֱוִינוּ, וְהִרְשַׁעְנוּ, זַדְנוּ, חָמַסְנוּ,

טָפַלְנוּ שֶׁקֶר. יָעַצְנוּ רָע, כִּזַּבְנוּ, לַצְנוּ, מָרַדְנוּ, נִאַצְנוּ, סָרַרְנוּ,

עָוִינוּ, פָּשַׁעְנוּ, צָרַרְנוּ, קִשִּׁינוּ עֹרֶף. רָשַׁעְנוּ, שִׁחַתְנוּ, תִּעַבְנוּ,

תָּעִינוּ, תִּעְתָּעְנוּ.

נחמיה ט סַרְנוּ מִמִּצְוֹתֶיךָ וּמִמִּשְׁפָּטֶיךָ הַטּוֹבִים, וְלֹא שָׁוָה לָנוּ. וְאַתָּה צַדִּיק עַל

כָּל-הַבָּא עָלֵינוּ, כִּי-אֱמֶת עָשִׂיתָ וַאֲנַחְנוּ הִרְשָׁעְנוּ.

הִרְשַׁעְנוּ וּפָשַׁעְנוּ לָכֵן לֹא נוֹשָׁעְנוּ. וְתֵן בְּלִבֵּנוּ לַעֲזֹב דֶּרֶךְ רֶשַׁע, וְחִישׁ

ישעיה נה לָנוּ יֶשַׁע, כַּכָּתוּב עַל יַד נְבִיאֶךָ: יַעֲזֹב רָשָׁע דַּרְכּוֹ וְאִישׁ אָוֶן מַחְשְׁבֹתָיו,

וְיָשֹׁב אֶל-יהוה וִירַחֲמֵהוּ וְאֶל-אֱלֹהֵינוּ כִּי-יַרְבֶּה לִסְלוֹחַ:

תהלים יט מְשִׁיחַ צִדְקְךָ אָמַר לְפָנֶיךָ: שְׁגִיאוֹת מִי-יָבִין, מִנִּסְתָּרוֹת נַקֵּנִי: נַקֵּנוּ יהוה

אֱלֹהֵינוּ מִכָּל-פְּשָׁעֵינוּ וְטַהֲרֵנוּ מִכָּל טֻמְאוֹתֵינוּ וּזְרֹק עָלֵינוּ מַיִם טְהוֹרִים

יחזקאל לו וְטַהֲרֵנוּ, כַּכָּתוּב עַל יַד נְבִיאֶךָ: וְזָרַקְתִּי עֲלֵיכֶם מַיִם טְהוֹרִים וּטְהַרְתֶּם,

מִכֹּל טֻמְאוֹתֵיכֶם וּמִכָּל-גִּלּוּלֵיכֶם אֲטַהֵר אֶתְכֶם: עַמְּךָ וְנַחֲלָתְךָ רְעֵבֵי

טוּבְךָ, צְמֵאֵי חַסְדֶּךָ, תְּאֵבֵי יִשְׁעֶךָ. יַכִּירוּ וְיֵדְעוּ, כִּי לַיהוה אֱלֹהֵינוּ

הָרַחֲמִים וְהַסְּלִיחוֹת.

On days when תחנון *is not said (such as on the morning of a* חתן, ברית מילה, *or when a* חתן
is present), continue with אבינו מלכנו *on page 195 followed by* חצי קדיש *(page 215).*

אֵל רַחוּם Compassionate God is Your name; Gracious God is Your name. We are called by Your name; LORD, act for the sake of Your name. Act for the sake of Your truth. Act for the sake of Your covenant. Act for the sake of Your greatness and glory. Act for the sake of Your Law. Act for the sake of Your majesty. Act for the sake of Your promise. Act for the sake of Your remembrance. Act for the sake of Your loving-kindness. Act for the sake of Your goodness. Act for the sake of Your oneness. Act for the sake of Your honor. Act for the sake of Your wisdom. Act for the sake of Your kingship. Act for the sake of Your eternity. Act for the sake of Your mystery. Act for the sake of Your might. Act for the sake of Your splendor. Act for the sake of Your righteousness. Act for the sake of Your holiness. Act for the sake of Your great compassion. Act for the sake of Your Presence. Act for the sake of Your praise. Act for the sake of those who loved You, who now dwell in the dust. Act for the sake of Abraham, Isaac and Jacob. Act for the sake of Moses and Aaron. Act for the sake of David and Solomon. Act for the sake of Jerusalem, Your holy city. Act for the sake of Zion, the dwelling place of Your glory. Act for the sake of the desolate site of Your Temple. Act for the sake of the ruins of Your altar. Act for the sake of those killed in sanctification of Your name. Act for the sake of those slaughtered over Your unity. Act for the sake of those who have gone through fire and water in sanctification of Your name. Act for the sake of suckling infants who have not sinned. Act for the sake of little ones just weaned who have done no wrong. Act for the sake of schoolchildren. Act for Your own sake if not for ours. Act for Your own sake, and save us.

עֲנֵנוּ Answer us, LORD, answer us. Answer us, our God, answer us. Answer us, our Father, answer us. Answer us, our Creator, answer us. Answer us, our Redeemer, answer us. Answer us, You who seek us, answer us. Answer us, God who is faithful, answer us. Answer us, You who are ancient and kind, answer us. Answer us, You who are pure and upright, answer us. Answer us, You who are alive and remain, answer us. Answer us, You who are good and do good, answer us. Answer us, You who know our impulses, answer us. Answer us, You who conquer rage, answer us. Answer us, You who clothe Yourself in righteousness, answer us. Answer us, Supreme King of kings, answer us. Answer us, You who are awesome and elevated, answer us. Answer us, You who forgive and pardon, answer us. Answer us, You who answer in times of trouble, answer us. Answer us, You who redeem and save, answer us. Answer us, You who are righteous and straightforward, answer us. Answer us, You who are close to those who call, answer us. Answer us, You who are compassionate and gracious, answer us. Answer us, You who listen to the destitute, answer us. Answer us, You who support the innocent, answer us. Answer us, God of our fathers, answer us. Answer us, God of Abraham, answer us. Answer us, Terror of Isaac, answer us. Answer us, Champion of Jacob, answer us. Answer us, Help of the tribes, answer us. Answer us, Stronghold of the mothers, answer us. Answer us, You who are slow to anger, answer us. Answer us, You who are lightly appeased, answer us. Answer us, You who answer at times of favor, answer us. Answer us, Father of orphans, answer us. Answer us, Justice of widows, answer us.

אֵל רַחוּם שְׁמֶךָ. אֵל חַנּוּן שְׁמֶךָ. בָּנוּ נִקְרָא שְׁמֶךָ. יהוה עֲשֵׂה לְמַעַן שְׁמֶךָ. עֲשֵׂה לְמַעַן אֲמִתֶּךָ. עֲשֵׂה לְמַעַן בְּרִיתֶךָ. עֲשֵׂה לְמַעַן גְּדָלְךָ וְתִפְאַרְתֶּךָ. עֲשֵׂה לְמַעַן דָּתֶךָ. עֲשֵׂה לְמַעַן הוֹדֶךָ. עֲשֵׂה לְמַעַן וְעוּדֶךָ. עֲשֵׂה לְמַעַן זִכְרֶךָ. עֲשֵׂה לְמַעַן חַסְדֶּךָ. עֲשֵׂה לְמַעַן טוּבֶךָ. עֲשֵׂה לְמַעַן יִחוּדֶךָ. עֲשֵׂה לְמַעַן כְּבוֹדֶךָ. עֲשֵׂה לְמַעַן לִמּוּדֶךָ. עֲשֵׂה לְמַעַן מַלְכוּתֶךָ. עֲשֵׂה לְמַעַן נִצְחֶךָ. עֲשֵׂה לְמַעַן סוֹדֶךָ. עֲשֵׂה לְמַעַן עֻזֶּךָ. עֲשֵׂה לְמַעַן פְּאֵרֶךָ. עֲשֵׂה לְמַעַן צִדְקָתֶךָ. עֲשֵׂה לְמַעַן קְדֻשָּׁתֶךָ. עֲשֵׂה לְמַעַן רַחֲמֶיךָ הָרַבִּים. עֲשֵׂה לְמַעַן שְׁכִינָתֶךָ. עֲשֵׂה לְמַעַן תְּהִלָּתֶךָ. עֲשֵׂה לְמַעַן אוֹהֲבֶיךָ שׁוֹכְנֵי עָפָר. עֲשֵׂה לְמַעַן אַבְרָהָם יִצְחָק וְיַעֲקֹב. עֲשֵׂה לְמַעַן מֹשֶׁה וְאַהֲרֹן. עֲשֵׂה לְמַעַן דָּוִד וּשְׁלֹמֹה. עֲשֵׂה לְמַעַן יְרוּשָׁלַיִם עִיר קָדְשֶׁךָ. עֲשֵׂה לְמַעַן צִיּוֹן מִשְׁכַּן כְּבוֹדֶךָ. עֲשֵׂה לְמַעַן שִׁמְמוֹת הֵיכָלֶךָ. עֲשֵׂה לְמַעַן הֲרִיסוֹת מִזְבְּחֶךָ. עֲשֵׂה לְמַעַן הֲרוּגִים עַל שֵׁם קָדְשֶׁךָ. עֲשֵׂה לְמַעַן טְבוּחִים עַל יִחוּדֶךָ. עֲשֵׂה לְמַעַן בָּאֵי בָאֵשׁ וּבַמַּיִם עַל קִדּוּשׁ שְׁמֶךָ. עֲשֵׂה לְמַעַן יוֹנְקֵי שָׁדַיִם שֶׁלֹּא חָטְאוּ. עֲשֵׂה לְמַעַן גְּמוּלֵי חָלָב שֶׁלֹּא פָשְׁעוּ. עֲשֵׂה לְמַעַן תִּינוֹקוֹת שֶׁל בֵּית רַבָּן. עֲשֵׂה לְמַעַנְךָ אִם לֹא לְמַעֲנֵנוּ. עֲשֵׂה לְמַעַנְךָ וְהוֹשִׁיעֵנוּ.

עֲנֵנוּ יהוה עֲנֵנוּ. עֲנֵנוּ אֱלֹהֵינוּ עֲנֵנוּ. עֲנֵנוּ אָבִינוּ עֲנֵנוּ. עֲנֵנוּ בּוֹרְאֵנוּ עֲנֵנוּ. עֲנֵנוּ גוֹאֲלֵנוּ עֲנֵנוּ. עֲנֵנוּ דוֹרְשֵׁנוּ עֲנֵנוּ. עֲנֵנוּ הָאֵל הַנֶּאֱמָן עֲנֵנוּ. עֲנֵנוּ וָתִיק וְחָסִיד עֲנֵנוּ. עֲנֵנוּ זַךְ וְיָשָׁר עֲנֵנוּ. עֲנֵנוּ חַי וְקַיָּם עֲנֵנוּ. עֲנֵנוּ טוֹב וּמֵטִיב עֲנֵנוּ. עֲנֵנוּ יוֹדֵעַ יֵצֶר עֲנֵנוּ. עֲנֵנוּ כּוֹבֵשׁ כְּעָסִים עֲנֵנוּ. עֲנֵנוּ לוֹבֵשׁ צְדָקוֹת עֲנֵנוּ. עֲנֵנוּ מֶלֶךְ מַלְכֵי הַמְּלָכִים עֲנֵנוּ. עֲנֵנוּ נוֹרָא וְנִשְׂגָּב עֲנֵנוּ. עֲנֵנוּ סוֹלֵחַ וּמוֹחֵל עֲנֵנוּ. עֲנֵנוּ עוֹנֶה בְּעֵת צָרָה עֲנֵנוּ. עֲנֵנוּ פּוֹדֶה וּמַצִּיל עֲנֵנוּ. עֲנֵנוּ צַדִּיק וְיָשָׁר עֲנֵנוּ. עֲנֵנוּ קָרוֹב לְקוֹרְאָיו עֲנֵנוּ. עֲנֵנוּ רַחוּם וְחַנּוּן עֲנֵנוּ. עֲנֵנוּ שׁוֹמֵעַ אֶל אֶבְיוֹנִים עֲנֵנוּ. עֲנֵנוּ תּוֹמֵךְ תְּמִימִים עֲנֵנוּ. עֲנֵנוּ אֱלֹהֵי אֲבוֹתֵינוּ עֲנֵנוּ. עֲנֵנוּ אֱלֹהֵי אַבְרָהָם עֲנֵנוּ. עֲנֵנוּ פַּחַד יִצְחָק עֲנֵנוּ. עֲנֵנוּ אֲבִיר יַעֲקֹב עֲנֵנוּ. עֲנֵנוּ עֶזְרַת הַשְּׁבָטִים עֲנֵנוּ. עֲנֵנוּ מִשְׂגַּב אִמָּהוֹת עֲנֵנוּ. עֲנֵנוּ קָשֶׁה לִכְעֹס עֲנֵנוּ. עֲנֵנוּ רַךְ לִרְצוֹת עֲנֵנוּ. עֲנֵנוּ עוֹנֶה בְּעֵת רָצוֹן עֲנֵנוּ. עֲנֵנוּ אֲבִי יְתוֹמִים עֲנֵנוּ. עֲנֵנוּ דַּיַּן אַלְמָנוֹת עֲנֵנוּ.

מִי שֶׁעָנָה The One who answered Abraham our father on Mount Moriah –
answer us.

The One who answered Isaac his son, when he was bound upon
the altar – answer us.

The One who answered Jacob in Beth-El – answer us.

The One who answered Joseph in prison – answer us.

The One who answered our fathers at the Reed Sea – answer us.

The One who answered Moses at Horeb – answer us.

The One who answered Aaron over his firepan – answer us.

The One who answered Pinehas when he stood up from among
the congregation – answer us.

The One who answered Joshua at Gilgal – answer us.

The One who answered Samuel at Mitzpah – answer us.

The One who answered David and Solomon his son in Jerusalem –
answer us.

The One who answered Elijah on Mount Carmel – answer us.

The One who answered Elisha at Jericho – answer us.

The One who answered Jonah in the belly of the fish – answer us.

The One who answered Hezekiah the king of Judah in his illness –
answer us.

The One who answered Hananiah, Mishael and Azariah in the
furnace of fire – answer us.

The One who answered Daniel in the lions' den – answer us.

The One who answered Mordekhai and Esther in Shushan the
capital city – answer us.

The One who answered Ezra in his exile – answer us.

The One who answered so many righteous, devoted, innocent
and upright people – answer us.

רַחֲמָנָא Loving God, who answers the oppressed: answer us.

Loving God, who answers the broken hearted: answer us.

Loving God, who answers those of humbled spirit: answer us.

Loving God, answer us.

Loving God, spare; Loving God, release; Loving God, save us.

Loving God, have compassion for us now, swiftly,
at a time soon coming.

Continue with "Avinu Malkenu" on page 194.

מִי שֶׁעָנָה לְאַבְרָהָם אָבִינוּ בְּהַר הַמּוֹרִיָּה, הוּא יַעֲנֵנוּ.

מִי שֶׁעָנָה לְיִצְחָק בְּנוֹ כְּשֶׁנֶּעֱקַד עַל גַּבֵּי הַמִּזְבֵּחַ, הוּא יַעֲנֵנוּ.

מִי שֶׁעָנָה לְיַעֲקֹב בְּבֵית אֵל, הוּא יַעֲנֵנוּ.

מִי שֶׁעָנָה לְיוֹסֵף בְּבֵית הָאֲסוּרִים, הוּא יַעֲנֵנוּ.

מִי שֶׁעָנָה לַאֲבוֹתֵינוּ עַל יַם סוּף, הוּא יַעֲנֵנוּ.

מִי שֶׁעָנָה לְמֹשֶׁה בְּחוֹרֵב, הוּא יַעֲנֵנוּ.

מִי שֶׁעָנָה לְאַהֲרֹן בַּמַּחְתָּה, הוּא יַעֲנֵנוּ.

מִי שֶׁעָנָה לְפִינְחָס בְּקוּמוֹ מִתּוֹךְ הָעֵדָה, הוּא יַעֲנֵנוּ.

מִי שֶׁעָנָה לִיהוֹשֻׁעַ בַּגִּלְגָּל, הוּא יַעֲנֵנוּ.

מִי שֶׁעָנָה לִשְׁמוּאֵל בַּמִּצְפָּה, הוּא יַעֲנֵנוּ.

מִי שֶׁעָנָה לְדָוִד וּשְׁלֹמֹה בְנוֹ בִירוּשָׁלַיִם, הוּא יַעֲנֵנוּ.

מִי שֶׁעָנָה לְאֵלִיָּהוּ בְּהַר הַכַּרְמֶל, הוּא יַעֲנֵנוּ.

מִי שֶׁעָנָה לֶאֱלִישָׁע בִּירִיחוֹ, הוּא יַעֲנֵנוּ.

מִי שֶׁעָנָה לְיוֹנָה בִּמְעֵי הַדָּגָה, הוּא יַעֲנֵנוּ.

מִי שֶׁעָנָה לְחִזְקִיָּהוּ מֶלֶךְ יְהוּדָה בְּחָלְיוֹ, הוּא יַעֲנֵנוּ.

מִי שֶׁעָנָה לַחֲנַנְיָה מִישָׁאֵל וַעֲזַרְיָה בְּתוֹךְ כִּבְשַׁן הָאֵשׁ, הוּא יַעֲנֵנוּ.

מִי שֶׁעָנָה לְדָנִיֵּאל בְּגוֹב הָאֲרָיוֹת, הוּא יַעֲנֵנוּ.

מִי שֶׁעָנָה לְמָרְדְּכַי וְאֶסְתֵּר בְּשׁוּשַׁן הַבִּירָה, הוּא יַעֲנֵנוּ.

מִי שֶׁעָנָה לְעֶזְרָא בַּגּוֹלָה, הוּא יַעֲנֵנוּ.

מִי שֶׁעָנָה לְכָל הַצַּדִּיקִים וְהַחֲסִידִים וְהַתְּמִימִים וְהַיְשָׁרִים, הוּא יַעֲנֵנוּ.

רַחֲמָנָא דְּעָנֵי לַעֲנִיֵּי עֲנֵינָן.

רַחֲמָנָא דְּעָנֵי לִתְבִירֵי לִבָּא עֲנֵינָן.

רַחֲמָנָא דְּעָנֵי לְמַכִּיכֵי רוּחָא עֲנֵינָן.

רַחֲמָנָא עֲנֵינָן.

רַחֲמָנָא חוּס, רַחֲמָנָא פְּרֹק, רַחֲמָנָא שֵׁיזִב.

רַחֲמָנָא רַחֵם עֲלָן, הַשְׁתָּא בַּעֲגָלָא וּבִזְמַן קָרִיב.

Continue with אבינו מלכנו *on page 195.*

ברכות

GIVING THANKS

THE MEAL AND ITS BLESSINGS

On washing hands before eating bread:

Blessed are You, LORD our God, King of the Universe,
who has made us holy through His commandments,
and has commanded us about washing hands.

Before eating bread:

Blessed are You, LORD our God, King of the Universe,
who brings forth bread from the earth.

BIRKAT HAMAZON / GRACE AFTER MEALS

On days when Taḥanun is said:

עַל־נַהֲרוֹת By the rivers of Babylon we sat and wept as we remembered Zion. There on *Ps. 137* the willow trees we hung up our harps, for there our captors asked us for songs, our tormentors, for amusement, said: "Sing us one of the songs of Zion!" How can we sing the LORD's song on foreign soil? If I forget you, Jerusalem, may my right hand forget its skill. May my tongue cling to the roof of my mouth if I do not remember you, if I do not set Jerusalem above my highest joy. Remember, LORD, what the Edomites did on the day Jerusalem fell. They said, "Tear it down, tear it down to its very foundations!" Daughter of Babylon, doomed to destruction, happy is he who repays you for what you have done to us, who seizes your infants and dashes them against the rocks.

On days when Taḥanun is omitted (see full list on page 200):

שִׁיר הַמַּעֲלוֹת A song of ascents. When the LORD brought back the exiles *Ps. 126* of Zion we were like people who dream. Then were our mouths filled with laughter, and our tongues with songs of joy. Then was it said among the nations, "The LORD has done great things for them." The LORD did do great things for us and we rejoiced. Bring back our exiles, LORD, like

special opportunity, when we sit together in a group, to have a *zimmun* – a calling together of everyone who has eaten in the same place. Rabbi S.R. Hirsch suggests one possible rationale: When we recognize Hashem as the Provider, Preserver, Sustainer of us all, whose goodness enables us all to live and remain alive, we acknowledge that

He is near to all of us, and so there is no reason to be envious of another's wealth. *Birkat HaMazon* is thus the great equalizer, reminding us that Hashem gives to each of us what is good and beneficial for us at any particular time. It makes us thankful, gives us perspective, and draws us closer to one another.

סדר סעודה וברכותיה

On washing hands before eating bread:

בָּרוּךְ אַתָּה יהוה אֱלֹהֵינוּ מֶלֶךְ הָעוֹלָם
אֲשֶׁר קִדְּשָׁנוּ בְּמִצְוֹתָיו וְצִוָּנוּ עַל נְטִילַת יָדָיִם.

Before eating bread:

בָּרוּךְ אַתָּה יהוה אֱלֹהֵינוּ מֶלֶךְ הָעוֹלָם
הַמּוֹצִיא לֶחֶם מִן הָאָרֶץ.

ברכת המזון

On days when תחנון is said:

תהלים קלז

עַל־נַהֲרוֹת בָּבֶל, שָׁם יָשַׁבְנוּ גַּם־בָּכִינוּ, בְּזָכְרֵנוּ אֶת־צִיּוֹן: עַל־עֲרָבִים בְּתוֹכָהּ תָּלִינוּ כִּנֹּרוֹתֵינוּ: כִּי שָׁם שְׁאֵלוּנוּ שׁוֹבֵינוּ דִּבְרֵי־שִׁיר וְתוֹלָלֵינוּ שִׂמְחָה, שִׁירוּ לָנוּ מִשִּׁיר צִיּוֹן: אֵיךְ נָשִׁיר אֶת־שִׁיר־יהוה עַל אַדְמַת נֵכָר: אִם־אֶשְׁכָּחֵךְ יְרוּשָׁלִָם, תִּשְׁכַּח יְמִינִי: תִּדְבַּק לְשׁוֹנִי לְחִכִּי אִם־לֹא אֶזְכְּרֵכִי, אִם־לֹא אַעֲלֶה אֶת־יְרוּשָׁלִַם עַל רֹאשׁ שִׂמְחָתִי: זְכֹר יהוה לִבְנֵי אֱדוֹם אֵת יוֹם יְרוּשָׁלִָם, הָאֹמְרִים עָרוּ עָרוּ עַד הַיְסוֹד בָּהּ: בַּת־בָּבֶל הַשְּׁדוּדָה, אַשְׁרֵי שֶׁיְשַׁלֶּם־לָךְ אֶת־גְּמוּלֵךְ שֶׁגָּמַלְתְּ לָנוּ: אַשְׁרֵי שֶׁיֹּאחֵז, וְנִפֵּץ אֶת־עֹלָלַיִךְ אֶל־הַסָּלַע:

On days when תחנון is omitted (see full list on page 201):

תהלים קכו

שִׁיר הַמַּעֲלוֹת, בְּשׁוּב יהוה אֶת־שִׁיבַת צִיּוֹן, הָיִינוּ כְּחֹלְמִים: אָז יִמָּלֵא שְׂחוֹק פִּינוּ וּלְשׁוֹנֵנוּ רִנָּה, אָז יֹאמְרוּ בַגּוֹיִם הִגְדִּיל יהוה לַעֲשׂוֹת עִם־אֵלֶּה: הִגְדִּיל יהוה לַעֲשׂוֹת עִמָּנוּ, הָיִינוּ שְׂמֵחִים: שׁוּבָה יהוה

INTRODUCTION TO BIRKAT HAMAZON

The Torah mandated that we say a blessing after our meal, apparently because it is precisely when our stomachs are full that we have a tendency to forget where the meal ultimately came from (*Devarim* 8:12–18). We tend to be very thankful at those moments when we are in need; we tend to forget to be thankful when the need has passed. *Berakhot* are a reminder not to forget.

In this particular mitzva there is also a

streams in a dry land. May those who sowed in tears, reap in joy. May one who goes out weeping, carrying a bag of seed, come back with songs of joy, carrying his sheaves.

Some say:

תְּהִלַּת My mouth shall speak the praise of God, and all creatures shall bless His holy name for ever and all time. We will bless God now and for ever. Halleluya! Thank the LORD for He is good; His loving-kindness is for ever. Who can tell of the LORD's mighty acts and make all His praise be heard?

Ps. 145
Ps. 115
Ps. 136
Ps. 106

ZIMMUN / INVITATION

When three or more men say Birkat HaMazon together, the following zimmun is said.
When three or more women say Birkat HaMazon, substitute "Friends" for "Gentlemen."
The leader should ask permission from those with precedence to lead the Birkat HaMazon.

Leader   Gentlemen, let us say grace.

Others   May the name of the LORD be blessed from now and for ever.   *Ps. 113*

Leader   May the name of the LORD be blessed from now and for ever.
       With your permission, (my father and teacher / my mother and
           teacher / the Kohanim present / our teacher the Rabbi /
           the master of this house / the mistress of this house)
       my masters and teachers,
       let us bless (*in a minyan:* our God,) the One
       from whose food we have eaten.

Others   Blessed be (*in a minyan:* our God,) the One
       from whose food we have eaten, and by whose goodness we live.

      *People present who have not taken part in the meal say:
      *Blessed be (in a minyan: our God,) the One
      whose name is continually blessed for ever and all time.

Leader   Blessed be (*in a minyan:* our God,) the One
       from whose food we have eaten, and by whose goodness we live.
       Blessed be He, and blessed be His name.

אֶת־שְׁבִיתֵנוּ, כַּאֲפִיקִים בַּנֶּגֶב: הַזֹּרְעִים בְּדִמְעָה בְּרִנָּה יִקְצֹרוּ: הָלוֹךְ
יֵלֵךְ וּבָכֹה נֹשֵׂא מֶשֶׁךְ־הַזֶּרַע, בֹּא־יָבֹא בְרִנָּה נֹשֵׂא אֲלֻמֹּתָיו:

Some say:

תהלים קמה
תהלים קטו תְּהִלַּת יהוה יְדַבֶּר־פִּי, וִיבָרֵךְ כָּל־בָּשָׂר שֵׁם קָדְשׁוֹ לְעוֹלָם וָעֶד: וַאֲנַחְנוּ
תהלים קלו נְבָרֵךְ יָהּ מֵעַתָּה וְעַד־עוֹלָם, הַלְלוּיָהּ: הוֹדוּ לַיהוה כִּי־טוֹב, כִּי לְעוֹלָם
תהלים קו חַסְדּוֹ: מִי יְמַלֵּל גְּבוּרוֹת יהוה, יַשְׁמִיעַ כָּל־תְּהִלָּתוֹ:

סדר הזימון

When three or more men say ברכת המזון *together, the following* זימון *is said.*
When three or more women say ברכת המזון, *substitute* רַבּוֹתַי *for* חֲבֵרוֹתַי.
The leader should ask permission from those with precedence to lead the ברכת המזון.

Leader רַבּוֹתַי, נְבָרֵךְ.

תהלים קיג **Others** יְהִי שֵׁם יהוה מְבֹרָךְ מֵעַתָּה וְעַד־עוֹלָם:

Leader יְהִי שֵׁם יהוה מְבֹרָךְ מֵעַתָּה וְעַד־עוֹלָם:
בִּרְשׁוּת (אָבִי מוֹרִי / אִמִּי מוֹרָתִי / כֹּהֲנִים / מוֹרֵנוּ הָרַב /
בַּעַל הַבַּיִת הַזֶּה / בַּעֲלַת הַבַּיִת הַזֶּה)
מָרָנָן וְרַבָּנָן וְרַבּוֹתַי
נְבָרֵךְ (במנין: אֱלֹהֵינוּ) שֶׁאָכַלְנוּ מִשֶּׁלּוֹ.

Others בָּרוּךְ (במנין: אֱלֹהֵינוּ) שֶׁאָכַלְנוּ מִשֶּׁלּוֹ וּבְטוּבוֹ חָיִינוּ.

People present who have not taken part in the meal say:
*בָּרוּךְ (במנין: אֱלֹהֵינוּ) וּמְבֹרָךְ שְׁמוֹ תָּמִיד לְעוֹלָם וָעֶד:

Leader בָּרוּךְ (במנין: אֱלֹהֵינוּ) שֶׁאָכַלְנוּ מִשֶּׁלּוֹ וּבְטוּבוֹ חָיִינוּ.
בָּרוּךְ הוּא וּבָרוּךְ שְׁמוֹ.

BLESSING OF NOURISHMENT

בָּרוּךְ Blessed are You, LORD our God, King of the Universe,
who in His goodness feeds the whole world
with grace, kindness and compassion.[B]
He gives food to all living things,
for His kindness is for ever.
Because of His continual great goodness,
we have never lacked food,
nor may we ever lack it,[A]
for the sake of His great name.
For He is God who feeds and sustains all,
does good to all,
and prepares food for all creatures He has created.
Blessed are You, LORD,
who feeds all.[A]

BLESSING OF LAND

נוֹדֶה We thank You,[A] LORD our God,
for having granted as a heritage to our ancestors
a desirable, good and spacious land;
for bringing us out, LORD our God, from the land of Egypt,
freeing us from the house of slavery;

לֹא חָסֵר לָנוּ וְאַל יֶחְסַר לָנוּ מָזוֹן לְעוֹלָם וָעֶד –
We have never lacked food, nor may we
ever lack it. The premise of the blessing
is that Hashem provides sufficient food
for the entire world. As such, the fact that
some people do not have enough to eat
is not a failure of God, but the failure
of man.

הַזָּן אֶת הַכֹּל – Who feeds all. There is a motif
word that is repeated six times in this paragraph. What is the word and what might be
the significance?

נוֹדֶה לְךָ – We thank You. There is one word
that appears in this blessing no less than
eleven times! What is the word and what is
its significance?

ברכת הזן

בָּרוּךְ אַתָּה יהוה אֱלֹהֵינוּ מֶלֶךְ הָעוֹלָם

הַזָּן אֶת הָעוֹלָם כֻּלּוֹ בְּטוּבוֹ

בְּחֵן בְּחֶסֶד וּבְרַחֲמִיםᵇ

הוּא נוֹתֵן לֶחֶם לְכָל בָּשָׂר

כִּי לְעוֹלָם חַסְדּוֹ.

וּבְטוּבוֹ הַגָּדוֹל, תָּמִיד לֹא חָסַר לָנוּ

וְאַל יֶחְסַר לָנוּ מָזוֹן לְעוֹלָם וָעֶדᵃ

בַּעֲבוּר שְׁמוֹ הַגָּדוֹל.

כִּי הוּא אֵל זָן וּמְפַרְנֵס לַכֹּל וּמֵטִיב לַכֹּל

וּמֵכִין מָזוֹן לְכָל בְּרִיּוֹתָיו אֲשֶׁר בָּרָא.

בָּרוּךְ אַתָּה יהוה, הַזָּן אֶת הַכֹּל.ᵃ

ברכת הארץ

נוֹדֶה לְּךָ,ᵃ יהוה אֱלֹהֵינוּ

עַל שֶׁהִנְחַלְתָּ לַאֲבוֹתֵינוּ אֶרֶץ חֶמְדָּה טוֹבָה וּרְחָבָה

וְעַל שֶׁהוֹצֵאתָנוּ יהוה אֱלֹהֵינוּ מֵאֶרֶץ מִצְרַיִם

וּפְדִיתָנוּ מִבֵּית עֲבָדִים

BIUR TEFILLA ⦁ ביאור תפילה

בְּחֵן בְּחֶסֶד וּבְרַחֲמִים – *With grace, kindness and compassion*. What might each of these three terms represent? Where does each manifest itself in your life?

The terms might refer to the different kinds of support that one needs from Hashem at different points in one's life (*Rabbi Yosef Albo*).

Alternatively, they might refer to different kinds of help depending on the merits of the receiver (*Rabbi S.R. Hirsch*).

Alternatively, they might refer to different people's economic status (*Arukh HaShulḥan*).

for Your covenant which You sealed in our flesh;
for Your Torah which You taught us;
for Your laws which You made known to us;
for the life, grace and kindness You have bestowed on us;
and for the food by which You continually feed and sustain us,
every day, every season, every hour.

On Ḥanukka:

עַל הַנִּסִּים [We thank You also] for the miracles, the redemption, the mighty deeds, the salvations, and the victories in battle which You performed for our ancestors in those days, at this time.

בִּימֵי מַתִּתְיָהוּ In the days of Mattityahu, son of Yoḥanan, the High Priest, the Hasmonean, and his sons, the wicked Greek kingdom rose up against Your people Israel to make them forget Your Torah and to force them to transgress the statutes of Your will. It was then that You in Your great compassion stood by them in the time of their distress. You championed their cause, judged their claim, and avenged their wrong. You delivered the strong into the hands of the weak, the many into the hands of the few, the impure into the hands of the pure, the wicked into the hands of the righteous, and the arrogant into the hands of those who were engaged in the study of Your Torah. You made for Yourself great and holy renown in Your world, and for Your people Israel You performed a great salvation and redemption as of this very day. Your children then entered the holiest part of Your House, cleansed Your Temple, purified Your Sanctuary, kindled lights in Your holy courts, and designated these eight days of Ḥanukka for giving thanks and praise to Your great name. *Continue with "For all this."*

On Purim:

עַל הַנִּסִּים [We thank You also] for the miracles, the redemption, the mighty deeds, the salvations, and the victories in battle which You performed for our ancestors in those days, at this time.

בִּימֵי מָרְדְּכַי In the days of Mordekhai and Esther, in Shushan the capital, the wicked Haman rose up against them and sought to destroy, slay and *Esther 3* exterminate all the Jews, young and old, children and women, on one day, the thirteenth day of the twelfth month, which is the month of Adar, and to plunder their possessions. Then You in Your great compassion thwarted his counsel, frustrated his plans, and caused his scheme to recoil on his own head, so that they hanged him and his sons on the gallows. *Continue with "For all this."*

וְעַל בְּרִיתְךָ שֶׁחָתַמְתָּ בִּבְשָׂרֵנוּ

וְעַל תּוֹרָתְךָ שֶׁלִּמַּדְתָּנוּ

וְעַל חֻקֶּיךָ שֶׁהוֹדַעְתָּנוּ

וְעַל חַיִּים חֵן וָחֶסֶד שֶׁחוֹנַנְתָּנוּ

וְעַל אֲכִילַת מָזוֹן שָׁאַתָּה זָן וּמְפַרְנֵס אוֹתָנוּ תָּמִיד

בְּכָל יוֹם וּבְכָל עֵת וּבְכָל שָׁעָה.

בחנוכה:

עַל הַנִּסִּים וְעַל הַפֻּרְקָן וְעַל הַגְּבוּרוֹת וְעַל הַתְּשׁוּעוֹת וְעַל הַמִּלְחָמוֹת שֶׁעָשִׂיתָ לַאֲבוֹתֵינוּ בַּיָּמִים הָהֵם בַּזְּמַן הַזֶּה.

בִּימֵי מַתִּתְיָהוּ בֶּן יוֹחָנָן כֹּהֵן גָּדוֹל חַשְׁמוֹנַאי וּבָנָיו, כְּשֶׁעָמְדָה מַלְכוּת יָוָן הָרְשָׁעָה עַל עַמְּךָ יִשְׂרָאֵל לְהַשְׁכִּיחָם תּוֹרָתֶךָ וּלְהַעֲבִירָם מֵחֻקֵּי רְצוֹנֶךָ, וְאַתָּה בְּרַחֲמֶיךָ הָרַבִּים עָמַדְתָּ לָהֶם בְּעֵת צָרָתָם, רַבְתָּ אֶת רִיבָם, דַּנְתָּ אֶת דִּינָם, נָקַמְתָּ אֶת נִקְמָתָם, מָסַרְתָּ גִבּוֹרִים בְּיַד חַלָּשִׁים, וְרַבִּים בְּיַד מְעַטִּים, וּטְמֵאִים בְּיַד טְהוֹרִים, וּרְשָׁעִים בְּיַד צַדִּיקִים, וְזֵדִים בְּיַד עוֹסְקֵי תוֹרָתֶךָ, וּלְךָ עָשִׂיתָ שֵׁם גָּדוֹל וְקָדוֹשׁ בְּעוֹלָמֶךָ, וּלְעַמְּךָ יִשְׂרָאֵל עָשִׂיתָ תְּשׁוּעָה גְדוֹלָה וּפֻרְקָן כְּהַיּוֹם הַזֶּה. וְאַחַר כֵּן בָּאוּ בָנֶיךָ לִדְבִיר בֵּיתֶךָ, וּפִנּוּ אֶת הֵיכָלֶךָ, וְטִהֲרוּ אֶת מִקְדָּשֶׁךָ, וְהִדְלִיקוּ נֵרוֹת בְּחַצְרוֹת קָדְשֶׁךָ, וְקָבְעוּ שְׁמוֹנַת יְמֵי חֲנֻכָּה אֵלּוּ, לְהוֹדוֹת וּלְהַלֵּל לְשִׁמְךָ הַגָּדוֹל.

Continue with וְעַל הַכֹּל.

בפורים:

עַל הַנִּסִּים וְעַל הַפֻּרְקָן וְעַל הַגְּבוּרוֹת וְעַל הַתְּשׁוּעוֹת וְעַל הַמִּלְחָמוֹת שֶׁעָשִׂיתָ לַאֲבוֹתֵינוּ בַּיָּמִים הָהֵם בַּזְּמַן הַזֶּה.

בִּימֵי מָרְדְּכַי וְאֶסְתֵּר בְּשׁוּשַׁן הַבִּירָה, כְּשֶׁעָמַד עֲלֵיהֶם הָמָן הָרָשָׁע, בִּקֵּשׁ לְהַשְׁמִיד לַהֲרֹג וּלְאַבֵּד אֶת־כָּל־הַיְּהוּדִים מִנַּעַר וְעַד־זָקֵן טַף וְנָשִׁים בְּיוֹם אֶחָד, בִּשְׁלוֹשָׁה עָשָׂר לְחֹדֶשׁ שְׁנֵים־עָשָׂר, הוּא־חֹדֶשׁ אֲדָר, וּשְׁלָלָם לָבוֹז. וְאַתָּה בְּרַחֲמֶיךָ הָרַבִּים הֵפַרְתָּ אֶת עֲצָתוֹ, וְקִלְקַלְתָּ אֶת מַחֲשַׁבְתּוֹ, וַהֲשֵׁבוֹתָ לּוֹ גְּמוּלוֹ בְּרֹאשׁוֹ, וְתָלוּ אוֹתוֹ וְאֶת בָּנָיו עַל הָעֵץ.

אסתר ג

Continue with וְעַל הַכֹּל.

וְעַל הַכֹּל For all this, LORD our God,
we thank and bless You.
May Your name be blessed continually
by the mouth of all that lives,
for ever and all time –
for so it is written:
"You will eat and be satisfied,
then you shall bless the LORD your God
for the good land He has given you."
Blessed are You, LORD,
for the land and for the food.[1]

Deut. 8

BLESSING FOR JERUSALEM

רַחֵם נָא Have compassion, please,
LORD our God,
on Israel Your people,[B]
on Jerusalem Your city,
on Zion the dwelling place of Your glory,
on the royal house of David Your anointed,
and on the great and holy House that bears Your name.

BIUR TEFILLA · ביאור תפילה

רַחֵם נָא, יהוה אֱלֹהֵינוּ, עַל יִשְׂרָאֵל עַמֶּךָ – *Have compassion, please, LORD our God, on Israel Your people.* Commentators have tried to explain the connection between the requests for the restoration of the *Beit HaMikdash* and the request that our food and material needs be provided. One suggestion cites the Gemara (*Ḥagiga* 27a) which says that the Altar in the *Beit HaMikdash* atoned for

the sins of mankind but, in its absence, the table where a person eats has the same impact. How might this connection be understood? Rashi suggests that it is because one has guests at one's table. How does this explain the Gemara's statement?

Can you suggest another connection between the themes of the *Beit HaMikdash* and the request for food?

וְעַל הַכֹּל, יהוה אֱלֹהֵינוּ
אֲנַחְנוּ מוֹדִים לָךְ וּמְבָרְכִים אוֹתָךְ
יִתְבָּרַךְ שִׁמְךָ בְּפִי כָּל חַי תָּמִיד לְעוֹלָם וָעֶד
כַּכָּתוּב:

דברים ח

וְאָכַלְתָּ וְשָׂבֶעְתָּ, וּבֵרַכְתָּ אֶת־יהוה אֱלֹהֶיךָ
עַל־הָאָרֶץ הַטֹּבָה אֲשֶׁר נָתַן־לָךְ:
בָּרוּךְ אַתָּה יהוה, עַל הָאָרֶץ וְעַל הַמָּזוֹן.ע

ברכת ירושלים

רַחֵם נָא, יהוה אֱלֹהֵינוּ
עַל יִשְׂרָאֵל עַמֶּךָ
וְעַל יְרוּשָׁלַיִם עִירֶךָ
וְעַל צִיּוֹן מִשְׁכַּן כְּבוֹדֶךָ
וְעַל מַלְכוּת בֵּית דָּוִד מְשִׁיחֶךָ
וְעַל הַבַּיִת הַגָּדוֹל וְהַקָּדוֹשׁ שֶׁנִּקְרָא שִׁמְךָ עָלָיו.

עיון תפילה • IYUN TEFILLA

עַל הָאָרֶץ וְעַל הַמָּזוֹן — *For the land and for the food.* The blessing enumerates a number of things for which we should be grateful: the Land, the Exodus, the covenant represented by Brit Mila, the Torah, the laws, the life, favor and *hesed* that Hashem bestowed upon us, our never-ending supply of food, and for everything. Yet the blessing's signature relates only to the Land and food.

(a) The Gemara (*Berakhot* 49a) says that the ending or signature of a blessing may not have two different themes in it. Yet here there are two mentioned. How might they be seen as the same?

(b) What might be the connection between those two things and all of the others? For which should we be grateful?

What reason can you suggest for the order of the eight things that are listed for which we should be grateful?

Our God, our Father,
tend us, feed us, sustain us and support us,
relieve us and send us relief,
LORD our God, swiftly from all our troubles.
Please, LORD our God, do not make us dependent
on the gifts or loans of other people,
but only on Your full, open, holy and generous hand
so that we may suffer neither shame nor humiliation
for ever and all time.

On Rosh Ḥodesh and Ḥol HaMo'ed, say:

אֱלֹהֵינוּ Our God and God of our ancestors,
may there rise, come, reach, appear,
be favored, heard, regarded
and remembered before You,
our recollection and remembrance,
as well as the remembrance of our ancestors,
and of the Messiah son of David Your servant,
and of Jerusalem Your holy city,
and of all Your people the house of Israel –
for deliverance and well-being,
grace, loving-kindness and compassion,
life and peace, on this day of:

On Rosh Ḥodesh: Rosh Ḥodesh.

On Pesaḥ: the Festival of Matzot.

On Sukkot: the Festival of Sukkot.

On it remember us, LORD our God, for good;
recollect us for blessing, and deliver us for life.
In accord with Your promise of salvation and compassion,
spare us and be gracious to us;
have compassion on us and deliver us,
for our eyes are turned to You because You are God,
gracious and compassionate.

וּבְנֵה And may Jerusalem the holy city be rebuilt soon, in our time.
Blessed are You, LORD, who in His compassion
will rebuild Jerusalem. Amen.[B]

אֱלֹהֵינוּ, אָבִינוּ

רְעֵנוּ, זוּנֵנוּ, פַּרְנְסֵנוּ וְכַלְכְּלֵנוּ

וְהַרְוִיחֵנוּ, וְהַרְוַח לָנוּ יהוה אֱלֹהֵינוּ מְהֵרָה מִכָּל צָרוֹתֵינוּ.

וְנָא אַל תַּצְרִיכֵנוּ, יהוה אֱלֹהֵינוּ

לֹא לִידֵי מַתְּנַת בָּשָׂר וָדָם וְלֹא לִידֵי הַלְוָאָתָם

כִּי אִם לְיָדְךָ הַמְּלֵאָה, הַפְּתוּחָה, הַקְּדוֹשָׁה וְהָרְחָבָה

שֶׁלֹּא נֵבוֹשׁ וְלֹא נִכָּלֵם לְעוֹלָם וָעֶד.

On ‏ראש חודש‏ and ‏חול המועד‏, say:

אֱלֹהֵינוּ וֵאלֹהֵי אֲבוֹתֵינוּ

יַעֲלֶה וְיָבוֹא וְיַגִּיעַ, וְיֵרָאֶה וְיֵרָצֶה וְיִשָּׁמַע

וְיִפָּקֵד וְיִזָּכֵר זִכְרוֹנֵנוּ וּפִקְדוֹנֵנוּ, וְזִכְרוֹן אֲבוֹתֵינוּ

וְזִכְרוֹן מָשִׁיחַ בֶּן דָּוִד עַבְדֶּךָ, וְזִכְרוֹן יְרוּשָׁלַיִם עִיר קָדְשֶׁךָ

וְזִכְרוֹן כָּל עַמְּךָ בֵּית יִשְׂרָאֵל

לְפָנֶיךָ, לִפְלֵיטָה לְטוֹבָה, לְחֵן וּלְחֶסֶד וּלְרַחֲמִים

לְחַיִּים וּלְשָׁלוֹם בְּיוֹם

‏בראש חודש:‏ רֹאשׁ הַחֹדֶשׁ הַזֶּה.

‏בפסח:‏ חַג הַמַּצּוֹת הַזֶּה.

‏בסוכות:‏ חַג הַסֻּכּוֹת הַזֶּה.

זָכְרֵנוּ יהוה אֱלֹהֵינוּ בּוֹ לְטוֹבָה

וּפָקְדֵנוּ בוֹ לִבְרָכָה, וְהוֹשִׁיעֵנוּ בוֹ לְחַיִּים.

וּבִדְבַר יְשׁוּעָה וְרַחֲמִים, חוּס וְחָנֵּנוּ וְרַחֵם עָלֵינוּ, וְהוֹשִׁיעֵנוּ

כִּי אֵלֶיךָ עֵינֵינוּ, כִּי אֵל חַנּוּן וְרַחוּם אָתָּה.

וּבְנֵה יְרוּשָׁלַיִם עִיר הַקֹּדֶשׁ בִּמְהֵרָה בְיָמֵינוּ.

בָּרוּךְ אַתָּה יהוה, בּוֹנֵה בְרַחֲמָיו יְרוּשָׁלָיִם, אָמֵן.׳

ביאור תפילה

BIUR TEFILLA

אָמֵן – *Amen.* Answering "Amen" to one's own blessing is rare. In this case it serves as a marker to separate the end of the three

blessings which are from the Torah and the beginning of the fourth blessing which is *deRabbanan,* instituted by the Rabbis.

BLESSING OF GOD'S GOODNESS

בָּרוּךְ Blessed are You, LORD our God, King of the Universe –
God our Father, our King, our Sovereign,
our Creator, our Redeemer, our Maker,
our Holy One, the Holy One of Jacob.
He is our Shepherd, Israel's Shepherd,
the good King who does good to all.
Every day He has done, is doing, and will do good to us.^B
He has acted, is acting, and will always act kindly
toward us for ever,
granting us grace, kindness and compassion,
relief and rescue,
prosperity, blessing, redemption and comfort,
sustenance and support,
compassion, life, peace and all good things,
and of all good things may He never let us lack.^B

ADDITIONAL REQUESTS

הָרַחֲמָן May the Compassionate One^A
    reign over us for ever and all time.

May the Compassionate One
    be blessed in heaven and on earth.

---

it is recited in a group. Despite its length, it does not end in the formula of *Barukh ata* because the entire blessing consists of one theme, which is the criteria for having only one blessing formula at the beginning (Rashi on *Berakhot* 49a).

ANI TEFILLA · אני תפילה

הָרַחֲמָן – *The Compassionate One.* This series of eight short requests are a later addition but they make room for one to add one's own related personal requests. The rationale is that since one's table is like an altar where atonement is granted, then the table is a particularly good place to have one's prayers heard, assuming one conducted oneself appropriately at the meal (*Piskei Teshuvot* 189:2).

What prayer would you like to add today?

ברכת הטוב והמטיב

בָּרוּךְ אַתָּה יהוה אֱלֹהֵינוּ מֶלֶךְ הָעוֹלָם
הָאֵל אָבִינוּ, מַלְכֵּנוּ, אַדִּירֵנוּ
בּוֹרְאֵנוּ, גּוֹאֲלֵנוּ, יוֹצְרֵנוּ, קְדוֹשֵׁנוּ, קְדוֹשׁ יַעֲקֹב
רוֹעֵנוּ, רוֹעֵה יִשְׂרָאֵל, הַמֶּלֶךְ הַטּוֹב וְהַמֵּיטִיב לַכֹּל
שֶׁבְּכָל יוֹם וָיוֹם
הוּא הֵיטִיב, הוּא מֵיטִיב, הוּא יֵיטִיב לָנוּ*
הוּא גְמָלָנוּ, הוּא גוֹמְלֵנוּ, הוּא יִגְמְלֵנוּ לָעַד
לְחֵן וּלְחֶסֶד וּלְרַחֲמִים, וּלְרֶוַח, הַצָּלָה וְהַצְלָחָה
בְּרָכָה וִישׁוּעָה
נֶחָמָה, פַּרְנָסָה וְכַלְכָּלָה
וְרַחֲמִים וְחַיִּים וְשָׁלוֹם וְכָל טוֹב
וּמִכָּל טוּב לְעוֹלָם אַל יְחַסְּרֵנוּ.*

בקשות נוספות

הָרַחֲמָן* הוּא יִמְלֹךְ עָלֵינוּ לְעוֹלָם וָעֶד.
הָרַחֲמָן הוּא יִתְבָּרַךְ בַּשָּׁמַיִם וּבָאָרֶץ.

BIUR TEFILLA · ביאור תפילה

הוא הֵיטִיב, הוא מֵיטִיב, הוא יֵיטִיב לָנוּ – *He has done, is doing, and will do good to us.* The first blessing is in the present tense, thanking Hashem for the food which He gives us; the second is in the past, thanking Hashem for the gifts of the Land; while the third blessing about the rebuilding of Yerushalayim is in the future

tense (Rabbi Munk). Here, we refer to Hashem's goodness toward us in all three tenses.

וּמִכָּל טוּב לְעוֹלָם אַל יְחַסְּרֵנוּ – *And of all good things may He never let us lack.* This is the end of the fourth blessing which is why it is appropriate to answer Amen when

May the Compassionate One
> be praised from generation to generation,
> be glorified by us to all eternity,
> and honored among us for ever and all time.

May the Compassionate One
> grant us an honorable livelihood.

May the Compassionate One
> break the yoke from our neck and lead us upright to our land.

May the Compassionate One
> send us many blessings to this house
> and this table at which we have eaten.

May the Compassionate One
> send us Elijah the prophet – may he be remembered for good –
> to bring us good tidings of salvation and consolation.

May the Compassionate One
> bless the State of Israel, first flowering of our redemption.

May the Compassionate One
> bless the members of Israel's Defense Forces,
> who stand guard over our land.

A guest says:

יְהִי רָצוֹן May it be Your will that the master of this house
shall not suffer shame in this world,
nor humiliation in the World to Come.
May all he owns prosper greatly,
and may his and our possessions be successful and close to hand.
Let not the Accuser hold sway over his deeds or ours,
and may no thought of sin, iniquity or transgression
enter him or us
from now and for evermore.

הָרַחֲמָן הוּא יִשְׁתַּבַּח לְדוֹר דּוֹרִים
וְיִתְפָּאַר בָּנוּ לָעַד וּלְנֵצַח נְצָחִים
וְיִתְהַדַּר בָּנוּ לָעַד וּלְעוֹלְמֵי עוֹלָמִים.

הָרַחֲמָן הוּא יְפַרְנְסֵנוּ בְּכָבוֹד.

הָרַחֲמָן הוּא יִשְׁבֹּר עֻלֵּנוּ מֵעַל צַוָּארֵנוּ
וְהוּא יוֹלִיכֵנוּ קוֹמְמִיּוּת לְאַרְצֵנוּ.

הָרַחֲמָן הוּא יִשְׁלַח לָנוּ בְּרָכָה מְרֻבָּה בַּבַּיִת הַזֶּה
וְעַל שֻׁלְחָן זֶה שֶׁאָכַלְנוּ עָלָיו.

הָרַחֲמָן הוּא יִשְׁלַח לָנוּ אֶת אֵלִיָּהוּ הַנָּבִיא זָכוּר לַטּוֹב
וִיבַשֶּׂר לָנוּ בְּשׂוֹרוֹת טוֹבוֹת יְשׁוּעוֹת וְנֶחָמוֹת.

הָרַחֲמָן הוּא יְבָרֵךְ אֶת מְדִינַת יִשְׂרָאֵל
רֵאשִׁית צְמִיחַת גְּאֻלָּתֵנוּ.

הָרַחֲמָן הוּא יְבָרֵךְ אֶת חַיָּלֵי צְבָא הַהֲגָנָה לְיִשְׂרָאֵל
הָעוֹמְדִים עַל מִשְׁמַר אַרְצֵנוּ.

A guest says:

יְהִי רָצוֹן שֶׁלֹּא יֵבוֹשׁ בַּעַל הַבַּיִת בָּעוֹלָם הַזֶּה
וְלֹא יִכָּלֵם לָעוֹלָם הַבָּא
וְיִצְלַח מְאֹד בְּכָל נְכָסָיו
וְיִהְיוּ נְכָסָיו וּנְכָסֵינוּ מֻצְלָחִים וּקְרוֹבִים לָעִיר
וְאַל יִשְׁלֹט שָׂטָן לֹא בְּמַעֲשֵׂה יָדָיו וְלֹא בְּמַעֲשֵׂה יָדֵינוּ.
וְאַל יִזְדַּקֵּר לֹא לְפָנָיו וְלֹא לְפָנֵינוּ שׁוּם דְּבַר הִרְהוּר חֵטְא
עֲבֵרָה וְעָוֹן, מֵעַתָּה וְעַד עוֹלָם.

הָרַחֲמָן May the Compassionate One bless –

When eating at one's own table, say (include the words in parentheses that apply):
me, (my wife/husband, / my father, my teacher / my mother,
my teacher/ my children,) and all that is mine,

A guest at someone else's table says (include the words in parentheses that apply):
the master of this house, him (and his wife,
the mistress of this house / and his children,) and all that is his,

Children at their parents' table say (include the words in parentheses that apply):
my father, my teacher, (master of this house,) and my mother,
my teacher, (mistress of this house,) them, their household,
their children, and all that is theirs.

For all other guests, add:
and all the diners here,

אוֹתָנוּ – together with us and all that is ours.
Just as our forefathers
Abraham, Isaac and Jacob were blessed in all, from all, with all,[1]
so may He bless all of us together
with a complete blessing,
and let us say: Amen.

בַּמָּרוֹם On high,
may grace be invoked for them and for us,
as a safeguard of peace.
May we receive a blessing from the LORD
and a just reward from the God of our salvation,
and may we find grace and good favor
in the eyes of God and man.

---

everything [I need]" (33:11). From here the Gemara
(*Bava Batra* 17a) concludes that the *yetzer hara*,
the evil inclination, had no power over the *Avot*.

**What do you think the Gemara means
by this? What is a lesson I can take
away from here whenever I say this?**

הָרַחֲמָן הוּא יְבָרֵךְ

When eating at one's own table, say (include the words in parentheses that apply):

אוֹתִי (וְאֶת אִשְׁתִּי / וְאֶת בַּעֲלִי / וְאֶת אָבִי מוֹרִי /
וְאֶת אִמִּי מוֹרָתִי / וְאֶת זַרְעִי) וְאֶת כָּל אֲשֶׁר לִי.

A guest at someone else's table says (include the words in parentheses that apply):

אֶת בַּעַל הַבַּיִת הַזֶּה, אוֹתוֹ (וְאֶת אִשְׁתּוֹ בַּעֲלַת הַבַּיִת הַזֶּה /
וְאֶת זַרְעוֹ) וְאֶת כָּל אֲשֶׁר לוֹ.

Children at their parents' table say (include the words in parentheses that apply):

אֶת אָבִי מוֹרִי (בַּעַל הַבַּיִת הַזֶּה), וְאֶת אִמִּי מוֹרָתִי (בַּעֲלַת הַבַּיִת
הַזֶּה), אוֹתָם וְאֶת בֵּיתָם וְאֶת זַרְעָם וְאֶת כָּל אֲשֶׁר לָהֶם

For all other guests, add:

וְאֶת כָּל הַמְּסֻבִּין כָּאן

אוֹתָנוּ וְאֶת כָּל אֲשֶׁר לָנוּ
כְּמוֹ שֶׁנִּתְבָּרְכוּ אֲבוֹתֵינוּ
אַבְרָהָם יִצְחָק וְיַעֲקֹב, בַּכֹּל, מִכֹּל, כֹּל,ᵛ
כֵּן יְבָרֵךְ אוֹתָנוּ כֻּלָּנוּ יַחַד בִּבְרָכָה שְׁלֵמָה, וְנֹאמַר אָמֵן.

בַּמָּרוֹם יְלַמְּדוּ עֲלֵיהֶם וְעָלֵינוּ זְכוּת
שֶׁתְּהֵא לְמִשְׁמֶרֶת שָׁלוֹם
וְנִשָּׂא בְרָכָה מֵאֵת יהוה וּצְדָקָה מֵאֱלֹהֵי יִשְׁעֵנוּ
וְנִמְצָא חֵן וְשֵׂכֶל טוֹב בְּעֵינֵי אֱלֹהִים וְאָדָם.

עיין תפילה

IYUN TEFILLA • עיין תפילה

בַּכֹּל, מִכֹּל, כֹּל – *In all, from all, with all.* Each of these words is a reference to one of the *Avot*: "And Hashem blessed Avraham with *every-*

thing" (*Bereshit* 24:1); "and I [Yitzhak] have eaten from *everything*" (27:33); "for Hashem has been kind to me [Yaakov] and I have

On Rosh Ḥodesh: May the Compassionate One renew this month for us,
for good and blessing.

On Sukkot: May the Compassionate One restore for us,
the fallen Tabernacle of David.

הָרַחֲמָן May the Compassionate One make us worthy
of the Messianic Age and life in the World to Come.
He gives great / *On Rosh Ḥodesh and Ḥol HaMo'ed:* He is a tower of /   *II Sam. 22*
salvation to His king, showing kindness to His anointed,
to David and his descendants for ever.
He who makes peace in His high places,
may He make peace for us and all Israel, and let us say: Amen.

יִרְאוּ Fear the LORD, you His holy ones;   *Ps. 34*
those who fear Him lack nothing.ᴬ
Young lions may grow weak and hungry,
but those who seek the LORD lack no good thing.
Thank the LORD for He is good;   *Ps. 118*
His loving-kindness is for ever.
You open Your hand, and satisfy every living thing with favor.   *Ps. 145*
Blessed is the person who trusts in the LORD,   *Jer. 17*
whose trust is in the LORD alone.
Once I was young, and now I am old,   *Ps. 37*
yet I have never watched a righteous man forsakenᴮ
or his children begging for bread.
The LORD will give His people strength.ᴬ   *Ps. 29*
The LORD will bless His people with peace.

BIUR TEFILLA · ביאור תפילה

נַעַר הָיִיתִי גַּם־זָקַנְתִּי, וְלֹא־רָאִיתִי צַדִּיק נֶעֱזָב –
*Once I was young, and now I am old, yet I
have never watched a righteous man forsaken.*
The word רָאִיתִי, "I saw," can be understood
instead as "I watched in silence" drawing
from a similar usage in Esther 8:6 – "For
how could I stand by silently and watch

the destruction of my people." If so, then
the translation here would be "I have never
stood by silently while a righteous man
was forsaken," that is, it is a call to us to not
be passive when others are in need, just
as Hashem has not stood by and let me
go hungry.

בראש חודש: הָרַחֲמָן הוּא יְחַדֵּשׁ עָלֵינוּ
אֶת הַחֹדֶשׁ הַזֶּה לְטוֹבָה וְלִבְרָכָה.

בסוכות: הָרַחֲמָן הוּא יָקִים לֵנוּ אֶת סֻכַּת דָּוִד הַנּוֹפֶלֶת.

הָרַחֲמָן הוּא יְזַכֵּנוּ לִימוֹת הַמָּשִׁיחַ וּלְחַיֵּי הָעוֹלָם הַבָּא

מַגְדִּל/ On חול המועד and ראש חודש מַגְדּוֹל/ יְשׁוּעוֹת מַלְכּוֹ

וְעֹשֶׂה־חֶסֶד לִמְשִׁיחוֹ, לְדָוִד וּלְזַרְעוֹ עַד־עוֹלָם:

עֹשֶׂה שָׁלוֹם בִּמְרוֹמָיו

הוּא יַעֲשֶׂה שָׁלוֹם עָלֵינוּ וְעַל כָּל יִשְׂרָאֵל, וְאִמְרוּ אָמֵן.

שמואל ב׳ כב

יְראוּ אֶת־יהוה קְדֹשָׁיו, כִּי־אֵין מַחְסוֹר לִירֵאָיו:א

כְּפִירִים רָשׁוּ וְרָעֵבוּ, וְדֹרְשֵׁי יהוה לֹא־יַחְסְרוּ כָל־טוֹב:

הוֹדוּ לַיהוה כִּי־טוֹב, כִּי לְעוֹלָם חַסְדּוֹ:

פּוֹתֵחַ אֶת־יָדֶךָ, וּמַשְׂבִּיעַ לְכָל־חַי רָצוֹן:

בָּרוּךְ הַגֶּבֶר אֲשֶׁר יִבְטַח בַּיהוה, וְהָיָה יהוה מִבְטַחוֹ:

נַעַר הָיִיתִי גַּם־זָקַנְתִּי, וְלֹא־רָאִיתִי צַדִּיק נֶעֱזָב, וְזַרְעוֹ מְבַקֶּשׁ־לָחֶם:

יהוה עֹז לְעַמּוֹ יִתֵּן,א יהוה יְבָרֵךְ אֶת־עַמּוֹ בַשָּׁלוֹם:

תהלים לד
תהלים קיח
תהלים קמה
ירמיה יז
תהלים לז
תהלים כט

אני תפילה · ANI TEFILLA

יְראוּ אֶת־יהוה קְדֹשָׁיו, כִּי־אֵין מַחְסוֹר לִירֵאָיו – *Fear the Lord, you His holy ones; those who fear Him lack nothing.* The blessing claims that those who fear or believe in Hashem are not lacking anything, yet we know that there are God-fearing people who are poor or who have needs. How might this seeming contradiction be reconciled?

יהוה עֹז לְעַמּוֹ יִתֵּן – *The Lord will give His people strength.* Rav Elimelekh of Lezajsk said:

Most people exert all of their energy in the time of prayer, to direct their heart and to ward off foreign thoughts. But when they eat they make no effort or exertion, since they eat only for their own pleasure – so where is there a place for effort or exertion? But as for the righteous, they have no need to exert themselves when they pray; then, their minds are always pure and clear. But during the time of eating, that is when they have to use their energy to exert themselves.

Before eating food, other than bread or matza,
made from the five species of grain (wheat, barley, rye, oats and spelt), or rice:

Blessed are You, the LORD our God, King of the Universe,
who creates the various kinds of nourishment.

Before drinking wine or grape juice:

Blessed are You, LORD our God, King of the Universe,
who creates the fruit of the vine.

Before eating fruit that grows on trees:

Blessed are You, LORD our God, King of the Universe,
who creates the fruit of the tree.

Before eating vegetables, or fruit that does not grow on trees:

Blessed are You, LORD our God, King of the Universe,
who creates the fruit of the ground.

Before eating other food or drinking other liquids:

Blessed are You, LORD our God, King of the Universe,
by whose word all things came to be.

Before eating fruit for the first time in a season, the following is said.
This blessing is also said when buying or wearing a new garment of significant value
(e.g. a dress or suit); entering a new home for the first time; or hearing personal good news.

Blessed are You, LORD our God, King of the Universe,
who has given us life, sustained us, and brought us to this time.

BLESSING AFTER FOOD – AL HAMIḤYA

Grace after eating from the "seven species" of produce with which Israel is blessed: food made from
the five grains (but not bread); wine or grape juice; grapes, figs, pomegranates, olives, or dates.

בָּרוּךְ Blessed are You, LORD our God, King of the Universe,

After grain products *(but not bread or matza):*	*After wine or grape juice:*	*After grapes, figs, olives,* *pomegranates or dates:*
for the nourishment and sustenance,	for the vine and the fruit of the vine,	for the tree and the fruit of the tree,

After grain products (but not bread or matza), and wine or grape juice:

for the nourishment and sustenance
and for the vine and the fruit of the vine,

and for the produce of the field; for the desirable, good and spacious land
that You willingly gave as heritage to our ancestors, that they might eat of
its fruit and be satisfied with its goodness. Have compassion, please, LORD

Before eating food, other than bread or מצה,
made from the five species of grain (wheat, barley, rye, oats and spelt), or rice:

בָּרוּךְ אַתָּה יהוה אֱלֹהֵינוּ מֶלֶךְ הָעוֹלָם, בּוֹרֵא מִינֵי מְזוֹנוֹת.

Before drinking wine or grape juice:

בָּרוּךְ אַתָּה יהוה אֱלֹהֵינוּ מֶלֶךְ הָעוֹלָם, בּוֹרֵא פְּרִי הַגָּפֶן.

Before eating fruit that grows on trees:

בָּרוּךְ אַתָּה יהוה אֱלֹהֵינוּ מֶלֶךְ הָעוֹלָם, בּוֹרֵא פְּרִי הָעֵץ.

Before eating vegetables, or fruit that does not grow on trees:

בָּרוּךְ אַתָּה יהוה אֱלֹהֵינוּ מֶלֶךְ הָעוֹלָם, בּוֹרֵא פְּרִי הָאֲדָמָה.

Before eating other food or drinking other liquids:

בָּרוּךְ אַתָּה יהוה אֱלֹהֵינוּ מֶלֶךְ הָעוֹלָם, שֶׁהַכֹּל נִהְיָה בִּדְבָרוֹ.

Before eating fruit for the first time in a season, the following שֶׁהֶחֱיָנוּ is said.
This blessing is also said when buying or wearing a new garment of significant value
(e.g. a dress or suit); entering a new home for the first time; or hearing personal good news.

בָּרוּךְ אַתָּה יהוה אֱלֹהֵינוּ מֶלֶךְ הָעוֹלָם
שֶׁהֶחֱיָנוּ וְקִיְּמָנוּ וְהִגִּיעָנוּ לַזְּמַן הַזֶּה.

ברכה מעין שלוש

Grace after eating from the "seven species" of produce with which Israel is blessed: food made from
the five grains (but not bread); wine or grape juice; grapes, figs, pomegranates, olives, or dates.

בָּרוּךְ אַתָּה יהוה אֱלֹהֵינוּ מֶלֶךְ הָעוֹלָם, עַל

		After grain products
After grapes, figs, olives,		*(but not bread or מצה):*
pomegranates or dates:	*After wine or grape juice:*	

הָעֵץ וְעַל פְּרִי הָעֵץ   הַגֶּפֶן וְעַל פְּרִי הַגֶּפֶן   הַמִּחְיָה וְעַל הַכַּלְכָּלָה

After grain products (but not bread or מצה), and wine or grape juice:

הַמִּחְיָה וְעַל הַכַּלְכָּלָה וְעַל הַגֶּפֶן וְעַל פְּרִי הַגֶּפֶן

וְעַל תְּנוּבַת הַשָּׂדֶה וְעַל אֶרֶץ חֶמְדָּה טוֹבָה וּרְחָבָה, שֶׁרָצִיתָ וְהִנְחַלְתָּ
לַאֲבוֹתֵינוּ לֶאֱכֹל מִפִּרְיָהּ וְלִשְׂבֹּעַ מִטּוּבָהּ. רַחֵם נָא יהוה אֱלֹהֵינוּ עַל יִשְׂרָאֵל
עַמֶּךְ וְעַל יְרוּשָׁלַיִם עִירֶךָ וְעַל צִיּוֹן מִשְׁכַּן כְּבוֹדֶךָ וְעַל מִזְבְּחֶךָ וְעַל הֵיכָלֶךָ.

our God, on Israel Your people, on Jerusalem, Your city, on Zion the home of Your glory, on Your altar and Your Temple. May You rebuild Jerusalem, the holy city swiftly in our time, and may You bring us back there, rejoicing in its rebuilding, eating from its fruit, satisfied by its goodness, and blessing You for it in holiness and purity.

On Rosh Ḥodesh: Remember us for good on this day of the New Moon.
On Pesaḥ: Grant us joy on this Festival of Matzot.
On Sukkot: Grant us joy on this Festival of Sukkot.

For You, God, are good and do good to all and we thank You for the land

After grain products (but not bread or matza):	*After wine or grape juice:*	*After grapes, figs, olives, pomegranates or dates:*
and for the nourishment. Blessed are You, Lord, for the land and for the nourishment.	and for the fruit of the vine. Blessed are You, Lord, for the land and for the fruit of the vine.	and for the fruit. Blessed are You, Lord, for the land and for the fruit.

After grain products (but not bread or matza), and wine or grape juice:
and for the nourishment and for the fruit of the vine.
Blessed are You, Lord, for the land and for the nourishment
and the fruit of the vine.

BLESSING AFTER FOOD – BOREH NEFASHOT

*After food or drink that does not require Birkat HaMazon or
Al HaMiḥya – such as meat, fish, dairy products, vegetables, beverages, or
fruit other than grapes, figs, pomegranates, olives or dates – say:*

בְּרוּךְ Blessed are You, Lord our God, King of the Universe, who creates the many forms of life and their needs. For all You have created to sustain the life of all that lives, blessed be He, Giver of life to the worlds.

The second opinion, however, sees this as one long blessing whose theme is Hashem's provision of our needs. As such, a comma after וְחֶסְרוֹנָן is unnecessary.

In any event, one sees that for all the focus on the spiritual, Judaism acknowledges the importance of the physical. The need to eat is a basic drive, no different from any other animal on the planet. But rather than succumbing to our bestial instincts, Judaism constantly raises the act of eating to a spiritual activity.

Have you ever seen people eating in a way that is more animalistic than human? How might the recitation of this blessing help me maintain my humanity?

וּבְנֵה יְרוּשָׁלַיִם עִיר הַקֹּדֶשׁ בִּמְהֵרָה בְיָמֵינוּ, וְהַעֲלֵנוּ לְתוֹכָהּ וְשַׂמְּחֵנוּ בְּבִנְיָנָהּ וְנֹאכַל מִפִּרְיָהּ וְנִשְׂבַּע מִטּוּבָהּ, וּנְבָרֶכְךָ עָלֶיהָ בִּקְדֻשָּׁה וּבְטָהֳרָה.

בראש חודש: וְזָכְרֵנוּ לְטוֹבָה בְּיוֹם רֹאשׁ הַחֹדֶשׁ הַזֶּה

בפסח: וְשַׂמְּחֵנוּ בְּיוֹם חַג הַמַּצּוֹת הַזֶּה

בסוכות: וְשַׂמְּחֵנוּ בְּיוֹם חַג הַסֻּכּוֹת הַזֶּה

כִּי אַתָּה יהוה טוֹב וּמֵטִיב לַכֹּל, וְנוֹדֶה לְּךָ עַל הָאָרֶץ

After grapes, figs, olives, pomegranates or dates:	*After wine or grape juice:*	*After grain products (but not bread or מצה):*
וְעַל הַפֵּרוֹת.**	וְעַל פְּרִי הַגָּפֶן.*	וְעַל הַמִּחְיָה.
בָּרוּךְ אַתָּה יהוה עַל הָאָרֶץ וְעַל הַפֵּרוֹת.**	בָּרוּךְ אַתָּה יהוה עַל הָאָרֶץ וְעַל פְּרִי הַגָּפֶן.*	בָּרוּךְ אַתָּה יהוה עַל הָאָרֶץ וְעַל הַמִּחְיָה.

After grain products (but not bread or מצה), and wine or grape juice:

וְעַל הַמִּחְיָה וְעַל פְּרִי הַגָּפֶן.*

בָּרוּךְ אַתָּה יהוה, עַל הָאָרֶץ וְעַל הַמִּחְיָה וְעַל פְּרִי הַגָּפֶן.*

*If the wine is from ארץ ישראל, then substitute גַּפְנָהּ for הַגָּפֶן.
**If the fruit is from ארץ ישראל, then substitute פֵּרוֹתֶיהָ for הַפֵּרוֹת.

בורא נפשות

After food or drink that does not require מעין שלוש or ברכת המזון – such as meat, fish, dairy products, vegetables, beverages, or fruit other than grapes, figs, pomegranates, olives or dates – say:

בָּרוּךְ אַתָּה יהוה אֱלֹהֵינוּ מֶלֶךְ הָעוֹלָם, בּוֹרֵא נְפָשׁוֹת רַבּוֹת וְחֶסְרוֹנָן, עַל כָּל מַה שֶּׁבָּרָאתָ, לְהַחֲיוֹת בָּהֶם נֶפֶשׁ כָּל חָי. בָּרוּךְ חֵי הָעוֹלָמִים.

BOREH NEFASHOT

There is a dispute among the Rishonim as to whether the text of the blessing is interpreted as having two themes or just one. According to the first opinion, there should be a comma after the word וְחֶסְרוֹנָן (needs). We thank Hashem for the fact that He created us (בּוֹרֵא נְפָשׁוֹת) and we acknowledge our deficiencies, that is, our need for bread and water, the staples that we need in order to survive. The second part of the blessing, referring to "all You have created," is therefore a reference to all other kinds of foods from which we derive pleasure, even if they are not staples. Alternatively, we thank Hashem even if we do not have those staples.

BLESSINGS

BLESSINGS ON MITZVOT

In Israel on separating teruma and first tithe (if there is doubt as to whether the teruma and first tithe have been taken, the following blessing is not said, but the subsequent declaration is):

Blessed are You, LORD our God, King of the Universe,
who has made us holy through His commandments,
and has commanded us to separate *terumot* and tithes.

Whatever [of the allocated portion] is more than one in a hundred of everything here, is hereby declared to be *teruma gedola* [the priestly portion] and is the northern portion. The one in a hundred that remains here, together with nine equal portions on the upper side of this produce are declared to be the first [levitical] tithe. The one in a hundred I have made first tithe is hereby declared to be *terumat maaser* [the tithe-of-the-tithe set aside for the priests]. Nine other equal portions on the lower side of the produce are declared to be second tithe, but if this produce must have the tithe of the poor separated from it, let them be the tithe of the poor.

In Israel on separating and redeeming the second tithe (if there is doubt as to whether the second tithe has been taken, the following blessing is not said, but the subsequent declaration is):

Blessed are You, LORD our God, King of the Universe,
who has made us holy through His commandments,
and has commanded us about the redemption of the second tithe.

This second tithe, together with its additional fifth, is hereby redeemed by one *peruta* of the coins I have set aside for the redemption of the second tithe.

On taking ḥalla:

Blessed are You, LORD our God, King of the Universe,
who has made us holy through His commandments,
and has commanded us to set aside ḥalla from the dough.

On redeeming fourth-year fruit:

Blessed are You, LORD our God, King of the Universe,
who has made us holy through His commandments,
and has commanded us about the redemption of fruit of the fourth year.

The Rabbis tell us that we should recite 100 blessings a day. If you imagine a 16-hour day, that would amount to a blessing about every ten minutes. While it is true that in practical terms, lots of those are clumped together (consider how many blessings we say in an average morning *Shaḥarit*), the point is that *Ḥazal* wanted us to be ever conscious of the miracle and Origin of life. *Berakhot* are about not taking life for granted. They take the ordinary and remind us of the extraordinary. They focus on the physical and make it spiritual.

ברכות

ברכות המצוות

In ארץ ישראל *on separating* תרומה *and* מעשר ראשון *(if there is doubt as to whether the* תרומה *and* מעשר ראשון *have been taken, the following blessing is not said, but the subsequent declaration is):*

בָּרוּךְ אַתָּה יהוה אֱלֹהֵינוּ מֶלֶךְ הָעוֹלָם, אֲשֶׁר קִדְּשָׁנוּ בְּמִצְוֹתָיו
וְצִוָּנוּ לְהַפְרִישׁ תְּרוּמוֹת וּמַעַשְׂרוֹת.

מַה שֶּׁהוּא יוֹתֵר מֵאֶחָד מִמֵּאָה מִן הַכֹּל שֶׁיֵּשׁ כָּאן, הֲרֵי הוּא תְּרוּמָה גְּדוֹלָה בִּצְפוֹנוֹ,
וְהָאֶחָד מִמֵּאָה שֶׁנִּשְׁאַר כָּאן עִם תִּשְׁעָה חֲלָקִים כְּמוֹהוּ בְּצַד הָעֶלְיוֹן שֶׁל הַפֵּרוֹת
הַלָּלוּ, הֲרֵי הֵם מַעֲשֵׂר רִאשׁוֹן. אוֹתוֹ הָאֶחָד מִמֵּאָה שֶׁעֲשִׂיתִיו מַעֲשֵׂר רִאשׁוֹן הֲרֵי
הוּא תְּרוּמַת מַעֲשֵׂר. עוֹד תִּשְׁעָה חֲלָקִים כְּאֵלֶּה בְּצַד הַתַּחְתּוֹן שֶׁל הַפֵּרוֹת הֲרֵי הֵם
מַעֲשֵׂר שֵׁנִי, וְאִם הֵם חַיָּבִים בְּמַעֲשַׂר עָנִי, הֲרֵי הֵם מַעֲשַׂר עָנִי.

In ארץ ישראל *on separating and redeeming the* מעשר שני *(if there is doubt as to whether the* מעשר שני *has been taken, the following blessing is not said, but the subsequent declaration is):*

בָּרוּךְ אַתָּה יהוה אֱלֹהֵינוּ מֶלֶךְ הָעוֹלָם, אֲשֶׁר קִדְּשָׁנוּ בְּמִצְוֹתָיו
וְצִוָּנוּ עַל פִּדְיוֹן מַעֲשֵׂר שֵׁנִי.

מַעֲשֵׂר שֵׁנִי זֶה, הוּא וְחֻמְשׁוֹ, הֲרֵי הוּא מְחֻלָּל עַל פְּרוּטָה אַחַת מִן הַמַּטְבֵּעַ שֶׁיִּחַדְתִּי
לְפִדְיוֹן מַעֲשֵׂר שֵׁנִי.

On taking חלה:

בָּרוּךְ אַתָּה יהוה אֱלֹהֵינוּ מֶלֶךְ הָעוֹלָם, אֲשֶׁר קִדְּשָׁנוּ בְּמִצְוֹתָיו
וְצִוָּנוּ לְהַפְרִישׁ חַלָּה מִן הָעִסָּה.

On redeeming נטע רבעי:

בָּרוּךְ אַתָּה יהוה אֱלֹהֵינוּ מֶלֶךְ הָעוֹלָם, אֲשֶׁר קִדְּשָׁנוּ בְּמִצְוֹתָיו
וְצִוָּנוּ עַל פִּדְיוֹן נֶטַע רְבָעִי.

INTRODUCTION TO BERAKHOT

A *berakha* is a kind of meditation, a reflective phrase designed to help us focus on the here and now, on an aspect of our lives that we might otherwise take for granted. It reminds us of the incredible miracle of nature or life that lies before us. It reminds us of the "Wow!" And it reminds us of the Ultimate Source.

On fixing a mezuza to the doorpost:
Blessed are You, Lord our God, King of the Universe,
who has made us holy through His commandments,
and has commanded us to affix the mezuza.

On making a protective railing around one's roof, or a fence around a pit:
Blessed are You, Lord our God, King of the Universe,
who has made us holy through His commandments,
and has commanded us to to affix a guard-rail.

On immersing utensils made by or bought from a gentile:
Blessed are You, Lord our God, King of the Universe,
who has made us holy through His commandments,
and has commanded us about immersing a vessel (vessels).

BLESSINGS ON PLEASURES, SIGHTS AND SOUNDS

On wearing new clothes:
Blessed are You, Lord our God, King of the Universe,
who clothes the naked.

On smelling fragrant shrubs or trees:
Blessed are You, Lord our God, King of the Universe,
who creates fragrant trees.

On smelling fragrant herbs, grasses or flowers:
Blessed are You, Lord our God, King of the Universe,
who creates fragrant plants.

On smelling fragrant fruit:
Blessed are You, Lord our God, King of the Universe,
who gives pleasant fragrance to fruits.

On smelling persimmon oil:
Blessed are You, Lord our God, King of the Universe,
who creates pleasing perfume.

On all other scents:
Blessed are You, Lord our God, King of the Universe,
who creates the various spices.

On fixing a מזוזה to the doorpost:

בָּרוּךְ אַתָּה יהוה אֱלֹהֵינוּ מֶלֶךְ הָעוֹלָם, אֲשֶׁר קִדְּשָׁנוּ בְּמִצְוֹתָיו
וְצִוָּנוּ לִקְבֹּעַ מְזוּזָה.

On making a protective railing around one's roof, or a fence around a pit:

בָּרוּךְ אַתָּה יהוה אֱלֹהֵינוּ מֶלֶךְ הָעוֹלָם, אֲשֶׁר קִדְּשָׁנוּ בְּמִצְוֹתָיו
וְצִוָּנוּ לַעֲשׂוֹת מַעֲקֶה.

On immersing utensils made by or bought from a gentile:

בָּרוּךְ אַתָּה יהוה אֱלֹהֵינוּ מֶלֶךְ הָעוֹלָם, אֲשֶׁר קִדְּשָׁנוּ בְּמִצְוֹתָיו
וְצִוָּנוּ עַל טְבִילַת כְּלִי (כֵּלִים).

ברכות הנהנין, הראייה והשמיעה

On wearing new clothes:

בָּרוּךְ אַתָּה יהוה אֱלֹהֵינוּ מֶלֶךְ הָעוֹלָם
מַלְבִּישׁ עֲרֻמִּים.

On smelling fragrant shrubs or trees:

בָּרוּךְ אַתָּה יהוה אֱלֹהֵינוּ מֶלֶךְ הָעוֹלָם
בּוֹרֵא עֲצֵי בְשָׂמִים.

On smelling fragrant herbs, grasses or flowers:

בָּרוּךְ אַתָּה יהוה אֱלֹהֵינוּ מֶלֶךְ הָעוֹלָם
בּוֹרֵא עִשְׂבֵי בְשָׂמִים.

On smelling fragrant fruit:

בָּרוּךְ אַתָּה יהוה אֱלֹהֵינוּ מֶלֶךְ הָעוֹלָם
הַנּוֹתֵן רֵיחַ טוֹב בַּפֵּרוֹת.

On smelling persimmon oil:

בָּרוּךְ אַתָּה יהוה אֱלֹהֵינוּ מֶלֶךְ הָעוֹלָם
בּוֹרֵא שֶׁמֶן עָרֵב.

On all other scents:

בָּרוּךְ אַתָּה יהוה אֱלֹהֵינוּ מֶלֶךְ הָעוֹלָם
בּוֹרֵא מִינֵי בְשָׂמִים.

On seeing the wonders of nature, such as lightning, and on the 28-year solar cycle:
Blessed are You, LORD our God, King of the Universe,
Author of creation.

On hearing thunder or experiencing a hurricane:
Blessed are You, LORD our God, King of the Universe,
whose power and might fill the world.

On seeing a rainbow:
Blessed are You, LORD our God, King of the Universe,
who remembers the covenant, is faithful to the covenant,
and fulfills His word.

On seeing the ocean or the Mediterranean Sea for the first time in thirty days:
Blessed are You, LORD our God, King of the Universe,
who has made the great sea.

On seeing trees blossoming for the first time in the year:
Blessed are You, LORD our God, King of the Universe,
who has withheld nothing from His world,
but has created in it beautiful creatures and trees
for human beings to enjoy.

On seeing beautiful scenes of nature:
Blessed are You, LORD our God, King of the Universe,
who has [created] such things in His world.

On seeing unusual people or animals:
Blessed are You, LORD our God, King of the Universe,
who makes [all] creatures different.

On hearing good news from which others as well as oneself will benefit:
Blessed are You, LORD our God, King of the Universe,
who is good and does good.

---

plan to do this. Yet the words flowed from my lips... It was a religious reaction to viewing the majesty of God's creation. When I recited the blessing upon seeing the sea, I did so with emotion and deep feeling. I experienced the words of the benediction "Blessed be He who wrought creation." Not all the blessings that I recite are said with such concentration. It was more than simply a blessing; it was an encounter with the Creator. I felt that the Shekhina [Divine Presence] was hidden in the darkness and vastness of the sea. The experience welled out of me. (Rav Soloveitchik)

On seeing the wonders of nature, such as lightning, and ברכת החמה:

בָּרוּךְ אַתָּה יהוה אֱלֹהֵינוּ מֶלֶךְ הָעוֹלָם, עוֹשֶׂה מַעֲשֵׂה בְרֵאשִׁית.

On hearing thunder or experiencing a hurricane:

בָּרוּךְ אַתָּה יהוה אֱלֹהֵינוּ מֶלֶךְ הָעוֹלָם, שֶׁכֹּחוֹ וּגְבוּרָתוֹ מָלֵא עוֹלָם.

On seeing a rainbow:

בָּרוּךְ אַתָּה יהוה אֱלֹהֵינוּ מֶלֶךְ הָעוֹלָם
זוֹכֵר הַבְּרִית וְנֶאֱמָן בִּבְרִיתוֹ וְקַיָּם בְּמַאֲמָרוֹ.

On seeing the ocean or the Mediterranean Sea for the first time in thirty days:

בָּרוּךְ אַתָּה יהוה אֱלֹהֵינוּ מֶלֶךְ הָעוֹלָם, שֶׁעָשָׂה אֶת הַיָּם הַגָּדוֹל.

On seeing trees blossoming for the first time in the year:

בָּרוּךְ אַתָּה יהוה אֱלֹהֵינוּ מֶלֶךְ הָעוֹלָם, שֶׁלֹּא חִסַּר בְּעוֹלָמוֹ כְּלוּם
וּבָרָא בוֹ בְּרִיּוֹת טוֹבוֹת וְאִילָנוֹת טוֹבִים לְהַנּוֹת בָּהֶם בְּנֵי אָדָם.

On seeing beautiful scenes of nature:

בָּרוּךְ אַתָּה יהוה אֱלֹהֵינוּ מֶלֶךְ הָעוֹלָם, שֶׁכָּכָה לוֹ בְּעוֹלָמוֹ.

On seeing unusual people or animals:

בָּרוּךְ אַתָּה יהוה אֱלֹהֵינוּ מֶלֶךְ הָעוֹלָם, מְשַׁנֶּה הַבְּרִיּוֹת.

On hearing good news from which others as well as oneself will benefit:

בָּרוּךְ אַתָּה יהוה אֱלֹהֵינוּ מֶלֶךְ הָעוֹלָם, הַטּוֹב וְהַמֵּטִיב.

ANI TEFILLA ・ אני תפילה

I remember how enthused I was the first time I saw the Baltic Sea. I was born in Russia and never saw a major body of water in my youth… I remember that the water was blue, deeply blue. From afar it looked like a blue forest. It resembles the aboriginal forests *near Pruzhana, where I was born. When I came close and realized it was the Baltic Sea, I was overwhelmed by its beauty. Spontaneously I began to recite the Psalm, "Bless the Lord, O my soul" [Barekhi Nafshi, Psalm 104 that is recited on Rosh Ḥodesh]. I did not*

On hearing bad news, and said by a mourner before the ritual tearing of the garment:
Blessed are You, Lᴏʀᴅ our God, King of the Universe,
the true Judge.ᴬ

On seeing an outstanding Torah scholar:
Blessed are You, Lᴏʀᴅ our God, King of the Universe,
who has shared of His wisdom with those who revere Him.

On seeing an outstanding secular scholar:
Blessed are You, Lᴏʀᴅ our God, King of the Universe,
who has given of His wisdom with human beings.

On seeing a Monarch or Head of State:
Blessed are You, Lᴏʀᴅ our God, King of the Universe,
who has given of His glory to human beings.

On seeing 600,000 Jews together in Israel:
Blessed are You, Lᴏʀᴅ our God, King of the Universe,
who knows all secrets.

On seeing Jewish settlements in Israel:
Blessed are You, Lᴏʀᴅ our God, King of the Universe,
who establishes the border of the widow.

On seeing the place where miracles occurred to the Jewish people:
Blessed are You, Lᴏʀᴅ our God, King of the Universe,
who performed miracles for our ancestors in this place.

*On seeing the place where miracles occurred to oneself
or one's family (insert the relevant words):*
Blessed are You, Lᴏʀᴅ our God, King of the Universe,
who performed a miracle for me (my father / my mother / my ancestors)
in this place.

---

and moved them all to Canada to start all over again, leaving behind all the members of his extended family. "How was I to know," he said, "that years later our enemies would come and destroy everyone I left behind, but I was left alive with my wife and children? Only then did I understand the Gemara's ad-monition that 'A person is obligated to say a blessing over the bad things that happen [like losing all of my money,] just like he is to say a blessing over the good.' For what seems to us like bad in the moment, may indeed be part of a bigger plan of HaKadosh Barukh Hu of which one is not and may not ever be aware."

On hearing bad news, and said by a mourner before the ritual tearing of the garment:

בָּרוּךְ אַתָּה יהוה אֱלֹהֵינוּ מֶלֶךְ הָעוֹלָם, דַּיַּן הָאֱמֶת.א

On seeing an outstanding Torah scholar:

בָּרוּךְ אַתָּה יהוה אֱלֹהֵינוּ מֶלֶךְ הָעוֹלָם, שֶׁחָלַק מֵחָכְמָתוֹ לִירֵאָיו.

On seeing an outstanding secular scholar:

בָּרוּךְ אַתָּה יהוה אֱלֹהֵינוּ מֶלֶךְ הָעוֹלָם, שֶׁנָּתַן מֵחָכְמָתוֹ לְבָשָׂר וָדָם.

On seeing a Monarch or Head of State:

בָּרוּךְ אַתָּה יהוה אֱלֹהֵינוּ מֶלֶךְ הָעוֹלָם, שֶׁנָּתַן מִכְּבוֹדוֹ לְבָשָׂר וָדָם.

On seeing 600,000 Jews together in אֶרֶץ יִשְׂרָאֵל:

בָּרוּךְ אַתָּה יהוה אֱלֹהֵינוּ מֶלֶךְ הָעוֹלָם, חֲכַם הָרָזִים.

On seeing Jewish settlements in אֶרֶץ יִשְׂרָאֵל:

בָּרוּךְ אַתָּה יהוה אֱלֹהֵינוּ מֶלֶךְ הָעוֹלָם
מַצִּיב גְּבוּל אַלְמָנָה.

On seeing the place where miracles occurred to the Jewish people:

בָּרוּךְ אַתָּה יהוה אֱלֹהֵינוּ מֶלֶךְ הָעוֹלָם
שֶׁעָשָׂה נִסִּים לַאֲבוֹתֵינוּ בַּמָּקוֹם הַזֶּה.

On seeing the place where miracles occurred to oneself
or one's family (insert the relevant words):

בָּרוּךְ אַתָּה יהוה אֱלֹהֵינוּ מֶלֶךְ הָעוֹלָם
שֶׁעָשָׂה לִי (לְאָבִי/לְאִמִּי/לַאֲבוֹתַי) נֵס בַּמָּקוֹם הַזֶּה.

ANI TEFILLA · אני תפילה

דַּיַּן הָאֱמֶת – *The true Judge.*
My grandfather, זלל״ה, emigrated from Eastern
Europe without his wife and child in order to
make some money, since the economy in Po-
land then was so poor. But after a few years,
World War I broke out and he could not get

back home and so he was separated from his
family for eight years! Upon his return with
his hard-earned savings, he invested it all but,
unfortunately, did so unwisely and lost it all.
"And for this," he said, "I am supposed to thank
God?!" So he picked up his immediate family

ADDITIONAL BLESSINGS

After relieving oneself and washing one's hands, say:

Blessed are You, LORD our God, King of the Universe, who formed man in wisdom and created in him many orifices and cavities. It is revealed and known before the throne of Your glory that were one of them to be ruptured or blocked, it would be impossible to survive and stand before You. Blessed are You, LORD, Healer of all flesh who does wondrous deeds.

On visiting a cemetery, or seeing a Jewish grave, for the first time in thirty days:

Blessed are You, LORD our God, King of the Universe, who formed you in judgment, who nourished and sustained you in judgment, who brought death on you in judgment, who knows the number of you all in judgment, and who in the future will restore you to life in judgment. Blessed are You, LORD, who revives the dead.

You are eternally mighty, LORD. You give life to the dead and have great power to save. He sustains the living with loving-kindness, and with great compassion revives the dead. He supports the fallen, heals the sick, sets captives free, and keeps His faith with those who sleep in the dust. Who is like You, Master of might, and who can compare to You, O King who brings death and gives life, and makes salvation grow? Faithful are You to revive the dead.

---

*In special cases of urgency only, the following short form
of the Amida may be said. First say the first three blessings of the Amida
from "O LORD" on page 138 until "the holy God" page 146, then say:*

הֲבִינֵנוּ Grant us understanding, LORD our God, to know Your ways. Sensitize our hearts so that we may revere You, and forgive us so that we may be redeemed. Keep us far from suffering and satisfy us with the pastures of Your land. Gather our scattered people from the four quarters of the earth. May those who go astray be judged according to Your will: raise Your hand against the wicked. May the righteous rejoice in the rebuilding of Your city, the restoration of Your Temple, the flowering of Your servant David's glory, and the radiant light of the son of Jesse, Your anointed. May You answer us even before we call. Blessed are You, LORD, who hears prayer.

Continue with the final three blessings from "Find favor" on page 176 until the end.

---

*In extreme cases where there is no time to say the abbreviated Amida above,
one may say the following. However, if prayer is then possible
at a later time, one should say the complete Amida.*

צָרְכֵי The needs of Your people Israel are many, and their patience is thin. May it be Your will, LORD our God and God of our ancestors, to give each one of them enough to sustain him, and to every single body, all that it lacks – and perform what is right in Your eyes. Blessed are You, LORD, who listens to prayer.

ברכות נוספות

After relieving oneself and washing one's hands, say:

בָּרוּךְ אַתָּה יהוה אֱלֹהֵינוּ מֶלֶךְ הָעוֹלָם, אֲשֶׁר יָצַר אֶת הָאָדָם בְּחָכְמָה, וּבָרָא בוֹ נְקָבִים נְקָבִים, חֲלוּלִים חֲלוּלִים. גָּלוּי וְיָדוּעַ לִפְנֵי כִסֵּא כְבוֹדֶךָ, שֶׁאִם יִפָּתֵחַ אֶחָד מֵהֶם אוֹ יִסָּתֵם אֶחָד מֵהֶם, אִי אֶפְשַׁר לְהִתְקַיֵּם וְלַעֲמֹד לְפָנֶיךָ. בָּרוּךְ אַתָּה יהוה, רוֹפֵא כָל בָּשָׂר וּמַפְלִיא לַעֲשׂוֹת.

On visiting a cemetery, or seeing a Jewish grave, for the first time in thirty days:

בָּרוּךְ אַתָּה יהוה אֱלֹהֵינוּ מֶלֶךְ הָעוֹלָם, אֲשֶׁר יָצַר אֶתְכֶם בַּדִּין, וְזָן וְכִלְכֵּל אֶתְכֶם בַּדִּין, וְהֵמִית אֶתְכֶם בַּדִּין, וְיוֹדֵעַ מִסְפַּר כֻּלְּכֶם בַּדִּין, וְהוּא עָתִיד לְהַחֲיוֹתְכֶם וּלְקַיֵּם אֶתְכֶם בַּדִּין. בָּרוּךְ אַתָּה יהוה, מְחַיֵּה הַמֵּתִים.

אַתָּה גִּבּוֹר לְעוֹלָם אֲדֹנָי, מְחַיֵּה מֵתִים אַתָּה, רַב לְהוֹשִׁיעַ, מְכַלְכֵּל חַיִּים בְּחֶסֶד, מְחַיֵּה מֵתִים בְּרַחֲמִים רַבִּים, סוֹמֵךְ נוֹפְלִים, וְרוֹפֵא חוֹלִים, וּמַתִּיר אֲסוּרִים, וּמְקַיֵּם אֱמוּנָתוֹ לִישֵׁנֵי עָפָר. מִי כָמְוֹךָ בַּעַל גְּבוּרוֹת וּמִי דּוֹמֶה לָּךְ, מֶלֶךְ מֵמִית וּמְחַיֶּה וּמַצְמִיחַ יְשׁוּעָה, וְנֶאֱמָן אַתָּה לְהַחֲיוֹת מֵתִים.

In special cases of urgency only, the following short form
of the עמידה ברכות of the עמידה may be said. First say the first three ברכות of the עמידה
on page 139 until הַקָּדוֹשׁ on page 147, then say:
from שְׂפָתַי תִּפְתָּח, אֲדֹנָי

הֲבִינֵנוּ יהוה אֱלֹהֵינוּ לָדַעַת דְּרָכֶיךָ, וּמוֹל אֶת לְבָבֵנוּ לְיִרְאָתֶךָ, וְתִסְלַח לָנוּ לִהְיוֹת גְּאוּלִים, וְרַחֲקֵנוּ מִמַּכְאוֹב, וְדַשְּׁנֵנוּ בִּנְאוֹת אַרְצֶךָ, וּנְפוּצוֹתֵינוּ מֵאַרְבַּע תְּקַבֵּץ, וְהַתּוֹעִים עַל דַּעְתְּךָ יִשָּׁפֵטוּ, וְעַל הָרְשָׁעִים תָּנִיף יָדֶךָ, וְיִשְׂמְחוּ צַדִּיקִים בְּבִנְיַן עִירְךָ וּבְתִקּוּן הֵיכָלֶךָ, וּבִצְמִיחַת קֶרֶן לְדָוִד עַבְדֶּךָ וּבַעֲרִיכַת נֵר לְבֶן יִשַׁי מְשִׁיחֶךָ, טֶרֶם נִקְרָא אַתָּה תַעֲנֶה. בָּרוּךְ אַתָּה יהוה, שׁוֹמֵעַ תְּפִלָּה.

Continue with the final three ברכות, from רְצֵה on page 177 until the end.

In extreme cases where there is no time to say the abbreviated עמידה above,
one may say the following. However, if prayer is possible
at a later time, one should say the complete עמידה.

צָרְכֵי עַמְּךָ יִשְׂרָאֵל מְרֻבִּים וְדַעְתָּם קְצָרָה. יְהִי רָצוֹן מִלְּפָנֶיךָ יהוה אֱלֹהֵינוּ וֵאלֹהֵי אֲבוֹתֵינוּ, שֶׁתִּתֵּן לְכָל אֶחָד וְאֶחָד כְּדֵי פַרְנָסָתוֹ, וּלְכָל גְּוִיָּה וּגְוִיָּה דֵּי מַחְסוֹרָהּ, וְהַטּוֹב בְּעֵינֶיךָ עֲשֵׂה. בָּרוּךְ אַתָּה יהוה, שׁוֹמֵעַ תְּפִלָּה.

*In times of drought in Israel, add:

וַעֲנֵנוּ And answer us through the attribute of compassion, Creator of the universe who chooses His people Israel to make known His greatness and majestic glory. You who listen to prayer, grant dew and rain on the face of the earth, satisfying the whole universe from Your goodness. Fill our hands from Your blessings and Your hand's rich gift. Guard and deliver this year from all evil, all kinds of destruction and punishment, and give it hope and a peaceful end. Spare us and have compassion on us and on all our produce and fruit, blessing us with bounteous rain. May we merit life, plenty and peace as in the good years. Remove from us plague, sword and famine, wild animals, captivity and plunder, the evil instinct and serious and dangerous illnesses and events. Decree for us goodly decrees, and may Your compassion prevail over Your other attributes, that You may act toward Your children through the attribute of compassion, and in compassion and favor accept our prayer.

BIRKAT KOHANIM IN ISRAEL

In Israel, the following is said by the Leader during the Repetition of the Amida when Kohanim bless the congregation. If there is more than one Kohen, a member of the congregation calls: (See laws 208–215.)

Kohanim!

The Kohanim respond:

Blessed are You, Lord our God, King of the Universe, who has made us holy with the holiness of Aaron, and has commanded us to bless His people Israel with love.

The Leader calls word by word, followed by the Kohanim:

יְבָרֶכְךָ May the LORD bless you and protect you. (*Cong:* Amen.)   Num. 6
     May the LORD make His face shine on you
     and be gracious to you. (*Cong:* Amen.)
     May the LORD turn His face toward you,
     and grant you peace. (*Cong:* Amen.)

The Leader continues with "Grant peace" below.

The congregation says:	*The Kohanim say:*
אַדִּיר Majestic One on high who dwells in power: You are peace and Your name is peace. May it be Your will to bestow on us and on Your people the house of Israel, life and blessing as a safeguard for peace.	רִבּוֹן Master of the Universe: we have done what You have decreed for us. So too may You deal with us as You have promised us. Look down from Your holy dwelling place, from heaven, and bless Your people Israel and the land You have given us as You promised on oath to our ancestors, a land flowing with milk and honey. *Deut. 26*

Go to Blessing of Peace, at Shaḥarit on page 186 and at Minḥa on page 324.

In times of drought in ארץ ישראל, add:

וְעַנֵּנוּ בּוֹרֵא עוֹלָם בְּמִדַּת הָרַחֲמִים, בּוֹחֵר בְּעַמּוֹ יִשְׂרָאֵל לְהוֹדִיעַ גָּדְלוֹ וְהַדְרַת כְּבוֹדוֹ. שׁוֹמֵעַ תְּפִלָּה, תֵּן טַל וּמָטָר עַל פְּנֵי הָאֲדָמָה, וְתַשְׂבִּיעַ אֶת הָעוֹלָם כֻּלּוֹ מִטּוּבֶךָ, וּמַלֵּא יָדֵינוּ מִבִּרְכוֹתֶיךָ וּמֵעֹשֶׁר מַתְּנַת יָדֶךָ. שְׁמוֹר וְהַצֵּל שָׁנָה זוֹ מִכָּל דָּבָר רָע, וּמִכָּל מִינֵי מַשְׁחִית וּמִכָּל מִינֵי פֻּרְעָנִיּוֹת, וַעֲשֵׂה לָהּ תִּקְוָה וְאַחֲרִית שָׁלוֹם. חוּס וְרַחֵם עָלֵינוּ וְעַל כָּל תְּבוּאָתֵנוּ וּפֵרוֹתֵינוּ, וּבָרְכֵנוּ בְּגִשְׁמֵי בְרָכָה, וְנִזְכֶּה לְחַיִּים וְשָׂבַע וְשָׁלוֹם כַּשָּׁנִים הַטּוֹבוֹת. וְהָסֵר מִמֶּנּוּ דֶּבֶר וְחֶרֶב וְרָעָב, וְחַיָּה רָעָה וּשְׁבִי וּבִזָּה, וְיֵצֶר הָרַע וָחֳלָיִים רָעִים וְקָשִׁים וּמְאֹרָעוֹת רָעִים וְקָשִׁים. גְּזוֹר עָלֵינוּ גְּזֵרוֹת טוֹבוֹת מִלְּפָנֶיךָ, וְיִגְלוּ רַחֲמֶיךָ עַל מִדּוֹתֶיךָ, וְתִתְנַהֵג עִם בָּנֶיךָ בְּמִדַּת הָרַחֲמִים, וְקַבֵּל בְּרַחֲמִים וּבְרָצוֹן אֶת תְּפִלָּתֵנוּ.

ברכת כהנים בארץ ישראל

In ארץ ישראל, *the following is said by the* שליח ציבור *during the* חזרת הש״ץ *when* כהנים *say* ברכת כהנים. *If there is more than one* כהן, *a member of the* קהל *calls: (See laws 208–215.)*

כֹּהֲנִים

The כהנים *respond:*

בָּרוּךְ אַתָּה יהוה אֱלֹהֵינוּ מֶלֶךְ הָעוֹלָם, אֲשֶׁר קִדְּשָׁנוּ בִּקְדֻשָּׁתוֹ שֶׁל אַהֲרֹן וְצִוָּנוּ לְבָרֵךְ אֶת עַמּוֹ יִשְׂרָאֵל בְּאַהֲבָה.

The שליח ציבור *calls word by word, followed by the* כהנים:

במדברו

יְבָרֶכְךָ יהוה וְיִשְׁמְרֶךָ: קהל אָמֵן

יָאֵר יהוה פָּנָיו אֵלֶיךָ וִיחֻנֶּךָ: קהל אָמֵן

יִשָּׂא יהוה פָּנָיו אֵלֶיךָ וְיָשֵׂם לְךָ שָׁלוֹם: קהל אָמֵן

The שליח ציבור *continues with* שים שלום *below.*

The קהל *says:*

אַדִּיר בַּמָּרוֹם שׁוֹכֵן בִּגְבוּרָה, אַתָּה שָׁלוֹם וְשִׁמְךָ שָׁלוֹם. יְהִי רָצוֹן שֶׁתָּשִׂים עָלֵינוּ וְעַל כָּל עַמְּךָ בֵּית יִשְׂרָאֵל חַיִּים וּבְרָכָה לְמִשְׁמֶרֶת שָׁלוֹם:

The כהנים *say:*

רִבּוֹנוֹ שֶׁל עוֹלָם, עָשִׂינוּ מַה שֶּׁגָּזַרְתָּ עָלֵינוּ, אַף אַתָּה עֲשֵׂה עִמָּנוּ כְּמוֹ שֶׁהִבְטַחְתָּנוּ. הַשְׁקִיפָה מִמְּעוֹן קָדְשְׁךָ מִן הַשָּׁמַיִם, וּבָרֵךְ אֶת עַמְּךָ אֶת יִשְׂרָאֵל, וְאֵת הָאֲדָמָה אֲשֶׁר נָתַתָּה לָנוּ, כַּאֲשֶׁר נִשְׁבַּעְתָּ לַאֲבֹתֵינוּ, אֶרֶץ זָבַת חָלָב וּדְבָשׁ:

דברים כו

Go to ברכת שלום, at שחרית *on page 187 and at* מנחה *on page 325.*

VIDUY

In Israel on days on which Taḥanun is said (see page 200), some say Viduy and the Thirteen Attributes of Divine Compassion. The congregation stands and says:

אֱלֹהֵינוּ Our God and God of our fathers, let our prayer come before You, and do not hide Yourself from our plea, for we are not so arrogant or obstinate as to say before You, Lord, our God and God of our fathers, we are righteous and have not sinned, for in truth, we and our fathers have sinned.

At each expression, strike the chest on the left side:

אָשַׁמְנוּ We have been guilty, we have acted treacherously, we have robbed, we have spoken slander. We have acted perversely, we have acted wickedly, we have acted presumptuously, we have been violent, we have framed lies. We have given bad advice, we have deceived, we have scorned, we have rebelled, we have provoked, we have turned away, we have committed iniquity, we have transgressed, we have persecuted, we have been obstinate. We have acted wickedly, we have corrupted, we have acted abominably, we have strayed, we have led others astray.

We have turned away from Your commandments and good laws, to no avail, for You are *Neh. 9* just in all that has befallen us, for You have acted faithfully while we have done wickedly.

When praying without a minyan continue with "He is compassionate" on page 200.

THIRTEEN ATTRIBUTES OF DIVINE COMPASSION

אֵל אֶרֶךְ You are a God slow to anger, You are called Master of Compassion, and You have taught the way of repentance. May You remember today and every day the greatness of Your compassion and loving-kindness for the sake of the descendants of Your beloved ones. Turn toward us in compassion, for You are the Master of Compassion. We come before You in plea and prayer, as You in ancient times showed the humble one [Moses]. Turn from Your fierce anger, as is written in Your Torah. In the shadow of Your wings may we shelter and abide, as on the day when the Lord descended in the cloud. ▸ Disregard transgression and erase guilt as on the day You stood with him [Moses] there. Hear our cry and heed our word, as on the day You proclaimed in the name of the Lord, and there it is written:

All say aloud:

וַיַּעֲבֹר And the Lord passed by before him and proclaimed: *Ex. 34*

The Lord, the Lord, compassionate and gracious God, slow to anger,
abounding in loving-kindness and truth, extending loving-kindness to a
thousand generations, forgiving iniquity, rebellion and sin,
and absolving [the guilty who repent]. Forgive us our iniquity and our sin,
and take us as Your inheritance. Forgive us, our Father, for we have sinned.
Pardon us, our King, for we have transgressed. For You, Lord, are good   *Ps. 86*
and forgiving, abounding in loving-kindness to all who call on You.

*On Mondays and Thursdays continue with "He is compassionate"
on page 200; on other days with "David said" on page 208.*

וידוי

In ארץ ישראל on days on which תחנון is said (see page 201),
some say וידוי and the י"ג מדות. The קהל stands and says:

אֱלֹהֵינוּ וֵאלֹהֵי אֲבוֹתֵינוּ, תָּבוֹא לְפָנֶיךָ תְּפִלָּתֵנוּ, וְאַל תִּתְעַלַּם מִתְּחִנָּתֵנוּ, שֶׁאֵין אֲנַחְנוּ עַזֵּי פָנִים וּקְשֵׁי עֹרֶף לוֹמַר לְפָנֶיךָ, יהוה אֱלֹהֵינוּ וֵאלֹהֵי אֲבוֹתֵינוּ, צַדִּיקִים אֲנַחְנוּ וְלֹא חָטָאנוּ, אֲבָל אֲנַחְנוּ וַאֲבוֹתֵינוּ חָטָאנוּ.

At each expression, strike the chest on the left side:

אָשַׁמְנוּ, בָּגַדְנוּ, גָּזַלְנוּ, דִּבַּרְנוּ דֹפִי, הֶעֱוִינוּ, וְהִרְשַׁעְנוּ, זַדְנוּ, חָמַסְנוּ, טָפַלְנוּ שֶׁקֶר, יָעַצְנוּ רָע, כִּזַּבְנוּ, לַצְנוּ, מָרַדְנוּ, נִאַצְנוּ, סָרַרְנוּ, עָוִינוּ, פָּשַׁעְנוּ, צָרַרְנוּ, קִשִּׁינוּ עֹרֶף, רָשַׁעְנוּ, שִׁחַתְנוּ, תִּעַבְנוּ, תָּעִינוּ, תִּעְתָּעְנוּ.

נחמיה ט · סַרְנוּ מִמִּצְוֹתֶיךָ וּמִמִּשְׁפָּטֶיךָ הַטּוֹבִים, וְלֹא שָׁוָה לָנוּ. וְאַתָּה צַדִּיק עַל כָּל־הַבָּא עָלֵינוּ, כִּי־אֱמֶת עָשִׂיתָ, וַאֲנַחְנוּ הִרְשָׁעְנוּ:

When praying without a מנין continue with וְהוּא רַחוּם on page 201.

י"ג מדות

אֵל אֶרֶךְ אַפַּיִם אַתָּה, וּבַעַל הָרַחֲמִים נִקְרֵאתָ, וְדֶרֶךְ תְּשׁוּבָה הוֹרֵיתָ. גְּדֻלַּת רַחֲמֶיךָ וַחֲסָדֶיךָ, תִּזְכֹּר הַיּוֹם וּבְכָל יוֹם לְזֶרַע יְדִידֶיךָ. תֵּפֶן אֵלֵינוּ בְּרַחֲמִים, כִּי אַתָּה הוּא בַּעַל הָרַחֲמִים. בְּתַחֲנוּן וּבִתְפִלָּה פָּנֶיךָ נְקַדֵּם, כְּהוֹדַעְתָּ לֶעָנָו מִקֶּדֶם. מֵחֲרוֹן אַפְּךָ שׁוּב, כְּמוֹ בְתוֹרָתְךָ כָּתוּב. וּבְצֵל כְּנָפֶיךָ נֶחֱסֶה וְנִתְלוֹנָן, כְּיוֹם וַיֵּרֶד יהוה בֶּעָנָן. ◀ תַּעֲבֹר עַל פֶּשַׁע וְתִמְחֶה אָשָׁם, כְּיוֹם וַיִּתְיַצֵּב עִמּוֹ שָׁם. תַּאֲזִין שַׁוְעָתֵנוּ וְתַקְשִׁיב מֶנּוּ מַאֲמָר, כְּיוֹם וַיִּקְרָא בְשֵׁם יהוה, וְשָׁם נֶאֱמַר:

All say aloud:

שמות לד · וַיַּעֲבֹר יהוה עַל־פָּנָיו וַיִּקְרָא

יהוה, יהוה, אֵל רַחוּם וְחַנּוּן, אֶרֶךְ אַפַּיִם וְרַב־חֶסֶד וֶאֱמֶת:
נֹצֵר חֶסֶד לָאֲלָפִים, נֹשֵׂא עָוֹן וָפֶשַׁע וְחַטָּאָה, וְנַקֵּה:
וְסָלַחְתָּ לַעֲוֹנֵנוּ וּלְחַטָּאתֵנוּ, וּנְחַלְתָּנוּ:
סְלַח לָנוּ אָבִינוּ כִּי חָטָאנוּ, מְחַל לָנוּ מַלְכֵּנוּ כִּי פָשָׁעְנוּ
תהלים פו · כִּי־אַתָּה אֲדֹנָי טוֹב וְסַלָּח, וְרַב־חֶסֶד לְכָל־קֹרְאֶיךָ:

On Mondays and Thursdays continue with וְהוּא רַחוּם
on page 201; on other days with וַיֹּאמֶר דָּוִד on page 209.

EIN KELOHEINU

In Israel the following through "Bless the LORD," on page 690, is said:

אֵין כֵּאלֹהֵֽינוּ There is none like our God, none like our LORD, none like our King, none like our Savior. Who is like our God? Like our LORD? Like our King? Like our Savior? We will thank our God, thank our LORD, thank our King, thank our Savior. Blessed is our God, blessed our LORD, blessed our King, blessed our Savior. You are our God, You are our LORD, You are our King, You are our Savior. You are He to whom our ancestors offered the fragrant incense.

פִּטּוּם הַקְּטֹֽרֶת The incense mixture consisted of balsam, onycha, galbanum and *Keritot 6a* frankincense, each weighing seventy manehs; myrrh, cassia, spikenard and saffron, each weighing sixteen manehs; twelve manehs of costus, three of aromatic bark; nine of cinnamon; nine kabs of Carsina lye; three seahs and three kabs of Cyprus wine. If Cyprus wine was not available, old white wine might be used. A quarter of a kab of Sodom salt, and a minute amount of a smoke-raising herb. Rabbi Nathan says: Also a minute amount of Jordan amber. If one added honey to the mixture, he rendered it unfit for sacred use. If he omitted any one of its ingredients, he is guilty of a capital offense.

Rabban Shimon ben Gamliel says: "Balsam" refers to the sap that drips from the balsam tree. The Carsina lye was used for bleaching the onycha to improve it. The Cyprus wine was used to soak the onycha in it to make it pungent. Though urine is suitable for this purpose, it is not brought into the Temple out of respect.

It was taught in the Academy of Elijah: Whoever studies [Torah] laws every day *Megilla 28b* is assured that he will be destined for the World to Come, as it is said, "The ways *Hab. 3* of the world are His" – read not, "ways" [*halikhot*] but "laws" [*halakhot*].

Rabbi Elazar said in the name of Rabbi Ḥanina: The disciples of the sages increase *Berakhot 64a* peace in the world, as it is said, "And all your children shall be taught of the LORD, *Is. 54* and great shall be the peace of your children [*banayikh*]." Read not *banayikh*, "your children," but *bonayikh*, "your builders." Those who love Your Torah have *Ps. 119* great peace; there is no stumbling block for them. May there be peace within your ramparts, prosperity in your palaces. For the sake of my brothers and friends, I *Ps. 122* shall say, "Peace be within you." For the sake of the House of the LORD our God, I will seek your good. ▸ May the LORD grant strength to His people; may the *Ps. 29* LORD bless His people with peace.

אין כאלהינו

In ארץ ישראל *the following through* בָּרְכוּ*, on the next page, is said:*

אֵין כֵּאלֹהֵֽינוּ, אֵין כַּאדוֹנֵֽינוּ, אֵין כְּמַלְכֵּֽנוּ, אֵין כְּמוֹשִׁיעֵֽנוּ. מִי כֵאלֹהֵֽינוּ, מִי כַאדוֹנֵֽינוּ, מִי כְמַלְכֵּֽנוּ, מִי כְמוֹשִׁיעֵֽנוּ. נוֹדֶה לֵאלֹהֵֽינוּ, נוֹדֶה לַאדוֹנֵֽינוּ, נוֹדֶה לְמַלְכֵּֽנוּ, נוֹדֶה לְמוֹשִׁיעֵֽנוּ. בָּרוּךְ אֱלֹהֵֽינוּ, בָּרוּךְ אֲדוֹנֵֽינוּ, בָּרוּךְ מַלְכֵּֽנוּ, בָּרוּךְ מוֹשִׁיעֵֽנוּ. אַתָּה הוּא אֱלֹהֵֽינוּ, אַתָּה הוּא אֲדוֹנֵֽינוּ, אַתָּה הוּא מַלְכֵּֽנוּ, אַתָּה הוּא מוֹשִׁיעֵֽנוּ. אַתָּה הוּא שֶׁהִקְטִֽירוּ אֲבוֹתֵֽינוּ לְפָנֶֽיךָ אֶת קְטֹֽרֶת הַסַּמִּים.

פִּטּוּם הַקְּטֹֽרֶת: הַצֳּרִי, וְהַצִּפֹּֽרֶן, וְהַחֶלְבְּנָה, וְהַלְּבוֹנָה מִשְׁקַל שִׁבְעִים שִׁבְעִים מָנֶה, מֹר, וּקְצִיעָה, שִׁבֹּֽלֶת נֵרְדְּ, וְכַרְכֹּם מִשְׁקַל שִׁשָּׁה עָשָׂר שִׁשָּׁה עָשָׂר מָנֶה, הַקֹּשְׁטְ שְׁנֵים עָשָׂר, קִלּוּפָה שְׁלֹשָׁה, וְקִנָּמוֹן תִּשְׁעָה, בֹּרִית כַּרְשִׁינָה תִּשְׁעָה קַבִּין, יֵין קַפְרִיסִין סְאִין תְּלָת וְקַבִּין תְּלָתָא, וְאִם אֵין לוֹ יֵין קַפְרִיסִין, מֵבִיא חֲמַר חִוַּרְיָן עַתִּיק. מֶֽלַח סְדוֹמִית רֹֽבַע, מַעֲלֶה עָשָׁן כָּל שֶׁהוּא. רַבִּי נָתָן הַבַּבְלִי אוֹמֵר: אַף כִּפַּת הַיַּרְדֵּן כָּל שֶׁהוּא, וְאִם נָתַן בָּהּ דְּבַשׁ פְּסָלָהּ, וְאִם חִסַּר אֶחָד מִכָּל סַמָּנֶֽיהָ, חַיָּב מִיתָה. כריתות ו.

רַבָּן שִׁמְעוֹן בֶּן גַּמְלִיאֵל אוֹמֵר: הַצֳּרִי אֵינוֹ אֶלָּא שְׂרָף הַנּוֹטֵף מֵעֲצֵי הַקְּטָף. בֹּרִית כַּרְשִׁינָה שֶׁשָּׁפִין בָּהּ אֶת הַצִּפֹּֽרֶן כְּדֵי שֶׁתְּהֵא נָאָה, יֵין קַפְרִיסִין שֶׁשּׁוֹרִין בּוֹ אֶת הַצִּפֹּֽרֶן כְּדֵי שֶׁתְּהֵא עַזָּה, וַהֲלֹא מֵי רַגְלַֽיִם יָפִין לָהּ, אֶלָּא שֶׁאֵין מַכְנִיסִין מֵי רַגְלַֽיִם בַּמִּקְדָּשׁ מִפְּנֵי הַכָּבוֹד.

תָּנָא דְבֵי אֵלִיָּֽהוּ: כָּל הַשּׁוֹנֶה הֲלָכוֹת בְּכָל יוֹם, מֻבְטָח לוֹ שֶׁהוּא בֶּן עוֹלָם הַבָּא, מגילה כח:
שֶׁנֶּאֱמַר הֲלִיכוֹת עוֹלָם לוֹ: אַל תִּקְרֵי הֲלִיכוֹת אֶלָּא הֲלָכוֹת. חבקוק ג

אָמַר רַבִּי אֶלְעָזָר, אָמַר רַבִּי חֲנִינָא: תַּלְמִידֵי חֲכָמִים מַרְבִּים שָׁלוֹם בָּעוֹלָם, שֶׁנֶּאֱמַר ברכות סד.
וְכָל־בָּנַֽיִךְ לִמּוּדֵי יהוה, וְרַב שְׁלוֹם בָּנָֽיִךְ: אַל תִּקְרֵי בָּנָֽיִךְ, אֶלָּא בּוֹנָֽיִךְ. שָׁלוֹם רָב ישעיה נד / תהלים קיט
לְאֹהֲבֵי תוֹרָתֶֽךָ, וְאֵין־לָֽמוֹ מִכְשׁוֹל: יְהִי־שָׁלוֹם בְּחֵילֵךְ, שַׁלְוָה בְּאַרְמְנוֹתָֽיִךְ: לְמַֽעַן תהלים קכב
אַחַי וְרֵעָי אֲדַבְּרָה־נָּא שָׁלוֹם בָּךְ: לְמַֽעַן בֵּית־יהוה אֱלֹהֵֽינוּ אֲבַקְשָׁה טוֹב לָךְ:
◂ יהוה עֹז לְעַמּוֹ יִתֵּן, יהוה יְבָרֵךְ אֶת־עַמּוֹ בַשָּׁלוֹם: תהלים כט

THE RABBIS' KADDISH

The following prayer, said by mourners, requires the presence of a minyan.
A transliteration can be found on page 920.

Mourner: יִתְגַּדַּל Magnified and sanctified
may His great name be, in the world He created by His will.
May He establish His kingdom in your lifetime
and in your days, and in the lifetime of all the house of Israel,
swiftly and soon – and say: Amen.

All: May His great name be blessed for ever and all time.

Mourner: Blessed and praised, glorified and exalted,
raised and honored, uplifted and lauded be
the name of the Holy One, blessed be He,
beyond any blessing,
song, praise and consolation
uttered in the world – and say: Amen.

To Israel, to the teachers,
their disciples and their disciples' disciples,
and to all who engage in the study of Torah,
in this (*in Israel add:* holy) place or elsewhere,
may there come to them and you great peace,
grace, kindness and compassion, long life, ample sustenance
and deliverance, from their Father in Heaven – and say: Amen.

May there be great peace from heaven,
and (good) life for us and all Israel – and say: Amen.

Bow, take three steps back, as if taking leave of the Divine Presence,
then bow, first left, then right, then center, while saying:
May He who makes peace in His high places,
in His compassion make peace for us and all Israel –
and say: Amen.

In Israel, on days when the Torah is not read, the person saying Kaddish adds:
Bless the LORD, the blessed One.

and the congregation responds:
Bless the LORD, the blessed One, for ever and all time.

In Israel during Elul, some congregations blow shofar and say Psalm 27
(page 270) at this point. In a house of mourning the service continues on page 272.

קדיש דרבנן

The following prayer, said by mourners, requires the presence of a מִנְיָן.
A transliteration can be found on page 920.

אבל: יִתְגַּדַּל וְיִתְקַדַּשׁ שְׁמֵהּ רַבָּא (קהל: אָמֵן)
בְּעָלְמָא דִּי בְרָא כִרְעוּתֵהּ
וְיַמְלִיךְ מַלְכוּתֵהּ
בְּחַיֵּיכוֹן וּבְיוֹמֵיכוֹן וּבְחַיֵּי דְכָל בֵּית יִשְׂרָאֵל
בַּעֲגָלָא וּבִזְמַן קָרִיב, וְאִמְרוּ אָמֵן. (קהל: אָמֵן)

קהל
ואבל: יְהֵא שְׁמֵהּ רַבָּא מְבָרַךְ לְעָלַם וּלְעָלְמֵי עָלְמַיָּא.

אבל: יִתְבָּרַךְ וְיִשְׁתַּבַּח וְיִתְפָּאַר וְיִתְרוֹמַם וְיִתְנַשֵּׂא
וְיִתְהַדָּר וְיִתְעַלֶּה וְיִתְהַלָּל, שְׁמֵהּ דְּקֻדְשָׁא בְּרִיךְ הוּא (קהל: בְּרִיךְ הוּא)
לְעֵלָּא מִן כָּל בִּרְכָתָא / בעשרת ימי תשובה: לְעֵלָּא לְעֵלָּא מִכָּל בִּרְכָתָא /
וְשִׁירָתָא, תֻּשְׁבְּחָתָא וְנֶחֱמָתָא, דַּאֲמִירָן בְּעָלְמָא, וְאִמְרוּ אָמֵן. (קהל: אָמֵן)

עַל יִשְׂרָאֵל וְעַל רַבָּנָן, וְעַל תַּלְמִידֵיהוֹן וְעַל כָּל תַּלְמִידֵי תַלְמִידֵיהוֹן
וְעַל כָּל מָאן דְּעָסְקִין בְּאוֹרַיְתָא
דִּי בְאַתְרָא (בארץ ישראל: קַדִּישָׁא) הָדֵין וְדִי בְּכָל אֲתַר וַאֲתַר
יְהֵא לְהוֹן וּלְכוֹן שְׁלָמָא רַבָּא, חִנָּא וְחִסְדָּא, וְרַחֲמֵי, וְחַיֵּי אֲרִיכֵי, וּמְזוֹנֵי רְוִיחֵי
וּפֻרְקָנָא מִן קֳדָם אֲבוּהוֹן דִּי בִשְׁמַיָּא, וְאִמְרוּ אָמֵן. (קהל: אָמֵן)

יְהֵא שְׁלָמָא רַבָּא מִן שְׁמַיָּא
וְחַיִּים (טוֹבִים) עָלֵינוּ וְעַל כָּל יִשְׂרָאֵל, וְאִמְרוּ אָמֵן. (קהל: אָמֵן)

Bow, take three steps back, as if taking leave of the Divine Presence,
then bow, first left, then right, then center, while saying:

עֹשֶׂה שָׁלוֹם/ בעשרת ימי תשובה: הַשָּׁלוֹם/ בִּמְרוֹמָיו
הוּא יַעֲשֶׂה בְרַחֲמָיו שָׁלוֹם, עָלֵינוּ וְעַל כָּל יִשְׂרָאֵל, וְאִמְרוּ אָמֵן. (קהל: אָמֵן)

In ארץ ישראל, on days when the תורה is not read, the person saying קדיש adds:

בָּרְכוּ אֶת יהוה הַמְבֹרָךְ.

and the קהל responds:

בָּרוּךְ יהוה הַמְבֹרָךְ לְעוֹלָם וָעֶד.

In ארץ ישראל during אלול, some congregations blow שופר and say לְדָוִד, יהוה אוֹרִי
(page 271) at this point. In a house of mourning the service continues on page 273.

THE TRAVELER'S PRAYER

If one intends to return home on the same day, add the words in parentheses:

יְהִי רָצוֹן May it be Your will,
Lord our God and God of our fathers,
to lead us to peace, direct our steps to peace,
guide us to peace, and bring us to our desired destination in life,
joy and peace
(and bring us back to our home in peace).
Rescue us from any enemy or ambush on the way,
and from all afflictions that trouble the world.
Send blessing to the work of our hands,
and let us find grace, kindness and compassion
from You and from all who see us.
Hear our pleas,
for You are a God who hears prayer and pleas.
Blessed are You, Lord, who listens to prayer.

May the Lord guard your going out and your return,   *Ps. 121*
from now and for all time.

Repeat three times:

וַיַּעֲקֹב And Jacob went on his way   *Gen. 32*
and angels of God met him.
When he saw them, Jacob said, "This is God's camp"
and he named the place Maḥanaim [two camps].

Repeat three times:

יְבָרֶכְךָ May the Lord bless you and protect you.   *Num. 6*
May the Lord make His face shine on you and be gracious to you.
May the Lord turn His face toward you and grant you peace.

שִׁיר לַמַּעֲלוֹת A song of ascents. I lift my eyes up to the hills; from where will   *Ps. 121*
my help come? My help comes from the Lord, Maker of heaven and earth.
He will not let your foot stumble; He who guards you does not slumber.
See: the Guardian of Israel neither slumbers nor sleeps. The Lord is your
Guardian; the Lord is your Shade at your right hand. The sun will not strike
you by day, nor the moon by night. The Lord will guard you from all harm;
He will guard your life. The Lord will guard your going and coming, now
and for evermore.

תְּפִלַּת הַדֶּרֶךְ

If one intends to return home on the same day, add the words in parentheses:

יְהִי רָצוֹן מִלְּפָנֶיךָ, יהוה אֱלֹהֵינוּ וֵאלֹהֵי אֲבוֹתֵינוּ
שֶׁתּוֹלִיכֵנוּ לְשָׁלוֹם, וְתַצְעִידֵנוּ לְשָׁלוֹם, וְתַדְרִיכֵנוּ לְשָׁלוֹם
וְתַגִּיעֵנוּ לִמְחוֹז חֶפְצֵנוּ לְחַיִּים וּלְשִׂמְחָה וּלְשָׁלוֹם
(וְתַחֲזִירֵנוּ לְבֵיתֵנוּ לְשָׁלוֹם)
וְתַצִּילֵנוּ מִכַּף כָּל אוֹיֵב וְאוֹרֵב בַּדֶּרֶךְ
וּמִכָּל מִינֵי פֻּרְעָנִיּוֹת הַמִּתְרַגְּשׁוֹת לָבוֹא לָעוֹלָם
וְתִשְׁלַח בְּרָכָה בְּמַעֲשֵׂה יָדֵינוּ
וְתִתְּנֵנוּ לְחֵן וּלְחֶסֶד וּלְרַחֲמִים בְּעֵינֶיךָ וּבְעֵינֵי כָל רוֹאֵינוּ
וְתִשְׁמַע קוֹל תַּחֲנוּנֵינוּ
כִּי אֵל שׁוֹמֵעַ תְּפִלָּה וְתַחֲנוּן אָתָּה.
בָּרוּךְ אַתָּה יהוה, שׁוֹמֵעַ תְּפִלָּה.

תהלים קכא יהוה יִשְׁמָר־צֵאתְךָ וּבוֹאֶךָ, מֵעַתָּה וְעַד־עוֹלָם:

Repeat three times:

בראשית לב וְיַעֲקֹב הָלַךְ לְדַרְכּוֹ, וַיִּפְגְּעוּ־בוֹ מַלְאֲכֵי אֱלֹהִים:
וַיֹּאמֶר יַעֲקֹב כַּאֲשֶׁר רָאָם, מַחֲנֵה אֱלֹהִים זֶה
וַיִּקְרָא שֵׁם־הַמָּקוֹם הַהוּא מַחֲנָיִם:

Repeat three times:

במדבר ו יְבָרֶכְךָ יהוה וְיִשְׁמְרֶךָ:
יָאֵר יהוה פָּנָיו אֵלֶיךָ וִיחֻנֶּךָּ:
יִשָּׂא יהוה פָּנָיו אֵלֶיךָ וְיָשֵׂם לְךָ שָׁלוֹם:

תהלים קכא שִׁיר לַמַּעֲלוֹת, אֶשָּׂא עֵינַי אֶל־הֶהָרִים, מֵאַיִן יָבֹא עֶזְרִי: עֶזְרִי מֵעִם יהוה,
עֹשֵׂה שָׁמַיִם וָאָרֶץ: אַל־יִתֵּן לַמּוֹט רַגְלֶךָ, אַל־יָנוּם שֹׁמְרֶךָ: הִנֵּה לֹא־יָנוּם
וְלֹא יִישָׁן, שׁוֹמֵר יִשְׂרָאֵל: יהוה שֹׁמְרֶךָ, יהוה צִלְּךָ עַל־יַד יְמִינֶךָ: יוֹמָם
הַשֶּׁמֶשׁ לֹא־יַכֶּכָּה, וְיָרֵחַ בַּלָּיְלָה: יהוה יִשְׁמָרְךָ מִכָּל־רָע, יִשְׁמֹר אֶת־נַפְשֶׁךָ:
יהוה יִשְׁמָר־צֵאתְךָ וּבוֹאֶךָ, מֵעַתָּה וְעַד־עוֹלָם:

קריאת התורה
TORAH READINGS

קריאת התורה לימי שני וחמישי

THE READING OF THE TORAH
FOR MONDAYS, THURSDAYS

BERESHIT   בראשית

בראשית א
א-ה

בְּרֵאשִׁ֖ית בָּרָ֣א אֱלֹהִ֑ים אֵ֥ת הַשָּׁמַ֖יִם וְאֵ֥ת הָאָֽרֶץ: וְהָאָ֗רֶץ הָיְתָ֥ה תֹ֙הוּ֙ וָבֹ֔הוּ וְחֹ֖שֶׁךְ עַל־פְּנֵ֣י תְה֑וֹם וְר֣וּחַ אֱלֹהִ֔ים מְרַחֶ֖פֶת עַל־פְּנֵ֥י הַמָּֽיִם: וַיֹּ֥אמֶר אֱלֹהִ֖ים יְהִ֣י א֑וֹר וַֽיְהִי־אֽוֹר: וַיַּ֧רְא אֱלֹהִ֛ים אֶת־הָא֖וֹר כִּי־ט֑וֹב וַיַּבְדֵּ֣ל אֱלֹהִ֔ים בֵּ֥ין הָא֖וֹר וּבֵ֥ין הַחֹֽשֶׁךְ: וַיִּקְרָ֨א אֱלֹהִ֤ים ׀ לָאוֹר֙ י֔וֹם וְלַחֹ֖שֶׁךְ קָ֣רָא לָ֑יְלָה וַֽיְהִי־עֶ֥רֶב וַֽיְהִי־בֹ֖קֶר י֥וֹם אֶחָֽד:

FIRST ALIYA: vv. 1–5
Based on this, some mistakenly thought there was more than one God. How do you think they came to that conclusion?

לוי   וַיֹּ֣אמֶר אֱלֹהִ֔ים יְהִ֥י רָקִ֖יעַ בְּת֣וֹךְ הַמָּ֑יִם וִיהִ֣י מַבְדִּ֔יל בֵּ֥ין מַ֖יִם לָמָֽיִם: וַיַּ֣עַשׂ אֱלֹהִים֮ אֶת־הָרָקִיעַ֒ וַיַּבְדֵּ֗ל בֵּ֤ין הַמַּ֙יִם֙ אֲשֶׁר֙ מִתַּ֣חַת לָרָקִ֔יעַ וּבֵ֣ין הַמַּ֔יִם אֲשֶׁ֖ר מֵעַ֣ל לָרָקִ֑יעַ וַֽיְהִי־כֵֽן: וַיִּקְרָ֧א אֱלֹהִ֛ים לָֽרָקִ֖יעַ שָׁמָ֑יִם וַֽיְהִי־עֶ֥רֶב וַֽיְהִי־בֹ֖קֶר י֥וֹם שֵׁנִֽי:

SECOND ALIYA: vv. 6–8
Find a word whose letters can be rearranged to spell the name of a Middle Eastern country situated on Nehar Perat.

ישראל   וַיֹּ֣אמֶר אֱלֹהִ֗ים יִקָּו֨וּ הַמַּ֜יִם מִתַּ֤חַת הַשָּׁמַ֙יִם֙ אֶל־מָק֣וֹם אֶחָ֔ד וְתֵרָאֶ֖ה הַיַּבָּשָׁ֑ה וַֽיְהִי־כֵֽן: וַיִּקְרָ֨א אֱלֹהִ֤ים ׀ לַיַּבָּשָׁה֙ אֶ֔רֶץ וּלְמִקְוֵ֥ה הַמַּ֖יִם קָרָ֣א יַמִּ֑ים וַיַּ֥רְא אֱלֹהִ֖ים כִּי־טֽוֹב: וַיֹּ֣אמֶר אֱלֹהִ֗ים תַּֽדְשֵׁ֤א הָאָ֙רֶץ֙ דֶּ֗שֶׁא עֵ֚שֶׂב מַזְרִ֣יעַ זֶ֔רַע עֵ֣ץ פְּרִ֞י עֹ֤שֶׂה פְּרִי֙ לְמִינ֔וֹ אֲשֶׁ֥ר זַרְעוֹ־ב֖וֹ עַל־הָאָ֑רֶץ וַֽיְהִי־כֵֽן: וַתּוֹצֵ֨א הָאָ֜רֶץ דֶּ֠שֶׁא עֵ֣שֶׂב מַזְרִ֤יעַ זֶ֙רַע֙ לְמִינֵ֔הוּ וְעֵ֧ץ עֹֽשֶׂה־פְּרִ֛י אֲשֶׁ֥ר זַרְעוֹ־ב֖וֹ לְמִינֵ֑הוּ וַיַּ֥רְא אֱלֹהִ֖ים כִּי־טֽוֹב: וַֽיְהִי־עֶ֥רֶב וַֽיְהִי־בֹ֖קֶר י֥וֹם שְׁלִישִֽׁי:

THIRD ALIYA: vv. 9–13
This day got something good that the previous day did not. What was it? As a result, it is a day that was common for people to get married on.

Some extend the ישראל *portion on the Thursday reading:*

וַיֹּ֣אמֶר אֱלֹהִ֗ים יְהִ֤י מְאֹרֹת֙ בִּרְקִ֣יעַ הַשָּׁמַ֔יִם לְהַבְדִּ֕יל בֵּ֥ין הַיּ֖וֹם וּבֵ֣ין הַלָּ֑יְלָה וְהָי֤וּ לְאֹתֹת֙ וּלְמ֣וֹעֲדִ֔ים וּלְיָמִ֖ים וְשָׁנִֽים:

וְהָיוּ לִמְאוֹרֹת בִּרְקִיעַ הַשָּׁמַיִם לְהָאִיר עַל־הָאָרֶץ וַיְהִי־כֵן: וַיַּעַשׂ אֱלֹהִים אֶת־שְׁנֵי הַמְּאֹרֹת הַגְּדֹלִים אֶת־הַמָּאוֹר הַגָּדֹל לְמֶמְשֶׁלֶת הַיּוֹם וְאֶת־הַמָּאוֹר הַקָּטֹן לְמֶמְשֶׁלֶת הַלַּיְלָה וְאֵת הַכּוֹכָבִים: וַיִּתֵּן אֹתָם אֱלֹהִים בִּרְקִיעַ הַשָּׁמָיִם לְהָאִיר עַל־הָאָרֶץ: וְלִמְשֹׁל בַּיּוֹם וּבַלַּיְלָה וּלֲהַבְדִּיל בֵּין הָאוֹר וּבֵין הַחֹשֶׁךְ וַיַּרְא אֱלֹהִים כִּי־טוֹב: וַיְהִי־עֶרֶב וַיְהִי־בֹקֶר יוֹם רְבִיעִי:

וַיֹּאמֶר אֱלֹהִים יִשְׁרְצוּ הַמַּיִם שֶׁרֶץ נֶפֶשׁ חַיָּה וְעוֹף יְעוֹפֵף עַל־הָאָרֶץ עַל־פְּנֵי רְקִיעַ הַשָּׁמָיִם: וַיִּבְרָא אֱלֹהִים אֶת־הַתַּנִּינִם הַגְּדֹלִים וְאֵת כָּל־נֶפֶשׁ הַחַיָּה ׀ הָרֹמֶשֶׂת אֲשֶׁר שָׁרְצוּ הַמַּיִם לְמִינֵהֶם וְאֵת כָּל־עוֹף כָּנָף לְמִינֵהוּ וַיַּרְא אֱלֹהִים כִּי־טוֹב: וַיְבָרֶךְ אֹתָם אֱלֹהִים לֵאמֹר פְּרוּ וּרְבוּ וּמִלְאוּ אֶת־הַמַּיִם בַּיַּמִּים וְהָעוֹף יִרֶב בָּאָרֶץ: וַיְהִי־עֶרֶב וַיְהִי־בֹקֶר יוֹם חֲמִישִׁי:

נח

NOAH

בראשית:
ט–כב

אֵלֶּה תּוֹלְדֹת נֹחַ נֹחַ אִישׁ צַדִּיק תָּמִים הָיָה בְּדֹרֹתָיו אֶת־הָאֱלֹהִים הִתְהַלֶּךְ־נֹחַ: וַיּוֹלֶד נֹחַ שְׁלֹשָׁה בָנִים אֶת־שֵׁם אֶת־חָם וְאֶת־יָפֶת: וַתִּשָּׁחֵת הָאָרֶץ לִפְנֵי הָאֱלֹהִים וַתִּמָּלֵא הָאָרֶץ חָמָס: וַיַּרְא אֱלֹהִים אֶת־הָאָרֶץ וְהִנֵּה נִשְׁחָתָה כִּי־הִשְׁחִית כָּל־בָּשָׂר אֶת־דַּרְכּוֹ עַל־הָאָרֶץ: וַיֹּאמֶר אֱלֹהִים לְנֹחַ קֵץ כָּל־בָּשָׂר בָּא לְפָנַי כִּי־מָלְאָה הָאָרֶץ חָמָס מִפְּנֵיהֶם וְהִנְנִי מַשְׁחִיתָם אֶת־הָאָרֶץ: עֲשֵׂה לְךָ תֵּבַת עֲצֵי־גֹפֶר קִנִּים תַּעֲשֶׂה אֶת־הַתֵּבָה וְכָפַרְתָּ אֹתָהּ מִבַּיִת וּמִחוּץ בַּכֹּפֶר: וְזֶה אֲשֶׁר תַּעֲשֶׂה אֹתָהּ שְׁלֹשׁ מֵאוֹת אַמָּה אֹרֶךְ הַתֵּבָה חֲמִשִּׁים אַמָּה רָחְבָּהּ וּשְׁלֹשִׁים אַמָּה קוֹמָתָהּ: צֹהַר ׀ תַּעֲשֶׂה לַתֵּבָה וְאֶל־אַמָּה תְּכַלֶּנָּה מִלְמַעְלָה וּפֶתַח הַתֵּבָה בְּצִדָּהּ תָּשִׂים תַּחְתִּיִּם שְׁנִיִּם וּשְׁלִשִׁים תַּעֲשֶׂהָ: וַאֲנִי הִנְנִי מֵבִיא אֶת־הַמַּבּוּל מַיִם עַל־הָאָרֶץ לְשַׁחֵת כָּל־בָּשָׂר אֲשֶׁר־בּוֹ רוּחַ חַיִּים מִתַּחַת

לוי

FIRST ALIYA: vv. 9–16
The one crime for which the generation of the flood was destroyed. Why do you think this sin was deemed more significant than any other, such that the world needed to be destroyed?

SECOND ALIYA:
vv. 17–19
Based on what clue in the text does Rashi

הַשָּׁמָיִם כֹּל אֲשֶׁר־בָּאָרֶץ יִגְוָע: וַהֲקִמֹתִי אֶת־בְּרִיתִי אִתָּךְ
וּבָאתָ אֶל־הַתֵּבָה אַתָּה וּבָנֶיךָ וְאִשְׁתְּךָ וּנְשֵׁי־בָנֶיךָ אִתָּךְ:
וּמִכָּל־הָחַי מִכָּל־בָּשָׂר שְׁנַיִם מִכֹּל תָּבִיא אֶל־הַתֵּבָה לְהַחֲיֹת
ישראל
אִתָּךְ זָכָר וּנְקֵבָה יִהְיוּ: מֵהָעוֹף לְמִינֵהוּ וּמִן־הַבְּהֵמָה לְמִינָהּ
מִכֹּל רֶמֶשׂ הָאֲדָמָה לְמִינֵהוּ שְׁנַיִם מִכֹּל יָבֹאוּ אֵלֶיךָ לְהַחֲיוֹת:
וְאַתָּה קַח־לְךָ מִכָּל־מַאֲכָל אֲשֶׁר יֵאָכֵל וְאָסַפְתָּ אֵלֶיךָ וְהָיָה
לְךָ וְלָהֶם לְאָכְלָה: וַיַּעַשׂ נֹחַ כְּכֹל אֲשֶׁר צִוָּה אֹתוֹ אֱלֹהִים
כֵּן עָשָׂה:

LEKH LEKHA

לך לך

בראשית יב
א–ג
וַיֹּאמֶר יְהוה אֶל־אַבְרָם לֶךְ־לְךָ מֵאַרְצְךָ וּמִמּוֹלַדְתְּךָ וּמִבֵּית
אָבִיךָ אֶל־הָאָרֶץ אֲשֶׁר אַרְאֶךָּ: וְאֶעֶשְׂךָ לְגוֹי גָּדוֹל וַאֲבָרֶכְךָ
וַאֲגַדְּלָה שְׁמֶךָ וֶהְיֵה בְּרָכָה: וַאֲבָרְכָה מְבָרְכֶיךָ וּמְקַלֶּלְךָ אָאֹר
וְנִבְרְכוּ בְךָ כֹּל מִשְׁפְּחֹת הָאֲדָמָה: וַיֵּלֶךְ אַבְרָם כַּאֲשֶׁר דִּבֶּר
לוי
אֵלָיו יְהוה וַיֵּלֶךְ אִתּוֹ לוֹט וְאַבְרָם בֶּן־חָמֵשׁ שָׁנִים וְשִׁבְעִים
שָׁנָה בְּצֵאתוֹ מֵחָרָן: וַיִּקַּח אַבְרָם אֶת־שָׂרַי אִשְׁתּוֹ וְאֶת־
לוֹט בֶּן־אָחִיו וְאֶת־כָּל־רְכוּשָׁם אֲשֶׁר רָכָשׁוּ וְאֶת־הַנֶּפֶשׁ
אֲשֶׁר־עָשׂוּ בְחָרָן וַיֵּצְאוּ לָלֶכֶת אַרְצָה כְּנַעַן וַיָּבֹאוּ אַרְצָה
כְּנָעַן: וַיַּעֲבֹר אַבְרָם בָּאָרֶץ עַד מְקוֹם שְׁכֶם עַד אֵלוֹן מוֹרֶה
וְהַכְּנַעֲנִי אָז בָּאָרֶץ: וַיֵּרָא יְהוה אֶל־אַבְרָם וַיֹּאמֶר לְזַרְעֲךָ
אֶתֵּן אֶת־הָאָרֶץ הַזֹּאת וַיִּבֶן שָׁם מִזְבֵּחַ לַיהוה הַנִּרְאֶה אֵלָיו:
וַיַּעְתֵּק מִשָּׁם הָהָרָה מִקֶּדֶם לְבֵית־אֵל וַיֵּט אָהֳלֹה בֵּית־אֵל
מִיָּם וְהָעַי מִקֶּדֶם וַיִּבֶן־שָׁם מִזְבֵּחַ לַיהוה וַיִּקְרָא בְּשֵׁם יְהוה:
וַיִּסַּע אַבְרָם הָלוֹךְ וְנָסוֹעַ הַנֶּגְבָּה:

ישראל
וַיְהִי רָעָב בָּאָרֶץ וַיֵּרֶד אַבְרָם מִצְרַיְמָה לָגוּר שָׁם כִּי־כָבֵד
הָרָעָב בָּאָרֶץ: וַיְהִי כַּאֲשֶׁר הִקְרִיב לָבוֹא מִצְרָיְמָה וַיֹּאמֶר
אֶל־שָׂרַי אִשְׁתּוֹ הִנֵּה־נָא יָדַעְתִּי כִּי אִשָּׁה יְפַת־מַרְאֶה אָתְּ:
וְהָיָה כִּי־יִרְאוּ אֹתָךְ הַמִּצְרִים וְאָמְרוּ אִשְׁתּוֹ זֹאת וְהָרְגוּ אֹתִי
וְאֹתָךְ יְחַיּוּ: אִמְרִי־נָא אֲחֹתִי אָתְּ לְמַעַן יִיטַב־לִי בַעֲבוּרֵךְ
וְחָיְתָה נַפְשִׁי בִּגְלָלֵךְ:

conclude that the men and women slept separately on the ark? Why do you think this arrangement was deemed necessary?

THIRD ALIYA: vv. 20–22
How do you know that Noah didn't have to go hunting the animals to find them?

FIRST ALIYA: vv. 1–3
The word אור appears five times at the very beginning of *Bereshit*, [indicating the beginning of a new world from darkness.] Someone once suggested that it parallels a word that appears in this *aliya* five times in different forms. What's the word? What's the connection?

SECOND ALIYA: vv. 4–9
From here one learns that Avram and Sarai converted a lot of people to monotheism. What do you think prompted them to do so?

THIRD ALIYA: vv. 10–13
According to Ramban, Avram committed a sin by doing this. Why do you think it was a sin?

VAYERA ‏וירא‏

FIRST ALIYA: vv. 1–5
From here one learns that
receiving guests is even
more important than
speaking to God. What is
the underlying value being
taught here?

SECOND ALIYA: vv. 6–8
There are three people
who moved quickly,
but one of them moved
more quickly than the
others. Prove it. What
lesson can one
learn from here?

‏לוי‏

THIRD ALIYA: vv. 9–14
God "lies" in these verses.
Where and why and what
are the implications for the
rest of us?

‏ישראל‏

‏וַיֵּרָ֤א אֵלָיו֙ יְהֹוָ֔ה בְּאֵלֹנֵ֖י מַמְרֵ֑א וְה֛וּא יֹשֵׁ֥ב פֶּֽתַח־הָאֹ֖הֶל‏
‏כְּחֹ֣ם הַיּֽוֹם: וַיִּשָּׂ֤א עֵינָיו֙ וַיַּ֔רְא וְהִנֵּה֙ שְׁלֹשָׁ֣ה אֲנָשִׁ֔ים נִצָּבִ֖ים‏
‏עָלָ֑יו וַיַּ֗רְא וַיָּ֤רׇץ לִקְרָאתָם֙ מִפֶּ֣תַח הָאֹ֔הֶל וַיִּשְׁתַּ֖חוּ אָֽרְצָה:‏
‏וַיֹּאמַ֑ר אֲדֹנָ֗י אִם־נָ֨א מָצָ֤אתִי חֵן֙ בְּעֵינֶ֔יךָ אַל־נָ֥א תַעֲבֹ֖ר מֵעַ֥ל‏
‏עַבְדֶּֽךָ: יֻקַּֽח־נָ֤א מְעַט־מַ֙יִם֙ וְרַחֲצ֖וּ רַגְלֵיכֶ֑ם וְהִֽשָּׁעֲנ֖וּ תַּ֥חַת‏
‏הָעֵֽץ: וְאֶקְחָ֨ה פַת־לֶ֜חֶם וְסַעֲד֤וּ לִבְּכֶם֙ אַחַ֣ר תַּעֲבֹ֔רוּ כִּֽי־עַל־‏
‏כֵּ֥ן עֲבַרְתֶּ֖ם עַֽל־עַבְדְּכֶ֑ם וַיֹּ֣אמְר֔וּ כֵּ֥ן תַּעֲשֶׂ֖ה כַּאֲשֶׁ֥ר דִּבַּֽרְתָּ:‏
‏*וַיְמַהֵ֧ר אַבְרָהָ֛ם הָאֹ֖הֱלָה אֶל־שָׂרָ֑ה וַיֹּ֗אמֶר מַהֲרִ֞י שְׁלֹ֤שׁ‏
‏סְאִים֙ קֶ֣מַח סֹ֔לֶת ל֖וּשִׁי וַעֲשִׂ֥י עֻגֽוֹת: וְאֶל־הַבָּקָ֖ר רָ֣ץ אַבְרָהָ֑ם‏
‏וַיִּקַּ֨ח בֶּן־בָּקָ֜ר רַ֤ךְ וָטוֹב֙ וַיִּתֵּ֣ן אֶל־הַנַּ֔עַר וַיְמַהֵ֖ר לַעֲשׂ֥וֹת אֹתֽוֹ:‏
‏וַיִּקַּ֨ח חֶמְאָ֜ה וְחָלָ֗ב וּבֶן־הַבָּקָר֙ אֲשֶׁ֣ר עָשָׂ֔ה וַיִּתֵּ֖ן לִפְנֵיהֶ֑ם‏
‏וְהֽוּא־עֹמֵ֧ד עֲלֵיהֶ֛ם תַּ֥חַת הָעֵ֖ץ וַיֹּאכֵֽלוּ: *וַיֹּאמְר֣וּ אֵלָ֔יו אַיֵּ֖ה‏
‏שָׂרָ֣ה אִשְׁתֶּ֑ךָ וַיֹּ֖אמֶר הִנֵּ֥ה בָאֹֽהֶל: וַיֹּ֗אמֶר שׁ֣וֹב אָשׁ֤וּב אֵלֶ֙יךָ֙‏
‏כָּעֵ֣ת חַיָּ֔ה וְהִנֵּה־בֵ֖ן לְשָׂרָ֣ה אִשְׁתֶּ֑ךָ וְשָׂרָ֥ה שֹׁמַ֛עַת פֶּ֥תַח‏
‏הָאֹ֖הֶל וְה֥וּא אַחֲרָֽיו: וְאַבְרָהָ֤ם וְשָׂרָה֙ זְקֵנִ֔ים בָּאִ֖ים בַּיָּמִ֑ים‏
‏חָדַל֙ לִהְי֣וֹת לְשָׂרָ֔ה אֹ֖רַח כַּנָּשִֽׁים: וַתִּצְחַ֥ק שָׂרָ֖ה בְּקִרְבָּ֣הּ‏
‏לֵאמֹ֑ר אַחֲרֵ֤י בְלֹתִי֙ הָֽיְתָה־לִּ֣י עֶדְנָ֔ה וַֽאדֹנִ֖י זָקֵֽן: וַיֹּ֥אמֶר יְהֹוָ֖ה‏
‏אֶל־אַבְרָהָ֑ם לָ֣מָּה זֶּה֩ צָחֲקָ֨ה שָׂרָ֜ה לֵאמֹ֗ר הַאַ֥ף אֻמְנָ֛ם אֵלֵ֖ד‏
‏וַאֲנִ֥י זָקַֽנְתִּי: הֲיִפָּלֵ֥א מֵֽיְהֹוָ֖ה דָּבָ֑ר לַמּוֹעֵ֞ד אָשׁ֥וּב אֵלֶ֛יךָ כָּעֵ֥ת‏
‏חַיָּ֖ה וּלְשָׂרָ֥ה בֵֽן:‏

HAYYEI SARA ‏חיי שרה‏

FIRST ALIYA: vv. 1–7
Avraham describes himself
in two ways. What are they
and what's the difference
between them?

‏וַיִּהְיוּ֙ חַיֵּ֣י שָׂרָ֔ה מֵאָ֥ה שָׁנָ֛ה וְעֶשְׂרִ֥ים שָׁנָ֖ה וְשֶׁ֣בַע שָׁנִ֑ים שְׁנֵ֖י‏
‏חַיֵּ֥י שָׂרָֽה: וַתָּ֣מׇת שָׂרָ֗ה בְּקִרְיַ֥ת אַרְבַּ֛ע הִ֥וא חֶבְר֖וֹן בְּאֶ֣רֶץ‏
‏כְּנָ֑עַן וַיָּבֹא֙ אַבְרָהָ֔ם לִסְפֹּ֥ד לְשָׂרָ֖ה וְלִבְכֹּתָֽהּ: וַיָּ֙קׇם֙ אַבְרָהָ֔ם‏
‏מֵעַ֖ל פְּנֵ֣י מֵת֑וֹ וַיְדַבֵּ֥ר אֶל־בְּנֵי־חֵ֖ת לֵאמֹֽר: גֵּר־וְתוֹשָׁ֥ב אָנֹכִ֖י‏
‏עִמָּכֶ֑ם תְּנ֨וּ לִ֤י אֲחֻזַּת־קֶ֙בֶר֙ עִמָּכֶ֔ם וְאֶקְבְּרָ֥ה מֵתִ֖י מִלְּפָנָֽי:‏
‏וַיַּעֲנ֧וּ בְנֵי־חֵ֛ת אֶת־אַבְרָהָ֖ם לֵאמֹ֥ר לֽוֹ: שְׁמָעֵ֣נוּ ׀ אֲדֹנִ֗י נְשִׂ֨יא‏
‏אֱלֹהִ֤ים אַתָּה֙ בְּתוֹכֵ֔נוּ בְּמִבְחַ֣ר קְבָרֵ֔ינוּ קְבֹ֖ר אֶת־מֵתֶ֑ךָ אִ֣ישׁ‏

מִמֶּ֫נּוּ אֶת־קִבְרְךָ֖ לֹֽא־יִכְלֶ֥ה מִמְּךָ֖ מִקְּבֹ֥ר מֵתֶֽךָ׃ וַיָּ֥קָם אַבְרָהָ֖ם
וַיִּשְׁתַּ֥חוּ לְעַם־הָאָ֖רֶץ לִבְנֵי־חֵֽת׃ וַיְדַבֵּ֥ר אִתָּ֖ם לֵאמֹ֑ר אִם־
יֵ֣שׁ אֶֽת־נַפְשְׁכֶ֗ם לִקְבֹּ֤ר אֶת־מֵתִי֙ מִלְּפָנַ֔י שְׁמָע֕וּנִי וּפִגְעוּ־לִ֖י
בְּעֶפְר֥וֹן בֶּן־צֹֽחַר׃ וְיִתֶּן־לִ֗י אֶת־מְעָרַ֤ת הַמַּכְפֵּלָה֙ אֲשֶׁר־ל֔וֹ
אֲשֶׁ֖ר בִּקְצֵ֣ה שָׂדֵ֑הוּ בְּכֶ֨סֶף מָלֵ֜א יִתְּנֶ֥נָּה לִּ֛י בְּתֽוֹכְכֶ֖ם לַאֲחֻזַּת־
קָֽבֶר׃ וְעֶפְר֥וֹן יֹשֵׁ֖ב בְּת֣וֹךְ בְּנֵי־חֵ֑ת וַיַּ֩עַן֩ עֶפְר֨וֹן הַחִתִּ֤י אֶת־
אַבְרָהָם֙ בְּאָזְנֵ֣י בְנֵי־חֵ֔ת לְכֹ֛ל בָּאֵ֥י שַֽׁעַר־עִיר֖וֹ לֵאמֹֽר׃ לֹֽא־
אֲדֹנִ֣י שְׁמָעֵ֔נִי הַשָּׂדֶה֙ נָתַ֣תִּי לָ֔ךְ וְהַמְּעָרָ֥ה אֲשֶׁר־בּ֖וֹ לְךָ֣ נְתַתִּ֑יהָ
לְעֵינֵ֧י בְנֵֽי־עַמִּ֛י נְתַתִּ֥יהָ לָּ֖ךְ קְבֹ֥ר מֵתֶֽךָ׃ וַיִּשְׁתַּ֙חוּ֙ אַבְרָהָ֔ם לִפְנֵ֖י
עַם־הָאָֽרֶץ׃ וַיְדַבֵּ֨ר אֶל־עֶפְר֜וֹן בְּאָזְנֵ֤י עַם־הָאָ֙רֶץ֙ לֵאמֹ֔ר אַ֛ךְ
אִם־אַתָּ֥ה ל֖וּ שְׁמָעֵ֑נִי נָתַ֜תִּי כֶּ֤סֶף הַשָּׂדֶה֙ קַ֣ח מִמֶּ֔נִּי וְאֶקְבְּרָ֥ה
אֶת־מֵתִ֖י שָֽׁמָּה׃ וַיַּ֧עַן עֶפְר֛וֹן אֶת־אַבְרָהָ֖ם לֵאמֹ֥ר לֽוֹ׃ אֲדֹנִ֣י
שְׁמָעֵ֔נִי אֶרֶץ֩ אַרְבַּ֨ע מֵאֹ֧ת שֶֽׁקֶל־כֶּ֛סֶף בֵּינִ֥י וּבֵֽינְךָ֖ מַה־הִ֑וא
וְאֶת־מֵתְךָ֖ קְבֹֽר׃ וַיִּשְׁמַ֣ע אַבְרָהָם֮ אֶל־עֶפְרוֹן֒ וַיִּשְׁקֹ֤ל אַבְרָהָם֙
לְעֶפְרֹ֔ן אֶת־הַכֶּ֕סֶף אֲשֶׁ֥ר דִּבֶּ֖ר בְּאָזְנֵ֣י בְנֵי־חֵ֑ת אַרְבַּ֤ע מֵאוֹת֙
שֶׁ֣קֶל כֶּ֔סֶף עֹבֵ֖ר לַסֹּחֵֽר׃

לוי

SECOND ALIYA: vv. 8–12
There is one major theme
word (motif) in this *aliya*
but it means something
different to Avraham than
it does to Efron. What is it?

ישראל

THIRD ALIYA: vv. 13–16
How much was it sold
for and why do you think
was it so important for
Avraham to pay for it
rather than accept
it as a gift?

תולדות

TOLEDOT

וְאֵ֛לֶּה תּוֹלְדֹ֥ת יִצְחָ֖ק בֶּן־אַבְרָהָ֑ם אַבְרָהָ֖ם הוֹלִ֥יד אֶת־יִצְחָֽק׃
וַיְהִ֤י יִצְחָק֙ בֶּן־אַרְבָּעִ֣ים שָׁנָ֔ה בְּקַחְתּ֣וֹ אֶת־רִבְקָ֗ה בַּת־בְּתוּאֵל֙
הָֽאֲרַמִּ֔י מִפַּדַּ֖ן אֲרָ֑ם אֲח֛וֹת לָבָ֥ן הָאֲרַמִּ֖י ל֥וֹ לְאִשָּֽׁה׃ וַיֶּעְתַּ֨ר
יִצְחָ֤ק לַֽיהוָה֙ לְנֹ֣כַח אִשְׁתּ֔וֹ כִּ֥י עֲקָרָ֖ה הִ֑וא וַיֵּעָ֤תֶר לוֹ֙ יְהוָ֔ה
וַתַּ֖הַר רִבְקָ֥ה אִשְׁתּֽוֹ׃ וַיִּתְרֹֽצֲצ֤וּ הַבָּנִים֙ בְּקִרְבָּ֔הּ וַתֹּ֣אמֶר אִם־
כֵּ֔ן לָ֥מָּה זֶּ֖ה אָנֹ֑כִי וַתֵּ֖לֶךְ לִדְרֹ֥שׁ אֶת־יְהוָֽה׃ וַיֹּ֨אמֶר יְהוָ֜ה לָ֗הּ
שְׁנֵ֤י גוֹיִם֙ בְּבִטְנֵ֔ךְ וּשְׁנֵ֣י לְאֻמִּ֔ים מִמֵּעַ֖יִךְ יִפָּרֵ֑דוּ וּלְאֹם֙ מִלְאֹ֣ם
יֶֽאֱמָ֔ץ וְרַ֖ב יַעֲבֹ֥ד צָעִֽיר׃ וַיִּמְלְא֥וּ יָמֶ֖יהָ לָלֶ֑דֶת וְהִנֵּ֥ה תוֹמִ֖ם
בְּבִטְנָֽהּ׃ וַיֵּצֵ֤א הָרִאשׁוֹן֙ אַדְמוֹנִ֔י כֻּלּ֖וֹ כְּאַדֶּ֣רֶת שֵׂעָ֑ר וַיִּקְרְא֥וּ
שְׁמ֖וֹ עֵשָֽׂו׃ וְאַֽחֲרֵי־כֵ֞ן יָצָ֣א אָחִ֗יו וְיָד֤וֹ אֹחֶ֙זֶת֙ בַּעֲקֵ֣ב עֵשָׂ֔ו
וַיִּקְרָ֥א שְׁמ֖וֹ יַעֲקֹ֑ב וְיִצְחָ֛ק בֶּן־שִׁשִּׁ֥ים שָׁנָ֖ה בְּלֶ֥דֶת אֹתָֽם׃

בראשית
כה:יט-כו:ה

FIRST ALIYA: vv. 19–22
What genealogical infor-
mation is provided here
and why?

לוי

SECOND ALIYA:
vv. 23–26
Who will work
for whom?

גוים

THIRD ALIYA: vv. 27–26:5

The Gemara (*Yoma* 28)
says that based on these
words Avraham kept all of
the mitzvot in the Torah.
What's the proof? What different explanations might
there be for how he knew
all of the mitzvot despite
the fact that the Torah had
not yet been given?

ישראל

*וַיִּגְדְּלוּ הַנְּעָרִים וַיְהִי עֵשָׂו אִישׁ יֹדֵעַ צַיִד אִישׁ שָׂדֶה וְיַעֲקֹב
אִישׁ תָּם יֹשֵׁב אֹהָלִים: וַיֶּאֱהַב יִצְחָק אֶת־עֵשָׂו כִּי־צַיִד בְּפִיו
וְרִבְקָה אֹהֶבֶת אֶת־יַעֲקֹב: וַיָּזֶד יַעֲקֹב נָזִיד וַיָּבֹא עֵשָׂו מִן־
הַשָּׂדֶה וְהוּא עָיֵף: וַיֹּאמֶר עֵשָׂו אֶל־יַעֲקֹב הַלְעִיטֵנִי נָא מִן־
הָאָדֹם הָאָדֹם הַזֶּה כִּי עָיֵף אָנֹכִי עַל־כֵּן קָרָא־שְׁמוֹ אֱדוֹם:
וַיֹּאמֶר יַעֲקֹב מִכְרָה כַיּוֹם אֶת־בְּכֹרָתְךָ לִי: וַיֹּאמֶר עֵשָׂו הִנֵּה
אָנֹכִי הוֹלֵךְ לָמוּת וְלָמָּה־זֶּה לִי בְּכֹרָה: וַיֹּאמֶר יַעֲקֹב הִשָּׁבְעָה
לִּי כַּיּוֹם וַיִּשָּׁבַע לוֹ וַיִּמְכֹּר אֶת־בְּכֹרָתוֹ לְיַעֲקֹב: וְיַעֲקֹב נָתַן
לְעֵשָׂו לֶחֶם וּנְזִיד עֲדָשִׁים וַיֹּאכַל וַיֵּשְׁתְּ וַיָּקָם וַיֵּלַךְ וַיִּבֶז עֵשָׂו
אֶת־הַבְּכֹרָה:

וַיְהִי רָעָב בָּאָרֶץ מִלְּבַד הָרָעָב הָרִאשׁוֹן אֲשֶׁר הָיָה בִּימֵי
אַבְרָהָם וַיֵּלֶךְ יִצְחָק אֶל־אֲבִימֶלֶךְ מֶלֶךְ־פְּלִשְׁתִּים גְּרָרָה:
וַיֵּרָא אֵלָיו יהוה וַיֹּאמֶר אַל־תֵּרֵד מִצְרָיְמָה שְׁכֹן בָּאָרֶץ אֲשֶׁר
אֹמַר אֵלֶיךָ: גּוּר בָּאָרֶץ הַזֹּאת וְאֶהְיֶה עִמְּךָ וַאֲבָרְכֶךָּ כִּי־לְךָ
וּלְזַרְעֲךָ אֶתֵּן אֶת־כָּל־הָאֲרָצֹת הָאֵל וַהֲקִמֹתִי אֶת־הַשְּׁבֻעָה
אֲשֶׁר נִשְׁבַּעְתִּי לְאַבְרָהָם אָבִיךָ: וְהִרְבֵּיתִי אֶת־זַרְעֲךָ כְּכוֹכְבֵי
הַשָּׁמַיִם וְנָתַתִּי לְזַרְעֲךָ אֵת כָּל־הָאֲרָצֹת הָאֵל וְהִתְבָּרְכוּ
בְזַרְעֲךָ כֹּל גּוֹיֵי הָאָרֶץ: עֵקֶב אֲשֶׁר־שָׁמַע אַבְרָהָם בְּקֹלִי
וַיִּשְׁמֹר מִשְׁמַרְתִּי מִצְוֺתַי חֻקּוֹתַי וְתוֹרֹתָי:

FIRST ALIYA: vv. 10–12

What was the
counterintuitive
image in Yaakov's
dream? What do you think
might be the significance?

SECOND ALIYA: vv. 13–17

From here tradition has
it that the place where
Yaakov had his dream was
the future site of the *Beit
HaMikdash*. Why would
that be appropriate?

VAYETZEH

ויצא

בראשית
כח:י–כב

לוי

וַיֵּצֵא יַעֲקֹב מִבְּאֵר שָׁבַע וַיֵּלֶךְ חָרָנָה: וַיִּפְגַּע בַּמָּקוֹם וַיָּלֶן שָׁם
כִּי־בָא הַשֶּׁמֶשׁ וַיִּקַּח מֵאַבְנֵי הַמָּקוֹם וַיָּשֶׂם מְרַאֲשֹׁתָיו וַיִּשְׁכַּב
בַּמָּקוֹם הַהוּא: וַיַּחֲלֹם וְהִנֵּה סֻלָּם מֻצָּב אַרְצָה וְרֹאשׁוֹ מַגִּיעַ
הַשָּׁמָיְמָה וְהִנֵּה מַלְאֲכֵי אֱלֹהִים עֹלִים וְיֹרְדִים בּוֹ: *וְהִנֵּה
יהוה נִצָּב עָלָיו וַיֹּאמַר אֲנִי יהוה אֱלֹהֵי אַבְרָהָם אָבִיךָ וֵאלֹהֵי
יִצְחָק הָאָרֶץ אֲשֶׁר אַתָּה שֹׁכֵב עָלֶיהָ לְךָ אֶתְּנֶנָּה וּלְזַרְעֶךָ:
וְהָיָה זַרְעֲךָ כַּעֲפַר הָאָרֶץ וּפָרַצְתָּ יָמָּה וָקֵדְמָה וְצָפֹנָה וָנֶגְבָּה
וְנִבְרְכוּ בְךָ כָּל־מִשְׁפְּחֹת הָאֲדָמָה וּבְזַרְעֶךָ: וְהִנֵּה אָנֹכִי עִמָּךְ

וּשְׁמַרְתִּ֙יךָ֙ בְּכֹ֣ל אֲשֶׁר־תֵּלֵ֔ךְ וַהֲשִֽׁבֹתִ֔יךָ אֶל־הָאֲדָמָ֖ה הַזֹּ֑את
כִּ֚י לֹ֣א אֶֽעֱזָבְךָ֔ עַ֚ד אֲשֶׁ֣ר אִם־עָשִׂ֔יתִי אֵ֛ת אֲשֶׁר־דִּבַּ֖רְתִּי לָֽךְ:
וַיִּיקַ֣ץ יַעֲקֹב֮ מִשְּׁנָתוֹ֒ וַיֹּ֕אמֶר אָכֵן֙ יֵ֣שׁ יהו֔ה בַּמָּק֖וֹם הַזֶּ֑ה
וְאָנֹכִ֖י לֹ֥א יָדָֽעְתִּי: וַיִּירָא֙ וַיֹּאמַ֔ר מַה־נּוֹרָ֖א הַמָּק֣וֹם הַזֶּ֑ה אֵ֣ין

ישראל

זֶ֗ה כִּ֚י אִם־בֵּ֣ית אֱלֹהִ֔ים וְזֶ֖ה שַׁ֥עַר הַשָּׁמָֽיִם: וַיַּשְׁכֵּ֨ם יַעֲקֹ֜ב
בַּבֹּ֗קֶר וַיִּקַּ֤ח אֶת־הָאֶ֙בֶן֙ אֲשֶׁר־שָׂ֣ם מְרַֽאֲשֹׁתָ֔יו וַיָּ֥שֶׂם אֹתָ֖הּ
מַצֵּבָ֑ה וַיִּצֹ֥ק שֶׁ֖מֶן עַל־רֹאשָֽׁהּ: וַיִּקְרָ֛א אֶת־שֵֽׁם־הַמָּק֥וֹם
הַה֖וּא בֵּֽית־אֵ֑ל וְאוּלָ֛ם ל֥וּז שֵׁם־הָעִ֖יר לָרִֽאשֹׁנָֽה: וַיִּדַּ֥ר יַעֲקֹ֖ב
נֶ֣דֶר לֵאמֹ֑ר אִם־יִֽהְיֶ֨ה אֱלֹהִ֜ים עִמָּדִ֗י וּשְׁמָרַ֙נִי֙ בַּדֶּ֤רֶךְ הַזֶּה֙
אֲשֶׁ֣ר אָֽנֹכִ֣י הוֹלֵ֔ךְ וְנָֽתַן־לִ֥י לֶ֛חֶם לֶֽאֱכֹ֖ל וּבֶ֥גֶד לִלְבֹּֽשׁ: וְשַׁבְתִּ֥י
בְשָׁל֖וֹם אֶל־בֵּ֣ית אָבִ֑י וְהָיָ֧ה יהו֛ה לִ֖י לֵאלֹהִֽים: וְהָאֶ֣בֶן הַזֹּ֗את
אֲשֶׁר־שַׂ֙מְתִּי֙ מַצֵּבָ֔ה יִהְיֶ֖ה בֵּ֣ית אֱלֹהִ֑ים וְכֹל֙ אֲשֶׁ֣ר תִּתֶּן־לִ֔י
עַשֵּׂ֖ר אֲעַשְּׂרֶ֥נּוּ לָֽךְ:

THIRD ALIYA: vv. 18–22
Based on this verse, the
Gemara suggests that one
should not give more than
20% of one's money to
tzedaka. Why do you think
this is so?

VAYISHLAH   וישלח

בראשית
לב:ד-יב

וַיִּשְׁלַ֨ח יַעֲקֹ֤ב מַלְאָכִים֙ לְפָנָ֔יו אֶל־עֵשָׂ֖ו אָחִ֑יו אַ֥רְצָה שֵׂעִ֖יר
שְׂדֵ֥ה אֱד֑וֹם: וַיְצַ֤ו אֹתָם֙ לֵאמֹ֔ר כֹּ֣ה תֹֽאמְר֔וּן לַֽאדֹנִ֖י לְעֵשָׂ֑ו
כֹּ֤ה אָמַר֙ עַבְדְּךָ֣ יַעֲקֹ֔ב עִם־לָבָ֣ן גַּ֔רְתִּי וָֽאֵחַ֖ר עַד־עָֽתָּה: וַֽיְהִי־
לִ֣י שׁ֣וֹר וַֽחֲמ֗וֹר צֹ֚אן וְעֶ֣בֶד וְשִׁפְחָ֔ה וָֽאֶשְׁלְחָה֙ לְהַגִּ֣יד לַֽאדֹנִ֔י

FIRST ALIYA: vv. 4–6
Why didn't Yaakov use
the word שַׁבְתִּי
instead of גַּרְתִּי?

לוי

לִמְצֹא־חֵ֖ן בְּעֵינֶֽיךָ: וַיָּשֻׁ֙בוּ֙ הַמַּלְאָכִ֔ים אֶֽל־יַעֲקֹ֖ב לֵאמֹ֑ר
בָּ֤אנוּ אֶל־אָחִ֙יךָ֙ אֶל־עֵשָׂ֔ו וְגַם֙ הֹלֵ֣ךְ לִקְרָֽאתְךָ֔ וְאַרְבַּע־
מֵא֥וֹת אִ֖ישׁ עִמּֽוֹ: וַיִּירָ֧א יַעֲקֹ֛ב מְאֹ֖ד וַיֵּ֣צֶר ל֑וֹ וַיַּ֣חַץ אֶת־
הָעָ֣ם אֲשֶׁר־אִתּ֗וֹ וְאֶת־הַצֹּ֧אן וְאֶת־הַבָּקָ֛ר וְהַגְּמַלִּ֖ים לִשְׁנֵ֥י
מַֽחֲנֽוֹת: וַיֹּ֕אמֶר אִם־יָב֥וֹא עֵשָׂ֛ו אֶל־הַמַּֽחֲנֶ֥ה הָֽאַחַ֖ת וְהִכָּ֑הוּ

SECOND ALIYA: vv. 7–9
Which word is both mas-
culine and feminine?

ישראל

וְהָיָ֛ה הַמַּֽחֲנֶ֥ה הַנִּשְׁאָ֖ר לִפְלֵיטָֽה: וַיֹּאמֶר֮ יַעֲקֹב֒ אֱלֹהֵי֙ אָבִ֣י
אַבְרָהָ֔ם וֵֽאלֹהֵ֖י אָבִ֣י יִצְחָ֑ק יהו֞ה הָֽאֹמֵ֣ר אֵלַ֗י שׁ֧וּב לְאַרְצְךָ֛
וּלְמֽוֹלַדְתְּךָ֖ וְאֵיטִ֥יבָה עִמָּֽךְ: קָטֹ֜נְתִּי מִכֹּ֤ל הַחֲסָדִים֙ וּמִכָּל־
הָ֣אֱמֶ֔ת אֲשֶׁ֥ר עָשִׂ֖יתָ אֶת־עַבְדֶּ֑ךָ כִּ֣י בְמַקְלִ֗י עָבַ֙רְתִּי֙ אֶת־
הַיַּרְדֵּ֣ן הַזֶּ֔ה וְעַתָּ֥ה הָיִ֖יתִי לִשְׁנֵ֥י מַֽחֲנֽוֹת: הַצִּילֵ֥נִי נָ֛א מִיַּ֥ד אָחִ֖י

THIRD ALIYA: vv. 10–13
Each *aliya* describes a
different method that
Yaakov used to defend his
family against Esav. What
are the three methods?

Why was there a need for
each of them?

מִיַּד עֵשָׂו כִּי־יָרֵא אָנֹכִי אֹתוֹ פֶּן־יָבוֹא וְהִכַּנִי אֵם עַל־בָּנִים:
וְאַתָּה אָמַרְתָּ הֵיטֵב אֵיטִיב עִמָּךְ וְשַׂמְתִּי אֶת־זַרְעֲךָ כְּחוֹל
הַיָּם אֲשֶׁר לֹא־יִסָּפֵר מֵרֹב:

VAYESHEV · וישב

FIRST ALIYA: vv. 1–3
According to some,
this is the reason
that the children
of Leah hated Yosef.
Why would Yosef
choose to act this way?

בראשית
לז:א-יא

וַיֵּשֶׁב יַעֲקֹב בְּאֶרֶץ מְגוּרֵי אָבִיו בְּאֶרֶץ כְּנָעַן: אֵלֶּה ׀ תֹּלְדוֹת
יַעֲקֹב יוֹסֵף בֶּן־שְׁבַע־עֶשְׂרֵה שָׁנָה הָיָה רֹעֶה אֶת־אֶחָיו בַּצֹּאן
וְהוּא נַעַר אֶת־בְּנֵי בִלְהָה וְאֶת־בְּנֵי זִלְפָּה נְשֵׁי אָבִיו וַיָּבֵא יוֹסֵף
אֶת־דִּבָּתָם רָעָה אֶל־אֲבִיהֶם: וְיִשְׂרָאֵל אָהַב אֶת־יוֹסֵף מִכָּל־

SECOND ALIYA: vv. 4–7
From a verse in this aliya,
Rashi learns the principle
that מִתּוֹךְ גְּנוּתָם לָמַדְנוּ
שִׁבְחָם – from something
bad that we learn about
them, we can also learn
some redeeming praise
about them. What can
we learn from here?

לוי

בָּנָיו כִּי־בֶן־זְקֻנִים הוּא לוֹ וְעָשָׂה לוֹ כְּתֹנֶת פַּסִּים: *וַיִּרְאוּ
אֶחָיו כִּי־אֹתוֹ אָהַב אֲבִיהֶם מִכָּל־אֶחָיו וַיִּשְׂנְאוּ אֹתוֹ וְלֹא
יָכְלוּ דַּבְּרוֹ לְשָׁלֹם: וַיַּחֲלֹם יוֹסֵף חֲלוֹם וַיַּגֵּד לְאֶחָיו וַיּוֹסִפוּ
עוֹד שְׂנֹא אֹתוֹ: וַיֹּאמֶר אֲלֵיהֶם שִׁמְעוּ־נָא הַחֲלוֹם הַזֶּה
אֲשֶׁר חָלָמְתִּי: וְהִנֵּה אֲנַחְנוּ מְאַלְּמִים אֲלֻמִּים בְּתוֹךְ הַשָּׂדֶה

ישראל

וְהִנֵּה קָמָה אֲלֻמָּתִי וְגַם־נִצָּבָה וְהִנֵּה תְסֻבֶּינָה אֲלֻמֹּתֵיכֶם
וַתִּשְׁתַּחֲוֶיןָ לַאֲלֻמָּתִי: *וַיֹּאמְרוּ לוֹ אֶחָיו הֲמָלֹךְ תִּמְלֹךְ עָלֵינוּ

THIRD ALIYA: vv. 8–11
How is this dream differ-
ent from the first?

אִם־מָשׁוֹל תִּמְשֹׁל בָּנוּ וַיּוֹסִפוּ עוֹד שְׂנֹא אֹתוֹ עַל־חֲלֹמֹתָיו
וְעַל־דְּבָרָיו: וַיַּחֲלֹם עוֹד חֲלוֹם אַחֵר וַיְסַפֵּר אֹתוֹ לְאֶחָיו
וַיֹּאמֶר הִנֵּה חָלַמְתִּי חֲלוֹם עוֹד וְהִנֵּה הַשֶּׁמֶשׁ וְהַיָּרֵחַ וְאַחַד
עָשָׂר כּוֹכָבִים מִשְׁתַּחֲוִים לִי: וַיְסַפֵּר אֶל־אָבִיו וְאֶל־אֶחָיו
וַיִּגְעַר־בּוֹ אָבִיו וַיֹּאמֶר לוֹ מָה הַחֲלוֹם הַזֶּה אֲשֶׁר חָלָמְתָּ
הֲבוֹא נָבוֹא אֲנִי וְאִמְּךָ וְאַחֶיךָ לְהִשְׁתַּחֲוֹת לְךָ אָרְצָה:
וַיְקַנְאוּ־בוֹ אֶחָיו וְאָבִיו שָׁמַר אֶת־הַדָּבָר:

MIKETZ · מקץ

FIRST ALIYA: vv. 1–4
Does the dream with
the cows contain
the prediction of
what would happen
or the solution for how
to survive what would
happen?

בראשית
מא:א-יד

וַיְהִי מִקֵּץ שְׁנָתַיִם יָמִים וּפַרְעֹה חֹלֵם וְהִנֵּה עֹמֵד עַל־הַיְאֹר:
וְהִנֵּה מִן־הַיְאֹר עֹלֹת שֶׁבַע פָּרוֹת יְפוֹת מַרְאֶה וּבְרִיאֹת
בָּשָׂר וַתִּרְעֶינָה בָּאָחוּ: וְהִנֵּה שֶׁבַע פָּרוֹת אֲחֵרוֹת עֹלוֹת
אַחֲרֵיהֶן מִן־הַיְאֹר רָעוֹת מַרְאֶה וְדַקּוֹת בָּשָׂר וַתַּעֲמֹדְנָה

אֵצֶל הַפָּרֹות עַל־שְׂפַת הַיְאֹר: וַתֹּאכַלְנָה הַפָּרֹות רָעֹות
הַמַּרְאֶה וְדַקֹּת הַבָּשָׂר אֵת שֶׁבַע הַפָּרֹות יְפֹת הַמַּרְאֶה
וְהַבְּרִיאֹת וַיִּיקַץ פַּרְעֹה: *וַיִּישָׁן וַיַּחֲלֹם שֵׁנִית וְהִנֵּה ׀ שֶׁבַע
שִׁבֳּלִים עֹלֹות בְּקָנֶה אֶחָד בְּרִיאֹות וְטֹבֹות: וְהִנֵּה שֶׁבַע
שִׁבֳּלִים דַּקֹּות וּשְׁדוּפֹת קָדִים צֹמְחֹות אַחֲרֵיהֶן: וַתִּבְלַעְנָה
הַשִּׁבֳּלִים הַדַּקֹּות אֵת שֶׁבַע הַשִּׁבֳּלִים הַבְּרִיאֹות וְהַמְּלֵאֹות
וַיִּיקַץ פַּרְעֹה וְהִנֵּה חֲלֹום: *וַיְהִי בַבֹּקֶר וַתִּפָּעֶם רוּחֹו וַיִּשְׁלַח
וַיִּקְרָא אֶת־כָּל־חַרְטֻמֵּי מִצְרַיִם וְאֶת־כָּל־חֲכָמֶיהָ וַיְסַפֵּר
פַּרְעֹה לָהֶם אֶת־חֲלֹמֹו וְאֵין־פֹּותֵר אֹותָם לְפַרְעֹה: וַיְדַבֵּר
שַׂר הַמַּשְׁקִים אֶת־פַּרְעֹה לֵאמֹר אֶת־חֲטָאַי אֲנִי מַזְכִּיר
הַיֹּום: פַּרְעֹה קָצַף עַל־עֲבָדָיו וַיִּתֵּן אֹתִי בְּמִשְׁמַר בֵּית שַׂר
הַטַּבָּחִים אֹתִי וְאֵת שַׂר הָאֹפִים: וַנַּחַלְמָה חֲלֹום בְּלַיְלָה
אֶחָד אֲנִי וָהוּא אִישׁ כְּפִתְרֹון חֲלֹמֹו חָלָמְנוּ: וְשָׁם אִתָּנוּ
נַעַר עִבְרִי עֶבֶד לְשַׂר הַטַּבָּחִים וַנְּסַפֶּר־לֹו וַיִּפְתָּר־לָנוּ אֶת־
חֲלֹמֹתֵינוּ אִישׁ כַּחֲלֹמֹו פָּתָר: וַיְהִי כַּאֲשֶׁר פָּתַר־לָנוּ כֵּן הָיָה
אֹתִי הֵשִׁיב עַל־כַּנִּי וְאֹתֹו תָלָה: וַיִּשְׁלַח פַּרְעֹה וַיִּקְרָא אֶת־
יֹוסֵף וַיְרִיצֻהוּ מִן־הַבֹּור וַיְגַלַּח וַיְחַלֵּף שִׂמְלֹתָיו וַיָּבֹא אֶל־
פַּרְעֹה:

VAYIGASH · ויגש

וַיִּגַּשׁ אֵלָיו יְהוּדָה וַיֹּאמֶר בִּי אֲדֹנִי יְדַבֶּר־נָא עַבְדְּךָ דָבָר
בְּאָזְנֵי אֲדֹנִי וְאַל־יִחַר אַפְּךָ בְּעַבְדֶּךָ כִּי כָמֹוךָ כְּפַרְעֹה: אֲדֹנִי
שָׁאַל אֶת־עֲבָדָיו לֵאמֹר הֲיֵשׁ־לָכֶם אָב אֹו־אָח: וַנֹּאמֶר אֶל־
אֲדֹנִי יֶשׁ־לָנוּ אָב זָקֵן וְיֶלֶד זְקֻנִים קָטָן וְאָחִיו מֵת וַיִּוָּתֵר הוּא
לְבַדֹּו לְאִמֹּו וְאָבִיו אֲהֵבֹו: *וַתֹּאמֶר אֶל־עֲבָדֶיךָ הֹורִדֻהוּ אֵלָי
וְאָשִׂימָה עֵינִי עָלָיו: וַנֹּאמֶר אֶל־אֲדֹנִי לֹא־יוּכַל הַנַּעַר לַעֲזֹב
אֶת־אָבִיו וְעָזַב אֶת־אָבִיו וָמֵת: וַתֹּאמֶר אֶל־עֲבָדֶיךָ אִם־לֹא
יֵרֵד אֲחִיכֶם הַקָּטֹן אִתְּכֶם לֹא תֹסִפוּן לִרְאֹות פָּנָי: וַיְהִי כִּי

SECOND ALIYA: vv. 5–7
Based on which words in the text does Ramban argue that Pharaoh knew that this was one long connected dream rather than two separate unrelated ones?

THIRD ALIYA: vv. 8–14
From which words in the *aliya* do we learn that "Cursed are the wicked, for the good deeds that they do are not complete," that is, that even when they try to do something good, they do so in a way which takes away from the good that they do?

FIRST ALIYA: vv. 18–20
What are the ways that Yehuda uses to try to gain the pity of Yosef?

SECOND ALIYA: vv. 21–24
According to *Hazal*, Yehuda said something so outrageous that Yosef should have stopped him and revealed himself at that moment. What?

לוי

ישראל

בראשית
מד:יח–ל

לוי

ישראל

THIRD ALIYA: vv. 25–30
Based on this, Rashi
reminds us that the *Satan*
attacks during moments
of danger. What do you
think he means by this
Talmudic concept?

עָלֵינוּ אֶל־עַבְדְּךָ אָבִי וַנַּגֶּד־לוֹ אֵת דִּבְרֵי אֲדֹנִי: ²⁵וַיֹּאמֶר
אָבִינוּ שֻׁבוּ שִׁבְרוּ־לָנוּ מְעַט־אֹכֶל: ²⁶וַנֹּאמֶר לֹא נוּכַל לָרֶדֶת
אִם־יֵשׁ אָחִינוּ הַקָּטֹן אִתָּנוּ וְיָרַדְנוּ כִּי־לֹא נוּכַל לִרְאוֹת פְּנֵי
הָאִישׁ וְאָחִינוּ הַקָּטֹן אֵינֶנּוּ אִתָּנוּ: ²⁷וַיֹּאמֶר עַבְדְּךָ אָבִי אֵלֵינוּ
אַתֶּם יְדַעְתֶּם כִּי שְׁנַיִם יָלְדָה־לִּי אִשְׁתִּי: ²⁸וַיֵּצֵא הָאֶחָד מֵאִתִּי
וָאֹמַר אַךְ טָרֹף טֹרָף וְלֹא רְאִיתִיו עַד־הֵנָּה: ²⁹וּלְקַחְתֶּם גַּם־
אֶת־זֶה מֵעִם פָּנַי וְקָרָהוּ אָסוֹן וְהוֹרַדְתֶּם אֶת־שֵׂיבָתִי בְּרָעָה
שְׁאֹלָה: ³⁰וְעַתָּה כְּבֹאִי אֶל־עַבְדְּךָ אָבִי וְהַנַּעַר אֵינֶנּוּ אִתָּנוּ
וְנַפְשׁוֹ קְשׁוּרָה בְנַפְשׁוֹ:

ויחי
VAYHI

בראשית
מז:כח–מח:ט

FIRST ALIYA: vv. 28–31
Why does it say וַיְחִי
instead of וַיֵּגַר?

²⁸וַיְחִי יַעֲקֹב בְּאֶרֶץ מִצְרַיִם שְׁבַע עֶשְׂרֵה שָׁנָה וַיְהִי יְמֵי־
יַעֲקֹב שְׁנֵי חַיָּיו שֶׁבַע שָׁנִים וְאַרְבָּעִים וּמְאַת שָׁנָה: ²⁹וַיִּקְרְבוּ
יְמֵי־יִשְׂרָאֵל לָמוּת וַיִּקְרָא ׀ לִבְנוֹ לְיוֹסֵף וַיֹּאמֶר לוֹ אִם־נָא
מָצָאתִי חֵן בְּעֵינֶיךָ שִׂים־נָא יָדְךָ תַּחַת יְרֵכִי וְעָשִׂיתָ עִמָּדִי
חֶסֶד וֶאֱמֶת אַל־נָא תִקְבְּרֵנִי בְּמִצְרָיִם: ³⁰וְשָׁכַבְתִּי עִם־אֲבֹתַי
וּנְשָׂאתַנִי מִמִּצְרַיִם וּקְבַרְתַּנִי בִּקְבֻרָתָם וַיֹּאמַר אָנֹכִי אֶעֱשֶׂה
כִדְבָרֶךָ: ³¹וַיֹּאמֶר הִשָּׁבְעָה לִי וַיִּשָּׁבַע לוֹ וַיִּשְׁתַּחוּ יִשְׂרָאֵל
עַל־רֹאשׁ הַמִּטָּה:

לוי

SECOND ALIYA: vv 1–3
In this *aliya* we hear of
a phenomenon for the
very first time in the Torah.
What is it?

¹וַיְהִי אַחֲרֵי הַדְּבָרִים הָאֵלֶּה וַיֹּאמֶר לְיוֹסֵף הִנֵּה אָבִיךָ חֹלֶה
וַיִּקַּח אֶת־שְׁנֵי בָנָיו עִמּוֹ אֶת־מְנַשֶּׁה וְאֶת־אֶפְרָיִם: ²וַיַּגֵּד
לְיַעֲקֹב וַיֹּאמֶר הִנֵּה בִּנְךָ יוֹסֵף בָּא אֵלֶיךָ וַיִּתְחַזֵּק יִשְׂרָאֵל
וַיֵּשֶׁב עַל־הַמִּטָּה: ³וַיֹּאמֶר יַעֲקֹב אֶל־יוֹסֵף אֵל שַׁדַּי נִרְאָה־

ישראל

THIRD ALIYA: vv. 4–9
Where is Rachel buried?

אֵלַי בְּלוּז בְּאֶרֶץ כְּנָעַן וַיְבָרֶךְ אֹתִי: ⁴וַיֹּאמֶר אֵלַי הִנְנִי מַפְרְךָ
וְהִרְבִּיתִךָ וּנְתַתִּיךָ לִקְהַל עַמִּים וְנָתַתִּי אֶת־הָאָרֶץ הַזֹּאת
לְזַרְעֲךָ אַחֲרֶיךָ אֲחֻזַּת עוֹלָם: ⁵וְעַתָּה שְׁנֵי־בָנֶיךָ הַנּוֹלָדִים
לְךָ בְּאֶרֶץ מִצְרַיִם עַד־בֹּאִי אֵלֶיךָ מִצְרַיְמָה לִי־הֵם אֶפְרַיִם
וּמְנַשֶּׁה כִּרְאוּבֵן וְשִׁמְעוֹן יִהְיוּ־לִי: ⁶וּמוֹלַדְתְּךָ אֲשֶׁר־הוֹלַדְתָּ

אַחֲרֵיהֶם לְךָ יִהְיֻ עַל שֵׁם אֲחֵיהֶם יִקָּרְאֻו בְּנַחֲלָתָם: וַאֲנִי ׀
בְּבֹאִי מִפַּדָּן מֵ֫תָה עָלַי רָחֵל בְּאֶרֶץ כְּנַעַן בַּדֶּרֶךְ בְּעֹוד כִּבְרַת־
אֶרֶץ לָבֹא אֶפְרָ֑תָה וָאֶקְבְּרֶ֫הָ שָּׁם בְּדֶרֶךְ אֶפְרָ֔ת הִוא בֵּית
לָחֶם: וַיַּרְא יִשְׂרָאֵל אֶת־בְּנֵי יֹוסֵף וַיֹּאמֶר מִי־אֵלֶּה: וַיֹּאמֶר
יֹוסֵף אֶל־אָבִיו בָּנַי הֵם אֲשֶׁר־נָתַן־לִי אֱלֹהִים בָּזֶה וַיֹּאמַר
קָחֶם־נָא אֵלַי וַאֲבָרֲכֵם:

SHEMOT

שמות

שמות
א:א–ה

וְאֵ֫לֶּה שְׁמֹות בְּנֵי יִשְׂרָאֵל הַבָּאִים מִצְרָ֑יְמָה אֵת יַעֲקֹב אִישׁ
וּבֵיתֹו בָּאוּ: רְאוּבֵן שִׁמְעֹון לֵוִי וִיהוּדָה: יִשָּׂשכָר זְבוּלֻן
וּבִנְיָמִן: דָּן וְנַפְתָּלִי גָּד וְאָשֵׁר: וַיְהִי כָּל־נֶפֶשׁ יֹצְאֵי יֶרֶךְ־יַעֲקֹב
שִׁבְעִים נָפֶשׁ וְיֹוסֵף הָיָה בְמִצְרָ֑יִם: וַיָּמָת יֹוסֵף וְכָל־אֶחָיו וְכֹל
הַדֹּור הַהוּא: וּבְנֵי יִשְׂרָאֵל פָּרוּ וַיִּשְׁרְצֻו וַיִּרְבֻּו וַיַּעַצְמֻו בִּמְאֹד
מְאֹד וַתִּמָּלֵא הָאָרֶץ אֹתָם:

לוי

וַיָּקָם מֶלֶךְ־חָדָשׁ עַל־מִצְרָ֑יִם אֲשֶׁר לֹא־יָדַע אֶת־יֹוסֵף:
וַיֹּאמֶר אֶל־עַמֹּו הִנֵּה עַם בְּנֵי יִשְׂרָאֵל רַב וְעָצֻום מִמֶּנּוּ:
הָבָה נִתְחַכְּמָה לֹו פֶּן־יִרְבֶּה וְהָיָה כִּי־תִקְרֶאנָה מִלְחָמָה
וְנֹוסַף גַּם־הוּא עַל־שֹׂנְאֵינוּ וְנִלְחַם־בָּנוּ וְעָלָה מִן־הָאָרֶץ:
וַיָּשִׂימוּ עָלָיו שָׂרֵי מִסִּים לְמַעַן עַנֹּתֹו בְּסִבְלֹתָ֑ם וַיִּבֶן עָרֵי
מִסְכְּנֹות לְפַרְעֹה אֶת־פִּתֹם וְאֶת־רַעַמְסֵס: וְכַאֲשֶׁר יְעַנֻּו

ישראל

אֹתֹו כֵּן יִרְבֶּה וְכֵן יִפְרֹ֑ץ וַיָּקֻ֫צוּ מִפְּנֵי בְּנֵי יִשְׂרָאֵל: וַיַּעֲבִדוּ
מִצְרַיִם אֶת־בְּנֵי יִשְׂרָאֵל בְּפָרֶךְ: וַיְמָרֲרֻו אֶת־חַיֵּיהֶם בַּעֲבֹדָה
קָשָׁה בְּחֹמֶר וּבִלְבֵנִים וּבְכָל־עֲבֹדָה בַּשָּׂדֶה אֵת כָּל־עֲבֹדָתָם
אֲשֶׁר־עָבְדוּ בָהֶם בְּפָרֶךְ: וַיֹּאמֶר מֶלֶךְ מִצְרַיִם לַמְיַלְּדֹת
הָעִבְרִיֹּת אֲשֶׁר שֵׁם הָאַחַת שִׁפְרָה וְשֵׁם הַשֵּׁנִית פּוּעָה:
וַיֹּאמֶר בְּיַלֶּדְכֶן אֶת־הָעִבְרִיֹּות וּרְאִיתֶן עַל־הָאָבְנָיִם אִם־בֵּן
הוּא וַהֲמִתֶּן אֹתֹו וְאִם־בַּת הִוא וָחָ֑יָה: וַתִּירֶאןָ הַמְיַלְּדֹת אֶת־

FIRST ALIYA: vv. 1–7
From here the Midrash learns that the women gave birth to six at a time. Where does the number six come from? Was this number intended to be literal? Why?

SECOND ALIYA: vv. 8–12
The letter מ can mean "from" or "than" and thereby changes the meaning of the verse. How so?

THIRD ALIYA: vv. 13–17
The phrase לַמְיַלְּדֹת הָעִבְרִיֹּת can mean the Hebrew midwives, or the midwives of the Hebrews (i.e., Egyptian midwives). How does each interpretation change one's understanding of the story?

הָאֱלֹהִ֑ים וְלֹ֤א עָשׂוּ֙ כַּאֲשֶׁ֣ר דִּבֶּ֣ר אֲלֵהֶ֔ן מֶ֖לֶךְ מִצְרָ֑יִם וַתְּחַיֶּ֖יןָ אֶת־הַיְלָדִֽים:

VA'ERA
וארא

שמות ו:ב–ג

וַיְדַבֵּ֥ר אֱלֹהִ֖ים אֶל־מֹשֶׁ֑ה וַיֹּ֥אמֶר אֵלָ֖יו אֲנִ֥י יְהוָֽה: וָאֵרָ֗א אֶל־אַבְרָהָ֛ם אֶל־יִצְחָ֥ק וְאֶֽל־יַעֲקֹ֖ב בְּאֵ֣ל שַׁדָּ֑י וּשְׁמִ֣י יְהוָ֔ה לֹ֥א נוֹדַ֖עְתִּי לָהֶֽם: וְגַ֨ם הֲקִמֹ֤תִי אֶת־בְּרִיתִי֙ אִתָּ֔ם לָתֵ֥ת לָהֶ֖ם אֶת־אֶ֣רֶץ כְּנָ֑עַן אֵ֛ת אֶ֥רֶץ מְגֻרֵיהֶ֖ם אֲשֶׁר־גָּ֥רוּ בָֽהּ: וְגַ֣ם ׀ אֲנִ֣י שָׁמַ֗עְתִּי אֶֽת־נַאֲקַת֙ בְּנֵ֣י יִשְׂרָאֵ֔ל אֲשֶׁ֥ר מִצְרַ֖יִם מַעֲבִדִ֣ים אֹתָ֑ם וָאֶזְכֹּ֖ר אֶת־בְּרִיתִֽי: *לָכֵ֞ן אֱמֹ֥ר לִבְנֵֽי־יִשְׂרָאֵל֮ אֲנִ֣י יְהוָה֒ וְהוֹצֵאתִ֣י אֶתְכֶ֗ם מִתַּ֨חַת֙ סִבְלֹ֣ת מִצְרַ֔יִם וְהִצַּלְתִּ֥י אֶתְכֶ֖ם מֵעֲבֹֽדָתָ֑ם וְגָאַלְתִּ֤י אֶתְכֶם֙ בִּזְר֣וֹעַ נְטוּיָ֔ה וּבִשְׁפָטִ֖ים גְּדֹלִֽים: וְלָקַחְתִּ֨י אֶתְכֶ֥ם לִי֙ לְעָ֔ם וְהָיִ֥יתִי לָכֶ֖ם לֵֽאלֹהִ֑ים וִֽידַעְתֶּ֗ם כִּ֣י אֲנִ֤י יְהוָה֙ אֱלֹ֣הֵיכֶ֔ם הַמּוֹצִ֣יא אֶתְכֶ֔ם מִתַּ֖חַת סִבְל֥וֹת מִצְרָֽיִם: וְהֵבֵאתִ֤י אֶתְכֶם֙ אֶל־הָאָ֔רֶץ אֲשֶׁ֤ר נָשָׂ֨אתִי֙ אֶת־יָדִ֔י לָתֵ֣ת אֹתָ֔הּ לְאַבְרָהָ֥ם לְיִצְחָ֖ק וּֽלְיַעֲקֹ֑ב וְנָתַתִּ֨י אֹתָ֥הּ לָכֶ֛ם מֽוֹרָשָׁ֖ה אֲנִ֥י יְהוָֽה: וַיְדַבֵּ֥ר מֹשֶׁ֛ה כֵּ֖ן אֶל־בְּנֵ֣י יִשְׂרָאֵ֑ל וְלֹ֤א שָֽׁמְעוּ֙ אֶל־מֹשֶׁ֔ה מִקֹּ֣צֶר ר֔וּחַ וּמֵעֲבֹדָ֖ה קָשָֽׁה:

לוי

ישראל

וַיְדַבֵּ֥ר יְהוָ֖ה אֶל־מֹשֶׁ֥ה לֵּאמֹֽר: בֹּ֣א דַבֵּ֔ר אֶל־פַּרְעֹ֖ה מֶ֣לֶךְ מִצְרָ֑יִם וִֽישַׁלַּ֥ח אֶת־בְּנֵֽי־יִשְׂרָאֵ֖ל מֵאַרְצֽוֹ: וַיְדַבֵּ֣ר מֹשֶׁ֔ה לִפְנֵ֥י יְהוָ֖ה לֵאמֹ֑ר הֵ֤ן בְּנֵֽי־יִשְׂרָאֵל֙ לֹֽא־שָׁמְע֣וּ אֵלַ֔י וְאֵיךְ֙ יִשְׁמָעֵ֣נִי פַרְעֹ֔ה וַאֲנִ֖י עֲרַ֥ל שְׂפָתָֽיִם: וַיְדַבֵּ֣ר יְהוָה֮ אֶל־מֹשֶׁ֣ה וְאֶֽל־אַהֲרֹן֒ וַיְצַוֵּם֙ אֶל־בְּנֵ֣י יִשְׂרָאֵ֔ל וְאֶל־פַּרְעֹ֖ה מֶ֣לֶךְ מִצְרָ֑יִם לְהוֹצִ֥יא אֶת־בְּנֵֽי־יִשְׂרָאֵ֖ל מֵאֶ֥רֶץ מִצְרָֽיִם:

BO
בא

שמות י:א–יא

וַיֹּ֤אמֶר יְהוָה֙ אֶל־מֹשֶׁ֔ה בֹּ֖א אֶל־פַּרְעֹ֑ה כִּֽי־אֲנִ֞י הִכְבַּ֤דְתִּי אֶת־לִבּוֹ֙ וְאֶת־לֵ֣ב עֲבָדָ֔יו לְמַ֗עַן שִׁתִ֥י אֹֽתֹתַ֛י אֵ֖לֶּה בְּקִרְבּֽוֹ: וּלְמַ֡עַן

FIRST ALIYA: vv. 2–5
What did Moshe learn that the *Avot* did not? Why do you think that was?

SECOND ALIYA: vv. 6–9
The one verse that is not highlighted at the Seder. Why?

THIRD ALIYA: vv. 10–13
The last verse answers Moshe's concern in the previous verse. How?

FIRST ALIYA: vv. 1–3
Which phrase here was used as a rallying cry for the Soviet Jewry movement?

תְּסַפֵּר בְּאָזְנֵי בִנְךָ וּבֶן־בִּנְךָ אֵת אֲשֶׁר הִתְעַלַּלְתִּי בְּמִצְרַיִם
וְאֶת־אֹתֹתַי אֲשֶׁר־שַׂמְתִּי בָם וִידַעְתֶּם כִּי־אֲנִי יהוה: וַיָּבֹא
מֹשֶׁה וְאַהֲרֹן אֶל־פַּרְעֹה וַיֹּאמְרוּ אֵלָיו כֹּה־אָמַר יהוה אֱלֹהֵי
הָעִבְרִים עַד־מָתַי מֵאַנְתָּ לֵעָנֹת מִפָּנָי שַׁלַּח עַמִּי וְיַעַבְדֻנִי:

לוי
כִּי אִם־מָאֵן אַתָּה לְשַׁלֵּחַ אֶת־עַמִּי הִנְנִי מֵבִיא מָחָר אַרְבֶּה
בִּגְבֻלֶךָ: וְכִסָּה אֶת־עֵין הָאָרֶץ וְלֹא יוּכַל לִרְאֹת אֶת־הָאָרֶץ
וְאָכַל ׀ אֶת־יֶתֶר הַפְּלֵטָה הַנִּשְׁאֶרֶת לָכֶם מִן־הַבָּרָד וְאָכַל
אֶת־כָּל־הָעֵץ הַצֹּמֵחַ לָכֶם מִן־הַשָּׂדֶה: וּמָלְאוּ בָתֶּיךָ וּבָתֵּי
כָל־עֲבָדֶיךָ וּבָתֵּי כָל־מִצְרַיִם אֲשֶׁר לֹא־רָאוּ אֲבֹתֶיךָ וַאֲבוֹת
אֲבֹתֶיךָ מִיּוֹם הֱיוֹתָם עַל־הָאֲדָמָה עַד הַיּוֹם הַזֶּה וַיִּפֶן וַיֵּצֵא
מֵעִם פַּרְעֹה:

ישראל
וַיֹּאמְרוּ עַבְדֵי פַרְעֹה אֵלָיו עַד־מָתַי יִהְיֶה זֶה
לָנוּ לְמוֹקֵשׁ שַׁלַּח אֶת־הָאֲנָשִׁים וְיַעַבְדוּ אֶת־יהוה אֱלֹהֵיהֶם
הֲטֶרֶם תֵּדַע כִּי אָבְדָה מִצְרָיִם: וַיּוּשַׁב אֶת־מֹשֶׁה וְאֶת־אַהֲרֹן
אֶל־פַּרְעֹה וַיֹּאמֶר אֲלֵהֶם לְכוּ עִבְדוּ אֶת־יהוה אֱלֹהֵיכֶם מִי
וָמִי הַהֹלְכִים: וַיֹּאמֶר מֹשֶׁה בִּנְעָרֵינוּ וּבִזְקֵנֵינוּ נֵלֵךְ בְּבָנֵינוּ
וּבִבְנוֹתֵנוּ בְּצֹאנֵנוּ וּבִבְקָרֵנוּ נֵלֵךְ כִּי חַג־יהוה לָנוּ: וַיֹּאמֶר
אֲלֵהֶם יְהִי כֵן יהוה עִמָּכֶם כַּאֲשֶׁר אֲשַׁלַּח אֶתְכֶם וְאֶת־טַפְּכֶם
רְאוּ כִּי רָעָה נֶגֶד פְּנֵיכֶם: לֹא כֵן לְכוּ־נָא הַגְּבָרִים וְעִבְדוּ אֶת־
יהוה כִּי אֹתָהּ אַתֶּם מְבַקְשִׁים וַיְגָרֶשׁ אֹתָם מֵאֵת פְּנֵי פַרְעֹה:

BESHALLAH   בשלח

וַיְהִי בְּשַׁלַּח פַּרְעֹה אֶת־הָעָם וְלֹא־נָחָם אֱלֹהִים דֶּרֶךְ אֶרֶץ
פְּלִשְׁתִּים כִּי קָרוֹב הוּא כִּי ׀ אָמַר אֱלֹהִים פֶּן־יִנָּחֵם הָעָם
בִּרְאֹתָם מִלְחָמָה וְשָׁבוּ מִצְרָיְמָה: וַיַּסֵּב אֱלֹהִים ׀ אֶת־הָעָם
דֶּרֶךְ הַמִּדְבָּר יַם־סוּף וַחֲמֻשִׁים עָלוּ בְנֵי־יִשְׂרָאֵל מֵאֶרֶץ
מִצְרָיִם: וַיִּקַּח מֹשֶׁה אֶת־עַצְמוֹת יוֹסֵף עִמּוֹ כִּי הַשְׁבֵּעַ
הִשְׁבִּיעַ אֶת־בְּנֵי יִשְׂרָאֵל לֵאמֹר פָּקֹד יִפְקֹד אֱלֹהִים אֶתְכֶם
וְהַעֲלִיתֶם אֶת־עַצְמֹתַי מִזֶּה אִתְּכֶם: וַיִּסְעוּ מִסֻּכֹּת וַיַּחֲנוּ
בְאֵתָם בִּקְצֵה הַמִּדְבָּר: וַיהוה הֹלֵךְ לִפְנֵיהֶם יוֹמָם בְּעַמּוּד

שמות י:ג:יז–
יד:ח

SECOND ALIYA: vv. 4–6
The plague mentioned
here has the same letters
as another one of the
plagues. Can you think
of a connection between
the two?

THIRD ALIYA: vv. 7–11
What are two possibilities
for the fear that Pharaoh
had about Israel's growing
strength?

FIRST ALIYA: vv. 17–22
How many words can
you find that are repeated
more than once?

עָנָן לַנְחֹתָם הַדֶּרֶךְ וְלַיְלָה בְּעַמּוּד אֵשׁ לְהָאִיר לָהֶם לָלֶכֶת
יוֹמָם וָלָיְלָה: לֹא־יָמִישׁ עַמּוּד הֶעָנָן יוֹמָם וְעַמּוּד הָאֵשׁ
לָיְלָה לִפְנֵי הָעָם:

SECOND ALIYA: vv. 1–4
It sounds like someone said something to someone but the listener didn't hear it even though he wasn't deaf and so it must mean something else.

וַיְדַבֵּר יהוה אֶל־מֹשֶׁה לֵּאמֹר: דַּבֵּר אֶל־בְּנֵי יִשְׂרָאֵל וְיָשֻׁבוּ
וְיַחֲנוּ לִפְנֵי פִּי הַחִירֹת בֵּין מִגְדֹּל וּבֵין הַיָּם לִפְנֵי בַּעַל צְפֹן
נִכְחוֹ תַחֲנוּ עַל־הַיָּם: וְאָמַר פַּרְעֹה לִבְנֵי יִשְׂרָאֵל נְבֻכִים
הֵם בָּאָרֶץ סָגַר עֲלֵיהֶם הַמִּדְבָּר: וְחִזַּקְתִּי אֶת־לֵב־פַּרְעֹה
וְרָדַף אַחֲרֵיהֶם וְאִכָּבְדָה בְּפַרְעֹה וּבְכָל־חֵילוֹ וְיָדְעוּ מִצְרַיִם
כִּי־אֲנִי יהוה וַיַּעֲשׂוּ־כֵן:

THIRD ALIYA: vv. 5–8
Ḥazal learn from here that people can do unusual things when they hate someone else.

וַיֻּגַּד לְמֶלֶךְ מִצְרַיִם כִּי בָרַח הָעָם
וַיֵּהָפֵךְ לְבַב פַּרְעֹה וַעֲבָדָיו אֶל־הָעָם וַיֹּאמְרוּ מַה־זֹּאת
עָשִׂינוּ כִּי־שִׁלַּחְנוּ אֶת־יִשְׂרָאֵל מֵעָבְדֵנוּ: וַיֶּאְסֹר אֶת־רִכְבּוֹ
וְאֶת־עַמּוֹ לָקַח עִמּוֹ: וַיִּקַּח שֵׁשׁ־מֵאוֹת רֶכֶב בָּחוּר וְכֹל
רֶכֶב מִצְרָיִם וְשָׁלִשִׁם עַל־כֻּלּוֹ: וַיְחַזֵּק יהוה אֶת־לֵב פַּרְעֹה
מֶלֶךְ מִצְרַיִם וַיִּרְדֹּף אַחֲרֵי בְּנֵי יִשְׂרָאֵל וּבְנֵי יִשְׂרָאֵל יֹצְאִים
בְּיָד רָמָה:

יתרו
YITRO

FIRST ALIYA: vv. 1–4
How many different names of individuals are mentioned in these verses?

שמות
יח:א–יב

וַיִּשְׁמַע יִתְרוֹ כֹהֵן מִדְיָן חֹתֵן מֹשֶׁה אֵת כָּל־אֲשֶׁר עָשָׂה
אֱלֹהִים לְמֹשֶׁה וּלְיִשְׂרָאֵל עַמּוֹ כִּי־הוֹצִיא יהוה אֶת־יִשְׂרָאֵל
מִמִּצְרָיִם: וַיִּקַּח יִתְרוֹ חֹתֵן מֹשֶׁה אֶת־צִפֹּרָה אֵשֶׁת מֹשֶׁה
אַחַר שִׁלּוּחֶיהָ: וְאֵת שְׁנֵי בָנֶיהָ אֲשֶׁר שֵׁם הָאֶחָד גֵּרְשֹׁם
כִּי אָמַר גֵּר הָיִיתִי בְּאֶרֶץ נָכְרִיָּה: וְשֵׁם הָאֶחָד אֱלִיעֶזֶר כִּי־
אֱלֹהֵי אָבִי בְּעֶזְרִי וַיַּצִּלֵנִי מֵחֶרֶב פַּרְעֹה:

SECOND ALIYA: vv. 5–8
Another name for the place where the Torah was given?

וַיָּבֹא יִתְרוֹ חֹתֵן
מֹשֶׁה וּבָנָיו וְאִשְׁתּוֹ אֶל־מֹשֶׁה אֶל־הַמִּדְבָּר אֲשֶׁר־הוּא חֹנֶה
שָׁם הַר הָאֱלֹהִים: וַיֹּאמֶר אֶל־מֹשֶׁה אֲנִי חֹתֶנְךָ יִתְרוֹ בָּא
אֵלֶיךָ וְאִשְׁתְּךָ וּשְׁנֵי בָנֶיהָ עִמָּהּ: וַיֵּצֵא מֹשֶׁה לִקְרַאת חֹתְנוֹ
וַיִּשְׁתַּחוּ וַיִּשַּׁק־לוֹ וַיִּשְׁאֲלוּ אִישׁ־לְרֵעֵהוּ לְשָׁלוֹם וַיָּבֹאוּ
הָאֹהֱלָה: וַיְסַפֵּר מֹשֶׁה לְחֹתְנוֹ אֵת כָּל־אֲשֶׁר עָשָׂה יהוה
לְפַרְעֹה וּלְמִצְרַיִם עַל אוֹדֹת יִשְׂרָאֵל אֵת כָּל־הַתְּלָאָה אֲשֶׁר

ישראל מְצֵאתֶם בַּדֶּרֶךְ וַיִּשְׁלַם יהוה: *וַיִּחַדְּ יִתְרוֹ עַל כָּל־הַטּוֹבָה אֲשֶׁר־עָשָׂה יהוה לְיִשְׂרָאֵל אֲשֶׁר הִצִּילוֹ מִיַּד מִצְרָיִם: וַיֹּאמֶר יִתְרוֹ בָּרוּךְ יהוה אֲשֶׁר הִצִּיל אֶתְכֶם מִיַּד מִצְרַיִם וּמִיַּד פַּרְעֹה אֲשֶׁר הִצִּיל אֶת־הָעָם מִתַּחַת יַד־מִצְרָיִם: עַתָּה יָדַעְתִּי כִּי־גָדוֹל יהוה מִכָּל־הָאֱלֹהִים כִּי בַדָּבָר אֲשֶׁר זָדוּ עֲלֵיהֶם: וַיִּקַּח יִתְרוֹ חֹתֵן מֹשֶׁה עֹלָה וּזְבָחִים לֵאלֹהִים וַיָּבֹא אַהֲרֹן וְכֹל ׀ זִקְנֵי יִשְׂרָאֵל לֶאֱכָל־לֶחֶם עִם־חֹתֵן מֹשֶׁה לִפְנֵי הָאֱלֹהִים:

THIRD ALIYA: vv. 9–12
Yitro says something here that only Noah and Eliezer said before him in the Torah. What is it, and what about the speaker makes it all the more noteworthy?

MISHPATIM / משפטים

שמות כא:א־יט וְאֵלֶּה הַמִּשְׁפָּטִים אֲשֶׁר תָּשִׂים לִפְנֵיהֶם: כִּי תִקְנֶה עֶבֶד עִבְרִי שֵׁשׁ שָׁנִים יַעֲבֹד וּבַשְּׁבִעִת יֵצֵא לַחָפְשִׁי חִנָּם: אִם־בְּגַפּוֹ יָבֹא בְּגַפּוֹ יֵצֵא אִם־בַּעַל אִשָּׁה הוּא וְיָצְאָה אִשְׁתּוֹ עִמּוֹ: אִם־אֲדֹנָיו יִתֶּן־לוֹ אִשָּׁה וְיָלְדָה־לוֹ בָנִים אוֹ בָנוֹת הָאִשָּׁה וִילָדֶיהָ תִּהְיֶה לַאדֹנֶיהָ וְהוּא יֵצֵא בְגַפּוֹ: וְאִם־אָמֹר יֹאמַר הָעֶבֶד אָהַבְתִּי אֶת־אֲדֹנִי אֶת־אִשְׁתִּי וְאֶת־בָּנָי לֹא אֵצֵא חָפְשִׁי: וְהִגִּישׁוֹ אֲדֹנָיו אֶל־הָאֱלֹהִים וְהִגִּישׁוֹ אֶל־הַדֶּלֶת אוֹ אֶל־הַמְּזוּזָה וְרָצַע

לוי אֲדֹנָיו אֶת־אָזְנוֹ בַּמַּרְצֵעַ וַעֲבָדוֹ לְעֹלָם: *וְכִי־ יִמְכֹּר אִישׁ אֶת־בִּתּוֹ לְאָמָה לֹא תֵצֵא כְּצֵאת הָעֲבָדִים:

לז אִם־רָעָה בְּעֵינֵי אֲדֹנֶיהָ אֲשֶׁר־לא יְעָדָהּ וְהֶפְדָּהּ לְעַם נָכְרִי לֹא־יִמְשֹׁל לְמָכְרָהּ בְּבִגְדוֹ־בָהּ: וְאִם־לִבְנוֹ יִיעָדֶנָּה כְּמִשְׁפַּט הַבָּנוֹת יַעֲשֶׂה־לָּהּ: אִם־אַחֶרֶת יִקַּח־לוֹ שְׁאֵרָהּ כְּסוּתָהּ וְעֹנָתָהּ לֹא יִגְרָע: וְאִם־שְׁלָשׁ־אֵלֶּה לֹא יַעֲשֶׂה לָהּ וְיָצְאָה

ישראל חִנָּם אֵין כָּסֶף: *מַכֵּה אִישׁ וָמֵת מוֹת יוּמָת: וַאֲשֶׁר לֹא צָדָה וְהָאֱלֹהִים אִנָּה לְיָדוֹ וְשַׂמְתִּי לְךָ מָקוֹם אֲשֶׁר יָנוּס שָׁמָּה: וְכִי־יָזִד אִישׁ עַל־רֵעֵהוּ

THIRD ALIYA: vv. 12–19
From which words do the Rabbis determine that you may not be your parents' dentist?

לְהָרְגוֹ בְעָרְמָה מֵעִם מִזְבְּחִי תִּקָּחֶנּוּ לָמוּת: וּמַכֵּה אָבִיו וְאִמּוֹ מוֹת יוּמָת: וְגֹנֵב אִישׁ וּמְכָרוֹ וְנִמְצָא בְיָדוֹ מוֹת יוּמָת: וּמְקַלֵּל אָבִיו וְאִמּוֹ מוֹת יוּמָת:

FIRST ALIYA: vv. 1–6
From here one learns that all of the mitzvot in this parasha and the following ones were given at Sinai, just as the Ten Commandments were. Why is that important to know?

SECOND ALIYA: vv. 7–11
Find the play on words.

יוּמָת: וְכִי־יְרִיבֻן אֲנָשִׁים וְהִכָּה־אִישׁ אֶת־
רֵעֵהוּ בְּאֶבֶן אוֹ בְאֶגְרֹף וְלֹא יָמוּת וְנָפַל לְמִשְׁכָּב: אִם־יָקוּם
וְהִתְהַלֵּךְ בַּחוּץ עַל־מִשְׁעַנְתּוֹ וְנִקָּה הַמַּכֶּה רַק שִׁבְתּוֹ יִתֵּן
וְרַפֹּא יְרַפֵּא:

TERUMA

תרומה

וַיְדַבֵּר יְהוָה אֶל־מֹשֶׁה לֵּאמֹר: דַּבֵּר אֶל־בְּנֵי יִשְׂרָאֵל וְיִקְחוּ־
לִי תְּרוּמָה מֵאֵת כָּל־אִישׁ אֲשֶׁר יִדְּבֶנּוּ לִבּוֹ תִּקְחוּ אֶת־
תְּרוּמָתִי: וְזֹאת הַתְּרוּמָה אֲשֶׁר תִּקְחוּ מֵאִתָּם זָהָב וָכֶסֶף
וּנְחֹשֶׁת: וּתְכֵלֶת וְאַרְגָּמָן וְתוֹלַעַת שָׁנִי וְשֵׁשׁ וְעִזִּים: וְעֹרֹת
אֵילִם מְאָדָּמִים וְעֹרֹת תְּחָשִׁים וַעֲצֵי שִׁטִּים: ‏*שֶׁמֶן לַמָּאֹר
בְּשָׂמִים לְשֶׁמֶן הַמִּשְׁחָה וְלִקְטֹרֶת הַסַּמִּים: אַבְנֵי־שֹׁהַם
וְאַבְנֵי מִלֻּאִים לָאֵפֹד וְלַחֹשֶׁן: וְעָשׂוּ לִי מִקְדָּשׁ וְשָׁכַנְתִּי
בְּתוֹכָם: כְּכֹל אֲשֶׁר אֲנִי מַרְאֶה אוֹתְךָ אֵת תַּבְנִית הַמִּשְׁכָּן
וְאֵת תַּבְנִית כָּל־כֵּלָיו וְכֵן תַּעֲשׂוּ: ‏*וְעָשׂוּ אֲרוֹן
עֲצֵי שִׁטִּים אַמָּתַיִם וָחֵצִי אָרְכּוֹ וְאַמָּה וָחֵצִי רָחְבּוֹ וְאַמָּה וָחֵצִי
קֹמָתוֹ: וְצִפִּיתָ אֹתוֹ זָהָב טָהוֹר מִבַּיִת וּמִחוּץ תְּצַפֶּנּוּ וְעָשִׂיתָ
עָלָיו זֵר זָהָב סָבִיב: וְיָצַקְתָּ לּוֹ אַרְבַּע טַבְּעֹת זָהָב וְנָתַתָּה
עַל אַרְבַּע פַּעֲמֹתָיו וּשְׁתֵּי טַבָּעֹת עַל־צַלְעוֹ הָאֶחָת וּשְׁתֵּי
טַבָּעֹת עַל־צַלְעוֹ הַשֵּׁנִית: וְעָשִׂיתָ בַדֵּי עֲצֵי שִׁטִּים וְצִפִּיתָ
אֹתָם זָהָב: וְהֵבֵאתָ אֶת־הַבַּדִּים בַּטַּבָּעֹת עַל צַלְעֹת הָאָרֹן
לָשֵׂאת אֶת־הָאָרֹן בָּהֶם: בְּטַבְּעֹת הָאָרֹן יִהְיוּ הַבַּדִּים לֹא
יָסֻרוּ מִמֶּנּוּ: וְנָתַתָּ אֶל־הָאָרֹן אֵת הָעֵדֻת אֲשֶׁר אֶתֵּן אֵלֶיךָ:

שמות
כה:א–טז

FIRST ALIYA: vv. 1–5
What are the two basic
materials that the kohen's
clothes were made from?

SECOND ALIYA: vv. 6–9
Find two words for the
structure that was to be
made. What do you think
is the significance of each?

THIRD ALIYA: vv. 10–16
What was contained in
the Aron? Why do you
think it was called that?

לוי

ישראל

TETZAVE

תצוה

וְאַתָּה תְּצַוֶּה ׀ אֶת־בְּנֵי יִשְׂרָאֵל וְיִקְחוּ אֵלֶיךָ שֶׁמֶן זַיִת זָךְ כָּתִית
לַמָּאוֹר לְהַעֲלֹת נֵר תָּמִיד: בְּאֹהֶל מוֹעֵד מִחוּץ לַפָּרֹכֶת אֲשֶׁר
עַל־הָעֵדֻת יַעֲרֹךְ אֹתוֹ אַהֲרֹן וּבָנָיו מֵעֶרֶב עַד־בֹּקֶר לִפְנֵי יְהוָה
חֻקַּת עוֹלָם לְדֹרֹתָם מֵאֵת בְּנֵי יִשְׂרָאֵל: וְאַתָּה

שמות
כז:כ–
כח:ה

FIRST ALIYA:
vv. 27:20–28:5
How do you know that
the word תָּמִיד here does
not mean "all of the time?"

הַקְרֵב אֵלֶיךָ אֶת־אַהֲרֹן אָחִיךָ וְאֶת־בָּנָיו אִתּוֹ מִתּוֹךְ בְּנֵי
יִשְׂרָאֵל לְכַהֲנוֹ־לִי אַהֲרֹן נָדָב וַאֲבִיהוּא אֶלְעָזָר וְאִיתָמָר בְּנֵי
אַהֲרֹן: וְעָשִׂיתָ בִגְדֵי־קֹדֶשׁ לְאַהֲרֹן אָחִיךָ לְכָבוֹד וּלְתִפְאָרֶת:
וְאַתָּה תְּדַבֵּר אֶל־כָּל־חַכְמֵי־לֵב אֲשֶׁר מִלֵּאתִיו רוּחַ חָכְמָה
וְעָשׂוּ אֶת־בִּגְדֵי אַהֲרֹן לְקַדְּשׁוֹ לְכַהֲנוֹ־לִי: וְאֵלֶּה הַבְּגָדִים
אֲשֶׁר יַעֲשׂוּ חֹשֶׁן וְאֵפוֹד וּמְעִיל וּכְתֹנֶת תַּשְׁבֵּץ מִצְנֶפֶת
וְאַבְנֵט וְעָשׂוּ בִגְדֵי־קֹדֶשׁ לְאַהֲרֹן אָחִיךָ וּלְבָנָיו לְכַהֲנוֹ־לִי:
וְהֵם יִקְחוּ אֶת־הַזָּהָב וְאֶת־הַתְּכֵלֶת וְאֶת־הָאַרְגָּמָן וְאֶת־
תּוֹלַעַת הַשָּׁנִי וְאֶת־הַשֵּׁשׁ:

לוי וְעָשׂוּ אֶת־הָאֵפֹד זָהָב תְּכֵלֶת וְאַרְגָּמָן תּוֹלַעַת שָׁנִי וְשֵׁשׁ
מָשְׁזָר מַעֲשֵׂה חֹשֵׁב: שְׁתֵּי כְתֵפֹת חֹבְרֹת יִהְיֶה־לּוֹ אֶל־
שְׁנֵי קְצוֹתָיו וְחֻבָּר: וְחֵשֶׁב אֲפֻדָּתוֹ אֲשֶׁר עָלָיו כְּמַעֲשֵׂהוּ
מִמֶּנּוּ יִהְיֶה זָהָב תְּכֵלֶת וְאַרְגָּמָן וְתוֹלַעַת שָׁנִי וְשֵׁשׁ מָשְׁזָר:
וְלָקַחְתָּ אֶת־שְׁתֵּי אַבְנֵי־שֹׁהַם וּפִתַּחְתָּ עֲלֵיהֶם שְׁמוֹת בְּנֵי
יִשְׂרָאֵל: *שִׁשָּׁה מִשְּׁמֹתָם עַל הָאֶבֶן הָאֶחָת וְאֶת־שְׁמוֹת
הַשִּׁשָּׁה הַנּוֹתָרִים עַל־הָאֶבֶן הַשֵּׁנִית כְּתוֹלְדֹתָם: מַעֲשֵׂה
חָרַשׁ אֶבֶן פִּתּוּחֵי חֹתָם תְּפַתַּח אֶת־שְׁתֵּי הָאֲבָנִים עַל־שְׁמֹת
בְּנֵי יִשְׂרָאֵל מֻסַבֹּת מִשְׁבְּצוֹת זָהָב תַּעֲשֶׂה אֹתָם: וְשַׂמְתָּ
אֶת־שְׁתֵּי הָאֲבָנִים עַל כִּתְפֹת הָאֵפֹד אַבְנֵי זִכָּרֹן לִבְנֵי יִשְׂרָאֵל
וְנָשָׂא אַהֲרֹן אֶת־שְׁמוֹתָם לִפְנֵי יהוה עַל־שְׁתֵּי כְתֵפָיו לְזִכָּרֹן:

ישראל

KI TISSA
כי תשא

וַיְדַבֵּר יהוה אֶל־מֹשֶׁה לֵּאמֹר: כִּי תִשָּׂא אֶת־רֹאשׁ בְּנֵי
יִשְׂרָאֵל לִפְקֻדֵיהֶם וְנָתְנוּ אִישׁ כֹּפֶר נַפְשׁוֹ לַיהוה בִּפְקֹד
אֹתָם וְלֹא־יִהְיֶה בָהֶם נֶגֶף בִּפְקֹד אֹתָם: זֶה ׀ יִתְּנוּ כָּל־הָעֹבֵר
עַל־הַפְּקֻדִים מַחֲצִית הַשֶּׁקֶל בְּשֶׁקֶל הַקֹּדֶשׁ עֶשְׂרִים גֵּרָה
הַשֶּׁקֶל מַחֲצִית הַשֶּׁקֶל תְּרוּמָה לַיהוה: *כֹּל הָעֹבֵר עַל־
הַפְּקֻדִים מִבֶּן עֶשְׂרִים שָׁנָה וָמָעְלָה יִתֵּן תְּרוּמַת יהוה:
הֶעָשִׁיר לֹא־יַרְבֶּה וְהַדַּל לֹא יַמְעִיט מִמַּחֲצִית הַשָּׁקֶל לָתֵת

שמות
לוי

SECOND ALIYA: vv. 6–9
This entire *parasha* is
known for one conspicu-
ous absence. What is it?
Why do you think that
might be?

THIRD ALIYA: vv. 10–12
There were two stones on
either shoulder strap of
the *ephod*, each with the
names of six of the twelve
tribes. According to what
order were the names ar-
ranged on the stones?

FIRST ALIYA: vv. 11–13
Based on *this* word,
Hazal understood
that Hashem actually
showed Moshe a coin
of fire. What do you think
might be the relationship
between the two?

SECOND ALIYA: vv. 14–16
What was the stated pur-
pose of the half-shekel?
What custom that we

אֶת־תְּרוּמַת יְהוֹה לְכַפֵּר עַל־נַפְשֹׁתֵיכֶם: וְלָקַחְתָּ אֶת־כֶּסֶף
הַכִּפֻּרִים מֵאֵת בְּנֵי יִשְׂרָאֵל וְנָתַתָּ אֹתוֹ עַל־עֲבֹדַת אֹהֶל
מוֹעֵד וְהָיָה לִבְנֵי יִשְׂרָאֵל לְזִכָּרוֹן לִפְנֵי יְהוֹה לְכַפֵּר עַל־
נַפְשֹׁתֵיכֶם:

ישראל

וַיְדַבֵּר יְהוֹה אֶל־מֹשֶׁה לֵּאמֹר: וְעָשִׂיתָ כִּיּוֹר נְחֹשֶׁת וְכַנּוֹ
נְחֹשֶׁת לְרָחְצָה וְנָתַתָּ אֹתוֹ בֵּין־אֹהֶל מוֹעֵד וּבֵין הַמִּזְבֵּחַ
וְנָתַתָּ שָׁמָּה מָיִם: וְרָחֲצוּ אַהֲרֹן וּבָנָיו מִמֶּנּוּ אֶת־יְדֵיהֶם וְאֶת־
רַגְלֵיהֶם: בְּבֹאָם אֶל־אֹהֶל מוֹעֵד יִרְחֲצוּ־מַיִם וְלֹא יָמֻתוּ
אוֹ בְגִשְׁתָּם אֶל־הַמִּזְבֵּחַ לְשָׁרֵת לְהַקְטִיר אִשֶּׁה לַיהוֹה:
וְרָחֲצוּ יְדֵיהֶם וְרַגְלֵיהֶם וְלֹא יָמֻתוּ וְהָיְתָה לָהֶם חָק־עוֹלָם
לוֹ וּלְזַרְעוֹ לְדֹרֹתָם:

ויקהל
VAYAK-HEL

שמות
לה:א-כ

וַיַּקְהֵל מֹשֶׁה אֶת־כָּל־עֲדַת בְּנֵי יִשְׂרָאֵל וַיֹּאמֶר אֲלֵהֶם אֵלֶּה
הַדְּבָרִים אֲשֶׁר־צִוָּה יְהוֹה לַעֲשֹׂת אֹתָם: שֵׁשֶׁת יָמִים תֵּעָשֶׂה
מְלָאכָה וּבַיּוֹם הַשְּׁבִיעִי יִהְיֶה לָכֶם קֹדֶשׁ שַׁבַּת שַׁבָּתוֹן
לַיהוֹה כָּל־הָעֹשֶׂה בוֹ מְלָאכָה יוּמָת: לֹא־תְבַעֲרוּ אֵשׁ בְּכֹל
מֹשְׁבֹתֵיכֶם בְּיוֹם הַשַּׁבָּת:

לוי

וַיֹּאמֶר מֹשֶׁה אֶל־כָּל־עֲדַת בְּנֵי־יִשְׂרָאֵל לֵאמֹר זֶה הַדָּבָר
אֲשֶׁר־צִוָּה יְהוֹה לֵאמֹר: קְחוּ מֵאִתְּכֶם תְּרוּמָה לַיהוֹה כֹּל
נְדִיב לִבּוֹ יְבִיאֶהָ אֵת תְּרוּמַת יְהוֹה זָהָב וָכֶסֶף וּנְחֹשֶׁת:
וּתְכֵלֶת וְאַרְגָּמָן וְתוֹלַעַת שָׁנִי וְשֵׁשׁ וְעִזִּים: וְעֹרֹת אֵילִם
מְאָדָּמִים וְעֹרֹת תְּחָשִׁים וַעֲצֵי שִׁטִּים: שֶׁמֶן לַמָּאוֹר וּבְשָׂמִים
לְשֶׁמֶן הַמִּשְׁחָה וְלִקְטֹרֶת הַסַּמִּים: וְאַבְנֵי־שֹׁהַם וְאַבְנֵי
מִלֻּאִים לָאֵפוֹד וְלַחֹשֶׁן: וְכָל־חֲכַם־לֵב בָּכֶם יָבֹאוּ וְיַעֲשׂוּ
אֵת כָּל־אֲשֶׁר צִוָּה יְהוֹה: *אֶת־הַמִּשְׁכָּן אֶת־אָהֳלוֹ וְאֶת־
מִכְסֵהוּ אֶת־קְרָסָיו וְאֶת־קְרָשָׁיו אֶת־בְּרִיחָו אֶת־עַמֻּדָיו
וְאֶת־אֲדָנָיו: אֶת־הָאָרֹן וְאֶת־בַּדָּיו אֶת־הַכַּפֹּרֶת וְאֵת פָּרֹכֶת
הַמָּסָךְ: אֶת־הַשֻּׁלְחָן וְאֶת־בַּדָּיו וְאֶת־כָּל־כֵּלָיו וְאֵת לֶחֶם

ישראל

have today evolved from
here? What do you think
should be done with the
money collected?

THIRD ALIYA: vv. 17–21
What is the punishment of
the *kohanim* for not using
the כִּיּוֹר?

FIRST ALIYA: vv. 1–3
Based on this verse,
the Karaites used to live
in the dark on Shabbat.
What can be learned
about the importance of
Torah Shebe'al Peh?

SECOND ALIYA: vv. 4–10
What is the expression
which indicates that contributions were voluntary?
Why do you think this
might be an appropriate
way to express this?

THIRD ALIYA: vv. 11–20
This is one of 14
parashot that are
frequently doubled
up so that the Torah
reading fits into one
year. What are the other
six doubles?

הַפָּנִים: וְאֶת־מְנֹרַת הַמָּאוֹר וְאֶת־כֵּלֶיהָ וְאֶת־נֵרֹתֶיהָ וְאֵת
שֶׁמֶן הַמָּאוֹר: וְאֵת ׀ מִזְבַּח הַזָּהָב וְאֶת־שֶׁמֶן הַמִּשְׁחָה וְאֵת שֶׁמֶן
הַמִּשְׁחָה וְאֵת קְטֹרֶת הַסַּמִּים וְאֵת מָסַךְ הַפֶּתַח לְפֶתַח
הַמִּשְׁכָּן: אֵת ׀ מִזְבַּח הַנְּחֹשֶׁת וְאֶת־מִכְבַּר הַנְּחֹשֶׁת אֲשֶׁר
לוֹ אֶת־בַּדָּיו וְאֶת־כָּל־כֵּלָיו אֶת־הַכִּיֹּר וְאֶת־כַּנּוֹ: אֵת קַלְעֵי
הֶחָצֵר אֶת־עַמֻּדֶיהָ וְאֶת־אֲדָנֶיהָ וְאֵת מָסַךְ שַׁעַר הֶחָצֵר:
אֶת־יִתְדֹת הַמִּשְׁכָּן וְאֶת־יִתְדֹת הֶחָצֵר וְאֶת־מֵיתְרֵיהֶם:
אֶת־בִּגְדֵי הַשְּׂרָד לְשָׁרֵת בַּקֹּדֶשׁ אֶת־בִּגְדֵי הַקֹּדֶשׁ לְאַהֲרֹן
הַכֹּהֵן וְאֶת־בִּגְדֵי בָנָיו לְכַהֵן: וַיֵּצְאוּ כָּל־עֲדַת בְּנֵי־יִשְׂרָאֵל
מִלִּפְנֵי מֹשֶׁה:

פקודי
PEKUDEI

שמות
לח:כא–לט:א

אֵלֶּה פְקוּדֵי הַמִּשְׁכָּן מִשְׁכַּן הָעֵדֻת אֲשֶׁר פֻּקַּד עַל־פִּי מֹשֶׁה
עֲבֹדַת הַלְוִיִּם בְּיַד אִיתָמָר בֶּן־אַהֲרֹן הַכֹּהֵן: וּבְצַלְאֵל בֶּן־
אוּרִי בֶן־חוּר לְמַטֵּה יְהוּדָה עָשָׂה אֵת כָּל־אֲשֶׁר־צִוָּה
יְהוָה אֶת־מֹשֶׁה: וְאִתּוֹ אָהֳלִיאָב בֶּן־אֲחִיסָמָךְ לְמַטֵּה־דָן
חָרָשׁ וְחֹשֵׁב וְרֹקֵם בַּתְּכֵלֶת וּבָאַרְגָּמָן וּבְתוֹלַעַת הַשָּׁנִי
וּבַשֵּׁשׁ: *כָּל־הַזָּהָב הֶעָשׂוּי לַמְּלָאכָה בְּכֹל

לוי

מְלֶאכֶת הַקֹּדֶשׁ וַיְהִי ׀ זְהַב הַתְּנוּפָה תֵּשַׁע וְעֶשְׂרִים כִּכָּר
וּשְׁבַע מֵאוֹת וּשְׁלֹשִׁים שֶׁקֶל בְּשֶׁקֶל הַקֹּדֶשׁ: וְכֶסֶף פְּקוּדֵי
הָעֵדָה מְאַת כִּכָּר וְאֶלֶף וּשְׁבַע מֵאוֹת וַחֲמִשָּׁה וְשִׁבְעִים
שֶׁקֶל בְּשֶׁקֶל הַקֹּדֶשׁ: בֶּקַע לַגֻּלְגֹּלֶת מַחֲצִית הַשֶּׁקֶל בְּשֶׁקֶל
הַקֹּדֶשׁ לְכֹל הָעֹבֵר עַל־הַפְּקֻדִים מִבֶּן עֶשְׂרִים שָׁנָה וָמַעְלָה
לְשֵׁשׁ־מֵאוֹת אֶלֶף וּשְׁלֹשֶׁת אֲלָפִים וַחֲמֵשׁ מֵאוֹת וַחֲמִשִּׁים:
וַיְהִי מְאַת כִּכַּר הַכֶּסֶף לָצֶקֶת אֵת אַדְנֵי הַקֹּדֶשׁ וְאֵת אַדְנֵי
הַפָּרֹכֶת מְאַת אֲדָנִים לִמְאַת הַכִּכָּר כִּכָּר לָאָדֶן: וְאֶת־

ישראל

הָאֶלֶף וּשְׁבַע הַמֵּאוֹת וַחֲמִשָּׁה וְשִׁבְעִים עָשָׂה וָוִים לָעַמּוּדִים
וְצִפָּה רָאשֵׁיהֶם וְחִשַּׁק אֹתָם: וּנְחֹשֶׁת הַתְּנוּפָה שִׁבְעִים כִּכָּר
וְאַלְפַּיִם וְאַרְבַּע־מֵאוֹת שָׁקֶל: וַיַּעַשׂ בָּהּ אֶת־אַדְנֵי פֶּתַח אֹהֶל

FIRST ALIYA: vv. 21–23
The *Mishkan* here is given
two names. What are
they? What might be the
significance of each?

SECOND ALIYA:
vv. 24–27
There were 3,000 shekel in
a כִּכָּר according to Rashi.
How many shekels worth
of gold and silver
were donated?

THIRD ALIYA: vv. 28–39:1
This phrase appears 18
times in the *parasha*,
which some say parallels

מוֹעֵד וְאֵת מִזְבַּח הַנְּחֹשֶׁת וְאֶת־מִכְבַּר הַנְּחֹשֶׁת אֲשֶׁר־לוֹ
וְאֶת־כָּל־כֵּלָיו הַמִּזְבֵּחַ׃ וְאֵת־אַדְנֵי הֶחָצֵר סָבִיב וְאֶת־אַדְנֵי
שַׁעַר הֶחָצֵר וְאֵת כָּל־יִתְדֹת הַמִּשְׁכָּן וְאֶת־כָּל־יִתְדֹת הֶחָצֵר
סָבִיב׃ וּמִן־הַתְּכֵלֶת וְהָאַרְגָּמָן וְתוֹלַעַת הַשָּׁנִי עָשׂוּ בִגְדֵי־
שְׂרָד לְשָׁרֵת בַּקֹּדֶשׁ וַיַּעֲשׂוּ אֶת־בִּגְדֵי הַקֹּדֶשׁ אֲשֶׁר לְאַהֲרֹן
כַּאֲשֶׁר צִוָּה יהוה אֶת־מֹשֶׁה׃

VAYIKRA

ויקרא

ויקרא
א:א–ד

וַיִּקְרָא אֶל־מֹשֶׁה וַיְדַבֵּר יהוה אֵלָיו מֵאֹהֶל מוֹעֵד לֵאמֹר׃
דַּבֵּר אֶל־בְּנֵי יִשְׂרָאֵל וְאָמַרְתָּ אֲלֵהֶם אָדָם כִּי־יַקְרִיב מִכֶּם
קָרְבָּן לַיהוה מִן־הַבְּהֵמָה מִן־הַבָּקָר וּמִן־הַצֹּאן תַּקְרִיבוּ אֶת־
קָרְבַּנְכֶם׃ אִם־עֹלָה קָרְבָּנוֹ מִן־הַבָּקָר זָכָר תָּמִים יַקְרִיבֶנּוּ
אֶל־פֶּתַח אֹהֶל מוֹעֵד יַקְרִיב אֹתוֹ לִרְצֹנוֹ לִפְנֵי יהוה׃ וְסָמַךְ

לוי

יָדוֹ עַל רֹאשׁ הָעֹלָה וְנִרְצָה לוֹ לְכַפֵּר עָלָיו׃ וְשָׁחַט אֶת־בֶּן־
הַבָּקָר לִפְנֵי יהוה וְהִקְרִיבוּ בְּנֵי אַהֲרֹן הַכֹּהֲנִים אֶת־הַדָּם
וְזָרְקוּ אֶת־הַדָּם עַל־הַמִּזְבֵּחַ סָבִיב אֲשֶׁר־פֶּתַח אֹהֶל מוֹעֵד׃
וְהִפְשִׁיט אֶת־הָעֹלָה וְנִתַּח אֹתָהּ לִנְתָחֶיהָ׃ וְנָתְנוּ בְּנֵי אַהֲרֹן
הַכֹּהֵן אֵשׁ עַל־הַמִּזְבֵּחַ וְעָרְכוּ עֵצִים עַל־הָאֵשׁ׃ וְעָרְכוּ בְּנֵי
אַהֲרֹן הַכֹּהֲנִים אֵת הַנְּתָחִים אֶת־הָרֹאשׁ וְאֶת־הַפָּדֶר עַל־
הָעֵצִים אֲשֶׁר עַל־הָאֵשׁ אֲשֶׁר עַל־הַמִּזְבֵּחַ׃ וְקִרְבּוֹ וּכְרָעָיו

ישראל

יִרְחַץ בַּמָּיִם וְהִקְטִיר הַכֹּהֵן אֶת־הַכֹּל הַמִּזְבֵּחָה עֹלָה אִשֵּׁה
רֵיחַ־נִיחוֹחַ לַיהוה׃ *וְאִם־מִן־הַצֹּאן קָרְבָּנוֹ מִן־
הַכְּשָׂבִים אוֹ מִן־הָעִזִּים לְעֹלָה זָכָר תָּמִים יַקְרִיבֶנּוּ׃ וְשָׁחַט
אֹתוֹ עַל יֶרֶךְ הַמִּזְבֵּחַ צָפֹנָה לִפְנֵי יהוה וְזָרְקוּ בְּנֵי אַהֲרֹן
הַכֹּהֲנִים אֶת־דָּמוֹ עַל־הַמִּזְבֵּחַ סָבִיב׃ וְנִתַּח אֹתוֹ לִנְתָחָיו
וְאֶת־רֹאשׁוֹ וְאֶת־פִּדְרוֹ וְעָרַךְ הַכֹּהֵן אֹתָם עַל־הָעֵצִים אֲשֶׁר
עַל־הָאֵשׁ אֲשֶׁר עַל־הַמִּזְבֵּחַ׃ וְהַקֶּרֶב וְהַכְּרָעַיִם יִרְחַץ בַּמָּיִם
וְהִקְרִיב הַכֹּהֵן אֶת־הַכֹּל וְהִקְטִיר הַמִּזְבֵּחָה עֹלָה הוּא אִשֵּׁה
רֵיחַ נִיחֹחַ לַיהוה׃

---

the 18 *berakhot* of the *Shemoneh Esreh* and the 18 bones in the vertebrae. What's the connection?

FIRST ALIYA: vv. 1–4
From here the Gemara (*Yoma* 4b) learns that one should not just begin to talk to a friend without some prelude of greeting that will give them a moment to turn their attention toward you. What message is contained here?

SECOND ALIYA: vv. 5–9
This particular kind of sacrifice is so called because it is totally burned (Rashi), or because it atones for sins which come up in one's mind (Ramban) or because it causes a person's spiritual status to rise up (Hirsch). Which of these interpretations speaks to you the most?

THIRD ALIYA: vv. 10–13
There are three types of *olah*, or elevated offerings. One of them involves birds. The other two can be found in this *aliya* and the first *aliya*. What are they?

TZAV

צו

וַיְדַבֵּר יהוָה אֶל־מֹשֶׁה לֵּאמֹר: צַו אֶת־אַהֲרֹן וְאֶת־בָּנָיו לֵאמֹר זֹאת תּוֹרַת הֶעֹלֶה הִוא הָעֹלָה עַל מוֹקְדָה עַל־הַמִּזְבֵּחַ כָּל־הַלַּיְלָה עַד־הַבֹּקֶר וְאֵשׁ הַמִּזְבֵּחַ תּוּקַד בּוֹ: וְלָבַשׁ הַכֹּהֵן מִדּוֹ בַד וּמִכְנְסֵי־בַד יִלְבַּשׁ עַל־בְּשָׂרוֹ וְהֵרִים אֶת־הַדֶּשֶׁן אֲשֶׁר תֹּאכַל הָאֵשׁ אֶת־הָעֹלָה עַל־הַמִּזְבֵּחַ וְשָׂמוֹ אֵצֶל הַמִּזְבֵּחַ: וּפָשַׁט אֶת־בְּגָדָיו וְלָבַשׁ בְּגָדִים אֲחֵרִים וְהוֹצִיא אֶת־הַדֶּשֶׁן אֶל־מִחוּץ לַמַּחֲנֶה אֶל־מָקוֹם טָהוֹר: וְהָאֵשׁ עַל־הַמִּזְבֵּחַ תּוּקַד־בּוֹ לֹא תִכְבֶּה וּבִעֵר עָלֶיהָ הַכֹּהֵן עֵצִים בַּבֹּקֶר בַּבֹּקֶר וְעָרַךְ עָלֶיהָ הָעֹלָה וְהִקְטִיר עָלֶיהָ חֶלְבֵי הַשְּׁלָמִים: אֵשׁ תָּמִיד תּוּקַד עַל־הַמִּזְבֵּחַ לֹא תִכְבֶּה: וְזֹאת תּוֹרַת הַמִּנְחָה הַקְרֵב אֹתָהּ בְּנֵי־אַהֲרֹן לִפְנֵי יהוה אֶל־פְּנֵי הַמִּזְבֵּחַ: וְהֵרִים מִמֶּנּוּ בְּקֻמְצוֹ מִסֹּלֶת הַמִּנְחָה וּמִשַּׁמְנָהּ וְאֵת כָּל־הַלְּבֹנָה אֲשֶׁר עַל־הַמִּנְחָה וְהִקְטִיר הַמִּזְבֵּחַ רֵיחַ נִיחֹחַ אַזְכָּרָתָהּ לַיהוה: וְהַנּוֹתֶרֶת מִמֶּנָּה יֹאכְלוּ אַהֲרֹן וּבָנָיו מַצּוֹת תֵּאָכֵל בְּמָקוֹם קָדֹשׁ בַּחֲצַר אֹהֶל־מוֹעֵד יֹאכְלוּהָ: לֹא תֵאָפֶה חָמֵץ חֶלְקָם נָתַתִּי אֹתָהּ מֵאִשָּׁי קֹדֶשׁ קָדָשִׁים הִוא כַּחַטָּאת וְכָאָשָׁם: כָּל־זָכָר בִּבְנֵי אַהֲרֹן יֹאכְלֶנָּה חָק־עוֹלָם לְדֹרֹתֵיכֶם מֵאִשֵּׁי יהוה כֹּל אֲשֶׁר־יִגַּע בָּהֶם יִקְדָּשׁ:

ויקרא ו:א–ג

FIRST ALIYA: vv. 1–3
How many garments of white linen did the *kohen* wear when removing the ashes from the previous day's sacrifices?

לוי

SECOND ALIYA: vv. 4–6
From here Rashi learns that one should not serve one's guest something to drink while wearing the same clothes that one wore when one was cooking food. What's the source and the reason?

ישראל

THIRD ALIYA: vv. 7–11
There are those who say that the name of the prayer comes from here because it too is a gift that we offer to Hashem. Which prayer? How is it a gift?

SHEMINI

שמיני

וַיְהִי בַּיּוֹם הַשְּׁמִינִי קָרָא מֹשֶׁה לְאַהֲרֹן וּלְבָנָיו וּלְזִקְנֵי יִשְׂרָאֵל: וַיֹּאמֶר אֶל־אַהֲרֹן קַח־לְךָ עֵגֶל בֶּן־בָּקָר לְחַטָּאת וְאַיִל לְעֹלָה תְּמִימִם וְהַקְרֵב לִפְנֵי יהוה: וְאֶל־בְּנֵי יִשְׂרָאֵל תְּדַבֵּר לֵאמֹר קְחוּ שְׂעִיר־עִזִּים לְחַטָּאת וְעֵגֶל וָכֶבֶשׂ בְּנֵי־שָׁנָה תְּמִימִם לְעֹלָה: וְשׁוֹר וָאַיִל לִשְׁלָמִים לִזְבֹּחַ לִפְנֵי יהוה וּמִנְחָה בְּלוּלָה בַשָּׁמֶן כִּי הַיּוֹם יהוה נִרְאָה אֲלֵיכֶם: וַיִּקְחוּ אֵת אֲשֶׁר צִוָּה מֹשֶׁה אֶל־פְּנֵי אֹהֶל מוֹעֵד וַיִּקְרְבוּ כָּל־הָעֵדָה וַיַּעַמְדוּ לִפְנֵי יהוה: וַיֹּאמֶר מֹשֶׁה זֶה הַדָּבָר אֲשֶׁר־צִוָּה יהוה

ויקרא ט:א–טז

FIRST ALIYA: vv. 1–5
For seven days Moshe had performed the inauguration service of the *Mishkan* by himself. But it was only on this, the eighth day, when Aharon and his sons took over, that Hashem made His Presence felt. Which words form the basis for this observation?

לוי

תַּעֲשׂוּ וְיֵרָא אֲלֵיכֶם כְּבוֹד יהוה: *וַיֹּאמֶר מֹשֶׁה אֶל־אַהֲרֹן
קְרַב אֶל־הַמִּזְבֵּחַ וַעֲשֵׂה אֶת־חַטָּאתְךָ וְאֶת־עֹלָתֶךָ וְכַפֵּר
בַּעַדְךָ וּבְעַד הָעָם וַעֲשֵׂה אֶת־קָרְבַּן הָעָם וְכַפֵּר בַּעֲדָם
כַּאֲשֶׁר צִוָּה יהוה: וַיִּקְרַב אַהֲרֹן אֶל־הַמִּזְבֵּחַ וַיִּשְׁחַט אֶת־
עֵגֶל הַחַטָּאת אֲשֶׁר־לוֹ: וַיַּקְרִבוּ בְּנֵי אַהֲרֹן אֶת־הַדָּם אֵלָיו
וַיִּטְבֹּל אֶצְבָּעוֹ בַּדָּם וַיִּתֵּן עַל־קַרְנוֹת הַמִּזְבֵּחַ וְאֶת־הַדָּם
יָצַק אֶל־יְסוֹד הַמִּזְבֵּחַ: וְאֶת־הַחֵלֶב וְאֶת־הַכְּלָיֹת וְאֶת־
הַיֹּתֶרֶת מִן־הַכָּבֵד מִן־הַחַטָּאת הִקְטִיר הַמִּזְבֵּחָה כַּאֲשֶׁר
צִוָּה יהוה אֶת־מֹשֶׁה: *וְאֶת־הַבָּשָׂר וְאֶת־הָעוֹר שָׂרַף בָּאֵשׁ
מִחוּץ לַמַּחֲנֶה: וַיִּשְׁחַט אֶת־הָעֹלָה וַיַּמְצִאוּ בְּנֵי אַהֲרֹן אֵלָיו
אֶת־הַדָּם וַיִּזְרְקֵהוּ עַל־הַמִּזְבֵּחַ סָבִיב: וְאֶת־הָעֹלָה הִמְצִיאוּ
אֵלָיו לִנְתָחֶיהָ וְאֶת־הָרֹאשׁ וַיַּקְטֵר עַל־הַמִּזְבֵּחַ: וַיִּרְחַץ
אֶת־הַקֶּרֶב וְאֶת־הַכְּרָעָיִם וַיַּקְטֵר עַל־הָעֹלָה הַמִּזְבֵּחָה:
וַיַּקְרֵב אֵת קָרְבַּן הָעָם וַיִּקַּח אֶת־שְׂעִיר הַחַטָּאת אֲשֶׁר לָעָם
וַיִּשְׁחָטֵהוּ וַיְחַטְּאֵהוּ כָּרִאשׁוֹן: וַיַּקְרֵב אֶת־הָעֹלָה וַיַּעֲשֶׂהָ
כַּמִּשְׁפָּט:

ישראל

לוי

SECOND ALIYA: vv. 6–10
The Gemara in *Bava Metzia* (107b) uses these words to say that one cannot atone for the sins of others until one atones for oneself. Why do you think this should be so?

THIRD ALIYA: vv. 11–16
Which Hebrew word means (a) feet, (b) entrails, (c) pieces?

TAZRIA

תזריע

וַיְרָא
יב:א-יג:ה

וַיְדַבֵּר יהוה אֶל־מֹשֶׁה לֵּאמֹר: דַּבֵּר אֶל־בְּנֵי יִשְׂרָאֵל לֵאמֹר
אִשָּׁה כִּי תַזְרִיעַ וְיָלְדָה זָכָר וְטָמְאָה שִׁבְעַת יָמִים כִּימֵי נִדַּת
דְּוֺתָהּ תִּטְמָא: וּבַיּוֹם הַשְּׁמִינִי יִמּוֹל בְּשַׂר עָרְלָתוֹ: וּשְׁלֹשִׁים
יוֹם וּשְׁלֹשֶׁת יָמִים תֵּשֵׁב בִּדְמֵי טָהֳרָה בְּכָל־קֹדֶשׁ לֹא־תִגָּע
וְאֶל־הַמִּקְדָּשׁ לֹא תָבֹא עַד־מְלֹאת יְמֵי טָהֳרָהּ: *וְאִם־נְקֵבָה
תֵלֵד וְטָמְאָה שְׁבֻעַיִם כְּנִדָּתָהּ וְשִׁשִּׁים יוֹם וְשֵׁשֶׁת יָמִים
תֵּשֵׁב עַל־דְּמֵי טָהֳרָה: וּבִמְלֹאת ׀ יְמֵי טָהֳרָהּ לְבֵן אוֹ לְבַת
תָּבִיא כֶּבֶשׂ בֶּן־שְׁנָתוֹ לְעֹלָה וּבֶן־יוֹנָה אוֹ־תֹר לְחַטָּאת
אֶל־פֶּתַח אֹהֶל־מוֹעֵד אֶל־הַכֹּהֵן: וְהִקְרִיבוֹ לִפְנֵי יהוה וְכִפֶּר
עָלֶיהָ וְטָהֲרָה מִמְּקֹר דָּמֶיהָ זֹאת תּוֹרַת הַיֹּלֶדֶת לַזָּכָר אוֹ
לַנְּקֵבָה: וְאִם־לֹא תִמְצָא יָדָהּ דֵּי שֶׂה וְלָקְחָה שְׁתֵּי־תֹרִים

FIRST ALIYA: vv. 1–4
From here the Rabbis learned that a *Brit Mila* must be performed during the day and not at night. Which is the critical word that teaches us this?

SECOND ALIYA: vv. 5–8
From here one could suggest that the Torah believes in progressive taxation. Why do you think that is?

אוֹ שְׁנֵי בְנֵי יוֹנָה אֶחָד לְעֹלָה וְאֶחָד לְחַטָּאת וְכִפֶּר עָלֶיהָ
הַכֹּהֵן וְטָהֵרָה:

ישראל וַיְדַבֵּר יְהוָה אֶל־מֹשֶׁה וְאֶל־אַהֲרֹן לֵאמֹר: אָדָם כִּי־יִהְיֶה
בְעוֹר־בְּשָׂרוֹ שְׂאֵת אֽוֹ־סַפַּחַת אוֹ בַהֶרֶת וְהָיָה בְעוֹר־בְּשָׂרוֹ
לְנֶגַע צָרָעַת וְהוּבָא אֶל־אַהֲרֹן הַכֹּהֵן אוֹ אֶל־אַחַד מִבָּנָיו
הַכֹּהֲנִים: וְרָאָה הַכֹּהֵן אֶת־הַנֶּגַע בְּעֽוֹר־הַבָּשָׂר וְשֵׂעָר בַּנֶּגַע
הָפַךְ ׀ לָבָן וּמַרְאֵה הַנֶּגַע עָמֹק מֵעוֹר בְּשָׂרוֹ נֶגַע צָרַעַת הוּא
וְרָאָהוּ הַכֹּהֵן וְטִמֵּא אֹתֽוֹ: וְאִם־בַּהֶרֶת לְבָנָה הִוא בְּעוֹר
בְּשָׂרוֹ וְעָמֹק אֵֽין־מַרְאֶהָ מִן־הָעוֹר וּשְׂעָרָה לֹא־הָפַךְ לָבָן
וְהִסְגִּיר הַכֹּהֵן אֶת־הַנֶּגַע שִׁבְעַת יָמִים: וְרָאָהוּ הַכֹּהֵן בַּיּוֹם
הַשְּׁבִיעִי וְהִנֵּה הַנֶּגַע עָמַד בְּעֵינָיו לֹֽא־פָשָׂה הַנֶּגַע בָּעוֹר
וְהִסְגִּירוֹ הַכֹּהֵן שִׁבְעַת יָמִים שֵׁנִֽית:

THIRD ALIYA: vv. 13:1–5
This phrase is one of more
than 70 in his commen-
tary on Tanakh that Rashi
says "I do not understand
its meaning." What can
this teach us?

METZORA מצורע

ויקרא
יד:א-יב
וַיְדַבֵּר יְהוָה אֶל־מֹשֶׁה לֵּאמֹר: זֹאת תִּהְיֶה תּוֹרַת הַמְּצֹרָע
בְּיוֹם טָהֳרָתוֹ וְהוּבָא אֶל־הַכֹּהֵן: וְיָצָא הַכֹּהֵן אֶל־מִחוּץ
לַמַּחֲנֶה וְרָאָה הַכֹּהֵן וְהִנֵּה נִרְפָּא נֶֽגַע־הַצָּרַעַת מִן־הַצָּרֽוּעַ:
וְצִוָּה הַכֹּהֵן וְלָקַח לַמִּטַּהֵר שְׁתֵּי־צִפֳּרִים חַיּוֹת טְהֹרוֹת
וְעֵץ אֶרֶז וּשְׁנִי תוֹלַעַת וְאֵזֹֽב: וְצִוָּה הַכֹּהֵן וְשָׁחַט אֶת־הַצִּפּוֹר
לוי הָאֶחָת אֶל־כְּלִי־חֶרֶשׂ עַל־מַיִם חַיִּים: *אֶת־הַצִּפֹּר הַֽחַיָּה
יִקַּח אֹתָהּ וְאֶת־עֵץ הָאֶרֶז וְאֶת־שְׁנִי הַתּוֹלַעַת וְאֶת־הָאֵזֹב
וְטָבַל אוֹתָם וְאֵת ׀ הַצִּפֹּר הַֽחַיָּה בְּדַם הַצִּפֹּר הַשְּׁחֻטָה
עַל הַמַּיִם הַחַיִּֽים: וְהִזָּה עַל הַמִּטַּהֵר מִן־הַצָּרַעַת שֶׁבַע
פְּעָמִים וְטִֽהֲרוֹ וְשִׁלַּח אֶת־הַצִּפֹּר הַֽחַיָּה עַל־פְּנֵי הַשָּׂדֶֽה:
וְכִבֶּס הַמִּטַּהֵר אֶת־בְּגָדָיו וְגִלַּח אֶת־כָּל־שְׂעָרוֹ וְרָחַץ בַּמַּיִם
וְטָהֵר וְאַחַר יָבוֹא אֶל־הַֽמַּחֲנֶה וְיָשַׁב מִחוּץ לְאָהֳלוֹ שִׁבְעַת
יָמִֽים: וְהָיָה בַיּוֹם הַשְּׁבִיעִי יְגַלַּח אֶת־כָּל־שְׂעָרוֹ אֶת־רֹאשׁוֹ
וְאֶת־זְקָנוֹ וְאֵת גַּבֹּת עֵינָיו וְאֶת־כָּל־שְׂעָרוֹ יְגַלֵּחַ וְכִבֶּס אֶת־
ישראל בְּגָדָיו וְרָחַץ אֶת־בְּשָׂרוֹ בַּמַּיִם וְטָהֵֽר: *וּבַיּוֹם הַשְּׁמִינִי יִקַּח

FIRST ALIYA: vv. 1–5
Since his punishment
came about because of
his twittering about
other people, his atone-
ment comes via sacrific-
ing these kinds of animals
(Arakhin 16b). Why do you
think the concept of מִדָּה
כְּנֶגֶד מִדָּה is important
in Torah law?

SECOND ALIYA: vv. 6–9
The person who gossiped
was punished by being
exiled to a place where no
other impure person was.
Where? Why do you think
this might be so?

THIRD ALIYA: vv. 10–12
In the *Beit HaMikdash* it took place at the gate of Nikanor. What was it?

שְׁנֵי־כְבָשִׂים תְּמִימִם וְכַבְשָׂה אַחַת בַּת־שְׁנָתָהּ תְּמִימָה
וּשְׁלֹשָׁה עֶשְׂרֹנִים סֹלֶת מִנְחָה בְּלוּלָה בַשֶּׁמֶן וְלֹג אֶחָד שָׁמֶן:
וְהֶעֱמִיד הַכֹּהֵן הַמְטַהֵר אֵת הָאִישׁ הַמִּטַּהֵר וְאֹתָם לִפְנֵי
יהוה פֶּתַח אֹהֶל מוֹעֵד: וְלָקַח הַכֹּהֵן אֶת־הַכֶּבֶשׂ הָאֶחָד
וְהִקְרִיב אֹתוֹ לְאָשָׁם וְאֶת־לֹג הַשָּׁמֶן וְהֵנִיף אֹתָם תְּנוּפָה
לִפְנֵי יהוה:

AHAREI MOT אַחֲרֵי מוֹת

וַיְדַבֵּר יהוה אֶל־מֹשֶׁה אַחֲרֵי מוֹת שְׁנֵי בְּנֵי אַהֲרֹן בְּקָרְבָתָם

FIRST ALIYA: vv. 1–6
Some say the custom of wearing a *kittel* on Yom Kippur comes from here. What impact may wearing a *kittel* have on the wearer?

לִפְנֵי־יהוה וַיָּמֻתוּ: וַיֹּאמֶר יהוה אֶל־מֹשֶׁה דַּבֵּר אֶל־אַהֲרֹן
אָחִיךָ וְאַל־יָבֹא בְכָל־עֵת אֶל־הַקֹּדֶשׁ מִבֵּית לַפָּרֹכֶת אֶל־
פְּנֵי הַכַּפֹּרֶת אֲשֶׁר עַל־הָאָרֹן וְלֹא יָמוּת כִּי בֶּעָנָן אֵרָאֶה
עַל־הַכַּפֹּרֶת: בְּזֹאת יָבֹא אַהֲרֹן אֶל־הַקֹּדֶשׁ בְּפַר בֶּן־בָּקָר
לְחַטָּאת וְאַיִל לְעֹלָה: כְּתֹנֶת־בַּד קֹדֶשׁ יִלְבָּשׁ וּמִכְנְסֵי־בַד
יִהְיוּ עַל־בְּשָׂרוֹ וּבְאַבְנֵט בַּד יַחְגֹּר וּבְמִצְנֶפֶת בַּד יִצְנֹף בִּגְדֵי־
קֹדֶשׁ הֵם וְרָחַץ בַּמַּיִם אֶת־בְּשָׂרוֹ וּלְבֵשָׁם: וּמֵאֵת עֲדַת בְּנֵי
יִשְׂרָאֵל יִקַּח שְׁנֵי־שְׂעִירֵי עִזִּים לְחַטָּאת וְאַיִל אֶחָד לְעֹלָה:
וְהִקְרִיב אַהֲרֹן אֶת־פַּר הַחַטָּאת אֲשֶׁר־לוֹ וְכִפֶּר בַּעֲדוֹ וּבְעַד

SECOND ALIYA: vv. 7–11
The lots were placed in a box, each with its own label. What was written on the labels?

בֵּיתוֹ: וְלָקַח אֶת־שְׁנֵי הַשְּׂעִירִם וְהֶעֱמִיד אֹתָם לִפְנֵי יהוה
פֶּתַח אֹהֶל מוֹעֵד: וְנָתַן אַהֲרֹן עַל־שְׁנֵי הַשְּׂעִירִם גֹּרָלוֹת
גּוֹרָל אֶחָד לַיהוה וְגוֹרָל אֶחָד לַעֲזָאזֵל: וְהִקְרִיב אַהֲרֹן
אֶת־הַשָּׂעִיר אֲשֶׁר עָלָה עָלָיו הַגּוֹרָל לַיהוה וְעָשָׂהוּ חַטָּאת:
וְהַשָּׂעִיר אֲשֶׁר עָלָה עָלָיו הַגּוֹרָל לַעֲזָאזֵל יָעֳמַד־חַי לִפְנֵי
יהוה לְכַפֵּר עָלָיו לְשַׁלַּח אֹתוֹ לַעֲזָאזֵל הַמִּדְבָּרָה: וְהִקְרִיב
אַהֲרֹן אֶת־פַּר הַחַטָּאת אֲשֶׁר־לוֹ וְכִפֶּר בַּעֲדוֹ וּבְעַד בֵּיתוֹ
וְשָׁחַט אֶת־פַּר הַחַטָּאת אֲשֶׁר־לוֹ: וְלָקַח מְלֹא־הַמַּחְתָּה

THIRD ALIYA: vv. 12–17
From these words one learns that Hashem's presence can be felt, even if one sins. Do you feel

גַּחֲלֵי־אֵשׁ מֵעַל הַמִּזְבֵּחַ מִלִּפְנֵי יהוה וּמְלֹא חָפְנָיו קְטֹרֶת
סַמִּים דַּקָּה וְהֵבִיא מִבֵּית לַפָּרֹכֶת: וְנָתַן אֶת־הַקְּטֹרֶת עַל־
הָאֵשׁ לִפְנֵי יהוה וְכִסָּה ׀ עֲנַן הַקְּטֹרֶת אֶת־הַכַּפֹּרֶת אֲשֶׁר

וַיִּקְרָא
טז: א–יז

עַל־הָעֵדֻת וְלֹא יָמוּת: וְלָקַח מִדַּם הַפָּר וְהִזָּה בְאֶצְבָּעוֹ
עַל־פְּנֵי הַכַּפֹּרֶת קֵדְמָה וְלִפְנֵי הַכַּפֹּרֶת יַזֶּה שֶׁבַע־פְּעָמִים
מִן־הַדָּם בְּאֶצְבָּעוֹ: וְשָׁחַט אֶת־שְׂעִיר הַחַטָּאת אֲשֶׁר לָעָם
וְהֵבִיא אֶת־דָּמוֹ אֶל־מִבֵּית לַפָּרֹכֶת וְעָשָׂה אֶת־דָּמוֹ כַּאֲשֶׁר
עָשָׂה לְדַם הַפָּר וְהִזָּה אֹתוֹ עַל־הַכַּפֹּרֶת וְלִפְנֵי הַכַּפֹּרֶת:
וְכִפֶּר עַל־הַקֹּדֶשׁ מִטֻּמְאֹת בְּנֵי יִשְׂרָאֵל וּמִפִּשְׁעֵיהֶם לְכָל־
חַטֹּאתָם וְכֵן יַעֲשֶׂה לְאֹהֶל מוֹעֵד הַשֹּׁכֵן אִתָּם בְּתוֹךְ
טֻמְאֹתָם: וְכָל־אָדָם לֹא־יִהְיֶה ׀ בְּאֹהֶל מוֹעֵד בְּבֹאוֹ לְכַפֵּר
בַּקֹּדֶשׁ עַד־צֵאתוֹ וְכִפֶּר בַּעֲדוֹ וּבְעַד בֵּיתוֹ וּבְעַד כָּל־קְהַל
יִשְׂרָאֵל:

KEDOSHIM

קדושים

ויקרא יט:א–ד וַיְדַבֵּר יְהוָה אֶל־מֹשֶׁה לֵּאמֹר: דַּבֵּר אֶל־כָּל־עֲדַת בְּנֵי
יִשְׂרָאֵל וְאָמַרְתָּ אֲלֵהֶם קְדֹשִׁים תִּהְיוּ כִּי קָדוֹשׁ אֲנִי יְהוָה
אֱלֹהֵיכֶם: אִישׁ אִמּוֹ וְאָבִיו תִּירָאוּ וְאֶת־שַׁבְּתֹתַי תִּשְׁמֹרוּ אֲנִי
יְהוָה אֱלֹהֵיכֶם: אַל־תִּפְנוּ אֶל־הָאֱלִילִם וֵאלֹהֵי מַסֵּכָה לֹא
תַעֲשׂוּ לָכֶם אֲנִי יְהוָה אֱלֹהֵיכֶם: *וְכִי תִזְבְּחוּ זֶבַח שְׁלָמִים
לוי
לַיהוָה לִרְצֹנְכֶם תִּזְבָּחֻהוּ: בְּיוֹם זִבְחֲכֶם יֵאָכֵל וּמִמָּחֳרָת
וְהַנּוֹתָר עַד־יוֹם הַשְּׁלִישִׁי בָּאֵשׁ יִשָּׂרֵף: וְאִם הֵאָכֹל יֵאָכֵל
בַּיּוֹם הַשְּׁלִישִׁי פִּגּוּל הוּא לֹא יֵרָצֶה: וְאֹכְלָיו עֲוֹנוֹ יִשָּׂא
כִּי־אֶת־קֹדֶשׁ יְהוָה חִלֵּל וְנִכְרְתָה הַנֶּפֶשׁ הַהִוא מֵעַמֶּיהָ:
וּבְקֻצְרְכֶם אֶת־קְצִיר אַרְצְכֶם לֹא תְכַלֶּה פְּאַת שָׂדְךָ לִקְצֹר
וְלֶקֶט קְצִירְךָ לֹא תְלַקֵּט: וְכַרְמְךָ לֹא תְעוֹלֵל וּפֶרֶט כַּרְמְךָ
לֹא תְלַקֵּט לֶעָנִי וְלַגֵּר תַּעֲזֹב אֹתָם אֲנִי יְהוָה אֱלֹהֵיכֶם:
ישראל *לֹא תִּגְנֹבוּ וְלֹא־תְכַחֲשׁוּ וְלֹא־תְשַׁקְּרוּ אִישׁ בַּעֲמִיתוֹ: וְלֹא־
תִשָּׁבְעוּ בִשְׁמִי לַשָּׁקֶר וְחִלַּלְתָּ אֶת־שֵׁם אֱלֹהֶיךָ אֲנִי יְהוָה:
לֹא־תַעֲשֹׁק אֶת־רֵעֲךָ וְלֹא תִגְזֹל לֹא־תָלִין פְּעֻלַּת שָׂכִיר
אִתְּךָ עַד־בֹּקֶר: לֹא־תְקַלֵּל חֵרֵשׁ וְלִפְנֵי עִוֵּר לֹא תִתֵּן מִכְשֹׁל
וְיָרֵאתָ מֵּאֱלֹהֶיךָ אֲנִי יְהוָה:

distant from Hashem after wrongdoing? How might this offer one comfort?

FIRST ALIYA: vv. 1–4
From here one learns that one need not obey a parent who commands you to transgress Shabbat. Do you think this is always applicable?

SECOND ALIYA: vv. 5–11
The Midrash suggests that the prohibitions in the last verse are interconnected. How?

THIRD ALIYA: vv. 12–14
From here it is understood that a teacher may generally not leave a room unsupervised, or that one may not give bad advice to someone, especially if you stand to benefit from it. What other examples can you think of where this rule would apply?

EMOR · אמור

ויקרא
כא:א-טו

וַיֹּאמֶר יהוה אֶל־מֹשֶׁה אֱמֹר אֶל־הַכֹּהֲנִים בְּנֵי אַהֲרֹן וְאָמַרְתָּ
אֲלֵהֶם לְנֶפֶשׁ לֹא־יִטַּמָּא בְּעַמָּיו: כִּי אִם־לִשְׁאֵרוֹ הַקָּרֹב אֵלָיו
לְאִמּוֹ וּלְאָבִיו וְלִבְנוֹ וּלְבִתּוֹ וּלְאָחִיו: וְלַאֲחֹתוֹ הַבְּתוּלָה
הַקְּרוֹבָה אֵלָיו אֲשֶׁר לֹא־הָיְתָה לְאִישׁ לָהּ יִטַּמָּא: לֹא יִטַּמָּא
בַּעַל בְּעַמָּיו לְהֵחַלּוֹ: לֹא־יִקְרְחֻה קָרְחָה בְּרֹאשָׁם וּפְאַת
זְקָנָם לֹא יְגַלֵּחוּ וּבִבְשָׂרָם לֹא יִשְׂרְטוּ שָׂרָטֶת: קְדֹשִׁים יִהְיוּ
לֵאלֹהֵיהֶם וְלֹא יְחַלְּלוּ שֵׁם אֱלֹהֵיהֶם כִּי אֶת־אִשֵּׁי יהוה לֶחֶם
אֱלֹהֵיהֶם הֵם מַקְרִיבִם וְהָיוּ קֹדֶשׁ: אִשָּׁה זֹנָה וַחֲלָלָה לֹא
יִקָּחוּ וְאִשָּׁה גְּרוּשָׁה מֵאִישָׁהּ לֹא יִקָּחוּ כִּי־קָדֹשׁ הוּא לֵאלֹהָיו:
וְקִדַּשְׁתּוֹ כִּי־אֶת־לֶחֶם אֱלֹהֶיךָ הוּא מַקְרִיב קָדֹשׁ יִהְיֶה־לָּךְ
כִּי קָדוֹשׁ אֲנִי יהוה מְקַדִּשְׁכֶם: וּבַת אִישׁ כֹּהֵן כִּי תֵחֵל לִזְנוֹת
אֶת־אָבִיהָ הִיא מְחַלֶּלֶת בָּאֵשׁ תִּשָּׂרֵף: וְהַכֹּהֵן
הַגָּדוֹל מֵאֶחָיו אֲשֶׁר־יוּצַק עַל־רֹאשׁוֹ ׀ שֶׁמֶן הַמִּשְׁחָה וּמִלֵּא
אֶת־יָדוֹ לִלְבֹּשׁ אֶת־הַבְּגָדִים אֶת־רֹאשׁוֹ לֹא יִפְרָע וּבְגָדָיו
לֹא יִפְרֹם: וְעַל כָּל־נַפְשֹׁת מֵת לֹא יָבֹא לְאָבִיו וּלְאִמּוֹ לֹא
יִטַּמָּא: וּמִן־הַמִּקְדָּשׁ לֹא יֵצֵא וְלֹא יְחַלֵּל אֵת מִקְדַּשׁ אֱלֹהָיו
כִּי נֵזֶר שֶׁמֶן מִשְׁחַת אֱלֹהָיו עָלָיו אֲנִי יהוה: ‏*הוּא אִשָּׁה
בִבְתוּלֶיהָ יִקָּח: אַלְמָנָה וּגְרוּשָׁה וַחֲלָלָה זֹנָה אֶת־אֵלֶּה לֹא
יִקָּח כִּי אִם־בְּתוּלָה מֵעַמָּיו יִקַּח אִשָּׁה: וְלֹא־יְחַלֵּל זַרְעוֹ
בְּעַמָּיו כִּי אֲנִי יהוה מְקַדְּשׁוֹ:

יקרחו

לוי

ישראל

BEHAR · בהר

ויקרא
כה:א-ג

וַיְדַבֵּר יהוה אֶל־מֹשֶׁה בְּהַר סִינַי לֵאמֹר: דַּבֵּר אֶל־בְּנֵי
יִשְׂרָאֵל וְאָמַרְתָּ אֲלֵהֶם כִּי תָבֹאוּ אֶל־הָאָרֶץ אֲשֶׁר אֲנִי נֹתֵן
לָכֶם וְשָׁבְתָה הָאָרֶץ שַׁבָּת לַיהוה: שֵׁשׁ שָׁנִים תִּזְרַע שָׂדֶךָ
וְשֵׁשׁ שָׁנִים תִּזְמֹר כַּרְמֶךָ וְאָסַפְתָּ אֶת־תְּבוּאָתָהּ: ‏*וּבַשָּׁנָה
הַשְּׁבִיעִת שַׁבַּת שַׁבָּתוֹן יִהְיֶה לָאָרֶץ שַׁבָּת לַיהוה שָׂדֶךָ
לֹא תִזְרָע וְכַרְמְךָ לֹא תִזְמֹר: אֵת סְפִיחַ קְצִירְךָ לֹא תִקְצוֹר

לוי

FIRST ALIYA: vv. 1–6
From this repetition, it is learned that the *kohanim* also had to teach their children the laws regarding the prohibition of becoming *tameh*. Why?

SECOND ALIYA: vv. 7–12
From here the Gemara learns that a *kohen* gets the first *aliya* and the *kohen* should be the first choice to lead *Birkat HaMazon*. Why do you think that is?

THIRD ALIYA: vv. 13–15
What is the name given to the children born of a forbidden marriage by a *kohen*?

FIRST ALIYA: vv. 1–3
Complete the famous question asked because of some unusual wording in the text: "What does *shemitta* have to do with ____?"

SECOND ALIYA: vv. 4–7
From this word one learns that the produce that

וְאֶת־עִנְּבֵי נְזִירֶךָ לֹא תִבְצֹר שְׁנַת שַׁבָּתוֹן יִהְיֶה לָאָרֶץ:
וְהָיְתָה שַׁבַּת הָאָרֶץ לָכֶם לְאָכְלָה לְךָ וּלְעַבְדְּךָ וְלַאֲמָתֶךָ
וְלִשְׂכִירְךָ וּלְתוֹשָׁבְךָ הַגָּרִים עִמָּךְ: וְלִבְהֶמְתְּךָ וְלַחַיָּה אֲשֶׁר
בְּאַרְצֶךָ תִּהְיֶה כָל־תְּבוּאָתָהּ לֶאֱכֹל: ‏*וְסָפַרְתָּ

ישראל

לְךָ שֶׁבַע שַׁבְּתֹת שָׁנִים שֶׁבַע שָׁנִים שֶׁבַע פְּעָמִים וְהָיוּ לְךָ
יְמֵי שֶׁבַע שַׁבְּתֹת הַשָּׁנִים תֵּשַׁע וְאַרְבָּעִים שָׁנָה: וְהַעֲבַרְתָּ
שׁוֹפַר תְּרוּעָה בַּחֹדֶשׁ הַשְּׁבִעִי בֶּעָשׂוֹר לַחֹדֶשׁ בְּיוֹם הַכִּפֻּרִים
תַּעֲבִירוּ שׁוֹפָר בְּכָל־אַרְצְכֶם: וְקִדַּשְׁתֶּם אֵת שְׁנַת הַחֲמִשִּׁים
שָׁנָה וּקְרָאתֶם דְּרוֹר בָּאָרֶץ לְכָל־יֹשְׁבֶיהָ יוֹבֵל הִוא תִּהְיֶה
לָכֶם וְשַׁבְתֶּם אִישׁ אֶל־אֲחֻזָּתוֹ וְאִישׁ אֶל־מִשְׁפַּחְתּוֹ תָּשֻׁבוּ:
יוֹבֵל הִוא שְׁנַת הַחֲמִשִּׁים שָׁנָה תִּהְיֶה לָכֶם לֹא תִזְרָעוּ וְלֹא
תִקְצְרוּ אֶת־סְפִיחֶיהָ וְלֹא תִבְצְרוּ אֶת־נְזִרֶיהָ: כִּי יוֹבֵל הִוא
קֹדֶשׁ תִּהְיֶה לָכֶם מִן־הַשָּׂדֶה תֹּאכְלוּ אֶת־תְּבוּאָתָהּ: בִּשְׁנַת
הַיּוֹבֵל הַזֹּאת תָּשֻׁבוּ אִישׁ אֶל־אֲחֻזָּתוֹ:

BEHUKKOTAI

בחוקותי

ויקרא
כו:ג-ג

אִם־בְּחֻקֹּתַי תֵּלֵכוּ וְאֶת־מִצְוֹתַי תִּשְׁמְרוּ וַעֲשִׂיתֶם אֹתָם:
וְנָתַתִּי גִשְׁמֵיכֶם בְּעִתָּם וְנָתְנָה הָאָרֶץ יְבוּלָהּ וְעֵץ הַשָּׂדֶה
יִתֵּן פִּרְיוֹ: וְהִשִּׂיג לָכֶם דַּיִשׁ אֶת־בָּצִיר וּבָצִיר יַשִּׂיג אֶת־
זֶרַע וַאֲכַלְתֶּם לַחְמְכֶם לָשֹׂבַע וִישַׁבְתֶּם לָבֶטַח בְּאַרְצְכֶם:
‏*וְנָתַתִּי שָׁלוֹם בָּאָרֶץ וּשְׁכַבְתֶּם וְאֵין מַחֲרִיד וְהִשְׁבַּתִּי חַיָּה

לוי

רָעָה מִן־הָאָרֶץ וְחֶרֶב לֹא־תַעֲבֹר בְּאַרְצְכֶם: וּרְדַפְתֶּם אֶת־
אֹיְבֵיכֶם וְנָפְלוּ לִפְנֵיכֶם לֶחָרֶב: וְרָדְפוּ מִכֶּם חֲמִשָּׁה מֵאָה
וּמֵאָה מִכֶּם רְבָבָה יִרְדֹּפוּ וְנָפְלוּ אֹיְבֵיכֶם לִפְנֵיכֶם לֶחָרֶב:
וּפָנִיתִי אֲלֵיכֶם וְהִפְרֵיתִי אֶתְכֶם וְהִרְבֵּיתִי אֶתְכֶם וַהֲקִימֹתִי
אֶת־בְּרִיתִי אִתְּכֶם: וַאֲכַלְתֶּם יָשָׁן נוֹשָׁן וְיָשָׁן מִפְּנֵי חָדָשׁ

ישראל

תּוֹצִיאוּ: וְנָתַתִּי מִשְׁכָּנִי בְּתוֹכְכֶם וְלֹא־תִגְעַל נַפְשִׁי אֶתְכֶם:
וְהִתְהַלַּכְתִּי בְּתוֹכְכֶם וְהָיִיתִי לָכֶם לֵאלֹהִים וְאַתֶּם תִּהְיוּ־
לִי לְעָם: אֲנִי יְהוָה אֱלֹהֵיכֶם אֲשֶׁר הוֹצֵאתִי אֶתְכֶם מֵאֶרֶץ

grows on its own is for
one thing only and cer-
tainly not for commercial
purposes. Is there a wider
lesson to learn here?

THIRD ALIYA: vv. 8–13
The words that appear on
the American Liberty Bell.

FIRST ALIYA: vv. 3–5
How can the first verse
be read so that it is
not repetitive?

SECOND ALIYA:
vv. 6–10
If you do the math,
you'll see that the more
people there are who
are united, the more that
they can accomplish.
Does that ring true
from your experience?

THIRD ALIYA:
vv. 11–13
Which of these words
may be the source for a
line in the blessing
before the *Shema* and in
Birkat HaMazon?

מִצְרַיִם מִהְיֹת לָהֶם עֲבָדִים וָאֶשְׁבֹּר מֹטֹת עֻלְּכֶם וָאוֹלֵךְ
אֶתְכֶם קוֹמְמִיּֽוּת:

BEMIDBAR
במדבר

וַיְדַבֵּר יְהוָה אֶל־מֹשֶׁה בְּמִדְבַּר סִינַי בְּאֹהֶל מוֹעֵד בְּאֶחָד

לַחֹדֶשׁ הַשֵּׁנִי בַּשָּׁנָה הַשֵּׁנִית לְצֵאתָם מֵאֶרֶץ מִצְרַיִם לֵאמֹֽר:
שְׂאוּ אֶת־רֹאשׁ כָּל־עֲדַת בְּנֵי־יִשְׂרָאֵל לְמִשְׁפְּחֹתָם לְבֵית
אֲבֹתָם בְּמִסְפַּר שֵׁמוֹת כָּל־זָכָר לְגֻלְגְּלֹתָֽם: מִבֶּן עֶשְׂרִים שָׁנָה
וָמַעְלָה כָּל־יֹצֵא צָבָא בְּיִשְׂרָאֵל תִּפְקְדוּ אֹתָם לְצִבְאֹתָם
אַתָּה וְאַהֲרֹֽן: וְאִתְּכֶם יִהְיוּ אִישׁ אִישׁ לַמַּטֶּה אִישׁ רֹאשׁ

לְבֵית־אֲבֹתָיו הֽוּא: וְאֵלֶּה שְׁמוֹת הָאֲנָשִׁים אֲשֶׁר יַעַמְדוּ

אִתְּכֶם לִרְאוּבֵן אֱלִיצוּר בֶּן־שְׁדֵיאֽוּר: לְשִׁמְעוֹן שְׁלֻמִיאֵל

בֶּן־צוּרִֽישַׁדָּֽי: לִיהוּדָה נַחְשׁוֹן בֶּן־עַמִּינָדָֽב: לְיִשָּׂשכָר נְתַנְאֵל
בֶּן־צוּעָֽר: לִזְבוּלֻן אֱלִיאָב בֶּן־חֵלֹֽן: לִבְנֵי יוֹסֵף לְאֶפְרַיִם
אֱלִישָׁמָע בֶּן־עַמִּיהוּד לִמְנַשֶּׁה גַּמְלִיאֵל בֶּן־פְּדָהצֽוּר: לְבִנְיָמִן
אֲבִידָן בֶּן־גִּדְעֹנִֽי: לְדָן אֲחִיעֶזֶר בֶּן־עַמִּֽישַׁדָּֽי: לְאָשֵׁר פַּגְעִיאֵל
בֶּן־עָכְרָֽן: לְגָד אֶלְיָסָף בֶּן־דְּעוּאֵֽל: לְנַפְתָּלִי אֲחִירַע בֶּן־עֵינָֽן:

אֵלֶּה קְרִיאֵי הָעֵדָה נְשִׂיאֵי מַטּוֹת אֲבוֹתָם רָאשֵׁי אַלְפֵי

יִשְׂרָאֵל הֵֽם: וַיִּקַּח מֹשֶׁה וְאַהֲרֹן אֵת הָאֲנָשִׁים הָאֵלֶּה אֲשֶׁר

נִקְּבוּ בְּשֵׁמֹֽת: וְאֵת כָּל־הָעֵדָה הִקְהִילוּ בְּאֶחָד לַחֹדֶשׁ הַשֵּׁנִי
וַיִּתְיַלְדוּ עַל־מִשְׁפְּחֹתָם לְבֵית אֲבֹתָם בְּמִסְפַּר שֵׁמוֹת מִבֶּן
עֶשְׂרִים שָׁנָה וָמַעְלָה לְגֻלְגְּלֹתָֽם: כַּאֲשֶׁר צִוָּה יְהוָה אֶת־מֹשֶׁה
וַֽיִּפְקְדֵם בְּמִדְבַּר סִינָֽי:

NASO
נשא

וַיְדַבֵּר יְהוָה אֶל־מֹשֶׁה לֵּאמֹֽר: נָשֹׂא אֶת־רֹאשׁ בְּנֵי גֵרְשׁוֹן גַּם־

הֵם לְבֵית אֲבֹתָם לְמִשְׁפְּחֹתָֽם: מִבֶּן שְׁלֹשִׁים שָׁנָה וָמַעְלָה
עַד בֶּן־חֲמִשִּׁים שָׁנָה תִּפְקֹד אוֹתָם כָּל־הַבָּא לִצְבֹא צָבָא
לַעֲבֹד עֲבֹדָה בְּאֹהֶל מוֹעֵֽד: זֹאת עֲבֹדַת מִשְׁפְּחֹת הַגֵּרְשֻׁנִּי

לוי לַעֲבֹד וְלַמַשָּׂא: *וְנָשְׂאוּ אֶת־יְרִיעֹת הַמִּשְׁכָּן וְאֶת־אֹהֶל
מוֹעֵד מִכְסֵהוּ וּמִכְסֵה הַתַּחַשׁ אֲשֶׁר־עָלָיו מִלְמָעְלָה וְאֶת־
מָסַךְ פֶּתַח אֹהֶל מוֹעֵד: וְאֵת קַלְעֵי הֶחָצֵר וְאֶת־מָסַךְ ׀
פֶּתַח ׀ שַׁעַר הֶחָצֵר אֲשֶׁר עַל־הַמִּשְׁכָּן וְעַל־הַמִּזְבֵּחַ סָבִיב
וְאֵת מֵיתְרֵיהֶם וְאֶת־כָּל־כְּלֵי עֲבֹדָתָם וְאֵת כָּל־אֲשֶׁר
יֵעָשֶׂה לָהֶם וְעָבָדוּ: עַל־פִּי אַהֲרֹן וּבָנָיו תִּהְיֶה כָּל־עֲבֹדַת
בְּנֵי הַגֵּרְשֻׁנִּי לְכָל־מַשָּׂאָם וּלְכֹל עֲבֹדָתָם וּפְקַדְתֶּם עֲלֵהֶם
בְּמִשְׁמֶרֶת אֵת כָּל־מַשָּׂאָם: זֹאת עֲבֹדַת מִשְׁפְּחֹת בְּנֵי
הַגֵּרְשֻׁנִּי בְּאֹהֶל מוֹעֵד וּמִשְׁמַרְתָּם בְּיַד אִיתָמָר בֶּן־אַהֲרֹן
הַכֹּהֵן: *בְּנֵי מְרָרִי לְמִשְׁפְּחֹתָם לְבֵית־אֲבֹתָם

SECOND ALIYA: vv. 25–28
What were *Benei Gershon*
responsible for?

ישראל תִּפְקֹד אֹתָם: מִבֶּן שְׁלֹשִׁים שָׁנָה וָמַעְלָה וְעַד בֶּן־חֲמִשִּׁים
שָׁנָה תִּפְקְדֵם כָּל־הַבָּא לַצָּבָא לַעֲבֹד אֶת־עֲבֹדַת אֹהֶל
מוֹעֵד: וְזֹאת מִשְׁמֶרֶת מַשָּׂאָם לְכָל־עֲבֹדָתָם בְּאֹהֶל מוֹעֵד
קַרְשֵׁי הַמִּשְׁכָּן וּבְרִיחָיו וְעַמּוּדָיו וַאֲדָנָיו: וְעַמּוּדֵי הֶחָצֵר
סָבִיב וְאַדְנֵיהֶם וִיתֵדֹתָם וּמֵיתְרֵיהֶם לְכָל־כְּלֵיהֶם וּלְכֹל
עֲבֹדָתָם וּבְשֵׁמֹת תִּפְקְדוּ אֶת־כְּלֵי מִשְׁמֶרֶת מַשָּׂאָם: זֹאת
עֲבֹדַת מִשְׁפְּחֹת בְּנֵי מְרָרִי לְכָל־עֲבֹדָתָם בְּאֹהֶל מוֹעֵד בְּיַד
אִיתָמָר בֶּן־אַהֲרֹן הַכֹּהֵן:

THIRD ALIYA: vv. 29–37
What were *Benei Merari*
responsible for?

Some extend the ישראל *portion:*

וַיִּפְקֹד מֹשֶׁה וְאַהֲרֹן וּנְשִׂיאֵי הָעֵדָה אֶת־בְּנֵי הַקְּהָתִי
לְמִשְׁפְּחֹתָם וּלְבֵית אֲבֹתָם: מִבֶּן שְׁלֹשִׁים שָׁנָה וָמַעְלָה וְעַד
בֶּן־חֲמִשִּׁים שָׁנָה כָּל־הַבָּא לַצָּבָא לַעֲבֹדָה בְּאֹהֶל מוֹעֵד:
וַיִּהְיוּ פְקֻדֵיהֶם לְמִשְׁפְּחֹתָם אַלְפַּיִם שְׁבַע מֵאוֹת וַחֲמִשִּׁים:
אֵלֶּה פְקוּדֵי מִשְׁפְּחֹת הַקְּהָתִי כָּל־הָעֹבֵד בְּאֹהֶל מוֹעֵד אֲשֶׁר
פָּקַד מֹשֶׁה וְאַהֲרֹן עַל־פִּי יהוה בְּיַד־מֹשֶׁה:

BEHAALOTEKHA

בהעלותך

במדבר
ח:א–ד
וַיְדַבֵּר יהוה אֶל־מֹשֶׁה לֵּאמֹר: דַּבֵּר אֶל־אַהֲרֹן וְאָמַרְתָּ אֵלָיו
בְּהַעֲלֹתְךָ אֶת־הַנֵּרֹת אֶל־מוּל פְּנֵי הַמְּנוֹרָה יָאִירוּ שִׁבְעַת

FIRST ALIYA: vv. 1–4
From here one learns
that the three
wicks on either side

faced the central wick. What is the message there?

הַנֵּרֽוֹת: וַיַּ֤עַשׂ כֵּן֙ אַֽהֲרֹ֔ן אֶל־מוּל֙ פְּנֵ֣י הַמְּנוֹרָ֔ה הֶעֱלָ֖ה נֵֽרֹתֶ֑יהָ
כַּֽאֲשֶׁ֛ר צִוָּ֥ה יְהוָֹ֖ה אֶת־מֹשֶֽׁה: וְזֶ֨ה מַֽעֲשֵׂ֤ה הַמְּנֹרָה֙ מִקְשָׁ֣ה
זָהָ֔ב עַד־יְרֵכָ֥הּ עַד־פִּרְחָ֖הּ מִקְשָׁ֣ה הִ֑וא כַּמַּרְאֶ֗ה אֲשֶׁ֨ר הֶרְאָ֤ה
יְהוָֹה֙ אֶת־מֹשֶׁ֔ה כֵּ֥ן עָשָׂ֖ה אֶת־הַמְּנֹרָֽה:

SECOND ALIYA: vv. 5–9
Besides bringing sacrifices, what were the three things that the *Levi'im* had to do in order to be consecrated for their new role in the *Mishkan*?

לוי

וַיְדַבֵּ֥ר יְהוָֹ֖ה אֶל־מֹשֶׁ֥ה לֵּאמֹֽר: קַ֚ח אֶת־הַֽלְוִיִּ֔ם מִתּ֖וֹךְ בְּנֵ֣י
יִשְׂרָאֵ֑ל וְטִֽהַרְתָּ֖ אֹתָֽם: וְכֹֽה־תַֽעֲשֶׂ֤ה לָהֶם֙ לְטַֽהֲרָ֔ם הַזֵּ֥ה
עֲלֵיהֶ֖ם מֵ֣י חַטָּ֑את וְהֶֽעֱבִ֤ירוּ תַ֨עַר֙ עַל־כָּל־בְּשָׂרָ֔ם וְכִבְּס֥וּ
בִגְדֵיהֶ֖ם וְהִטֶּהָֽרוּ: וְלָֽקְחוּ֙ פַּ֣ר בֶּן־בָּקָ֔ר וּמִנְחָת֖וֹ סֹ֣לֶת
בְּלוּלָ֣ה בַשָּׁ֑מֶן וּפַר־שֵׁנִ֥י בֶן־בָּקָ֖ר תִּקַּ֥ח לְחַטָּֽאת: וְהִקְרַבְתָּ֙
אֶת־הַ֣לְוִיִּ֔ם לִפְנֵ֖י אֹ֣הֶל מוֹעֵ֑ד וְהִ֨קְהַלְתָּ֔ אֶֽת־כָּל־עֲדַ֖ת בְּנֵ֥י

THIRD ALIYA: vv. 10–14
Why might the people have been required to lean their hands upon the *Levi'im*?

ישראל

יִשְׂרָאֵֽל: *וְהִקְרַבְתָּ֥ אֶת־הַֽלְוִיִּ֖ם לִפְנֵ֣י יְהוָֹ֑ה וְסָֽמְכ֧וּ בְנֵֽי־
יִשְׂרָאֵ֛ל אֶת־יְדֵיהֶ֖ם עַל־הַֽלְוִיִּֽם: וְהֵנִ֣יף אַֽהֲרֹן֩ אֶת־הַֽלְוִיִּ֨ם
תְּנוּפָ֜ה לִפְנֵ֣י יְהוָֹ֗ה מֵאֵ֖ת בְּנֵ֣י יִשְׂרָאֵ֑ל וְהָי֕וּ לַֽעֲבֹ֖ד אֶת־
עֲבֹדַ֥ת יְהוָֹֽה: וְהַ֨לְוִיִּ֔ם יִסְמְכ֥וּ אֶת־יְדֵיהֶ֖ם עַ֣ל רֹ֣אשׁ הַפָּרִ֑ים
וַֽ֠עֲשֵׂ֠ה אֶת־הָֽאֶחָ֨ד חַטָּ֜את וְאֶת־הָֽאֶחָ֤ד עֹלָה֙ לַֽיהוָֹ֔ה לְכַפֵּ֖ר
עַל־הַֽלְוִיִּֽם: וְהַֽעֲמַדְתָּ֙ אֶת־הַ֣לְוִיִּ֔ם לִפְנֵ֥י אַֽהֲרֹ֖ן וְלִפְנֵ֣י בָנָ֑יו
וְהֵֽנַפְתָּ֥ אֹתָ֛ם תְּנוּפָ֖ה לַֽיהוָֹֽה: וְהִבְדַּלְתָּ֙ אֶת־הַ֣לְוִיִּ֔ם מִתּ֖וֹךְ בְּנֵ֣י
יִשְׂרָאֵ֑ל וְהָ֥יוּ לִ֖י הַֽלְוִיִּֽם:

FIRST ALIYA: vv. 1–3
From this word one could learn that the idea for sending the spies did not come from God, in which case three other words need explanation. How might this change one's understanding of the story?

SECOND ALIYA: vv. 4–16
Which tribe was not represented among the spies?

SHELAH

שלח

במדבר
י״ג:א־כ

וַיְדַבֵּ֥ר יְהוָֹ֖ה אֶל־מֹשֶׁ֥ה לֵּאמֹֽר: שְׁלַח־לְךָ֣ אֲנָשִׁ֗ים וְיָתֻ֨רוּ֙
אֶת־אֶ֣רֶץ כְּנַ֔עַן אֲשֶׁר־אֲנִ֥י נֹתֵ֖ן לִבְנֵ֣י יִשְׂרָאֵ֑ל אִ֣ישׁ אֶחָד֩
אִ֨ישׁ אֶחָ֜ד לְמַטֵּ֤ה אֲבֹתָיו֙ תִּשְׁלָ֔חוּ כֹּ֖ל נָשִׂ֥יא בָהֶֽם: וַיִּשְׁלַ֨ח
אֹתָ֥ם מֹשֶׁ֛ה מִמִּדְבַּ֥ר פָּארָ֖ן עַל־פִּ֣י יְהוָֹ֑ה כֻּלָּ֣ם אֲנָשִׁ֔ים רָאשֵׁ֥י
בְנֵֽי־יִשְׂרָאֵ֖ל הֵֽמָּה: *וְאֵ֖לֶּה שְׁמוֹתָ֑ם לְמַטֵּ֣ה רְאוּבֵ֔ן שַׁמּ֖וּעַ

לוי

בֶּן־זַכּֽוּר: לְמַטֵּ֣ה שִׁמְע֔וֹן שָׁפָ֖ט בֶּן־חוֹרִֽי: לְמַטֵּ֣ה יְהוּדָ֔ה כָּלֵ֖ב
בֶּן־יְפֻנֶּֽה: לְמַטֵּ֣ה יִשָּׂשכָ֔ר יִגְאָ֖ל בֶּן־יוֹסֵֽף: לְמַטֵּ֣ה אֶפְרָ֔יִם
הוֹשֵׁ֖עַ בִּן־נֽוּן: לְמַטֵּ֣ה בִנְיָמִ֔ן פַּלְטִ֖י בֶּן־רָפֽוּא: לְמַטֵּ֣ה זְבוּלֻ֔ן
גַּדִּיאֵ֖ל בֶּן־סוֹדִֽי: לְמַטֵּ֣ה יוֹסֵ֖ף לְמַטֵּ֣ה מְנַשֶּׁ֔ה גַּדִּ֖י בֶּן־סוּסִֽי:

לְמַטֵּה דָן עַמִּיאֵל בֶּן־גְּמַלִּי: לְמַטֵּה אָשֵׁר סְתוּר בֶּן־מִיכָאֵל:
לְמַטֵּה נַפְתָּלִי נַחְבִּי בֶּן־וָפְסִי: לְמַטֵּה גָד גְּאוּאֵל בֶּן־מָכִי:
אֵלֶּה שְׁמוֹת הָאֲנָשִׁים אֲשֶׁר־שָׁלַח מֹשֶׁה לָתוּר אֶת־הָאָרֶץ
וַיִּקְרָא מֹשֶׁה לְהוֹשֵׁעַ בִּן־נוּן יְהוֹשֻׁעַ: *וַיִּשְׁלַח אֹתָם מֹשֶׁה
לָתוּר אֶת־אֶרֶץ כְּנָעַן וַיֹּאמֶר אֲלֵהֶם עֲלוּ זֶה בַּנֶּגֶב וַעֲלִיתֶם
אֶת־הָהָר: וּרְאִיתֶם אֶת־הָאָרֶץ מַה־הִוא וְאֶת־הָעָם
הַיֹּשֵׁב עָלֶיהָ הֶחָזָק הוּא הֲרָפֶה הַמְעַט הוּא אִם־רָב: וּמָה
הָאָרֶץ אֲשֶׁר־הוּא יֹשֵׁב בָּהּ הֲטוֹבָה הִוא אִם־רָעָה וּמָה
הֶעָרִים אֲשֶׁר־הוּא יוֹשֵׁב בָּהֵנָּה הַבְּמַחֲנִים אִם בְּמִבְצָרִים:
וּמָה הָאָרֶץ הַשְּׁמֵנָה הִוא אִם־רָזָה הֲיֵשׁ־בָּהּ עֵץ אִם־אַיִן
וְהִתְחַזַּקְתֶּם וּלְקַחְתֶּם מִפְּרִי הָאָרֶץ וְהַיָּמִים יְמֵי בִּכּוּרֵי
עֲנָבִים:

THIRD ALIYA: vv. 17–20
How many objectives did
the spies have?

KORAH   קורח

וַיִּקַּח קֹרַח בֶּן־יִצְהָר בֶּן־קְהָת בֶּן־לֵוִי וְדָתָן וַאֲבִירָם בְּנֵי
אֱלִיאָב וְאוֹן בֶּן־פֶּלֶת בְּנֵי רְאוּבֵן: וַיָּקֻמוּ לִפְנֵי מֹשֶׁה וַאֲנָשִׁים
מִבְּנֵי־יִשְׂרָאֵל חֲמִשִּׁים וּמָאתָיִם נְשִׂיאֵי עֵדָה קְרִאֵי מוֹעֵד
אַנְשֵׁי־שֵׁם: וַיִּקָּהֲלוּ עַל־מֹשֶׁה וְעַל־אַהֲרֹן וַיֹּאמְרוּ אֲלֵהֶם
רַב־לָכֶם כִּי כָל־הָעֵדָה כֻּלָּם קְדֹשִׁים וּבְתוֹכָם יהוה וּמַדּוּעַ
תִּתְנַשְּׂאוּ עַל־קְהַל יהוה: *וַיִּשְׁמַע מֹשֶׁה וַיִּפֹּל עַל־פָּנָיו:
וַיְדַבֵּר אֶל־קֹרַח וְאֶל־כָּל־עֲדָתוֹ לֵאמֹר בֹּקֶר וְיֹדַע יהוה אֶת־
אֲשֶׁר־לוֹ וְאֶת־הַקָּדוֹשׁ וְהִקְרִיב אֵלָיו וְאֵת אֲשֶׁר יִבְחַר־בּוֹ
יַקְרִיב אֵלָיו: זֹאת עֲשׂוּ קְחוּ־לָכֶם מַחְתּוֹת קֹרַח וְכָל־עֲדָתוֹ:
וּתְנוּ־בָהֵן אֵשׁ וְשִׂימוּ עֲלֵיהֶן קְטֹרֶת לִפְנֵי יהוה מָחָר וְהָיָה
הָאִישׁ אֲשֶׁר־יִבְחַר יהוה הוּא הַקָּדוֹשׁ רַב־לָכֶם בְּנֵי לֵוִי:
*וַיֹּאמֶר מֹשֶׁה אֶל־קֹרַח שִׁמְעוּ־נָא בְּנֵי לֵוִי: הַמְעַט מִכֶּם
כִּי־הִבְדִּיל אֱלֹהֵי יִשְׂרָאֵל אֶתְכֶם מֵעֲדַת יִשְׂרָאֵל לְהַקְרִיב
אֶתְכֶם אֵלָיו לַעֲבֹד אֶת־עֲבֹדַת מִשְׁכַּן יהוה וְלַעֲמֹד לִפְנֵי
הָעֵדָה לְשָׁרְתָם: וַיַּקְרֵב אֹתְךָ וְאֶת־כָּל־אַחֶיךָ בְנֵי־לֵוִי אִתָּךְ

במדבר
טז:א–יג

לוי

ישראל

FIRST ALIYA: vv. 1–3
It is said that Koraḥ
made two state-
ments – one was a
direct attack on Moshe
and Aharon, while the
other was intended to
appeal to the masses by
stroking their egos. What
were the two arguments?
What might be learned
from here about
Koraḥ's intentions?

SECOND ALIYA: vv. 4–7
Moshe uses Koraḥ's own
words against him. What
were they?

THIRD ALIYA: vv. 8–13
Datan and Aviram use
Moshe's own words against
him. What were they?

וּבִקַּשְׁתֶּם גַּם־כְּהֻנָּה: לָכֵן אַתָּה וְכָל־עֲדָתְךָ הַנְּעָדִים עַל־
יהוה וְאַהֲרֹן מַה־הוּא כִּי תַלִּינוּ עָלָיו: וַיִּשְׁלַח מֹשֶׁה לִקְרֹא תַּלֵּינוּ
לְדָתָן וְלַאֲבִירָם בְּנֵי אֱלִיאָב וַיֹּאמְרוּ לֹא נַעֲלֶה: הַמְעַט כִּי
הֶעֱלִיתָנוּ מֵאֶרֶץ זָבַת חָלָב וּדְבַשׁ לַהֲמִיתֵנוּ בַּמִּדְבָּר כִּי־
תִשְׂתָּרֵר עָלֵינוּ גַּם־הִשְׂתָּרֵר:

HUKAT
חוקת

וַיְדַבֵּר יהוה אֶל־מֹשֶׁה וְאֶל־אַהֲרֹן לֵאמֹר: זֹאת חֻקַּת הַתּוֹרָה במדבר
אֲשֶׁר־צִוָּה יהוה לֵאמֹר דַּבֵּר ׀ אֶל־בְּנֵי יִשְׂרָאֵל וְיִקְחוּ אֵלֶיךָ יט:א-יז
פָרָה אֲדֻמָּה תְּמִימָה אֲשֶׁר אֵין־בָּהּ מוּם אֲשֶׁר לֹא־עָלָה
עָלֶיהָ עֹל: וּנְתַתֶּם אֹתָהּ אֶל־אֶלְעָזָר הַכֹּהֵן וְהוֹצִיא אֹתָהּ
אֶל־מִחוּץ לַמַּחֲנֶה וְשָׁחַט אֹתָהּ לְפָנָיו: וְלָקַח אֶלְעָזָר הַכֹּהֵן
מִדָּמָהּ בְּאֶצְבָּעוֹ וְהִזָּה אֶל־נֹכַח פְּנֵי אֹהֶל־מוֹעֵד מִדָּמָהּ שֶׁבַע
פְּעָמִים: וְשָׂרַף אֶת־הַפָּרָה לְעֵינָיו אֶת־עֹרָהּ וְאֶת־בְּשָׂרָהּ
וְאֶת־דָּמָהּ עַל־פִּרְשָׁהּ יִשְׂרֹף: וְלָקַח הַכֹּהֵן עֵץ אֶרֶז וְאֵזוֹב
וּשְׁנִי תוֹלָעַת וְהִשְׁלִיךְ אֶל־תּוֹךְ שְׂרֵפַת הַפָּרָה: וְכִבֶּס בְּגָדָיו לוי
הַכֹּהֵן וְרָחַץ בְּשָׂרוֹ בַּמַּיִם וְאַחַר יָבֹא אֶל־הַמַּחֲנֶה וְטָמֵא
הַכֹּהֵן עַד־הָעָרֶב: וְהַשֹּׂרֵף אֹתָהּ יְכַבֵּס בְּגָדָיו בַּמַּיִם וְרָחַץ
בְּשָׂרוֹ בַּמָּיִם וְטָמֵא עַד־הָעָרֶב: וְאָסַף ׀ אִישׁ טָהוֹר אֵת
אֵפֶר הַפָּרָה וְהִנִּיחַ מִחוּץ לַמַּחֲנֶה בְּמָקוֹם טָהוֹר וְהָיְתָה
לַעֲדַת בְּנֵי־יִשְׂרָאֵל לְמִשְׁמֶרֶת לְמֵי נִדָּה חַטָּאת הִוא:
וְכִבֶּס הָאֹסֵף אֶת־אֵפֶר הַפָּרָה אֶת־בְּגָדָיו וְטָמֵא עַד־הָעָרֶב יִשְׂרָאֵל
וְהָיְתָה לִבְנֵי יִשְׂרָאֵל וְלַגֵּר הַגָּר בְּתוֹכָם לְחֻקַּת עוֹלָם: הַנֹּגֵעַ
בְּמֵת לְכָל־נֶפֶשׁ אָדָם וְטָמֵא שִׁבְעַת יָמִים: הוּא יִתְחַטָּא־
בוֹ בַּיּוֹם הַשְּׁלִישִׁי וּבַיּוֹם הַשְּׁבִיעִי יִטְהָר וְאִם־לֹא יִתְחַטָּא
בַּיּוֹם הַשְּׁלִישִׁי וּבַיּוֹם הַשְּׁבִיעִי לֹא יִטְהָר: כָּל־הַנֹּגֵעַ בְּמֵת
בְּנֶפֶשׁ הָאָדָם אֲשֶׁר־יָמוּת וְלֹא יִתְחַטָּא אֶת־מִשְׁכַּן יהוה
טִמֵּא וְנִכְרְתָה הַנֶּפֶשׁ הַהִוא מִיִּשְׂרָאֵל כִּי מֵי נִדָּה לֹא־זֹרַק
עָלָיו טָמֵא יִהְיֶה עוֹד טֻמְאָתוֹ בוֹ: זֹאת הַתּוֹרָה אָדָם כִּי־

FIRST ALIYA: vv. 1–6
What does the adjective *temima* (whole, complete) describe – the cow or the red color?

SECOND ALIYA: vv. 7–10
In the times of the *Beit HaMikdash*, some ash was kept on the Mount of Olives for future use, some was kept among the 24 divisions of the *kohanim* and some was stored in an area next to the courtyard for safe-keeping. Which is alluded to here?

THIRD ALIYA: vv. 11–17
The Red Heifer ceremony is used for what kind of *tuma*?

יָמוּת בְּאֹהֶל כָּל־הַבָּא אֶל־הָאֹהֶל וְכָל־אֲשֶׁר בָּאֹהֶל יִטְמָא
שִׁבְעַת יָמִים: וְכֹל כְּלִי פָתוּחַ אֲשֶׁר אֵין־צָמִיד פָּתִיל עָלָיו
טָמֵא הוּא: וְכֹל אֲשֶׁר־יִגַּע עַל־פְּנֵי הַשָּׂדֶה בַּחֲלַל־חֶרֶב
אוֹ בְמֵת אוֹ־בְעֶצֶם אָדָם אוֹ בְקָבֶר יִטְמָא שִׁבְעַת יָמִים:
וְלָקְחוּ לַטָּמֵא מֵעֲפַר שְׂרֵפַת הַחַטָּאת וְנָתַן עָלָיו מַיִם חַיִּים
אֶל־כֶּלִי:

BALAK

בלק

וַיַּרְא בָּלָק בֶּן־צִפּוֹר אֵת כָּל־אֲשֶׁר־עָשָׂה יִשְׂרָאֵל לָאֱמֹרִי:
וַיָּגָר מוֹאָב מִפְּנֵי הָעָם מְאֹד כִּי רַב־הוּא וַיָּקָץ מוֹאָב מִפְּנֵי
בְּנֵי יִשְׂרָאֵל: וַיֹּאמֶר מוֹאָב אֶל־זִקְנֵי מִדְיָן עַתָּה יְלַחֲכוּ הַקָּהָל
אֶת־כָּל־סְבִיבֹתֵינוּ כִּלְחֹךְ הַשּׁוֹר אֵת יֶרֶק הַשָּׂדֶה וּבָלָק
בֶּן־צִפּוֹר מֶלֶךְ לְמוֹאָב בָּעֵת הַהִוא: וַיִּשְׁלַח מַלְאָכִים

לוי

אֶל־בִּלְעָם בֶּן־בְּעוֹר פְּתוֹרָה אֲשֶׁר עַל־הַנָּהָר אֶרֶץ בְּנֵי־
עַמּוֹ לִקְרֹא־לוֹ לֵאמֹר הִנֵּה עַם יָצָא מִמִּצְרַיִם הִנֵּה כִסָּה
אֶת־עֵין הָאָרֶץ וְהוּא יֹשֵׁב מִמֻּלִי: וְעַתָּה לְכָה־נָּא אָרָה־לִי
אֶת־הָעָם הַזֶּה כִּי־עָצוּם הוּא מִמֶּנִּי אוּלַי אוּכַל נַכֶּה־בּוֹ
וַאֲגָרְשֶׁנּוּ מִן־הָאָרֶץ כִּי יָדַעְתִּי אֵת אֲשֶׁר־תְּבָרֵךְ מְבֹרָךְ
וַאֲשֶׁר תָּאֹר יוּאָר: וַיֵּלְכוּ זִקְנֵי מוֹאָב וְזִקְנֵי מִדְיָן וּקְסָמִים
בְּיָדָם וַיָּבֹאוּ אֶל־בִּלְעָם וַיְדַבְּרוּ אֵלָיו דִּבְרֵי בָלָק: וַיֹּאמֶר

ישראל

אֲלֵיהֶם לִינוּ פֹה הַלַּיְלָה וַהֲשִׁבֹתִי אֶתְכֶם דָּבָר כַּאֲשֶׁר יְדַבֵּר
יהוה אֵלָי וַיֵּשְׁבוּ שָׂרֵי־מוֹאָב עִם־בִּלְעָם: וַיָּבֹא אֱלֹהִים אֶל־
בִּלְעָם וַיֹּאמֶר מִי הָאֲנָשִׁים הָאֵלֶּה עִמָּךְ: וַיֹּאמֶר בִּלְעָם
אֶל־הָאֱלֹהִים בָּלָק בֶּן־צִפֹּר מֶלֶךְ מוֹאָב שָׁלַח אֵלָי: הִנֵּה
הָעָם הַיֹּצֵא מִמִּצְרַיִם וַיְכַס אֶת־עֵין הָאָרֶץ עַתָּה לְכָה
קָבָה־לִּי אֹתוֹ אוּלַי אוּכַל לְהִלָּחֶם בּוֹ וְגֵרַשְׁתִּיו: וַיֹּאמֶר
אֱלֹהִים אֶל־בִּלְעָם לֹא תֵלֵךְ עִמָּהֶם לֹא תָאֹר אֶת־הָעָם כִּי
בָרוּךְ הוּא:

FIRST ALIYA: vv. 2–4
What biographical infor-
mation is not revealed at
first about Balak?

SECOND ALIYA: vv. 5–7
Its other name is the
Euphrates. Why do you
think it is referred to in
this way?

THIRD ALIYA: vv. 8–12
According to Rashi,
Hashem told Bilam in
the last verse not to go
with the messengers, to
which Bilam responded
something not explicit
in the text, to which
Hashem responded, to
which Bilam responded,
to which Hashem
responded. Assuming
Hashem's three state-
ments are all in the last
verse, what are the things
that Bilam was saying?

PINEHAS

FIRST ALIYA:
vv. 10–12
There are two
synonyms for anger
here. What are they
and what else does
each convey?

פינחס

וַיְדַבֵּר יהוה אֶל־מֹשֶׁה לֵּאמֹר: פִּינְחָס בֶּן־אֶלְעָזָר בֶּן־אַהֲרֹן
הַכֹּהֵן הֵשִׁיב אֶת־חֲמָתִי מֵעַל בְּנֵי־יִשְׂרָאֵל בְּקַנְאוֹ אֶת־
קִנְאָתִי בְּתוֹכָם וְלֹא־כִלִּיתִי אֶת־בְּנֵי־יִשְׂרָאֵל בְּקִנְאָתִי: לָכֵן
אֱמֹר הִנְנִי נֹתֵן לוֹ אֶת־בְּרִיתִי שָׁלוֹם: וְהָיְתָה לּוֹ וּלְזַרְעוֹ
אַחֲרָיו בְּרִית כְּהֻנַּת עוֹלָם תַּחַת אֲשֶׁר קִנֵּא לֵאלֹהָיו וַיְכַפֵּר
עַל־בְּנֵי יִשְׂרָאֵל: וְשֵׁם אִישׁ יִשְׂרָאֵל הַמֻּכֶּה אֲשֶׁר הֻכָּה אֶת־
הַמִּדְיָנִית זִמְרִי בֶּן־סָלוּא נְשִׂיא בֵית־אָב לַשִּׁמְעֹנִי: וְשֵׁם
הָאִשָּׁה הַמֻּכָּה הַמִּדְיָנִית כָּזְבִּי בַת־צוּר רֹאשׁ אֻמּוֹת בֵּית־
אָב בְּמִדְיָן הוּא:

SECOND ALIYA: vv. 13–18
There are two command-
ments concerning Midyan;
what are they?

במדבר
כה:י–כ:ד

לוי

ישראל

וַיְדַבֵּר יהוה אֶל־מֹשֶׁה לֵּאמֹר: צָרוֹר אֶת־הַמִּדְיָנִים וְהִכִּיתֶם
אוֹתָם: כִּי־צֹרְרִים הֵם לָכֶם בְּנִכְלֵיהֶם אֲשֶׁר־נִכְּלוּ לָכֶם עַל־
דְּבַר פְּעוֹר וְעַל־דְּבַר כָּזְבִּי בַת־נְשִׂיא מִדְיָן אֲחֹתָם הַמֻּכָּה
בְיוֹם־הַמַּגֵּפָה עַל־דְּבַר פְּעוֹר: וַיְהִי אַחֲרֵי הַמַּגֵּפָה
וַיֹּאמֶר יהוה אֶל־מֹשֶׁה וְאֶל אֶלְעָזָר בֶּן־אַהֲרֹן הַכֹּהֵן לֵאמֹר:
שְׂאוּ אֶת־רֹאשׁ ׀ כָּל־עֲדַת בְּנֵי־יִשְׂרָאֵל מִבֶּן עֶשְׂרִים שָׁנָה
וָמַעְלָה לְבֵית אֲבֹתָם כָּל־יֹצֵא צָבָא בְּיִשְׂרָאֵל: וַיְדַבֵּר מֹשֶׁה
וְאֶלְעָזָר הַכֹּהֵן אֹתָם בְּעַרְבֹת מוֹאָב עַל־יַרְדֵּן יְרֵחוֹ לֵאמֹר:
מִבֶּן עֶשְׂרִים שָׁנָה וָמַעְלָה כַּאֲשֶׁר צִוָּה יהוה אֶת־מֹשֶׁה וּבְנֵי
יִשְׂרָאֵל הַיֹּצְאִים מֵאֶרֶץ מִצְרָיִם:

THIRD ALIYA: vv. 26:1–4
Rashi mentions here the
analogy "Like a shepherd
whose flock was attacked
by wolves." What is he
referring to?

MATOT

FIRST ALIYA: vv. 2–9
From here one learns
that a vow which
permits that which is
otherwise forbidden is
not a binding vow, e.g.,
one may not say "I vow
that I will eat non-kosher
food from now on." What
message to us is con-
tained in this law?

מטות

וַיְדַבֵּר מֹשֶׁה אֶל־רָאשֵׁי הַמַּטּוֹת לִבְנֵי יִשְׂרָאֵל לֵאמֹר זֶה
הַדָּבָר אֲשֶׁר צִוָּה יהוה: אִישׁ כִּי־יִדֹּר נֶדֶר לַיהוה אוֹ־הִשָּׁבַע
שְׁבֻעָה לֶאְסֹר אִסָּר עַל־נַפְשׁוֹ לֹא יַחֵל דְּבָרוֹ כְּכָל־הַיֹּצֵא
מִפִּיו יַעֲשֶׂה: וְאִשָּׁה כִּי־תִדֹּר נֶדֶר לַיהוה וְאָסְרָה אִסָּר
בְּבֵית אָבִיהָ בִּנְעֻרֶיהָ: וְשָׁמַע אָבִיהָ אֶת־נִדְרָהּ וֶאֱסָרָהּ
אֲשֶׁר אָסְרָה עַל־נַפְשָׁהּ וְהֶחֱרִישׁ לָהּ אָבִיהָ וְקָמוּ כָּל־נְדָרֶיהָ

במדבר
לב:ב–ט

וְכָל־אִסָּר אֲשֶׁר־אָסְרָה עַל־נַפְשָׁהּ יָקוּם: וְאִם־הֵנִיא אָבִיהָ אֹתָהּ בְּיוֹם שָׁמְעוֹ כָּל־נְדָרֶיהָ וֶאֱסָרֶיהָ אֲשֶׁר־אָסְרָה עַל־נַפְשָׁהּ לֹא יָקוּם וַיהוה יִסְלַח־לָהּ כִּי־הֵנִיא אָבִיהָ אֹתָהּ: וְאִם־הָיוֹ תִהְיֶה לְאִישׁ וּנְדָרֶיהָ עָלֶיהָ אוֹ מִבְטָא שְׂפָתֶיהָ אֲשֶׁר אָסְרָה עַל־נַפְשָׁהּ: וְשָׁמַע אִישָׁהּ בְּיוֹם שָׁמְעוֹ וְהֶחֱרִישׁ לָהּ וְקָמוּ נְדָרֶיהָ וֶאֱסָרֶהָ אֲשֶׁר־אָסְרָה עַל־נַפְשָׁהּ יָקֻמוּ: וְאִם בְּיוֹם שְׁמֹעַ אִישָׁהּ יָנִיא אוֹתָהּ וְהֵפֵר אֶת־נִדְרָהּ אֲשֶׁר עָלֶיהָ וְאֵת מִבְטָא שְׂפָתֶיהָ אֲשֶׁר אָסְרָה עַל־נַפְשָׁהּ וַיהוה

לוי יִסְלַח־לָהּ: וְנֵדֶר אַלְמָנָה וּגְרוּשָׁה כֹּל אֲשֶׁר־אָסְרָה עַל־ נַפְשָׁהּ יָקוּם עָלֶיהָ: וְאִם־בֵּית אִישָׁהּ נָדָרָה אוֹ־אָסְרָה אִסָּר עַל־נַפְשָׁהּ בִּשְׁבֻעָה: וְשָׁמַע אִישָׁהּ וְהֶחֱרִשׁ לָהּ לֹא הֵנִיא אֹתָהּ וְקָמוּ כָּל־נְדָרֶיהָ וְכָל־אִסָּר אֲשֶׁר־אָסְרָה עַל־ נַפְשָׁהּ יָקוּם: וְאִם־הָפֵר יָפֵר אֹתָם ׀ אִישָׁהּ בְּיוֹם שָׁמְעוֹ כָּל־מוֹצָא שְׂפָתֶיהָ לִנְדָרֶיהָ וּלְאִסַּר נַפְשָׁהּ לֹא יָקוּם אִישָׁהּ

ישראל הֲפֵרָם וַיהוה יִסְלַח־לָהּ: כָּל־נֵדֶר וְכָל־שְׁבֻעַת אִסָּר לְעַנֹּת נָפֶשׁ אִישָׁהּ יְקִימֶנּוּ וְאִישָׁהּ יְפֵרֶנּוּ: וְאִם־הַחֲרֵשׁ יַחֲרִישׁ לָהּ אִישָׁהּ מִיּוֹם אֶל־יוֹם וְהֵקִים אֶת־כָּל־נְדָרֶיהָ אוֹ אֶת־ כָּל־אֱסָרֶיהָ אֲשֶׁר עָלֶיהָ הֵקִים אֹתָם כִּי־הֶחֱרִשׁ לָהּ בְּיוֹם שָׁמְעוֹ: וְאִם־הָפֵר יָפֵר אֹתָם אַחֲרֵי שָׁמְעוֹ וְנָשָׂא אֶת־עֲוֹנָהּ: אֵלֶּה הַחֻקִּים אֲשֶׁר צִוָּה יהוה אֶת־מֹשֶׁה בֵּין אִישׁ לְאִשְׁתּוֹ בֵּין־אָב לְבִתּוֹ בִּנְעֻרֶיהָ בֵּית אָבִיהָ:

SECOND ALIYA: vv. 10–13
What is the maximum amount of time by when a husband can revoke his wife's vow?

THIRD ALIYA: vv. 14–17
From here one learns that he can only revoke the vow by sunset of the day he learns about it. Why do you think there would be a time limit?

MASEI · מסעי

בְּמִדְבַּר
לג: א–נג

אֵלֶּה מַסְעֵי בְנֵי־יִשְׂרָאֵל אֲשֶׁר יָצְאוּ מֵאֶרֶץ מִצְרַיִם לְצִבְאֹתָם בְּיַד־מֹשֶׁה וְאַהֲרֹן: וַיִּכְתֹּב מֹשֶׁה אֶת־מוֹצָאֵיהֶם לְמַסְעֵיהֶם עַל־פִּי יהוה וְאֵלֶּה מַסְעֵיהֶם לְמוֹצָאֵיהֶם: וַיִּסְעוּ מֵרַעְמְסֵס בַּחֹדֶשׁ הָרִאשׁוֹן בַּחֲמִשָּׁה עָשָׂר יוֹם לַחֹדֶשׁ הָרִאשׁוֹן מִמָּחֳרַת הַפֶּסַח יָצְאוּ בְנֵי־יִשְׂרָאֵל בְּיָד רָמָה לְעֵינֵי כָּל־

לוי מִצְרָיִם: וּמִצְרַיִם מְקַבְּרִים אֵת אֲשֶׁר הִכָּה יהוה בָּהֶם כָּל־

FIRST ALIYA: vv. 1–3
Moshe does something here that he does nowhere else in *Bemidbar* but twice in *Devarim*. What is it?

SECOND ALIYA: vv. 4–6
Which is the place where
they first encountered
the clouds of glory or
ישראל *ananei hakavod?*

THIRD ALIYA: vv. 7–10
What extended to both
sides of the Reed Sea?

בְּכוֹר וּבֵאלֹהֵיהֶם עָשָׂה יהוה שְׁפָטִים: וַיִּסְעוּ בְנֵי־יִשְׂרָאֵל
מֵרַעְמְסֵס וַיַּחֲנוּ בְּסֻכֹּת: וַיִּסְעוּ מִסֻּכֹּת וַיַּחֲנוּ בְאֵתָם אֲשֶׁר
בִּקְצֵה הַמִּדְבָּר: *וַיִּסְעוּ מֵאֵתָם וַיָּשָׁב עַל־פִּי הַחִירֹת אֲשֶׁר
עַל־פְּנֵי בַּעַל צְפוֹן וַיַּחֲנוּ לִפְנֵי מִגְדֹּל: וַיִּסְעוּ מִפְּנֵי הַחִירֹת
וַיַּעַבְרוּ בְתוֹךְ־הַיָּם הַמִּדְבָּרָה וַיֵּלְכוּ דֶּרֶךְ שְׁלֹשֶׁת יָמִים
בְּמִדְבַּר אֵתָם וַיַּחֲנוּ בְּמָרָה: וַיִּסְעוּ מִמָּרָה וַיָּבֹאוּ אֵילִמָה
וּבְאֵילִם שְׁתֵּים עֶשְׂרֵה עֵינֹת מַיִם וְשִׁבְעִים תְּמָרִים וַיַּחֲנוּ־
שָׁם: וַיִּסְעוּ מֵאֵילִם וַיַּחֲנוּ עַל־יַם־סוּף:

Some extend the לוי *portion:*

וַיִּסְעוּ מִיַּם־סוּף וַיַּחֲנוּ בְּמִדְבַּר־סִין: וַיִּסְעוּ מִמִּדְבַּר־סִין וַיַּחֲנוּ
בְּדָפְקָה: וַיִּסְעוּ מִדָּפְקָה וַיַּחֲנוּ בְּאָלוּשׁ: וַיִּסְעוּ מֵאָלוּשׁ וַיַּחֲנוּ
בִּרְפִידִם וְלֹא־הָיָה שָׁם מַיִם לָעָם לִשְׁתּוֹת: וַיִּסְעוּ מֵרְפִידִם
וַיַּחֲנוּ בְּמִדְבַּר סִינָי: וַיִּסְעוּ מִמִּדְבַּר סִינָי וַיַּחֲנוּ בְּקִבְרֹת
הַתַּאֲוָה: וַיִּסְעוּ מִקִּבְרֹת הַתַּאֲוָה וַיַּחֲנוּ בַּחֲצֵרֹת: וַיִּסְעוּ
מֵחֲצֵרֹת וַיַּחֲנוּ בְּרִתְמָה: וַיִּסְעוּ מֵרִתְמָה וַיַּחֲנוּ בְּרִמֹּן פָּרֶץ:
וַיִּסְעוּ מֵרִמֹּן פָּרֶץ וַיַּחֲנוּ בְּלִבְנָה: וַיִּסְעוּ מִלִּבְנָה וַיַּחֲנוּ בְּרִסָּה:
וַיִּסְעוּ מֵרִסָּה וַיַּחֲנוּ בִּקְהֵלָתָה: וַיִּסְעוּ מִקְּהֵלָתָה וַיַּחֲנוּ בְּהַר־
שָׁפֶר: וַיִּסְעוּ מֵהַר־שָׁפֶר וַיַּחֲנוּ בַּחֲרָדָה: וַיִּסְעוּ מֵחֲרָדָה וַיַּחֲנוּ
בְּמַקְהֵלֹת: וַיִּסְעוּ מִמַּקְהֵלֹת וַיַּחֲנוּ בְּתָחַת: וַיִּסְעוּ מִתָּחַת
וַיַּחֲנוּ בְּתָרַח: וַיִּסְעוּ מִתָּרַח וַיַּחֲנוּ בְּמִתְקָה: וַיִּסְעוּ מִמִּתְקָה
וַיַּחֲנוּ בְּחַשְׁמֹנָה: וַיִּסְעוּ מֵחַשְׁמֹנָה וַיַּחֲנוּ בְּמֹסֵרוֹת: וַיִּסְעוּ
מִמֹּסֵרוֹת וַיַּחֲנוּ בִּבְנֵי יַעֲקָן: וַיִּסְעוּ מִבְּנֵי יַעֲקָן וַיַּחֲנוּ בְּחֹר
הַגִּדְגָּד: וַיִּסְעוּ מֵחֹר הַגִּדְגָּד וַיַּחֲנוּ בְּיָטְבָתָה: וַיִּסְעוּ מִיָּטְבָתָה
וַיַּחֲנוּ בְּעַבְרֹנָה: וַיִּסְעוּ מֵעַבְרֹנָה וַיַּחֲנוּ בְּעֶצְיוֹן גָּבֶר: וַיִּסְעוּ
מֵעֶצְיוֹן גָּבֶר וַיַּחֲנוּ בְמִדְבַּר־צִן הִוא קָדֵשׁ: וַיִּסְעוּ מִקָּדֵשׁ
וַיַּחֲנוּ בְּהֹר הָהָר בִּקְצֵה אֶרֶץ אֱדוֹם: וַיַּעַל אַהֲרֹן הַכֹּהֵן
אֶל־הֹר הָהָר עַל־פִּי יהוה וַיָּמָת שָׁם בִּשְׁנַת הָאַרְבָּעִים
לְצֵאת בְּנֵי־יִשְׂרָאֵל מֵאֶרֶץ מִצְרַיִם בַּחֹדֶשׁ הַחֲמִישִׁי בְּאֶחָד
לַחֹדֶשׁ: וְאַהֲרֹן בֶּן־שָׁלֹשׁ וְעֶשְׂרִים וּמְאַת שָׁנָה בְּמֹתוֹ בְּהֹר

הָהָר: וַיִּשְׁמַע הַכְּנַעֲנִי מֶלֶךְ־עֲרָד וְהוּא־יֹשֵׁב
בַּנֶּגֶב בְּאֶרֶץ כְּנָעַן בְּבֹא בְּנֵי יִשְׂרָאֵל: וַיִּסְעוּ מֵהֹר הָהָר וַיַּחֲנוּ
בְּצַלְמֹנָה: וַיִּסְעוּ מִצַּלְמֹנָה וַיַּחֲנוּ בְּפוּנֹן: וַיִּסְעוּ מִפּוּנֹן וַיַּחֲנוּ
בְּאֹבֹת: וַיִּסְעוּ מֵאֹבֹת וַיַּחֲנוּ בְּעִיֵּי הָעֲבָרִים בִּגְבוּל מוֹאָב:
וַיִּסְעוּ מֵעִיִּים וַיַּחֲנוּ בְּדִיבֹן גָּד: וַיִּסְעוּ מִדִּיבֹן גָּד וַיַּחֲנוּ בְּעַלְמֹן
דִּבְלָתָיְמָה: וַיִּסְעוּ מֵעַלְמֹן דִּבְלָתָיְמָה וַיַּחֲנוּ בְּהָרֵי הָעֲבָרִים
לִפְנֵי נְבוֹ: וַיִּסְעוּ מֵהָרֵי הָעֲבָרִים וַיַּחֲנוּ בְּעַרְבֹת מוֹאָב עַל
יַרְדֵּן יְרֵחוֹ: וַיַּחֲנוּ עַל־הַיַּרְדֵּן מִבֵּית הַיְשִׁמֹת עַד אָבֵל הַשִּׁטִּים

ישראל בְּעַרְבֹת מוֹאָב: *וַיְדַבֵּר יְהוָה אֶל־מֹשֶׁה
בְּעַרְבֹת מוֹאָב עַל־יַרְדֵּן יְרֵחוֹ לֵאמֹר: דַּבֵּר אֶל־בְּנֵי יִשְׂרָאֵל
וְאָמַרְתָּ אֲלֵהֶם כִּי אַתֶּם עֹבְרִים אֶת־הַיַּרְדֵּן אֶל־אֶרֶץ כְּנָעַן:
וְהוֹרַשְׁתֶּם אֶת־כָּל־יֹשְׁבֵי הָאָרֶץ מִפְּנֵיכֶם וְאִבַּדְתֶּם אֵת כָּל־
מַשְׂכִּיֹּתָם וְאֵת כָּל־צַלְמֵי מַסֵּכֹתָם תְּאַבֵּדוּ וְאֵת כָּל־בָּמוֹתָם
תַּשְׁמִידוּ: וְהוֹרַשְׁתֶּם אֶת־הָאָרֶץ וִישַׁבְתֶּם־בָּהּ כִּי לָכֶם נָתַתִּי
אֶת־הָאָרֶץ לָרֶשֶׁת אֹתָהּ:

DEVARIM

דברים

אֵלֶּה הַדְּבָרִים אֲשֶׁר דִּבֶּר מֹשֶׁה אֶל־כָּל־יִשְׂרָאֵל בְּעֵבֶר
הַיַּרְדֵּן בַּמִּדְבָּר בָּעֲרָבָה מוֹל סוּף בֵּין־פָּארָן וּבֵין־תֹּפֶל וְלָבָן
וַחֲצֵרֹת וְדִי זָהָב: אַחַד עָשָׂר יוֹם מֵחֹרֵב דֶּרֶךְ הַר־שֵׂעִיר
עַד קָדֵשׁ בַּרְנֵעַ: וַיְהִי בְּאַרְבָּעִים שָׁנָה בְּעַשְׁתֵּי־עָשָׂר חֹדֶשׁ
בְּאֶחָד לַחֹדֶשׁ דִּבֶּר מֹשֶׁה אֶל־בְּנֵי יִשְׂרָאֵל כְּכֹל אֲשֶׁר צִוָּה
לוי יְהוָה אֹתוֹ אֲלֵהֶם: *אַחֲרֵי הַכֹּתוֹ אֵת סִיחֹן מֶלֶךְ הָאֱמֹרִי
אֲשֶׁר יוֹשֵׁב בְּחֶשְׁבּוֹן וְאֵת עוֹג מֶלֶךְ הַבָּשָׁן אֲשֶׁר־יוֹשֵׁב
בְּעַשְׁתָּרֹת בְּאֶדְרֶעִי: בְּעֵבֶר הַיַּרְדֵּן בְּאֶרֶץ מוֹאָב הוֹאִיל
מֹשֶׁה בֵּאֵר אֶת־הַתּוֹרָה הַזֹּאת לֵאמֹר: יְהוָה אֱלֹהֵינוּ דִּבֶּר
אֵלֵינוּ בְּחֹרֵב לֵאמֹר רַב־לָכֶם שֶׁבֶת בָּהָר הַזֶּה: פְּנוּ וּסְעוּ
לָכֶם וּבֹאוּ הַר הָאֱמֹרִי וְאֶל־כָּל־שְׁכֵנָיו בָּעֲרָבָה בָהָר וּבַשְּׁפֵלָה
וּבַנֶּגֶב וּבְחוֹף הַיָּם אֶרֶץ הַכְּנַעֲנִי וְהַלְּבָנוֹן עַד־הַנָּהָר הַגָּדֹל

דברים
א:א–ג

FIRST ALIYA: vv. 1–3
There are those who say that each of these places alludes to a different sin that took place there. Can you identify the sin?

SECOND ALIYA: vv. 4–7
From here the Midrash teaches that Moshe explained the Torah in many languages, from which one could learn that the Torah may be learned in any language. Does this take away from the holiness and importance of Hebrew?

נְהַר־פְּרָת: *רְאֵה נָתַתִּי לִפְנֵיכֶם אֶת־הָאָרֶץ בֹּאוּ וּרְשׁוּ
אֶת־הָאָרֶץ אֲשֶׁר נִשְׁבַּע יהוה לַאֲבֹתֵיכֶם לְאַבְרָהָם לְיִצְחָק
וּלְיַעֲקֹב לָתֵת לָהֶם וּלְזַרְעָם אַחֲרֵיהֶם: וָאֹמַר אֲלֵכֶם בָּעֵת
הַהִוא לֵאמֹר לֹא־אוּכַל לְבַדִּי שְׂאֵת אֶתְכֶם: יהוה אֱלֹהֵיכֶם
הִרְבָּה אֶתְכֶם וְהִנְּכֶם הַיּוֹם כְּכוֹכְבֵי הַשָּׁמַיִם לָרֹב: יהוה
אֱלֹהֵי אֲבוֹתֵכֶם יֹסֵף עֲלֵיכֶם כָּכֶם אֶלֶף פְּעָמִים וִיבָרֵךְ אֶתְכֶם
כַּאֲשֶׁר דִּבֶּר לָכֶם:

THIRD ALIYA: vv. 8–11
It refers not to their number but to their quality.
What do you think that
quality might be?

ישראל

VA'ET-HANAN
ואתחנן

וָאֶתְחַנַּן אֶל־יהוה בָּעֵת הַהִוא לֵאמֹר: אֲדֹנָי יהוה אַתָּה
הַחִלּוֹתָ לְהַרְאוֹת אֶת־עַבְדְּךָ אֶת־גָּדְלְךָ וְאֶת־יָדְךָ הַחֲזָקָה
אֲשֶׁר מִי־אֵל בַּשָּׁמַיִם וּבָאָרֶץ אֲשֶׁר־יַעֲשֶׂה כְמַעֲשֶׂיךָ
וְכִגְבוּרֹתֶךָ: אֶעְבְּרָה־נָּא וְאֶרְאֶה אֶת־הָאָרֶץ הַטּוֹבָה אֲשֶׁר
בְּעֵבֶר הַיַּרְדֵּן הָהָר הַטּוֹב הַזֶּה וְהַלְּבָנֹן: *וַיִּתְעַבֵּר יהוה בִּי
לְמַעַנְכֶם וְלֹא שָׁמַע אֵלָי וַיֹּאמֶר יהוה אֵלַי רַב־לָךְ אַל־תּוֹסֶף
דַּבֵּר אֵלַי עוֹד בַּדָּבָר הַזֶּה: עֲלֵה ׀ רֹאשׁ הַפִּסְגָּה וְשָׂא עֵינֶיךָ
יָמָּה וְצָפֹנָה וְתֵימָנָה וּמִזְרָחָה וּרְאֵה בְעֵינֶיךָ כִּי־לֹא תַעֲבֹר
אֶת־הַיַּרְדֵּן הַזֶּה: וְצַו אֶת־יְהוֹשֻׁעַ וְחַזְּקֵהוּ וְאַמְּצֵהוּ כִּי־הוּא
יַעֲבֹר לִפְנֵי הָעָם הַזֶּה וְהוּא יַנְחִיל אוֹתָם אֶת־הָאָרֶץ אֲשֶׁר
תִּרְאֶה: וַנֵּשֶׁב בַּגָּיְא מוּל בֵּית פְּעוֹר:

FIRST ALIYA: vv. 23–29
From here one learns
that one should first
praise Hashem and
only afterwards make
one's personal requests.
Where is this principle
reflected in the siddur?

דברים
ג:כג–ד:ח

לוי

וְעַתָּה יִשְׂרָאֵל שְׁמַע אֶל־הַחֻקִּים וְאֶל־הַמִּשְׁפָּטִים אֲשֶׁר
אָנֹכִי מְלַמֵּד אֶתְכֶם לַעֲשׂוֹת לְמַעַן תִּחְיוּ וּבָאתֶם וִירִשְׁתֶּם
אֶת־הָאָרֶץ אֲשֶׁר יהוה אֱלֹהֵי אֲבֹתֵיכֶם נֹתֵן לָכֶם: לֹא
תֹסִפוּ עַל־הַדָּבָר אֲשֶׁר אָנֹכִי מְצַוֶּה אֶתְכֶם וְלֹא תִגְרְעוּ
מִמֶּנּוּ לִשְׁמֹר אֶת־מִצְוֹת יהוה אֱלֹהֵיכֶם אֲשֶׁר אָנֹכִי מְצַוֶּה
אֶתְכֶם: עֵינֵיכֶם הָרֹאוֹת אֵת אֲשֶׁר־עָשָׂה יהוה בְּבַעַל פְּעוֹר
כִּי כָל־הָאִישׁ אֲשֶׁר הָלַךְ אַחֲרֵי בַעַל־פְּעוֹר הִשְׁמִידוֹ יהוה
אֱלֹהֶיךָ מִקִּרְבֶּךָ: וְאַתֶּם הַדְּבֵקִים בַּיהוה אֱלֹהֵיכֶם חַיִּים
כֻּלְּכֶם הַיּוֹם: *רְאֵה ׀ לִמַּדְתִּי אֶתְכֶם חֻקִּים וּמִשְׁפָּטִים

SECOND ALIYA: vv. 4:1–4
From here one learns that
one may not have five
strings on one's *tzitzit* or
five species with one's
lulav or five chapters in
one's *tefillin*. Why can't
we add to the mitzvot
to show how important
they are to us?

ישראל

כַּאֲשֶׁר צִוַּנִי יהוה אֱלֹהָי לַעֲשׂוֹת כֵּן בְּקֶרֶב הָאָרֶץ אֲשֶׁר אַתֶּם בָּאִים שָׁמָּה לְרִשְׁתָּהּ: וּשְׁמַרְתֶּם וַעֲשִׂיתֶם כִּי הִוא חָכְמַתְכֶם וּבִינַתְכֶם לְעֵינֵי הָעַמִּים אֲשֶׁר יִשְׁמְעוּן אֵת כָּל־הַחֻקִּים הָאֵלֶּה וְאָמְרוּ רַק עַם־חָכָם וְנָבוֹן הַגּוֹי הַגָּדוֹל הַזֶּה: כִּי מִי־גוֹי גָּדוֹל אֲשֶׁר־לוֹ אֱלֹהִים קְרֹבִים אֵלָיו כַּיהוה אֱלֹהֵינוּ בְּכָל־קָרְאֵנוּ אֵלָיו: וּמִי גּוֹי גָּדוֹל אֲשֶׁר־לוֹ חֻקִּים וּמִשְׁפָּטִים צַדִּיקִם כְּכֹל הַתּוֹרָה הַזֹּאת אֲשֶׁר אָנֹכִי נֹתֵן לִפְנֵיכֶם הַיּוֹם:

THIRD ALIYA: vv. 5–8
What is it that the non-Jews will admire us for? Can you think of any specific examples that might be representative?

EKEV עקב

וְהָיָה | עֵקֶב תִּשְׁמְעוּן אֵת הַמִּשְׁפָּטִים הָאֵלֶּה וּשְׁמַרְתֶּם וַעֲשִׂיתֶם אֹתָם וְשָׁמַר יהוה אֱלֹהֶיךָ לְךָ אֶת־הַבְּרִית וְאֶת־הַחֶסֶד אֲשֶׁר נִשְׁבַּע לַאֲבֹתֶיךָ: וַאֲהֵבְךָ וּבֵרַכְךָ וְהִרְבֶּךָ וּבֵרַךְ פְּרִי־בִטְנְךָ וּפְרִי־אַדְמָתֶךָ דְּגָנְךָ וְתִירֹשְׁךָ וְיִצְהָרֶךָ שְׁגַר־אֲלָפֶיךָ וְעַשְׁתְּרֹת צֹאנֶךָ עַל הָאֲדָמָה אֲשֶׁר־נִשְׁבַּע לַאֲבֹתֶיךָ לָתֶת לָךְ: בָּרוּךְ תִּהְיֶה מִכָּל־הָעַמִּים לֹא־יִהְיֶה בְךָ עָקָר וַעֲקָרָה וּבִבְהֶמְתֶּךָ: וְהֵסִיר יהוה מִמְּךָ כָּל־חֹלִי וְכָל־מַדְוֵי מִצְרַיִם הָרָעִים אֲשֶׁר יָדַעְתָּ לֹא יְשִׂימָם בָּךְ וּנְתָנָם בְּכָל־שֹׂנְאֶיךָ: וְאָכַלְתָּ אֶת־כָּל־הָעַמִּים אֲשֶׁר יהוה אֱלֹהֶיךָ נֹתֵן לָךְ לֹא־תָחוֹס עֵינְךָ עֲלֵיהֶם וְלֹא תַעֲבֹד אֶת־אֱלֹהֵיהֶם כִּי־מוֹקֵשׁ הוּא לָךְ: כִּי תֹאמַר בִּלְבָבְךָ רַבִּים הַגּוֹיִם הָאֵלֶּה מִמֶּנִּי אֵיכָה אוּכַל לְהוֹרִישָׁם: לֹא תִירָא מֵהֶם זָכֹר תִּזְכֹּר אֵת אֲשֶׁר־עָשָׂה יהוה אֱלֹהֶיךָ לְפַרְעֹה וּלְכָל־מִצְרָיִם: הַמַּסֹּת הַגְּדֹלֹת אֲשֶׁר־רָאוּ עֵינֶיךָ וְהָאֹתֹת וְהַמֹּפְתִים וְהַיָּד הַחֲזָקָה וְהַזְּרֹעַ הַנְּטוּיָה אֲשֶׁר הוֹצִאֲךָ יהוה אֱלֹהֶיךָ כֵּן־יַעֲשֶׂה יהוה אֱלֹהֶיךָ לְכָל־הָעַמִּים אֲשֶׁר־אַתָּה יָרֵא מִפְּנֵיהֶם: וְגַם אֶת־הַצִּרְעָה יְשַׁלַּח יהוה אֱלֹהֶיךָ בָּם עַד־אֲבֹד הַנִּשְׁאָרִים וְהַנִּסְתָּרִים מִפָּנֶיךָ: לֹא תַעֲרֹץ מִפְּנֵיהֶם

דברים
ד:יב–ח:י

FIRST ALIYA: vv. 12–21
How many rewards are mentioned here?

SECOND ALIYA:
vv. 7:22–8:3
What was the test referred
to here? Can you think of
a modern day equivalent
that would have the same
effect?

כִּי־יהוה אֱלֹהֶיךָ בְּקִרְבֶּךָ אֵל גָּדוֹל וְנוֹרָא: ⋆וְנָשַׁל יהוה לוי
אֱלֹהֶיךָ אֶת־הַגּוֹיִם הָאֵל מִפָּנֶיךָ מְעַט מְעָט לֹא תוּכַל כַּלֹּתָם
מַהֵר פֶּן־תִּרְבֶּה עָלֶיךָ חַיַּת הַשָּׂדֶה: וּנְתָנָם יהוה אֱלֹהֶיךָ
לְפָנֶיךָ וְהָמָם מְהוּמָה גְדֹלָה עַד הִשָּׁמְדָם: וְנָתַן מַלְכֵיהֶם
בְּיָדֶךָ וְהַאֲבַדְתָּ אֶת־שְׁמָם מִתַּחַת הַשָּׁמָיִם לֹא־יִתְיַצֵּב אִישׁ
בְּפָנֶיךָ עַד הִשְׁמִדְךָ אֹתָם: פְּסִילֵי אֱלֹהֵיהֶם תִּשְׂרְפוּן בָּאֵשׁ
לֹא־תַחְמֹד כֶּסֶף וְזָהָב עֲלֵיהֶם וְלָקַחְתָּ לָךְ פֶּן תִּוָּקֵשׁ בּוֹ כִּי
תוֹעֲבַת יהוה אֱלֹהֶיךָ הוּא: וְלֹא־תָבִיא תוֹעֵבָה אֶל־בֵּיתֶךָ
וְהָיִיתָ חֵרֶם כָּמֹהוּ שַׁקֵּץ ׀ תְּשַׁקְּצֶנּוּ וְתַעֵב ׀ תְּתַעֲבֶנּוּ כִּי־חֵרֶם
הוּא:

כָּל־הַמִּצְוָה אֲשֶׁר אָנֹכִי מְצַוְּךָ הַיּוֹם תִּשְׁמְרוּן לַעֲשׂוֹת לְמַעַן
תִּחְיוּן וּרְבִיתֶם וּבָאתֶם וִירִשְׁתֶּם אֶת־הָאָרֶץ אֲשֶׁר־נִשְׁבַּע
יהוה לַאֲבֹתֵיכֶם: וְזָכַרְתָּ אֶת־כָּל־הַדֶּרֶךְ אֲשֶׁר הוֹלִיכְךָ
יהוה אֱלֹהֶיךָ זֶה אַרְבָּעִים שָׁנָה בַּמִּדְבָּר לְמַעַן עַנֹּתְךָ
לְנַסֹּתְךָ לָדַעַת אֶת־אֲשֶׁר בִּלְבָבְךָ הֲתִשְׁמֹר מִצְוֹתָו אִם־
לֹא: וַיְעַנְּךָ וַיַּרְעִבֶךָ וַיַּאֲכִלְךָ אֶת־הַמָּן אֲשֶׁר לֹא־יָדַעְתָּ וְלֹא
יָדְעוּן אֲבֹתֶיךָ לְמַעַן הוֹדִיעֲךָ כִּי לֹא עַל־הַלֶּחֶם לְבַדּוֹ יִחְיֶה
הָאָדָם כִּי עַל־כָּל־מוֹצָא פִי־יהוה יִחְיֶה הָאָדָם: ⋆שִׂמְלָתְךָ ישראל
לֹא בָלְתָה מֵעָלֶיךָ וְרַגְלְךָ לֹא בָצֵקָה זֶה אַרְבָּעִים שָׁנָה:
וְיָדַעְתָּ עִם־לְבָבֶךָ כִּי כַּאֲשֶׁר יְיַסֵּר אִישׁ אֶת־בְּנוֹ יהוה אֱלֹהֶיךָ
מְיַסְּרֶךָּ: וְשָׁמַרְתָּ אֶת־מִצְוֹת יהוה אֱלֹהֶיךָ לָלֶכֶת בִּדְרָכָיו
וּלְיִרְאָה אֹתוֹ: כִּי יהוה אֱלֹהֶיךָ מְבִיאֲךָ אֶל־אֶרֶץ טוֹבָה אֶרֶץ
נַחֲלֵי מָיִם עֲיָנֹת וּתְהֹמֹת יֹצְאִים בַּבִּקְעָה וּבָהָר: אֶרֶץ
חִטָּה וּשְׂעֹרָה וְגֶפֶן וּתְאֵנָה וְרִמּוֹן אֶרֶץ־זֵית שֶׁמֶן וּדְבָשׁ:
אֶרֶץ אֲשֶׁר לֹא בְמִסְכֵּנֻת תֹּאכַל־בָּהּ לֶחֶם לֹא־תֶחְסַר כֹּל
בָּהּ אֶרֶץ אֲשֶׁר אֲבָנֶיהָ בַרְזֶל וּמֵהֲרָרֶיהָ תַּחְצֹב נְחֹשֶׁת:
וְאָכַלְתָּ וְשָׂבָעְתָּ וּבֵרַכְתָּ אֶת־יהוה אֱלֹהֶיךָ עַל־הָאָרֶץ הַטֹּבָה
אֲשֶׁר נָתַן־לָךְ:

THIRD ALIYA: vv. 4–10
From here one learns the
mitzva of Birkat HaMazon.
Is this mitzva limited to
produce from Eretz Yisrael?
If not, why does the verse
mention the Land of
Israel?

RE'EH

ראה

ראה

דברים
יא:כו–יב:י

רְאֵ֗ה אָנֹכִ֛י נֹתֵ֥ן לִפְנֵיכֶ֖ם הַיּ֑וֹם בְּרָכָ֖ה וּקְלָלָֽה: אֶת־
הַבְּרָכָ֔ה אֲשֶׁ֣ר תִּשְׁמְע֔וּ אֶל־מִצְוֺת֙ יהוה אֱלֹ֣הֵיכֶ֔ם אֲשֶׁ֧ר
אָנֹכִ֛י מְצַוֶּ֥ה אֶתְכֶ֖ם הַיּֽוֹם: וְהַקְּלָלָ֗ה אִם־לֹ֤א תִשְׁמְעוּ֙
אֶל־מִצְוֺת֙ יהוה אֱלֹ֣הֵיכֶ֔ם וְסַרְתֶּ֣ם מִן־הַדֶּ֔רֶךְ אֲשֶׁ֧ר אָנֹכִ֛י
מְצַוֶּ֥ה אֶתְכֶ֖ם הַיּ֑וֹם לָלֶ֗כֶת אַֽחֲרֵ֛י אֱלֹהִ֥ים אֲחֵרִ֖ים אֲשֶׁ֥ר
לֹֽא־יְדַעְתֶּֽם: וְהָיָ֗ה כִּֽי יְבִֽיאֲךָ֞ יהוה אֱלֹהֶ֘יךָ֮ אֶל־
הָאָ֗רֶץ אֲשֶׁר־אַתָּ֥ה בָא־שָׁ֖מָּה לְרִשְׁתָּ֑הּ וְנָֽתַתָּ֤ה אֶת־הַבְּרָכָה֙
עַל־הַ֣ר גְּרִזִ֔ים וְאֶת־הַקְּלָלָ֖ה עַל־הַ֥ר עֵיבָֽל: הֲלֹא־הֵ֜מָּה
בְּעֵ֣בֶר הַיַּרְדֵּ֗ן אַֽחֲרֵי֙ דֶּ֚רֶךְ מְב֣וֹא הַשֶּׁ֔מֶשׁ בְּאֶ֨רֶץ֙ הַֽכְּנַֽעֲנִ֔י
הַיֹּשֵׁ֖ב בָּעֲרָבָ֑ה מ֚וּל הַגִּלְגָּ֔ל אֵ֖צֶל אֵֽלוֹנֵ֥י מֹרֶֽה: כִּ֣י אַתֶּ֗ם
עֹֽבְרִים֙ אֶת־הַיַּרְדֵּ֔ן לָבֹא֙ לָרֶ֣שֶׁת אֶת־הָאָ֔רֶץ אֲשֶׁר־יהוה

לוי

אֱלֹֽהֵיכֶ֖ם נֹתֵ֣ן לָכֶ֑ם וִֽירִשְׁתֶּ֥ם אֹתָ֖הּ וִֽישַׁבְתֶּם־בָּֽהּ: וּשְׁמַרְתֶּ֣ם
לַעֲשׂ֔וֹת אֵ֥ת כָּל־הַֽחֻקִּ֖ים וְאֶת־הַמִּשְׁפָּטִ֑ים אֲשֶׁ֧ר אָנֹכִ֛י נֹתֵ֥ן
לִפְנֵיכֶ֖ם הַיּֽוֹם: אֵ֣לֶּה הַֽחֻקִּ֣ים וְהַמִּשְׁפָּטִ֗ים אֲשֶׁ֤ר תִּשְׁמְרוּן֙
לַעֲשׂ֔וֹת בָּאָ֕רֶץ אֲשֶׁר֩ נָתַ֨ן יהוה אֱלֹהֵ֧י אֲבֹתֶ֛יךָ לְךָ֖ לְרִשְׁתָּ֑הּ
כָּל־הַ֨יָּמִ֔ים אֲשֶׁר־אַתֶּ֥ם חַיִּ֖ים עַל־הָֽאֲדָמָֽה: אַבֵּ֣ד תְּאַבְּד֠וּן
אֶֽת־כָּל־הַמְּקֹמ֞וֹת אֲשֶׁ֧ר עָֽבְדוּ־שָׁ֣ם הַגּוֹיִ֗ם אֲשֶׁ֥ר אַתֶּ֛ם
יֹֽרְשִׁ֥ים אֹתָ֖ם אֶת־אֱלֹֽהֵיהֶ֑ם עַל־הֶֽהָרִ֤ים הָֽרָמִים֙ וְעַל־
הַגְּבָע֔וֹת וְתַ֖חַת כָּל־עֵ֥ץ רַֽעֲנָֽן: וְנִתַּצְתֶּ֣ם אֶת־מִזְבְּחֹתָ֗ם
וְשִׁבַּרְתֶּם֙ אֶת־מַצֵּ֣בֹתָ֔ם וַֽאֲשֵֽׁרֵיהֶם֙ תִּשְׂרְפ֣וּן בָּאֵ֔שׁ וּפְסִילֵ֥י
אֱלֹֽהֵיהֶ֖ם תְּגַדֵּע֑וּן וְאִבַּדְתֶּ֣ם אֶת־שְׁמָ֔ם מִן־הַמָּק֖וֹם הַהֽוּא:
לֹֽא־תַֽעֲשׂ֣וּן כֵּ֔ן לַֽיהוה אֱלֹֽהֵיכֶֽם: כִּ֠י אִֽם־אֶל־הַמָּק֞וֹם אֲשֶׁר־

ישראל

יִבְחַ֨ר יהוה אֱלֹֽהֵיכֶ֤ם מִכָּל־שִׁבְטֵיכֶם֙ לָשׂ֥וּם אֶת־שְׁמ֖וֹ שָׁ֑ם
לְשִׁכְנ֥וֹ תִדְרְשׁ֖וּ וּבָ֥אתָ שָֽׁמָּה: וַֽהֲבֵאתֶ֣ם שָׁ֗מָּה עֹלֹֽתֵיכֶם֙
וְזִבְחֵיכֶ֔ם וְאֵת֙ מַעְשְׂרֹ֣תֵיכֶ֔ם וְאֵ֖ת תְּרוּמַ֣ת יֶדְכֶ֑ם וְנִדְרֵיכֶם֙
וְנִדְבֹ֣תֵיכֶ֔ם וּבְכֹרֹ֥ת בְּקַרְכֶ֖ם וְצֹֽאנְכֶֽם: וַֽאֲכַלְתֶּם־שָׁ֗ם לִפְנֵי֙
יהוה אֱלֹֽהֵיכֶ֔ם וּשְׂמַחְתֶּ֗ם בְּכֹל֙ מִשְׁלַ֣ח יֶדְכֶ֔ם אַתֶּ֖ם וּבָֽתֵּיכֶ֑ם
אֲשֶׁ֥ר בֵּֽרַכְךָ֖ יהוה אֱלֹהֶֽיךָ: לֹ֣א תַֽעֲשׂ֔וּן כְּכֹ֛ל אֲשֶׁ֥ר אֲנַ֛חְנוּ

FIRST ALIYA: vv. 26–31
The verb at the outset
doesn't seem to fit. Why
not? How can this never-
theless be explained? How
might one fulfill it today?

SECOND ALIYA:
vv. 11:32–12:5
From here one may learn
that one cannot erase the
name of Hashem.
What are some of the
practical implications of
this law today?

THIRD ALIYA: vv. 6–10
This phrase has become
an expression today for
people who do the
opposite of what
should be done.

עֹשִׂים פֹּה הַיּוֹם אִישׁ כָּל־הַיָּשָׁר בְּעֵינָיו: כִּי לֹא־בָּאתֶם
עַד־עָתָּה אֶל־הַמְּנוּחָה וְאֶל־הַנַּחֲלָה אֲשֶׁר־יְהוָה אֱלֹהֶיךָ
נֹתֵן לָךְ: וַעֲבַרְתֶּם אֶת־הַיַּרְדֵּן וִישַׁבְתֶּם בָּאָרֶץ אֲשֶׁר־יְהוָה
אֱלֹהֵיכֶם מַנְחִיל אֶתְכֶם וְהֵנִיחַ לָכֶם מִכָּל־אֹיְבֵיכֶם מִסָּבִיב
וִישַׁבְתֶּם־בֶּטַח:

SHOFETIM

שופטים

דברים
טז:יח–יז:י

שֹׁפְטִים וְשֹׁטְרִים תִּתֶּן־לְךָ בְּכָל־שְׁעָרֶיךָ אֲשֶׁר יְהוָה אֱלֹהֶיךָ
נֹתֵן לְךָ לִשְׁבָטֶיךָ וְשָׁפְטוּ אֶת־הָעָם מִשְׁפַּט־צֶדֶק: לֹא־
תַטֶּה מִשְׁפָּט לֹא תַכִּיר פָּנִים וְלֹא־תִקַּח שֹׁחַד כִּי הַשֹּׁחַד
יְעַוֵּר עֵינֵי חֲכָמִים וִיסַלֵּף דִּבְרֵי צַדִּיקִם: צֶדֶק צֶדֶק תִּרְדֹּף
לְמַעַן תִּחְיֶה וְיָרַשְׁתָּ אֶת־הָאָרֶץ אֲשֶׁר־יְהוָה אֱלֹהֶיךָ נֹתֵן
לָךְ: לֹא־תִטַּע לְךָ אֲשֵׁרָה כָּל־עֵץ אֵצֶל מִזְבַּח
יְהוָה אֱלֹהֶיךָ אֲשֶׁר תַּעֲשֶׂה־לָּךְ: וְלֹא־תָקִים לְךָ מַצֵּבָה אֲשֶׁר
שָׂנֵא יְהוָה אֱלֹהֶיךָ: לֹא־תִזְבַּח לַיהוָה אֱלֹהֶיךָ
שׁוֹר וָשֶׂה אֲשֶׁר יִהְיֶה בוֹ מוּם כֹּל דָּבָר רָע כִּי תוֹעֲבַת יְהוָה
אֱלֹהֶיךָ הוּא: כִּי־יִמָּצֵא בְקִרְבְּךָ בְּאַחַד שְׁעָרֶיךָ
אֲשֶׁר־יְהוָה אֱלֹהֶיךָ נֹתֵן לָךְ אִישׁ אוֹ־אִשָּׁה אֲשֶׁר יַעֲשֶׂה
אֶת־הָרַע בְּעֵינֵי יְהוָה־אֱלֹהֶיךָ לַעֲבֹר בְּרִיתוֹ: וַיֵּלֶךְ וַיַּעֲבֹד
אֱלֹהִים אֲחֵרִים וַיִּשְׁתַּחוּ לָהֶם וְלַשֶּׁמֶשׁ אוֹ לַיָּרֵחַ אוֹ לְכָל־
צְבָא הַשָּׁמַיִם אֲשֶׁר לֹא־צִוִּיתִי: וְהֻגַּד־לְךָ וְשָׁמָעְתָּ וְדָרַשְׁתָּ
הֵיטֵב וְהִנֵּה אֱמֶת נָכוֹן הַדָּבָר נֶעֶשְׂתָה הַתּוֹעֵבָה הַזֹּאת
בְּיִשְׂרָאֵל: וְהוֹצֵאתָ אֶת־הָאִישׁ הַהוּא אוֹ אֶת־הָאִשָּׁה הַהִוא
אֲשֶׁר עָשׂוּ אֶת־הַדָּבָר הָרָע הַזֶּה אֶל־שְׁעָרֶיךָ אֶת־הָאִישׁ אוֹ
אֶת־הָאִשָּׁה וּסְקַלְתָּם בָּאֲבָנִים וָמֵתוּ: עַל־פִּי שְׁנַיִם עֵדִים
אוֹ שְׁלֹשָׁה עֵדִים יוּמַת הַמֵּת לֹא יוּמַת עַל־פִּי עֵד אֶחָד: יַד
הָעֵדִים תִּהְיֶה־בּוֹ בָרִאשֹׁנָה לַהֲמִיתוֹ וְיַד כָּל־הָעָם בָּאַחֲרֹנָה
וּבִעַרְתָּ הָרָע מִקִּרְבֶּךָ:

לוי

FIRST ALIYA: vv. 18–20
From here one
might learn that
(a) it's not enough
to be righteous – one
also needs to proactively
seek out righteousness,
(b) that righteous acts
must be committed
through honest means,
(c) that a judge must be
thorough regardless of
the circumstances.
Where have you seen any
of these implemented
or ignored?

SECOND ALIYA: vv.
16:21–17:10
The word Torah is derived
from here. What does the
root of the word mean?

כִּי יִפָּלֵא מִמְּךָ דָבָר לַמִּשְׁפָּט בֵּין־דָּם ׀ לְדָם בֵּין־דִּין לְדִין וּבֵין
נֶגַע לָנֶגַע דִּבְרֵי רִיבֹת בִּשְׁעָרֶיךָ וְקַמְתָּ וְעָלִיתָ אֶל־הַמָּקוֹם
אֲשֶׁר יִבְחַר יְהוָה אֱלֹהֶיךָ בּוֹ: וּבָאתָ אֶל־הַכֹּהֲנִים הַלְוִיִּם
וְאֶל־הַשֹּׁפֵט אֲשֶׁר יִהְיֶה בַּיָּמִים הָהֵם וְדָרַשְׁתָּ וְהִגִּידוּ לְךָ
אֵת דְּבַר הַמִּשְׁפָּט: וְעָשִׂיתָ עַל־פִּי הַדָּבָר אֲשֶׁר יַגִּידוּ לְךָ
מִן־הַמָּקוֹם הַהוּא אֲשֶׁר יִבְחַר יְהוָה וְשָׁמַרְתָּ לַעֲשׂוֹת כְּכֹל
אֲשֶׁר יוֹרוּךָ: *עַל־פִּי הַתּוֹרָה אֲשֶׁר יוֹרוּךָ וְעַל־הַמִּשְׁפָּט
אֲשֶׁר־יֹאמְרוּ לְךָ תַּעֲשֶׂה לֹא תָסוּר מִן־הַדָּבָר אֲשֶׁר־יַגִּידוּ
לְךָ יָמִין וּשְׂמֹאל: וְהָאִישׁ אֲשֶׁר־יַעֲשֶׂה בְזָדוֹן לְבִלְתִּי שְׁמֹעַ
אֶל־הַכֹּהֵן הָעֹמֵד לְשָׁרֶת שָׁם אֶת־יְהוָה אֱלֹהֶיךָ אוֹ אֶל־
הַשֹּׁפֵט וּמֵת הָאִישׁ הַהוּא וּבִעַרְתָּ הָרָע מִיִּשְׂרָאֵל: וְכָל־הָעָם
יִשְׁמְעוּ וְיִרָאוּ וְלֹא יְזִידוּן עוֹד:

ישראל THIRD ALIYA: vv. 11–13
From here one learns
that one may say
"He commanded us" (צִוָּנוּ)
even when saying a bless-
ing over a mitzva that is
not from the Torah, e.g.,
Ḥanukka candles. How
can we reconcile this?

KI TETZEH
כי תצא

כִּי־תֵצֵא לַמִּלְחָמָה עַל־אֹיְבֶיךָ וּנְתָנוֹ יְהוָה אֱלֹהֶיךָ בְּיָדֶךָ
וְשָׁבִיתָ שִׁבְיוֹ: וְרָאִיתָ בַּשִּׁבְיָה אֵשֶׁת יְפַת־תֹּאַר וְחָשַׁקְתָּ
בָהּ וְלָקַחְתָּ לְךָ לְאִשָּׁה: וַהֲבֵאתָהּ אֶל־תּוֹךְ בֵּיתֶךָ וְגִלְּחָה
אֶת־רֹאשָׁהּ וְעָשְׂתָה אֶת־צִפָּרְנֶיהָ: וְהֵסִירָה אֶת־שִׂמְלַת
שִׁבְיָהּ מֵעָלֶיהָ וְיָשְׁבָה בְּבֵיתֶךָ וּבָכְתָה אֶת־אָבִיהָ וְאֶת־
אִמָּהּ יֶרַח יָמִים וְאַחַר כֵּן תָּבוֹא אֵלֶיהָ וּבְעַלְתָּהּ וְהָיְתָה
לְךָ לְאִשָּׁה: וְהָיָה אִם־לֹא חָפַצְתָּ בָּהּ וְשִׁלַּחְתָּהּ לְנַפְשָׁהּ
וּמָכֹר לֹא־תִמְכְּרֶנָּה בַּכָּסֶף לֹא־תִתְעַמֵּר בָּהּ תַּחַת אֲשֶׁר
עִנִּיתָהּ: *כִּי־תִהְיֶיןָ לְאִישׁ שְׁתֵּי נָשִׁים הָאַחַת
אֲהוּבָה וְהָאַחַת שְׂנוּאָה וְיָלְדוּ־לוֹ בָנִים הָאֲהוּבָה וְהַשְּׂנוּאָה
וְהָיָה הַבֵּן הַבְּכֹר לַשְּׂנִיאָה: וְהָיָה בְּיוֹם הַנְחִילוֹ אֶת־בָּנָיו אֵת
אֲשֶׁר־יִהְיֶה לוֹ לֹא יוּכַל לְבַכֵּר אֶת־בֶּן־הָאֲהוּבָה עַל־פְּנֵי בֶן־
הַשְּׂנוּאָה הַבְּכֹר: כִּי אֶת־הַבְּכֹר בֶּן־הַשְּׂנוּאָה יַכִּיר לָתֶת לוֹ פִּי
שְׁנַיִם בְּכֹל אֲשֶׁר־יִמָּצֵא לוֹ כִּי־הוּא רֵאשִׁית אֹנוֹ לוֹ מִשְׁפַּט
הַבְּכֹרָה: *כִּי־יִהְיֶה לְאִישׁ בֵּן סוֹרֵר וּמוֹרֶה אֵינֶנּוּ

דברים FIRST ALIYA:
כא:י–יא vv. 10–14
Of this the Rabbis said:
לֹא דִבְּרָה תּוֹרָה אֶלָּא כְּנֶגֶד
יֵצֶר הָרָע – the Torah spoke
only in response to
one's evil inclination.
Are there any other
mitzvot that you think can
be seen in this light?

לוי SECOND ALIYA: vv. 15–17
Rearrange the letters of
one of the wives to determine how she got there
in the first place.

ישראל THIRD ALIYA: vv. 18–21
The Gemara (Sanhedrin
71a) says that there
never was and never
will be a capital case
involving a wayward
son (ben sorer

umoreh) as described here, because there are so many requirements for a conviction dictated by Oral Law as to make it impossible. If so, what is the purpose of the law?

שֹׁמֵעַ בְּקוֹל אָבִיו וּבְקוֹל אִמּוֹ וְיִסְּרוּ אֹתוֹ וְלֹא יִשְׁמַע אֲלֵיהֶם:
וְתָפְשׂוּ בוֹ אָבִיו וְאִמּוֹ וְהוֹצִיאוּ אֹתוֹ אֶל־זִקְנֵי עִירוֹ וְאֶל־שַׁעַר
מְקֹמוֹ: וְאָמְרוּ אֶל־זִקְנֵי עִירוֹ בְּנֵנוּ זֶה סוֹרֵר וּמֹרֶה אֵינֶנּוּ שֹׁמֵעַ
בְּקֹלֵנוּ זוֹלֵל וְסֹבֵא: וּרְגָמֻהוּ כָּל־אַנְשֵׁי עִירוֹ בָאֲבָנִים וָמֵת
וּבִעַרְתָּ הָרָע מִקִּרְבֶּךָ וְכָל־יִשְׂרָאֵל יִשְׁמְעוּ וְיִרָאוּ:

KI TAVO

כי תבוא

FIRST ALIYA: vv. 1–3
A hint to the Pesah Seder can be found in this word. Once you find it, can you provide an explanation for a possible connection?

דברים
כו: א-טו

וְהָיָה כִּי־תָבוֹא אֶל־הָאָרֶץ אֲשֶׁר יהוה אֱלֹהֶיךָ נֹתֵן לְךָ נַחֲלָה
וִירִשְׁתָּהּ וְיָשַׁבְתָּ בָּהּ: וְלָקַחְתָּ מֵרֵאשִׁית ׀ כָּל־פְּרִי הָאֲדָמָה
אֲשֶׁר תָּבִיא מֵאַרְצְךָ אֲשֶׁר יהוה אֱלֹהֶיךָ נֹתֵן לָךְ וְשַׂמְתָּ
בַטֶּנֶא וְהָלַכְתָּ אֶל־הַמָּקוֹם אֲשֶׁר יִבְחַר יהוה אֱלֹהֶיךָ לְשַׁכֵּן
שְׁמוֹ שָׁם: וּבָאתָ אֶל־הַכֹּהֵן אֲשֶׁר יִהְיֶה בַּיָּמִים הָהֵם וְאָמַרְתָּ
אֵלָיו הִגַּדְתִּי הַיּוֹם לַיהוה אֱלֹהֶיךָ כִּי־בָאתִי אֶל־הָאָרֶץ אֲשֶׁר
נִשְׁבַּע יהוה לַאֲבֹתֵינוּ לָתֶת לָנוּ: *וְלָקַח הַכֹּהֵן הַטֶּנֶא מִיָּדֶךָ

SECOND ALIYA: vv. 4–11
Half the verses included here are recited on the night of Pesah and half are not. Which half? Why and why not?

לוי

וְהִנִּיחוֹ לִפְנֵי מִזְבַּח יהוה אֱלֹהֶיךָ: וְעָנִיתָ וְאָמַרְתָּ לִפְנֵי ׀ יהוה
אֱלֹהֶיךָ אֲרַמִּי אֹבֵד אָבִי וַיֵּרֶד מִצְרַיְמָה וַיָּגָר שָׁם בִּמְתֵי מְעָט
וַיְהִי־שָׁם לְגוֹי גָּדוֹל עָצוּם וָרָב: וַיָּרֵעוּ אֹתָנוּ הַמִּצְרִים וַיְעַנּוּנוּ
וַיִּתְּנוּ עָלֵינוּ עֲבֹדָה קָשָׁה: וַנִּצְעַק אֶל־יהוה אֱלֹהֵי אֲבֹתֵינוּ
וַיִּשְׁמַע יהוה אֶת־קֹלֵנוּ וַיַּרְא אֶת־עָנְיֵנוּ וְאֶת־עֲמָלֵנוּ וְאֶת־
לַחֲצֵנוּ: וַיּוֹצִאֵנוּ יהוה מִמִּצְרַיִם בְּיָד חֲזָקָה וּבִזְרֹעַ נְטוּיָה
וּבְמֹרָא גָּדֹל וּבְאֹתוֹת וּבְמֹפְתִים: וַיְבִאֵנוּ אֶל־הַמָּקוֹם הַזֶּה
וַיִּתֶּן־לָנוּ אֶת־הָאָרֶץ הַזֹּאת אֶרֶץ זָבַת חָלָב וּדְבָשׁ: וְעַתָּה
הִנֵּה הֵבֵאתִי אֶת־רֵאשִׁית פְּרִי הָאֲדָמָה אֲשֶׁר־נָתַתָּה לִּי
יהוה וְהִנַּחְתּוֹ לִפְנֵי יהוה אֱלֹהֶיךָ וְהִשְׁתַּחֲוִיתָ לִפְנֵי יהוה
אֱלֹהֶיךָ: וְשָׂמַחְתָּ בְכָל־הַטּוֹב אֲשֶׁר נָתַן־לְךָ יהוה אֱלֹהֶיךָ
וּלְבֵיתֶךָ אַתָּה וְהַלֵּוִי וְהַגֵּר אֲשֶׁר בְּקִרְבֶּךָ: *כִּי

THIRD ALIYA:
vv. 12–15
The tithe of the first year, *ma'aser rishon*, went to the Levi, the second tithe was generally eaten

ישראל

תְכַלֶּה לַעְשֵׂר אֶת־כָּל־מַעְשַׂר תְּבוּאָתְךָ בַּשָּׁנָה הַשְּׁלִישִׁת
שְׁנַת הַמַּעֲשֵׂר וְנָתַתָּה לַלֵּוִי לַגֵּר לַיָּתוֹם וְלָאַלְמָנָה וְאָכְלוּ
בִשְׁעָרֶיךָ וְשָׂבֵעוּ: וְאָמַרְתָּ לִפְנֵי יהוה אֱלֹהֶיךָ בִּעַרְתִּי הַקֹּדֶשׁ

מִן־הַבַּ֜יִת וְגַ֣ם נְתַתִּ֣יו לַלֵּוִ֣י וְלַגֵּ֗ר לַיָּת֣וֹם וְלָֽאַלְמָנָה֮ כְּכָל־
מִצְוָֽתְךָ֮ אֲשֶׁ֣ר צִוִּיתָ֒נִי לֹֽא־עָבַ֥רְתִּי מִמִּצְוֺתֶ֖יךָ וְלֹ֥א שָׁכָֽחְתִּי:
לֹֽא־אָכַ֨לְתִּי בְאֹנִ֜י מִמֶּ֗נּוּ וְלֹֽא־בִעַ֤רְתִּי מִמֶּ֨נּוּ֙ בְּטָמֵ֔א וְלֹֽא־נָתַ֥תִּי
מִמֶּ֖נּוּ לְמֵ֑ת שָׁמַ֗עְתִּי בְּקוֹל֙ יְהֹוָ֣ה אֱלֹהָ֔י עָשִׂ֕יתִי כְּכֹ֖ל אֲשֶׁ֥ר
צִוִּיתָֽנִי: הַשְׁקִ֩יפָה֩ מִמְּע֨וֹן קׇדְשְׁךָ֜ מִן־הַשָּׁמַ֗יִם וּבָרֵ֤ךְ אֶֽת־עַמְּךָ֙
אֶת־יִשְׂרָאֵ֔ל וְאֵת֙ הָֽאֲדָמָ֔ה אֲשֶׁ֥ר נָתַ֖תָּה לָ֑נוּ כַּֽאֲשֶׁ֤ר נִשְׁבַּ֨עְתָּ֙
לַֽאֲבֹתֵ֔ינוּ אֶ֛רֶץ זָבַ֥ת חָלָ֖ב וּדְבָֽשׁ:

NITZAVIM / נצבים

אַתֶּ֨ם נִצָּבִ֤ים הַיּוֹם֙ כֻּלְּכֶ֔ם לִפְנֵ֖י יְהֹוָ֣ה אֱלֹֽהֵיכֶ֑ם רָֽאשֵׁיכֶ֣ם
שִׁבְטֵיכֶ֗ם זִקְנֵיכֶם֙ וְשֹׁ֣טְרֵיכֶ֔ם כֹּ֖ל אִ֥ישׁ יִשְׂרָאֵֽל: טַפְּכֶ֣ם נְשֵׁיכֶ֔ם
וְגֵ֣רְךָ֔ אֲשֶׁ֖ר בְּקֶ֣רֶב מַֽחֲנֶ֑יךָ מֵֽחֹטֵ֣ב עֵצֶ֔יךָ עַ֖ד שֹׁאֵ֥ב מֵימֶֽיךָ:
לְעׇבְרְךָ֗ בִּבְרִ֛ית יְהֹוָ֥ה אֱלֹהֶ֖יךָ וּבְאָֽלָת֑וֹ אֲשֶׁר֙ יְהֹוָ֣ה אֱלֹהֶ֔יךָ
לוי כֹּרֵ֥ת עִמְּךָ֖ הַיּֽוֹם: *לְמַ֣עַן הָקִֽים־אֹֽתְךָ֩ הַיּ֨וֹם ׀ ל֜וֹ לְעָ֗ם וְה֤וּא
יִֽהְיֶה־לְּךָ֙ לֵֽאלֹהִ֔ים כַּֽאֲשֶׁ֖ר דִּבֶּר־לָ֑ךְ וְכַֽאֲשֶׁ֤ר נִשְׁבַּע֙ לַֽאֲבֹתֶ֔יךָ
לְאַבְרָהָ֥ם לְיִצְחָ֖ק וּֽלְיַֽעֲקֹֽב: וְלֹ֥א אִתְּכֶ֖ם לְבַדְּכֶ֑ם אָֽנֹכִ֗י כֹּרֵת֙
אֶת־הַבְּרִ֣ית הַזֹּ֔את וְאֶת־הָֽאָלָ֖ה הַזֹּֽאת: כִּי֩ אֶת־אֲשֶׁ֨ר יֶשְׁנ֜וֹ
פֹּ֗ה עִמָּ֨נוּ֙ עֹמֵ֣ד הַיּ֔וֹם לִפְנֵ֖י יְהֹוָ֣ה אֱלֹהֵ֑ינוּ וְאֵ֨ת אֲשֶׁ֥ר אֵינֶ֛נּוּ
ישראל פֹּ֖ה עִמָּ֥נוּ הַיּֽוֹם: *כִּֽי־אַתֶּ֣ם יְדַעְתֶּ֔ם אֵ֥ת אֲשֶׁר־יָשַׁ֖בְנוּ בְּאֶ֣רֶץ
מִצְרָ֑יִם וְאֵ֧ת אֲשֶׁר־עָבַ֛רְנוּ בְּקֶ֥רֶב הַגּוֹיִ֖ם אֲשֶׁ֥ר עֲבַרְתֶּֽם:
וַתִּרְאוּ֙ אֶת־שִׁקּ֣וּצֵיהֶ֔ם וְאֵ֖ת גִּלֻּֽלֵיהֶ֑ם עֵ֣ץ וָאֶ֔בֶן כֶּ֥סֶף וְזָהָ֖ב
אֲשֶׁ֥ר עִמָּהֶֽם: פֶּן־יֵ֣שׁ בָּ֠כֶ֠ם אִ֣ישׁ אֽוֹ־אִשָּׁ֞ה א֧וֹ מִשְׁפָּחָ֣ה אֽוֹ־
שֵׁ֗בֶט אֲשֶׁר֩ לְבָב֨וֹ פֹנֶ֤ה הַיּוֹם֙ מֵעִם֙ יְהֹוָ֣ה אֱלֹהֵ֔ינוּ לָלֶ֣כֶת
לַֽעֲבֹ֔ד אֶת־אֱלֹהֵ֖י הַגּוֹיִ֣ם הָהֵ֑ם פֶּן־יֵ֣שׁ בָּכֶ֗ם שֹׁ֛רֶשׁ פֹּרֶ֥ה רֹ֖אשׁ
וְלַֽעֲנָֽה: וְהָיָ֡ה בְּשׇׁמְעוֹ֩ אֶת־דִּבְרֵ֨י הָֽאָלָ֜ה הַזֹּ֗את וְהִתְבָּרֵ֤ךְ
בִּלְבָבוֹ֙ לֵאמֹר֙ שָׁל֣וֹם יִֽהְיֶה־לִּ֔י כִּ֛י בִּשְׁרִר֥וּת לִבִּ֖י אֵלֵ֑ךְ לְמַ֛עַן
סְפ֥וֹת הָֽרָוָ֖ה אֶת־הַצְּמֵאָֽה: לֹֽא־יֹאבֶ֣ה יְהֹוָה֮ סְלֹ֣חַֽ לוֹ֒ כִּ֣י
אָ֠ז יֶעְשַׁ֨ן אַף־יְהֹוָ֤ה וְקִנְאָתוֹ֙ בָּאִ֣ישׁ הַה֔וּא וְרָ֤בְצָה בּוֹ֙ כׇּל־
הָ֣אָלָ֔ה הַכְּתוּבָ֖ה בַּסֵּ֣פֶר הַזֶּ֑ה וּמָחָ֤ה יְהֹוָה֙ אֶת־שְׁמ֔וֹ מִתַּ֖חַת

by the owner in Jerusalem, while the third tithe, *ma'aser ani*, was given to the poor. Not every tithe was given in every year. Which was/were given in the third year?

FIRST ALIYA: vv. 9–11
The verses describe the renewal of the covenant between God and Israel. One group mentioned could not legally participate. Which? Why, then, do you think it was important for them to be present?

SECOND ALIYA: vv. 12–14
From here some conclude that all of our souls were present at Sinai even if we were not yet born. What are the implications of this for us today?

THIRD ALIYA: vv. 15–28
From here one learns that we as a society are responsible for the sins of others that we are aware of. If we are not aware of them, then Hashem does not hold us accountable. What actions in today's society do you think would fall into each category?

הַשָּׁמָיִם: וְהִבְדִּילוֹ יהוה לְרָעָה מִכֹּל שִׁבְטֵי יִשְׂרָאֵל כְּכֹל
אָלוֹת הַבְּרִית הַכְּתוּבָה בְּסֵפֶר הַתּוֹרָה הַזֶּה: וְאָמַר הַדּוֹר
הָאַחֲרוֹן בְּנֵיכֶם אֲשֶׁר יָקוּמוּ מֵאַחֲרֵיכֶם וְהַנָּכְרִי אֲשֶׁר יָבֹא
מֵאֶרֶץ רְחוֹקָה וְרָאוּ אֶת־מַכּוֹת הָאָרֶץ הַהִוא וְאֶת־תַּחֲלֻאֶיהָ
אֲשֶׁר־חִלָּה יהוה בָּהּ: גָּפְרִית וָמֶלַח שְׂרֵפָה כָל־אַרְצָהּ לֹא
תִזָּרַע וְלֹא תַצְמִחַ וְלֹא־יַעֲלֶה בָהּ כָּל־עֵשֶׂב כְּמַהְפֵּכַת סְדֹם
וַעֲמֹרָה אַדְמָה וּצְבֹיִים אֲשֶׁר הָפַךְ יהוה בְּאַפּוֹ וּבַחֲמָתוֹ: וְצְבֹיִים
וְאָמְרוּ כָּל־הַגּוֹיִם עַל־מֶה עָשָׂה יהוה כָּכָה לָאָרֶץ הַזֹּאת
מֶה חֳרִי הָאַף הַגָּדוֹל הַזֶּה: וְאָמְרוּ עַל אֲשֶׁר עָזְבוּ אֶת־בְּרִית
יהוה אֱלֹהֵי אֲבֹתָם אֲשֶׁר כָּרַת עִמָּם בְּהוֹצִיאוֹ אֹתָם מֵאֶרֶץ
מִצְרָיִם: וַיֵּלְכוּ וַיַּעַבְדוּ אֱלֹהִים אֲחֵרִים וַיִּשְׁתַּחֲווּ לָהֶם אֱלֹהִים
אֲשֶׁר לֹא־יְדָעוּם וְלֹא חָלַק לָהֶם: וַיִּחַר־אַף יהוה בָּאָרֶץ
הַהִוא לְהָבִיא עָלֶיהָ אֶת־כָּל־הַקְּלָלָה הַכְּתוּבָה בַּסֵּפֶר הַזֶּה:
וַיִּתְּשֵׁם יהוה מֵעַל אַדְמָתָם בְּאַף וּבְחֵמָה וּבְקֶצֶף גָּדוֹל
וַיַּשְׁלִכֵם אֶל־אֶרֶץ אַחֶרֶת כַּיּוֹם הַזֶּה: הַנִּסְתָּרֹת לַיהוה
אֱלֹהֵינוּ וְהַנִּגְלֹת לָנוּ וּלְבָנֵינוּ עַד־עוֹלָם לַעֲשׂוֹת אֶת־כָּל־
דִּבְרֵי הַתּוֹרָה הַזֹּאת:

VAYELEKH
וילך

דברים
לא, א–ג

וַיֵּלֶךְ מֹשֶׁה וַיְדַבֵּר אֶת־הַדְּבָרִים הָאֵלֶּה אֶל־כָּל־יִשְׂרָאֵל:
וַיֹּאמֶר אֲלֵהֶם בֶּן־מֵאָה וְעֶשְׂרִים שָׁנָה אָנֹכִי הַיּוֹם לֹא־אוּכַל
עוֹד לָצֵאת וְלָבוֹא וַיהוה אָמַר אֵלַי לֹא תַעֲבֹר אֶת־הַיַּרְדֵּן
הַזֶּה: יהוה אֱלֹהֶיךָ הוּא ׀ עֹבֵר לְפָנֶיךָ הוּא־יַשְׁמִיד אֶת־הַגּוֹיִם
הָאֵלֶּה מִלְּפָנֶיךָ וִירִשְׁתָּם יְהוֹשֻׁעַ הוּא עֹבֵר לְפָנֶיךָ כַּאֲשֶׁר דִּבֶּר
יהוה: *וְעָשָׂה יהוה לָהֶם כַּאֲשֶׁר עָשָׂה לְסִיחוֹן וּלְעוֹג מַלְכֵי לוי
הָאֱמֹרִי וּלְאַרְצָם אֲשֶׁר הִשְׁמִיד אֹתָם: וּנְתָנָם יהוה לִפְנֵיכֶם
וַעֲשִׂיתֶם לָהֶם כְּכָל־הַמִּצְוָה אֲשֶׁר צִוִּיתִי אֶתְכֶם: חִזְקוּ וְאִמְצוּ
אַל־תִּירְאוּ וְאַל־תַּעַרְצוּ מִפְּנֵיהֶם כִּי ׀ יהוה אֱלֹהֶיךָ הוּא
הַהֹלֵךְ עִמָּךְ לֹא יַרְפְּךָ וְלֹא יַעַזְבֶךָּ: *וַיִּקְרָא ישראל

FIRST ALIYA: vv. 1–3
From this word, one may learn that Moshe was born and died on the same day. What do you think is the significance in this fact?

SECOND ALIYA: vv. 4–6
In this *aliya* and the next, there are four words of encouragement which are repeated, one pair negative, one pair positive. What are they?

מֹשֶׁה לִיהוֹשֻׁעַ וַיֹּאמֶר אֵלָיו לְעֵינֵי כָל־יִשְׂרָאֵל חֲזַק וֶאֱמָץ
כִּי אַתָּה תָּבוֹא אֶת־הָעָם הַזֶּה אֶל־הָאָרֶץ אֲשֶׁר נִשְׁבַּע
יְהֹוָה לַאֲבֹתָם לָתֵת לָהֶם וְאַתָּה תַּנְחִילֶנָּה אוֹתָם: וַיהוָה
הוּא ׀ הַהֹלֵךְ לְפָנֶיךָ הוּא יִהְיֶה עִמָּךְ לֹא יַרְפְּךָ וְלֹא יַעַזְבֶךָּ
לֹא תִירָא וְלֹא תֵחָת: וַיִּכְתֹּב מֹשֶׁה אֶת־הַתּוֹרָה הַזֹּאת
וַיִּתְּנָהּ אֶל־הַכֹּהֲנִים בְּנֵי לֵוִי הַנֹּשְׂאִים אֶת־אֲרוֹן בְּרִית יְהֹוָה
וְאֶל־כָּל־זִקְנֵי יִשְׂרָאֵל: וַיְצַו מֹשֶׁה אוֹתָם לֵאמֹר מִקֵּץ ׀ שֶׁבַע
שָׁנִים בְּמֹעֵד שְׁנַת הַשְּׁמִטָּה בְּחַג הַסֻּכּוֹת: בְּבוֹא כָל־יִשְׂרָאֵל
לֵרָאוֹת אֶת־פְּנֵי יְהֹוָה אֱלֹהֶיךָ בַּמָּקוֹם אֲשֶׁר יִבְחָר תִּקְרָא
אֶת־הַתּוֹרָה הַזֹּאת נֶגֶד כָּל־יִשְׂרָאֵל בְּאָזְנֵיהֶם: הַקְהֵל אֶת־
הָעָם הָאֲנָשִׁים וְהַנָּשִׁים וְהַטַּף וְגֵרְךָ אֲשֶׁר בִּשְׁעָרֶיךָ לְמַעַן
יִשְׁמְעוּ וּלְמַעַן יִלְמְדוּ וְיָרְאוּ אֶת־יְהֹוָה אֱלֹהֵיכֶם וְשָׁמְרוּ
לַעֲשׂוֹת אֶת־כָּל־דִּבְרֵי הַתּוֹרָה הַזֹּאת: וּבְנֵיהֶם אֲשֶׁר לֹא־
יָדְעוּ יִשְׁמְעוּ וְלָמְדוּ לְיִרְאָה אֶת־יְהֹוָה אֱלֹהֵיכֶם כָּל־הַיָּמִים
אֲשֶׁר אַתֶּם חַיִּים עַל־הָאֲדָמָה אֲשֶׁר אַתֶּם עֹבְרִים אֶת־הַיַּרְדֵּן
שָׁמָּה לְרִשְׁתָּהּ:

THIRD ALIYA: vv. 7–13
For the *Hak-hel* ceremony, one group's participation is strange. Why and how might their participation be explained?

HA'AZINU / האזינו

וְתִשְׁמַע הָאָרֶץ אִמְרֵי־פִי:	הַאֲזִינוּ הַשָּׁמַיִם וַאֲדַבֵּרָה
תִּזַּל כַּטַּל אִמְרָתִי	יַעֲרֹף כַּמָּטָר לִקְחִי
וְכִרְבִיבִים עֲלֵי־עֵשֶׂב:	כִּשְׂעִירִם עֲלֵי־דֶשֶׁא
הָבוּ גֹדֶל לֵאלֹהֵינוּ:	כִּי שֵׁם יְהֹוָה אֶקְרָא
כִּי כָל־דְּרָכָיו מִשְׁפָּט	*הַצּוּר תָּמִים פָּעֳלוֹ
צַדִּיק וְיָשָׁר הוּא:	אֵל אֱמוּנָה וְאֵין עָוֶל
דּוֹר עִקֵּשׁ וּפְתַלְתֹּל:	שִׁחֵת לוֹ לֹא בָּנָיו מוּמָם
עַם נָבָל וְלֹא חָכָם	הֲ לַיהֹוָה תִּגְמְלוּ־זֹאת
הוּא עָשְׂךָ וַיְכֹנְנֶךָ:	הֲלוֹא־הוּא אָבִיךָ קָּנֶךָ

Some start the לוי *portion here:*

בִּינוּ שְׁנוֹת דֹּר־וָדֹר	*זְכֹר יְמוֹת עוֹלָם

דברים
לב:א–יח

לוי

ישראל

FIRST ALIYA: vv. 1–3
From here one learns (a) that a blessing is recited before one studies Torah, (b) that when three people eat together, one calls out to the others (*zimmun*) to join in *Birkat HaMazon*, (c) that when Hashem's name was uttered on Yom Kippur in the *Beit HaMikdash*, everyone responded with the words *Barukh Shem Kevod...*, (d) that when one hears someone recite the beginning of a blessing, *Barukh ata Hashem...*, one should respond, *Barukh Hu uvarukh shemo?*

SECOND ALIYA: vv. 4–6
Two words that sound the same but together blame man not God.

THIRD ALIYA: vv. 7–12

From here one might learn that there is great value in knowing history. Why might this be a value?

שְׁאַל אָבִיךָ וְיַגֵּדְךָ	זְקֵנֶיךָ וְיֹאמְרוּ לָךְ:
בְּהַנְחֵל עֶלְיוֹן גּוֹיִם	בְּהַפְרִידוֹ בְּנֵי אָדָם
יַצֵּב גְּבֻלֹת עַמִּים	לְמִסְפַּר בְּנֵי יִשְׂרָאֵל:
כִּי חֵלֶק יְהוָה עַמּוֹ	יַעֲקֹב חֶבֶל נַחֲלָתוֹ:
יִמְצָאֵהוּ בְּאֶרֶץ מִדְבָּר	וּבְתֹהוּ יְלֵל יְשִׁמֹן
יְסֹבְבֶנְהוּ יְבוֹנְנֵהוּ	יִצְּרֶנְהוּ כְּאִישׁוֹן עֵינוֹ:
כְּנֶשֶׁר יָעִיר קִנּוֹ	עַל־גּוֹזָלָיו יְרַחֵף
יִפְרֹשׂ כְּנָפָיו יִקָּחֵהוּ	יִשָּׂאֵהוּ עַל־אֶבְרָתוֹ:
יְהוָה בָּדָד יַנְחֶנּוּ	וְאֵין עִמּוֹ אֵל נֵכָר:

Most finish here; some start the ישראל *portion here:*

*יַרְכִּבֵהוּ עַל־בָּמֳתֵי אָרֶץ	וַיֹּאכַל תְּנוּבֹת שָׂדָי
וַיֵּנִקֵהוּ דְבַשׁ מִסֶּלַע	וְשֶׁמֶן מֵחַלְמִישׁ צוּר:
חֶמְאַת בָּקָר וַחֲלֵב צֹאן	עִם־חֵלֶב כָּרִים
וְאֵילִים בְּנֵי־בָשָׁן וְעַתּוּדִים	עִם־חֵלֶב כִּלְיוֹת חִטָּה
וְדַם־עֵנָב תִּשְׁתֶּה־חָמֶר:	וַיִּשְׁמַן יְשֻׁרוּן וַיִּבְעָט
שָׁמַנְתָּ עָבִיתָ כָּשִׂיתָ	וַיִּטֹּשׁ אֱלוֹהַּ עָשָׂהוּ
וַיְנַבֵּל צוּר יְשֻׁעָתוֹ:	יַקְנִאֻהוּ בְּזָרִים
בְּתוֹעֵבֹת יַכְעִיסֻהוּ:	יִזְבְּחוּ לַשֵּׁדִים לֹא אֱלֹהַּ
אֱלֹהִים לֹא יְדָעוּם	חֲדָשִׁים מִקָּרֹב בָּאוּ
לֹא שְׂעָרוּם אֲבֹתֵיכֶם:	צוּר יְלָדְךָ תֶּשִׁי
וַתִּשְׁכַּח אֵל מְחֹלְלֶךָ:	

VEZOT HABERAKHA — וְזֹאת הַבְּרָכָה

FIRST ALIYA: vv. 1–7

The Gemara says that when one's child begins to speak, the fourth verse here is the first verse that he should be taught to recite. Why do you think this one was chosen of all of the verses in the Torah?

וְזֹאת הַבְּרָכָה אֲשֶׁר בֵּרַךְ מֹשֶׁה אִישׁ הָאֱלֹהִים אֶת־בְּנֵי
יִשְׂרָאֵל לִפְנֵי מוֹתוֹ: וַיֹּאמַר יְהוָה מִסִּינַי בָּא וְזָרַח מִשֵּׂעִיר
לָמוֹ הוֹפִיעַ מֵהַר פָּארָן וְאָתָה מֵרִבְבֹת קֹדֶשׁ מִימִינוֹ אֵשׁ דָּת
לָמוֹ: אַף חֹבֵב עַמִּים כָּל־קְדֹשָׁיו בְּיָדֶךָ וְהֵם תֻּכּוּ לְרַגְלֶךָ יִשָּׂא
מִדַּבְּרֹתֶיךָ: תּוֹרָה צִוָּה־לָנוּ מֹשֶׁה מוֹרָשָׁה קְהִלַּת יַעֲקֹב:
וַיְהִי בִישֻׁרוּן מֶלֶךְ בְּהִתְאַסֵּף רָאשֵׁי עָם יַחַד שִׁבְטֵי יִשְׂרָאֵל:

דברים
לג,א-ז

יְחִי רְאוּבֵן וְאַל־יָמֹת וִיהִי מְתָיו מִסְפָּר: וְזֹאת
לִיהוּדָה וַיֹּאמַר שְׁמַע יהוה קוֹל יְהוּדָה וְאֶל־עַמּוֹ תְּבִיאֶנּוּ
יָדָיו רָב לוֹ וְעֵזֶר מִצָּרָיו תִּהְיֶה:

לוי
SECOND ALIYA: vv. 8–12
Which four relatives can
be found in a single verse?

וּלְלֵוִי אָמַר תֻּמֶּיךָ וְאוּרֶיךָ לְאִישׁ חֲסִידֶךָ אֲשֶׁר נִסִּיתוֹ בְּמַסָּה
תְּרִיבֵהוּ עַל־מֵי מְרִיבָה: הָאֹמֵר לְאָבִיו וּלְאִמּוֹ לֹא רְאִיתִיו
וְאֶת־אֶחָיו לֹא הִכִּיר וְאֶת־בָּנָו לֹא יָדָע כִּי שָׁמְרוּ אִמְרָתֶךָ
וּבְרִיתְךָ יִנְצֹרוּ: יוֹרוּ מִשְׁפָּטֶיךָ לְיַעֲקֹב וְתוֹרָתְךָ לְיִשְׂרָאֵל
יָשִׂימוּ קְטוֹרָה בְּאַפֶּךָ וְכָלִיל עַל־מִזְבְּחֶךָ: בָּרֵךְ יהוה
חֵילוֹ וּפֹעַל יָדָיו תִּרְצֶה מְחַץ מָתְנַיִם קָמָיו וּמְשַׂנְאָיו מִן־
יְקוּמוּן: לְבִנְיָמִן אָמַר יְדִיד יהוה יִשְׁכֹּן לָבֶטַח עָלָיו
חֹפֵף עָלָיו כָּל־הַיּוֹם וּבֵין כְּתֵפָיו שָׁכֵן: *וּלְיוֹסֵף

ישראל
THIRD ALIYA: vv. 13–17
Which word is repeated
five times?

אָמַר מְבֹרֶכֶת יהוה אַרְצוֹ מִמֶּגֶד שָׁמַיִם מִטָּל וּמִתְּהוֹם רֹבֶצֶת
תָּחַת: וּמִמֶּגֶד תְּבוּאֹת שָׁמֶשׁ וּמִמֶּגֶד גֶּרֶשׁ יְרָחִים: וּמֵרֹאשׁ
הַרְרֵי־קֶדֶם וּמִמֶּגֶד גִּבְעוֹת עוֹלָם: וּמִמֶּגֶד אֶרֶץ וּמְלֹאָהּ
וּרְצוֹן שֹׁכְנִי סְנֶה תָּבוֹאתָה לְרֹאשׁ יוֹסֵף וּלְקָדְקֹד נְזִיר אֶחָיו:
בְּכוֹר שׁוֹרוֹ הָדָר לוֹ וְקַרְנֵי רְאֵם קַרְנָיו בָּהֶם עַמִּים יְנַגַּח יַחְדָּו
אַפְסֵי־אָרֶץ וְהֵם רִבְבוֹת אֶפְרַיִם וְהֵם אַלְפֵי מְנַשֶּׁה:

קריאת התורה לראש חודש,
לתעניות ציבור, לחנוכה ולפורים

THE READING OF THE TORAH FOR
ROSH ḤODESH, FAST DAYS, ḤANUKKA
AND PURIM

ROSH ḤODESH　　　　קריאה לראש חודש

For the כהן, *the first three verses are read up to* עֹלָה תָמִיד. *For the* לֵוִי, *the third verse is repeated and starts with* וְאָמַרְתָּ לָהֶם. *For* שְׁלִישִׁי, *continue from* וּנְסָכָּהּ *up to* עֹלַת תָּמִיד. *For* רְבִיעִי, *read from* וּבְרָאשֵׁי חָדְשֵׁיכֶם *until the end. In* אֶרֶץ יִשְׂרָאֵל, *some read as follows: For the* כהן *read until* אֶת־הַכֶּבֶשׂ *the* רְבִיעַת הַהִין, *for the* לֵוִי *read from* וַעֲשִׂירִת הָאֵיפָה *until* רְבִיעִת הַהִין, *for* שְׁלִישִׁי, *the last verse is repeated and starts at* עֹלַת תָּמִיד *up to* וּנְסָכָּהּ, *and for* רְבִיעִי, *from* וּבְרָאשֵׁי חָדְשֵׁיכֶם *until the end. On* רֹאשׁ חוֹדֶשׁ טבת, *the* כהן *reads until* רְבִיעַת הַהִין, *the* לֵוִי *reads the portion for* שְׁלִישִׁי *and the* שְׁלִישִׁי *the portion of* רְבִיעִי; *the fourth* עוֹלֶה *reads the appropriate day of* חנוכה *on page 756.*

the fourth עוֹלֶה *reads the appropriate day of* חנוכה *on page 756.*

במדבר
כח:א-טו

וַיְדַבֵּר יְהוָה אֶל־מֹשֶׁה לֵּאמֹר: צַו אֶת־בְּנֵי יִשְׂרָאֵל וְאָמַרְתָּ אֲלֵהֶם אֶת־קָרְבָּנִי לַחְמִי לְאִשַּׁי רֵיחַ נִיחֹחִי תִּשְׁמְרוּ לְהַקְרִיב לִי בְּמוֹעֲדוֹ: *וְאָמַרְתָּ לָהֶם זֶה הָאִשֶּׁה אֲשֶׁר תַּקְרִיבוּ לַיהוָה

לֵוִי
עַד כָּאן
לכהן

כְּבָשִׂים בְּנֵי־שָׁנָה תְמִימִם שְׁנַיִם לַיּוֹם עֹלָה תָמִיד: אֶת־הַכֶּבֶשׂ אֶחָד תַּעֲשֶׂה בַבֹּקֶר וְאֵת הַכֶּבֶשׂ הַשֵּׁנִי תַּעֲשֶׂה בֵּין הָעַרְבָּיִם: וַעֲשִׂירִת הָאֵיפָה סֹלֶת לְמִנְחָה בְּלוּלָה בְּשֶׁמֶן כָּתִית רְבִיעִת הַהִין: *עֹלַת תָּמִיד הָעֲשֻׂיָה בְּהַר סִינַי לְרֵיחַ נִיחֹחַ אִשֶּׁה לַיהוָה: וְנִסְכּוֹ רְבִיעִת הַהִין לַכֶּבֶשׂ הָאֶחָד בַּקֹּדֶשׁ הַסֵּךְ נֶסֶךְ שֵׁכָר לַיהוָה: וְאֵת הַכֶּבֶשׂ הַשֵּׁנִי תַּעֲשֶׂה בֵּין הָעַרְבָּיִם כְּמִנְחַת הַבֹּקֶר וּכְנִסְכּוֹ תַּעֲשֶׂה אִשֵּׁה רֵיחַ נִיחֹחַ לַיהוָה:

שְׁלִישִׁי

וּבְיוֹם הַשַּׁבָּת שְׁנֵי־כְבָשִׂים בְּנֵי־שָׁנָה תְּמִימִם וּשְׁנֵי עֶשְׂרֹנִים סֹלֶת מִנְחָה בְּלוּלָה בַשֶּׁמֶן וְנִסְכּוֹ: עֹלַת שַׁבַּת בְּשַׁבַּתּוֹ עַל־עֹלַת הַתָּמִיד וְנִסְכָּהּ:

FIRST ALIYA: vv. 1–3
Commentators often find symbolic meaning in aspects of the sacrifices and the *Mishkan*. What might be the significance of the word לַחְמִי in this context?

SECOND ALIYA: vv. 3–5
In all of the references in the Torah to this *Tamid* sacrifice every morning, the Torah simply says בַּבֹּקֶר. Based on this word, however, there are those who say that it's the source for sleeping later on Shabbat.

THIRD ALIYA: vv. 6–10
There are two different occasions for sacrificial offerings described here. What are they?

רביעי וּבְרָאשֵׁי חָדְשֵׁיכֶם תַּקְרִיבוּ עֹלָה לַיהוה פָּרִים בְּנֵי־בָקָר
שְׁנַיִם וְאַיִל אֶחָד כְּבָשִׂים בְּנֵי־שָׁנָה שִׁבְעָה תְּמִימִם: וּשְׁלֹשָׁה
עֶשְׂרֹנִים סֹלֶת מִנְחָה בְּלוּלָה בַשֶּׁמֶן לַפָּר הָאֶחָד וּשְׁנֵי
עֶשְׂרֹנִים סֹלֶת מִנְחָה בְּלוּלָה בַשֶּׁמֶן לָאַיִל הָאֶחָד: וְעִשָּׂרֹן
עִשָּׂרוֹן סֹלֶת מִנְחָה בְּלוּלָה בַשֶּׁמֶן לַכֶּבֶשׂ הָאֶחָד עֹלָה רֵיחַ
נִיחֹחַ אִשֶּׁה לַיהוה: וְנִסְכֵּיהֶם חֲצִי הַהִין יִהְיֶה לַפָּר וּשְׁלִישִׁת
הַהִין לָאַיִל וּרְבִיעִת הַהִין לַכֶּבֶשׂ יָיִן זֹאת עֹלַת חֹדֶשׁ בְּחָדְשׁוֹ
לְחָדְשֵׁי הַשָּׁנָה: וּשְׂעִיר עִזִּים אֶחָד לְחַטָּאת לַיהוה עַל־עֹלַת
הַתָּמִיד יֵעָשֶׂה וְנִסְכּוֹ:

FOURTH ALIYA: 11–15
Compare the way that
Shabbat is referred to in
the previous *aliya* with
the way that Rosh Ḥodesh
is referred to in this one.
Why is there a difference
and what do you think a
reason might be?

READING FOR FAST DAYS

קריאה לתענית ציבור

The following is read on a תענית ציבור *(except* תשעה באב*) in both*
שחרית *and* מנחה.
At מנחה*, the person called up for* שלישי *also reads the* הפטרה.

It is customary for the קהל *to say aloud the passages*
marked by arrows, followed by the קורא.

◄ וַיְחַל מֹשֶׁה אֶת־פְּנֵי יהוה אֱלֹהָיו וַיֹּאמֶר לָמָה יהוה יֶחֱרֶה
אַפְּךָ בְּעַמֶּךָ אֲשֶׁר הוֹצֵאתָ מֵאֶרֶץ מִצְרַיִם בְּכֹחַ גָּדוֹל וּבְיָד
חֲזָקָה: לָמָּה יֹאמְרוּ מִצְרַיִם לֵאמֹר בְּרָעָה הוֹצִיאָם לַהֲרֹג
אֹתָם בֶּהָרִים וּלְכַלֹּתָם מֵעַל פְּנֵי הָאֲדָמָה ◄ שׁוּב מֵחֲרוֹן אַפֶּךָ
וְהִנָּחֵם עַל־הָרָעָה לְעַמֶּךָ: זְכֹר לְאַבְרָהָם לְיִצְחָק וּלְיִשְׂרָאֵל
עֲבָדֶיךָ אֲשֶׁר נִשְׁבַּעְתָּ לָהֶם בָּךְ וַתְּדַבֵּר אֲלֵהֶם אַרְבֶּה אֶת־
זַרְעֲכֶם כְּכוֹכְבֵי הַשָּׁמָיִם וְכָל־הָאָרֶץ הַזֹּאת אֲשֶׁר אָמַרְתִּי
אֶתֵּן לְזַרְעֲכֶם וְנָחֲלוּ לְעֹלָם: וַיִּנָּחֶם יהוה עַל־הָרָעָה אֲשֶׁר
דִּבֶּר לַעֲשׂוֹת לְעַמּוֹ:

שמות לב:
יא–יד

FIRST ALIYA: vv. 32:11–14
How many different
arguments does Moshe
use here for why Hashem
should not destroy
Benei Yisrael?

וַיֹּאמֶר יהוה אֶל־מֹשֶׁה פְּסָל־לְךָ שְׁנֵי־לֻחֹת אֲבָנִים כָּרִאשֹׁנִים
וְכָתַבְתִּי עַל־הַלֻּחֹת אֶת־הַדְּבָרִים אֲשֶׁר הָיוּ עַל־הַלֻּחֹת
הָרִאשֹׁנִים אֲשֶׁר שִׁבַּרְתָּ: וֶהְיֵה נָכוֹן לַבֹּקֶר וְעָלִיתָ בַבֹּקֶר אֶל־
הַר סִינַי וְנִצַּבְתָּ לִי שָׁם עַל־רֹאשׁ הָהָר: וְאִישׁ לֹא־יַעֲלֶה עִמָּךְ
וְגַם־אִישׁ אַל־יֵרָא בְּכָל־הָהָר גַּם־הַצֹּאן וְהַבָּקָר אַל־יִרְעוּ

שמות לג:א–
לוי

SECOND ALIYA:
vv. 34:1–3
Unlike the first time the
commandments were
received, there are certain
restrictions and changes
this time. What are they
and how might this over-
all change be explained?

ישראל

אֶל־מוּל הָהָר הַהוּא: *וַיִּפְסֹל שְׁנֵי־לֻחֹת אֲבָנִים כָּרִאשֹׁנִים
וַיַּשְׁכֵּם מֹשֶׁה בַבֹּקֶר וַיַּעַל אֶל־הַר סִינַי כַּאֲשֶׁר צִוָּה יהוה אֹתוֹ
וַיִּקַּח בְּיָדוֹ שְׁנֵי לֻחֹת אֲבָנִים: וַיֵּרֶד יהוה בֶּעָנָן וַיִּתְיַצֵּב עִמּוֹ
שָׁם וַיִּקְרָא בְשֵׁם יהוה: ◂ וַיַּעֲבֹר יהוה ׀ עַל־פָּנָיו וַיִּקְרָא ◂ יהוה ׀
יהוה אֵל רַחוּם וְחַנּוּן אֶרֶךְ אַפַּיִם וְרַב־חֶסֶד וֶאֱמֶת: נֹצֵר חֶסֶד
לָאֲלָפִים נֹשֵׂא עָוֺן וָפֶשַׁע וְחַטָּאָה וְנַקֵּה ◂ לֹא יְנַקֶּה פֹּקֵד ׀ עֲוֺן
אָבוֹת עַל־בָּנִים וְעַל־בְּנֵי בָנִים עַל־שִׁלֵּשִׁים וְעַל־רִבֵּעִים:
וַיְמַהֵר מֹשֶׁה וַיִּקֹּד אַרְצָה וַיִּשְׁתָּחוּ: וַיֹּאמֶר אִם־נָא מָצָאתִי
חֵן בְּעֵינֶיךָ אֲדֹנָי יֵלֶךְ־נָא אֲדֹנָי בְּקִרְבֵּנוּ כִּי עַם־קְשֵׁה־עֹרֶף
הוּא ◂ וְסָלַחְתָּ לַעֲוֺנֵנוּ וּלְחַטָּאתֵנוּ וּנְחַלְתָּנוּ: וַיֹּאמֶר הִנֵּה
אָנֹכִי כֹּרֵת בְּרִית נֶגֶד כָּל־עַמְּךָ אֶעֱשֶׂה נִפְלָאֹת אֲשֶׁר לֹא־
נִבְרְאוּ בְכָל־הָאָרֶץ וּבְכָל־הַגּוֹיִם וְרָאָה כָל־הָעָם אֲשֶׁר־אַתָּה
בְקִרְבּוֹ אֶת־מַעֲשֵׂה יהוה כִּי־נוֹרָא הוּא אֲשֶׁר אֲנִי עֹשֶׂה עִמָּךְ:

ברכות ההפטרה

Before reading the הפטרה, *the person called up for* מפטיר *says:*

בָּרוּךְ אַתָּה יהוה אֱלֹהֵינוּ מֶלֶךְ הָעוֹלָם אֲשֶׁר בָּחַר בִּנְבִיאִים
טוֹבִים, וְרָצָה בְדִבְרֵיהֶם הַנֶּאֱמָרִים בֶּאֱמֶת. בָּרוּךְ אַתָּה יהוה,
הַבּוֹחֵר בַּתּוֹרָה וּבְמֹשֶׁה עַבְדּוֹ וּבְיִשְׂרָאֵל עַמּוֹ וּבִנְבִיאֵי הָאֱמֶת
וָצֶדֶק.

הפטרה לתענית ציבור　　HAFTARA – FAST DAYS

ישעיה
נה:ו–נו:ח

דִּרְשׁוּ יהוה בְּהִמָּצְאוֹ קְרָאֻהוּ בִּהְיוֹתוֹ קָרוֹב: יַעֲזֹב רָשָׁע
דַּרְכּוֹ וְאִישׁ אָוֶן מַחְשְׁבֹתָיו וְיָשֹׁב אֶל־יהוה וִירַחֲמֵהוּ וְאֶל־
אֱלֹהֵינוּ כִּי־יַרְבֶּה לִסְלוֹחַ: כִּי לֹא מַחְשְׁבוֹתַי מַחְשְׁבוֹתֵיכֶם
וְלֹא דַרְכֵיכֶם דְּרָכָי נְאֻם יהוה: כִּי־גָבְהוּ שָׁמַיִם מֵאָרֶץ כֵּן
גָּבְהוּ דְרָכַי מִדַּרְכֵיכֶם וּמַחְשְׁבֹתַי מִמַּחְשְׁבֹתֵיכֶם: כִּי כַּאֲשֶׁר
יֵרֵד הַגֶּשֶׁם וְהַשֶּׁלֶג מִן־הַשָּׁמַיִם וְשָׁמָּה לֹא יָשׁוּב כִּי אִם־
הִרְוָה אֶת־הָאָרֶץ וְהוֹלִידָהּ וְהִצְמִיחָהּ וְנָתַן זֶרַע לַזֹּרֵעַ וְלֶחֶם

THIRD ALIYA: vv. 4–10
What might be different
ways of counting the 13
Attributes of Hashem
mentioned here and how
might you distinguish the
meanings of each?

HAFTARA – FAST DAYS
The first verse is under-
stood in different
ways by the
commentators:

a. Seek Hashem
when He is near. But
isn't He always near?!
Rather, this refers to
the days between Rosh
HaShana and Yom Kippur.
(*Yevamot* 49b)

b. Seek out Hashem to ask
for forgiveness before you

לֶאֱכֹל: כֵּן יִהְיֶה דְבָרִי אֲשֶׁר יֵצֵא מִפִּי לֹא־יָשׁוּב אֵלַי רֵיקָם כִּי אִם־עָשָׂה אֶת־אֲשֶׁר חָפַצְתִּי וְהִצְלִיחַ אֲשֶׁר שְׁלַחְתִּיו: כִּי־בְשִׂמְחָה תֵצֵאוּ וּבְשָׁלוֹם תּוּבָלוּן הֶהָרִים וְהַגְּבָעוֹת יִפְצְחוּ לִפְנֵיכֶם רִנָּה וְכָל־עֲצֵי הַשָּׂדֶה יִמְחֲאוּ־כָף: תַּחַת הַנַּעֲצוּץ יַעֲלֶה בְרוֹשׁ תַּחַת הַסִּרְפַּד יַעֲלֶה הֲדַס וְהָיָה לַיהוה לְשֵׁם לְאוֹת עוֹלָם לֹא יִכָּרֵת:

כֹּה אָמַר יהוה שִׁמְרוּ מִשְׁפָּט וַעֲשׂוּ צְדָקָה כִּי־קְרוֹבָה יְשׁוּעָתִי לָבוֹא וְצִדְקָתִי לְהִגָּלוֹת: אַשְׁרֵי אֱנוֹשׁ יַעֲשֶׂה־זֹּאת וּבֶן־אָדָם יַחֲזִיק בָּהּ שֹׁמֵר שַׁבָּת מֵחַלְּלוֹ וְשֹׁמֵר יָדוֹ מֵעֲשׂוֹת כָּל־רָע: וְאַל־יֹאמַר בֶּן־הַנֵּכָר הַנִּלְוָה אֶל־יהוה לֵאמֹר הַבְדֵּל יַבְדִּילַנִי יהוה מֵעַל עַמּוֹ וְאַל־יֹאמַר הַסָּרִיס הֵן אֲנִי עֵץ יָבֵשׁ: כִּי־כֹה אָמַר יהוה לַסָּרִיסִים אֲשֶׁר יִשְׁמְרוּ אֶת־שַׁבְּתוֹתַי וּבָחֲרוּ בַּאֲשֶׁר חָפָצְתִּי וּמַחֲזִיקִים בִּבְרִיתִי: וְנָתַתִּי לָהֶם בְּבֵיתִי וּבְחוֹמֹתַי יָד וָשֵׁם טוֹב מִבָּנִים וּמִבָּנוֹת שֵׁם עוֹלָם אֶתֶּן־לוֹ אֲשֶׁר לֹא יִכָּרֵת: וּבְנֵי הַנֵּכָר הַנִּלְוִים עַל־יהוה לְשָׁרְתוֹ וּלְאַהֲבָה אֶת־שֵׁם יהוה לִהְיוֹת לוֹ לַעֲבָדִים כָּל־שֹׁמֵר שַׁבָּת מֵחַלְּלוֹ וּמַחֲזִיקִים בִּבְרִיתִי: וַהֲבִיאוֹתִים אֶל־הַר קָדְשִׁי וְשִׂמַּחְתִּים בְּבֵית תְּפִלָּתִי עוֹלֹתֵיהֶם וְזִבְחֵיהֶם לְרָצוֹן עַל־מִזְבְּחִי כִּי בֵיתִי בֵּית־תְּפִלָּה יִקָּרֵא לְכָל־הָעַמִּים: נְאֻם אֲדֹנָי יהוה מְקַבֵּץ נִדְחֵי יִשְׂרָאֵל עוֹד אֲקַבֵּץ עָלָיו לְנִקְבָּצָיו:

After the הפטרה, the person called up for מפטיר says the following blessings:

בָּרוּךְ אַתָּה יהוה אֱלֹהֵינוּ מֶלֶךְ הָעוֹלָם, צוּר כָּל הָעוֹלָמִים, צַדִּיק בְּכָל הַדּוֹרוֹת, הָאֵל הַנֶּאֱמָן, הָאוֹמֵר וְעוֹשֶׂה, הַמְדַבֵּר וּמְקַיֵּם, שֶׁכָּל דְּבָרָיו אֱמֶת וָצֶדֶק. נֶאֱמָן אַתָּה הוּא יהוה אֱלֹהֵינוּ וְנֶאֱמָנִים דְּבָרֶיךָ, וְדָבָר אֶחָד מִדְּבָרֶיךָ אָחוֹר לֹא יָשׁוּב רֵיקָם, כִּי אֵל מֶלֶךְ נֶאֱמָן (וְרַחֲמָן) אָתָּה. בָּרוּךְ אַתָּה יהוה, הָאֵל הַנֶּאֱמָן בְּכָל דְּבָרָיו.

are judged, for afterwards it will be too late. (Rashi)

c. Seek out Hashem while you are still alive, for afterwards it will not be possible. (Targum Yonatan)

וְתַחַת d. Seek out Hashem before you are exiled, while the *Shekhina* is still with you. (Metzudat David)

e. Seek out Hashem even if you have sinned, call out to Him as you would to someone you love who is angry with you, and don't wait until they become distant to you. (Malbim)

1. Which of these interpretations appeals to you most on this fast day?

2. Which one interprets the word בְּהִמָּצְאוֹ differently from the rest?

3. What is the difference between the opinion of Rashi and that of Malbim?

4. The letter בּ can be used to designate a time ("when He is found/close") but it can also be used to designate a place ("where He is found/close"). The commentaries selected above all interpret it as the former. How would you interpret it as the latter?

5. The letter בּ can also be used to denote "for the purpose of" or "so that." How might that fit our verse and change its meaning?

רַחֵם עַל צִיּוֹן כִּי הִיא בֵּית חַיֵּינוּ, וְלַעֲלוּבַת נֶפֶשׁ תּוֹשִׁיעַ בִּמְהֵרָה בְיָמֵינוּ. בָּרוּךְ אַתָּה יהוה, מְשַׂמֵּחַ צִיּוֹן בְּבָנֶיהָ.

שַׂמְּחֵנוּ יהוה אֱלֹהֵינוּ בְּאֵלִיָּהוּ הַנָּבִיא עַבְדֶּךָ, וּבְמַלְכוּת בֵּית דָּוִד מְשִׁיחֶךָ, בִּמְהֵרָה יָבוֹא וְיָגֵל לִבֵּנוּ. עַל כִּסְאוֹ לֹא יֵשֶׁב זָר, וְלֹא יִנְחֲלוּ עוֹד אֲחֵרִים אֶת כְּבוֹדוֹ, כִּי בְשֵׁם קָדְשְׁךָ נִשְׁבַּעְתָּ לּוֹ שֶׁלֹּא יִכְבֶּה נֵרוֹ לְעוֹלָם וָעֶד. בָּרוּךְ אַתָּה יהוה, מָגֵן דָּוִד.

קריאה לתשעה באב   READING FOR TISHA B'AV

The following is read during שחרית *of* תשעה באב*. The person*
called up for שלישי *also reads the* הפטרה*. At* מנחה*, the* קריאה
and הפטרה *are those for regular Fast Days.*

דברים
ד:כה-מ

FIRST ALIYA: vv. 25–29
Most of the references to
Israel used here are in the
plural except for the ones
at the end. What might be
the reason?

כִּי־תוֹלִיד בָּנִים וּבְנֵי בָנִים וְנוֹשַׁנְתֶּם בָּאָרֶץ וְהִשְׁחַתֶּם וַעֲשִׂיתֶם פֶּסֶל תְּמוּנַת כֹּל וַעֲשִׂיתֶם הָרַע בְּעֵינֵי־יהוה אֱלֹהֶיךָ לְהַכְעִיסוֹ: הַעִידֹתִי בָכֶם הַיּוֹם אֶת־הַשָּׁמַיִם וְאֶת־הָאָרֶץ כִּי־אָבֹד תֹּאבֵדוּן מַהֵר מֵעַל הָאָרֶץ אֲשֶׁר אַתֶּם עֹבְרִים אֶת־הַיַּרְדֵּן שָׁמָּה לְרִשְׁתָּהּ לֹא־תַאֲרִיכֻן יָמִים עָלֶיהָ כִּי הִשָּׁמֵד תִּשָּׁמֵדוּן: וְהֵפִיץ יהוה אֶתְכֶם בָּעַמִּים וְנִשְׁאַרְתֶּם מְתֵי מִסְפָּר בַּגּוֹיִם אֲשֶׁר יְנַהֵג יהוה אֶתְכֶם שָׁמָּה: וַעֲבַדְתֶּם־שָׁם אֱלֹהִים מַעֲשֵׂה יְדֵי אָדָם עֵץ וָאֶבֶן אֲשֶׁר לֹא־יִרְאוּן וְלֹא יִשְׁמְעוּן וְלֹא יֹאכְלוּן וְלֹא יְרִיחֻן: וּבִקַּשְׁתֶּם מִשָּׁם אֶת־יהוה אֱלֹהֶיךָ וּמָצָאתָ כִּי תִדְרְשֶׁנּוּ בְּכָל־לְבָבְךָ וּבְכָל־נַפְשֶׁךָ:

לוי

בַּצַּר לְךָ וּמְצָאוּךָ כֹּל הַדְּבָרִים הָאֵלֶּה בְּאַחֲרִית הַיָּמִים וְשַׁבְתָּ עַד־ יהוה אֱלֹהֶיךָ וְשָׁמַעְתָּ בְּקֹלוֹ: כִּי אֵל רַחוּם יהוה אֱלֹהֶיךָ לֹא יַרְפְּךָ וְלֹא יַשְׁחִיתֶךָ וְלֹא יִשְׁכַּח אֶת־בְּרִית אֲבֹתֶיךָ אֲשֶׁר נִשְׁבַּע לָהֶם: כִּי שְׁאַל־נָא לְיָמִים רִאשֹׁנִים אֲשֶׁר־הָיוּ לְפָנֶיךָ לְמִן־הַיּוֹם אֲשֶׁר בָּרָא אֱלֹהִים ׀ אָדָם עַל־הָאָרֶץ וּלְמִקְצֵה הַשָּׁמַיִם וְעַד־קְצֵה הַשָּׁמָיִם הֲנִהְיָה כַּדָּבָר הַגָּדוֹל הַזֶּה אוֹ הֲנִשְׁמַע כָּמֹהוּ: הֲשָׁמַע עָם קוֹל אֱלֹהִים מְדַבֵּר מִתּוֹךְ־הָאֵשׁ כַּאֲשֶׁר־שָׁמַעְתָּ אַתָּה וַיֶּחִי: אוֹ ׀ הֲנִסָּה אֱלֹהִים

SECOND ALIYA: vv. 30–34
What possible proofs for
God's existence might
be alluded to in the
verses here?

לָבוֹא לָקַחַת לוֹ גוֹי מִקֶּרֶב גּוֹי בְּמַסֹּת בְּאֹתֹת וּבְמוֹפְתִים
וּבְמִלְחָמָה וּבְיָד חֲזָקָה וּבִזְרוֹעַ נְטוּיָה וּבְמוֹרָאִים גְּדֹלִים
כְּכֹל אֲשֶׁר־עָשָׂה לָכֶם יְהוָה אֱלֹהֵיכֶם בְּמִצְרַיִם לְעֵינֶיךָ:
אַתָּה הָרְאֵתָ לָדַעַת כִּי יְהוָה הוּא הָאֱלֹהִים אֵין עוֹד מִלְבַדּוֹ:

ישראל *מִן־הַשָּׁמַיִם הִשְׁמִיעֲךָ אֶת־קֹלוֹ לְיַסְּרֶךָּ וְעַל־הָאָרֶץ
הֶרְאֲךָ אֶת־אִשּׁוֹ הַגְּדוֹלָה וּדְבָרָיו שָׁמַעְתָּ מִתּוֹךְ הָאֵשׁ: וְתַחַת כִּי
אָהַב אֶת־אֲבֹתֶיךָ וַיִּבְחַר בְּזַרְעוֹ אַחֲרָיו וַיּוֹצִאֲךָ בְּפָנָיו בְּכֹחוֹ
הַגָּדֹל מִמִּצְרָיִם: לְהוֹרִישׁ גּוֹיִם גְּדֹלִים וַעֲצֻמִים מִמְּךָ מִפָּנֶיךָ
לַהֲבִיאֲךָ לָתֶת־לְךָ אֶת־אַרְצָם נַחֲלָה כַּיּוֹם הַזֶּה: וְיָדַעְתָּ
הַיּוֹם וַהֲשֵׁבֹתָ אֶל־לְבָבֶךָ כִּי יְהוָה הוּא הָאֱלֹהִים בַּשָּׁמַיִם
מִמַּעַל וְעַל־הָאָרֶץ מִתָּחַת אֵין עוֹד: וְשָׁמַרְתָּ אֶת־חֻקָּיו
וְאֶת־מִצְוֺתָיו אֲשֶׁר אָנֹכִי מְצַוְּךָ הַיּוֹם אֲשֶׁר יִיטַב לְךָ וּלְבָנֶיךָ
אַחֲרֶיךָ וּלְמַעַן תַּאֲרִיךְ יָמִים עַל־הָאֲדָמָה אֲשֶׁר יְהוָה אֱלֹהֶיךָ
נֹתֵן לְךָ כָּל־הַיָּמִים:

THIRD ALIYA: vv. 35–40
What words are used here for one of the prayers we say daily and what do the words mean?

HAFTARA FOR TISHA B'AV
הפטרה לתשעה באב

The blessings before the הפטרה *can be found on page 747.*

ירמיהו
ח:יג–ט:כג

אָסֹף אֲסִיפֵם נְאֻם־יְהוָֹה אֵין עֲנָבִים בַּגֶּפֶן וְאֵין תְּאֵנִים
בַּתְּאֵנָה וְהֶעָלֶה נָבֵל וָאֶתֵּן לָהֶם יַעַבְרוּם: עַל־מָה אֲנַחְנוּ
יֹשְׁבִים הֵאָסְפוּ וְנָבוֹא אֶל־עָרֵי הַמִּבְצָר וְנִדְּמָה־שָּׁם כִּי יְהוָֹה
אֱלֹהֵינוּ הֲדִמָּנוּ וַיַּשְׁקֵנוּ מֵי־רֹאשׁ כִּי חָטָאנוּ לַיהוָֹה: קַוֵּה
לְשָׁלוֹם וְאֵין טוֹב לְעֵת מַרְפֵּה וְהִנֵּה בְעָתָה: מִדָּן נִשְׁמַע
נַחְרַת סוּסָיו מִקּוֹל מִצְהֲלוֹת אַבִּירָיו רָעֲשָׁה כָּל־הָאָרֶץ
וַיָּבוֹאוּ וַיֹּאכְלוּ אֶרֶץ וּמְלוֹאָהּ עִיר וְיֹשְׁבֵי בָהּ: כִּי הִנְנִי
מְשַׁלֵּחַ בָּכֶם נְחָשִׁים צִפְעֹנִים אֲשֶׁר אֵין־לָהֶם לָחַשׁ וְנִשְּׁכוּ
אֶתְכֶם נְאֻם־יְהוָֹה: מַבְלִיגִיתִי עֲלֵי יָגוֹן עָלַי לִבִּי
דַוָּי: הִנֵּה־קוֹל שַׁוְעַת בַּת־עַמִּי מֵאֶרֶץ מַרְחַקִּים הַיהוָֹה
אֵין בְּצִיּוֹן אִם־מַלְכָּהּ אֵין בָּהּ מַדּוּעַ הִכְעִסוּנִי בִּפְסִלֵיהֶם

HAFTARA FOR TISHA B'AV

1. The *Haftara* consists of a number of different themes regarding the destruction of the *Beit HaMikdash*. The first 11 verses speak of the inevitable victory of the enemy and a lamentation about the death and exile that have already taken place and that are yet to come. Among these verses there is only one explicit sin that is mentioned. What is it?

2. The next ten verses revolve around one category of sin. What is it and why do you think it gets so much more mention than the first one?

3. The next five verses (beginning with the words מִי הָאִישׁ הֶחָכָם) refer to a different sin. What is it? (See commentary at the beginning of the Siddur in the section on the blessings on the Torah). What is it and how might it fit in with the rest of the Haftara?

4. The last two verses warn against human pride in which areas? Why do you think these were chosen?

5. Which part of the Haftara speaks most to you on this Tisha B'Av?

בְּהַבְלֵיהֶם נֵכָר: עָבַר קָצִיר כָּלָה קָיִץ וַאֲנַחְנוּ לוֹא נוֹשָׁעְנוּ:
עַל־שֶׁבֶר בַּת־עַמִּי הָשְׁבָּרְתִּי קָדַרְתִּי שַׁמָּה הֶחֱזִקָתְנִי: הַצֳּרִי
אֵין בְּגִלְעָד אִם־רֹפֵא אֵין שָׁם כִּי מַדּוּעַ לֹא עָלְתָה אֲרֻכַת
בַּת־עַמִּי: מִי־יִתֵּן רֹאשִׁי מַיִם וְעֵינִי מְקוֹר דִּמְעָה
וְאֶבְכֶּה יוֹמָם וָלַיְלָה אֵת חַלְלֵי בַת־עַמִּי: מִי־יִתְּנֵנִי בַמִּדְבָּר
מְלוֹן אֹרְחִים וְאֶעֶזְבָה אֶת־עַמִּי וְאֵלְכָה מֵאִתָּם כִּי כֻלָּם
מְנָאֲפִים עֲצֶרֶת בֹּגְדִים: וַיַּדְרְכוּ אֶת־לְשׁוֹנָם קַשְׁתָּם שֶׁקֶר
וְלֹא לֶאֱמוּנָה גָּבְרוּ בָאָרֶץ כִּי מֵרָעָה אֶל־רָעָה יָצָאוּ וְאֹתִי
לֹא־יָדָעוּ נְאֻם־יְהוֹה: אִישׁ מֵרֵעֵהוּ הִשָּׁמֵרוּ וְעַל־כָּל־אָח אַל־
תִּבְטָחוּ כִּי כָל־אָח עָקוֹב יַעְקֹב וְכָל־רֵעַ רָכִיל יַהֲלֹךְ: וְאִישׁ
בְּרֵעֵהוּ יְהָתֵלּוּ וֶאֱמֶת לֹא יְדַבֵּרוּ לִמְּדוּ לְשׁוֹנָם דַּבֶּר־שֶׁקֶר
הַעֲוֵה נִלְאוּ: שִׁבְתְּךָ בְּתוֹךְ מִרְמָה בְּמִרְמָה מֵאֲנוּ דַעַת־אוֹתִי
נְאֻם־יְהוֹה: לָכֵן כֹּה אָמַר יְהוֹה צְבָאוֹת הִנְנִי
צוֹרְפָם וּבְחַנְתִּים כִּי־אֵיךְ אֶעֱשֶׂה מִפְּנֵי בַּת־עַמִּי: חֵץ שׁוֹחֵט שָׁחוּט
לְשׁוֹנָם מִרְמָה דִבֵּר בְּפִיו שָׁלוֹם אֶת־רֵעֵהוּ יְדַבֵּר וּבְקִרְבּוֹ
יָשִׂים אָרְבּוֹ: הַעַל־אֵלֶּה לֹא־אֶפְקָד־בָּם נְאֻם־יְהוֹה אִם בְּגוֹי
אֲשֶׁר־כָּזֶה לֹא תִתְנַקֵּם נַפְשִׁי: עַל־הֶהָרִים אֶשָּׂא
בְכִי וָנֶהִי וְעַל־נְאוֹת מִדְבָּר קִינָה כִּי נִצְּתוּ מִבְּלִי־אִישׁ עֹבֵר
וְלֹא שָׁמְעוּ קוֹל מִקְנֶה מֵעוֹף הַשָּׁמַיִם וְעַד־בְּהֵמָה נָדְדוּ
הָלָכוּ: וְנָתַתִּי אֶת־יְרוּשָׁלַם לְגַלִּים מְעוֹן תַּנִּים וְאֶת־עָרֵי
יְהוּדָה אֶתֵּן שְׁמָמָה מִבְּלִי יוֹשֵׁב: מִי־הָאִישׁ
הֶחָכָם וְיָבֵן אֶת־זֹאת וַאֲשֶׁר דִּבֶּר פִּי־יְהוֹה אֵלָיו וְיַגִּדָהּ עַל־מָה
אָבְדָה הָאָרֶץ נִצְּתָה כַמִּדְבָּר מִבְּלִי עֹבֵר: וַיֹּאמֶר
יְהוֹה עַל־עָזְבָם אֶת־תּוֹרָתִי אֲשֶׁר נָתַתִּי לִפְנֵיהֶם וְלֹא־
שָׁמְעוּ בְקוֹלִי וְלֹא־הָלְכוּ בָהּ: וַיֵּלְכוּ אַחֲרֵי שְׁרִרוּת לִבָּם
וְאַחֲרֵי הַבְּעָלִים אֲשֶׁר לִמְּדוּם אֲבוֹתָם: לָכֵן
כֹּה־אָמַר יְהוֹה צְבָאוֹת אֱלֹהֵי יִשְׂרָאֵל הִנְנִי מַאֲכִילָם
אֶת־הָעָם הַזֶּה לַעֲנָה וְהִשְׁקִיתִים מֵי־רֹאשׁ: וַהֲפִצוֹתִים

בַּגּוֹיִם אֲשֶׁר לֹא־יְדָעוּ הֵמָּה וַאֲבוֹתָם וְשִׁלַּחְתִּי אַחֲרֵיהֶם
אֶת־הַחֶרֶב עַד כַּלּוֹתִי אוֹתָם:　　כֹּה אָמַר יְהוָה
צְבָאוֹת הִתְבּוֹנְנוּ וְקִרְאוּ לַמְקוֹנְנוֹת וּתְבוֹאֶינָה וְאֶל־
הַחֲכָמוֹת שִׁלְחוּ וְתָבוֹאנָה: וּתְמַהֵרְנָה וְתִשֶּׂנָה עָלֵינוּ נֶהִי
וְתֵרַדְנָה עֵינֵינוּ דִּמְעָה וְעַפְעַפֵּינוּ יִזְּלוּ־מָיִם: כִּי קוֹל נְהִי
נִשְׁמַע מִצִּיּוֹן אֵיךְ שֻׁדָּדְנוּ בֹּשְׁנוּ מְאֹד כִּי־עָזַבְנוּ אָרֶץ כִּי
הִשְׁלִיכוּ מִשְׁכְּנוֹתֵינוּ:　　כִּי־שְׁמַעְנָה נָשִׁים דְּבַר־
יְהוָה וְתִקַּח אָזְנְכֶם דְּבַר־פִּיו וְלַמֵּדְנָה בְנוֹתֵיכֶם נֶהִי וְאִשָּׁה
רְעוּתָהּ קִינָה: כִּי־עָלָה מָוֶת בְּחַלּוֹנֵינוּ בָּא בְּאַרְמְנוֹתֵינוּ
לְהַכְרִית עוֹלָל מִחוּץ בַּחוּרִים מֵרְחֹבוֹת: דַּבֵּר כֹּה נְאֻם־
יְהוָה וְנָפְלָה נִבְלַת הָאָדָם כְּדֹמֶן עַל־פְּנֵי הַשָּׂדֶה וּכְעָמִיר
מֵאַחֲרֵי הַקֹּצֵר וְאֵין מְאַסֵּף:　　כֹּה ׀ אָמַר יְהוָה
אַל־יִתְהַלֵּל חָכָם בְּחָכְמָתוֹ וְאַל־יִתְהַלֵּל הַגִּבּוֹר בִּגְבוּרָתוֹ
אַל־יִתְהַלֵּל עָשִׁיר בְּעָשְׁרוֹ: כִּי אִם־בְּזֹאת יִתְהַלֵּל הַמִּתְהַלֵּל
הַשְׂכֵּל וְיָדֹעַ אוֹתִי כִּי אֲנִי יְהוָה עֹשֶׂה חֶסֶד מִשְׁפָּט וּצְדָקָה
בָּאָרֶץ כִּי־בְאֵלֶּה חָפַצְתִּי נְאֻם־יְהוָה:

The blessings after the הפטרה can be found on page 748.

The blessings after the הפטרה *can be found on page 748.*

FIRST DAY OF 　 קריאה ליום הראשון של חנוכה
HANUKKA

HANUKKA — EIGHT
QUESTIONS FOR
EIGHT DAYS

וַיְהִי בְּיוֹם כַּלּוֹת מֹשֶׁה לְהָקִים אֶת־הַמִּשְׁכָּן וַיִּמְשַׁח אֹתוֹ
וַיְקַדֵּשׁ אֹתוֹ וְאֶת־כָּל־כֵּלָיו וְאֶת־הַמִּזְבֵּחַ וְאֶת־כָּל־כֵּלָיו
וַיִּמְשָׁחֵם וַיְקַדֵּשׁ אֹתָם: וַיַּקְרִיבוּ נְשִׂיאֵי יִשְׂרָאֵל רָאשֵׁי בֵּית
אֲבֹתָם הֵם נְשִׂיאֵי הַמַּטֹּת הֵם הָעֹמְדִים עַל־הַפְּקֻדִים: וַיָּבִיאוּ
אֶת־קָרְבָּנָם לִפְנֵי יְהוָה שֵׁשׁ־עֶגְלֹת צָב וּשְׁנֵי עָשָׂר בָּקָר עֲגָלָה
עַל־שְׁנֵי הַנְּשִׂאִים וְשׁוֹר לְאֶחָד וַיַּקְרִיבוּ אוֹתָם לִפְנֵי הַמִּשְׁכָּן:
וַיֹּאמֶר יְהוָה אֶל־מֹשֶׁה לֵּאמֹר: קַח מֵאִתָּם וְהָיוּ לַעֲבֹד
אֶת־עֲבֹדַת אֹהֶל מוֹעֵד וְנָתַתָּה אוֹתָם אֶל־הַלְוִיִּם אִישׁ כְּפִי
עֲבֹדָתוֹ: וַיִּקַּח מֹשֶׁה אֶת־הָעֲגָלֹת וְאֶת־הַבָּקָר וַיִּתֵּן אוֹתָם

בְּמִדְבַּר
ז:א-ו

1. FIRST DAY:
There is one letter that
appears in the description
of the first sacrifice that is
not found in any of
the others on
subsequent days.
What is it?

אֶל־הַלְוִיֶּם: אֵת ׀ שְׁתֵּי הָעֲגָלֹת וְאֵת אַרְבַּעַת הַבָּקָר נָתַן
לִבְנֵי גֵרְשׁוֹן כְּפִי עֲבֹדָתָם: וְאֵת ׀ אַרְבַּע הָעֲגָלֹת וְאֵת שְׁמֹנַת
הַבָּקָר נָתַן לִבְנֵי מְרָרִי כְּפִי עֲבֹדָתָם בְּיַד אִיתָמָר בֶּן־אַהֲרֹן
הַכֹּהֵן: וְלִבְנֵי קְהָת לֹא נָתָן כִּי־עֲבֹדַת הַקֹּדֶשׁ עֲלֵהֶם בַּכָּתֵף
יִשָּׂאוּ: וַיַּקְרִיבוּ הַנְּשִׂאִים אֵת חֲנֻכַּת הַמִּזְבֵּחַ בְּיוֹם הִמָּשַׁח
אֹתוֹ וַיַּקְרִיבוּ הַנְּשִׂיאִם אֶת־קָרְבָּנָם לִפְנֵי הַמִּזְבֵּחַ: וַיֹּאמֶר
יְהוָה אֶל־מֹשֶׁה נָשִׂיא אֶחָד לַיּוֹם נָשִׂיא אֶחָד לַיּוֹם יַקְרִיבוּ
אֶת־קָרְבָּנָם לַחֲנֻכַּת הַמִּזְבֵּחַ: ***וַיְהִי הַמַּקְרִיב** לוי

בַּיּוֹם הָרִאשׁוֹן אֶת־קָרְבָּנוֹ נַחְשׁוֹן בֶּן־עַמִּינָדָב לְמַטֵּה יְהוּדָה:
וְקָרְבָּנוֹ קַעֲרַת־כֶּסֶף אַחַת שְׁלֹשִׁים וּמֵאָה מִשְׁקָלָהּ מִזְרָק
אֶחָד כֶּסֶף שִׁבְעִים שֶׁקֶל בְּשֶׁקֶל הַקֹּדֶשׁ שְׁנֵיהֶם ׀ מְלֵאִים
סֹלֶת בְּלוּלָה בַשֶּׁמֶן לְמִנְחָה: כַּף אַחַת עֲשָׂרָה זָהָב מְלֵאָה
קְטֹרֶת: ***פַּר** אֶחָד בֶּן־בָּקָר אַיִל אֶחָד כֶּבֶשׂ־אֶחָד בֶּן־שְׁנָתוֹ ישראל
לְעֹלָה: שְׂעִיר־עִזִּים אֶחָד לְחַטָּאת: וּלְזֶבַח הַשְּׁלָמִים בָּקָר
שְׁנַיִם אֵילִם חֲמִשָּׁה עַתּוּדִים חֲמִשָּׁה כְּבָשִׂים בְּנֵי־שָׁנָה
חֲמִשָּׁה זֶה קָרְבַּן נַחְשׁוֹן בֶּן־עַמִּינָדָב:

SECOND DAY OF HANUKKA
קריאה ליום השני של חנוכה

In אֶרֶץ יִשְׂרָאֵל, *for* שְׁלִישִׁי *repeat the first paragraph:*
נְתַנְאֵל בֶּן־צוּעָר *until* בַּיּוֹם הַשֵּׁנִי

בַּיּוֹם הַשֵּׁנִי הִקְרִיב נְתַנְאֵל בֶּן־צוּעָר נְשִׂיא יִשָּׂשכָר: הִקְרִב במדבר
אֶת־קָרְבָּנוֹ קַעֲרַת־כֶּסֶף אַחַת שְׁלֹשִׁים וּמֵאָה מִשְׁקָלָהּ מִזְרָק ז:יח-כט
אֶחָד כֶּסֶף שִׁבְעִים שֶׁקֶל בְּשֶׁקֶל הַקֹּדֶשׁ שְׁנֵיהֶם ׀ מְלֵאִים
סֹלֶת בְּלוּלָה בַשֶּׁמֶן לְמִנְחָה: כַּף אַחַת עֲשָׂרָה זָהָב מְלֵאָה
קְטֹרֶת: ***פַּר** אֶחָד בֶּן־בָּקָר אַיִל אֶחָד כֶּבֶשׂ־אֶחָד בֶּן־שְׁנָתוֹ לוי
לְעֹלָה: שְׂעִיר־עִזִּים אֶחָד לְחַטָּאת: וּלְזֶבַח הַשְּׁלָמִים בָּקָר
שְׁנַיִם אֵילִם חֲמִשָּׁה עַתּוּדִים חֲמִשָּׁה כְּבָשִׂים בְּנֵי־שָׁנָה חֲמִשָּׁה
זֶה קָרְבַּן נְתַנְאֵל בֶּן־צוּעָר:

2. SECOND DAY:
There is one verse here
that is particularly different from the verses on
the other days.
Which is it?

ישראל בַּיּוֹם הַשְּׁלִישִׁי נָשִׂיא לִבְנֵי זְבוּלֻן אֱלִיאָב בֶּן־חֵלֹן: קָרְבָּנוֹ
קַעֲרַת־כֶּסֶף אַחַת שְׁלֹשִׁים וּמֵאָה מִשְׁקָלָהּ מִזְרָק אֶחָד
כֶּסֶף שִׁבְעִים שֶׁקֶל בְּשֶׁקֶל הַקֹּדֶשׁ שְׁנֵיהֶם מְלֵאִים סֹלֶת
בְּלוּלָה בַשֶּׁמֶן לְמִנְחָה: כַּף אַחַת עֲשָׂרָה זָהָב מְלֵאָה קְטֹרֶת:
פַּר אֶחָד בֶּן־בָּקָר אַיִל אֶחָד כֶּבֶשׂ־אֶחָד בֶּן־שְׁנָתוֹ לְעֹלָה:
שְׂעִיר־עִזִּים אֶחָד לְחַטָּאת: וּלְזֶבַח הַשְּׁלָמִים בָּקָר שְׁנַיִם
אֵילִם חֲמִשָּׁה עַתֻּדִים חֲמִשָּׁה כְּבָשִׂים בְּנֵי־שָׁנָה חֲמִשָּׁה זֶה
קָרְבַּן אֱלִיאָב בֶּן־חֵלֹן:

THIRD DAY OF HANUKKA
קריאה ליום השלישי של חנוכה

In ארץ ישראל, for שלישי *repeat the first paragraph:*
אֱלִיאָב בֶּן־חֵלֹן *until* בַּיּוֹם הַשְּׁלִישִׁי.

במדבר בַּיּוֹם הַשְּׁלִישִׁי נָשִׂיא לִבְנֵי זְבוּלֻן אֱלִיאָב בֶּן־חֵלֹן: קָרְבָּנוֹ
ז:כד-לה קַעֲרַת־כֶּסֶף אַחַת שְׁלֹשִׁים וּמֵאָה מִשְׁקָלָהּ מִזְרָק אֶחָד
כֶּסֶף שִׁבְעִים שֶׁקֶל בְּשֶׁקֶל הַקֹּדֶשׁ שְׁנֵיהֶם מְלֵאִים סֹלֶת
בְּלוּלָה בַשֶּׁמֶן לְמִנְחָה: כַּף אַחַת עֲשָׂרָה זָהָב מְלֵאָה קְטֹרֶת:
לוי *פַּר אֶחָד בֶּן־בָּקָר אַיִל אֶחָד כֶּבֶשׂ־אֶחָד בֶּן־שְׁנָתוֹ לְעֹלָה:
שְׂעִיר־עִזִּים אֶחָד לְחַטָּאת: וּלְזֶבַח הַשְּׁלָמִים בָּקָר שְׁנַיִם
אֵילִם חֲמִשָּׁה עַתֻּדִים חֲמִשָּׁה כְּבָשִׂים בְּנֵי־שָׁנָה חֲמִשָּׁה זֶה
קָרְבַּן אֱלִיאָב בֶּן־חֵלֹן:

ישראל בַּיּוֹם הָרְבִיעִי נָשִׂיא לִבְנֵי רְאוּבֵן אֱלִיצוּר בֶּן־שְׁדֵיאוּר: קָרְבָּנוֹ
קַעֲרַת־כֶּסֶף אַחַת שְׁלֹשִׁים וּמֵאָה מִשְׁקָלָהּ מִזְרָק אֶחָד
כֶּסֶף שִׁבְעִים שֶׁקֶל בְּשֶׁקֶל הַקֹּדֶשׁ שְׁנֵיהֶם מְלֵאִים סֹלֶת
בְּלוּלָה בַשֶּׁמֶן לְמִנְחָה: כַּף אַחַת עֲשָׂרָה זָהָב מְלֵאָה קְטֹרֶת:
פַּר אֶחָד בֶּן־בָּקָר אַיִל אֶחָד כֶּבֶשׂ־אֶחָד בֶּן־שְׁנָתוֹ לְעֹלָה:
שְׂעִיר־עִזִּים אֶחָד לְחַטָּאת: וּלְזֶבַח הַשְּׁלָמִים בָּקָר שְׁנַיִם
אֵילִם חֲמִשָּׁה עַתֻּדִים חֲמִשָּׁה כְּבָשִׂים בְּנֵי־שָׁנָה חֲמִשָּׁה זֶה
קָרְבַּן אֱלִיצוּר בֶּן־שְׁדֵיאוּר:

3. THIRD DAY: From where in these verses may one learn that there is no need to try to "show up" someone else.

קריאה ליום הרביעי של חנוכה FOURTH DAY OF ḤANUKKA

In ארץ ישראל*, for* שלישי *repeat the first paragraph:* בַּיּוֹם הָרְבִיעִי *until* אֱלִיצוּר בֶּן־שְׁדֵיאוּר.

במדבר ז:ל–מא
בַּיּוֹם הָרְבִיעִי נָשִׂיא לִבְנֵי רְאוּבֵן אֱלִיצוּר בֶּן־שְׁדֵיאוּר׃ קָרְבָּנוֹ
קַעֲרַת־כֶּסֶף אַחַת שְׁלֹשִׁים וּמֵאָה מִשְׁקָלָהּ מִזְרָק אֶחָד
כֶּסֶף שִׁבְעִים שֶׁקֶל בְּשֶׁקֶל הַקֹּדֶשׁ שְׁנֵיהֶם ׀ מְלֵאִים סֹלֶת
בְּלוּלָה בַשֶּׁמֶן לְמִנְחָה׃ כַּף אַחַת עֲשָׂרָה זָהָב מְלֵאָה קְטֹרֶת׃
לוי *פַּר אֶחָד בֶּן־בָּקָר אַיִל אֶחָד כֶּבֶשׂ־אֶחָד בֶּן־שְׁנָתוֹ לְעֹלָה׃
שְׂעִיר־עִזִּים אֶחָד לְחַטָּאת׃ וּלְזֶבַח הַשְּׁלָמִים בָּקָר שְׁנַיִם
אֵילִם חֲמִשָּׁה עַתֻּדִים חֲמִשָּׁה כְּבָשִׂים בְּנֵי־שָׁנָה חֲמִשָּׁה זֶה
קָרְבַּן אֱלִיצוּר בֶּן־שְׁדֵיאוּר׃
ישראל בַּיּוֹם הַחֲמִישִׁי נָשִׂיא לִבְנֵי שִׁמְעוֹן שְׁלֻמִיאֵל בֶּן־צוּרִישַׁדָּי׃
קָרְבָּנוֹ קַעֲרַת־כֶּסֶף אַחַת שְׁלֹשִׁים וּמֵאָה מִשְׁקָלָהּ מִזְרָק
אֶחָד כֶּסֶף שִׁבְעִים שֶׁקֶל בְּשֶׁקֶל הַקֹּדֶשׁ שְׁנֵיהֶם ׀ מְלֵאִים
סֹלֶת בְּלוּלָה בַשֶּׁמֶן לְמִנְחָה׃ כַּף אַחַת עֲשָׂרָה זָהָב מְלֵאָה
קְטֹרֶת׃ פַּר אֶחָד בֶּן־בָּקָר אַיִל אֶחָד כֶּבֶשׂ־אֶחָד בֶּן־שְׁנָתוֹ
לְעֹלָה׃ שְׂעִיר־עִזִּים אֶחָד לְחַטָּאת׃ וּלְזֶבַח הַשְּׁלָמִים בָּקָר
שְׁנַיִם אֵילִם חֲמִשָּׁה עַתֻּדִים חֲמִשָּׁה כְּבָשִׂים בְּנֵי־שָׁנָה חֲמִשָּׁה
זֶה קָרְבַּן שְׁלֻמִיאֵל בֶּן־צוּרִישַׁדָּי׃

4. FOURTH DAY: The commentator Rabbi Yitzḥak Arama explains that the sacrifices of the heads of the tribes are reminiscent of the verse we read in *Pesukei DeZimra* from *Tehillim* 147: "He counts all of the stars; He knows each by name." What's the connection?

קריאה ליום החמישי של חנוכה FIFTH DAY OF ḤANUKKA

In ארץ ישראל*, for* שלישי *repeat the first paragraph:* בַּיּוֹם הַחֲמִישִׁי *until* שְׁלֻמִיאֵל בֶּן־צוּרִישַׁדָּי.

במדבר ז:לו–מז
בַּיּוֹם הַחֲמִישִׁי נָשִׂיא לִבְנֵי שִׁמְעוֹן שְׁלֻמִיאֵל בֶּן־צוּרִישַׁדָּי׃
קָרְבָּנוֹ קַעֲרַת־כֶּסֶף אַחַת שְׁלֹשִׁים וּמֵאָה מִשְׁקָלָהּ מִזְרָק
אֶחָד כֶּסֶף שִׁבְעִים שֶׁקֶל בְּשֶׁקֶל הַקֹּדֶשׁ שְׁנֵיהֶם ׀ מְלֵאִים
סֹלֶת בְּלוּלָה בַשֶּׁמֶן לְמִנְחָה׃ כַּף אַחַת עֲשָׂרָה זָהָב מְלֵאָה

5. FIFTH DAY: The commentator Ibn Caspi says that the purpose of this is to teach us how great was the voluntary spirit of the Jewish People at the time. What is it?

לוי קְטֹרֶת: *פַּר אֶחָד בֶּן־בָּקָר אַיִל אֶחָד כֶּבֶשׂ־אֶחָד בֶּן־שְׁנָתוֹ
לְעֹלָה: שְׂעִיר־עִזִּים אֶחָד לְחַטָּאת: וּלְזֶבַח הַשְּׁלָמִים בָּקָר
שְׁנַיִם אֵילִם חֲמִשָּׁה עַתֻּדִים חֲמִשָּׁה כְּבָשִׂים בְּנֵי־שָׁנָה חֲמִשָּׁה
זֶה קָרְבַּן שְׁלֻמִיאֵל בֶּן־צוּרִישַׁדָּי:

ישראל בַּיּוֹם הַשִּׁשִּׁי נָשִׂיא לִבְנֵי גָד אֶלְיָסָף בֶּן־דְּעוּאֵל: קָרְבָּנוֹ
קַעֲרַת־כֶּסֶף אַחַת שְׁלֹשִׁים וּמֵאָה מִשְׁקָלָהּ מִזְרָק אֶחָד
כֶּסֶף שִׁבְעִים שֶׁקֶל בְּשֶׁקֶל הַקֹּדֶשׁ שְׁנֵיהֶם מְלֵאִים סֹלֶת
בְּלוּלָה בַשֶּׁמֶן לְמִנְחָה: כַּף אַחַת עֲשָׂרָה זָהָב מְלֵאָה קְטֹרֶת:
פַּר אֶחָד בֶּן־בָּקָר אַיִל אֶחָד כֶּבֶשׂ־אֶחָד בֶּן־שְׁנָתוֹ לְעֹלָה:
שְׂעִיר־עִזִּים אֶחָד לְחַטָּאת: וּלְזֶבַח הַשְּׁלָמִים בָּקָר שְׁנַיִם
אֵלִם חֲמִשָּׁה עַתֻּדִים חֲמִשָּׁה כְּבָשִׂים בְּנֵי־שָׁנָה חֲמִשָּׁה זֶה
קָרְבַּן אֶלְיָסָף בֶּן־דְּעוּאֵל:

קריאה ליום הששי של חנוכה וראש חודש

SIXTH DAY OF ḤANUKKA AND ROSH
ḤODESH

The sixth day is ראש חודש טבת. *Two* ספרי תורה *are taken
out of the* ארון קודש. *From the first, read the* קריאת התורה *for*
ביום הששי *(page 745), from the second, read* ראש חודש:

(page 745)

במדבר בַּיּוֹם הַשִּׁשִּׁי נָשִׂיא לִבְנֵי גָד אֶלְיָסָף בֶּן־דְּעוּאֵל: קָרְבָּנוֹ
ז:מב-מז קַעֲרַת־כֶּסֶף אַחַת שְׁלֹשִׁים וּמֵאָה מִשְׁקָלָהּ מִזְרָק אֶחָד
כֶּסֶף שִׁבְעִים שֶׁקֶל בְּשֶׁקֶל הַקֹּדֶשׁ שְׁנֵיהֶם מְלֵאִים סֹלֶת
בְּלוּלָה בַשֶּׁמֶן לְמִנְחָה: כַּף אַחַת עֲשָׂרָה זָהָב מְלֵאָה קְטֹרֶת:
פַּר אֶחָד בֶּן־בָּקָר אַיִל אֶחָד כֶּבֶשׂ־אֶחָד בֶּן־שְׁנָתוֹ לְעֹלָה:
שְׂעִיר־עִזִּים אֶחָד לְחַטָּאת: וּלְזֶבַח הַשְּׁלָמִים בָּקָר שְׁנַיִם
אֵילִם חֲמִשָּׁה עַתֻּדִים חֲמִשָּׁה כְּבָשִׂים בְּנֵי־שָׁנָה חֲמִשָּׁה זֶה
קָרְבַּן אֶלְיָסָף בֶּן־דְּעוּאֵל:

6. SIXTH DAY:
Ramban says that
each head of tribe had
something different in
mind when he brought
his sacrifice. What is the
significance of this for
religious life?

קריאה ליום השביעי של חנוכה וראש חודש

SEVENTH DAY OF ḤANUKKA AND ROSH ḤODESH

If the seventh day is also ראש חודש, then two ספרי תורה are taken out of the ark. From the first, read the קריאת התורה for ראש חודש (page 745), from the second, read בים השביעי:

במדבר
ז:מח-נג

בַּיּוֹם הַשְּׁבִיעִי נָשִׂיא לִבְנֵי אֶפְרָיִם אֱלִישָׁמָע בֶּן־עַמִּיהוּד:
קָרְבָּנוֹ קַעֲרַת־כֶּסֶף אַחַת שְׁלֹשִׁים וּמֵאָה מִשְׁקָלָהּ מִזְרָק
אֶחָד כֶּסֶף שִׁבְעִים שֶׁקֶל בְּשֶׁקֶל הַקֹּדֶשׁ שְׁנֵיהֶם ׀ מְלֵאִים
סֹלֶת בְּלוּלָה בַשֶּׁמֶן לְמִנְחָה: כַּף אַחַת עֲשָׂרָה זָהָב מְלֵאָה
קְטֹרֶת: פַּר אֶחָד בֶּן־בָּקָר אַיִל אֶחָד כֶּבֶשׂ־אֶחָד בֶּן־שְׁנָתוֹ
לְעֹלָה: שְׂעִיר־עִזִּים אֶחָד לְחַטָּאת: וּלְזֶבַח הַשְּׁלָמִים בָּקָר
שְׁנַיִם אֵילִם חֲמִשָּׁה עַתֻּדִים חֲמִשָּׁה כְּבָשִׂים בְּנֵי־שָׁנָה חֲמִשָּׁה
זֶה קָרְבַּן אֱלִישָׁמָע בֶּן־עַמִּיהוּד:

קריאה ליום השביעי של חנוכה

SEVENTH DAY OF ḤANUKKA

If the seventh day is not ראש חודש, then read as below. In ארץ ישראל, for שליש repeat the first paragraph: בים השביעי until אֱלִישָׁמָע בֶּן־עַמִּיהוּד.

במדבר
ז:מח-נט

בַּיּוֹם הַשְּׁבִיעִי נָשִׂיא לִבְנֵי אֶפְרָיִם אֱלִישָׁמָע בֶּן־עַמִּיהוּד:
קָרְבָּנוֹ קַעֲרַת־כֶּסֶף אַחַת שְׁלֹשִׁים וּמֵאָה מִשְׁקָלָהּ מִזְרָק
אֶחָד כֶּסֶף שִׁבְעִים שֶׁקֶל בְּשֶׁקֶל הַקֹּדֶשׁ שְׁנֵיהֶם ׀ מְלֵאִים
סֹלֶת בְּלוּלָה בַשֶּׁמֶן לְמִנְחָה: כַּף אַחַת עֲשָׂרָה זָהָב מְלֵאָה
קְטֹרֶת: *פַּר אֶחָד בֶּן־בָּקָר אַיִל אֶחָד כֶּבֶשׂ־אֶחָד בֶּן־שְׁנָתוֹ לוי
לְעֹלָה: שְׂעִיר־עִזִּים אֶחָד לְחַטָּאת: וּלְזֶבַח הַשְּׁלָמִים בָּקָר
שְׁנַיִם אֵילִם חֲמִשָּׁה עַתֻּדִים חֲמִשָּׁה כְּבָשִׂים בְּנֵי־שָׁנָה חֲמִשָּׁה
זֶה קָרְבַּן אֱלִישָׁמָע בֶּן־עַמִּיהוּד:

7. SEVENTH DAY: According to Rashi, each of the heads of the tribes personally paid for the sacrifice that he brought. What proof may be brought for this and what lesson may be learned?

ישראל בַּיּוֹם הַשְּׁמִינִי נָשִׂיא לִבְנֵי מְנַשֶּׁה גַּמְלִיאֵל בֶּן־פְּדָהצוּר: קָרְבָּנוֹ קַעֲרַת־כֶּסֶף אַחַת שְׁלֹשִׁים וּמֵאָה מִשְׁקָלָהּ מִזְרָק אֶחָד כֶּסֶף שִׁבְעִים שֶׁקֶל בְּשֶׁקֶל הַקֹּדֶשׁ שְׁנֵיהֶם ׀ מְלֵאִים סֹלֶת בְּלוּלָה בַשֶּׁמֶן לְמִנְחָה: כַּף אַחַת עֲשָׂרָה זָהָב מְלֵאָה קְטֹרֶת: פַּר אֶחָד בֶּן־בָּקָר אַיִל אֶחָד כֶּבֶשׂ־אֶחָד בֶּן־שְׁנָתוֹ לְעֹלָה: שְׂעִיר־עִזִּים אֶחָד לְחַטָּאת: וּלְזֶבַח הַשְּׁלָמִים בָּקָר שְׁנַיִם אֵילִם חֲמִשָּׁה עַתֻּדִים חֲמִשָּׁה כְּבָשִׂים בְּנֵי־שָׁנָה חֲמִשָּׁה זֶה קָרְבַּן גַּמְלִיאֵל בֶּן־פְּדָהצוּר:

EIGHTH DAY OF HANUKKA

קריאה ליום השמיני של חנוכה

במדבר ז:נד–ח:ד

בַּיּוֹם הַשְּׁמִינִי נָשִׂיא לִבְנֵי מְנַשֶּׁה גַּמְלִיאֵל בֶּן־פְּדָהצוּר: קָרְבָּנוֹ קַעֲרַת־כֶּסֶף אַחַת שְׁלֹשִׁים וּמֵאָה מִשְׁקָלָהּ מִזְרָק אֶחָד כֶּסֶף שִׁבְעִים שֶׁקֶל בְּשֶׁקֶל הַקֹּדֶשׁ שְׁנֵיהֶם ׀ מְלֵאִים סֹלֶת בְּלוּלָה בַשֶּׁמֶן לְמִנְחָה: כַּף אַחַת עֲשָׂרָה זָהָב מְלֵאָה קְטֹרֶת: *פַּר אֶחָד

לוי בֶּן־בָּקָר אַיִל אֶחָד כֶּבֶשׂ־אֶחָד בֶּן־שְׁנָתוֹ לְעֹלָה: שְׂעִיר־עִזִּים אֶחָד לְחַטָּאת: וּלְזֶבַח הַשְּׁלָמִים בָּקָר שְׁנַיִם אֵילִם חֲמִשָּׁה עַתֻּדִים חֲמִשָּׁה כְּבָשִׂים בְּנֵי־שָׁנָה חֲמִשָּׁה זֶה קָרְבַּן גַּמְלִיאֵל בֶּן־פְּדָהצוּר:

ישראל בַּיּוֹם הַתְּשִׁיעִי נָשִׂיא לִבְנֵי בִנְיָמִן אֲבִידָן בֶּן־גִּדְעֹנִי: קָרְבָּנוֹ קַעֲרַת־כֶּסֶף אַחַת שְׁלֹשִׁים וּמֵאָה מִשְׁקָלָהּ מִזְרָק אֶחָד כֶּסֶף שִׁבְעִים שֶׁקֶל בְּשֶׁקֶל הַקֹּדֶשׁ שְׁנֵיהֶם ׀ מְלֵאִים סֹלֶת בְּלוּלָה בַשֶּׁמֶן לְמִנְחָה: כַּף אַחַת עֲשָׂרָה זָהָב מְלֵאָה קְטֹרֶת: פַּר אֶחָד בֶּן־בָּקָר אַיִל אֶחָד כֶּבֶשׂ־אֶחָד בֶּן־שְׁנָתוֹ לְעֹלָה: שְׂעִיר־עִזִּים אֶחָד לְחַטָּאת: וּלְזֶבַח הַשְּׁלָמִים בָּקָר שְׁנַיִם אֵילִם חֲמִשָּׁה עַתֻּדִים חֲמִשָּׁה כְּבָשִׂים בְּנֵי־שָׁנָה חֲמִשָּׁה זֶה קָרְבַּן אֲבִידָן בֶּן־גִּדְעֹנִי: בַּיּוֹם הָעֲשִׂירִי נָשִׂיא לִבְנֵי דָן אֲחִיעֶזֶר בֶּן־עַמִּישַׁדָּי: קָרְבָּנוֹ קַעֲרַת־כֶּסֶף אַחַת שְׁלֹשִׁים וּמֵאָה מִשְׁקָלָהּ מִזְרָק אֶחָד

8. EIGHTH DAY: The eighth day of Ḥanukka is often referred to as *"vezot Ḥanukka."* Why?

כֶּסֶף שִׁבְעִים שֶׁקֶל בְּשֶׁקֶל הַקֹּדֶשׁ שְׁנֵיהֶם ׀ מְלֵאִים סֹלֶת
בְּלוּלָה בַשֶּׁמֶן לְמִנְחָה: כַּף אַחַת עֲשָׂרָה זָהָב מְלֵאָה קְטֹרֶת:
פַּר אֶחָד בֶּן־בָּקָר אַיִל אֶחָד כֶּבֶשׂ־אֶחָד בֶּן־שְׁנָתוֹ לְעֹלָה:
שְׂעִיר־עִזִּים אֶחָד לְחַטָּאת: וּלְזֶבַח הַשְּׁלָמִים בָּקָר שְׁנַיִם
אֵילִם חֲמִשָּׁה עַתֻּדִים חֲמִשָּׁה כְּבָשִׂים בְּנֵי־שָׁנָה חֲמִשָּׁה זֶה
קָרְבַּן אֲחִיעֶזֶר בֶּן־עַמִּישַׁדָּי:

בְּיוֹם עַשְׁתֵּי עָשָׂר יוֹם נָשִׂיא לִבְנֵי אָשֵׁר פַּגְעִיאֵל בֶּן־עָכְרָן:
קָרְבָּנוֹ קַעֲרַת־כֶּסֶף אַחַת שְׁלֹשִׁים וּמֵאָה מִשְׁקָלָהּ מִזְרָק
אֶחָד כֶּסֶף שִׁבְעִים שֶׁקֶל בְּשֶׁקֶל הַקֹּדֶשׁ שְׁנֵיהֶם ׀ מְלֵאִים
סֹלֶת בְּלוּלָה בַשֶּׁמֶן לְמִנְחָה: כַּף אַחַת עֲשָׂרָה זָהָב מְלֵאָה
קְטֹרֶת: פַּר אֶחָד בֶּן־בָּקָר אַיִל אֶחָד כֶּבֶשׂ־אֶחָד בֶּן־שְׁנָתוֹ
לְעֹלָה: שְׂעִיר־עִזִּים אֶחָד לְחַטָּאת: וּלְזֶבַח הַשְּׁלָמִים בָּקָר
שְׁנַיִם אֵילִם חֲמִשָּׁה עַתֻּדִים חֲמִשָּׁה כְּבָשִׂים בְּנֵי־שָׁנָה חֲמִשָּׁה
זֶה קָרְבַּן פַּגְעִיאֵל בֶּן־עָכְרָן:

בְּיוֹם שְׁנֵים עָשָׂר יוֹם נָשִׂיא לִבְנֵי נַפְתָּלִי אֲחִירַע בֶּן־עֵינָן:
קָרְבָּנוֹ קַעֲרַת־כֶּסֶף אַחַת שְׁלֹשִׁים וּמֵאָה מִשְׁקָלָהּ מִזְרָק
אֶחָד כֶּסֶף שִׁבְעִים שֶׁקֶל בְּשֶׁקֶל הַקֹּדֶשׁ שְׁנֵיהֶם ׀ מְלֵאִים
סֹלֶת בְּלוּלָה בַשֶּׁמֶן לְמִנְחָה: כַּף אַחַת עֲשָׂרָה זָהָב מְלֵאָה
קְטֹרֶת: פַּר אֶחָד בֶּן־בָּקָר אַיִל אֶחָד כֶּבֶשׂ־אֶחָד בֶּן־שְׁנָתוֹ
לְעֹלָה: שְׂעִיר־עִזִּים אֶחָד לְחַטָּאת: וּלְזֶבַח הַשְּׁלָמִים בָּקָר
שְׁנַיִם אֵילִם חֲמִשָּׁה עַתֻּדִים חֲמִשָּׁה כְּבָשִׂים בְּנֵי־שָׁנָה חֲמִשָּׁה
זֶה קָרְבַּן אֲחִירַע בֶּן־עֵינָן:

זֹאת ׀ חֲנֻכַּת הַמִּזְבֵּחַ בְּיוֹם הִמָּשַׁח אֹתוֹ מֵאֵת נְשִׂיאֵי יִשְׂרָאֵל
קַעֲרֹת כֶּסֶף שְׁתֵּים עֶשְׂרֵה מִזְרְקֵי־כֶסֶף שְׁנֵים עָשָׂר כַּפּוֹת
זָהָב שְׁתֵּים עֶשְׂרֵה: שְׁלֹשִׁים וּמֵאָה הַקְּעָרָה הָאַחַת כֶּסֶף
וְשִׁבְעִים הַמִּזְרָק הָאֶחָד כֹּל כֶּסֶף הַכֵּלִים אַלְפַּיִם וְאַרְבַּע־
מֵאוֹת בְּשֶׁקֶל הַקֹּדֶשׁ: כַּפּוֹת זָהָב שְׁתֵּים־עֶשְׂרֵה מְלֵאֹת
קְטֹרֶת עֲשָׂרָה עֲשָׂרָה הַכַּף בְּשֶׁקֶל הַקֹּדֶשׁ כָּל־זְהַב הַכַּפּוֹת
עֶשְׂרִים וּמֵאָה: כָּל־הַבָּקָר לָעֹלָה שְׁנֵים עָשָׂר פָּרִים אֵילִם

שְׁנֵים־עָשָׂר כְּבָשִׂים בְּנֵי־שָׁנָה שְׁנֵים עָשָׂר וּמִנְחָתָם וְשָׂעִירֵי
עִזִּים שְׁנֵים עָשָׂר לְחַטָּאת: וְכֹל בָּקָר וּזֶבַח הַשְּׁלָמִים עֶשְׂרִים
וְאַרְבָּעָה פָּרִים אֵילִם שִׁשִּׁים עַתֻּדִים שִׁשִּׁים כְּבָשִׂים בְּנֵי־
שָׁנָה שִׁשִּׁים זֹאת חֲנֻכַּת הַמִּזְבֵּחַ אַחֲרֵי הִמָּשַׁח אֹתוֹ: וּבְבֹא
מֹשֶׁה אֶל־אֹהֶל מוֹעֵד לְדַבֵּר אִתּוֹ וַיִּשְׁמַע אֶת־הַקּוֹל מִדַּבֵּר
אֵלָיו מֵעַל הַכַּפֹּרֶת אֲשֶׁר עַל־אֲרֹן הָעֵדֻת מִבֵּין שְׁנֵי הַכְּרֻבִים
וַיְדַבֵּר אֵלָיו:

וַיְדַבֵּר יהוה אֶל־מֹשֶׁה לֵּאמֹר: דַּבֵּר אֶל־אַהֲרֹן וְאָמַרְתָּ אֵלָיו
בְּהַעֲלֹתְךָ אֶת־הַנֵּרֹת אֶל־מוּל פְּנֵי הַמְּנוֹרָה יָאִירוּ שִׁבְעַת
הַנֵּרוֹת: וַיַּעַשׂ כֵּן אַהֲרֹן אֶל־מוּל פְּנֵי הַמְּנוֹרָה הֶעֱלָה נֵרֹתֶיהָ
כַּאֲשֶׁר צִוָּה יהוה אֶת־מֹשֶׁה: וְזֶה מַעֲשֵׂה הַמְּנֹרָה מִקְשָׁה
זָהָב עַד־יְרֵכָהּ עַד־פִּרְחָהּ מִקְשָׁה הִוא כַּמַּרְאֶה אֲשֶׁר הֶרְאָה
יהוה אֶת־מֹשֶׁה כֵּן עָשָׂה אֶת־הַמְּנֹרָה:

קריאה לפורים

וַיָּבֹא עֲמָלֵק וַיִּלָּחֶם עִם־יִשְׂרָאֵל בִּרְפִידִם: וַיֹּאמֶר מֹשֶׁה
אֶל־יְהוֹשֻׁעַ בְּחַר־לָנוּ אֲנָשִׁים וְצֵא הִלָּחֵם בַּעֲמָלֵק מָחָר
אָנֹכִי נִצָּב עַל־רֹאשׁ הַגִּבְעָה וּמַטֵּה הָאֱלֹהִים בְּיָדִי: וַיַּעַשׂ
יְהוֹשֻׁעַ כַּאֲשֶׁר אָמַר־לוֹ מֹשֶׁה לְהִלָּחֵם בַּעֲמָלֵק וּמֹשֶׁה אַהֲרֹן
וְחוּר עָלוּ רֹאשׁ הַגִּבְעָה: וְהָיָה כַּאֲשֶׁר יָרִים מֹשֶׁה יָדוֹ
וְגָבַר יִשְׂרָאֵל וְכַאֲשֶׁר יָנִיחַ יָדוֹ וְגָבַר עֲמָלֵק: וִידֵי מֹשֶׁה
כְּבֵדִים וַיִּקְחוּ־אֶבֶן וַיָּשִׂימוּ תַחְתָּיו וַיֵּשֶׁב עָלֶיהָ וְאַהֲרֹן וְחוּר
תָּמְכוּ בְיָדָיו מִזֶּה אֶחָד וּמִזֶּה אֶחָד וַיְהִי יָדָיו אֱמוּנָה עַד־
בֹּא הַשָּׁמֶשׁ: וַיַּחֲלֹשׁ יְהוֹשֻׁעַ אֶת־עֲמָלֵק וְאֶת־עַמּוֹ לְפִי־
חָרֶב:

וַיֹּאמֶר יהוה אֶל־מֹשֶׁה כְּתֹב זֹאת זִכָּרוֹן בַּסֵּפֶר וְשִׂים בְּאָזְנֵי
יְהוֹשֻׁעַ כִּי־מָחֹה אֶמְחֶה אֶת־זֵכֶר עֲמָלֵק מִתַּחַת הַשָּׁמָיִם:
וַיִּבֶן מֹשֶׁה מִזְבֵּחַ וַיִּקְרָא שְׁמוֹ יהוה נִסִּי: וַיֹּאמֶר כִּי־יָד
עַל־כֵּס יָהּ מִלְחָמָה לַיהוה בַּעֲמָלֵק מִדֹּר דֹּר:

שמות
יז:ח–טז

FIRST ALIYA: vv. 8–10
From here the Sages
stated: "Your disciple's
honor shall be as dear
to you as your own
honor" (*Avot* 4:12).

לוי

SECOND ALIYA: vv. 11–13
What function did
Moshe's raising his hands
serve? What lessons can
be learned from here?

ישראל

THIRD ALIYA: vv. 14–16
This indicates that
Hashem's hand and
throne are dimin-
ished as long as Amalek
exists. Does Amalek still
exist? Is Amalek a tribe
or an ideology? What are
the implications of each?

קריאת התורה לחול המועד
THE READING OF THE TORAH
FOR ḤOL HAMO'ED

חול המועד פסח
ḤOL HAMO'ED PESAḤ

קריאה ליום ראשון דחול המועד בארץ ישראל
FIRST DAY OF ḤOL HAMO'ED IN ISRAEL

Two ספרי תורה are taken out of the ארון קודש. The following
קריאת התורה is read from the first scroll; the fourth עליה
(page 740) is read from the second scroll.

ויקרא כב:
כו-כג:מד

FIRST ALIYA: vv.
22:26–23:8
What reasons can you
think of to explain why
the Torah prohibits the
slaughtering of a parent
animal and its offspring
on the same day?

וַיְדַבֵּ֥ר יְהֹוָ֖ה אֶל־מֹשֶׁ֥ה לֵּאמֹֽר: שׁ֣וֹר אוֹ־כֶ֤שֶׂב אוֹ־עֵז֙ כִּ֣י
יִוָּלֵ֔ד וְהָיָ֛ה שִׁבְעַ֥ת יָמִ֖ים תַּ֣חַת אִמּ֑וֹ וּמִיּ֣וֹם הַשְּׁמִינִי֙ וָהָ֔לְאָה
יֵרָצֶ֕ה לְקָרְבַּ֥ן אִשֶּׁ֖ה לַיהֹוָֽה: וְשׁ֖וֹר אוֹ־שֶׂ֑ה אֹת֣וֹ וְאֶת־בְּנ֗וֹ
לֹ֥א תִשְׁחֲט֖וּ בְּי֥וֹם אֶחָֽד: וְכִֽי־תִזְבְּח֥וּ זֶֽבַח־תּוֹדָ֖ה לַֽיהֹוָ֑ה
לִֽרְצֹנְכֶ֖ם תִּזְבָּֽחוּ: בַּיּ֤וֹם הַהוּא֙ יֵֽאָכֵ֔ל לֹֽא־תוֹתִ֥ירוּ מִמֶּ֖נּוּ עַד־
בֹּ֑קֶר אֲנִ֖י יְהֹוָֽה: וּשְׁמַרְתֶּם֙ מִצְוֺתַ֔י וַֽעֲשִׂיתֶ֖ם אֹתָ֑ם אֲנִ֖י יְהֹוָֽה:
וְלֹ֤א תְחַלְּלוּ֙ אֶת־שֵׁ֣ם קׇדְשִׁ֔י וְנִ֨קְדַּשְׁתִּ֔י בְּת֖וֹךְ בְּנֵ֣י יִשְׂרָאֵ֑ל
אֲנִ֥י יְהֹוָ֖ה מְקַדִּשְׁכֶֽם: הַמּוֹצִ֤יא אֶתְכֶם֙ מֵאֶ֣רֶץ מִצְרַ֔יִם לִֽהְי֥וֹת
לָכֶ֖ם לֵֽאלֹהִ֑ים אֲנִ֖י יְהֹוָֽה:

וַיְדַבֵּ֥ר יְהֹוָ֖ה אֶל־מֹשֶׁ֥ה לֵּאמֹֽר: דַּבֵּ֞ר אֶל־בְּנֵ֤י יִשְׂרָאֵל֙ וְאָֽמַרְתָּ֣
אֲלֵהֶ֔ם מֽוֹעֲדֵ֣י יְהֹוָ֔ה אֲשֶׁר־תִּקְרְא֥וּ אֹתָ֖ם מִקְרָאֵ֣י קֹ֑דֶשׁ אֵ֥לֶּה
הֵ֖ם מֽוֹעֲדָֽי: שֵׁ֣שֶׁת יָמִים֮ תֵּֽעָשֶׂ֣ה מְלָאכָה֒ וּבַיּ֣וֹם הַשְּׁבִיעִ֗י
שַׁבַּ֤ת שַׁבָּתוֹן֙ מִקְרָא־קֹ֔דֶשׁ כׇּל־מְלָאכָ֖ה לֹ֣א תַֽעֲשׂ֑וּ שַׁבָּ֥ת
הִוא֙ לַֽיהֹוָ֔ה בְּכֹ֖ל מֽוֹשְׁבֹֽתֵיכֶֽם:

אֵ֚לֶּה מֽוֹעֲדֵ֣י יְהֹוָ֔ה מִקְרָאֵ֖י קֹ֑דֶשׁ אֲשֶׁר־תִּקְרְא֥וּ אֹתָ֖ם בְּמֽוֹעֲדָֽם:
בַּחֹ֣דֶשׁ הָֽרִאשׁ֗וֹן בְּאַרְבָּעָ֥ה עָשָׂ֛ר לַחֹ֖דֶשׁ בֵּ֣ין הָֽעַרְבָּ֑יִם פֶּ֖סַח
לַֽיהֹוָֽה: וּבַֽחֲמִשָּׁ֨ה עָשָׂ֥ר יוֹם֙ לַחֹ֣דֶשׁ הַזֶּ֔ה חַ֥ג הַמַּצּ֖וֹת לַֽיהֹוָ֑ה
שִׁבְעַ֥ת יָמִ֖ים מַצּ֥וֹת תֹּאכֵֽלוּ: בַּיּוֹם֙ הָֽרִאשׁ֔וֹן מִקְרָא־קֹ֖דֶשׁ

יִהְיֶה לָכֶם כָּל־מְלֶאכֶת עֲבֹדָה לֹא תַעֲשׂוּ: וְהִקְרַבְתֶּם אִשֶּׁה
לַיהוה שִׁבְעַת יָמִים בַּיּוֹם הַשְּׁבִיעִי מִקְרָא־קֹדֶשׁ כָּל־מְלֶאכֶת
עֲבֹדָה לֹא תַעֲשׂוּ:

לוי וַיְדַבֵּר יהוה אֶל־מֹשֶׁה לֵּאמֹר: דַּבֵּר אֶל־בְּנֵי יִשְׂרָאֵל וְאָמַרְתָּ
אֲלֵהֶם כִּי־תָבֹאוּ אֶל־הָאָרֶץ אֲשֶׁר אֲנִי נֹתֵן לָכֶם וּקְצַרְתֶּם
אֶת־קְצִירָהּ וַהֲבֵאתֶם אֶת־עֹמֶר רֵאשִׁית קְצִירְכֶם אֶל־
הַכֹּהֵן: וְהֵנִיף אֶת־הָעֹמֶר לִפְנֵי יהוה לִרְצֹנְכֶם מִמָּחֳרַת
הַשַּׁבָּת יְנִיפֶנּוּ הַכֹּהֵן: וַעֲשִׂיתֶם בְּיוֹם הֲנִיפְכֶם אֶת־הָעֹמֶר
כֶּבֶשׂ תָּמִים בֶּן־שְׁנָתוֹ לְעֹלָה לַיהוה: וּמִנְחָתוֹ שְׁנֵי עֶשְׂרֹנִים
סֹלֶת בְּלוּלָה בַשֶּׁמֶן אִשֶּׁה לַיהוה רֵיחַ נִיחֹחַ וְנִסְכֹּה יַיִן רְבִיעִת
הַהִין: וְלֶחֶם וְקָלִי וְכַרְמֶל לֹא תֹאכְלוּ עַד־עֶצֶם הַיּוֹם הַזֶּה
עַד הֲבִיאֲכֶם אֶת־קָרְבַּן אֱלֹהֵיכֶם חֻקַּת עוֹלָם לְדֹרֹתֵיכֶם
בְּכֹל מֹשְׁבֹתֵיכֶם: *וּסְפַרְתֶּם לָכֶם מִמָּחֳרַת

שלישי הַשַּׁבָּת מִיּוֹם הֲבִיאֲכֶם אֶת־עֹמֶר הַתְּנוּפָה שֶׁבַע שַׁבָּתוֹת
תְּמִימֹת תִּהְיֶינָה: עַד מִמָּחֳרַת הַשַּׁבָּת הַשְּׁבִיעִת תִּסְפְּרוּ
חֲמִשִּׁים יוֹם וְהִקְרַבְתֶּם מִנְחָה חֲדָשָׁה לַיהוה: מִמּוֹשְׁבֹתֵיכֶם
תָּבִיאוּ לֶחֶם תְּנוּפָה שְׁתַּיִם שְׁנֵי עֶשְׂרֹנִים סֹלֶת תִּהְיֶינָה חָמֵץ
תֵּאָפֶינָה בִּכּוּרִים לַיהוה: וְהִקְרַבְתֶּם עַל־הַלֶּחֶם שִׁבְעַת
כְּבָשִׂים תְּמִימִם בְּנֵי שָׁנָה וּפַר בֶּן־בָּקָר אֶחָד וְאֵילִם שְׁנָיִם
יִהְיוּ עֹלָה לַיהוה וּמִנְחָתָם וְנִסְכֵּיהֶם אִשֵּׁה רֵיחַ־נִיחֹחַ לַיהוה:
וַעֲשִׂיתֶם שְׂעִיר־עִזִּים אֶחָד לְחַטָּאת וּשְׁנֵי כְבָשִׂים בְּנֵי
שָׁנָה לְזֶבַח שְׁלָמִים: וְהֵנִיף הַכֹּהֵן אֹתָם עַל לֶחֶם הַבִּכּוּרִים
תְּנוּפָה לִפְנֵי יהוה עַל־שְׁנֵי כְּבָשִׂים קֹדֶשׁ יִהְיוּ לַיהוה לַכֹּהֵן:
וּקְרָאתֶם בְּעֶצֶם הַיּוֹם הַזֶּה מִקְרָא־קֹדֶשׁ יִהְיֶה לָכֶם כָּל־
מְלֶאכֶת עֲבֹדָה לֹא תַעֲשׂוּ חֻקַּת עוֹלָם בְּכָל־מוֹשְׁבֹתֵיכֶם
לְדֹרֹתֵיכֶם: וּבְקֻצְרְכֶם אֶת־קְצִיר אַרְצְכֶם לֹא־תְכַלֶּה פְּאַת
שָׂדְךָ בְּקֻצְרֶךָ וְלֶקֶט קְצִירְךָ לֹא תְלַקֵּט לֶעָנִי וְלַגֵּר תַּעֲזֹב
אֹתָם אֲנִי יהוה אֱלֹהֵיכֶם:

וַיְדַבֵּר יהוה אֶל־מֹשֶׁה לֵּאמֹר: דַּבֵּר אֶל־בְּנֵי יִשְׂרָאֵל

SECOND ALIYA: vv. 9–14
מִמָּחֳרַת הַשַּׁבָּת can be interpreted in different ways
and represents a historical
argument with massive
implications. How
so, and which way of
reading these words
won the day?

THIRD ALIYA: vv. 15–44
How many times can you
find the number seven
featured here? What do
you think the message
of this is?

לֵאמֹר בַּחֹדֶשׁ הַשְּׁבִיעִי בְּאֶחָד לַחֹדֶשׁ יִהְיֶה לָכֶם שַׁבָּתוֹן
זִכְרוֹן תְּרוּעָה מִקְרָא־קֹדֶשׁ: כָּל־מְלֶאכֶת עֲבֹדָה לֹא
תַעֲשׂוּ וְהִקְרַבְתֶּם אִשֶּׁה לַיהוָה: וַיְדַבֵּר
יְהוָה אֶל־מֹשֶׁה לֵּאמֹר: אַךְ בֶּעָשׂוֹר לַחֹדֶשׁ הַשְּׁבִיעִי הַזֶּה
יוֹם הַכִּפֻּרִים הוּא מִקְרָא־קֹדֶשׁ יִהְיֶה לָכֶם וְעִנִּיתֶם אֶת־
נַפְשֹׁתֵיכֶם וְהִקְרַבְתֶּם אִשֶּׁה לַיהוָה: וְכָל־מְלָאכָה לֹא
תַעֲשׂוּ בְּעֶצֶם הַיּוֹם הַזֶּה כִּי יוֹם כִּפֻּרִים הוּא לְכַפֵּר עֲלֵיכֶם
לִפְנֵי יְהוָה אֱלֹהֵיכֶם: כִּי כָל־הַנֶּפֶשׁ אֲשֶׁר לֹא־תְעֻנֶּה בְּעֶצֶם
הַיּוֹם הַזֶּה וְנִכְרְתָה מֵעַמֶּיהָ: וְכָל־הַנֶּפֶשׁ אֲשֶׁר תַּעֲשֶׂה כָּל־
מְלָאכָה בְּעֶצֶם הַיּוֹם הַזֶּה וְהַאֲבַדְתִּי אֶת־הַנֶּפֶשׁ הַהִוא
מִקֶּרֶב עַמָּהּ: כָּל־מְלָאכָה לֹא תַעֲשׂוּ חֻקַּת עוֹלָם לְדֹרֹתֵיכֶם
בְּכֹל מֹשְׁבֹתֵיכֶם: שַׁבַּת שַׁבָּתוֹן הוּא לָכֶם וְעִנִּיתֶם אֶת־
נַפְשֹׁתֵיכֶם בְּתִשְׁעָה לַחֹדֶשׁ בָּעֶרֶב מֵעֶרֶב עַד־עֶרֶב תִּשְׁבְּתוּ
שַׁבַּתְּכֶם:

וַיְדַבֵּר יְהוָה אֶל־מֹשֶׁה לֵּאמֹר: דַּבֵּר אֶל־בְּנֵי יִשְׂרָאֵל לֵאמֹר
בַּחֲמִשָּׁה עָשָׂר יוֹם לַחֹדֶשׁ הַשְּׁבִיעִי הַזֶּה חַג הַסֻּכּוֹת שִׁבְעַת
יָמִים לַיהוָה: בַּיּוֹם הָרִאשׁוֹן מִקְרָא־קֹדֶשׁ כָּל־מְלֶאכֶת עֲבֹדָה
לֹא תַעֲשׂוּ: שִׁבְעַת יָמִים תַּקְרִיבוּ אִשֶּׁה לַיהוָה בַּיּוֹם הַשְּׁמִינִי
מִקְרָא־קֹדֶשׁ יִהְיֶה לָכֶם וְהִקְרַבְתֶּם אִשֶּׁה לַיהוָה עֲצֶרֶת
הִוא כָּל־מְלֶאכֶת עֲבֹדָה לֹא תַעֲשׂוּ: אֵלֶּה מוֹעֲדֵי יְהוָה
אֲשֶׁר־תִּקְרְאוּ אֹתָם מִקְרָאֵי קֹדֶשׁ לְהַקְרִיב אִשֶּׁה לַיהוָה
עֹלָה וּמִנְחָה זֶבַח וּנְסָכִים דְּבַר־יוֹם בְּיוֹמוֹ: מִלְּבַד שַׁבְּתֹת
יְהוָה וּמִלְּבַד מַתְּנוֹתֵיכֶם וּמִלְּבַד כָּל־נִדְרֵיכֶם וּמִלְּבַד כָּל־
נִדְבֹתֵיכֶם אֲשֶׁר תִּתְּנוּ לַיהוָה: אַךְ בַּחֲמִשָּׁה עָשָׂר יוֹם לַחֹדֶשׁ
הַשְּׁבִיעִי בְּאָסְפְּכֶם אֶת־תְּבוּאַת הָאָרֶץ תָּחֹגּוּ אֶת־חַג־יְהוָה
שִׁבְעַת יָמִים בַּיּוֹם הָרִאשׁוֹן שַׁבָּתוֹן וּבַיּוֹם הַשְּׁמִינִי שַׁבָּתוֹן:
וּלְקַחְתֶּם לָכֶם בַּיּוֹם הָרִאשׁוֹן פְּרִי עֵץ הָדָר כַּפֹּת תְּמָרִים
וַעֲנַף עֵץ־עָבֹת וְעַרְבֵי־נָחַל וּשְׂמַחְתֶּם לִפְנֵי יְהוָה אֱלֹהֵיכֶם
שִׁבְעַת יָמִים: וְחַגֹּתֶם אֹתוֹ חַג לַיהוָה שִׁבְעַת יָמִים בַּשָּׁנָה

חֻקַּת עוֹלָם לְדֹרֹתֵיכֶם בְּחֹדֶשׁ הַשְּׁבִיעִי תָּחֹגּוּ אֹתוֹ: בַּסֻּכֹּת
תֵּשְׁבוּ שִׁבְעַת יָמִים כָּל־הָאֶזְרָח בְּיִשְׂרָאֵל יֵשְׁבוּ בַּסֻּכֹּת:
לְמַעַן יֵדְעוּ דֹרֹתֵיכֶם כִּי בַסֻּכּוֹת הוֹשַׁבְתִּי אֶת־בְּנֵי יִשְׂרָאֵל
בְּהוֹצִיאִי אוֹתָם מֵאֶרֶץ מִצְרָיִם אֲנִי יְהוָה אֱלֹהֵיכֶם: וַיְדַבֵּר
מֹשֶׁה אֶת־מֹעֲדֵי יְהוָה אֶל־בְּנֵי יִשְׂרָאֵל:

רביעי *is read from the second* ספר תורה:

במדבר כח:
יט־כה

וְהִקְרַבְתֶּם אִשֶּׁה עֹלָה לַיהוָה פָּרִים בְּנֵי־בָקָר שְׁנַיִם וְאַיִל
אֶחָד וְשִׁבְעָה כְבָשִׂים בְּנֵי שָׁנָה תְּמִימִם יִהְיוּ לָכֶם: וּמִנְחָתָם
סֹלֶת בְּלוּלָה בַשָּׁמֶן שְׁלֹשָׁה עֶשְׂרֹנִים לַפָּר וּשְׁנֵי עֶשְׂרֹנִים
לָאַיִל תַּעֲשׂוּ: עִשָּׂרוֹן עִשָּׂרוֹן תַּעֲשֶׂה לַכֶּבֶשׂ הָאֶחָד לְשִׁבְעַת
הַכְּבָשִׂים: וּשְׂעִיר חַטָּאת אֶחָד לְכַפֵּר עֲלֵיכֶם: מִלְּבַד עֹלַת
הַבֹּקֶר אֲשֶׁר לְעֹלַת הַתָּמִיד תַּעֲשׂוּ אֶת־אֵלֶּה: כָּאֵלֶּה תַּעֲשׂוּ
לַיּוֹם שִׁבְעַת יָמִים לֶחֶם אִשֵּׁה רֵיחַ־נִיחֹחַ לַיהוָה עַל־עוֹלַת
הַתָּמִיד יֵעָשֶׂה וְנִסְכּוֹ: וּבַיּוֹם הַשְּׁבִיעִי מִקְרָא־קֹדֶשׁ יִהְיֶה
לָכֶם כָּל־מְלֶאכֶת עֲבֹדָה לֹא תַעֲשׂוּ:

Continue with חצי קדיש *(page 227).*

קריאה ליום ראשון דחול המועד (ב׳ בארץ ישראל)
FIRST DAY OF ḤOL HAMO'ED
(SECOND DAY IN ISRAEL)

שמות
יג:א־טז

וַיְדַבֵּר יְהוָה אֶל־מֹשֶׁה לֵּאמֹר: קַדֶּשׁ־לִי כָל־בְּכוֹר פֶּטֶר כָּל־
רֶחֶם בִּבְנֵי יִשְׂרָאֵל בָּאָדָם וּבַבְּהֵמָה לִי הוּא: וַיֹּאמֶר מֹשֶׁה
אֶל־הָעָם זָכוֹר אֶת־הַיּוֹם הַזֶּה אֲשֶׁר יְצָאתֶם מִמִּצְרַיִם מִבֵּית
עֲבָדִים כִּי בְּחֹזֶק יָד הוֹצִיא יְהוָה אֶתְכֶם מִזֶּה וְלֹא יֵאָכֵל
חָמֵץ: הַיּוֹם אַתֶּם יֹצְאִים בְּחֹדֶשׁ הָאָבִיב: *וְהָיָה כִי־יְבִיאֲךָ*

לוי

יְהוָה אֶל־אֶרֶץ הַכְּנַעֲנִי וְהַחִתִּי וְהָאֱמֹרִי וְהַחִוִּי וְהַיְבוּסִי אֲשֶׁר
נִשְׁבַּע לַאֲבֹתֶיךָ לָתֶת לָךְ אֶרֶץ זָבַת חָלָב וּדְבָשׁ וְעָבַדְתָּ
אֶת־הָעֲבֹדָה הַזֹּאת בַּחֹדֶשׁ הַזֶּה: שִׁבְעַת יָמִים תֹּאכַל מַצֹּת
וּבַיּוֹם הַשְּׁבִיעִי חַג לַיהוָה: מַצּוֹת יֵאָכֵל אֵת שִׁבְעַת הַיָּמִים

FOURTH ALIYA:
BEMIDBAR 28:19–25
What is the significance of
reading about the order
of the animal sacrifices
on the festivals?

FIRST ALIYA: vv. 1–4
How and when do we
remember "this day"?

SECOND ALIYA: vv. 5–10
"It is because of what
the LORD did for me when
I went out of Egypt" is the
source for one of the an-
swers given to one of the
four sons in the Haggada.
Which one? And why?

וְלֹא־יֵרָאֶה לְךָ חָמֵץ וְלֹא־יֵרָאֶה לְךָ שְׂאֹר בְּכָל־גְּבֻלֶךָ: וְהִגַּדְתָּ לְבִנְךָ בַּיּוֹם הַהוּא לֵאמֹר בַּעֲבוּר זֶה עָשָׂה יהוה לִי בְּצֵאתִי מִמִּצְרָיִם: וְהָיָה לְךָ לְאוֹת עַל־יָדְךָ וּלְזִכָּרוֹן בֵּין עֵינֶיךָ לְמַעַן תִּהְיֶה תּוֹרַת יהוה בְּפִיךָ כִּי בְּיָד חֲזָקָה הוֹצִאֲךָ יהוה מִמִּצְרָיִם: וְשָׁמַרְתָּ אֶת־הַחֻקָּה הַזֹּאת לְמוֹעֲדָהּ מִיָּמִים יָמִימָה:

שלישי
וְהָיָה כִּי־יְבִאֲךָ יהוה אֶל־אֶרֶץ הַכְּנַעֲנִי כַּאֲשֶׁר נִשְׁבַּע לְךָ וְלַאֲבֹתֶיךָ וּנְתָנָהּ לָךְ: וְהַעֲבַרְתָּ כָל־פֶּטֶר־רֶחֶם לַיהוה וְכָל־פֶּטֶר ׀ שֶׁגֶר בְּהֵמָה אֲשֶׁר יִהְיֶה לְךָ הַזְּכָרִים לַיהוה: וְכָל־פֶּטֶר חֲמֹר תִּפְדֶּה בְשֶׂה וְאִם־לֹא תִפְדֶּה וַעֲרַפְתּוֹ וְכֹל בְּכוֹר אָדָם בְּבָנֶיךָ תִּפְדֶּה: וְהָיָה כִּי־יִשְׁאָלְךָ בִנְךָ מָחָר לֵאמֹר מַה־זֹּאת וְאָמַרְתָּ אֵלָיו בְּחֹזֶק יָד הוֹצִיאָנוּ יהוה מִמִּצְרַיִם מִבֵּית עֲבָדִים: וַיְהִי כִּי־הִקְשָׁה פַרְעֹה לְשַׁלְּחֵנוּ וַיַּהֲרֹג יהוה כָּל־בְּכוֹר בְּאֶרֶץ מִצְרַיִם מִבְּכֹר אָדָם וְעַד־בְּכוֹר בְּהֵמָה עַל־כֵּן אֲנִי זֹבֵחַ לַיהוה כָּל־פֶּטֶר רֶחֶם הַזְּכָרִים וְכָל־בְּכוֹר בָּנַי אֶפְדֶּה: וְהָיָה לְאוֹת עַל־יָדְכָה וּלְטוֹטָפֹת בֵּין עֵינֶיךָ כִּי בְּחֹזֶק יָד הוֹצִיאָנוּ יהוה מִמִּצְרָיִם:

For רביעי *read* וְהִקְרַבְתֶּם *from the second* ספר תורה *(page 764).*

קריאה ליום שני דחול המועד (ג' בארץ ישראל)
SECOND DAY OF ḤOL HAMO'ED
(THIRD DAY IN ISRAEL)

If the second day of חול המועד פסח *falls on Sunday, the* קריאת התורה *for the first day of* חול המועד *is read (page 764).*

שמות כב:
כד–כג:ט
אִם־כֶּסֶף ׀ תַּלְוֶה אֶת־עַמִּי אֶת־הֶעָנִי עִמָּךְ לֹא־תִהְיֶה לוֹ כְּנֹשֶׁה לֹא־תְשִׂימוּן עָלָיו נֶשֶׁךְ: אִם־חָבֹל תַּחְבֹּל שַׂלְמַת רֵעֶךָ עַד־בֹּא הַשֶּׁמֶשׁ תְּשִׁיבֶנּוּ לוֹ: כִּי הִוא כְסוּתֹה לְבַדָּהּ הִוא שִׂמְלָתוֹ לְעֹרוֹ בַּמֶּה יִשְׁכָּב וְהָיָה כִּי־יִצְעַק אֵלַי וְשָׁמַעְתִּי כִּי־חַנּוּן אָנִי:

לוי
*אֱלֹהִים לֹא תְקַלֵּל וְנָשִׂיא בְעַמְּךָ לֹא תָאֹר: מְלֵאָתְךָ וְדִמְעֲךָ לֹא תְאַחֵר בְּכוֹר בָּנֶיךָ תִּתֶּן־לִי: כֵּן־תַּעֲשֶׂה

THIRD ALIYA: vv. 11–16
"Your child will ask you
'What is this?' is the
source for another of the
four sons in the Haggada.
Which one? And why
do you think the answer
provided is appropriate
for that son?

FIRST ALIYA:
vv. 22:24–26
Where can you see the
theme of dignity
in this section?

SECOND ALIYA:
vv. 27–23:5
A warning against
being influenced by
peer pressure. Where
is it and why warn
against it?

לְשֹׁרֶךָ לֹא־יִגְאָל לְצֵאנְךָ שִׁבְעַת יָמִים יִהְיֶה עִם־אִמּוֹ בַּיּוֹם הַשְּׁמִינִי
תִּתְּנוֹ־לִי: וְאַנְשֵׁי־קֹדֶשׁ תִּהְיוּן לִי וּבָשָׂר בַּשָּׂדֶה טְרֵפָה לֹא
תֹאכֵלוּ לַכֶּלֶב תַּשְׁלִכוּן אֹתוֹ: לֹא תִשָּׂא שֵׁמַע
שָׁוְא אַל־תָּשֶׁת יָדְךָ עִם־רָשָׁע לִהְיֹת עֵד חָמָס: לֹא־תִהְיֶה
אַחֲרֵי־רַבִּים לְרָעֹת וְלֹא־תַעֲנֶה עַל־רִב לִנְטֹת אַחֲרֵי רַבִּים
לְהַטֹּת: וְדָל לֹא תֶהְדַּר בְּרִיבוֹ: כִּי תִפְגַּע שׁוֹר
אֹיִבְךָ אוֹ חֲמֹרוֹ תֹּעֶה הָשֵׁב תְּשִׁיבֶנּוּ לוֹ: כִּי־
תִרְאֶה חֲמוֹר שֹׂנַאֲךָ רֹבֵץ תַּחַת מַשָּׂאוֹ וְחָדַלְתָּ מֵעֲזֹב לוֹ
עָזֹב תַּעֲזֹב עִמּוֹ: *לֹא תַטֶּה מִשְׁפַּט אֶבְיֹנְךָ בְּרִיבוֹ: שלישי
מִדְּבַר־שֶׁקֶר תִּרְחָק וְנָקִי וְצַדִּיק אַל־תַּהֲרֹג כִּי לֹא־אַצְדִּיק
רָשָׁע: וְשֹׁחַד לֹא תִקָּח כִּי הַשֹּׁחַד יְעַוֵּר פִּקְחִים וִיסַלֵּף דִּבְרֵי
צַדִּיקִים: וְגֵר לֹא תִלְחָץ וְאַתֶּם יְדַעְתֶּם אֶת־נֶפֶשׁ הַגֵּר כִּי־
גֵרִים הֱיִיתֶם בְּאֶרֶץ מִצְרָיִם: וְשֵׁשׁ שָׁנִים תִּזְרַע אֶת־אַרְצֶךָ
וְאָסַפְתָּ אֶת־תְּבוּאָתָהּ: וְהַשְּׁבִיעִת תִּשְׁמְטֶנָּה וּנְטַשְׁתָּהּ
וְאָכְלוּ אֶבְיֹנֵי עַמֶּךָ וְיִתְרָם תֹּאכַל חַיַּת הַשָּׂדֶה כֵּן־תַּעֲשֶׂה
לְכַרְמְךָ לְזֵיתֶךָ: שֵׁשֶׁת יָמִים תַּעֲשֶׂה מַעֲשֶׂיךָ וּבַיּוֹם הַשְּׁבִיעִי
תִּשְׁבֹּת לְמַעַן יָנוּחַ שׁוֹרְךָ וַחֲמֹרֶךָ וְיִנָּפֵשׁ בֶּן־אֲמָתְךָ וְהַגֵּר:
וּבְכֹל אֲשֶׁר־אָמַרְתִּי אֲלֵיכֶם תִּשָּׁמֵרוּ וְשֵׁם אֱלֹהִים אֲחֵרִים
לֹא תַזְכִּירוּ לֹא יִשָּׁמַע עַל־פִּיךָ: שָׁלֹשׁ רְגָלִים תָּחֹג לִי בַּשָּׁנָה:
אֶת־חַג הַמַּצּוֹת תִּשְׁמֹר שִׁבְעַת יָמִים תֹּאכַל מַצּוֹת כַּאֲשֶׁר
צִוִּיתִךָ לְמוֹעֵד חֹדֶשׁ הָאָבִיב כִּי־בוֹ יָצָאתָ מִמִּצְרָיִם וְלֹא־יֵרָאוּ
פָנַי רֵיקָם: וְחַג הַקָּצִיר בִּכּוּרֵי מַעֲשֶׂיךָ אֲשֶׁר תִּזְרַע בַּשָּׂדֶה
וְחַג הָאָסִף בְּצֵאת הַשָּׁנָה בְּאָסְפְּךָ אֶת־מַעֲשֶׂיךָ מִן־הַשָּׂדֶה:
שָׁלֹשׁ פְּעָמִים בַּשָּׁנָה יֵרָאֶה כָּל־זְכוּרְךָ אֶל־פְּנֵי הָאָדֹן יְהוָה:
לֹא־תִזְבַּח עַל־חָמֵץ דַּם־זִבְחִי וְלֹא־יָלִין חֵלֶב־חַגִּי עַד־בֹּקֶר:
רֵאשִׁית בִּכּוּרֵי אַדְמָתְךָ תָּבִיא בֵּית יְהוָה אֱלֹהֶיךָ לֹא־תְבַשֵּׁל
גְּדִי בַּחֲלֵב אִמּוֹ:

THIRD ALIYA: vv. 5–19
"You have known the soul
of the stranger" – how do
we know that? And how
has this affected us
as a nation?

For ספר תורה *from the second* read וְהִקְרַבְתֶּם רביעי *(page 764).*

קריאה ליום ג׳ ליום שלישי דחול המועד
THIRD DAY OF ḤOL HAMO'ED
(ד׳ בארץ ישראל)
(FOURTH DAY IN ISRAEL)

If the third day of חול המועד פסח *falls on a Monday, the* קריאת
התורה *for the second day of* חול המועד *is read* (*page 765*).

FIRST ALIYA: vv. 1–3
These second stone
tablets were carved by
Moshe himself, with
God inscribing them
with the command-
ments, something
that was not the case
for the first pair that
were broken. What do
you think the message
of this is?

שמות
לד:א-כט

וַיֹּאמֶר יְהוָה אֶל־מֹשֶׁה פְּסָל־לְךָ שְׁנֵי־לֻחֹת אֲבָנִים כָּרִאשֹׁנִים
וְכָתַבְתִּי עַל־הַלֻּחֹת אֶת־הַדְּבָרִים אֲשֶׁר הָיוּ עַל־הַלֻּחֹת
הָרִאשֹׁנִים אֲשֶׁר שִׁבַּרְתָּ: וֶהְיֵה נָכוֹן לַבֹּקֶר וְעָלִיתָ בַבֹּקֶר
אֶל־הַר סִינַי וְנִצַּבְתָּ לִי שָׁם עַל־רֹאשׁ הָהָר: וְאִישׁ לֹא־
יַעֲלֶה עִמָּךְ וְגַם־אִישׁ אַל־יֵרָא בְּכָל־הָהָר גַּם־הַצֹּאן וְהַבָּקָר
אַל־יִרְעוּ אֶל־מוּל הָהָר הַהוּא: *וַיִּפְסֹל שְׁנֵי־לֻחֹת אֲבָנִים

SECOND ALIYA: vv. 4–10
Which word in this *aliya*
has the same root as the
word for womb (רֶחֶם)?
What lesson do you think
can be learned about God
from this connection?

לוי

כָּרִאשֹׁנִים וַיַּשְׁכֵּם מֹשֶׁה בַבֹּקֶר וַיַּעַל אֶל־הַר סִינַי כַּאֲשֶׁר צִוָּה
יְהוָה אֹתוֹ וַיִּקַּח בְּיָדוֹ שְׁנֵי לֻחֹת אֲבָנִים: וַיֵּרֶד יְהוָה בֶּעָנָן
וַיִּתְיַצֵּב עִמּוֹ שָׁם וַיִּקְרָא בְשֵׁם יְהוָה: וַיַּעֲבֹר יְהוָה ׀ עַל־פָּנָיו
וַיִּקְרָא יְהוָה ׀ יְהוָה אֵל רַחוּם וְחַנּוּן אֶרֶךְ אַפַּיִם וְרַב־חֶסֶד
וֶאֱמֶת: נֹצֵר חֶסֶד לָאֲלָפִים נֹשֵׂא עָוֹן וָפֶשַׁע וְחַטָּאָה וְנַקֵּה
לֹא יְנַקֶּה פֹּקֵד ׀ עֲוֹן אָבוֹת עַל־בָּנִים וְעַל־בְּנֵי בָנִים עַל־
שִׁלֵּשִׁים וְעַל־רִבֵּעִים: וַיְמַהֵר מֹשֶׁה וַיִּקֹּד אַרְצָה וַיִּשְׁתָּחוּ:
וַיֹּאמֶר אִם־נָא מָצָאתִי חֵן בְּעֵינֶיךָ אֲדֹנָי יֵלֶךְ־נָא אֲדֹנָי
בְּקִרְבֵּנוּ כִּי עַם־קְשֵׁה־עֹרֶף הוּא וְסָלַחְתָּ לַעֲוֹנֵנוּ וּלְחַטָּאתֵנוּ
וּנְחַלְתָּנוּ: וַיֹּאמֶר הִנֵּה אָנֹכִי כֹּרֵת בְּרִית נֶגֶד כָּל־עַמְּךָ
אֶעֱשֶׂה נִפְלָאֹת אֲשֶׁר לֹא־נִבְרְאוּ בְכָל־הָאָרֶץ וּבְכָל־הַגּוֹיִם

THIRD ALIYA:
vv. 11–26
What is the under-
lying theme behind all
of these mitzvot and
why do you think they
are found here (directly
after Moshe received the
tablets on Mount Sinai)?

שלישי

וְרָאָה כָל־הָעָם אֲשֶׁר־אַתָּה בְקִרְבּוֹ אֶת־מַעֲשֵׂה יְהוָה כִּי־
נוֹרָא הוּא אֲשֶׁר אֲנִי עֹשֶׂה עִמָּךְ: *שְׁמָר־לְךָ אֵת אֲשֶׁר אָנֹכִי
מְצַוְּךָ הַיּוֹם הִנְנִי גֹרֵשׁ מִפָּנֶיךָ אֶת־הָאֱמֹרִי וְהַכְּנַעֲנִי וְהַחִתִּי
וְהַפְּרִזִּי וְהַחִוִּי וְהַיְבוּסִי: הִשָּׁמֶר לְךָ פֶּן־תִּכְרֹת בְּרִית לְיוֹשֵׁב
הָאָרֶץ אֲשֶׁר אַתָּה בָּא עָלֶיהָ פֶּן־יִהְיֶה לְמוֹקֵשׁ בְּקִרְבֶּךָ:
כִּי אֶת־מִזְבְּחֹתָם תִּתֹּצוּן וְאֶת־מַצֵּבֹתָם תְּשַׁבֵּרוּן וְאֶת־

אַשֶׁרָיו תַּכְרָעוּן: כִּי לֹא תִּשְׁתַּחֲוֶה לְאֵל אַחֵר כִּי יהוה קַנָּא
שְׁמוֹ אֵל קַנָּא הוּא: פֶּן־תִּכְרֹת בְּרִית לְיוֹשֵׁב הָאָרֶץ וְזָנוּ ׀
אַחֲרֵי אֱלֹהֵיהֶם וְזָבְחוּ לֵאלֹהֵיהֶם וְקָרָא לְךָ וְאָכַלְתָּ מִזִּבְחוֹ:
וְלָקַחְתָּ מִבְּנֹתָיו לְבָנֶיךָ וְזָנוּ בְנֹתָיו אַחֲרֵי אֱלֹהֵיהֶן וְהִזְנוּ
אֶת־בָּנֶיךָ אַחֲרֵי אֱלֹהֵיהֶן: אֱלֹהֵי מַסֵּכָה לֹא תַעֲשֶׂה־לָּךְ:
אֶת־חַג הַמַּצּוֹת תִּשְׁמֹר שִׁבְעַת יָמִים תֹּאכַל מַצּוֹת אֲשֶׁר
צִוִּיתִךָ לְמוֹעֵד חֹדֶשׁ הָאָבִיב כִּי בְּחֹדֶשׁ הָאָבִיב יָצָאתָ
מִמִּצְרָיִם: כָּל־פֶּטֶר רֶחֶם לִי וְכָל־מִקְנְךָ תִּזָּכָר פֶּטֶר שׁוֹר
וָשֶׂה: וּפֶטֶר חֲמוֹר תִּפְדֶּה בְשֶׂה וְאִם־לֹא תִפְדֶּה וַעֲרַפְתּוֹ
כֹּל בְּכוֹר בָּנֶיךָ תִּפְדֶּה וְלֹא־יֵרָאוּ פָנַי רֵיקָם: שֵׁשֶׁת יָמִים
תַּעֲבֹד וּבַיּוֹם הַשְּׁבִיעִי תִּשְׁבֹּת בֶּחָרִישׁ וּבַקָּצִיר תִּשְׁבֹּת:
וְחַג שָׁבֻעֹת תַּעֲשֶׂה לְךָ בִּכּוּרֵי קְצִיר חִטִּים וְחַג הָאָסִיף
תְּקוּפַת הַשָּׁנָה: שָׁלֹשׁ פְּעָמִים בַּשָּׁנָה יֵרָאֶה כָּל־זְכוּרְךָ אֶת־
פְּנֵי הָאָדֹן ׀ יהוה אֱלֹהֵי יִשְׂרָאֵל: כִּי־אוֹרִישׁ גּוֹיִם מִפָּנֶיךָ
וְהִרְחַבְתִּי אֶת־גְּבֻלֶךָ וְלֹא־יַחְמֹד אִישׁ אֶת־אַרְצְךָ בַּעֲלֹתְךָ
לֵרָאוֹת אֶת־פְּנֵי יהוה אֱלֹהֶיךָ שָׁלֹשׁ פְּעָמִים בַּשָּׁנָה: לֹא־
תִשְׁחַט עַל־חָמֵץ דַּם־זִבְחִי וְלֹא־יָלִין לַבֹּקֶר זֶבַח חַג הַפָּסַח:
רֵאשִׁית בִּכּוּרֵי אַדְמָתְךָ תָּבִיא בֵּית יהוה אֱלֹהֶיךָ לֹא־תְבַשֵּׁל
גְּדִי בַּחֲלֵב אִמּוֹ:

For רביעי *read* וְהִקְרַבְתֶּם *from the second* ספר תורה (*page* 764).

קריאה ליום ד׳ דחול המועד פסח (ה׳ בארץ ישראל)

קריאה ליום רביעי דחול המועד (ה׳ בארץ ישראל)
FOURTH DAY OF ḤOL HAMO'ED
(FIFTH DAY IN ISRAEL)

במדבר
ט:א-יד

וַיְדַבֵּר יהוה אֶל־מֹשֶׁה בְמִדְבַּר־סִינַי בַּשָּׁנָה הַשֵּׁנִית לְצֵאתָם
מֵאֶרֶץ מִצְרַיִם בַּחֹדֶשׁ הָרִאשׁוֹן לֵאמֹר: וְיַעֲשׂוּ בְנֵי־יִשְׂרָאֵל
אֶת־הַפָּסַח בְּמוֹעֲדוֹ: בְּאַרְבָּעָה עָשָׂר־יוֹם בַּחֹדֶשׁ הַזֶּה בֵּין
הָעַרְבַּיִם תַּעֲשׂוּ אֹתוֹ בְּמֹעֲדוֹ כְּכָל־חֻקֹּתָיו וּכְכָל־מִשְׁפָּטָיו

FIRST ALIYA:
vv. 1–5
Why do you think
the Torah stresses
that the mitzva of
Korban Pesaḥ must be
"at its appointed time"?

תֵּעֲשׂוּ אֹתוֹ: וַיְדַבֵּר מֹשֶׁה אֶל־בְּנֵי יִשְׂרָאֵל לַעֲשֹׂת הַפָּסַח:
וַיַּעֲשׂוּ אֶת־הַפֶּסַח בָּרִאשׁוֹן בְּאַרְבָּעָה עָשָׂר יוֹם לַחֹדֶשׁ בֵּין
הָעַרְבַּיִם בְּמִדְבַּר סִינָי כְּכֹל אֲשֶׁר צִוָּה יְהוָֹה אֶת־מֹשֶׁה כֵּן
עָשׂוּ בְּנֵי יִשְׂרָאֵל: וַיְהִי אֲנָשִׁים אֲשֶׁר הָיוּ טְמֵאִים לְנֶפֶשׁ
אָדָם וְלֹא־יָכְלוּ לַעֲשֹׂת־הַפֶּסַח בַּיּוֹם הַהוּא וַיִּקְרְבוּ לִפְנֵי
מֹשֶׁה וְלִפְנֵי אַהֲרֹן בַּיּוֹם הַהוּא: וַיֹּאמְרוּ הָאֲנָשִׁים הָהֵמָּה
אֵלָיו אֲנַחְנוּ טְמֵאִים לְנֶפֶשׁ אָדָם לָמָּה נִגָּרַע לְבִלְתִּי הַקְרִב
אֶת־קָרְבַּן יְהוָֹה בְּמֹעֲדוֹ בְּתוֹךְ בְּנֵי יִשְׂרָאֵל: וַיֹּאמֶר אֲלֵהֶם
מֹשֶׁה עִמְדוּ וְאֶשְׁמְעָה מַה־יְצַוֶּה יְהוָֹה לָכֶם:

שְׁלִישִׁי
וַיְדַבֵּר יְהוָֹה אֶל־מֹשֶׁה לֵּאמֹר: דַּבֵּר אֶל־בְּנֵי יִשְׂרָאֵל לֵאמֹר
אִישׁ אִישׁ כִּי־יִהְיֶה טָמֵא ׀ לָנֶפֶשׁ אוֹ בְדֶרֶךְ רְחֹקָה לָכֶם אוֹ
לְדֹרֹתֵיכֶם וְעָשָׂה פֶסַח לַיהוָֹה: בַּחֹדֶשׁ הַשֵּׁנִי בְּאַרְבָּעָה עָשָׂר
יוֹם בֵּין הָעַרְבַּיִם יַעֲשׂוּ אֹתוֹ עַל־מַצּוֹת וּמְרֹרִים יֹאכְלֻהוּ:
לֹא־יַשְׁאִירוּ מִמֶּנּוּ עַד־בֹּקֶר וְעֶצֶם לֹא יִשְׁבְּרוּ־בוֹ כְּכָל־חֻקַּת
הַפֶּסַח יַעֲשׂוּ אֹתוֹ: וְהָאִישׁ אֲשֶׁר־הוּא טָהוֹר וּבְדֶרֶךְ לֹא־
הָיָה וְחָדַל לַעֲשׂוֹת הַפֶּסַח וְנִכְרְתָה הַנֶּפֶשׁ הַהִוא מֵעַמֶּיהָ
כִּי ׀ קָרְבַּן יְהוָֹה לֹא הִקְרִיב בְּמֹעֲדוֹ חֶטְאוֹ יִשָּׂא הָאִישׁ
הַהוּא: וְכִי־יָגוּר אִתְּכֶם גֵּר וְעָשָׂה פֶסַח לַיהוָֹה כְּחֻקַּת הַפֶּסַח
וּכְמִשְׁפָּטוֹ כֵּן יַעֲשֶׂה חֻקָּה אַחַת יִהְיֶה לָכֶם וְלַגֵּר וּלְאֶזְרַח
הָאָרֶץ:

For רביעי *read* וְהִקְרַבְתֶּם *from the second* ספר תורה *(page 764)*.

SECOND ALIYA: vv. 6–8 לוי
What leadership qualities can we see Moshe demonstrate in this section?

THIRD ALIYA: vv. 9–14
Why would you think a convert to Judaism would not have to bring this sacrifice, necessitating the Torah to clarify they were also required to do this mitzva?

קריאה לחול המועד סוכות
ḤOL HAMO'ED SUKKOT

קריאה ליום ראשון דחול המועד סוכות
FIRST DAY OF ḤOL HAMO'ED SUKKOT

In ארץ ישראל, *the first three verses,* וּבַיּוֹם הַשֵּׁנִי *through* וְנִסְכֵּיהֶם, *are read for each of the four* עליות.

במדבר
כט:יז–כה

וּבַיּוֹם הַשֵּׁנִי פָּרִים בְּנֵי־בָקָר שְׁנֵים עָשָׂר אֵילִם שְׁנָיִם
כְּבָשִׂים בְּנֵי־שָׁנָה אַרְבָּעָה עָשָׂר תְּמִימִם: וּמִנְחָתָם
וְנִסְכֵּיהֶם לַפָּרִים לָאֵילִם וְלַכְּבָשִׂים בְּמִסְפָּרָם כַּמִּשְׁפָּט:
וּשְׂעִיר־עִזִּים אֶחָד חַטָּאת מִלְּבַד עֹלַת הַתָּמִיד וּמִנְחָתָהּ
וְנִסְכֵּיהֶם:

לוי

*וּבַיּוֹם הַשְּׁלִישִׁי פָּרִים עַשְׁתֵּי־עָשָׂר
אֵילִם שְׁנָיִם כְּבָשִׂים בְּנֵי־שָׁנָה אַרְבָּעָה עָשָׂר תְּמִימִם:
וּמִנְחָתָם וְנִסְכֵּיהֶם לַפָּרִים לָאֵילִם וְלַכְּבָשִׂים בְּמִסְפָּרָם
כַּמִּשְׁפָּט: וּשְׂעִיר חַטָּאת אֶחָד מִלְּבַד עֹלַת הַתָּמִיד וּמִנְחָתָהּ
וְנִסְכָּהּ:

שלישי

*וּבַיּוֹם הָרְבִיעִי פָּרִים עֲשָׂרָה אֵילִם
שְׁנָיִם כְּבָשִׂים בְּנֵי־שָׁנָה אַרְבָּעָה עָשָׂר תְּמִימִם: מִנְחָתָם
וְנִסְכֵּיהֶם לַפָּרִים לָאֵילִם וְלַכְּבָשִׂים בְּמִסְפָּרָם כַּמִּשְׁפָּט:
וּשְׂעִיר־עִזִּים אֶחָד חַטָּאת מִלְּבַד עֹלַת הַתָּמִיד מִנְחָתָהּ
וְנִסְכָּהּ:

רביעי

וּבַיּוֹם הַשֵּׁנִי פָּרִים בְּנֵי־בָקָר שְׁנֵים עָשָׂר אֵילִם שְׁנָיִם
כְּבָשִׂים בְּנֵי־שָׁנָה אַרְבָּעָה עָשָׂר תְּמִימִם: וּמִנְחָתָם
וְנִסְכֵּיהֶם לַפָּרִים לָאֵילִם וְלַכְּבָשִׂים בְּמִסְפָּרָם כַּמִּשְׁפָּט:
וּשְׂעִיר־עִזִּים אֶחָד חַטָּאת מִלְּבַד עֹלַת הַתָּמִיד וּמִנְחָתָהּ
וְנִסְכֵּיהֶם: וּבַיּוֹם הַשְּׁלִישִׁי פָּרִים עַשְׁתֵּי־עָשָׂר
אֵילִם שְׁנָיִם כְּבָשִׂים בְּנֵי־שָׁנָה אַרְבָּעָה עָשָׂר תְּמִימִם:
וּמִנְחָתָם וְנִסְכֵּיהֶם לַפָּרִים לָאֵילִם וְלַכְּבָשִׂים בְּמִסְפָּרָם
כַּמִּשְׁפָּט: וּשְׂעִיר חַטָּאת אֶחָד מִלְּבַד עֹלַת הַתָּמִיד וּמִנְחָתָהּ
וְנִסְכָּהּ:

FIRST DAY
ḤOL HAMO'ED:
BEMIDBAR 29:17–25
The word וְנִסְכֵּיהֶם has
an extra letter.
What is it? Put it
aside until verse 33.

קריאה ליום שני דחול המועד סוכות
SECOND DAY OF HOL HAMO'ED SUKKOT

In ארץ ישראל, *the first three verses,* ובַיּוֹם הַשְּׁלִישִׁי through וּמִנְחָתָהּ וְנִסְכָּהּ, *are read for each of the four* עֲלִיּוֹת.

במדבר
כט:כ-כח

וּבַיּוֹם הַשְּׁלִישִׁי פָּרִים עַשְׁתֵּי־עָשָׂר אֵילִם שְׁנָיִם כְּבָשִׂים בְּנֵי־שָׁנָה אַרְבָּעָה עָשָׂר תְּמִימִם: וּמִנְחָתָם וְנִסְכֵּיהֶם לַפָּרִים לָאֵילִם וְלַכְּבָשִׂים בְּמִסְפָּרָם כַּמִּשְׁפָּט: וּשְׂעִיר חַטָּאת אֶחָד

לוי
מִלְּבַד עֹלַת הַתָּמִיד וּמִנְחָתָהּ וְנִסְכָּהּ: *וּבַיּוֹם הָרְבִיעִי פָּרִים עֲשָׂרָה אֵילִם שְׁנָיִם כְּבָשִׂים בְּנֵי־שָׁנָה אַרְבָּעָה עָשָׂר תְּמִימִם: מִנְחָתָם וְנִסְכֵּיהֶם לַפָּרִים לָאֵילִם וְלַכְּבָשִׂים בְּמִסְפָּרָם כַּמִּשְׁפָּט: וּשְׂעִיר־עִזִּים אֶחָד חַטָּאת מִלְּבַד עֹלַת

שלישי
הַתָּמִיד מִנְחָתָהּ וְנִסְכָּהּ: *וּבַיּוֹם הַחֲמִישִׁי פָּרִים תִּשְׁעָה אֵילִם שְׁנָיִם כְּבָשִׂים בְּנֵי־שָׁנָה אַרְבָּעָה עָשָׂר תְּמִימִם: וּמִנְחָתָם וְנִסְכֵּיהֶם לַפָּרִים לָאֵילִם וְלַכְּבָשִׂים בְּמִסְפָּרָם כַּמִּשְׁפָּט: וּשְׂעִיר חַטָּאת אֶחָד מִלְּבַד עֹלַת הַתָּמִיד וּמִנְחָתָהּ וְנִסְכָּהּ:

רביעי
וּבַיּוֹם הַשְּׁלִישִׁי פָּרִים עַשְׁתֵּי־עָשָׂר אֵילִם שְׁנָיִם כְּבָשִׂים בְּנֵי־שָׁנָה אַרְבָּעָה עָשָׂר תְּמִימִם: וּמִנְחָתָם וְנִסְכֵּיהֶם לַפָּרִים לָאֵילִם וְלַכְּבָשִׂים בְּמִסְפָּרָם כַּמִּשְׁפָּט: וּשְׂעִיר חַטָּאת אֶחָד מִלְּבַד עֹלַת הַתָּמִיד וּמִנְחָתָהּ וְנִסְכָּהּ:

וּבַיּוֹם
הָרְבִיעִי פָּרִים עֲשָׂרָה אֵילִם שְׁנָיִם כְּבָשִׂים בְּנֵי־שָׁנָה אַרְבָּעָה עָשָׂר תְּמִימִם: מִנְחָתָם וְנִסְכֵּיהֶם לַפָּרִים לָאֵילִם וְלַכְּבָשִׂים בְּמִסְפָּרָם כַּמִּשְׁפָּט: וּשְׂעִיר־עִזִּים אֶחָד חַטָּאת מִלְּבַד עֹלַת הַתָּמִיד מִנְחָתָהּ וְנִסְכָּהּ:

קריאה ליום שלישי דחול המועד סוכות
THIRD DAY OF HOL HAMO'ED SUKKOT

In ארץ ישראל, *the first three verses,* ובַיּוֹם הָרְבִיעִי through מִנְחָתָהּ וְנִסְכָּהּ, *are read for each of the four* עֲלִיּוֹת.

במדבר
כט:כג-לא

וּבַיּוֹם הָרְבִיעִי פָּרִים עֲשָׂרָה אֵילִם שְׁנָיִם כְּבָשִׂים בְּנֵי־שָׁנָה אַרְבָּעָה עָשָׂר תְּמִימִם: מִנְחָתָם וְנִסְכֵּיהֶם לַפָּרִים לָאֵילִם

SECOND DAY
HOL HAMO'ED:
BEMIDBAR 29:20–28
On the first day of Sukkot, 13 bulls were sacrificed. How many bulls were sacrificed on each day thereafter?

THIRD DAY
HOL HAMO'ED:
BEMIDBAR 29:23–31
The word וְנִסְכֵּיהֶ has an extra letter. What is it? Put it aside until verse 33.

וְלִכְבָשִׂים בְּמִסְפָּרָם כַּמִּשְׁפָּט: וּשְׂעִיר־עִזִּים אֶחָד חַטָּאת

לֵוִי   מִלְּבַד עֹלַת הַתָּמִיד מִנְחָתָהּ וְנִסְכָּהּ:   *וּבַיּוֹם

הַחֲמִישִׁי פָּרִים תִּשְׁעָה אֵילִם שְׁנָיִם כְּבָשִׂים בְּנֵי־שָׁנָה

אַרְבָּעָה עָשָׂר תְּמִימִם: וּמִנְחָתָם וְנִסְכֵּיהֶם לַפָּרִים לָאֵילִם

וְלִכְבָשִׂים בְּמִסְפָּרָם כַּמִּשְׁפָּט: וּשְׂעִיר חַטָּאת אֶחָד מִלְּבַד

שְׁלִישִׁי   עֹלַת הַתָּמִיד וּמִנְחָתָהּ וְנִסְכָּהּ:   *וּבַיּוֹם הַשִּׁשִּׁי

פָּרִים שְׁמֹנָה אֵילִם שְׁנָיִם כְּבָשִׂים בְּנֵי־שָׁנָה אַרְבָּעָה עָשָׂר

תְּמִימִם: וּמִנְחָתָם וְנִסְכֵּיהֶם לַפָּרִים לָאֵילִם וְלַכְּבָשִׂים

בְּמִסְפָּרָם כַּמִּשְׁפָּט: וּשְׂעִיר חַטָּאת אֶחָד מִלְּבַד עֹלַת

הַתָּמִיד מִנְחָתָהּ וְנִסְכָּהּ:

רְבִיעִי   וּבַיּוֹם הָרְבִיעִי פָּרִים עֲשָׂרָה אֵילִם שְׁנָיִם כְּבָשִׂים בְּנֵי־שָׁנָה

אַרְבָּעָה עָשָׂר תְּמִימִם: מִנְחָתָם וְנִסְכֵּיהֶם לַפָּרִים לָאֵילִם

וְלִכְבָשִׂים בְּמִסְפָּרָם כַּמִּשְׁפָּט: וּשְׂעִיר־עִזִּים אֶחָד חַטָּאת

מִלְּבַד עֹלַת הַתָּמִיד מִנְחָתָהּ וְנִסְכָּהּ:   וּבַיּוֹם

הַחֲמִישִׁי פָּרִים תִּשְׁעָה אֵילִם שְׁנָיִם כְּבָשִׂים בְּנֵי־שָׁנָה

אַרְבָּעָה עָשָׂר תְּמִימִם: וּמִנְחָתָם וְנִסְכֵּיהֶם לַפָּרִים לָאֵילִם

וְלִכְבָשִׂים בְּמִסְפָּרָם כַּמִּשְׁפָּט: וּשְׂעִיר חַטָּאת אֶחָד מִלְּבַד

עֹלַת הַתָּמִיד וּמִנְחָתָהּ וְנִסְכָּהּ:

קריאה ליום רביעי דחול המועד סוכות

FOURTH DAY OF ḤOL HAMO'ED SUKKOT

In ארץ ישראל, *the first three verses,* וּבַיּוֹם הַחֲמִישִׁי *through* וּמִנְחָתָהּ וְנִסְכָּהּ *are read for each of the four* עֲלִיּוֹת.

במדבר   וּבַיּוֹם הַחֲמִישִׁי פָּרִים תִּשְׁעָה אֵילִם שְׁנָיִם כְּבָשִׂים בְּנֵי־
כט:כו־לד   שָׁנָה אַרְבָּעָה עָשָׂר תְּמִימִם: וּמִנְחָתָם וְנִסְכֵּיהֶם לַפָּרִים

לָאֵילִם וְלִכְבָשִׂים בְּמִסְפָּרָם כַּמִּשְׁפָּט: וּשְׂעִיר חַטָּאת אֶחָד

לֵוִי   מִלְּבַד עֹלַת הַתָּמִיד מִנְחָתָהּ וְנִסְכָּהּ:   *וּבַיּוֹם

הַשִּׁשִּׁי פָּרִים שְׁמֹנָה אֵילִם שְׁנָיִם כְּבָשִׂים בְּנֵי־שָׁנָה אַרְבָּעָה

עָשָׂר תְּמִימִם: וּמִנְחָתָם וְנִסְכֵּיהֶם לַפָּרִים לָאֵילִם וְלִכְבָשִׂים

The word כַּמִּשְׁפָּט has an extra letter. What is it? Now put it together with the other extra letters and what do you get? What is the connection between this word and Sukkot?

בְּמִסְפָּרָם כַּמִּשְׁפָּט: וּשְׂעִיר חַטָּאת אֶחָד מִלְּבַד עֹלַת הַתָּמִיד
מִנְחָתָהּ וְנִסְכָּהּ: ‏*וּבַיּוֹם הַשְּׁבִיעִי פָּרִים שִׁבְעָה שלישי
אֵילִם שְׁנָיִם כְּבָשִׂים בְּנֵי־שָׁנָה אַרְבָּעָה עָשָׂר תְּמִימִם:
וּמִנְחָתָם וְנִסְכֵּהֶם לַפָּרִים לָאֵילִם וְלַכְּבָשִׂים בְּמִסְפָּרָם
כְּמִשְׁפָּטָם: וּשְׂעִיר חַטָּאת אֶחָד מִלְּבַד עֹלַת הַתָּמִיד
מִנְחָתָהּ וְנִסְכָּהּ:

וּבַיּוֹם הַחֲמִישִׁי פָּרִים תִּשְׁעָה אֵילִם שְׁנָיִם כְּבָשִׂים בְּנֵי־שָׁנָה רביעי
אַרְבָּעָה עָשָׂר תְּמִימִם: וּמִנְחָתָם וְנִסְכֵּיהֶם לַפָּרִים לָאֵילִם
וְלַכְּבָשִׂים בְּמִסְפָּרָם כַּמִּשְׁפָּט: וּשְׂעִיר חַטָּאת אֶחָד מִלְּבַד
עֹלַת הַתָּמִיד וּמִנְחָתָהּ וְנִסְכָּהּ: ‏וּבַיּוֹם הַשִּׁשִּׁי
פָּרִים שְׁמֹנָה אֵילִם שְׁנָיִם כְּבָשִׂים בְּנֵי־שָׁנָה אַרְבָּעָה עָשָׂר
תְּמִימִם: וּמִנְחָתָם וְנִסְכֵּיהֶם לַפָּרִים לָאֵילִם וְלַכְּבָשִׂים
בְּמִסְפָּרָם כַּמִּשְׁפָּט: וּשְׂעִיר חַטָּאת אֶחָד מִלְּבַד עֹלַת הַתָּמִיד
מִנְחָתָהּ וְנִסְכָּהּ:

קריאה ליום החמישי דחול המועד סוכות בארץ ישראל

FIFTH DAY OF ḤOL HAMO'ED IN ISRAEL

In ארץ ישראל, *the following is read for each of the four* עליות.

וּבַיּוֹם הַשִּׁשִּׁי פָּרִים שְׁמֹנָה אֵילִם שְׁנָיִם כְּבָשִׂים בְּנֵי־שָׁנָה
אַרְבָּעָה עָשָׂר תְּמִימִם: וּמִנְחָתָם וְנִסְכֵּיהֶם לַפָּרִים לָאֵילִם
וְלַכְּבָשִׂים בְּמִסְפָּרָם כַּמִּשְׁפָּט: וּשְׂעִיר חַטָּאת אֶחָד מִלְּבַד
עֹלַת הַתָּמִיד מִנְחָתָהּ וְנִסְכָּהּ:

קריאה להושענא רבה

HOSHANA RABA

In ארץ ישראל, *the three verses from* וּבַיּוֹם הַשְּׁבִיעִי *through* וּמִנְחָתָהּ וְנִסְכָּהּ
are read for each of the four עליות.

וּבַיּוֹם הַחֲמִישִׁי פָּרִים תִּשְׁעָה אֵילִם שְׁנָיִם כְּבָשִׂים בְּנֵי־
שָׁנָה אַרְבָּעָה עָשָׂר תְּמִימִם: וּמִנְחָתָם וְנִסְכֵּיהֶם לַפָּרִים

FIFTH DAY ḤOL HAMO'ED
IN ISRAEL:
BEMIDBAR 29:29–31
How many bulls were
sacrificed altogether
over Sukkot? What
significance does that
number (and its
multiples) have
in Jewish life?
How many can
you think of?

במדבר
כט:כט–לא

HOSHANA RABA:
BEMIDBAR 29:26–34
Ḥazal say this corres-
ponds to the number
of non-Jewish nations
of the world. What
would be the
connection to the
themes of Sukkot?

במדבר
כט:כו–לד

לָאֵילִם וְלַכְּבָשִׂים בְּמִסְפָּרָם כַּמִּשְׁפָּט: וּשְׂעִיר חַטָּאת אֶחָד

לוי מִלְּבַד עֹלַת הַתָּמִיד וּמִנְחָתָהּ וְנִסְכָּהּ: ⁕וּבַיּוֹם

הַשִּׁשִּׁי פָּרִים שְׁמֹנָה אֵילִם שְׁנָיִם כְּבָשִׂים בְּנֵי־שָׁנָה אַרְבָּעָה

עָשָׂר תְּמִימִם: וּמִנְחָתָם וְנִסְכֵּיהֶם לַפָּרִים לָאֵילִם וְלַכְּבָשִׂים

בְּמִסְפָּרָם כַּמִּשְׁפָּט: וּשְׂעִיר חַטָּאת אֶחָד מִלְּבַד עֹלַת הַתָּמִיד

שלישי מִנְחָתָהּ וְנִסְכָּהּ: ⁕וּבַיּוֹם הַשְּׁבִיעִי פָּרִים שִׁבְעָה

אֵילִם שְׁנָיִם כְּבָשִׂים בְּנֵי־שָׁנָה אַרְבָּעָה עָשָׂר תְּמִימִם: וּמִנְחָתָם

וְנִסְכֵּהֶם לַפָּרִים לָאֵילִם וְלַכְּבָשִׂים בְּמִסְפָּרָם כְּמִשְׁפָּטָם:

וּשְׂעִיר חַטָּאת אֶחָד מִלְּבַד עֹלַת הַתָּמִיד מִנְחָתָהּ וְנִסְכָּהּ:

רביעי וּבַיּוֹם הַשִּׁשִּׁי פָּרִים שְׁמֹנָה אֵילִם שְׁנַיִם כְּבָשִׂים בְּנֵי־שָׁנָה

אַרְבָּעָה עָשָׂר תְּמִימִם: וּמִנְחָתָם וְנִסְכֵּיהֶם לַפָּרִים לָאֵילִם

וְלַכְּבָשִׂים בְּמִסְפָּרָם כַּמִּשְׁפָּט: וּשְׂעִיר חַטָּאת אֶחָד מִלְּבַד

עֹלַת הַתָּמִיד מִנְחָתָהּ וְנִסְכָּהּ: וּבַיּוֹם הַשְּׁבִיעִי

פָּרִים שִׁבְעָה אֵילִם שְׁנַיִם כְּבָשִׂים בְּנֵי־שָׁנָה אַרְבָּעָה עָשָׂר

תְּמִימִם: וּמִנְחָתָם וְנִסְכֵּהֶם לַפָּרִים לָאֵילִם וְלַכְּבָשִׂים

בְּמִסְפָּרָם כְּמִשְׁפָּטָם: וּשְׂעִיר חַטָּאת אֶחָד מִלְּבַד עֹלַת

הַתָּמִיד מִנְחָתָהּ וְנִסְכָּהּ:

תהלים

TEHILLIM

תהלים

Before saying Tehillim it is customary to recite:

יְהִי רָצוֹן מִלְּפָנֶיךָ, יהוה אֱלֹהֵינוּ וֵאלֹהֵי אֲבוֹתֵינוּ, הַבּוֹחֵר בְּדָוִד עַבְדּוֹ וּבְזַרְעוֹ אַחֲרָיו, וְהַבּוֹחֵר בְּשִׁירוֹת וְתִשְׁבָּחוֹת, שֶׁתֵּפֶן בְּרַחֲמִים אֶל קְרִיאַת מִזְמוֹרֵי תְהִלִּים שֶׁאֶקְרָא כְּאִלּוּ אֲמָרָם דָּוִד הַמֶּלֶךְ עָלָיו הַשָּׁלוֹם בְּעַצְמוֹ, זְכוּתוֹ תָּגֵן עָלֵינוּ, וְתַעֲמֹד לָנוּ זְכוּת פְּסוּקֵי תְהִלִּים וּזְכוּת תֵּבוֹתֵיהֶם וְאוֹתִיּוֹתֵיהֶם וּנְקֻדּוֹתֵיהֶם וְטַעֲמֵיהֶם וְהַשֵּׁמוֹת הַיּוֹצְאִים מֵהֶם מֵרָאשֵׁי תֵבוֹת וּמִסּוֹפֵי תֵבוֹת לְכַפֵּר פְּשָׁעֵינוּ וַעֲוֹנוֹתֵינוּ וְחַטֹּאתֵינוּ, וּלְזַמֵּר עָרִיצִים וּלְהַכְרִית כָּל הַחוֹחִים וְהַקּוֹצִים הַסּוֹבְבִים אֶת הַשּׁוֹשַׁנָּה הָעֶלְיוֹנָה וּלְחַבֵּר אֵשֶׁת נְעוּרִים עִם דּוֹדָהּ בְּאַהֲבָה וְאַחֲוָה וְרֵעוּת, וּמִשָּׁם יִמָּשֵׁךְ לָנוּ שֶׁפַע לְנֶפֶשׁ רוּחַ וּנְשָׁמָה לְטַהֲרֵנוּ מֵעֲוֹנוֹתֵינוּ וְלִסְלֹחַ חַטֹּאתֵינוּ וּלְכַפֵּר פְּשָׁעֵינוּ, כְּמוֹ שֶׁסָּלַחְתָּ לְדָוִד שֶׁאָמַר מִזְמוֹרִים אֵלּוּ לְפָנֶיךָ, כְּמוֹ שֶׁנֶּאֱמַר, גַּם־יהוה הֶעֱבִיר חַטָּאתְךָ לֹא תָמוּת: שמואל ב׳ י״ב וְאַל תִּקָּחֵנוּ מֵהָעוֹלָם הַזֶּה קֹדֶם זְמַנֵּנוּ עַד מְלֹאת שְׁנוֹתֵינוּ בָּהֶם שִׁבְעִים שָׁנָה, בְּאוֹפָן שֶׁנּוּכַל לְתַקֵּן אֶת אֲשֶׁר שִׁחַתְנוּ, וּזְכוּת דָּוִד הַמֶּלֶךְ עָלָיו הַשָּׁלוֹם תָּגֵן עָלֵינוּ וּבַעֲדֵנוּ, שֶׁתַּאֲרִיךְ אַפְּךָ עַד שׁוּבֵנוּ אֵלֶיךָ בִּתְשׁוּבָה שְׁלֵמָה לְפָנֶיךָ, וּמֵאוֹצַר מַתְּנַת חִנָּם חָנֵּנוּ, כִּדְכְתִיב, וְחַנֹּתִי אֶת־אֲשֶׁר אָחֹן וְרִחַמְתִּי אֶת־אֲשֶׁר שמות ל״ג אֲרַחֵם: וּכְשֵׁם שֶׁאָנוּ אוֹמְרִים לְפָנֶיךָ שִׁירָה בָּעוֹלָם הַזֶּה, כָּךְ נִזְכֶּה לוֹמַר לְפָנֶיךָ יהוה אֱלֹהֵינוּ שִׁיר וּשְׁבָחָה לָעוֹלָם הַבָּא. וְעַל יְדֵי אֲמִירַת תְּהִלִּים, תִּתְעוֹרֵר חֲבַצֶּלֶת הַשָּׁרוֹן וְלָשִׁיר בְּקוֹל נָעִים בְּגִילַת וְרַנֵּן, כְּבוֹד הַלְּבָנוֹן נִתַּן לָהּ, הוֹד וְהָדָר בְּבֵית אֱלֹהֵינוּ בִּמְהֵרָה בְיָמֵינוּ, אָמֵן סֶלָה.

תהלים צה לְכוּ נְרַנְּנָה לַיהוה, נָרִיעָה לְצוּר יִשְׁעֵנוּ:
נְקַדְּמָה פָנָיו בְּתוֹדָה, בִּזְמִרוֹת נָרִיעַ לוֹ:
כִּי אֵל גָּדוֹל יהוה, וּמֶלֶךְ גָּדוֹל עַל־כָּל־אֱלֹהִים:

ספר ראשון

א*
*א אַשְׁרֵי־הָאִישׁ אֲשֶׁר ׀ לֹא הָלַךְ בַּעֲצַת רְשָׁעִים וּבְדֶרֶךְ חַטָּאִים לֹא עָמָד וּבְמוֹשַׁב לֵצִים לֹא יָשָׁב: כִּי אִם בְּתוֹרַת יהוה חֶפְצוֹ וּבְתוֹרָתוֹ יֶהְגֶּה יוֹמָם וָלָיְלָה: וְהָיָה כְּעֵץ שָׁתוּל עַל־פַּלְגֵי מָיִם אֲשֶׁר פִּרְיוֹ ׀ יִתֵּן בְּעִתּוֹ וְעָלֵהוּ לֹא־יִבּוֹל וְכֹל אֲשֶׁר־יַעֲשֶׂה יַצְלִיחַ: לֹא־כֵן הָרְשָׁעִים כִּי אִם־כַּמֹּץ אֲשֶׁר־תִּדְּפֶנּוּ רוּחַ: עַל־כֵּן ׀ לֹא־יָקֻמוּ רְשָׁעִים בַּמִּשְׁפָּט וְחַטָּאִים בַּעֲדַת צַדִּיקִים: כִּי־יוֹדֵעַ יהוה דֶּרֶךְ צַדִּיקִים וְדֶרֶךְ רְשָׁעִים תֹּאבֵד:

ב לָמָּה רָגְשׁוּ גוֹיִם וּלְאֻמִּים יֶהְגּוּ־רִיק: יִתְיַצְּבוּ ׀ מַלְכֵי־אֶרֶץ וְרוֹזְנִים נוֹסְדוּ־יָחַד עַל־יהוה וְעַל־מְשִׁיחוֹ: נְנַתְּקָה אֶת־מוֹסְרוֹתֵימוֹ וְנַשְׁלִיכָה מִמֶּנּוּ עֲבֹתֵימוֹ: יוֹשֵׁב בַּשָּׁמַיִם יִשְׂחָק אֲדֹנָי יִלְעַג־לָמוֹ: אָז יְדַבֵּר אֵלֵימוֹ בְאַפּוֹ וּבַחֲרוֹנוֹ יְבַהֲלֵמוֹ: וַאֲנִי נָסַכְתִּי מַלְכִּי עַל־צִיּוֹן הַר־קָדְשִׁי: אֲסַפְּרָה אֶל חֹק יהוה אָמַר אֵלַי בְּנִי אַתָּה אֲנִי הַיּוֹם יְלִדְתִּיךָ: שְׁאַל מִמֶּנִּי וְאֶתְּנָה גוֹיִם נַחֲלָתֶךָ וַאֲחֻזָּתְךָ אַפְסֵי־אָרֶץ: תְּרֹעֵם בְּשֵׁבֶט בַּרְזֶל כִּכְלִי יוֹצֵר תְּנַפְּצֵם: וְעַתָּה מְלָכִים הַשְׂכִּילוּ הִוָּסְרוּ שֹׁפְטֵי אָרֶץ: עִבְדוּ אֶת־יהוה בְּיִרְאָה וְגִילוּ בִּרְעָדָה: נַשְּׁקוּ־בַר פֶּן־יֶאֱנַף ׀ וְתֹאבְדוּ דֶרֶךְ כִּי־יִבְעַר כִּמְעַט אַפּוֹ אַשְׁרֵי כָּל־חוֹסֵי בוֹ:

ג מִזְמוֹר לְדָוִד בְּבָרְחוֹ מִפְּנֵי ׀ אַבְשָׁלוֹם בְּנוֹ: יהוה מָה־רַבּוּ צָרָי רַבִּים קָמִים עָלָי: רַבִּים אֹמְרִים לְנַפְשִׁי אֵין יְשׁוּעָתָה לּוֹ בֵאלֹהִים סֶלָה: וְאַתָּה יהוה מָגֵן בַּעֲדִי כְּבוֹדִי וּמֵרִים רֹאשִׁי: קוֹלִי אֶל־יהוה אֶקְרָא וַיַּעֲנֵנִי מֵהַר קָדְשׁוֹ סֶלָה: אֲנִי שָׁכַבְתִּי וָאִישָׁנָה הֱקִיצוֹתִי כִּי יהוה יִסְמְכֵנִי: לֹא־אִירָא מֵרִבְבוֹת עָם אֲשֶׁר סָבִיב שָׁתוּ עָלָי: קוּמָה יהוה ׀ הוֹשִׁיעֵנִי אֱלֹהַי כִּי־הִכִּיתָ אֶת־כָּל־אֹיְבַי לֶחִי שִׁנֵּי רְשָׁעִים שִׁבַּרְתָּ: לַיהוה הַיְשׁוּעָה עַל־עַמְּךָ בִרְכָתֶךָ סֶּלָה:

ד לַמְנַצֵּחַ בִּנְגִינוֹת מִזְמוֹר לְדָוִד: בְּקָרְאִי עֲנֵנִי ׀ אֱלֹהֵי צִדְקִי בַּצָּר הִרְחַבְתָּ לִּי חָנֵּנִי וּשְׁמַע תְּפִלָּתִי: בְּנֵי אִישׁ עַד־מֶה כְבוֹדִי לִכְלִמָּה תֶּאֱהָבוּן רִיק תְּבַקְשׁוּ כָזָב סֶלָה: וּדְעוּ כִּי־הִפְלָה יהוה חָסִיד לוֹ יהוה יִשְׁמַע בְּקָרְאִי אֵלָיו: רִגְזוּ וְאַל־תֶּחֱטָאוּ אִמְרוּ בִלְבַבְכֶם עַל־מִשְׁכַּבְכֶם וְדֹמּוּ סֶלָה: זִבְחוּ זִבְחֵי־צֶדֶק וּבִטְחוּ אֶל־יהוה: רַבִּים אֹמְרִים מִי־יַרְאֵנוּ טוֹב נְסָה־עָלֵינוּ אוֹר פָּנֶיךָ יהוה: נָתַתָּה שִׂמְחָה בְלִבִּי מֵעֵת דְּגָנָם וְתִירוֹשָׁם רָבּוּ: בְּשָׁלוֹם יַחְדָּו אֶשְׁכְּבָה וְאִישָׁן כִּי־אַתָּה יהוה לְבָדָד לָבֶטַח תּוֹשִׁיבֵנִי:

ה לַמְנַצֵּחַ אֶל־הַנְּחִילוֹת מִזְמוֹר לְדָוִד: אֲמָרַי הַאֲזִינָה ׀ יהוה בִּינָה הֲגִיגִי:

הַקְשִׁיבָה ׀ לְקוֹל שַׁוְעִי מַלְכִּי וֵאלֹהָי כִּי־אֵלֶיךָ אֶתְפַּלָּל: יְהֹוָה בֹּקֶר תִּשְׁמַע
קוֹלִי בֹּקֶר אֶעֱרָךְ־לְךָ וַאֲצַפֶּה: כִּי ׀ לֹא אֵל־חָפֵץ רֶשַׁע ׀ אָתָּה לֹא יְגֻרְךָ רָע:
לֹא־יִתְיַצְּבוּ הוֹלְלִים לְנֶגֶד עֵינֶיךָ שָׂנֵאתָ כָּל־פֹּעֲלֵי אָוֶן: תְּאַבֵּד דֹּבְרֵי כָזָב
אִישׁ־דָּמִים וּמִרְמָה יְתָעֵב ׀ יְהֹוָה: וַאֲנִי ׀ בְּרֹב חַסְדְּךָ אָבוֹא בֵיתֶךָ אֶשְׁתַּחֲוֶה
אֶל־הֵיכַל־קָדְשְׁךָ בְּיִרְאָתֶךָ: יְהֹוָה ׀ נְחֵנִי בְצִדְקָתֶךָ לְמַעַן שׁוֹרְרָי הַיְשַׁר הֽוֹשֵׁר
לְפָנַי דַּרְכֶּךָ: כִּי אֵין בְּפִיהוּ נְכוֹנָה קִרְבָּם הַוּוֹת קֶבֶר־פָּתוּחַ גְּרוֹנָם לְשׁוֹנָם יַחֲלִיקוּן:
הַאֲשִׁימֵם ׀ אֱלֹהִים יִפְּלוּ מִמֹּעֲצוֹתֵיהֶם בְּרֹב פִּשְׁעֵיהֶם הַדִּיחֵמוֹ כִּי־מָרוּ בָךְ:
וְיִשְׂמְחוּ כָל־חוֹסֵי בָךְ לְעוֹלָם יְרַנֵּנוּ וְתָסֵךְ עָלֵימוֹ וְיַעְלְצוּ בְךָ אֹהֲבֵי שְׁמֶךָ:
כִּי־אַתָּה תְּבָרֵךְ צַדִּיק יְהֹוָה כַּצִּנָּה רָצוֹן תַּעְטְרֶנּוּ:

ו לַמְנַצֵּחַ בִּנְגִינוֹת עַל־הַשְּׁמִינִית מִזְמוֹר לְדָוִד: יְהֹוָה אַל־בְּאַפְּךָ תוֹכִיחֵנִי
וְאַל־בַּחֲמָתְךָ תְיַסְּרֵנִי: חָנֵּנִי יְהֹוָה כִּי אֻמְלַל אָנִי רְפָאֵנִי יְהֹוָה כִּי נִבְהֲלוּ עֲצָמָי:
וְנַפְשִׁי נִבְהֲלָה מְאֹד וְאַתָּ יְהֹוָה עַד־מָתָי: שׁוּבָה יְהֹוָה חַלְּצָה נַפְשִׁי הוֹשִׁיעֵנִי
לְמַעַן חַסְדֶּךָ: כִּי אֵין בַּמָּוֶת זִכְרֶךָ בִּשְׁאוֹל מִי יוֹדֶה־לָּךְ: יָגַעְתִּי ׀ בְּאַנְחָתִי
אַשְׂחֶה בְכָל־לַיְלָה מִטָּתִי בְּדִמְעָתִי עַרְשִׂי אַמְסֶה: עָשְׁשָׁה מִכַּעַס עֵינִי
עָתְקָה בְּכָל־צוֹרְרָי: סוּרוּ מִמֶּנִּי כָּל־פֹּעֲלֵי אָוֶן כִּי־שָׁמַע יְהֹוָה קוֹל בִּכְיִי:
שָׁמַע יְהֹוָה תְּחִנָּתִי יְהֹוָה תְּפִלָּתִי יִקָּח: יֵבֹשׁוּ ׀ וְיִבָּהֲלוּ מְאֹד כָּל־אֹיְבָי יָשֻׁבוּ
יֵבֹשׁוּ רָגַע:

ז שִׁגָּיוֹן לְדָוִד אֲשֶׁר־שָׁר לַיהֹוָה עַל־דִּבְרֵי־כוּשׁ בֶּן־יְמִינִי: יְהֹוָה אֱלֹהַי בְּךָ חָסִיתִי
הוֹשִׁיעֵנִי מִכָּל־רֹדְפַי וְהַצִּילֵנִי: פֶּן־יִטְרֹף כְּאַרְיֵה נַפְשִׁי פֹּרֵק וְאֵין מַצִּיל: יְהֹוָה
אֱלֹהַי אִם־עָשִׂיתִי זֹאת אִם־יֶשׁ־עָוֶל בְּכַפָּי: אִם־גָּמַלְתִּי שׁוֹלְמִי רָע וָאֲחַלְּצָה
צוֹרְרִי רֵיקָם: יִרַדֹּף אוֹיֵב ׀ נַפְשִׁי וְיַשֵּׂג וְיִרְמֹס לָאָרֶץ חַיָּי וּכְבוֹדִי ׀ לֶעָפָר יַשְׁכֵּן
סֶלָה: קוּמָה יְהֹוָה ׀ בְּאַפֶּךָ הִנָּשֵׂא בְּעַבְרוֹת צוֹרְרָי וְעוּרָה אֵלַי מִשְׁפָּט צִוִּיתָ:
וַעֲדַת לְאֻמִּים תְּסוֹבְבֶךָּ וְעָלֶיהָ לַמָּרוֹם שׁוּבָה: יְהֹוָה יָדִין עַמִּים שָׁפְטֵנִי יְהֹוָה
כְּצִדְקִי וּכְתֻמִּי עָלָי: יִגְמָר־נָא רַע ׀ רְשָׁעִים וּתְכוֹנֵן צַדִּיק וּבֹחֵן לִבּוֹת וּכְלָיוֹת
אֱלֹהִים צַדִּיק: מָגִנִּי עַל־אֱלֹהִים מוֹשִׁיעַ יִשְׁרֵי־לֵב: אֱלֹהִים שׁוֹפֵט צַדִּיק וְאֵל
זֹעֵם בְּכָל־יוֹם: אִם־לֹא יָשׁוּב חַרְבּוֹ יִלְטוֹשׁ קַשְׁתּוֹ דָרַךְ וַיְכוֹנְנֶהָ: וְלוֹ הֵכִין
כְּלֵי־מָוֶת חִצָּיו לְדֹלְקִים יִפְעָל: הִנֵּה יְחַבֶּל־אָוֶן וְהָרָה עָמָל וְיָלַד שָׁקֶר: בּוֹר
כָּרָה וַיַּחְפְּרֵהוּ וַיִּפֹּל בְּשַׁחַת יִפְעָל: יָשׁוּב עֲמָלוֹ בְרֹאשׁוֹ וְעַל קָדְקֳדוֹ חֲמָסוֹ
יֵרֵד: אוֹדֶה יְהֹוָה כְּצִדְקוֹ וַאֲזַמְּרָה שֵׁם־יְהֹוָה עֶלְיוֹן:

ח לַמְנַצֵּחַ עַל־הַגִּתִּית מִזְמוֹר לְדָוִד: יְהוָה אֲדֹנֵינוּ מָה־אַדִּיר שִׁמְךָ בְּכָל־הָאָרֶץ
אֲשֶׁר־תְּנָה הוֹדְךָ עַל־הַשָּׁמָיִם: מִפִּי עוֹלְלִים וְיֹנְקִים יִסַּדְתָּ עֹז לְמַעַן צוֹרְרֶיךָ
לְהַשְׁבִּית אוֹיֵב וּמִתְנַקֵּם: כִּי־אֶרְאֶה שָׁמֶיךָ מַעֲשֵׂה אֶצְבְּעֹתֶיךָ יָרֵחַ וְכוֹכָבִים
אֲשֶׁר כּוֹנָנְתָּה: מָה־אֱנוֹשׁ כִּי־תִזְכְּרֶנּוּ וּבֶן־אָדָם כִּי תִפְקְדֶנּוּ: וַתְּחַסְּרֵהוּ מְּעַט
מֵאֱלֹהִים וְכָבוֹד וְהָדָר תְּעַטְּרֵהוּ: תַּמְשִׁילֵהוּ בְּמַעֲשֵׂי יָדֶיךָ כֹּל שַׁתָּה תַחַת־
רַגְלָיו: צֹנֶה וַאֲלָפִים כֻּלָּם וְגַם בַּהֲמוֹת שָׂדָי: צִפּוֹר שָׁמַיִם וּדְגֵי הַיָּם עֹבֵר אָרְחוֹת
יַמִּים: יְהוָה אֲדֹנֵינוּ מָה־אַדִּיר שִׁמְךָ בְּכָל־הָאָרֶץ:

ט לַמְנַצֵּחַ עַל־מוּת לַבֵּן מִזְמוֹר לְדָוִד: אוֹדֶה יְהוָה בְּכָל־לִבִּי אֲסַפְּרָה כָּל־
נִפְלְאוֹתֶיךָ: אֶשְׂמְחָה וְאֶעֶלְצָה בָךְ אֲזַמְּרָה שִׁמְךָ עֶלְיוֹן: בְּשׁוּב־אוֹיְבַי אָחוֹר
יִכָּשְׁלוּ וְיֹאבְדוּ מִפָּנֶיךָ: כִּי־עָשִׂיתָ מִשְׁפָּטִי וְדִינִי יָשַׁבְתָּ לְכִסֵּא שׁוֹפֵט צֶדֶק:
גָּעַרְתָּ גוֹיִם אִבַּדְתָּ רָשָׁע שְׁמָם מָחִיתָ לְעוֹלָם וָעֶד: הָאוֹיֵב תַּמּוּ חֳרָבוֹת
לָנֶצַח וְעָרִים נָתַשְׁתָּ אָבַד זִכְרָם הֵמָּה: וַיהוָה לְעוֹלָם יֵשֵׁב כּוֹנֵן לַמִּשְׁפָּט
כִּסְאוֹ: וְהוּא יִשְׁפֹּט־תֵּבֵל בְּצֶדֶק יָדִין לְאֻמִּים בְּמֵישָׁרִים: וִיהִי יְהוָה מִשְׂגָּב
לַדָּךְ מִשְׂגָּב לְעִתּוֹת בַּצָּרָה: וְיִבְטְחוּ בְךָ יוֹדְעֵי שְׁמֶךָ כִּי לֹא־עָזַבְתָּ דֹרְשֶׁיךָ
יְהוָה: זַמְּרוּ לַיהוָה יֹשֵׁב צִיּוֹן הַגִּידוּ בָעַמִּים עֲלִילוֹתָיו: כִּי־דֹרֵשׁ דָּמִים אוֹתָם
זָכָר לֹא־שָׁכַח צַעֲקַת עֲנָוִים: חָנְנֵנִי יְהוָה רְאֵה עָנְיִי מִשֹּׂנְאָי מְרוֹמְמִי מִשַּׁעֲרֵי־ עֲנָוִים
מָוֶת: לְמַעַן אֲסַפְּרָה כָּל־תְּהִלָּתֶיךָ בְּשַׁעֲרֵי בַת־צִיּוֹן אָגִילָה בִּישׁוּעָתֶךָ: טָבְעוּ
גוֹיִם בְּשַׁחַת עָשׂוּ בְּרֶשֶׁת־זוּ טָמָנוּ נִלְכְּדָה רַגְלָם: נוֹדַע יְהוָה מִשְׁפָּט עָשָׂה
בְּפֹעַל כַּפָּיו נוֹקֵשׁ רָשָׁע הִגָּיוֹן סֶלָה: יָשׁוּבוּ רְשָׁעִים לִשְׁאוֹלָה כָּל־גּוֹיִם שְׁכֵחֵי
אֱלֹהִים: כִּי לֹא לָנֶצַח יִשָּׁכַח אֶבְיוֹן תִּקְוַת עֲנָוִים תֹּאבַד לָעַד: קוּמָה יְהוָה עֲנָוִים
אַל־יָעֹז אֱנוֹשׁ יִשָּׁפְטוּ גוֹיִם עַל־פָּנֶיךָ: שִׁיתָה יְהוָה מוֹרָה לָהֶם יֵדְעוּ גוֹיִם
אֱנוֹשׁ הֵמָּה סֶּלָה:

י לָמָה יְהוָה תַּעֲמֹד בְּרָחוֹק תַּעְלִים לְעִתּוֹת בַּצָּרָה: בְּגַאֲוַת רָשָׁע יִדְלַק עָנִי
יִתָּפְשׂוּ בִּמְזִמּוֹת זוּ חָשָׁבוּ: כִּי־הִלֵּל רָשָׁע עַל־תַּאֲוַת נַפְשׁוֹ וּבֹצֵעַ בֵּרֵךְ נִאֵץ
יְהוָה: רָשָׁע כְּגֹבַהּ אַפּוֹ בַּל־יִדְרֹשׁ אֵין אֱלֹהִים כָּל־מְזִמּוֹתָיו: יָחִילוּ דְרָכָו
בְּכָל־עֵת מָרוֹם מִשְׁפָּטֶיךָ מִנֶּגְדּוֹ כָּל־צוֹרְרָיו יָפִיחַ בָּהֶם: אָמַר בְּלִבּוֹ בַּל־אֶמּוֹט
לְדֹר וָדֹר אֲשֶׁר לֹא־בְרָע: אָלָה פִּיהוּ מָלֵא וּמִרְמוֹת וָתֹךְ תַּחַת לְשׁוֹנוֹ עָמָל
וָאָוֶן: יֵשֵׁב בְּמַאְרַב חֲצֵרִים בַּמִּסְתָּרִים יַהֲרֹג נָקִי עֵינָיו לְחֵלְכָה יִצְפֹּנוּ: יֶאֱרֹב
בַּמִּסְתָּר כְּאַרְיֵה בְסֻכֹּה יֶאֱרֹב לַחֲטוֹף עָנִי יַחְטֹף עָנִי בְּמָשְׁכוֹ בְרִשְׁתּוֹ: וְדֹכֶּה יִדְכֶּה

חָל כָּאִים יִשְׁחַ וְנָפַל בַּעֲצוּמָיו חֵלְכָּאִים: אָמַר בְּלִבּוֹ שָׁכַח אֵל הִסְתִּיר פָּנָיו בַּל־רָאָה לָנֶצַח: קוּמָה יְהוָה אֵל נְשָׂא יָדֶךָ אַל־תִּשְׁכַּח עֲנָיִים: עַל־מֶה ׀ נִאֵץ רָשָׁע ׀ אֱלֹהִים אָמַר בְּלִבּוֹ לֹא תִדְרֹשׁ: רָאִתָה כִּי־אַתָּה ׀ עָמָל וָכַעַס ׀ תַּבִּיט לָתֵת בְּיָדֶךָ עָלֶיךָ יַעֲזֹב חֵלְכָה יָתוֹם אַתָּה ׀ הָיִיתָ עוֹזֵר: שְׁבֹר זְרוֹעַ רָשָׁע וָרָע תִּדְרוֹשׁ־רִשְׁעוֹ בַל־תִּמְצָא: יְהוָה מֶלֶךְ עוֹלָם וָעֶד אָבְדוּ גוֹיִם מֵאַרְצוֹ: תַּאֲוַת עֲנָוִים שָׁמַעְתָּ יְהוָה תָּכִין לִבָּם תַּקְשִׁיב אָזְנֶךָ: לִשְׁפֹּט יָתוֹם וָדָךְ בַּל־יוֹסִיף עוֹד לַעֲרֹץ אֱנוֹשׁ מִן־הָאָרֶץ:

יא לַמְנַצֵּחַ לְדָוִד בַּיהוָה ׀ חָסִיתִי אֵיךְ תֹּאמְרוּ לְנַפְשִׁי נוּדִי הַרְכֶם צִפּוֹר: כִּי הִנֵּה הָרְשָׁעִים יִדְרְכוּן קֶשֶׁת כּוֹנְנוּ חִצָּם עַל־יֶתֶר לִירוֹת בְּמוֹ־אֹפֶל לְיִשְׁרֵי־לֵב: כִּי הַשָּׁתוֹת יֵהָרֵסוּן צַדִּיק מַה־פָּעָל: יְהוָה ׀ בְּהֵיכַל קָדְשׁוֹ יְהוָה בַּשָּׁמַיִם כִּסְאוֹ עֵינָיו יֶחֱזוּ עַפְעַפָּיו יִבְחֲנוּ בְּנֵי אָדָם: יְהוָה צַדִּיק יִבְחָן וְרָשָׁע וְאֹהֵב חָמָס שָׂנְאָה נַפְשׁוֹ: יַמְטֵר עַל־רְשָׁעִים פַּחִים אֵשׁ וְגָפְרִית וְרוּחַ זִלְעָפוֹת מְנָת כּוֹסָם: כִּי־צַדִּיק יְהוָה צְדָקוֹת אָהֵב יָשָׁר יֶחֱזוּ פָנֵימוֹ:

יב לַמְנַצֵּחַ עַל־הַשְּׁמִינִית מִזְמוֹר לְדָוִד: הוֹשִׁיעָה יְהוָה כִּי־גָמַר חָסִיד כִּי־פַסּוּ אֱמוּנִים מִבְּנֵי אָדָם: שָׁוְא ׀ יְדַבְּרוּ אִישׁ אֶת־רֵעֵהוּ שְׂפַת חֲלָקוֹת בְּלֵב וָלֵב יְדַבֵּרוּ: יַכְרֵת יְהוָה כָּל־שִׂפְתֵי חֲלָקוֹת לָשׁוֹן מְדַבֶּרֶת גְּדֹלוֹת: אֲשֶׁר אָמְרוּ ׀ לִלְשֹׁנֵנוּ נַגְבִּיר שְׂפָתֵינוּ אִתָּנוּ מִי אָדוֹן לָנוּ: מִשֹּׁד עֲנִיִּים מֵאַנְקַת אֶבְיוֹנִים עַתָּה אָקוּם יֹאמַר יְהוָה אָשִׁית בְּיֵשַׁע יָפִיחַ לוֹ: אִמֲרוֹת יְהוָה אֲמָרוֹת טְהֹרוֹת כֶּסֶף צָרוּף בַּעֲלִיל לָאָרֶץ מְזֻקָּק שִׁבְעָתָיִם: אַתָּה־יְהוָה תִּשְׁמְרֵם תִּצְּרֶנּוּ ׀ מִן־הַדּוֹר זוּ לְעוֹלָם: סָבִיב רְשָׁעִים יִתְהַלָּכוּן כְּרֻם זֻלּוּת לִבְנֵי אָדָם:

יג לַמְנַצֵּחַ מִזְמוֹר לְדָוִד: עַד־אָנָה יְהוָה תִּשְׁכָּחֵנִי נֶצַח עַד־אָנָה ׀ תַּסְתִּיר אֶת־פָּנֶיךָ מִמֶּנִּי: עַד־אָנָה אָשִׁית עֵצוֹת בְּנַפְשִׁי יָגוֹן בִּלְבָבִי יוֹמָם עַד־אָנָה ׀ יָרוּם אֹיְבִי עָלָי: הַבִּיטָה עֲנֵנִי יְהוָה אֱלֹהָי הָאִירָה עֵינַי פֶּן־אִישַׁן הַמָּוֶת: פֶּן־יֹאמַר אֹיְבִי יְכָלְתִּיו צָרַי יָגִילוּ כִּי אֶמּוֹט: וַאֲנִי ׀ בְּחַסְדְּךָ בָטַחְתִּי יָגֵל לִבִּי בִּישׁוּעָתֶךָ אָשִׁירָה לַיהוָה כִּי גָמַל עָלָי:

יד לַמְנַצֵּחַ לְדָוִד אָמַר נָבָל בְּלִבּוֹ אֵין אֱלֹהִים הִשְׁחִיתוּ הִתְעִיבוּ עֲלִילָה אֵין עֹשֵׂה־טוֹב: יְהוָה מִשָּׁמַיִם הִשְׁקִיף עַל־בְּנֵי־אָדָם לִרְאוֹת הֲיֵשׁ מַשְׂכִּיל דֹּרֵשׁ אֶת־אֱלֹהִים: הַכֹּל סָר יַחְדָּו נֶאֱלָחוּ אֵין עֹשֵׂה־טוֹב אֵין גַּם־אֶחָד: הֲלֹא יָדְעוּ כָּל־פֹּעֲלֵי אָוֶן אֹכְלֵי עַמִּי אָכְלוּ לֶחֶם יְהוָה לֹא קָרָאוּ: שָׁם ׀ פָּחֲדוּ פַחַד כִּי

אֱלֹהִים בְּדוֹר צַדִּיק: עֲצַת־עָנִי תָבִישׁוּ כִּי יְהֹוָה מַחְסֵהוּ: מִי יִתֵּן מִצִּיּוֹן יְשׁוּעַת
יִשְׂרָאֵל בְּשׁוּב יְהֹוָה שְׁבוּת עַמּוֹ יָגֵל יַעֲקֹב יִשְׂמַח יִשְׂרָאֵל:

טו מִזְמוֹר לְדָוִד יְהֹוָה מִי־יָגוּר בְּאָהֳלֶךָ מִי־יִשְׁכֹּן בְּהַר קָדְשֶׁךָ: הוֹלֵךְ תָּמִים
וּפֹעֵל צֶדֶק וְדֹבֵר אֱמֶת בִּלְבָבוֹ: לֹא־רָגַל עַל־לְשֹׁנוֹ לֹא־עָשָׂה לְרֵעֵהוּ רָעָה
וְחֶרְפָּה לֹא־נָשָׂא עַל־קְרֹבוֹ: נִבְזֶה בְּעֵינָיו נִמְאָס וְאֶת־יִרְאֵי יְהֹוָה יְכַבֵּד נִשְׁבַּע
לְהָרַע וְלֹא יָמִר: כַּסְפּוֹ לֹא־נָתַן בְּנֶשֶׁךְ וְשֹׁחַד עַל־נָקִי לֹא־לָקָח עֹשֵׂה אֵלֶּה
לֹא יִמּוֹט לְעוֹלָם:

טז מִכְתָּם לְדָוִד שָׁמְרֵנִי אֵל כִּי־חָסִיתִי בָךְ: אָמַרְתְּ לַיהֹוָה אֲדֹנָי אָתָּה טוֹבָתִי
בַּל־עָלֶיךָ: לִקְדוֹשִׁים אֲשֶׁר־בָּאָרֶץ הֵמָּה וְאַדִּירֵי כָּל־חֶפְצִי־בָם: יִרְבּוּ עַצְּבוֹתָם
אַחֵר מָהָרוּ בַּל־אַסִּיךְ נִסְכֵּיהֶם מִדָּם וּבַל־אֶשָּׂא אֶת־שְׁמוֹתָם עַל־שְׂפָתָי:
יְהֹוָה מְנָת־חֶלְקִי וְכוֹסִי אַתָּה תּוֹמִיךְ גּוֹרָלִי: חֲבָלִים נָפְלוּ־לִי בַּנְּעִמִים אַף־
נַחֲלָת שָׁפְרָה עָלָי: אֲבָרֵךְ אֶת־יְהֹוָה אֲשֶׁר יְעָצָנִי אַף־לֵילוֹת יִסְּרוּנִי כִלְיוֹתָי:
שִׁוִּיתִי יְהֹוָה לְנֶגְדִּי תָמִיד כִּי מִימִינִי בַּל־אֶמּוֹט: לָכֵן שָׂמַח לִבִּי וַיָּגֶל כְּבוֹדִי
אַף־בְּשָׂרִי יִשְׁכֹּן לָבֶטַח: כִּי לֹא־תַעֲזֹב נַפְשִׁי לִשְׁאוֹל לֹא־תִתֵּן חֲסִידְךָ
לִרְאוֹת שָׁחַת: תּוֹדִיעֵנִי אֹרַח חַיִּים שֹׂבַע שְׂמָחוֹת אֶת־פָּנֶיךָ נְעִמוֹת בִּימִינְךָ
נֶצַח:

יז תְּפִלָּה לְדָוִד שִׁמְעָה יְהֹוָה צֶדֶק הַקְשִׁיבָה רִנָּתִי הַאֲזִינָה תְפִלָּתִי בְּלֹא שִׂפְתֵי
מִרְמָה: מִלְּפָנֶיךָ מִשְׁפָּטִי יֵצֵא עֵינֶיךָ תֶּחֱזֶינָה מֵישָׁרִים: בָּחַנְתָּ לִבִּי ׀ פָּקַדְתָּ
לַּיְלָה צְרַפְתַּנִי בַל־תִּמְצָא זַמֹּתִי בַּל־יַעֲבָר־פִּי: לִפְעֻלּוֹת אָדָם בִּדְבַר שְׂפָתֶיךָ
אֲנִי שָׁמַרְתִּי אָרְחוֹת פָּרִיץ: תָּמֹךְ אֲשֻׁרַי בְּמַעְגְּלוֹתֶיךָ בַּל־נָמוֹטּוּ פְעָמָי:
אֲנִי־קְרָאתִיךָ כִי־תַעֲנֵנִי אֵל הַט־אָזְנְךָ לִי שְׁמַע אִמְרָתִי: הַפְלֵה חֲסָדֶיךָ מוֹשִׁיעַ
חוֹסִים מִמִּתְקוֹמְמִים בִּימִינֶךָ: שָׁמְרֵנִי כְּאִישׁוֹן בַּת־עָיִן בְּצֵל כְּנָפֶיךָ תַּסְתִּירֵנִי:
מִפְּנֵי רְשָׁעִים זוּ שַׁדּוּנִי אֹיְבַי בְּנֶפֶשׁ יַקִּיפוּ עָלָי: חֶלְבָּמוֹ סָגְרוּ פִּימוֹ דִּבְּרוּ
בְגֵאוּת: אַשֻּׁרֵינוּ עַתָּה סְבָבוּנִי עֵינֵיהֶם יָשִׁיתוּ לִנְטוֹת בָּאָרֶץ: דִּמְיֹנוֹ כְּאַרְיֵה
יִכְסוֹף לִטְרוֹף וְכִכְפִיר יֹשֵׁב בְּמִסְתָּרִים: קוּמָה יְהֹוָה קַדְּמָה פָנָיו הַכְרִיעֵהוּ
פַּלְּטָה נַפְשִׁי מֵרָשָׁע חַרְבֶּךָ: מִמְתִים יָדְךָ ׀ יְהֹוָה מִמְתִים מֵחֶלֶד חֶלְקָם בַּחַיִּים
וּצְפוּנְךָ תְּמַלֵּא בִטְנָם יִשְׂבְּעוּ בָנִים וְהִנִּיחוּ יִתְרָם לְעוֹלְלֵיהֶם: אֲנִי בְּצֶדֶק אֶחֱזֶה
פָנֶיךָ אֶשְׂבְּעָה בְהָקִיץ תְּמוּנָתֶךָ:

יח לַמְנַצֵּחַ ׀ לְעֶבֶד יְהֹוָה לְדָוִד אֲשֶׁר דִּבֶּר ׀ לַיהֹוָה אֶת־דִּבְרֵי הַשִּׁירָה הַזֹּאת בְּיוֹם ׀

חֲסִידְךָ

סְבָבוּנִי

וְצִפּוּנְךָ

הִצִּיל־יְהֹוָה אוֹתוֹ מִכַּף כָּל־אֹיְבָיו וּמִיַּד שָׁאוּל: וַיֹּאמַר אֶרְחָמְךָ יְהֹוָה חִזְקִי:
יְהֹוָה ׀ סַלְעִי וּמְצוּדָתִי וּמְפַלְטִי אֵלִי צוּרִי אֶחֱסֶה־בּוֹ מָגִנִּי וְקֶרֶן־יִשְׁעִי מִשְׂגַּבִּי:
מְהֻלָּל אֶקְרָא יְהֹוָה וּמִן־אֹיְבַי אִוָּשֵׁעַ: אֲפָפוּנִי חֶבְלֵי־מָוֶת וְנַחֲלֵי בְלִיַּעַל
יְבַעֲתוּנִי: חֶבְלֵי שְׁאוֹל סְבָבוּנִי קִדְּמוּנִי מוֹקְשֵׁי מָוֶת: בַּצַּר־לִי ׀ אֶקְרָא יְהֹוָה
וְאֶל־אֱלֹהַי אֲשַׁוֵּעַ יִשְׁמַע מֵהֵיכָלוֹ קוֹלִי וְשַׁוְעָתִי לְפָנָיו ׀ תָּבוֹא בְאָזְנָיו: וַתִּגְעַשׁ
וַתִּרְעַשׁ ׀ הָאָרֶץ וּמוֹסְדֵי הָרִים יִרְגָּזוּ וַיִּתְגָּעֲשׁוּ כִּי־חָרָה לוֹ: עָלָה עָשָׁן ׀ בְּאַפּוֹ
וְאֵשׁ־מִפִּיו תֹּאכֵל גֶּחָלִים בָּעֲרוּ מִמֶּנּוּ: וַיֵּט שָׁמַיִם וַיֵּרַד וַעֲרָפֶל תַּחַת רַגְלָיו:
וַיִּרְכַּב עַל־כְּרוּב וַיָּעֹף וַיֵּדֶא עַל־כַּנְפֵי־רוּחַ: יָשֶׁת חֹשֶׁךְ ׀ סִתְרוֹ סְבִיבוֹתָיו סֻכָּתוֹ
חֶשְׁכַת־מַיִם עָבֵי שְׁחָקִים: מִנֹּגַהּ נֶגְדּוֹ עָבָיו עָבְרוּ בָּרָד וְגַחֲלֵי־אֵשׁ: וַיַּרְעֵם
בַּשָּׁמַיִם ׀ יְהֹוָה וְעֶלְיוֹן יִתֵּן קֹלוֹ בָּרָד וְגַחֲלֵי־אֵשׁ: וַיִּשְׁלַח חִצָּיו וַיְפִיצֵם וּבְרָקִים
רָב וַיְהֻמֵּם: וַיֵּרָאוּ ׀ אֲפִיקֵי מַיִם וַיִּגָּלוּ מוֹסְדוֹת תֵּבֵל מִגַּעֲרָתְךָ יְהֹוָה מִנִּשְׁמַת
רוּחַ אַפֶּךָ: יִשְׁלַח מִמָּרוֹם יִקָּחֵנִי יַמְשֵׁנִי מִמַּיִם רַבִּים: יַצִּילֵנִי מֵאֹיְבִי עָז וּמִשֹּׂנְאַי
כִּי־אָמְצוּ מִמֶּנִּי: יְקַדְּמוּנִי בְיוֹם־אֵידִי וַיְהִי־יְהֹוָה לְמִשְׁעָן לִי: וַיּוֹצִיאֵנִי לַמֶּרְחָב
יְחַלְּצֵנִי כִּי חָפֵץ בִּי: יִגְמְלֵנִי יְהֹוָה כְּצִדְקִי כְּבֹר יָדַי יָשִׁיב לִי: כִּי־שָׁמַרְתִּי דַּרְכֵי
יְהֹוָה וְלֹא־רָשַׁעְתִּי מֵאֱלֹהָי: כִּי כָל־מִשְׁפָּטָיו לְנֶגְדִּי וְחֻקֹּתָיו לֹא־אָסִיר מֶנִּי:
וָאֱהִי תָמִים עִמּוֹ וָאֶשְׁתַּמֵּר מֵעֲוֹנִי: וַיָּשֶׁב־יְהֹוָה לִי כְצִדְקִי כְּבֹר יָדַי לְנֶגֶד עֵינָיו:
עִם־חָסִיד תִּתְחַסָּד עִם־גְּבַר תָּמִים תִּתַּמָּם: עִם־נָבָר תִּתְבָּרָר וְעִם־עִקֵּשׁ
תִּתְפַּתָּל: כִּי־אַתָּה עַם־עָנִי תוֹשִׁיעַ וְעֵינַיִם רָמוֹת תַּשְׁפִּיל: כִּי־אַתָּה תָּאִיר נֵרִי
יְהֹוָה אֱלֹהַי יַגִּיהַּ חָשְׁכִּי: כִּי־בְךָ אָרֻץ גְּדוּד וּבֵאלֹהַי אֲדַלֶּג־שׁוּר: הָאֵל תָּמִים
דַּרְכּוֹ אִמְרַת־יְהֹוָה צְרוּפָה מָגֵן הוּא לְכֹל ׀ הַחֹסִים בּוֹ: כִּי מִי אֱלוֹהַּ מִבַּלְעֲדֵי
יְהֹוָה וּמִי צוּר זוּלָתִי אֱלֹהֵינוּ: הָאֵל הַמְאַזְּרֵנִי חָיִל וַיִּתֵּן תָּמִים דַּרְכִּי: מְשַׁוֶּה
רַגְלַי כָּאַיָּלוֹת וְעַל בָּמֹתַי יַעֲמִידֵנִי: מְלַמֵּד יָדַי לַמִּלְחָמָה וְנִחֲתָה קֶשֶׁת־נְחוּשָׁה
זְרוֹעֹתָי: וַתִּתֶּן־לִי מָגֵן יִשְׁעֶךָ וִימִינְךָ תִסְעָדֵנִי וְעַנְוַתְךָ תַרְבֵּנִי: תַּרְחִיב צַעֲדִי
תַחְתָּי וְלֹא מָעֲדוּ קַרְסֻלָּי: אֶרְדּוֹף אוֹיְבַי וְאַשִּׂיגֵם וְלֹא־אָשׁוּב עַד־כַּלּוֹתָם:
אֶמְחָצֵם וְלֹא־יֻכְלוּ קוּם יִפְּלוּ תַּחַת רַגְלָי: וַתְּאַזְּרֵנִי חַיִל לַמִּלְחָמָה תַּכְרִיעַ
קָמַי תַּחְתָּי: וְאֹיְבַי נָתַתָּה לִּי עֹרֶף וּמְשַׂנְאַי אַצְמִיתֵם: יְשַׁוְּעוּ וְאֵין־מוֹשִׁיעַ
עַל־יְהֹוָה וְלֹא עָנָם: וְאֶשְׁחָקֵם כְּעָפָר עַל־פְּנֵי־רוּחַ כְּטִיט חוּצוֹת אֲרִיקֵם:
תְּפַלְּטֵנִי מֵרִיבֵי עָם תְּשִׂימֵנִי לְרֹאשׁ גּוֹיִם עַם לֹא־יָדַעְתִּי יַעַבְדוּנִי: לְשֵׁמַע אֹזֶן
יִשָּׁמְעוּ לִי בְּנֵי־נֵכָר יְכַחֲשׁוּ־לִי: בְּנֵי־נֵכָר יִבֹּלוּ וְיַחְרְגוּ מִמִּסְגְּרוֹתֵיהֶם: חַי־יְהֹוָה

וּבְרִית צוּרִי וְיָדוֹם אֱלוֹהֵי יִשְׁעִי: הָאֵל הַנּוֹתֵן נְקָמוֹת לִי וַיַּדְבֵּר עַמִּים תַּחְתָּי: מְפַלְּטִי מֵאֹיְבָי אַף מִן־קָמַי תְּרוֹמְמֵנִי מֵאִישׁ חָמָס תַּצִּילֵנִי: עַל־כֵּן ׀ אוֹדְךָ בַגּוֹיִם יְהוָה וּלְשִׁמְךָ אֲזַמֵּרָה: מַגְדִּל יְשׁוּעוֹת מַלְכּוֹ וְעֹשֶׂה חֶסֶד ׀ לִמְשִׁיחוֹ לְדָוִד וּלְזַרְעוֹ עַד־עוֹלָם:

יט לַמְנַצֵּחַ מִזְמוֹר לְדָוִד: הַשָּׁמַיִם מְסַפְּרִים כְּבוֹד־אֵל וּמַעֲשֵׂה יָדָיו מַגִּיד הָרָקִיעַ: יוֹם לְיוֹם יַבִּיעַ אֹמֶר וְלַיְלָה לְּלַיְלָה יְחַוֶּה־דָּעַת: אֵין־אֹמֶר וְאֵין דְּבָרִים בְּלִי נִשְׁמָע קוֹלָם: בְּכָל־הָאָרֶץ ׀ יָצָא קַוָּם וּבִקְצֵה תֵבֵל מִלֵּיהֶם לַשֶּׁמֶשׁ שָׂם־ אֹהֶל בָּהֶם: וְהוּא כְּחָתָן יֹצֵא מֵחֻפָּתוֹ יָשִׂישׂ כְּגִבּוֹר לָרוּץ אֹרַח: מִקְצֵה הַשָּׁמַיִם ׀ מוֹצָאוֹ וּתְקוּפָתוֹ עַל־קְצוֹתָם וְאֵין נִסְתָּר מֵחַמָּתוֹ: תּוֹרַת יְהוָה תְּמִימָה מְשִׁיבַת נָפֶשׁ עֵדוּת יְהוָה נֶאֱמָנָה מַחְכִּימַת פֶּתִי: פִּקּוּדֵי יְהוָה יְשָׁרִים מְשַׂמְּחֵי־לֵב מִצְוַת יְהוָה בָּרָה מְאִירַת עֵינָיִם: יִרְאַת יְהוָה ׀ טְהוֹרָה עוֹמֶדֶת לָעַד מִשְׁפְּטֵי־יְהוָה אֱמֶת צָדְקוּ יַחְדָּו: הַנֶּחֱמָדִים מִזָּהָב וּמִפַּז רָב וּמְתוּקִים מִדְּבַשׁ וְנֹפֶת צוּפִים: גַּם־עַבְדְּךָ נִזְהָר בָּהֶם בְּשָׁמְרָם עֵקֶב רָב: שְׁגִיאוֹת מִי־יָבִין מִנִּסְתָּרוֹת נַקֵּנִי: גַּם מִזֵּדִים ׀ חֲשֹׂךְ עַבְדֶּךָ אַל־יִמְשְׁלוּ־בִי אָז אֵיתָם וְנִקֵּיתִי מִפֶּשַׁע רָב: יִהְיוּ לְרָצוֹן ׀ אִמְרֵי־פִי וְהֶגְיוֹן לִבִּי לְפָנֶיךָ יְהוָה צוּרִי וְגֹאֲלִי:

כ לַמְנַצֵּחַ מִזְמוֹר לְדָוִד: יַעַנְךָ יְהוָה בְּיוֹם צָרָה יְשַׂגֶּבְךָ שֵׁם ׀ אֱלֹהֵי יַעֲקֹב: יִשְׁלַח־ עֶזְרְךָ מִקֹּדֶשׁ וּמִצִּיּוֹן יִסְעָדֶךָּ: יִזְכֹּר כָּל־מִנְחֹתֶךָ וְעוֹלָתְךָ יְדַשְּׁנֶה סֶלָה: יִתֶּן־ לְךָ כִלְבָבֶךָ וְכָל־עֲצָתְךָ יְמַלֵּא: נְרַנְּנָה ׀ בִּישׁוּעָתֶךָ וּבְשֵׁם־אֱלֹהֵינוּ נִדְגֹּל יְמַלֵּא יְהוָה כָּל־מִשְׁאֲלוֹתֶיךָ: עַתָּה יָדַעְתִּי כִּי הוֹשִׁיעַ ׀ יְהוָה מְשִׁיחוֹ יַעֲנֵהוּ מִשְּׁמֵי קָדְשׁוֹ בִּגְבֻרוֹת יֵשַׁע יְמִינוֹ: אֵלֶּה בָרֶכֶב וְאֵלֶּה בַסּוּסִים וַאֲנַחְנוּ ׀ בְּשֵׁם־יְהוָה אֱלֹהֵינוּ נַזְכִּיר: הֵמָּה כָּרְעוּ וְנָפָלוּ וַאֲנַחְנוּ קַּמְנוּ וַנִּתְעוֹדָד: יְהוָה הוֹשִׁיעָה הַמֶּלֶךְ יַעֲנֵנוּ בְיוֹם־קָרְאֵנוּ:

כא לַמְנַצֵּחַ מִזְמוֹר לְדָוִד: יְהוָה בְּעָזְּךָ יִשְׂמַח־מֶלֶךְ וּבִישׁוּעָתְךָ מַה־יָּגֶל מְאֹד: תַּאֲוַת לִבּוֹ נָתַתָּה לּוֹ וַאֲרֶשֶׁת שְׂפָתָיו בַּל־מָנַעְתָּ סֶּלָה: כִּי־תְקַדְּמֶנּוּ בִּרְכוֹת טוֹב תָּשִׁית לְרֹאשׁוֹ עֲטֶרֶת פָּז: חַיִּים ׀ שָׁאַל מִמְּךָ נָתַתָּה לּוֹ אֹרֶךְ יָמִים עוֹלָם וָעֶד: גָּדוֹל כְּבוֹדוֹ בִּישׁוּעָתֶךָ הוֹד וְהָדָר תְּשַׁוֶּה עָלָיו: כִּי־תְשִׁיתֵהוּ בְרָכוֹת לָעַד תְּחַדֵּהוּ בְשִׂמְחָה אֶת־פָּנֶיךָ: כִּי־הַמֶּלֶךְ בֹּטֵחַ בַּיהוָה וּבְחֶסֶד עֶלְיוֹן בַּל־יִמּוֹט: תִּמְצָא יָדְךָ לְכָל־אֹיְבֶיךָ יְמִינְךָ תִּמְצָא שֹׂנְאֶיךָ: תְּשִׁיתֵמוֹ ׀ כְּתַנּוּר אֵשׁ לְעֵת פָּנֶיךָ יְהוָה בְּאַפּוֹ יְבַלְּעֵם וְתֹאכְלֵם אֵשׁ: פִּרְיָמוֹ מֵאֶרֶץ תְּאַבֵּד וְזַרְעָם מִבְּנֵי

אָדָם: כִּי-נָטוּ עָלֶיךָ רָעָה חָשְׁבוּ מְזִמָּה בַּל-יוּכָלוּ: כִּי תְּשִׁיתֵמוֹ שֶׁכֶם בְּמֵיתָרֶיךָ תְּכוֹנֵן עַל-פְּנֵיהֶם: רוּמָה יְהוָה בְּעֻזֶּךָ נָשִׁירָה וּנְזַמְּרָה גְּבוּרָתֶךָ:

כב לַמְנַצֵּחַ עַל-אַיֶּלֶת הַשַּׁחַר מִזְמוֹר לְדָוִד: אֵלִי אֵלִי לָמָה עֲזַבְתָּנִי רָחוֹק מִישׁוּעָתִי דִּבְרֵי שַׁאֲגָתִי: אֱלֹהַי אֶקְרָא יוֹמָם וְלֹא תַעֲנֶה וְלַיְלָה וְלֹא-דוּמִיָּה לִי: וְאַתָּה קָדוֹשׁ יוֹשֵׁב תְּהִלּוֹת יִשְׂרָאֵל: בְּךָ בָּטְחוּ אֲבֹתֵינוּ בָּטְחוּ וַתְּפַלְּטֵמוֹ: אֵלֶיךָ זָעֲקוּ וְנִמְלָטוּ בְּךָ בָטְחוּ וְלֹא-בוֹשׁוּ: וְאָנֹכִי תוֹלַעַת וְלֹא-אִישׁ חֶרְפַּת אָדָם וּבְזוּי עָם: כָּל-רֹאַי יַלְעִגוּ לִי יַפְטִירוּ בְשָׂפָה יָנִיעוּ רֹאשׁ: גֹּל אֶל-יְהוָה יְפַלְּטֵהוּ יַצִּילֵהוּ כִּי חָפֵץ בּוֹ: כִּי-אַתָּה גֹחִי מִבָּטֶן מַבְטִיחִי עַל-שְׁדֵי אִמִּי: עָלֶיךָ הָשְׁלַכְתִּי מֵרָחֶם מִבֶּטֶן אִמִּי אֵלִי אָתָּה: אַל-תִּרְחַק מִמֶּנִּי כִּי-צָרָה קְרוֹבָה כִּי-אֵין עוֹזֵר: סְבָבוּנִי פָּרִים רַבִּים אַבִּירֵי בָשָׁן כִּתְּרוּנִי: פָּצוּ עָלַי פִּיהֶם אַרְיֵה טֹרֵף וְשֹׁאֵג: כַּמַּיִם נִשְׁפַּכְתִּי וְהִתְפָּרְדוּ כָּל-עַצְמוֹתָי הָיָה לִבִּי כַּדּוֹנָג נָמֵס בְּתוֹךְ מֵעָי: יָבֵשׁ כַּחֶרֶשׂ כֹּחִי וּלְשׁוֹנִי מֻדְבָּק מַלְקוֹחָי וְלַעֲפַר-מָוֶת תִּשְׁפְּתֵנִי: כִּי סְבָבוּנִי כְּלָבִים עֲדַת מְרֵעִים הִקִּיפוּנִי כָּאֲרִי יָדַי וְרַגְלָי: אֲסַפֵּר כָּל-עַצְמוֹתָי הֵמָּה יַבִּיטוּ יִרְאוּ-בִי: יְחַלְּקוּ בְגָדַי לָהֶם וְעַל-לְבוּשִׁי יַפִּילוּ גוֹרָל: וְאַתָּה יְהוָה אַל-תִּרְחָק אֱיָלוּתִי לְעֶזְרָתִי חוּשָׁה: הַצִּילָה מֵחֶרֶב נַפְשִׁי מִיַּד-כֶּלֶב יְחִידָתִי: הוֹשִׁיעֵנִי מִפִּי אַרְיֵה וּמִקַּרְנֵי רֵמִים עֲנִיתָנִי: אֲסַפְּרָה שִׁמְךָ לְאֶחָי בְּתוֹךְ קָהָל אֲהַלְלֶךָּ: יִרְאֵי יְהוָה הַלְלוּהוּ כָּל-זֶרַע יַעֲקֹב כַּבְּדוּהוּ וְגוּרוּ מִמֶּנּוּ כָּל-זֶרַע יִשְׂרָאֵל: כִּי לֹא-בָזָה וְלֹא שִׁקַּץ עֱנוּת עָנִי וְלֹא-הִסְתִּיר פָּנָיו מִמֶּנּוּ וּבְשַׁוְּעוֹ אֵלָיו שָׁמֵעַ: מֵאִתְּךָ תְהִלָּתִי בְּקָהָל רָב נְדָרַי אֲשַׁלֵּם נֶגֶד יְרֵאָיו: יֹאכְלוּ עֲנָוִים וְיִשְׂבָּעוּ יְהַלְלוּ יְהוָה דֹּרְשָׁיו יְחִי לְבַבְכֶם לָעַד: יִזְכְּרוּ וְיָשֻׁבוּ אֶל-יְהוָה כָּל-אַפְסֵי-אָרֶץ וְיִשְׁתַּחֲווּ לְפָנֶיךָ כָּל-מִשְׁפְּחוֹת גּוֹיִם: כִּי לַיהוָה הַמְּלוּכָה וּמֹשֵׁל בַּגּוֹיִם: אָכְלוּ וַיִּשְׁתַּחֲווּ כָּל-דִּשְׁנֵי-אֶרֶץ לְפָנָיו יִכְרְעוּ כָּל-יוֹרְדֵי עָפָר וְנַפְשׁוֹ לֹא חִיָּה: זֶרַע יַעַבְדֶנּוּ יְסֻפַּר לַאדֹנָי לַדּוֹר: יָבֹאוּ וְיַגִּידוּ צִדְקָתוֹ לְעַם נוֹלָד כִּי עָשָׂה:

כג מִזְמוֹר לְדָוִד יְהוָה רֹעִי לֹא אֶחְסָר: בִּנְאוֹת דֶּשֶׁא יַרְבִּיצֵנִי עַל-מֵי מְנֻחוֹת יְנַהֲלֵנִי: נַפְשִׁי יְשׁוֹבֵב יַנְחֵנִי בְמַעְגְּלֵי-צֶדֶק לְמַעַן שְׁמוֹ: גַּם כִּי-אֵלֵךְ בְּגֵיא צַלְמָוֶת לֹא-אִירָא רָע כִּי-אַתָּה עִמָּדִי שִׁבְטְךָ וּמִשְׁעַנְתֶּךָ הֵמָּה יְנַחֲמֻנִי: תַּעֲרֹךְ לְפָנַי שֻׁלְחָן נֶגֶד צֹרְרָי דִּשַּׁנְתָּ בַשֶּׁמֶן רֹאשִׁי כּוֹסִי רְוָיָה: אַךְ טוֹב וָחֶסֶד יִרְדְּפוּנִי כָּל-יְמֵי חַיָּי וְשַׁבְתִּי בְּבֵית-יְהוָה לְאֹרֶךְ יָמִים:

כד לְדָוִד מִזְמוֹר לַיהוָה הָאָרֶץ וּמְלוֹאָהּ תֵּבֵל וְיֹשְׁבֵי בָהּ: כִּי-הוּא עַל-יַמִּים יְסָדָהּ

*כד לחודש

וְעַל־נְהָרוֹת יְכוֹנְנֶהָ: מִי־יַעֲלֶה בְהַר־יְהֹוָה וּמִי־יָקוּם בִּמְקוֹם קָדְשׁוֹ: נְקִי
כַפַּיִם וּבַר־לֵבָב אֲשֶׁר לֹא־נָשָׂא לַשָּׁוְא נַפְשִׁי וְלֹא נִשְׁבַּע לְמִרְמָה: יִשָּׂא בְרָכָה
מֵאֵת יְהֹוָה וּצְדָקָה מֵאֱלֹהֵי יִשְׁעוֹ: זֶה דּוֹר דֹּרְשָׁיו מְבַקְשֵׁי פָנֶיךָ יַעֲקֹב סֶלָה:
שְׂאוּ שְׁעָרִים ׀ רָאשֵׁיכֶם וְהִנָּשְׂאוּ פִּתְחֵי עוֹלָם וְיָבוֹא מֶלֶךְ הַכָּבוֹד: מִי זֶה
מֶלֶךְ הַכָּבוֹד יְהֹוָה עִזּוּז וְגִבּוֹר יְהֹוָה גִּבּוֹר מִלְחָמָה: שְׂאוּ שְׁעָרִים ׀ רָאשֵׁיכֶם
וּשְׂאוּ פִּתְחֵי עוֹלָם וְיָבֹא מֶלֶךְ הַכָּבוֹד: מִי הוּא זֶה מֶלֶךְ הַכָּבוֹד יְהֹוָה צְבָאוֹת
הוּא מֶלֶךְ הַכָּבוֹד סֶלָה:

כה לְדָוִד אֵלֶיךָ יְהֹוָה נַפְשִׁי אֶשָּׂא: אֱלֹהַי בְּךָ בָטַחְתִּי אַל־אֵבוֹשָׁה אַל־יַעַלְצוּ
אֹיְבַי לִי: גַּם כָּל־קֹוֶיךָ לֹא יֵבֹשׁוּ יֵבֹשׁוּ הַבּוֹגְדִים רֵיקָם: דְּרָכֶיךָ יְהֹוָה הוֹדִיעֵנִי
אֹרְחוֹתֶיךָ לַמְּדֵנִי: הַדְרִיכֵנִי בַאֲמִתֶּךָ ׀ וְלַמְּדֵנִי כִּי־אַתָּה אֱלֹהֵי יִשְׁעִי אוֹתְךָ
קִוִּיתִי כָּל־הַיּוֹם: זְכֹר־רַחֲמֶיךָ יְהֹוָה וַחֲסָדֶיךָ כִּי מֵעוֹלָם הֵמָּה: חַטֹּאות נְעוּרַי ׀
וּפְשָׁעַי אַל־תִּזְכֹּר כְּחַסְדְּךָ זְכָר־לִי־אַתָּה לְמַעַן טוּבְךָ יְהֹוָה: טוֹב־וְיָשָׁר יְהֹוָה
עַל־כֵּן יוֹרֶה חַטָּאִים בַּדָּרֶךְ: יַדְרֵךְ עֲנָוִים בַּמִּשְׁפָּט וִילַמֵּד עֲנָוִים דַּרְכּוֹ: כָּל־
אָרְחוֹת יְהֹוָה חֶסֶד וֶאֱמֶת לְנֹצְרֵי בְרִיתוֹ וְעֵדֹתָיו: לְמַעַן־שִׁמְךָ יְהֹוָה וְסָלַחְתָּ
לַעֲוֹנִי כִּי רַב־הוּא: מִי־זֶה הָאִישׁ יְרֵא יְהֹוָה יוֹרֶנּוּ בְּדֶרֶךְ יִבְחָר: נַפְשׁוֹ בְּטוֹב תָּלִין
וְזַרְעוֹ יִירַשׁ אָרֶץ: סוֹד יְהֹוָה לִירֵאָיו וּבְרִיתוֹ לְהוֹדִיעָם: עֵינַי תָּמִיד אֶל־יְהֹוָה
כִּי הוּא־יוֹצִיא מֵרֶשֶׁת רַגְלָי: פְּנֵה־אֵלַי וְחָנֵּנִי כִּי־יָחִיד וְעָנִי אָנִי: צָרוֹת לְבָבִי
הִרְחִיבוּ מִמְּצוּקוֹתַי הוֹצִיאֵנִי: רְאֵה עָנְיִי וַעֲמָלִי וְשָׂא לְכָל־חַטֹּאותָי: רְאֵה־אֹיְבַי
כִּי־רָבּוּ וְשִׂנְאַת חָמָס שְׂנֵאוּנִי: שָׁמְרָה נַפְשִׁי וְהַצִּילֵנִי אַל־אֵבוֹשׁ כִּי־חָסִיתִי
בָךְ: תֹּם־וָיֹשֶׁר יִצְּרוּנִי כִּי קִוִּיתִיךָ: פְּדֵה אֱלֹהִים אֶת־יִשְׂרָאֵל מִכֹּל צָרוֹתָיו:

כו לְדָוִד ׀ שָׁפְטֵנִי יְהֹוָה כִּי־אֲנִי בְּתֻמִּי הָלַכְתִּי וּבַיהֹוָה בָּטַחְתִּי לֹא אֶמְעָד: בְּחָנֵנִי
יְהֹוָה וְנַסֵּנִי צָרְפָה כִלְיוֹתַי וְלִבִּי: כִּי־חַסְדְּךָ לְנֶגֶד עֵינָי וְהִתְהַלַּכְתִּי בַּאֲמִתֶּךָ: צָרְפָה
לֹא־יָשַׁבְתִּי עִם־מְתֵי־שָׁוְא וְעִם נַעֲלָמִים לֹא אָבוֹא: שָׂנֵאתִי קְהַל מְרֵעִים
וְעִם־רְשָׁעִים לֹא אֵשֵׁב: אֶרְחַץ בְּנִקָּיוֹן כַּפָּי וַאֲסֹבְבָה אֶת־מִזְבַּחֲךָ יְהֹוָה: לַשְׁמִעַ
בְּקוֹל תּוֹדָה וּלְסַפֵּר כָּל־נִפְלְאוֹתֶיךָ: יְהֹוָה אָהַבְתִּי מְעוֹן בֵּיתֶךָ וּמְקוֹם מִשְׁכַּן
כְּבוֹדֶךָ: אַל־תֶּאֱסֹף עִם־חַטָּאִים נַפְשִׁי וְעִם־אַנְשֵׁי דָמִים חַיָּי: אֲשֶׁר־בִּידֵיהֶם
זִמָּה וִימִינָם מָלְאָה שֹּׁחַד: וַאֲנִי בְּתֻמִּי אֵלֵךְ פְּדֵנִי וְחָנֵּנִי: רַגְלִי עָמְדָה בְמִישׁוֹר
בְּמַקְהֵלִים אֲבָרֵךְ יְהֹוָה:

כז לְדָוִד ׀ יְהֹוָה ׀ אוֹרִי וְיִשְׁעִי מִמִּי אִירָא יְהֹוָה מָעוֹז־חַיַּי מִמִּי אֶפְחָד: בִּקְרֹב

עָלַי ׀ מְרֵעִים לֶאֱכֹל אֶת־בְּשָׂרִי צָרַי וְאֹיְבַי לִי הֵמָּה כָשְׁלוּ וְנָפָלוּ: אִם־תַּחֲנֶה
עָלַי ׀ מַחֲנֶה לֹא־יִירָא לִבִּי אִם־תָּקוּם עָלַי מִלְחָמָה בְּזֹאת אֲנִי בוֹטֵחַ: אַחַת ׀
שָׁאַלְתִּי מֵאֵת־יְהוָה אוֹתָהּ אֲבַקֵּשׁ שִׁבְתִּי בְּבֵית־יְהוָה כָּל־יְמֵי חַיַּי לַחֲזוֹת
בְּנֹעַם־יְהוָה וּלְבַקֵּר בְּהֵיכָלוֹ: כִּי יִצְפְּנֵנִי ׀ בְּסֻכֹּה בְּיוֹם רָעָה יַסְתִּרֵנִי בְּסֵתֶר
אָהֳלוֹ בְּצוּר יְרוֹמְמֵנִי: וְעַתָּה יָרוּם רֹאשִׁי עַל אֹיְבַי סְבִיבוֹתַי וְאֶזְבְּחָה בְאָהֳלוֹ
זִבְחֵי תְרוּעָה אָשִׁירָה וַאֲזַמְּרָה לַיהוָה: שְׁמַע־יְהוָה קוֹלִי אֶקְרָא וְחָנֵּנִי וַעֲנֵנִי:
לְךָ ׀ אָמַר לִבִּי בַּקְּשׁוּ פָנָי אֶת־פָּנֶיךָ יְהוָה אֲבַקֵּשׁ: אַל־תַּסְתֵּר פָּנֶיךָ ׀ מִמֶּנִּי
אַל תַּט־בְּאַף עַבְדֶּךָ עֶזְרָתִי הָיִיתָ אַל־תִּטְּשֵׁנִי וְאַל־תַּעַזְבֵנִי אֱלֹהֵי יִשְׁעִי:
כִּי־אָבִי וְאִמִּי עֲזָבוּנִי וַיהוָה יַאַסְפֵנִי: הוֹרֵנִי יְהוָה דַּרְכֶּךָ וּנְחֵנִי בְּאֹרַח מִישׁוֹר
לְמַעַן שׁוֹרְרָי: אַל־תִּתְּנֵנִי בְּנֶפֶשׁ צָרָי כִּי קָמוּ־בִי עֵדֵי־שֶׁקֶר וִיפֵחַ חָמָס:
לׅׄוּׅׄלֵׅׄאׅׄ הֶאֱמַנְתִּי לִרְאוֹת בְּטוּב־יְהוָה בְּאֶרֶץ חַיִּים: קַוֵּה אֶל־יְהוָה חֲזַק וְיַאֲמֵץ לִבֶּךָ
וְקַוֵּה אֶל־יְהוָה:

כח לְדָוִד אֵלֶיךָ יְהוָה ׀ אֶקְרָא צוּרִי אַל־תֶּחֱרַשׁ מִמֶּנִּי פֶּן־תֶּחֱשֶׁה מִמֶּנִּי וְנִמְשַׁלְתִּי
עִם־יוֹרְדֵי בוֹר: שְׁמַע קוֹל תַּחֲנוּנַי בְּשַׁוְּעִי אֵלֶיךָ בְּנָשְׂאִי יָדַי אֶל־דְּבִיר קָדְשֶׁךָ:
אַל־תִּמְשְׁכֵנִי עִם־רְשָׁעִים וְעִם־פֹּעֲלֵי אָוֶן דֹּבְרֵי שָׁלוֹם עִם־רֵעֵיהֶם וְרָעָה
בִּלְבָבָם: תֶּן־לָהֶם כְּפָעֳלָם וּכְרֹעַ מַעַלְלֵיהֶם כְּמַעֲשֵׂה יְדֵיהֶם תֵּן לָהֶם הָשֵׁב
גְּמוּלָם לָהֶם: כִּי לֹא יָבִינוּ אֶל־פְּעֻלֹּת יְהוָה וְאֶל־מַעֲשֵׂה יָדָיו יֶהֶרְסֵם וְלֹא יִבְנֵם:
בָּרוּךְ יְהוָה כִּי־שָׁמַע קוֹל תַּחֲנוּנָי: יְהוָה ׀ עֻזִּי וּמָגִנִּי בּוֹ בָטַח לִבִּי וְנֶעֱזָרְתִּי וַיַּעֲלֹז
לִבִּי וּמִשִּׁירִי אֲהוֹדֶנּוּ: יְהוָה עֹז־לָמוֹ וּמָעוֹז יְשׁוּעוֹת מְשִׁיחוֹ הוּא: הוֹשִׁיעָה ׀
אֶת־עַמֶּךָ וּבָרֵךְ אֶת־נַחֲלָתֶךָ וּרְעֵם וְנַשְּׂאֵם עַד־הָעוֹלָם:

כט* מִזְמוֹר לְדָוִד הָבוּ לַיהוָה בְּנֵי אֵלִים הָבוּ לַיהוָה כָּבוֹד וָעֹז: הָבוּ לַיהוָה כְּבוֹד
שְׁמוֹ הִשְׁתַּחֲווּ לַיהוָה בְּהַדְרַת־קֹדֶשׁ: קוֹל יְהוָה עַל־הַמָּיִם אֵל־הַכָּבוֹד הִרְעִים
יְהוָה עַל־מַיִם רַבִּים: קוֹל־יְהוָה בַּכֹּחַ קוֹל יְהוָה בֶּהָדָר: קוֹל יְהוָה שֹׁבֵר אֲרָזִים
וַיְשַׁבֵּר יְהוָה אֶת־אַרְזֵי הַלְּבָנוֹן: וַיַּרְקִידֵם כְּמוֹ־עֵגֶל לְבָנוֹן וְשִׂרְיֹן כְּמוֹ בֶן־
רְאֵמִים: קוֹל־יְהוָה חֹצֵב לַהֲבוֹת אֵשׁ: קוֹל יְהוָה יָחִיל מִדְבָּר יָחִיל יְהוָה מִדְבַּר
קָדֵשׁ: קוֹל יְהוָה ׀ יְחוֹלֵל אַיָּלוֹת וַיֶּחֱשֹׂף יְעָרוֹת וּבְהֵיכָלוֹ כֻּלּוֹ אֹמֵר כָּבוֹד:
יְהוָה לַמַּבּוּל יָשָׁב וַיֵּשֶׁב יְהוָה מֶלֶךְ לְעוֹלָם: יְהוָה עֹז לְעַמּוֹ יִתֵּן יְהוָה ׀ יְבָרֵךְ
אֶת־עַמּוֹ בַשָּׁלוֹם:

ל** מִזְמוֹר שִׁיר־חֲנֻכַּת הַבַּיִת לְדָוִד: אֲרוֹמִמְךָ יְהוָה כִּי דִלִּיתָנִי וְלֹא־שִׂמַּחְתָּ אֹיְבַי לִי

לִי: יְהוָה אֱלֹהַי שִׁוַּעְתִּי אֵלֶיךָ וַתִּרְפָּאֵנִי: יְהוָה הֶעֱלִיתָ מִן־שְׁאוֹל נַפְשִׁי חִיִּיתַנִי מִיָּרְדִי־בוֹר: זַמְּרוּ לַיהוָה חֲסִידָיו וְהוֹדוּ לְזֵכֶר קָדְשׁוֹ: כִּי רֶגַע בְּאַפּוֹ חַיִּים מִיָּרְדִי בְּרְצוֹנוֹ בָּעֶרֶב יָלִין בֶּכִי וְלַבֹּקֶר רִנָּה: וַאֲנִי אָמַרְתִּי בְשַׁלְוִי בַּל־אֶמּוֹט לְעוֹלָם: יְהוָה בִּרְצוֹנְךָ הֶעֱמַדְתָּה לְהַרְרִי עֹז הִסְתַּרְתָּ פָנֶיךָ הָיִיתִי נִבְהָל: אֵלֶיךָ יְהוָה אֶקְרָא וְאֶל־אֲדֹנָי אֶתְחַנָּן: מַה־בֶּצַע בְּדָמִי בְּרִדְתִּי אֶל־שָׁחַת הֲיוֹדְךָ עָפָר הֲיַגִּיד אֲמִתֶּךָ: שְׁמַע־יְהוָה וְחָנֵּנִי יְהוָה הֱיֵה־עֹזֵר לִי: הָפַכְתָּ מִסְפְּדִי לְמָחוֹל לִי פִּתַּחְתָּ שַׂקִּי וַתְּאַזְּרֵנִי שִׂמְחָה: לְמַעַן יְזַמֶּרְךָ כָבוֹד וְלֹא יִדֹּם יְהוָה אֱלֹהַי לְעוֹלָם אוֹדֶךָּ:

לא לַמְנַצֵּחַ מִזְמוֹר לְדָוִד: בְּךָ־יְהוָה חָסִיתִי אַל־אֵבוֹשָׁה לְעוֹלָם בְּצִדְקָתְךָ פַלְּטֵנִי: הַטֵּה אֵלַי אָזְנְךָ מְהֵרָה הַצִּילֵנִי הֱיֵה לִי לְצוּר־מָעוֹז לְבֵית מְצוּדוֹת לְהוֹשִׁיעֵנִי: כִּי־סַלְעִי וּמְצוּדָתִי אָתָּה וּלְמַעַן שִׁמְךָ תַּנְחֵנִי וּתְנַהֲלֵנִי: תּוֹצִיאֵנִי מֵרֶשֶׁת זוּ טָמְנוּ לִי כִּי־אַתָּה מָעוּזִּי: בְּיָדְךָ אַפְקִיד רוּחִי פָּדִיתָה אוֹתִי יְהוָה אֵל אֱמֶת: שָׂנֵאתִי הַשֹּׁמְרִים הַבְלֵי־שָׁוְא וַאֲנִי אֶל־יְהוָה בָּטָחְתִּי: אָגִילָה וְאֶשְׂמְחָה בְּחַסְדֶּךָ אֲשֶׁר רָאִיתָ אֶת־עָנְיִי יָדַעְתָּ בְּצָרוֹת נַפְשִׁי: וְלֹא הִסְגַּרְתַּנִי בְּיַד־אוֹיֵב הֶעֱמַדְתָּ בַמֶּרְחָב רַגְלָי: חָנֵּנִי יְהוָה כִּי צַר לִי עָשְׁשָׁה בְכַעַס עֵינִי נַפְשִׁי וּבִטְנִי: כִּי כָלוּ בְיָגוֹן חַיַּי וּשְׁנוֹתַי בַּאֲנָחָה כָּשַׁל בַּעֲוֹנִי כֹחִי וַעֲצָמַי עָשֵׁשׁוּ: מִכָּל־צֹרְרַי הָיִיתִי חֶרְפָּה וְלִשֲׁכֵנַי מְאֹד וּפַחַד לִמְיֻדָּעָי רֹאַי בַּחוּץ נָדְדוּ מִמֶּנִּי: נִשְׁכַּחְתִּי כְּמֵת מִלֵּב הָיִיתִי כִּכְלִי אֹבֵד: כִּי שָׁמַעְתִּי דִּבַּת רַבִּים מָגוֹר מִסָּבִיב בְּהִוָּסְדָם יַחַד עָלַי לָקַחַת נַפְשִׁי זָמָמוּ: וַאֲנִי עָלֶיךָ בָטַחְתִּי יְהוָה אָמַרְתִּי אֱלֹהַי אָתָּה: בְּיָדְךָ עִתֹּתָי הַצִּילֵנִי מִיַּד־אוֹיְבַי וּמֵרֹדְפָי: הָאִירָה פָנֶיךָ עַל־עַבְדֶּךָ הוֹשִׁיעֵנִי בְחַסְדֶּךָ: יְהוָה אַל־אֵבוֹשָׁה כִּי קְרָאתִיךָ יֵבֹשׁוּ רְשָׁעִים יִדְּמוּ לִשְׁאוֹל: תֵּאָלַמְנָה שִׂפְתֵי שָׁקֶר הַדֹּבְרוֹת עַל־צַדִּיק עָתָק בְּגַאֲוָה וָבוּז: מָה רַב־טוּבְךָ אֲשֶׁר־צָפַנְתָּ לִּירֵאֶיךָ פָּעַלְתָּ לַחֹסִים בָּךְ נֶגֶד בְּנֵי אָדָם: תַּסְתִּירֵם בְּסֵתֶר פָּנֶיךָ מֵרֻכְסֵי אִישׁ תִּצְפְּנֵם בְּסֻכָּה מֵרִיב לְשֹׁנוֹת: בָּרוּךְ יְהוָה כִּי הִפְלִיא חַסְדּוֹ לִי בְּעִיר מָצוֹר: וַאֲנִי אָמַרְתִּי בְחָפְזִי נִגְרַזְתִּי מִנֶּגֶד עֵינֶיךָ אָכֵן שָׁמַעְתָּ קוֹל תַּחֲנוּנַי בְּשַׁוְּעִי אֵלֶיךָ: אֶהֱבוּ אֶת־יְהוָה כָּל־חֲסִידָיו אֱמוּנִים נֹצֵר יְהוָה וּמְשַׁלֵּם עַל־יֶתֶר עֹשֵׂה גַאֲוָה: חִזְקוּ וְיַאֲמֵץ לְבַבְכֶם כָּל־הַמְיַחֲלִים לַיהוָה:

לב לְדָוִד מַשְׂכִּיל אַשְׁרֵי נְשׂוּי־פֶּשַׁע כְּסוּי חֲטָאָה: אַשְׁרֵי אָדָם לֹא יַחְשֹׁב יְהוָה לוֹ עָוֹן וְאֵין בְּרוּחוֹ רְמִיָּה: כִּי־הֶחֱרַשְׁתִּי בָּלוּ עֲצָמָי בְּשַׁאֲגָתִי כָּל־הַיּוֹם: כִּי יוֹמָם

וְלַיְלָה תִּכְבַּד עָלַי יָדֶךָ נֶהְפַּךְ לְשַׁדִּי בְּחַרְבֹנֵי קַיִץ סֶלָה: חַטָּאתִי אוֹדִיעֲךָ וַעֲוֹנִי
לֹא־כִסִּיתִי אָמַרְתִּי אוֹדֶה עֲלֵי פְשָׁעַי לַיהוָה וְאַתָּה נָשָׂאתָ עֲוֹן חַטָּאתִי סֶלָה:
עַל־זֹאת יִתְפַּלֵּל כָּל־חָסִיד ׀ אֵלֶיךָ לְעֵת מְצֹא רַק לְשֵׁטֶף מַיִם רַבִּים אֵלָיו
לֹא יַגִּיעוּ: אַתָּה ׀ סֵתֶר לִי מִצַּר תִּצְּרֵנִי רָנֵּי פַלֵּט תְּסוֹבְבֵנִי סֶלָה: אַשְׂכִּילְךָ ׀
וְאוֹרְךָ בְּדֶרֶךְ־זוּ תֵלֵךְ אִיעֲצָה עָלֶיךָ עֵינִי: אַל־תִּהְיוּ ׀ כְּסוּס כְּפֶרֶד אֵין הָבִין
בְּמֶתֶג־וָרֶסֶן עֶדְיוֹ לִבְלוֹם בַּל קְרֹב אֵלֶיךָ: רַבִּים מַכְאוֹבִים לָרָשָׁע וְהַבּוֹטֵחַ
בַּיהוָה חֶסֶד יְסוֹבְבֶנּוּ: שִׂמְחוּ בַיהוָה וְגִילוּ צַדִּיקִים וְהַרְנִינוּ כָּל־יִשְׁרֵי־לֵב:

לג רַנְּנוּ צַדִּיקִים בַּיהוָה לַיְשָׁרִים נָאוָה תְהִלָּה: הוֹדוּ לַיהוָה בְּכִנּוֹר בְּנֵבֶל עָשׂוֹר
זַמְּרוּ־לוֹ: שִׁירוּ־לוֹ שִׁיר חָדָשׁ הֵיטִיבוּ נַגֵּן בִּתְרוּעָה: כִּי־יָשָׁר דְּבַר־יְהוָה וְכָל־
מַעֲשֵׂהוּ בֶּאֱמוּנָה: אֹהֵב צְדָקָה וּמִשְׁפָּט חֶסֶד יְהוָה מָלְאָה הָאָרֶץ: בִּדְבַר יְהוָה
שָׁמַיִם נַעֲשׂוּ וּבְרוּחַ פִּיו כָּל־צְבָאָם: כֹּנֵס כַּנֵּד מֵי הַיָּם נֹתֵן בְּאֹצָרוֹת תְּהוֹמוֹת:
יִירְאוּ מֵיהוָה כָּל־הָאָרֶץ מִמֶּנּוּ יָגוּרוּ כָּל־יֹשְׁבֵי תֵבֵל: כִּי הוּא אָמַר וַיֶּהִי הוּא־
צִוָּה וַיַּעֲמֹד: יְהוָה הֵפִיר עֲצַת־גּוֹיִם הֵנִיא מַחְשְׁבוֹת עַמִּים: עֲצַת יְהוָה לְעוֹלָם
תַּעֲמֹד מַחְשְׁבוֹת לִבּוֹ לְדֹר וָדֹר: אַשְׁרֵי הַגּוֹי אֲשֶׁר־יְהוָה אֱלֹהָיו הָעָם ׀ בָּחַר
לְנַחֲלָה לוֹ: מִשָּׁמַיִם הִבִּיט יְהוָה רָאָה אֶת־כָּל־בְּנֵי הָאָדָם: מִמְּכוֹן־שִׁבְתּוֹ
הִשְׁגִּיחַ אֶל כָּל־יֹשְׁבֵי הָאָרֶץ: הַיֹּצֵר יַחַד לִבָּם הַמֵּבִין אֶל־כָּל־מַעֲשֵׂיהֶם: אֵין־
הַמֶּלֶךְ נוֹשָׁע בְּרָב־חָיִל גִּבּוֹר לֹא־יִנָּצֵל בְּרָב־כֹּחַ: שֶׁקֶר הַסּוּס לִתְשׁוּעָה וּבְרֹב
חֵילוֹ לֹא יְמַלֵּט: הִנֵּה עֵין יְהוָה אֶל־יְרֵאָיו לַמְיַחֲלִים לְחַסְדּוֹ: לְהַצִּיל מִמָּוֶת
נַפְשָׁם וּלְחַיּוֹתָם בָּרָעָב: נַפְשֵׁנוּ חִכְּתָה לַיהוָה עֶזְרֵנוּ וּמָגִנֵּנוּ הוּא: כִּי־בוֹ יִשְׂמַח
לִבֵּנוּ כִּי בְשֵׁם קָדְשׁוֹ בָטָחְנוּ: יְהִי־חַסְדְּךָ יְהוָה עָלֵינוּ כַּאֲשֶׁר יִחַלְנוּ לָךְ:

לד לְדָוִד בְּשַׁנּוֹתוֹ אֶת־טַעְמוֹ לִפְנֵי אֲבִימֶלֶךְ וַיְגָרֲשֵׁהוּ וַיֵּלַךְ: אֲבָרֲכָה אֶת־יְהוָה
בְּכָל־עֵת תָּמִיד תְּהִלָּתוֹ בְּפִי: בַּיהוָה תִּתְהַלֵּל נַפְשִׁי יִשְׁמְעוּ עֲנָוִים וְיִשְׂמָחוּ:
גַּדְּלוּ לַיהוָה אִתִּי וּנְרוֹמְמָה שְׁמוֹ יַחְדָּו: דָּרַשְׁתִּי אֶת־יְהוָה וְעָנָנִי וּמִכָּל־מְגוּרוֹתַי
הִצִּילָנִי: הִבִּיטוּ אֵלָיו וְנָהָרוּ וּפְנֵיהֶם אַל־יֶחְפָּרוּ: זֶה עָנִי קָרָא וַיהוָה שָׁמֵעַ
וּמִכָּל־צָרוֹתָיו הוֹשִׁיעוֹ: חֹנֶה מַלְאַךְ־יְהוָה סָבִיב לִירֵאָיו וַיְחַלְּצֵם: טַעֲמוּ וּרְאוּ
כִּי־טוֹב יְהוָה אַשְׁרֵי הַגֶּבֶר יֶחֱסֶה־בּוֹ: יְראוּ אֶת־יְהוָה קְדֹשָׁיו כִּי־אֵין מַחְסוֹר
לִירֵאָיו: כְּפִירִים רָשׁוּ וְרָעֵבוּ וְדֹרְשֵׁי יְהוָה לֹא־יַחְסְרוּ כָל־טוֹב: לְכוּ־בָנִים
שִׁמְעוּ־לִי יִרְאַת יְהוָה אֲלַמֶּדְכֶם: מִי־הָאִישׁ הֶחָפֵץ חַיִּים אֹהֵב יָמִים לִרְאוֹת
טוֹב: נְצֹר לְשׁוֹנְךָ מֵרָע וּשְׂפָתֶיךָ מִדַּבֵּר מִרְמָה: סוּר מֵרָע וַעֲשֵׂה־טוֹב בַּקֵּשׁ

שָׁלוֹם וְרָדְפֵהוּ: עֵינֵי יְהוָה אֶל־צַדִּיקִים וְאָזְנָיו אֶל־שַׁוְעָתָם: פְּנֵי יְהוָה בְּעֹשֵׂי רָע לְהַכְרִית מֵאֶרֶץ זִכְרָם: צָעֲקוּ וַיהוָה שָׁמֵעַ וּמִכָּל־צָרוֹתָם הִצִּילָם: קָרוֹב יְהוָה לְנִשְׁבְּרֵי־לֵב וְאֶת־דַּכְּאֵי־רוּחַ יוֹשִׁיעַ: רַבּוֹת רָעוֹת צַדִּיק וּמִכֻּלָּם יַצִּילֶנּוּ יְהוָה: שֹׁמֵר כָּל־עַצְמוֹתָיו אַחַת מֵהֵנָּה לֹא נִשְׁבָּרָה: תְּמוֹתֵת רָשָׁע רָעָה וְשֹׂנְאֵי צַדִּיק יֶאְשָׁמוּ: פּוֹדֶה יְהוָה נֶפֶשׁ עֲבָדָיו וְלֹא יֶאְשְׁמוּ כָּל־הַחֹסִים בּוֹ:

לה לְדָוִד ׀ רִיבָה יְהוָה אֶת־יְרִיבַי לְחַם אֶת־לֹחֲמָי: הַחֲזֵק מָגֵן וְצִנָּה וְקוּמָה בְּעֶזְרָתִי: וְהָרֵק חֲנִית וּסְגֹר לִקְרַאת רֹדְפָי אֱמֹר לְנַפְשִׁי יְשֻׁעָתֵךְ אָנִי: יֵבֹשׁוּ וְיִכָּלְמוּ מְבַקְשֵׁי נַפְשִׁי יִסֹּגוּ אָחוֹר וְיַחְפְּרוּ חֹשְׁבֵי רָעָתִי: יִהְיוּ כְּמֹץ לִפְנֵי־רוּחַ וּמַלְאַךְ יְהוָה דּוֹחֶה: יְהִי־דַרְכָּם חֹשֶׁךְ וַחֲלַקְלַקֹּת וּמַלְאַךְ יְהוָה רֹדְפָם: כִּי־חִנָּם טָמְנוּ־לִי שַׁחַת רִשְׁתָּם חִנָּם חָפְרוּ לְנַפְשִׁי: תְּבוֹאֵהוּ שׁוֹאָה לֹא־יֵדָע וְרִשְׁתּוֹ אֲשֶׁר־טָמַן תִּלְכְּדוֹ בְּשׁוֹאָה יִפָּל־בָּהּ: וְנַפְשִׁי תָּגִיל בַּיהוָה תָּשִׂישׂ בִּישׁוּעָתוֹ: כָּל עַצְמוֹתַי ׀ תֹּאמַרְנָה יְהוָה מִי כָמוֹךָ מַצִּיל עָנִי מֵחָזָק מִמֶּנּוּ וְעָנִי וְאֶבְיוֹן מִגֹּזְלוֹ: יְקוּמוּן עֵדֵי חָמָס אֲשֶׁר לֹא־יָדַעְתִּי יִשְׁאָלוּנִי: יְשַׁלְּמוּנִי רָעָה תַּחַת טוֹבָה שְׁכוֹל לְנַפְשִׁי: וַאֲנִי ׀ בַּחֲלוֹתָם לְבוּשִׁי שָׂק עִנֵּיתִי בַצּוֹם נַפְשִׁי וּתְפִלָּתִי עַל־חֵיקִי תָשׁוּב: כְּרֵעַ־כְּאָח לִי הִתְהַלָּכְתִּי כַּאֲבֶל־אֵם קֹדֵר שַׁחוֹתִי: וּבְצַלְעִי שָׂמְחוּ וְנֶאֱסָפוּ נֶאֶסְפוּ עָלַי נֵכִים וְלֹא יָדַעְתִּי קָרְעוּ וְלֹא־דָמּוּ: בְּחַנְפֵי לַעֲגֵי מָעוֹג חָרֹק עָלַי שִׁנֵּימוֹ: אֲדֹנָי כַּמָּה תִּרְאֶה הָשִׁיבָה נַפְשִׁי מִשֹּׁאֵיהֶם מִכְּפִירִים יְחִידָתִי: אוֹדְךָ בְּקָהָל רָב בְּעַם עָצוּם אֲהַלְלֶךָּ: אַל־יִשְׂמְחוּ־לִי אֹיְבַי שֶׁקֶר שֹׂנְאַי חִנָּם יִקְרְצוּ־עָיִן: כִּי לֹא שָׁלוֹם יְדַבֵּרוּ וְעַל רִגְעֵי־אֶרֶץ דִּבְרֵי מִרְמוֹת יַחֲשֹׁבוּן: וַיַּרְחִיבוּ עָלַי פִּיהֶם אָמְרוּ הֶאָח ׀ הֶאָח רָאֲתָה עֵינֵנוּ: רָאִיתָה יְהוָה אַל־תֶּחֱרַשׁ אֲדֹנָי אַל־תִּרְחַק מִמֶּנִּי: הָעִירָה וְהָקִיצָה לְמִשְׁפָּטִי אֱלֹהַי וַאדֹנָי לְרִיבִי: שָׁפְטֵנִי כְצִדְקְךָ יְהוָה אֱלֹהָי וְאַל־יִשְׂמְחוּ־לִי: אַל־יֹאמְרוּ בְלִבָּם הֶאָח נַפְשֵׁנוּ אַל־יֹאמְרוּ בִּלַּעֲנוּהוּ: יֵבֹשׁוּ וְיַחְפְּרוּ ׀ יַחְדָּו שְׂמֵחֵי רָעָתִי יִלְבְּשׁוּ־בֹשֶׁת וּכְלִמָּה הַמַּגְדִּילִים עָלָי: יָרֹנּוּ וְיִשְׂמְחוּ חֲפֵצֵי צִדְקִי וְיֹאמְרוּ תָמִיד יִגְדַּל יְהוָה הֶחָפֵץ שְׁלוֹם עַבְדּוֹ: וּלְשׁוֹנִי תֶּהְגֶּה צִדְקֶךָ כָּל־הַיּוֹם תְּהִלָּתֶךָ:

לו לַמְנַצֵּחַ ׀ לְעֶבֶד־יְהוָה לְדָוִד: נְאֻם־פֶּשַׁע לָרָשָׁע בְּקֶרֶב לִבִּי אֵין־פַּחַד אֱלֹהִים לְנֶגֶד עֵינָיו: כִּי־הֶחֱלִיק אֵלָיו בְּעֵינָיו לִמְצֹא עֲוֹנוֹ לִשְׂנֹא: דִּבְרֵי־פִיו אָוֶן וּמִרְמָה חָדַל לְהַשְׂכִּיל לְהֵיטִיב: אָוֶן ׀ יַחְשֹׁב עַל־מִשְׁכָּבוֹ יִתְיַצֵּב עַל־דֶּרֶךְ לֹא־טוֹב רָע לֹא יִמְאָס: יְהוָה בְּהַשָּׁמַיִם חַסְדֶּךָ אֱמוּנָתְךָ עַד־שְׁחָקִים: צִדְקָתְךָ ׀ כְּהַרְרֵי־אֵל

מִשְׁפָּטֶיךָ תְּהוֹם רַבָּה אָדָם וּבְהֵמָה תוֹשִׁיעַ יְהֹוָה: מַה־יָּקָר חַסְדְּךָ אֱלֹהִים וּבְנֵי אָדָם בְּצֵל כְּנָפֶיךָ יֶחֱסָיוּן: יִרְוְיֻן מִדֶּשֶׁן בֵּיתֶךָ וְנַחַל עֲדָנֶיךָ תַשְׁקֵם: כִּי־עִמְּךָ מְקוֹר חַיִּים בְּאוֹרְךָ נִרְאֶה־אוֹר: מְשֹׁךְ חַסְדְּךָ לְיֹדְעֶיךָ וְצִדְקָתְךָ לְיִשְׁרֵי־לֵב: אַל־תְּבוֹאֵנִי רֶגֶל גַּאֲוָה וְיַד־רְשָׁעִים אַל־תְּנִדֵנִי: שָׁם נָפְלוּ פֹּעֲלֵי אָוֶן דֹּחוּ וְלֹא־יָכְלוּ קוּם:

לְדָוִד ׀ אַל־תִּתְחַר בַּמְּרֵעִים אַל־תְּקַנֵּא בְּעֹשֵׂי עַוְלָה: כִּי כֶחָצִיר מְהֵרָה יִמָּלוּ וּכְיֶרֶק דֶּשֶׁא יִבּוֹלוּן: בְּטַח בַּיהֹוָה וַעֲשֵׂה־טוֹב שְׁכָן־אֶרֶץ וּרְעֵה אֱמוּנָה: וְהִתְעַנַּג עַל־יְהֹוָה וְיִתֶּן־לְךָ מִשְׁאֲלֹת לִבֶּךָ: גּוֹל עַל־יְהֹוָה דַּרְכֶּךָ וּבְטַח עָלָיו וְהוּא יַעֲשֶׂה: וְהוֹצִיא כָאוֹר צִדְקֶךָ וּמִשְׁפָּטֶךָ כַּצָּהֳרָיִם: דּוֹם ׀ לַיהֹוָה וְהִתְחוֹלֵל לוֹ אַל־תִּתְחַר בְּמַצְלִיחַ דַּרְכּוֹ בְּאִישׁ עֹשֶׂה מְזִמּוֹת: הֶרֶף מֵאַף וַעֲזֹב חֵמָה אַל־תִּתְחַר אַךְ־לְהָרֵעַ: כִּי־מְרֵעִים יִכָּרֵתוּן וְקֹוֵי יְהֹוָה הֵמָּה יִירְשׁוּ־אָרֶץ: וְעוֹד מְעַט וְאֵין רָשָׁע וְהִתְבּוֹנַנְתָּ עַל־מְקוֹמוֹ וְאֵינֶנּוּ: וַעֲנָוִים יִירְשׁוּ־אָרֶץ וְהִתְעַנְּגוּ עַל־רֹב שָׁלוֹם: זֹמֵם רָשָׁע לַצַּדִּיק וְחֹרֵק עָלָיו שִׁנָּיו: אֲדֹנָי יִשְׂחַק־לוֹ כִּי־רָאָה כִּי־יָבֹא יוֹמוֹ: חֶרֶב ׀ פָּתְחוּ רְשָׁעִים וְדָרְכוּ קַשְׁתָּם לְהַפִּיל עָנִי וְאֶבְיוֹן לִטְבוֹחַ יִשְׁרֵי־דָרֶךְ: חַרְבָּם תָּבוֹא בְלִבָּם וְקַשְּׁתוֹתָם תִּשָּׁבַרְנָה: טוֹב־מְעַט לַצַּדִּיק מֵהֲמוֹן רְשָׁעִים רַבִּים: כִּי זְרוֹעוֹת רְשָׁעִים תִּשָּׁבַרְנָה וְסוֹמֵךְ צַדִּיקִים יְהֹוָה: יוֹדֵעַ יְהֹוָה יְמֵי תְמִימִם וְנַחֲלָתָם לְעוֹלָם תִּהְיֶה: לֹא־יֵבֹשׁוּ בְּעֵת רָעָה וּבִימֵי רְעָבוֹן יִשְׂבָּעוּ: כִּי רְשָׁעִים ׀ יֹאבֵדוּ וְאֹיְבֵי יְהֹוָה כִּיקַר כָּרִים כָּלוּ בֶעָשָׁן כָּלוּ: לֹוֶה רָשָׁע וְלֹא יְשַׁלֵּם וְצַדִּיק חוֹנֵן וְנוֹתֵן: כִּי מְבֹרָכָיו יִירְשׁוּ אָרֶץ וּמְקֻלָּלָיו יִכָּרֵתוּ: מֵיְהֹוָה מִצְעֲדֵי־גֶבֶר כּוֹנָנוּ וְדַרְכּוֹ יֶחְפָּץ: כִּי־יִפֹּל לֹא־יוּטָל כִּי־יְהֹוָה סוֹמֵךְ יָדוֹ: נַעַר ׀ הָיִיתִי גַּם־זָקַנְתִּי וְלֹא־רָאִיתִי צַדִּיק נֶעֱזָב וְזַרְעוֹ מְבַקֶּשׁ־לָחֶם: כָּל־הַיּוֹם חוֹנֵן וּמַלְוֶה וְזַרְעוֹ לִבְרָכָה: סוּר מֵרָע וַעֲשֵׂה־טוֹב וּשְׁכֹן לְעוֹלָם: כִּי יְהֹוָה ׀ אֹהֵב מִשְׁפָּט וְלֹא־יַעֲזֹב אֶת־חֲסִידָיו לְעוֹלָם נִשְׁמָרוּ וְזֶרַע רְשָׁעִים נִכְרָת: צַדִּיקִים יִירְשׁוּ־אָרֶץ וְיִשְׁכְּנוּ לָעַד עָלֶיהָ: פִּי־צַדִּיק יֶהְגֶּה חָכְמָה וּלְשׁוֹנוֹ תְּדַבֵּר מִשְׁפָּט: תּוֹרַת אֱלֹהָיו בְּלִבּוֹ לֹא תִמְעַד אֲשֻׁרָיו: צוֹפֶה רָשָׁע לַצַּדִּיק וּמְבַקֵּשׁ לַהֲמִיתוֹ: יְהֹוָה לֹא־יַעַזְבֶנּוּ בְיָדוֹ וְלֹא יַרְשִׁיעֶנּוּ בְּהִשָּׁפְטוֹ: קַוֵּה אֶל־יְהֹוָה ׀ וּשְׁמֹר דַּרְכּוֹ וִירוֹמִמְךָ לָרֶשֶׁת אָרֶץ בְּהִכָּרֵת רְשָׁעִים תִּרְאֶה: רָאִיתִי רָשָׁע עָרִיץ וּמִתְעָרֶה כְּאֶזְרָח רַעֲנָן: וַיַּעֲבֹר וְהִנֵּה אֵינֶנּוּ וָאֲבַקְשֵׁהוּ וְלֹא נִמְצָא: שְׁמָר־תָּם וּרְאֵה יָשָׁר כִּי־אַחֲרִית לְאִישׁ שָׁלוֹם: וּפֹשְׁעִים נִשְׁמְדוּ יַחְדָּו אַחֲרִית רְשָׁעִים נִכְרָתָה:

וּתְשׁוּעַת צַדִּיקִים מֵיהוָה מָעוּזָּם בְּעֵת צָרָה: וַיַּעְזְרֵם יְהוָה וַיְפַלְּטֵם יְפַלְּטֵם
מֵרְשָׁעִים וְיוֹשִׁיעֵם כִּי־חָסוּ בוֹ:

לח מִזְמוֹר לְדָוִד לְהַזְכִּיר: יְהוָה אַל־בְּקֶצְפְּךָ תוֹכִיחֵנִי וּבַחֲמָתְךָ תְיַסְּרֵנִי: כִּי־חִצֶּיךָ
נִחֲתוּ בִי וַתִּנְחַת עָלַי יָדֶךָ: אֵין־מְתֹם בִּבְשָׂרִי מִפְּנֵי זַעְמֶךָ אֵין־שָׁלוֹם בַּעֲצָמַי
מִפְּנֵי חַטָּאתִי: כִּי עֲוֺנֹתַי עָבְרוּ רֹאשִׁי כְּמַשָּׂא כָבֵד יִכְבְּדוּ מִמֶּנִּי: הִבְאִישׁוּ
נָמַקּוּ חַבּוּרֹתָי מִפְּנֵי אִוַּלְתִּי: נַעֲוֵיתִי שַׁחֹתִי עַד־מְאֹד כָּל־הַיּוֹם קֹדֵר הִלָּכְתִּי:
כִּי־כְסָלַי מָלְאוּ נִקְלֶה וְאֵין מְתֹם בִּבְשָׂרִי: נְפוּגוֹתִי וְנִדְכֵּיתִי עַד־מְאֹד שָׁאַגְתִּי
מִנַּהֲמַת לִבִּי: אֲדֹנָי נֶגְדְּךָ כָל־תַּאֲוָתִי וְאַנְחָתִי מִמְּךָ לֹא־נִסְתָּרָה: לִבִּי סְחַרְחַר
עֲזָבַנִי כֹחִי וְאוֹר־עֵינַי גַּם־הֵם אֵין אִתִּי: אֹהֲבַי וְרֵעַי מִנֶּגֶד נִגְעִי יַעֲמֹדוּ וּקְרוֹבַי
מֵרָחֹק עָמָדוּ: וַיְנַקְשׁוּ מְבַקְשֵׁי נַפְשִׁי וְדֹרְשֵׁי רָעָתִי דִּבְּרוּ הַוּוֹת וּמִרְמוֹת כָּל־
הַיּוֹם יֶהְגּוּ: וַאֲנִי כְחֵרֵשׁ לֹא אֶשְׁמָע וּכְאִלֵּם לֹא יִפְתַּח־פִּיו: וָאֱהִי כְּאִישׁ אֲשֶׁר
לֹא־שֹׁמֵעַ וְאֵין בְּפִיו תּוֹכָחוֹת: כִּי־לְךָ יְהוָה הוֹחָלְתִּי אַתָּה תַעֲנֶה אֲדֹנָי אֱלֹהָי:
כִּי־אָמַרְתִּי פֶּן־יִשְׂמְחוּ־לִי בְּמוֹט רַגְלִי עָלַי הִגְדִּילוּ: כִּי־אֲנִי לְצֶלַע נָכוֹן וּמַכְאוֹבִי
נֶגְדִּי תָמִיד: כִּי־עֲוֺנִי אַגִּיד אֶדְאַג מֵחַטָּאתִי: וְאֹיְבַי חַיִּים עָצֵמוּ וְרַבּוּ שֹׂנְאַי
שָׁקֶר: וּמְשַׁלְּמֵי רָעָה תַּחַת טוֹבָה יִשְׂטְנוּנִי תַּחַת רדופי־טוֹב: אַל־תַּעַזְבֵנִי דָפִי
יְהוָה אֱלֹהַי אַל־תִּרְחַק מִמֶּנִּי: חוּשָׁה לְעֶזְרָתִי אֲדֹנָי תְּשׁוּעָתִי:

לט לַמְנַצֵּחַ לידיתון לִידוּתוּן מִזְמוֹר לְדָוִד: אָמַרְתִּי אֶשְׁמְרָה דְרָכַי מֵחֲטוֹא בִלְשׁוֹנִי לידותון
אֶשְׁמְרָה לְפִי מַחְסוֹם בְּעֹד רָשָׁע לְנֶגְדִּי: נֶאֱלַמְתִּי דוּמִיָּה הֶחֱשֵׁיתִי מִטּוֹב
וּכְאֵבִי נֶעְכָּר: חַם־לִבִּי בְּקִרְבִּי בַּהֲגִיגִי תִבְעַר־אֵשׁ דִּבַּרְתִּי בִּלְשׁוֹנִי: הוֹדִיעֵנִי
יְהוָה קִצִּי וּמִדַּת יָמַי מַה־הִיא אֵדְעָה מֶה־חָדֵל אָנִי: הִנֵּה טְפָחוֹת נָתַתָּה
יָמַי וְחֶלְדִּי כְאַיִן נֶגְדֶּךָ אַךְ כָּל־הֶבֶל כָּל־אָדָם נִצָּב סֶלָה: אַךְ־בְּצֶלֶם יִתְהַלֶּךְ־
אִישׁ אַךְ־הֶבֶל יֶהֱמָיוּן יִצְבֹּר וְלֹא־יֵדַע מִי־אֹסְפָם: וְעַתָּה מַה־קִּוִּיתִי אֲדֹנָי
תּוֹחַלְתִּי לְךָ הִיא: מִכָּל־פְּשָׁעַי הַצִּילֵנִי חֶרְפַּת נָבָל אַל־תְּשִׂימֵנִי: נֶאֱלַמְתִּי לֹא
אֶפְתַּח־פִּי כִּי אַתָּה עָשִׂיתָ: הָסֵר מֵעָלַי נִגְעֶךָ מִתִּגְרַת יָדְךָ אֲנִי כָלִיתִי:
בְּתוֹכָחוֹת עַל־עָוֺן יִסַּרְתָּ אִישׁ וַתֶּמֶס כָּעָשׁ חֲמוּדוֹ אַךְ הֶבֶל כָּל־אָדָם סֶלָה:
שִׁמְעָה תְפִלָּתִי יְהוָה וְשַׁוְעָתִי הַאֲזִינָה אֶל־דִּמְעָתִי אַל־תֶּחֱרַשׁ כִּי גֵר אָנֹכִי
עִמָּךְ תּוֹשָׁב כְּכָל־אֲבוֹתָי: הָשַׁע מִמֶּנִּי וְאַבְלִיגָה בְּטֶרֶם אֵלֵךְ וְאֵינֶנִּי:

מ לַמְנַצֵּחַ לְדָוִד מִזְמוֹר: קַוֺּה קִוִּיתִי יְהוָה וַיֵּט אֵלַי וַיִּשְׁמַע שַׁוְעָתִי: וַיַּעֲלֵנִי
מִבּוֹר שָׁאוֹן מִטִּיט הַיָּוֵן וַיָּקֶם עַל־סֶלַע רַגְלַי כּוֹנֵן אֲשֻׁרָי: וַיִּתֵּן בְּפִי שִׁיר חָדָשׁ

תְּהִלָּה לֵאלֹהֵינוּ יִרְאוּ רַבִּים וְיִירָאוּ וְיִבְטְחוּ בַּיהוָה: אַשְׁרֵי הַגֶּבֶר אֲשֶׁר־שָׂם יְהוָה מִבְטַחוֹ וְלֹא־פָנָה אֶל־רְהָבִים וְשָׂטֵי כָזָב: רַבּוֹת עָשִׂיתָ אַתָּה יְהוָה אֱלֹהַי נִפְלְאֹתֶיךָ וּמַחְשְׁבֹתֶיךָ אֵלֵינוּ אֵין עֲרֹךְ אֵלֶיךָ אַגִּידָה וַאֲדַבֵּרָה עָצְמוּ מִסַּפֵּר: זֶבַח וּמִנְחָה לֹא־חָפַצְתָּ אָזְנַיִם כָּרִיתָ לִּי עוֹלָה וַחֲטָאָה לֹא שָׁאָלְתָּ: אָז אָמַרְתִּי הִנֵּה־בָאתִי בִּמְגִלַּת־סֵפֶר כָּתוּב עָלָי: לַעֲשׂוֹת־רְצוֹנְךָ אֱלֹהַי חָפָצְתִּי וְתוֹרָתְךָ בְּתוֹךְ מֵעָי: בִּשַּׂרְתִּי צֶדֶק בְּקָהָל רָב הִנֵּה שְׂפָתַי לֹא אֶכְלָא יְהוָה אַתָּה יָדָעְתָּ: צִדְקָתְךָ לֹא־כִסִּיתִי בְּתוֹךְ לִבִּי אֱמוּנָתְךָ וּתְשׁוּעָתְךָ אָמָרְתִּי לֹא־כִחַדְתִּי חַסְדְּךָ וַאֲמִתְּךָ לְקָהָל רָב: אַתָּה יְהוָה לֹא־תִכְלָא רַחֲמֶיךָ מִמֶּנִּי חַסְדְּךָ וַאֲמִתְּךָ תָּמִיד יִצְּרוּנִי: כִּי אָפְפוּ־עָלַי רָעוֹת עַד־אֵין מִסְפָּר הִשִּׂיגוּנִי עֲוֹנֹתַי וְלֹא־יָכֹלְתִּי לִרְאוֹת עָצְמוּ מִשַּׂעֲרוֹת רֹאשִׁי וְלִבִּי עֲזָבָנִי: רְצֵה יְהוָה לְהַצִּילֵנִי יְהוָה לְעֶזְרָתִי חוּשָׁה: יֵבֹשׁוּ וְיַחְפְּרוּ יַחַד מְבַקְשֵׁי נַפְשִׁי לִסְפּוֹתָהּ יִסֹּגוּ אָחוֹר וְיִכָּלְמוּ חֲפֵצֵי רָעָתִי: יָשֹׁמּוּ עַל־עֵקֶב בָּשְׁתָּם הָאֹמְרִים לִי הֶאָח הֶאָח: יָשִׂישׂוּ וְיִשְׂמְחוּ בְּךָ כָּל־מְבַקְשֶׁיךָ יֹאמְרוּ תָמִיד יִגְדַּל יְהוָה אֹהֲבֵי תְּשׁוּעָתֶךָ: וַאֲנִי עָנִי וְאֶבְיוֹן אֲדֹנָי יַחֲשָׁב לִי עֶזְרָתִי וּמְפַלְטִי אַתָּה אֱלֹהַי אַל־תְּאַחַר:

מא לַמְנַצֵּחַ מִזְמוֹר לְדָוִד: אַשְׁרֵי מַשְׂכִּיל אֶל־דָּל בְּיוֹם רָעָה יְמַלְּטֵהוּ יְהוָה: יְהוָה יִשְׁמְרֵהוּ וִיחַיֵּהוּ יֻאֻשַּׁר בָּאָרֶץ וְאַל־תִּתְּנֵהוּ בְּנֶפֶשׁ אֹיְבָיו: יְהוָה יִסְעָדֶנּוּ עַל־עֶרֶשׂ דְּוָי כָּל־מִשְׁכָּבוֹ הָפַכְתָּ בְחָלְיוֹ: אֲנִי־אָמַרְתִּי יְהוָה חָנֵּנִי רְפָאָה נַפְשִׁי כִּי־חָטָאתִי לָךְ: אוֹיְבַי יֹאמְרוּ רַע לִי מָתַי יָמוּת וְאָבַד שְׁמוֹ: וְאִם־בָּא לִרְאוֹת שָׁוְא יְדַבֵּר לִבּוֹ יִקְבָּץ־אָוֶן לוֹ יֵצֵא לַחוּץ יְדַבֵּר: יַחַד עָלַי יִתְלַחֲשׁוּ כָּל־שֹׂנְאָי עָלַי יַחְשְׁבוּ רָעָה לִי: דְּבַר־בְּלִיַּעַל יָצוּק בּוֹ וַאֲשֶׁר שָׁכַב לֹא־יוֹסִיף לָקוּם: גַּם־אִישׁ שְׁלוֹמִי אֲשֶׁר־בָּטַחְתִּי בוֹ אוֹכֵל לַחְמִי הִגְדִּיל עָלַי עָקֵב: וְאַתָּה יְהוָה חָנֵּנִי וַהֲקִימֵנִי וַאֲשַׁלְּמָה לָהֶם: בְּזֹאת יָדַעְתִּי כִּי־חָפַצְתָּ בִּי כִּי לֹא־יָרִיעַ אֹיְבִי עָלָי: וַאֲנִי בְּתֻמִּי תָּמַכְתָּ בִּי וַתַּצִּיבֵנִי לְפָנֶיךָ לְעוֹלָם: בָּרוּךְ יְהוָה אֱלֹהֵי יִשְׂרָאֵל מֵהָעוֹלָם וְעַד הָעוֹלָם אָמֵן וְאָמֵן:

ספר שני

מב לַמְנַצֵּחַ מַשְׂכִּיל לִבְנֵי־קֹרַח: כְּאַיָּל תַּעֲרֹג עַל־אֲפִיקֵי־מָיִם כֵּן נַפְשִׁי תַעֲרֹג אֵלֶיךָ אֱלֹהִים: צָמְאָה נַפְשִׁי לֵאלֹהִים לְאֵל חָי מָתַי אָבוֹא וְאֵרָאֶה פְּנֵי אֱלֹהִים: הָיְתָה־לִּי דִמְעָתִי לֶחֶם יוֹמָם וָלָיְלָה בֶּאֱמֹר אֵלַי כָּל־הַיּוֹם אַיֵּה אֱלֹהֶיךָ: אֵלֶּה אֶזְכְּרָה וְאֶשְׁפְּכָה עָלַי נַפְשִׁי כִּי אֶעֱבֹר בַּסָּךְ אֶדַּדֵּם עַד־בֵּית אֱלֹהִים

בְּקוֹל־רִנָּה וְתוֹדָה הָמוֹן חוֹגֵג: מַה־תִּשְׁתּוֹחֲחִי ׀ נַפְשִׁי וַתֶּהֱמִי עָלָי הוֹחִלִי
לֵאלֹהִים כִּי־עוֹד אוֹדֶנּוּ יְשׁוּעוֹת פָּנָיו: אֱלֹהַי עָלַי נַפְשִׁי תִשְׁתּוֹחָח עַל־כֵּן
אֶזְכָּרְךָ מֵאֶרֶץ יַרְדֵּן וְחֶרְמוֹנִים מֵהַר מִצְעָר: תְּהוֹם־אֶל־תְּהוֹם קוֹרֵא לְקוֹל
צִנּוֹרֶיךָ כָּל־מִשְׁבָּרֶיךָ וְגַלֶּיךָ עָלַי עָבָרוּ: יוֹמָם ׀ יְצַוֶּה יְהֹוָה ׀ חַסְדּוֹ וּבַלַּיְלָה
שִׁירֹה עִמִּי תְּפִלָּה לְאֵל חַיָּי: אוֹמְרָה ׀ לְאֵל סַלְעִי לָמָה שְׁכַחְתָּנִי לָמָּה־קֹדֵר
אֵלֵךְ בְּלַחַץ אוֹיֵב: בְּרֶצַח ׀ בְּעַצְמוֹתַי חֵרְפוּנִי צוֹרְרָי בְּאָמְרָם אֵלַי כָּל־הַיּוֹם
אַיֵּה אֱלֹהֶיךָ: מַה־תִּשְׁתּוֹחֲחִי ׀ נַפְשִׁי וּמַה־תֶּהֱמִי עָלָי הוֹחִילִי לֵאלֹהִים כִּי־
עוֹד אוֹדֶנּוּ יְשׁוּעֹת פָּנַי וֵאלֹהָי:

מג שָׁפְטֵנִי אֱלֹהִים ׀ וְרִיבָה רִיבִי מִגּוֹי לֹא־חָסִיד מֵאִישׁ־מִרְמָה וְעַוְלָה תְפַלְּטֵנִי:
כִּי־אַתָּה ׀ אֱלֹהֵי מָעוּזִּי לָמָה זְנַחְתָּנִי לָמָּה־קֹדֵר אֶתְהַלֵּךְ בְּלַחַץ אוֹיֵב:
שְׁלַח־אוֹרְךָ וַאֲמִתְּךָ הֵמָּה יַנְחוּנִי יְבִיאוּנִי אֶל־הַר־קָדְשְׁךָ וְאֶל־מִשְׁכְּנוֹתֶיךָ:
וְאָבוֹאָה ׀ אֶל־מִזְבַּח אֱלֹהִים אֶל־אֵל שִׂמְחַת גִּילִי וְאוֹדְךָ בְכִנּוֹר אֱלֹהִים
אֱלֹהָי: מַה־תִּשְׁתּוֹחֲחִי ׀ נַפְשִׁי וּמַה־תֶּהֱמִי עָלָי הוֹחִילִי לֵאלֹהִים כִּי־עוֹד
אוֹדֶנּוּ יְשׁוּעֹת פָּנַי וֵאלֹהָי:

מד לַמְנַצֵּחַ לִבְנֵי־קֹרַח מַשְׂכִּיל: אֱלֹהִים ׀ בְּאָזְנֵינוּ שָׁמַעְנוּ אֲבוֹתֵינוּ סִפְּרוּ־לָנוּ
פֹּעַל־פָּעַלְתָּ בִימֵיהֶם בִּימֵי קֶדֶם: אַתָּה ׀ יָדְךָ גּוֹיִם הוֹרַשְׁתָּ וַתִּטָּעֵם תָּרַע
לְאֻמִּים וַתְּשַׁלְּחֵם: כִּי לֹא בְחַרְבָּם יָרְשׁוּ אָרֶץ וּזְרוֹעָם לֹא־הוֹשִׁיעָה לָּמוֹ כִּי־
יְמִינְךָ וּזְרוֹעֲךָ וְאוֹר פָּנֶיךָ כִּי רְצִיתָם: אַתָּה־הוּא מַלְכִּי אֱלֹהִים צַוֵּה יְשׁוּעוֹת
יַעֲקֹב: בְּךָ צָרֵינוּ נְנַגֵּחַ בְּשִׁמְךָ נָבוּס קָמֵינוּ: כִּי לֹא בְקַשְׁתִּי אֶבְטָח וְחַרְבִּי לֹא
תוֹשִׁיעֵנִי: כִּי הוֹשַׁעְתָּנוּ מִצָּרֵינוּ וּמְשַׂנְאֵינוּ הֱבִישׁוֹתָ: בֵּאלֹהִים הִלַּלְנוּ כָל־
הַיּוֹם וְשִׁמְךָ ׀ לְעוֹלָם נוֹדֶה סֶלָה: אַף־זָנַחְתָּ וַתַּכְלִימֵנוּ וְלֹא־תֵצֵא בְּצִבְאוֹתֵינוּ:
תְּשִׁיבֵנוּ אָחוֹר מִנִּי־צָר וּמְשַׂנְאֵינוּ שָׁסוּ לָמוֹ: תִּתְּנֵנוּ כְּצֹאן מַאֲכָל וּבַגּוֹיִם
זֵרִיתָנוּ: תִּמְכֹּר־עַמְּךָ בְלֹא־הוֹן וְלֹא־רִבִּיתָ בִּמְחִירֵיהֶם: תְּשִׂימֵנוּ חֶרְפָּה
לִשְׁכֵנֵינוּ לַעַג וָקֶלֶס לִסְבִיבוֹתֵינוּ: תְּשִׂימֵנוּ מָשָׁל בַּגּוֹיִם מְנוֹד־רֹאשׁ בַּלְאֻמִּים:
כָּל־הַיּוֹם כְּלִמָּתִי נֶגְדִּי וּבֹשֶׁת פָּנַי כִּסָּתְנִי: מִקּוֹל מְחָרֵף וּמְגַדֵּף מִפְּנֵי אוֹיֵב
וּמִתְנַקֵּם: כָּל־זֹאת בָּאַתְנוּ וְלֹא שְׁכַחֲנוּךָ וְלֹא־שִׁקַּרְנוּ בִּבְרִיתֶךָ: לֹא־נָסוֹג
אָחוֹר לִבֵּנוּ וַתֵּט אֲשֻׁרֵינוּ מִנִּי אָרְחֶךָ: כִּי דִכִּיתָנוּ בִּמְקוֹם תַּנִּים וַתְּכַס עָלֵינוּ
בְצַלְמָוֶת: אִם־שָׁכַחְנוּ שֵׁם אֱלֹהֵינוּ וַנִּפְרֹשׂ כַּפֵּינוּ לְאֵל זָר: הֲלֹא אֱלֹהִים
יַחֲקָר־זֹאת כִּי־הוּא יֹדֵעַ תַּעֲלֻמוֹת לֵב: כִּי־עָלֶיךָ הֹרַגְנוּ כָל־הַיּוֹם נֶחְשַׁבְנוּ

כְּצֹאן טִבְחָה: עוּרָה ו לָמָּה תִישַׁן ו אֲדֹנָי הָקִיצָה אַל־תִּזְנַח לָנֶצַח: לָמָּה־פָנֶיךָ
תַסְתִּיר תִּשְׁכַּח עָנְיֵנוּ וְלַחֲצֵנוּ: כִּי שָׁחָה לֶעָפָר נַפְשֵׁנוּ דָּבְקָה לָאָרֶץ בִּטְנֵנוּ:
קוּמָה עֶזְרָתָה לָּנוּ וּפְדֵנוּ לְמַעַן חַסְדֶּךָ:

לַמְנַצֵּחַ עַל־שֹׁשַׁנִּים לִבְנֵי־קֹרַח מַשְׂכִּיל שִׁיר יְדִידֹת: רָחַשׁ לִבִּי ו דָּבָר טוֹב מה
אֹמֵר אָנִי מַעֲשַׂי לְמֶלֶךְ לְשׁוֹנִי עֵט ו סוֹפֵר מָהִיר: יָפְיָפִיתָ מִבְּנֵי אָדָם הוּצַק חֵן
בְּשִׂפְתוֹתֶיךָ עַל־כֵּן בֵּרַכְךָ אֱלֹהִים לְעוֹלָם: חֲגוֹר־חַרְבְּךָ עַל־יָרֵךְ גִּבּוֹר הוֹדְךָ
וַהֲדָרֶךָ: וַהֲדָרְךָ ו צְלַח רְכַב עַל־דְּבַר־אֱמֶת וְעַנְוָה־צֶדֶק וְתוֹרְךָ נוֹרָאוֹת יְמִינֶךָ:
חִצֶּיךָ שְׁנוּנִים עַמִּים תַּחְתֶּיךָ יִפְּלוּ בְּלֵב אוֹיְבֵי הַמֶּלֶךְ: כִּסְאֲךָ אֱלֹהִים עוֹלָם
וָעֶד שֵׁבֶט מִישֹׁר שֵׁבֶט מַלְכוּתֶךָ: אָהַבְתָּ צֶּדֶק וַתִּשְׂנָא רֶשַׁע עַל־כֵּן ו מְשָׁחֲךָ
אֱלֹהִים אֱלֹהֶיךָ שֶׁמֶן שָׂשׂוֹן מֵחֲבֵרֶךָ: מֹר־וַאֲהָלוֹת קְצִיעוֹת כָּל־בִּגְדֹתֶיךָ מִן־
הֵיכְלֵי שֵׁן מִנִּי שִׂמְּחוּךָ: בְּנוֹת מְלָכִים בְּיִקְּרוֹתֶיךָ נִצְּבָה שֵׁגַל לִימִינְךָ בְּכֶתֶם
אוֹפִיר: שִׁמְעִי־בַת וּרְאִי וְהַטִּי אָזְנֵךְ וְשִׁכְחִי עַמֵּךְ וּבֵית אָבִיךְ: וְיִתְאָו הַמֶּלֶךְ
יָפְיֵךְ כִּי־הוּא אֲדֹנַיִךְ וְהִשְׁתַּחֲוִי־לוֹ: וּבַת־צֹר ו בְּמִנְחָה פָּנַיִךְ יְחַלּוּ עֲשִׁירֵי עָם:
כָּל־כְּבוּדָּה בַת־מֶלֶךְ פְּנִימָה מִמִּשְׁבְּצוֹת זָהָב לְבוּשָׁהּ: לִרְקָמוֹת תּוּבַל לַמֶּלֶךְ
בְּתוּלוֹת אַחֲרֶיהָ רֵעוֹתֶיהָ מוּבָאוֹת לָךְ: תּוּבַלְנָה בִּשְׂמָחֹת וָגִיל תְּבֹאֶינָה
בְּהֵיכַל מֶלֶךְ: תַּחַת אֲבֹתֶיךָ יִהְיוּ בָנֶיךָ תְּשִׁיתֵמוֹ לְשָׂרִים בְּכָל־הָאָרֶץ: אַזְכִּירָה
שִׁמְךָ בְּכָל־דֹּר וָדֹר עַל־כֵּן עַמִּים יְהוֹדֻךָ לְעוֹלָם וָעֶד:

לַמְנַצֵּחַ לִבְנֵי־קֹרַח עַל־עֲלָמוֹת שִׁיר: אֱלֹהִים לָנוּ מַחֲסֶה וָעֹז עֶזְרָה בְצָרוֹת מו
נִמְצָא מְאֹד: עַל־כֵּן לֹא־נִירָא בְּהָמִיר אָרֶץ וּבְמוֹט הָרִים בְּלֵב יַמִּים: יֶהֱמוּ
יֶחְמְרוּ מֵימָיו יִרְעֲשׁוּ־הָרִים בְּגַאֲוָתוֹ סֶלָה: נָהָר פְּלָגָיו יְשַׂמְּחוּ עִיר־אֱלֹהִים
קְדֹשׁ מִשְׁכְּנֵי עֶלְיוֹן: אֱלֹהִים בְּקִרְבָּהּ בַּל־תִּמּוֹט יַעְזְרֶהָ אֱלֹהִים לִפְנוֹת בֹּקֶר:
הָמוּ גוֹיִם מָטוּ מַמְלָכוֹת נָתַן בְּקוֹלוֹ תָּמוּג אָרֶץ: יְהוָה צְבָאוֹת עִמָּנוּ מִשְׂגָּב
לָנוּ אֱלֹהֵי יַעֲקֹב סֶלָה: לְכוּ־חֲזוּ מִפְעֲלוֹת יְהוָה אֲשֶׁר־שָׂם שַׁמּוֹת בָּאָרֶץ:
מַשְׁבִּית מִלְחָמוֹת עַד־קְצֵה הָאָרֶץ קֶשֶׁת יְשַׁבֵּר וְקִצֵּץ חֲנִית עֲגָלוֹת יִשְׂרֹף
בָּאֵשׁ: הַרְפּוּ וּדְעוּ כִּי־אָנֹכִי אֱלֹהִים אָרוּם בַּגּוֹיִם אָרוּם בָּאָרֶץ: יְהוָה צְבָאוֹת
עִמָּנוּ מִשְׂגָּב לָנוּ אֱלֹהֵי יַעֲקֹב סֶלָה:

לַמְנַצֵּחַ לִבְנֵי־קֹרַח מִזְמוֹר: כָּל־הָעַמִּים תִּקְעוּ־כָף הָרִיעוּ לֵאלֹהִים בְּקוֹל רִנָּה: מז
כִּי־יְהוָה עֶלְיוֹן נוֹרָא מֶלֶךְ גָּדוֹל עַל־כָּל־הָאָרֶץ: יַדְבֵּר עַמִּים תַּחְתֵּינוּ וּלְאֻמִּים
תַּחַת רַגְלֵינוּ: יִבְחַר־לָנוּ אֶת־נַחֲלָתֵנוּ אֶת גְּאוֹן יַעֲקֹב אֲשֶׁר־אָהֵב סֶלָה: עָלָה

אֱלֹהִים בִּתְרוּעָה יְהֹוָה בְּקוֹל שׁוֹפָר: זַמְּרוּ אֱלֹהִים זַמֵּרוּ זַמְּרוּ לְמַלְכֵּנוּ זַמֵּרוּ: כִּי מֶלֶךְ כָּל־הָאָרֶץ אֱלֹהִים זַמְּרוּ מַשְׂכִּיל: מָלַךְ אֱלֹהִים עַל־גּוֹיִם אֱלֹהִים יָשַׁב ׀ עַל־כִּסֵּא קָדְשׁוֹ: נְדִיבֵי עַמִּים ׀ נֶאֱסָפוּ עַם אֱלֹהֵי אַבְרָהָם כִּי לֵאלֹהִים מָגִנֵּי־אֶרֶץ מְאֹד נַעֲלָה:

מה שִׁיר מִזְמוֹר לִבְנֵי־קֹרַח: גָּדוֹל יְהֹוָה וּמְהֻלָּל מְאֹד בְּעִיר אֱלֹהֵינוּ הַר־קָדְשׁוֹ: יְפֵה נוֹף מְשׂוֹשׂ כָּל־הָאָרֶץ הַר־צִיּוֹן יַרְכְּתֵי צָפוֹן קִרְיַת מֶלֶךְ רָב: אֱלֹהִים בְּאַרְמְנוֹתֶיהָ נוֹדַע לְמִשְׂגָּב: כִּי־הִנֵּה הַמְּלָכִים נוֹעֲדוּ עָבְרוּ יַחְדָּו: הֵמָּה רָאוּ כֵּן תָּמָהוּ נִבְהֲלוּ נֶחְפָּזוּ: רְעָדָה אֲחָזָתַם שָׁם חִיל כַּיּוֹלֵדָה: בְּרוּחַ קָדִים תְּשַׁבֵּר אֳנִיּוֹת תַּרְשִׁישׁ: כַּאֲשֶׁר שָׁמַעְנוּ ׀ כֵּן רָאִינוּ בְּעִיר־יְהֹוָה צְבָאוֹת בְּעִיר אֱלֹהֵינוּ אֱלֹהִים יְכוֹנְנֶהָ עַד־עוֹלָם סֶלָה: דִּמִּינוּ אֱלֹהִים חַסְדֶּךָ בְּקֶרֶב הֵיכָלֶךָ: כְּשִׁמְךָ ׀ אֱלֹהִים כֵּן תְּהִלָּתְךָ עַל־קַצְוֵי־אֶרֶץ צֶדֶק מָלְאָה יְמִינֶךָ: יִשְׂמַח ׀ הַר־צִיּוֹן תָּגֵלְנָה בְּנוֹת יְהוּדָה לְמַעַן מִשְׁפָּטֶיךָ: סֹבּוּ צִיּוֹן וְהַקִּיפוּהָ סִפְרוּ מִגְדָּלֶיהָ: שִׁיתוּ לִבְּכֶם ׀ לְחֵילָה פַּסְּגוּ אַרְמְנוֹתֶיהָ לְמַעַן תְּסַפְּרוּ לְדוֹר אַחֲרוֹן: כִּי זֶה ׀ אֱלֹהִים אֱלֹהֵינוּ עוֹלָם וָעֶד הוּא יְנַהֲגֵנוּ עַל־מוּת:

מט *לַמְנַצֵּחַ לִבְנֵי־קֹרַח מִזְמוֹר: שִׁמְעוּ־זֹאת כָּל־הָעַמִּים הַאֲזִינוּ כָּל־יֹשְׁבֵי חָלֶד: גַּם־בְּנֵי אָדָם גַּם־בְּנֵי־אִישׁ יַחַד עָשִׁיר וְאֶבְיוֹן: פִּי יְדַבֵּר חָכְמוֹת וְהָגוּת לִבִּי תְבוּנוֹת: אַטֶּה לְמָשָׁל אָזְנִי אֶפְתַּח בְּכִנּוֹר חִידָתִי: לָמָּה אִירָא בִּימֵי רָע עֲוֹן עֲקֵבַי יְסוּבֵּנִי: הַבֹּטְחִים עַל־חֵילָם וּבְרֹב עָשְׁרָם יִתְהַלָּלוּ: אָח לֹא־פָדֹה יִפְדֶּה אִישׁ לֹא־יִתֵּן לֵאלֹהִים כָּפְרוֹ: וְיֵקַר פִּדְיוֹן נַפְשָׁם וְחָדַל לְעוֹלָם: וִיחִי־עוֹד לָנֶצַח לֹא יִרְאֶה הַשָּׁחַת: כִּי יִרְאֶה ׀ חֲכָמִים יָמוּתוּ יַחַד כְּסִיל וָבַעַר יֹאבֵדוּ וְעָזְבוּ לַאֲחֵרִים חֵילָם: קִרְבָּם בָּתֵּימוֹ ׀ לְעוֹלָם מִשְׁכְּנֹתָם לְדֹר וָדֹר קָרְאוּ בִשְׁמוֹתָם עֲלֵי אֲדָמוֹת: וְאָדָם בִּיקָר בַּל־יָלִין נִמְשַׁל כַּבְּהֵמוֹת נִדְמוּ: זֶה דַרְכָּם כֵּסֶל לָמוֹ וְאַחֲרֵיהֶם ׀ בְּפִיהֶם יִרְצוּ סֶלָה: כַּצֹּאן ׀ לִשְׁאוֹל שַׁתּוּ מָוֶת יִרְעֵם וַיִּרְדּוּ בָם יְשָׁרִים ׀ לַבֹּקֶר וְצִירָם לְבַלּוֹת שְׁאוֹל מִזְּבֻל לוֹ: אַךְ־אֱלֹהִים יִפְדֶּה נַפְשִׁי וְצוּרָם מִיַּד שְׁאוֹל כִּי יִקָּחֵנִי סֶלָה: אַל־תִּירָא כִּי־יַעֲשִׁר אִישׁ כִּי־יִרְבֶּה כְּבוֹד בֵּיתוֹ: כִּי לֹא בְמוֹתוֹ יִקַּח הַכֹּל לֹא־יֵרֵד אַחֲרָיו כְּבוֹדוֹ: כִּי־נַפְשׁוֹ בְּחַיָּיו יְבָרֵךְ וְיוֹדֻךָ כִּי־תֵיטִיב לָךְ: תָּבוֹא עַד־דּוֹר אֲבוֹתָיו עַד־נֵצַח לֹא יִרְאוּ־אוֹר: אָדָם בִּיקָר וְלֹא יָבִין נִמְשַׁל כַּבְּהֵמוֹת נִדְמוּ:

נ מִזְמוֹר לְאָסָף אֵל ׀ אֱלֹהִים יְהֹוָה דִּבֶּר וַיִּקְרָא־אָרֶץ מִמִּזְרַח־שֶׁמֶשׁ עַד־מְבֹאוֹ:

*ט לחודש

מִצִּיּוֹן מִכְלַל־יֹ֫פִי אֱלֹהִ֥ים הוֹפִֽיעַ: יָבֹ֤א אֱלֹהֵ֨ינוּ וְֽאַל־יֶ֫חֱרַ֥שׁ אֵשׁ־לְפָנָ֥יו תֹּאכֵ֑ל
וּ֝סְבִיבָ֗יו נִשְׂעֲרָ֥ה מְאֹֽד: יִקְרָ֣א אֶל־הַשָּׁמַ֣יִם מֵעָ֑ל וְאֶל־הָ֝אָ֗רֶץ לָדִ֥ין עַמּֽוֹ: אִסְפוּ־
לִ֥י חֲסִידָ֑י כֹּרְתֵ֖י בְרִיתִ֣י עֲלֵי־זָֽבַח: וַיַּגִּ֖ידוּ שָׁמַ֣יִם צִדְק֑וֹ כִּֽי־אֱלֹהִ֓ים ׀ שֹׁפֵ֖ט ה֣וּא
סֶֽלָה: שִׁמְעָ֤ה עַמִּ֨י ׀ וַאֲדַבֵּ֗רָה יִ֭שְׂרָאֵל וְאָעִ֣ידָה בָּ֑ךְ אֱלֹהִ֖ים אֱלֹהֶ֣יךָ אָנֹֽכִי: לֹ֤א
עַל־זְבָחֶ֥יךָ אוֹכִיחֶ֑ךָ וְעוֹלֹתֶ֖יךָ לְנֶגְדִּ֣י תָמִֽיד: לֹא־אֶקַּ֣ח מִבֵּיתְךָ֣ פָ֑ר מִ֝מִּכְלְאֹתֶ֗יךָ
עַתּוּדִֽים: כִּי־לִ֥י כׇל־חַיְתוֹ־יָ֑עַר בְּ֝הֵמ֗וֹת בְּהַרְרֵי־אָֽלֶף: יָ֭דַעְתִּי כׇּל־ע֣וֹף הָרִ֑ים
וְזִ֥יז שָׂ֝דַ֗י עִמָּדִֽי: אִם־אֶ֭רְעַב לֹא־אֹ֣מַר לָ֑ךְ כִּי־לִ֥י תֵ֝בֵ֗ל וּמְלֹאָֽהּ: הַֽאוֹכַ֗ל בְּשַׂ֥ר
אַבִּירִ֑ים וְדַ֖ם עַתּוּדִ֣ים אֶשְׁתֶּֽה: זְבַ֣ח לֵאלֹהִ֣ים תּוֹדָ֑ה וְשַׁלֵּ֖ם לְעֶלְי֣וֹן נְדָרֶֽיךָ:
וּ֭קְרָאֵנִי בְּי֣וֹם צָרָ֑ה אֲ֝חַלֶּצְךָ֗ וּֽתְכַבְּדֵֽנִי: וְלָ֤רָשָׁ֨ע ׀ אָ֘מַ֤ר אֱלֹהִ֗ים מַה־לְּ֭ךָ לְסַפֵּ֣ר
חֻקָּ֑י וַתִּשָּׂ֖א בְרִיתִ֣י עֲלֵי־פִֽיךָ: וְ֭אַתָּה שָׂנֵ֣אתָ מוּסָ֑ר וַתַּשְׁלֵ֖ךְ דְּבָרַ֣י אַחֲרֶֽיךָ:
אִם־רָאִ֣יתָ גַ֭נָּב וַתִּ֣רֶץ עִמּ֑וֹ וְעִ֖ם מְנָאֲפִ֣ים חֶלְקֶֽךָ: פִּ֭יךָ שָׁלַ֣חְתָּ בְרָעָ֑ה וּ֝לְשׁוֹנְךָ֗
תַּצְמִ֥יד מִרְמָֽה: תֵּ֭שֵׁב בְּאָחִ֣יךָ תְדַבֵּ֑ר בְּבֶֽן־אִ֝מְּךָ֗ תִּתֶּן־דֹּֽפִי: אֵ֤לֶּה עָשִׂ֨יתָ ׀
וְֽהֶחֱרַ֗שְׁתִּי דִּמִּ֗יתָ הֱֽיוֹת־אֶֽהְיֶ֥ה כָמ֑וֹךָ אוֹכִיחֲךָ֖ וְאֶֽעֶרְכָ֣ה לְעֵינֶֽיךָ: בִּֽינוּ־נָ֣א זֹ֭את
שֹׁכְחֵ֣י אֱל֑וֹהַּ פֶּן־אֶ֝טְרֹ֗ף וְאֵ֣ין מַצִּֽיל: זֹבֵ֥חַ תּוֹדָ֗ה יְֽכַבְּדָ֥נְנִי וְשָׂ֥ם דֶּ֑רֶךְ אַ֝רְאֶ֗נּוּ
בְּיֵ֣שַׁע אֱלֹהִֽים:

לַמְנַצֵּ֗חַ מִזְמ֥וֹר לְדָוִֽד: בְּֽבוֹא־אֵ֭לָיו נָתָ֣ן הַנָּבִ֑יא כַּֽאֲשֶׁר־בָּ֝֗א אֶל־בַּת־שָֽׁבַע:‎ נא*

הרב‎ חָנֵּ֣נִי אֱלֹהִ֣ים כְּחַסְדֶּ֑ךָ כְּרֹ֥ב רַ֝חֲמֶ֗יךָ מְחֵ֣ה פְשָׁעָֽי: הֶ֭רֶב כַּבְּסֵ֣נִי מֵעֲוֺנִ֑י וּֽמֵחַטָּאתִ֥י
טַהֲרֵֽנִי: כִּֽי־פְ֭שָׁעַי אֲנִ֣י אֵדָ֑ע וְחַטָּאתִ֖י נֶגְדִּ֣י תָמִֽיד: לְךָ֤ לְבַדְּךָ֨ ׀ חָטָ֗אתִי וְהָרַ֥ע
בְּעֵינֶ֗יךָ עָ֫שִׂ֥יתִי לְמַ֤עַן תִּצְדַּ֥ק בְּדׇבְרֶ֗ךָ תִּזְכֶּ֥ה בְשׇׁפְטֶֽךָ: הֵן־בְּעָו֥וֹן חוֹלָ֑לְתִּי
וּ֝בְחֵ֗טְא יֶֽחֱמַ֥תְנִי אִמִּֽי: הֵן־אֱ֭מֶת חָפַ֣צְתָּ בַטֻּח֑וֹת וּ֝בְסָתֻ֗ם חׇכְמָ֥ה תוֹדִיעֵֽנִי:
תְּחַטְּאֵ֣נִי בְאֵז֣וֹב וְאֶטְהָ֑ר תְּ֝כַבְּסֵ֗נִי וּמִשֶּׁ֥לֶג אַלְבִּֽין: תַּ֭שְׁמִיעֵנִי שָׂשׂ֣וֹן וְשִׂמְחָ֑ה
תָּ֝גֵ֗לְנָה עֲצָמ֥וֹת דִּכִּֽיתָ: הַסְתֵּ֣ר פָּ֭נֶיךָ מֵחֲטָאָ֑י וְֽכׇל־עֲוֺנֹתַ֥י מְחֵֽה: לֵ֣ב טָ֭הוֹר
בְּרָא־לִ֣י אֱלֹהִ֑ים וְר֥וּחַ נָ֝כ֗וֹן חַדֵּ֥שׁ בְּקִרְבִּֽי: אַל־תַּשְׁלִיכֵ֥נִי מִלְּפָנֶ֑יךָ וְר֥וּחַ קׇ֝דְשְׁךָ֗
אַל־תִּקַּ֥ח מִמֶּֽנִּי: הָשִׁ֣יבָה לִּ֭י שְׂשׂ֣וֹן יִשְׁעֶ֑ךָ וְר֖וּחַ נְדִיבָ֣ה תִסְמְכֵֽנִי: אֲלַמְּדָ֣ה
פֹשְׁעִ֣ים דְּרָכֶ֑יךָ וְ֝חַטָּאִ֗ים אֵלֶ֥יךָ יָשֽׁוּבוּ: הַצִּ֘ילֵ֤נִי מִדָּמִ֨ים ׀ אֱֽלֹהִ֗ים אֱלֹהֵ֥י תְּשׁוּעָתִ֑י
תְּרַנֵּ֥ן לְ֝שׁוֹנִ֗י צִדְקָתֶֽךָ: אֲ֭דֹנָי שְׂפָתַ֣י תִּפְתָּ֑ח וּ֝פִ֗י יַגִּ֥יד תְּהִלָּתֶֽךָ: כִּ֤י ׀ לֹא־תַחְפֹּ֣ץ
זֶ֣בַח וְאֶתֵּ֑נָה עֹ֝לָ֗ה לֹ֣א תִרְצֶֽה: זִֽבְחֵ֣י אֱלֹהִים֮ ר֤וּחַ נִשְׁבָּ֫רָ֥ה לֵב־נִשְׁבָּ֥ר וְנִדְכֶּ֑ה
אֱ֝לֹהִ֗ים לֹ֣א תִבְזֶֽה: הֵיטִ֣יבָה בִ֭רְצוֹנְךָ אֶת־צִיּ֑וֹן תִּ֝בְנֶ֗ה חוֹמ֥וֹת יְרוּשָׁלָֽ͏ִם: אָ֤ז
תַּחְפֹּ֣ץ זִבְחֵי־צֶ֭דֶק עוֹלָ֣ה וְכָלִ֑יל אָ֤ז יַעֲל֖וּ עַל־מִזְבַּחֲךָ֣ פָרִֽים:

*לַיּוֹם הַשְּׁלִישִׁי‎

נב לַמְנַצֵּחַ מַשְׂכִּיל לְדָוִד: בְּבוֹא ׀ דּוֹאֵג הָאֲדֹמִי וַיַּגֵּד לְשָׁאוּל וַיֹּאמֶר לוֹ בָּא דָוִד
אֶל־בֵּית אֲחִימֶלֶךְ: מַה־תִּתְהַלֵּל בְּרָעָה הַגִּבּוֹר חֶסֶד אֵל כָּל־הַיּוֹם: הַוּוֹת
תַּחְשֹׁב לְשׁוֹנֶךָ כְּתַעַר מְלֻטָּשׁ עֹשֵׂה רְמִיָּה: אָהַבְתָּ רָּע מִטּוֹב שֶׁקֶר ׀ מִדַּבֵּר
צֶדֶק סֶלָה: אָהַבְתָּ כָל־דִּבְרֵי־בָלַע לְשׁוֹן מִרְמָה: גַּם־אֵל יִתָּצְךָ לָנֶצַח יַחְתְּךָ
וְיִסָּחֲךָ מֵאֹהֶל וְשֵׁרֶשְׁךָ מֵאֶרֶץ חַיִּים סֶלָה: וְיִרְאוּ צַדִּיקִים וְיִירָאוּ וְעָלָיו יִשְׂחָקוּ:
הִנֵּה הַגֶּבֶר לֹא יָשִׂים אֱלֹהִים מָעוּזּוֹ וַיִּבְטַח בְּרֹב עָשְׁרוֹ יָעֹז בְּהַוָּתוֹ: וַאֲנִי ׀
כְּזַיִת רַעֲנָן בְּבֵית אֱלֹהִים בָּטַחְתִּי בְחֶסֶד־אֱלֹהִים עוֹלָם וָעֶד: אוֹדְךָ לְעוֹלָם
כִּי עָשִׂיתָ וַאֲקַוֶּה שִׁמְךָ כִי־טוֹב נֶגֶד חֲסִידֶיךָ:

נג לַמְנַצֵּחַ עַל־מָחֲלַת מַשְׂכִּיל לְדָוִד: אָמַר נָבָל בְּלִבּוֹ אֵין אֱלֹהִים הִשְׁחִיתוּ
וְהִתְעִיבוּ עָוֶל אֵין עֹשֵׂה־טוֹב: אֱלֹהִים מִשָּׁמַיִם הִשְׁקִיף עַל־בְּנֵי־אָדָם לִרְאוֹת
הֲיֵשׁ מַשְׂכִּיל דֹּרֵשׁ אֶת־אֱלֹהִים: כֻּלּוֹ סָג יַחְדָּו נֶאֱלָחוּ אֵין עֹשֵׂה־טוֹב אֵין
גַּם־אֶחָד: הֲלֹא יָדְעוּ פֹּעֲלֵי אָוֶן אֹכְלֵי עַמִּי אָכְלוּ לֶחֶם אֱלֹהִים לֹא קָרָאוּ:
שָׁם ׀ פָּחֲדוּ־פַחַד לֹא־הָיָה פָחַד כִּי־אֱלֹהִים פִּזַּר עַצְמוֹת חֹנָךְ הֱבִשֹׁתָה כִּי־
אֱלֹהִים מְאָסָם: מִי יִתֵּן מִצִּיּוֹן יְשֻׁעוֹת יִשְׂרָאֵל בְּשׁוּב אֱלֹהִים שְׁבוּת עַמּוֹ יָגֵל
יַעֲקֹב יִשְׂמַח יִשְׂרָאֵל:

נד לַמְנַצֵּחַ בִּנְגִינֹת מַשְׂכִּיל לְדָוִד: בְּבוֹא הַזִּיפִים וַיֹּאמְרוּ לְשָׁאוּל הֲלֹא דָוִד
מִסְתַּתֵּר עִמָּנוּ: אֱלֹהִים בְּשִׁמְךָ הוֹשִׁיעֵנִי וּבִגְבוּרָתְךָ תְדִינֵנִי: אֱלֹהִים שְׁמַע
תְּפִלָּתִי הַאֲזִינָה לְאִמְרֵי־פִי: כִּי זָרִים ׀ קָמוּ עָלַי וְעָרִיצִים בִּקְשׁוּ נַפְשִׁי לֹא שָׂמוּ
אֱלֹהִים לְנֶגְדָּם סֶלָה: הִנֵּה אֱלֹהִים עֹזֵר לִי אֲדֹנָי בְּסֹמְכֵי נַפְשִׁי: יָשׁוֹב הָרַע יָשִׁיב
לְשֹׁרְרָי בַּאֲמִתְּךָ הַצְמִיתֵם: בִּנְדָבָה אֶזְבְּחָה־לָּךְ אוֹדֶה שִּׁמְךָ יְהוָה כִּי־טוֹב:
כִּי מִכָּל־צָרָה הִצִּילָנִי וּבְאֹיְבַי רָאֲתָה עֵינִי:

*נה לַמְנַצֵּחַ בִּנְגִינֹת מַשְׂכִּיל לְדָוִד: הַאֲזִינָה אֱלֹהִים תְּפִלָּתִי וְאַל־תִּתְעַלַּם
מִתְּחִנָּתִי: הַקְשִׁיבָה לִּי וַעֲנֵנִי אָרִיד בְּשִׂיחִי וְאָהִימָה: מִקּוֹל אוֹיֵב מִפְּנֵי עָקַת
רָשָׁע כִּי־יָמִיטוּ עָלַי אָוֶן וּבְאַף יִשְׂטְמוּנִי: לִבִּי יָחִיל בְּקִרְבִּי וְאֵימוֹת מָוֶת נָפְלוּ
עָלָי: יִרְאָה וָרַעַד יָבֹא בִי וַתְּכַסֵּנִי פַּלָּצוּת: וָאֹמַר מִי־יִתֶּן־לִי אֵבֶר כַּיּוֹנָה אָעוּפָה
וְאֶשְׁכֹּנָה: הִנֵּה אַרְחִיק נְדֹד אָלִין בַּמִּדְבָּר סֶלָה: אָחִישָׁה מִפְלָט לִי מֵרוּחַ
סֹעָה מִסָּעַר: בַּלַּע אֲדֹנָי פַּלַּג לְשׁוֹנָם כִּי־רָאִיתִי חָמָס וְרִיב בָּעִיר: יוֹמָם וָלַיְלָה
יְסוֹבְבֻהָ עַל־חוֹמֹתֶיהָ וְאָוֶן וְעָמָל בְּקִרְבָּהּ: הַוּוֹת בְּקִרְבָּהּ וְלֹא־יָמִישׁ מֵרְחֹבָהּ
תֹּךְ וּמִרְמָה: כִּי לֹא־אוֹיֵב יְחָרְפֵנִי וְאֶשָּׂא לֹא־מְשַׂנְאִי עָלַי הִגְדִּיל וְאֶסָּתֵר

מִמֶּנּוּ: וְאַתָּה אֱנוֹשׁ כְּעֶרְכִּי אַלּוּפִי וּמְיֻדָּעִי: אֲשֶׁר יַחְדָּו נַמְתִּיק סוֹד בְּבֵית
אֱלֹהִים נְהַלֵּךְ בְּרָגֶשׁ: יַשִּׁימָוֶת יַשִּׁי מָוֶת עָלֵימוֹ יֵרְדוּ שְׁאוֹל חַיִּים כִּי־רָעוֹת בִּמְגוּרָם
בְּקִרְבָּם: אֲנִי אֶל־אֱלֹהִים אֶקְרָא וַיהוָה יוֹשִׁיעֵנִי: עֶרֶב וָבֹקֶר וְצָהֳרַיִם אָשִׂיחָה
וְאֶהֱמֶה וַיִּשְׁמַע קוֹלִי: פָּדָה בְשָׁלוֹם נַפְשִׁי מִקְּרָב־לִי כִּי־בְרַבִּים הָיוּ עִמָּדִי:
יִשְׁמַע אֵל וְיַעֲנֵם וְיֹשֵׁב קֶדֶם סֶלָה אֲשֶׁר אֵין חֲלִיפוֹת לָמוֹ וְלֹא יָרְאוּ אֱלֹהִים:
שָׁלַח יָדָיו בִּשְׁלֹמָיו חִלֵּל בְּרִיתוֹ: חָלְקוּ מַחְמָאֹת פִּיו וּקְרָב־לִבּוֹ רַכּוּ דְבָרָיו
מִשֶּׁמֶן וְהֵמָּה פְתִחוֹת: הַשְׁלֵךְ עַל־יְהוָה יְהָבְךָ וְהוּא יְכַלְכְּלֶךָ לֹא־יִתֵּן
לְעוֹלָם מוֹט לַצַּדִּיק: וְאַתָּה אֱלֹהִים תּוֹרִדֵם לִבְאֵר שַׁחַת אַנְשֵׁי דָמִים
וּמִרְמָה לֹא־יֶחֱצוּ יְמֵיהֶם וַאֲנִי אֶבְטַח־בָּךְ:

נו לַמְנַצֵּחַ עַל־יוֹנַת אֵלֶם רְחֹקִים לְדָוִד מִכְתָּם בֶּאֱחֹז אֹתוֹ פְלִשְׁתִּים בְּגַת:
חָנֵּנִי אֱלֹהִים כִּי־שְׁאָפַנִי אֱנוֹשׁ כָּל־הַיּוֹם לֹחֵם יִלְחָצֵנִי: שָׁאֲפוּ שׁוֹרְרַי כָּל־הַיּוֹם
כִּי־רַבִּים לֹחֲמִים לִי מָרוֹם: יוֹם אִירָא אֲנִי אֵלֶיךָ אֶבְטָח: בֵּאלֹהִים אֲהַלֵּל דְּבָרוֹ
בֵּאלֹהִים בָּטַחְתִּי לֹא אִירָא מַה־יַּעֲשֶׂה בָשָׂר לִי: כָּל־הַיּוֹם דְּבָרַי יְעַצֵּבוּ עָלַי
כָּל־מַחְשְׁבֹתָם לָרָע: יָגוּרוּ יִצְפּוֹנוּ הֵמָּה עֲקֵבַי יִשְׁמֹרוּ כַּאֲשֶׁר קִוּוּ נַפְשִׁי: עַל־
אָוֶן פַּלֶּט־לָמוֹ בְּאַף עַמִּים הוֹרֵד אֱלֹהִים: נֹדִי סָפַרְתָּה אָתָּה שִׂימָה דִמְעָתִי
בְנֹאדֶךָ הֲלֹא בְּסִפְרָתֶךָ: אָז יָשׁוּבוּ אוֹיְבַי אָחוֹר בְּיוֹם אֶקְרָא זֶה־יָדַעְתִּי כִּי־
אֱלֹהִים לִי: בֵּאלֹהִים אֲהַלֵּל דָּבָר בַּיהוָה אֲהַלֵּל דָּבָר: בֵּאלֹהִים בָּטַחְתִּי לֹא
אִירָא מַה־יַּעֲשֶׂה אָדָם לִי: עָלַי אֱלֹהִים נְדָרֶיךָ אֲשַׁלֵּם תּוֹדֹת לָךְ: כִּי הִצַּלְתָּ
נַפְשִׁי מִמָּוֶת הֲלֹא רַגְלַי מִדֶּחִי לְהִתְהַלֵּךְ לִפְנֵי אֱלֹהִים בְּאוֹר הַחַיִּים:

נז לַמְנַצֵּחַ אַל־תַּשְׁחֵת לְדָוִד מִכְתָּם בְּבָרְחוֹ מִפְּנֵי־שָׁאוּל בַּמְּעָרָה: חָנֵּנִי אֱלֹהִים
חָנֵּנִי כִּי בְךָ חָסָיָה נַפְשִׁי וּבְצֵל־כְּנָפֶיךָ אֶחְסֶה עַד יַעֲבֹר הַוּוֹת: אֶקְרָא לֵאלֹהִים
עֶלְיוֹן לָאֵל גֹּמֵר עָלָי: יִשְׁלַח מִשָּׁמַיִם וְיוֹשִׁיעֵנִי חֵרֵף שֹׁאֲפִי סֶלָה יִשְׁלַח אֱלֹהִים
חַסְדּוֹ וַאֲמִתּוֹ: נַפְשִׁי בְּתוֹךְ לְבָאִם אֶשְׁכְּבָה לֹהֲטִים בְּנֵי־אָדָם שִׁנֵּיהֶם חֲנִית
וְחִצִּים וּלְשׁוֹנָם חֶרֶב חַדָּה: רוּמָה עַל־הַשָּׁמַיִם אֱלֹהִים עַל כָּל־הָאָרֶץ כְּבוֹדֶךָ:
רֶשֶׁת הֵכִינוּ לִפְעָמַי כָּפַף נַפְשִׁי כָּרוּ לְפָנַי שִׁיחָה נָפְלוּ בְתוֹכָהּ סֶלָה: נָכוֹן לִבִּי
אֱלֹהִים נָכוֹן לִבִּי אָשִׁירָה וַאֲזַמֵּרָה: עוּרָה כְבוֹדִי עוּרָה הַנֵּבֶל וְכִנּוֹר אָעִירָה
שָּׁחַר: אוֹדְךָ בָעַמִּים אֲדֹנָי אֲזַמֶּרְךָ בַּל־אֻמִּים: כִּי־גָדֹל עַד־שָׁמַיִם חַסְדֶּךָ
וְעַד־שְׁחָקִים אֲמִתֶּךָ: רוּמָה עַל־שָׁמַיִם אֱלֹהִים עַל כָּל־הָאָרֶץ כְּבוֹדֶךָ:

נח לַמְנַצֵּחַ אַל־תַּשְׁחֵת לְדָוִד מִכְתָּם: הַאֻמְנָם אֵלֶם צֶדֶק תְּדַבֵּרוּן מֵישָׁרִים

תִּשְׁפְּטוּ בְּנֵי אָדָם: אַף־בְּלֵב עוֹלֹת תִּפְעָלוּן בָּאָרֶץ חֲמַס יְדֵיכֶם תְּפַלֵּסוּן: זֹרוּ
רְשָׁעִים מֵרָחֶם תָּעוּ מִבֶּטֶן דֹּבְרֵי כָזָב: חֲמַת־לָמוֹ כִּדְמוּת חֲמַת־נָחָשׁ כְּמוֹ־פֶתֶן
חֵרֵשׁ יַאְטֵם אָזְנוֹ: אֲשֶׁר לֹא־יִשְׁמַע לְקוֹל מְלַחֲשִׁים חוֹבֵר חֲבָרִים מְחֻכָּם:
אֱלֹהִים הֲרָס־שִׁנֵּימוֹ בְּפִימוֹ מַלְתְּעוֹת כְּפִירִים נְתֹץ ׀ יְהוָה: יִמָּאֲסוּ כְמוֹ־מַיִם
יִתְהַלְּכוּ־לָמוֹ יִדְרֹךְ חִצָּו כְּמוֹ יִתְמֹלָלוּ: כְּמוֹ שַׁבְּלוּל תֶּמֶס יַהֲלֹךְ נֵפֶל אֵשֶׁת
בַּל־חָזוּ שָׁמֶשׁ: בְּטֶרֶם יָבִינוּ סִּירֹתֵכֶם אָטָד כְּמוֹ־חַי כְּמוֹ־חָרוֹן יִשְׂעָרֶנּוּ: יִשְׂמַח
צַדִּיק כִּי־חָזָה נָקָם פְּעָמָיו יִרְחַץ בְּדַם הָרָשָׁע: וְיֹאמַר אָדָם אַךְ־פְּרִי לַצַּדִּיק
אַךְ יֵשׁ־אֱלֹהִים שֹׁפְטִים בָּאָרֶץ:

נט לַמְנַצֵּחַ אַל־תַּשְׁחֵת לְדָוִד מִכְתָּם בִּשְׁלֹחַ שָׁאוּל וַיִּשְׁמְרוּ אֶת־הַבַּיִת לַהֲמִיתוֹ:
הַצִּילֵנִי מֵאֹיְבַי ׀ אֱלֹהָי מִמִּתְקוֹמְמַי תְּשַׂגְּבֵנִי: הַצִּילֵנִי מִפֹּעֲלֵי אָוֶן וּמֵאַנְשֵׁי דָמִים
הוֹשִׁיעֵנִי: כִּי הִנֵּה אָרְבוּ לְנַפְשִׁי יָגוּרוּ עָלַי עַזִּים לֹא־פִשְׁעִי וְלֹא־חַטָּאתִי יְהוָה:
בְּלִי־עָו‍ֹן יְרֻצוּן וְיִכּוֹנָנוּ עוּרָה לִקְרָאתִי וּרְאֵה: וְאַתָּה יְהוָה־אֱלֹהִים ׀ צְבָאוֹת
אֱלֹהֵי יִשְׂרָאֵל הָקִיצָה לִפְקֹד כָּל־הַגּוֹיִם אַל־תָּחֹן כָּל־בֹּגְדֵי אָוֶן סֶלָה: יָשׁוּבוּ
לָעֶרֶב יֶהֱמוּ כַכָּלֶב וִיסוֹבְבוּ עִיר: הִנֵּה ׀ יַבִּיעוּן בְּפִיהֶם חֲרָבוֹת בְּשִׂפְתוֹתֵיהֶם
כִּי־מִי שֹׁמֵעַ: וְאַתָּה יְהוָה תִּשְׂחַק־לָמוֹ תִּלְעַג לְכָל־גּוֹיִם: עֻזּוֹ אֵלֶיךָ אֶשְׁמֹרָה
כִּי־אֱלֹהִים מִשְׂגַּבִּי: אֱלֹהֵי חַסְדִּי יְקַדְּמֵנִי אֱלֹהִים יַרְאֵנִי בְשֹׁרְרָי: אַל־תַּהַרְגֵם ׀ חַסְדִּי
פֶּן־יִשְׁכְּחוּ עַמִּי הֲנִיעֵמוֹ בְחֵילְךָ וְהוֹרִידֵמוֹ מָגִנֵּנוּ אֲדֹנָי: חַטַּאת־פִּימוֹ דְּבַר־
שְׂפָתֵימוֹ וְיִלָּכְדוּ בִגְאוֹנָם וּמֵאָלָה וּמִכַּחַשׁ יְסַפֵּרוּ: כַּלֵּה בְחֵמָה כַּלֵּה וְאֵינֵמוֹ
וְיֵדְעוּ כִּי־אֱלֹהִים מֹשֵׁל בְּיַעֲקֹב לְאַפְסֵי הָאָרֶץ סֶלָה: וְיָשֻׁבוּ לָעֶרֶב יֶהֱמוּ כַכָּלֶב
וִיסוֹבְבוּ עִיר: הֵמָּה יְנִיעוּן לֶאֱכֹל אִם־לֹא יִשְׂבְּעוּ וַיָּלִינוּ: וַאֲנִי ׀ אָשִׁיר עֻזֶּךָ יְמִינֶךָ
וַאֲרַנֵּן לַבֹּקֶר חַסְדֶּךָ כִּי־הָיִיתָ מִשְׂגָּב לִי וּמָנוֹס בְּיוֹם צַר־לִי: עֻזִּי אֵלֶיךָ אֲזַמֵּרָה
כִּי־אֱלֹהִים מִשְׂגַּבִּי אֱלֹהֵי חַסְדִּי:

ס* לַמְנַצֵּחַ עַל־שׁוּשַׁן עֵדוּת מִכְתָּם לְדָוִד לְלַמֵּד: בְּהַצּוֹתוֹ ׀ אֶת אֲרַם נַהֲרַיִם
וְאֶת־אֲרַם צוֹבָה וַיָּשָׁב יוֹאָב וַיַּךְ אֶת־אֱדוֹם בְּגֵיא־מֶלַח שְׁנֵים עָשָׂר אָלֶף:
אֱלֹהִים זְנַחְתָּנוּ פְרַצְתָּנוּ אָנַפְתָּ תְּשׁוֹבֵב לָנוּ: הִרְעַשְׁתָּה אֶרֶץ פְּצַמְתָּהּ רְפָה
שְׁבָרֶיהָ כִי־מָטָה: הִרְאִיתָ עַמְּךָ קָשָׁה הִשְׁקִיתָנוּ יַיִן תַּרְעֵלָה: נָתַתָּה לִּירֵאֶיךָ וַעֲנֵנִי
נֵּס לְהִתְנוֹסֵס מִפְּנֵי קֹשֶׁט סֶלָה: לְמַעַן יֵחָלְצוּן יְדִידֶיךָ הוֹשִׁיעָה יְמִינְךָ וַעֲנֵנִי: וַעֲנֵנִי
אֱלֹהִים ׀ דִּבֶּר בְּקָדְשׁוֹ אֶעְלֹזָה אֲחַלְּקָה שְׁכֶם וְעֵמֶק סֻכּוֹת אֲמַדֵּד: לִי גִלְעָד ׀
וְלִי מְנַשֶּׁה וְאֶפְרַיִם מָעוֹז רֹאשִׁי יְהוּדָה מְחֹקְקִי: מוֹאָב ׀ סִיר רַחְצִי עַל־אֱדוֹם

*יא לחודש

אַשְׁלִיךְ נַעֲלִי עַל־פְּלֶשֶׁת עָלַי הִתְרֹעָעִי: מִי יֹבִלֵנִי עִיר מָצוֹר מִי נָחַנִי עַד־אֱדוֹם: הֲלֹא־אַתָּה אֱלֹהִים זְנַחְתָּנוּ וְלֹא־תֵצֵא אֱלֹהִים בְּצִבְאוֹתֵינוּ: הָבָה־לָּנוּ עֶזְרָת מִצָּר וְשָׁוְא תְּשׁוּעַת אָדָם: בֵּאלֹהִים נַעֲשֶׂה־חָיִל וְהוּא יָבוּס צָרֵינוּ:

סא לַמְנַצֵּחַ ׀ עַל־נְגִינַת לְדָוִד: שִׁמְעָה אֱלֹהִים רִנָּתִי הַקְשִׁיבָה תְּפִלָּתִי: מִקְצֵה הָאָרֶץ ׀ אֵלֶיךָ אֶקְרָא בַּעֲטֹף לִבִּי בְּצוּר־יָרוּם מִמֶּנִּי תַנְחֵנִי: כִּי־הָיִיתָ מַחְסֶה לִי מִגְדַּל־עֹז מִפְּנֵי אוֹיֵב: אָגוּרָה בְאָהׇלְךָ עוֹלָמִים אֶחֱסֶה בְסֵתֶר כְּנָפֶיךָ סֶּלָה: כִּי־אַתָּה אֱלֹהִים שָׁמַעְתָּ לִנְדָרָי נָתַתָּ יְרֻשַּׁת יִרְאֵי שְׁמֶךָ: יָמִים עַל־יְמֵי־מֶלֶךְ תּוֹסִיף שְׁנוֹתָיו כְּמוֹ־דֹר וָדֹר: יֵשֵׁב עוֹלָם לִפְנֵי אֱלֹהִים חֶסֶד וֶאֱמֶת מַן יִנְצְרֻהוּ: כֵּן אֲזַמְּרָה שִׁמְךָ לָעַד לְשַׁלְּמִי נְדָרַי יוֹם ׀ יוֹם:

סב לַמְנַצֵּחַ עַל־יְדוּתוּן מִזְמוֹר לְדָוִד: אַךְ אֶל־אֱלֹהִים דּוּמִיָּה נַפְשִׁי מִמֶּנּוּ יְשׁוּעָתִי: אַךְ־הוּא צוּרִי וִישׁוּעָתִי מִשְׂגַּבִּי לֹא־אֶמּוֹט רַבָּה: עַד־אָנָה ׀ תְּהוֹתְתוּ עַל־אִישׁ תְּרָצְּחוּ כֻלְּכֶם כְּקִיר נָטוּי גָּדֵר הַדְּחוּיָה: אַךְ מִשְּׂאֵתוֹ ׀ יָעֲצוּ לְהַדִּיחַ יִרְצוּ כָזָב בְּפִיו יְבָרֵכוּ וּבְקִרְבָּם יְקַלְלוּ־סֶלָה: אַךְ לֵאלֹהִים דּוֹמִּי נַפְשִׁי כִּי־מִמֶּנּוּ תִּקְוָתִי: אַךְ־הוּא צוּרִי וִישׁוּעָתִי מִשְׂגַּבִּי לֹא אֶמּוֹט: עַל־אֱלֹהִים יִשְׁעִי וּכְבוֹדִי צוּר־עֻזִּי מַחְסִי בֵּאלֹהִים: בִּטְחוּ בוֹ בְכׇל־עֵת ׀ עָם שִׁפְכוּ־לְפָנָיו לְבַבְכֶם אֱלֹהִים מַחֲסֶה־לָּנוּ סֶלָה: אַךְ ׀ הֶבֶל בְּנֵי־אָדָם כָּזָב בְּנֵי אִישׁ בְּמֹאזְנַיִם לַעֲלוֹת הֵמָּה מֵהֶבֶל יָחַד: אַל־תִּבְטְחוּ בְעֹשֶׁק וּבְגָזֵל אַל־תֶּהְבָּלוּ חַיִל ׀ כִּי־יָנוּב אַל־תָּשִׁיתוּ לֵב: אַחַת ׀ דִּבֶּר אֱלֹהִים שְׁתַּיִם־זוּ שָׁמָעְתִּי כִּי עֹז לֵאלֹהִים: וּלְךָ־אֲדֹנָי חָסֶד כִּי־אַתָּה תְשַׁלֵּם לְאִישׁ כְּמַעֲשֵׂהוּ:

סג מִזְמוֹר לְדָוִד בִּהְיוֹתוֹ בְּמִדְבַּר יְהוּדָה: אֱלֹהִים ׀ אֵלִי אַתָּה אֲשַׁחֲרֶךָּ צָמְאָה לְךָ ׀ נַפְשִׁי כָּמַהּ לְךָ בְשָׂרִי בְּאֶרֶץ־צִיָּה וְעָיֵף בְּלִי־מָיִם: כֵּן בַּקֹּדֶשׁ חֲזִיתִךָ לִרְאוֹת עֻזְּךָ וּכְבוֹדֶךָ: כִּי־טוֹב חַסְדְּךָ מֵחַיִּים שְׂפָתַי יְשַׁבְּחוּנְךָ: כֵּן אֲבָרֶכְךָ בְחַיָּי בְּשִׁמְךָ אֶשָּׂא כַפָּי: כְּמוֹ חֵלֶב וָדֶשֶׁן תִּשְׂבַּע נַפְשִׁי וְשִׂפְתֵי רְנָנוֹת יְהַלֶּל־פִּי: אִם־זְכַרְתִּיךָ עַל־יְצוּעָי בְּאַשְׁמֻרוֹת אֶהְגֶּה־בָּךְ: כִּי־הָיִיתָ עֶזְרָתָה לִּי וּבְצֵל כְּנָפֶיךָ אֲרַנֵּן: דָּבְקָה נַפְשִׁי אַחֲרֶיךָ בִּי תָּמְכָה יְמִינֶךָ: וְהֵמָּה לְשׁוֹאָה יְבַקְשׁוּ נַפְשִׁי יָבֹאוּ בְּתַחְתִּיּוֹת הָאָרֶץ: יַגִּירֻהוּ עַל־יְדֵי־חָרֶב מְנָת שֻׁעָלִים יִהְיוּ: וְהַמֶּלֶךְ יִשְׂמַח בֵּאלֹהִים יִתְהַלֵּל כָּל־הַנִּשְׁבָּע בּוֹ כִּי יִסָּכֵר פִּי דוֹבְרֵי־שָׁקֶר:

סד לַמְנַצֵּחַ מִזְמוֹר לְדָוִד: שְׁמַע־אֱלֹהִים קוֹלִי בְשִׂיחִי מִפַּחַד אוֹיֵב תִּצֹּר חַיָּי: תַּסְתִּירֵנִי מִסּוֹד מְרֵעִים מֵרִגְשַׁת פֹּעֲלֵי אָוֶן: אֲשֶׁר שָׁנְנוּ כַחֶרֶב לְשׁוֹנָם דָּרְכוּ

חִצָּם דָּבָר מָר: לִירוֹת בַּמִּסְתָּרִים תָּם פִּתְאֹם יֹרֻהוּ וְלֹא יִירָאוּ ׀ יְחַזְּקוּ־לָמוֹ ׀ דָּבָר רָע יְסַפְּרוּ לִטְמוֹן מוֹקְשִׁים אָמְרוּ מִי יִרְאֶה־לָּמוֹ: יַחְפְּשׂוּ־עוֹלֹת תַּמְנוּ חֵפֶשׂ מְחֻפָּשׂ וְקֶרֶב אִישׁ וְלֵב עָמֹק: וַיֹּרֵם אֱלֹהִים חֵץ פִּתְאֹם הָיוּ מַכּוֹתָם: וַיַּכְשִׁילוּהוּ עָלֵימוֹ לְשׁוֹנָם יִתְנֹדְדוּ כָּל־רֹאֵה בָם: וַיִּירְאוּ כָּל־אָדָם וַיַּגִּידוּ פֹּעַל אֱלֹהִים וּמַעֲשֵׂהוּ הִשְׂכִּילוּ: יִשְׂמַח צַדִּיק בַּיהוָה וְחָסָה בוֹ וְיִתְהַלְלוּ כָּל־יִשְׁרֵי־לֵב:

סה לַמְנַצֵּחַ מִזְמוֹר לְדָוִד שִׁיר: לְךָ דֻמִיָּה תְהִלָּה אֱלֹהִים בְּצִיּוֹן וּלְךָ יְשֻׁלַּם־נֶדֶר: שֹׁמֵעַ תְּפִלָּה עָדֶיךָ כָּל־בָּשָׂר יָבֹאוּ: דִּבְרֵי עֲוֹנֹת גָּבְרוּ מֶנִּי פְּשָׁעֵינוּ אַתָּה תְכַפְּרֵם: אַשְׁרֵי ׀ תִּבְחַר וּתְקָרֵב יִשְׁכֹּן חֲצֵרֶיךָ נִשְׂבְּעָה בְּטוּב בֵּיתֶךָ קְדֹשׁ הֵיכָלֶךָ: נוֹרָאוֹת ׀ בְּצֶדֶק תַּעֲנֵנוּ אֱלֹהֵי יִשְׁעֵנוּ מִבְטָח כָּל־קַצְוֵי־אֶרֶץ וְיָם רְחֹקִים: מֵכִין הָרִים בְּכֹחוֹ נֶאְזָר בִּגְבוּרָה: מַשְׁבִּיחַ ׀ שְׁאוֹן יַמִּים שְׁאוֹן גַּלֵּיהֶם וַהֲמוֹן לְאֻמִּים: וַיִּירְאוּ ׀ יֹשְׁבֵי קְצָוֹת מֵאוֹתֹתֶיךָ מוֹצָאֵי־בֹקֶר וָעֶרֶב תַּרְנִין: פָּקַדְתָּ הָאָרֶץ ׀ וַתְּשֹׁקְקֶהָ רַבַּת תַּעְשְׁרֶנָּה פֶּלֶג אֱלֹהִים מָלֵא מָיִם תָּכִין דְּגָנָם כִּי־כֵן תְּכִינֶהָ: תְּלָמֶיהָ רַוֵּה נַחֵת גְּדוּדֶהָ בִּרְבִיבִים תְּמֹגְגֶנָּה צִמְחָהּ תְּבָרֵךְ: עִטַּרְתָּ שְׁנַת טוֹבָתֶךָ וּמַעְגָּלֶיךָ יִרְעֲפוּן דָּשֶׁן: יִרְעֲפוּ נְאוֹת מִדְבָּר וְגִיל גְּבָעוֹת תַּחְגֹּרְנָה: לָבְשׁוּ כָרִים ׀ הַצֹּאן וַעֲמָקִים יַעַטְפוּ־בָר יִתְרוֹעֲעוּ אַף־יָשִׁירוּ:

סו ׀ לַמְנַצֵּחַ שִׁיר מִזְמוֹר הָרִיעוּ לֵאלֹהִים כָּל־הָאָרֶץ: זַמְּרוּ כְבוֹד־שְׁמוֹ שִׂימוּ כָבוֹד תְּהִלָּתוֹ: אִמְרוּ לֵאלֹהִים מַה־נּוֹרָא מַעֲשֶׂיךָ בְּרֹב עֻזְּךָ יְכַחֲשׁוּ־לְךָ אֹיְבֶיךָ: כָּל־הָאָרֶץ ׀ יִשְׁתַּחֲווּ לְךָ וִיזַמְּרוּ־לָךְ יְזַמְּרוּ שִׁמְךָ סֶלָה: לְכוּ וּרְאוּ מִפְעֲלוֹת אֱלֹהִים נוֹרָא עֲלִילָה עַל־בְּנֵי אָדָם: הָפַךְ יָם ׀ לְיַבָּשָׁה בַּנָּהָר יַעַבְרוּ בְרָגֶל שָׁם נִשְׂמְחָה־בּוֹ: מֹשֵׁל בִּגְבוּרָתוֹ ׀ עוֹלָם עֵינָיו בַּגּוֹיִם תִּצְפֶּינָה הַסּוֹרְרִים ׀ אַל־יָרִימוּ לָמוֹ סֶלָה: בָּרְכוּ עַמִּים ׀ אֱלֹהֵינוּ וְהַשְׁמִיעוּ קוֹל תְּהִלָּתוֹ: הַשָּׂם נַפְשֵׁנוּ בַּחַיִּים וְלֹא־נָתַן לַמּוֹט רַגְלֵנוּ: כִּי־בְחַנְתָּנוּ אֱלֹהִים צְרַפְתָּנוּ כִּצְרָף־כָּסֶף: הֲבֵאתָנוּ בַמְּצוּדָה שַׂמְתָּ מוּעָקָה בְמָתְנֵינוּ: הִרְכַּבְתָּ אֱנוֹשׁ לְרֹאשֵׁנוּ בָּאנוּ־בָאֵשׁ וּבַמַּיִם וַתּוֹצִיאֵנוּ לָרְוָיָה: אָבוֹא בֵיתְךָ בְעוֹלוֹת אֲשַׁלֵּם לְךָ נְדָרָי: אֲשֶׁר־פָּצוּ שְׂפָתָי וְדִבֶּר־פִּי בַּצַּר־לִי: עֹלוֹת מֵחִים אַעֲלֶה־לָּךְ עִם־קְטֹרֶת אֵילִים אֶעֱשֶׂה בָקָר עִם־עַתּוּדִים סֶלָה: לְכוּ־שִׁמְעוּ וַאֲסַפְּרָה כָּל־יִרְאֵי אֱלֹהִים אֲשֶׁר עָשָׂה לְנַפְשִׁי: אֵלָיו פִּי־קָרָאתִי וְרוֹמַם תַּחַת לְשׁוֹנִי: אָוֶן אִם־רָאִיתִי בְלִבִּי לֹא יִשְׁמַע ׀ אֲדֹנָי:

*יב לחודש

אָכֵן שָׁמַע אֱלֹהִים הִקְשִׁיב בְּקוֹל תְּפִלָּתִי: בָּרוּךְ אֱלֹהִים אֲשֶׁר לֹא־הֵסִיר
תְּפִלָּתִי וְחַסְדּוֹ מֵאִתִּי:

סז לַמְנַצֵּחַ בִּנְגִינֹת מִזְמוֹר שִׁיר: אֱלֹהִים יְחָנֵּנוּ וִיבָרְכֵנוּ יָאֵר פָּנָיו אִתָּנוּ סֶלָה:
לָדַעַת בָּאָרֶץ דַּרְכֶּךָ בְּכָל־גּוֹיִם יְשׁוּעָתֶךָ: יוֹדוּךָ עַמִּים ׀ אֱלֹהִים יוֹדוּךָ עַמִּים
כֻּלָּם: יִשְׂמְחוּ וִירַנְּנוּ לְאֻמִּים כִּי־תִשְׁפֹּט עַמִּים מִישֹׁר וּלְאֻמִּים ׀ בָּאָרֶץ תַּנְחֵם
סֶלָה: יוֹדוּךָ עַמִּים ׀ אֱלֹהִים יוֹדוּךָ עַמִּים כֻּלָּם: אֶרֶץ נָתְנָה יְבוּלָהּ יְבָרְכֵנוּ
אֱלֹהִים אֱלֹהֵינוּ: יְבָרְכֵנוּ אֱלֹהִים וְיִירְאוּ אוֹתוֹ כָּל־אַפְסֵי־אָרֶץ:

סח לַמְנַצֵּחַ לְדָוִד מִזְמוֹר שִׁיר: יָקוּם אֱלֹהִים יָפוּצוּ אוֹיְבָיו וְיָנוּסוּ מְשַׂנְאָיו מִפָּנָיו:
כְּהִנְדֹּף עָשָׁן תִּנְדֹּף כְּהִמֵּס דּוֹנַג מִפְּנֵי־אֵשׁ יֹאבְדוּ רְשָׁעִים מִפְּנֵי אֱלֹהִים:
וְצַדִּיקִים יִשְׂמְחוּ יַעַלְצוּ לִפְנֵי אֱלֹהִים וְיָשִׂישׂוּ בְשִׂמְחָה: שִׁירוּ ׀ לֵאלֹהִים
זַמְּרוּ שְׁמוֹ סֹלּוּ לָרֹכֵב בָּעֲרָבוֹת בְּיָהּ שְׁמוֹ וְעִלְזוּ לְפָנָיו: אֲבִי יְתוֹמִים וְדַיַּן
אַלְמָנוֹת אֱלֹהִים בִּמְעוֹן קָדְשׁוֹ: אֱלֹהִים ׀ מוֹשִׁיב יְחִידִים ׀ בַּיְתָה מוֹצִיא
אֲסִירִים בַּכּוֹשָׁרוֹת אַךְ סוֹרְרִים שָׁכְנוּ צְחִיחָה: אֱלֹהִים בְּצֵאתְךָ לִפְנֵי עַמֶּךָ
בְּצַעְדְּךָ בִישִׁימוֹן סֶלָה: אֶרֶץ רָעָשָׁה ׀ אַף־שָׁמַיִם נָטְפוּ מִפְּנֵי אֱלֹהִים זֶה
סִינַי מִפְּנֵי אֱלֹהִים אֱלֹהֵי יִשְׂרָאֵל: גֶּשֶׁם נְדָבוֹת תָּנִיף אֱלֹהִים נַחֲלָתְךָ וְנִלְאָה
אַתָּה כוֹנַנְתָּהּ: חַיָּתְךָ יָשְׁבוּ־בָהּ תָּכִין בְּטוֹבָתְךָ לֶעָנִי אֱלֹהִים: אֲדֹנָי יִתֶּן־אֹמֶר
הַמְבַשְּׂרוֹת צָבָא רָב: מַלְכֵי צְבָאוֹת יִדֹּדוּן יִדֹּדוּן וּנְוַת־בַּיִת תְּחַלֵּק שָׁלָל:
אִם־תִּשְׁכְּבוּן בֵּין שְׁפַתָּיִם כַּנְפֵי יוֹנָה נֶחְפָּה בַכֶּסֶף וְאֶבְרוֹתֶיהָ בִּירַקְרַק חָרוּץ:
בְּפָרֵשׂ שַׁדַּי מְלָכִים בָּהּ תַּשְׁלֵג בְּצַלְמוֹן: הַר־אֱלֹהִים הַר־בָּשָׁן הַר גַּבְנֻנִּים
הַר־בָּשָׁן: לָמָּה ׀ תְּרַצְּדוּן הָרִים גַּבְנֻנִּים הָהָר חָמַד אֱלֹהִים לְשִׁבְתּוֹ אַף־יְהוָה
יִשְׁכֹּן לָנֶצַח: רֶכֶב אֱלֹהִים רִבֹּתַיִם אַלְפֵי שִׁנְאָן אֲדֹנָי בָם סִינַי בַּקֹּדֶשׁ: עָלִיתָ
לַמָּרוֹם ׀ שָׁבִיתָ שֶּׁבִי לָקַחְתָּ מַתָּנוֹת בָּאָדָם וְאַף סוֹרְרִים לִשְׁכֹּן ׀ יָהּ אֱלֹהִים:
בָּרוּךְ אֲדֹנָי יוֹם ׀ יוֹם יַעֲמָס־לָנוּ הָאֵל יְשׁוּעָתֵנוּ סֶלָה: הָאֵל ׀ לָנוּ אֵל לְמוֹשָׁעוֹת
וְלֵיהוָה אֲדֹנָי לַמָּוֶת תּוֹצָאוֹת: אַךְ־אֱלֹהִים יִמְחַץ רֹאשׁ אֹיְבָיו קָדְקֹד שֵׂעָר
מִתְהַלֵּךְ בַּאֲשָׁמָיו: אָמַר אֲדֹנָי מִבָּשָׁן אָשִׁיב אָשִׁיב מִמְּצֻלוֹת יָם: לְמַעַן ׀ תִּמְחַץ
רַגְלְךָ בְּדָם לְשׁוֹן כְּלָבֶיךָ מֵאֹיְבִים מִנֵּהוּ: רָאוּ הֲלִיכוֹתֶיךָ אֱלֹהִים הֲלִיכוֹת אֵלִי
מַלְכִּי בַקֹּדֶשׁ: קִדְּמוּ שָׁרִים אַחַר נֹגְנִים בְּתוֹךְ עֲלָמוֹת תּוֹפֵפוֹת: בְּמַקְהֵלוֹת
בָּרְכוּ אֱלֹהִים אֲדֹנָי מִמְּקוֹר יִשְׂרָאֵל: שָׁם בִּנְיָמִן ׀ צָעִיר רֹדֵם שָׂרֵי יְהוּדָה
רִגְמָתָם שָׂרֵי זְבֻלוּן שָׂרֵי נַפְתָּלִי: צִוָּה אֱלֹהֶיךָ עֻזֶּךָ עוּזָּה אֱלֹהִים זוּ פָּעַלְתָּ לָּנוּ:

מֵהֵיכָלֶךָ עַל־יְרוּשָׁלִָם לְךָ יוֹבִילוּ מְלָכִים שָׁי: גְּעַר חַיַּת קָנֶה עֲדַת אַבִּירִים ׀
בְּעֶגְלֵי עַמִּים מִתְרַפֵּס בְּרַצֵּי־כָסֶף בִּזַּר עַמִּים קְרָבוֹת יֶחְפָּצוּ: יֶאֱתָיוּ חַשְׁמַנִּים
מִנִּי מִצְרָיִם כּוּשׁ תָּרִיץ יָדָיו לֵאלֹהִים: מַמְלְכוֹת הָאָרֶץ שִׁירוּ לֵאלֹהִים זַמְּרוּ
אֲדֹנָי סֶלָה: לָרֹכֵב בִּשְׁמֵי שְׁמֵי־קֶדֶם הֵן יִתֵּן בְּקוֹלוֹ קוֹל עֹז: תְּנוּ עֹז לֵאלֹהִים
עַל־יִשְׂרָאֵל גַּאֲוָתוֹ וְעֻזּוֹ בַּשְּׁחָקִים: נוֹרָא אֱלֹהִים ׀ מִמִּקְדָּשֶׁיךָ אֵל יִשְׂרָאֵל
הוּא נֹתֵן ׀ עֹז וְתַעֲצֻמוֹת לָעָם בָּרוּךְ אֱלֹהִים:

*סט לַמְנַצֵּחַ עַל־שׁוֹשַׁנִּים לְדָוִד: הוֹשִׁיעֵנִי אֱלֹהִים כִּי בָאוּ מַיִם עַד־נָפֶשׁ: טָבַעְתִּי ׀
בִּיוֵן מְצוּלָה וְאֵין מָעֳמָד בָּאתִי בְמַעֲמַקֵּי־מַיִם וְשִׁבֹּלֶת שְׁטָפָתְנִי: יָגַעְתִּי בְקָרְאִי
נִחַר גְּרוֹנִי כָּלוּ עֵינַי מְיַחֵל לֵאלֹהָי: רַבּוּ ׀ מִשַּׂעֲרוֹת רֹאשִׁי שֹׂנְאַי חִנָּם עָצְמוּ
מַצְמִיתַי אֹיְבַי שֶׁקֶר אֲשֶׁר לֹא־גָזַלְתִּי אָז אָשִׁיב: אֱלֹהִים אַתָּה יָדַעְתָּ לְאִוַּלְתִּי
וְאַשְׁמוֹתַי מִמְּךָ לֹא־נִכְחָדוּ: אַל־יֵבֹשׁוּ בִי ׀ קֹוֶיךָ אֲדֹנָי יֱהֹוִה צְבָאוֹת אַל־יִכָּלְמוּ
בִי מְבַקְשֶׁיךָ אֱלֹהֵי יִשְׂרָאֵל: כִּי־עָלֶיךָ נָשָׂאתִי חֶרְפָּה כִּסְּתָה כְלִמָּה פָנָי: מוּזָר
הָיִיתִי לְאֶחָי וְנָכְרִי לִבְנֵי אִמִּי: כִּי־קִנְאַת בֵּיתְךָ אֲכָלָתְנִי וְחֶרְפּוֹת חוֹרְפֶיךָ נָפְלוּ
עָלָי: וָאֶבְכֶּה בַצּוֹם נַפְשִׁי וַתְּהִי לַחֲרָפוֹת לִי: וָאֶתְּנָה לְבוּשִׁי שָׂק וָאֱהִי לָהֶם
לְמָשָׁל: יָשִׂיחוּ בִי יֹשְׁבֵי שָׁעַר וּנְגִינוֹת שׁוֹתֵי שֵׁכָר: וַאֲנִי תְפִלָּתִי־לְךָ ׀ יְהֹוָה
עֵת רָצוֹן אֱלֹהִים בְּרָב־חַסְדֶּךָ עֲנֵנִי בֶּאֱמֶת יִשְׁעֶךָ: הַצִּילֵנִי מִטִּיט וְאַל־אֶטְבָּעָה
אִנָּצְלָה מִשֹּׂנְאַי וּמִמַּעֲמַקֵּי־מָיִם: אַל־תִּשְׁטְפֵנִי ׀ שִׁבֹּלֶת מַיִם וְאַל־תִּבְלָעֵנִי
מְצוּלָה וְאַל־תֶּאְטַר־עָלַי בְּאֵר פִּיהָ: עֲנֵנִי יְהֹוָה כִּי־טוֹב חַסְדֶּךָ כְּרֹב רַחֲמֶיךָ
פְּנֵה אֵלָי: וְאַל־תַּסְתֵּר פָּנֶיךָ מֵעַבְדֶּךָ כִּי־צַר־לִי מַהֵר עֲנֵנִי: קָרְבָה אֶל־נַפְשִׁי
גְאָלָהּ לְמַעַן אֹיְבַי פְּדֵנִי: אַתָּה יָדַעְתָּ חֶרְפָּתִי וּבָשְׁתִּי וּכְלִמָּתִי נֶגְדְּךָ כָּל־צוֹרְרָי:
חֶרְפָּה ׀ שָׁבְרָה לִבִּי וָאָנוּשָׁה וָאֲקַוֶּה לָנוּד וָאַיִן וְלַמְנַחֲמִים וְלֹא מָצָאתִי:
וַיִּתְּנוּ בְּבָרוּתִי רֹאשׁ וְלִצְמָאִי יַשְׁקוּנִי חֹמֶץ: יְהִי־שֻׁלְחָנָם לִפְנֵיהֶם לְפָח
וְלִשְׁלוֹמִים לְמוֹקֵשׁ: תֶּחְשַׁכְנָה עֵינֵיהֶם מֵרְאוֹת וּמָתְנֵיהֶם תָּמִיד הַמְעַד:
שְׁפָךְ־עֲלֵיהֶם זַעְמֶךָ וַחֲרוֹן אַפְּךָ יַשִּׂיגֵם: תְּהִי־טִירָתָם נְשַׁמָּה בְּאָהֳלֵיהֶם אַל־
יְהִי יֹשֵׁב: כִּי־אַתָּה אֲשֶׁר־הִכִּיתָ רָדָפוּ וְאֶל־מַכְאוֹב חֲלָלֶיךָ יְסַפֵּרוּ: תְּנָה־עָוֹן
עַל־עֲוֹנָם וְאַל־יָבֹאוּ בְּצִדְקָתֶךָ: יִמָּחוּ מִסֵּפֶר חַיִּים וְעִם צַדִּיקִים אַל־יִכָּתֵבוּ:
וַאֲנִי עָנִי וְכוֹאֵב יְשׁוּעָתְךָ אֱלֹהִים תְּשַׂגְּבֵנִי: אֲהַלְלָה שֵׁם־אֱלֹהִים בְּשִׁיר
וַאֲגַדְּלֶנּוּ בְתוֹדָה: וְתִיטַב לַיהֹוָה מִשּׁוֹר פָּר מַקְרִן מַפְרִיס: רָאוּ עֲנָוִים יִשְׂמָחוּ
דֹּרְשֵׁי אֱלֹהִים וִיחִי לְבַבְכֶם: כִּי־שֹׁמֵעַ אֶל־אֶבְיוֹנִים יְהֹוָה וְאֶת־אֲסִירָיו לֹא

*סט לחודש

בָזֶה: יְהַלְלוּהוּ שָׁמַיִם וָאָרֶץ יַמִּים וְכָל־רֹמֵשׂ בָּם: כִּי אֱלֹהִים ׀ יוֹשִׁיעַ צִיּוֹן
וְיִבְנֶה עָרֵי יְהוּדָה וְיָשְׁבוּ שָׁם וִירֵשׁוּהָ: וְזֶרַע עֲבָדָיו יִנְחָלוּהָ וְאֹהֲבֵי שְׁמוֹ
יִשְׁכְּנוּ־בָהּ:

ע לַמְנַצֵּחַ לְדָוִד לְהַזְכִּיר: אֱלֹהִים לְהַצִּילֵנִי יְהוָה לְעֶזְרָתִי חוּשָׁה: יֵבֹשׁוּ וְיַחְפְּרוּ
מְבַקְשֵׁי נַפְשִׁי יִסֹּגוּ אָחוֹר וְיִכָּלְמוּ חֲפֵצֵי רָעָתִי: יָשׁוּבוּ עַל־עֵקֶב בָּשְׁתָּם
הָאֹמְרִים הֶאָח ׀ הֶאָח: יָשִׂישׂוּ וְיִשְׂמְחוּ ׀ בְּךָ כָּל־מְבַקְשֶׁיךָ וְיֹאמְרוּ תָמִיד
יִגְדַּל אֱלֹהִים אֹהֲבֵי יְשׁוּעָתֶךָ: וַאֲנִי ׀ עָנִי וְאֶבְיוֹן אֱלֹהִים חוּשָׁה־לִּי עֶזְרִי וּמְפַלְטִי
אַתָּה יְהוָה אַל־תְּאַחַר:

עא בְּךָ־יְהוָה חָסִיתִי אַל־אֵבוֹשָׁה לְעוֹלָם: בְּצִדְקָתְךָ תַּצִּילֵנִי וּתְפַלְּטֵנִי הַטֵּה־אֵלַי
אָזְנְךָ וְהוֹשִׁיעֵנִי: הֱיֵה לִי ׀ לְצוּר מָעוֹן לָבוֹא תָּמִיד צִוִּיתָ לְהוֹשִׁיעֵנִי כִּי־סַלְעִי
וּמְצוּדָתִי אָתָּה: אֱלֹהַי פַּלְּטֵנִי מִיַּד רָשָׁע מִכַּף מְעַוֵּל וְחוֹמֵץ: כִּי־אַתָּה תִקְוָתִי
אֲדֹנָי יְהוִה מִבְטַחִי מִנְּעוּרָי: עָלֶיךָ ׀ נִסְמַכְתִּי מִבֶּטֶן מִמְּעֵי אִמִּי אַתָּה גוֹזִי בְּךָ
תְהִלָּתִי תָמִיד: כְּמוֹפֵת הָיִיתִי לְרַבִּים וְאַתָּה מַחֲסִי־עֹז: יִמָּלֵא פִי תְּהִלָּתֶךָ
כָּל־הַיּוֹם תִּפְאַרְתֶּךָ: אַל־תַּשְׁלִיכֵנִי לְעֵת זִקְנָה כִּכְלוֹת כֹּחִי אַל־תַּעַזְבֵנִי:
כִּי־אָמְרוּ אוֹיְבַי לִי וְשֹׁמְרֵי נַפְשִׁי נוֹעֲצוּ יַחְדָּו: לֵאמֹר אֱלֹהִים עֲזָבוֹ רִדְפוּ
וְתִפְשׂוּהוּ כִּי־אֵין מַצִּיל: אֱלֹהִים אַל־תִּרְחַק מִמֶּנִּי אֱלֹהַי לְעֶזְרָתִי חישה [חוּשָׁה]:
יֵבֹשׁוּ יִכְלוּ שֹׂטְנֵי נַפְשִׁי יַעֲטוּ חֶרְפָּה וּכְלִמָּה מְבַקְשֵׁי רָעָתִי: וַאֲנִי תָּמִיד אֲיַחֵל
וְהוֹסַפְתִּי עַל־כָּל־תְּהִלָּתֶךָ: פִּי ׀ יְסַפֵּר צִדְקָתֶךָ כָּל־הַיּוֹם תְּשׁוּעָתֶךָ כִּי לֹא
יָדַעְתִּי סְפֹרוֹת: אָבוֹא בִּגְבֻרוֹת אֲדֹנָי יְהוִה אַזְכִּיר צִדְקָתְךָ לְבַדֶּךָ: אֱלֹהִים
לִמַּדְתַּנִי מִנְּעוּרָי וְעַד־הֵנָּה אַגִּיד נִפְלְאוֹתֶיךָ: וְגַם עַד־זִקְנָה ׀ וְשֵׂיבָה אֱלֹהִים
אַל־תַּעַזְבֵנִי עַד־אַגִּיד זְרוֹעֲךָ לְדוֹר לְכָל־יָבוֹא גְּבוּרָתֶךָ: וְצִדְקָתְךָ אֱלֹהִים
עַד־מָרוֹם אֲשֶׁר־עָשִׂיתָ גְדֹלוֹת אֱלֹהִים מִי כָמוֹךָ: אֲשֶׁר הראיתנו [הִרְאִיתַנִי] ׀ צָרוֹת
רַבּוֹת וְרָעוֹת תָּשׁוּב תחיינו [תְּחַיֵּנִי] וּמִתְּהֹמוֹת הָאָרֶץ תָּשׁוּב תעלני [תַּעֲלֵנִי]: תֶּרֶב ׀ גְּדֻלָּתִי
וְתִסֹּב תְּנַחֲמֵנִי: גַּם־אֲנִי ׀ אוֹדְךָ בִכְלִי־נֶבֶל אֲמִתְּךָ אֱלֹהַי אֲזַמְּרָה לְךָ בְכִנּוֹר
קְדוֹשׁ יִשְׂרָאֵל: תְּרַנֵּנָּה שְׂפָתַי כִּי אֲזַמְּרָה־לָּךְ וְנַפְשִׁי אֲשֶׁר פָּדִיתָ: גַּם־לְשׁוֹנִי
כָּל־הַיּוֹם תֶּהְגֶּה צִדְקָתֶךָ כִּי־בֹשׁוּ כִי־חָפְרוּ מְבַקְשֵׁי רָעָתִי:

עב לִשְׁלֹמֹה ׀ אֱלֹהִים מִשְׁפָּטֶיךָ לְמֶלֶךְ תֵּן וְצִדְקָתְךָ לְבֶן־מֶלֶךְ: יָדִין עַמְּךָ בְצֶדֶק
וַעֲנִיֶּיךָ בְמִשְׁפָּט: יִשְׂאוּ הָרִים שָׁלוֹם לָעָם וּגְבָעוֹת בִּצְדָקָה: יִשְׁפֹּט ׀ עֲנִיֵּי־עָם
יוֹשִׁיעַ לִבְנֵי אֶבְיוֹן וִידַכֵּא עוֹשֵׁק: יִירָאוּךָ עִם־שָׁמֶשׁ וְלִפְנֵי יָרֵחַ דּוֹר דּוֹרִים:

יֵרְד כְּמָטָר עַל־גֵּז כִּרְבִיבִים זַרְזִיף אָרֶץ: יִפְרַח־בְּיָמָיו צַדִּיק וְרֹב שָׁלוֹם עַד־בְּלִי־
יָרֵחַ: וְיֵרְדְּ מִיָּם עַד־יָם וּמִנָּהָר עַד־אַפְסֵי־אָרֶץ: לְפָנָיו יִכְרְעוּ צִיִּים וְאֹיְבָיו עָפָר
יְלַחֵכוּ: מַלְכֵי תַרְשִׁישׁ וְאִיִּים מִנְחָה יָשִׁיבוּ מַלְכֵי שְׁבָא וּסְבָא אֶשְׁכָּר יַקְרִיבוּ:
וְיִשְׁתַּחֲווּ־לוֹ כָל־מְלָכִים כָּל־גּוֹיִם יַעַבְדוּהוּ: כִּי־יַצִּיל אֶבְיוֹן מְשַׁוֵּעַ וְעָנִי וְאֵין־
עֹזֵר לוֹ: יָחֹס עַל־דַּל וְאֶבְיוֹן וְנַפְשׁוֹת אֶבְיוֹנִים יוֹשִׁיעַ: מִתּוֹךְ וּמֵחָמָס יִגְאַל
נַפְשָׁם וְיֵיקַר דָּמָם בְּעֵינָיו: וִיחִי וְיִתֶּן־לוֹ מִזְּהַב שְׁבָא וְיִתְפַּלֵּל בַּעֲדוֹ תָמִיד
כָּל־הַיּוֹם יְבָרֲכֶנְהוּ: יְהִי פִסַּת־בַּר בָּאָרֶץ בְּרֹאשׁ הָרִים יִרְעַשׁ כַּלְּבָנוֹן פִּרְיוֹ
וְיָצִיצוּ מֵעִיר כְּעֵשֶׂב הָאָרֶץ: יְהִי שְׁמוֹ לְעוֹלָם לִפְנֵי־שֶׁמֶשׁ יִנּוֹן שְׁמוֹ וְיִתְבָּרֲכוּ **יִנּוֹן**
בוֹ כָּל־גּוֹיִם יְאַשְּׁרוּהוּ: בָּרוּךְ יְהוָה אֱלֹהִים אֱלֹהֵי יִשְׂרָאֵל עֹשֵׂה נִפְלָאוֹת
לְבַדּוֹ: וּבָרוּךְ שֵׁם כְּבוֹדוֹ לְעוֹלָם וְיִמָּלֵא כְבוֹדוֹ אֶת־כֹּל הָאָרֶץ אָמֵן וְאָמֵן:
כָּלּוּ תְפִלּוֹת דָּוִד בֶּן־יִשָׁי:

סֵפֶר שְׁלִישִׁי

עג ★ מִזְמוֹר לְאָסָף אַךְ טוֹב לְיִשְׂרָאֵל אֱלֹהִים לְבָרֵי לֵבָב: וַאֲנִי כִּמְעַט נָטוּי רַגְלָי **נָטָיוּ**
כְּאַיִן שֻׁפְּכָה אֲשֻׁרָי: כִּי־קִנֵּאתִי בַּהוֹלְלִים שְׁלוֹם רְשָׁעִים אֶרְאֶה: כִּי אֵין **שֻׁפְּכוּ**
חַרְצֻבּוֹת לְמוֹתָם וּבָרִיא אוּלָם: בַּעֲמַל אֱנוֹשׁ אֵינֵמוֹ וְעִם־אָדָם לֹא יְנֻגָּעוּ:
לָכֵן עֲנָקַתְמוֹ גַאֲוָה יַעֲטָף־שִׁית חָמָס לָמוֹ: יָצָא מֵחֵלֶב עֵינֵמוֹ עָבְרוּ מַשְׂכִּיּוֹת
לֵבָב: יָמִיקוּ וִידַבְּרוּ בְרָע עֹשֶׁק מִמָּרוֹם יְדַבֵּרוּ: שַׁתּוּ בַשָּׁמַיִם פִּיהֶם וּלְשׁוֹנָם
תִּהֲלַךְ בָּאָרֶץ: לָכֵן יָשׁוּב עַמּוֹ הֲלֹם וּמֵי מָלֵא יִמָּצוּ לָמוֹ: וְאָמְרוּ אֵיכָה יָדַע־ **יָשׁוּב**
אֵל וְיֵשׁ דֵּעָה בְעֶלְיוֹן: הִנֵּה־אֵלֶּה רְשָׁעִים וְשַׁלְוֵי עוֹלָם הִשְׂגּוּ־חָיִל: אַךְ־רִיק
זִכִּיתִי לְבָבִי וָאֶרְחַץ בְּנִקָּיוֹן כַּפָּי: וָאֱהִי נָגוּעַ כָּל־הַיּוֹם וְתוֹכַחְתִּי לַבְּקָרִים:
אִם־אָמַרְתִּי אֲסַפְּרָה כְמוֹ הִנֵּה דוֹר בָּנֶיךָ בָגָדְתִּי: וָאֲחַשְּׁבָה לָדַעַת זֹאת עָמָל
הִיא בְעֵינָי: עַד־אָבוֹא אֶל־מִקְדְּשֵׁי־אֵל אָבִינָה לְאַחֲרִיתָם: אַךְ בַּחֲלָקוֹת **הִיא**
תָּשִׁית לָמוֹ הִפַּלְתָּם לְמַשּׁוּאוֹת: אֵיךְ הָיוּ לְשַׁמָּה כְרָגַע סָפוּ תַמּוּ מִן־בַּלָּהוֹת:
כַּחֲלוֹם מֵהָקִיץ אֲדֹנָי בָּעִיר צַלְמָם תִּבְזֶה: כִּי יִתְחַמֵּץ לְבָבִי וְכִלְיוֹתַי אֶשְׁתּוֹנָן:
וַאֲנִי־בַעַר וְלֹא אֵדָע בְּהֵמוֹת הָיִיתִי עִמָּךְ: וַאֲנִי תָמִיד עִמָּךְ אָחַזְתָּ בְּיַד־יְמִינִי:
בַּעֲצָתְךָ תַנְחֵנִי וְאַחַר כָּבוֹד תִּקָּחֵנִי: מִי־לִי בַשָּׁמָיִם וְעִמְּךָ לֹא־חָפַצְתִּי בָאָרֶץ:
כָּלָה שְׁאֵרִי וּלְבָבִי צוּר־לְבָבִי וְחֶלְקִי אֱלֹהִים לְעוֹלָם: כִּי־הִנֵּה רְחֵקֶיךָ יֹאבֵדוּ
הִצְמַתָּה כָּל־זוֹנֶה מִמֶּךָּ: וַאֲנִי קִרֲבַת אֱלֹהִים לִי־טוֹב שַׁתִּי בַּאדֹנָי יְהוִה
מַחְסִי לְסַפֵּר כָּל־מַלְאֲכוֹתֶיךָ:

עד מַשְׂכִּיל לְאָסָף לָמָה אֱלֹהִים זָנַחְתָּ לָנֶצַח יֶעְשַׁן אַפְּךָ בְּצֹאן מַרְעִיתֶךָ: זְכֹר עֲדָתְךָ ׀ קָנִיתָ קֶּדֶם גָּאַלְתָּ שֵׁבֶט נַחֲלָתֶךָ הַר-צִיּוֹן זֶה ׀ שָׁכַנְתָּ בּוֹ: הָרִימָה פְעָמֶיךָ לְמַשֻּׁאוֹת נֶצַח כָּל-הֵרַע אוֹיֵב בַּקֹּדֶשׁ: שָׁאֲגוּ צֹרְרֶיךָ בְּקֶרֶב מוֹעֲדֶךָ שָׂמוּ אוֹתֹתָם אֹתוֹת: יִוָּדַע כְּמֵבִיא לְמָעְלָה בִּסְבָךְ-עֵץ קַרְדֻּמּוֹת: וְעֵת פִּתּוּחֶיהָ יָּחַד בְּכַשִּׁיל וְכֵילַפּוֹת יַהֲלֹמוּן: שִׁלְחוּ בָאֵשׁ מִקְדָּשֶׁךָ לָאָרֶץ חִלְּלוּ מִשְׁכַּן-שְׁמֶךָ: אָמְרוּ בְלִבָּם נִינָם יָחַד שָׂרְפוּ כָל-מוֹעֲדֵי-אֵל בָּאָרֶץ: אוֹתֹתֵינוּ לֹא-רָאִינוּ אֵין-עוֹד נָבִיא וְלֹא-אִתָּנוּ יֹדֵעַ עַד-מָה: עַד-מָתַי אֱלֹהִים יְחָרֶף

חֵיקֶךָ צָר יְנָאֵץ אוֹיֵב שִׁמְךָ לָנֶצַח: לָמָּה תָשִׁיב יָדְךָ וִימִינֶךָ מִקֶּרֶב חוקך כַלֵּה: וֵאלֹהִים מַלְכִּי מִקֶּדֶם פֹּעֵל יְשׁוּעוֹת בְּקֶרֶב הָאָרֶץ: אַתָּה פוֹרַרְתָּ בְעָזְּךָ יָם שִׁבַּרְתָּ רָאשֵׁי תַנִּינִים עַל-הַמָּיִם: אַתָּה רִצַּצְתָּ רָאשֵׁי לִוְיָתָן תִּתְּנֶנּוּ מַאֲכָל לְעָם לְצִיִּים: אַתָּה בָקַעְתָּ מַעְיָן וָנָחַל אַתָּה הוֹבַשְׁתָּ נַהֲרוֹת אֵיתָן: לְךָ יוֹם אַף-לְךָ לָיְלָה אַתָּה הֲכִינוֹתָ מָאוֹר וָשָׁמֶשׁ: אַתָּה הִצַּבְתָּ כָּל-גְּבוּלוֹת אָרֶץ קַיִץ וָחֹרֶף אַתָּה יְצַרְתָּם: זְכָר-זֹאת אוֹיֵב חֵרֵף ׀ יְהוָה וְעַם-נָבָל נִאֲצוּ שְׁמֶךָ: אַל-תִּתֵּן לְחַיַּת נֶפֶשׁ תּוֹרֶךָ חַיַּת עֲנִיֶּיךָ אַל-תִּשְׁכַּח לָנֶצַח: הַבֵּט לַבְּרִית כִּי מָלְאוּ מַחֲשַׁכֵּי-אֶרֶץ נְאוֹת חָמָס: אַל-יָשֹׁב דַּךְ נִכְלָם עָנִי וְאֶבְיוֹן יְהַלְלוּ שְׁמֶךָ: קוּמָה אֱלֹהִים רִיבָה רִיבֶךָ זְכֹר חֶרְפָּתְךָ מִנִּי-נָבָל כָּל-הַיּוֹם: אַל-תִּשְׁכַּח קוֹל צֹרְרֶיךָ שְׁאוֹן קָמֶיךָ עֹלֶה תָמִיד:

עה לַמְנַצֵּחַ אַל-תַּשְׁחֵת מִזְמוֹר לְאָסָף שִׁיר: הוֹדִינוּ לְּךָ ׀ אֱלֹהִים הוֹדִינוּ וְקָרוֹב שְׁמֶךָ סִפְּרוּ נִפְלְאוֹתֶיךָ: כִּי אֶקַּח מוֹעֵד אֲנִי מֵישָׁרִים אֶשְׁפֹּט: נְמֹגִים אֶרֶץ וְכָל-יֹשְׁבֶיהָ אָנֹכִי תִכַּנְתִּי עַמּוּדֶיהָ סֶּלָה: אָמַרְתִּי לַהוֹלְלִים אַל-תָּהֹלּוּ וְלָרְשָׁעִים אַל-תָּרִימוּ קָרֶן: אַל-תָּרִימוּ לַמָּרוֹם קַרְנְכֶם תְּדַבְּרוּ בְצַוָּאר עָתָק: כִּי לֹא מִמּוֹצָא וּמִמַּעֲרָב וְלֹא מִמִּדְבַּר הָרִים: כִּי-אֱלֹהִים שֹׁפֵט זֶה יַשְׁפִּיל וְזֶה יָרִים: כִּי כוֹס בְּיַד-יְהוָה וְיַיִן חָמַר ׀ מָלֵא מֶסֶךְ וַיַּגֵּר מִזֶּה אַךְ-שְׁמָרֶיהָ יִמְצוּ יִשְׁתּוּ כֹּל רִשְׁעֵי-אָרֶץ: וַאֲנִי אַגִּיד לְעֹלָם אֲזַמְּרָה לֵאלֹהֵי יַעֲקֹב: וְכָל-קַרְנֵי רְשָׁעִים אֲגַדֵּעַ תְּרוֹמַמְנָה קַרְנוֹת צַדִּיק:

עו לַמְנַצֵּחַ בִּנְגִינֹת מִזְמוֹר לְאָסָף שִׁיר: נוֹדָע בִּיהוּדָה אֱלֹהִים בְּיִשְׂרָאֵל גָּדוֹל שְׁמוֹ: וַיְהִי בְשָׁלֵם סֻכּוֹ וּמְעוֹנָתוֹ בְצִיּוֹן: שָׁמָּה שִׁבַּר רִשְׁפֵי-קָשֶׁת מָגֵן וְחֶרֶב וּמִלְחָמָה סֶלָה: נָאוֹר אַתָּה אַדִּיר מֵהַרְרֵי-טָרֶף: אֶשְׁתּוֹלְלוּ ׀ אַבִּירֵי לֵב נָמוּ שְׁנָתָם וְלֹא-מָצְאוּ כָל-אַנְשֵׁי-חַיִל יְדֵיהֶם: מִגַּעֲרָתְךָ אֱלֹהֵי יַעֲקֹב נִרְדָּם וָרֶכֶב

וָסֻס: אַתָּה ׀ נוֹרָא אַתָּה וּמִי־יַעֲמֹד לְפָנֶיךָ מֵאָז אַפֶּךָ: מִשָּׁמַיִם הִשְׁמַעְתָּ דִּין
אֶרֶץ יָרְאָה וְשָׁקָטָה: בְּקוּם־לַמִּשְׁפָּט אֱלֹהִים לְהוֹשִׁיעַ כָּל־עַנְוֵי־אֶרֶץ סֶלָה:
כִּי־חֲמַת אָדָם תּוֹדֶךָּ שְׁאֵרִית חֵמֹת תַּחְגֹּר: נִדְרוּ וְשַׁלְּמוּ לַיהוָה אֱלֹהֵיכֶם כָּל־
סְבִיבָיו יֹבִילוּ שַׁי לַמּוֹרָא: יִבְצֹר רוּחַ נְגִידִים נוֹרָא לְמַלְכֵי־אָרֶץ:

עז ‎*לַמְנַצֵּחַ עַל־יְדוּתוּן לְאָסָף מִזְמוֹר: קוֹלִי אֶל־אֱלֹהִים וְאֶצְעָקָה קוֹלִי אֶל־אֱלֹהִים ‎לִידוּתוּן
וְהַאֲזִין אֵלָי: בְּיוֹם צָרָתִי אֲדֹנָי דָּרָשְׁתִּי יָדִי ׀ לַיְלָה נִגְּרָה וְלֹא תָפוּג מֵאֲנָה
הִנָּחֵם נַפְשִׁי: אֶזְכְּרָה אֱלֹהִים וְאֶהֱמָיָה אָשִׂיחָה ׀ וְתִתְעַטֵּף רוּחִי סֶלָה: אָחַזְתָּ
שְׁמֻרוֹת עֵינָי נִפְעַמְתִּי וְלֹא אֲדַבֵּר: חִשַּׁבְתִּי יָמִים מִקֶּדֶם שְׁנוֹת עוֹלָמִים:
אֶזְכְּרָה נְגִינָתִי בַּלָּיְלָה עִם־לְבָבִי אָשִׂיחָה וַיְחַפֵּשׂ רוּחִי: הַלְעוֹלָמִים יִזְנַח ׀
אֲדֹנָי וְלֹא־יֹסִיף לִרְצוֹת עוֹד: הֶאָפֵס לָנֶצַח חַסְדּוֹ גָּמַר אֹמֶר לְדֹר וָדֹר: הֲשָׁכַח
חַנּוֹת אֵל אִם־קָפַץ בְּאַף רַחֲמָיו סֶלָה: וָאֹמַר חַלּוֹתִי הִיא שְׁנוֹת יְמִין עֶלְיוֹן:
אזכיר מַעַלְלֵי־יָהּ כִּי־אֶזְכְּרָה מִקֶּדֶם פִּלְאֶךָ: וְהָגִיתִי בְכָל־פָּעֳלֶךָ וּבַעֲלִילוֹתֶיךָ ‎אֶזְכּוֹר
אָשִׂיחָה: אֱלֹהִים בַּקֹּדֶשׁ דַּרְכֶּךָ מִי־אֵל גָּדוֹל כֵּאלֹהִים: אַתָּה הָאֵל עֹשֵׂה
פֶלֶא הוֹדַעְתָּ בָעַמִּים עֻזֶּךָ: גָּאַלְתָּ בִּזְרוֹעַ עַמֶּךָ בְּנֵי־יַעֲקֹב וְיוֹסֵף סֶלָה: רָאוּךָ
מַּיִם ׀ אֱלֹהִים רָאוּךָ מַּיִם יָחִילוּ אַף יִרְגְּזוּ תְהֹמוֹת: זֹרְמוּ מַיִם ׀ עָבוֹת קוֹל נָתְנוּ
שְׁחָקִים אַף־חֲצָצֶיךָ יִתְהַלָּכוּ: קוֹל רַעַמְךָ ׀ בַּגַּלְגַּל הֵאִירוּ בְרָקִים תֵּבֵל רָגְזָה
וַתִּרְעַשׁ הָאָרֶץ: בַּיָּם דַּרְכֶּךָ וּשְׁבִילְךָ בְּמַיִם רַבִּים וְעִקְּבוֹתֶיךָ לֹא נֹדָעוּ: ‎וּשְׁבִילְךָ
נָחִיתָ כַצֹּאן עַמֶּךָ בְּיַד־מֹשֶׁה וְאַהֲרֹן:

עח מַשְׂכִּיל לְאָסָף הַאֲזִינָה עַמִּי תּוֹרָתִי הַטּוּ אָזְנְכֶם לְאִמְרֵי־פִי: אֶפְתְּחָה בְמָשָׁל
פִּי אַבִּיעָה חִידוֹת מִנִּי־קֶדֶם: אֲשֶׁר שָׁמַעְנוּ וַנֵּדָעֵם וַאֲבוֹתֵינוּ סִפְּרוּ־לָנוּ: לֹא
נְכַחֵד ׀ מִבְּנֵיהֶם לְדוֹר אַחֲרוֹן מְסַפְּרִים תְּהִלּוֹת יְהוָה וֶעֱזוּזוֹ וְנִפְלְאוֹתָיו אֲשֶׁר
עָשָׂה: וַיָּקֶם עֵדוּת ׀ בְּיַעֲקֹב וְתוֹרָה שָׂם בְּיִשְׂרָאֵל אֲשֶׁר צִוָּה אֶת־אֲבוֹתֵינוּ
לְהוֹדִיעָם לִבְנֵיהֶם: לְמַעַן יֵדְעוּ ׀ דּוֹר אַחֲרוֹן בָּנִים יִוָּלֵדוּ יָקֻמוּ וִיסַפְּרוּ לִבְנֵיהֶם:
וְיָשִׂימוּ בֵאלֹהִים כִּסְלָם וְלֹא יִשְׁכְּחוּ מַעַלְלֵי־אֵל וּמִצְוֹתָיו יִנְצֹרוּ: וְלֹא יִהְיוּ ׀
כַּאֲבוֹתָם דּוֹר סוֹרֵר וּמֹרֶה דּוֹר לֹא־הֵכִין לִבּוֹ וְלֹא־נֶאֶמְנָה אֶת־אֵל רוּחוֹ:
בְּנֵי־אֶפְרַיִם נוֹשְׁקֵי רוֹמֵי־קָשֶׁת הָפְכוּ בְּיוֹם קְרָב: לֹא שָׁמְרוּ בְּרִית אֱלֹהִים
וּבְתוֹרָתוֹ מֵאֲנוּ לָלֶכֶת: וַיִּשְׁכְּחוּ עֲלִילוֹתָיו וְנִפְלְאוֹתָיו אֲשֶׁר הֶרְאָם: נֶגֶד
אֲבוֹתָם עָשָׂה פֶלֶא בְּאֶרֶץ מִצְרַיִם שְׂדֵה־צֹעַן: בָּקַע יָם וַיַּעֲבִירֵם וַיַּצֶּב־מַיִם
כְּמוֹ־נֵד: וַיַּנְחֵם בֶּעָנָן יוֹמָם וְכָל־הַלַּיְלָה בְּאוֹר אֵשׁ: יְבַקַּע צֻרִים בַּמִּדְבָּר

וַיִּשְׁקְ כִּתְהֹמוֹת רַבָּה: וַיּוֹצִא נוֹזְלִים מִסָּלַע וַיּוֹרֶד כַּנְּהָרוֹת מָיִם: וַיּוֹסִיפוּ עוֹד
לַחֲטֹא־לוֹ לַמְרוֹת עֶלְיוֹן בַּצִּיָּה: וַיְנַסּוּ־אֵל בִּלְבָבָם לִשְׁאָל־אֹכֶל לְנַפְשָׁם:
וַיְדַבְּרוּ בֵּאלֹהִים אָמְרוּ הֲיוּכַל אֵל לַעֲרֹךְ שֻׁלְחָן בַּמִּדְבָּר: הֵן הִכָּה־צוּר וַיָּזוּבוּ
מַיִם וּנְחָלִים יִשְׁטֹפוּ הֲגַם־לֶחֶם יוּכַל תֵּת אִם־יָכִין שְׁאֵר לְעַמּוֹ: לָכֵן שָׁמַע
יְהוָה וַיִּתְעַבָּר וְאֵשׁ נִשְּׂקָה בְיַעֲקֹב וְגַם־אַף עָלָה בְיִשְׂרָאֵל: כִּי לֹא הֶאֱמִינוּ
בֵּאלֹהִים וְלֹא בָטְחוּ בִּישׁוּעָתוֹ: וַיְצַו שְׁחָקִים מִמָּעַל וְדַלְתֵי שָׁמַיִם פָּתָח:
וַיַּמְטֵר עֲלֵיהֶם מָן לֶאֱכֹל וּדְגַן־שָׁמַיִם נָתַן לָמוֹ: לֶחֶם אַבִּירִים אָכַל אִישׁ צֵידָה
שָׁלַח לָהֶם לָשֹׂבַע: יַסַּע קָדִים בַּשָּׁמָיִם וַיְנַהֵג בְּעֻזּוֹ תֵימָן: וַיַּמְטֵר עֲלֵיהֶם
כֶּעָפָר שְׁאֵר וּכְחוֹל יַמִּים עוֹף כָּנָף: וַיַּפֵּל בְּקֶרֶב מַחֲנֵהוּ סָבִיב לְמִשְׁכְּנֹתָיו:
וַיֹּאכְלוּ וַיִּשְׂבְּעוּ מְאֹד וְתַאֲוָתָם יָבִא לָהֶם: לֹא־זָרוּ מִתַּאֲוָתָם עוֹד אָכְלָם
בְּפִיהֶם: וְאַף אֱלֹהִים עָלָה בָהֶם וַיַּהֲרֹג בְּמִשְׁמַנֵּיהֶם וּבַחוּרֵי יִשְׂרָאֵל הִכְרִיעַ:
בְּכָל־זֹאת חָטְאוּ־עוֹד וְלֹא הֶאֱמִינוּ בְּנִפְלְאוֹתָיו: וַיְכַל־בַּהֶבֶל יְמֵיהֶם וּשְׁנוֹתָם
בַּבֶּהָלָה: אִם־הֲרָגָם וּדְרָשׁוּהוּ וְשָׁבוּ וְשִׁחֲרוּ־אֵל: וַיִּזְכְּרוּ כִּי־אֱלֹהִים צוּרָם
וְאֵל עֶלְיוֹן גֹּאֲלָם: וַיְפַתּוּהוּ בְּפִיהֶם וּבִלְשׁוֹנָם יְכַזְּבוּ־לוֹ: וְלִבָּם לֹא־נָכוֹן עִמּוֹ
וְלֹא נֶאֶמְנוּ בִּבְרִיתוֹ: וְהוּא רַחוּם יְכַפֵּר עָוֹן וְלֹא־יַשְׁחִית וְהִרְבָּה לְהָשִׁיב
אַפּוֹ וְלֹא־יָעִיר כָּל־חֲמָתוֹ: וַיִּזְכֹּר כִּי־בָשָׂר הֵמָּה רוּחַ הוֹלֵךְ וְלֹא יָשׁוּב: כַּמָּה
יַמְרוּהוּ בַמִּדְבָּר יַעֲצִיבוּהוּ בִּישִׁימוֹן: וַיָּשׁוּבוּ וַיְנַסּוּ אֵל וּקְדוֹשׁ יִשְׂרָאֵל הִתְווּ:
לֹא־זָכְרוּ אֶת־יָדוֹ יוֹם אֲשֶׁר־פָּדָם מִנִּי־צָר: אֲשֶׁר־שָׂם בְּמִצְרַיִם אֹתוֹתָיו וּמוֹפְתָיו
בִּשְׂדֵה־צֹעַן: וַיַּהֲפֹךְ לְדָם יְאֹרֵיהֶם וְנֹזְלֵיהֶם בַּל־יִשְׁתָּיוּן: יְשַׁלַּח בָּהֶם עָרֹב
וַיֹּאכְלֵם וּצְפַרְדֵּעַ וַתַּשְׁחִיתֵם: וַיִּתֵּן לֶחָסִיל יְבוּלָם וִיגִיעָם לָאַרְבֶּה: יַהֲרֹג
בַּבָּרָד גַּפְנָם וְשִׁקְמוֹתָם בַּחֲנָמַל: וַיַּסְגֵּר לַבָּרָד בְּעִירָם וּמִקְנֵיהֶם לָרְשָׁפִים:
יְשַׁלַּח־בָּם חֲרוֹן אַפּוֹ עֶבְרָה וָזַעַם וְצָרָה מִשְׁלַחַת מַלְאֲכֵי רָעִים: יְפַלֵּס נָתִיב
לְאַפּוֹ לֹא־חָשַׂךְ מִמָּוֶת נַפְשָׁם וְחַיָּתָם לַדֶּבֶר הִסְגִּיר: וַיַּךְ כָּל־בְּכוֹר בְּמִצְרָיִם
רֵאשִׁית אוֹנִים בְּאָהֳלֵי־חָם: וַיַּסַּע כַּצֹּאן עַמּוֹ וַיְנַהֲגֵם כַּעֵדֶר בַּמִּדְבָּר: וַיַּנְחֵם
לָבֶטַח וְלֹא פָחָדוּ וְאֶת־אוֹיְבֵיהֶם כִּסָּה הַיָּם: וַיְבִיאֵם אֶל־גְּבוּל קָדְשׁוֹ הַר־זֶה
קָנְתָה יְמִינוֹ: וַיְגָרֶשׁ מִפְּנֵיהֶם גּוֹיִם וַיַּפִּילֵם בְּחֶבֶל נַחֲלָה וַיַּשְׁכֵּן בְּאָהֳלֵיהֶם
שִׁבְטֵי יִשְׂרָאֵל: וַיְנַסּוּ וַיַּמְרוּ אֶת־אֱלֹהִים עֶלְיוֹן וְעֵדוֹתָיו לֹא שָׁמָרוּ: וַיִּסֹּגוּ
וַיִּבְגְּדוּ כַּאֲבוֹתָם נֶהְפְּכוּ כְּקֶשֶׁת רְמִיָּה: וַיַּכְעִיסוּהוּ בְּבָמוֹתָם וּבִפְסִילֵיהֶם
יַקְנִיאוּהוּ: שָׁמַע אֱלֹהִים וַיִּתְעַבָּר וַיִּמְאַס מְאֹד בְּיִשְׂרָאֵל: וַיִּטֹּשׁ מִשְׁכַּן שִׁלוֹ

אֹהֶל שִׁכֵּן בָּאָדָם: וַיִּתֵּן לַשְּׁבִי עֻזּוֹ וְתִפְאַרְתּוֹ בְיַד־צָר: וַיַּסְגֵּר לַחֶרֶב עַמּוֹ וּבְנַחֲלָתוֹ הִתְעַבָּר: בַּחוּרָיו אָכְלָה־אֵשׁ וּבְתוּלֹתָיו לֹא הוּלָּלוּ: כֹּהֲנָיו בַּחֶרֶב נָפָלוּ וְאַלְמְנֹתָיו לֹא תִבְכֶּינָה: וַיִּקַץ כְּיָשֵׁן אֲדֹנָי כְּגִבּוֹר מִתְרוֹנֵן מִיָּיִן: וַיַּךְ־צָרָיו אָחוֹר חֶרְפַּת עוֹלָם נָתַן לָמוֹ: וַיִּמְאַס בְּאֹהֶל יוֹסֵף וּבְשֵׁבֶט אֶפְרַיִם לֹא בָחָר: וַיִּבְחַר אֶת־שֵׁבֶט יְהוּדָה אֶת־הַר צִיּוֹן אֲשֶׁר אָהֵב: וַיִּבֶן כְּמוֹ־רָמִים מִקְדָּשׁוֹ כְּאֶרֶץ יְסָדָהּ לְעוֹלָם: וַיִּבְחַר בְּדָוִד עַבְדּוֹ וַיִּקָּחֵהוּ מִמִּכְלְאֹת צֹאן: מֵאַחַר עָלוֹת הֱבִיאוֹ לִרְעוֹת בְּיַעֲקֹב עַמּוֹ וּבְיִשְׂרָאֵל נַחֲלָתוֹ: וַיִּרְעֵם כְּתֹם לְבָבוֹ וּבִתְבוּנוֹת כַּפָּיו יַנְחֵם:

*עט מִזְמוֹר לְאָסָף אֱלֹהִים בָּאוּ גוֹיִם ׀ בְּנַחֲלָתֶךָ טִמְּאוּ אֶת־הֵיכַל קָדְשֶׁךָ שָׂמוּ אֶת־יְרוּשָׁלַ‍ִם לְעִיִּים: נָתְנוּ אֶת־נִבְלַת עֲבָדֶיךָ מַאֲכָל לְעוֹף הַשָּׁמָיִם בְּשַׂר חֲסִידֶיךָ לְחַיְתוֹ־אָרֶץ: שָׁפְכוּ דָמָם ׀ כַּמַּיִם סְבִיבוֹת יְרוּשָׁלַ‍ִם וְאֵין קוֹבֵר: הָיִינוּ חֶרְפָּה לִשְׁכֵנֵינוּ לַעַג וָקֶלֶס לִסְבִיבוֹתֵינוּ: עַד־מָה יְהוָה תֶּאֱנַף לָנֶצַח תִּבְעַר כְּמוֹ־אֵשׁ קִנְאָתֶךָ: שְׁפֹךְ חֲמָתְךָ ׀ אֶל־הַגּוֹיִם אֲשֶׁר לֹא־יְדָעוּךָ וְעַל מַמְלָכוֹת אֲשֶׁר בְּשִׁמְךָ לֹא קָרָאוּ: כִּי אָכַל אֶת־יַעֲקֹב וְאֶת־נָוֵהוּ הֵשַׁמּוּ: אַל־תִּזְכָּר־לָנוּ עֲוֹנֹת רִאשֹׁנִים מַהֵר יְקַדְּמוּנוּ רַחֲמֶיךָ כִּי דַלּוֹנוּ מְאֹד: עָזְרֵנוּ ׀ אֱלֹהֵי יִשְׁעֵנוּ עַל־דְּבַר כְּבוֹד־שְׁמֶךָ וְהַצִּילֵנוּ וְכַפֵּר עַל־חַטֹּאתֵינוּ לְמַעַן שְׁמֶךָ: לָמָּה ׀ יֹאמְרוּ בגוים הַגּוֹיִם אַיֵּה אֱלֹהֵיהֶם יִוָּדַע בַּגֹּיִים לְעֵינֵינוּ נִקְמַת דַּם־עֲבָדֶיךָ הַשָּׁפוּךְ: תָּבוֹא לְפָנֶיךָ אֶנְקַת אָסִיר כְּגֹדֶל זְרוֹעֲךָ הוֹתֵר בְּנֵי תְמוּתָה: וְהָשֵׁב לִשְׁכֵנֵינוּ שִׁבְעָתַיִם אֶל־חֵיקָם חֶרְפָּתָם אֲשֶׁר חֵרְפוּךָ אֲדֹנָי: וַאֲנַחְנוּ עַמְּךָ ׀ וְצֹאן מַרְעִיתֶךָ נוֹדֶה לְּךָ לְעוֹלָם לְדוֹר וָדֹר נְסַפֵּר תְּהִלָּתֶךָ:

פ לַמְנַצֵּחַ אֶל־שֹׁשַׁנִּים עֵדוּת לְאָסָף מִזְמוֹר: רֹעֵה יִשְׂרָאֵל ׀ הַאֲזִינָה נֹהֵג כַּצֹּאן יוֹסֵף יֹשֵׁב הַכְּרוּבִים הוֹפִיעָה: לִפְנֵי אֶפְרַיִם ׀ וּבִנְיָמִן וּמְנַשֶּׁה עוֹרְרָה אֶת־גְּבוּרָתֶךָ וּלְכָה לִישֻׁעָתָה לָּנוּ: אֱלֹהִים הֲשִׁיבֵנוּ וְהָאֵר פָּנֶיךָ וְנִוָּשֵׁעָה: יְהוָה אֱלֹהִים צְבָאוֹת עַד־מָתַי עָשַׁנְתָּ בִּתְפִלַּת עַמֶּךָ: הֶאֱכַלְתָּם לֶחֶם דִּמְעָה וַתַּשְׁקֵמוֹ בִּדְמָעוֹת שָׁלִישׁ: תְּשִׂימֵנוּ מָדוֹן לִשְׁכֵנֵינוּ וְאֹיְבֵינוּ יִלְעֲגוּ־לָמוֹ: אֱלֹהִים צְבָאוֹת הֲשִׁיבֵנוּ וְהָאֵר פָּנֶיךָ וְנִוָּשֵׁעָה: גֶּפֶן מִמִּצְרַיִם תַּסִּיעַ תְּגָרֵשׁ גּוֹיִם וַתִּטָּעֶהָ: פִּנִּיתָ לְפָנֶיהָ וַתַּשְׁרֵשׁ שָׁרָשֶׁיהָ וַתְּמַלֵּא־אָרֶץ: כָּסּוּ הָרִים צִלָּהּ וַעֲנָפֶיהָ אַרְזֵי־אֵל: תְּשַׁלַּח קְצִירֶהָ עַד־יָם וְאֶל־נָהָר יוֹנְקוֹתֶיהָ: לָמָּה פָּרַצְתָּ גְדֵרֶיהָ וְאָרוּהָ כָּל־עֹבְרֵי דָרֶךְ: יְכַרְסְמֶנָּה חֲזִיר מִיָּעַר וְזִיז שָׂדַי יִרְעֶנָּה: אֱלֹהִים צְבָאוֹת שׁוּב

נָא הַבֵּט מִשָּׁמַיִם וּרְאֵה וּפְקֹד גֶּפֶן זֹאת: וְכַנָּה אֲשֶׁר־נָטְעָה יְמִינֶךָ וְעַל־בֵּן אִמַּצְתָּה לָּךְ: שְׂרֻפָה בָאֵשׁ כְּסוּחָה מִגַּעֲרַת פָּנֶיךָ יֹאבֵדוּ: תְּהִי־יָדְךָ עַל־אִישׁ יְמִינֶךָ עַל־בֶּן־אָדָם אִמַּצְתָּ לָּךְ: וְלֹא־נָסוֹג מִמֶּךָּ תְּחַיֵּנוּ וּבְשִׁמְךָ נִקְרָא: יְהוָה אֱלֹהִים צְבָאוֹת הֲשִׁיבֵנוּ הָאֵר פָּנֶיךָ וְנִוָּשֵׁעָה:

פא לַמְנַצֵּחַ ׀ עַל־הַגִּתִּית לְאָסָף: הַרְנִינוּ לֵאלֹהִים עוּזֵּנוּ הָרִיעוּ לֵאלֹהֵי יַעֲקֹב: שְׂאוּ־זִמְרָה וּתְנוּ־תֹף כִּנּוֹר נָעִים עִם־נָבֶל: תִּקְעוּ בַחֹדֶשׁ שׁוֹפָר בַּכֵּסֶה לְיוֹם חַגֵּנוּ: כִּי חֹק לְיִשְׂרָאֵל הוּא מִשְׁפָּט לֵאלֹהֵי יַעֲקֹב: עֵדוּת ׀ בִּיהוֹסֵף שָׂמוֹ בְּצֵאתוֹ עַל־אֶרֶץ מִצְרָיִם שְׂפַת לֹא־יָדַעְתִּי אֶשְׁמָע: הֲסִירוֹתִי מִסֵּבֶל שִׁכְמוֹ כַּפָּיו מִדּוּד תַּעֲבֹרְנָה: בַּצָּרָה קָרָאתָ וָאֲחַלְּצֶךָּ אֶעֶנְךָ בְּסֵתֶר רַעַם אֶבְחָנְךָ עַל־מֵי מְרִיבָה סֶלָה: שְׁמַע עַמִּי וְאָעִידָה בָּךְ יִשְׂרָאֵל אִם־תִּשְׁמַע־לִי: לֹא־יִהְיֶה בְךָ אֵל זָר וְלֹא תִשְׁתַּחֲוֶה לְאֵל נֵכָר: אָנֹכִי ׀ יְהוָה אֱלֹהֶיךָ הַמַּעַלְךָ מֵאֶרֶץ מִצְרָיִם הַרְחֶב־פִּיךָ וַאֲמַלְאֵהוּ: וְלֹא־שָׁמַע עַמִּי לְקוֹלִי וְיִשְׂרָאֵל לֹא־אָבָה לִי: וָאֲשַׁלְּחֵהוּ בִּשְׁרִירוּת לִבָּם יֵלְכוּ בְּמוֹעֲצוֹתֵיהֶם: לוּ עַמִּי שֹׁמֵעַ לִי יִשְׂרָאֵל בִּדְרָכַי יְהַלֵּכוּ: כִּמְעַט אוֹיְבֵיהֶם אַכְנִיעַ וְעַל־צָרֵיהֶם אָשִׁיב יָדִי: מְשַׂנְאֵי יְהוָה יְכַחֲשׁוּ־לוֹ וִיהִי עִתָּם לְעוֹלָם: וַיַּאֲכִילֵהוּ מֵחֵלֶב חִטָּה וּמִצּוּר דְּבַשׁ אַשְׂבִּיעֶךָ:

פב מִזְמוֹר לְאָסָף אֱלֹהִים נִצָּב בַּעֲדַת־אֵל בְּקֶרֶב אֱלֹהִים יִשְׁפֹּט: עַד־מָתַי תִּשְׁפְּטוּ־עָוֶל וּפְנֵי רְשָׁעִים תִּשְׂאוּ־סֶלָה: שִׁפְטוּ־דַל וְיָתוֹם עָנִי וָרָשׁ הַצְדִּיקוּ: פַּלְּטוּ־דַל וְאֶבְיוֹן מִיַּד רְשָׁעִים הַצִּילוּ: לֹא יָדְעוּ ׀ וְלֹא יָבִינוּ בַּחֲשֵׁכָה יִתְהַלָּכוּ יִמּוֹטוּ כָּל־מוֹסְדֵי אָרֶץ: אֲנִי־אָמַרְתִּי אֱלֹהִים אַתֶּם וּבְנֵי עֶלְיוֹן כֻּלְּכֶם: אָכֵן כְּאָדָם תְּמוּתוּן וּכְאַחַד הַשָּׂרִים תִּפֹּלוּ: קוּמָה אֱלֹהִים שָׁפְטָה הָאָרֶץ כִּי־אַתָּה תִנְחַל בְּכָל־הַגּוֹיִם:

פג* שִׁיר מִזְמוֹר לְאָסָף: אֱלֹהִים אַל־דֳּמִי־לָךְ אַל־תֶּחֱרַשׁ וְאַל־תִּשְׁקֹט אֵל: כִּי־הִנֵּה אוֹיְבֶיךָ יֶהֱמָיוּן וּמְשַׂנְאֶיךָ נָשְׂאוּ רֹאשׁ: עַל־עַמְּךָ יַעֲרִימוּ סוֹד וְיִתְיָעֲצוּ עַל־צְפוּנֶיךָ: אָמְרוּ לְכוּ וְנַכְחִידֵם מִגּוֹי וְלֹא־יִזָּכֵר שֵׁם־יִשְׂרָאֵל עוֹד: כִּי נוֹעֲצוּ לֵב יַחְדָּו עָלֶיךָ בְּרִית יִכְרֹתוּ: אָהֳלֵי אֱדוֹם וְיִשְׁמְעֵאלִים מוֹאָב וְהַגְרִים: גְּבָל וְעַמּוֹן וַעֲמָלֵק פְּלֶשֶׁת עִם־יֹשְׁבֵי צוֹר: גַּם־אַשּׁוּר נִלְוָה עִמָּם הָיוּ זְרוֹעַ לִבְנֵי־לוֹט סֶלָה: עֲשֵׂה־לָהֶם כְּמִדְיָן כְּסִיסְרָא כְיָבִין בְּנַחַל קִישׁוֹן: נִשְׁמְדוּ בְעֵין־דֹּאר הָיוּ דֹּמֶן לָאֲדָמָה: שִׁיתֵמוֹ נְדִיבֵמוֹ כְּעֹרֵב וְכִזְאֵב וּכְזֶבַח וּכְצַלְמֻנָּע כָּל־נְסִיכֵמוֹ: אֲשֶׁר אָמְרוּ נִירֲשָׁה לָּנוּ אֵת נְאוֹת אֱלֹהִים: אֱלֹהַי שִׁיתֵמוֹ כַגַּלְגַּל כְּקַשׁ לִפְנֵי

רוּחַ: כְּאֵשׁ תִּבְעַר־יָעַר וּכְלֶהָבָה תְּלַהֵט הָרִים: כֵּן תִּרְדְּפֵם בְּסַעֲרֶךָ וּבְסוּפָתְךָ
תְבַהֲלֵם: מַלֵּא פְנֵיהֶם קָלוֹן וִיבַקְשׁוּ שִׁמְךָ יְהוָה: יֵבֹשׁוּ וְיִבָּהֲלוּ עֲדֵי־עַד וְיַחְפְּרוּ
וְיֹאבֵדוּ: וְיֵדְעוּ כִּי־אַתָּה שִׁמְךָ יְהוָה לְבַדֶּךָ עֶלְיוֹן עַל־כָּל־הָאָרֶץ:

פד לַמְנַצֵּחַ עַל־הַגִּתִּית לִבְנֵי־קֹרַח מִזְמוֹר: מַה־יְּדִידוֹת מִשְׁכְּנוֹתֶיךָ יְהוָה צְבָאוֹת:
נִכְסְפָה וְגַם־כָּלְתָה ׀ נַפְשִׁי לְחַצְרוֹת יְהוָה לִבִּי וּבְשָׂרִי יְרַנְּנוּ אֶל אֵל־חָי: גַּם־
צִפּוֹר ׀ מָצְאָה בַיִת וּדְרוֹר ׀ קֵן לָהּ אֲשֶׁר־שָׁתָה אֶפְרֹחֶיהָ אֶת־מִזְבְּחוֹתֶיךָ
יְהוָה צְבָאוֹת מַלְכִּי וֵאלֹהָי: אַשְׁרֵי יוֹשְׁבֵי בֵיתֶךָ עוֹד יְהַלְלוּךָ סֶּלָה: אַשְׁרֵי אָדָם
עוֹז־לוֹ בָךְ מְסִלּוֹת בִּלְבָבָם: עֹבְרֵי ׀ בְּעֵמֶק הַבָּכָא מַעְיָן יְשִׁיתוּהוּ גַּם־בְּרָכוֹת
יַעְטֶה מוֹרֶה: יֵלְכוּ מֵחַיִל אֶל־חָיִל יֵרָאֶה אֶל־אֱלֹהִים בְּצִיּוֹן: יְהוָה אֱלֹהִים
צְבָאוֹת שִׁמְעָה תְפִלָּתִי הַאֲזִינָה אֱלֹהֵי יַעֲקֹב סֶלָה: מָגִנֵּנוּ רְאֵה אֱלֹהִים וְהַבֵּט
פְּנֵי מְשִׁיחֶךָ: כִּי טוֹב־יוֹם בַּחֲצֵרֶיךָ מֵאָלֶף בָּחַרְתִּי הִסְתּוֹפֵף בְּבֵית אֱלֹהַי מִדּוּר
בְּאָהֳלֵי־רֶשַׁע: כִּי שֶׁמֶשׁ ׀ וּמָגֵן יְהוָה אֱלֹהִים חֵן וְכָבוֹד יִתֵּן יְהוָה לֹא יִמְנַע־טוֹב
לַהֹלְכִים בְּתָמִים: יְהוָה צְבָאוֹת אַשְׁרֵי אָדָם בֹּטֵחַ בָּךְ:

פה לַמְנַצֵּחַ לִבְנֵי־קֹרַח מִזְמוֹר: רָצִיתָ יְהוָה אַרְצֶךָ שַׁבְתָּ שְׁבִית יַעֲקֹב: נָשָׂאתָ
עֲוֹן עַמֶּךָ כִּסִּיתָ כָל־חַטָּאתָם סֶלָה: אָסַפְתָּ כָל־עֶבְרָתֶךָ הֱשִׁיבוֹתָ מֵחֲרוֹן
אַפֶּךָ: שׁוּבֵנוּ אֱלֹהֵי יִשְׁעֵנוּ וְהָפֵר כַּעַסְךָ עִמָּנוּ: הַלְעוֹלָם תֶּאֱנַף־בָּנוּ תִּמְשֹׁךְ
אַפְּךָ לְדֹר וָדֹר: הֲלֹא־אַתָּה תָּשׁוּב תְּחַיֵּנוּ וְעַמְּךָ יִשְׂמְחוּ־בָךְ: הַרְאֵנוּ יְהוָה
חַסְדֶּךָ וְיֶשְׁעֲךָ תִּתֶּן־לָנוּ: אֶשְׁמְעָה מַה־יְדַבֵּר הָאֵל ׀ יְהוָה כִּי ׀ יְדַבֵּר שָׁלוֹם
אֶל־עַמּוֹ וְאֶל־חֲסִידָיו וְאַל־יָשׁוּבוּ לְכִסְלָה: אַךְ ׀ קָרוֹב לִירֵאָיו יִשְׁעוֹ לִשְׁכֹּן
כָּבוֹד בְּאַרְצֵנוּ: חֶסֶד־וֶאֱמֶת נִפְגָּשׁוּ צֶדֶק וְשָׁלוֹם נָשָׁקוּ: אֱמֶת מֵאֶרֶץ תִּצְמָח
וְצֶדֶק מִשָּׁמַיִם נִשְׁקָף: גַּם־יְהוָה יִתֵּן הַטּוֹב וְאַרְצֵנוּ תִּתֵּן יְבוּלָהּ: צֶדֶק לְפָנָיו
יְהַלֵּךְ וְיָשֵׂם לְדֶרֶךְ פְּעָמָיו:

שְׁבִית

פו תְּפִלָּה לְדָוִד הַטֵּה־יְהוָה אָזְנְךָ עֲנֵנִי כִּי־עָנִי וְאֶבְיוֹן אָנִי: שָׁמְרָה נַפְשִׁי כִּי־
חָסִיד אָנִי הוֹשַׁע עַבְדְּךָ אַתָּה אֱלֹהַי הַבּוֹטֵחַ אֵלֶיךָ: חָנֵּנִי אֲדֹנָי כִּי־אֵלֶיךָ
אֶקְרָא כָּל־הַיּוֹם: שַׂמֵּחַ נֶפֶשׁ עַבְדֶּךָ כִּי־אֵלֶיךָ אֲדֹנָי נַפְשִׁי אֶשָּׂא: כִּי־אַתָּה
אֲדֹנָי טוֹב וְסַלָּח וְרַב־חֶסֶד לְכָל־קֹרְאֶיךָ: הַאֲזִינָה יְהוָה תְּפִלָּתִי וְהַקְשִׁיבָה
בְּקוֹל תַּחֲנוּנוֹתָי: בְּיוֹם צָרָתִי אֶקְרָאֶךָּ כִּי תַעֲנֵנִי: אֵין־כָּמוֹךָ בָאֱלֹהִים ׀ אֲדֹנָי
וְאֵין כְּמַעֲשֶׂיךָ: כָּל־גּוֹיִם ׀ אֲשֶׁר עָשִׂיתָ יָבוֹאוּ ׀ וְיִשְׁתַּחֲווּ לְפָנֶיךָ אֲדֹנָי וִיכַבְּדוּ
לִשְׁמֶךָ: כִּי־גָדוֹל אַתָּה וְעֹשֵׂה נִפְלָאוֹת אַתָּה אֱלֹהִים לְבַדֶּךָ: הוֹרֵנִי יְהוָה ׀

דַּרְכֶּךָ אֲהַלֵּךְ בַּאֲמִתֶּךָ יַחֵד לְבָבִי לְיִרְאָה שְׁמֶךָ: אוֹדְךָ ׀ אֲדֹנָי אֱלֹהַי בְּכָל־לְבָבִי וַאֲכַבְּדָה שִׁמְךָ לְעוֹלָם: כִּי־חַסְדְּךָ גָּדוֹל עָלָי וְהִצַּלְתָּ נַפְשִׁי מִשְּׁאוֹל תַּחְתִּיָּה: אֱלֹהִים ׀ זֵדִים קָמוּ־עָלַי וַעֲדַת עָרִיצִים בִּקְשׁוּ נַפְשִׁי וְלֹא שָׂמוּךָ לְנֶגְדָּם: וְאַתָּה אֲדֹנָי אֵל־רַחוּם וְחַנּוּן אֶרֶךְ אַפַּיִם וְרַב־חֶסֶד וֶאֱמֶת: פְּנֵה אֵלַי וְחָנֵּנִי תְּנָה־עֻזְּךָ לְעַבְדֶּךָ וְהוֹשִׁיעָה לְבֶן־אֲמָתֶךָ: עֲשֵׂה־עִמִּי אוֹת לְטוֹבָה וְיִרְאוּ שֹׂנְאַי וְיֵבֹשׁוּ כִּי־אַתָּה יְהוָה עֲזַרְתַּנִי וְנִחַמְתָּנִי:

פז לִבְנֵי־קֹרַח מִזְמוֹר שִׁיר יְסוּדָתוֹ בְּהַרְרֵי־קֹדֶשׁ: אֹהֵב יְהוָה שַׁעֲרֵי צִיּוֹן מִכֹּל מִשְׁכְּנוֹת יַעֲקֹב: נִכְבָּדוֹת מְדֻבָּר בָּךְ עִיר הָאֱלֹהִים סֶלָה: אַזְכִּיר ׀ רַהַב וּבָבֶל לְיֹדְעָי הִנֵּה פְלֶשֶׁת וְצוֹר עִם־כּוּשׁ זֶה יֻלַּד־שָׁם: וּלְצִיּוֹן ׀ יֵאָמַר אִישׁ וְאִישׁ יֻלַּד־בָּהּ וְהוּא יְכוֹנְנֶהָ עֶלְיוֹן: יְהוָה יִסְפֹּר בִּכְתוֹב עַמִּים זֶה יֻלַּד־שָׁם סֶלָה: וְשָׁרִים כְּחֹלְלִים כָּל־מַעְיָנַי בָּךְ:

פח* שִׁיר מִזְמוֹר לִבְנֵי קֹרַח לַמְנַצֵּחַ עַל־מָחֲלַת לְעַנּוֹת מַשְׂכִּיל לְהֵימָן הָאֶזְרָחִי: יְהוָה אֱלֹהֵי יְשׁוּעָתִי יוֹם־צָעַקְתִּי בַלַּיְלָה נֶגְדֶּךָ: תָּבוֹא לְפָנֶיךָ תְּפִלָּתִי הַטֵּה אָזְנְךָ לְרִנָּתִי: כִּי־שָׂבְעָה בְרָעוֹת נַפְשִׁי וְחַיַּי לִשְׁאוֹל הִגִּיעוּ: נֶחְשַׁבְתִּי עִם־יוֹרְדֵי בוֹר הָיִיתִי כְּגֶבֶר אֵין־אֱיָל: בַּמֵּתִים חָפְשִׁי כְּמוֹ חֲלָלִים ׀ שֹׁכְבֵי קֶבֶר אֲשֶׁר לֹא זְכַרְתָּם עוֹד וְהֵמָּה מִיָּדְךָ נִגְזָרוּ: שַׁתַּנִי בְּבוֹר תַּחְתִּיּוֹת בְּמַחֲשַׁכִּים בִּמְצֹלוֹת: עָלַי סָמְכָה חֲמָתֶךָ וְכָל־מִשְׁבָּרֶיךָ עִנִּיתָ סֶּלָה: הִרְחַקְתָּ מְיֻדָּעַי מִמֶּנִּי שַׁתַּנִי תוֹעֵבוֹת לָמוֹ כָּלֻא וְלֹא אֵצֵא: עֵינִי דָאֲבָה מִנִּי עֹנִי קְרָאתִיךָ יְהוָה בְּכָל־יוֹם שִׁטַּחְתִּי אֵלֶיךָ כַפָּי: הֲלַמֵּתִים תַּעֲשֶׂה־פֶּלֶא אִם־רְפָאִים יָקוּמוּ ׀ יוֹדוּךָ סֶּלָה: הַיְסֻפַּר בַּקֶּבֶר חַסְדֶּךָ אֱמוּנָתְךָ בָּאֲבַדּוֹן: הֲיִוָּדַע בַּחֹשֶׁךְ פִּלְאֶךָ וְצִדְקָתְךָ בְּאֶרֶץ נְשִׁיָּה: וַאֲנִי ׀ אֵלֶיךָ יְהוָה שִׁוַּעְתִּי וּבַבֹּקֶר תְּפִלָּתִי תְקַדְּמֶךָּ: לָמָה יְהוָה תִּזְנַח נַפְשִׁי תַּסְתִּיר פָּנֶיךָ מִמֶּנִּי: עָנִי אֲנִי וְגֹוֵעַ מִנֹּעַר נָשָׂאתִי אֵמֶיךָ אָפוּנָה: עָלַי עָבְרוּ חֲרוֹנֶיךָ בִּעוּתֶיךָ צִמְּתֻתֻנִי: סַבּוּנִי כַמַּיִם כָּל־הַיּוֹם הִקִּיפוּ עָלַי יָחַד: הִרְחַקְתָּ מִמֶּנִּי אֹהֵב וָרֵעַ מְיֻדָּעַי מַחְשָׁךְ:

פט מַשְׂכִּיל לְאֵיתָן הָאֶזְרָחִי: חַסְדֵי יְהוָה עוֹלָם אָשִׁירָה לְדֹר וָדֹר ׀ אוֹדִיעַ אֱמוּנָתְךָ בְּפִי: כִּי־אָמַרְתִּי עוֹלָם חֶסֶד יִבָּנֶה שָׁמַיִם ׀ תָּכִן אֱמוּנָתְךָ בָהֶם: כָּרַתִּי בְרִית לִבְחִירִי נִשְׁבַּעְתִּי לְדָוִד עַבְדִּי: עַד־עוֹלָם אָכִין זַרְעֶךָ וּבָנִיתִי לְדֹר־וָדוֹר כִּסְאֲךָ סֶּלָה: וְיוֹדוּ שָׁמַיִם פִּלְאֲךָ יְהוָה אַף־אֱמוּנָתְךָ בִּקְהַל קְדֹשִׁים: כִּי מִי בַשַּׁחַק יַעֲרֹךְ לַיהוָה יִדְמֶה לַיהוָה בִּבְנֵי אֵלִים: אֵל נַעֲרָץ בְּסוֹד־קְדֹשִׁים רַבָּה וְנוֹרָא

---

*יח לחודש

עַל־כָּל־סְבִיבָיו: יְהוָה ו אֱלֹהֵי צְבָאוֹת מִי־כָמוֹךָ חֲסִין ו יָהּ וֶאֱמוּנָתְךָ סְבִיבוֹתֶיךָ:
אַתָּה מוֹשֵׁל בְּגֵאוּת הַיָּם בְּשׂוֹא גַלָּיו אַתָּה תְשַׁבְּחֵם: אַתָּה דִכִּאתָ כֶחָלָל
רָהַב בִּזְרוֹעַ עֻזְּךָ פִּזַּרְתָּ אוֹיְבֶיךָ: לְךָ שָׁמַיִם אַף־לְךָ אָרֶץ תֵּבֵל וּמְלֹאָהּ אַתָּה
יְסַדְתָּם: צָפוֹן וְיָמִין אַתָּה בְרָאתָם תָּבוֹר וְחֶרְמוֹן בְּשִׁמְךָ יְרַנֵּנוּ: לְךָ זְרוֹעַ
עִם־גְּבוּרָה תָּעֹז יָדְךָ תָּרוּם יְמִינֶךָ: צֶדֶק וּמִשְׁפָּט מְכוֹן כִּסְאֶךָ חֶסֶד וֶאֱמֶת
יְקַדְּמוּ פָנֶיךָ: אַשְׁרֵי הָעָם יוֹדְעֵי תְרוּעָה יְהוָה בְּאוֹר־פָּנֶיךָ יְהַלֵּכוּן: בְּשִׁמְךָ
יְגִילוּן כָּל־הַיּוֹם וּבְצִדְקָתְךָ יָרוּמוּ: כִּי־תִפְאֶרֶת עֻזָּמוֹ אָתָּה וּבִרְצֹנְךָ תרים **תָּרוּם**
קַרְנֵנוּ: כִּי לַיהוָה מָגִנֵּנוּ וְלִקְדוֹשׁ יִשְׂרָאֵל מַלְכֵּנוּ: אָז דִּבַּרְתָּ בְחָזוֹן לַחֲסִידֶיךָ
וַתֹּאמֶר שִׁוִּיתִי עֵזֶר עַל־גִּבּוֹר הֲרִימוֹתִי בָחוּר מֵעָם: מָצָאתִי דָּוִד עַבְדִּי בְּשֶׁמֶן
קָדְשִׁי מְשַׁחְתִּיו: אֲשֶׁר יָדִי תִּכּוֹן עִמּוֹ אַף־זְרוֹעִי תְאַמְּצֶנּוּ: לֹא־יַשִּׁיא אוֹיֵב בּוֹ
וּבֶן־עַוְלָה לֹא יְעַנֶּנּוּ: וְכַתּוֹתִי מִפָּנָיו צָרָיו וּמְשַׂנְאָיו אֶגּוֹף: וֶאֱמוּנָתִי וְחַסְדִּי
עִמּוֹ וּבִשְׁמִי תָּרוּם קַרְנוֹ: וְשַׂמְתִּי בַיָּם יָדוֹ וּבַנְּהָרוֹת יְמִינוֹ: הוּא יִקְרָאֵנִי אָבִי
אָתָּה אֵלִי וְצוּר יְשׁוּעָתִי: אַף־אָנִי בְּכוֹר אֶתְּנֵהוּ עֶלְיוֹן לְמַלְכֵי־אָרֶץ: לְעוֹלָם
אֶשְׁמָר־ **אֶשְׁמוֹר**־לוֹ חַסְדִּי וּבְרִיתִי נֶאֱמֶנֶת לוֹ: וְשַׂמְתִּי לָעַד זַרְעוֹ וְכִסְאוֹ כִּימֵי שָׁמָיִם:
אִם־יַעַזְבוּ בָנָיו תּוֹרָתִי וּבְמִשְׁפָּטַי לֹא יֵלֵכוּן: אִם־חֻקֹּתַי יְחַלֵּלוּ וּמִצְוֹתַי לֹא
יִשְׁמֹרוּ: וּפָקַדְתִּי בְשֵׁבֶט פִּשְׁעָם וּבִנְגָעִים עֲוֺנָם: וְחַסְדִּי לֹא־אָפִיר מֵעִמּוֹ
וְלֹא אֲשַׁקֵּר בֶּאֱמוּנָתִי: לֹא־אֲחַלֵּל בְּרִיתִי וּמוֹצָא שְׂפָתַי לֹא אֲשַׁנֶּה: אַחַת
נִשְׁבַּעְתִּי בְקָדְשִׁי אִם־לְדָוִד אֲכַזֵּב: זַרְעוֹ לְעוֹלָם יִהְיֶה וְכִסְאוֹ כַשֶּׁמֶשׁ נֶגְדִּי:
כְּיָרֵחַ יִכּוֹן עוֹלָם וְעֵד בַּשַּׁחַק נֶאֱמָן סֶלָה: וְאַתָּה זָנַחְתָּ וַתִּמְאָס הִתְעַבַּרְתָּ
עִם־מְשִׁיחֶךָ: נֵאַרְתָּה בְּרִית עַבְדֶּךָ חִלַּלְתָּ לָאָרֶץ נִזְרוֹ: פָּרַצְתָּ כָל־גְּדֵרֹתָיו
שַׂמְתָּ מִבְצָרָיו מְחִתָּה: שַׁסֻּהוּ כָּל־עֹבְרֵי דָרֶךְ הָיָה חֶרְפָּה לִשְׁכֵנָיו: הֲרִימוֹתָ
יְמִין צָרָיו הִשְׂמַחְתָּ כָּל־אוֹיְבָיו: אַף־תָּשִׁיב צוּר חַרְבּוֹ וְלֹא הֲקֵמֹתוֹ בַּמִּלְחָמָה:
הִשְׁבַּתָּ מִטְּהָרוֹ וְכִסְאוֹ לָאָרֶץ מִגַּרְתָּה: הִקְצַרְתָּ יְמֵי עֲלוּמָיו הֶעֱטִיתָ עָלָיו
בּוּשָׁה סֶלָה: עַד־מָה יְהוָה תִּסָּתֵר לָנֶצַח תִּבְעַר כְּמוֹ־אֵשׁ חֲמָתֶךָ: זְכָר־אֲנִי
מֶה־חָלֶד עַל־מַה־שָּׁוְא בָּרָאתָ כָל־בְּנֵי־אָדָם: מִי גֶבֶר יִחְיֶה וְלֹא יִרְאֶה־מָּוֶת
יְמַלֵּט נַפְשׁוֹ מִיַּד־שְׁאוֹל סֶלָה: אַיֵּה ו חֲסָדֶיךָ הָרִאשֹׁנִים ו אֲדֹנָי נִשְׁבַּעְתָּ
לְדָוִד בֶּאֱמוּנָתֶךָ: זְכֹר אֲדֹנָי חֶרְפַּת עֲבָדֶיךָ שְׂאֵתִי בְחֵיקִי כָּל־רַבִּים עַמִּים:
אֲשֶׁר חֵרְפוּ אוֹיְבֶיךָ ו יְהוָה אֲשֶׁר חֵרְפוּ עִקְּבוֹת מְשִׁיחֶךָ: בָּרוּךְ יְהוָה לְעוֹלָם
אָמֵן ו וְאָמֵן:

ספר רביעי

צ תְּפִלָּה לְמֹשֶׁה אִישׁ־הָאֱלֹהִים אֲדֹנָי מָעוֹן אַתָּה הָיִיתָ לָּנוּ בְּדֹר וָדֹר: בְּטֶרֶם
הָרִים יֻלָּדוּ וַתְּחוֹלֵל אֶרֶץ וְתֵבֵל וּמֵעוֹלָם עַד־עוֹלָם אַתָּה אֵל: תָּשֵׁב אֱנוֹשׁ
עַד־דַּכָּא וַתֹּאמֶר שׁוּבוּ בְנֵי־אָדָם: כִּי אֶלֶף שָׁנִים בְּעֵינֶיךָ כְּיוֹם אֶתְמוֹל כִּי
יַעֲבֹר וְאַשְׁמוּרָה בַלָּיְלָה: זְרַמְתָּם שֵׁנָה יִהְיוּ בַּבֹּקֶר כֶּחָצִיר יַחֲלֹף: בַּבֹּקֶר יָצִיץ
וְחָלָף לָעֶרֶב יְמוֹלֵל וְיָבֵשׁ: כִּי־כָלִינוּ בְאַפֶּךָ וּבַחֲמָתְךָ נִבְהָלְנוּ: שַׁתָּ עֲוֺנֹתֵינוּ
לְנֶגְדֶּךָ עֲלֻמֵנוּ לִמְאוֹר פָּנֶיךָ: כִּי כָל־יָמֵינוּ פָּנוּ בְעֶבְרָתֶךָ כִּלִּינוּ שָׁנֵינוּ כְמוֹ־
הֶגֶה: יְמֵי־שְׁנוֹתֵינוּ בָהֶם שִׁבְעִים שָׁנָה וְאִם בִּגְבוּרֹת שְׁמוֹנִים שָׁנָה וְרָהְבָּם
עָמָל וָאָוֶן כִּי־גָז חִישׁ וַנָּעֻפָה: מִי־יוֹדֵעַ עֹז אַפֶּךָ וּכְיִרְאָתְךָ עֶבְרָתֶךָ: לִמְנוֹת
יָמֵינוּ כֵּן הוֹדַע וְנָבִא לְבַב חָכְמָה: שׁוּבָה יְהוָה עַד־מָתָי וְהִנָּחֵם עַל־עֲבָדֶיךָ:
שַׂבְּעֵנוּ בַבֹּקֶר חַסְדֶּךָ וּנְרַנְּנָה וְנִשְׂמְחָה בְּכָל־יָמֵינוּ: שַׂמְּחֵנוּ כִּימוֹת עִנִּיתָנוּ
שְׁנוֹת רָאִינוּ רָעָה: יֵרָאֶה אֶל־עֲבָדֶיךָ פָעֳלֶךָ וַהֲדָרְךָ עַל־בְּנֵיהֶם: וִיהִי
נֹעַם אֲדֹנָי אֱלֹהֵינוּ עָלֵינוּ וּמַעֲשֵׂה יָדֵינוּ כּוֹנְנָה עָלֵינוּ וּמַעֲשֵׂה יָדֵינוּ
כּוֹנְנֵהוּ:

צא יֹשֵׁב בְּסֵתֶר עֶלְיוֹן בְּצֵל שַׁדַּי יִתְלוֹנָן: אֹמַר לַיהוָה מַחְסִי וּמְצוּדָתִי אֱלֹהַי
אֶבְטַח־בּוֹ: כִּי הוּא יַצִּילְךָ מִפַּח יָקוּשׁ מִדֶּבֶר הַוּוֹת: בְּאֶבְרָתוֹ יָסֶךְ לָךְ וְתַחַת־
כְּנָפָיו תֶּחְסֶה צִנָּה וְסֹחֵרָה אֲמִתּוֹ: לֹא־תִירָא מִפַּחַד לָיְלָה מֵחֵץ יָעוּף יוֹמָם:
מִדֶּבֶר בָּאֹפֶל יַהֲלֹךְ מִקֶּטֶב יָשׁוּד צָהֳרָיִם: יִפֹּל מִצִּדְּךָ אֶלֶף וּרְבָבָה מִימִינֶךָ
אֵלֶיךָ לֹא יִגָּשׁ: רַק בְּעֵינֶיךָ תַבִּיט וְשִׁלֻּמַת רְשָׁעִים תִּרְאֶה: כִּי־אַתָּה יְהוָה
מַחְסִי עֶלְיוֹן שַׂמְתָּ מְעוֹנֶךָ: לֹא־תְאֻנֶּה אֵלֶיךָ רָעָה וְנֶגַע לֹא־יִקְרַב בְּאָהֳלֶךָ:
כִּי מַלְאָכָיו יְצַוֶּה־לָּךְ לִשְׁמָרְךָ בְּכָל־דְּרָכֶיךָ: עַל־כַּפַּיִם יִשָּׂאוּנְךָ פֶּן־תִּגֹּף בָּאֶבֶן
רַגְלֶךָ: עַל־שַׁחַל וָפֶתֶן תִּדְרֹךְ תִּרְמֹס כְּפִיר וְתַנִּין: כִּי בִי חָשַׁק וַאֲפַלְּטֵהוּ
אֲשַׂגְּבֵהוּ כִּי־יָדַע שְׁמִי: יִקְרָאֵנִי וְאֶעֱנֵהוּ עִמּוֹ־אָנֹכִי בְצָרָה אֲחַלְּצֵהוּ וַאֲכַבְּדֵהוּ:
אֹרֶךְ יָמִים אַשְׂבִּיעֵהוּ וְאַרְאֵהוּ בִּישׁוּעָתִי:

צב מִזְמוֹר שִׁיר לְיוֹם הַשַּׁבָּת: טוֹב לְהֹדוֹת לַיהוָה וּלְזַמֵּר לְשִׁמְךָ עֶלְיוֹן: לְהַגִּיד
בַּבֹּקֶר חַסְדֶּךָ וֶאֱמוּנָתְךָ בַּלֵּילוֹת: עֲלֵי־עָשׂוֹר וַעֲלֵי־נָבֶל עֲלֵי הִגָּיוֹן בְּכִנּוֹר:
כִּי שִׂמַּחְתַּנִי יְהוָה בְּפָעֳלֶךָ בְּמַעֲשֵׂי יָדֶיךָ אֲרַנֵּן: מַה־גָּדְלוּ מַעֲשֶׂיךָ יְהוָה מְאֹד
עָמְקוּ מַחְשְׁבֹתֶיךָ: אִישׁ־בַּעַר לֹא יֵדָע וּכְסִיל לֹא־יָבִין אֶת־זֹאת: בִּפְרֹחַ
רְשָׁעִים כְּמוֹ עֵשֶׂב וַיָּצִיצוּ כָּל־פֹּעֲלֵי אָוֶן לְהִשָּׁמְדָם עֲדֵי־עַד: וְאַתָּה מָרוֹם

לְעָלָם יְהוָה: כִּי הִנֵּה אֹיְבֶיךָ יְהוָה כִּי־הִנֵּה אֹיְבֶיךָ יֹאבֵדוּ יִתְפָּרְדוּ כָּל־פֹּעֲלֵי
אָוֶן: וַתָּרֶם כִּרְאֵים קַרְנִי בַּלֹּתִי בְּשֶׁמֶן רַעֲנָן: וַתַּבֵּט עֵינִי בְּשׁוּרָי בַּקָּמִים עָלַי
מְרֵעִים תִּשְׁמַעְנָה אָזְנָי: צַדִּיק כַּתָּמָר יִפְרָח כְּאֶרֶז בַּלְּבָנוֹן יִשְׂגֶּה: שְׁתוּלִים
בְּבֵית יְהוָה בְּחַצְרוֹת אֱלֹהֵינוּ יַפְרִיחוּ: עוֹד יְנוּבוּן בְּשֵׂיבָה דְּשֵׁנִים וְרַעֲנַנִּים
יִהְיוּ: לְהַגִּיד כִּי־יָשָׁר יְהוָה צוּרִי וְלֹא־עַוְלָתָה בּוֹ: עַוְלָתָה

צג יְהוָה מָלָךְ גֵּאוּת לָבֵשׁ לָבֵשׁ יְהוָה עֹז הִתְאַזָּר אַף־תִּכּוֹן תֵּבֵל בַּל־תִּמּוֹט:
נָכוֹן כִּסְאֲךָ מֵאָז מֵעוֹלָם אָתָּה: נָשְׂאוּ נְהָרוֹת יְהוָה נָשְׂאוּ נְהָרוֹת קוֹלָם יִשְׂאוּ
נְהָרוֹת דָּכְיָם: מִקֹּלוֹת מַיִם רַבִּים אַדִּירִים מִשְׁבְּרֵי־יָם אַדִּיר בַּמָּרוֹם יְהוָה:
עֵדֹתֶיךָ נֶאֶמְנוּ מְאֹד לְבֵיתְךָ נַאֲוָה־קֹדֶשׁ יְהוָה לְאֹרֶךְ יָמִים:

צד אֵל־נְקָמוֹת יְהוָה אֵל נְקָמוֹת הוֹפִיעַ: הִנָּשֵׂא שֹׁפֵט הָאָרֶץ הָשֵׁב גְּמוּל עַל־
גֵּאִים: עַד־מָתַי רְשָׁעִים יְהוָה עַד־מָתַי רְשָׁעִים יַעֲלֹזוּ: יַבִּיעוּ יְדַבְּרוּ עָתָק
יִתְאַמְּרוּ כָּל־פֹּעֲלֵי אָוֶן: עַמְּךָ יְהוָה יְדַכְּאוּ וְנַחֲלָתְךָ יְעַנּוּ: אַלְמָנָה וְגֵר יַהֲרֹגוּ
וִיתוֹמִים יְרַצֵּחוּ: וַיֹּאמְרוּ לֹא יִרְאֶה־יָּהּ וְלֹא־יָבִין אֱלֹהֵי יַעֲקֹב: בִּינוּ בֹּעֲרִים
בָּעָם וּכְסִילִים מָתַי תַּשְׂכִּילוּ: הֲנֹטַע אֹזֶן הֲלֹא יִשְׁמָע אִם־יֹצֵר עַיִן הֲלֹא יַבִּיט:
הֲיֹסֵר גּוֹיִם הֲלֹא יוֹכִיחַ הַמְלַמֵּד אָדָם דָּעַת: יְהוָה יֹדֵעַ מַחְשְׁבוֹת אָדָם כִּי־
הֵמָּה הָבֶל: אַשְׁרֵי הַגֶּבֶר אֲשֶׁר־תְּיַסְּרֶנּוּ יָּהּ וּמִתּוֹרָתְךָ תְלַמְּדֶנּוּ: לְהַשְׁקִיט לוֹ
מִימֵי רָע עַד יִכָּרֶה לָרָשָׁע שָׁחַת: כִּי לֹא־יִטֹּשׁ יְהוָה עַמּוֹ וְנַחֲלָתוֹ לֹא יַעֲזֹב:
כִּי־עַד־צֶדֶק יָשׁוּב מִשְׁפָּט וְאַחֲרָיו כָּל־יִשְׁרֵי־לֵב: מִי־יָקוּם לִי עִם־מְרֵעִים מִי־
יִתְיַצֵּב לִי עִם־פֹּעֲלֵי אָוֶן: לוּלֵי יְהוָה עֶזְרָתָה לִּי כִּמְעַט שָׁכְנָה דוּמָה נַפְשִׁי:
אִם־אָמַרְתִּי מָטָה רַגְלִי חַסְדְּךָ יְהוָה יִסְעָדֵנִי: בְּרֹב שַׂרְעַפַּי בְּקִרְבִּי תַּנְחוּמֶיךָ
יְשַׁעַשְׁעוּ נַפְשִׁי: הַיְחָבְרְךָ כִּסֵּא הַוּוֹת יֹצֵר עָמָל עֲלֵי־חֹק: יָגוֹדּוּ עַל־נֶפֶשׁ צַדִּיק
וְדָם נָקִי יַרְשִׁיעוּ: וַיְהִי יְהוָה לִי לְמִשְׂגָּב וֵאלֹהַי לְצוּר מַחְסִי: וַיָּשֶׁב עֲלֵיהֶם
אֶת־אוֹנָם וּבְרָעָתָם יַצְמִיתֵם יַצְמִיתֵם יְהוָה אֱלֹהֵינוּ:

צה לְכוּ נְרַנְּנָה לַיהוָה נָרִיעָה לְצוּר יִשְׁעֵנוּ: נְקַדְּמָה פָנָיו בְּתוֹדָה בִּזְמִרוֹת נָרִיעַ
לוֹ: כִּי אֵל גָּדוֹל יְהוָה וּמֶלֶךְ גָּדוֹל עַל־כָּל־אֱלֹהִים: אֲשֶׁר בְּיָדוֹ מֶחְקְרֵי־אָרֶץ
וְתוֹעֲפֹת הָרִים לוֹ: אֲשֶׁר־לוֹ הַיָּם וְהוּא עָשָׂהוּ וְיַבֶּשֶׁת יָדָיו יָצָרוּ: בֹּאוּ נִשְׁתַּחֲוֶה
וְנִכְרָעָה נִבְרְכָה לִפְנֵי־יְהוָה עֹשֵׂנוּ: כִּי הוּא אֱלֹהֵינוּ וַאֲנַחְנוּ עַם מַרְעִיתוֹ
וְצֹאן יָדוֹ הַיּוֹם אִם־בְּקֹלוֹ תִשְׁמָעוּ: אַל־תַּקְשׁוּ לְבַבְכֶם כִּמְרִיבָה כְּיוֹם מַסָּה
בַּמִּדְבָּר: אֲשֶׁר נִסּוּנִי אֲבוֹתֵיכֶם בְּחָנוּנִי גַּם־רָאוּ פָעֳלִי: אַרְבָּעִים שָׁנָה אָקוּט

בְּדוֹר וָאֹמַר עַם תֹּעֵי לֵבָב הֵם וְהֵם לֹא־יָדְעוּ דְרָכָי: אֲשֶׁר־נִשְׁבַּעְתִּי בְאַפִּי אִם־יְבֹאוּן אֶל־מְנוּחָתִי:

‏צו שִׁירוּ לַיהוָה שִׁיר חָדָשׁ שִׁירוּ לַיהוָה כָּל־הָאָרֶץ: שִׁירוּ לַיהוָה בָּרְכוּ שְׁמוֹ בַּשְּׂרוּ מִיּוֹם־לְיוֹם יְשׁוּעָתוֹ: סַפְּרוּ בַגּוֹיִם כְּבוֹדוֹ בְּכָל־הָעַמִּים נִפְלְאוֹתָיו: כִּי גָדוֹל יְהוָה וּמְהֻלָּל מְאֹד נוֹרָא הוּא עַל־כָּל־אֱלֹהִים: כִּי כָּל־אֱלֹהֵי הָעַמִּים אֱלִילִים וַיהוָה שָׁמַיִם עָשָׂה: הוֹד־וְהָדָר לְפָנָיו עֹז וְתִפְאֶרֶת בְּמִקְדָּשׁוֹ: הָבוּ לַיהוָה מִשְׁפְּחוֹת עַמִּים הָבוּ לַיהוָה כָּבוֹד וָעֹז: הָבוּ לַיהוָה כְּבוֹד שְׁמוֹ שְׂאוּ־מִנְחָה וּבֹאוּ לְחַצְרוֹתָיו: הִשְׁתַּחֲווּ לַיהוָה בְּהַדְרַת־קֹדֶשׁ חִילוּ מִפָּנָיו כָּל־הָאָרֶץ: אִמְרוּ בַגּוֹיִם יְהוָה מָלָךְ אַף־תִּכּוֹן תֵּבֵל בַּל־תִּמּוֹט יָדִין עַמִּים בְּמֵישָׁרִים: יִשְׂמְחוּ הַשָּׁמַיִם וְתָגֵל הָאָרֶץ יִרְעַם הַיָּם וּמְלֹאוֹ: יַעֲלֹז שָׂדַי וְכָל־אֲשֶׁר־בּוֹ אָז יְרַנְּנוּ כָּל־עֲצֵי־יָעַר: לִפְנֵי יְהוָה כִּי בָא כִּי בָא לִשְׁפֹּט הָאָרֶץ יִשְׁפֹּט־תֵּבֵל בְּצֶדֶק וְעַמִּים בֶּאֱמוּנָתוֹ:

‏צז* יְהוָה מָלָךְ תָּגֵל הָאָרֶץ יִשְׂמְחוּ אִיִּים רַבִּים: עָנָן וַעֲרָפֶל סְבִיבָיו צֶדֶק וּמִשְׁפָּט מְכוֹן כִּסְאוֹ: אֵשׁ לְפָנָיו תֵּלֵךְ וּתְלַהֵט סָבִיב צָרָיו: הֵאִירוּ בְרָקָיו תֵּבֵל רָאֲתָה וַתָּחֵל הָאָרֶץ: הָרִים כַּדּוֹנַג נָמַסּוּ מִלִּפְנֵי יְהוָה מִלִּפְנֵי אֲדוֹן כָּל־הָאָרֶץ: הִגִּידוּ הַשָּׁמַיִם צִדְקוֹ וְרָאוּ כָל־הָעַמִּים כְּבוֹדוֹ: יֵבֹשׁוּ כָּל־עֹבְדֵי פֶסֶל הַמִּתְהַלְלִים בָּאֱלִילִים הִשְׁתַּחֲווּ־לוֹ כָּל־אֱלֹהִים: שָׁמְעָה וַתִּשְׂמַח צִיּוֹן וַתָּגֵלְנָה בְּנוֹת יְהוּדָה לְמַעַן מִשְׁפָּטֶיךָ יְהוָה: כִּי־אַתָּה יְהוָה עֶלְיוֹן עַל־כָּל־הָאָרֶץ מְאֹד נַעֲלֵיתָ עַל־כָּל־אֱלֹהִים: אֹהֲבֵי יְהוָה שִׂנְאוּ רָע שֹׁמֵר נַפְשׁוֹת חֲסִידָיו מִיַּד רְשָׁעִים יַצִּילֵם: אוֹר זָרֻעַ לַצַּדִּיק וּלְיִשְׁרֵי־לֵב שִׂמְחָה: שִׂמְחוּ צַדִּיקִים בַּיהוָה וְהוֹדוּ לְזֵכֶר קָדְשׁוֹ:

‏צח מִזְמוֹר שִׁירוּ לַיהוָה שִׁיר חָדָשׁ כִּי־נִפְלָאוֹת עָשָׂה הוֹשִׁיעָה־לּוֹ יְמִינוֹ וּזְרוֹעַ קָדְשׁוֹ: הוֹדִיעַ יְהוָה יְשׁוּעָתוֹ לְעֵינֵי הַגּוֹיִם גִּלָּה צִדְקָתוֹ: זָכַר חַסְדּוֹ וֶאֱמוּנָתוֹ לְבֵית יִשְׂרָאֵל רָאוּ כָל־אַפְסֵי־אָרֶץ אֵת יְשׁוּעַת אֱלֹהֵינוּ: הָרִיעוּ לַיהוָה כָּל־הָאָרֶץ פִּצְחוּ וְרַנְּנוּ וְזַמֵּרוּ: זַמְּרוּ לַיהוָה בְּכִנּוֹר בְּכִנּוֹר וְקוֹל זִמְרָה: בַּחֲצֹצְרוֹת וְקוֹל שׁוֹפָר הָרִיעוּ לִפְנֵי הַמֶּלֶךְ יְהוָה: יִרְעַם הַיָּם וּמְלֹאוֹ תֵּבֵל וְיֹשְׁבֵי בָהּ: נְהָרוֹת יִמְחֲאוּ־כָף יַחַד הָרִים יְרַנֵּנוּ: לִפְנֵי־יְהוָה כִּי בָא לִשְׁפֹּט הָאָרֶץ יִשְׁפֹּט־תֵּבֵל בְּצֶדֶק וְעַמִּים בְּמֵישָׁרִים:

‏צט יְהוָה מָלָךְ יִרְגְּזוּ עַמִּים יֹשֵׁב כְּרוּבִים תָּנוּט הָאָרֶץ: יְהוָה בְּצִיּוֹן גָּדוֹל וְרָם

*כ לחודש

הוּא עַל־כָּל־הָעַמִּים: יוֹדוּ שִׁמְךָ גָּדוֹל וְנוֹרָא קָדוֹשׁ הוּא: וְעֹז מֶלֶךְ מִשְׁפָּט
אָהֵב אַתָּה כּוֹנַנְתָּ מֵישָׁרִים מִשְׁפָּט וּצְדָקָה בְּיַעֲקֹב אַתָּה עָשִׂיתָ: רוֹמְמוּ
יְהוָה אֱלֹהֵינוּ וְהִשְׁתַּחֲווּ לַהֲדֹם רַגְלָיו קָדוֹשׁ הוּא: מֹשֶׁה וְאַהֲרֹן בְּכֹהֲנָיו
וּשְׁמוּאֵל בְּקֹרְאֵי שְׁמוֹ קֹרִאים אֶל־יְהוָה וְהוּא יַעֲנֵם: בְּעַמּוּד עָנָן יְדַבֵּר אֲלֵיהֶם
שָׁמְרוּ עֵדֹתָיו וְחֹק נָתַן־לָמוֹ: יְהוָה אֱלֹהֵינוּ אַתָּה עֲנִיתָם אֵל נֹשֵׂא הָיִיתָ לָהֶם
וְנֹקֵם עַל־עֲלִילוֹתָם: רוֹמְמוּ יְהוָה אֱלֹהֵינוּ וְהִשְׁתַּחֲווּ לְהַר קָדְשׁוֹ כִּי־קָדוֹשׁ
יְהוָה אֱלֹהֵינוּ:

ק מִזְמוֹר לְתוֹדָה הָרִיעוּ לַיהוָה כָּל־הָאָרֶץ: עִבְדוּ אֶת־יְהוָה בְּשִׂמְחָה בֹּאוּ
לְפָנָיו בִּרְנָנָה: דְּעוּ כִּי־יְהוָה הוּא אֱלֹהִים הוּא עָשָׂנוּ וְלֹא אֲנַחְנוּ עַמּוֹ וְצֹאן
מַרְעִיתוֹ: בֹּאוּ שְׁעָרָיו בְּתוֹדָה חֲצֵרֹתָיו בִּתְהִלָּה הוֹדוּ לוֹ בָּרְכוּ שְׁמוֹ: כִּי־טוֹב
יְהוָה לְעוֹלָם חַסְדּוֹ וְעַד־דֹּר וָדֹר אֱמוּנָתוֹ:

קא לְדָוִד מִזְמוֹר חֶסֶד־וּמִשְׁפָּט אָשִׁירָה לְךָ יְהוָה אֲזַמֵּרָה: אַשְׂכִּילָה בְּדֶרֶךְ
תָּמִים מָתַי תָּבוֹא אֵלָי אֶתְהַלֵּךְ בְּתָם־לְבָבִי בְּקֶרֶב בֵּיתִי: לֹא־אָשִׁית לְנֶגֶד
עֵינַי דְּבַר־בְּלִיָּעַל עֲשֹׂה־סֵטִים שָׂנֵאתִי לֹא יִדְבַּק בִּי: לֵבָב עִקֵּשׁ יָסוּר מִמֶּנִּי
רָע לֹא אֵדָע: מְלָשְׁנִי בַסֵּתֶר רֵעֵהוּ אוֹתוֹ אַצְמִית גְּבַהּ־עֵינַיִם וּרְחַב לֵבָב
אֹתוֹ לֹא אוּכָל: עֵינַי בְּנֶאֶמְנֵי־אֶרֶץ לָשֶׁבֶת עִמָּדִי הֹלֵךְ בְּדֶרֶךְ תָּמִים הוּא
יְשָׁרְתֵנִי: לֹא־יֵשֵׁב בְּקֶרֶב בֵּיתִי עֹשֵׂה רְמִיָּה דֹּבֵר שְׁקָרִים לֹא־יִכּוֹן לְנֶגֶד עֵינָי:
לַבְּקָרִים אַצְמִית כָּל־רִשְׁעֵי־אָרֶץ לְהַכְרִית מֵעִיר־יְהוָה כָּל־פֹּעֲלֵי אָוֶן:

קב תְּפִלָּה לְעָנִי כִי־יַעֲטֹף וְלִפְנֵי יְהוָה יִשְׁפֹּךְ שִׂיחוֹ: יְהוָה שִׁמְעָה תְפִלָּתִי וְשַׁוְעָתִי
אֵלֶיךָ תָבוֹא: אַל־תַּסְתֵּר פָּנֶיךָ מִמֶּנִּי בְּיוֹם צַר לִי הַטֵּה־אֵלַי אָזְנֶךָ בְּיוֹם אֶקְרָא
מַהֵר עֲנֵנִי: כִּי־כָלוּ בְעָשָׁן יָמָי וְעַצְמוֹתַי כְּמוֹ־קֵד נִחָרוּ: הוּכָּה כָעֵשֶׂב וַיִּבַשׁ לִבִּי
כִּי־שָׁכַחְתִּי מֵאֲכֹל לַחְמִי: מִקּוֹל אַנְחָתִי דָּבְקָה עַצְמִי לִבְשָׂרִי: דָּמִיתִי לִקְאַת
מִדְבָּר הָיִיתִי כְּכוֹס חֳרָבוֹת: שָׁקַדְתִּי וָאֶהְיֶה כְּצִפּוֹר בּוֹדֵד עַל־גָּג: כָּל־הַיּוֹם
חֵרְפוּנִי אוֹיְבָי מְהוֹלָלַי בִּי נִשְׁבָּעוּ: כִּי־אֵפֶר כַּלֶּחֶם אָכָלְתִּי וְשִׁקֻּוַי בִּבְכִי מָסָכְתִּי:
מִפְּנֵי־זַעַמְךָ וְקִצְפֶּךָ כִּי נְשָׂאתַנִי וַתַּשְׁלִיכֵנִי: יָמַי כְּצֵל נָטוּי וַאֲנִי כָּעֵשֶׂב אִיבָשׁ:
וְאַתָּה יְהוָה לְעוֹלָם תֵּשֵׁב וְזִכְרְךָ לְדֹר וָדֹר: אַתָּה תָקוּם תְּרַחֵם צִיּוֹן כִּי־עֵת
לְחֶנְנָהּ כִּי־בָא מוֹעֵד: כִּי־רָצוּ עֲבָדֶיךָ אֶת־אֲבָנֶיהָ וְאֶת־עֲפָרָהּ יְחֹנֵנוּ: וְיִירְאוּ
גוֹיִם אֶת־שֵׁם יְהוָה וְכָל־מַלְכֵי הָאָרֶץ אֶת־כְּבוֹדֶךָ: כִּי־בָנָה יְהוָה צִיּוֹן נִרְאָה
בִּכְבוֹדוֹ: פָּנָה אֶל־תְּפִלַּת הָעַרְעָר וְלֹא־בָזָה אֶת־תְּפִלָּתָם: תִּכָּתֶב זֹאת לְדוֹר

אַהֲרוֹן וְעַם נִבְרָא יְהַלֶּל־יָהּ ׃ כִּי־הִשְׁקִיף מִמְּרוֹם קָדְשׁוֹ יְהוָה מִשָּׁמַיִם ׀ אֶל־
אֶרֶץ הִבִּיט ׃ לִשְׁמֹעַ אֶנְקַת אָסִיר לְפַתֵּחַ בְּנֵי תְמוּתָה ׃ לְסַפֵּר בְּצִיּוֹן שֵׁם יְהוָה
וּתְהִלָּתוֹ בִּירוּשָׁלִָם ׃ בְּהִקָּבֵץ עַמִּים יַחְדָּו וּמַמְלָכוֹת לַעֲבֹד אֶת־יְהוָה ׃ עִנָּה
בַדֶּרֶךְ כֹּחוֹ קִצַּר יָמָי ׃ אֹמַר אֵלִי אַל־תַּעֲלֵנִי בַּחֲצִי יָמָי בְּדוֹר דּוֹרִים שְׁנוֹתֶיךָ ׃ כֹּחִי
לְפָנִים הָאָרֶץ יָסַדְתָּ וּמַעֲשֵׂה יָדֶיךָ שָׁמָיִם ׃ הֵמָּה ׀ יֹאבֵדוּ וְאַתָּה תַעֲמֹד וְכֻלָּם
כַּבֶּגֶד יִבְלוּ כַּלְּבוּשׁ תַּחֲלִיפֵם וְיַחֲלֹפוּ ׃ וְאַתָּה־הוּא וּשְׁנוֹתֶיךָ לֹא יִתָּמּוּ ׃ בְּנֵי־
עֲבָדֶיךָ יִשְׁכּוֹנוּ וְזַרְעָם לְפָנֶיךָ יִכּוֹן ׃

קג לְדָוִד ׀ בָּרֲכִי נַפְשִׁי אֶת־יְהוָה וְכָל־קְרָבַי אֶת־שֵׁם קָדְשׁוֹ ׃ בָּרֲכִי נַפְשִׁי אֶת־יְהוָה
וְאַל־תִּשְׁכְּחִי כָּל־גְּמוּלָיו ׃ הַסֹּלֵחַ לְכָל־עֲוֺנֵכִי הָרֹפֵא לְכָל־תַּחֲלֻאָיְכִי ׃ הַגּוֹאֵל
מִשַּׁחַת חַיָּיְכִי הַמְעַטְּרֵכִי חֶסֶד וְרַחֲמִים ׃ הַמַּשְׂבִּיעַ בַּטּוֹב עֶדְיֵךְ תִּתְחַדֵּשׁ כַּנֶּשֶׁר
נְעוּרָיְכִי ׃ עֹשֵׂה צְדָקוֹת יְהוָה וּמִשְׁפָּטִים לְכָל־עֲשׁוּקִים ׃ יוֹדִיעַ דְּרָכָיו לְמֹשֶׁה
לִבְנֵי יִשְׂרָאֵל עֲלִילוֹתָיו ׃ רַחוּם וְחַנּוּן יְהוָה אֶרֶךְ אַפַּיִם וְרַב־חָסֶד ׃ לֹא־לָנֶצַח
יָרִיב וְלֹא לְעוֹלָם יִטּוֹר ׃ לֹא כַחֲטָאֵינוּ עָשָׂה לָנוּ וְלֹא כַעֲוֺנֹתֵינוּ גָּמַל עָלֵינוּ ׃ כִּי
כִגְבֹהַּ שָׁמַיִם עַל־הָאָרֶץ גָּבַר חַסְדּוֹ עַל־יְרֵאָיו ׃ כִּרְחֹק מִזְרָח מִמַּעֲרָב הִרְחִיק
מִמֶּנּוּ אֶת־פְּשָׁעֵינוּ ׃ כְּרַחֵם אָב עַל־בָּנִים רִחַם יְהוָה עַל־יְרֵאָיו ׃ כִּי־הוּא יָדַע
יִצְרֵנוּ זָכוּר כִּי־עָפָר אֲנָחְנוּ ׃ אֱנוֹשׁ כֶּחָצִיר יָמָיו כְּצִיץ הַשָּׂדֶה כֵּן יָצִיץ ׃ כִּי רוּחַ
עָבְרָה־בּוֹ וְאֵינֶנּוּ וְלֹא־יַכִּירֶנּוּ עוֹד מְקוֹמוֹ ׃ וְחֶסֶד יְהוָה ׀ מֵעוֹלָם וְעַד־עוֹלָם
עַל־יְרֵאָיו וְצִדְקָתוֹ לִבְנֵי בָנִים ׃ לְשֹׁמְרֵי בְרִיתוֹ וּלְזֹכְרֵי פִקֻּדָיו לַעֲשׂוֹתָם ׃ יְהוָה
בַּשָּׁמַיִם הֵכִין כִּסְאוֹ וּמַלְכוּתוֹ בַּכֹּל מָשָׁלָה ׃ בָּרֲכוּ יְהוָה מַלְאָכָיו גִּבֹּרֵי כֹחַ
עֹשֵׂי דְבָרוֹ לִשְׁמֹעַ בְּקוֹל דְּבָרוֹ ׃ בָּרֲכוּ יְהוָה כָּל־צְבָאָיו מְשָׁרְתָיו עֹשֵׂי רְצוֹנוֹ ׃
בָּרֲכוּ יְהוָה ׀ כָּל־מַעֲשָׂיו בְּכָל־מְקֹמוֹת מֶמְשַׁלְתּוֹ בָּרֲכִי נַפְשִׁי אֶת־יְהוָה ׃

קד* בָּרֲכִי נַפְשִׁי אֶת־יְהוָה יְהוָה אֱלֹהַי גָּדַלְתָּ מְּאֹד הוֹד וְהָדָר לָבָשְׁתָּ ׃ עֹטֶה־אוֹר
כַּשַּׂלְמָה נוֹטֶה שָׁמַיִם כַּיְרִיעָה ׃ הַמְקָרֶה בַמַּיִם עֲלִיּוֹתָיו הַשָּׂם־עָבִים רְכוּבוֹ
הַמְהַלֵּךְ עַל־כַּנְפֵי־רוּחַ ׃ עֹשֶׂה מַלְאָכָיו רוּחוֹת מְשָׁרְתָיו אֵשׁ לֹהֵט ׃ יָסַד־אֶרֶץ
עַל־מְכוֹנֶיהָ בַּל־תִּמּוֹט עוֹלָם וָעֶד ׃ תְּהוֹם כַּלְּבוּשׁ כִּסִּיתוֹ עַל־הָרִים יַעַמְדוּ־
מָיִם ׃ מִן־גַּעֲרָתְךָ יְנוּסוּן מִן־קוֹל רַעַמְךָ יֵחָפֵזוּן ׃ יַעֲלוּ הָרִים יֵרְדוּ בְקָעוֹת
אֶל־מְקוֹם זֶה ׀ יָסַדְתָּ לָהֶם ׃ גְּבוּל־שַׂמְתָּ בַּל־יַעֲבֹרוּן בַּל־יְשׁוּבוּן לְכַסּוֹת הָאָרֶץ ׃
הַמְשַׁלֵּחַ מַעְיָנִים בַּנְּחָלִים בֵּין הָרִים יְהַלֵּכוּן ׃ יַשְׁקוּ כָּל־חַיְתוֹ שָׂדָי יִשְׁבְּרוּ
פְרָאִים צְמָאָם ׃ עֲלֵיהֶם עוֹף־הַשָּׁמַיִם יִשְׁכּוֹן מִבֵּין עֳפָאיִם יִתְּנוּ־קוֹל ׃ מַשְׁקֶה

הָרִים מֵעֲלִיּוֹתָיו מִפְּרִי מַעֲשֶׂיךָ תִּשְׂבַּע הָאָרֶץ: מַצְמִיחַ חָצִיר ׀ לַבְּהֵמָה וְעֵשֶׂב
לַעֲבֹדַת הָאָדָם לְהוֹצִיא לֶחֶם מִן־הָאָרֶץ: וְיַיִן ׀ יְשַׂמַּח לְבַב־אֱנוֹשׁ לְהַצְהִיל
פָּנִים מִשָּׁמֶן וְלֶחֶם לְבַב־אֱנוֹשׁ יִסְעָד: יִשְׂבְּעוּ עֲצֵי יְהוָה אַרְזֵי לְבָנוֹן אֲשֶׁר
נָטָע: אֲשֶׁר־שָׁם צִפֳּרִים יְקַנֵּנוּ חֲסִידָה בְּרוֹשִׁים בֵּיתָהּ: הָרִים הַגְּבֹהִים לַיְּעֵלִים
סְלָעִים מַחְסֶה לַשְׁפַנִּים: עָשָׂה יָרֵחַ לְמוֹעֲדִים שֶׁמֶשׁ יָדַע מְבוֹאוֹ: תָּשֶׁת־חֹשֶׁךְ
וִיהִי לָיְלָה בּוֹ־תִרְמֹשׂ כָּל־חַיְתוֹ־יָעַר: הַכְּפִירִים שֹׁאֲגִים לַטָּרֶף וּלְבַקֵּשׁ מֵאֵל
אָכְלָם: תִּזְרַח הַשֶּׁמֶשׁ יֵאָסֵפוּן וְאֶל־מְעוֹנֹתָם יִרְבָּצוּן: יֵצֵא אָדָם לְפָעֳלוֹ
וְלַעֲבֹדָתוֹ עֲדֵי־עָרֶב: מָה־רַבּוּ מַעֲשֶׂיךָ ׀ יְהוָה כֻּלָּם בְּחָכְמָה עָשִׂיתָ מָלְאָה
הָאָרֶץ קִנְיָנֶךָ: זֶה ׀ הַיָּם גָּדוֹל וּרְחַב יָדָיִם שָׁם־רֶמֶשׂ וְאֵין מִסְפָּר חַיּוֹת קְטַנּוֹת
עִם־גְּדֹלוֹת: שָׁם אֳנִיּוֹת יְהַלֵּכוּן לִוְיָתָן זֶה־יָצַרְתָּ לְשַׂחֶק־בּוֹ: כֻּלָּם אֵלֶיךָ יְשַׂבֵּרוּן
לָתֵת אָכְלָם בְּעִתּוֹ: תִּתֵּן לָהֶם יִלְקֹטוּן תִּפְתַּח יָדְךָ יִשְׂבְּעוּן טוֹב: תַּסְתִּיר פָּנֶיךָ
יִבָּהֵלוּן תֹּסֵף רוּחָם יִגְוָעוּן וְאֶל־עֲפָרָם יְשׁוּבוּן: תְּשַׁלַּח רוּחֲךָ יִבָּרֵאוּן וּתְחַדֵּשׁ
פְּנֵי אֲדָמָה: יְהִי כְבוֹד יְהוָה לְעוֹלָם יִשְׂמַח יְהוָה בְּמַעֲשָׂיו: הַמַּבִּיט לָאָרֶץ
וַתִּרְעָד יִגַּע בֶּהָרִים וְיֶעֱשָׁנוּ: אָשִׁירָה לַיהוָה בְּחַיָּי אֲזַמְּרָה לֵאלֹהַי בְּעוֹדִי:
יֶעֱרַב עָלָיו שִׂיחִי אָנֹכִי אֶשְׂמַח בַּיהוָה: יִתַּמּוּ חַטָּאִים ׀ מִן־הָאָרֶץ וּרְשָׁעִים ׀
עוֹד אֵינָם בָּרֲכִי נַפְשִׁי אֶת־יְהוָה הַלְלוּיָהּ:

קה הוֹדוּ לַיהוָה קִרְאוּ בִשְׁמוֹ הוֹדִיעוּ בָעַמִּים עֲלִילוֹתָיו: שִׁירוּ־לוֹ זַמְּרוּ־לוֹ שִׂיחוּ
בְּכָל־נִפְלְאוֹתָיו: הִתְהַלְלוּ בְּשֵׁם קָדְשׁוֹ יִשְׂמַח לֵב ׀ מְבַקְשֵׁי יְהוָה: דִּרְשׁוּ יְהוָה
וְעֻזּוֹ בַּקְשׁוּ פָנָיו תָּמִיד: זִכְרוּ נִפְלְאוֹתָיו אֲשֶׁר־עָשָׂה מֹפְתָיו וּמִשְׁפְּטֵי־פִיו: זֶרַע
אַבְרָהָם עַבְדּוֹ בְּנֵי יַעֲקֹב בְּחִירָיו: הוּא יְהוָה אֱלֹהֵינוּ בְּכָל־הָאָרֶץ מִשְׁפָּטָיו:
זָכַר לְעוֹלָם בְּרִיתוֹ דָּבָר צִוָּה לְאֶלֶף דּוֹר: אֲשֶׁר כָּרַת אֶת־אַבְרָהָם וּשְׁבוּעָתוֹ
לְיִשְׂחָק: וַיַּעֲמִידֶהָ לְיַעֲקֹב לְחֹק לְיִשְׂרָאֵל בְּרִית עוֹלָם: לֵאמֹר לְךָ אֶתֵּן אֶת־
אֶרֶץ־כְּנָעַן חֶבֶל נַחֲלַתְכֶם: בִּהְיוֹתָם מְתֵי מִסְפָּר כִּמְעַט וְגָרִים בָּהּ: וַיִּתְהַלְּכוּ
מִגּוֹי אֶל־גּוֹי מִמַּמְלָכָה אֶל־עַם אַחֵר: לֹא־הִנִּיחַ אָדָם לְעָשְׁקָם וַיּוֹכַח עֲלֵיהֶם
מְלָכִים: אַל־תִּגְּעוּ בִמְשִׁיחָי וְלִנְבִיאַי אַל־תָּרֵעוּ: וַיִּקְרָא רָעָב עַל־הָאָרֶץ כָּל־
מַטֵּה־לֶחֶם שָׁבָר: שָׁלַח לִפְנֵיהֶם אִישׁ לְעֶבֶד נִמְכַּר יוֹסֵף: עִנּוּ בַכֶּבֶל רַגְלָיו [רַגְלוֹ]
בַּרְזֶל בָּאָה נַפְשׁוֹ: עַד־עֵת בֹּא־דְבָרוֹ אִמְרַת יְהוָה צְרָפָתְהוּ: שָׁלַח מֶלֶךְ
וַיַתִּירֵהוּ מֹשֵׁל עַמִּים וַיְפַתְּחֵהוּ: שָׂמוֹ אָדוֹן לְבֵיתוֹ וּמֹשֵׁל בְּכָל־קִנְיָנוֹ: לֶאְסֹר
שָׂרָיו בְּנַפְשׁוֹ וּזְקֵנָיו יְחַכֵּם: וַיָּבֹא יִשְׂרָאֵל מִצְרָיִם וְיַעֲקֹב גָּר בְּאֶרֶץ־חָם: וַיֶּפֶר

אֶת־עַמּוֹ מְאֹד וַיַּעֲצִמֵהוּ מִצָּרָיו: הָפַךְ לִבָּם לִשְׂנֹא עַמּוֹ לְהִתְנַכֵּל בַּעֲבָדָיו:
שָׁלַח מֹשֶׁה עַבְדּוֹ אַהֲרֹן אֲשֶׁר בָּחַר־בּוֹ: שָׂמוּ־בָם דִּבְרֵי אֹתוֹתָיו וּמֹפְתִים
דברו בְּאֶרֶץ חָם: שָׁלַח חֹשֶׁךְ וַיַּחְשִׁךְ וְלֹא־מָרוּ אֶת־דְּבָרָיו: הָפַךְ אֶת־מֵימֵיהֶם
לְדָם וַיָּמֶת אֶת־דְּגָתָם: שָׁרַץ אַרְצָם צְפַרְדְּעִים בְּחַדְרֵי מַלְכֵיהֶם: אָמַר וַיָּבֹא
עָרֹב כִּנִּים בְּכָל־גְּבוּלָם: נָתַן גִּשְׁמֵיהֶם בָּרָד אֵשׁ לֶהָבוֹת בְּאַרְצָם: וַיַּךְ גַּפְנָם
וּתְאֵנָתָם וַיְשַׁבֵּר עֵץ גְּבוּלָם: אָמַר וַיָּבֹא אַרְבֶּה וְיֶלֶק וְאֵין מִסְפָּר: וַיֹּאכַל כָּל־
עֵשֶׂב בְּאַרְצָם וַיֹּאכַל פְּרִי אַדְמָתָם: וַיַּךְ כָּל־בְּכוֹר בְּאַרְצָם רֵאשִׁית לְכָל־אוֹנָם:
וַיּוֹצִיאֵם בְּכֶסֶף וְזָהָב וְאֵין בִּשְׁבָטָיו כּוֹשֵׁל: שָׂמַח מִצְרַיִם בְּצֵאתָם כִּי־נָפַל
פַּחְדָּם עֲלֵיהֶם: פָּרַשׂ עָנָן לְמָסָךְ וְאֵשׁ לְהָאִיר לָיְלָה: שָׁאַל וַיָּבֵא שְׂלָו וְלֶחֶם
שָׁמַיִם יַשְׂבִּיעֵם: פָּתַח צוּר וַיָּזוּבוּ מָיִם הָלְכוּ בַּצִּיּוֹת נָהָר: כִּי־זָכַר אֶת־דְּבַר
קָדְשׁוֹ אֶת־אַבְרָהָם עַבְדּוֹ: וַיּוֹצִא עַמּוֹ בְשָׂשׂוֹן בְּרִנָּה אֶת־בְּחִירָיו: וַיִּתֵּן לָהֶם
אַרְצוֹת גּוֹיִם וַעֲמַל לְאֻמִּים יִירָשׁוּ: בַּעֲבוּר ׀ יִשְׁמְרוּ חֻקָּיו וְתוֹרֹתָיו יִנְצֹרוּ
הַלְלוּיָהּ:

קו הַלְלוּיָהּ ׀ הוֹדוּ לַיהוָה כִּי־טוֹב כִּי לְעוֹלָם חַסְדּוֹ: מִי יְמַלֵּל גְּבוּרוֹת יְהוָה יַשְׁמִיעַ *
כָּל־תְּהִלָּתוֹ: אַשְׁרֵי שֹׁמְרֵי מִשְׁפָּט עֹשֵׂה צְדָקָה בְכָל־עֵת: זָכְרֵנִי יְהוָה בִּרְצוֹן
עַמֶּךָ פָּקְדֵנִי בִּישׁוּעָתֶךָ: לִרְאוֹת ׀ בְּטוֹבַת בְּחִירֶיךָ לִשְׂמֹחַ בְּשִׂמְחַת גּוֹיֶךָ
לְהִתְהַלֵּל עִם־נַחֲלָתֶךָ: חָטָאנוּ עִם־אֲבוֹתֵינוּ הֶעֱוִינוּ הִרְשָׁעְנוּ: אֲבוֹתֵינוּ
בְמִצְרַיִם ׀ לֹא־הִשְׂכִּילוּ נִפְלְאוֹתֶיךָ לֹא זָכְרוּ אֶת־רֹב חֲסָדֶיךָ וַיַּמְרוּ עַל־יָם
בְּיַם־סוּף: וַיּוֹשִׁיעֵם לְמַעַן שְׁמוֹ לְהוֹדִיעַ אֶת־גְּבוּרָתוֹ: וַיִּגְעַר בְּיַם־סוּף וַיֶּחֱרָב
וַיּוֹלִיכֵם בַּתְּהֹמוֹת כַּמִּדְבָּר: וַיּוֹשִׁיעֵם מִיַּד שׂוֹנֵא וַיִּגְאָלֵם מִיַּד אוֹיֵב: וַיְכַסּוּ־מַיִם
צָרֵיהֶם אֶחָד מֵהֶם לֹא נוֹתָר: וַיַּאֲמִינוּ בִדְבָרָיו יָשִׁירוּ תְּהִלָּתוֹ: מִהֲרוּ שָׁכְחוּ
מַעֲשָׂיו לֹא־חִכּוּ לַעֲצָתוֹ: וַיִּתְאַוּוּ תַאֲוָה בַּמִּדְבָּר וַיְנַסּוּ־אֵל בִּישִׁימוֹן: וַיִּתֵּן
לָהֶם שֶׁאֱלָתָם וַיְשַׁלַּח רָזוֹן בְּנַפְשָׁם: וַיְקַנְאוּ לְמֹשֶׁה בַּמַּחֲנֶה לְאַהֲרֹן קְדוֹשׁ
יְהוָה: תִּפְתַּח־אֶרֶץ וַתִּבְלַע דָּתָן וַתְּכַס עַל־עֲדַת אֲבִירָם: וַתִּבְעַר־אֵשׁ בַּעֲדָתָם
לֶהָבָה תְּלַהֵט רְשָׁעִים: יַעֲשׂוּ־עֵגֶל בְּחֹרֵב וַיִּשְׁתַּחֲווּ לְמַסֵּכָה: וַיָּמִירוּ אֶת־
כְּבוֹדָם בְּתַבְנִית שׁוֹר אֹכֵל עֵשֶׂב: שָׁכְחוּ אֵל מוֹשִׁיעָם עֹשֶׂה גְדֹלוֹת בְּמִצְרָיִם:
נִפְלָאוֹת בְּאֶרֶץ חָם נוֹרָאוֹת עַל־יַם־סוּף: וַיֹּאמֶר לְהַשְׁמִידָם לוּלֵי מֹשֶׁה בְחִירוֹ
עָמַד בַּפֶּרֶץ לְפָנָיו לְהָשִׁיב חֲמָתוֹ מֵהַשְׁחִית: וַיִּמְאֲסוּ בְּאֶרֶץ חֶמְדָּה לֹא־
הֶאֱמִינוּ לִדְבָרוֹ: וַיֵּרָגְנוּ בְאָהֳלֵיהֶם לֹא שָׁמְעוּ בְּקוֹל יְהוָה: וַיִּשָּׂא יָדוֹ לָהֶם

*כב לחודש

לְהַפִּיל אוֹתָם בַּמִּדְבָּר: וּלְהַפִּיל זַרְעָם בַּגּוֹיִם וּלְזָרוֹתָם בָּאֲרָצוֹת: וַיִּצָּמְדוּ
לְבַעַל פְּעוֹר וַיֹּאכְלוּ זִבְחֵי מֵתִים: וַיַּכְעִיסוּ בְּמַעַלְלֵיהֶם וַתִּפְרָץ־בָּם מַגֵּפָה:
וַיַּעֲמֹד פִּינְחָס וַיְפַלֵּל וַתֵּעָצַר הַמַּגֵּפָה: וַתֵּחָשֶׁב לוֹ לִצְדָקָה לְדֹר וָדֹר עַד־עוֹלָם:
וַיַּקְצִיפוּ עַל־מֵי מְרִיבָה וַיֵּרַע לְמֹשֶׁה בַּעֲבוּרָם: כִּי־הִמְרוּ אֶת־רוּחוֹ וַיְבַטֵּא
בִּשְׂפָתָיו: לֹא־הִשְׁמִידוּ אֶת־הָעַמִּים אֲשֶׁר אָמַר יְהֹוָה לָהֶם: וַיִּתְעָרְבוּ בַגּוֹיִם
וַיִּלְמְדוּ מַעֲשֵׂיהֶם: וַיַּעַבְדוּ אֶת־עֲצַבֵּיהֶם וַיִּהְיוּ לָהֶם לְמוֹקֵשׁ: וַיִּזְבְּחוּ אֶת־
בְּנֵיהֶם וְאֶת־בְּנוֹתֵיהֶם לַשֵּׁדִים: וַיִּשְׁפְּכוּ דָם נָקִי דַּם־בְּנֵיהֶם וּבְנוֹתֵיהֶם אֲשֶׁר
זִבְּחוּ לַעֲצַבֵּי כְנָעַן וַתֶּחֱנַף הָאָרֶץ בַּדָּמִים: וַיִּטְמְאוּ בְמַעֲשֵׂיהֶם וַיִּזְנוּ
בְּמַעַלְלֵיהֶם: וַיִּחַר־אַף יְהֹוָה בְּעַמּוֹ וַיְתָעֵב אֶת־נַחֲלָתוֹ: וַיִּתְּנֵם בְּיַד־גּוֹיִם
וַיִּמְשְׁלוּ בָהֶם שֹׂנְאֵיהֶם: וַיִּלְחָצוּם אוֹיְבֵיהֶם וַיִּכָּנְעוּ תַּחַת יָדָם: פְּעָמִים רַבּוֹת
יַצִּילֵם וְהֵמָּה יַמְרוּ בַעֲצָתָם וַיָּמֹכּוּ בַּעֲוֺנָם: וַיַּרְא בַּצַּר לָהֶם בְּשָׁמְעוֹ אֶת־רִנָּתָם:
וַיִּזְכֹּר לָהֶם בְּרִיתוֹ וַיִּנָּחֵם כְּרֹב חֲסָדָיו: וַיִּתֵּן אוֹתָם לְרַחֲמִים לִפְנֵי כָּל־שׁוֹבֵיהֶם:
הוֹשִׁיעֵנוּ ׀ יְהֹוָה אֱלֹהֵינוּ וְקַבְּצֵנוּ מִן־הַגּוֹיִם לְהֹדוֹת לְשֵׁם קָדְשֶׁךָ לְהִשְׁתַּבֵּחַ
בִּתְהִלָּתֶךָ: בָּרוּךְ יְהֹוָה אֱלֹהֵי יִשְׂרָאֵל מִן־הָעוֹלָם ׀ וְעַד הָעוֹלָם וְאָמַר כָּל־הָעָם
אָמֵן הַלְלוּיָהּ:

ספר חמישי

*קו הֹדוּ לַיהֹוָה כִּי־טוֹב כִּי לְעוֹלָם חַסְדּוֹ: יֹאמְרוּ גְּאוּלֵי יְהֹוָה אֲשֶׁר גְּאָלָם מִיַּד־
צָר: וּמֵאֲרָצוֹת קִבְּצָם מִמִּזְרָח וּמִמַּעֲרָב מִצָּפוֹן וּמִיָּם: תָּעוּ בַמִּדְבָּר בִּישִׁימוֹן
דָּרֶךְ עִיר מוֹשָׁב לֹא מָצָאוּ: רְעֵבִים גַּם־צְמֵאִים נַפְשָׁם בָּהֶם תִּתְעַטָּף: וַיִּצְעֲקוּ
אֶל־יְהֹוָה בַּצַּר לָהֶם מִמְּצוּקוֹתֵיהֶם יַצִּילֵם: וַיַּדְרִיכֵם בְּדֶרֶךְ יְשָׁרָה לָלֶכֶת
אֶל־עִיר מוֹשָׁב: יוֹדוּ לַיהֹוָה חַסְדּוֹ וְנִפְלְאוֹתָיו לִבְנֵי אָדָם: כִּי־הִשְׂבִּיעַ נֶפֶשׁ
שֹׁקֵקָה וְנֶפֶשׁ רְעֵבָה מִלֵּא־טוֹב: יֹשְׁבֵי חֹשֶׁךְ וְצַלְמָוֶת אֲסִירֵי עֳנִי וּבַרְזֶל:
כִּי־הִמְרוּ אִמְרֵי־אֵל וַעֲצַת עֶלְיוֹן נָאָצוּ: וַיַּכְנַע בֶּעָמָל לִבָּם כָּשְׁלוּ וְאֵין
עֹזֵר: וַיִּזְעֲקוּ אֶל־יְהֹוָה בַּצַּר לָהֶם מִמְּצֻקוֹתֵיהֶם יוֹשִׁיעֵם: יוֹצִיאֵם מֵחֹשֶׁךְ
וְצַלְמָוֶת וּמוֹסְרוֹתֵיהֶם יְנַתֵּק: יוֹדוּ לַיהֹוָה חַסְדּוֹ וְנִפְלְאוֹתָיו לִבְנֵי אָדָם: כִּי־
שִׁבַּר דַּלְתוֹת נְחֹשֶׁת וּבְרִיחֵי בַרְזֶל גִּדֵּעַ: אֱוִלִים מִדֶּרֶךְ פִּשְׁעָם וּמֵעֲוֺנֹתֵיהֶם
יִתְעַנּוּ: כָּל־אֹכֶל תְּתַעֵב נַפְשָׁם וַיַּגִּיעוּ עַד־שַׁעֲרֵי מָוֶת: וַיִּזְעֲקוּ אֶל־יְהֹוָה בַּצַּר
לָהֶם מִמְּצֻקוֹתֵיהֶם יוֹשִׁיעֵם: יִשְׁלַח דְּבָרוֹ וְיִרְפָּאֵם וִימַלֵּט מִשְּׁחִיתוֹתָם: יוֹדוּ
לַיהֹוָה חַסְדּוֹ וְנִפְלְאוֹתָיו לִבְנֵי אָדָם: וְיִזְבְּחוּ זִבְחֵי תוֹדָה וִיסַפְּרוּ מַעֲשָׂיו

בְרֹגֶז: ד יוֹרְדֵי הַיָּם בָּאֳנִיּוֹת עֹשֵׂי מְלָאכָה בְּמַיִם רַבִּים: ד הֵמָּה רָאוּ
מַעֲשֵׂי יְהֹוָה וְנִפְלְאוֹתָיו בִּמְצוּלָה: ד וַיֹּאמֶר וַיַּעֲמֵד רוּחַ סְעָרָה וַתְּרוֹמֵם
גַּלָּיו: ד יַעֲלוּ שָׁמַיִם יֵרְדוּ תְהוֹמוֹת נַפְשָׁם בְּרָעָה תִתְמוֹגָג: ד יָחוֹגּוּ
וְיָנוּעוּ כַּשִּׁכּוֹר וְכָל־חָכְמָתָם תִּתְבַּלָּע: ד וַיִּצְעֲקוּ אֶל־יְהֹוָה בַּצַּר לָהֶם
וּמִמְּצוּקֹתֵיהֶם יוֹצִיאֵם: יָקֵם סְעָרָה לִדְמָמָה וַיֶּחֱשׁוּ גַּלֵּיהֶם: וַיִּשְׂמְחוּ כִי־יִשְׁתֹּקוּ
וַיַּנְחֵם אֶל־מְחוֹז חֶפְצָם: יוֹדוּ לַיהֹוָה חַסְדּוֹ וְנִפְלְאוֹתָיו לִבְנֵי אָדָם: וִירֹמְמוּהוּ
בִּקְהַל־עָם וּבְמוֹשַׁב זְקֵנִים יְהַלְלוּהוּ: יָשֵׂם נְהָרוֹת לְמִדְבָּר וּמֹצָאֵי מַיִם
לְצִמָּאוֹן: אֶרֶץ פְּרִי לִמְלֵחָה מֵרָעַת יֹשְׁבֵי בָהּ: יָשֵׂם מִדְבָּר לַאֲגַם־מַיִם וְאֶרֶץ
צִיָּה לְמֹצָאֵי מָיִם: וַיּוֹשֶׁב שָׁם רְעֵבִים וַיְכוֹנְנוּ עִיר מוֹשָׁב: וַיִּזְרְעוּ שָׂדוֹת וַיִּטְּעוּ
כְרָמִים וַיַּעֲשׂוּ פְּרִי תְבוּאָה: וַיְבָרֲכֵם וַיִּרְבּוּ מְאֹד וּבְהֶמְתָּם לֹא יַמְעִיט: וַיִּמְעֲטוּ
וַיָּשֹׁחוּ מֵעֹצֶר רָעָה וְיָגוֹן: ד שֹׁפֵךְ בּוּז עַל־נְדִיבִים וַיַּתְעֵם בְּתֹהוּ לֹא־דָרֶךְ:
וַיְשַׂגֵּב אֶבְיוֹן מֵעוֹנִי וַיָּשֶׂם כַּצֹּאן מִשְׁפָּחוֹת: יִרְאוּ יְשָׁרִים וְיִשְׂמָחוּ וְכָל־עַוְלָה
קָפְצָה פִּיהָ: מִי־חָכָם וְיִשְׁמָר־אֵלֶּה וְיִתְבּוֹנְנוּ חַסְדֵי יְהֹוָה:

קח* שִׁיר מִזְמוֹר לְדָוִד: נָכוֹן לִבִּי אֱלֹהִים אָשִׁירָה וַאֲזַמְּרָה אַף־כְּבוֹדִי: עוּרָה הַנֵּבֶל
וְכִנּוֹר אָעִירָה שָּׁחַר: אוֹדְךָ בָעַמִּים יְהֹוָה וַאֲזַמֶּרְךָ בַּלְאֻמִּים: כִּי־גָדוֹל מֵעַל־
שָׁמַיִם חַסְדֶּךָ וְעַד־שְׁחָקִים אֲמִתֶּךָ: רוּמָה עַל־שָׁמַיִם אֱלֹהִים וְעַל כָּל־הָאָרֶץ
כְּבוֹדֶךָ: לְמַעַן יֵחָלְצוּן יְדִידֶיךָ הוֹשִׁיעָה יְמִינְךָ וַעֲנֵנִי: אֱלֹהִים דִּבֶּר בְּקָדְשׁוֹ
אֶעְלֹזָה אֲחַלְּקָה שְׁכֶם וְעֵמֶק סֻכּוֹת אֲמַדֵּד: לִי גִלְעָד לִי מְנַשֶּׁה וְאֶפְרַיִם מָעוֹז
רֹאשִׁי יְהוּדָה מְחֹקְקִי: מוֹאָב סִיר רַחְצִי עַל־אֱדוֹם אַשְׁלִיךְ נַעֲלִי עֲלֵי־פְלֶשֶׁת
אֶתְרוֹעָע: מִי יֹבִלֵנִי עִיר מִבְצָר מִי נָחַנִי עַד־אֱדוֹם: הֲלֹא־אֱלֹהִים זְנַחְתָּנוּ
וְלֹא־תֵצֵא אֱלֹהִים בְּצִבְאֹתֵינוּ: הָבָה־לָּנוּ עֶזְרָת מִצָּר וְשָׁוְא תְּשׁוּעַת אָדָם:
בֵּאלֹהִים נַעֲשֶׂה־חָיִל וְהוּא יָבוּס צָרֵינוּ:

קט לַמְנַצֵּחַ לְדָוִד מִזְמוֹר אֱלֹהֵי תְהִלָּתִי אַל־תֶּחֱרַשׁ: כִּי פִי רָשָׁע וּפִי־מִרְמָה עָלַי
פָּתָחוּ דִּבְּרוּ אִתִּי לְשׁוֹן שָׁקֶר: וְדִבְרֵי שִׂנְאָה סְבָבוּנִי וַיִּלָּחֲמוּנִי חִנָּם: תַּחַת
אַהֲבָתִי יִשְׂטְנוּנִי וַאֲנִי תְפִלָּה: וַיָּשִׂימוּ עָלַי רָעָה תַּחַת טוֹבָה וְשִׂנְאָה תַּחַת
אַהֲבָתִי: הַפְקֵד עָלָיו רָשָׁע וְשָׂטָן יַעֲמֹד עַל־יְמִינוֹ: בְּהִשָּׁפְטוֹ יֵצֵא רָשָׁע
וּתְפִלָּתוֹ תִּהְיֶה לַחֲטָאָה: יִהְיוּ־יָמָיו מְעַטִּים פְּקֻדָּתוֹ יִקַּח אַחֵר: יִהְיוּ־בָנָיו
יְתוֹמִים וְאִשְׁתּוֹ אַלְמָנָה: וְנוֹעַ יָנוּעוּ בָנָיו וְשִׁאֵלוּ וְדָרְשׁוּ מֵחָרְבוֹתֵיהֶם: יְנַקֵּשׁ
נוֹשֶׁה לְכָל־אֲשֶׁר־לוֹ וְיָבֹזּוּ זָרִים יְגִיעוֹ: אַל־יְהִי־לוֹ מֹשֵׁךְ חָסֶד וְאַל־יְהִי חוֹנֵן

*כג לחודש

לִיתוֹמָיו: יְהִי-אַחֲרִיתוֹ לְהַכְרִית בְּדוֹר אַחֵר יִמַּח שְׁמָם: יִזָּכֵר ׀ עֲוֹן אֲבֹתָיו אֶל-יְהוָה וְחַטַּאת אִמּוֹ אַל-תִּמָּח: יִהְיוּ נֶגֶד-יְהוָה תָּמִיד וְיַכְרֵת מֵאֶרֶץ זִכְרָם: יַעַן אֲשֶׁר ׀ לֹא זָכַר עֲשׂוֹת חָסֶד וַיִּרְדֹּף אִישׁ-עָנִי וְאֶבְיוֹן וְנִכְאֵה לֵבָב לְמוֹתֵת: וַיֶּאֱהַב קְלָלָה וַתְּבוֹאֵהוּ וְלֹא-חָפֵץ בִּבְרָכָה וַתִּרְחַק מִמֶּנּוּ: וַיִּלְבַּשׁ קְלָלָה כְּמַדּוֹ וַתָּבֹא כַמַּיִם בְּקִרְבּוֹ וְכַשֶּׁמֶן בְּעַצְמוֹתָיו: תְּהִי-לוֹ כְּבֶגֶד יַעְטֶה וּלְמֵזַח תָּמִיד יַחְגְּרֶהָ: זֹאת פְּעֻלַּת שֹׂטְנַי מֵאֵת יְהוָה וְהַדֹּבְרִים רָע עַל-נַפְשִׁי: וְאַתָּה ׀ יְהוָה אֲדֹנָי עֲשֵׂה-אִתִּי לְמַעַן שְׁמֶךָ כִּי-טוֹב חַסְדְּךָ הַצִּילֵנִי: כִּי-עָנִי וְאֶבְיוֹן אָנֹכִי וְלִבִּי חָלַל בְּקִרְבִּי: כְּצֵל-כִּנְטוֹתוֹ נֶהֱלָכְתִּי נִנְעַרְתִּי כָּאַרְבֶּה: בִּרְכַּי כָּשְׁלוּ מִצּוֹם וּבְשָׂרִי כָּחַשׁ מִשָּׁמֶן: וַאֲנִי ׀ הָיִיתִי חֶרְפָּה לָהֶם יִרְאוּנִי יְנִיעוּן רֹאשָׁם: עָזְרֵנִי יְהוָה אֱלֹהָי הוֹשִׁיעֵנִי כְחַסְדֶּךָ: וְיֵדְעוּ כִּי-יָדְךָ זֹּאת אַתָּה יְהוָה עֲשִׂיתָהּ: יְקַלְלוּ-הֵמָּה וְאַתָּה תְבָרֵךְ קָמוּ ׀ וַיֵּבֹשׁוּ וְעַבְדְּךָ יִשְׂמָח: יִלְבְּשׁוּ שׂוֹטְנַי כְּלִמָּה וְיַעֲטוּ כַמְעִיל בָּשְׁתָּם: אוֹדֶה יְהוָה מְאֹד בְּפִי וּבְתוֹךְ רַבִּים אֲהַלְלֶנּוּ: כִּי-יַעֲמֹד לִימִין אֶבְיוֹן לְהוֹשִׁיעַ מִשֹּׁפְטֵי נַפְשׁוֹ:

קי לְדָוִד מִזְמוֹר נְאֻם יְהוָה ׀ לַאדֹנִי שֵׁב לִימִינִי עַד-אָשִׁית אֹיְבֶיךָ הֲדֹם לְרַגְלֶיךָ: מַטֵּה עֻזְּךָ יִשְׁלַח יְהוָה מִצִּיּוֹן רְדֵה בְּקֶרֶב אֹיְבֶיךָ: עַמְּךָ נְדָבֹת בְּיוֹם חֵילֶךָ בְּהַדְרֵי-קֹדֶשׁ מֵרֶחֶם מִשְׁחָר לְךָ טַל יַלְדֻתֶיךָ: נִשְׁבַּע יְהוָה ׀ וְלֹא יִנָּחֵם אַתָּה-כֹהֵן לְעוֹלָם עַל-דִּבְרָתִי מַלְכִּי-צֶדֶק: אֲדֹנָי עַל-יְמִינְךָ מָחַץ בְּיוֹם-אַפּוֹ מְלָכִים: יָדִין בַּגּוֹיִם מָלֵא גְוִיּוֹת מָחַץ רֹאשׁ עַל-אֶרֶץ רַבָּה: מִנַּחַל בַּדֶּרֶךְ יִשְׁתֶּה עַל-כֵּן יָרִים רֹאשׁ:

קיא הַלְלוּיָהּ ׀ אוֹדֶה יְהוָה בְּכָל-לֵבָב בְּסוֹד יְשָׁרִים וְעֵדָה: גְּדֹלִים מַעֲשֵׂי יְהוָה דְּרוּשִׁים לְכָל-חֶפְצֵיהֶם: הוֹד-וְהָדָר פָּעֳלוֹ וְצִדְקָתוֹ עֹמֶדֶת לָעַד: זֵכֶר עָשָׂה לְנִפְלְאֹתָיו חַנּוּן וְרַחוּם יְהוָה: טֶרֶף נָתַן לִירֵאָיו יִזְכֹּר לְעוֹלָם בְּרִיתוֹ: כֹּחַ מַעֲשָׂיו הִגִּיד לְעַמּוֹ לָתֵת לָהֶם נַחֲלַת גּוֹיִם: מַעֲשֵׂי יָדָיו אֱמֶת וּמִשְׁפָּט נֶאֱמָנִים כָּל-פִּקּוּדָיו: סְמוּכִים לָעַד לְעוֹלָם עֲשׂוּיִם בֶּאֱמֶת וְיָשָׁר: פְּדוּת ׀ שָׁלַח לְעַמּוֹ צִוָּה-לְעוֹלָם בְּרִיתוֹ קָדוֹשׁ וְנוֹרָא שְׁמוֹ: רֵאשִׁית חָכְמָה ׀ יִרְאַת יְהוָה שֵׂכֶל טוֹב לְכָל-עֹשֵׂיהֶם תְּהִלָּתוֹ עֹמֶדֶת לָעַד:

קיב הַלְלוּיָהּ ׀ אַשְׁרֵי-אִישׁ יָרֵא אֶת-יְהוָה בְּמִצְוֹתָיו חָפֵץ מְאֹד: גִּבּוֹר בָּאָרֶץ יִהְיֶה זַרְעוֹ דּוֹר יְשָׁרִים יְבֹרָךְ: הוֹן-וָעֹשֶׁר בְּבֵיתוֹ וְצִדְקָתוֹ עֹמֶדֶת לָעַד: זָרַח בַּחֹשֶׁךְ אוֹר לַיְשָׁרִים חַנּוּן וְרַחוּם וְצַדִּיק: טוֹב-אִישׁ חוֹנֵן וּמַלְוֶה יְכַלְכֵּל דְּבָרָיו

בְּמִשְׁפָּט: כִּי־לְעוֹלָם לֹא־יִמּוֹט לְזֵכֶר עוֹלָם יִהְיֶה צַדִּיק: מִשְּׁמוּעָה רָעָה לֹא
יִירָא נָכוֹן לִבּוֹ בָּטֻחַ בַּיהוה: סָמוּךְ לִבּוֹ לֹא יִירָא עַד אֲשֶׁר־יִרְאֶה בְצָרָיו: פִּזַּר ׀
נָתַן לָאֶבְיוֹנִים צִדְקָתוֹ עֹמֶדֶת לָעַד קַרְנוֹ תָּרוּם בְּכָבוֹד: רָשָׁע יִרְאֶה ׀ וְכָעָס
שִׁנָּיו יַחֲרֹק וְנָמָס תַּאֲוַת רְשָׁעִים תֹּאבֵד:

הַלְלוּיָהּ ׀ הַלְלוּ עַבְדֵי יהוה הַלְלוּ אֶת־שֵׁם יהוה: יְהִי שֵׁם יהוה מְבֹרָךְ מֵעַתָּה **קיג***
וְעַד־עוֹלָם: מִמִּזְרַח־שֶׁמֶשׁ עַד־מְבוֹאוֹ מְהֻלָּל שֵׁם יהוה: רָם עַל־כָּל־גּוֹיִם ׀
יהוה עַל הַשָּׁמַיִם כְּבוֹדוֹ: מִי כַּיהוה אֱלֹהֵינוּ הַמַּגְבִּיהִי לָשָׁבֶת: הַמַּשְׁפִּילִי
לִרְאוֹת בַּשָּׁמַיִם וּבָאָרֶץ: מְקִימִי מֵעָפָר דָּל מֵאַשְׁפֹּת יָרִים אֶבְיוֹן: לְהוֹשִׁיבִי
עִם־נְדִיבִים עִם נְדִיבֵי עַמּוֹ: מוֹשִׁיבִי ׀ עֲקֶרֶת הַבַּיִת אֵם־הַבָּנִים שְׂמֵחָה
הַלְלוּיָהּ:

בְּצֵאת יִשְׂרָאֵל מִמִּצְרָיִם בֵּית יַעֲקֹב מֵעַם לֹעֵז: הָיְתָה יְהוּדָה לְקָדְשׁוֹ יִשְׂרָאֵל **קיד**
מַמְשְׁלוֹתָיו: הַיָּם רָאָה וַיָּנֹס הַיַּרְדֵּן יִסֹּב לְאָחוֹר: הֶהָרִים רָקְדוּ כְאֵילִים גְּבָעוֹת
כִּבְנֵי־צֹאן: מַה־לְּךָ הַיָּם כִּי תָנוּס הַיַּרְדֵּן תִּסֹּב לְאָחוֹר: הֶהָרִים תִּרְקְדוּ כְאֵילִים
גְּבָעוֹת כִּבְנֵי־צֹאן: מִלִּפְנֵי אָדוֹן חוּלִי אָרֶץ מִלִּפְנֵי אֱלוֹהַּ יַעֲקֹב: הַהֹפְכִי הַצּוּר
אֲגַם־מָיִם חַלָּמִישׁ לְמַעְיְנוֹ־מָיִם:

לֹא לָנוּ יהוה לֹא לָנוּ כִּי־לְשִׁמְךָ תֵּן כָּבוֹד עַל־חַסְדְּךָ עַל־אֲמִתֶּךָ: לָמָּה יֹאמְרוּ **קטו**
הַגּוֹיִם אַיֵּה־נָא אֱלֹהֵיהֶם: וֵאלֹהֵינוּ בַשָּׁמָיִם כֹּל אֲשֶׁר־חָפֵץ עָשָׂה: עֲצַבֵּיהֶם
כֶּסֶף וְזָהָב מַעֲשֵׂה יְדֵי אָדָם: פֶּה־לָהֶם וְלֹא יְדַבֵּרוּ עֵינַיִם לָהֶם וְלֹא יִרְאוּ: אָזְנַיִם
לָהֶם וְלֹא יִשְׁמָעוּ אַף לָהֶם וְלֹא יְרִיחוּן: יְדֵיהֶם ׀ וְלֹא יְמִישׁוּן רַגְלֵיהֶם וְלֹא
יְהַלֵּכוּ לֹא־יֶהְגּוּ בִּגְרוֹנָם: כְּמוֹהֶם יִהְיוּ עֹשֵׂיהֶם כֹּל אֲשֶׁר־בֹּטֵחַ בָּהֶם: יִשְׂרָאֵל
בְּטַח בַּיהוה עֶזְרָם וּמָגִנָּם הוּא: בֵּית אַהֲרֹן בִּטְחוּ בַיהוה עֶזְרָם וּמָגִנָּם הוּא:
יִרְאֵי יהוה בִּטְחוּ בַיהוה עֶזְרָם וּמָגִנָּם הוּא: יהוה זְכָרָנוּ יְבָרֵךְ יְבָרֵךְ אֶת־בֵּית
יִשְׂרָאֵל יְבָרֵךְ אֶת־בֵּית אַהֲרֹן: יְבָרֵךְ יִרְאֵי יהוה הַקְּטַנִּים עִם־הַגְּדֹלִים: יֹסֵף
יהוה עֲלֵיכֶם עֲלֵיכֶם וְעַל־בְּנֵיכֶם: בְּרוּכִים אַתֶּם לַיהוה עֹשֵׂה שָׁמַיִם וָאָרֶץ:
הַשָּׁמַיִם שָׁמַיִם לַיהוה וְהָאָרֶץ נָתַן לִבְנֵי־אָדָם: לֹא הַמֵּתִים יְהַלְלוּ־יָהּ וְלֹא
כָּל־יֹרְדֵי דוּמָה: וַאֲנַחְנוּ ׀ נְבָרֵךְ יָהּ מֵעַתָּה וְעַד־עוֹלָם הַלְלוּיָהּ:

אָהַבְתִּי כִּי־יִשְׁמַע ׀ יהוה אֶת־קוֹלִי תַּחֲנוּנָי: כִּי־הִטָּה אָזְנוֹ לִי וּבְיָמַי אֶקְרָא: **קטז**
אֲפָפוּנִי ׀ חֶבְלֵי־מָוֶת וּמְצָרֵי שְׁאוֹל מְצָאוּנִי צָרָה וְיָגוֹן אֶמְצָא: וּבְשֵׁם־יהוה
אֶקְרָא אָנָּה יהוה מַלְּטָה נַפְשִׁי: חַנּוּן יהוה וְצַדִּיק וֵאלֹהֵינוּ מְרַחֵם: שֹׁמֵר

פְּתָאיִם יְהוָה דַּלּוֹתִי וְלִי יְהוֹשִֽׁיעַ: שׁוּבִי נַפְשִׁי לִמְנוּחָיְכִי כִּי־יְהוָה גָּמַל עָלָֽיְכִי: כִּי חִלַּצְתָּ נַפְשִׁי מִמָּוֶת אֶת־עֵינִי מִן־דִּמְעָה אֶת־רַגְלִי מִדֶּֽחִי: אֶתְהַלֵּךְ לִפְנֵי יְהוָה בְּאַרְצוֹת הַֽחַיִּים: הֶֽאֱמַנְתִּי כִּי אֲדַבֵּר אֲנִי עָנִיתִי מְאֹֽד: אֲנִי אָמַרְתִּי בְחָפְזִי כָּל־הָאָדָם כֹּזֵֽב: מָֽה־אָשִׁיב לַיהוָה כָּל־תַּגְמוּלוֹהִי עָלָֽי: כּוֹס־יְשׁוּעוֹת אֶשָּׂא וּבְשֵׁם יְהוָה אֶקְרָֽא: נְדָרַי לַיהוָה אֲשַׁלֵּם נֶגְדָה־נָּא לְכָל־עַמּֽוֹ: יָקָר בְּעֵינֵי יְהוָה הַמָּוְתָה לַחֲסִידָֽיו: אָֽנָּה יְהוָה כִּי־אֲנִי עַבְדֶּךָ אֲֽנִי־עַבְדְּךָ בֶּן־אֲמָתֶךָ פִּתַּחְתָּ לְמֽוֹסֵרָֽי: לְךָֽ־אֶזְבַּח זֶבַח תּוֹדָה וּבְשֵׁם יְהוָה אֶקְרָֽא: נְדָרַי לַיהוָה אֲשַׁלֵּם נֶגְדָה־נָּא לְכָל־עַמּֽוֹ: בְּחַצְרוֹת ׀ בֵּית יְהוָה בְּתוֹכֵכִי יְרֽוּשָׁלִַם הַֽלְלוּ־יָֽהּ:

קטז הַֽלְלוּ אֶת־יְהוָה כָּל־גּוֹיִם שַׁבְּחוּהוּ כָּל־הָֽאֻמִּים: כִּי גָבַר עָלֵינוּ ׀ חַסְדּוֹ וֶֽאֱמֶת־יְהוָה לְעוֹלָם הַֽלְלוּ־יָֽהּ:

קיח הוֹדוּ לַיהוָה כִּי־טוֹב כִּי לְעוֹלָם חַסְדּֽוֹ: יֹֽאמַר־נָא יִשְׂרָאֵל כִּי לְעוֹלָם חַסְדּֽוֹ: יֹֽאמְרוּ־נָא בֵית־אַהֲרֹן כִּי לְעוֹלָם חַסְדּֽוֹ: יֹֽאמְרוּ־נָא יִרְאֵי יְהוָה כִּי לְעוֹלָם חַסְדּֽוֹ: מִֽן־הַמֵּצַ֗ר קָרָאתִי יָּהּ עָנָנִי בַמֶּרְחָב יָֽהּ: יְהוָה לִי לֹא אִירָא מַה־יַּעֲשֶׂה לִי אָדָֽם: יְהוָה לִי בְּעֹזְרָי וַאֲנִי אֶרְאֶה בְשֹׂנְאָֽי: טוֹב לַחֲסוֹת בַּיהוָה מִבְּטֹחַ בָּֽאָדָֽם: טוֹב לַחֲסוֹת בַּיהוָה מִבְּטֹחַ בִּנְדִיבִֽים: כָּל־גּוֹיִם סְבָבוּנִי בְּשֵׁם יְהוָה כִּי אֲמִילַֽם: סַבּוּנִי גַם־סְבָבוּנִי בְּשֵׁם יְהוָה כִּי אֲמִילַֽם: סַבּוּנִי כִדְבוֹרִים דֹּֽעֲכוּ כְּאֵשׁ קוֹצִים בְּשֵׁם יְהוָה כִּי אֲמִילַֽם: דָּחֹה דְחִיתַנִי לִנְפֹּל וַיהוָה עֲזָרָֽנִי: עָזִּי וְזִמְרָת יָהּ וַֽיְהִי־לִי לִֽישׁוּעָֽה: קוֹל ׀ רִנָּה וִֽישׁוּעָה בְּאָהֳלֵי צַדִּיקִים יְמִין יְהוָה עֹ֥שָׂה חָֽיִל: יְמִין יְהוָה רֽוֹמֵמָה יְמִין יְהוָה עֹשָׂה חָֽיִל: לֹֽא־אָמוּת כִּֽי־אֶחְיֶה וַאֲסַפֵּר מַֽעֲשֵׂי יָֽהּ: יַסֹּר יִסְּרַנִּי יָּהּ וְלַמָּוֶת לֹא נְתָנָֽנִי: פִּתְחוּ־לִי שַׁעֲרֵי־צֶדֶק אָֽבֹא־בָם אוֹדֶה יָֽהּ: זֶֽה־הַשַּׁעַר לַיהוָה צַדִּיקִים יָבֹאוּ בֽוֹ: אוֹדְךָ כִּי עֲנִיתָנִי וַתְּהִי־לִי לִֽישׁוּעָֽה: אֶבֶן מָאֲסוּ הַבּוֹנִים הָֽיְתָה לְרֹאשׁ פִּנָּֽה: מֵאֵת יְהוָה הָיְתָה זֹּאת הִיא נִפְלָאת בְּעֵינֵֽינוּ: זֶה־הַיּוֹם עָשָׂה יְהוָה נָגִילָה וְנִשְׂמְחָה בֽוֹ: אָֽנָּא יְהוָה הוֹשִׁיעָה נָּא אָֽנָּא יְהוָה הַצְלִיחָה נָּֽא: בָּרוּךְ הַבָּא בְּשֵׁם יְהוָה בֵּרַכְנוּכֶם מִבֵּית יְהוָֽה: אֵל ׀ יְהוָה וַיָּאֶר לָנוּ אִסְרוּ־חַג בַּעֲבֹתִים עַד־קַרְנוֹת הַמִּזְבֵּֽחַ: אֵלִי אַתָּה וְאוֹדֶךָּ אֱלֹהַי אֲרֽוֹמְמֶֽךָּ: הוֹדוּ לַיהוָה כִּי־טוֹב כִּי לְעוֹלָם חַסְדּֽוֹ:

קיט אַשְׁרֵי תְמִֽימֵי־דָרֶךְ הַֽהֹלְכִים בְּתוֹרַת יְהוָֽה: אַשְׁרֵי נֹֽצְרֵי עֵֽדֹתָיו בְּכָל־לֵב יִדְרְשֽׁוּהוּ: אַף לֹֽא־פָעֲלוּ עַוְלָה בִּדְרָכָיו הָלָֽכוּ: אַתָּה צִוִּיתָה פִקֻּדֶיךָ לִשְׁמֹר מְאֹֽד: אַֽחֲלַי יִכֹּנוּ דְרָכָי לִשְׁמֹר חֻקֶּֽיךָ: אָז לֹא־אֵבוֹשׁ בְּהַבִּיטִי אֶל־כָּל־מִצְוֺתֶֽיךָ:

*כה לחודש

אוֹדְךָ בְּיֹשֶׁר לֵבָב בְּלָמְדִי מִשְׁפְּטֵי צִדְקֶךָ: אֶת־חֻקֶּיךָ אֶשְׁמֹר אַל־תַּעַזְבֵנִי
עַד־מְאֹד:

בַּמֶּה יְזַכֶּה־נַּעַר אֶת־אָרְחוֹ לִשְׁמֹר כִּדְבָרֶךָ: בְּכָל־לִבִּי דְרַשְׁתִּיךָ אַל־תַּשְׁגֵּנִי
מִמִּצְוֹתֶיךָ: בְּלִבִּי צָפַנְתִּי אִמְרָתֶךָ לְמַעַן לֹא אֶחֱטָא־לָךְ: בָּרוּךְ אַתָּה יְהֹוָה
לַמְּדֵנִי חֻקֶּיךָ: בִּשְׂפָתַי סִפַּרְתִּי כֹּל מִשְׁפְּטֵי־פִיךָ: בְּדֶרֶךְ עֵדְוֹתֶיךָ שַׂשְׂתִּי כְּעַל
כָּל־הוֹן: בְּפִקּוּדֶיךָ אָשִׂיחָה וְאַבִּיטָה אֹרְחֹתֶיךָ: בְּחֻקֹּתֶיךָ אֶשְׁתַּעֲשָׁע לֹא
אֶשְׁכַּח דְּבָרֶךָ:

גְּמֹל עַל־עַבְדְּךָ אֶחְיֶה וְאֶשְׁמְרָה דְבָרֶךָ: גַּל־עֵינַי וְאַבִּיטָה נִפְלָאוֹת מִתּוֹרָתֶךָ:
גֵּר אָנֹכִי בָאָרֶץ אַל־תַּסְתֵּר מִמֶּנִּי מִצְוֹתֶיךָ: גָּרְסָה נַפְשִׁי לְתַאֲבָה אֶל־מִשְׁפָּטֶיךָ
בְכָל־עֵת: גָּעַרְתָּ זֵדִים אֲרוּרִים הַשֹּׁגִים מִמִּצְוֹתֶיךָ: גַּל מֵעָלַי חֶרְפָּה וָבוּז כִּי
עֵדֹתֶיךָ נָצָרְתִּי: גַּם יָשְׁבוּ שָׂרִים בִּי נִדְבָּרוּ עַבְדְּךָ יָשִׂיחַ בְּחֻקֶּיךָ: גַּם־עֵדֹתֶיךָ
שַׁעֲשֻׁעָי אַנְשֵׁי עֲצָתִי:

דָּבְקָה לֶעָפָר נַפְשִׁי חַיֵּנִי כִּדְבָרֶךָ: דְּרָכַי סִפַּרְתִּי וַתַּעֲנֵנִי לַמְּדֵנִי חֻקֶּיךָ: דֶּרֶךְ־
פִּקּוּדֶיךָ הֲבִינֵנִי וְאָשִׂיחָה בְּנִפְלְאוֹתֶיךָ: דָּלְפָה נַפְשִׁי מִתּוּגָה קַיְּמֵנִי כִּדְבָרֶךָ:
דֶּרֶךְ־שֶׁקֶר הָסֵר מִמֶּנִּי וְתוֹרָתְךָ חָנֵּנִי: דֶּרֶךְ־אֱמוּנָה בָחָרְתִּי מִשְׁפָּטֶיךָ שִׁוִּיתִי:
דָּבַקְתִּי בְעֵדְוֹתֶיךָ יְהֹוָה אַל־תְּבִישֵׁנִי: דֶּרֶךְ־מִצְוֹתֶיךָ אָרוּץ כִּי תַרְחִיב לִבִּי:

הוֹרֵנִי יְהֹוָה דֶּרֶךְ חֻקֶּיךָ וְאֶצְּרֶנָּה עֵקֶב: הֲבִינֵנִי וְאֶצְּרָה תוֹרָתֶךָ וְאֶשְׁמְרֶנָּה
בְכָל־לֵב: הַדְרִיכֵנִי בִּנְתִיב מִצְוֹתֶיךָ כִּי־בוֹ חָפָצְתִּי: הַט־לִבִּי אֶל־עֵדְוֹתֶיךָ
וְאַל אֶל־בָּצַע: הַעֲבֵר עֵינַי מֵרְאוֹת שָׁוְא בִּדְרָכֶךָ חַיֵּנִי: הָקֵם לְעַבְדְּךָ אִמְרָתֶךָ
אֲשֶׁר לְיִרְאָתֶךָ: הַעֲבֵר חֶרְפָּתִי אֲשֶׁר יָגֹרְתִּי כִּי מִשְׁפָּטֶיךָ טוֹבִים: הִנֵּה תָּאַבְתִּי
לְפִקֻּדֶיךָ בְּצִדְקָתְךָ חַיֵּנִי:

וִיבֹאֻנִי חֲסָדֶךָ יְהֹוָה תְּשׁוּעָתְךָ כְּאִמְרָתֶךָ: וְאֶעֱנֶה חֹרְפִי דָבָר כִּי־בָטַחְתִּי
בִדְבָרֶךָ: וְאַל־תַּצֵּל מִפִּי דְבַר־אֱמֶת עַד־מְאֹד כִּי לְמִשְׁפָּטֶךָ יִחָלְתִּי: וְאֶשְׁמְרָה
תוֹרָתְךָ תָמִיד לְעוֹלָם וָעֶד: וְאֶתְהַלְּכָה בָרְחָבָה כִּי פִקֻּדֶיךָ דָרָשְׁתִּי: וַאֲדַבְּרָה
בְעֵדֹתֶיךָ נֶגֶד מְלָכִים וְלֹא אֵבוֹשׁ: וְאֶשְׁתַּעֲשַׁע בְּמִצְוֹתֶיךָ אֲשֶׁר אָהָבְתִּי: וְאֶשָּׂא־
כַפַּי אֶל־מִצְוֹתֶיךָ אֲשֶׁר אָהָבְתִּי וְאָשִׂיחָה בְחֻקֶּיךָ:

זְכֹר־דָּבָר לְעַבְדֶּךָ עַל אֲשֶׁר יִחַלְתָּנִי: זֹאת נֶחָמָתִי בְעָנְיִי כִּי אִמְרָתְךָ חִיָּתְנִי:
זֵדִים הֱלִיצֻנִי עַד־מְאֹד מִתּוֹרָתְךָ לֹא נָטִיתִי: זָכַרְתִּי מִשְׁפָּטֶיךָ מֵעוֹלָם ׀ יְהֹוָה
וָאֶתְנֶחָם: וְלְעָפָה אֲחָזַתְנִי מֵרְשָׁעִים עֹזְבֵי תּוֹרָתֶךָ: זְמִרוֹת הָיוּ־לִי חֻקֶּיךָ

בְּבֵית מְגוּרָי: זָכַרְתִּי בַלַּיְלָה שִׁמְךָ יהוה וָאֶשְׁמְרָה תּוֹרָתֶךָ: זֹאת הָיְתָה־לִּי
כִּי פִקֻּדֶיךָ נָצָרְתִּי:

חֶלְקִי יהוה אָמַרְתִּי לִשְׁמֹר דְּבָרֶיךָ: חִלִּיתִי פָנֶיךָ בְכָל־לֵב חָנֵּנִי כְּאִמְרָתֶךָ:
חִשַּׁבְתִּי דְרָכָי וָאָשִׁיבָה רַגְלַי אֶל־עֵדֹתֶיךָ: חַשְׁתִּי וְלֹא הִתְמַהְמָהְתִּי לִשְׁמֹר
מִצְוֹתֶיךָ: חֶבְלֵי רְשָׁעִים עִוְּדֻנִי תּוֹרָתְךָ לֹא שָׁכָחְתִּי: חֲצוֹת־לַיְלָה אָקוּם
לְהוֹדוֹת לָךְ עַל מִשְׁפְּטֵי צִדְקֶךָ: חָבֵר אָנִי לְכָל־אֲשֶׁר יְרֵאוּךָ וּלְשֹׁמְרֵי פִּקּוּדֶיךָ:
חַסְדְּךָ יהוה מָלְאָה הָאָרֶץ חֻקֶּיךָ לַמְּדֵנִי:

טוֹב עָשִׂיתָ עִם־עַבְדְּךָ יהוה כִּדְבָרֶךָ: טוּב טַעַם וָדַעַת לַמְּדֵנִי כִּי בְמִצְוֹתֶיךָ
הֶאֱמָנְתִּי: טֶרֶם אֶעֱנֶה אֲנִי שֹׁגֵג וְעַתָּה אִמְרָתְךָ שָׁמָרְתִּי: טוֹב־אַתָּה וּמֵטִיב
לַמְּדֵנִי חֻקֶּיךָ: טָפְלוּ עָלַי שֶׁקֶר זֵדִים אֲנִי בְּכָל־לֵב ׀ אֶצֹּר פִּקּוּדֶיךָ: טָפַשׁ כַּחֵלֶב
לִבָּם אֲנִי תּוֹרָתְךָ שִׁעֲשָׁעְתִּי: טוֹב־לִי כִי־עֻנֵּיתִי לְמַעַן אֶלְמַד חֻקֶּיךָ: טוֹב־לִי
תוֹרַת־פִּיךָ מֵאַלְפֵי זָהָב וָכָסֶף:

יָדֶיךָ עָשׂוּנִי וַיְכוֹנְנוּנִי הֲבִינֵנִי וְאֶלְמְדָה מִצְוֹתֶיךָ: יְרֵאֶיךָ יִרְאוּנִי וְיִשְׂמָחוּ כִּי
לִדְבָרְךָ יִחָלְתִּי: יָדַעְתִּי יהוה כִּי־צֶדֶק מִשְׁפָּטֶיךָ וֶאֱמוּנָה עִנִּיתָנִי: יְהִי־נָא
חַסְדְּךָ לְנַחֲמֵנִי כְּאִמְרָתְךָ לְעַבְדֶּךָ: יְבֹאוּנִי רַחֲמֶיךָ וְאֶחְיֶה כִּי־תוֹרָתְךָ שַׁעֲשֻׁעָי: וְיֹדְעֵי
יֵבֹשׁוּ זֵדִים כִּי־שֶׁקֶר עִוְּתוּנִי אֲנִי אָשִׂיחַ בְּפִקּוּדֶיךָ: יָשׁוּבוּ לִי יְרֵאֶיךָ וְיֹדְעֵי
עֵדֹתֶיךָ: יְהִי־לִבִּי תָמִים בְּחֻקֶּיךָ לְמַעַן לֹא אֵבוֹשׁ:

כָּלְתָה לִתְשׁוּעָתְךָ נַפְשִׁי לִדְבָרְךָ יִחָלְתִּי: כָּלוּ עֵינַי לְאִמְרָתֶךָ לֵאמֹר מָתַי
תְּנַחֲמֵנִי: כִּי־הָיִיתִי כְּנֹאד בְּקִיטוֹר חֻקֶּיךָ לֹא שָׁכָחְתִּי: כַּמָּה יְמֵי־עַבְדֶּךָ מָתַי
תַּעֲשֶׂה בְרֹדְפַי מִשְׁפָּט: כָּרוּ־לִי זֵדִים שִׁיחוֹת אֲשֶׁר לֹא כְתוֹרָתֶךָ: כָּל־מִצְוֹתֶיךָ
אֱמוּנָה שֶׁקֶר רְדָפוּנִי עָזְרֵנִי: כִּמְעַט כִּלּוּנִי בָאָרֶץ וַאֲנִי לֹא־עָזַבְתִּי פִקֻּדֶיךָ:
כְּחַסְדְּךָ חַיֵּנִי וְאֶשְׁמְרָה עֵדוּת פִּיךָ:

לְעוֹלָם יהוה דְּבָרְךָ נִצָּב בַּשָּׁמָיִם: לְדֹר וָדֹר אֱמוּנָתֶךָ כּוֹנַנְתָּ אֶרֶץ וַתַּעֲמֹד:
לְמִשְׁפָּטֶיךָ עָמְדוּ הַיּוֹם כִּי הַכֹּל עֲבָדֶיךָ: לוּלֵי תוֹרָתְךָ שַׁעֲשֻׁעָי אָז אָבַדְתִּי
בְעָנְיִי: לְעוֹלָם לֹא־אֶשְׁכַּח פִּקּוּדֶיךָ כִּי בָם חִיִּיתָנִי: לְךָ־אֲנִי הוֹשִׁיעֵנִי כִּי פִקּוּדֶיךָ
דָרָשְׁתִּי: לִי קִוּוּ רְשָׁעִים לְאַבְּדֵנִי עֵדֹתֶיךָ אֶתְבּוֹנָן: לְכָל־תִּכְלָה רָאִיתִי קֵץ
רְחָבָה מִצְוָתְךָ מְאֹד:

* מָה־אָהַבְתִּי תוֹרָתֶךָ כָּל־הַיּוֹם הִיא שִׂיחָתִי: מֵאֹיְבַי תְּחַכְּמֵנִי מִצְוֹתֶךָ כִּי לְעוֹלָם
הִיא־לִי: מִכָּל־מְלַמְּדַי הִשְׂכַּלְתִּי כִּי עֵדְוֹתֶיךָ שִׂיחָה לִי: מִזְּקֵנִים אֶתְבּוֹנָן כִּי

*כ׳ לַחֹדֶשׁ

פִּקּוּדֶיךָ נָצָרְתִּי: מִכָּל־אֹרַח רָע כָּלִאתִי רַגְלָי לְמַעַן אֶשְׁמֹר דְּבָרֶךָ: מִמִּשְׁפָּטֶיךָ
לֹא־סָרְתִּי כִּי־אַתָּה הוֹרֵתָנִי: מַה־נִּמְלְצוּ לְחִכִּי אִמְרָתֶךָ מִדְּבַשׁ לְפִי: מִפִּקּוּדֶיךָ
אֶתְבּוֹנָן עַל־כֵּן שָׂנֵאתִי ׀ כָּל־אֹרַח שָׁקֶר:

נֵר־לְרַגְלִי דְבָרֶךָ וְאוֹר לִנְתִיבָתִי: נִשְׁבַּעְתִּי וָאֲקַיֵּמָה לִשְׁמֹר מִשְׁפְּטֵי צִדְקֶךָ:
נַעֲנֵיתִי עַד־מְאֹד יְהוָה חַיֵּנִי כִדְבָרֶךָ: נִדְבוֹת פִּי רְצֵה־נָא יְהוָה וּמִשְׁפָּטֶיךָ
לַמְּדֵנִי: נַפְשִׁי בְכַפִּי תָמִיד וְתוֹרָתְךָ לֹא שָׁכָחְתִּי: נָתְנוּ רְשָׁעִים פַּח לִי וּמִפִּקּוּדֶיךָ
לֹא תָעִיתִי: נָחַלְתִּי עֵדְוֺתֶיךָ לְעוֹלָם כִּי־שְׂשׂוֹן לִבִּי הֵמָּה: נָטִיתִי לִבִּי לַעֲשׂוֹת
חֻקֶּיךָ לְעוֹלָם עֵקֶב:

סֵעֲפִים שָׂנֵאתִי וְתוֹרָתְךָ אָהָבְתִּי: סִתְרִי וּמָגִנִּי אָתָּה לִדְבָרְךָ יִחָלְתִּי: סוּרוּ
מִמֶּנִּי מְרֵעִים וְאֶצְּרָה מִצְוֺת אֱלֹהָי: סָמְכֵנִי כְאִמְרָתְךָ וְאֶחְיֶה וְאַל־תְּבִישֵׁנִי
מִשִּׂבְרִי: סְעָדֵנִי וְאִוָּשֵׁעָה וְאֶשְׁעָה בְחֻקֶּיךָ תָמִיד: סָלִיתָ כָּל־שׁוֹגִים מֵחֻקֶּיךָ
כִּי־שֶׁקֶר תַּרְמִיתָם: סִגִים הִשְׁבַּתָּ כָל־רִשְׁעֵי־אָרֶץ לָכֵן אָהַבְתִּי עֵדֹתֶיךָ:
סָמַר מִפַּחְדְּךָ בְשָׂרִי וּמִמִּשְׁפָּטֶיךָ יָרֵאתִי:

עָשִׂיתִי מִשְׁפָּט וָצֶדֶק בַּל־תַּנִּיחֵנִי לְעֹשְׁקָי: עֲרֹב עַבְדְּךָ לְטוֹב אַל־יַעַשְׁקֻנִי
זֵדִים: עֵינַי כָּלוּ לִישׁוּעָתֶךָ וּלְאִמְרַת צִדְקֶךָ: עֲשֵׂה עִם־עַבְדְּךָ כְחַסְדֶּךָ וְחֻקֶּיךָ
לַמְּדֵנִי: עַבְדְּךָ־אָנִי הֲבִינֵנִי וְאֵדְעָה עֵדֹתֶיךָ: עֵת לַעֲשׂוֹת לַיהוָה הֵפֵרוּ תּוֹרָתֶךָ:
עַל־כֵּן אָהַבְתִּי מִצְוֺתֶיךָ מִזָּהָב וּמִפָּז: עַל־כֵּן ׀ כָּל־פִּקּוּדֵי כֹל יִשָּׁרְתִּי כָּל־אֹרַח
שֶׁקֶר שָׂנֵאתִי:

פְּלָאוֹת עֵדְוֺתֶיךָ עַל־כֵּן נְצָרָתַם נַפְשִׁי: פֵּתַח־דְּבָרֶיךָ יָאִיר מֵבִין פְּתָיִים:
פִּי־פָעַרְתִּי וָאֶשְׁאָפָה כִּי לְמִצְוֺתֶיךָ יָאָבְתִּי: פְּנֵה־אֵלַי וְחָנֵּנִי כְּמִשְׁפָּט לְאֹהֲבֵי
שְׁמֶךָ: פְּעָמַי הָכֵן בְּאִמְרָתֶךָ וְאַל־תַּשְׁלֶט־בִּי כָל־אָוֶן: פְּדֵנִי מֵעֹשֶׁק אָדָם
וְאֶשְׁמְרָה פִּקּוּדֶיךָ: פָּנֶיךָ הָאֵר בְּעַבְדֶּךָ וְלַמְּדֵנִי אֶת־חֻקֶּיךָ: פַּלְגֵי־מַיִם יָרְדוּ
עֵינָי עַל לֹא־שָׁמְרוּ תוֹרָתֶךָ:

צַדִּיק אַתָּה יְהוָה וְיָשָׁר מִשְׁפָּטֶיךָ: צִוִּיתָ צֶדֶק עֵדֹתֶיךָ וֶאֱמוּנָה מְאֹד: צִמְּתַתְנִי
קִנְאָתִי כִּי־שָׁכְחוּ דְבָרֶיךָ צָרָי: צְרוּפָה אִמְרָתְךָ מְאֹד וְעַבְדְּךָ אֲהֵבָהּ: צָעִיר
אָנֹכִי וְנִבְזֶה פִּקֻּדֶיךָ לֹא שָׁכָחְתִּי: צִדְקָתְךָ צֶדֶק לְעוֹלָם וְתוֹרָתְךָ אֱמֶת: צַר־
וּמָצוֹק מְצָאוּנִי מִצְוֺתֶיךָ שַׁעֲשֻׁעָי: צֶדֶק עֵדְוֺתֶיךָ לְעוֹלָם הֲבִינֵנִי וְאֶחְיֶה:

קָרָאתִי בְכָל־לֵב עֲנֵנִי יְהוָה חֻקֶּיךָ אֶצֹּרָה: קְרָאתִיךָ הוֹשִׁיעֵנִי וְאֶשְׁמְרָה
עֵדֹתֶיךָ: קִדַּמְתִּי בַנֶּשֶׁף וָאֲשַׁוֵּעָה לִדְבָרְךָ יִחָלְתִּי: קִדְּמוּ עֵינַי אַשְׁמֻרוֹת לִדְבָר

לָשִׂיחַ בְּאִמְרָתֶךָ: קוֹלִי שִׁמְעָה כְחַסְדֶּךָ יְהוָה כְּמִשְׁפָּטֶךָ חַיֵּנִי: קָרְבוּ רֹדְפֵי
זִמָּה מִתּוֹרָתְךָ רָחָקוּ: קָרוֹב אַתָּה יְהוָה וְכָל-מִצְוֺתֶיךָ אֱמֶת: קֶדֶם יָדַעְתִּי
מֵעֵדֹתֶיךָ כִּי לְעוֹלָם יְסַדְתָּם:
רְאֵה-עָנְיִי וְחַלְּצֵנִי כִּי-תוֹרָתְךָ לֹא שָׁכָחְתִּי: רִיבָה רִיבִי וּגְאָלֵנִי לְאִמְרָתְךָ חַיֵּנִי:
רָחוֹק מֵרְשָׁעִים יְשׁוּעָה כִּי-חֻקֶּיךָ לֹא דָרָשׁוּ: רַחֲמֶיךָ רַבִּים יְהוָה כְּמִשְׁפָּטֶיךָ
חַיֵּנִי: רַבִּים רֹדְפַי וְצָרָי מֵעֵדְוֺתֶיךָ לֹא נָטִיתִי: רָאִיתִי בֹגְדִים וָאֶתְקוֹטָטָה
אֲשֶׁר אִמְרָתְךָ לֹא שָׁמָרוּ: רְאֵה כִּי-פִקּוּדֶיךָ אָהָבְתִּי יְהוָה כְּחַסְדְּךָ חַיֵּנִי:
רֹאשׁ-דְּבָרְךָ אֱמֶת וּלְעוֹלָם כָּל-מִשְׁפַּט צִדְקֶךָ:
שָׂרִים רְדָפוּנִי חִנָּם וּמִדְּבָרְךָ פָּחַד לִבִּי: שָׂשׂ אָנֹכִי עַל-אִמְרָתֶךָ כְּמוֹצֵא שָׁלָל   וּמִדְּבָרְךָ
רָב: שֶׁקֶר שָׂנֵאתִי וַאֲתַעֵבָה תּוֹרָתְךָ אָהָבְתִּי: שֶׁבַע בַּיּוֹם הִלַּלְתִּיךָ עַל מִשְׁפְּטֵי
צִדְקֶךָ: שָׁלוֹם רָב לְאֹהֲבֵי תוֹרָתֶךָ וְאֵין-לָמוֹ מִכְשׁוֹל: שִׂבַּרְתִּי לִישׁוּעָתְךָ
יְהוָה וּמִצְוֺתֶיךָ עָשִׂיתִי: שָׁמְרָה נַפְשִׁי עֵדֹתֶיךָ וָאֹהֲבֵם מְאֹד: שָׁמַרְתִּי פִקּוּדֶיךָ
וְעֵדֹתֶיךָ כִּי כָל-דְּרָכַי נֶגְדֶּךָ:
תִּקְרַב רִנָּתִי לְפָנֶיךָ יְהוָה כִּדְבָרְךָ הֲבִינֵנִי: תָּבוֹא תְּחִנָּתִי לְפָנֶיךָ כְּאִמְרָתְךָ
הַצִּילֵנִי: תַּבַּעְנָה שְׂפָתַי תְּהִלָּה כִּי תְלַמְּדֵנִי חֻקֶּיךָ: תַּעַן לְשׁוֹנִי אִמְרָתֶךָ כִּי
כָל-מִצְוֺתֶיךָ צֶּדֶק: תְּהִי-יָדְךָ לְעָזְרֵנִי כִּי פִקּוּדֶיךָ בָחָרְתִּי: תָּאַבְתִּי לִישׁוּעָתְךָ
יְהוָה וְתוֹרָתְךָ שַׁעֲשֻׁעָי: תְּחִי-נַפְשִׁי וּתְהַלְלֶךָּ וּמִשְׁפָּטֶךָ יַעְזְרֻנִי: תָּעִיתִי כְּשֶׂה
אֹבֵד בַּקֵּשׁ עַבְדֶּךָ כִּי מִצְוֺתֶיךָ לֹא שָׁכָחְתִּי:

קכ *שִׁיר הַמַּעֲלוֹת אֶל-יְהוָה בַּצָּרָתָה לִּי קָרָאתִי וַיַּעֲנֵנִי: יְהוָה הַצִּילָה נַפְשִׁי
מִשְּׂפַת-שֶׁקֶר מִלָּשׁוֹן רְמִיָּה: מַה-יִּתֵּן לְךָ וּמַה-יֹּסִיף לָךְ לָשׁוֹן רְמִיָּה: חִצֵּי
גִבּוֹר שְׁנוּנִים עִם גַּחֲלֵי רְתָמִים: אוֹיָה-לִי כִּי-גַרְתִּי מֶשֶׁךְ שָׁכַנְתִּי עִם-אָהֳלֵי
קֵדָר: רַבַּת שָׁכְנָה-לָּהּ נַפְשִׁי עִם שׂוֹנֵא שָׁלוֹם: אֲנִי-שָׁלוֹם וְכִי אֲדַבֵּר הֵמָּה
לַמִּלְחָמָה:

קכא שִׁיר לַמַּעֲלוֹת אֶשָּׂא עֵינַי אֶל-הֶהָרִים מֵאַיִן יָבֹא עֶזְרִי: עֶזְרִי מֵעִם יְהוָה עֹשֵׂה
שָׁמַיִם וָאָרֶץ: אַל-יִתֵּן לַמּוֹט רַגְלֶךָ אַל-יָנוּם שֹׁמְרֶךָ: הִנֵּה לֹא-יָנוּם וְלֹא
יִישָׁן שׁוֹמֵר יִשְׂרָאֵל: יְהוָה שֹׁמְרֶךָ יְהוָה צִלְּךָ עַל-יַד יְמִינֶךָ: יוֹמָם הַשֶּׁמֶשׁ
לֹא-יַכֶּכָּה וְיָרֵחַ בַּלָּיְלָה: יְהוָה יִשְׁמָרְךָ מִכָּל-רָע יִשְׁמֹר אֶת-נַפְשֶׁךָ: יְהוָה
יִשְׁמָר-צֵאתְךָ וּבוֹאֶךָ מֵעַתָּה וְעַד-עוֹלָם:

קכב שִׁיר הַמַּעֲלוֹת לְדָוִד שָׂמַחְתִּי בְּאֹמְרִים לִי בֵּית יְהוָה נֵלֵךְ: עֹמְדוֹת הָיוּ רַגְלֵינוּ

בִּשְׁעָרַ֗יִךְ יְר֫וּשָׁלִָ֥ם: יְרוּשָׁלִַ֥ם הַבְּנוּיָ֑ה כְּ֝עִ֗יר שֶׁחֻבְּרָה־לָּ֥הּ יַחְדָּֽו: שֶׁשָּׁ֨ם עָל֪וּ
שְׁבָטִ֡ים שִׁבְטֵי־יָ֭הּ עֵד֣וּת לְיִשְׂרָאֵ֑ל לְ֝הֹד֗וֹת לְשֵׁ֣ם יְהֹוָֽה: כִּ֤י שָׁ֨מָּה ׀ יָשְׁב֣וּ
כִסְא֣וֹת לְמִשְׁפָּ֑ט כִּ֝סְא֗וֹת לְבֵ֣ית דָּוִֽד: שַׁ֭אֲלוּ שְׁל֣וֹם יְרוּשָׁלִָ֑ם יִ֝שְׁלָ֗יוּ אֹהֲבָֽיִךְ:
יְהִֽי־שָׁל֥וֹם בְּחֵילֵ֑ךְ שַׁ֝לְוָ֗ה בְּאַרְמְנוֹתָֽיִךְ: לְ֭מַעַן אַחַ֣י וְרֵעָ֑י אֲדַבְּרָה־נָּ֖א שָׁל֣וֹם
בָּֽךְ: לְ֭מַעַן בֵּית־יְהֹוָ֣ה אֱלֹהֵ֑ינוּ אֲבַקְשָׁ֖ה ט֣וֹב לָֽךְ:

קכג שִׁ֗יר הַֽמַּ֫עֲל֥וֹת אֵ֭לֶיךָ נָשָׂ֣אתִי אֶת־עֵינַ֑י הַ֝יֹּשְׁבִ֗י בַּשָּׁמָֽיִם: הִנֵּ֨ה כְעֵינֵ֪י עֲבָדִ֡ים
אֶל־יַ֤ד אֲֽדוֹנֵיהֶ֗ם כְּעֵינֵ֣י שִׁפְחָה֮ אֶל־יַ֪ד גְּבִ֫רְתָּ֥הּ כֵּ֣ן עֵ֭ינֵינוּ אֶל־יְהֹוָ֣ה אֱלֹהֵ֑ינוּ
עַ֝֗ד שֶׁיְּחׇנֵּֽנוּ: חׇנֵּ֣נוּ יְהֹוָ֣ה חׇנֵּ֑נוּ כִּי־רַ֝֗ב שָׂבַ֥עְנוּ בֽוּז: רַבַּת֮ שָֽׂבְעָה־לָּ֢הּ נַ֫פְשֵׁ֥נוּ
לְגַאֵי יוֹנִים הַלַּ֥עַג הַשַּׁאֲנַנִּ֑ים הַ֝בּ֗וּז לִגְאֵ֥י(יוֹנִֽים:

קכד שִׁ֥יר הַֽמַּעֲל֗וֹת לְדָ֫וִ֥ד לוּלֵ֣י יְ֭הֹוָה שֶׁהָ֣יָה לָ֑נוּ יֹאמַר־נָ֝֗א יִשְׂרָאֵֽל: לוּלֵ֣י יְ֭הֹוָה
שֶׁהָ֣יָה לָ֑נוּ בְּק֖וּם עָלֵ֣ינוּ אָדָֽם: אֲ֭זַי חַיִּ֣ים בְּלָע֑וּנוּ בַּחֲר֖וֹת אַפָּ֣ם בָּֽנוּ: אֲ֭זַי הַמַּ֣יִם
שְׁטָפ֑וּנוּ נַ֝֗חְלָה עָבַ֥ר עַל־נַפְשֵֽׁנוּ: אֲ֭זַי עָבַ֣ר עַל־נַפְשֵׁ֑נוּ הַ֝מַּ֗יִם הַזֵּֽידוֹנִֽים: בָּר֥וּךְ
יְהֹוָ֑ה שֶׁלֹּ֥א נְתָנָ֥נוּ טֶ֝֗רֶף לְשִׁנֵּיהֶֽם: נַפְשֵׁ֗נוּ כְּצִפּ֥וֹר נִמְלְטָה֮ מִפַּ֢ח י֫וֹקְשִׁ֥ים הַפַּ֥ח
נִשְׁבָּ֗ר וַאֲנַ֥חְנוּ נִמְלָֽטְנוּ: עֶ֭זְרֵנוּ בְּשֵׁ֣ם יְהֹוָ֑ה עֹ֝שֵׂ֗ה שָׁמַ֥יִם וָאָֽרֶץ:

קכה שִׁ֗יר הַֽמַּ֫עֲל֥וֹת הַבֹּטְחִ֥ים בַּיהֹוָ֑ה כְּֽהַר־צִיּ֥וֹן לֹא־יִ֝מּ֗וֹט לְעוֹלָ֥ם יֵשֵֽׁב: יְֽרוּשָׁלִַ֗ם
הָרִים֮ סָבִ֢יב לָ֥הּ וַֽיהֹוָ֗ה סָבִ֥יב לְעַמּ֑וֹ מֵ֝עַתָּ֗ה וְעַד־עוֹלָֽם: כִּ֤י לֹ֪א יָנ֡וּחַ שֵׁ֤בֶט
הָרֶ֗שַׁע עַל֮ גּוֹרַ֢ל הַֽצַּדִּ֫יקִ֥ים לְמַ֡עַן לֹא־יִשְׁלְח֖וּ הַצַּדִּיקִ֗ים בְּעַוְלָ֥תָה יְדֵיהֶֽם:
הֵיטִ֣יבָה יְ֭הֹוָה לַטּוֹבִ֑ים וְ֝לִֽישָׁרִ֗ים בְּלִבּוֹתָֽם: וְהַמַּטִּ֤ים עֲ֝קַלְקַלּוֹתָ֗ם יוֹלִיכֵ֣ם יְהֹוָה֮
אֶת־פֹּעֲלֵ֪י הָ֫אָ֥וֶן שָׁ֝ל֗וֹם עַל־יִשְׂרָאֵֽל:

קכו שִׁ֗יר הַֽמַּ֫עֲל֥וֹת בְּשׁ֣וּב יְ֭הֹוָה אֶת־שִׁיבַ֣ת צִיּ֑וֹן הָ֝יִ֗ינוּ כְּחֹלְמִֽים: אָ֤ז יִמָּלֵ֪א שְׂח֡וֹק
פִּינוּ֮ וּלְשׁוֹנֵ֢נוּ רִ֫נָּ֥ה אָ֭ז יֹאמְר֣וּ בַגּוֹיִ֑ם הִגְדִּ֥יל יְ֝הֹוָ֗ה לַעֲשׂ֥וֹת עִם־אֵֽלֶּה: הִגְדִּ֣יל
שביתנו יְ֭הֹוָה לַעֲשׂ֣וֹת עִמָּ֑נוּ הָ֝יִ֗ינוּ שְׂמֵחִֽים: שׁוּבָ֣ה יְ֭הֹוָה אֶת־*שְׁבִיתֵ֑נוּ* כַּאֲפִיקִ֥ים בַּנֶּֽגֶב:
הַזֹּרְעִ֥ים בְּדִמְעָ֗ה בְּרִנָּ֥ה יִקְצֹֽרוּ: הָ֘ל֤וֹךְ יֵלֵ֨ךְ ׀ וּבָכֹה֮ נֹשֵׂ֢א מֶֽשֶׁךְ־הַ֫זָּ֥רַע בֹּא־יָב֥וֹא
בְרִנָּ֑ה נֹ֝שֵׂ֗א אֲלֻמֹּתָֽיו:

קכז שִׁ֥יר הַֽמַּעֲל֗וֹת לִשְׁלֹ֫מֹ֥ה אִם־יְהֹוָ֤ה ׀ לֹא־יִבְנֶ֬ה בַ֗יִת שָׁ֤וְא ׀ עָמְל֣וּ בוֹנָ֣יו בּ֑וֹ אִם־
יְהֹוָ֥ה לֹֽא־יִשְׁמׇר־עִ֝֗יר שָׁ֤וְא ׀ שָׁקַ֬ד שׁוֹמֵֽר: שָׁ֤וְא לָכֶ֨ם ׀ מַשְׁכִּ֪ימֵי ק֡וּם מְאַֽחֲרֵי־
שֶׁ֗בֶת אֹֽכְלֵ֗י לֶ֣חֶם הָעֲצָבִ֑ים כֵּ֤ן יִתֵּ֖ן לִֽידִיד֣וֹ שֵׁנָֽא: הִנֵּ֤ה נַחֲלַ֣ת יְהֹוָ֣ה בָּנִ֑ים
שָׂ֝כָ֗ר פְּרִ֣י הַבָּֽטֶן: כְּחִצִּ֥ים בְּיַד־גִּבּ֑וֹר כֵּ֝֗ן בְּנֵ֣י הַנְּעוּרִֽים: אַשְׁרֵ֤י הַגֶּ֗בֶר אֲשֶׁ֤ר מִלֵּ֥א
אֶת־אַשְׁפָּת֗וֹ מֵ֫הֶ֥ם לֹֽא־יֵבֹ֑שׁוּ כִּֽי־יְדַבְּר֖וּ אֶת־אוֹיְבִ֣ים בַּשָּֽׁעַר:

קכח שִׁיר הַמַּעֲלוֹת אַשְׁרֵי כָּל־יְרֵא יְהוָה הַהֹלֵךְ בִּדְרָכָיו: יְגִיעַ כַּפֶּיךָ כִּי תֹאכֵל
אַשְׁרֶיךָ וְטוֹב לָךְ: אֶשְׁתְּךָ ׀ כְּגֶפֶן פֹּרִיָּה בְּיַרְכְּתֵי בֵיתֶךָ בָּנֶיךָ כִּשְׁתִלֵי זֵיתִים
סָבִיב לְשֻׁלְחָנֶךָ: הִנֵּה כִי־כֵן יְבֹרַךְ גָּבֶר יְרֵא יְהוָה: יְבָרֶכְךָ יְהוָה מִצִּיּוֹן וּרְאֵה
בְּטוּב יְרוּשָׁלָ͏ִם כֹּל יְמֵי חַיֶּיךָ: וּרְאֵה־בָנִים לְבָנֶיךָ שָׁלוֹם עַל־יִשְׂרָאֵל:

קכט שִׁיר הַמַּעֲלוֹת רַבַּת צְרָרוּנִי מִנְּעוּרַי יֹאמַר־נָא יִשְׂרָאֵל: רַבַּת צְרָרוּנִי מִנְּעוּרָי
גַּם לֹא־יָכְלוּ לִי: עַל־גַּבִּי חָרְשׁוּ חֹרְשִׁים הֶאֱרִיכוּ לְמַעֲנוֹתָם: יְהוָה צַדִּיק קִצֵּץ לְמַעֲנִיתָם
עֲבוֹת רְשָׁעִים: יֵבֹשׁוּ וְיִסֹּגוּ אָחוֹר כֹּל שֹׂנְאֵי צִיּוֹן: יִהְיוּ כַּחֲצִיר גַּגּוֹת שֶׁקַּדְמַת
שָׁלַף יָבֵשׁ: שֶׁלֹּא מִלֵּא כַפּוֹ קוֹצֵר וְחִצְנוֹ מְעַמֵּר: וְלֹא אָמְרוּ ׀ הָעֹבְרִים בִּרְכַּת־
יְהוָה אֲלֵיכֶם בֵּרַכְנוּ אֶתְכֶם בְּשֵׁם יְהוָה:

קל שִׁיר הַמַּעֲלוֹת מִמַּעֲמַקִּים קְרָאתִיךָ יְהוָה: אֲדֹנָי שִׁמְעָה בְקוֹלִי תִּהְיֶינָה
אָזְנֶיךָ קַשֻּׁבוֹת לְקוֹל תַּחֲנוּנָי: אִם־עֲוֹנוֹת תִּשְׁמָר־יָהּ אֲדֹנָי מִי יַעֲמֹד: כִּי־עִמְּךָ
הַסְּלִיחָה לְמַעַן תִּוָּרֵא: קִוִּיתִי יְהוָה קִוְּתָה נַפְשִׁי וְלִדְבָרוֹ הוֹחָלְתִּי: נַפְשִׁי לַאדֹנָי
מִשֹּׁמְרִים לַבֹּקֶר שֹׁמְרִים לַבֹּקֶר: יַחֵל יִשְׂרָאֵל אֶל־יְהוָה כִּי־עִם־יְהוָה הַחֶסֶד
וְהַרְבֵּה עִמּוֹ פְדוּת: וְהוּא יִפְדֶּה אֶת־יִשְׂרָאֵל מִכֹּל עֲוֹנֹתָיו:

קלא שִׁיר הַמַּעֲלוֹת לְדָוִד יְהוָה ׀ לֹא־גָבַהּ לִבִּי וְלֹא־רָמוּ עֵינַי וְלֹא־הִלַּכְתִּי ׀ בִּגְדֹלוֹת
וּבְנִפְלָאוֹת מִמֶּנִּי: אִם־לֹא שִׁוִּיתִי ׀ וְדוֹמַמְתִּי נַפְשִׁי כְּגָמֻל עֲלֵי אִמּוֹ כַּגָּמֻל עָלַי
נַפְשִׁי: יַחֵל יִשְׂרָאֵל אֶל־יְהוָה מֵעַתָּה וְעַד־עוֹלָם:

קלב שִׁיר הַמַּעֲלוֹת זְכוֹר־יְהוָה לְדָוִד אֵת כָּל־עֻנּוֹתוֹ: אֲשֶׁר נִשְׁבַּע לַיהוָה נָדַר
לַאֲבִיר יַעֲקֹב: אִם־אָבֹא בְּאֹהֶל בֵּיתִי אִם־אֶעֱלֶה עַל־עֶרֶשׂ יְצוּעָי: אִם־אֶתֵּן
שְׁנַת לְעֵינָי לְעַפְעַפַּי תְּנוּמָה: עַד־אֶמְצָא מָקוֹם לַיהוָה מִשְׁכָּנוֹת לַאֲבִיר יַעֲקֹב:
הִנֵּה־שְׁמַעֲנוּהָ בְאֶפְרָתָה מְצָאנוּהָ בִּשְׂדֵי־יָעַר: נָבוֹאָה לְמִשְׁכְּנוֹתָיו נִשְׁתַּחֲוֶה
לַהֲדֹם רַגְלָיו: קוּמָה יְהוָה לִמְנוּחָתֶךָ אַתָּה וַאֲרוֹן עֻזֶּךָ: כֹּהֲנֶיךָ יִלְבְּשׁוּ־צֶדֶק
וַחֲסִידֶיךָ יְרַנֵּנוּ: בַּעֲבוּר דָּוִד עַבְדֶּךָ אַל־תָּשֵׁב פְּנֵי מְשִׁיחֶךָ: נִשְׁבַּע־יְהוָה ׀ לְדָוִד
אֱמֶת לֹא־יָשׁוּב מִמֶּנָּה מִפְּרִי בִטְנְךָ אָשִׁית לְכִסֵּא־לָךְ: אִם־יִשְׁמְרוּ בָנֶיךָ ׀ בְּרִיתִי
וְעֵדֹתִי זוֹ אֲלַמְּדֵם גַּם־בְּנֵיהֶם עֲדֵי־עַד יֵשְׁבוּ לְכִסֵּא־לָךְ: כִּי־בָחַר יְהוָה בְּצִיּוֹן
אִוָּהּ לְמוֹשָׁב לוֹ: זֹאת־מְנוּחָתִי עֲדֵי־עַד פֹּה־אֵשֵׁב כִּי אִוִּתִיהָ: צֵידָהּ בָּרֵךְ אֲבָרֵךְ
אֶבְיוֹנֶיהָ אַשְׂבִּיעַ לָחֶם: וְכֹהֲנֶיהָ אַלְבִּישׁ יֶשַׁע וַחֲסִידֶיהָ רַנֵּן יְרַנֵּנוּ: שָׁם אַצְמִיחַ
קֶרֶן לְדָוִד עָרַכְתִּי נֵר לִמְשִׁיחִי: אוֹיְבָיו אַלְבִּישׁ בֹּשֶׁת וְעָלָיו יָצִיץ נִזְרוֹ:

קלג שִׁיר הַמַּעֲלוֹת לְדָוִד הִנֵּה מַה־טּוֹב וּמַה־נָּעִים שֶׁבֶת אַחִים גַּם־יָחַד: כַּשֶּׁמֶן

הַטּוֹב ׀ עַל־הָרֹאשׁ יֹרֵד עַל־הַזָּקָן זְקַן־אַהֲרֹן שֶׁיֹּרֵד עַל־פִּי מִדּוֹתָיו: כְּטַל־חֶרְמוֹן שֶׁיֹּרֵד עַל־הַרְרֵי צִיּוֹן כִּי שָׁם ׀ צִוָּה יְהוָה אֶת־הַבְּרָכָה חַיִּים עַד־הָעוֹלָם:

שִׁיר הַמַּעֲלוֹת הִנֵּה ׀ בָּרְכוּ אֶת־יְהוָה כָּל־עַבְדֵי יְהוָה הָעֹמְדִים בְּבֵית־יְהוָה **קלד** בַּלֵּילוֹת: שְׂאוּ־יְדֵכֶם קֹדֶשׁ וּבָרְכוּ אֶת־יְהוָה: יְבָרֶכְךָ יְהוָה מִצִּיּוֹן עֹשֵׂה שָׁמַיִם וָאָרֶץ:

הַלְלוּיָהּ ׀ הַלְלוּ אֶת־שֵׁם יְהוָה הַלְלוּ עַבְדֵי יְהוָה: שֶׁעֹמְדִים בְּבֵית יְהוָה **קלה** בְּחַצְרוֹת בֵּית אֱלֹהֵינוּ: הַלְלוּיָהּ כִּי־טוֹב יְהוָה זַמְּרוּ לִשְׁמוֹ כִּי נָעִים: כִּי־יַעֲקֹב בָּחַר לוֹ יָהּ יִשְׂרָאֵל לִסְגֻלָּתוֹ: כִּי אֲנִי יָדַעְתִּי כִּי־גָדוֹל יְהוָה וַאֲדֹנֵינוּ מִכָּל־אֱלֹהִים: כֹּל אֲשֶׁר־חָפֵץ יְהוָה עָשָׂה בַּשָּׁמַיִם וּבָאָרֶץ בַּיַּמִּים וְכָל־תְּהֹמוֹת: מַעֲלֶה נְשִׂאִים מִקְצֵה הָאָרֶץ בְּרָקִים לַמָּטָר עָשָׂה מוֹצֵא־רוּחַ מֵאוֹצְרוֹתָיו: שֶׁהִכָּה בְּכוֹרֵי מִצְרָיִם מֵאָדָם עַד־בְּהֵמָה: שָׁלַח ׀ אֹתוֹת וּמֹפְתִים בְּתוֹכֵכִי מִצְרָיִם בְּפַרְעֹה וּבְכָל־עֲבָדָיו: שֶׁהִכָּה גּוֹיִם רַבִּים וְהָרַג מְלָכִים עֲצוּמִים: לְסִיחוֹן ׀ מֶלֶךְ הָאֱמֹרִי וּלְעוֹג מֶלֶךְ הַבָּשָׁן וּלְכֹל מַמְלְכוֹת כְּנָעַן: וְנָתַן אַרְצָם נַחֲלָה נַחֲלָה לְיִשְׂרָאֵל עַמּוֹ: יְהוָה שִׁמְךָ לְעוֹלָם יְהוָה זִכְרְךָ לְדֹר־וָדֹר: כִּי־יָדִין יְהוָה עַמּוֹ וְעַל־עֲבָדָיו יִתְנֶחָם: עֲצַבֵּי הַגּוֹיִם כֶּסֶף וְזָהָב מַעֲשֵׂה יְדֵי אָדָם: פֶּה־לָהֶם וְלֹא יְדַבֵּרוּ עֵינַיִם לָהֶם וְלֹא יִרְאוּ: אָזְנַיִם לָהֶם וְלֹא יַאֲזִינוּ אַף אֵין־יֶשׁ־רוּחַ בְּפִיהֶם: כְּמוֹהֶם יִהְיוּ עֹשֵׂיהֶם כֹּל אֲשֶׁר־בֹּטֵחַ בָּהֶם: בֵּית יִשְׂרָאֵל בָּרְכוּ אֶת־יְהוָה בֵּית אַהֲרֹן בָּרְכוּ אֶת־יְהוָה: בֵּית הַלֵּוִי בָּרְכוּ אֶת־יְהוָה יִרְאֵי יְהוָה בָּרְכוּ אֶת־יְהוָה: בָּרוּךְ יְהוָה ׀ מִצִּיּוֹן שֹׁכֵן יְרוּשָׁלִָם הַלְלוּיָהּ:

הוֹדוּ לַיהוָה כִּי־טוֹב כִּי לְעוֹלָם חַסְדּוֹ: הוֹדוּ לֵאלֹהֵי הָאֱלֹהִים כִּי לְעוֹלָם **קלו** חַסְדּוֹ: הוֹדוּ לַאֲדֹנֵי הָאֲדֹנִים כִּי לְעוֹלָם חַסְדּוֹ: לְעֹשֵׂה נִפְלָאוֹת גְּדֹלוֹת לְבַדּוֹ כִּי לְעוֹלָם חַסְדּוֹ: לְעֹשֵׂה הַשָּׁמַיִם בִּתְבוּנָה כִּי לְעוֹלָם חַסְדּוֹ: לְרֹקַע הָאָרֶץ עַל־הַמָּיִם כִּי לְעוֹלָם חַסְדּוֹ: לְעֹשֵׂה אוֹרִים גְּדֹלִים כִּי לְעוֹלָם חַסְדּוֹ: אֶת־הַשֶּׁמֶשׁ לְמֶמְשֶׁלֶת בַּיּוֹם כִּי לְעוֹלָם חַסְדּוֹ: אֶת־הַיָּרֵחַ וְכוֹכָבִים לְמֶמְשְׁלוֹת בַּלָּיְלָה כִּי לְעוֹלָם חַסְדּוֹ: לְמַכֵּה מִצְרַיִם בִּבְכוֹרֵיהֶם כִּי לְעוֹלָם חַסְדּוֹ: וַיּוֹצֵא יִשְׂרָאֵל מִתּוֹכָם כִּי לְעוֹלָם חַסְדּוֹ: בְּיָד חֲזָקָה וּבִזְרוֹעַ נְטוּיָה כִּי לְעוֹלָם חַסְדּוֹ: לְגֹזֵר יַם־סוּף לִגְזָרִים כִּי לְעוֹלָם חַסְדּוֹ: וְהֶעֱבִיר יִשְׂרָאֵל בְּתוֹכוֹ כִּי לְעוֹלָם חַסְדּוֹ: וְנִעֵר פַּרְעֹה וְחֵילוֹ בְיַם־סוּף כִּי לְעוֹלָם חַסְדּוֹ: לְמוֹלִיךְ עַמּוֹ בַּמִּדְבָּר כִּי לְעוֹלָם חַסְדּוֹ: לְמַכֵּה מְלָכִים גְּדֹלִים כִּי לְעוֹלָם חַסְדּוֹ: וַיַּהֲרֹג מְלָכִים אַדִּירִים

כִּי לְעוֹלָם חַסְדּוֹ: לְסִיחוֹן מֶלֶךְ הָאֱמֹרִי כִּי לְעוֹלָם חַסְדּוֹ: וּלְעוֹג מֶלֶךְ הַבָּשָׁן כִּי לְעוֹלָם חַסְדּוֹ: וְנָתַן אַרְצָם לְנַחֲלָה כִּי לְעוֹלָם חַסְדּוֹ: נַחֲלָה לְיִשְׂרָאֵל עַבְדּוֹ כִּי לְעוֹלָם חַסְדּוֹ: שֶׁבְּשִׁפְלֵנוּ זָכַר לָנוּ כִּי לְעוֹלָם חַסְדּוֹ: וַיִּפְרְקֵנוּ מִצָּרֵינוּ כִּי לְעוֹלָם חַסְדּוֹ: נֹתֵן לֶחֶם לְכָל־בָּשָׂר כִּי לְעוֹלָם חַסְדּוֹ: הוֹדוּ לְאֵל הַשָּׁמָיִם כִּי לְעוֹלָם חַסְדּוֹ:

קלז עַל־נַהֲרוֹת ׀ בָּבֶל שָׁם יָשַׁבְנוּ גַּם־בָּכִינוּ בְּזָכְרֵנוּ אֶת־צִיּוֹן: עַל־עֲרָבִים בְּתוֹכָהּ תָּלִינוּ כִּנֹּרוֹתֵינוּ: כִּי שָׁם שְׁאֵלוּנוּ שׁוֹבֵינוּ דִּבְרֵי־שִׁיר וְתוֹלָלֵינוּ שִׂמְחָה שִׁירוּ לָנוּ מִשִּׁיר צִיּוֹן: אֵיךְ נָשִׁיר אֶת־שִׁיר־יְהוָה עַל אַדְמַת נֵכָר: אִם־אֶשְׁכָּחֵךְ יְרוּשָׁלִָם תִּשְׁכַּח יְמִינִי: תִּדְבַּק־לְשׁוֹנִי ׀ לְחִכִּי אִם־לֹא אֶזְכְּרֵכִי אִם־לֹא אַעֲלֶה אֶת־יְרוּשָׁלִַם עַל רֹאשׁ שִׂמְחָתִי: זְכֹר יְהוָה ׀ לִבְנֵי אֱדוֹם אֵת יוֹם יְרוּשָׁלִָם הָאֹמְרִים עָרוּ ׀ עָרוּ עַד הַיְסוֹד בָּהּ: בַּת־בָּבֶל הַשְּׁדוּדָה אַשְׁרֵי שֶׁיְשַׁלֶּם־לָךְ אֶת־גְּמוּלֵךְ שֶׁגָּמַלְתְּ לָנוּ: אַשְׁרֵי ׀ שֶׁיֹּאחֵז וְנִפֵּץ אֶת־עֹלָלַיִךְ אֶל־הַסָּלַע:

קלח לְדָוִד ׀ אוֹדְךָ בְכָל־לִבִּי נֶגֶד אֱלֹהִים אֲזַמְּרֶךָּ: אֶשְׁתַּחֲוֶה אֶל־הֵיכַל קָדְשְׁךָ וְאוֹדֶה אֶת־שְׁמֶךָ עַל־חַסְדְּךָ וְעַל־אֲמִתֶּךָ כִּי־הִגְדַּלְתָּ עַל־כָּל־שִׁמְךָ אִמְרָתֶךָ: בְּיוֹם קָרָאתִי וַתַּעֲנֵנִי תַּרְהִבֵנִי בְנַפְשִׁי עֹז: יוֹדוּךָ יְהוָה כָּל־מַלְכֵי־אָרֶץ כִּי שָׁמְעוּ אִמְרֵי־פִיךָ: וְיָשִׁירוּ בְּדַרְכֵי יְהוָה כִּי־גָדוֹל כְּבוֹד יְהוָה: כִּי־רָם יְהוָה וְשָׁפָל יִרְאֶה וְגָבֹהַּ מִמֶּרְחָק יְיֵדָע: אִם־אֵלֵךְ ׀ בְּקֶרֶב צָרָה תְּחַיֵּנִי עַל אַף אֹיְבַי תִּשְׁלַח יָדֶךָ וְתוֹשִׁיעֵנִי יְמִינֶךָ: יְהוָה יִגְמֹר בַּעֲדִי יְהוָה חַסְדְּךָ לְעוֹלָם מַעֲשֵׂי יָדֶיךָ אַל־תֶּרֶף:

קלט לַמְנַצֵּחַ לְדָוִד מִזְמוֹר יְהוָה חֲקַרְתַּנִי וַתֵּדָע: אַתָּה יָדַעְתָּ שִׁבְתִּי וְקוּמִי בַּנְתָּה לְרֵעִי מֵרָחוֹק: אָרְחִי וְרִבְעִי זֵרִיתָ וְכָל־דְּרָכַי הִסְכַּנְתָּה: כִּי אֵין מִלָּה בִּלְשׁוֹנִי הֵן יְהוָה יָדַעְתָּ כֻלָּהּ: אָחוֹר וָקֶדֶם צַרְתָּנִי וַתָּשֶׁת עָלַי כַּפֶּכָה: פְּלִיאָה **פליאה** דַעַת מִמֶּנִּי נִשְׂגְּבָה לֹא־אוּכַל לָהּ: אָנָה אֵלֵךְ מֵרוּחֶךָ וְאָנָה מִפָּנֶיךָ אֶבְרָח: אִם־אֶסַּק שָׁמַיִם שָׁם אָתָּה וְאַצִּיעָה שְּׁאוֹל הִנֶּךָּ: אֶשָּׂא כַנְפֵי־שָׁחַר אֶשְׁכְּנָה בְּאַחֲרִית יָם: גַּם־שָׁם יָדְךָ תַנְחֵנִי וְתֹאחֲזֵנִי יְמִינֶךָ: וָאֹמַר אַךְ־חֹשֶׁךְ יְשׁוּפֵנִי וְלַיְלָה אוֹר בַּעֲדֵנִי: גַּם־חֹשֶׁךְ לֹא־יַחְשִׁיךְ מִמֶּךָ וְלַיְלָה כַּיּוֹם יָאִיר כַּחֲשֵׁיכָה כָּאוֹרָה: כִּי־אַתָּה קָנִיתָ כִלְיֹתָי תְּסֻכֵּנִי בְּבֶטֶן אִמִּי: אוֹדְךָ עַל כִּי נוֹרָאוֹת נִפְלֵיתִי נִפְלָאִים מַעֲשֶׂיךָ וְנַפְשִׁי יֹדַעַת מְאֹד: לֹא־נִכְחַד עָצְמִי מִמֶּךָּ אֲשֶׁר־עֻשֵּׂיתִי בַסֵּתֶר רֻקַּמְתִּי בְּתַחְתִּיּוֹת אָרֶץ: גָּלְמִי ׀ רָאוּ עֵינֶיךָ וְעַל־סִפְרְךָ כֻּלָּם יִכָּתֵבוּ יָמִים

וְלִי יָצְרוּ וְלֹא אֶחָד בָּהֶם: וְלִי מַה־יָּקְרוּ רֵעֶיךָ אֵל מֶה עָצְמוּ רָאשֵׁיהֶם: אֶסְפְּרֵם מֵחוֹל יִרְבּוּן הֱקִיצֹתִי וְעוֹדִי עִמָּךְ: אִם־תִּקְטֹל אֱלוֹהַּ ׀ רָשָׁע וְאַנְשֵׁי דָמִים סוּרוּ מֶנִּי: אֲשֶׁר יֹאמְרֻךָ לִמְזִמָּה נָשֻׂא לַשָּׁוְא עָרֶיךָ: הֲלוֹא־מְשַׂנְאֶיךָ יְהוָה ׀ אֶשְׂנָא וּבִתְקוֹמְמֶיךָ אֶתְקוֹטָט: תַּכְלִית שִׂנְאָה שְׂנֵאתִים לְאוֹיְבִים הָיוּ לִי: חָקְרֵנִי אֵל וְדַע לְבָבִי בְּחָנֵנִי וְדַע שַׂרְעַפָּי: וּרְאֵה אִם־דֶּרֶךְ־עֹצֶב בִּי וּנְחֵנִי בְּדֶרֶךְ עוֹלָם:

קמ* לַמְנַצֵּחַ מִזְמוֹר לְדָוִד: חַלְּצֵנִי יְהוָה מֵאָדָם רָע מֵאִישׁ חֲמָסִים תִּנְצְרֵנִי: אֲשֶׁר חָשְׁבוּ רָעוֹת בְּלֵב כָּל־יוֹם יָגוּרוּ מִלְחָמוֹת: שָׁנֲנוּ לְשׁוֹנָם כְּמוֹ־נָחָשׁ חֲמַת עַכְשׁוּב תַּחַת שְׂפָתֵימוֹ סֶלָה: שָׁמְרֵנִי יְהוָה ׀ מִידֵי רָשָׁע מֵאִישׁ חֲמָסִים תִּנְצְרֵנִי אֲשֶׁר חָשְׁבוּ לִדְחוֹת פְּעָמָי: טָמְנוּ־גֵאִים ׀ פַּח לִי וַחֲבָלִים פָּרְשׂוּ רֶשֶׁת לְיַד־מַעְגָּל מֹקְשִׁים שָׁתוּ־לִי סֶלָה: אָמַרְתִּי לַיהוָה אֵלִי אָתָּה הַאֲזִינָה יְהוָה קוֹל תַּחֲנוּנָי: יְהוִה אֲדֹנָי עֹז יְשׁוּעָתִי סַכֹּתָה לְרֹאשִׁי בְּיוֹם נָשֶׁק: אַל־תִּתֵּן יְהוָה מַאֲוַיֵּי רָשָׁע זְמָמוֹ אַל־תָּפֵק יָרוּמוּ סֶלָה: רֹאשׁ מְסִבָּי עֲמַל שְׂפָתֵימוֹ יְכַסֵּימוֹ **יְכַסְמוֹ** [יְכַסֵּימוֹ]: יִמּוֹטוּ עֲלֵיהֶם גֶּחָלִים בָּאֵשׁ יַפִּלֵם בְּמַהֲמֹרוֹת בַּל־יָקוּמוּ: אִישׁ לָשׁוֹן בַּל־ **יִמּוֹטוּ** [יִכּוֹן] בָּאָרֶץ אִישׁ־חָמָס רָע יְצוּדֶנּוּ לְמַדְחֵפֹת: יָדַעְתִּי כִּי־יַעֲשֶׂה יְהוָה דִּין עָנִי מִשְׁפַּט אֶבְיֹנִים: אַךְ צַדִּיקִים יוֹדוּ לִשְׁמֶךָ יֵשְׁבוּ יְשָׁרִים אֶת־פָּנֶיךָ:

קמא מִזְמוֹר לְדָוִד יְהוָה קְרָאתִיךָ חוּשָׁה לִּי הַאֲזִינָה קוֹלִי בְּקָרְאִי־לָךְ: תִּכּוֹן תְּפִלָּתִי קְטֹרֶת לְפָנֶיךָ מַשְׂאַת כַּפַּי מִנְחַת־עָרֶב: שִׁיתָה יְהוָה שָׁמְרָה לְפִי נִצְּרָה עַל־דַּל שְׂפָתָי: אַל־תַּט־לִבִּי לְדָבָר ׀ רָע לְהִתְעוֹלֵל עֲלִלוֹת בְּרֶשַׁע אֶת־אִישִׁים פֹּעֲלֵי־אָוֶן וּבַל־אֶלְחַם בְּמַנְעַמֵּיהֶם: יֶהֶלְמֵנִי צַדִּיק ׀ חֶסֶד וְיוֹכִיחֵנִי שֶׁמֶן רֹאשׁ אַל־יָנִי רֹאשִׁי כִּי־עוֹד וּתְפִלָּתִי בְּרָעוֹתֵיהֶם: נִשְׁמְטוּ בִידֵי־סֶלַע שֹׁפְטֵיהֶם וְשָׁמְעוּ אֲמָרַי כִּי נָעֵמוּ: כְּמוֹ פֹלֵחַ וּבֹקֵעַ בָּאָרֶץ נִפְזְרוּ עֲצָמֵינוּ לְפִי שְׁאוֹל: כִּי אֵלֶיךָ ׀ יְהוִה אֲדֹנָי עֵינָי בְּכָה חָסִיתִי אַל־תְּעַר נַפְשִׁי: שָׁמְרֵנִי מִידֵי פַח יָקְשׁוּ לִי וּמֹקְשׁוֹת פֹּעֲלֵי אָוֶן: יִפְּלוּ בְמַכְמֹרָיו רְשָׁעִים יַחַד אָנֹכִי עַד־אֶעֱבוֹר:

קמב מַשְׂכִּיל לְדָוִד בִּהְיוֹתוֹ בַמְּעָרָה תְפִלָּה: קוֹלִי אֶל־יְהוָה אֶזְעָק קוֹלִי אֶל־יְהוָה אֶתְחַנָּן: אֶשְׁפֹּךְ לְפָנָיו שִׂיחִי צָרָתִי לְפָנָיו אַגִּיד: בְּהִתְעַטֵּף עָלַי ׀ רוּחִי וְאַתָּה יָדַעְתָּ נְתִיבָתִי בְּאֹרַח־זוּ אֲהַלֵּךְ טָמְנוּ פַח לִי: הַבֵּיט יָמִין ׀ וּרְאֵה וְאֵין־לִי מַכִּיר אָבַד מָנוֹס מִמֶּנִּי אֵין דּוֹרֵשׁ לְנַפְשִׁי: זָעַקְתִּי אֵלֶיךָ יְהוָה אָמַרְתִּי אַתָּה מַחְסִי חֶלְקִי בְּאֶרֶץ הַחַיִּים: הַקְשִׁיבָה ׀ אֶל־רִנָּתִי כִּי־דַלּוֹתִי מְאֹד הַצִּילֵנִי מֵרֹדְפַי כִּי

אָמְצוּ מִמֶּנִּי: הוֹצִיאָה מִמַּסְגֵּר ׀ נַפְשִׁי לְהוֹדוֹת אֶת־שְׁמֶךָ בִּי יַכְתִּרוּ צַדִּיקִים כִּי תִגְמֹל עָלָי:

קמג מִזְמוֹר לְדָוִד ׀ יְהוָה ׀ שְׁמַע תְּפִלָּתִי הַאֲזִינָה אֶל־תַּחֲנוּנַי בֶּאֱמֻנָתְךָ עֲנֵנִי בְּצִדְקָתֶךָ: וְאַל־תָּבוֹא בְמִשְׁפָּט אֶת־עַבְדֶּךָ כִּי לֹא־יִצְדַּק לְפָנֶיךָ כָל־חָי: כִּי רָדַף אוֹיֵב ׀ נַפְשִׁי דִּכָּא לָאָרֶץ חַיָּתִי הוֹשִׁיבַנִי בְמַחֲשַׁכִּים כְּמֵתֵי עוֹלָם: וַתִּתְעַטֵּף עָלַי רוּחִי בְּתוֹכִי יִשְׁתּוֹמֵם לִבִּי: זָכַרְתִּי יָמִים ׀ מִקֶּדֶם הָגִיתִי בְכָל־פָּעֳלֶךָ בְּמַעֲשֵׂה יָדֶיךָ אֲשׂוֹחֵחַ: פֵּרַשְׂתִּי יָדַי אֵלֶיךָ נַפְשִׁי ׀ כְּאֶרֶץ־עֲיֵפָה לְךָ סֶלָה: מַהֵר עֲנֵנִי ׀ יְהוָה כָּלְתָה רוּחִי אַל־תַּסְתֵּר פָּנֶיךָ מִמֶּנִּי וְנִמְשַׁלְתִּי עִם־יֹרְדֵי בוֹר: הַשְׁמִיעֵנִי בַבֹּקֶר ׀ חַסְדֶּךָ כִּי־בְךָ בָטָחְתִּי הוֹדִיעֵנִי דֶּרֶךְ־זוּ אֵלֵךְ כִּי־אֵלֶיךָ נָשָׂאתִי נַפְשִׁי: הַצִּילֵנִי מֵאֹיְבַי ׀ יְהוָה אֵלֶיךָ כִסִּתִי: לַמְּדֵנִי ׀ לַעֲשׂוֹת רְצוֹנֶךָ כִּי־אַתָּה אֱלוֹהָי רוּחֲךָ טוֹבָה תַּנְחֵנִי בְּאֶרֶץ מִישׁוֹר: לְמַעַן־שִׁמְךָ יְהוָה תְּחַיֵּנִי בְּצִדְקָתְךָ ׀ תּוֹצִיא מִצָּרָה נַפְשִׁי: וּבְחַסְדְּךָ תַּצְמִית אֹיְבָי וְהַאֲבַדְתָּ כָּל־צֹרְרֵי נַפְשִׁי כִּי אֲנִי עַבְדֶּךָ:

קמד לְדָוִד ׀ בָּרוּךְ יְהוָה ׀ צוּרִי הַמְלַמֵּד יָדַי לַקְרָב אֶצְבְּעוֹתַי לַמִּלְחָמָה: חַסְדִּי וּמְצוּדָתִי מִשְׂגַּבִּי וּמְפַלְטִי־לִי מָגִנִּי וּבוֹ חָסִיתִי הָרוֹדֵד עַמִּי תַחְתָּי: יְהוָה מָה־אָדָם וַתֵּדָעֵהוּ בֶּן־אֱנוֹשׁ וַתְּחַשְּׁבֵהוּ: אָדָם לַהֶבֶל דָּמָה יָמָיו כְּצֵל עוֹבֵר: יְהוָה הַט־שָׁמֶיךָ וְתֵרֵד גַּע בֶּהָרִים וְיֶעֱשָׁנוּ: בְּרוֹק בָּרָק וּתְפִיצֵם שְׁלַח חִצֶּיךָ וּתְהֻמֵּם: שְׁלַח יָדֶיךָ מִמָּרוֹם פְּצֵנִי וְהַצִּילֵנִי מִמַּיִם רַבִּים מִיַּד בְּנֵי נֵכָר: אֲשֶׁר פִּיהֶם דִּבֶּר־שָׁוְא וִימִינָם יְמִין שָׁקֶר: אֱלֹהִים שִׁיר חָדָשׁ אָשִׁירָה לָּךְ בְּנֵבֶל עָשׂוֹר אֲזַמְּרָה־לָּךְ: הַנּוֹתֵן תְּשׁוּעָה לַמְּלָכִים הַפּוֹצֶה אֶת־דָּוִד עַבְדּוֹ מֵחֶרֶב רָעָה: פְּצֵנִי וְהַצִּילֵנִי מִיַּד בְּנֵי־נֵכָר אֲשֶׁר פִּיהֶם דִּבֶּר־שָׁוְא וִימִינָם יְמִין שָׁקֶר: אֲשֶׁר בָּנֵינוּ ׀ כִּנְטִעִים מְגֻדָּלִים בִּנְעוּרֵיהֶם בְּנוֹתֵינוּ כְזָוִיֹּת מְחֻטָּבוֹת תַּבְנִית הֵיכָל: מְזָוֵינוּ מְלֵאִים מְפִיקִים מִזַּן אֶל זַן צֹאונֵנוּ מַאֲלִיפוֹת מְרֻבָּבוֹת בְּחוּצוֹתֵינוּ: אַלּוּפֵינוּ מְסֻבָּלִים אֵין פֶּרֶץ וְאֵין יוֹצֵאת וְאֵין צְוָחָה בִּרְחֹבֹתֵינוּ: אַשְׁרֵי הָעָם שֶׁכָּכָה לּוֹ אַשְׁרֵי הָעָם שֶׁיְּהוָה אֱלֹהָיו:

קמה תְּהִלָּה לְדָוִד אֲרוֹמִמְךָ אֱלוֹהַי הַמֶּלֶךְ וַאֲבָרֲכָה שִׁמְךָ לְעוֹלָם וָעֶד: בְּכָל־יוֹם אֲבָרֲכֶךָּ וַאֲהַלְלָה שִׁמְךָ לְעוֹלָם וָעֶד: גָּדוֹל יְהוָה וּמְהֻלָּל מְאֹד וְלִגְדֻלָּתוֹ אֵין חֵקֶר: דּוֹר לְדוֹר יְשַׁבַּח מַעֲשֶׂיךָ וּגְבוּרֹתֶיךָ יַגִּידוּ: הֲדַר כְּבוֹד הוֹדֶךָ וְדִבְרֵי נִפְלְאֹתֶיךָ אָשִׂיחָה: וֶעֱזוּז נוֹרְאֹתֶיךָ יֹאמֵרוּ וּגְדוּלָּתְךָ אֲסַפְּרֶנָּה: זֵכֶר רַב־טוּבְךָ וּגְדוּלָּתְךָ

יַבִּיעוּ וְצִדְקָתְךָ יְרַנֵּנוּ: חַנּוּן וְרַחוּם יהוה אֶרֶךְ אַפַּיִם וּגְדָל־חָסֶד: טוֹב־יהוה
לַכֹּל וְרַחֲמָיו עַל־כָּל־מַעֲשָׂיו: יוֹדוּךָ יהוה כָּל־מַעֲשֶׂיךָ וַחֲסִידֶיךָ יְבָרְכוּכָה:
כְּבוֹד מַלְכוּתְךָ יֹאמֵרוּ וּגְבוּרָתְךָ יְדַבֵּרוּ: לְהוֹדִיעַ ׀ לִבְנֵי הָאָדָם גְּבוּרֹתָיו וּכְבוֹד
הֲדַר מַלְכוּתוֹ: מַלְכוּתְךָ מַלְכוּת כָּל־עֹלָמִים וּמֶמְשַׁלְתְּךָ בְּכָל־דּוֹר וָדֹר: סוֹמֵךְ
יהוה לְכָל־הַנֹּפְלִים וְזוֹקֵף לְכָל־הַכְּפוּפִים: עֵינֵי־כֹל אֵלֶיךָ יְשַׂבֵּרוּ וְאַתָּה נוֹתֵן־
לָהֶם אֶת־אָכְלָם בְּעִתּוֹ: פּוֹתֵחַ אֶת־יָדֶךָ וּמַשְׂבִּיעַ לְכָל־חַי רָצוֹן: צַדִּיק יהוה
בְּכָל־דְּרָכָיו וְחָסִיד בְּכָל־מַעֲשָׂיו: קָרוֹב יהוה לְכָל־קֹרְאָיו לְכֹל אֲשֶׁר יִקְרָאֻהוּ
בֶאֱמֶת: רְצוֹן־יְרֵאָיו יַעֲשֶׂה וְאֶת־שַׁוְעָתָם יִשְׁמַע וְיוֹשִׁיעֵם: שׁוֹמֵר יהוה אֶת־
כָּל־אֹהֲבָיו וְאֵת כָּל־הָרְשָׁעִים יַשְׁמִיד: תְּהִלַּת יהוה יְדַבֶּר־פִּי וִיבָרֵךְ כָּל־
בָּשָׂר שֵׁם קָדְשׁוֹ לְעוֹלָם וָעֶד:

קמו הַלְלוּיָהּ הַלְלִי נַפְשִׁי אֶת־יהוה: אֲהַלְלָה יהוה בְּחַיָּי אֲזַמְּרָה לֵאלֹהַי בְּעוֹדִי:
אַל־תִּבְטְחוּ בִנְדִיבִים בְּבֶן־אָדָם שֶׁאֵין לוֹ תְשׁוּעָה: תֵּצֵא רוּחוֹ יָשֻׁב לְאַדְמָתוֹ
בַּיּוֹם הַהוּא אָבְדוּ עֶשְׁתֹּנֹתָיו: אַשְׁרֵי שֶׁאֵל יַעֲקֹב בְּעֶזְרוֹ שִׂבְרוֹ עַל־יהוה
אֱלֹהָיו: עֹשֶׂה ׀ שָׁמַיִם וָאָרֶץ אֶת־הַיָּם וְאֶת־כָּל־אֲשֶׁר־בָּם הַשֹּׁמֵר אֱמֶת לְעוֹלָם:
עֹשֶׂה מִשְׁפָּט ׀ לָעֲשׁוּקִים נֹתֵן לֶחֶם לָרְעֵבִים יהוה מַתִּיר אֲסוּרִים: יהוה ׀
פֹּקֵחַ עִוְרִים יהוה זֹקֵף כְּפוּפִים יהוה אֹהֵב צַדִּיקִים: יהוה ׀ שֹׁמֵר אֶת־גֵּרִים
יָתוֹם וְאַלְמָנָה יְעוֹדֵד וְדֶרֶךְ רְשָׁעִים יְעַוֵּת: יִמְלֹךְ יהוה ׀ לְעוֹלָם אֱלֹהַיִךְ צִיּוֹן
לְדֹר וָדֹר הַלְלוּיָהּ:

קמז הַלְלוּיָהּ ׀ כִּי־טוֹב זַמְּרָה אֱלֹהֵינוּ כִּי־נָעִים נָאוָה תְהִלָּה: בּוֹנֵה יְרוּשָׁלִַם יהוה
נִדְחֵי יִשְׂרָאֵל יְכַנֵּס: הָרֹפֵא לִשְׁבוּרֵי לֵב וּמְחַבֵּשׁ לְעַצְּבוֹתָם: מוֹנֶה מִסְפָּר
לַכּוֹכָבִים לְכֻלָּם שֵׁמוֹת יִקְרָא: גָּדוֹל אֲדוֹנֵינוּ וְרַב־כֹּחַ לִתְבוּנָתוֹ אֵין מִסְפָּר:
מְעוֹדֵד עֲנָוִים יהוה מַשְׁפִּיל רְשָׁעִים עֲדֵי־אָרֶץ: עֱנוּ לַיהוה בְּתוֹדָה זַמְּרוּ
לֵאלֹהֵינוּ בְכִנּוֹר: הַמְכַסֶּה שָׁמַיִם ׀ בְּעָבִים הַמֵּכִין לָאָרֶץ מָטָר הַמַּצְמִיחַ
הָרִים חָצִיר: נוֹתֵן לִבְהֵמָה לַחְמָהּ לִבְנֵי עֹרֵב אֲשֶׁר יִקְרָאוּ: לֹא בִגְבוּרַת הַסּוּס
יֶחְפָּץ לֹא־בְשׁוֹקֵי הָאִישׁ יִרְצֶה: רוֹצֶה יהוה אֶת־יְרֵאָיו אֶת־הַמְיַחֲלִים לְחַסְדּוֹ:
שַׁבְּחִי יְרוּשָׁלִַם אֶת־יהוה הַלְלִי אֱלֹהַיִךְ צִיּוֹן: כִּי־חִזַּק בְּרִיחֵי שְׁעָרָיִךְ בֵּרַךְ
בָּנַיִךְ בְּקִרְבֵּךְ: הַשָּׂם־גְּבוּלֵךְ שָׁלוֹם חֵלֶב חִטִּים יַשְׂבִּיעֵךְ: הַשֹּׁלֵחַ אִמְרָתוֹ אָרֶץ
עַד־מְהֵרָה יָרוּץ דְּבָרוֹ: הַנֹּתֵן שֶׁלֶג כַּצָּמֶר כְּפוֹר כָּאֵפֶר יְפַזֵּר: מַשְׁלִיךְ קַרְחוֹ
כְפִתִּים לִפְנֵי קָרָתוֹ מִי יַעֲמֹד: יִשְׁלַח דְּבָרוֹ וְיַמְסֵם יַשֵּׁב רוּחוֹ יִזְּלוּ־מָיִם: מַגִּיד

דְּבָרָו לְיַעֲקֹב חֻקָּיו וּמִשְׁפָּטָיו לְיִשְׂרָאֵל: לֹא עָשָׂה כֵן ׀ לְכָל־גּוֹי וּמִשְׁפָּטִים
בַּל־יְדָעוּם הַלְלוּיָהּ:

קמח הַלְלוּיָהּ ׀ הַלְלוּ אֶת־יְהוָה מִן־הַשָּׁמַיִם הַלְלוּהוּ בַּמְּרוֹמִים: הַלְלוּהוּ כָל־
מַלְאָכָיו הַלְלוּהוּ כָּל־צְבָאָו: הַלְלוּהוּ שֶׁמֶשׁ וְיָרֵחַ הַלְלוּהוּ כָּל־כּוֹכְבֵי אוֹר:
הַלְלוּהוּ שְׁמֵי הַשָּׁמָיִם וְהַמַּיִם אֲשֶׁר ׀ מֵעַל הַשָּׁמָיִם: יְהַלְלוּ אֶת־שֵׁם יְהוָה כִּי
הוּא צִוָּה וְנִבְרָאוּ: וַיַּעֲמִידֵם לָעַד לְעוֹלָם חָק־נָתַן וְלֹא יַעֲבוֹר: הַלְלוּ אֶת־
יְהוָה מִן־הָאָרֶץ תַּנִּינִים וְכָל־תְּהֹמוֹת: אֵשׁ וּבָרָד שֶׁלֶג וְקִיטוֹר רוּחַ סְעָרָה
עֹשָׂה דְבָרוֹ: הֶהָרִים וְכָל־גְּבָעוֹת עֵץ פְּרִי וְכָל־אֲרָזִים: הַחַיָּה וְכָל־בְּהֵמָה
רֶמֶשׂ וְצִפּוֹר כָּנָף: מַלְכֵי־אֶרֶץ וְכָל־לְאֻמִּים שָׂרִים וְכָל־שֹׁפְטֵי אָרֶץ: בַּחוּרִים
וְגַם־בְּתוּלוֹת זְקֵנִים עִם־נְעָרִים: יְהַלְלוּ ׀ אֶת־שֵׁם יְהוָה כִּי־נִשְׂגָּב שְׁמוֹ לְבַדּוֹ
הוֹדוֹ עַל־אֶרֶץ וְשָׁמָיִם: וַיָּרֶם קֶרֶן ׀ לְעַמּוֹ תְּהִלָּה לְכָל־חֲסִידָיו לִבְנֵי יִשְׂרָאֵל
עַם קְרֹבוֹ הַלְלוּיָהּ:

קמט הַלְלוּיָהּ ׀ שִׁירוּ לַיהוָה שִׁיר חָדָשׁ תְּהִלָּתוֹ בִּקְהַל חֲסִידִים: יִשְׂמַח יִשְׂרָאֵל
בְּעֹשָׂיו בְּנֵי־צִיּוֹן יָגִילוּ בְמַלְכָּם: יְהַלְלוּ שְׁמוֹ בְמָחוֹל בְּתֹף וְכִנּוֹר יְזַמְּרוּ־לוֹ:
כִּי־רוֹצֶה יְהוָה בְּעַמּוֹ יְפָאֵר עֲנָוִים בִּישׁוּעָה: יַעְלְזוּ חֲסִידִים בְּכָבוֹד יְרַנְּנוּ
עַל־מִשְׁכְּבוֹתָם: רוֹמְמוֹת אֵל בִּגְרוֹנָם וְחֶרֶב פִּיפִיּוֹת בְּיָדָם: לַעֲשׂוֹת נְקָמָה
בַּגּוֹיִם תּוֹכֵחוֹת בַּל־אֻמִּים: לֶאְסֹר מַלְכֵיהֶם בְּזִקִּים וְנִכְבְּדֵיהֶם בְּכַבְלֵי בַרְזֶל:
לַעֲשׂוֹת בָּהֶם ׀ מִשְׁפָּט כָּתוּב הָדָר הוּא לְכָל־חֲסִידָיו הַלְלוּיָהּ:

קנ הַלְלוּיָהּ ׀ הַלְלוּ־אֵל בְּקָדְשׁוֹ הַלְלוּהוּ בִּרְקִיעַ עֻזּוֹ: הַלְלוּהוּ בִגְבוּרֹתָיו הַלְלוּהוּ
כְּרֹב גֻּדְלוֹ: הַלְלוּהוּ בְּתֵקַע שׁוֹפָר הַלְלוּהוּ בְּנֵבֶל וְכִנּוֹר: הַלְלוּהוּ בְתֹף וּמָחוֹל
הַלְלוּהוּ בְּמִנִּים וְעֻגָב: הַלְלוּהוּ בְצִלְצְלֵי־שָׁמַע הַלְלוּהוּ בְּצִלְצְלֵי תְרוּעָה:
כֹּל הַנְּשָׁמָה תְּהַלֵּל יָהּ הַלְלוּיָהּ:

After saying Tehillim it is customary to recite:

תהלים יד

מִי יִתֵּן מִצִּיּוֹן יְשׁוּעַת יִשְׂרָאֵל
בְּשׁוּב יהוה שְׁבוּת עַמּוֹ
יָגֵל יַעֲקֹב, יִשְׂמַח יִשְׂרָאֵל:

תהלים לז

וּתְשׁוּעַת צַדִּיקִים מֵיהוה
מָעוּזָּם בְּעֵת צָרָה:
וַיַּעְזְרֵם יהוה וַיְפַלְּטֵם
יְפַלְּטֵם מֵרְשָׁעִים וְיוֹשִׁיעֵם
כִּי חָסוּ בוֹ:

On weekdays:

יְהִי רָצוֹן מִלְּפָנֶיךָ יהוה אֱלֹהֵינוּ וֵאלֹהֵי אֲבוֹתֵינוּ, בִּזְכוּת סֵפֶר רִאשׁוֹן / שֵׁנִי /
שְׁלִישִׁי / רְבִיעִי / חֲמִישִׁי / שֶׁבַּתְּהִלִּים שֶׁקְּרָאנוּ לְפָנֶיךָ שֶׁהוּא כְּנֶגֶד סֵפֶר
בְּרֵאשִׁית / שְׁמוֹת / וַיִּקְרָא / בְּמִדְבַּר / דְּבָרִים / בִּזְכוּת מִזְמוֹרָיו וּבִזְכוּת
פְּסוּקָיו וּבִזְכוּת תֵּבוֹתָיו וּבִזְכוּת שְׁמוֹתֶיךָ הַקְּדוֹשִׁים וְהַטְּהוֹרִים הַיּוֹצְאִים
מִמֶּנּוּ, שֶׁתְּכַפֵּר לָנוּ עַל כָּל חַטֹּאתֵינוּ, וְתִסְלַח לָנוּ עַל כָּל פְּשָׁעֵינוּ שֶׁחָטָאנוּ
וְשֶׁעָוִינוּ וְשֶׁפָּשַׁעְנוּ לְפָנֶיךָ, וְהַחֲזִירֵנוּ בִּתְשׁוּבָה שְׁלֵמָה לְפָנֶיךָ, וְהַדְרִיכֵנוּ
לַעֲבוֹדָתֶךָ, וְתִפְתַּח לִבֵּנוּ בְּתַלְמוּד תּוֹרָתֶךָ, וְתִשְׁלַח רְפוּאָה שְׁלֵמָה לְחוֹלֵי
ישעיה סא עַמֶּךָ (לְחוֹלֶה/לְחוֹלָה פלוני/ת בֶּן/בַּת פלונית), וְתִקְרָא לִשְׁבוּיִם דְּרוֹר, וְלָאֲסוּרִים
פְּקַח קוֹחַ. וּלְכָל הוֹלְכֵי דְרָכִים וְעוֹבְרֵי יַמִּים וּנְהָרוֹת מֵעַמְּךָ יִשְׂרָאֵל תַּצִּילֵם
מִכָּל צַעַר וָנֶזֶק, וְתַגִּיעֵם לִמְחוֹז חֶפְצָם לְחַיִּים וּלְשָׁלוֹם. וְתִפְקֹד לְכָל חֲשׂוּכֵי
בָנִים בְּזֶרַע שֶׁל קַיָּמָא לַעֲבוֹדָתֶךָ וּלְיִרְאָתֶךָ, וְעֻבָּרוֹת שֶׁל עַמְּךָ בֵּית יִשְׂרָאֵל
תַּצִּילֵן שֶׁלֹּא תַפֵּלְנָה וַלְדוֹתֵיהֶן, וְהַיּוֹשְׁבוֹת עַל הַמַּשְׁבֵּר בְּרַחֲמֶיךָ הָרַבִּים תַּצִּילֵן
מִכָּל רָע, וְאֶל הַמֵּינִיקוֹת תַּשְׁפִּיעַ שֶׁלֹּא יֶחְסַר חָלָב מִדַּדֵּיהֶן, וְאַל יִמְשֹׁל אַסְכְּרָה
וְשֵׁדִין וְרוּחִין וְלִילִין וְכָל פְּגָעִים וּמַרְעִין בִּישִׁין בְּכָל יַלְדֵי עַמְּךָ בֵּית יִשְׂרָאֵל,
וּתְגַדְּלֵם לְתוֹרָתֶךָ לִלְמֹד תּוֹרָה לִשְׁמָהּ, וְתַצִּילֵם מֵעַיִן הָרָע וּמִדֶּבֶר וּמִמַּגֵּפָה
וּמִשָּׂטָן וּמִיֵּצֶר הָרָע. וּתְבַטֵּל מֵעָלֵינוּ וּמִכָּל עַמְּךָ בֵּית יִשְׂרָאֵל בְּכָל מָקוֹם
שֶׁהֵם כָּל גְּזֵרוֹת קָשׁוֹת וְרָעוֹת, וְתַטֶּה לֵב הַמַּלְכוּת עָלֵינוּ לְטוֹבָה, וְתִגְזֹר עָלֵינוּ
גְּזֵרוֹת טוֹבוֹת, וְתִשְׁלַח בְּרָכָה וְהַצְלָחָה בְּכָל מַעֲשֵׂה יָדֵינוּ, וְהָכֵן פַּרְנָסָתֵנוּ מִיָּדְךָ

הָרְחָבָה וְהַמְּלֵאָה, וְלֹא יִצְטָרְכוּ עַמְּךָ בֵּית יִשְׂרָאֵל זֶה לָזֶה וְלֹא לְעַם אַחֵר, וְתֵן לְכָל אִישׁ וָאִישׁ דֵּי פַּרְנָסָתוֹ וּלְכָל גְּוִיָּה וּגְוִיָּה דֵּי מַחְסוֹרָהּ וּתְמַהֵר וְתָחִישׁ לְגָאֳלֵנוּ, וְתִבְנֶה בֵּית מִקְדָּשֵׁנוּ וְתִפְאַרְתֵּנוּ. וּבִזְכוּת שְׁלֹשׁ עֶשְׂרֵה מִדּוֹתֶיךָ שֶׁל

שמות לד
רַחֲמִים הַכְּתוּבוֹת בְּתוֹרָתֶךָ, כְּמוֹ שֶׁנֶּאֱמַר: יהוה, יהוה, אֵל רַחוּם וְחַנּוּן, אֶרֶךְ אַפַּיִם וְרַב־חֶסֶד וֶאֱמֶת: נֹצֵר חֶסֶד לָאֲלָפִים, נֹשֵׂא עָוֹן וָפֶשַׁע וְחַטָּאָה, וְנַקֵּה:
תהלים עט
שֶׁאֵינָן חוֹזְרוֹת רֵיקָם מִלְּפָנֶיךָ. עָזְרֵנוּ אֱלֹהֵי יִשְׁעֵנוּ עַל־דְּבַר כְּבוֹד־שְׁמֶךָ, וְהַצִּילֵנוּ
תהלים עט
וְכַפֵּר עַל־חַטֹּאתֵינוּ לְמַעַן שְׁמֶךָ: בָּרוּךְ יהוה לְעוֹלָם אָמֵן וְאָמֵן:

On Shabbat and Yom Tov:

יְהִי רָצוֹן מִלְּפָנֶיךָ יהוה אֱלֹהֵינוּ וֵאלֹהֵי אֲבוֹתֵינוּ, בִּזְכוּת סֵפֶר רִאשׁוֹן / שֵׁנִי / שְׁלִישִׁי / רְבִיעִי / חֲמִישִׁי / שֶׁבַּתְּהִלִּים שֶׁקְּרָאנוּ לְפָנֶיךָ שֶׁהוּא כְּנֶגֶד סֵפֶר בְּרֵאשִׁית / שְׁמוֹת / וַיִּקְרָא / בְּמִדְבַּר / דְּבָרִים / בִּזְכוּת מִזְמוֹרָיו וּבִזְכוּת פְּסוּקָיו וּבִזְכוּת תֵּבוֹתָיו וּבִזְכוּת שְׁמוֹתֶיךָ הַקְּדוֹשִׁים וְהַטְּהוֹרִים הַיּוֹצְאִים מִמֶּנּוּ שֶׁתְּהֵא נֶחְשֶׁבֶת לָנוּ אֲמִירַת מִזְמוֹרֵי תְהִלִּים אֵלּוּ כְּאִלּוּ אֲמָרָם דָּוִד מֶלֶךְ יִשְׂרָאֵל בְּעַצְמוֹ, זְכוּתוֹ תָּגֵן עָלֵינוּ. וְיַעֲמָד לָנוּ לְחַבֵּר אֵשֶׁת נְעוּרִים עִם דּוֹדָהּ בְּאַהֲבָה וְאַחֲוָה וְרֵעוּת, וּמִשָּׁם יִמָּשֵׁךְ לָנוּ שֶׁפַע לְנֶפֶשׁ רוּחַ וּנְשָׁמָה. וּכְשֵׁם שֶׁאֲנַחְנוּ אוֹמְרִים שִׁירִים בָּעוֹלָם הַזֶּה, כָּךְ נִזְכֶּה לוֹמַר לְפָנֶיךָ יהוה אֱלֹהֵינוּ וֵאלֹהֵי אֲבוֹתֵינוּ, שִׁיר וּשְׁבָחָה לָעוֹלָם הַבָּא. וְעַל יְדֵי אֲמִירַת תְּהִלִּים תִּתְעוֹרֵר חֲבַצֶּלֶת

ישעיה לה
הַשָּׁרוֹן לָשִׁיר בְּקוֹל נָעִים גִּילַת וְרַנֵּן, כְּבוֹד הַלְּבָנוֹן נִתַּן־לָהּ הוֹד וְהָדָר בְּבֵית אֱלֹהֵינוּ בִּמְהֵרָה בְיָמֵינוּ, אָמֵן סֶלָה.

שערי תפילה
GATES TO PRAYER

GUIDE TO THE JEWISH YEAR

ELUL

1 Beginning on the first day of Elul (the second day of Rosh Ḥodesh) and for the entire month of Elul, it is customary to say לְדָוִד, יהוה אוֹרִי (page 271) in the evening at the end of Ma'ariv and in the morning after saying the Psalm of the Day [אשי ישראל, פמ״ה:ג].

2 In addition, four shofar blasts are sounded at the end of weekday morning prayers, prior to (or following) recitation of לְדָוִד, יהוה אוֹרִי [רמ״א אריח, תקפא:א].

Pre-Rosh HaShana Customs

3 On the Motza'ei Shabbat prior to Rosh HaShana, the congregation gathers at midnight to say *Seliḥot*. This is often preceded by a sermon from the rabbi. If Rosh HaShana falls on Monday or Tuesday, the first recitation of *Seliḥot* is moved back to the preceding Motza'ei Shabbat [רמ״א אריח, תקפא:א].

4 The congregation says *Seliḥot* each weekday thereafter through Erev Yom Kippur. Although the original custom was to say *Seliḥot* every night after midnight and before dawn, most congregations today say them prior to Shaḥarit; some say them during the preceding evening [עוּוֹהיש שם, ב-ד].

5 The *Shaliaḥ Tzibbur* chosen to lead the *Seliḥot* should preferably be distinguished in Torah scholarship and personal virtue, over the age of thirty and married [רמ״א אריח, תקפא:א].

6 One who is praying alone is permitted to say *Seliḥot* without a *minyan*, provided one omits the י״ג מידות ("Thirteen Attributes of Mercy") and the Aramaic passages [תקפא:ד]. However, one who is alone may read the י״ג מידות with *ta'amei hamikra* [שרע אריח תקפה:ה].

Erev Rosh HaShana (29th of Elul)

7 The recitation of *Seliḥot* (the longest of the year) precedes regular Shaḥarit for weekdays. The congregation omits *Taḥanun* and shofar blowing [שרע ורמ״א, אור״ח, תקפא:ג].

8 It is customary to say the formula of התרת נדרים, the Annulment of Vows (page 547), in front of three adult males after Shaḥarit [חיי אדם, קלח:ח]. The formula may be said at any time of the day [שרע יו״ד, רלד:נו] and may be said any day prior to Yom Kippur.

9 Some have the custom to immerse in the mikveh. Other customs include fasting and visiting the graves of departed relatives [שרע אור״ח, תקפא:ב; רמ״א, שם:ד].

TISHREI

Laws of Aseret Yemei Teshuva (the Ten Days of Repentance)

10 Changes to the Kaddish: It is customary to replace the phrase לְעֵלָּא מִן כָּל ("beyond any") with לְעֵלָּא לְעֵלָּא מִכָּל ("above and beyond any") [משנ״ב, נו:ב] and to change the phrase עֹשֶׂה שָׁלוֹם ("He who makes peace") to עֹשֶׂה הַשָּׁלוֹם ("He who makes the peace") [עזוה״ש אור״ח, תקפב:ח]. One who forgets either of these changes is not required to repeat the Kaddish.

11 Special additions to the Amida: Between Rosh HaShana and Yom Kippur, additional phrases are added to the Amida: זָכְרֵנוּ לְחַיִּים is added in the first blessing; מִי כָמוֹךָ in the second; the ending of the third is changed to הַמֶּלֶךְ הַקָּדוֹשׁ; the ending of the eleventh blessing is changed from הַמֶּלֶךְ הַמִּשְׁפָּט; וּכְתֹב to מֶלֶךְ אוֹהֵב צְדָקָה וּמִשְׁפָּט is added in the penultimate blessing; and בְּסֵפֶר חַיִּים is added to the final blessing, and the ending is changed to עֹשֶׂה הַשָּׁלוֹם (some do not change the ending of the blessing).

12 One who forgets to say any of the additional passages is not required to repeat the Amida with the forgotten additions [שרע ורמ״א אור״ח, תקפב:ה]. Likewise one who forgets to change the ending of the eleventh blessing to הַמֶּלֶךְ הַמִּשְׁפָּט need not repeat [רמ״א אור״ח, קיח:א]. However, one who forgets to change the ending of the third blessing to הַמֶּלֶךְ הַקָּדוֹשׁ must repeat the Amida from the beginning, unless one corrects the error תוך כדי דיבור (see source in the *Shulḥan Arukh* for a discussion of this rule.) [שרע אור״ח, תקפב:ג].

13 During the morning prayers, it is customary, after *Yishtabaḥ*, to open the Ark

and say Psalm 130 responsively (page 107) [משיב ארח, נד: נ]. Some say Psalm 130 before *Yishtabaḥ*.

14 In Shaḥarit and Minḥa, after the Amida, the Ark is opened and the congregation says *Avinu Malkenu*. This is omitted on Friday afternoon [רמ״א ארח, תרב: א].

Fast of Gedalya (3rd of Tishrei)

15 This fast commemorates the slaying of Gedalya ben Aḥikam by Yishmael ben Netanya, at the behest of Ba'alis, the king of Amon (circa 586 BCE). Shortly after the Babylonian conquest of Jerusalem, Gedalya was appointed governor of Judea. His assassination just months after the appointment spelled the end of Jewish self-government in the land of Israel in that era and led to the dispersion of the Jews who remained in the land of Israel after the destruction of the First Temple [II Kings 25:22–26; Jer. 40:4–41:18].

16 If the 3rd of Tishrei falls on Shabbat, the fast is postponed to Sunday.

17 The fast begins at dawn [שו״ע ארח, תקנ: ב]. One is permitted to wake before dawn to eat and drink, but only if one had the intention to do so before going to sleep [שו״ע ארח, תקסד: א].

18 Eating and drinking are forbidden, but other activities (bathing, wearing leather shoes) are permitted [שו״ע ארח, תקנ: ב]. Pregnant and nursing women are exempt from fasting [רמ״א, שם: א].

19 Shaḥarit: The recitation of *Seliḥot* precedes Shaḥarit for weekdays. The additions for *Aseret Yemei Teshuva* are said. During the Repetition of the Amida, the *Shaliaḥ Tzibbur* says the paragraph עֲנֵנוּ between the seventh and eighth blessings (page 157) [שו״ע ארח, תקסו: א]. This is followed by *Avinu Malkenu* and *Taḥanun*.

20 Torah Reading (page 746): The Torah is read only if at least six people (according to some: three people) are fasting. Only people who are fasting are called up. It is customary for the congregation to say the following passages aloud: the last seven words of Ex. 32:12: שׁוּב מֵחֲרוֹן אַפֶּךָ, וְהִנָּחֵם עַל-הָרָעָה לְעַמֶּךָ, the "Thirteen Attributes of Mercy": יהוה יהוה אֵל רַחוּם וְחַנּוּן אֶרֶךְ אַפַּיִם וְרַב-חֶסֶד וֶאֱמֶת: נֹצֵר חֶסֶד לָאֲלָפִים נֹשֵׂא עָוֺן וָפֶשַׁע וְחַטָּאָה וְנַקֵּה, and the last four words of Ex. 34:9: "וְסָלַחְתָּ לַעֲוֺנֵנוּ וּלְחַטָּאתֵנוּ וּנְחַלְתָּנוּ" [משיב, שם (ג)].

21 Minḥa: After *Ashrei* and Half Kaddish, the Torah is read. The reading is the same as that of the morning. The third *oleh* reads the Haftara (page 747) [רמ״א, שם]. After the Torah is returned to the Ark, the *Shaliaḥ Tzibbur* says Half Kaddish, and Minḥa Amida for weekdays is said.

22 During the silent recitation of the Amida, those who are fasting say the paragraph עֲנֵנוּ as part of the sixteenth blessing, שׁוֹמֵעַ תְּפִלָּה (page 315); during the Repetition of the Amida, the *Shaliaḥ Tzibbur* says עֲנֵנוּ between the seventh and eighth blessings, as in the morning (page 297). After the blessing הַטּוֹב שִׁמְךָ וּלְךָ נָאֶה לְהוֹדוֹת, the *Shaliaḥ Tzibbur* says the paragraph relating to *Birkat Kohanim* (page 323). For the final blessings of the Amida, שִׂים שָׁלוֹם is said instead of שָׁלוֹם רָב. After the Amida, the congregation says *Avinu Malkenu*. This is followed by *Taḥanun*, Full Kaddish and *Aleinu*.

Erev Yom Kippur (9th of Tishrei)

23 It is a mitzva to eat and drink on the day before Yom Kippur [שו״ע אור״ח, תר״ד:א].

24 Every person should ask forgiveness from others, because Yom Kippur atones for sins against one's fellows only if the wronged individual has offered his or her forgiveness [שו״ע אור״ח, תר״ו:א].

25 It is customary to say *Kaparot* (page 551) [רמ״א אור״ח, תר״ה:א], and for males to immerse in the mikveh [שו״ע ורמ״א אור״ח, תר״ו:ד].

26 In the morning, an abbreviated *Seliḥot* is said, followed by Shaḥarit for weekdays. During *Pesukei DeZimra*, the congregation omits Psalm 100. Similarly, *Avinu Malkenu*, *Taḥanun* and לַמְנַצֵּחַ (Psalm 20) are omitted. However, if Erev Yom Kippur falls on Friday, the congregation does not omit *Avinu Malkenu* [שו״ע ורמ״א אור״ח, תר״ד:ב].

27 Minḥa: Most communities schedule an early recitation of Minḥa, to allow time for the congregants to return home and eat a final meal (*Se'uda Mafseket*) prior to the fast. Minḥa for weekdays is said with additions for *Aseret Yemei Teshuva*. Before saying the paragraph אֱלֹהַי, נְצֹר at the conclusion of the Amida, each individual says *Viduy* (page 553) [שו״ע אור״ח, תר״ז:א]. *Viduy* is not said by the *Shaliaḥ Tzibbur* during the Repetition of the Amida. As in the morning, both *Avinu Malkenu* and *Taḥanun* are omitted.

28 The *Se'uda Mafseket* (final meal) must be finished a few minutes before sunset [שו״ע אור״ח, תר״ח:א]. It is customary for parents to say a special blessing for their children after the meal [חיי אדם, קמ״ד:יט].

Motza'ei Yom Kippur till Sukkot (11th–13th of Tishrei)

29 *Taḥanun* is not said between Yom Kippur and Sukkot [שו״ע אור״ח, קל״א:ו].

Erev Sukkot (14th of Tishrei)

30 The construction and decoration of the sukka should be completed before Sukkot begins. Likewise, the myrtle (*hadasim*) and willow (*aravot*) should be bound to the lulav before the holiday begins [שו״ע אויח, תרנא: א].

Ḥol HaMo'ed Sukkot

31 During Shaḥarit, Minḥa and Ma'ariv, יַעֲלֶה וְיָבוֹא is added to the seventeenth blessing of the Amida (רְצֵה). It is also added during *Birkat HaMazon* (page 661) [שו״ע אויח, תצ: ב]. If one forgets to say יַעֲלֶה וְיָבוֹא in its proper place, see law 265.

32 The traditional Ashkenazi practice is to wear tefillin during Shaḥarit until the recitation of Hallel. However, some congregations follow the Sephardi custom, in which tefillin are not worn on Ḥol HaMo'ed; this is also the practice in Israel [שו״ע ורמ״א אויח, לא: ב].

33 First Evening of Ḥol HaMo'ed: Ma'ariv for weekdays (page 342). אַתָּה חוֹנַנְתָּנוּ is added in the fourth blessing of the Amida. Havdala is said in the sukka (unless Ḥol HaMo'ed begins on Friday night). No blessing is made over spices or a flame (unless Ḥol HaMo'ed begins on Saturday night), but one says the blessing לֵישֵׁב בַּסֻּכָּה before drinking (page 415).

34 Shaḥarit: for weekdays. After the *Shaliaḥ Tzibbur* repeats the Amida, the congregation takes the lulav and says the blessing עַל נְטִילַת לוּלָב [שו״ע אויח, תרמג: א]. Hallel is said, and some congregations say *Hoshanot* after Hallel instead of after Musaf. This is followed by Full Kaddish.

35 Torah Reading: Pages 770–774. Four men are called up. Each day's reading is nine verses long. For each of the first three *aliyot*, one reads three verses. The fourth *oleh* goes back to the beginning and reads the first six verses a second time [רמ״א אויח, תרסג: א].

36 After the Torah reading, Half Kaddish is said, the Torah is returned to the Ark, and *Ashrei* and וּבָא לְצִיּוֹן are said. The *Shaliaḥ Tzibbur* then says Half Kaddish.

37 Musaf: for Festivals (page 503). The *Kedusha* for weekdays is said; no *Birkat Kohanim* is said. After the Repetition of the Amida, the congregation takes the lulav, the Ark is opened and one Torah scroll is taken out. The *Shaliaḥ Tzibbur* leads the congregation in saying the *Hoshanot* of the day (see table on page 522), while making a circuit around the *bima*. The Torah scroll is returned to the Ark, and the *Shaliaḥ Tzibbur* says Full Kaddish. This is followed by *Aleinu* (page 381), and the conclusion of the weekday service.

Hoshana Raba (21st of Tishrei)

38 Shaḥarit: It is customary for the *Shaliaḥ Tzibbur* to wear a *kittel*. *Pesukei DeZimra* for Shabbat and Yom Tov is said, including Psalm 100 (מִזְמוֹר לְתוֹדָה, page 485). After Psalm 93 (page 495), prayers continue with Shaḥarit for weekdays (page 79) [שו"ע ורמ"א אוי"ח, תרסד:א]. Some have the custom to open the Ark after *Yishtabaḥ*, and say Psalm 130 responsively (some say Psalm 130 before *Yishtabaḥ*). After the *Shaliaḥ Tzibbur* repeats the Amida, the congregation takes the lulav and says the blessing עַל נְטִילַת לוּלָב. Hallel is said, and some congregations say *Hoshanot* after Hallel instead of after Musaf. This is followed Full Kaddish.

39 While the Torah is taken from the Ark, the congregation says *Ein Kamokha* (page 497) [רמ"א, שם]. Most congregations say the "Thirteen Attributes of Mercy" and a special supplication (page 497). Torah Reading: page 773. Some have the custom to read in the melody of *Yamim Nora'im*.

40 After the Torah reading, Half Kaddish is said, the Torah is returned to the Ark, and *Ashrei* and וּבָא לְצִיּוֹן are said. The *Shaliaḥ Tzibbur* says Half Kaddish.

41 Musaf: for Festivals (page 503). It is customary for the *Shaliaḥ Tzibbur* to wear a *kittel* [רמ"א שם]. The *Kedusha* for Yom Tov is said, but *Birkat Kohanim* is not. After the Repetition of the Amida, the congregation takes the lulav, the Ark is opened and seven Torah scrolls are taken out to the *bima*. Many congregations have the custom of taking out all the Torah scrolls [רמ"א אוי"ח, תרס:א]. The *Shaliaḥ Tzibbur* leads the congregation in saying the *Hoshanot* while making seven circuits around the *bima* (page 526) [רמ"א אוי"ח, תרסד:א]. These are followed by special *piyutim* asking for rain. Then five willow branches (*aravot*) are taken and beaten five times before the Torah scrolls are returned to the Ark (page 539). Some have the custom of beating the *aravot* after the *Shaliaḥ Tzibbur* says the Full Kaddish [רמ"א, שם:ו]. This is followed by *Ein Keloheinu*, Rabbis' Kaddish, *Aleinu*, Mourner's Kaddish, the Daily Psalm, Psalm 27 and Mourner's Kaddish.

Laws of מַשִּׁיב הָרוּחַ

42 One begins saying מַשִּׁיב הָרוּחַ in Musaf of Shemini Atzeret and continues until Musaf of the first day of Pesaḥ [שו"ע אוי"ח, קיד:ד].

43 If one forgets to say מַשִּׁיב הָרוּחַ in its proper place but realizes before beginning the words of the blessing מְחַיֵּה הַמֵּתִים, one should immediately say מַשִּׁיב הָרוּחַ and continue with the rest of the blessing. If one realizes the omission immediately after completing the blessing מְחַיֵּה הַמֵּתִים, one should say מַשִּׁיב הָרוּחַ and continue

with the following blessing. If one realizes the omission after beginning the words אַתָּה קָדוֹשׁ, one must repeat the Amida from the beginning [שוע אריח, קיד:ו].

44 If one forgets to say מַשִּׁיב הָרוּחַ but says מוֹרִיד הַטָּל (as is the custom in Israel, and that of *Nusaḥ Sepharad*, in the spring and summer months), one need not repeat the Amida [שוע אריח, קיד:ה]. If there is doubt whether one said מַשִּׁיב הָרוּחַ, the presumption is as follows: within the first thirty days from *Shemini Atzeret*, one should assume that one forgot to say מַשִּׁיב הָרוּחַ. After thirty days, one should assume that one said מַשִּׁיב הָרוּחַ [שוע אריח, קיד:ח].

MARHESHVAN

Laws of BaHaB (בה״ב)

45 Some have the custom to say special *Seliḥot* after the Repetition of the Amida of Shaḥarit on the first Monday, the first Thursday and the second Monday of Marḥeshvan. Historically, these days were dedicated to fasting to atone for overstepping halakhic limits during the celebration of the Yom Tov. This custom is also observed on the first Monday, the first Thursday and the second Monday of Iyar [שוע ורמ״א אריח, תצב: א].

KISLEV

4th–5th of December

46 In most years, during Ma'ariv on the evening of the 4th of December, one begins to say וְתֵן טַל וּמָטָר לִבְרָכָה in the ninth blessing of the Amida. In the year preceding a civil leap year, one begins to say וְתֵן טַל וּמָטָר לִבְרָכָה one day later, on the night of the 5th of December [שוע אריח, קיז:א].

47 If one forgets to say וְתֵן טַל וּמָטָר לִבְרָכָה in its proper place but realizes before saying God's name in the ninth blessing (מְבָרֵךְ הַשָּׁנִים), one should immediately say וְתֵן טַל וּמָטָר לִבְרָכָה and continue with the rest of the blessing. If one realizes the omission after completing the blessing מְבָרֵךְ הַשָּׁנִים, one should say וְתֵן טַל וּמָטָר לִבְרָכָה prior to the words כִּי אַתָּה שׁוֹמֵעַ in the sixteenth blessing (שׁוֹמֵעַ תְּפִלָּה). If one realizes the omission after beginning the seventeenth blessing (רְצֵה), one must repeat the Amida from the beginning of the ninth blessing (מְבָרֵךְ הַשָּׁנִים). If one realizes the omission after completing the Amida, one must repeat the entire Amida [שוע אריח, קיז:ה].

48 If there is doubt whether one properly said וְתֵן טַל וּמָטָר לִבְרָכָה, the presumption is
as follows: within the first thirty days from December 4th (or 5th), one should
assume that one forgot to say וְתֵן טַל וּמָטָר לִבְרָכָה. After thirty days, one should assume that one said וְתֵן טַל וּמָטָר לִבְרָכָה.

Ḥanukka (25th of Kislev–2nd of Tevet)

49 On Ḥanukka, עַל הַנִּסִּים is added to the Amida in Maʿariv, Shaḥarit and Minḥa, as
well as the second blessing of *Birkat HaMazon*. If one forgets to say עַל הַנִּסִּים, one
does not repeat the Amida or *Birkat HaMazon* [שו"ע או"ח, תרפ"ב:א].

50 It is customary to light Ḥanukka lights in the synagogue, either before or after
Maʿariv of each evening. The procedure is identical to that of lighting
in the home, as described below, except that the lights should be placed along
the southern wall of the synagogue.

51 After Maʿariv, Ḥanukka lights are lit in the home. On the first night, three blessings are said: (1) לְהַדְלִיק נֵר שֶׁל חֲנֻכָּה, (2) שֶׁעָשָׂה נִסִּים ("Who performed miracles")
and (3) שֶׁהֶחֱיָנוּ (page 563). On subsequent nights, only the first two blessings
are said [שו"ע או"ח, תרע"א:א]. When adding lights each night, the new light is always
added to the left. The newest candle is lit first, and one then lights the rest of
the lights from left to right.

52 The lights must burn for at least half an hour after nightfall [שו"ע או"ח, תרע"ב:
ב; משנ"ב, שם: ד]. If one did not light during this time, one is permitted to light
any time before daybreak. In such a case, one says the appropriate blessings when lighting, but only if other household members are awake [שו"ע, שם;
משנ"ב, שם: יא].

53 Most have the custom for each member of the household to light separately,
but the head of household may light one menora for the entire family
[שו"ע ורמ"א או"ח, תרע"א:ב].

54 Women are obligated to light Ḥanukka lights [שו"ע או"ח, תרע"ה:ג]. Hence, a woman
can light for herself, on behalf of her household, and on behalf of an adult male
[משנ"ב, שם: ט].

55 The menora is generally lit indoors, but near a window, so that the lights are
visible to the general public as well [שו"ע או"ח, תרע"א:ה].

56 After the lighting, it is customary to sing הַנֵּרוֹת הַלָּלוּ and מָעוֹז צוּר (pages 563–565)
[שו"ע או"ח, תרע"א:ד].

57 Shaḥarit: It is customary to light the menora in the synagogue without a blessing before the prayers begin. Shaḥarit for weekdays is said. עַל הַנִּסִּים is added to
the Amida, as discussed above. After the Repetition of the Amida, *Taḥanun* is

omitted and the *Shaliaḥ Tzibbur* leads the congregation in saying Full Hallel (page 443) [שו"ע אורח, תרפג: א]. This is followed by Half Kaddish and taking the Torah from the Ark (page 217).

58 Torah reading: pages 752–760. Three men are called up [שו"ע אורח, תרפד: א]. The Torah is returned to the Ark, *Ashrei* and וּבָא לְצִיּוֹן are said, but לַמְנַצֵּחַ is omitted, and the *Shaliaḥ Tzibbur* says Full Kaddish. This is followed by *Aleinu*, Mourner's Kaddish, the Daily Psalm, Psalm 30 (page 63), and Mourner's Kaddish.

TEVET

Rosh Ḥodesh Tevet

59 On a weekday, Shaharit for weekdays is said. יַעֲלֶה וְיָבֹא and עַל הַנִּסִּים are added to the Amida. After the Repetition of the Amida, *Taḥanun* is omitted and the *Shaliaḥ Tzibbur* leads the congregation in saying Hallel. This is followed by Full Kaddish.

60 Torah reading: Two scrolls are removed from the Ark. Three men are called up to the first scroll, and Num. 28:1–15 (page 745) is read. A fourth man is called up to the second scroll, from which the appropriate day's reading from Num. 7:42–53 (page 756–757) is read. The *Shaliaḥ Tzibbur* then says Half Kaddish. Prayers continue as on a regular Rosh Ḥodesh, except that עַל הַנִּסִּים is added to the Amida of Musaf.

Asara B'Tevet (10th of Tevet)

61 This fast commemorates the besieging of Jerusalem by Nebuchadnezzar, which led to the capture of the city and the destruction of the First Temple (Ezek. 24:1–2).

62 The fast begins at dawn (see laws 17–18) [שו"ע אורח, תקנ: ב].

63 Shaharit: for weekdays. During the Repetition of the Amida, the *Shaliaḥ Tzibbur* says עֲנֵנוּ between the seventh and eighth blessings (page 157) [שו"ע אורח, תקסו: א]. This is followed by *Seliḥot, Avinu Malkenu* and *Taḥanun* [עירוה"ש אורח, תקסו:ח].

64 Torah Reading: Page 746 (see law 20) [שו"ע אורח, תקסו: א].

65 Minḥa: for weekdays, except that after *Ashrei* and Half Kaddish, the Torah is read. The reading is the same as that of the morning. The third *oleh* reads the Haftara (page 747) [רמ"א שם]. After the Torah is returned to the Ark, the *Shaliaḥ Tzibbur* says Half Kaddish, and continues with the rest of Minḥa for weekdays.

66 During the silent recitation of the Amida, those who are fasting say עֲנֵנוּ as part of the sixteenth blessing, שׁוֹמֵעַ תְּפִלָּה (page 315). During the Repetition of the Amida, the *Shaliaḥ Tzibbur* says עֲנֵנוּ between the seventh and eighth blessings, as in the morning (page 297). After the eighteenth blessing (מוֹדִים), the *Shaliaḥ Tzibbur* says the paragraph relating to *Birkat Kohanim* (page 323). For the final blessing of the Amida, שִׂים שָׁלוֹם is said instead of שָׁלוֹם רָב. After the Amida, the congregation says *Avinu Malkenu*. This is followed by *Taḥanun*, Full Kaddish and *Aleinu*. If the fast falls on Friday, *Avinu Malkenu* and *Taḥanun* are omitted [משנ״ב, תקנ״א].

SHEVAT

Tu BiShevat (15th of Shevat)

67 *Taḥanun* is omitted [שו״ע או״ח, קל״א:ו].

68 It is customary to eat many different fruits, especially fruits that are among the Seven Species associated with the land of Israel, namely, grapes, figs, pomegranates, olives and dates [משנ״ב, שם: לא].

ADAR

Purim Katan (14th–15th of Adar I)

69 In a leap year, on the dates during Adar I corresponding to Purim and Shushan Purim, both *Taḥanun* and לַמְנַצֵּחַ are omitted [שו״ע או״ח, תרצ״ז:א].

Fast of Esther (13th of Adar)

70 This fast commemorates Esther's fast prior to going to see King Ahasuerus without an invitation (Esther 4:15–16). Unlike other fast days, the fast of Esther is considered a custom, and anyone who experiences serious discomfort is permitted to eat or drink [רמ״א או״ח, תרפ״ו:ב].

71 If the 13th of Adar falls on Shabbat, the fast is observed on the preceding Thursday [שו״ע, שם].

72 The fast begins at dawn (see laws 17–18).

73 Prayers as for the 10th of Tevet (see laws 63–66), except that *Avinu Malkenu* and *Taḥanun* are not said during Minḥa. However, if the 13th of Adar falls on Shabbat and the fast is moved back to Thursday, *Avinu Malkenu* and *Taḥanun* are said.

Purim (14th of Adar)

74 On Purim, עַל הַנִּסִּים is added to the Amida in Ma'ariv, Shaḥarit and Minḥa, as well as the second blessing of *Birkat HaMazon*. If one forgets to say עַל הַנִּסִּים, one does not repeat the Amida or *Birkat HaMazon* [שוע אורח, תרנג: ב].

75 Ma'ariv: for weekdays. After recitation of the Amida, the *Shaliaḥ Tzibbur* says the Full Kaddish. The Reader of the Megilla says three blessings: (1) עַל מִקְרָא מְגִלָּה ("about reading the Megilla"), (2) שֶׁעָשָׂה נִסִּים ("Who performed miracles") and (3) שֶׁהֶחֱיָנוּ (page 567). The Megilla is read and the concluding blessing, הָרָב אֶת רִיבֵנוּ, is said. The congregation says אֲשֶׁר הֵנִיא and concludes with a joyous singing of שׁוֹשַׁנַּת יַעֲקֹב. The *Shaliaḥ Tzibbur* leads the congregation in saying וְאַתָּה קָדוֹשׁ at the first arrow, page 247 [שוע אורח, תרצג: א]. This is followed by Full Kaddish (omitting the sentence beginning תִּתְקַבֵּל), and *Aleinu* [משבצ, שם: א].

76 Women are obligated to hear the reading of the Megilla [שוע אורח, תרפט: א].

77 Shaḥarit: for weekdays. After the Repetition of the Amida, the *Shaliaḥ Tzibbur* says Half Kaddish and the Torah is taken from the Ark. The Torah reading (page 760) is followed by Half Kaddish and returning the Torah to the Ark [שוע אורח, תרצג: ד]. The Megilla reading is repeated, with the introductory blessings and the concluding blessing. אֲשֶׁר הֵנִיא is not said a second time, but שׁוֹשַׁנַּת יַעֲקֹב is. The congregation says *Ashrei* and לַצִּיּוֹן וּבָא, followed by Full Kaddish, *Aleinu*, the Daily Psalm and Mourner's Kaddish.

78 On Purim day, one is commanded to fulfill the mitzvot of מַתָּנוֹת לָאֶבְיוֹנִים (gifts to the poor – *tzedaka* given to at least two poor people) [שוע אורח, תרצד: א]; מִשְׁלוֹחַ מָנוֹת (sending at least two portions of food to one person) [שם, תרצה: ד]; and סְעוּדַת פּוּרִים (the Purim feast), at which one should drink "until he cannot distinguish between 'Cursed be Haman' and 'Blessed be Mordekhai'" [שם, תרצה: ב].

Shushan Purim (15th of Adar)

79 Both *Taḥanun* and לַמְנַצֵּחַ are omitted [שוע אורח, תרצו: א].

NISAN

80 During the month of Nisan, *Taḥanun* is omitted [שו״ע ורמ״א אורח, תכט:ב].

81 Many have the custom not to eat matza from Rosh Ḥodesh Nisan [משנ״ב, שם:יב]. Some refrain from eating matza from Purim.

82 One may not eat matza on Erev Pesaḥ [רמ״א אורח, תעא:ב]. On Erev Pesaḥ it is per-missible to eat certain kinds of matza which are not considered proper matza, such as matza made with juice instead of water, or which was cooked or fried after it was baked [שו״ע אורח תעא,ב].

Erev Pesaḥ (14th of Nisan)

83 Shaḥarit: for weekdays. לַמְנַצֵּחַ and מִזְמוֹר לְתוֹדָה are omitted [רמ״א אורח, נא:ט].

84 First born males are required to fast (תענית בכורות), unless they attend a *siyum* (celebratory meal to mark the completion of a unit of Torah study), which is traditionally held immediately following Shaḥarit [שו״ע אורח, תע:א].

85 One is forbidden from eating *ḥametz* from the end of the first third of the day [שו״ע אורח, תמג:א]. There is a dispute between halakhic authorities whether the day is measured from daybreak to nightfall (Magen Avraham), or from sunrise to sunset (Vilna Gaon). One should follow local communal practice in this regard.

86 One is forbidden from owning *ḥametz* from the end of the first 5/12 of the day, by which time one should burn or otherwise destroy any *ḥametz* remaining in one's possession [שם].

87 After Minḥa, some have the custom to say the biblical verses describing the sacrifice of the Pesaḥ lamb (Ex. 12:1–13) [משנ״ב אורח, תעא:כב].

88 If Pesaḥ eve falls on Motza'ei Shabbat, the Fast of the Firstborn is held on the preceding Thursday [שו״ע ורמ״א אורח, תע:ב]. *Bedikat Ḥametz* is done on Thursday night, and the *ḥametz* is burned (see law 86) on Friday morning, while leav-ing enough *ḥametz* for Shabbat. On Shabbat morning, after eating the last of one's *ḥametz*, any leftovers must be given to a non-Jew or made inedible (e.g. by flushing it down the toilet), by the end of the first 5/12 of the day [שו״ע אורח, תמד:ב].

Ḥol HaMo'ed Pesaḥ

89 During Shaḥarit, Minḥa and Ma'ariv, יַעֲלֶה וְיָבוֹא is added to the seventeenth bless-ing of the Amida (רְצֵה). It is also added to *Birkat HaMazon* (page 661) [שו״ע אורח,

ב:תצ]. If יַעֲלֶה וְיָבוֹא is forgotten in the Amida, one should repeat the Amida, but if forgotten in *Birkat HaMazon*, one need not repeat it [שם].

90 The traditional Ashkenazi practice is to wear tefillin during Shaḥarit until the recitation of Hallel. However, some congregations follow the Sephardi custom, in which tefillin are not worn on Ḥol HaMo'ed; this is also the practice in Israel [שו"ע ורמ"א או"ח, לא:ב].

91 First Evening of Ḥol HaMo'ed: Ma'ariv for weekdays (page 343) is said. In the fourth blessing of the Amida, the paragraph of אַתָּה חוֹנַנְתָּנוּ (page 363) is said. In the ninth blessing of the Amida (ברכת השנים), one begins to say וְתֵן בְּרָכָה, a practice which will continue until December 4th (or, in some years, December 5th) (see law 46). If one erroneously says וְתֵן טַל וּמָטָר לִבְרָכָה in the spring and summer months, one must repeat the Amida. If one realizes the error before completing the Amida, one must repeat the Amida from the beginning of ברכת השנים [שו"ע או"ח, קיז:ג]. In the seventeenth blessing of the Amida (רצה), יַעֲלֶה וְיָבוֹא is added.

92 The Omer is counted prior to *Aleinu*. Havdala is said over a cup of wine or grape juice; no blessing is made over spices or a flame (except on Motza'ei Shabbat).

93 Shaḥarit: for weekdays. מִזְמוֹר לְתוֹדָה is omitted. After the Repetition of the Amida, the congregation says Half Hallel [שו"ע או"ח, תצ:ד]. The *Shaliaḥ Tzibbur* says Full Kaddish, and two Torah scrolls are taken from the Ark.

94 Torah Reading: Pages 761 – 769. Four men are called up, the fourth *aliya* is read from the second scroll [שו"ע או"ח, תצ:ד-ה]. If the first day of Pesaḥ falls on Shabbat or Sunday, such that there is no Shabbat Ḥol HaMo'ed, the readings are as listed on pages 761–769. Otherwise, the portions of the first, second and fourth day are read on the weekdays of Ḥol HaMo'ed, as the portion for the third day is included in the reading for Shabbat Ḥol HaMo'ed.

95 After the Torah reading, Half Kaddish is said, the Torah is returned to the Ark, and *Ashrei* and וּבָא לְצִיּוֹן are said. The *Shaliaḥ Tzibbur* says Half Kaddish.

96 Musaf: for Festivals (page 503). The *Kedusha* for weekdays is said; *Birkat Kohanim* is omitted. After the Repetition of the Amida, the *Shaliaḥ Tzibbur* says Full Kaddish. This is followed by *Aleinu*, Mourner's Kaddish, the Daily Psalm, and Mourner's Kaddish.

Laws of Sefirat HaOmer

97 One counts the Omer for a given day after nightfall. The custom is to count standing up [שו"ע או"ח, תפט:א].

98 One who forgets to count at night may count prior to nightfall of the following day, although no blessing is said when counting during daylight hours [שם:ו].

99 One who forgets to count for an entire 24-hour period continues counting the Omer from the following day, but without the blessing [שם:ח].

Laws of the Sefirat HaOmer Period

100 During the period of counting the Omer, certain mourning rituals are observed: one does not cut one's hair, shave, listen to music, or hold weddings and other parties [שו״ע ורמ״א או״ח, תצג א-ג]. Some permit shaving during this period. These practices commemorate a plague that killed twelve thousand pairs of students of Rabbi Akiva who, the Talmud says, did not honor one another properly. The Ashkenazi community intensified these mourning customs in the wake of the pogroms of the First Crusade, which took place in Iyar and Sivan in the year 1096 (4856).

101 Different communities observe these customs during different periods: (1) from the end of Pesaḥ to the 18th of Iyar (Lag BaOmer), (2) from the 1st of Iyar until the 3rd of Sivan, (3) during the entire period from the end of Pesaḥ until the 3rd of Sivan.

IYAR

Laws of BaHaB (בה״ב)

102 Some have the custom to say special Seliḥot on the first Monday, the first Thursday and the second Monday of Iyar (see law 45). If one of these days falls on Yom HaAtzma'ut or Pesaḥ Sheni, no Seliḥot are said.

Yom HaZikaron (4th of Iyar)

103 This day commemorates the Jews who gave their lives in defense of the Jewish settlement in the land of Israel, including soldiers of the Israel Defense Forces killed in the line of duty and civilians murdered in acts of terror. On Yom HaZikaron eve, a yahrzeit candle is lit and the Mourner's Kaddish is said by a bereaved parent, spouse or child. At the end of Shaḥarit, some congregations say special prayers (see pages 571–573).

104 Many communities hold special memorial ceremonies after Minḥa. These are generally planned to end at nightfall, when the celebrations of Yom HaAtzma'ut begin.

Yom HaAtzma'ut (5th of Iyar)

105 If the 5th of Iyar falls on Friday or Shabbat, Yom HaAtzma'ut is moved back to the preceding Thursday. If the 5th of Iyar falls on a Monday, Yom HaAtzma'ut is postponed to Tuesday.

106 On Yom HaAtzma'ut, the mourning customs of *Sefirat HaOmer* are suspended. It is permissible to cut one's hair, shave, attend parties, celebrate weddings and bar/bat mitzvas, and listen to music. The custom is to permit shaving and cutting one's hair before nightfall in honor of the holiday.

107 Ma'ariv: Customs differ (see pages 575–583). The service adopted by the Israeli Chief Rabbinate is as follows: selections from Psalms and other readings precede Ma'ariv for weekdays. It is customary for the *Shaliaḥ Tzibbur* to lead Ma'ariv using melodies associated with Yom Tov. After the Amida, the *Shaliaḥ Tzibbur* says Full Kaddish. Responsive readings and Psalm 126 to the tune of *"HaTikva"* follow. The service concludes with the counting of the Omer, *Aleinu*, Mourner's Kaddish and communal singing of אֲנִי מַאֲמִין.

108 Shaḥarit: *Pesukei DeZimra* as for Shabbat and Yom Tov, with the addition of מִזְמוֹר לְתוֹדָה (page 475). נִשְׁמַת is not said. After psalm 93 (page 495), prayers continue with Shaḥarit for weekdays (page 79). The Repetition of the Amida by the *Shaliaḥ Tzibbur* is followed by Hallel and Half Kaddish. On a Thursday the Torah is taken from the Ark and the appropriate section of the Torah is read. After the Torah reading, Half Kaddish is said. Haftara is said without blessings (page 585). The Prayer for the State of Israel is said, followed by the Memorial Prayer for fallen soldiers (page 573). Shaḥarit continues as for weekdays (page 241). At the end of the service, the congregation sings אֲנִי מַאֲמִין (page 589).

109 *Taḥanun* is omitted during Shaḥarit and Minḥa on the 5th of Iyar, even if Yom HaAtzma'ut is celebrated on a different day.

Pesaḥ Sheni (14th of Iyar)

110 *Taḥanun* is omitted during Shaḥarit and Minḥa but not on Minḥa of the preceding day.

Lag BaOmer (18th of Iyar)

111 The mourning customs of *Sefirat HaOmer* are suspended. It is permissible to cut one's hair, shave, attend parties, celebrate weddings and bar/bat mitzvas, and listen to music [שרע ורמיא אורח, תצג:ב].

112 For some communites, the mourning period that started at Pesaḥ, ends after Lag BaOmer. For others, it continues until three days before Shavuot [שם].

113 When Lag BaOmer falls on Sunday, shaving and cutting one's hair are permitted on the preceding Friday, in honor of Shabbat.

114 *Taḥanun* is omitted during Shaḥarit and Minḥa [משנ״ב או״ח תצג:ט].

Yom Yerushalayim (28th of Iyar)

115 The mourning customs of *Sefirat HaOmer* are suspended. It is permissible to cut one's hair, shave, attend parties, celebrate weddings and bar/bat mitzvas, and listen to music.

116 Shaḥarit: *Pesukei DeZimra* as for Shabbat and Yom Tov, with the addition of מִזְמוֹר לְתוֹדָה (page 475). נִשְׁמַת is not said. After psalm 93 (page 495), prayers continue with Shaḥarit for weekdays (page 79). The Repetition of the Amida by the *Shaliaḥ Tzibbur* is followed by Hallel and Half Kaddish. On a Thursday the Torah is taken from the Ark and the appropriate section of the Torah is read. After the Torah reading, Half Kaddish is said. Haftara is said without blessings (page 585). The Prayer for the State of Israel (page 587) is said, followed by the Memorial Prayer for fallen soldiers (page 573). Shaḥarit continues as for weekdays (page 241). At the end of the service, the congregation sings אֲנִי מַאֲמִין (page 589). The Repetition of the Amida is followed by Hallel and Half Kaddish. On Monday or Thursday, the Torah is taken from the Ark and the appropriate section of the Torah is read. After the Torah reading, Half Kaddish is said, followed by the Prayer for the State of Israel. On Monday or Thursday, the Torah is returned to the Ark. *Ashrei* and וּבָא לְצִיּוֹן are said, followed by Full Kaddish, *Aleinu*, Mourner's Kaddish, the Daily Psalm, and Mourner's Kaddish.

117 *Taḥanun* is omitted during Shaḥarit and Minḥa.

SIVAN

118 From Rosh Ḥodesh Sivan until the day after Shavuot, *Taḥanun* is omitted in Shaḥarit and Minḥa [רמ״א או״ח, תצד:ג].

Sheloshet Yemei Hagbala (3rd–5th of Sivan)

119 The three days prior to Shavuot commemorate the three days before the Torah was given at Sinai, when the Jewish people were enjoined to prepare themselves for the Divine Revelation.

120 For those who observe the customs of mourning after Lag BaOmer, the mourning period ends on the 3rd of Sivan.

TAMMUZ

Shiva Asar B'Tammuz (17th of Tammuz)

121 According to the Mishna (*Ta'anit* 4:6), the fast of the 17th of Tammuz commemorates five calamities that befell the Jewish people on that date: (1) Moses broke the tablets, (2) the daily *Tamid* sacrifice was interrupted (in Second Temple times), (3) the walls of Jerusalem were breached by Titus, (4) Apostemus burned the Torah, and (5) an idol was introduced to the Temple.

122 The fast begins at dawn (see laws 17–18) [שו"ע אורח, תקסד:א]. If the 17th of Tammuz falls on Shabbat, the fast is postponed to Sunday [שו"ע אורח תקנ,ג].

123 Shaḥarit: for weekdays. During the Repetition of the Amida, the *Shaliaḥ Tzibbur* says עֲנֵנוּ between the seventh and eighth blessings (page 157) [שו"ע אורח, תקסו:א]. This is followed by *Seliḥot, Avinu Malkenu* and *Taḥanun* [עֲרוּהיש אורח, תקסו:ח].

124 Torah Reading: Page 746 (see law 20).

125 Minḥa: for weekdays, except that after *Ashrei* and Half Kaddish, the Torah is read. The reading is the same as that of the morning. The third *oleh* reads the Haftara (page 747) [רמ"א, אורח, תקסו:א]. After the Torah is returned to the Ark, the *Shaliaḥ Tzibbur* says Half Kaddish, and Minḥa continues as for weekdays.

126 During the silent Amida, those who are fasting say עֲנֵנוּ as part of the sixteenth blessing, שׁוֹמֵעַ תְּפִלָּה (page 315). During the Repetition of the Amida, the *Shaliaḥ Tzibbur* says עֲנֵנוּ between the seventh and eighth blessings, as in the morning (page 297). After the eighteenth blessing (מוֹדִים), the *Shaliaḥ Tzibbur* says the paragraph relating to *Birkat Kohanim* (page 323). For the final blessing of the Amida, שִׂים שָׁלוֹם is said instead of שָׁלוֹם רָב. After the Amida, the congregation says *Avinu Malkenu*. This is followed by *Taḥanun*, Full Kaddish and *Aleinu*.

127 From the 17th of Tammuz until Tisha B'Av (the "Three Weeks"), certain mourning rituals are observed: one does not cut one's hair, shave, listen to music, buy new things, or hold weddings and other parties [שו"ע אורח תקנא,א]. Some permit shaving during this period.

AV

128 From Rosh Ḥodesh Av through Tisha B'Av (the "Nine Days") additional mourning rituals are observed: one abstains from eating meat or drinking wine, clothes are not laundered or pressed, and one generally minimizes joyful activities [שו"ע ורמ"א אורח, תקנא].

Erev Tisha B'Av (8th of Av)

129 *Taḥanun* is omitted from Minḥa.

130 The *Se'uda Mafseket* (final meal) is eaten after Minḥa. The custom is to eat no more than one cooked item. Three adult males should not eat together, so that no *zimmun* is said. Some have the custom to sit on the floor and eat eggs with ashes [שרע ורמיא אריח, תקנב].

131 When the final meal is eaten on Shabbat afternoon, these restrictions do not apply; however, the meal must be finished before sunset [שם: י].

Tisha B'Av (9th of Av)

132 According to the Mishna (*Ta'anit* 4:6), the fast of the 9th of Av commemorates five calamities that befell the Jewish people on that date: (1) God decreed that the children of Israel would not be allowed to enter the land of Israel, (2) the First Temple was destroyed, (3) the Second Temple was destroyed, (4) Beitar was captured, and (5) Jerusalem was plowed over.

133 The fast begins at sunset. In addition to eating and drinking, one is prohibited from washing and anointing oneself and from wearing leather shoes. Marital relations are likewise forbidden. One abstains from Torah study, except for topics such as mourning laws, *Eikha*, Job, and the unhappy portions of Jeremiah [שרע אריח, תקנד:א-ב]. One does not greet other people or inquire after their welfare [כ: שם].

134 Ma'ariv: for weekdays. The Amida is followed by Full Kaddish, the reading of *Eikha* and the recitation of *Kinot*. The congregation says וְאַתָּה קָדוֹשׁ (at the first arrow, page 247), followed by Full Kaddish (omitting the line beginning תִּתְקַבֵּל), *Aleinu*, and Mourner's Kaddish.

135 Shaḥarit: Neither tallit nor tefillin is worn in the morning [שרע אריח, תקנא: א]. During the Repetition of the Amida, the *Shaliaḥ Tzibbur* says עֲנֵנוּ between the seventh and eighth blessings (page 157). *Taḥanun* is omitted.

136 Torah Reading: page 746. Three men are called up. The third *oleh* reads the Haftara: page 747 [ד, ורמיא אריח תקנד:]. Afterwards, the first three blessings following the Haftara are said. After the Torah is returned to the Ark, *Kinot* are said. This is followed by *Ashrei*, וּבָא לְצִיּוֹן (omitting the verse וַאֲנִי זֹאת בְּרִיתִי, see page 247), Full Kaddish (omitting the line beginning תִּתְקַבֵּל), *Aleinu*, and Mourner's Kaddish.

137 During Minḥa both tallit and tefillin are worn.

138 Minḥa starts with the Daily Psalm (pages 259–267), *Ashrei* and Half Kaddish. The Torah is read: page 746. Three men are called up; the third reads the

Haftara: page 747. After the Torah is returned to the Ark, the *Shaliaḥ Tzibbur* says Half Kaddish.

139 During the silent recitation of the Amida (page 281), the congregation says נַחֵם as part of the fourteenth blessing (בּוֹנֵה יְרוּשָׁלַיִם), עֲנֵנוּ as part of the sixteenth blessing (שׁוֹמֵעַ תְּפִלָּה) (unless one is not fasting), and שִׂים שָׁלוֹם in place of שָׁלוֹם רָב (page 325). During the Repetition of the Amida, the *Shaliaḥ Tzibbur* says עֲנֵנוּ between the seventh (גּוֹאֵל יִשְׂרָאֵל) and eighth (רוֹפֵא חוֹלֵי עַמּוֹ יִשְׂרָאֵל) blessings, נַחֵם as part of the fourteenth blessing, the paragraph relating to *Birkat Kohanim* [שו״ע ורמ״א אוֹרַח, תקנו:א], and שִׂים שָׁלוֹם. Minḥa ends with Full Kaddish and *Aleinu*.

140 After Ma'ariv, *Kiddush Levana* is said (page 423). When Tisha B'Av begins on Motza'ei Shabbat, Havdala is said on Sunday night, preferably over a cup of wine or grape juice; no blessing is made over spices or a flame.

141 Although the fast is broken after nightfall, it is customary to continue the other mourning customs until midday of the 10th of Av. However, if the 10th of Av falls on Friday, one is permitted to bathe and otherwise prepare for Shabbat prior to midday [רמ״א אוֹרַח, תקנח:א].

Tu B'Av (15th of Av)

142 According to the Mishna (*Ta'anit* 4:8), on the 15th of Av, the young women of Jerusalem would put on borrowed white dresses and dance together in the vineyards. Young men would come out to watch them, and the women would urge the men not to be swayed by beauty, but to be drawn to women of good family.

143 *Taḥanun* is omitted during Shaḥarit and Minḥa.

DAILY PRAYER

ON WAKING

144 The custom is to say מוֹדֶה אֲנִי immediately on waking, even before washing hands [משנ"ב אורח, א: ח].

Laws of Washing Hands; בִּרְכַּת אֲשֶׁר יָצַר; אֱלֹהַי נְשָׁמָה

145 Upon waking, one is obligated to wash hands [שבת, קח]. Some hold that one should not walk four *amot* (around six feet) prior to washing hands [משנ"ב אורח, א:ב (בשם הזוהר)].

146 According to some authorities, there is a separate obligation to wash hands prior to prayer [עזוה"ש אורח, ד: ה]. One who washes and says the blessing of עַל נְטִילַת יָדַיִם after waking, does not repeat the blessing when washing prior to prayer [רמ"א אורח, ו: ב].

147 Hands should preferably be washed using a cup, but a cup is not required [שו"ע ורמ"א, אורח: ד, ז]. The custom is to pour water from the cup onto the right hand, then the left, and repeat a total of three times [משנ"ב, שם: י]. Where water is unavailable, one may clean one's hands using any appropriate material; in that case, the blessing is changed to עַל נְקִיּוּת יָדַיִם [שו"ע אורח, ד: כב].

148 The blessing of עַל נְטִילַת יָדַיִם may be said before drying one's hands or afterward [משנ"ב, ד: ב].

149 A number of reasons have been offered for washing hands upon waking. The Gemara states that, during the night, hands are enveloped by an "evil vapor," רוּחַ רָעָה, which is removed by washing one's hands [שבת, קח]. In addition, there is a concern that, while sleeping, one's hands may have touched an unclean part of the body [ראו"ש ברכות, פ"ט: כג]. Finally, it is noted that a person who wakes is like a newborn; therefore, one needs to sanctify oneself by washing [שו״ת רשב״א ח״א, קצא].

150 The blessing of אֲשֶׁר יָצַר should be said each time after relieving oneself. It is recommended that one should go to the bathroom immediately after washing hands, then say the blessings of עַל נְטִילַת יָדַיִם followed by אֲשֶׁר יָצַר. However, even if one does not relieve oneself, one is permitted to say אֲשֶׁר יָצַר after washing hands [רמ״א אורח, ד:א]. One should not postpone going to the bathroom [שו״ע אורח, ג:יז].

151 According to the Gemara, the blessing of אֱלֹהַי נְשָׁמָה should be said upon waking [ברכות, ס]. The contemporary custom is to say אֱלֹהַי נְשָׁמָה immediately after אֲשֶׁר יָצַר [משנ״ב, שם יב]. However, some rule that one who stays up all night should not say אֱלֹהַי נְשָׁמָה and the blessing of הַמַּעֲבִיר שֵׁנָה מֵעֵינָי, and should instead hear them from others [משנ״ב, מו:כד].

152 The custom is to say the *Birkhot HaTorah* after אֲשֶׁר יָצַר, because one should not read or recite Torah verses before making the requisite blessings on Torah study [שו״ע ורמ״א, אורח:מו, ט].

Laws of Tzitzit

153 Putting on a four-cornered garment with tzitzit attached fulfills an affirmative mitzva from the Torah. The obligation applies only during the daytime [מנחות, מג]. Since wearing tzitzit is a time-bound mitzva, women are exempt [שו״ע אורח, יז: ב].

154 The accepted practice is to wear a *tallit katan* all day long and to wear a *tallit gadol* during Shaḥarit [שו״ע אורח, כד: א]. The dominant Ashkenazi custom is to begin wearing a *tallit gadol* when one marries [משנ״ב, יז:י], but Jews of German and Sephardi descent begin wearing the *tallit gadol* at an earlier age. Nevertheless, the custom is to wear a *tallit gadol* – even if unmarried – when acting as *Shaliaḥ Tzibbur*, reading from or being called up to the Torah, opening the Ark or performing *hagbaha* or *gelila*.

155 One should put on the *tallit katan* immediately upon dressing. One should first examine the strings of the tzitzit to ensure that they are not torn [שו״ע אורח, ח:ט]. Then, while standing [שו״ע אורח, ח:א], one should say the blessing of עַל מִצְוַת צִיצִית and immediately put on the garment [רמ״א אורח, ח:ו]. One does not say the blessing if (a) one is about to put on a *tallit gadol*, and (b) one will have in mind the *tallit katan* when saying the blessing on the *tallit gadol*. On the other hand, if there is a substantial interruption between the time one puts on the *tallit katan* and one puts on the *tallit gadol*, one should say the separate blessing on the *tallit katan* [שו״ע אורח, ח:יג].

156 The blessing on tzitzit may be said at daybreak, but not before [רמ״א אורח, יח:ג].

157 Similarly with the *tallit gadol*, one should first examine the strings, then while standing, say the blessing לְהִתְעַטֵּף בַּצִּיצִית and put on the *tallit gadol*. The word לְהִתְעַטֵּף means to wrap oneself; one should initially wrap the *tallit gadol* around to cover one's head and face for a few moments, after which it is sufficient that it cover the torso [מגא, ח:ב].

158 If one removes the *tallit gadol* for any reason, one should repeat the blessing when putting the tallit back on [שו״ע אורח, ח:יד]. The blessing is not repeated if the *tallit gadol* is put back on soon after taking it off, and either (a) one was wearing a *tallit katan* all along, or (b) one's original intention was to put the tallit back on shortly [משבצ, שם:לז].

159 If one's head is otherwise covered, there is no requirement to cover one's head with the *tallit gadol* [טורא אורח, ח:ג]. Some authorities nevertheless require married men to cover their heads with the *tallit gadol* throughout Shaḥarit, because it promotes reverence in prayer [בהיט אורח, ח:ג (בשם הרדב״ז)]. Others have the custom to cover their heads during the Amida only, or from *Barekhu* through the end of the Amida. Unmarried persons should not wear the *tallit gadol* over their heads [קידושין, כט:].

Laws of Tefillin

160 Putting on tefillin fulfills an affirmative mitzva from the Torah. The obligation applies only on weekdays [שו״ע אורח, לא]. Since wearing tefillin is a time-bound mitzva, women are exempt [שו״ע אורח, לח:ג].

161 One puts on tefillin after the tallit, because the former are more sacred, and we follow the principle of "ascending in sanctity" (מעלין בקודש) [שו״ע אורח, כה:א].

162 The *tefillin shel yad* is worn on the weaker arm, meaning that right-handed people wear it on the left arm, and left-handed people wear it on the right arm [שו״ע אורח, כז:ו].

163 The *tefillin shel yad* is put on first, by placing the box on the biceps near the elbow joint, angled toward the heart, and saying the blessing לְהָנִיחַ תְּפִלִּין. One then tightens the strap around the muscle and wraps the strap around the forearm seven times. Without speaking or otherwise becoming distracted [שו״ע אורח, כה:ט-י], one places the *tefillin shel rosh* on the head above the hairline, centered over the nose, and says the blessing עַל מִצְוַת תְּפִלִּין. One then adjusts the straps, so that the knot rests at the base of the skull and the two straps hang down the front of one's chest, and says בָּרוּךְ שֵׁם כְּבוֹד מַלְכוּתוֹ לְעוֹלָם וָעֶד [רמ״א אורח, כה:ה].

Finally, one wraps the strap of the *tefillin shel yad* around the fingers, while saying וְאֵרַשְׂתִּיךְ (See page 17).

164 The box of the *tefillin shel yad* and the *tefillin shel rosh* must rest directly on the arm and head respectively, without any barrier between them [שו"ע או"ח, כו:ד]. This rule does not apply to the straps of the tefillin [רמ"א, שם].

165 One should regularly touch first the *tefillin shel yad*, then the *tefillin shel rosh*, so as to remain conscious that one is wearing them. In particular, one should touch the appropriate tefillin when saying the relevant verses of the Shema [שו"ע או"ח, כח:א] (see law 182). It is also customary to touch them when saying the verse פּוֹתֵחַ אֶת־יָדֶךָ during *Ashrei*.

166 At a minimum, tefillin should be worn while saying the Shema and the Amida [שו"ע או"ח, כה:ד]. The custom is to keep them on until one has heard the *Kedusha* three times and Kaddish four times [רמ"א, שם:ג], which means that one should not remove the tefillin until after the Mourner's Kaddish following *Aleinu* [משנ"ב, שם:ו]. In theory, one should wear tefillin all day. The custom, however, is to take the tefillin off after praying, because it is difficult to maintain a constant awareness of the tefillin and the requisite purity of mind and body throughout the day [שו"ע או"ח, לז:ב].

167 The order in which one removes tefillin is the reverse of the order in which they were put on. Thus, one first unwinds the strap of the *tefillin shel yad* from one's fingers, then removes the *tefillin shel rosh* and wraps it in its case. One then unwinds the *tefillin shel yad* from the arm, removes the box from the muscle and wraps the tefillin in its case [שו"ע או"ח, כח:ב]. This entire process should be performed standing up [משנ"ב, כח:ו].

SERVICES

Laws of Birkhot HaShaḥar and Pesukei DeZimra

168 According to the Gemara [ברכות, ס:], *Birkhot HaShaḥar* (Morning Blessings) were originally said separately, in conjunction with the performance of the associated activity. Thus, upon dressing one would say the blessing of מַלְבִּישׁ עֲרֻמִּים, and upon standing up one would say the blessing of זוֹקֵף כְּפוּפִים. However, the custom now is to say all of the blessings together in the synagogue [שו"ע או"ח, מו:ב].

169 The insertion of the verse (or verses) of Shema after *Birkhot HaShaḥar* was not meant to satisfy the individual's obligation to say the Shema every morning [רמ"א, שם:ט]. However, as discussed in further detail in law 176, the three paragraphs of Shema must be said within the first half of the morning (measured as ¼ of the time from daybreak to nightfall). Since some congregations hold Shaḥarit services late, especially on Shabbat, and as such the communal recitation of the Shema in Shaḥarit may take place too late to fulfill the halakhic obligation, under such circumstances it is recommended to say all three paragraphs of Shema after *Birkhot HaShaḥar* [משנ"ב, שם: לא].

170 One should say the biblical verses describing the קרבן תמיד (page 47), preferably with the congregation [רמ"א אורח, מח]. Some authorities require one to stand [משנ"ב, שם: ב].

171 The fifth chapter of מסכת זבחים and the ברייתא דרבי ישמעאל were added after the biblical passages regarding sacrifices to institutionalize the daily study of Scripture, Mishna and Gemara [שו"ע אורח, נ: א].

172 Saying Kaddish, *Barekhu* or *Kedusha* requires the presence of a *minyan* (ten adult males) [שו"ע אורח, נה: א].

173 One should not utter idle speech from the beginning of the words בָּרוּךְ אַתָּה יהוה in *Barukh SheAmar* until one completes the Amida [שו"ע אורח, נא: ד].

174 If one comes late to the synagogue, one may skip all, or portions, of *Pesukei DeZimra*, as follows:

   a If there is sufficient time, say *Barukh SheAmar*, Psalms 145–150, and *Yishtabaḥ*.

   b If there is less time, say *Barukh SheAmar*, Psalms 145, 148, 150, and *Yishtabaḥ*.

   c If there is less time, say *Barukh SheAmar*, Psalm 145, and *Yishtabaḥ*.

   d If there is less time, omit *Pesukei DeZimra* altogether. Complete the rest of the service with the congregation, then say *Pesukei DeZimra* privately, omitting *Barukh SheAmar* and *Yishtabaḥ* [רמ"א ושו"ע אורח, נב].

Morning Shema – קריאת שמע של שחרית

175 Saying the three paragraphs of the Shema each morning and each night fulfills an affirmative mitzva from the Torah. Since saying the Shema is a time-bound mitzva, women are exempt [שו"ע אורח, ע:א]. Nevertheless, women are required to say the first verse to express their acceptance of עול מלכות שמים ("the yoke of the kingdom of Heaven") [ב"ח, שם]. Women are permitted to say the Shema and its preceding and following blessings [משנ"ב, שם: ב].

176 There is a set time period every morning during which the Shema may be

said. The optimal time is immediately before sunrise, when there is assumed to be sufficient light to recognize an acquaintance from a distance of four *amot* (around 6 feet). If necessary, the Shema may be said from daybreak [שו״ע אר״ח, נ:ג]. After sunrise, the earlier the Shema is said, the better [שם: ב]. At the latest, the Shema must be said during the first quarter of the day (in halakhic terminology, three halakhic "hours," where each hour represents 1/12 of the day; regarding the measure of a "day," see law 85) [שם: א]. After that time, one is permitted to say the Shema with the blessings during the fourth halakhic "hour," that is, until the end of the first third of the day. After that, the Shema may be said without the blessings, but this does not fulfill the mitzva [שם].

177 If one says the Shema without its preceding and following blessings, one has still fulfilled the mitzva. However, one should say the blessings afterward, preferably repeating the Shema as well [שו״ע אר״ח, ס: ב].

178 Given the emphasis on the *reading* of the Shema and the importance of its content, the practice is that each of the letters and words be pronounced and enunciated clearly, without slurring from one letter or word to the next. So, for example, when a word ends with the same letter as the beginning of the next word, one should enunciate them separately; for example, על לבבכם or ואבדתם מהרה, so that they do not sound like one word. Similarly, if one were to slur the words *veḥara af*, which means "will be angry," it would sound like *ḥaraf*, which means "blasphemed"! Similarly, when a word ends with the letter *mem* and the next begins with an *alef*, like וכרתם את or ושמתם את, reading them quickly would make it sound like "death" – מת. So, too, one should be careful not to confuse letters that have similar sounds; for example, the word תזכרו, "you will remember," should not be made to sound like תשכרו, "you will be rewarded." (For further examples, see *Shulḥan Arukh* 61.) Because of this, people tend to slow down when they read the Shema, being very deliberate and exacting. Indeed, when one is in a *minyan*, the rabbi often sets a slower pace so that people will not feel rushed.

179 Because of the special importance of the first line of the Shema, the custom is to pause for a moment to collect one's thoughts and to have the intention to accept Hashem as King in one's life. For this reason, too, there is a custom to cover one's eyes so that one is not distracted, and to say the first verse louder than one might usually recite one's prayers, for the command here, after all, is *Shema* – Hear!

180 So important is the first line, that if one does not have the proper intention, then one should repeat it (*Shulḥan Arukh* 60:5).

181 The second line, however, is recited quietly since, unlike the other verses here, it does not derive from the Torah but was instituted by the Rabbis (*Pesahim* 56a) as an extension of the theme of the first verse. Among the reasons offered for its inclusion is that in the days of the *Beit HaMikdash*, when on Yom Kippur the *Kohen Gadol* invoked the special Name of Hashem, the priests and the people did not answer "Amen" but rather they answered with this phrase. Today, in the absence of the *Beit HaMikdash* and in the absence of the Name, our reciting this phrase achieves the same purpose.

182 As discussed in law 165 above, the custom is to touch the *tefillin shel yad* when saying וּקְשַׁרְתָּם לְאוֹת עַל־יָדֶךָ and to touch the *tefillin shel rosh* when saying וְהָיוּ לְטֹטָפֹת בֵּין עֵינֶיךָ [שו״ע אורח, כח:א].

183 If one enters the synagogue and hears the congregation about to begin saying the Shema, one is required to say the first verse of the Shema together with the congregation [שו״ע אורח, סה:ב].

Laws of the Shaharit Amida

184 There is a set time period every morning during which the Amida may be said. In general, the Amida should be said at or after sunrise. At the latest, the Amida should be said during the first third of the day, (four halakhic "hours"; regarding the measure of a "day," see law 85). If the Amida was said between daybreak and sunrise, the mitzva has been fulfilled. If necessary, it is permissible to say the Amida after the first third of the day, but before midday [שו״ע אורח, פט:א].

185 One who must leave for work (or a journey) before sunrise is permitted to say the Amida from daybreak [שו״ע שם סעיז]. If one did not say the Shaharit Amida prior to midday, one should say the Minha Amida twice [משנ״ב, שם סיקז].

186 One should not eat or drink before saying the Amida, although drinking water is permitted. Moreover, anyone who needs to eat or drink in order to concentrate on his prayers is permitted to do so [שו״ע אורח, פט:ג-ד].

187 The Amida is said facing the site of the Temple in Jerusalem. Thus, outside Israel, one faces the land of Israel; inside Israel, one faces Jerusalem; and inside Jerusalem, one faces the Temple Mount [שו״ע אורח, צד:א]. If one is praying in a synagogue, one should pray facing the Ark [משנ״ב, שם סיק י].

188 One who is traveling in a vehicle should, if possible, say the Amida standing; if this is not possible, one is permitted to sit [שו״ע אורח, צד:ה].

189 When saying the Shaharit Amida, one may not allow any interruption or disruption between the conclusion of the blessing גָּאַל יִשְׂרָאֵל and the introductory

words to the Amida [שו"ע או"ח, ס: ח; שם, קיא: א]. This includes not responding to Kaddish, *Barekhu*, *Kedusha* or *Modim*, although on Shabbat one may do so [רמ"א, שם]. One may also answer "Amen" if one hears someone else concluding the blessing גָּאַל יִשְׂרָאֵל [רמ"א או"ח, ס: ו].

The Sacred Choreography of Tefilla –
An Introduction to the Mechanics of the Amida

▸ THREE STEPS FORWARDS AND BACKWARDS

190 Rema (Rabbi Moshe Isserles) writes in his gloss on the *Shulḥan Arukh* (95:1) that before beginning the *Shemoneh Esreh*, one should take three steps forwards as a way of "coming close and approaching." This is derived from the three places in the Tanakh where the word וַיִּגַּשׁ, *vayigash*, is used just before prayer (Gen. 18:23; 44:18; Kings I 18:36). This action makes sense given that the *Shemoneh Esreh* is the culmination of our movement in Shaḥarit toward a meeting with Hashem. Some (*Mishna Berura* 95:3) suggest that one should first take three steps backwards since "all actions of holiness require preparation," and some even suggest that this take place during the sentences preceding the beginning of the *Shemoneh Esreh* (i.e., ...תְּהִלּוֹת לְאֵל עֶלְיוֹן). That is to say, if one has not yet come to the realization that he is about to address the King of kings in a personal encounter, one takes a moment to get into the right frame of mind by preparing oneself – body and soul.

▸ STANDING

191 One is required to stand (*Shulḥan Arukh* 94:8). Hence one of the names of *Shemoneh Esreh* is *Amida* which means standing. The prayer is supposed to be said with awe or reverence, and such emotions are rarely associated with sitting or leaning (*Hagahot Maimoniot Tefilla* 5:7). One may not lean against a chair or wall or the like in such a way that if the object were to be removed, one would lose one's balance. There are some rare exceptions, for example, if you are not feeling well (*Mishna Berura* 94:22), or if you need to pray on an airplane and standing is impossible or unsafe.

▸ FEET TOGETHER

192 One should stand with one's feet close together. This is supposed to imitate the stance of the angels whom the prophet Ezekiel (1:7) described in one of the most mystical visions in Tanakh as: "their legs were as one straight leg." The *Shemoneh Esreh* is the pinnacle of our prayers, and so we try to emulate those

who always stand in His presence. MahaRi Aboab (fl. late-fourteenth century, quoted in *Beit Yosef* 95:1) suggests that we thus make ourselves like someone who cannot escape; we are rooted in place in order to focus on our standing before Hashem. The *Beit Yosef* suggests further that since we are standing before God, we should try to see ourselves as purely spiritual creatures, and thereby rid ourselves of physical concerns.

▸ SWAYING OR STANDING STILL

193 There is a difference of opinion about the need to sway or *shokel* when one is praying. There are those who say it adds to one's experience and others who say it detracts. Do whatever works for you. Try praying with or without movement, or alternate from time to time (*Mishna Berura* 48:5; 95:7).

▸ SILENTLY OR IN A WHISPER

194 Many of the practices of prayer are learned from Hannah (Sam. I 1:9-16). You might recall that she was seen praying silently by Eli, who thought she was drunk, because "only her lips moved." From here emerged support for the value of articulating the words by whispering (hence the Amida is also sometimes referred to as תפילה בלחש – *Tefilla beLaḥash*) instead of just reading them in your mind; words said aloud are often different than words just said in your head. Moreover, whispering is a form of communication that connotes closeness and intimacy, precisely the way one is supposed to feel toward Hashem at this point. Hence, when praying with others, the practice is to say the prayer in a whisper, loud enough that you can hear your own voice but not so loud that you will disturb the concentration of anyone near you. Should you prefer to say the prayer silently, you can do that too – after all it worked for Hannah, who ultimately gave birth to a prophet.

▸ BOWING – AVOT AND MODIM

195 The Gemara (*Berakhot* 34a) says that one should bow at only two points: at the beginning and end of the first blessing, *Avot*, and at the beginning and end of *Modim*. Apparently these two blessings were singled out because of their central importance to the *Shemoneh Esreh*. "Bowing" minimally consists of bending over at the waist, and this indeed is the Sephardi custom. Ashkenazi practice is to also bend one's knees for *Avot* as follows: ברוך – bend one's knees (the Hebrew words "bless" and "knee" are related); אתה – bend at the waist; יהוה – stand up straight (*Magen Avraham* 113:4). At *Modim*, however, the custom

is fairly universal to simply bend at the waist. A common practice is to follow the opinion in the Gemara (*Berakhot* 28b) which suggests that one bend "until all of the vertebrae in the spinal column protrude."

▸ BOWING AT THE CONCLUSION

196 The Gemara (*Yoma* 53b) explains that upon concluding one's prayer, one should take three steps backwards and bid farewell to the King. If one fails to do so, it says, "it would have been better had he not prayed at all," presumably because one lacked the proper intent and posture to begin with. Furthermore, the prescribed manner of taking leave is by bowing first to Hashem's right side (symbolic of His might) and then to His left (which is our right). From here derives the practice to take three steps back, bow to our left while reciting עשה שלום במרומיו; then to our right while saying הוא יעשה שלום עלינו; and then bowing forward when concluding ועל כל ישראל. If one does not have enough space to retreat directly backwards, one may do so diagonally.

▸ STANDING IN PLACE

197 The Gemara (*Yoma* 53b) also suggests that one should wait a few moments in the place to which one has retreated rather than rushing forward or away. Rif (Rabbi Yitzḥak ben Yaakov Alfasi HaKohen) suggests that one should remain there until the Ḥazan begins the *Kedusha* (*Berakhot* 24b). If one is praying alone, it is suggested that one wait for the amount of time it takes to walk four *amot* (about six feet).

Laws of Havinenu

198 When circumstances require, one is permitted to substitute a special paragraph (*Havinenu*, page 683) for the thirteen middle blessings of the Amida. This is only permitted in exceptional cases, such as when one is incapable of concentrating during a full-length Amida or expects interruptions. One says this abbreviated form of the Amida while standing, and one does not need to repeat the full-length Amida afterward. *Havinenu* is not said during the winter months or on Motza'ei Shabbat [שו"ע אורח, קי:א].

Laws of חזרת הש"ץ

199 The Gemara (*Rosh HaShana* 34b) says that the *Shemoneh Esreh* is repeated so that the Ḥazan can help fulfill the obligation of those who were not learned enough to have said the *Shemoneh Esreh* on their own. Hence, all they needed

to do was wait for the repetition and respond "Amen." If so, then why repeat the *Shemoneh Esreh* today, when all of us have siddurim (which they did not have in those days), and all of us can read and thereby fulfill the obligation on our own during the silent *Shemoneh Esreh*? Rav Soloveitchik maintained that while the repetition served a functional purpose, that was not its ultimate goal. Rather the goal was to have another *Shemoneh Esreh* that was recited not by individuals but by the community. The *Ḥazan* serves as the duly appointed emissary and our presence as a *minyan* responding Amen to every blessing is what makes it into a communal prayer. This is the reason that during the *Ḥazarat HaShatz* many replicate the silent *Shemoneh Esreh* by standing at all times and not speaking, lest the blessings, and the communal nature of the prayer, be rendered invalid. And this is the reason, too, why it is so important for everyone to respond Amen.

200 During the Repetition of the Amida, the congregation is required to listen attentively to the blessings and respond "Amen" [שו"ע אורח, קכד: ד].

201 In order to begin the Repetition of the Amida, at least nine men are required to be listening attentively [שם].

202 Some require the congregation to stand during the Repetition of the Amida [רמ"א, שם].

203 Under extenuating circumstances, the *Shaliaḥ Tzibbur* may begin saying the Amida aloud, while the congregation says the Amida quietly along with him. The *Kedusha* is said aloud in the customary fashion and, after the *Shaliaḥ Tzibbur* finishes the blessing הָאֵל הַקָּדוֹשׁ, he and the congregation continue saying the Amida quietly [רמ"א, שם: ב].

204 At the conclusion of the Repetition of the Amida, it is recommended that the *Shaliaḥ Tzibbur* say quietly the verse יִהְיוּ לְרָצוֹן אִמְרֵי פִי, except when Full Kaddish immediately follows the Repetition of the Amida [משנ"ב קנג:נ]. Some also say this verse during the individual's silent Amida.

Laws of Kedusha

205 There are different customs regarding what the congregation says during the *Kedusha*: (1) The congregation says only the biblical verses (...בָּרוּךְ...; קָדוֹשׁ...; יִמְלֹךְ) [שו"ע אורח, קכה:א]; (2) The congregation says every word of the *Kedusha*, with the *Shaliaḥ Tzibbur* repeating each sentence [בה"ט, שם (בשם האר"י)]; (3) The congregation says נְקַדֵּשׁ and all the biblical verses [ערוה"ש, שם: ב].

206 *Kedusha* belongs to a category of prayers in which we sanctify God's name. Like

Barekhu and *Kaddish*, it requires a *minyan*, we must be summoned or invited to say them by a *Ḥazan*, and (according to Ashkenazic practice), they are all said while standing.

207 Hashem is seen as surrounded by His angels sanctifying His name, and here we try to recreate that scene as we ourselves mirror the words and actions of the angels. Before *Keriat Shema*, we recited these verses as a description of what took place; but here we reenact it and so we stand, feet together, rising on our toes like angels (Ezek. 1:7 – "and their legs were as one straight leg").

Laws of Birkat Kohanim

208 The Kohen has an affirmative obligation from the Torah to bless the congregation, provided there are at least ten males aged 13 or over (including the Kohen himself) [שרע' אורח, קכח: א-ב].

209 The Kohen is required to wash his hands (without a blessing) before saying *Birkat Kohanim*. It is customary for a Levi to pour the water [שם, ו]. If there is no water, or if the Kohen did not have enough time to wash, he may say *Birkat Kohanim*, provided that: (a) he washed his hands before Shaḥarit, and (b) since washing for Shaḥarit he has not touched anything unclean, even his own shoes [משנב, שם:כ].

210 Each Kohen removes his shoes before ascending to say *Birkat Kohanim* [שם,ה]. When the *Shaliaḥ Tzibbur* begins רצה, the Kohanim ascend to the Ark and stand with their backs to the congregation [שם, ח:ו-ז]. After the congregation answers "Amen" to the blessing הטוב שמך ולך נאה להודות, if there is more than one Kohen, the *Shaliaḥ Tzibbur* calls out "Kohanim," and they turn around and say the blessing. If only one Kohen has ascended to the Ark, he starts the blessing without being prompted [שם:י-יא]. The *Shaliaḥ Tzibbur* does not answer "Amen" at the end of the blessing [משנב, שם: עא].

211 The *Shaliaḥ Tzibbur* reads each word of *Birkat Kohanim* and the Kohanim repeat it in unison. At the end of each verse, the congregation answers "Amen" [שרע' ורמ"א, שם: יג]. The *Shaliaḥ Tzibbur* does not answer "Amen" at the end of each verse [שרע', שם: ט].

212 If the *Shaliaḥ Tzibbur* is himself a Kohen, some rule that he should not say the blessing, unless no other Kohanim are in the synagogue [שרע', שם:ט]. However, the custom today is for the *Shaliaḥ Tzibbur* to participate in the blessing [משנב, שם: עה].

213 During *Birkat Kohanim*, the congregation should stand silently with eyes lowered and concentrate on the words of the Kohanim. One should not look at the faces or hands of the Kohanim [שו״ע, שם:כג].

214 In most congregations in Israel, *Birkat Kohanim* is said every day in Shaḥarit and, where applicable, in Musaf, as well as in *Ne'ila* on Yom Kippur. It is also said in Minḥa on a fast day [שו״ע אורח, קכט:א]. *Birkat Kohanim* is not said in Shaḥarit of Tisha B'Av or in a mourner's house [משנב, קכא:י], although in Jerusalem, the custom is to say *Birkat Kohanim* even in a mourner's house [גשר החיים, כ:ה]. On those occasions and when no Kohen is present, the *Shaliaḥ Tzibbur* says אֱלֹהֵינוּ וֵאלֹהֵי אֲבוֹתֵינוּ (page 185).

215 The custom outside Israel and in certain northern Israeli congregations, is for the *Shaliaḥ Tzibbur* to say אֱלֹהֵינוּ וֵאלֹהֵי אֲבוֹתֵינוּ instead of the Kohanim saying *Birkat Kohanim*, except in Musaf of Yom Tov [רמ״א אורח, קכח:מד].

Laws of Taḥanun

216 נפילת אפיים ("Lowering the Head," pages 209/333) is said immediately after the Shaḥarit Amida on Sundays, Tuesdays, Wednesdays and Thursdays, and after the Minḥa Amida on every weekday except for Friday. In Shaḥarit on Mondays and Thursdays, *Taḥanun* begins with וְהוּא רַחוּם (page 201), and יהוה אֱלֹהֵי יִשְׂרָאֵל (page 213) is added.

217 On fast days (except on Tisha B'Av, when neither *Avinu Malkenu* nor *Taḥanun* is said) and during the *Aseret Yemei Teshuva*, *Avinu Malkenu* (page 195) is said before *Taḥanun*.

218 One should not speak between the Amida and נפילת אפיים [שו״ע אורח, קלא:א].

219 נפילת אפיים should be said while sitting [שם:ב], with one's head lowered against one's weaker forearm. If one is wearing tefillin however, one lays one's head against the arm lacking tefillin [שו״ע ורמ״א, שם:א]. The head is lowered only where there is a Sefer Torah [רמ״א, שם:ב], except in Jerusalem, where the custom is to lower the head in any case [שרית אגרות משה יורד חיג, קכט:ב].

220 For days on which *Taḥanun* is not said, see list on page 201 [שו״ע ורמ״א אורח, קלא:ד; משנב, שם:ט].

Laws of Torah Reading

221 To ensure that the Torah is read at least once every three days, Moses established the public reading of the Torah on Shabbat, Yom Tov, Ḥol HaMo'ed, Rosh

Ḥodesh, and Monday and Thursday mornings. Ezra added the public reading in Shabbat Minḥa [רמב״ם הלכות תפילה פי״ב ה״א].

222 On weekdays and Shabbat Minḥa, three people are called up [שו״ע או״ח, קלה:א]. On Shabbat morning, seven are called up, though additional individuals (*hosafot*) may also be called [שו״ע או״ח, רפב:א]. On Yom Kippur morning, six are called up, five on Yom Tov, and four on Ḥol HaMo'ed and Rosh Ḥodesh.

223 If a Kohen is present, he is called up first. If a Levi is also present, he is called up second; for subsequent *aliyot*, one calls up a Yisrael [שו״ע או״ח, קלה:ג]. If a Kohen is present but a Levi is not, the same Kohen is called up for the first two *aliyot* [שם:ח]. If a Levi is present and a Kohen is not, the Levi need not be called up, but if the Levi is called up, he should be first [שו״ע ורמ״א או״ח, קלה:ו].

224 The custom is to avoid calling up a Kohen after a Yisrael, except for Maftir and, in some communities, for אחרון, provided it is a *hosafa* [רמ״א, שם:י].

225 Other individuals who are given priority for an *aliya* include: a bridegroom on his wedding day and the Shabbat preceding and following the wedding; a Bar Mitzva; the father of a newborn baby; one commemorating a parent's *yahrzeit*; and a person obligated to say *Birkat HaGomel* [בהל, קלו:דיה יבשבת].

226 It is considered bad luck to call up two brothers or a father and son one after the other [שו״ע או״ח, קמא:ו]. While the custom is to avoid the practice, if one is called up after one's brother or father, one should accept the *aliya*.

227 One who is called up to the Torah should take the shortest route to the *bima* [שו״ע, שם:ו]. He should open the scroll to locate where the *aliya* begins. Still holding the handle, he should say the blessing, taking care to look away from the Torah (or close the scroll or his eyes), so as not to appear to be reading the blessing from the scroll itself [שו״ע ורמ״א או״ח, קלט:ד].

228 If, after the blessing is said, the *ba'al koreh* discovers that the blessing was said over the wrong passage of the Torah, the scroll is rolled to the correct location and the *oleh* repeats the blessing. The blessing does not need to be repeated if the correct passage was visible when the blessing was said [שו״ע או״ח, קמ:ג; משנ״ב, שם:ט].

229 The Torah is read standing [שו״ע או״ח, קמא:א]. The *oleh* is also required to stand. The rest of the congregation is not obligated to stand, but it is proper to do so [ערוהי״ש, שם:ב].

230 The *oleh* should read the words quietly along with the *ba'al koreh* [שו״ע או״ח, קמא:ב].

231 If the *ba'al koreh* makes an error that affects the meaning of the words, he needs to reread the Torah portion from the location of the error [שו״ע ורמ״א או״ח, קמב:א].

232 If an error is found in the Torah scroll, the reading is stopped, a new scroll is brought out, and the reading is continued from the location of the error [שו״ע או״ח, קמ״ג: ד]. It is not required to call up all of the *aliyot* a second time to read from the new scroll, but if the remainder of the reading can be divided into the appropriate number of *aliyot* for that day, it is preferable to do so [משנ״ב שם: טו].

233 It is customary to say a prayer for a sick person (מִי שֶׁבֵּרַךְ, page 225) at the conclusion of the Torah reading, or between *aliyot*.

234 After completing the reading from a Torah scroll, the open scroll is raised and displayed to the entire congregation. The congregation says וְזֹאת הַתּוֹרָה (page 227) [שו״ע ורמ״א או״ח, קל״ד: ב].

Laws of Birkat HaGomel

235 After being saved from mortal danger, one should say *Birkat HaGomel* on page 225 [שו״ע או״ח, ריש, סי׳: א ו-ט; משנ״ב, שם: לב]. The blessing should be said no later than three days after the event [שו״ע, שם]. *Birkat HaGomel* is said only in the presence of a *minyan*; the custom is to say the blessing after the Torah reading [שם: ג]. If one will not be in the presence of *minyan* within three days, one is permitted to say the blessing without a *minyan* [משנ״ב, שם: ח].

236 A husband may say *Birkat HaGomel* for his wife, or a father for his children [משנ״ב, שם: ז]. But, according to most authorities, it is preferable that a woman say *Birkat HaGomel* for herself in the presence of a *minyan*.

Laws of Mourner's Kaddish

237 The Mourner's Kaddish is generally said after specific chapters of Psalms at the beginning and end of a service. It is said by one who is either (a) in mourning for a relative, or (b) commemorating the *yahrzeit* of a relative. When no such person is present, the Mourner's Kaddish is generally omitted, except after *Aleinu* at the end of Shaḥarit [רמ״א או״ח, קל״ב: ב], when it is said by one whose parents have died or whose parents do not object to their child saying the Mourner's Kaddish [שם].

238 Historically, the Mourner's Kaddish was said by one individual. A set of rules developed for allocating among different mourners the various opportunities for saying it [ביאור הלכה, שם, קונטרס מאמר קדישין, י]. Today, most congregations allow group recitation of the Mourner's Kaddish. In such cases, they should say the words in unison [סידור יעב״ץ].

Laws of the Minḥa Amida

239 There is a set time period every afternoon during which the Minḥa Amida may be said. At the earliest, one may say the Amida one half of a halakhic "hour" from midday (a halakhic hour is ¹⁄₁₂ of the day measured from daybreak to nightfall). At the latest, the Amida must be said before nightfall. It is preferable to say the Amida at least 3½ halakhic "hours" after midday [שו״ע אורח, רלג:א].

240 One should wash hands before saying Minḥa, even if they are not dirty; but if no water is available, one need not wash [שו״ע אורח, רלג:ב]. No blessing is said on the hand-washing.

Laws of the Evening Shema and Ma'ariv

241 There is a set time period every night during which the Shema may be said. At the earliest, one may say the Shema from nightfall [שו״ע אורח, רלה:א]. It is preferable to say the Shema before midnight (measured from nightfall to daybreak), but one is permitted to say the Shema until daybreak [שם:ג].

242 Some congregations hold Ma'ariv services early, with the result that the communal recitation of the Shema in Ma'ariv may take place too early to fulfill the halakhic obligation. Under such circumstances, one should repeat all three paragraphs of Shema after nightfall [שו״ע, שם:א].

243 If one enters the synagogue and hears the congregation about to begin saying the Amida, one should say the Amida together with the congregation, then afterward say the Shema with its preceding and following blessings [שו״ע אורח, רלו:ג].

244 After the blessings of the Shema, the congregation says בָּרוּךְ יהוה לְעוֹלָם (page 355), except in Israel. One who begins Ma'ariv late should omit בָּרוּךְ יהוה לְעוֹלָם in order to say the Amida with the congregation, then say בָּרוּךְ יהוה לְעוֹלָם after Ma'ariv, without the final blessing [משנ״ב, שם:יא].

Laws of Motza'ei Shabbat

245 In some congregations, Psalms 144 and 67 (page 399) are sung before Ma'ariv.

246 Ma'ariv: as for weekdays (page 343). In the fourth blessing of the Amida, אַתָּה חוֹנַנְתָּנוּ (page 363) is added [שו״ע אורח, רצד:א]. On Rosh Ḥodesh, יַעֲלֶה וְיָבוֹא (page 371) is added in the seventeenth blessing. If one forgets either of these additions, one does not repeat the Amida [שם]. After the silent Amida, unless Yom Tov falls in the following week, the Shaliaḥ Tzibbur says Half Kaddish and the

congregation says וַיְהִי נֹעַם and אַתָּה קָדוֹשׁ (pages 401–403) [רמ״א אור״ח, רצב: א]. The *Shaliaḥ Tzibbur* then says Full Kaddish. From the second day of Pesaḥ until Shavuot, the Omer is counted (page 389). Some have the custom to say וִיתֶּן־לְךָ (page 409) [שם]. In most congregations, the *Shaliaḥ Tzibbur* says Havdala [שו״ע, שם]. The congregation says *Aleinu*, followed by Mourner's Kaddish. From the 1st of Elul to Shemini Azeret, Psalm 27 is said (page 421).

247 After nightfall, one may not perform labor until one says Havdala or hears it said. If one says אַתָּה חוֹנַנְתָּנוּ in Ma'ariv (page 363), one may perform labor after nightfall prior to Havdala [רמ״א אור״ח, רצב: י].

248 Each month, one says Kiddush Levana (page 423) on seeing the New Moon at night. Kiddush Levana may be said from the eve of the fourth day of the new month until the middle day of the month. By custom, it is said on the first Motza'ei Shabbat that falls within the time span, preferably outdoors with a *minyan*. [שו״ע ורמ״א אור״ח, תכו].

249 Havdala is said at home if (a) one did not say אַתָּה חוֹנַנְתָּנוּ or hear Havdala in the synagogue; (b) one said אַתָּה חוֹנַנְתָּנוּ or heard Havdala, but intended not to fulfill one's obligation; or (c) someone at home did not yet hear Havdala [שו״ע אור״ח, רצ: לב; משנ״ב, שם: לב]. Women may say Havdala for themselves [משנ״ב, שם: לה–לו]. If one forgets to say Havdala on Motza'ei Shabbat, one may say it as late as Tuesday night.

250 After Shabbat, one should eat a meal, the *Melaveh Malka*, as a way of marking the end of Shabbat [שו״ע אור״ח, ש: א].

Laws of Keri'at Shema al HaMita
(the Shema Before Sleep at Night)

251 *Keri'at Shema al HaMita* should be said before retiring, when one is feeling sleepy [משכ״ב אור״ח, רלט: ג], after which one should not eat, drink or speak [רמ״א, שם: א].

LAWS OF HAND-WASHING
HAMOTZI AND BIRKAT HAMAZON

252 Before eating bread, one is required to wash one's hands [שו״ע אורח, קנח:א]. After washing but before drying the hands, one says the blessing עַל נְטִילַת יָדַיִם; however, if one forgot, one may say the blessing after one's hands are dry [רמ״א, שם:יא]. One should dry one's hands carefully before touching the bread [שו״ע, שם:יב].

253 Hands should be washed using a cup or other container that holds at least a *revi'it* (about 4.4 ounces) of liquid [שו״ע אורח, קנט:א]. Holding one's hands under flowing water is not valid [שו״ע, שם:ו].

254 One should wash each hand up to the wrist, although the minimum requirement is to wash the fingers up to the knuckle furthest from the nail [שו״ע אורח, קסא:ד]. Hands should be free of dirt or other material that one normally removes. In addition, rings should be removed before washing [שם:א-ג].

255 If the hands are clean, it is sufficient to pour water once on each hand [שו״ע אורח, but twice on each hand is preferable [מ״ב שם, כא] ;[קסב:ב].

256 After washing, one should take care not to allow one's wet hands to touch the unwashed hands of another. If they do so, one must dry them and wash them again [שו״ע שם, ד].

257 If one makes the blessing הַמּוֹצִיא לֶחֶם מִן הָאָרֶץ on bread, no blessing need be said on foods that are part of the meal. If one eats foods that are not eaten with bread or are not part of the meal, such as fruit eaten as dessert, they require a separate blessing [שו״ע, קעז:א].

258 If wine is served during the meal, the blessing בּוֹרֵא פְּרִי הַגָּפֶן must be said, as the blessing on bread does not cover wine [שו״ע אורח, קעד:א]. But if wine is drunk before the meal (or as part of Kiddush), the blessing need not be repeated when drinking wine during the meal [שם:ד].

259 One should not remove bread from the table until after *Birkat HaMazon* is said [שו״ע אורח, קפ:א].

260 Prior to saying *Birkat HaMazon*, one should wash the grime off one's fingers with *mayim aharonim* [שו״ע אורח, קפא:א]. Some have the custom not to wash with *mayim aharonim*, because the original reasons for the practice no longer apply [שם, ר; משנ״ב שם, כב], but a fastidious person who washes after a meal should wash with *mayim aharonim* before *Birkat HaMazon* [שו״ע שם].

261 Women are obligated to say *Birkat HaMazon* [שו״ע אורח, קפו: א].

262 *Birkat HaMazon* should be said where one ate. If one forgot to say *Birkat HaMazon* and went elsewhere, one should return to the site of the meal to say *Birkat HaMazon*. If one cannot return to the site of the meal, one is permitted to say *Birkat HaMazon* as soon as one remembers to do so [שו״ע ורמ״א אורח, קפד: א; משנ״ב, שם: ו].

263 If one forgets to say *Birkat HaMazon* at the end of the meal, it must be said afterward, so long as one does not feel hungry [שו״ע אורח, קפד: ד]. If one wants to eat again, one may wash hands and say הַמּוֹצִיא again; the subsequent *Birkat HaMazon* then covers the first meal as well [רמ״א אורח, קעח: ב].

264 On Ḥanukka or Purim, one adds עַל הַנִּסִּים (page 657) to the second blessing. If one forgets עַל הַנִּסִּים, one is not required to repeat *Birkat HaMazon* [שו״ע אורח, תרפב: א; שו״ע ורמ״א אורח, תרצה: ג].

265 On Rosh Ḥodesh and Ḥol HaMo'ed, one adds יַעֲלֶה וְיָבוֹא (page 661) to the third blessing. If one forgets the required addition on Rosh Ḥodesh, one is not required to repeat *Birkat HaMazon* [שם: ו].

266 If one started eating while it was Rosh Ḥodesh or other days on which additions to *Birkat HaMazon* are said, and continued the meal after sunset, one still says the additions to *Birkat HaMazon* [שם: י].

267 If three adult males eat a meal together, they are required to preface *Birkat HaMazon* with *zimmun* (page 653). If women are present, they are required to join in the *zimmun* as well. Three adult females may also form a *zimmun*, but are not obligated to do so. If ten or more males are present, the word אֱלֹהֵינוּ is added to the formula [שו״ע אורח, קצב: א].

268 *Zimmun* is required if all three participants ate bread. If only two participants ate bread, but a third person either eats a *kezayit* (about 1.5 ounces) of any food, or drinks a *revi'it* (about 4.4 ounces) of any beverage (other than water), the three should say *zimmun* [שו״ע אורח, קצו: ג; משנ״ב, שם: כב].

269 Even if the participants are not sitting together, as long as some of the participants can see each other, they can join together in a *zimmun* [שו״ע אורח, קצה: א].

270 If one of the three participants said *Birkat HaMazon* by himself, he may still join the other two to make a *zimmun*, but if two of them (or all three) said *Birkat HaMazon* by themselves, then no *zimmun* may be said [שו״ע אורח, קצה: א].

PRAYER IN A HOUSE OF MOURNING

271 The following prayers are omitted when praying in a house of mourning during the days of *shiva*:

 a *Korbanot* (Offerings) – omitted only by the mourners themselves [משנ״ב, אורח, א: ט]

 b *Taḥanun* [שו״ע אורח, קל״א: ד]

 c Hallel, except when Rosh Ḥodesh falls on Shabbat [משנ״ב, שם: כ]. On Ḥanukka, those who are not mourning should say Hallel on returning home.

 d אֵל אֶרֶךְ אַפַּיִם [משנ״ב, שם: לה]

 e Psalm 20 (לַמְנַצֵּחַ) [שם]

 f *Pirkei Avot* or *Barekhi Nafshi* on Shabbat – omitted only by the mourners themselves [אשי ישראל, לו: צו]

 g *Birkat Kohanim* in Israel (see law 214)

272 In a house of mourning, it is customary to say Psalm 49 after the Daily Psalm; on days on which no *Taḥanun* is said, Psalm 16 is said instead (page 273).

ROSH ḤODESH PRAYER

273 On Rosh Ḥodesh, יַעֲלֶה וְיָבֹא is added to the seventeenth blessing of the Amida (רְצֵה) in Maʿariv, Shaḥarit and Minḥa [שו״ע אורח, תכב: א], and to the third blessing of *Birkat HaMazon* (page 661) [שם, תרד: א].

274 If one forgets to say יַעֲלֶה וְיָבֹא in its proper place in the Amida, but realizes before beginning the blessing הַמַּחֲזִיר שְׁכִינָתוֹ לְצִיּוֹן, one should immediately say יַעֲלֶה וְיָבֹא and continue with the rest of the blessing. If one realizes the omission immediately after completing the blessing הַמַּחֲזִיר שְׁכִינָתוֹ לְצִיּוֹן, one should say יַעֲלֶה וְיָבֹא and continue with the following blessing. If one realizes the omission after beginning the words מוֹדִים אֲנַחְנוּ לָךְ, one must repeat the Amida from the beginning of the seventeenth blessing (from the word רְצֵה). If one realizes the omission after completing the Amida, one must repeat the Amida from the beginning [שו״ע אורח, תכב: א].

275 If one forgets to say יַעֲלֶה וְיָבֹא in Maʿariv, one does not repeat the Amida [שם].

276 Shaḥarit: as for weekdays, although one adds special verses for Rosh Ḥodesh in the *Korbanot* (page 53) [שו״ע אורח, תכא: א]. יַעֲלֶה וְיָבֹא is added to the Amida (see

laws 273–274). After the Repetition of the Amida, *Taḥanun* is omitted, and the congregation says Half Hallel [שו״ע או״ח, תכב: ב], followed by Full Kaddish.

277 Torah reading: page 745. Four men are called up [שו״ע או״ח, תכב: א]. Note that the second *aliya* begins by repeating the last verse of the first *aliya* [שו״ע או״ח, תכג: ג]. Half Kaddish is said before the Torah is returned to the Ark. The service continues with *Ashrei*, וּבָא לְצִיּוֹן and Half Kaddish. The tefillin are then removed [שו״ע או״ח, תכג: ד], and the congregation says Musaf for Rosh Ḥodesh. This is followed by *Aleinu*, Mourner's Kaddish, the Daily Psalm, Psalm 104 (בָּרְכִי נַפְשִׁי), and Mourner's Kaddish.

Laws of Hallel

278 Hallel is said standing [שו״ע או״ח, תכב: ו]. On Rosh Ḥodesh and the last six days of Pesaḥ, the abridged form, Half Hallel, is said [שו״ע או״ח, תכב: ב; תצ: ד], omitting the first halves of Psalm 115 (לֹא לָנוּ) and Psalm 116 (אָהַבְתִּי כִּי יִשְׁמַע).

279 At the beginning of Psalm 118 (הוֹדוּ לַיהוה כִּי־טוֹב, page 451), it is customary for the *Shaliaḥ Tzibbur* to say each of the four verses out loud, and the congregation responds with [משיב תכב, כ] הוֹדוּ לַיהוה כִּי־טוֹב, כִּי לְעוֹלָם חַסְדּוֹ. Some advise the congregation to quietly say each verse with the *Shaliaḥ Tzibbur*.

SOME FREQUENTLY ASKED QUESTIONS
ABOUT TEFILLA

Why pray?

- I pray because I want a connection with God. If you consider the gap that exists between an all-knowing, all-powerful God and a limited finite human being, it would be absurd to imagine that any connection is even possible. Yet God revealed to us that through prayer contact is possible. The difference is that when God initiated contact with man, He did so through prophecy; when man initiates the contact it is through prayer.

- I believe that I am made up of a body and a soul. I'm not really sure what the soul is. I do know that it is something that makes up who I am, the inner essence of me, the part of me that others cannot see. It longs to be nourished. I therefore pray for the sake of nourishing my soul, no less than I eat in order to nourish my body. The body needs to be fed else it will wither; the soul needs to be fed else it, too, will wither. Prayer is the vitamin for the soul.

- The Rabbis tell us that each person is unique; there are no two people in the world who are the same, either in body or soul. As much as I celebrate my uniqueness, there is also a part of me that is sometimes lonely, when my inner essence makes me feel like I am so different from anyone else that there is no one else who truly understands me, no one else who knows my innermost thoughts, feelings, fears. The only One who truly can is God, since my uniqueness comes from Him. Prayer enables me to connect and overcome my loneliness.

- I pray because it is a mitzva to do so.

- There have been times when I was so happy that I could burst. Something great happened to me or I saw something so amazing or so

◄ beautiful

beautiful that I just needed to express myself besides saying "Wow!" Prayer enables me to express my feelings of wonder, awe, amazement, gratitude, appreciation or humility. Similarly, there have been times when I have been very sad or when I am so overcome by the distress or sadness around me that I just want to scream. Prayer provides me with the opportunity and the language with which to express myself when words fail, when I want to express my anger, my sorrow, my pain. It also enables me to encounter Hashem at those moments for He is the source for the goodness, and often the source of the sadness that I am experiencing.

- There are things that I need. Whether it's a better grade, a material possession, help with an activity, a job or a relationship. In prayer, I turn to Hashem to ask for the things that I need.

- There are things that I am afraid of. In prayer I can ask for help with my fears and insecurities, my anxieties and my worries. Sometimes, when I can just share those feelings with Someone who understands, it provides relief.

- One opinion says that the Hebrew word for prayer *lehitpalel* comes from the root *pilel* which means to judge. The reflexive form, *hitpalel*, therefore means to judge oneself. *Tefilla* is about holding up a mirror to oneself a few times a day. It's about reminding oneself of what's important and what one's values are, and how one can use the hours ahead most productively.

- Similarly, when I assess my own needs, I become conscious of the needs of others. When I ask God for something or become conscious of the ethics which guide His behavior as indicated by the prayers, then I grow more sensitive to the ethics that I should live by, the responsibilities I have toward others. Prayer makes me a better person.

- When I pray, I connect myself with the Jewish people of the past. I use the same words they did, I refer to experiences they had, I recall the beliefs that we all share, in the same language that has been used for thousands of years. In prayer, I become a part of the chain of tradition.

- When I pray, I connect myself to my fellow Jews in the present wherever they may be. Prayers are almost always in the plural, reminding

◀ me that

me that I am concerned not only with myself but with my extended family, just as they are concerned with me in their prayers. I join with the people around me to form a cohesive group and am thus provided with a constant source of community, even if the people around me are strangers.

- Prayer heightens awareness. When I recite a blessing regarding a particular event, it raises the event to something more transcendent.

- The very act of prayer, mandated as it is by halakha to specific times, forces me to take time out of my day to be conscious of all of the above, even if it doesn't always succeed in doing so. Prayer provides me with self-discipline.

- I pray because I cannot not pray.

Why do I need to use a Siddur?

- EXPRESSING YOUR FEELINGS CAN BE DIFFICULT. WE ALL NEED HELP

  One practical reason is that we're not so good at coming up with ways to express our feelings. Consider the fact that when you go to the store to buy a birthday card for someone, you usually have two choices: one card is blank, while the other has a pre-printed message. The vast majority of us choose the card with the message. Filling a blank card can be too difficult, especially if you do it every day.

- YOUR PRAYERS SHOULD BE JEWISH

  One of the things that distinguish our prayers from those of other faiths or spiritual practices, is that our prayers are Jewish. They are based upon things in our belief system and in our history. These are uniquely Jewish beliefs and Jewish history. Were we to only use our own prayers, it is likely that our prayers would not have this dimension.

- JEWISH PRAYER HAS A PARTICULAR STRUCTURE

  The most famous example is the structure of שבח, בקשה, הודאה – *praise, request, thanks*. Were we to only use our own prayers, we probably would not think to use that structure. Yet we are told that praying this way can be particularly meaningful and powerful.

- ◆ **JEWISH PRAYER CONSISTS OF PARTICULAR CONTENTS**

  The prospect of finite man being able to communicate with an infinite God would be an absurd impossibility if not for the fact that the Torah says that such a thing is possible. From the Tanakh we learn the way that God can be approached, the kinds of things that can be said and the way that they can be said. These are incorporated in the Siddur. Were we only to use our own prayers, we would probably not speak to God in these uniquely Jewish terms.

- ◆ **JEWISH PRAYER CONSISTS OF VARIOUS FORMS OF COMMUNICATION**

  There are verses from the Torah and teachings of the Talmud; there are texts based upon deep philosophical thoughts and mysterious kabbalistic insights; there is complex poetry and lyrical prose. Were we only to use our own prayers, we would most likely use but one form, and lose the rich opportunities provided by the Siddur.

- ◆ **JEWISH PRAYER IS RECITED IN HEBREW**

  While this is not an absolute requirement (*Shulḥan Arukh* 60:2, 101:4 and *Mishna Berura* there), praying in Hebrew can be much more enriching and meaningful than in English. This is both because of the nuanced meaning of Hebrew and because it is לשון קודש, the mystical holy language that Jews have used to communicate with God for millennia. Were we to only use our own prayers, we would probably just use English rather than our uniquely Jewish language. Consider, for example, the famous expression אדון עולם, used in the song that is sung at the conclusion of services or said early in the morning. Most often it is translated as Master of the Universe. But the word עולם can also mean "world" and so the expression can also mean "Master of the Planet." Alternatively, the word עולם is related to the word נעלם meaning "hidden," thus rendering the expression to mean that God is hidden or mysterious. One could have one of these meanings or any combination of them in mind when you say this expression, depending on your mood or what you want to convey. English limits you to only one possibility.

- **JEWISH PRAYER IS USUALLY IN THE PLURAL**
  In Judaism, you seldom are praying for yourself alone. We see ourselves as part of a quorum, a community, a people. Being a part of these groups is a critical part of Jewish prayer. Were we to only use our own prayers, we probably would only use the self-centered and often selfish singular. If there are things which I need but am not thinking about for myself, there's a pretty good chance that someone else in the *minyan* will have them in mind. I get included in his prayers simply because he's saying it in the plural and we join our prayers to one another.

- **JEWISH PRAYER ATTACHES YOU TO JEWISH HISTORY**
  Jewish prayer is the composite work of thousands of years of Jewish history. The Siddur contains whole sections from the Torah and Nevi'im and Ketuvim. Other prayers and blessings were composed during Mishnaic and Talmudic times. פיוטים (liturgical poems) were composed and included in the liturgy of the Middle Ages in all countries of Europe and North Africa and the Middle East. In our own era, contemporary concerns and sensitivities have been added, such as the prayers for the welfare of Israeli soldiers, American soldiers, and the State of Israel. When we use the Siddur, we thus join ourselves to thousands of years of Jewish history and the Jewish people, we utter words that have been used for millenia and words that join us to Jews around the world. Were we to only use our own prayers, we probably would think most of the time only about ourselves and our own time.

- **JEWISH PRAYER JOINS YOU TO OTHER JEWS**
  When I was in the ninth grade I went to Belarus with my school to visit the Jewish community there. Although we could barely communicate with the people there, the words of the *Shema* and *Tefilla* connected us. Two completely different people with completely different languages and histories came together as one. (Ethan Stein)

So how do I make prayer more personal?

- **BRING YOUR OWN FEELINGS TO THE WORDS ON THE PAGE**
  Always remember that one of the most important (if not *the* most important) things about *tefilla* is *kavana*, the intent that you bring

◄ important

to the task. The words in the Siddur serve multiple purposes as we described above. While the literal meaning of the words is important, there is nothing wrong with bringing your own meaning to them. In other words (excuse the pun), the words can be understood metaphorically as well.

For example, in the *Shemoneh Esreh*, we say the prayer for the revival of the dead. This is considered the supreme example of Hashem's mastery over nature, which is the theme of that particular blessing (*Gevurot*) in *Shemoneh Esreh*. Now when we say this blessing, we should certainly try to bear in mind the belief that Hashem can perform the miraculous act of revival of the dead. But if that's not where your head is that day, then consider other possibilities that have been suggested: (1) He supports and cures those who were at death's door whom doctors said could not be cured. Hashem thus revives the dead in this way. (2) Hashem has mercy on the evil, who are called "dead" in their lifetimes. (3) Hashem grants life to those who are downcast or enveloped by sadness, who may feel like they are dead. (4) Hashem sends rain on a regular basis which revives life on earth. (5) Hashem enables us to awake every morning when we are otherwise like dead people.

Each of these is in keeping with the theme of the blessing of *Gevurot*, His mastery over the world, but they are not limited to the literal meaning alone. Be creative. Acknowledge the literal meaning but let your heart be free.

+ ADD YOUR OWN REQUESTS

Contrary perhaps to popular belief, you are allowed, in fact encouraged, to add your own prayers. If *tefilla* is supposed to be service of the heart, then let your heart do the talking. The *Shulḥan Arukh* (119:1) specifically says that if you have individual requests in *Shemoneh Esreh* then you should add them in the appropriate place. If you want to ask for material things, then ask in the blessing of *Barekh Aleinu*; if you want to pray on behalf of someone who is ill, then do so in the blessing of *Refa'enu*. Every blessing has a theme; find the theme appropriate for your particular request and add it in before you conclude the blessing. Alternatively, insert your own prayer into the blessing of *Shema Kolenu*,

◀ a catch-all

a catch-all blessing where anything goes. Or, insert it toward the end of the blessing of *Elokai Netzor*.

In short, it's a mistake to think that the Siddur is impersonal. It's as personal as you want to make it using the guidelines it provides. The Gemara (*Berakhot 28b*) suggests that one should not make his prayer the same every day. Yet how does one do that if in fact the prayers are the same every day?! The answer: you are different every day and therefore what you bring to the prayer makes it a different prayer. Whether prayer is the same old thing day in and day out or whether it is a way to express new feelings or hopes or needs depends entirely upon you.

What if I'm not in the mood to pray?

• This is one of the biggest misconceptions about *tefilla*. Ḥazal absolutely understood that people were not always in the mood to *daven*. Precisely because we can too often take life and the beauty of the world around us for granted, precisely because we can forget to be thankful for what we have or fail to note our dependency on God, precisely because we can so easily get lost in our own fatigue or our own concerns about the day, Ḥazal forced us to stop in our tracks three times a day and take note of these things. In other words, the Siddur is not there only for when we are in the mood; rather, the Siddur is there to help put us in the mood.

What if prayer really doesn't do it for me?

• An artist was once asked: "How long did it take to produce this remarkable painting?" He replied: "Ten hours to apply the paints, but forty years to learn how." Prayer is an art, not only a mechanical act. It takes time and patience and persistence. It's the exercise of a muscle, the development of a relationship, the cultivation of love.

What value is there to saying something even if you don't mean it?

• The story is told of a small town where the only watchmaker passed away. Over time, the clocks in the town failed to tell the correct time and so the people didn't bother with them any more. Yet one man

◀ continued

continued to wind his clock every day, even though it continued to tell the wrong time. Finally, a new watchmaker came to town. When everyone brought their clocks to be fixed he told them that each was too difficult to fix for the mechanisms had rusted and run down. Only the person who had kept winding his clock had a machine that could be easily restored to working order.

Moreover, there is something to be said for the very act of going to *shul* even if one is not in the mood and even if one's prayers amount to just mumbling the words. The very act of attending *shul* is itself a statement to Hashem that I'm committed and I recognize that You are a part of my life. In addition, it is a statement to myself that I see myself as part of the community and that the community needs my presence.

What value is there to saying something I don't understand?

- Pray in English if you need to. While Hebrew is richer, the most important thing is *kavana,* so say it in whatever language you want. And if at times you don't have a translation available, let the very act of praying serve as a prayer.

  (When you can, try to focus on one blessing in Hebrew. Learn the translation. Think about the meaning. The added beauty and significance of the words will come in time, one blessing at a time.)

Does God really answer prayers?

- In the *Shemoneh Esreh*, we declare that Hashem is a *Shome'a Tefilla*: He *hears* prayer. Sometimes, that's like having a cell phone conversation with someone when the signal isn't so strong; the other person hears you even though you cannot hear them, and so you continue to speak, knowing that their very act of listening is response enough. As Rabbi Sacks once wrote, "Prayer is the place where speaking meets God's listening, and in ways we will never understand, we are transformed."

- Maybe He did answer you. It was just in another form, which was perhaps far more worthwhile than your original intention.

◀ Maybe He

- Maybe He yet will answer. Prayer, as someone said, is not a slot machine where you put in a coin and you get the jackpot. Sometimes, you need to have the patience to wait...and keep trying.

- Maybe what you asked for was not appropriate. You may think it would be good for you or for another person but really it is not. Maybe it would be bad for someone else. Maybe it would be bad for you.

- Maybe you asked in an inappropriate way. Were you just paying lip service to what you said? Were you testing God to see if He really exists? Were you testing prayer to see if it really works? Were you really praying?

- Maybe you need to do something to change yourself before you are deemed suitable for what you want.

- Sometimes the answer is "no." That may not be the answer to our prayers that we wanted, but it still means that our prayer was answered.

  Moreover, as Rav Noaḥ Weinberg once wrote, if a billionaire father handed over unlimited cash on a silver platter, his child would grow up spoiled and irresponsible. So too, if God gave us everything automatically, we may never define for ourselves what we want in life. True, life would be easy. But we would not grow. Since God has our best interests at heart, He wants us to earn it. Because that's what will make us great.

SUGGESTIONS FOR ENHANCING ONE'S KAVANA[1,2]

PART I

Choose the right physical place and stick with it. Psychologists say that you are better able to focus on an activity (e.g., homework) when you dedicate a space to that activity and only that activity. The mind grows accustomed to associating that place with the thoughts and actions developed in that place, thus making it easier to dedicate oneself to the task at hand. This is wisdom that Ḥazal had long ago when they said that one should establish a קבוע מקום, a fixed place for prayer.[3] Keep that seat and keep the experience around it pure. If you find yourself slipping too often, try another seat for a while.

Prepare yourself mentally and emotionally.[4] The Mishna (*Berakhot* 30b)

---

1   What exactly is *kavana*? "The word has variously been translated as "feeling," "emotion," "concentration," or "devotion." Its root, however, is *kiven*, which means "to aim," suggesting "directed *consciousness*" as perhaps the most literal translation of *kavana*. Indeed, it does consist of directing all of one's thoughts toward a single goal. (Rabbi Aryeh Kaplan)

2   Many of the citations which appear in the footnotes of this section were translated by Rabbi David Derovan. See his wonderful anthology and strategies on his website at davidderovan.com.

3   One should have a [set] place where one prays, that one should not change unless it is necessary. It is not sufficient for one to select a [specific] synagogue to pray in, but inside that [selected] synagogue, one should also have a set place. (*Shulḥan Arukh* 90:19, based on *Berakhot* 6b)

4   One should prepare one's heart for [prayer] with *kavana*. How do you prepare the heart? Before standing to pray, sit quietly, do nothing, for a short while. Remove all other thoughts from your heart. Begin to think about the greatness of the Creator, His wonders and the great feats and kindnesses that He performed for His people. Think about the goodness and kindness that He, who does goodness for those who deserve it, did for you... Think that now you wish to stand before the King, to petition

◄ relates

relates that the first pious ones would wait an hour before praying, that is, they psyched themselves beforehand, just like an athlete before a game or a student before a test or a musician or actor before a performance. Pause for a moment or two before you even enter the *shul*. Rid yourself of any baggage you have, physical (an electronic device) or mental. Someone once suggested that it is like crossing the border between two countries. Check your baggage and throw away whatever contraband might get in your way. Take a moment or two before you start praying to close your eyes and collect your thoughts.

Recall the custom to face Jerusalem whenever and wherever we pray. Visualize yourself standing at the *Kotel* if that is a place that is meaningful to you. Feel the rays of the sun and the coolness of the stones. Listen to the sounds of the prayers of others around you. Imagine that the *Beit HaMikdash* is just on the other side of the Wall. Now pray.[5]

Visualize yourself in a place in nature or somewhere else that has always

---

Him and to ask of Him all that you desire and request … Afterwards, stand and pray [*Shemoneh Esreh*]. This is what our Sages said, "Only stand for *Tefilla* with seriousness." (Rabbi Yeshayahu Horowitz)

5   The Rabbis taught: A blind person or whoever cannot determine directions should direct his heart to his Father in heaven, as it says, "They will pray to God" (*Melakhim* I 8:44). If one is standing outside of *Eretz Yisrael*, he should direct his heart to *Eretz Yisrael*, as it says, "They will pray to You via their land" (*Melakhim* I 8:48). If one is standing in *Eretz Yisrael*, then he directs his heart to Jerusalem, as it says, "They will pray to God via the city You have chosen" (*Melakhim* I 8:44). If one is standing in Jerusalem, then he should direct his heart to the *Beit HaMikdash*, as it says, "They will pray toward this house" (*Divrei HaYamim* II 6:32). If one was standing in the *Beit HaMikdash*, he should direct his heart to the Holy of Holies (*Beit Kodesh HaKodashim*), as it says, "They will pray toward this place" (*Melakhim* I 8:35). If one is standing inside the Holy of Holies, he should direct his heart toward the *Beit HaKaporet*. If one was standing behind the *Beit HaKaporet*, he should think of himself as standing in front of the *Beit HaKaporet*. Thus: If you are standing in the east, turn to face the west. In the west, turn to face the east. In the south, turn to face the north. In the north, turn to face the south. Rabbi Avin said – and some say [it was] Rabbi Avina: What is the scriptural source? "Your neck is like Tower of David, built like *Talpiot*" (*Shir HaShirim* 4:4). A *tel* (hill) that all the *piot* (mouths) turn toward. (*Berakhot* 30a)

There is a place where heaven and earth touch like no other place. Your heart can be there, regardless of where you are now standing.

◂ given you

given you a sense of calm and peace, and perhaps even a place where you once prayed with enormous feeling. Now pray.

Know that you are standing in front of Hashem. It's not "as if" you are standing in front of Hashem but rather He is there, in front of you, now. Many synagogues have words posted above the *Aron Kodesh*, such as *Shiviti Hashem Lenegdi Tamid*, "I place Hashem before me always" (*Tehillim* 16:8). Use that as a way to focus before you start to pray; use it as a way of regaining focus if you lose it. Hashem is real.[6]

Think of something new that you want to tell God. Ḥazal long ago realized that the routine of praying the same thing every day can cause one to lose sight of the personal element of prayer. Hence when the Gemara says that "one who makes his prayer routine (קבע) does not make his *tefilla* into petitions" (*Mishna Berakhot* 28b), Rabba and Rav Yosef explain that it means that he did not make any requests in his prayer. Think about something new you want to say.[7]

---

6   There are three things that a person needs to look at and consider well in order to arrive at this awe. The first is that he is actually standing before the Creator, and conducting a conversation with Him, even though He is not visible. You should note that this is the hardest thing to envision effectively in one's heart, since the senses do not assist in it at all.

However, with a little reflection and attention, a person can implant in his heart the truth of this matter: that he comes and literally enters into conversation with Him, and he pleads to Him and asks of Him; and that Hashem listens to him and pays attention to his words, as a person listens to his friend while his friend pays attention and listens to him. (Ramḥal, *Mesilat Yesharim* 19)

7   "When you pray, you should add what you need to each and every *berakha*, for this helps greatly with *kavana*. And if you cannot add to every *berakha*, because the congregation will finish before you [because you are adding so much] then add to [only] one or two *berakhot* so you will not have to rush through a different *berakha*. (*Sefer Ḥasidim*, R. Margoliot, § 158)

If one wants to add something that fits the theme of the *berakha* to one of the middle *berakhot*, one is [allowed] to add. How [should one do this]? If one knows of a sick person, one asks for *raḥamim* (a combination of God's compassion, sensitivity, love and help) [for that person] in the *berakha* of Refa'enu – רפאנו. If one needs financial help, one is to ask for it in the *berakha* of Birkat HaShanim – ברכת השנים. Note: When he does add [to a *berakha*], he should first begin the *berakha* and then add. But he should not say the addition and then begin the *berakha*. (*Mishna Berura* 119:3, 7); One can ask for all of one's needs in the *berakha* of Shome'a Tefilla – שומע

◂ *Feel*

Feel the need to pray. When we cannot relate to prayer or are distracted by other things, we tend to forget the dependence that we have on Hashem. Think about something that you really need (as opposed to really want) and use the depth of that feeling as a catalyst to energize your prayer.[8]

Mean what you say. Don't just read the words – mean the words. When a verse is about joy, be joyful, when it focuses on God's greatness, feel awe, etc. When it speaks about the sun and the moon and the stars, visualize them. When you mention the trees and the plants, imagine them silently in praise of Hashem (Y. Buxbaum).

Choose carefully whom you sit with. There is certainly a communal element to *shul* attendance but *shul* is primarily about talking to God, not to your neighbor. Sitting in a class with a bunch of friends who aren't serious, or trying to be a fan at a game where the people around you aren't paying attention or don't care, inevitably has an impact on your own interest and enthusiasm. Because an important part of prayer is the communal experience, whom you sit with can be critical to your own experience.[9] If you find that you need to talk, do not do so in your usual seat.

Keep up your involvement. In order to maintain focus it helps to stay on task. If there are moments in the service when people tend to zone out or talk, e.g., *Kaddish, Berikh Shemeh, Ḥazarat HaShatz*, then just

---

תפילה, which [is a general *berakha*] containing all petitions. (*Shulḥan Arukh, Oraḥ Ḥayyim*, 119)

8   Need. When a person has a great need for something and prays for it, then he will have much *kavana*, especially if it is a very great need. For instance, if his child is dying or he is suffering from some illness or if he is at sea and there is a great storm and the ship feels like it will sink, then one should pray and petition [God] with all one's heart, and shed tears and pour out his heart before God. However, if a person has no great need for what he asks for in his prayers, then it makes it more difficult to have *kavana* … The bottom line is that the greater the need for what the person is asking in his *Tefilla*, then the greater the *kavana*. The less the need, then the *kavana* is less. (Rabbi Yeshayahu Horowitz)

9   Neighbor. When a person's neighbors – I mean those sitting next to him – pray with *kavana*, this makes it easier for him to have proper *kavana* as well. However, if those sitting next to him are not serious and are not praying with *kavana*, then it is hard for him to have *kavana*. About this [situation] it is said, "Woe to the evil one and woe to his neighbor." (Rabbi Yeshayahu Horowitz)

◀ try to

try to give those prayers your attention. Keep your head and heart engaged. [10]

Use your voice (without bothering your neighbors). Our brains are the first computer; they can multitask. Ever notice how your eyes can read pages of a text but your brain is occupied elsewhere? You have some vague notion that you have been reading but can't remember a word you've read. When we speak the words out loud, however, it can force us to focus more on what we are saying. Similarly, song has a way of transforming words into emotion. Speak the words so that your mind can hear them. Say the words so that your soul can feel them. [11]

Sing (without bothering your neighbors). A famous composer once said "music can name the unnamable and communicate the unknowable." There is something about music that draws us in and lets us feel and allows us to let go and to express emotions which are not always accessible with spoken words. Yes, singing can sometimes make you feel silly, but we do it all the time at birthday parties, large crowd events, in the shower, etc. Our heads may think it's silly but our hearts feel it. Let your heart give your mind the permission to loosen up.

Use your body. Sometimes one needs to get one's body in tune with one's soul. For some people that means *shokeling* or rocking one's body back and forth. Rabbi Levi Yitzḥak of Berditchev was once criticized for swaying back and forth too much. He asked: "Would you say the same

---

10   A parable explains that if a person sleeps fitfully, half asleep, half awake, waking and sleeping on and off, she cannot reach the peaceful state of deep sleep that powerfully refreshes the mind. Only by continuous uninterrupted sleep can she sink into a profound refreshing slumber. Similarly, if a person prays fitfully, on and off, concentrating for awhile and then turning her attention elsewhere, she cannot reach the state of profound God-consciousness that transforms and refreshes her mind by its peace and joy. (Y. Buxbaum)

11   How should one modulate the voice [during the *Shemoneh Esreh*]? The voice should not be raised during prayer nor should one pray in thought alone. Rather, the words should be pronounced with the lips, but softly, audible to one's ears. (Rambam, *Mishneh Torah, Tefilla* 5:9)

Imagine composing a beautiful piece of music or singing a melody in one's head. Imagine feeling a tremendous amount of love for someone but never expressing it out loud. Imagine that someone feels sorry and apologetic about something they did to you but never utters a word of remorse out loud. So, too, with prayer.

◀ thing if

thing if you saw a person drowning in the water, motioning wildly for help? Well, when I pray, I too am fighting for my life." Others maintain that such movements are a distraction and suggest that one should calm one's body so that it is at peace with itself. They use the techniques of meditation or mindfulness to help focus on the words which can act as a kind of mantra for becoming prayerful.[12]

Use your eyes. The eyes wander. Don't let them. There are those who suggest that one should keep one's eyes closed as much as possible. Alternatively, one should keep one's eyes glued to the Siddur so that one can maintain one's focus. Alternatively, there is a custom to have windows in *shul* so that, when necessary, one can look up to the sky to maintain one's focus. The key is to not let one's eyes go aimlessly on a tour of the room, for wherever they go, your *kavana* is sure to follow.[13]

Learn the meaning of the prayers. There is much to be said for praying even if one does not understand every word. Standing in the presence of Hashem, feeling the power of the words and their history, joining yourself to the community and to tradition, to name but a few, are all reasons that one can pray without understanding. But there are scores of books available in English and Hebrew that can help you figure out not only the meanings of the words but also the history of the prayers, for there is no

---

12   Those who are careful about mitzvot sway during prayer in keeping with the verse "all of my bones will declare: who is like You Hashem?" (Rema *Shulḥan Arukh Oraḥ Ḥayyim* 48). It all depends on one's own personal nature. If one applies himself well to his prayer by moving to and fro, he should in fact do so but, if not, he should keep still so that he should be able just to apply his heart to praying" (*Mishna Berura*, 48:4).

13   Ideally one should pray in such a way that there is nothing that stands between himself and the wall. Something permanent, like a cabinet or a chest, is not a problem in this regard (*Shulḥan Arukh* 90:21). One should close his eyes or pray from a siddur without looking outside [the siddur] so that he will not come to destroy his *kavana* as a result of the interposing object in front of him (*Mishna Berura* 90:63). It is stated in the *Zohar Va'et-ḥanan*: "One who stands in prayer is required to cover his head and eyes so he will not look at the *Shekhina*" (*Mishna Berura* 91:6).

A person should only pray in a place that has windows (*Berakhot* 34b). According to Rashi, this is because by looking at the sky through the windows one will better be able to direct one's heart by thinking of God and being humbled.

◀ other book

other book that so reflects Jewish history, philosophy, law and custom as the Siddur does.[14]

Change it up from time to time. Recall the excitement when you came to *shul* for the first time or actually felt something in *shul* for the first time. Recreate that. Do something different once in a while. Dress differently – wear a different *kippa* or article of clothing. Sit in a different seat. Use a different siddur. Pray by heart without a siddur. Stand most of the time even when everyone else is sitting. Say it all in English. Say it all in Hebrew. Say some in Hebrew and some in English. Pray one prayer more slowly. Find one sentence upon which you will reflect a little more. And always remember before Whom you stand.[15]

Most of these suggestions presume one thing – you need to slow down! There is an inherent tension in most of our services between the needs of the community and the needs of the individual. One of the hallmarks of Jewish prayer is that we want to do both. The problem is that, depending on where you pray on any given day, it can often be impossible. The unfortunate reality is that we can only apportion a certain amount of our day to *tefilla*. More often than not, that means that *minyanim* can rush along often at breakneck speed making participants feel like they need to mumble all of the words as quickly as possible. One solution: don't try to keep up. Go for quality instead of quantity.

---

14 A small child doesn't know the difference between a hundred dollar bill and a scrap of green paper. If he were given the currency to hold, he might drop it out the window or cut it into pieces; he would never understand what he had lost. To value something, you have to know what it is and how much it is worth. (*Praying with Fire*, p. 181)

15 When Rabbi Eliezer fell ill, his students came to visit him. They said, "Rabbi, teach us a way to conduct ourselves, that we may thereby merit eternal life." He answered: "Be careful with the honor of your friends...and when you pray know in front of Whom you stand. By this means, you will merit eternal life. (*Berakhot* 28b)

Is this supposed to be some kind of revelation? If a person doesn't know in front of Whom he is standing, surely he wouldn't pray at all!? But Rabbi Eliezer emphasized "Know" – don't be satisfied simply with kavana, for that can be artificial and external. "Know in front of Whom you are standing" – then, out of that "knowledge," your prayer will be natural. (Rabbi Yehuda Amital)

◀ Inevitably

Inevitably this means that you will have to skip certain parts of the service. So be it. But that is why it is important to know which parts can be skipped and which cannot. The *Shemoneh Esreh*, for example, is not only the most important *tefilla* but ideally it is also important that it be said at the same time that everyone else is saying it so that the communal nature of the *tefilla* is operative. The goal should therefore be to get to the *Shemoneh Esreh* at the same time as everyone else. *Keriat Shema* and its blessings (everything after *Barekhu* and before the *Shemoneh Esreh*) are considered a whole unit and none of its component parts can be deleted, but you need not necessarily say it at the same time as everyone else. And *Pesukei DeZimra* is there to help prepare you for the later parts of *tefilla*, so that would be a perfect place to slow down and focus more in order to create more personal meaning for yourself. After all, each day you are a different person, and different *tefillot* or lines within them will appeal to you more. You need the time to find them and feel them. Mumble a lot or really mean a little? The choice seems pretty clear.

Even once you get to the *Shemoneh Esreh*, there is no obligation to go as fast as everyone else seems to be. It is true that there are halakhic opinions which suggest that you should try to finish your own *Shemoneh Esreh* in time to recite the *Kedusha* with the congregation during the repetition of the *Shemoneh Esreh*, but it is hard to imagine that what they had in mind was to completely sacrifice your *kavana* during the *Shemoneh Esreh* in order to do so.

In short, slow down. Like anything we do well in life, learning to pray with *kavana* can take time and lots of practice. There are moments of inspiration and intimacy and other moments of difficulty and distance. There are times when one can be alone with *HaKadosh Barukh Hu* even in a roomful of people, and other times when He seems harder to find. But the more one prays, the more one creates meaning for oneself, the more one attaches oneself to the words, the verses, the themes, the rhythms of the Siddur and its different component parts, the easier it becomes, the more meaningful it becomes, the more satisfying it becomes to one's body and soul. Don't feel the peer pressure if there is any. Matters of the heart cannot be rushed.

* * *

◀ Some followers

Some followers of the Ba'al Shem Tov came to ask him for permission to go to a famous *tzaddik* who was known for the *segulot*, or mystical remedies, that he would give to his followers. The Ba'al Shem Tov replied, "If you want to go, then go." They asked him for a sign that would help them to discern whether the man was a true *tzaddik* or a fake. The Ba'al Shem Tov replied: "I will give you a sign. He is supposed to be an expert in remedies for all sorts of maladies. Ask him for a *segula* for foreign thoughts in prayer. If he offers you one, then know that he is a fake."

SUGGESTIONS FOR ENHANCING ONE'S KAVANA
PART II

A special note on mindfulness, meditation and tefilla

When the pious men of old, the Ḥasidim Rishonim, would spend an hour preparing themselves for prayer, what did they do during that hour? Rabbi Aryeh Kaplan has suggested that they meditated. Indeed, there is some evidence to suggest that even the biblical prophets used meditation of some sort to prepare themselves to hear the word of God.

Meditation and mindfulness are ways of enhancing an experience. Imagine being so totally focused on an act, say eating a raisin or looking at a rose, that you are oblivious to everything else around you. Most of us have experienced what it is like to be so totally engrossed in a book that you don't know what's going on around you. So, too, have we experienced the opposite: the total inability to focus on reading such that we keep reading the same words over and over again or, worse, we find ourselves a few paragraphs or pages ahead and have no idea how we got there, with no awareness of anything we read. Mindfulness and meditation are designed to address that and, as such, they can be powerful tools in bringing more focus to one's prayer. In fact, there are those who say that prayer itself is a form of meditative practice.

The greater our focus, the greater is the experience. Rabbi Kaplan suggests that this can be done in two ways. In the first, we train the mind to simply block out other stimuli. This enables us to home in on the subject of our attention. It's like listening to a radio or a phone call that has a lot of static. Get rid of the static and you can pay more attention to the message. We'll call this mindfulness, and it enables one to bring one's entire attention, moment to moment, to the task at hand. The other technique

◀ is to focu

is to focus more of the mind on the object, so much so, that one has an increased awareness of it and its essence. It takes on properties that one would not necessarily have noticed before; one experiences it in a more intense way. This latter technique requires more practice and expertise.

Rabbi Kaplan explains that if one has never experienced these things then it is hard to understand a description of them. And so he provides an analogy:

> For the average sighted person, a page of braille feels like bumpy paper and nothing more. A blind person, however, does not have his sense of sight competing with his sense of touch, and hence experiences less "static." Furthermore, since he uses his sense of touch more often, his tactile sense is enhanced. With practice, he learns to decipher the patterns of raised dots as letters and words. It is true that a sighted person can also learn to read braille, but those who have mastered it usually read with their eyes closed, so that their faculty of sight will not interfere with their sense of touch.
>
> Reading braille is a good example of an experience that is meaningless to a non-sensitized person but has a world of meaning for a sensitized person. Many such experiences may exist in the world, and meditation can teach one to "read" these messages.

Jewish meditation has a long history that should not be confused with its forms in other cultures and religions. Rabbi Kaplan's book *Jewish Meditation* is a good introduction. Mindfulness is a practice that has also come to be adopted and adapted by the mental health profession, which has found it to be a powerful force in the reduction of stress, anxiety, pain and other conditions. It can be a powerful force, too, in helping make one's *tefilla* more meaningful.

Mindfulness is something that you can teach yourself but ideally it is best to find a competent guide who can help direct you and can provide support. Here's an example of a mindfulness exercise:

Establish concentration by sitting in a comfortable position in a straight-backed chair and focus on your breathing, either by paying attention to the air going into your nostrils and out of your mouth, or to the way in which your stomach rises and falls with each breath.

◀ Then begin

Then begin to widen your attention. Observe the flow of your inner thoughts, emotions and bodily sensations without actually judging any of them as good or bad.

Outside stimuli will also intrude but acknowledge them and then gently push them aside.

Watch what comes and goes in your mind and then begin to identify which mental habits bring a feeling of well being and which do not.

If your mind starts to wander (it inevitably will at the beginning) then go back to focusing on your breathing.

Don't just try this once and then get frustrated and give up. It's a practice that needs training. And *minyan* is not necessarily the place to become proficient. Rather, try to train yourself to be mindful during the course of the day (focus on one task at a time and savor it) and set a few minutes aside each morning and/or evening. Eventually, when you bring it to *tefilla*, it will make a huge difference to your *kavana*.

IN CONCLUSION
A STORY FROM THE BA'AL SHEM TOV

A king, by magic, surrounded his palace with many walls. Then he hid himself within the palace. The formidable walls were arranged in concentric circles, one inside the other, and they grew increasingly larger – higher and thicker – as one approached the center. They had fortified battlements and were manned by fierce soldiers who guarded from above; wild animals – lions and bears – ran loose below. All of this was so that people would have proper awe and fear of the king, and not all who desired to approach would be allowed to do as they pleased.

The king then had proclamations sent throughout the kingdom saying that whoever came to see him in his palace would be richly rewarded and given a rank second to none in the king's service. Who would not desire this? But when many came and saw the outer wall's awesome size and the terrifying soldiers and animals, most were afraid and turned back. There were some, however, who succeeded in scaling that wall and fighting past the soldiers and animals, but then the second wall loomed before their eyes, even more imposing than the first, and its guards even more terrible. Seeing that, many others turned back.

Moreover, the king had appointed servants to stand behind the walls to give money and precious stones to whoever got beyond each wall. Those who had crossed one or a few walls soon found themselves very rich and satisfied with what they had gained from their efforts; so they too turned back. For one reason or another, either from fear at the increasing obstacles or satisfaction with the accumulated rewards, none reached the king...

Except for the king's son. He had only one desire: to see the face of his beloved father. When he came and saw the walls, soldiers, and wild

◄ animals

animals, he was astonished. He could not understand how his dear father could hide himself behind all these terrifying barriers and obstacles. "How can I ever reach him?" he thought. Then he began to weep and cried out, "Father, Father, have compassion on me; don't keep me away from you!" His longing was so intense that he had no interest in any rewards. Indeed, he was willing to risk his life to attain his goal. By the courage of his broken heart, which burned to see his father, he ran forward with reckless abandon and self-sacrifice. He scaled one wall and then another, fought past soldiers and wild animals. After crossing the walls, he was offered money and jewels, but he threw them down in disgust. His only desire was to see his father. Again and again he called out to him.

His father the king, hearing his son's pathetic cries and seeing his total self-sacrifice, suddenly, instantaneously, removed the walls and other obstacles. In a moment they vanished as if they had never existed. Then his son saw that there were no walls, soldiers, or animals. His father the king was right before him, sitting on his majestic throne, while multitudes of servants stood near to serve him and heavenly choirs sang his praises. Gardens and orchards surrounded the palace on all sides. And the whole earth shone from the king's glory. Everything was tranquil, and there was nothing bad or terrible at all. Then the son realized that the walls and obstacles were a magical illusion and that his father the king had never really been hidden or concealed, but was with him all the time. It was all just a test to see who truly loved the king. (Cited in Yitzhak Buxbaum, *The Light and Fire of the Baal Shem Tov*. New York: Continuum, 2006.)

LIST OF AUTHORS REFERENCED

Aaron, Rabbi David, b. 1957, Jerusalem. Founder of Isralight and the post-high-school Yeshivat Orayta, Rabbi Aaron writes extensively on issues related to Jewish spirituality, including a book about prayer called *Tefillah Training*. See Bibliography.

Aboab, Rabbi Isaac (Menorat HaMaor), fourteenth century, Spain. The name comes from the title of his very influential and popular work on the beauty of Jewish life and ethics. He also wrote a commentary on the Siddur.

Abudarham, Rabbi David, c. 1340, Spain. He wrote an important commentary on the siddur (*Abudarham HaShalem*) which includes comments and laws gathered from the Geonim, the Jerusalem and Babylonian Talmuds in addition to including customs and laws prevalent in his native Spain.

Agnon, Shmuel Yosef (Shai), 1888–1970, Ukraine and Israel. Author of Hebrew fiction who won the Nobel Prize for literature.

Albo, Rabbi Yosef, c. 1380–1444, Spain. Important philosopher especially known for his *Sefer HaIkkarim*, much of which is dedicated to the issue of prayer.

Amiḥai, Yehuda, 1924–2000, Israel. Originally from Germany, he went on to become one of Israel's great modern poets, receiving numerous national and international awards.

Angel, Rabbi Marc, b. 1945. Rabbi and communal leader in the U.S.A. Author of more than a dozen books, especially about Sephardic life, and the founder of the Institute for Jewish Ideas and Ideals. He is the author of an article called "Thoughts on Prayer" which appears in *Seeking Good, Speaking Peace*, Angel, H. ed. Ktav Publishing House, Hoboken, 1994.

Arama, Rabbi Yitzḥak, 1420–1494, Spain. He is especially known for his philosophical commentary on the Torah, *Akeidat Yitzḥak*, parts of which have been translated.

Asevilli, Rabbi Yom Tov ben Avraham (Ritva), 1250–1330, Spain. His last name is a derivation of the town he came from, Seville. A leading student of Rashba and Ra'ah, he wrote a concise but oft-cited commentary on the Torah.

Aviner, Rav Shlomo Ḥayyim HaKohen, b. 1943. French-born Israeli rabbi who is one of the leaders of the Religious Zionist community. He has written numerous works on a wide variety of subjects including a three-volume commentary on the Siddur. See Bibliography.

Ba'al HaTanya – Rabbi Shneur Zalman of Liadi, 1745–1812. The first Lubavitcher rebbe. He is called the Ba'al HaTanya after the name of his famous work on Hasidic philosophy titled *Tanya* which has been translated.

Ba'al Shem Tov – Rabbi Yisrael ben Eliezer, 1698–1760, Ukraine. The founder of Hasidism.

Beit Yosef – See *Shulḥan Arukh*.

Bick, Rabbi Ezra, Har Etzion. Rabbi Bick made *aliya* in 1977 and is a teacher at Yeshivat Har Etzion (the Gush) where he is also in charge of their Virtual Beit Midrash: www.vbm-torah.org.

Da'at Soferim – See Rabbi Ḥayyim Dov Rabinowitz.

Da'at Zekenim – A collection of commentaries on the Torah by the Tosafists. See Tosafot.

Danzig, Rabbi Avraham (Ḥayyei Adam), 1748–1820, Poland. A digest of the *Oraḥ Ḥayyim* section of the *Shulḥan Arukh* intended for the informed layman as opposed to the scholar. Often cited by the *Mishna Berura*, it became popular for its conciseness and scholarship.

Eidels, Rabbi Shmuel (Maharsha), 1555–1631, Poland. Communal rabbi who wrote an important commentary on the Talmud, Rashi and Tosafot, including a commentary on the aggadic portions of the Talmud.

Elimelekh of Grodzhisk – See Szapira, Rabbi Elimelekh of Grodzhisk.

Elimelekh of Lezajsk – See Weisblum, Rabbi Elimelekh of Lezajsk.

Emden, Rabbi Yaakov (Ya'avetz), 1697–1776, Germany. A halakhic authority and communal leader who wrote more than two dozen works including a three-part commentary on the Siddur, known collectively as *Siddur Ya'avetz*, incorporating grammatical notes, laws, and a number of essays on prayer.

Etz Yosef – Rabbi Ḥanokh Zundel ben Yosef, d. 1859, Poland. Wrote this commentary on the Siddur, in addition to numerous other commentaries on collections of Midrash and Aggada. Found in the collection *Otzar HaTefillot*.

Eybeschutz, Rabbi Yonatan (Ye'orot Devash), 1690–1764, Prague and Germany. A prominent rabbinic leader who was expert in Talmud, Kabbala, and Jewish law. Known also by this title of his collection of sermons.

Falk, Rabbi Yehoshua ben Alexander HaKohen (Perisha), 1555–1614. The *Perisha* and *Derisha* are two parts of a commentary he wrote on the *Tur* called *Beit Yisrael*.

Gerondi, Yona ben Avraham (Rabbeinu Yona), d. 1263, Gerona, Spain. Teacher of the Rashba. Known for his commentary on the Talmud and his various ethical works.

Gombiner, Rabbi Avraham (Magen Avraham), c. 1635–1682, Poland. He is known by the name of this indispensable commentary to the *Shulḥan Arukh*.

Ḥafetz Ḥayyim – See Rabbi Yisrael Meir HaKohen Kagan.

Hai Gaon, Rav, 939–1038, Babylonia. The last, and some would say the greatest, of the Geonim of Pumbedita.

Ḥayyei Adam – See Rabbi Avraham Danzig.

Ḥayyim of Volozhin, Rabbi, 1749–1821, Lithuania. One of the prominent students of the Vilna Gaon, he established the model of Lithuanian *yeshivot* whose influence is still felt today. Among his works is *Nefesh HaḤayyim*, a book about prayer, Torah and the nature of God, which has been translated.

Hertz, Rabbi Joseph, 1872–1946, England. Chief Rabbi of the United Kingdom. Wrote a commentary on the Siddur called *The Authorized Daily Prayer Book*.

Herzog, Rabbi Yitzḥak HaLevi, 1838–1959. Chief Rabbi of Ireland and then the first Ashkenazic Chief Rabbi of the State of Israel.

Hirsch, Rabbi Shimshon Raphael, 1808–1888, Germany. Leader of Orthodox German Jewry, best known for his philosophy of *Torah im Derekh Eretz*. He wrote numerous works including commentaries on *Tehillim* and the Siddur. See Bibliography.

Horowitz, Rabbi Naftali Tzvi of Ropshitz, 1760–1827, Galicia. A leading Hasidic rebbe who was a student of Rabbi Elimelekh of Lezajsk.

Horowitz, Rabbi Shmuel (Shmelke HaLevi) of Nikolsburg, 1726–1778, Moravia. A hassidic rabbi and communal leader, student of the Maggid of Mezeritch and teacher of a number of other Hasidic rebbes including the Ḥozeh of Lublin.

Ibn Ezra – Rabbi Avraham ibn Ezra, 1089–1164, Spain. A poet, astronomer, and philosopher best known for his commentaries on Tanakh including *Tehillim*.

Isserles, Rabbi Moshe (Rema), 1520–1572, Poland. Leading rabbi, Talmudist and philosopher, known especially as the authoritative Ashkenazic halakhic commentator on the *Shulḥan Arukh*.

Iyyun Tefilla – Rabbi Yaakov Tzvi Mecklenburg, 1785–1865, Prussia. A communal leader, he wrote this commentary on the Siddur in addition to a famous commentary on the Torah, *HaKtav VeHaKabbala*.

Kagan, Rabbi Yisrael Meir HaKohen (Ḥafetz Ḥayyim), 1838–1933, Lithuania. One of the leading Ashkenazic halakhic authorities of modern times and an ethicist known for his work on gossip called the *Ḥafetz Ḥayyim*. His halakhic magnum opus is the *Mishna Berura* on that part of the *Shulḥan Arukh* dealing with everyday life including *tefilla*.

Kaplan, Rabbi Aryeh, 1934–1983, U.S.A. A prolific writer on Jewish subjects, able to integrate physics and Kabbala. Among his works were those directed to the newly religious, as well as a new translation of the Torah, *The Living Torah*, a translation of the *Me'am Loez*, and books on Jewish meditation. See Bibliography.

Kimḥi, Rabbi David (Radak), 1160–1235, Provence. Rabbinic authority, biblical commentator, philosopher and grammarian.

Kook, Rabbi Avraham Yitzḥak HaKohen, 1865–1935. First Ashkenazic Chief Rabbi of British Mandatory Palestine. In addition to being a halakhic authority and communal leader, he was a profound thinker whose influence on the Religious Zionist community continues today through his writings. He wrote a commentary on the Siddur called *Olat Re'iya*.

Kotzker Rebbe – See Menaḥem Mendel Morgensztern.

Kremer, Rabbi Eliyahu ben Shlomo (Vilna) 1720–1797, Lithuania. One of the foremost leaders of non-Hasidic Jewry who wrote numerous commentaries especially on *Shulḥan Arukh* and the Talmud. A siddur reflecting his views was also published and known as *Siddur HaGra*.

Leibowitz, Nechama, 1905–1997, Jerusalem. Nechama, as she was called by her students, revolutionized the way that Tanakh was studied. Her weekly study pages and her books on studies of the weekly *parasha* earned her an international reputation. In her classes, she frequently would point to the meaning of words and phrases in the Siddur.

Magen Avraham – See Rabbi Avraham Gombiner.

Maggid of Mezeritch – Rabbi Dov Ber of Mezeritch, d. 1772. One of the leading disciples of the Ba'al Shem Tov.

Maharal – Rabbi Yehuda Loew ben Betzalel, c. 1520–1609. Known as the Maharal (Moreinu HaRav Loew) of Prague. Leading communal rabbi, scholar and mystic. Author of over a dozen works.

Maharam Alsheikh – Rav Moshe Alsheikh HaKadosh, c. 1508–1600, Safed. He was a student of Rav Yosef Karo and is best known for his popular homiletic commentaries on Tanakh, some of which have been translated.

Maharsha – See Rabbi Shmuel Eidels.

Malbim – See Meir Leibush ben Yeḥiel Mikhel Wisser.

Me'am Loez – a commentary on the Torah in Ladino begun by Rabbi Yaakov Culi in 1730; others subsequently adopted his style and completed the work on all of Tanakh. The commentary draws heavily from Midrash and Talmud and went through periods of being immensely popular. The sections on Torah have been translated.

Meir Simḥa of Dvinsk, Rabbi, 1843–1926, Latvia. Rabbinic leader and author of a major commentary on the Torah called *Meshekh Ḥokhma* and on the Rambam's *Mishneh Torah* called *Ohr Same'aḥ*.

Meiri, Rabbi Menaḥem, 1249–1315, Provence. In addition to his interest in philosophy, he is known especially for his monumental work on the Talmud which was only revived in modern times. He also wrote commentaries on *Mishlei* and *Tehillim*.

Menorat HaMaor – See Rabbi Isaac Aboab.

Metzudot. A popular commentary on *Nevi'im* and *Ketuvim* begun by Rabbi David Altschuler (1687–1769, Galicia) and completed by his son Yeḥiel. His son divided the commentary into two parts called *Metzudat David* and *Metzudat Tziyon*. His father sought to write a commentary that would be more accessible to the masses who had a more difficult time understanding Rashi and Biblical Hebrew.

Mishna Berura – see Ḥafetz Ḥayyim.

Modena, Rabbi Leon, or Yehuda Aryeh MiModena, 1571–1648, Italy. A controversial personality, he wrote numerous works including responsa, anti-Christian polemics, a work on ethics and a collection of poetry.

Moltzin, Rabbi Yitzḥak (Siaḥ Yitzḥak), 1854–1917, Lithuania and Israel. Wrote a number of works including a commentary on the Siddur of the Vilna Gaon.

Morgensztern, Rabbi Menaḥem Mendel (Kotzker Rebbe), 1787–1859, Poland. Better known as the Kotzker Rebbe, he was a student of Rav Simḥa Bunim and is considered a spiritual founder of Ger Hasidism.

Munk, Rabbi Elie, 1900–1981, Paris and Germany. Communal rabbi and author who wrote a popular two-volume commentary on the Siddur called *The World of Prayer*. See Bibliography.

Naftali Tzvi of Ropshitz – See Horowitz, Rabbi Naftali Tzvi of Ropshitz.

Otto, Rudolph, 1869–1937. An eminent German Lutheran theologian and scholar of comparative religion. Wrote numerous works including *The Idea of the Holy*.

Papo, Rabbi Eliezer, 1785–1828, Bulgaria. Most well known for writing a book on *musar* called *Peleh Yoetz*, he also wrote a commentary on the Siddur called *Beit Tefilla* or *Beit Tefilla HaHadash*.

Perisha – See Rabbi Yehoshua ben Alexander HaKohen Falk.

Rabbeinu Tam – Yaakov ben Meir, 1100–1171, France. A grandson of Rashi, one of the leading Tosafists and halakhists of his day.

Rabbeinu Yona – See Yona ben Avraham Gerondi.

Rabinowitz, Rabbi Hayyim Dov (Da'at Soferim), 1909–2001, Lithuania, Tel Aviv. The *Da'at Soferim* is a multivolume commentary on all of Tanakh that distinguishes itself for the way in which it addresses difficult issues from a very traditionalist perspective as well as emphasizing the hand of God in human history.

Rabinowitz, Rav Tzaddok HaKohen of Lublin, 1823–1900, Poland. A famous child prodigy who went on to become a leading Hasidic thinker in halakha, Hasidism, Kabbala, and ethics.

Radak – See Rabbi David Kimhi.

Rambam – Rabbi Moshe ben Maimon, 1135–1204, Spain and Egypt. One of the pivotal figures in Jewish intellectual history. His halakhic code, *Mishneh Torah*, remains a foundation for Jewish law today.

Rashba – Rabbi Shlomo ben Aderet, 1235–1310, Spain. Known for his thousands of halakhic responsa and a commentary on the Talmud.

Rashi – Rabbi Shlomo Yitzhaki, 1040–1104, France. One of the most influential intellectual giants in Jewish life. Among his works in addition to his extensive commentaries on almost all of Tanakh and Talmud there is a *Siddur Rashi* compiled by one of his students.

Rav Tzaddok – See Rabinowitz, Rav Tzaddok HaKohen of Lublin.

Rema – See Isserles, Rabbi Moshe.

Ritva – See Asevilli, Rabbi Yom Tov ben Avraham.

Roke'ah – Rabbi Elazar of Worms, 1176–1238, Germany. Wrote a number of works but best known for his book *HaRoke'ah*, on Jewish ethics and halakha.

Sa'adia Gaon, Rav, c. 882–942, Egypt. Rabbi, philosopher and biblical commentator. One of the first rabbinic figures to write in Arabic and to integrate elements of Greek philosophy with Judaism. Also wrote a copy of the text of the Siddur including his own poetry called *Siddur Rav Sa'adia Gaon*.

Sacks, Rabbi Lord Jonathan, b. 1948. Former Chief Rabbi of the United Hebrew Congregations of the Commonwealth. A renowned author of philosophical and popular writings including a commentary on the Siddur published by Koren. See Bibliography.

Schwab, Rabbi Shimon, 1908–1995. A German-born rabbi who became the communal leader of the German community in Washington Heights in New York City. In addition to numerous books and articles published in his lifetime, a collection of his lectures on prayer were published posthumously, called *Rav Schwab on Prayer*. See Bibliography.

Sefat Emet – Yehuda Aryeh Leib Alter, 1847–1905, Poland. He was the second rebbe of the dynasty of Gerer Hasidim. He composed commentaries on a number of tractates on the Talmud but is known more widely for his homilies on the Torah, collectively called the *Sfat Emet*.

Seforno – Rabbi Ovadia ben Yaakov, 1475–1550, Italy. A rabbi, philosopher, and medical doctor best known for his biblical commentaries.

Sharansky, Natan, b. 1948. He was known for years as a Soviet refusenik who spent more than nine years in a Soviet prison for his advocacy for human rights and for his desire to make *aliya*. He was subsequently released and has gone on to become a politician, cabinet member, and human rights activist in Israel. His book, *Fear No Evil*, describes his experiences in prison.

Shmuel (Shmelke HaLevi) of Nikolsburg – See Horowitz, Rabbi Shmuel (Shmelke HaLevi) of Nikolsburg.

Shulḥan Arukh. The authoritative code of law written by Rabbi Yosef Karo, 1488–1575, Safed. He first wrote an extensive commentary on the *Tur* called the *Beit Yosef*, and he also authored a commentary on Rambam's *Mishneh Torah* entitled the *Kesef Mishneh*. The core of his rulings are accepted by all, while the work also includes traditions and customs unique to Sephardic communities.

Siaḥ Yitzḥak – See Moltzin, Rabbi Yitzḥak, 1854–1917, Lithuania and Israel. Wrote a number of works including a commentary on the Siddur of the Vilna Gaon.

Simḥa Bunim of Peshischa, Rabbi, 1765–1827, Poland. A businessman and pharmacist but most especially a major Hasidic rebbe who was a student of the Ḥozeh of Lublin and the Yid HaKadosh. Among his students were some of the leaders of Hasidism of the next generation including the Kotzker, the Gerer and the Alexander rebbes.

Soloveitchik, Rabbi Joseph B., 1903–1993. A descendent of the famous Lithuanian Soloveitchik dynasty, he was the leading figure in modern Orthodox Jewish life in America in the twentieth century. His interpretations of *tefilla* are found throughout his writings and a representative compendium was published by Koren. See Bibliography.

Szapira, Rabbi Elimelekh of Grodzhisk, 1823–1892, Poland. A leading Hasidic rebbe. Father of Rabbi Kalonymous Kalman Szapira, the Piaseczner Rebbe.

Tehillot HaShem – Rabbi Eliyahu ben Avraham Shlomo HaKohen HaItamari, 1659– c. 1729, Turkey. This is a commentary on *Tehillim* that the author wrote in addition to tens of other books, including a popular work on *musar* called *Shevet Musar*.

Tosafot. Not a single author but a collection of commentaries written primarily on the Talmud during the twelfth and thirteenth centuries in Western Europe. Some of these comments or glosses have been incorporated into the standard page of Talmud opposite Rashi's commentary, while others exist as independent collections.

Tur – See Rabbi Yaakov ben Asher.

Twerski, Rabbi Abraham Joshua, b. 1930. An American scion of the Chernobyl Hasidic dynasty, and a psychiatrist specializing in substance abuse. Has written dozens of books, a number of which focus on *tefilla*.

Twerski, Rabbi Menaḥem Noḥum of Chernobyl, 1730–1797, Ukraine. A disciple of the Ba'al Shem Tov and the Maggid of Mezeritch, and founder of the Chernobyl Hasidic dynasty. Wrote a book on the Torah called *Me'or Einayim*.

Tzeluta DeAvraham – a siddur incorporating the customs of Hasidic Rabbi Avraham Landau of Tshechnov (1784–1875) with commentaries on the content and text by his grandson Rabbi Menaḥem Mendel of Zawiercie and Rabbi Yaakov Wyrdiger. See Bibliography.

Uziel, Rabbi Ben-Tziyon Meir Ḥai, 1880–1953. The first Sephardic Chief Rabbi of the State of Israel.

Vilna Gaon – Rabbi Eliyahu ben Shlomo, 1720–1797, Lithuania. One of the foremost leaders of non-Hasidic Jewry who wrote numerous commentaries especially on *Shulḥan Arukh* and the Talmud. A siddur reflecting his views was also published and known as *Siddur HaGra*.

Weinberg, Rabbi Avraham, 1884–1933, Belarus. Rebbe of Slonim Hasidim and author of *Beit Avraham*.

Weisblum, Rabbi Elimelekh of Lezajsk, 1717–1787, Galicia. One of the founders of the Hasidic movement. He was a student of the Maggid of Mezeritch and thus became a leader of the third generation of Hasidic dynasties together with his brother Rabbi Zushya.

Wiesel, Elie, b. 1928 in Romania. Nobel Prize winner and renowned writer on the Holocaust. He delivered a paper called "Prayer and Modern Man" published in *Prayer in Judaism: Continuity and Change* (Cohn, G.H. and Fish, H. eds., NJ: Jason Aronson, 1996).

Wisser, Meir Leibush ben Yeḥiel Mikhel (Malbim), 1809–1879, Russia. A communal rabbinic leader, he is best known for his unique commentary on Tanakh, some of which has been translated.

Wohlgemuth, Rabbi Isaiah, 1915–2008. European-born beloved teacher at the Maimonides High School in Boston where he taught a course on *Bi'ur Tefilla*. His notes were subsequently published in a volume called *A Guide to Jewish Prayer*. See Bibliography.

Yaakov ben Asher, Rabbi, c. 1269–1343, Germany and Spain. Known by the title of his work on Jewish law called the *Arba'a Turim* or simply the *Tur*, a predecessor and basis for the *Shulḥan Arukh* as well as a commentary on the Torah called the *Ba'al Turim*.

Ya'avetz – See Emden, Rabbi Yaakov.

Yeḥiel Mikhel of Zlotchov, Rabbi, 1721–1786, Poland. One of the prominent students of the Ba'al Shem Tov and the Maggid of Mezeritch. Helped introduce Hasidism into Poland.

Ye'orot Devash – See Eybeschutz, Rabbi Yonatan.

BIBLIOGRAPHY

Numerous sources were used in this work. The following is a more limited list for those who are interested in further reading and study.

Aaron, David. *Tefillah Training: An In-Depth User Friendly Understanding of the Daily Amidah Prayer.* Jerusalem: Isralight, 2008.

> The subtitle of the book explains its purpose and its orientation. There is a short essay on each blessing of the *Shemoneh Esreh* that is designed to provide both meaning and spiritual inspiration based upon the author's own insights.

Buxbaum, Yitzhak. *Real Davvening: Jewish Prayer as a Spiritual Practice and a Form of Meditation for Beginning and Experienced Davveners.* New York: Jewish Spirit Booklet Series, 1996.

> A short pamphlet filled with some lovely practical ideas for how to improve one's focus and *kavana.*

Derovan, David Jay. *Strategies and Tactics for Improving the Spiritual Experience of Prayer.* Ramat Beit Shemesh: 2007. www.davidderovan.com.

> The title speaks for itself. Rooted in classic texts and contemporary experience.

Hirsch, Samson Raphael. *The Hirsch Siddur.* Jerusalem/NY: Feldheim, 1978.

> Despite the fact that it was written in a rather heavy nineteenth-century German style, Rav Hirsch's sensitivity to language and the broader perspective lent by his philosophy of *Torah im Derekh Eretz* made this an early classic that still stands the test of time. The comments tend to be more of an overview than line-by-line analysis. It can be supplemented by his commentary on *Tehillim*, which is still only available in Hebrew.

Jacobson, B.S. *Meditations on the Siddur: Studies in the Essential Problems and Ideas of Jewish Worship.* Tel Aviv: Sinai, 1978.

One of the first major works available in English. This is a translation of volume one of his series in Hebrew called *Netiv Bina*. This volume speaks on more philosophical issues related to *tefilla* primarily by compiling short selections from rabbis through the ages. Other volumes such as *The Weekday Siddur* and *The Sabbath Service* were published subsequently. The approach is one that is more of a compendium of what commentators say about different elements of individual prayers with additional attention paid to their historical development.

Kaplan, Aryeh. *Jewish Meditation: A Practical Guide.* NY: Schocken, 1995.

Rabbi Kaplan was a prolific writer in his relatively short lifetime including a number of works on spirituality that have direct relevance to *tefilla*.

Katz, Abe. *The Beurei Hatefila Institute.* http://www.beureihatefila.com.

This is a very rich and very deep collection of primary and secondary sources about individual prayers, as well as numerous lessons and lectures on the siddur. The emphasis is primarily on the historical origins of the different prayers and their development.

Kleinman, Heshy. *Praying With Fire.* Brooklyn: Mesorah Publications, 2006/2008. Two volumes.

Both volumes together have over two hundred brief essays (intended to be read in five minutes a day) that focus on meaning, inspiration and strategies for improving one's prayer.

Leff, Zev. *Shemoneh Esrei: The Depth and Beauty of Our Daily Tefillah.* Southfield: Targum Press, 2008.

An entire book of over five hundred pages just on Shemoneh Esreh! It can be read more as a collection of traditional *shiurim* than a running commentary, organized thematically and drawing from a variety of traditional sources.

Munk, Elie. *The World of Prayer.* New York: Feldheim, 1961. Two volumes.

One of the first books to appear on prayer in English, this is a classic. It has some great content but feels a little outdated because of the flowery language used, due in no small measure to the fact that it was translated from the original German. Still, lots of treasures here.

Pincus, Rav Shimshon Dovid. *Gates of Prayer.* Jerusalem and Nanuet, NY: Feldheim, 2013.

> A translation of the author's Hebrew work *She'arim BeTefilla* published in 1993 and extremely popular in the yeshiva world. The book is organized according to ten different Hebrew words for prayer, each with its own emphasis and *kavana.*

Sacks, Jonathan. *The Koren Siddur: with introduction, translation and commentary by Rabbi Jonathan Sacks.* Jerusalem: Koren, 2009.

> Rabbi Sacks has earned an international reputation as a scholarly and articulate spokesman for Judaism. His brief commentary supplements his many writings on the *parasha* available in books and online.

Schwab, Shimon. *Rav Schwab on Prayer.* Brooklyn: Mesorah, 2001.

> A detailed explanation of *Shaḥarit* and selections on the Pesaḥ Haggada by the former leader of the Breuer's Community in New York. One of the more extensive commentaries available in English.

Soloveitchik, Joseph B. *Koren Mesorat HaRav Siddur.* Edited by A. Lustiger, G. Student, S. Posner. Jerusalem: OU Press/Koren, 2011.

> Contains a commentary based upon the teachings of Rav Soloveitchik gleaned from his various writings. One volume dedicated to the philosophy of *tefilla* by Rav Soloveitchik, published posthumously, is *Worship of the Heart: Essays on Jewish Prayer.* Ed. Shalom Carmy. Hoboken, NJ: Ktav, 2003.

Wohlgemuth, Isaiah. *A Guide to Jewish Prayer.* Transcribed by A. Reichert. Lakewood, NJ: J. Robinson, 1999.

> A commentary primarily on *Shaḥarit* by a beloved teacher at the Maimonides School in Boston who taught a course on the Siddur for many years. It includes a number of insights from Rav Soloveitchik.

הרב ש״ח הכהן אבינר, תפלת עמך: פירוש על סידור התפלה, ירושלים תשס״ט.

A contemporary, almost line-by-line commentary by one of the leaders of the religious Zionist community in Israel.

ח׳ זונדל בהר״ר יוסף, אוצר התפלות – שני סידורים כתבי יד: ׳ערוגת הבושם׳ ו׳ראשי בשמים׳ יכילו: א. עץ יוסף ב. ענף יוסף.

שלמה גורדון, סידור כתב יד ׳עבודת הלב׳ יכיל: א. עיון תפלה ב. תקון תפלה.

A collection of what amounts to four commentaries on the siddur set up in a similar fashion to a *Mikraot Gedolot*. The commentaries cover the history of the text of individual prayers as well as explorations into the meanings of individual words and phrases.

א׳ טרגין ומ׳ רובינשטיין, תפלה כמפגש, בית אל 2010.

A work that explores the ideational content of the *halakhot* of *tefilla*, i.e., the ways in which the laws of prayer help direct one to the goals of prayer.

הרב י׳ יעקבסון, נתיב בינה, תל אביב: סיני, 1994–1978.

See the description in the English section above. The Hebrew edition has the original as well as further volumes on the holidays, Rosh Ḥodesh and the like, some of which were published posthumously.

צלותא דאברהם – סידור על פי נוסח הרבי מטשכנוב, נערך על ידי נכדו ותלמידו רבי מנחם מנדל חיים מזאוויירצא. נקרא ׳שומע תפילה׳, ונחלק לשני חלקים: ׳עמק ברכה׳ ו׳ויעש אברהם׳. אליו נלווה ׳שירותא דצלותא׳ – הערות והארות, מאת י׳ ורדיגר, תל-אביב תשכ״ג.

A siddur which follows the customs of Hasidic Rabbi Avraham Landau of Ciechanow but whose broader value is in the four commentaries which accompany it on the text and meaning of the prayers.

RABBIS' KADDISH

Mourner: Yitgadal ve-yitkadash shemeh raba. (*Cong:* Amen)
Be-alema di vera khir'uteh, ve-yamlikh malkhuteh,
be-ḥayyeikhon, uv-yomeikhon,
uv-ḥayyei de-khol beit Yisrael,
ba-agala uvi-zman kariv,
ve-imru Amen. (*Cong:* Amen)

All: Yeheh shemeh raba mevarakh le'alam ul-alemei alemaya.

Mourner: Yitbarakh ve-yishtabaḥ ve-yitpa'ar ve-yitromam ve-yitnaseh
ve-yit-hadar ve-yit'aleh ve-yit-hallal
shemeh dekudsha, berikh hu. (*Cong:* Berikh hu)
Le-ela min kol birkhata
/*Between Rosh HaShana & Yom Kippur:* Le-ela le-ela mi-kol birkhata/
ve-shirata, tushbeḥata ve-neḥemata, da-amiran be-alema,
ve-imru, Amen. (*Cong:* Amen)

Al Yisrael, ve-al rabanan,
ve-al talmideihon, ve-al kol talmidei talmideihon,
ve-al kol man de-asekin be-oraita
di be-atra (*In Israel:* kadisha) ha-dein ve-di be-khol atar va-atar,
yeheh lehon ul-khon shelama raba,
ḥina ve-ḥisda, ve-raḥamei,
ve-ḥayyei arikhei, um-zonei re-viḥei,
u-furkana min kodam avuhon di vish-maya,
ve-imru Amen. (*Cong:* Amen)

Yeheh shelama raba min shemaya
ve-ḥayyim (tovim) aleinu ve-al kol Yisrael,
ve-imru Amen. (*Cong:* Amen)

Bow, take three steps back, as if taking leave of the Divine Presence, then bow, first left, then right, then center, while saying:
Oseh shalom/*Between Rosh HaShana & Yom Kippur:* ha-shalom/
bim-romav,
hu ya'aseh ve-raḥamav shalom aleinu, ve-al kol Yisrael,
ve-imru Amen. (*Cong:* Amen)

MOURNER'S KADDISH

Mourner: Yitgadal ve-yitkadash shemeh raba. (*Cong:* Amen)
Be-alema di vera khir'uteh, ve-yamlikh malkhuteh,
be-ḥayyeikhon, uv-yomeikhon,
uv-ḥayyei de-khol beit Yisrael,
ba-agala uvi-zman kariv, ve-imru Amen. (*Cong:* Amen)

All: Yeheh shemeh raba mevarakh le'alam ul-alemei alemaya.

Mourner: Yitbarakh ve-yishtabaḥ ve-yitpa'ar ve-yitromam ve-yitnaseh
ve-yit-hadar ve-yit'aleh ve-yit-hallal
shemeh dekudsha, berikh hu. (*Cong:* Berikh hu)
Le-ela min kol birkhata
/*Between Rosh HaShana & Yom Kippur:* Le-ela le-ela mi-kol birkhata/
ve-shirata, tushbeḥata ve-neḥemata, da-amiran be-alema,
ve-imru, Amen. (*Cong:* Amen)

Yeheh shelama raba min shemaya
ve-ḥayyim aleinu ve-al kol Yisrael,
ve-imru Amen. (*Cong:* Amen)

Bow, take three steps back, as if taking leave of the Divine Presence, then bow, first left, then right, then center, while saying:

Oseh shalom/*Between Rosh HaShana & Yom Kippur:* ha-shalom/
bim-romav,
hu ya'aseh shalom aleinu, ve-al kol Yisrael,
ve-imru Amen. (*Cong:* Amen)